About the Cover Image

Jiao Bingzhen, Ladies at a Pavilion Taking Tea, Qing Dynasty

In this image by the prominent court painter Jiao Bingzhen (1689–1726), a group of high-ranking Chinese ladies have gathered for tea in a pavilion, probably at the imperial court in Beijing. Such women were honored members of the imperial household. Often literate and well-educated, they enjoyed music, poetry, painting, calligraphy and board games. The painting also reflects China's early interaction with the West, for the painter had encountered highly educated Jesuit missionaries at the Directorate of Astronomy, where both he and the missionaries were employed. From them he learned something of Western styles of painting, especially techniques of shading, perspective, and mathematical precision in depicting buildings. Jiao Bingzhen was also impressed by European astronomy, and he eventually converted to Roman Catholicism.

Ladies at a pavilion taking tea. Qing Dynasty painter Jiao Bingzhen (1689–1726) / Pictures from History / Bridgeman Images

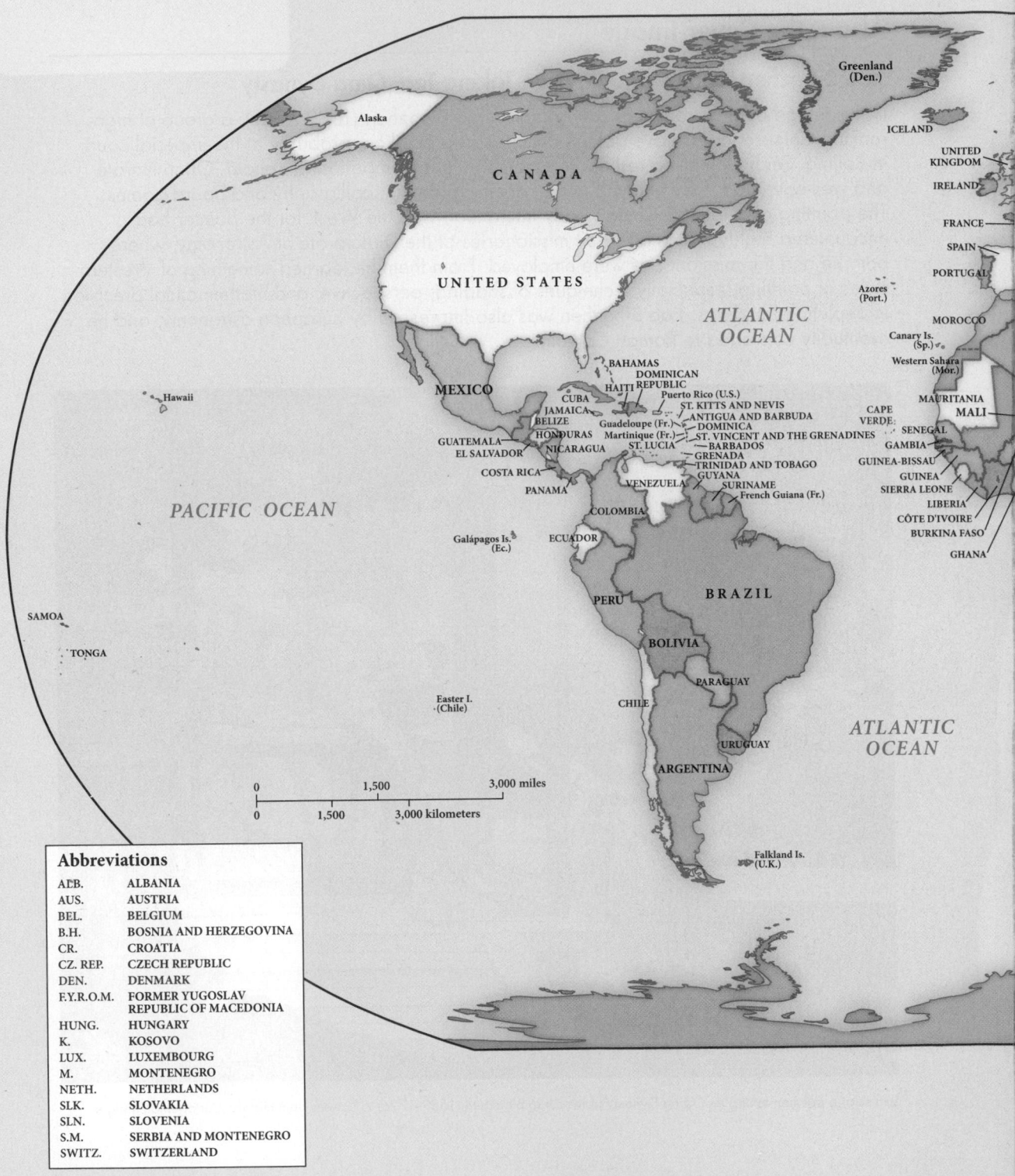

Greenland (Den.)

ICELAND

UNITED KINGDOM

IRELAND

FRANCE

SPAIN

PORTUGAL

Alaska

CANADA

UNITED STATES

ATLANTIC OCEAN

Azores (Port.)

MOROCCO

Canary Is. (Sp.)

Western Sahara (Mor.)

MAURITANIA

MALI

Hawaii

MEXICO

BAHAMAS

DOMINICAN REPUBLIC

HAITI

CUBA

JAMAICA

BELIZE

HONDURAS

GUATEMALA

EL SALVADOR

NICARAGUA

COSTA RICA

PANAMA

Puerto Rico (U.S.)

ST. KITTS AND NEVIS

ANTIGUA AND BARBUDA

Guadeloupe (Fr.)

DOMINICA

Martinique (Fr.)

ST. VINCENT AND THE GRENADINES

ST. LUCIA

BARBADOS

GRENADA

TRINIDAD AND TOBAGO

GUYANA

SURINAME

French Guiana (Fr.)

CAPE VERDE

SENEGAL

GAMBIA

GUINEA-BISSAU

GUINEA

SIERRA LEONE

LIBERIA

CÔTE D'IVOIRE

BURKINA FASO

GHANA

VENEZUELA

COLOMBIA

PACIFIC OCEAN

Galápagos Is. (Ec.)

ECUADOR

PERU

BRAZIL

BOLIVIA

PARAGUAY

SAMOA

TONGA

Easter I. (Chile)

CHILE

URUGUAY

ARGENTINA

ATLANTIC OCEAN

0		1,500		3,000 miles
0	1,500		3,000 kilometers	

Falkland Is. (U.K.)

Abbreviations

ALB.	ALBANIA
AUS.	AUSTRIA
BEL.	BELGIUM
B.H.	BOSNIA AND HERZEGOVINA
CR.	CROATIA
CZ. REP.	CZECH REPUBLIC
DEN.	DENMARK
F.Y.R.O.M.	FORMER YUGOSLAV REPUBLIC OF MACEDONIA
HUNG.	HUNGARY
K.	KOSOVO
LUX.	LUXEMBOURG
M.	MONTENEGRO
NETH.	NETHERLANDS
SLK.	SLOVAKIA
SLN.	SLOVENIA
S.M.	SERBIA AND MONTENEGRO
SWITZ.	SWITZERLAND

ARCTIC OCEAN

NORWAY
SWEDEN
FINLAND
DEN.
ESTONIA
LATVIA
LITHUANIA
NETH. POLAND BELARUS
GERMANY
BEL.
CZ. REP.
LUX. AUS. SLK.
SWITZ.
SLN.
HUNG.
B.H.
CR.
S.
MFYR.O.M.
ITALY ALB.
GREECE

RUSSIAN FEDERATION

UKRAINE
MOLDOVA
ROMANIA
BULGARIA
GEORGIA
ARMENIA
TURKEY
AZERBAIJAN

KAZAKHSTAN

UZBEKISTAN
TURKMENISTAN
TAJIKISTAN
KYRGYZSTAN

MONGOLIA

N. KOREA
S. KOREA

JAPAN

PACIFIC OCEAN

MALTA
TUNISIA

CYPRUS
SYRIA
LEBANON
ISRAEL
West Bank
IRAQ
JORDAN
KUWAIT
AFGHANISTAN
IRAN
BAHRAIN

CHINA

TAIWAN

ALGERIA

LIBYA

EGYPT

Gaza
Strip

SAUDI
ARABIA
QATAR
UNITED ARAB
EMIRATES
OMAN

PAKISTAN

NEPAL

BHUTAN

BANGLADESH

INDIA

MYANMAR
(BURMA)

LAOS
THAILAND
CAMBODIA

VIETNAM

PHILIPPINES

Mariana Is.
(U.S.)

Guam
(U.S.)

MARSHALL
IS.

NIGER
CHAD
SUDAN
ERITREA
YEMEN
DJIBOUTI

BRUNEI

PALAU

FEDERATED STATES
OF MICRONESIA

NIGERIA
BENIN
TOGO
CAMEROON
CENTRAL
AFRICAN REP.
SOUTH
SUDAN
ETHIOPIA
SOMALIA

MALDIVES

SRI
LANKA

MALAYSIA

SINGAPORE

NAURU

KIRIBATI

TUVALU

EQ. GUINEA
GABON
CONGO
RWANDA
UGANDA
KENYA
DEM. REP. OF
THE CONGO
SÃO
TOMÉ
&
PRÍNCIPE
BURUNDI
TANZANIA

COMOROS
SEYCHELLES

INDIAN OCEAN

INDONESIA

PAPUA
NEW
GUINEA

SOLOMON
IS.

EAST
TIMOR

ANGOLA
ZAMBIA
MALAWI
NAMIBIA
ZIMBABWE
BOTSWANA
MADAGASCAR

MAURITIUS

VANUATU

New Caledonia
(Fr.)

FIJI

AUSTRALIA

SOUTH
AFRICA
MOZAMBIQUE
SWAZILAND
LESOTHO

NEW
ZEALAND

Tasmania
(Aust.)

ANTARCTICA

ROCKY MTS.

Mississippi R.

APPALACHIAN MTS.

ATLANTIC
OCEAN

Gulf of
Mexico

Tropic of Cancer

PACIFIC OCEAN

Niger R.

Equator

Amazon R.

ANDES MTS.

Tropic of Capricorn

ATLANTIC
OCEAN

ALPS

URAL MTS.

Volga R.

Ob R.

GOBI

Yellow R.

SYRIAN
DESERT

Mediterranean Sea

HIMALAYA MTS.

Yangzi R.

SAHARA

Ganges R.

Nile R.

Tropic of Cancer

PACIFIC OCEAN

Arabian
Sea

Bay of
Bengal

South
China
Sea

Congo R.

Equator

INDIAN OCEAN

Zambezi R.

KALAHARI
DESERT

Tropic of Capricorn

Vegetation Zones

Tundra
Northern forest
Temperate forest
Temperate grassland
Desert and dry shrub
Mediterranean shrub
Mountain grassland
Tropical grassland
and savanna
Tropical forest
Permanent ice cover

Ways of the World

A Brief Global History with Sources

Ways of the World

A Brief Global History with Sources

FOURTH EDITION

Robert W. Strayer

The College at Brockport: State University of New York

Eric W. Nelson

Missouri State University

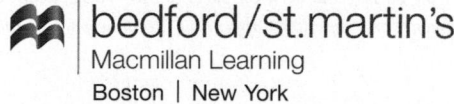

bedford/st.martin's
Macmillan Learning
Boston | New York

FOR EVELYN RHIANNON WITH LOVE

For Bedford/St. Martin's

Vice President, Editorial, Macmillan Learning Humanities:
Edwin Hill
Program Director for History: Michael Rosenberg
Senior Program Manager for History: William J. Lombardo
History Marketing Manager: Melissa Rodriguez
Director of Content Development, Humanities: Jane Knetzger
Senior Developmental Editor: Heidi L. Hood
Senior Content Project Manager: Christina M. Horn
Workflow Project Supervisor: Joe Ford
Production Supervisor: Robin Besofsky
Senior Media Project Manager: Michelle Camisa
Media Editor: Tess Fletcher
Editorial Assistant: Stephanie Sosa
Copy Editor: Susan Zorn
Indexer: Leoni Z. McVey
Editorial Services: Lumina Datamatics, Inc.

Composition: Lumina Datamatics, Inc.
Cartographer: Mapping Specialists, Ltd.
Photo Editor: Christine Buese
Photo Researcher: Bruce Carson
Permissions Editor: Eve Lehmann
Design Director, Content Management: Diana Blume
Text Design: Lisa Buckley
Cover Design: William Boardman
Printing and Binding: LSC Communications

Cover Image: top, Carpet decorated with animals, Indian, 16th century (wool and needlepoint), Indian School (16th century)/Musée des Arts Décoratifs, Paris, France/ Bridgeman Images; bottom, Ladies at a pavilion taking tea. Qing Dynasty painter Jiao Bingzhen (1689–1726)/Pictures from History/Bridgeman Images

Manufactured in the United States of America.

1 2 3 4 5 6   23 22 21 20 19 18

For information, write: Bedford/St. Martin's, 75 Arlington Street, Boston, MA 02116

ISBN 978-1-319-10972-1 (Combined Edition)
ISBN 978-1-319-10975-2 (Volume 1)
ISBN 978-1-319-10978-3 (Volume 2)

Acknowledgments

Text acknowledgments and copyrights appear at the back of the book on pages 1080–1081, which constitute an extension of the copyright page. Art acknowledgments and copyrights appear on the same page as the art selections they cover.

Preface

About *Ways of the World*

Ways of the World is an intentionally brief global history of the human experience that focuses on the big pictures of world history, using examples selectively rather than cluttering the narrative with endless details. It repeatedly highlights issues of change, of comparison, and of connection among culturally different peoples, both in the narrative text and in the book's innovative primary and secondary source features.

The main title of the book, *Ways of the World*, evokes three dimensions of its distinctive character and outlook, all of them based on our experience as teachers and scholars. The first is **diversity** or **variation**, for the "ways of the world," or the ways of being human in the world, have been many and constantly changing. This book seeks to embrace the global experience of humankind, both in its common features and in its vast diversity, while noticing the changing location of particular centers of innovation and wider influence.

Second, the title *Ways of the World* invokes major **panoramas**, **patterns**, or **pathways** in world history rather than a highly detailed narrative, which can often overwhelm students. Thus, most chapters are organized in terms of broad global or transregional themes, illustrated by a limited number of specific examples.

A third implication of the book's title lies in a certain **reflective quality** that appears in the Big Picture essays that introduce each Part, in the Reflections section at the end of each chapter, and periodically in the narrative itself. This dimension of the book offers many opportunities for pondering larger questions about how historians operate, about the dilemmas they face in reconstructing the human journey, and about the relationship of the past to the present.

These elements of *Ways of the World* find expression repeatedly in what we call the **four Cs** of world history: context, change, comparison, and connection. The first "C," **context**, refers to the larger frameworks within which particular historical figures, events, societies, and civilizations take shape. In our telling of the human past, context is central, for in world history nothing stands alone. Like Russian nesting dolls, every story finds a place in some more inclusive narrative. European empires in the Americas, for example, take on new meaning when they are understood as part of a global process of imperial expansion that included the growth of the Inca, Russian, Chinese, and Ottoman empires at the same time.

The second "C," large-scale **change**, both within and especially across major regions of the world, represents another prominent emphasis in *Ways of the World*. Examples include the peopling of the planet, the emergence of "civilization," the linking of Eastern and Western hemispheres in the wake of Columbus's voyages, the Industrial Revolution, and many other significant changes during the course of human history. The flip side of change, of course, is continuity, implying a focus on what persists over long periods of time. And so *Ways of the World* seeks to juxtapose these contrasting elements of human experience. While civilizations have changed dramatically over time, some of their essential features—cities, states, patriarchy, and class inequality, for example—have long endured.

A third "C" involves frequent **comparison**, bringing several regions or cultures into our field of vision at the same time. It means constantly asking "what's the difference?" Thus this book makes comparisons between the Agricultural Revolution in the Eastern and Western hemispheres; between the beginnings of Buddhism and the early history of Christianity and Islam; between the Russian and Chinese revolutions; and between feminism in the Global North and the Global South. These and many more comparisons frequently punctuate our account of the global past.

The final "C" emphasizes **connections**, networks of communication and exchange that increasingly shaped the character of the societies that participated in them. In our account of the human story, world history is less about what happened within particular civilizations or cultures than about the processes and outcomes of their meetings with one another. Cross-cultural encounters then become one of the major motors of historical transformation. Examples include the clash of the ancient Greeks and the Persians; the long-distance commercial networks that linked the Afro-Eurasian world; the numerous cross-cultural interactions spawned by the spread of Islam; the trans-hemispheric Columbian exchange of the early modern era; and the more recent growth of a thoroughly entangled global economy.

These emphases have remained at the heart of *Ways of the World* since its initial publication in 2008. But the book has also changed, grown, and matured. Originally a brief account of the global past by a single author, Robert Strayer, it has acquired a fine co-author in Eric Nelson from Missouri State University.

Along the way, it also began to combine a brief narrative text with thematically based sets of primary sources followed by paired secondary sources at the end of each chapter. What has emerged is a new kind of book for the world history survey, one that enables students to "do history," using the kind of evidence that historians work with. Each of the **Working with Evidence** primary source collections now includes both documents and images and is organized around a particular theme, issue, or question that derives from the chapter narrative. As the title of these features suggests, they enable students to "work with evidence" and thus begin to understand the craft of historians as well as their conclusions. They include brief headnotes that provide context for the sources, and they are accompanied by a series of probing Doing History questions appropriate for in-class discussion and writing assignments. Furthermore, Working with Evidence is now followed by a new **Historians' Voices** secondary source feature that presents two brief extracts from scholarly works, aligned with the theme of the Working with Evidence feature. Thus it can be used in conjunction with that feature or assigned on its own.

Further changes in the book have derived from new scholarship in the rapidly expanding field of World History. Thus we have increasingly integrated issues of gender, the environment, and technology into this account of the human journey. Coverage of particular areas of the world, such as Southeast Asia, Latin America, and Pacific Oceania, has likewise been strengthened. This fourth edition in particular has completely reimagined our treatment of the past century in a more global fashion, moving beyond the cold war framework of earlier editions. And over time the book has more often highlighted individual people and particular events, which sometimes get lost in the broad sweep of world history. Finally, *Ways of the World* has acquired a very substantial electronic and online presence with an impressive array of innovative pedagogical and learning aids.

These changes remind us that textbooks are not fixed and finished compilations of what happened in the past. Rather, such books develop as they respond to new technologies, to new historical research, and to the evolving political, social, and economic conditions of the contemporary world. As authors, we are acutely aware of how much debate and controversy lie behind many of the issues that are explored in *Ways of the World*. This book, then, is a snapshot of our current understanding of World History, shaped by the particular time (the early twenty-first century) and place (the United States) in which it was composed. Such a book written fifty years ago, or in contemporary China, Nigeria, Iran, or Brazil, or in the mid-twenty-first century, would surely be very different. Thus *Ways of the World* can and should be criticized, assessed, and argued with, not simply accepted as a definitive account of the global past.

What Else Is New in the Fourth Edition?

In this new edition, *Ways of the World* continues to change, most notably in a **revision of Part 6**, which deals with the past century. Previously the several chapters of that Part were organized regionally and in terms deriving from the cold war: the Western capitalist world, the communist world, and the third world of developing countries. But with the cold war now more than a quarter of a century in the past, it seemed appropriate to reorganize our treatment of the past century in more global terms. We have done so by distinguishing between major events or milestones and longer-term historical processes. Thus the first two chapters of Part 6, Chapters 20 and 21, focus on milestone events such as the world wars, revolutions, the cold war, decolonization, the demise of communism, and much more. With these "milestones" of the past century in mind, Chapters 22 and 23 turn to the larger and perhaps even more consequential processes occurring beneath the surface of major public events. Chapter 22 treats the enormous acceleration of technological innovation as a decisive driver of a deeply interconnected world economy and of pervasive social change. Chapter 23 then turns the spotlight on the explosive growth of human numbers, on the movement of many people to cities and to new lives abroad, and on the cultural transformations that accompanied modern life during the past century. The chapter—and the book—conclude by examining the enormous and continuing impact of human activity on the entire biosphere, which represents by far the most significant long-term process of this new era and the most critical challenge of the next century.

Another new element in this fourth edition is a feature titled **Controversies**, intended to highlight the debates that accompany so many historical inquiries. These Controversies, which appear in one chapter of each Part of the book, explore debates about key historical issues: when history begins; the origins of major religious traditions; the nature of empires; the idea of the Atlantic world; why the Industrial Revolution began in Europe; and the concept of globalization. We believe these brief essays will counteract any remaining notion of a textbook as an authoritative, encyclopedia-like tome to be assimilated, while conveying an understanding of World History as a frequently contested conversation.

Furthermore, the **Working with Evidence** primary source collections that accompany each chapter now incorporate both documents and images, many of them new to this edition. Thus the visual sources illustrating Pompeii in Chapter 5 are now enriched with a collection of graffiti inscriptions deriving from that ancient Italian city. And the documents that reflect the rise of fascism in Chapter 20 are now combined with propaganda posters and images showing how those ideas were visually presented to the public.

The new **Historians' Voices** feature now supplies a range of secondary sources for students to consider. In Chapter 9, for example, two prominent scholars, Francis Robinson and Karen Armstrong, explore the significance of the life of Muhammad. And in Chapter 22, Peter Stearns and Merry Wiesner-Hanks, both major world historians, offer assessments of global feminism during the past century. Historians' Voices has also been added to the book's companion source reader *Thinking through Sources for Ways of the World*, which is available as a print supplement or online in LaunchPad, adding another dimension to these alternate source collections.

The book's features are rounded out by the popular **Zooming In** essays, which were new to the third edition and call attention to particular people, places, and events, situating them in a larger global context. Appearing once in each chapter, Zooming In addresses topics such as Göbekli Tepe and monumental construction before agriculture, Trung Trac and resistance to the Chinese empire, gunpowder, the end of the Byzantine Empire, feminism and nationalism in Java, the Cuban Revolution, and many more.

A number of pedagogical aids in *Ways of the World* have also been updated or enhanced. New **Landmarks** visual timelines for each Part and each chapter allow students to see at a glance what was happening in various regions of the world during the same period of time. Many of the maps included in this fourth edition now feature a **Mapping History** exercise accompanied by two levels of questions. The first requires students to read the map carefully, and the second asks them to interpret its implications.

Promoting Active Learning

As all instructors know, students can often "do the assignment" or read the required chapter and yet have little understanding of it when they come to class. The problem, frequently, is passive studying—a quick once-over, perhaps some highlighting of the text—but little sustained involvement with the material. A central pedagogical problem in all teaching is how to encourage more active, engaged styles of learning. We want to enable students to manipulate the information of the book, using its ideas and data to answer questions, to make comparisons, to draw conclusions, to criticize assumptions, and to infer implications that are not explicitly disclosed in the text itself.

Ways of the World seeks to promote active learning in various ways. Most obviously, the source-based features in the book itself (Working with Evidence and the new Historians' Voices) and those in the companion reader *Thinking through Sources for Ways of the World* (also available on LaunchPad) invite students to engage actively with documents and images alike, assisted by abundant questions to guide that engagement.

In addition, whenever an instructor assigns the **LaunchPad e-book** (which can be bundled for free with the print book), students have at their disposal all the resources of the print text, including its special features and its primary and secondary sources. But they also gain access to **LearningCurve**, an online adaptive learning tool that helps students actively rehearse what they have read and foster a deeper understanding and retention of the material. With this adaptive quizzing, students accumulate points toward a target score as they go, giving the interaction a game-like feel. Feedback for incorrect responses explains why the answer is incorrect and directs students back to the text to review before they attempt to answer the question again. The end result is a better understanding of the key elements of the text. Instructors who actively assign LearningCurve report that their students come to class prepared for discussion and their students enjoy using it. In addition, LearningCurve's reporting feature allows instructors to quickly diagnose which concepts students are struggling with so they can adjust lectures and activities accordingly.

Further opportunities for active learning are available with the special online activities accompanying *Thinking through Sources for Ways of the World* in LaunchPad. When required by instructors, the wrap-around pedagogy that accompanies the sources virtually ensures active learning. LaunchPad is thus a rich asset for instructors who want to support students in all settings, from traditional lectures to "flipped" classrooms.

For instructors who need a mobile and accessible option for delivering adaptive quizzing with the narrative alone, Macmillan's new **Achieve Read & Practice** e-book platform offers an exceptionally easy-to-use and affordable option. This simple product pairs the Value Edition—a two-color narrative-only text (no sources)—with the power of LearningCurve's quizzing, all in a format that is mobile-friendly, allowing students to complete their assignments on the bus or in the library.

Another aspect of the book important for the promotion of active learning involves the stimulation of curiosity. A **contemporary vignette** opens each chapter with a story that links the past and the present to show the continuing resonance of history in the lives of contemporary people. Chapter 6, for example, begins by describing the inauguration in 2010 of Bolivian president Evo Morales at an impressive ceremony at Tiwanaku, the center of an ancient Andean empire, thus emphasizing the continuing cultural significance of this ancient civilization in contemporary Bolivian culture. At the end of each chapter, a short **Reflections** section raises provocative, sometimes quasi-philosophical, questions about the craft of the historian and the unfolding of the human story. We believe that these brief essays can motivate our students' curiosity, stimulate their own pondering, and provide grist for the mill of vigorous class discussions.

A further technique for encouraging active learning lies in the provision of frequent contextual markers. Student readers need to know where they are going and where they have been. Thus Part-opening **Big Picture essays** preview what follows in the subsequent chapters, while a **chapter outline** suggests what is coming in each chapter. A new **Landmarks** visual timeline, providing a chronological overview of major events and processes, appears at the beginning of each Part and each chapter. **Snapshot boxes** present succinct glimpses of particular themes, regions, or time periods, adding some trees to the forest of world history. A **list of terms** at the end of each chapter invites students to check their grasp of the material. As usual with books published by Bedford/St. Martin's, a **rich illustration program** provides striking visual markers that enhance the narrative.

Active learning also means approaching the text with something to look for, rather than simply dutifully completing the assignment. *Ways of the World* provides such cues in abundance. A **Seeking the Main Point** question helps students focus on the central theme of the chapter. Each chapter also has at least one **Practicing Historical Thinking** question that invites students to reflect on what they have learned to that point in the chapter. A series of **Guided Reading Questions in the margins**, with labels such as "change," "comparison," or "connection," allows students to read the adjacent material with a clear purpose in mind. **Big Picture Questions** at the end of each chapter deal with matters not directly addressed in the text. Instead, they provide opportunities for integration, comparison, analysis, and sometimes speculation. New **Mapping History** exercises invite students to read maps carefully and to interpret their implications.

Teaching History in the Digital Age

Because the teaching of history is changing rapidly, we have created online interactive complements for *Ways of the World* via Macmillan's premier learning platform, **LaunchPad**, an intuitive and interactive e-book and course space. Free when packaged with the print book or available at a low price when used on its own, LaunchPad grants students and instructors access to a wealth of online tools and resources built specifically for this text to enhance reading comprehension and promote in-depth study. LaunchPad's course space and interactive e-book are ready to use "as is," or they can be edited and customized with your own material and assigned right away.

Developed with extensive feedback from history instructors and students, LaunchPad for *Ways of the World* includes the complete narrative and special features of the print book plus the companion reader, *Thinking through Sources for Ways of the World*, and **LearningCurve**, an adaptive learning tool designed to get students to read before they come to class. With **an expanded set of source-based questions in the test bank and in LearningCurve**, instructors now have more ways to test students on their understanding of sources and narrative in the book. The addition of the **new Bedford Document Collections modules in LaunchPad** means instructors have a flexible repository of discovery-oriented primary source projects to assign. This makes LaunchPad for *Ways of the World* a one-stop shop for working with sources and thinking critically in a multitude of modes.

LaunchPad also includes additional **primary source online activities** for each chapter of the *Thinking through Sources* companion reader. These activities supply a distinctive and sophisticated pedagogy of self-grading exercises that help students not only understand the sources but also think critically about them. More specifically, a short **quiz after each source** offers students the opportunity to check their understanding of materials that often derive from quite distant times and places. Some questions focus on audience, purpose, point of view, limitations, or context, while others challenge students to draw conclusions about the source or to compare one source with another. And a **Draw Conclusions from the Evidence activity** challenges students to assess whether a specific piece of evidence drawn from the sources supports or challenges a stated conclusion. Collectively these assignments create an active learning environment where reading with a purpose is reinforced by immediate feedback and support. This feedback for each rejoinder creates an active learning environment where students are rewarded for reaching the correct answer through their own process of investigation.

More broadly, in this interactive learning environment, students will enhance their ability to build arguments and to practice historical reasoning. Thus, this LaunchPad pedagogy does for skill development what LearningCurve does for content mastery and reading comprehension.

LaunchPad also provides a simple, user-friendly platform for individual instructors to add their own voice, materials, and assignments to the text, guiding their students' learning outside of the traditional classroom setting. Available with training and support, LaunchPad can help take history teaching and learning into a new era.

For instructors who need a mobile and accessible option for delivering adaptive quizzing with the narrative alone, Macmillan's new **Achieve Read & Practice** e-book platform offers an exceptionally easy-to-use and affordable option. This simple product pairs the Value Edition—a two-color narrative-only text (no sources)—with the power of LearningCurve's quizzing, all in a format that students can use wherever they go. Available for the first time with this edition, Achieve Read & Practice's interactive e-book, adaptive quizzing, and gradebook are built with an intuitive interface that can be read on mobile devices and are fully accessible and available at an affordable price.

To learn more about the benefits of LearningCurve, LaunchPad, Achieve Read & Practice, and the different versions to package with these digital tools, see the Versions and Supplements section on page xxi.

"It Takes a Village"

In any enterprise of significance, "it takes a village," as they say. Bringing *Ways of the World* to life in this new edition, it seems, has occupied the energies of several villages. Among the privileges and delights of writing and revising this book has been the opportunity to interact with our fellow villagers.

We are grateful to the community of fellow historians who contributed their expertise to this revision. For this edition, they include Andreas Agocs, University of the Pacific; Tonio Andrade, Emory University; Monty Armstrong, Cerritos High School; Melanie Bailey, Piedmont Virginia Community College; Djene Bajalan, Missouri State University; Anthony Barbieri-Low, University of California, Santa Barbara; Christine Bond, Edmond Memorial High School; Mike Burns, Concordia International School, Hanoi; Elizabeth Campbell, Daemen College; Theodore Cohen, Lindenwood University; Bradley Davis, Eastern Connecticut State University; Denis Gainty, Georgia State University; Duane Galloway, Rowan-Cabarrus Community College; Jay Harmon, Houston Christian High School; Michael Hunt, University of North Carolina at Chapel Hill; Ane Lintvedt, McDonogh School; Aran MacKinnon, Georgia College and State University; Harold Marcuse, University of California, Santa Barbara; Merritt McKinney, Volunteer State Community College; Erin O'Donnell, East Stroudsburg University; Sarah Panzer, Missouri State University; Charmayne Patterson, Clark Atlanta University; Dean Pavlakis, Carroll College; Chris Peek, Bellaire High School; Tracie Provost, Middle Georgia State University; Masako Racel, Kennesaw State University; and Eddie Supratman, Arkansas State University-Beebe.

We also offer our gratitude to reviewers of earlier editions: Maria S. Arbelaez, University of Nebraska–Omaha; Veronica L. Bale, Mira Costa College; Christopher Bellitto, Kean University; Monica Bord-Lamberty, Northwood High School; Stanley Burstein, California State University–Los Angeles; Ralph Croizier, University of

Victoria; Gregory Cushman, the University of Kansas; Edward Dandrow, University of Central Florida; Peter L. de Rosa, Bridgewater State University; Carter Findley, Ohio State University; Amy Forss, Metropolitan Community College; Denis Gainty, Georgia State University; Steven A. Glazer, Graceland University; Sue Gronewald, Kean University; Andrew Hamilton, Viterbo University; J. Laurence Hare, University of Arkansas; Michael Hinckley, Northern Kentucky University; Bram Hubbell, Friends Seminary; Ronald Huch, Eastern Kentucky University; Elizabeth Hyde, Kean University; Mark Lentz, University of Louisiana–Lafayette; Kate McGrath, Central Connecticut State University; C. Brid Nicholson, Kean University; Donna Patch, Westside High School; Jonathan T. Reynolds, Northern Kentucky University; James Sabathne, Hononegah High School; Christopher Sleeper, Mira Costa College; Ira Spar, Ramapo College and Metropolitan Museum of Art; Kristen Strobel, Lexington High School; Michael Vann, Sacramento State University; Peter Winn, Tufts University; and Judith Zinsser, Miami University of Ohio.

The fine people at Bedford/St. Martin's (Macmillan Learning) have provided a second community sustaining this enterprise and the one most directly responsible for the book's fourth edition. It would be difficult for any author to imagine a more supportive and professional publishing team. Our chief point of contact with the Bedford village has been Heidi Hood, our development editor. She has coordinated the immensely complex task of assembling a new edition of the book and has done so with great professional care, with timely responses to our many queries, and with sensitivity to the needs and feelings of authors, even when she found it necessary to decline our suggestions.

Others on the team have also exhibited that lovely combination of personal kindness and professional competence that is so characteristic of the Bedford way. Editorial director Edwin Hill, program director Michael Rosenberg, and program manager William Lombardo have kept an eye on the project amid many duties. Christina Horn, our content project manager, managed the process of turning a manuscript into a published book and did so with both grace and efficiency. Editorial assistant Stephanie Sosa has efficiently and thoughtfully directed the revision of the *Thinking through Sources* companion reader and handled countless other project details. Operating behind the scenes in the Bedford village, a series of highly competent and always supportive people have shepherded this revised edition along its way. Photo researcher Bruce Carson identified and acquired the many images that grace this new edition of *Ways of the World* and did so with a keen eye and courtesy. Copy editor Susan Zorn polished the prose and sorted out our many inconsistent usages with a seasoned and perceptive eye. Melissa Rodriguez has overseen the marketing process, while Bedford's sales representatives have reintroduced the book to the academic world. Media editor Tess Fletcher supervised the development of supplements and media products to support the book, and William Boardman ably coordinated research for the lovely covers that mark *Ways of the World*. Eve Lehmann conducted the always-difficult negotiations surrounding permissions with more equanimity than we could have imagined.

A final and much smaller community sustained this project and its authors. It is that most intimate of villages that we know as a marriage. Sharing that village with me (Robert Strayer) is my wife, Suzanne Sturn. It is her work to bring ideas and people to life onstage, even as I try to do so between these covers. She knows how I feel about her love and support, and no one else needs to. And across the street, I (Eric Nelson) would also like to thank two other residents of this village: my wife, Alice Victoria, and our little girl, Evelyn Rhiannon, to whom this new edition is dedicated. Without their patience and support, I could not have become part of such an interesting journey.

To all of our fellow villagers, we offer deep thanks for an immensely rewarding experience. We are grateful beyond measure.

Robert Strayer, La Selva Beach, California
Eric Nelson, Springfield, Missouri

Versions and Supplements

Adopters of *Ways of the World* and their students have access to abundant print and digital resources and tools, the acclaimed *Bedford Series in History and Culture* volumes, and much more. The LaunchPad course space for *Ways of the World* provides access to the narrative as well as a wealth of primary sources and other features, along with assignment and assessment opportunities at the ready. Achieve Read & Practice supplies adaptive quizzing and our mobile, accessible Value Edition e-book in one easy-to-use, affordable product. See below for more information, visit the book's catalog site at **macmillanlearning.com**, or contact your local Bedford/St. Martin's sales representative.

Get the Right Version for Your Class

To accommodate different course lengths and course budgets, *Ways of the World* is available in several different versions and formats to best suit your course needs. The comprehensive *Ways of the World* includes a full-color art program and a robust set of features. Offered now for the first time, *Ways of the World*, Value Edition, offers a trade-sized two-color option with the full narrative and selected art and maps at a steep discount. The Value Edition is also offered at the lowest price point in loose-leaf format, and these versions are available as e-books. To get the best values of all, package a new print book with LaunchPad or Achieve Read & Practice at no additional charge to get the best each format offers. LaunchPad users get a print version for easy portability with an interactive e-book for the full-feature text and course space, along with LearningCurve and loads of additional assignment and assessment options; Achieve Read & Practice users get a print version with a mobile, interactive Value Edition e-book plus LearningCurve adaptive quizzing in one exceptionally affordable, easy-to-use product.

- **Combined Volume** (Chapters 1–23): available in paperback, Value, loose-leaf, and e-book formats and in LaunchPad and Achieve Read & Practice
- **Volume 1: To the Fifteenth Century** (Chapters 1–12): available in paperback, Value, loose-leaf, and e-book formats and in LaunchPad and Achieve Read & Practice
- **Volume 2: Since the Fifteenth Century** (Chapters 12–23): available in paperback, Value, loose-leaf, and e-book formats and in LaunchPad and Achieve Read & Practice

As noted below, any of these volumes can be packaged with additional titles for a discount. To get ISBNs for discount packages, visit **macmillanlearning.com** or contact your Bedford/St. Martin's representative.

LaunchPad
macmillan learning

Assign LaunchPad—an Assessment-Ready Interactive E-book and Course Space

Available for discount purchase on its own or for packaging with new books at no additional charge, LaunchPad is a breakthrough solution for history courses. Intuitive and easy to use for students and instructors alike, LaunchPad is ready to use as is and can be edited, customized with your own material, and assigned quickly. LaunchPad for *Ways of the World* includes Bedford/St. Martin's high-quality content all in one place, including the full interactive e-book and the companion reader *Thinking through Sources for Ways of the World*, plus LearningCurve adaptive quizzing, guided reading activities designed to help students read actively for key concepts, auto-graded quizzes for each primary source, and chapter summative quizzes. Through a wealth of formative and summative assessments, including the adaptive learning program of LearningCurve (see the full description ahead), students gain confidence and get into their reading before class. Through the Bedford Document Collections for World History (see full description ahead), embedded within LaunchPad, instructors get a flexible set of primary source projects ready to assign. These features, plus additional primary source documents, video sources and tools for making video assignments, map activities, flashcards, and customizable test banks, make LaunchPad an invaluable asset for any instructor.

LaunchPad easily integrates with course management systems, and with fast ways to build assignments, rearrange chapters, and add new pages, sections, or links, it lets teachers build the courses they want to teach and hold students accountable. For more information, visit **launchpadworks.com**, or to arrange a demo, contact us at **historymktg@macmillan.com**.

LearningCurve
macmillan learning

Assign LearningCurve So Your Students Come to Class Prepared

Students using LaunchPad or Achieve Read & Practice receive access to LearningCurve for *Ways of the World*. Assigning LearningCurve in place of reading quizzes is easy for instructors, and the reporting features help instructors track overall class trends and spot topics that are giving students trouble so they can adjust their lectures and class activities. This online learning tool is popular with students because it was designed to help them rehearse content at their own pace in a nonthreatening, game-like environment. The feedback for wrong answers provides instructional coaching and sends students back to the book for review. Students answer as many questions as necessary to reach a target score, with repeated chances to revisit material they haven't mastered. When Learning-Curve is assigned, students come to class better prepared.

Assign Achieve Read & Practice So Your Students Can Read and Study Wherever They Go

Available for discount purchase on its own or for packaging with new books at no additional charge, Achieve Read & Practice is Bedford/St. Martin's most affordable digital solution for history courses. Intuitive and easy to use for students and instructors alike, Achieve Read & Practice is ready to use as is and can be assigned quickly. Achieve Read & Practice for *Ways of the World* includes the Value Edition interactive e-book, LearningCurve formative quizzing, assignment tools, and a gradebook. All this is built with an intuitive interface that can be read on mobile devices and is fully accessible and available at a discounted price so anyone can use it. Instructors can set due dates for reading assignments and LearningCurve quizzes in just a few clicks, making it a simple and affordable way to engage students with the narrative and hold students accountable for course reading so they will come to class better prepared. For more information, visit **macmillanlearning.com/ReadandPractice**, or to arrange a demo, contact us at **historymktg@macmillan.com**.

▷ iClicker
iClicker, Active Learning Simplified

iClicker offers simple, flexible tools to help you give students a voice and facilitate active learning in the classroom. Students can participate with the devices they already bring to class using our iClicker Reef mobile apps (which work with smartphones, tablets, or laptops) or iClicker remotes. We've now integrated iClicker with Macmillan's LaunchPad to make it easier than ever to synchronize grades and promote engagement—both in and out of class. iClicker Reef access cards can also be packaged with LaunchPad or your textbook at a significant savings for your students. To learn more, talk to your Macmillan Learning representative or visit us at **www.iclicker.com**.

Take Advantage of Instructor Resources

Bedford/St. Martin's has developed a rich array of teaching resources for this book and for this course. They range from lecture and presentation materials and assessment tools to course management options. Most can be found in LaunchPad or can be downloaded or ordered at **macmillanlearning.com**.

Bedford Coursepack for Blackboard, Canvas, Brightspace by D2L, or Moodle. We can help you integrate our rich content into your course management system. Registered instructors can download coursepacks that include our popular free resources and book-specific content for *Ways of the World*. Visit **macmillanlearning.com** to find your version or download your coursepack.

Instructor's Resource Manual. The instructor's manual offers both experienced and first-time instructors tools for presenting textbook material in engaging ways. It includes content learning objectives, annotated chapter outlines, and strategies for teaching with the textbook, plus suggestions on how to get the most out of LearningCurve and a survival guide for first-time teaching assistants.

Guide to Changing Editions. Designed to facilitate an instructor's transition from the previous edition of *Ways of the World* to this new edition, this guide presents an overview of major changes as well as of changes in each chapter.

Online Test Bank. The test bank includes a mix of fresh, carefully crafted multiple-choice, matching, short-answer, and essay questions for each chapter. Many of the multiple-choice questions feature a map, an image, or a primary source excerpt as the prompt. All questions appear in Microsoft Word format and in easy-to-use test bank software that allows instructors to add, edit, re-sequence, filter by question type or learning objective, and print questions and answers. Instructors can also export questions into a variety of course management systems.

The Bedford Lecture Kit: *Lecture Outlines, Maps, and Images.* Look good and save time with *The Bedford Lecture Kit*. These presentation materials include fully customizable multimedia presentations built around chapter outlines that are embedded with maps, figures, and images from the textbook and are supplemented by more detailed instructor notes on key points and concepts.

Print, Digital, and Custom Options for More Choice and Value

For information on free packages and discounts up to 50%, visit **macmillanlearning .com**, or contact your local Bedford/St. Martin's sales representative.

NEW *Thinking through Sources for Ways of the World*, **Fourth Edition.** Designed to accompany *Ways of the World*, each chapter of this reader contains approximately five to eight written and visual primary sources organized around a particular theme, issue, or question. Each of these projects is followed by a related **Historians' Voices** secondary source feature that pairs two brief excerpts from historians who comment on some aspect of the topics covered in the primary sources. *Thinking through Sources for Ways of the World* provides a broad selection of over 140 primary source documents and images as well as editorial apparatus to help students understand the sources. This companion reader is an exceptional value for students and offers plenty of assignment options for instructors. Available free when packaged with the print text and included in the LaunchPad e-book with auto-graded quizzes for each source. In LaunchPad each chapter of the reader includes special primary source online activities—self-graded exercises that challenge students to assess whether a specific piece of evidence drawn from the sources supports or challenges a conclusion related to a guiding question. Also available on its own as a downloadable e-book.

NEW Bedford Select for History. Create the ideal textbook for your course with only the chapters you need. Starting from one of our Value Edition history texts, you can rearrange chapters, delete unnecessary chapters, select chapters of primary sources from *Thinking through Sources for Ways of the World* and add document projects from the Bedford Document Collections, or choose to improve your students' historical thinking skills with the Bedford Tutorials for History. In addition, you can add your own original content to create just the book you're looking for. With Bedford Select, students pay only for material that will be assigned in the course, and nothing more. Order your textbook every semester, or modify from one term to the next. It is easy to build your customized textbook, without compromising the quality and affordability you've come to expect from Bedford/St. Martin's.

NEW The Bedford Document Collections for World History. Found in the LaunchPad for *Ways of the World* and available to customize the print text, this collection provides a flexible repository of discovery-oriented primary source projects ready to assign. Each curated project—written by a historian about a favorite topic—poses a historical question and guides students through analysis of the sources. Examples include "The Silk Road: Travel and Trade in Pre-Modern Inner Asia," "The Spread of Christianity in the Sixteenth and Early Seventeenth Centuries," "The Singapore Mutiny of 1915: Understanding World War I from a Global Perspective," and "Living through Perestroika: The Soviet Union in Upheaval, 1985–1991." For more information, visit **macmillanlearning.com**.

NEW The Bedford Document Collections for World History Print Modules. Choose one or two document projects from the collection (see above) and add them in print to a Bedford/St. Martin's title, or select several to be bound together in a custom reader created specifically for your course. Either way, the modules are affordably priced. For more information, contact your Bedford/St. Martin's representative.

NEW Bedford Tutorials for History. Designed to customize textbooks with resources relevant to individual courses, this collection of brief units, each 16 pages long and loaded with examples, guides students through basic skills such as using historical evidence effectively, working with primary sources, taking effective notes, avoiding plagiarism and citing sources, and more. Up to two tutorials can be added to a Bedford/St. Martin's history survey title at no additional charge, freeing you to spend your class time focusing on content and interpretation. For more information, visit **macmillanlearning.com/historytutorials**.

The Bedford Series in History and Culture. More than 100 titles in this highly praised series combine first-rate scholarship, historical narrative, and important primary documents for undergraduate courses. Each book is brief, inexpensive, and focused on a specific topic or period. Recent titles in the series include *Apartheid in South Africa: A Brief History with Documents* by David M. Gordon; *Politics and Society in Japan's Meiji Restoration: A Brief History with Documents* by Anne Walthall and M. William Steele; and *The Congo Free State and the New Imperialism: A Brief History with Documents* by Kevin Grant. For a complete list of titles, visit **macmillan learning.com**. Package discounts are available.

Rand McNally Atlas of World History. This collection of almost 70 full-color maps illustrates the eras and civilizations in world history from the emergence of human societies to the present. Free when packaged.

The Bedford Glossary for World History. This handy supplement for the survey course gives students historically contextualized definitions for hundreds of terms—from *abolitionism* to *Zoroastrianism*—that they will encounter in lectures, reading, and exams. Free when packaged.

Trade Books. Titles published by sister companies Hill and Wang; Farrar, Straus and Giroux; Henry Holt and Company; St. Martin's Press; Picador; and Palgrave Macmillan are available at a 50% discount when packaged with Bedford/St. Martin's textbooks. For more information, visit **macmillanlearning.com/tradeup**.

A Pocket Guide to Writing in History. Updated to reflect changes made in the 2017 *Chicago Manual of Style* revision, this portable and affordable reference tool by Mary Lynn Rampolla provides reading, writing, and research advice useful to students in all history courses. Concise yet comprehensive advice on approaching typical history assignments, developing critical reading skills, writing effective history papers, conducting research, using and documenting sources, and avoiding plagiarism—enhanced with practical tips and examples throughout—has made this slim reference a best seller. Package discounts are available.

A Student's Guide to History. This complete guide to success in any history course provides the practical help students need to be successful. In addition to introducing students to the nature of the discipline, author Jules Benjamin teaches a wide range of skills, from preparing for exams to approaching common writing assignments, and explains the research and documentation process with plentiful examples. Package discounts are available.

Brief Contents

Contents

photo: © De Agostini Picture Library/AGF Fotostock

2 First Civilizations: Cities, States, and Unequal Societies 3500 B.C.E.–600 B.C.E.

PART 2

Continuity and Change in the Second-Wave Era

3 State and Empire in Eurasia / North Africa

4 Culture and Religion in Eurasia / North Africa 600 B.C.E.–600 C.E.   141

photo: © Peter M. Wilson/Alamy

photo: Martha Avery/Getty
Images

8 China and the World: East Asian Connections 600–1300   317

9 The Worlds of Islam: Afro-Eurasian Connections 600–1450

photo: From "Grandes Chroniques
de France," 1375–1379/
Bibliothèque Municipale, Castres,
France/Bridgeman Images

photo: Moghul court painting,
ca.1596/Pictures from History/
Bridgeman Images

photo: Illustration from the Padshahnama, ca. 1630–40/ Royal Collection/Royal Collection Trust © Her Majesty Queen Elizabeth II, 2017/Bridgeman Images

photo: Slave Merchant in
Gorée Island, Senegal, from
Encyclopédie des Voyages,
engraved by L. F. Labrousse,
1796/Bibliothèque des Arts
Decoratifs, Paris, France/Archives
Charmet/Bridgeman Images

photo: Gianni Dagli Orti/REX/ Shutterstock

---

photos: Musée de la Ville de
Paris, Musée Carnavalet, Paris,
France/© RMN-Grand Palais/Art
Resource, NY; Gianni Dagli Orti/
REX/Shutterstock

18 Colonial Encounters in Asia, Africa, and Oceania 1750–1950

19 Empires in Collision: Europe, the Middle East, and East Asia 1800–1900   827

Reversal of Fortune: China's Century of Crisis   828
    The Crisis Within ▪ Western Pressures ▪ The Failure of Conservative
    Modernization

The Ottoman Empire and the West in the Nineteenth Century   838
    "The Sick Man of Europe" ▪ Reform and Its Opponents ▪ Outcomes:
    Comparing China and the Ottoman Empire

The Japanese Difference: The Rise of a New East Asian Power   844
    The Tokugawa Background ▪ American Intrusion and the Meiji
    Restoration ▪ Modernization Japanese-Style ▪ Japan and the World

Reflections: Success and Failure in History   854

Second Thoughts   855
    What's the Significance? ▪ Big Picture Questions ▪ Next Steps: For
    Further Study

photo: From "Le Petit Journal,"
1898, lithograph by Henri Meyer
(1844–1899)/Private Collection/
Roger-Viollet, Paris, France/
Bridgeman Images

PART 6

The Long Twentieth Century 1900–PRESENT   866

1778   1943

20 Milestones of the Past Century: War and Revolution 1900–1950   873

photo: Library of Congress,
Prints and Photographs Division,
LC-USZC4-2119

21 Milestones of the Past Century: A Changing Global Landscape 1950–PRESENT

photo: "West Africa Awakes"
(gouache on paper) by Angus
McBride (1931–2007)/Look and
Learn (A & B Images)/Private
Collection/Bridgeman Images

22 Global Processes: Technology, Economy, and Society 1900–PRESENT   971

photo: Peter Langer/Design Pics/ UIG/Bridgeman Images

23 Global Processes: Demography, Culture, and the Environment 1900–PRESENT   1019

photo: Image created by Reto Stockli, Nazmi El Saleous, and Marit Jentoft-Nilsen, NASA GSFC

Maps

Features

CONTROVERSIES

HISTORIANS' VOICES

MAPPING HISTORY

SNAPSHOT

WORKING WITH EVIDENCE

ZOOMING IN

Working with Primary Sources

wo sets of primary sources accompany each chapter of *Ways of the World*. **Working with Evidence** collections appear at the end of each chapter in the book, while *Thinking through Sources* sets are available either as a print supplement or in LaunchPad—the interactive course space for this text. Both collections typically feature written sources, such as inscriptions, letters, diaries, law codes, official records, and sacred texts, alongside visual sources—paintings, sculptures, engravings, photographs, posters, cartoons, buildings, and artifacts. Both collections are followed by a pair of secondary sources—short extracts from the writings of modern historians, archeologists, and other scholars. Collectively these sources provide an opportunity for you to practice the work of historians in a kind of guided "history laboratory." In working with this evidence, you are "doing history," much as students conducting lab experiments in chemistry or biology courses are "doing science."

Since each feature explores a theme of a particular chapter, the chapter narrative itself provides a broad context for analyzing these sources. Furthermore, brief introductions to each feature and to each document or image offer more specific context or background information, while questions provide things to look for as you examine each source. Other more integrative questions offer a focus for using those sources together to probe larger historical issues. What follows are a few more specific suggestions for assessing these raw materials of history.

Working with Documents

Written sources or documents are the most common type of primary source that historians use. For example, a number of ancient religious texts are sampled in the Working with Evidence feature of Chapter 4, while the documents in Chapter 13 present ideas about political authority in Mughal India, France, and the Inca Empire.

Analysis of such documents usually begins with the basics:

- Who wrote the document?
- When and where was it written?
- What type of document is it (for example, a letter to a friend, a political decree, an exposition of a religious teaching)?

Sometimes the document itself will provide answers to these questions. On other occasions, you may need to rely on the introductions.

Once these basics have been established, a historian is then likely to consider several further questions that situate the document in its particular historical context:

- Why was the document written, for what audience, and under what circumstances?
- What point of view does it reflect? What other views or opinions is the document arguing against? Can you get a sense of the larger conversation in which this document is participating?

Inspiration and intention are crucial factors that shape the form and content of a source. For instance, one might examine a document differently depending on whether it was composed for a private or a public readership, or whether it was intended to be read by a small elite or a wider audience.

Still another level of analysis seeks to elicit useful information from the document.

- What material in the document is believable, and what is not?
- What might historians learn from this document?
- What can the document tell us about the individual who produced it and the society from which he or she came?

In all of this, historical imagination is essential. Informed by knowledge of the context and the content of the document, your imagination will help you read it through the eyes of its author and its audience. You should ask yourself: how might this document have been understood at the time it was written? But in using your imagination, you must take care not to read into the documents your own assumptions and understandings. It is a delicate balance, a kind of dance that historians constantly undertake. Even documents that contain material that historians find unbelievable can be useful, for we seek not only to know what actually happened in the past but also to grasp the world as the people who lived that past understood it. And so historians sometimes speak about reading documents "against the grain," looking for meanings that the author might not have intended to convey.

Working with Images

Visual sources derive from the material culture of the past—religious icons or paintings that add to our understanding of belief systems, a family portrait that provides insight into presentations of self in a particular time and place, a building or sculpture that reveals how power and authority were displayed in a specific empire. These kinds of evidence represent another category of primary source material that historians can use to re-create and understand the past. But such visual sources can be even more difficult to interpret than written documents. The ideas that animated the creators of particular images or artifacts are often not obvious. Nor are the meanings they conveyed to those who viewed or used them. The lovely images from the ancient Indus River valley civilization contained in the Working with Evidence feature for Chapter 2, for example, remain enigmatic although still engaging to twenty-first-century viewers. Propaganda posters, frequently used in the source features for Volume 2, convey vividly how various groups or governments understood their own times. Despite the difficulties of interpretation, visual sources can provide insights not offered by written documents.

To use visual sources, we must try as best we can to see these pieces of evidence through the eyes of the societies that produced them and to decode the symbols and other features that imbue them with meaning. Thus context is, if anything, even more crucial for analyzing visual evidence than it is for documents. For example, understanding artistic depictions from the life of Muhammad, featured in Chapter 9, depends heavily on some knowledge of Islamic history and culture. A set of basic questions, similar to those you would ask about a written document, provides a starting point for analyzing visual sources:

- When and where was the image or artifact created?
- Who made the image or artifact? Who paid for or commissioned it? For what audience(s) was it intended?
- Where was the image or artifact originally displayed or used?

Having established this basic information about the image or artifact, you may simply want to describe it, as if to someone who had never seen it before.

- If the source is an image, who or what is depicted? What activities are shown? How might you describe the positioning of figures, their clothing, hairstyles, and other visual cues?
- If the source is an object or building, how would you describe its major features?

Finally, you will want to take a stab at more interpretive issues, making use of what you know about the context in which the visual source was created.

- What likely purpose or function did the image or artifact serve?
- What message(s) does it seek to convey?

- How could it be interpreted differently depending on who viewed or used it?
- What are the meanings of any symbols or other abstract features in the visual source?
- What can the image or artifact tell us about the society that produced it and the time period in which it was created?

Beyond analyzing particular sources, you will be invited to draw conclusions from sets of related sources—both visual and written—that address a central theme in the chapter. What can you learn, for example, about the life of Chinese elites from the sources in Chapter 8? And what do the images and documents in the Working with Evidence feature of Chapter 15 disclose about the reception of Christianity in various cultural settings?

Alongside these primary sources, the **Historians' Voices** features offer you the opportunity to consider how contemporary scholars make historical arguments and draw sound conclusions. While primary sources—documentary and visual alike—are the foundation for all historical accounts, students and scholars gain further perspective from reading the analysis of modern experts who use their deep knowledge of the sources to examine and explain the past. Immersing yourself in documents, images, and the writings of modern scholars allows you to catch a glimpse of the messiness, the ambiguity, the heartaches, and the achievements of history as it was lived and as it has been recorded.

Using these sources effectively, however, is no easy task. In fact, the work of historians might well be compared with that of Sisyphus, the ancient Greek king who, having offended the gods, was condemned to eternally roll a large rock up a mountain, only to have it ceaselessly fall back down. Like Sisyphus, historians work at a mission that can never be completely successful—to recapture the past before it is lost forever in the mists of time and fading memory. The evidence available is always partial and fragmentary. Historians and students of history alike are limited and fallible, for we operate often at a great distance—in both time and culture—from those we are studying. And we rarely agree on important matters, divided as we are by sex, nationality, religion, race, and values, all of which shape our understandings of the past.

Despite these challenges, scholars and students have long found their revisiting of the past a compelling project—intensely interesting, personally meaningful, and even fun—particularly when working with "primary" or "original" sources, which are the building blocks of all historical accounts. Such sources are windows into the lives of our ancestors, though these windows are often smudged and foggy. We hope that working with the evidence contained in these sources will enrich your own life as you listen in on multiple conversations from the past, eavesdropping, as it were, on our ancestors.

Prologue
From Cosmic History to Human History

History books in general, and world history textbooks in particular, share something in common with those Russian nested dolls in which a series of carved figures fit inside one another. In much the same fashion, all historical accounts take place within some larger context, as stories within stories unfold. Individual biographies and histories of local communities, particularly modern ones, occur within the context of one nation or another. Nations often find a place in some more encompassing civilization, such as the Islamic world or the West, or in a regional or continental context such as Southeast Asia, Latin America, or Africa. And those civilizational or regional histories in turn take on richer meaning when they are understood within the even broader story of world history, which embraces humankind as a whole.

In recent decades, some world historians have begun to situate that remarkable story of the human journey in the much larger framework of both cosmic and planetary history, an approach that has come to be called "big history." It is really the "history of everything" from the big bang to the present, and it extends over the enormous, almost unimaginable timescale of some 13.8 billion years, the current rough estimate of the age of the universe.[1]

The History of the Universe

To make this vast expanse of time even remotely comprehensible, some scholars have depicted the history of the cosmos as if it were a single calendar year (see Snapshot). On that cosmic calendar, most of the action took place in the first few milliseconds of January 1. As astronomers, physicists, and chemists tell it, the universe that we know began in an eruption of inconceivable power and heat. Out of that explosion of creation emerged matter, energy, gravity, electromagnetism, and the "strong" and "weak" forces that govern the behavior of atomic nuclei. As gravity pulled the rapidly expanding cosmic gases into increasingly dense masses, stars formed, with the first ones lighting up around 1 to 2 billion years after the big bang, or the end of January to mid-February on the cosmic calendar.

Hundreds of billions of stars followed, each with its own history, though following common patterns. They emerge, flourish for a time, and then collapse and die. In their final stages, they sometimes generate supernovae, black holes, and pulsars—phenomena at least as fantastic as the most exotic of earlier creation stories. Within the stars, enormous nuclear reactions gave rise to the elements that are reflected in the periodic table known to all students of chemistry. Over eons, these stars came together in galaxies, such as our own Milky Way, which probably emerged in March or early April, and in even larger structures called groups, clusters, and superclusters. Adding to the strangeness of our picture of the cosmos is the recent and controversial notion that perhaps 90 percent or more of the total mass of the universe is invisible to us, consisting of a mysterious and mathematically predicted substance known to scholars only as "dark matter."

The contemplation of cosmic history has prompted profound religious or philosophical questions about the meaning of human life. For some, it has engendered a sense of great insignificance in the face of cosmic vastness. In disputing the earth- and human-centered view of the cosmos, long held by the Catholic Church, the eighteenth-century French thinker Voltaire wrote: "This little globe, nothing more than a point, rolls in space like so many other globes; we are lost in this immensity."[2] Nonetheless, human consciousness and our awareness of the mystery of this immeasurable

SNAPSHOT The History of the Universe as a Cosmic Calendar

Big bang	January 1	13.7 billion years ago
Stars and galaxies begin to form	End of January / mid-February	12 billion years ago
Milky Way galaxy forms	March / early April	10 billion years ago
Origin of the solar system	September 9	4.7 billion years ago
Formation of the earth	September 15	4.5 billion years ago
Earliest life on earth	Late September / early October	4 billion years ago
Oxygen forms on earth	December 1	1.3 billion years ago
First worms	December 16	658 million years ago
First fish, first vertebrates	December 19	534 million years ago
First reptiles, first trees	December 23	370 million years ago
Age of dinosaurs	December 24–28	66 to 240 million years ago
First human-like creatures	December 31 (late evening)	2.7 million years ago
First agriculture	December 31: 11:59:35	12,000 years ago
Birth of the Buddha / Greek civilization	December 31: 11:59:55	2,500 years ago
Birth of Jesus	December 31: 11:59:56	2,000 years ago

Adapted from Carl Sagan, *The Dragons of Eden* (New York: Random House, 1977), 13–17.

universe render us unique and generate for many people feelings of awe, gratitude, and humility that are almost religious. As tiny but knowing observers of this majestic cosmos, we have found ourselves living in a grander home than ever we knew before.

The History of a Planet

For most of us, one star, our own sun, is far more important than all the others, despite its quite ordinary standing among the billions of stars in the universe and its somewhat remote location on the outer edge of the Milky Way galaxy. Circling that star is a series of planets, formed of leftover materials from the sun's birth. One of those planets, the third from the sun and the fifth largest, is home to all of us. Human history—our history—takes place not only on the earth but also as part of the planet's history.

That history began with the emergence of the entire solar system about two-thirds of the way through the history of the universe, some 4.7 billion years ago, or early September on the cosmic calendar. Geologists have learned a great deal about the history of the earth: the formation of its rocks and atmosphere; the movement of its continents; the collision of the tectonic plates that make up its crust; and the constant changes of its landscape as mountains formed, volcanoes erupted, and erosion transformed the surface of the planet. All of this has been happening for more than 4 billion years and continues still.

The most remarkable feature of the earth's history—and so far as we know unrepeated elsewhere—was the emergence of life from the chemical soup of the early planet. It happened rather quickly, only about 600 million years after the earth itself took shape, or late September on the cosmic calendar. Then for some 3 billion years, life remained at the level of microscopic single-celled organisms. According to biologists, the many species of larger multicelled creatures—all of the flowers, shrubs, and trees as well as all of the animals of land, sea, and air—have evolved in an explosive proliferation of life-forms over the past 600 million years, or since mid-December on the cosmic calendar. The history of life on earth has, however, been periodically punctuated by massive die-offs, at least five of them, in which very large numbers of animal or plant species have perished. The most widespread of these "extinction events," known to scholars as the Permian mass extinction, occurred around 250 million years ago and eliminated some 96 percent of living species on the planet. That catastrophic diminution of life-forms on the earth has been associated with massive volcanic eruptions, the release of huge quantities of carbon dioxide and methane into the atmosphere, and a degree of global warming that came close to extinguishing all life on the planet. Much later, around 66 million years ago, another such extinction event decimated about 75 percent of plant and animal species, including what was left of the dinosaurs. Most scientists now believe that it was caused primarily by the impact of a huge asteroid that landed near the Yucatán Peninsula off the coast of southern Mexico, generating enormous earthquakes, tsunamis, fireballs, and a cloud of toxic dust and debris. Many scholars believe we are currently in the midst of a sixth extinction event, driven, like the others, by major climate change, but which, unlike the others, is the product of human actions.

So life on earth has been and remains both fragile and resilient. Within these conditions, every species has had a history as its members struggled to find resources, cope with changing environments, and deal with competitors. Egocentric creatures that we are, however, human beings have usually focused their history books and history courses entirely on a single species—our own, *Homo sapiens*, humankind. On the cosmic calendar, *Homo sapiens* is an upstart primate whose entire history occurred in the last few minutes of December 31. Almost all of what we normally study in history courses—agriculture, writing, civilizations, empires, industrialization—took place in the very last minute of that cosmic year. The entire history of the United States occurred in the last second.

Yet during that very brief time, humankind has had a career more remarkable and arguably more consequential for the planet than any other species. At the heart of human uniqueness lies our amazing capacity for accumulating knowledge and skills. Other animals learn, of course, but for the most part they learn the same things over and over again. Twenty-first-century chimpanzees in the wild master much the same set of skills as their ancestors did a million years ago. But the exceptional communication abilities provided by human language allow us to learn from one another, to express that learning in abstract symbols, and then to pass it on, cumulatively, to future generations. Thus we have moved from stone axes to lasers, from spears to nuclear weapons, from "talking drums" to the Internet, from grass huts to the pyramids of Egypt, the Taj Mahal of India, and the skyscrapers of modern cities.

This extraordinary ability has translated into a human impact on the earth that is unprecedented among all living species.[3] Human populations have multiplied far more extensively and have come to occupy a far greater range of environments than has any other large animal. Through our ingenious technologies, we have appropriated for ourselves, according to recent calculations, some 25 to 40 percent of the solar energy that enters the food chain. We have recently gained access to the stored solar energy of coal, gas, and oil, all of which have been many millions of years in the making, and we have the capacity to deplete these resources in a few hundred or a few thousand years. Other forms of life have felt the impact of human activity, as numerous extinct or threatened species testify. Human beings have even affected the atmosphere and the oceans as carbon dioxide and other emissions of the industrial age have warmed the climate of the planet in ways that broadly resemble the conditions that triggered earlier extinction events. Thus human history has been, and remains, of great significance, not for ourselves alone, but also for the earth itself and for the many other living creatures with which we share it.

The History of the Human Species . . . in a Single Paragraph

The history of our species has occurred during roughly the last 200,000–300,000 years, conventionally divided into three major phases, based on the kind of technology that was most widely practiced. The enormously long Paleolithic age, with its gathering and hunting way of life, accounts for 95 percent or more of the time that humans have occupied the planet. People utilizing a stone-age Paleolithic technology initially settled every major landmass on the earth and constructed the first human societies (see Chapter 1). Then beginning about 12,000 years ago with the first Agricultural Revolution, the domestication of plants and animals increasingly became the primary means of sustaining human life and societies. In giving rise to agricultural villages and chiefdoms, to pastoral communities depending on their herds of animals, and to state- and city-based civilizations, this agrarian way of life changed virtually everything and fundamentally reshaped human societies and their relationship to the natural order. Finally, around 1750 a quite sudden spurt in the rate of technological change, which we know as the Industrial Revolution, began to take hold. That vast increase in productivity, wealth, and human control over nature once again transformed almost every aspect of human life and gave rise to new kinds of societies that we call "modern."

Here then, in a single paragraph, is the history of humankind—the Paleolithic era, the agricultural era, and, most recently and briefly, the modern industrial era. Clearly this is a big picture perspective, based on the notion that the human species as a whole has a history that transcends any of its particular and distinctive cultures. That perspective—known variously as planetary, global, or world history—has become increasingly prominent among those who study the past. Why should this be so?

Why World History?

Not long ago—in the mid-twentieth century, for example—virtually all college-level history courses were organized in terms of particular civilizations or nations. In the United States, courses such as Western Civilization or some version of American History served to introduce students to the study of the past. Since then, however, a set of profound changes has pushed much of the historical profession in a different direction.

The world wars of the twentieth century, revealing as they did the horrendous consequences of unchecked nationalism, persuaded some historians that a broader view of the past might contribute to a sense of global citizenship. Economic and cultural globalization has highlighted both the interdependence of the world's peoples and their very unequal positions within that world. Moreover, we are aware as never before that our problems—whether they involve economic well-being, global warming, disease, or terrorism—respect no national boundaries. To many thoughtful people, a global present seemed to call for a global past. Furthermore, as colonial empires shrank and new nations asserted themselves on the world stage, these peoples also insisted that their histories be accorded equivalent treatment with those of Europe and North America. An explosion of new knowledge about the histories of Asia, Africa, and pre-Columbian America erupted from the research of scholars around the world. All of this has generated a "world history movement," reflected in college and high school curricula, in numerous conferences and specialized studies, and in a proliferation of textbooks, of which this is one.

This world history movement has attempted to create a global understanding of the human past that highlights broad patterns cutting across particular civilizations and countries, while acknowledging in an inclusive fashion the distinctive histories of its many peoples. This is, to put it mildly, a tall order. How is it possible to encompass within a single book or course the separate stories of the world's various peoples? Surely it must be something more than just recounting the history of one civilization or culture after another. How can we distill a common history of humankind as a whole from the distinct trajectories of particular peoples? Because no world history book or course can cover everything, what criteria should we use for deciding what to include and what to leave out? Such questions have ensured no end of controversy among students, teachers, and scholars of world history, making it one of the most exciting fields of historical inquiry.

Context, Change, Comparison, and Connection: The Four Cs of World History

Despite much debate and argument, most scholars and teachers of world history would probably agree on four major emphases of this remarkable field of study. The first lies in the observation that in world history, nothing stands alone. Every event, every historical figure, every culture, society, or civilization gains significance from its inclusion in some larger framework. This means that **context** is central to world history and that contextual thinking is the essential skill that world history teaches. And so we ask the same question about every particular occurrence: where does it fit in the larger scheme of things?

A second common theme in world history involves **change** over time. Most often, it is the "big picture" changes—those that affect large segments of humankind—that are of greatest interest. How did the transition from a gathering and hunting economy to one based on agriculture take place? How did cities, empires, and civilizations take shape in various parts of the world? What impact did the growing prominence of Europe have on the rest of the world in recent centuries? A focus on change provides an antidote to a persistent tendency of human thinking that historians call "essentialism." A more common term is "stereotyping." It refers to our inclination to define particular groups of people with an unchanging or essential set of characteristics. Women are nurturing; peasants are conservative; Americans are aggressive; Hindus are religious. Serious students of history soon become aware that every significant category of people contains endless divisions and conflicts and that those human communities are constantly in flux. Peasants may often accept the status quo, except of course when they rebel, as they frequently have. Americans have experienced periods of isolationism and withdrawal from the world as well as times of aggressive engagement with it. Things change.

But some things persist, even if they also change. We should not allow an emphasis on change to blind us to the continuities of human experience.

A recognizably Chinese state has operated for more than 2,000 years. Slavery and patriarchy persisted as human institutions for thousands of years until they were challenged in recent centuries, and in various forms they exist still. The teachings of Buddhism, Christianity, and Islam have endured for centuries, though with endless variations and transformations.

A third element that operates constantly in world history books and courses is that of **comparison**. Whatever else it may be, world history is a comparative discipline, seeking to identify similarities and differences in the experience of the world's peoples. What is the difference between the development of agriculture in the Middle East and in Mesoamerica? Was the experience of women largely the same in all patriarchal societies? Why did the Industrial Revolution and a modern way of life evolve first in Western Europe rather than somewhere else? What distinguished the French, Russian, and Chinese revolutions from one another? Describing and, if possible, explaining such similarities and differences are among the major tasks of world history. Comparison has proven an effective tool in efforts to counteract Eurocentrism, the notion that Europeans or people of European descent have long been the primary movers and shakers of the historical process. That notion arose in recent centuries when Europeans were in fact the major source of innovation in the world and did for a time exercise something close to world domination. But comparative world history sets this recent European prominence in a global and historical context, helping us to sort out what was distinctive about the development of Europe and what similarities it bore to other major regions of the world. Puncturing the pretensions of Eurocentrism has been high on the agenda of world history.

A fourth emphasis within world history, and in this book, involves the interactions, encounters, and **connections** among different and often distant peoples. Focusing on cross-cultural connections—whether those of conflict or more peaceful exchange—represents an effort to counteract a habit of thinking about particular peoples, states, or cultures as self-contained or isolated communities. Despite the historical emergence of many separate and distinct societies, none of them developed alone. Each was embedded in a network of relationships with both near and more distant peoples.

Moreover, these cross-cultural connections did not begin with Columbus. The Chinese, for example, interacted continuously with the nomadic peoples on their northern border; generated technologies that diffused across all of Eurasia; transmitted elements of their culture to Japan, Korea, and Vietnam; and assimilated a foreign religious tradition, Buddhism, that had originated in India. Though clearly distinctive, China was not a self-contained or isolated civilization. Thus world history remains always alert to the networks, webs, and encounters in which particular civilizations or peoples were enmeshed.

Context, change, comparison, and connection—all of them operating on a global scale—represent various ways of bringing some coherence to the multiple and complex stories of world history. They will recur repeatedly in the pages that follow.

A final observation about this account of world history: *Ways of the World*, like all other world history textbooks, is radically unbalanced in terms of coverage. Chapter 1, for example, takes on some 95 percent of the human story, well over 200,000 years of our history. By contrast, the last century alone occupies four entire chapters. In fact, the six major sections of the book deal with progressively shorter time periods, in progressively greater detail. This imbalance owes much to the relative scarcity of information about earlier periods of our history. But it also reflects a certain "present mindedness," for we look to history, always, to make sense of our current needs and circumstances. And in doing so, we often assume that more recent events have a greater significance for our own lives in the here and now than those that occurred in more distant times. Whether you agree with this assumption or not, you will have occasion to ponder it as you consider the many and various "ways of the world" that have emerged in the course of the human journey and as you contemplate their relevance for your own journey.

Ways of the World

A Brief Global History with Sources

PART 1

First Things First:
Beginnings in History

to 600 B.C.E.

THE BIG PICTURE

Turning Points in Early World History

Human beings have long been inveterate storytellers, and so too are contemporary historians. They tell stories about individuals, communities, nations, civilizations, and, in the case of world history, about humankind as a whole. All tellers of stories—ancient and modern alike—have to decide where to begin their accounts and what major turning points in those narratives to highlight. For world historians seeking to tell the story of "all under Heaven," as the Chinese put it, four major "beginnings," each of them an extended historical process, have marked the initial stages of the human journey.

The Emergence of Humankind

The first large-scale process in the human story lies in biological evolution. According to archeologists and anthropologists, the evolutionary line of descent leading to *Homo sapiens* separated from that of chimpanzees, our closest primate relatives, some 5 to 6 million years ago, and it happened in eastern and southern Africa. There, perhaps twenty or thirty different species emerged, all of them members of the Homininae (or hominid) family of human-like creatures. What they all shared was bipedalism, the ability to walk upright on two legs. Over time, these hominid species changed. Their brains grew larger; they began to make and use simple stone tools; some started to eat meat, at least occasionally; eventually they learned to control fire. By 1 million years ago, some hominid species, especially *Homo erectus*, began to migrate out of Africa, and their remains have been found in various parts of Eurasia.

But all of these earlier hominid species finally died out, except one: *Homo sapiens*, ourselves. With a remarkable capacity for symbolic language that permitted the accumulation and transmission of learning, our species too appeared first in Africa and quite recently, probably no more than 250,000 years ago. For a long time, all of the small number of *Homo sapiens* lived in Africa, but sometime after 100,000 years ago, they too began to migrate out of Africa onto the Eurasian landmass, then to Australia, and ultimately into the Western Hemisphere and the Pacific islands.

The Globalization of Humankind

This amazing journey represents the second major turning point in the human story. Our ancient ancestors—small in stature, not fast on foot, and armed with a very limited technology of stone tools—were able to adapt to almost every environmental setting on the planet. The phase of human history during which these initial migrations took place is known to scholars as the Paleolithic era. The word "Paleolithic" literally means the "old stone age," but it refers more generally to a gathering, hunting, and fishing way of life, before agriculture allowed people to grow crops or raise animals deliberately. Lasting until roughly 12,000 years ago, and in many places much longer, the Paleolithic era represents over 95 percent of the time that human beings have inhabited the earth. Although often neglected by historians and history textbooks, this long period of the human experience merits greater attention and is the focus of the initial sections of Chapter 1.

The Revolution of Farming and Herding

Then, a third process began to completely reshape the human experience. Around 12,000 years ago, human communities in parts of the Middle East, Asia, Africa, and the Americas began the laborious process of domesticating animals and selecting seeds to be planted. This momentous accomplishment, often called the Agricultural Revolution, surely marks the single most significant and enduring transformation of our history. Now our species learned to exploit and manipulate particular organisms, both plant and animal. Farming and raising animals allowed for a substantial increase in human numbers and over many centuries generated a profound transformation of the environment. Forests were felled, arid lands irrigated, meadows plowed, and mountains terraced. Increasingly, the landscape reflected human intentions and actions.

The Turning Point of Civilization

The most prominent and powerful human communities to emerge from this Agricultural Revolution were those often designated as "civilizations," more complex societies that were based in bustling cities and governed by formal states. Their emergence in Eurasia, Africa, and the Americas marked the fourth major transformation in human history. Because almost all of the world's people now live in such societies, states and cities have come to seem almost natural. In world history terms, however, their appearance is quite recent. Not until several thousand years *after* the beginning of agriculture did the first cities and states emerge, around 3500 B.C.E. Well after 1000 C.E., substantial numbers of people still lived in communities without any state or urban structures. Nonetheless, people living in state- and city-based societies or civilizations have long constituted the most powerful and innovative human communities on the planet. They have given rise to empires of increasing size, enduring cultural and religious traditions, new technologies, sharper

class and gender inequalities, new conceptions of masculinity and femininity, and large-scale warfare. The earliest of these civilizations provide the focus of Chapter 2.

Time and World History

Reckoning time is central to all historical study, for history is essentially the story of change over time. Recently it has become standard in the Western world to refer to dates prior to the birth of Christ as B.C.E. (before the Common Era), replacing the earlier B.C. (before Christ) usage. This convention is an effort to become less Christian-centered and Eurocentric in our use of language, although the chronology remains linked to the birth of Jesus. Similarly, the time following the birth of Christ is referred to as C.E. (the Common Era) rather than A.D. (*Anno Domini*, Latin for "year of the Lord"). Dates in the more distant past are designated in this book as B.P. (before the present), or simply as so many "years ago." Of course, these conventions are only some of the many ways that human societies have charted time, and they reflect the global dominance of Europeans in recent centuries. But the Chinese frequently dated important events in terms of the reign of particular emperors, while Muslims created a new calendar beginning with Year 1, marking Muhammad's forced relocation from Mecca to Medina in 622 C.E. As with so much else, the ways we represent change over time reflect the cultures in which we have been born and the historical experience of our societies.

World history frequently deals with very long periods of time, often encompassing many millennia or centuries in a single paragraph or even in a single sentence. This panoramic perspective provides context, a big picture framework in which we can situate particular events, societies, and individual experiences. Doing so allows us to discern patterns and trends that may be invisible from the viewpoint of a local community, a single nation, or one civilization. In the narrative that follows, there will be plenty of particulars — events, places, people — but always embedded in some larger setting that heightens their significance.

	27,000	26,000	25,000	24,000	23,000	22,000	21,000	20,000	19,000	18,000	17,000	16,000	15,000

AFRICA

◄ **250,000–200,000** Emergence of *Homo Sapiens*

◄ **100,000–70,000** Earliest evidence of human symbolic behavior

◄ **100,000–60,000** Human migration out of Africa into Eurasia

EURASIA

◄ **70,000** Human entry into Asia

◄ **45,000** Human entry into Europe

◄ **35,000** Earliest female figurines from Germany

◄───

33,000–15,000 Paleolithic cave art in Europe

■ **25,000** Extinction of Neanderthals

THE AMERICAS AND PACIFIC OCEANIA

◄ **60,000–40,000** Human entry into Australia

◄ **30,000** Extinction of large mammals in Australia

◄───

30,000–15,000 Human entry into the Americas

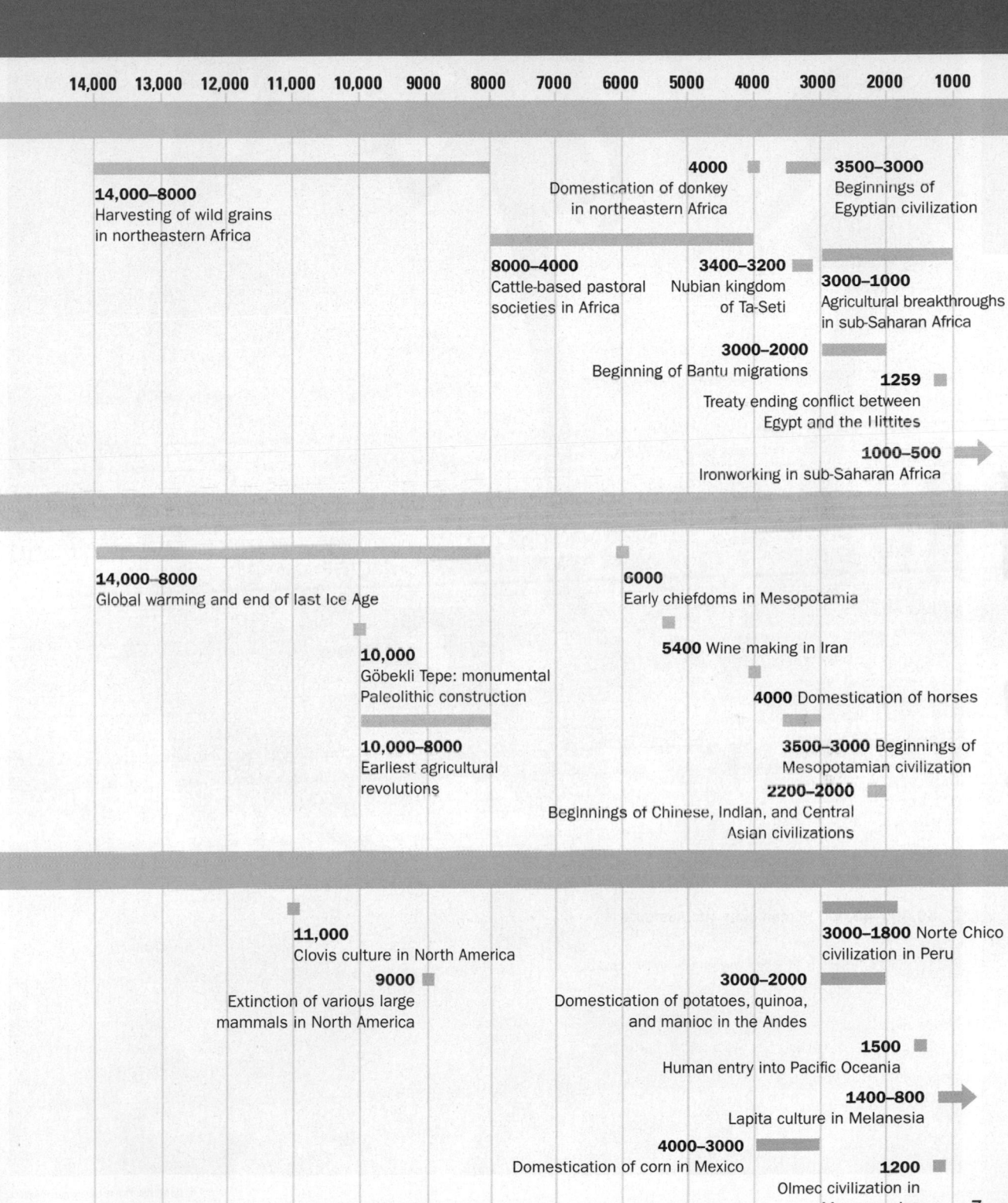

14,000 13,000 12,000 11,000 10,000 9000 8000 7000 6000 5000 4000 3000 2000 1000

14,000–8000
Harvesting of wild grains
in northeastern Africa

4000
Domestication of donkey
in northeastern Africa

3500–3000
Beginnings of
Egyptian civilization

8000–4000
Cattle-based pastoral
societies in Africa

3400–3200
Nubian kingdom
of Ta-Seti

3000–1000
Agricultural breakthroughs
in sub-Saharan Africa

3000–2000
Beginning of Bantu migrations

1259
Treaty ending conflict between
Egypt and the Hittites

1000–500
Ironworking in sub-Saharan Africa

14,000–8000
Global warming and end of last Ice Age

6000
Early chiefdoms in Mesopotamia

10,000
Göbekli Tepe: monumental
Paleolithic construction

5400 Wine making in Iran

4000 Domestication of horses

10,000–8000
Earliest agricultural
revolutions

3500–3000 Beginnings of
Mesopotamian civilization

2200–2000
Beginnings of Chinese, Indian, and Central
Asian civilizations

11,000
Clovis culture in North America

3000–1800 Norte Chico
civilization in Peru

9000
Extinction of various large
mammals in North America

3000–2000
Domestication of potatoes, quinoa,
and manioc in the Andes

1500
Human entry into Pacific Oceania

1400–800
Lapita culture in Melanesia

4000–3000
Domestication of corn in Mexico

1200
Olmec civilization in
Mesoamerica

7

1

First Peoples;
First Farmers

Most of History in a Single Chapter

to 3500 B.C.E.

"We do not want cattle, just wild animals to hunt and water that we can drink."[1] That was the view of Gudo Mahiya, a prominent member of the Hadza people of northern Tanzania, when he was questioned in 1997 about his interest in a settled life of farming and cattle raising. The Hadza represent one of the very last peoples on earth to continue a way of life that was universal among humankind until 10,000 to 12,000 years ago. In 2014, only about 1,300 Hadza survived, and of these just several hundred still made a living by hunting game, collecting honey, digging up roots, and gathering berries and fruit. Almost certainly, Gudo Mahiya's way of life is doomed, as farmers, cattle herders, governments, missionaries, and now tourists push the Hadza toward extinction. The likely disappearance of the Hadza people and their culture is among the final chapters of a very long story in which gathering, hunting, and fishing peoples have been unsuccessfully on the defensive against more numerous and powerful neighbors for 10,000 years. ∎

N onetheless, that way of life sustained humankind for more than 95 percent of our time on the earth. During countless centuries, human beings successfully adapted to a wide variety of environments without benefit of deliberate farming or animal husbandry. Instead, our early ancestors wrested a livelihood by gathering wild foods such as berries, nuts, roots, and grain; by scavenging dead animals; by hunting live animals; and by fishing. Known to scholars as "gathering and hunting" peoples, they were foragers or food collectors

《 Paleolithic Art The rock art of gathering and hunting peoples has been found in Africa, Europe, Australia, and elsewhere. This image from the San people of southern Africa represents aspects of their outer life in the form of wild animals and hunters with bows as well as the inner life of their shamans during a trance, reflected in the elongated figures with both human and animal features.

rather than food producers. Because they used stone rather than metal tools, they also have been labeled Paleolithic, or Old Stone Age, peoples.

Then, around 12,000 years ago, an enormous transformation began to unfold as a few human societies—in Eurasia, Africa, and the Americas alike—started to practice the deliberate cultivation of plants and the domestication of animals. This Agricultural or **Neolithic** (New Stone Age) **Revolution** marked a technological breakthrough of immense significance, with implications for every aspect of human life. This chapter, dealing with the long **Paleolithic era** and the initial transition to an agricultural way of life, represents most of human history—everything, in fact, before the advent of urban-based civilizations, which began only 5,500 years ago.

And yet history courses and history books often neglect this long phase of the human journey and instead choose to begin the story with the early civilizations of Egypt, Mesopotamia, China, and elsewhere. Some historians identify "real history" with writing and so dismiss the Paleolithic and Neolithic eras as largely unknowable because their peoples did not write. (See Controversies: Debating the Timescales of History, page 12.) Others, impressed with the rapid pace of change in human affairs in more recent times, assume that nothing much of real significance happened during the long Paleolithic era—and that no change meant no history.

But does it make sense to ignore the first 200,000 years or more of human experience? The achievements of Paleolithic peoples—the initial settlement of the planet, the creation of the earliest human societies, the beginnings of reflection on the great questions of life and death—surely deserve our attention. And the breakthrough to agriculture arguably represents the single most profound transformation of human life in all of history. Our grasp of the human past is incomplete—massively so—if we choose to disregard the Paleolithic and Neolithic eras.

SEEKING THE MAIN POINT

What arguments does this chapter make for paying serious attention to human history before the coming of "civilization"?

Out of Africa: First Migrations

The first 150,000 years or more of human experience was an exclusively African story. Around 200,000 to 250,000 years ago, in the grasslands of eastern and southern Africa, *Homo sapiens* first emerged, following in the footsteps of many other hominid or human-like species before it. Time and climate have erased much of the record of these early people, and Africa has witnessed much less archeological research than other parts of the world. Nonetheless, scholars have turned up evidence of distinctly human behavior in Africa long before its appearance elsewhere. Africa, almost certainly, was the place where the "human revolution" occurred, where "culture," defined as learned or invented ways of living, became more important than biology in shaping behavior.

What kinds of uniquely human activity show up in the early African record?[2] In the first place, our ancient African ancestors began to create new technologies as stone blades and points fastened to shafts replaced the earlier hand axes; tools made

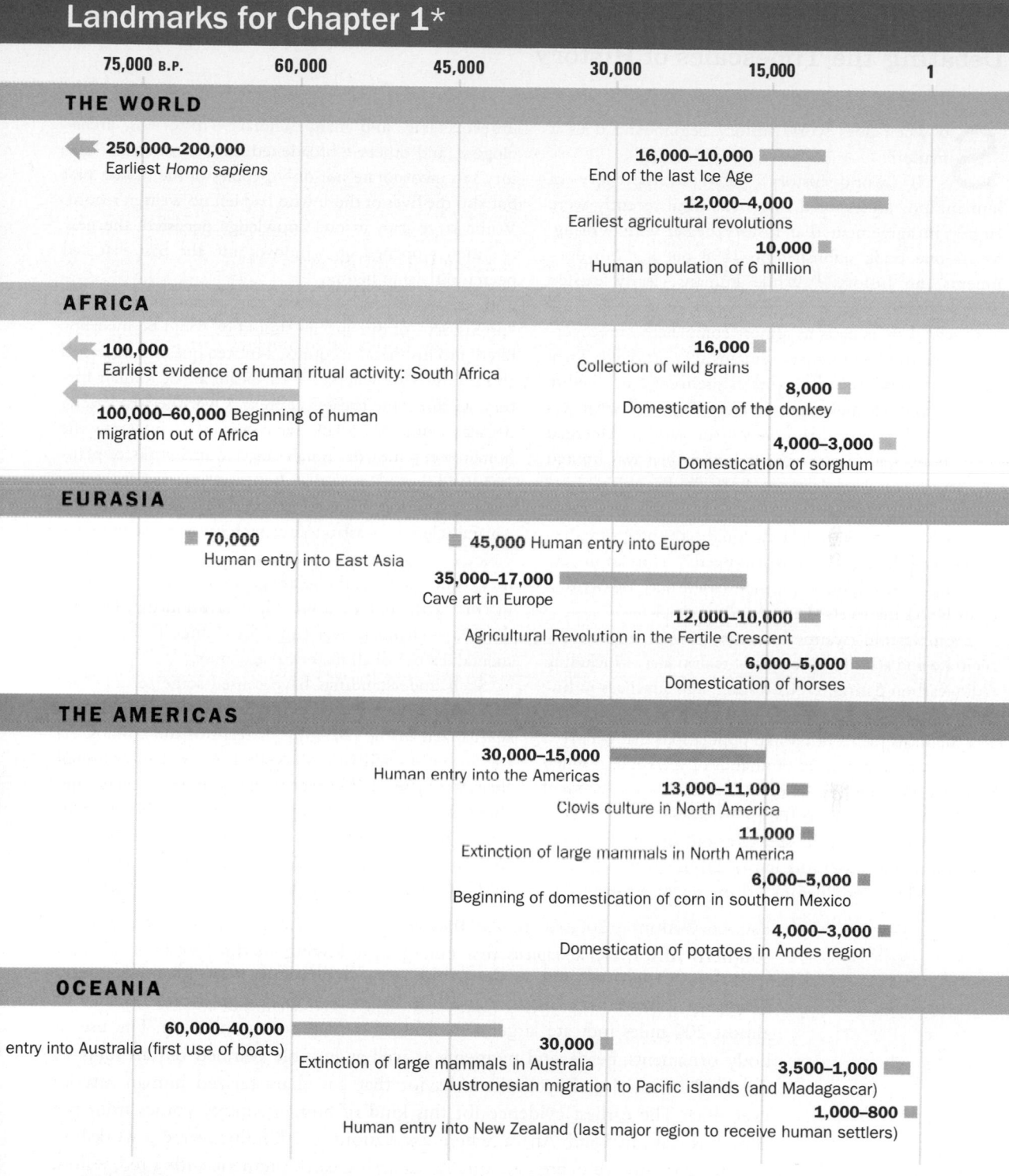

Landmarks for Chapter 1*

| | 75,000 B.P. | 60,000 | 45,000 | 30,000 | 15,000 | 1 |

THE WORLD

250,000–200,000
Earliest *Homo sapiens*

16,000–10,000
End of the last Ice Age

12,000–4,000
Earliest agricultural revolutions

10,000
Human population of 6 million

AFRICA

100,000
Earliest evidence of human ritual activity: South Africa

100,000–60,000 Beginning of human migration out of Africa

16,000
Collection of wild grains

8,000
Domestication of the donkey

4,000–3,000
Domestication of sorghum

EURASIA

70,000
Human entry into East Asia

45,000 Human entry into Europe

35,000–17,000
Cave art in Europe

12,000–10,000
Agricultural Revolution in the Fertile Crescent

6,000–5,000
Domestication of horses

THE AMERICAS

30,000–15,000
Human entry into the Americas

13,000–11,000
Clovis culture in North America

11,000
Extinction of large mammals in North America

6,000–5,000
Beginning of domestication of corn in southern Mexico

4,000–3,000
Domestication of potatoes in Andes region

OCEANIA

60,000–40,000
an entry into Australia (first use of boats)

30,000
Extinction of large mammals in Australia

3,500–1,000
Austronesian migration to Pacific islands (and Madagascar)

1,000–800
Human entry into New Zealand (last major region to receive human settlers)

*All dates are B.P. or Before the Present, and all dates are approximate.

Debating the Timescales of History

So when does world history begin? And does it matter?

If "world history" refers to the story of humankind, professional historians until recently were largely in agreement that history began with writing, for as one book published in 1898 put it, "No documents, no history."[3] While humans clearly existed before writing—some 200,000 years, in fact—historians viewed their pasts as almost completely unrecoverable from the few physical remains that survived. They described these earlier peoples as prehistoric or "before history" and left their study to archeology and what was later called paleoanthropology. But writing emerged only about 5,500 years ago, and even then was limited to a few places. Furthermore, until the last several centuries writing was confined largely to elites, who wrote primarily about "the wars they fought, the literature they wrote, and the gods they worshipped."[4] Thus an understanding of the human journey based only on written records was massively skewed and incomplete.

From the mid-twentieth century onward, increasingly accurate and affordable scientific techniques—including radio-carbon dating, DNA testing, and advances in linguistics and archeology—allowed scholars to date artifacts and the movements of human populations that occurred tens or even hundreds of thousands of years ago. A much clearer understanding of early human history emerged as scholars were able to trace chronologically such crucial developments as the spread of our species across the planet and the dissemination of bronze-working technologies. The world before writing no longer seemed so unrecoverable, and many scholars—historians, archeologists, and others—broadened the definition of "history" to incorporate not only peoples of the distant past but also the lives of those who had left no written record. While large gaps in our knowledge persisted, the new techniques opened up windows into the past that had been mostly shut before.

Even as historians debated the extent to which the "prehistory" of our species should or could be incorporated into historical accounts, a related question emerged about how—or whether—to locate all of human history within some greater context. Over the past several decades, some historians have begun to integrate the human story into the much larger frameworks of planetary and cosmic evolution, an approach that has come to be called "big history." Remarkable advances in the natural sciences—astronomy, geology, and evolutionary biology—suggest that the cosmos as a whole has a history, as do the stars, the solar system, the planets, including the earth, and life itself. They have a history because they have changed over time, for change is the fundamental feature of all historical accounts.

Such understandings have caused some to conclude that human history can be fully understood only if contextualized in the changing patterns of the cosmos. As the historian William McNeill has written, "Human beings, it appears, do indeed belong to the universe and share its unstable, evolving character . . . what happens among human beings and what happens among the stars looks to be part of a grand, evolving story."[5] Supporters of this view assert that big history "offers a powerful way

from bones appeared, and so did grindstones. Settlements were planned around the seasonal movement of game and fish. Patterns of exchange over a distance of almost 200 miles indicate larger networks of human communication. The use of body ornaments, beads, and pigments as well as possible planned burials suggests the kind of social and symbolic behavior that has characterized human activity ever since. The earliest evidence for this kind of human activity comes from the Blombos Cave in South Africa, where excavations in 2008 uncovered a workshop for the processing of ochre (a naturally occurring earth pigment with a red, yellow, or brown color) dating to around 100,000 years ago, well before such behavior surfaced elsewhere in the world.

of understanding the place of our own species, *homo sapiens,* within the universe. By doing so it helps us to understand better what human history is all about."[6]

But not all historians agree with this perspective. Some critics of "big history" argue that its almost unimaginable timescales, measured in billions or many millions of years, leave too little room for the human story, reducing it to insignificance. The types of problems or questions that have long occupied professional historians, such as the legacies of the Chinese warring states period or World War I, are worthy of little more than a mention in big history timescales. Others complain that the careful reading and analysis of documents have been replaced by scientific forms of inquiry. Is "big history," they ask, really history at all?

Whatever one may think of these debates, big history represents the latest chapter in a remarkable rethinking of when world history begins. At the turn of the twentieth century few historians could conceive of history beginning more than 6,000 years ago, but by the early twenty-first century some argue that the human story finds its most appropriate place in a process that began over thirteen billion years earlier.

Clearly the timescales of human history matter, because they shape the questions we ask and the techniques of inquiry that we employ. If we seek to understand the ups and downs of civilizations over the past five millennia, written records are essential. Without them, we would know little about the evolution of Buddhism, the rise and fall of empires, the Industrial Revolution, and much more. But if we want to know something of the process by which humans came to occupy almost every environmental niche on the earth, then written

records are of little help, because almost all of that process took place long before writing was invented anywhere. So we must rely on DNA analysis, carbon dating, and linguistics.

Finally, when historians turn to the cosmic or "big history" timescale, they are motivated by still other concerns. For David Christian, one of the leading practitioners of "big history," that grand scale of things offers a "creation myth" for our times, a coherent and scientifically informed explanation of the origins and evolution of our universe and the place of humankind within it.[7] For those more philosophically or spiritually inclined, the "big history" outlook raises profound questions about the relationship of human history to the larger narrative of cosmic and planetary evolution. Does the human experiment represent the story of just one more species thrown up by the ceaseless transformations of the web of life on this planet? Or is human consciousness distinctive, representing perhaps the cosmos becoming aware of itself? In these perspectives the human story is solidly anchored within the unfolding of the universe, the geological transformations of the planet, and the evolution of life on the earth.

QUESTIONS TO CONSIDER

1. How might your understanding of world history change if you subscribed to the idea that history began with writing, began with the emergence of our species, or began at the start of the universe?

2. In what specific ways have advancements in science affected how historians understand world history?

The development and spread of human culture were highly uncertain and took place amid immense obstacles. Around 70,000 years ago an enormous volcanic eruption on the island of Sumatra in present-day Indonesia resulted in a cooler and drier global climate and, scholars speculate, something close to human extinction. But human numbers recovered, growing slowly to perhaps 500,000 by 30,000 years ago and then to 6 million by 10,000 years ago.[8] As this recovery took shape, sometime between 100,000 and 60,000 years ago, human beings began their long trek out of Africa and into Eurasia, Australia, the Americas, and, much later, the islands of the Pacific, where they encountered vastly different environments (see Map 1.1). Much of this long journey occurred during the difficult climatic conditions of the

GREENLAND

(15,000–30,000 years ago)

NORTH AMERICA

ATLANTIC OCEAN

PACIFIC OCEAN

Equator

Easter Island (Rapa Nui) (800–1,000 years ago)

SOUTH AMERICA

(by 12,500 years ago)

| 0 | 1,000 | 2,000 miles |
| 0 | 1,000 2,000 kilometers | |

MAPPING HISTORY

Map 1.1 The Global Dispersion of Humankind

With origins in Africa perhaps 250,000 years ago, members of our species (*Homo sapiens*) have migrated to every environmental setting on the planet over the past 100,000 years.

EUROPE

(45,000 years ago)

ASIA

(70,000 years ago)

(100,000 years ago)

PACIFIC OCEAN

AFRICA

Equator

(1,500 years ago)

(3,500 years ago)

INDIAN OCEAN

(40,000–60,000 years ago)

AUSTRALIA

(1,000 years ago)

NEW ZEALAND

Ice sheet (20,000 years ago)
Land bridges (20,000 years ago)
Human expansion (dates for earliest human occupation)

ANTARCTICA

READING THE MAP: Trace the routes of human migration and settlement from the point where our species first left Africa. In what order were the regions of the world settled, and how long did it take for that settlement to unfold?

INTERPRETING THE MAP: Identify those regions where humans settled last. What geographic factors may have delayed the settlement of these regions?

last Ice Age (at its peak around 20,000 years ago), when thick ice sheets covered much of the Northern Hemisphere. The Ice Age did give these outward-bound human beings one advantage, however: the amount of water frozen in northern glaciers lowered sea levels around the planet, creating land bridges among various regions that were separated after the glaciers melted. Britain was then joined to Europe; eastern Siberia was connected to Alaska; and parts of what is now Indonesia were linked to mainland Southeast Asia.

Into Eurasia

Human migration out of Africa led first to the Middle East and from there to Asia about 70,000 years ago and to Europe about 45,000 years ago. Among the most carefully researched areas of early human settlement in Eurasia are those in southern France and northern Spain. There, around 35,000 to 17,000 years ago, Paleolithic peoples left a record of their world in hundreds of cave paintings depicting bulls, horses, and other animals, brilliantly portrayed in colors of red, yellow, brown, and black. Images of human beings, impressions of human hands, and various abstract designs sometimes accompanied these cave paintings.

Farther east, archeologists have uncovered still other remarkable Paleolithic adaptations to Ice Age conditions. Across the vast plains of Central Europe, Ukraine, and Russia, new technologies emerged, including bone needles, multilayered clothing, weaving, nets, storage pits, baskets, and pottery. Partially underground dwellings constructed from the bones and tusks of mammoths compensated for the absence of caves and rock shelters. All of this suggests that some of these people had lived in more permanent settlements, at least temporarily abandoning their nomadic journeys. Associated with these Eastern European peoples were numerous female figurines, the oldest of which was uncovered in 2008 in Germany and dated to at least 35,000 years ago. Carved from stone, antlers, mammoth tusks, or, occasionally, baked clay, these so-called **Venus figurines** depict the female form, often with exaggerated breasts, buttocks, hips, and stomachs. Similar figurines have been found all across Eurasia, raising any number of controversial questions. (See the image of the Willendorf Venus, page 23.) Does their widespread distribution suggest a network of human communication and cultural diffusion over a wide area? If so, did they move from west to east or vice versa? What do they mean in terms of women's roles and status in Paleolithic societies?

Into Australia

Early human migration to Australia, perhaps 60,000 years ago, came from Indonesia and involved another first in human affairs—the use of boats. Over time, people settled in most regions of this huge continent, though quite sparsely. Scholars estimate the population of Australia at about 300,000 in 1788, when the first Europeans arrived. Over tens of thousands of years, the peoples of Australia had developed perhaps 250 languages; learned to collect a wide variety of bulbs, tubers, roots, seeds, and cereal grasses; and become proficient hunters of large and small animals, as well as birds, fish,

Guided Reading Question

■ **CHANGE**

What was the sequence of human migration across the planet?

and other marine life. A relatively simple technology, appropriate to a gathering and hunting economy, sustained Australia's Aboriginal people into modern times.

Accompanying Aboriginals' technological simplicity and traditionalism was the development of an elaborate and complex outlook on the world, known as the **Dreamtime**. (See Working with Evidence, page 44, for more on the Dreamtime.) Expressed in endless stories, in extended ceremonies, and in the evocative rock art of the continent's peoples, the Dreamtime recounted the beginning of things: how ancestral beings crisscrossed the land, creating its rivers, hills, rocks, and waterholes; how various peoples came to inhabit the land; and how they related to animals and to one another. In this view of the world, everything in the natural order was a vibration, an echo, a footprint of

Australian Rock Art: The Rainbow Serpent Associated with creation, fertility, and social harmony, the Rainbow Serpent has figured prominently in Australian Aboriginal mythology and in its rock art. See a story associated with the Rainbow Serpent in Working with Evidence, Source 1.2. (Prisma by Dukas Presseagentur GmbH/Alamy)

these ancient happenings, which linked the current inhabitants intimately to particular places and to timeless events in the past.

The journeys of the Dreamtime's ancestral beings reflect the networks of migration, communication, and exchange that linked the continent's many Paleolithic peoples. Far from living as isolated groups, they had long exchanged particular stones, pigments, materials for ropes and baskets, wood for spears, feathers and shells for ornaments, and an addictive psychoactive drug known as *pituri* over distances of hundreds of miles. Songs, dances, stories, and rituals likewise circulated. Precisely how far back in time these networks extend is difficult to pinpoint, but it seems clear that Paleolithic Australia, like ancient Europe, was both many separate worlds and, at the same time, one loosely connected world.

Into the Americas

The earliest settlement of the Western Hemisphere occurred much later than that of Australia, for it took some time for human beings to penetrate the frigid lands of eastern Siberia, which was the jumping-off point for the move into the Americas. Experts continue to argue about precisely when the first migrations occurred (somewhere between 30,000 and 15,000 years ago), about the route of migration (by land across the Bering Strait or by sea down the west coast of North America), about how many separate migrations took place, and about how long it took to penetrate to the tip of South America. Some DNA evidence suggests a possible separate migration by sea from Pacific Polynesia.

Whenever the earliest migrations occurred, one of the first clearly defined and widespread cultural traditions in the Americas is associated with people who made a distinctive projectile point, known to archeologists as a Clovis point. Scattered all over North America, **Clovis culture** first emerged around 13,000 years ago and spread rapidly across much of North America. Scattered bands of Clovis people ranged over this huge area, camping along rivers, springs, and waterholes, where large animals congregated. Although they certainly hunted smaller animals and gathered many wild plants, Clovis men show up in the archeological record most dramatically as hunters of very large mammals, such as mammoths and bison. Killing a single mammoth could provide food for many weeks or, in cold weather, for much of the winter. The wide distribution of Clovis point technology suggests yet again a regional pattern of cultural diffusion and at least indirect communication over a large area.

Then, rather abruptly, by roughly 11,000 years ago, all trace of the Clovis culture disappeared from the archeological record at about the same time that many species of large animals, including the mammoth and several species of horses and camels, also became extinct. Did the Clovis people hunt these animals to extinction and then vanish themselves as their source of food disappeared? Or did the drier climate that came with the end of the Ice Age cause this **megafaunal extinction** (extinction of large animals)? Experts disagree, but what happened next was the creation of a much greater diversity of cultures as people adapted to this new situation in various ways. Hunters on the Great Plains continued to pursue bison, which largely avoided the fate of the mammoths. Others learned to live in the desert, taking advantage of seasonal plants and smaller animals, while those who lived near the sea, lakes, or streams drew on local fish and birds. Many peoples of the Americas retained their gathering and hunting way of life into modern times, while others became farmers and, in a few favored regions, later developed cities and large-scale states.

Into the Pacific

The last phase of the great human migration took place in the Pacific Ocean and was distinctive in many ways. It occurred quite recently, jumping off only about 3,500 years ago from the Bismarck and Solomon Islands near New Guinea as well as from the islands of the Philippines. It was everywhere a waterborne migration, making use of oceangoing canoes and remarkable navigational skills, and it happened very quickly and over a huge area of the planet. Speaking Austronesian languages that trace back to southern China, these oceanic voyagers had settled every habitable piece of land in the Pacific basin within about 2,500 years. Other Austronesians had sailed west from Indonesia across the Indian Ocean to settle the island of Madagascar off the coast of eastern Africa. These extraordinary **Austronesian migrations** made the Austronesian family of languages the most geographically widespread in the world and Austronesian trading networks, reaching some

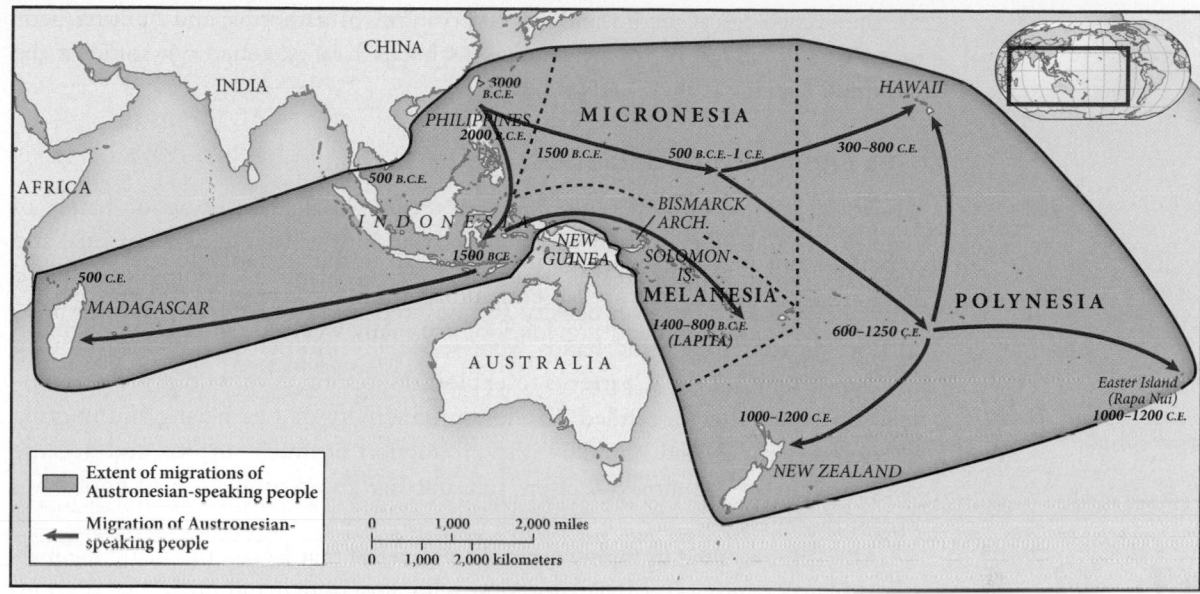

Map 1.2 Migration of Austronesian-Speaking Peoples
People speaking Austronesian languages completed the human settlement of the earth quite recently as they settled the islands of the vast Pacific and penetrated the Indian Ocean to Madagascar, off the coast of southeast Africa.

5,000 miles from western Indonesia to the mid-Pacific, the most extensive. With the occupation of Aotearoa (New Zealand) and Rapa Nui (Easter Island) around 1000 to 1200 C.E., the initial human settlement of the planet was finally complete (see Map 1.2).

In contrast with all of the other initial migrations, these Pacific voyages were undertaken by agricultural people who carried both domesticated plants and animals in their canoes. Both men and women made these journeys, suggesting a deliberate intention to colonize new lands. Virtually everywhere they went, two developments followed. One was the creation of highly stratified societies or chiefdoms, of which ancient Hawaiian society is a prime example. The other development was extensive deforestation and the quick extinction of many species of animals, especially large flightless birds such as the *moa* of New Zealand, which largely vanished within a century of this human intrusion into a pristine environment.

Guided Reading Question
....
■ **COMPARISON**
How did Austronesian migrations differ from other early patterns of human movement?

Paleolithic Lifeways

During their long journeys across the earth, Paleolithic people created a multitude of separate and distinct societies, each with its own history, culture, language, identity, stories, and rituals, but the limitations of a gathering and hunting technology using stone tools also imposed some commonalities on these ancient people. Based on the archeological record and on observations of gathering and hunting peoples that still existed in recent centuries, scholars have sketched out some of the common features of these early societies.

The First Human Societies

Above all else, these Paleolithic societies were small, consisting of bands of twenty-five to fifty people, in which all relationships were intensely personal and normally understood in terms of kinship. The available technology permitted only a very low population density and ensured an extremely slow rate of population growth. Paleolithic bands were seasonally mobile or nomadic, moving frequently and in regular patterns to exploit the resources of wild plants and animals on which they depended. The low productivity of a gathering and hunting economy normally did not allow the production of much surplus, and because people were on the move so often, transporting an accumulation of goods was out of the question.

All of this resulted in highly egalitarian societies that lacked the many inequalities of wealth and power that came later with agricultural and urban life. With no formal chiefs, kings, bureaucrats, soldiers, nobles, or priests, Paleolithic men and women were perhaps freer of human tyranny and oppression than any later kind of human society, even if they were more constrained by the forces of nature. Without specialists, most people possessed the same set of skills, although male and female tasks often differed sharply. The male role as hunter, especially of big game, perhaps gave rise to one of the first criteria of masculine identity: success in killing large animals.

Contemporary Gathering and Hunting Peoples: The San of Southern Africa A very small number of gathering and hunting peoples have maintained their ancient way of life into the twenty-first century. Here two young men from the Jul'hoan !Kung San of southern Africa set a trap for small animals in 2009. (robertharding/Alamy)

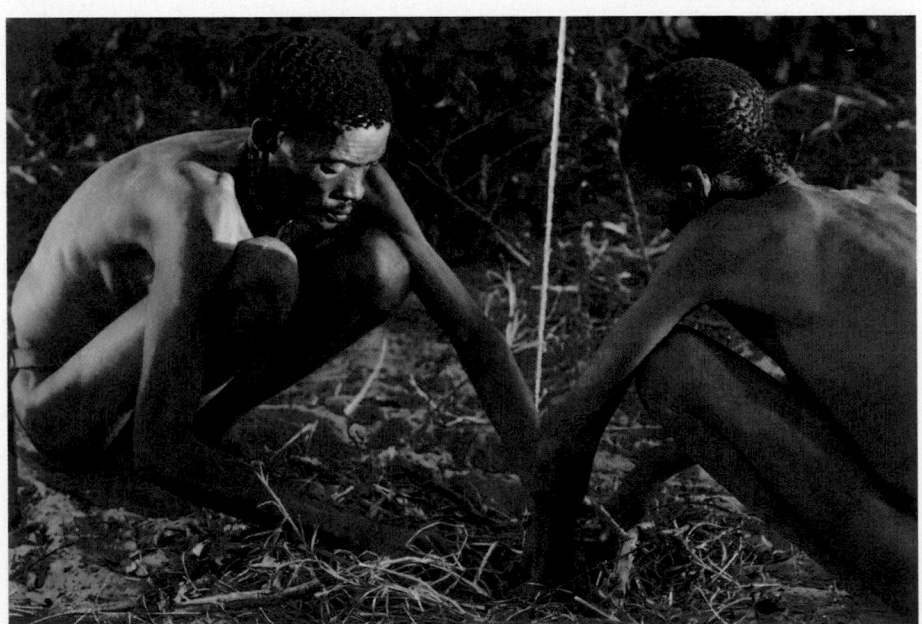

Relationships between women and men usually were far more equal than in later societies. As the primary food gatherers, women provided the bulk of the family's sustenance. One study undertaken during the 1960s of the San people, a surviving gathering and hunting society in southern Africa, found that plants, normally gathered by women, provided 70 percent of the diet, while meat, hunted by men, accounted for just 30 percent. This division of labor underpinned what anthropologist Richard Lee called "relative equality between the sexes with no-one having the upper hand." Among the San, teenagers engaged quite freely in sex play, and the concept of female virginity was apparently unknown, as were rape, wife beating, and the sexual double standard. Although polygamy was permitted, most marriages were in fact monogamous because women strongly resisted sharing a husband with another wife. Frequent divorce among very young couples allowed women to leave unsatisfactory marriages easily. Lee found that longer-term marriages seemed to be generally fulfilling and stable. Both men and women expected a satisfying sexual relationship, and both occasionally took lovers, although discreetly.[9]

When the British navigator and explorer Captain James Cook first encountered the gathering and hunting peoples of Australia in 1770, he described them, perhaps a little enviously, in this way:

> They live in a Tranquillity which is not disturb'd by the Inequality of Conditions: The Earth and sea of their own accord furnishes them with all things necessary for life, they covet not Magnificent houses, Household-stuff. . . .
> In short they seem'd to set no value upon any thing we gave them. . . . They think themselves provided with all the necessarys of Life.[10]

The Europeans who settled permanently among such people some twenty years later, however, found a society in which physical competition among men was expressed in frequent one-on-one combat and in formalized but bloody battles. It also meant recurrent, public, and quite brutal beatings of wives by their husbands.[11] This evidence coincides with Richard Lee's observations about conflict and violence among the San of southern Africa, where frequent arguments about the distribution of meat or the laziness or stinginess of particular people generated serious disputes, as did rivalries among men over women. More generally, recent studies have found that in Paleolithic societies some 15 percent of deaths occurred through violence at the hands of other people, a rate far higher than in later civilizations, where violence was largely monopolized by the state.[12] Although sometimes romanticized by outsiders, the relative equality of Paleolithic societies did not always ensure a utopia of social harmony.

Like all other human cultures, Paleolithic societies had rules and structures. A gender-based division of labor usually cast men as hunters and women as gatherers. Values emphasizing reciprocal sharing of goods resulted in clearly defined rules about distributing the meat from an animal kill. Various rules about incest and adultery governed sexual behavior, while understandings about who could hunt or gather in particular territories regulated economic activity. Leaders arose as needed

Guided Reading Question

■ **CHANGE**

In what ways did a gathering and hunting economy shape other aspects of Paleolithic societies?

to organize a task such as a hunt, but permanent power was not conferred on individuals.

Economy and the Environment

For a long time, modern people viewed their gathering and hunting ancestors as primitive and impoverished, barely eking out a living from the land. In more recent decades, anthropologists studying contemporary Paleolithic societies—those that survived into the twentieth century—began to paint a different picture. They noted that gathering and hunting people frequently worked fewer hours to meet their material needs than did people in agricultural or industrial societies and so had more leisure time. One scholar referred to them as **"the original affluent society,"** not because they had so much but because they wanted or needed so little.[13] Nonetheless, life expectancy was low, probably little more than thirty-five years on average. Life in the wild was surely dangerous, and dependency on the vagaries of nature rendered it insecure as well.

But Paleolithic people also acted to alter the natural environment substantially. The use of deliberately set fires in the landscape to encourage the growth of par-ticular plants certainly changed the environment and in Australia led to the pro-liferation of fire-resistant eucalyptus trees at the expense of other plant species. In many ecosystems, especially small ones like Pacific islands, the arrival of humans resulted in the rapid extinction of some native plants and animals. In Australia and North America the majority of large animals disappeared long before our ancestors learned to farm or fashion weapons from metal. Other hominid, or human-like, species (such as the Neanderthals in Europe or "Flores man," discovered in 2003 in Indonesia) also perished after living side by side with *Homo sapiens* for millennia. Whether their disappearance occurred through massacre, interbreeding, peaceful competition, or something unrelated to the human presence, ultimately they did not survive the rise of humankind. Thus the biological environment inhabited by gathering and hunting peoples was not wholly natural but was shaped in part by their own hands.

The Realm of the Spirit

The religious or spiritual dimension of Paleolithic culture has been hard to pin down, because bones and stones tell us little about what people thought, art is sub-ject to many interpretations, and the experience of contemporary gathering and hunting peoples may not reflect the distant past. Clear evidence exists, however, for a rich and distinctive spiritual life. The presence of rock art deep inside caves and far from living spaces suggests a "ceremonial space" separate from ordinary life. The extended rituals of contemporary Australian Aboriginals, which sometimes last for weeks, confirm this impression, as do numerous and elaborate burial sites found throughout the world. No full-time religious specialists or priests led these cere-monies, but part-time **shamans** (people believed to be especially skilled at dealing with the spirit world) emerged as the need arose. Such people sometimes entered an altered state of consciousness or a trance while performing the ceremonies, often with the aid of psychoactive drugs.

Precisely how Paleolithic people understood the nonmaterial world is hard to reconstruct, and speculation abounds. Linguistic evidence from ancient Africa suggests a variety of understandings: some Paleolithic societies were apparently monotheistic; others saw several levels of supernatural beings, including a creator deity, various territorial spirits, and the spirits of dead ancestors; still others believed in an impersonal force suffused throughout the natural order that could be accessed by shamans during a trance dance.[14] The prevalence of Venus figurines and other symbols all across Europe has convinced some, but not all, scholars that Paleolithic religious thought had a strongly feminine dimension, embodied in a Great Goddess and concerned with the regeneration and renewal of life.[15] Many gathering and hunting peoples likely developed a cyclical view of time derived from recurring natural cycles: sunrise and sunset; changing seasons; the phases of the moon; patterns of female fertility—birth, menstruation, pregnancy, new birth—and, of course, life, death, and new life. These understandings of the cosmos, which saw endlessly repeated patterns of regeneration and disintegration, differed from later Western views, which saw time moving in a straight line toward some predetermined goal. Nor did Paleolithic people make sharp distinctions between the material and spiritual worlds, for they understood that animals, rocks, trees, mountains, and much more were animated by spirits or possessed souls of their own.

Settling Down: The Great Transition

Though glacially slow by contemporary standards, changes in Paleolithic cultures occurred over time as people moved into new environments, as populations grew, as climates altered, and as different human groups interacted with one another. For example, all over the Afro-Eurasian world after 25,000 years ago, a tendency toward the miniaturization of stone tools is evident, analogous perhaps to the miniaturization of electronic components in the twentieth century. Known as micro-blades, these smaller and more refined spear points, arrowheads, knives, and scrapers were carefully struck from larger cores and often mounted in antler, bone, or wooden handles. Another important change involved the collection of wild grains. This innovation originated in northeastern Africa around 16,000 years ago and represented a major addition to the food supply beyond the use of roots, berries, and nuts.

But the most striking and significant change in the lives of Paleolithic peoples occurred as the last Ice Age came to an end between 16,000 and 10,000 years ago. What followed was a general global warming, though one with periodic fluctuations and cold snaps. Unlike the contemporary global warming, generated by human activity and especially the burning of fossil fuels, this ancient warming phase was a wholly natural phenomenon, part of a long cycle of repeated heating and cooling characteristic of the earth's climatic history. Plants and animals that had

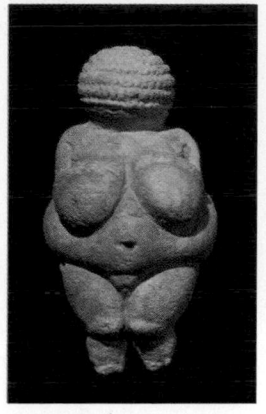

The Willendorf Venus Less than four and a half inches in height and dating to about 25,000 years ago, this female figure, which was found near the town of Willendorf in Austria, has become the most famous of the many Venus figurines. Certain features—the absence of both face and feet, the coils of hair around her head, the prominence of her breasts and sexual organs—have prompted much speculation among scholars about the significance of these intriguing carvings. (Naturhistorisches Museum, Vienna, Austria/ Ali Meyer/Bridgeman Images)

Guided Reading Question

■ **CHANGE**
Why did some Paleolithic peoples abandon earlier, more nomadic ways and begin to live a more settled life?

struggled in the Ice Age climate now flourished and increased their range, providing a much richer and more diverse environment for many human societies. Under these improved conditions, human populations grew, and some previously nomadic gathering and hunting communities, but not all of them, found it possible to settle down and live in more permanent settlements or villages. These societies were becoming both larger and more complex, and it was less possible to simply move away if trouble struck. Settlement also meant that households could store and accumulate goods to a greater degree than previously. Because some people were more energetic, more talented, or luckier than others, the thin edge of inequality gradually began to wear away the egalitarianism of Paleolithic communities.

Changes along these lines emerged in many places. Paleolithic societies in Japan, known as Jomon, settled down in villages by the sea, where they greatly expanded the number of animals, both land and marine, that they consumed. They also created some of the world's first pottery, along with dugout canoes, paddles, bows, bowls, and tool handles, all made from wood. A similar pattern of permanent settlement, a broader range of food sources, and specialized technologies is evident in parts of Scandinavia, Southeast Asia, North America, and the Middle East between 12,000 and 4,000 years ago. In Labrador, longhouses appear in the archeological record between 7,500 and 3,500 years ago, some of them accommodating 100 people. Far more elaborate burial sites in many places testify to the growing complexity of human communities and the kinship systems that bound them together. Separate cemeteries for dogs suggest that humankind's best friend was also our first domesticated animal friend. Some of the most stunning and unexpected achievements of such sedentary Paleolithic people come from the archeological complex of **Göbekli Tepe** (goh-BEHK-lee TEH-peh) in southeastern Turkey, described more fully in the Zooming In feature on page 25.

Studies of more recent gathering and hunting societies, which were able to settle permanently in particular resource-rich areas, show marked differences from their more nomadic counterparts. Among the Chumash of southern California, for example, early Spanish settlers found peoples who had developed substantial and permanent structures accommodating up to seventy persons; hereditary political elites; elements of a market economy, including the use of money and private ownership of some property; and the beginnings of class distinctions.

This **Paleolithic settling down**—and the changes that followed from it—marked a major turn in human history, away from countless millennia of nomadic journeys by very small communities. It also provided the setting within which the next great transition would occur. Growing numbers of men and women, living in settled communities, placed a much greater demand on the environment than did small bands of people on the move. Therefore, it is perhaps not surprising that among the innovations that emerged in some of these more complex gathering and hunting societies was yet another way for increasing the food supply—agriculture.

PRACTICING HISTORICAL THINKING

How do you understand the significance of the long Paleolithic era in the larger context of world history?

Göbekli Tepe: Monumental Construction before Agriculture

Perhaps the most stunning archeological discovery of recent decades comes from the site known as Göbekli Tepe, or "potbelly hill," in southeastern Turkey, which has been under excavation since the mid-1990s. Dating to almost 12,000 years ago, this twenty-five-acre complex currently consists of about 200 massive limestone pillars, some as tall as eighteen feet and weighing as much as fifty tons. Carved in a T shape, perhaps to represent human beings with arms outstretched, they were arranged in a set of walled circles or rings. Five such circles have been unearthed so far, with another twenty or so awaiting excavation. Gracefully carved wild animals—gazelles, snakes, boars, foxes, lions, scorpions, vultures—decorate the pillars. Göbekli Tepe was probably a ceremonial or religious site, for little evidence of long-term human habitation has been found. Dubbed "the world's oldest temple," it likely attracted worshippers or pilgrims from many miles around and may well have served as a place of ritual burials, although no actual graves have yet been found.

Göbekli Tepe.

Carved Lion on a Stone Pillar at Göbekli Tepe.

The most amazing feature of Göbekli Tepe involves those who constructed it, for they were clearly gathering and hunting peoples, living at least part of the year in settled villages. No evidence of agriculture or domesticated animals has emerged. Rather, the tens of thousands of animal bone fragments found at the site suggest that those who built the complex dined on wild gazelles, pigs, sheep, deer, vultures, and ducks, as well as wild plants native to the area. Thus Göbekli Tepe represents a kind of monumental construction long associated only with agricultural societies and civilizations, forcing scholars to rethink their understanding of the late Paleolithic era.

How did such pre-agricultural peoples with only the simplest of stone tools carve, transport, and erect such enormous structures? What kind of social organization facilitated their remarkable achievement? What did this complex mean to those who created it? Since stones and bones tell us little about these matters, many mysteries remain.

Although Göbekli Tepe was the product of pre-agricultural peoples, the process of its construction may well have played a role in the breakthrough to farming in this region. Klaus Schmidt, the chief archeologist at the site for many years, argued that the need for food to supply those who built and maintained this massive religious complex may well have triggered the development of agriculture in the area. Certainly, some of the earliest domesticated wheat has been located just twenty miles away and at roughly the same date. If this connection holds, it suggests that the human impulse to worship collectively played a significant role in generating the epic transformation of the Agricultural Revolution.

Scholars have long believed that large-scale construction, settled village life, and institutional religion were generated by agricultural societies. The finds at Göbekli Tepe and elsewhere now suggest that these achievements may have figured in the creation of those farming communities. Perhaps they were precursors to agriculture rather than products of it.

QUESTIONS

In what ways has Göbekli Tepe forced historians to rethink earlier views? How does this archeological discovery affect your own understanding of the Paleolithic era?

Breakthroughs to Agriculture

The chief feature of the long Paleolithic era—and the first human process to operate on a global scale—was the initial settlement of the earth. Then, beginning around 12,000 years ago, a second global pattern began to unfold—agriculture. The terms "Neolithic (New Stone Age) Revolution" and "Agricultural Revolution" both refer to the deliberate cultivation of particular plants as well as the taming and breeding of particular animals. Thus a whole new way of life gradually replaced the earlier practices of gathering and hunting in most parts of the world. Although it took place over centuries and millennia, the coming of agriculture represented a genuinely revolutionary transformation of human life all across the planet and provided the foundation for almost everything that followed: growing populations, settled villages, animal-borne diseases, horse-drawn chariot warfare, cities, states, empires, civilizations, writing, literature, and much more.

Among the most revolutionary aspects of the age of agriculture was a new relationship between humankind and other living things, for now men and women were not simply using what they found in nature but actively changing nature as well. They were consciously "directing" the process of evolution. The actions of farmers in the Americas, for example, transformed corn from a plant with a cob of an inch or so to one measuring about six inches by 1500. Later efforts more than doubled that length. Farmers everywhere stamped the landscape with a human imprint in the form of fields with boundaries, terraced hillsides, irrigation ditches, and canals. Animals too were transformed, as selective breeding produced sheep that grew more wool, cows that gave more milk, and chickens that laid more eggs than their wild counterparts. This was "domestication"—the taming, and the changing, of nature for the benefit of humankind. In many agricultural communities, however, gathering, hunting, and fishing did not quickly disappear, but long continued to supplement agriculture and animal husbandry as food sources.

A further revolutionary aspect of the agricultural age is summed up in the term "intensification." It means getting more for less, in this case more food and resources—far more—from a much smaller area of land than was possible with a gathering and hunting technology. More food meant more people. Growing populations in turn required an even more intensive exploitation of the environment. Thus was launched the continuing human effort to "fill the earth and subdue it," as the biblical story in Genesis recorded God's command to Adam and Eve.

Common Patterns

Perhaps the most extraordinary feature of the Neolithic or Agricultural Revolution was that it occurred, separately and independently, in many widely scattered parts of the world: the Fertile Crescent of Southwest Asia, several places in sub-Saharan Africa, China, Southeast Asia, New Guinea, Mesoamerica, the Andes, and eastern North America (see Map 1.3). Even more remarkably, all of this took place at roughly the same time (at least as measured by the 250,000-year span of human history on the planet)—between 12,000 and 4,000 years ago. So why was the Agricultural Revolution so late in the history of humankind? What was unique about the period after 10,000 B.C.E. that may have triggered or facilitated this vast upheaval? In what different ways did the Agricultural Revolution take shape in its various locations? How did it spread from its several points of origin to the rest of the earth? And what impact did it have on the making of human societies?

It is surely no accident that the Agricultural Revolution coincided with the end of the last Ice Age, a process of global warming that began some 16,000 years ago. By about 11,000 years ago, the Ice Age was over, and climatic conditions similar to those of our own time generally prevailed. Ice ages had come and gone earlier in the earth's history, caused by minor periodic changes in the earth's orbit around the sun. The end of the last Ice Age, however, coincided with the migration of *Homo sapiens* across the planet and created new conditions that made agriculture more possible in some areas, even as rising sea levels inundated other regions (see Map 1.1). Combined perhaps with active hunting by human societies, climate change in some places helped to push into extinction various species of large mammals on which Paleolithic people had depended, thus adding to the pressure to find new food sources. The warmer, wetter, and more stable conditions, particularly in the tropical and temperate regions of the earth, also permitted the flourishing of more wild plants, especially cereal grasses, which were the ancestors of many domesticated crops. What climate change took away with one hand, it apparently gave back with the other.

Over their long history, gathering and hunting peoples had already developed a deep knowledge of the natural world and, in some cases, the ability to manage it actively. They had learned to make use of a large number of plants and to hunt and eat both small and large animals, creating what archeologists call a "broad-spectrum diet." In the Middle East, people had developed sickles for cutting newly available wild grain, baskets to carry it, mortars and pestles to remove the husk, and storage pits to preserve it. In hindsight, much of this looks like a kind of unintentional preparation for agriculture. Because women in particular had long been intimately associated with collecting wild plants, they were the likely innovators who led the way to deliberate farming, with men perhaps taking the lead in domesticating animals.

Using available technologies, and benefiting from the global warming at the end of the last Ice Age, gathering and hunting peoples in various resource-rich areas were able to settle down and establish more permanent villages, abandoning their nomadic ways and more intensively exploiting the local area. In settling down, however, they found themselves now required to support growing populations. Evidence for increasing human numbers around the world during this period of global warming has persuaded some scholars that agriculture was a response to the need for additional food, perhaps even a "food crisis." Such conditions surely motivated people to experiment and to innovate in an effort to increase the food supply. Clearly, many of the breakthroughs to agriculture occurred only *after* gathering and hunting peoples had already grown substantially in numbers and had established a sedentary way of life.

Guided Reading Question

■ CHANGE
What accounts for the emergence of agriculture after countless millennia of human life without it?

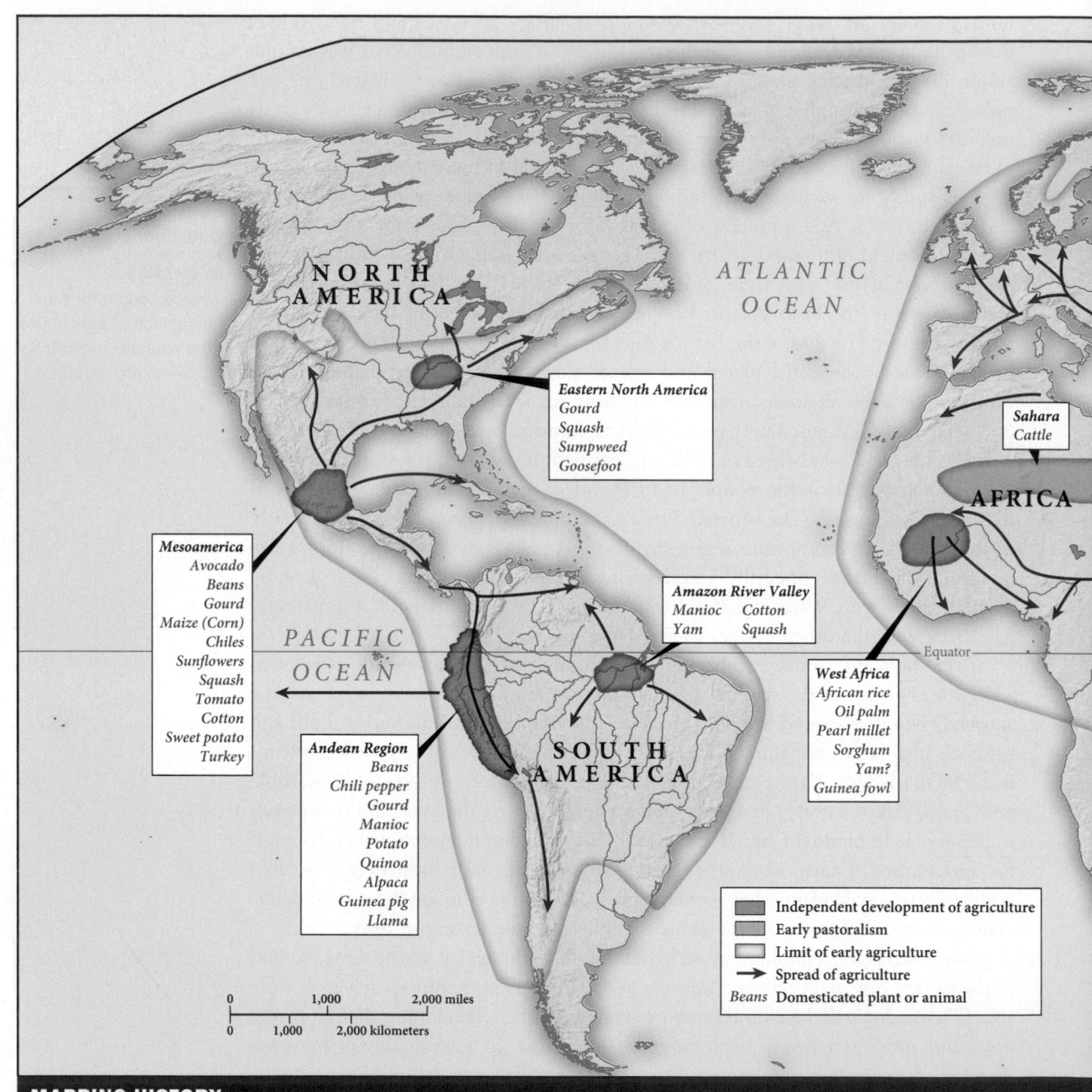

MAPPING HISTORY

Map 1.3 The Global Spread of Agriculture and Pastoralism

From ten or more separate points of origin, agriculture spread to adjacent areas, eventually
encompassing almost all of the world's peoples.

READING THE MAP: On which continents did early pastoral societies develop? Which
continents fostered no early pastoral societies? ➡

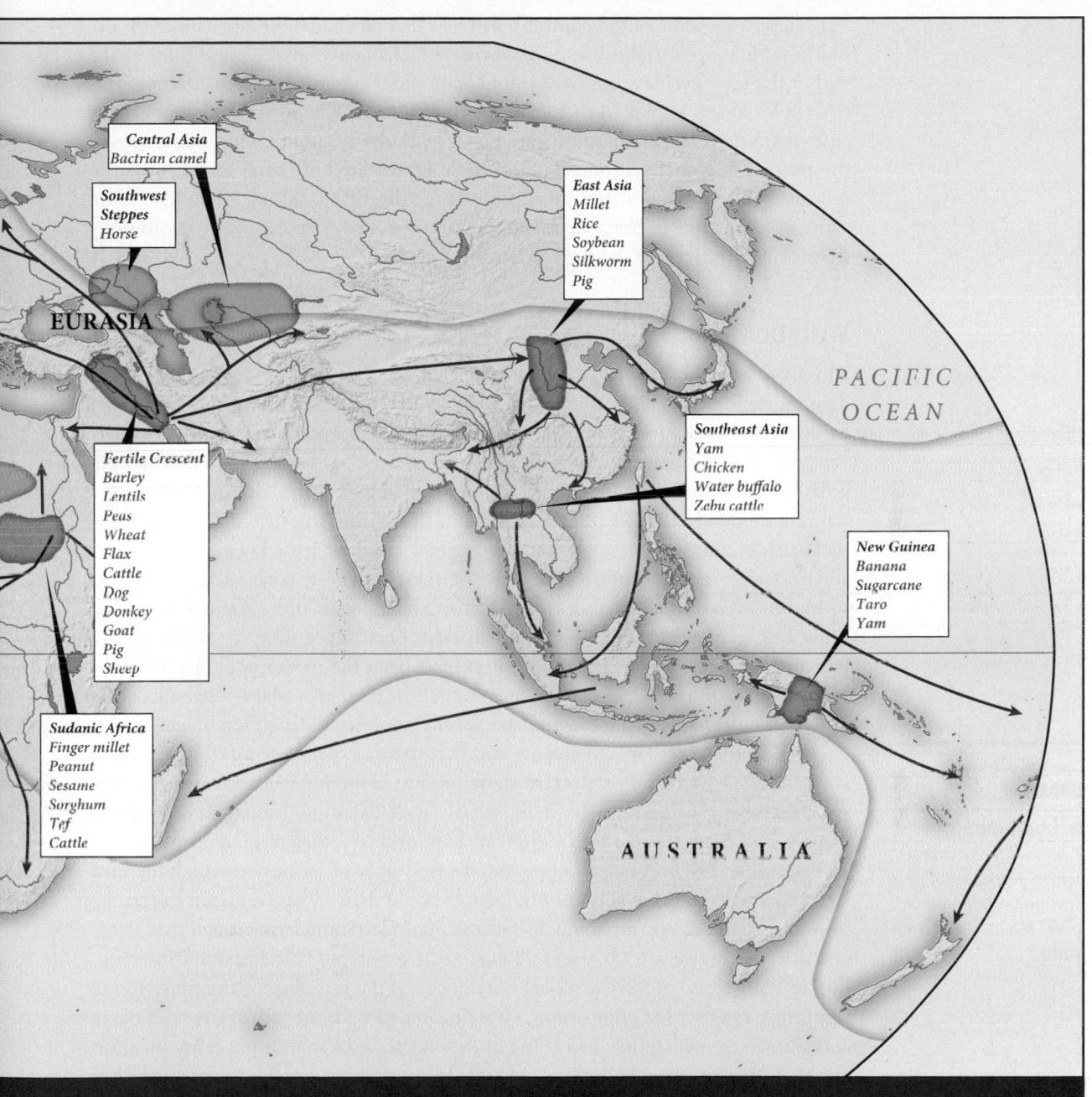

Central Asia
Bactrian camel

Southwest Steppes
Horse

East Asia
Millet
Rice
Soybean
Silkworm
Pig

EURASIA

PACIFIC OCEAN

Fertile Crescent
Barley
Lentils
Peas
Wheat
Flax
Cattle
Dog
Donkey
Goat
Pig
Sheep

Southeast Asia
Yam
Chicken
Water buffalo
Zebu cattle

New Guinea
Banana
Sugarcane
Taro
Yam

Sudanic Africa
Finger millet
Peanut
Sesame
Sorghum
Tef
Cattle

AUSTRALIA

INTERPRETING THE MAP: How might you describe the climatic regions where agriculture developed independently? Were they in equatorial tropical zones, arctic zones, and/or in regions in between called temperate zones? What factors might explain this distribution?

These were some of the common patterns that facilitated the Agricultural Revolution. New opportunities appeared with the changed climatic conditions at the end of the Ice Age. New knowledge and technology emerged as human communities explored and exploited that changed environment. The disappearance of many large mammals, growing populations, newly settled ways of life, and fluctuations in the process of global warming—all of these represented pressures or incentives to increase food production and thus to minimize the risks of life in a new era. From some combination of these opportunities and incentives emerged the profoundly transforming process of the Agricultural Revolution.

Variations

This new way of life initially operated everywhere with a simple technology—the digging stick or hoe. Plows were developed much later. But the several transitions to this hoe-based agriculture, commonly known as horticulture, varied considerably, depending on what plants and animals were available locally. For example, potatoes were found in the Andes region, but not in Africa or Asia; wheat and wild pigs existed in the Fertile Crescent, but not in the Americas. Furthermore, of the world's 200,000 plant species, only several hundred have been domesticated, and in more recent centuries just five of these—wheat, corn, rice, barley, and sorghum—have supplied more than half of the calories that sustain human life. Only fourteen species of large mammals have been successfully domesticated, of which sheep, pigs, goats, cattle, and horses have been the most important. Thus the kind of Agricultural Revolution that unfolded in particular places depended very much on what happened to be available locally; in short, it depended on sheer luck.

Among the most favored areas—and the first to experience a full Agricultural Revolution—was the **Fertile Crescent**, an area sometimes known as Southwest Asia, consisting of present-day Iraq, Syria, Israel/Palestine, Jordan, and southern Turkey (see Map 1.4). In this region, an extraordinary variety of wild plants and animals capable of domestication provided a rich array of species on which the now largely settled gathering and hunting people could draw. What triggered the transition to agriculture remains a much-debated question. Some have argued that a cold and dry spell between 11,000 and 9500 B.C.E., a very rapid but temporary interruption in the general process of global warming, was the stimulus for the transition to farming. Larger settled populations, now threatened with the loss of the wild plants and animals on which they had come to depend, found a solution in domestication, either during or soon after this cold and dry period passed. Figs were apparently the first cultivated crop, dating to about 9400 B.C.E. In the millennium or so that followed, wheat, barley, rye, peas, lentils, sheep, goats, pigs, and cattle all came under human control, providing the foundation for the world's first agricultural societies.

Archeological evidence suggests that the transition to a fully agricultural way of life in parts of this region took place quite quickly, within as few as 500 years. Signs of that transformation included large increases in the size of settlements, which now

Guided Reading Question

■ **COMPARISON**
In what different ways did the Agricultural Revolution take shape in various parts of the world?

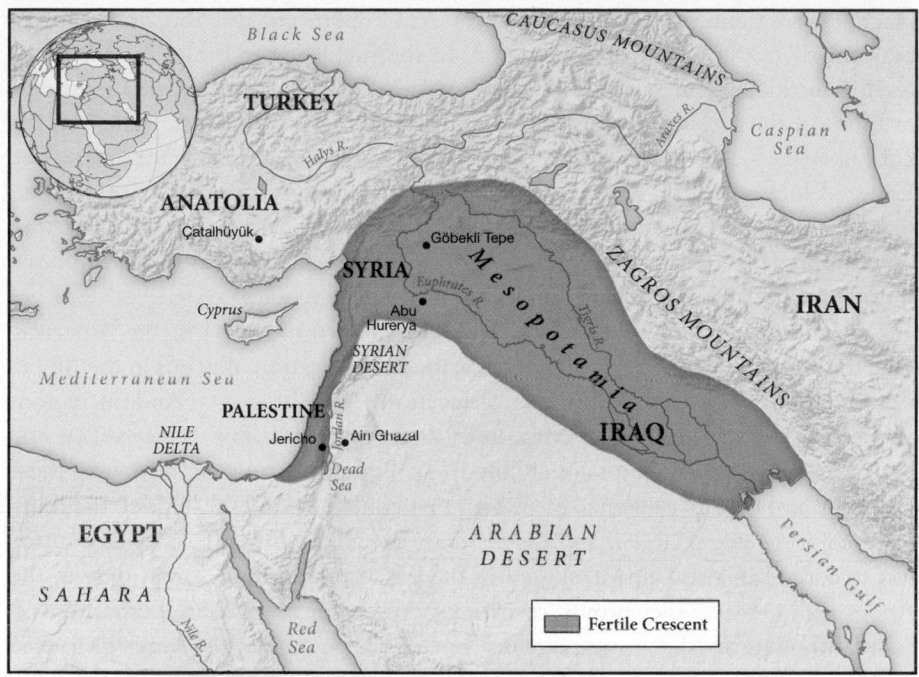

Map 1.4 The Fertile Crescent
Located in what is now called the Middle East, the Fertile Crescent was the site of many significant processes in early world history, including a major breakthrough to agriculture and later the development of one of the First Civilizations.

housed as many as several thousand people. In these agricultural settings, archeologists have found major innovations: the use of sun-dried mud bricks; the appearance of monuments or shrine-like buildings; displays of cattle skulls; more elaborate human burials, including the removal of the skull; and more sophisticated tools, such as sickles, polished axes, and awls.

At roughly the same time, or perhaps a bit later, another process of domestication was unfolding on the African continent in the eastern part of what is now the Sahara in present-day Sudan. Between 10,000 and 5,000 years ago, this region received more rainfall than it currently does, had extensive grassland vegetation, and was "relatively hospitable to human life."[16] During these millennia, domesticated cattle appeared in the region, though whether they were tamed locally or were introduced from the Fertile Crescent is still debated. Around 6,000 years ago, the donkey was also domesticated in northeastern Africa near the Red Sea and spread from there into Southwest Asia, even as the practice of raising sheep and goats moved in the other direction.

In terms of farming, the African pattern again was somewhat different. Unlike the Fertile Crescent, where a number of plants were domesticated in a small area, sub-Saharan Africa witnessed the emergence of several widely scattered farming practices. Sorghum, which grows well in arid conditions, was the first grain to be "tamed" in the eastern Sahara region. In the highlands of Ethiopia, teff, a tiny, highly nutritious grain, as well as enset, a relative of the banana, came under cultivation. In the forested region of West Africa, yams, oil palm trees, okra, and the kola nut (used as a flavoring for cola drinks) emerged as important crops. The scattered location of these domestications generated a less productive agriculture than in the more favored and compact Fertile Crescent, but a number of African domesticates—sorghum, castor beans, gourds, millet, the donkey—subsequently spread to enrich the agricultural practices of Eurasian peoples.

Yet another pattern of agricultural development took shape in the Americas. Like the Agricultural Revolution in Africa, the domestication of plants in the Americas occurred separately in a number of locations—in the coastal Andean regions of western South America, in Mesoamerica, in the Mississippi River valley, and perhaps in the Amazon basin. Surely the most distinctive common feature of these regions was the relative absence of animals that could be domesticated. Of the fourteen major species of large mammals that have been brought under human control, just two, the llama and alpaca, existed in the Western Hemisphere, and only in the Andes region, where they proved enormously useful for food, fiber, and transportation. Without goats, sheep, pigs, cattle, or horses, the peoples of the Americas lacked sources of protein, manure (for fertilizer), and power (to draw plows or pull carts, for example) that were widely available to societies in the Afro-Eurasian world. Because they could not depend on domesticated animals for meat, many agricultural peoples in the Americas relied more on hunting and fishing than did peoples in the Eastern Hemisphere. While the Americas lacked the cereal grains that were widely available in Afro-Eurasia, they had **maize** or corn, first domesticated in southern Mexico by 4000 to 3000 B.C.E. Unlike the cereal grains of the Fertile Crescent, which closely resemble their wild predecessors, the ancestor of corn was a mountain grass that looks nothing like what we now know as corn or maize. Thousands of years of selective adaptation were required to develop a sufficiently large cob and number of kernels to sustain a productive agriculture, an achievement that one geneticist has called "arguably man's first, and perhaps his greatest, feat of genetic engineering."[17] Thus while Middle Eastern societies quite rapidly replaced their gathering and hunting economy with agriculture, that process took several thousand years in Mesoamerica. Beyond maize, Native American farmers domesticated squash, beans, potatoes, sunflowers, quinoa, pigweed, and goosefoot, which were harvested on a large scale.

Another difference in the unfolding of the Agricultural Revolution lay in the north/south orientation of the Americas, which required agricultural practices to move through, and adapt to, quite distinct climatic and vegetation zones if they were to spread. The east/west axis of North Africa / Eurasia meant that agricultural innovations could spread more rapidly because they were entering roughly similar environments. Thus corn, beans, and squash, which were first domesticated in Mesoamerica, took several thousand years to travel the few hundred miles from their Mexican

The Statues of Ain Ghazal Among the largest of the early agricultural settlements investigated by archeologists is that of Ain Ghazal, located in the modern state of Jordan. Inhabited from about 7200 to 5000 B.C.E., in its prime it was home to some 3,000 people, who lived in multiroomed stone houses; cultivated barley, wheat, peas, beans, and lentils; and herded domesticated goats. These remarkable statues, around three feet tall and made of limestone plaster applied to a core of bundled reeds, were among the most startling finds at that site. Did they represent heroes, gods, goddesses, or ordinary people? No one really knows. (Courtesy, Department of Antiquities of Jordan [DoA]/Photo by John Tsantesi, Courtesy, Dr. Gary O. Rollefson)

homeland to the southwestern United States and another thousand years or more to arrive in eastern North America. The llama, guinea pig, quinoa, and potato, which were domesticated in the Andean highlands, never reached Mesoamerica.

The Globalization of Agriculture

From the various places where it originated, agriculture spread gradually to much of the rest of the earth, although for a long time it coexisted with gathering and hunting ways of life, even as it eroded and diminished those practices. Broadly speaking, this extension of farming occurred in two ways. The first, known as diffusion, refers to the gradual spread of agricultural techniques, and perhaps of the plants and animals themselves, but without the extensive movement of agricultural people. Neighboring groups exchanged ideas and products in a down-the-line pattern of communication. A second process involved the slow colonization or migration of agricultural peoples as growing populations pushed them outward.

Triumph and Resistance

Guided Reading Question

■ CONNECTION

In what ways did agriculture spread? Where and why was it sometimes resisted?

Some combination of diffusion and migration underpinned the spread of agriculture to new regions, and the adoption of farming practices was at times accompanied by the spread of languages as well. For instance, between 6500 and 4000 B.C.E. the agricultural package of Southwest Asia spread into Europe, Central Asia, Egypt, and North Africa. In the case of Europe, the adoption of agriculture was accompanied by the spread into the region of Indo-European languages, which had originated further east in Anatolia or, as some scholars suggest, in the area north of the Black and Caspian Seas. Within Africa, the development of agricultural societies in the southern half of the continent is associated with the **Bantu migration**, the movement of peoples speaking one or another of the some 400 Bantu languages. Beginning from what is now southern Nigeria or Cameroon around 3000 B.C.E., Bantu-speaking people moved east and south over the next several millennia, taking with them their agricultural, cattle-raising, and, later, ironworking skills, as well as their languages. They generally absorbed, killed, or drove away the indigenous Paleolithic peoples or exposed them to animal-borne diseases to which they had no immunities. A similar process brought agricultural Austronesian-speaking people, who originated in southern China, to the Philippine and Indonesian islands, with similar consequences for their earlier inhabitants (see Map 1.2, page 19).

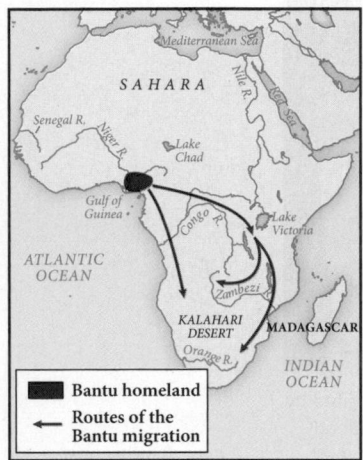

Bantu Migration

The globalization of agriculture was a prolonged process, lasting 10,000 years or more after its first emergence in the Fertile Crescent, but it did not take hold everywhere. The Agricultural Revolution in highland New Guinea, for example, generated a number of domesticated plants including yams, taro, bananas, and sugarcane. But while these spread to parts of Island Southeast Asia, they did not pass to the nearby peoples of Australia, who remained steadfastly committed to gathering and hunting ways of life. The people of the west coast of North America, arctic regions, and southwestern Africa also maintained their gathering and hunting economies into the modern era.

Some of those who resisted the swelling tide of agriculture lived in areas unsuitable to farming, such as harsh desert or arctic environments; others lived in regions of particular natural abundance, so they felt little need for agriculture. Such societies found it easier to resist agriculture if they were not in the direct line of advancing, more powerful farming people. But many of the remaining gathering and hunting peoples knew about agricultural practices from nearby neighbors, suggesting that they quite deliberately chose to resist it in favor of the freer life of their Paleolithic ancestors. Nonetheless, by the beginning of the Common Era, the global spread of agriculture had reduced gathering and hunting peoples to a small and dwindling minority of humankind.

Guided Reading Question

■ CHANGE

What changes did the Agricultural Revolution bring in its wake?

The Culture of Agriculture

In many accounts, the Agricultural Revolution is presented as "progress"—a great leap forward—for humankind. If evolutionary success or an increase in numbers is a measure of progress, then the Agricultural Revolution certainly fits that description, for it led to a substantial increase in human population, as the greater productivity of agriculture was able to support many more people. By 8000 B.C.E. an early agricultural settlement uncovered near Jericho in present-day Israel probably had 2,000 to 3,000 people, a vast increase in the size of human communities compared to much smaller Paleolithic bands. On a global level, scholars estimate that the world's population was about 6 million around 10,000 years ago, before the Agricultural Revolution had a pervasive impact, and shot up to some 50 million by 5,000 years ago and 250 million by the beginning of the Common Era. Here was the real beginning of the human dominance over other forms of life on the planet.

That dominance was reflected in major environmental transformations. In a growing number of places, forests and grasslands became cultivated fields and grazing lands. Human selection modified the genetic composition of numerous plants and animals. In parts of the Middle East, within a thousand years after the beginning of settled agricultural life, some villages were abandoned when soil erosion and deforestation led to declining crop yields, which could not support mounting populations. Human life too changed dramatically in farming communities, for agriculture usually required a settled, village-based way of life. An example of such an early agricultural settlement, now called **Banpo**, has been uncovered in northern China, dating to around 6,000 years ago. Millet, pigs, and dogs had been domesticated, but diets were supplemented with wild plants, animals, and fish. Some forty-five houses covered with thatch laid over wooden beams provided homes to perhaps 500 people. More than 200 storage pits permitted the accumulation of grain, and six kilns and pottery wheels enabled the production of various pots, vases, and dishes, many decorated with geometric designs and human and animal images. A large central space suggests an area for public religious or political activity, and a trench surrounding the village indicates some common effort to defend the community.

But beyond growing populations, did such villages represent "progress," so often associated with the Agricultural Revolution? Farming involved hard work and more of it than in many earlier gathering and hunting societies. The remains of early agricultural people show some deterioration in health—more tooth decay, malnutrition, anemia, slipped disks, arthritis, and hernias; a shorter physical stature; and diminished life expectancy. Living close to animals subjected humans to new diseases—smallpox, flu, measles, chicken pox, malaria, tuberculosis, rabies—while living in larger communities generated epidemics for the first time in human history. Furthermore, since farming peoples often relied heavily on a single plant (rice, wheat, or potatoes), they were vulnerable to famine in case of crop failure, drought, or other catastrophes, while their foraging ancestors had drawn on a much wider range of food resources. The advent of agriculture bore costs as well as benefits.

Agricultural villages, however, also generated an explosion of technological innovation. Mobile Paleolithic peoples had little use for pots, but such vessels were essential for settled societies, and their creation and elaboration accompanied agriculture everywhere. So too did the weaving of textiles, made possible by collecting the fibers of domesticated plants (cotton and flax, for example) and raising animals such as sheep. Evidence for the invention of looms of several kinds dates back to 7,000 years ago, and textiles, some elaborately decorated, show up in Peru, Switzerland, China, and Egypt. Like agriculture itself, weaving was a technology in which women were probably the primary innovators, as it was a task compatible with their childbearing and child-rearing responsibilities. Another technology associated with the Agricultural Revolution was metallurgy. The working of gold and copper, then bronze, and, later, iron became part of the jewelry-, tool-, and weapon-making skill set of humankind. The long "stone age" of human technological history was coming to an end, and the age of metals was beginning.

A further set of technological changes, beginning around 4000 B.C.E., has been labeled the **secondary products revolution**.[18] These technological innovations involved new uses for domesticated animals, beyond their meat and hides. Agricultural people in parts of Europe, Asia, and Africa learned to milk their animals, to harvest their wool, and to enrich the soil with their manure. Even more important, they learned to ride horses and camels and to hitch various animals to plows and carts. Because these animals did not exist in the Americas, this revolutionary new source of power and transportation was available only in the Eastern Hemisphere.

Finally, the Agricultural Revolution presented to humankind the gift of wine and beer, often a blessing, sometimes a curse. As barley, wheat, rice, and grapes were domesticated, their potential for generating alcoholic beverages soon became apparent. The Chinese were making a rice-based wine combined with honey and fruit by about 7000 B.C.E., while grape wine was consumed in Iran by 5400 B.C.E., only 600 years after grapes were domesticated in nearby regions. The precise origins of beer are unclear, but its use was already quite widespread in the Middle East by 4000 B.C.E., when a pictogram on a seal from Mesopotamia showed two figures using straws to drink beer from a large pottery jar. Regarded as a gift from the gods, beer, like bread, was understood in Mesopotamia as something that could turn a savage into a fully human and civilized person.[19] In the Americas, an alcoholic beverage known as *chicha* had been produced from maize, manioc, honey, and various fruits from ancient times and was the drink of choice in the Inca court.

If the Agricultural Revolution meant "progress" in certain ways, it also claimed many victims. While the farming frontier expanded relentlessly,

Nok Culture The agricultural and iron-using Nok culture of northern Nigeria in West Africa generated a remarkable artistic tradition of terra-cotta, or fired-clay, figures depicting animals and, especially, people. This one dates to somewhere between 500 B.C.E. and 50 C.E. Some scholars have dubbed this and many similar Nok sculptures "thinkers." Does this notion reflect a present-day sensibility, or is it an insight into the mentality of the ancient artist who created the image? (Werner Forman Archive/Bridgeman Images) gathering and hunting societies were almost everywhere eroded as foragers became farmers or married into farming communities; as diseases spread from agricultural neighbors; and as more powerful farming communities violently displaced Paleolithic peoples. The plaintive cry of Gudo Mahiya, recorded at the beginning of this chapter, was certainly an echo of many such laments over many centuries.

And what of the animals? Like their human counterparts, certain animals such as cattle, pigs, sheep, and chickens greatly increased their numbers as their habitats became global. But they lost, of course, the freedom of the wild as they lived under the constraint, and often the lash, of their human masters. Many suffered a much shortened life-span as they were slaughtered at a young age for human consumption. Others were required to pull carts and plows or to transport humans on their backs, while some were castrated or branded. Mothers and their offspring were frequently separated shortly after birth. No wonder one scholar has called the Agricultural Revolution a "terrible catastrophe" for the majority of domesticated animals. For humans and animals alike, reproductive success for the species often translated into great suffering for many individuals.[20]

Social Variation in the Age of Agriculture

The resources generated by the Agricultural Revolution opened up vast new possibilities for the construction of human societies, but they led to no single or common outcome. Differences in the natural environment, the encounter with strangers, and, sometimes, deliberate choices gave rise to several distinct kinds of societies early on in the age of agriculture, all of which have endured into modern times.

Pastoral Societies

One variation of great significance grew out of the difference between the domestication of plants and the domestication of animals. Many societies made use of both, but in regions where farming was difficult or impossible — arctic tundra, certain grasslands, and deserts — some people came to depend far more extensively on their animals, such as sheep, goats, cattle, horses, camels, or reindeer. Animal husbandry was a "distinct form of food-producing economy," relying on the products of animals.[21] Those animals could turn grass or waste products into meat, fiber, hides, and milk; they were useful for transport and warfare; and they could walk to market. Known as herders, pastoralists, or nomads, peoples largely dependent on their domesticated animals emerged most prominently in Central Asia, the Arabian Peninsula, the Sahara, and parts of eastern and southern Africa. What they had in common was mobility, for they moved seasonally as they followed the changing patterns of the vegetation necessary as pasture for their animals. Some lived a nomadic existence of constant seasonal movement, but for others it was possible to combine permanent settlements in lowland areas and the movement of animals to more mountainous pasturelands in the summer.

Guided Reading Question

■ COMPARISON
What different kinds of societies emerged out of the Agricultural Revolution?

The Domestication of Animals Although farming often gets top billing in discussions of the Agricultural Revolution, the raising of animals was equally important, for they provided meat, pulling power, transportation (in the case of horses and camels), and manure. Animal husbandry also made possible pastoral societies, which were largely dependent on their domesticated animals. This rock art painting from the Sahara (now southeastern Algeria) dates to somewhere around 4000 B.C.E. and depicts an early pastoral community. The white ovals represent a group of huts. (Musée de l'Homme, Paris, France/Erich Lessing/ Art Resource, NY)

The particular animals central to pastoral economies differed from region to region. The domestication of horses by 4000 B.C.E. and the mastery of horseback-riding skills several thousand years later enabled the growth of pastoral peoples all across the steppes of Central Asia by the first millennium B.C.E. Although organized primarily in kinship-based clans or tribes, these nomads periodically created powerful military confederations, which played a major role in the history of Eurasia for thousands of years. In the Inner Asian, Arabian, and Saharan deserts, domesticated camels made possible the human occupation of forbidding environments. (See Zooming In: The Arabian Camel, Chapter 7, page 296.) The grasslands south of the Sahara and in parts of eastern Africa supported cattle-raising pastoralists. In the Americas, llamas and alpacas were tremendously important in the economy of Andean civilizations, but only in a few pockets in the Andes did human communities rely as heavily on their domesticated animals as did the pastoral peoples of the Afro-Eurasian world.

The relationship between nomadic herders and their farming neighbors has been one of the enduring themes of Afro-Eurasian history. Frequently, it was a relationship of conflict, as pastoral peoples, unable to produce their own agricultural products, were attracted to the wealth and sophistication of agrarian societies and sought access to their richer grazing lands as well as their food crops and manufactured products. The biblical story of the deadly rivalry between two brothers—Cain, a "tiller of the ground," and Abel, a "keeper of sheep"—reflects this ancient conflict, which persisted well into modern times. But not all was conflict between pastoral and agricultural peoples. The more peaceful exchange of technologies, ideas, products, and people across the ecological frontier of pastoral and agricultural societies also served to enrich and to change both sides.

Within **pastoral societies**, the relative equality of men and women, characteristic of most Paleolithic societies, persisted, perhaps because women's work was so essential. Women were centrally involved in milking animals, in processing that milk, and in producing textiles such as felt, which was widely used in Central Asia for tents, beds, rugs, and clothing. Among the Saka pastoralists in what is now Azerbaijan, women rode horses and participated in battles along with men.

A number of archeological sites around the Black Sea have revealed high-status women buried with armor, swords, daggers, and arrows. In the Xinjiang region of western China, still other women were buried with the apparatus of healers and shamans, strongly suggesting an important female role in religious life.

Agricultural Village Societies

For thousands of years, people practiced agriculture using digging sticks or hoes, rather than plows, and even after plows came into use, many societies continued with hoe-based or horticultural farming. Most such hoe-based agricultural peoples lived in settled villages such as Banpo or Jericho, but to varying degrees they continued to augment their agricultural livelihood with gathering, hunting, and fishing. They also retained much of the social and gender equality of gathering and hunting communities, as they continued to do without kings, chiefs, bureaucrats, or aristocracies.

An example of this type of social order can be found at **Çatalhüyük** (cha-TAHL-hoo-YOOK), a very early agricultural village in southern Turkey, which flourished between 7400 and 6000 B.C.E. A careful excavation of the site revealed a population of several thousand people who buried their dead under their houses and then filled the houses with dirt and built new ones on top, layer upon layer. No streets divided the houses, which were constructed adjacent to one another. People moved about the village on adjoining rooftops, from which they entered their homes. Despite the presence of many specialized crafts, few signs of inherited social inequality have surfaced. Nor is there any indication of male or female dominance, although men were more closely associated with hunting wild animals and women with plants and agriculture. "Both men and women," concludes one scholar, "could carry out a series of roles and enjoy a range of positions, from making tools to grinding grain and baking to heading a household."[22]

In many horticultural villages, women's critical role as farmers as well as their work in the spinning and weaving of textiles no doubt contributed to a social position of relative equality with men. Some such societies traced their descent through the female line and practiced marriage patterns in which men left their homes to live with their wives' families. Archeologist Marija Gimbutas has highlighted the prevalence of female imagery in the art of early agricultural societies in Europe and Anatolia, which has suggested to her a widespread cult of the Goddess, focused on "the mystery of birth, death and the renewal of life."[23] But early agriculture did not produce identical gender systems everywhere. Some societies practiced patrilineal descent and required a woman to live in the household of her husband. Grave sites in early Eastern European farming communities reveal fewer adult females than males, indicating perhaps the practice of female infanticide. Some early written evidence from China suggests a long-term preference for male children. These variations in practice suggest that gender roles were likely determined more by cultural preference than by any biological need for a sexual division of labor and power.

In all of their diversity, many village-based agricultural societies flourished well into the modern era, usually organizing themselves in terms of kinship groups or lineages, which incorporated large numbers of people well beyond the immediate or extended family. Such a system provided the framework within which large numbers of people could make and enforce rules, maintain order, and settle disputes without going to war. In short, the lineage system performed the functions of government, but without the formal apparatus of government, and thus did not require kings or queens, chiefs, or permanent officials associated with a state organization. Despite their democratic qualities and the absence of centralized authority, village-based lineage societies sometimes developed modest social and economic inequalities. Elders could exploit the labor of junior members of the community and sought particularly to control women's reproductive powers, which were essential for the growth of the lineage. People with special knowledge, skills, or experience could achieve higher status and greater influence. Among the Igbo of southern Nigeria well into the twentieth century, "title societies" enabled men and women of wealth and character to earn a series of increasingly prestigious "titles" that set them apart from other members of their community, although these honors could not be inherited. Lineages also sought to expand their numbers, and hence their prestige and power, by incorporating war captives or migrants in subordinate positions, sometimes as slaves.

Cahokia: A Nursing Mother Effigy Bottle Among the artifacts uncovered in the North American chiefdom of Cahokia is this effigy bottle in the shape of a nursing mother, dating from 1200 to 1400 C.E. (Photo © The Detroit Institute of Arts/St. Louis Museum of Science & Natural History, Missouri, USA/Bridgeman Images)

Given the frequent oppressiveness of organized political power in human history, agricultural village societies represent an intriguing alternative to the states, kingdoms, and empires so often highlighted in the historical record. They pioneered the human settlement of vast areas; adapted to a variety of environments; maintained a substantial degree of social and gender equality; created numerous cultural, artistic, and religious traditions; and interacted continuously with their neighbors.

Chiefdoms

In other places, agricultural village societies came to be organized politically as **chiefdoms**, in which inherited positions of power and privilege introduced a more distinct element of inequality, but unlike later kings, chiefs could seldom use force to compel the obedience of their subjects. Instead, chiefs relied on their generosity or gift giving, their ritual status, or their personal charisma to persuade their followers. The earliest such chiefdoms seem to have emerged in the Tigris-Euphrates river valley called Mesopotamia (present–day Iraq), sometime after 6000 B.C.E., when temple priests may have organized irrigation systems and controlled trade with nearby societies.

Many chiefdoms followed in all parts of the world, and the more recent ones have been much studied by anthropologists. For example, chiefdoms emerged everywhere in the Pacific islands, which had been colonized by agricultural Poly-nesian peoples. Chiefs usually derived from a senior lineage, tracing their descent to the first son of an imagined ancestor. With both religious and secular func-tions, chiefs led important rituals and ceremonies, organized the community for warfare, directed its economic life, and sought to resolve internal conflicts. They collected tribute from commoners in the form of food, manufactured goods, and raw materials. These items in turn were redistributed to warriors, craftsmen, reli-gious specialists, and other subordinates, while chiefs kept enough to maintain their prestigious positions and imposing lifestyle. In North America as well, a remarkable series of chiefdoms emerged in the eastern woodlands, where an extensive array of large earthen mounds testify to the organizational capacity of these early societies. The largest of them, known as Cahokia, flourished around 1100 C.E. (See "North America: Ancestral Pueblo and Mound Builders" in Chapter 6.)

Thus the Agricultural Revolution radically transformed both the trajectory of the human journey and the evolution of life on the planet. This epic process granted to one species, *Homo sapiens*, a growing power over many other species of plants and animals and made possible an increase in human numbers far beyond what a gathering and hunting economy could support.

But if agriculture provided humankind with the power to dominate nature, it also, increasingly, enabled some people to dominate others. This was not imme-diately apparent, and for several thousand years, and much longer in some places, agricultural villages and pastoral communities retained elements of the social equal-ity that had characterized Paleolithic life. Slowly, though, many of the resources released by the Agricultural Revolution accumulated in the hands of a few. Rich and poor, chiefs and commoners, landowners and dependent peasants, rulers and subjects, dominant men and subordinate women, slaves and free people—these distinctions, so common in the record of world history, took shape most extensively in highly productive agricultural settings, which generated a substantial economic surplus. There the endless elaboration of such differences, for better or worse, became a major fea-ture of those distinctive agricultural societies known to us as "civilizations."

PRACTICING HISTORICAL THINKING

What was revolutionary about the Agricultural Revolution?

REFLECTIONS

The Uses of the Paleolithic

Even when it is about the distant past, history is also about those who tell it in the present. We search the past, always, for our own purposes. For example, mod-ern people were long inclined to view their Paleolithic or gathering and hunting ancestors as primitive or superstitious, unable to exercise control over nature, and ignorant of its workings. Such a view was, of course, a kind of self-congratulation, designed to highlight the "progress" of modern humankind. It was a way of saying, "Look how far we have come."

In more recent decades, however, growing numbers of people, disillusioned with modernity, have looked to the Paleolithic era for material with which to criticize, rather than celebrate, contemporary life. Feminists have found in gathering and hunting peoples a much more gender-equal society and religious thinking that featured the divine feminine, qualities that encouragingly suggested that patriarchy was neither inevitable nor eternal. Environmentalists have sometimes identified peoples in the distant past who were uniquely in tune with the natural environment rather than seeking to dominate it. Some nutritionists have advocated a "Paleolithic diet" of wild plants and animals as well suited to our physiology. Critics of modern materialism and competitive capitalism have been delighted to discover societies in which values of sharing and equality predominated over those of accumulation and hierarchy. Still others have asked, in light of the long Paleolithic era, whether the explosive population and economic growth of recent centuries should be considered normal or natural. Perhaps they are better seen as extraordinary, possibly even pathological. All of these uses of the Paleolithic have been a way of asking, "What have we lost in the mad rush to modernity, and how can we recover it?"

Both those who look with disdain on Paleolithic "backwardness" and those who praise, often quite romantically, its simplicity and equality seek to use these ancient people for their own purposes. None of us can be entirely detached when we view the past, but this is not necessarily a matter for regret. What we may lose in objectivity, we gain in passionate involvement with the historical record and with the many men and women who have inhabited it. Despite its remoteness from us in time and manner of living, the Paleolithic era resonates still in the twenty-first century, reminding us of our kinship with these distant people and the significance of that kinship to finding our own way in a very different world.

Second Thoughts

What's the Significance?

Big Picture Questions

1. In what ways did various Paleolithic societies differ from one another, and how did they change over time?
2. The Agricultural Revolution marked a decisive and progressive turning point in human history. What evidence might you offer to support this claim, and how might you argue against it?
3. How did early agricultural societies differ from those of the Paleolithic era?
4. Was the Agricultural Revolution inevitable? Why did it occur so late in the story of humankind?
5. In what different ways did human beings relate to the natural world during the early and long phases of our history explored in the chapter?

Next Steps: For Further Study

Elizabeth Wayland Barber, *Women's Work: The First 20,000 Years* (1994). Explores the role of women in early technological development, particularly textile making.

David Christian, *This Fleeting World: A Short History of Humanity* (2008). A lovely essay by a leading world historian, which condenses parts of his earlier *Maps of Time* (2004).

Jean Clottes, *What Is Paleolithic Art?*, 2016. A personal and contemplative examination of Paleolithic art and its relationship to shamanism by a prominent French archeologist.

Steven Mithen, *After the Ice: A Global Human History, 20,000–5000 B.C.* (2004). An imaginative tour of world archeological sites during the Agricultural Revolution.

Lauren Ristvet, *In the Beginning* (2007). A brief account of human evolution, Paleolithic life, the origins of agriculture, and the First Civilizations, informed by recent archeological discoveries.

Fred Spier, *Big History and the Future of Humanity* (2011). An effort to place human history in the context of cosmic, geological, and biological history with a focus on the growth of complexity.

James Suzman, *Affluence without Abundance: The Disappearing World of the Bushmen* (2017). A thoughtful and readable account of the Bushmen, a gathering and hunting society in southern Africa, and their encounter with the modern world.

Mark B. Tauger, *Agriculture in World History* (2011). An overview of the origins and significance of farming on a global scale.

"The Agricultural Revolution," http://www.youtube.com/watch?v=Yocja_N5s1I. An eleven-minute animated survey from John Green's *Crash Course World History* series.

The Bradshaw Foundation, "The Cave Paintings of the Lascaux Cave," http://www.bradshawfoundation.com/lascaux/index.php. Text, images, and videos introduce the Paleolithic paintings from the Lascaux Cave in France.

The Australian Dreamtime

The Aboriginal, or native, peoples of Australia have inhabited their continent for tens of thousands of years, living in hundreds of distinct social and linguistic groups. Until the arrival of Europeans in the late eighteenth century, they practiced a gathering and hunting way of life. These peoples have persisted into the twenty-first century as a small minority in modern Australia, and a dwindling few of them still practice their ancient culture. Over an enormously long period of time, they developed an elaborate cosmology, or understanding of the world. Known collectively as the Dreamtime, this cosmology found expression in an evolving body of orally transmitted traditions or stories and in numerous rock art paintings scattered across Australia and frequently retouched or painted over. These stories and images linked the landscape and its human and animal inhabitants to distant events and ancient ancestors.

A contemporary Aboriginal artist, Semon Deeb, explains:

> Around the beginning the Ancestral Beings rose from the folds of the earth and stretching up to the scorching sun they called, "I am!" As each Ancestor sang out their name, "I am Snake," "I am Honey Ant," they created the most sacred of their songs. Slowly they began to move across the barren land naming all things and thus bringing them into being. Their words forming verses as the Ancestors walked about, they sang mountains, rivers and deserts into existence. Wherever they went, their songs remained, creating a web of Songlines over the Country. As they traveled, the Ancestors hunted, ate, made love, sang and danced leaving a trail of Dreaming along the songlines. Finally at the end of their journey the Ancestral Beings sang "back into" the earth where they can be seen as land formations, sleeping.[24]

Over the past two centuries, many Dreamtime stories have been collected and set down in writing, even as new versions have emerged. And the prolific rock art of ancient Aboriginal peoples, which also expressed the Dreamtime outlook, has attracted the attention of many scholars. The tales and images presented here illustrate these Aboriginal efforts to give meaning and shape to their experience.

SOURCE 1.1 Understanding Creation

People everywhere have sought to understand the beginnings of things and in doing so to frame human life in some larger and more meaningful context. In this and other stories from Australia, creation occurred in the Dreamtime, or the "time before time," when ancient ancestral beings brought into existence the latent possibilities of a world that was frozen or asleep. Then they disappeared when their work was finished. But they remained present in the sun, moon, and stars, in the features of the landscape, in the animals of the world, and in paintings on the surface of large rock formations.

- How might you compare this story to creation accounts in other societies?
- What is the relationship between Yhi and Baiame in creating and sustaining the world? Do they play equal roles, or is one superior to the other?
- In what ways are human beings and other living creatures made aware of their connection to the spirit world?

Yhi Brings Life to the World | Oral tradition recorded in 20th century

In the beginning the world lay quiet, in utter darkness. There was no vegetation, no living or moving thing on the bare bones of the mountains. No wind blew across the peaks. There was no sound to break the silence.

The world was not dead. It was asleep, waiting for the soft touch of life and light. . . . Somewhere in the immensity of space Yhi [a sun goddess of light and creation] stirred in her sleep, waiting for the whisper of Baiame, the Great Spirit [a creator deity, Sky Father], to come to her.

Then the whisper came, the whisper that woke the world. . . . Yhi floated down to earth and began a pilgrimage that took her far to the west, to the east, to north, and south. Where her feet rested on the ground, there the earth leaped in ecstasy. Grass, shrubs, trees, and flowers sprang from it, lifting themselves towards the radiant source of light. Yhi's tracks crossed and recrossed until the whole earth was clothed with vegetation.

Her first joyous task completed, Yhi, the sun goddess, rested on the Nullarbor Plain. . . .

"The work of creation is well begun," Baiame said, "but it has only begun. . . . Take your light into the caverns of earth and see what will happen."

Yhi rose and made her way into the gloomy spaces beneath the surface. There were no seeds there to spring to life at her touch. Harsh shadows lurked behind the light. . . . "Sleep, sleep, sleep," the evil spirits wailed, but the shapes had been waiting for the caressing warmth of the sun goddess. Filmy wings opened, bodies raised themselves on long legs. . . . Soon Yhi was surrounded by myriads of insects, creeping, flying, swarming from every dark corner. . . . They followed her out into the world, into the sunshine, into the embrace of the waiting grass and leaves and flowers. . . . [Now] Yhi sped up the hill slopes. . . . She disappeared into the caverns, chilled by the black ice that hung from the roofs and walls. . . . Birds and animals gathered round her, singing in their own voices, racing down the slopes, choosing homes for themselves, drinking in a new world of light, colour, sound, and movement.

"It is good. My world is alive," Baiame said.

Yhi took his hand and called in a golden voice to all the things she had brought to life. "This is the land of Baiame. It is yours forever, to enjoy. Baiame is the Great Spirit. He will guard you and listen to your requests. I have nearly finished my work, so you must listen to my words."

"I shall send you the seasons of summer and winter—summer with warmth which ripens fruit ready for eating, winter for sleeping while the cold winds sweep through the world and blow away the refuse of summer. These are changes that I shall send you . . . , the creatures of my love. Soon I shall leave you and live far above in the sky. When you die your bodies will remain here, but your spirits will come to live with me."

One by one the birds and animals woke up, as they have done every morning since the first dawn. After the first shock of darkness they knew that day would succeed night, that there would always be a new sunrise and sunset, giving hours of daylight for work and play, and night for sleeping. . . .

One last deed remained to be done, because the dark hours of night were frightening for some of the creatures. Yhi sent the Morning Star to herald her coming each day. Then, feeling sorry for the star in her loneliness, she gave her Bahloo, the Moon, for her husband. A sigh of satisfaction arose from the earth when the white moon sailed majestically across the sky, giving birth to myriads of stars, making a new glory in the heavens.

Source: "Yhi Brings Life to the World," in A. W. Reed, *Aboriginal Stories of Australia* (Chatsworth, New South Wales: New Holland, 1980), 11–14.

■ ■ ■

SOURCE 1.2 **The Rainbow Serpent**

A common theme of many Dreamtime stories involved the Rainbow Serpent, which was usually associated with creation, fertility, or social harmony. Images of the Rainbow Serpent in the rock art of Australia date back many thousands of years. (See an image of the Rainbow Serpent on page 17.)

■ What does this version of the Rainbow Serpent story seek to explain?

■ In what ways does the story relate to social problems of Aboriginal peoples?

The Rainbow Serpent Awakens | Oral tradition recorded in 20th century

In the Dreamtime all earth lay sleeping. Nothing moved. Nothing grew. One day the Rainbow Serpent awoke from her slumber and came out from under the ground. She travelled far and wide and eventually grew tired and curled up and slept. She left marks of her sleeping body and her winding tracks. Then she returned to the place where she had first appeared, and called to the frogs, "Come out!"

The frogs came out slow because their bellies were heavy with water, which they had stored in their sleep. The Rainbow Serpent tickled their stomachs and when the frogs laughed, water ran all over the earth to fill the tracks of the Rainbow Serpents' wanderings. This is how lakes and rivers were formed.

With water, grass and trees sprang up. Also all animals awoke and followed the Rainbow Serpent across the land. They were happy on earth and each lived and gathered food with his own tribe. Some animals live in rocks, others on the plains and others in trees and in the air.

The Rainbow Serpent made laws that they all were to obey, but some became quarrelsome and made trouble. The Rainbow Serpent said, "Those who keep my laws will be rewarded; I shall give them human form. Those who break my laws will be punished and turned to stone, never to walk the earth again."

The lawbreakers became stone and turned to mountains and hills, but those who kept the laws were turned into human form. The Rainbow Serpent gave each of them their own totem of the animal, bird or reptile from whence they came. The tribes knew themselves by their totems. Kangaroo, emu, carpet snake, and many, many more. So no one would starve, the Rainbow Serpent ruled that no man should eat of his totem, but only of other totems. This way there was food for everyone.

The tribes lived together on the land given to them by the Rainbow Serpent or Mother of Life and knew the land would always be theirs, and no one should ever take it from them.

Source: http://www.expedition360.com/australia_lessons_literacy/2001/09/dreamtime_stories_the_rainbow.html

■ ■ ■

SOURCE 1.3 **Explaining the World in Aboriginal Rock Art** ▶

The Dreamtime found expression, not only in orally transmitted stories, but also in the rock art of the Aboriginal peoples all across Australia. Created in the unrecorded past by unknown artists, some of these paintings date to 20,000 or more years ago, and many have been repainted or touched up repeatedly over the centuries. Aboriginal peoples have understood these images, not as the work of human artists, but as the actual ancestral beings themselves, able to convey their spiritual energy to their descendants. By engaging with these paintings, Aboriginal peoples "explain and map the landscape. . . . Rock-art is a tangible expression of the continuing presence of Ancestral Beings who moulded and humanized the landscape."[25]

In Source 1.3, painted on a rock face in northern Australia's Kakudu National Park, the largest and main figure at the top is Namondjok, a Creation Ancestor, who according to some accounts can be seen in the sky at night as a dark spot in the Milky Way galaxy. To the right is Namarrgon, or Lightning Man, who generates the tremendous lightning storms that occur during the rainy season. The arc around his body represents the lightning, while the axes on his head, elbow, and feet are used to split the dark clouds, creating thunder and lightning. The female figure beneath Namondjok is Barrginj, the wife of Lightning Man, while below her is a group of elaborately dressed people.

- What might an Aboriginal viewer learn about nature from this painting?

- What might he or she understand about the cosmic hierarchy and the position of human beings within it?

- Why do you think the artist positioned ordinary people at the bottom of the picture? What might they be doing? Could the positioning of Barrginj have meaning as well?

- Notice the distinctive X-ray style, which depicts the internal bones and organs of the figures while also showing their outward appearance. What intentions might lie behind such a style?

Namondjok and the Lightning Man

Kakadu National Park, Northern Territory, Australia/
Werner Forman Archive/Bridgeman Images

■ ■ ■

SOURCE 1.4 Understanding Death

Death marks the end of a life, but an awareness of death shapes much of the living of our lives. And so humans everywhere have sought to understand death, with an eye perhaps to avoiding or delaying it. In the Australian Dreamtime, the immortal ancestor Purukapali was responsible for the introduction of death into the world. The story that follows is one version of this event.

■ How does this story account for the entry of death into human life?

■ What responses to death are suggested in the story?

■ Does such a story carry any meaning to people today?

How Death Came: The Purukapali Myth │ **Oral tradition recorded in 20th century**

In the pleasant land of the Tiwi people, Purukapali lived with his wife, Bima, and their infant son, Djinini. This was in the earliest days when spirits became men and death had not yet come to the earth. In their camp also lived Purukapali's younger brother, Tjapara, strong and handsome. Many times the brothers stalked wallaby together, but most often it was Purukapali who carried game into the camp and received the women's praise.

Tjapara had no wife and he hungered for Bima. One morning after the brothers had returned from the hunt, Bima rose and placed the sleeping Djinini beside her husband, who was skinning a slain wallaby.

"I go find yams," she said. "Guard the child. He will sleep now and will have my milk when I return."

She picked up a net bag and walked off into the bush. Tjapara watched her swinging hips and said, "I saw shellfish at the shore. I will go gather them," and he strode off toward the beach, leaving Puru-kapali with the sleeping child.

As soon as he was well out of sight, Tjapara quickly circled back through the bush and came upon Bima as she bent over her digging stick. Softly he crept upon her and clasped her from behind. "Lie with me," he urged.

[*And so she did, spending the entire day with Tjapara. Meanwhile, her young child died for lack of his mother's milk. When she finally returned to her home*], she found Djinini on the grass, cold and still. Death had come to him in the early darkness. . . . Now Purukapali turned on his wife. "He was hungry. He cried for you and you did not come. Now he is gone from us and will not return," said the father. . . . Bima began to moan and beat her breast. "I am a bad woman, for I let my son die," she cried. . . .

Bima lashed out at Tjapara in despair. "You killed him!" she accused, "for you would not let me go." Now did Purukapali understand. . . . He picked up a forked fighting stick and attacked. "You, too, shall die!" he screamed at his brother. . . . Tjapara fled to a tall tree and frantically began to climb. When he reached the top limb, he let out a great shout and leaped into the sky, rising higher and higher until he reached the moon.

Purukapali returned to camp and took Djinini's body in his arms. "I shall die with my son," he announced to the Tiwi people. "And all who now live also shall die." Then he danced the first ceremony of death and sang of the events that led to it. "This shall be your pukamani [funeral] ceremony," he decreed, "and you shall dance it to remember those who die." Purukapali wrapped his son in paperbark, walked backward into the sea, and disappeared. As he sank beneath the surface, a whirlpool formed which marks the spot to this day.

Bima lived on, but grief soon made her haggard and old. She too wandered about the camp, complaining in a shrill voice until she too died. Her spirit lived on as the curlew bird, which still flits and cries mournfully about the beaches.

Tjapara became the Moon Man. He can be seen in the night sky, his face marked by the bruises and wounds that Purukapali inflicted. He still feels Purukapali at his heels, for he never ceases his restless journey. Hungry from his travels, he gorges on crabmeat, growing rounder and fatter each day until he has feasted so much he falls sick. His wasting body is the waning moon. Each month he dies, but after three days he comes back to life and begins his journey once again. His loneliness is over, for he has found many wives, the planets, who accompany him on his journey across the sky.

So death comes to the people of earth, the Tiwi say, but always life returns.

Source: Louis A. Allen, *Time before Morning* (New York: Thomas Y. Crowell, 1975), 215–19.

■ ■ ■

SOURCE 1.5 **Hunting in Aboriginal Rock Art** ▶

This painting depicts a hunting scene, featuring either ordinary people or the thin Mimi spirits, said to inhabit the nooks and crannies of the area's rock formations and credited with teaching humans how to paint, hunt, and cook kangaroo meat. Notice the spears that the hunters carry. Various kinds of spears and spear-throwing devices had earlier replaced or supplemented the boomerang. The painting is located at the Ubirr art site in Australia's Kakadu National Park, where rock art dates to many thousands of years ago.

- If the painting depicts real people or hunters, what purposes might it serve?

- What different understandings might emerge if the painting is seen as portraying Mimi spirits?

- How do Sources 1.3 and 1.5 reflect the outlook of the Dreamtime stories?

Aboriginal Hunters

Kakadu National Park, Northern Territory, Australia/ullstein bild/Getty Images

DOING HISTORY

1. **Considering human commonality and diversity:** The study of world history highlights both the common humanity of people from all times and places and the vast differences that have separated particular cultures from one another. How might these sources illustrate both of these perspectives?

2. **Linking sources and text narrative:** How do these sources support or amplify the narrative account of the Paleolithic era in Chapter 1? How might they challenge or contradict that narrative?

3. **Considering the relationship of technology and culture:** How might the gathering and hunting technology of these Australian peoples have shaped their cultural understandings as expressed in these stories and paintings? Does it make sense to evaluate technology as more or less "advanced"? Should culture be assessed in the same way?

4. **Pondering relevance:** How might these sources from a very different time and place speak to us in the modern world of the twenty-first century? Or are they only of historical interest?

5. **Thinking about sources:** These stories were only committed to writing over the past two centuries and the paintings may have been redone many times; how does this affect their usefulness as historical sources for the distant past?

Australian Aboriginal Culture

Since written sources are absent, stories and art are often ambiguous, and the dating of events is uncertain, scholars interested in ancient Aboriginal culture have relied heavily on observations and accounts from more recent times. What follows are two such descriptions of ancient Aboriginal life. Voice 1.1, focusing on economic and social life, comes from a historian, Dale Kerwin, who is himself an Aboriginal Australian. Voice 1.2, from an anthropologist, Barbara West, examines the Dreamtime cosmology of Aboriginal peoples.

■ To what extent do these selections emphasize broad similarities between Aboriginal and more modern societies, and in what ways do they stress the differences?

■ What conception of "time" is conveyed in Voice 1.2 and its notion of "the everywhen"? In what ways does this Aboriginal understanding compare with how modern historians approach time?

■ How do these selections complement or challenge the narrative description of Paleolithic life in Chapter 1?

■ **Integrating Primary and Secondary Sources:** How might evidence from the Dreamtime stories and rock art support or challenge the ideas contained in these selections?

VOICE 1.1

Dale Kerwin on the Economic and Social Life of Aboriginal Australians | 2012

Aboriginal people mastered the environment and because of this had ample spare time to pursue other activities such as the arts and political gatherings. Not all people were engaged in food gathering activities; some were engaged in ceremonial activities and trade. . . . [S]ome Aboriginal people choose to travel long distances to trade nuts, stories, and material goods. . . . There is much evidence that Aboriginal society was, and is, dynamic with the sharing of ceremonies and songs with each other and the adoption of various creator spirits. . . . The dynamic nature of Aboriginal society can also be seen in the development of technologies that master the environment. The spearthrower

is a multipurpose tool, which when used as a launcher would extend the throwing range of a spear. It would also be used for carrying tools, so that it became a toolbox. The spearthrower was also used as digging tool and a bowl for food and the stone adze attached to one end would be used as a knife. . . . Aboriginal societies had some members who toiled and collected sufficient food to sustain people in specialized positions such as religious practitioners, specialized craft practitioners, . . . or merchants.

Source: Dale Kerwin, *Aboriginal Dreaming Paths and Trading Routes* (Eastbourne: Sussex Academic Press, 2012), 8, 9, 14.

VOICE 1.2

Barbara West on Aboriginal Dreamtime Cosmology | 2010

Dreaming stories form the basis of Australian Aboriginal religion. They provide explanations for why the world is the way it is. They usually relate to the actions of ancestors, who created the world. The world depicted in these stories is much more complex than that of most westerners for whom the natural and supernatural, past and present, sacred and profane are separate. For Aboriginal Australians, these planes of existence are intertwined. Ancient ancestors created the world and everything in it including rocks, lakes, animals, humans, the wind, and rain, but are also active in the present. Their past actions cannot be separated from present actions especially in ritual which remakes the world each time it is undertaken. The songlines or footprints of these ancient ancestors continue to cross the Australian continent and carry information back and forth from one community to another. Sacred spaces along these lines coexist with everyday or profane spaces, often materialize in rocks, rivers, and other geological features. . . . Anthropologists sometimes use "the everywhen" to refer to the context of the Dreaming stories in order to indicate their timelessness.

Source: Barbara A. West and Francis Murphy, *A Brief History of Australia* (New York: Facts on File, 2010), 27.

First Civilizations

Cities, States, and Unequal Societies

3500 B.C.E.–600 B.C.E.

"Sometimes the weight of civilization can be overwhelming. The fast pace . . . the burdens of relationships . . . the political strife . . . the technological complexity — it's enough to make you dream of escaping to a simpler life more in touch with nature."[1] Found on the website of an organization called Mother Nature Network, this expression of discontent with modernity, written in 2010, reflects the perspectives of the back-to-the-land movement that began in the mid-1960s as an alternative to the pervasive materialism of modern life. Growing numbers of urban dwellers, perhaps as many as a million in North America, exchanged their busy city lives for a few acres of rural land and a very different way of living.

This urge to "escape from civilization" has long been a central feature in modern life. It found expression in Henry David Thoreau's musings on his sojourn at Walden Pond. It is a large part of the "cowboy" image in American culture, and it permeates environmentalist efforts to protect the remaining wilderness areas of the country. Nor has this impulse been limited to modern societies and the Western world. The ancient Chinese teachers of Daoism likewise urged their followers to abandon the structured and demanding world of urban and civilized life and to immerse themselves in the eternal patterns of the natural order. It is a strange paradox that we count the creation of civilizations among the major achievements of humankind and yet people within them have often sought to escape the constraints, artificiality, hierarchies, and other discontents of civilized living. ▪

《 Raherka and Mersankh Writing was among the defining features of civilizations almost everywhere. In ancient Egyptian civilization, the scribes who possessed this skill enjoyed both social prestige and political influence. This famous statue shows Raherka, an "inspector of the scribes" during Egypt's Fifth Dynasty (ca. 2350 B.C.E.), in an affectionate pose with his wife, Mersankh.

So what exactly are these civilizations that have generated such ambivalent responses among their inhabitants? When, where, and how did they first arise in human history? What changes did they bring to the people who lived within them? Why might some people criticize or seek to escape from them?

As historians commonly use the term, "civilization" represents a new and particular type of human society, made possible by the immense productivity of the Agricultural Revolution. Such societies encompassed far larger populations than any earlier form of human community and for the first time concentrated some of those people in sizable cities. Both within and beyond these cities, people were organized and controlled by states whose leaders could use force to compel obedience. Profound differences in economic function, skill, wealth, and status sharply divided the people of civilizations, making them far less equal and

SEEKING THE MAIN POINT

What distinguished "civilizations" from earlier Paleolithic and Neolithic societies? And in what ways did these "civilizations" differ from one another?

subject to much greater oppression than had been the case in earlier Paleolithic communities, agricultural villages, pastoral societies, or chiefdoms. Pyramids, temples, palaces, elaborate sculptures, written literature, and complex calendars, as well as more elaborate class and gender hierarchies, slavery, and large-scale warfare—all of these have been among the cultural products of civilization.

Something New: The Emergence of Civilizations

Like agriculture, civilization was a global phenomenon, showing up independently in seven major locations scattered around the world during the several millennia after 3500 B.C.E. and in a number of other smaller expressions as well (see Map 2.1). In the long run of human history, these civilizations—small breakthroughs to new city- and state-based societies—gradually absorbed, overran, or displaced people practicing other ways of living. Over the next 5,000 years, civilization, as a unique kind of human community, gradually encompassed ever-larger numbers of people and extended over ever-larger territories, even as particular civilizations rose, fell, revived, and changed.

Introducing the First Civilizations

Guided Reading Question

■ **CHANGE**

When and where did the First Civilizations emerge?

The earliest of these civilizations emerged around 3500 B.C.E. to 3000 B.C.E. in three places. One was the "cradle" of Middle Eastern civilization, expressed in the many and competing city-states of **Sumer**. Sumer was located in the southern reaches of Mesopotamia, a term referring to the region between the Tigris and Euphrates rivers, mostly in present-day Iraq. Much studied by archeologists and historians, Sumerian civilization likely gave rise to the world's earliest written language, which was used initially by officials to record the goods received by various temples. Later, Sumerian cities were absorbed into the larger empires of Akkad, Babylon, and Assyria, which encompassed much of Mesopotamia. Almost simultaneously, the Nile River valley in northeastern Africa witnessed the emergence

Landmarks for Chapter 2*

	2500	2000	1500	1000	500	1 B.C.E.

MESOPOTAMIA

3500–3000
Beginnings of
Sumerian civilization

ca. 2000
Epic of Gilgamesh compiled

900–612 Assyrian Empire

ca. 1775
Code of Hammurabi

ca. 500
Persian Empire established

EGYPT

3500–3000
Beginnings of Egyptian civilization

1550–1064 New Kingdom

ca. 1500 Creation of Egyptian empire

2663–2195
Old Kingdom; high point of pharaoh's
power and pyramid building

760 660 Kush conquest of Egypt

CHINA

2200–2000
Beginnings of Chinese civilization

2070–1600
Xia dynasty

1600–1046
Shang dynasty

1046–771 Zhou dynasty

INDUS VALLEY / CENTRAL ASIA

2200–2000
Beginnings of civilization in Indus Valley and Central Asia (Oxus Valley)

ca. 2000
Flourishing of the cities of Mohenjo Dara and Harappa

ca. 1700
Abandonment of Indus Valley and Central Asian cities

THE AMERICAS

3000–1800
Norte Chico civilization

ca. 1200
Beginnings of Olmec civilization

ca. 3000 Quipu in use in Norte Chico

ca. 900
Writing in Olmec civilization

*All dates are B.C.E. or Before the Common Era, and all dates are approximate.

MAPPING HISTORY

Map 2.1 First Civilizations

Seven First Civilizations emerged independently in locations scattered across the planet, all within a few thousand years, from 3500 to 600 B.C.E.

Caspian Sea

Ninevah

Euphrates R.

Tigris R.

Babylon

Nippur

Lagash

SUMER

Ur

A R A B I A N
D E S E R T

Persian Gulf

Aral Sea

Caspian Sea

Amu Darya R.

Anau

Gonur

Murgab R.

Xiangtai

Anyang

Yellow R.

Zhengzhou

Yellow Sea

Yangzi R.

East China Sea

EUROPE

Mesopotamian Civilization

Nile Valley Civilizations

AFRICA

Chinese Civilization: Shang Dynasty

Oxus Civilization

ASIA

Indus Valley Civilization

PACIFIC OCEAN

INDIAN OCEAN

AUSTRALIA

Mediterranean Sea

Jericho

Dead Sea

LOWER EGYPT

Giza

Memphis

SINAI PENINSULA

Akhetaten

Red Sea

UPPER EGYPT

Thebes

Aswan

First Cataract

Second Cataract

NUBIA

Third Cataract

Kerma

Fifth Cataract

Fourth Cataract

Meroë

Sixth Cataract

Indus R.

Harappa

Mohenjo Daro

Arabian Sea

READING THE MAP: Which First Civilizations both emerged along major river valleys and built major urban centers along those rivers?

MAKING CONNECTIONS: Compare this map with Map 1.3, which shows areas where agriculture emerged independently. To what extent did First Civilizations take shape in the same regions where agriculture also emerged?

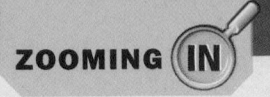

Caral, a City of Norte Chico

Stonework at Caral.

In early 2001, published reports of archeological excavations at a site called Caral set off a firestorm of amazed commentary in both academic circles and the popular media. And no wonder! Archeologists had uncovered, about fourteen miles inland from the coast of Peru, an urban center dating to the time of the Egyptian pyramids, around 2600 B.C.E., far earlier than any previously known urban settlements in the Americas. Thus Egyptian and Mesopotamian claims to the status of "First Civilizations" were now joined by those of Peru.

Most obviously impressive about Caral was its elaborate and monumental architecture. One of its six pyramids stood sixty feet tall and occupied an area the size of four football fields. Circular sunken plazas, temples, an amphitheater, stairways, and many residential spaces, including apartment-style complexes, likewise emerged from the excavations. An intricate irrigation system funneled water from the nearby Supe River to agricultural fields.

Smaller finds at the site convey something about ordinary life in Caral. A clay figure with long hair, a colorful costume, and a decorative necklace suggested a shaman, who served as an intermediary between the gods and humans at Caral. The skeleton of a baby, wrapped in layers of fine cloth, had been carefully buried with a necklace of stone beads. Dozens of beautifully carved flutes and cornets made of condor, pelican, deer, and llama bones revealed an instrumental musical tradition. A *quipu*, consisting of knotted cords and later widely used by the Incas for accounting purposes, pointed to an element of cultural continuity in the Andes region that spanned over 4,000 years.

Archeologists also discovered remains of plants that enhanced sexual performance, as well as hallucinogenic drugs, long used in the Andes and elsewhere in religious

of the civilization of **Egypt**, famous for its pharaohs and pyramids, as well as a separate civilization known as **Nubia**, farther south along the Nile. Unlike the city-states of Sumer, Egyptian civilization took shape as a unified territorial state in which cities were rather less prominent. Later in this chapter, we will compare these two First Civilizations in greater detail.

Less well known and only recently investigated by scholars was a third early civilization that was developing along the central coast of Peru from roughly 3000 B.C.E. to 1800 B.C.E., at about the same time as the civilizations of Egypt and Sumer. This desert region received very little rainfall, but it was punctuated by dozens of rivers that brought the snowmelt of the adjacent Andes Mountains to the Pacific Ocean. Along a thirty-mile stretch of that coast and in the nearby interior, a series of some twenty-five urban centers emerged in an area known as **Norte Chico**, the largest of which was **Caral**, in the Supe River valley. (See Zooming In: Caral, a City of Norte Chico, above.)

Norte Chico was a distinctive civilization in many ways. Its cities were smaller than those of Sumer and show less evidence of economic specialization.

ceremonies. A possible hint about Caral's religious outlook derives from a drawing etched on a gourd, which shows a sharp-toothed figure wearing a hat and holding long sticks or rods in each hand. It clearly resembles the Staff God prevalent in later Andean civilizations. And the remains of a young man found in a ceremonial place suggest the possibility of human sacrifice.

The bone flutes found at Caral.

Nor was Caral an isolated instance of urban living. More than twenty other related sites in the river valleys of the area make up what scholars are now calling the Norte Chico civilization. Caral and other inland cities had close relationships with coastal communities, exchanging their agricultural products such as cotton, beans, squash, and sweet potatoes for sardines and anchovies, whose bones have been found in abundance in Caral. Goods from as far away as present-day Ecuador, the high Andes, and the rain forests that lay to the east suggest a network of wider relationships.

But what was missing from Caral has proved equally intriguing. Grain-based agriculture, pottery, metallurgy, and writing—all features of urban life in Egypt and Mesopotamia—were noticeably absent in Caral. Do we therefore need to revisit the criteria for defining a "First Civilization"? Warfare too apparently played little role in Caral, as no walls, fortresses, weapons, or signs of violent destruction have appeared in the archeological record. Does this mean that Caral uniquely enjoyed "a thousand years of peace," as one of the lead excavators suggested? Was trade rather than warfare the stimulus to creating a complex society? Perhaps so, but it is early in the study of this distinctive civilization.

QUESTIONS

In what ways do recent discoveries at Caral invite reconsideration of Andean civilization and of the history of the earliest civilizations generally? What do you find most surprising about Caral?

The economy was based to an unusual degree on an extremely rich fishing industry in anchovies and sardines along the coast. These items apparently were exchanged for cotton, essential for fishing nets, as well as food crops such as squash, beans, and guava, all of which were grown by inland people in the river valleys using irrigation agriculture. Unlike Egyptian and Sumerian societies, this Peruvian civilization did not rest on grain-based farming; its people did not develop pottery or writing; and few sculptures, carvings, or drawings have been uncovered so far. Furthermore, the cities of Norte Chico lacked defensive walls, and archeologists have discovered little evidence of warfare, such as burned buildings and mutilated corpses. Norte Chico apparently "lighted a cultural fire" in the Andes and established a pattern for the many Andean civilizations that followed—Chavín, Moche, Wari, Tiwanaku, and Inca.[2]

Somewhat later, at least four additional First Civilizations made their appearance. In the Indus and Saraswati river valleys of what is now Pakistan, a remarkable civilization arose during the third millennium B.C.E. By 2000 B.C.E., it embraced a far larger area than Sumer, Egypt, or coastal Peru and was expressed primarily in its elaborately planned cities. All across this huge area, common patterns prevailed: standardized weights, measures, architectural styles, even the size of bricks. As elsewhere, irrigated agriculture provided the economic foundation for the civilization, and a written language, thus far undeciphered, provides evidence of a literate culture for the few.

Unlike its Middle Eastern counterparts, the **Indus Valley civilization** apparently generated no palaces, temples, elaborate graves, kings, or warrior classes. In short, the archeological evidence provides little indication of a political hierarchy or centralized state. This absence of evidence has sent scholars scrambling to provide an explanation for the obvious specialization, coordination, and complexity that the Indus Valley civilization exhibited. A series of small republics, rule by priests, an early form of the caste system—all of these have been suggested as alternative mechanisms of integration in this first South Asian civilization. Although no one knows for sure, the possibility that the Indus Valley may have housed a sophisticated civilization without a corresponding state has excited the imagination of scholars. (See Working with Evidence: Indus Valley Civilization, page 84.)

Whatever its organization, the local environmental impact of the Indus Valley civilization, as of many others, was heavy and eventually undermined its ecological foundations. Repeated irrigation increased the amount of salt in the soil and lowered crop yields. The making of mud bricks, dried in ovens, required an enormous amount of wood for fuel, generating large-scale deforestation and soil erosion. Thus environmental degradation contributed significantly to the abandonment of these magnificent cities by about 1700 B.C.E. Nonetheless, many features of this early civilization—ceremonial bathing, burning of incense, ritual fire altars, yoga positions, bulls and elephants as religious symbols, styles of clothing and jewelry—continued to nourish the later civilization of the Indian subcontinent.[3]

The early Chinese civilization, dating to perhaps 2200 B.C.E., was very different from that of the Indus Valley. The ideal—if not always the reality—of a centralized state was evident from the days of the Xia (shyah) dynasty (2070–1600 B.C.E.), whose legendary monarch Wu organized flood control projects that "mastered the waters and made them to flow in great channels." Subsequent dynasties—the Shang (1600–1046 B.C.E.) and the Zhou (JOH) (1046–771 B.C.E.)—substantially enlarged the Chinese state, erected lavish tombs for their rulers, and buried thousands of

Shang Dynasty Bronze This bronze tiger, created around 1100 B.C.E., illustrates Chinese skill in working with bronze and the mythological or religious significance of the tiger as a messenger between heaven and the human world. (© Martha Avery/Getty Images)

human sacrificial victims to accompany them in the next world. By the Zhou dynasty, a distinctive Chinese political ideology had emerged, featuring a ruler, known as the Son of Heaven. This monarch served as an intermediary between Heaven and Earth and ruled by the Mandate of Heaven only so long as he governed with benevolence and maintained social harmony among his people. This civilization also had writing; an early form of written Chinese has been discovered on numerous oracle bones, which were intended to predict the future and to assist China's rulers in the task of governing. Like Egypt, China has experienced an impressive continuity of identity as a distinct civilization from its earliest expression into modern times.

Central Asia was the site of yet another First Civilization. In the Oxus or Amu Darya River valley and nearby desert oases (what is now northern Afghanistan and southern Turkmenistan), a quite distinctive and separate civilization took shape very quickly after 2200 B.C.E.

An Oxus Valley Axe Head Dating to around 2000 B.C.E., this exquisitely wrought axe head derives from the Oxus Valley civilization. It features in the center a heroic human figure with a bird's head and talons fighting with a wild boar on the upper right and a winged dragon on the lower left. (The Metropolitan Museum of Art, New York, NY, USA/Purchase, Harris Brisbane Dick Fund and James N. Spear and Schimmel Foundation Inc. Gifts, 1982/agefotostock Art Collection/AGE Fotostock)

Within two centuries, a number of substantial fortified centers had emerged, containing residential compounds, artisan workshops, and temples, all surrounded by impressive walls and gates. Economically based on irrigation agriculture and stock raising, this **Central Asian** or **Oxus civilization** had a distinctive cultural style, expressed in its architecture, ceramics, burial techniques, seals, and more, though it did not develop a literate culture. Evidence for an aristocratic social hierarchy comes from depictions of gods and men in widely differing dress performing various functions, from eating at a banquet to driving chariots to carrying heavy burdens. Visitors to this civilization would have found occasional goods from China, India, and Mesopotamia, as well as products from pastoral nomads of the steppe land and the forest dwellers of Siberia. According to a leading historian, this Central Asian civilization was the focal point of a "Eurasian-wide system of intellectual and commercial exchange."[4] Compared to Egyptian and Mesopotamian civilizations, however, it had a relatively brief history, for by 1700 B.C.E., it had faded away as a civilization, at about the same time as a similar fate befell its Indus Valley counterpart. Its cities were abandoned and apparently forgotten until their resurrection by archeologists in the twentieth century. And yet its influence persisted, as elements of this civilization's cultural style show up much later in Iran, India, and the eastern Mediterranean world.

A final First Civilization, known as the Olmec, took shape around 1200 B.C.E. along the coast of the Gulf of Mexico near present-day Veracruz in southern Mexico. Based on an agricultural economy of maize, beans, and squash, Olmec cities arose from a series of competing chiefdoms and became ceremonial centers filled with elaborately decorated temples, altars, pyramids, and tombs of rulers. The most famous artistic legacy of the Olmecs lay in some seventeen colossal basalt heads, weighing twenty tons or more (see the "Olmec Head" image, page 73). Recent discoveries suggest that the Olmecs may well have created the first written language in the Americas by about 900 B.C.E. Sometimes regarded as the "mother civilization" of Mesoamerica, **Olmec civilization** generated cultural patterns—mound building, artistic styles, urban planning, a game played with a rubber ball, ritual sacrifice, and bloodletting by rulers—that spread widely throughout the region and influenced subsequent civilizations, such as the Maya and Teotihuacán.

Beyond these seven First Civilizations, other smaller civilizations also flourished. Lying south of Egypt in the Nile Valley, an early Nubian civilization (3400–3200 B.C.E.) known as Ta-Seti was clearly distinctive and independent of its northern neighbor, although Nubia was later involved in a long and often contentious relationship with Egypt. Likewise in China, a large city known as Sanxingdui, rich in bronze sculptures and much else, arose separately but at the same time as the more well-known Shang dynasty. As a new form of human society, civilization was beginning its long march toward encompassing almost all of humankind by the twentieth century. At the time, however, these breakthroughs to new forms of culture and society were small islands of innovation in a sea of people living in much older ways.

The Question of Origins

Scholars of all kinds—archeologists, anthropologists, sociologists, and historians—have been arguing about the origins of civilization for a very long time, with no end in sight. Amid all the controversy, one thing seems reasonably clear: civilizations had their roots in the Agricultural Revolution. That is the reason they appeared so late in the human story, for only an agricultural technology permitted human communities to produce sufficient surplus to support large populations and the specialized or elite minorities who did not themselves produce food. But not all agricultural societies or chiefdoms developed into civilizations, so something else must have been involved. It is the search for this "something else" that has provoked such great debate among scholars.

The need to organize large-scale irrigation projects, growing populations, the desire to protect favored groups, the stimulus of trade, the demands of warfare—all of these have figured in the debate about the origins of civilization. Geography surely played a role as well, for civilizations often took shape in biologically rich and productive environments such as wetlands, estuaries, and river basins. Anthropologist Robert

Guided Reading Question

■ **CHANGE**
What accounts for the initial breakthroughs to civilization?

Carneiro combined several of these factors in a thoughtful approach to the question. He argued that a growing density of population, producing more congested and competitive societies, was a fundamental motor of change, especially in areas where rich agricultural land was limited, either by geography (oceans, deserts, mountains) or by powerful neighboring societies. Such settings provided incentives for innovations, such as irrigation or plows that could produce more food, because opportunities for territorial expansion were not readily available. But circumscribed environments with dense populations also generated intense competition among rival groups, which led to repeated warfare. A strong and highly organized state was a decided advantage in such competition. Because losers could not easily flee to new lands, they were absorbed into the winner's society as a lower class. Successful leaders of the winning side emerged as elites with an enlarged base of land, a class of subordinated workers, and a powerful state at their disposal—in short, a civilization.[5]

Although such a process was relatively rapid by world history standards, it took many generations, centuries, or perhaps millennia to evolve. It was, of course, an unconscious undertaking in which the participants had little sense of the long-term outcome as they coped with the practical problems of life on a day-to-day basis. What is surprising, though, is the rough similarity of the outcome in many widely separated places from about 3500 B.C.E. to the beginning of the Common Era.

However they got started (and much about this is still guesswork), the First Civilizations, once established, represented a very different kind of human society than anything that came before. All of them were based on highly productive agricultural economies. Various forms of irrigation, drainage, terracing, and flood control enabled these early civilizations to tap the food-producing potential of their regions more intensively. All across the Afro-Eurasian hemisphere, though not in the Americas, animal-drawn plows and metalworking greatly enhanced the productivity of farming. Ritual sacrifice, sometimes including people, accompanied the growth of civilization, and the new rulers normally served as high priests, their right to rule legitimated by association with the sacred.

An Urban Revolution

It was the resources from agriculture that made possible one of the most distinctive features of the First Civilizations—cities. What would an agricultural villager have made of **Uruk**, ancient Mesopotamia's largest city? Uruk had walls more than twenty feet tall and a population around 50,000 in the third millennium B.C.E. At the city's center, visible for miles around, was a stepped pyramid, or ziggurat, topped with a temple (see the photo of a ziggurat on page 71). Inside the city, this village visitor would have found other temples as well, serving as centers of ritual performance and as places for the redistribution of stored food. Numerous craftspeople labored as masons, copper workers, and weavers and in many other specialties, while bureaucrats helped administer the city. It was, surely, a "vibrant, noisy, smelly, sometimes bewildering and dangerous, but also exciting place."[6] Here is how the

Epic of Gilgamesh, Mesopotamia's ancient epic poem dating to around 2000 B.C.E., describes the city:

> Come then, Enkidu, to ramparted Uruk, / Where fellows are resplendent in
>   holiday clothing,
> Where every day is set for celebration, / Where harps and drums are played.
> And the harlots too, they are fairest of form, / Rich in beauty, full of delights,
> Even the great gods are kept from sleeping at night.[7]

Guided Reading Question

■ **CHANGE**

What was the role of cities in the early civilizations?

Equally impressive to a village visitor would have been the city of **Mohenjo Daro** (moe-hen-joe DAHR-oh), which flourished along the banks of the Indus River around 2000 B.C.E. With a population of perhaps 40,000, Mohenjo Daro and its sister city of **Harappa** featured large, richly built houses of two or three stories, complete with indoor plumbing, luxurious bathrooms, and private wells. Streets were laid out in a grid-like pattern, and beneath the streets ran a complex sewage system. Workers lived in row upon row of standardized two-room houses. Grand public buildings, including what seems to be a huge public bath, graced the city, while an enormous citadel was surrounded by a brick wall some forty-five feet high.

Even larger, though considerably later, was the Mesoamerican city of Teotihuacán (tay-uh-tee-wah-KAHN), located in the central valley of Mexico. It housed perhaps 150,000 people in the middle of the first millennium C.E. Broad avenues, dozens of temples, two huge pyramids, endless stone carvings and many bright frescoes, small apartments for the ordinary, palatial homes for the wealthy—all of this must have seemed another world for a new visitor from a distant village. In shopping for obsidian blades, how was she to decide among the 350 workshops in the city? In seeking relatives, how could she find her way among many different compounds, each surrounded by a wall and housing a different lineage? And what would she make of a neighborhood composed entirely of Maya merchants from the distant coastal lowlands?

Cities, then, were central to most of the First Civilizations, though to varying degrees. They were political/administrative capitals; they functioned as centers for the production of culture, including art, architecture, literature, ritual, and ceremony; they served as marketplaces for both local and long-distance exchange; and they housed most manufacturing activity. Everywhere they generated a unique kind of society, compared to earlier agricultural villages or Paleolithic camps. Urban society was impersonal, for it was no

A Mask from Teotihuacán This mask illustrates the kind of facial adornment—a nose pendant and ear spools—often worn by members of the nobility in Teotihuacán. (Museo Nacional de Antropología, Mexico City, Mexico/Bridgeman Images)

longer possible to know everyone. Relationships of class and occupation emerged alongside those of kinship and village loyalty. Most notably, the degree of specialization and inequality far surpassed that of all preceding human communities.

The Erosion of Equality

Among the most novel features of early urban life, at least to our imaginary village visitor, was the amazing specialization of work outside of agriculture—scholars, officials, merchants, priests, and artisans of all kinds. In ancient Sumer, even scribes were subdivided into many categories: junior and senior scribes, temple scribes and royal scribes, scribes for particular administrative or official functions. None of these people, of course, grew their own food; they were supported by the highly productive agriculture of farmers.

Hierarchies of Class

Alongside the occupational specialization of the First Civilizations lay their vast inequalities—in wealth, status, and power. As ingenuity and technology created more productive economies, the greater wealth now available was everywhere piled up rather than spread out. Early signs of this erosion of equality were evident in the more settled and complex gathering and hunting societies and in agricultural chiefdoms, but the advent of urban-based civilizations multiplied and magnified these inequalities many times over, as the more egalitarian values of earlier cultures were everywhere displaced. This transition represents one of the major turning points in the social history of humankind.

As the First Civilizations took shape, inequality and hierarchy soon came to be regarded as normal and natural. Upper classes everywhere enjoyed great wealth in land or salaries, were able to avoid physical labor, had the finest of everything, and occupied the top positions in political, military, and religious life. Frequently, they were distinguished by the clothing they wore, the houses they lived in, and the manner of their burial. Early Chinese monarchs bestowed special robes, banners, chariots, weapons, and ornaments on their regional officials, and all of these items were graded according to the officials' precise location in the hierarchy. In the Babylonian Empire the punishments prescribed in the famous **Code of Hammurabi** (hahm-moo-RAH-bee) (ca. 1775 B.C.E.) depended on social status. A free-born commoner who struck a person of equal rank had to pay a small fine, but if he struck "a man who is his superior, he [would] receive 60 strokes with an oxtail whip in public." Clearly, class had consequences.

In all of the First Civilizations, free commoners represented the vast majority of the population and included artisans of all kinds, lower-level officials, soldiers and police, servants, and, most numerous of all, farmers. It was their surplus production—appropriated through a variety of taxes, rents, required labor, and tribute payments—that supported the upper classes. At least some of these people were aware of, and resented, these forced extractions and their position in the social hierarchy.

Guided Reading Question

■ **CHANGE**
In what ways was social inequality expressed in early civilizations?

Most Chinese peasants, for example, owned little land of their own and worked on plots granted to them by royal or aristocratic landowners. An ancient poem compared the exploiting landlords to rats and expressed the farmers' vision of a better life:

Large rats! Large rats! / Do not eat our spring grain!
Three years have we had to do with you. / And you have not been willing to
    think of our toil.
We will leave you, / And go to those happy borders.
Happy borders, happy borders! / Who will there make us always to groan?[8]

At the bottom of social hierarchies everywhere were slaves. Evidence for slavery dates to well before the emergence of civilization and was clearly present in some gathering and hunting societies and early agricultural communities. But the practice of "people owning people" flourished on a larger scale in urban- and state-based civilizations. Female slaves, captured in the many wars among rival Mesopotamian cities, were put to work in large-scale semi-industrial weaving enterprises, while males helped to maintain irrigation canals and construct ziggurats. Others worked as domestic servants in the households of their owners. In all of the First Civilizations, slaves—derived from prisoners of war, criminals, and debtors—were available for sale; for work in the fields, mines, homes, and shops of their owners; or on occasion for sacrifice. From the days of the earliest civilizations until the nineteenth century, slavery was everywhere an enduring feature of these more complex societies.

Its practice in ancient times, however, varied considerably from place to place. Egypt and the Indus Valley civilizations initially had far fewer slaves than did Mesopotamia, which was highly militarized. Later, the Greeks of Athens and the Romans employed slaves far more extensively than did the Chinese or Indians (see "The Making of Roman Slavery" in Chapter 5). Furthermore, most ancient slavery differed from the type of slavery practiced in the Americas during recent centuries: in the early civilizations, slaves were not a primary agricultural labor force; many children of slaves could become free people; and slavery was not associated primarily with "blackness" or with Africa.

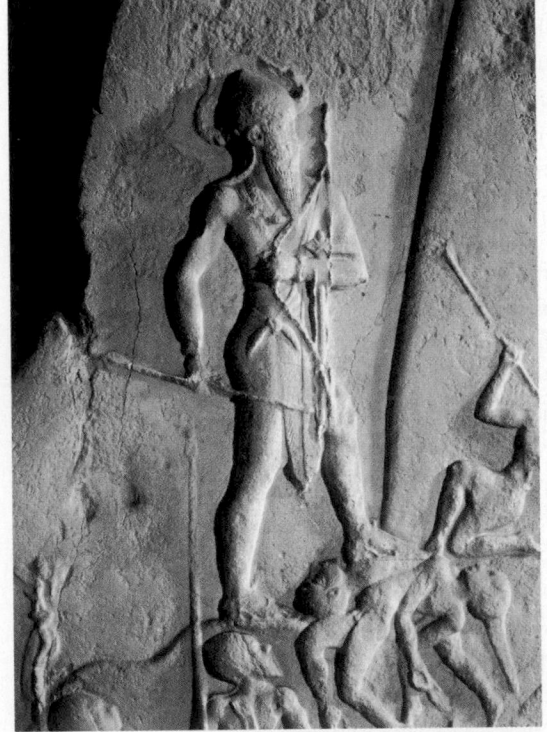

War and Slavery This Mesopotamian victory monument, dating to about 2200 B.C.E., shows the Akkadian ruler Naram-Sin crushing his enemies. Prisoners taken in such wars were a major source of slaves in the ancient world. (Musée du Louvre, Paris, France/Bridgeman Images)

Hierarchies of Gender

No divisions of human society have held greater significance for the lives of individuals than those of sex and gender. Sex describes the obvious biological differences between males and females. More important to historians, however, has been gender, which refers to the many and varied ways that cultures have assigned meaning to those sexual differences. To be gendered as masculine or feminine defines the roles and behavior considered appropriate for men and women in every human community. At least since the emergence of the First Civilizations, and in some cases even earlier, gender systems have supported **patriarchy**, which refers to a social system in which women have been made markedly subordinate to men in the family and in society generally. The inequalities of gender, like those of class, decisively shaped the character of the First Civilizations and of those that followed.

The patriarchal ideal regarded men as superior to women and sons preferable to daughters. Men had legal and property rights unknown to most women. Public life in general was associated with masculinity, which defined men as rulers, warriors, scholars, and heads of households. Women's roles—both productive and reproductive—took place in the home, mostly within a heterosexual family, where women were defined largely by their relationship to a man: as a daughter, wife, mother, or widow. Frequently men could marry more than one woman and claim the right to regulate the social and sexual lives of the wives, daughters, and sisters in their families. Widely seen as weak but feared as potentially disruptive, women required both the protection and control of men.

For men and women alike, gender and class intersected to shape the lives of individuals. Most men, of course, were far from prominent and exercised little power, except perhaps over the women and children of their own families. Upper-class women often experienced a privileged but highly restricted life, for they were largely limited to the home and the management of servants or slaves. By contrast, the vast majority of women always had to be out in public, working in the fields, tending livestock, buying and selling in the streets, or serving in the homes of their social superiors. A few women also operated in roles defined as masculine, acting as rulers, priests, and scholars, while others pushed against the limits and restrictions assigned to women. But most women no doubt accepted their assigned roles, unable to imagine anything approaching gender equality, even as most men genuinely believed that they were protecting and providing for their women.

The big question for historians lies in trying to explain the origins of this kind of pervasive patriarchy. Clearly it was neither natural nor of long standing. For millennia beyond measure, gathering and hunting societies had developed gender systems without the sharp restrictions and vast inequalities that characterized civilizations. Early farming societies, those using a hoe or digging stick for cultivation, continued the relative gender equality that had characterized Paleolithic peoples. What was it, then, about civilization that seemed to generate a more explicit and restrictive patriarchy?

One approach to answering this question highlights the role of a new and more intensive form of agriculture, involving the use of animal-drawn plows and the keeping and milking of large herds of animals. Unlike earlier farming practices that relied on a hoe or digging stick, plow-based agriculture meant heavier work, which men were better able to perform. Taking place at a distance from the village, this

Guided Reading Question

■ **CHANGE**

In what ways have historians tried to explain the origins of patriarchy?

new form of agriculture was perhaps less compatible with women's primary responsibility for child rearing and food preparation. Furthermore, the growing population of civilizations meant that women were more often pregnant and thus more deeply involved in child care than before. Hence, in plow-based communities, men took over most of the farming work, and the status of women declined correspondingly, even though their other productive activities—weaving and food preparation, for example—continued. "As women were increasingly relegated to secondary tasks," writes archeologist Margaret Ehrenberg, "they had fewer personal resources with which to assert their status."[9] But in much of Africa, all of the agricultural areas of the Americas, and parts of Southeast Asia, hoe-based farming persisted and with it, arguably, less restrictive lives for women.

Women have long been identified not only with the home but also with nature, for they are central to the primordial natural process of reproduction. But civilization seemed to highlight culture, or the human mastery of nature, through agriculture, monumental art and architecture, and creation of large-scale cities and states. Did this mean, as some scholars have suggested, that women were now associated with an inferior dimension of human life (nature), while men assumed responsibility for the higher order of culture?[10]

Warfare and professionally led armies, central to many of the First Civilizations, surely contributed to patriarchy. With military service largely restricted to men, its growing prominence in the affairs of civilizations enhanced the values, power, and prestige of a male warrior class and cemented the association of masculinity with organized violence and with the protection of society, especially its women.

Private property and commerce, also prominent among the First Civilizations, may have helped to shape early patriarchies. Without sharp restrictions on women's sexual activity, how could a father be certain that family property would be inherited by his offspring? In addition, the buying and selling associated with commerce were soon applied to male rights over women, as female slaves, concubines, and wives were exchanged among men.

Patriarchy in Practice

Whatever the precise origins of patriarchy, women's subordination permeated the First Civilizations, marking a gradual change from the more equal relationships of men and women within agricultural villages or Paleolithic bands. By the second millennium B.C.E. in Mesopotamia, various written laws codified and sought to enforce a patriarchal family life that offered women a measure of paternalistic protection while insisting on their submission to the unquestioned authority of men. Central to these laws was the regulation of female sexuality. A wife caught sleeping with another man might be drowned at her husband's discretion, whereas he was permitted to enjoy sexual relations with his female servants, though not with another man's wife. Divorce was far easier for the husband than for the wife. Rape was a serious offense, but the injured party was primarily the father or the husband of the victim, rather than the violated woman herself. While wealthy women might own and operate their own businesses or act on behalf of their powerful husbands, they too saw themselves as dependent. "Let all be well with [my husband]," prayed one such wife, "that I may prosper under his protection."[11]

Furthermore, women in Mesopotamian civilization were sometimes divided into two sharply distinguished categories. Under an Assyrian law code that was in effect between the fifteenth and eleventh centuries B.C.E., respectable women, those under the protection and sexual control of one man, were required to be veiled when outside the home, whereas nonrespectable women, such as slaves and prostitutes, were forbidden to wear veils and were subject to severe punishment if they presumed to cover their heads.

Finally, in some places, the powerful goddesses of earlier times were gradually relegated to the home and hearth. They were replaced in the public arena by dominant male deities, who now were credited with the power of creation and fertility and viewed as the patrons of wisdom and learning. This "demotion of the goddess," argued historian Gerda Lerner, found expression in the Hebrew Scriptures, in which a single male deity, Yahweh (YAH-way), alone undertakes the act of creation without any participation of a female counterpart. Yet this demotion did not occur always or everywhere; in Mesopotamia, for example, the prominent goddess Inanna, or Ishtar, long held her own against male gods and was regarded as a goddess of love and sexuality as well as a war deity.

Thus expressions of patriarchy varied among the First Civilizations. Egypt, while clearly patriarchal, afforded its women greater opportunities than did most other First Civilizations. In Egypt, women were recognized as legal equals to men, able to own property and slaves, to administer and sell land, to make their own wills, to sign their own marriage contracts, and to initiate divorce. Moreover, married women in Egypt were not veiled as they were at times in Mesopotamia. Royal women occasionally exercised significant political power, acting as regents for their young sons or, more rarely, as queens in their own right. Clearly, though, this was seen as abnormal, for Egypt's most famous queen, Hatshepsut (r. 1472–1457 B.C.E.), was sometimes portrayed in statues as a man, dressed in male clothing and sporting the traditional false beard of the pharaoh.

The Rise of the State

What, we might reasonably ask, held ancient civilizations together despite the many tensions and complexities of urban living and the vast inequalities of civilized societies? The answer, in large part, lay in yet another distinctive feature of the First Civilizations—states. Organized around particular cities or larger territories, early states were headed almost everywhere by kings, who employed a variety of ranked officials, exercised a measure of control over society, and defended against external enemies. The state is a quite recent invention in human history, replacing, or at least supplementing, kinship as the basic organizing principle of society and exercising

Guided Reading Question

■ **COMPARISON**
How did Mesopotamian and Egyptian patriarchy differ from each other?

far greater power than earlier chiefdoms. But the power of central states in the First Civilizations was limited and certainly not "totalitarian" in the modern sense of that term. The temple and the private economy rivaled and checked the power of rulers, and most authority was local rather than directed from the capital.

Coercion and Consent

Early states in Mesopotamia, Egypt, China, Mesoamerica, and elsewhere drew their power from various sources, all of which helped to integrate their societies. One basis of authority lay in the recognition that the complexity of life in cities or densely populated territories required some authority to coordinate and regulate the community. Someone had to organize the irrigation systems of river valley civilizations. Someone had to direct efforts to defend the city or territory against aggressive outsiders. Someone had to adjudicate conflicts among the many different peoples, unrelated to one another, who rubbed elbows in the streets of early cities. The state, in short, solved certain widely shared problems and therefore had a measure of voluntary support among the population. For many people, it was surely useful.

The state, however, was more useful for some people than for others, for it also served to protect the privileges of the upper classes, to require farmers to give up a portion of their product to support city-dwellers, and to demand work on large public projects such as pyramids and fortifications. If necessary, state authorities had the ability, and the willingness, to use force to compel obedience. As recorded in the Jewish scriptures of the Old Testament, the prophet Samuel warned the ancient people of Israel about the "ways of the king":

> He will take your sons and make them serve with his chariots and horses. . . .
> Some he will assign to be commanders . . . and others to plow his ground and
> reap his harvest, and still others to make weapons of war and equipment for his
> chariots. He will take your daughters to be perfumers and cooks and bakers. He
> will take the best of your fields and vineyards and olive groves and give them to
> his attendants. He will take a tenth of your grain and of your vintage and give
> it to his officials and attendants. Your male and female servants and the best of
> your cattle and donkeys he will take for his own use. He will take a tenth of
> your flocks, and you yourselves will become his slaves.[12]

Such was the power of the state, as rulers accumulated the resources to pay for officials, soldiers, police, and attendants. This capacity for violence and coercion marked off the states of the First Civilizations from earlier chiefdoms, whose leaders had only persuasion, prestige, and gifts to back up their authority. But as states increasingly monopolized the legitimate right to use violence, rates of death from interpersonal violence declined as compared to earlier nonstate communities.[13]

Force, however, was not always necessary, for the First Civilizations soon generated ideas suggesting that state authority as well as class and gender inequalities were normal, natural, and ordained by the gods. Rulers in many places were thought

Guided Reading Question

■ **CHANGE**

What were the sources of state authority in the First Civilizations?

to be morally responsible for the care of their subjects, especially in times of crisis or catastrophe. Kingship everywhere was associated with the sacred. Ancient Chinese kings were known as the Son of Heaven, and only they or their authorized priests could perform the rituals and sacrifices necessary to keep the cosmos in balance, thus preventing war, pestilence, and natural disaster. Egyptians, most of all, invested their pharaohs with divine qualities. Rulers claimed to embody all the major gods of Egypt, and their supernatural power ensured the regular flooding of the Nile and the defeat of the country's enemies.

But if religion served most often to justify unequal power and privilege, it might also on occasion be used to restrain, or even undermine, the established order. Hammurabi claimed that his law code was inspired by Marduk, the chief god of Babylon, and was intended to "bring about the rule of righteousness in the land, to destroy the wicked and the evildoers; so that the strong should not harm the weak."[14] Another Mesopotamian monarch, Urukagina from the city of Lagash, claimed authority from the city's patron god for reforms aimed at ending the corruption and tyranny of a previous ruler. In China during the Western Zhou dynasty (1046–771 B.C.E.), emperors ruled by the Mandate of Heaven, but their bad behavior could result in the removal of that mandate and their overthrow.

A Mesopotamian Ziggurat This massive ziggurat/temple to the Mesopotamian moon god Nanna was built around 2100 B.C.E. in the city of Ur. The solitary figure standing atop the staircase illustrates the size of this huge structure. (© Richard Ashworth/Robert Harding)

Writing and Accounting

A further support for state authority lay in the remarkable invention of writing. It was a powerful and transforming innovation, regarded almost everywhere as a gift from the gods, while people without writing often saw it as something magical or supernatural. Distinctive forms of writing emerged in most of the First Civilizations (see Snapshot, page 72), sustaining them and their successors in many ways. Literacy defined elite status and conveyed enormous prestige to those who possessed it. For Egyptians, a scribe earned a kind of immortality through his writing, for it persisted long after his death. Because it can be learned, writing also provided a means for some commoners to join the charmed circle of the literate. Writing as propaganda, celebrating the great deeds of the kings, was prominent, especially among the Egyptians

SNAPSHOT   Writing in Ancient Civilizations

Most of the early writing systems were logophonetic, using symbols to designate both whole words and particular sounds or syllables. Chinese characters, which indicated only words, were an exception. None of the early writing systems employed alphabets.

Location	Type	Initial Use	Example	Comment
Sumer	Cuneiform: wedge-shaped symbols on clay tablets representing objects, abstract ideas, sounds, and syllables	Records of economic transactions, such as temple payments and taxes	bird	Regarded as the world's first written language; other languages such as Babylonian and Assyrian were written with Sumerian script
Egypt	Hieroglyphs ("sacred carvings"): a series of signs that denote words and consonants (but not vowels or syllables)	Business and administrative purposes; later used for religious inscriptions, stories, poetry, hymns, and mathematics	rain, dew, storm	For everyday use, less formal systems of cursive writing (known as hieratic and demotic) were developed
Andes	Quipu: a complex system of knotted cords in which the color, length, type, and location of knots conveyed mostly numerical meaning	Various accounting functions; perhaps also used to express words	numerical data (possibly in codes), words, and ideas	Widely used in the Inca Empire; recent discoveries place quipus in Caral some 4,600 years ago
Indus River Valley	Some 400 pictographic symbols representing sounds and words, probably expressing a Dravidian language currently spoken in southern India	Found on thousands of clay seals and pottery; probably used to mark merchandise	6 fish	As yet undeciphered
China	Oracle bone script: pictographs (stylized drawings) with no phonetic meaning	Inscribed on turtle shells or animal bones; used for divination (predicting the future) in the royal court of Shang dynasty rulers	horse	Direct ancestor of contemporary Chinese characters
Olmec	Signs that represent sounds (syllables) and words; numbering system using bars and dots	Used to record the names and deeds of rulers and shamans, as well as battles and astronomical data	jaguar	Structurally similar to later Mayan script; Olmec calendars were highly accurate and the basis for later Mesoamerican calendars

and later among the Maya. A hymn to the pharaoh, dating to about 1850 B.C.E., extravagantly praised the Egyptian ruler:

> He has come unto us . . . and has given peace to the two Riverbanks and has made Egypt to live; he hath banished its suffering; he has caused the throat of the subjects to breathe and has trodden down foreign countries; he has delivered them that were robbed; he has come unto us, that we may [nurture up?] our children and bury our aged ones.[15]

In Mesopotamia and elsewhere, writing served an accounting function, recording who had paid their taxes, who owed what to the temple, and how much workers had earned. Thus it immensely strengthened bureaucracy. Complex calendars indicated precisely when certain rituals should be performed. Writing also gave weight and specificity to orders, regulations, and laws. Hammurabi's famous law code, while correcting certain abuses, made crystal clear that fundamental distinctions divided men and women and separated slaves, commoners, and people of higher rank.

Once it had been developed, writing, like religion, proved hard to control and operated as a wild card in human affairs. It gave rise to literature and philosophy, to astronomy and mathematics, and, in some places, to history, often recording what had long been oral traditions. On occasion, the written word proved threatening, rather than supportive, to rulers. China's so-called First Emperor, Qin Shihuangdi (r. 221–210 B.C.E.), allegedly buried alive some 460 scholars and burned their books when they challenged his brutal efforts to unify China's many warring states, or so his later critics claimed (see "China: From Warring States to Empire," Chapter 3). Thus writing became a major arena for social and political conflict, and rulers have always sought to control it.

The Grandeur of Kings

Yet another source of state authority derived from the lavish lifestyle of elites, the impressive rituals they arranged, and the imposing structures they created. Everywhere, kings, high officials, and their families lived in luxurious palaces or homes, dressed in splendid clothing, bedecked themselves with the loveliest jewelry, and were attended by endless servants. Their deaths triggered elaborate burials, of which the pyramids of the Egyptian pharaohs were perhaps the most ostentatious. Monumental palaces, temples, ziggurats, pyramids, and statues conveyed the imposing power of the state

Olmec Head This colossal statue, some eight feet high and weighing twenty-four tons, is one of seventeen such carvings, dating to the first millennium B.C.E., that were discovered in the territory of the ancient Olmec civilization. Thought to represent individual rulers, each of the statues has a distinct and realistically portrayed face. (© Danny Lehman/Corbis/VCG/Getty Images)

PRACTICING HISTORICAL THINKING

In what ways might the advent of "civilization" have marked a revolutionary change in the human condition? And in what ways did it carry on earlier patterns from the past?

and its elite rulers. The Olmec civilization of Mesoamerica (1200–400 B.C.E.) erected enormous human heads, some more than ten feet tall and weighing at least twenty tons, carved from blocks of basalt and probably representing particular rulers. Somewhat later, the Maya Temple of the Great Jaguar, 154 feet tall, was the most impressive among many temples, pyramids, and palaces that graced the city of Tikal. All of this must have seemed overwhelming to common people in the cities and villages of the First Civilizations.

Comparing Mesopotamia and Egypt

A productive agricultural technology, city living, distinct class and gender inequalities, the emerging power of states—all of these were common features of First Civilizations across the world and also of those that followed. Still, these civilizations were not everywhere the same, for differences in political organization, religious beliefs and practices, the role of women, and much more gave rise to distinctive traditions. Nor were they static. Like all human communities, they changed over the centuries. Finally, these civilizations did not exist in complete isolation, for they participated in networks of interactions with near and sometimes more distant neighbors. In looking more closely at two of these First Civilizations—Mesopotamia and Egypt—we can catch a glimpse of the differences, changes, and connections that characterized early civilizations.

Environment and Culture

Guided Reading Question

■ **COMPARISON**
In what ways did Mesopotamian and Egyptian civilizations differ from each other?

The civilizations of both Mesopotamia and Egypt grew up in river valleys and depended on their rivers to sustain a productive agriculture in otherwise-arid lands. Those rivers, however, were radically different. At the heart of Egyptian life was the Nile, "that green gash of teeming life," which rose predictably every year to bring the soil and water that nurtured a rich Egyptian agriculture. The Tigris and Euphrates rivers, which gave life to Mesopotamian civilization, also rose annually, but "unpredictably and fitfully, breaking man's dikes and submerging his crops"[16] (see Map 2.2). Furthermore, an open environment without serious obstacles to travel made Mesopotamia far more vulnerable to invasion than the much more protected space of Egypt, which was surrounded by deserts, mountains, seas, and to its south by unnavigable stretches of the Nile. For long periods of its history, Egypt enjoyed a kind of "free security" from external attack that Mesopotamians clearly lacked.

But does the physical environment shape the human cultures that develop within it? Most historians are reluctant to endorse a "geography is destiny" outlook, but in the case of Mesopotamia and Egypt, it is hard to deny some relationship between the physical setting and culture. Mesopotamia's location within a precarious, unpredictable, and often-violent environment arguably contributed to an

Map 2.2 Mesopotamia

After about 1,000 years of independent and competitive existence, the city-states of Sumer were incorporated into a number of larger imperial states based in Akkad, Babylon, and then Assyria.

outlook suggesting that humankind was caught in an inherently disorderly world, was subject to the whims of capricious and quarreling gods, and had to face death without much hope of a blessed life beyond. A Mesopotamian poet complained: "I have prayed to the gods and sacrificed, but who can understand the gods in heaven? Who knows what they plan for us? Who has ever been able to understand a god's conduct?"[17]

By contrast, elite literate culture in Egypt, developing in a more stable, predictable, and beneficent environment, produced a rather more cheerful and hopeful outlook on the world. The rebirth of the sun every day and of the river every year seemed to assure Egyptians that life would prevail over death. The amazing pyramids, constructed during Egypt's Old Kingdom (2663–2195 B.C.E.), reflected the firm belief that at least the pharaohs and other high-ranking people could successfully make the journey to eternal life in the Land of the West. Incantations for the dead describe an afterlife of abundance and tranquillity that Gilgamesh could only have envied. Over time, larger groups of people, beyond the pharaoh and his entourage, came to believe that they too could gain access to the afterlife if they followed proper procedures and lived a morally upright life. Thus Egyptian civilization not only affirmed the possibility of eternal life but also expanded access to it.

If the different environments of Mesopotamia and Egypt shaped their societies and cultures, those civilizations, with their mounting populations and growing demand for resources, likewise had an impact on the environment.[18] The *Epic of Gilgamesh* inscribed in mythology the deforestation of Mesopotamia. When the ruler Gilgamesh sought to make for himself "a name that endures" by building walls, ramparts, and temples, he required much timber. But to acquire it, he had first to kill Humbaba, appointed by the gods to guard the forests. The epic describes what happened next: "Then there followed confusion. . . . Now the mountains were moved and all the hills, for the guardian of the forest was killed. They attacked the cedars. . . . So they pressed on into the forest . . . and while Gilgamesh felled the first of the trees of the forest, Enkidu [the friend of Gilgamesh] cleared their roots as far as the banks of Euphrates."[19]

In Sumer (southern Mesopotamia), such deforestation and the soil erosion that followed from it sharply decreased crop yields between 2400 and 1700 B.C.E. Also contributing to this disaster was the increasing salinization of the soil, a long-term outcome of intensive irrigation. By 2000 B.C.E., there were reports that "the earth turned white" as salt accumulated in the soil. As a result, wheat was largely replaced by barley, which is far more tolerant of salty conditions. This ecological deterioration clearly weakened Sumerian city-states, facilitated their conquest by foreigners, and shifted the center of Mesopotamian civilization permanently to the north.

Egypt, by contrast, created a more sustainable agricultural system, which lasted for thousands of years and contributed to the remarkable continuity of its civilization. Whereas Sumerian irrigation involved a complex and artificial network of canals and dikes that led to the salinization of the soil, its Egyptian counterpart was much less intrusive, simply regulating the natural flow of the Nile. Such a system avoided the problem of salty soils, allowing Egyptian agriculture to emphasize wheat production, but it depended on the general regularity and relative gentleness of the Nile's annual flooding. On occasion, that pattern was interrupted, with serious consequences for Egyptian society. An extended period of low floods between 2250 and 1950 B.C.E. led to sharply reduced agricultural output, large-scale starvation, the loss of livestock, and, consequently, social upheaval and political disruption. Nonetheless, Egypt's ability to work *with* its more favorable natural environment enabled a degree of stability and continuity that proved impossible in Sumer, where human action intruded more heavily into a less benevolent natural setting.

Cities and States

Politically as well as culturally and environmentally, Mesopotamian and Egyptian civilizations differed sharply. For its first thousand years (3200–2350 B.C.E.), Mesopotamian civilization, located in the southern Tigris-Euphrates region known as Sumer, was organized in a dozen or more separate and independent city-states. Each city-state was ruled by a king, who claimed to represent the city's patron deity and who controlled the affairs of the walled city and surrounding rural area. Quite remarkably, some 80 percent of the population of Sumer lived in one or another of these city-states, making Mesopotamia the most thoroughly urbanized society of ancient times. The chief reason for this massive urbanization, however, lay in the great flaw of this system, for frequent warfare among these Sumerian city-states caused people living in rural areas to flee to the walled cities for protection. With no overarching authority, rivalry over land and water often led to violent conflict.

These conflicts, together with environmental devastation, eventually left Sumerian cities vulnerable to outside forces, and after about 2350 B.C.E., stronger peoples from northern Mesopotamia conquered Sumer's warring cities, bringing an end to the Sumerian phase of Mesopotamian civilization. First the Akkadians (2350–2000 B.C.E.), and later the Babylonians (1900–1500 B.C.E.) and the Assyrians (900–612 B.C.E.), created larger territorial states or bureaucratic empires that encompassed all or most of Mesopotamia. Periods of political unity now descended upon this First Civilization, but it was unity imposed from outside.

Egyptian civilization, by contrast, began its history around 3100 B.C.E., with the merger of several earlier states or chiefdoms into a unified territory that stretched some 1,000 miles along the Nile. For an amazing 3,000 years, the Egypt of the pharaohs maintained its unity and independence, though with occasional interruptions. A combination of wind patterns that made it easy to sail south along the Nile and a current flowing north facilitated communication, exchange, unity, and stability within the Nile Valley. Here was a record of political longevity and continuity that the Mesopotamians and many other ancient peoples could not replicate. An Egyptian territorial state and cultural identity persist still in northeastern Africa.

Cities in Egypt were less important than in Mesopotamia, although political capitals, market centers, and major burial sites gave Egypt an urban presence as well. Most people lived in agricultural villages along the river rather than in urban centers, perhaps because Egypt's greater security made it less necessary for people to gather in fortified towns. The focus of the Egyptian state resided in the pharaoh, believed to be a god in human form. He alone ensured the daily rising of the sun and the annual flooding of the Nile. All of the country's many officials served at his pleasure, and access to the afterlife lay in proximity to him and burial in or near his towering pyramids.

This image of the pharaoh and his role as an enduring symbol of a unified Egyptian civilization persisted over the course of three millennia, but the realities of Egyptian political life did not always match these ideals. By 2400 B.C.E., the power of the pharaoh had diminished, as local officials and nobles assumed greater authority. Having been been awarded their own land, they were able to pass their positions on to their sons. When changes in the weather resulted in the Nile's repeated failure to flood properly around 2200 B.C.E., the authority of the pharaoh was severely discredited, and Egypt dissolved for several centuries into a series of local principalities.

Even when centralized rule was restored around 2000 B.C.E., the pharaohs never regained their old power and prestige. Kings were now warned that they too would have to account for their actions at the Day of Judgment. Nobles no longer sought to be buried near the pharaoh's pyramid but instead created their own more modest tombs in their own areas. Osiris, the god of the dead, became increasingly prominent, and all worthy men, not only those who had been close to the pharaoh in life, could aspire to immortality in his realm.

Interaction and Exchange

Although Mesopotamia and Egypt represented separate and distinct civilizations, they interacted frequently with each other and with both near and more distant neighbors. Even in these ancient times, the First Civilizations were embedded in larger networks of commerce, culture, and power. None of them stood alone.

Guided Reading Question

┄┄┄┄┄┄┄┄┄┄┄┄┄┄┄┄┄

■ **CONNECTION**

In what ways were Mesopotamian and Egyptian civilizations shaped by their interactions with near and distant neighbors?

Egypt's early agriculture, for example, drew upon wheat and barley, which likely reached Egypt from Mesopotamia, as well as gourds, watermelon, domesticated donkeys, and cattle, which came from the Sudan to the south. The practice of "divine kingship" probably derived from the central or eastern Sudan, where small-scale agricultural communities had long viewed their rulers as sacred and buried them with various servants and officials. From this complex of influences, the Egyptians created something distinct and unique, but that civilization had roots in both Africa and Southwest Asia.

Furthermore, once they were established, both Mesopotamia and Egypt carried on long-distance trade, mostly in luxury goods destined for the elite. Sumerian merchants had established seaborne contact with the Indus Valley civilization as early as 2300 B.C.E., while Indus Valley traders and their interpreters had taken up residence in Mesopotamia. Other trade routes connected Mesopotamia to Anatolia (present-day Turkey), Egypt, Iran, and Afghanistan. During Akkadian rule over Mesopotamia, a Sumerian poet described its capital of Agade:

> In those days the dwellings of Agade were filled with gold, / its bright-shining
>   houses were filled with silver,
> into its granaries were brought copper, tin, slabs of lapis lazuli [a blue gemstone],
> its silos bulged at the sides . . . / its quay where the boats docked were all bustle.[20]

All of this and more came from far away.

Egyptian trade likewise extended far afield. In addition to being involved with the Mediterranean and the Middle East, Egyptian trading journeys extended deep into Africa, including Nubia, south of Egypt in the Nile Valley, and Punt, along the East African coast of Ethiopia and Somalia. One Egyptian official described his return from an expedition to Nubia: "I came down with three hundred donkeys laden with incense, ebony, . . . panther skins, elephant tusks, throw sticks, and all sorts of good products."[21]

Along with trade goods went cultural influence from the civilizations of Mesopotamia and Egypt. Among the smaller societies of the region to feel this influence were the Hebrews. Their sacred writings, recorded in the Old Testament, showed the influence of Mesopotamia in the "eye for an eye" principle of their legal system and in the story of a flood that destroyed the world. The Phoenicians, who were commercially active in the Mediterranean basin from their homeland in present-day Lebanon, also were influenced by Mesopotamian civilization. They venerated Astarte, a local form of the Mesopotamian fertility goddess Ishtar. They also adapted the Sumerian cuneiform method of writing to a much easier alphabetic system, which later became the basis for Greek and Latin writing. Various Indo-European peoples, dispersing probably from north-central Anatolia (the site of contemporary Turkey), also incorporated Sumerian deities into their own religions as well as bronze metallurgy and the wheel into their economies. When their widespread migrations carried them across much of Eurasia, they took these Sumerian cultural artifacts with them.

Egyptian cultural influence likewise spread in several directions. Nubia, located to the south of Egypt in the Nile Valley, not only traded with its more powerful neighbor but also was subject to periodic military intervention and political control from Egypt. Skilled Nubian archers were actively recruited for service as mercenaries in Egyptian armies. They often married Egyptian women and were buried in Egyptian style. All of this led to the diffusion of Egyptian culture in Nubia, expressed in building Egyptian-style pyramids, worshipping Egyptian gods and goddesses, and making use of Egyptian hieroglyphic writing. Despite this cultural borrowing, Nubia remained a distinct civilization, developing its own alphabetic script, retaining many of its own gods, developing a major ironworking industry by 500 B.C.E., and asserting its political independence whenever possible. The Nubian kingdom of Kush, in fact, invaded Egypt in 760 B.C.E. and ruled it for about 100 years.

In the Mediterranean basin, clear Egyptian influence is visible in the art of the Minoan civilization, which emerged on the island of Crete about 2500 B.C.E. More controversial has been the claim by some scholars that ancient Greek culture — its

Egypt and Nubia This wall painting from the tomb of an Egyptian court official, dating to the fifteenth century B.C.E., shows Nubians bringing animals as tribute to Egyptian authorities. (James Morris/AKG Images)

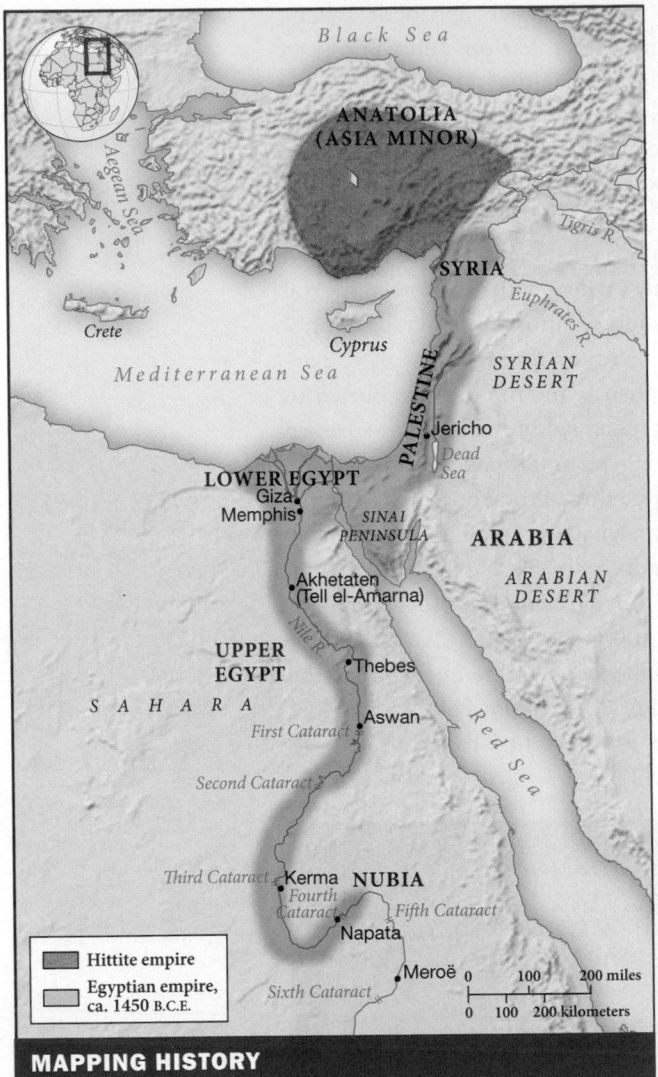

MAPPING HISTORY

Map 2.3 An Egyptian Empire
During the New Kingdom period after 1550 B.C.E., Egypt became for several centuries an empire, extending its political control southward into Nubia and northward into Palestine and Syria.

READING THE MAP: What geographical features and political realities influenced the extent and shape of the Egyptian New Kingdom empire?

INTERPRETING THE MAP: What geographic factors might have made it difficult for Egyptian pharaohs to expand their empire farther or even maintain its New Kingdom borders?

art, religion, philosophy, and language—drew heavily upon Egyptian as well as Mesopotamian precedents. Influence was not a one-way street, however, as Egypt and Mesopotamia likewise felt the impact of neighboring peoples. Pastoral peoples, speaking Indo-European languages and living in what is now southern Russia, had domesticated the horse by perhaps 4000 B.C.E. and later learned to tie that powerful animal to wheeled carts and chariots. This new technology provided a fearsome military potential that enabled various chariot-driving peoples, such as the Hittites, to threaten ancient civilizations. Based in Anatolia, the Hittites sacked the city of Babylon in 1595 B.C.E. Several centuries later, conflict between the Hittites and Egypt over control of Syria resulted in the world's first written peace treaty. But chariot technology was portable, and soon both the Egyptians and the Mesopotamians incorporated it into their own military forces. In fact, this powerful military innovation, together with the knowledge of bronze metallurgy, spread quickly and widely, reaching China by 1200 B.C.E. There it enabled the creation of a strong Chinese state ruled by the Shang dynasty. All of these developments provide evidence of at least indirect connections across parts of the Afro-Eurasian landmass in ancient times. Even then, no civilization was wholly isolated from larger patterns of interaction.

In Egypt, the centuries following 1650 B.C.E. witnessed the migration of foreigners from surrounding regions and conflict with neighboring peoples, shaking the sense of security that this Nile Valley civilization had long enjoyed. It also stimulated the normally complacent Egyptians to adopt a number of technologies pioneered earlier in Asia, including the horse-drawn chariot; new kinds of armor, bows, daggers, and swords; improved methods of spinning and weaving; new musical instruments; and olive and pomegranate trees. Absorbing these foreign innovations, Egyptians went on to create their own empire, both in Nubia and in the eastern Mediterranean regions of Syria and Palestine. By 1500 B.C.E., the previously self-contained Egypt became for several centuries an imperial state bridging Africa and Asia, ruling over substantial numbers of non-Egyptian peoples (see Map 2.3). It also became part of an international political system that included the Babylonian and later Assyrian empires of Mesopotamia as well as many other peoples of the region. Egyptian and Babylonian rulers engaged in regular diplomatic correspondence, referred to one another as "brother," exchanged gifts, and married their daughters into one another's families. Or at least they tried to. While Babylonian rulers were willing to send their daughters to Egypt, the Egyptians were exceedingly reluctant to return the favor, claiming that "from ancient times the daughter of the king of Egypt has not been given to anyone." To this rebuff, the disappointed Babylonian monarch replied: "You are a king and you can do as pleases you. . . . Send me [any] beautiful woman as if she were your daughter. Who is to say this woman is not the daughter of the king?"[22]

REFLECTIONS

"Civilization": What's in a Word?

In examining the First Civilizations, we are worlds away from life in agricultural villages or Paleolithic camps. Strangely enough, historians have been somewhat uncertain as to how to refer to these new forms of human community. Following common practice, we have called them "civilizations," but scholars have reservations about the term for two reasons. The first is its implication of superiority. In popular usage, "civilization" suggests refined behavior, a "higher" form of society, something unreservedly positive. The opposite of "civilized"—"barbarian," "savage," or "uncivilized"—is normally understood as an insult implying inferiority. That, of course, is precisely how the inhabitants of many civilizations have viewed outsiders, particularly those neighboring peoples living without the alleged benefit of cities and states.

Modern assessments of the First Civilizations reveal a profound ambiguity about these new, larger, and more complex societies. On the one hand, these civilizations have given us inspiring art, profound reflections on the meaning of life, more productive technologies, increased control over nature, and the art of writing—all of which have been cause for celebration. On the other hand, as anthropologist Marvin Harris noted, "human beings learned for the first time how to bow, grovel, kneel, and kowtow."[23] Massive inequalities, state oppression, slavery, large-scale warfare, the subordination of women, and epidemic disease also accompanied the rise of civilization, generating discontent, rebellion, and sometimes the urge to escape. This ambiguity about the character of civilizations has led some historians to avoid the word, referring to early Egypt, Mesopotamia, and other regions instead as complex societies, urban-based societies, or state-organized societies.

A second reservation about using the term "civilization" derives from its implication of solidity—the idea that civilizations represent distinct and widely shared identities with clear boundaries that mark them off from other such units. It is unlikely, however, that many people living in Mesopotamia, Norte Chico, or ancient China felt themselves part of a shared culture. Local identities defined by occupation, clan affiliation, village, city, or region were surely more important for most people than those of some larger civilization. At best, members of an educated upper class who shared a common literary tradition may have felt themselves part of some more inclusive civilization, but that left out most of the population. Moreover, unlike modern nations, none of the earlier civilizations had definite borders. Any identification with that civilization surely faded as distance from its core region increased. Finally, the line between civilizations and other kinds of societies is not always clear. Just when does a village or town become a city? At what point does a chiefdom become a state?

Despite these reservations, this book continues to use the term "civilization," both because it is so deeply embedded in our way of thinking about the world and because no alternative concept has achieved widespread acceptance. For historians, however, "civilization" is a purely descriptive term, referring to a distinctive type of human society—one with cities and states—without implying any judgment or assessment, any sense of superiority or inferiority. Furthermore "civilization" serves to define broad cultural patterns in particular geographic regions—Mesopotamia, the Peruvian coast, or China, for example—even though many people living in those regions may have been more aware of differences and conflicts than of those commonalities.

Second Thoughts

What's the Significance?

Big Picture Questions

1. How does historians' use of the term "civilization" differ from popular usage? How do you use it?
2. "Civilizations were held together largely by force." Do you agree with this assessment, or were there other mechanisms of integration as well?
3. How did the various First Civilizations differ from one another?
4. **Looking Back:** To what extent did civilizations represent "progress" in comparison with earlier Paleolithic and Neolithic societies? And in what ways did they constitute a setback for humankind?

Next Steps: For Further Study

Cyril Aldred, *The Egyptians* (1998). A brief account from a widely recognized expert.

Jonathan M. Kenoyer, *Ancient Cities of the Indus Valley Civilization* (1998). A thorough and beautifully illustrated study by a leading archeologist of the area.

Samuel Noah Kramer, *History Begins at Sumer* (1981). A classic account of Sumerian civilization, filled with wonderful stories and anecdotes.

David B. O'Connor, *Ancient Nubia: Egypt's Rival in Africa* (1994). An overview of this ancient African civilization, with lovely illustrations based on a museum exhibit.

Christopher A. Pool, *Olmec Archeology and Early Mesoamerica* (2007). A scholarly and up-to-date account of the earliest civilization in Mesoamerica.

James C. Scott, *Against the Grain: The Deep History of the Earliest States* (2017). An up-to-date review of the scholarship on the origins of agrarian state-based civilizations with an emphasis on the many negative consequences of that landmark development.

Robert Thorp, *China in the Early Bronze Age: Shang Civilization* (2006). An accessible and scholarly account of early Chinese civilization informed by recent archeological discoveries.

"The Ancient Indus Valley Civilization 3500–1700 B.C.E.," http://www.harappa.com. Everything you want to know about the Indus Valley civilization in hundreds of vivid pictures, videos, essays, books, and articles.

The British Museum, "Ancient Egypt," http://www.ancientegypt.co.uk/menu.html. An interactive exploration of Egyptian civilization from the British Museum.

Indus Valley Civilization

In most accounts of the First Civilizations, Egypt and Mesopotamia hold center stage. And yet the civilization of the Indus River valley was much larger, and its archeological treasures have been equally impressive, though clearly distinctive. This civilization flourished around 2000 B.C.E., about a thousand years later than its better-known counterparts in the Middle East and Northeast Africa. By 1700 B.C.E., Indus Valley civilization was in decline, as the center of Indian or South Asian civilization shifted gradually eastward to the plains of the Ganges River. In the process, all distinct memory of the earlier Indus Valley civilization vanished, to be rediscovered only in the early twentieth century as archeologists uncovered its remarkable remains. Here is yet another contrast with Egypt and Mesopotamia, where conscious memory of earlier achievements persisted long after those civilizations had passed into history. The images that follow are drawn from archeological investigations of the Indus Valley civilization and offer us a glimpse of its achievements and unique features. Since its written language was limited in extent and has not yet been deciphered, scholars have been highly dependent on its physical remains for understanding this First Civilization.

SOURCE 2.1 Cityscape of Mohenjo Daro ▶

Among the most distinctive elements of the Indus Valley civilization were its cities, of which Mohenjo Daro and Harappa were the largest and are the most thoroughly investigated. Laid out systematically on a grid pattern and clearly planned, they were surrounded by substantial walls made from mud bricks of a standardized size and interrupted by imposing gateways. Inside the walls, public buildings, market areas, large and small houses, and craft workshops stood in each of the cities' various neighborhoods. Many houses had indoor latrines, while wide main streets and narrow side lanes had drains to carry away polluted water and sewage. Source 2.1 is a modern drawing of ancient Mohenjo Daro.

■ Based on this image, how would you describe Mohenjo Daro to someone who had never seen it?

■ How useful are such modern reconstructions in understanding ancient civilizations?

Wall Painting of Mohenjo Daro Reconstruction | **20th century**

Mohenjo-Daro Archeological Museum, Sindh Province, Pakistan/Roland and Sabrina Michaud/akg-images

■ ■ ■

SOURCE 2.2 A Seal from the Indus Valley ▶

In many ancient and more recent societies, seals have been used for imprinting an image on a document or a product. Archeologists have frequently found such seals in Indus Valley cities. They often incorporate the image of an animal——a bull, an elephant, a crocodile, a buffalo, or even a mythic creature such as a unicorn—and a title or inscription in a still-undeciphered script. Thus the seals were accessible to an illiterate worker loading goods on a boat as well as to literate merchants or officials. Particular seals may well have represented a specific clan, a high official, a particular business, or a prominent individual. Unicorn seals have been the most numerous finds and were often used to make impressions on clay tags attached to bundled goods, suggesting that their owners were involved in trade or commerce. Because bull seals, such as the one shown in Source 2.2, were rarer, their owners may have been high-ranking officials or members of a particularly powerful clan. The bull, speculates archeologist Jonathan Kenoyer, "may symbolize the leader of the herd, whose strength and virility protects the herd and ensures the procreation of the species, or it may stand for a sacrificial animal."[24] Indus Valley seals, as well as pottery, have been found in Mesopotamia, indicating an established trade between these two First Civilizations.

■ How might a prominent landowner, a leading official, a clan head, or a merchant make use of such a seal?

■ What meaning might you attach to the use of animals as totems or symbols of a particular group or individual?

■ Notice the five characters of the Indus Valley script at the top of the seal. Do a little research on the script with an eye to understanding why it has proved so difficult to decipher.

A Humped Cattle Seal from Mohenjo Daro | **19th century** B.C.E.

National Museum of Pakistan, Karachi, Pakistan/De Agostini Picture Library/A. Dagli Orti/Bridgeman Images

■ ■ ■

SOURCE 2.3 Man from Mohenjo Daro ▶

The most intriguing features of the Indus Valley civilization involve what is missing, at least in comparison with ancient Egypt and Mesopotamia. Archeologists have found no grand temples or palaces; no elite burial places filled with great wealth; no images of warfare, conquest, or the seizing of captives; no monuments to celebrate powerful rulers. These absences have left scholars guessing about the social and political organization of this civilization. Nonetheless, the archeology reveals a social hierarchy that included some elite groups. Source 2.3, a statue seven inches tall and found in Mohenjo Daro, likely depicts one of these elite men.

■ What specific features of the statue can you point out?

■ What possible indication of elite status can you identify?

■ What overall impression does the statue convey?

■ In the past some scholars have argued that this statue depicts a "priest king." Do you see any evidence that he is either a priest or a king? To what extent is such speculation helpful? In what ways might it be problematic?

Statue of an Elite Man | **3rd millennium B.C.E.**

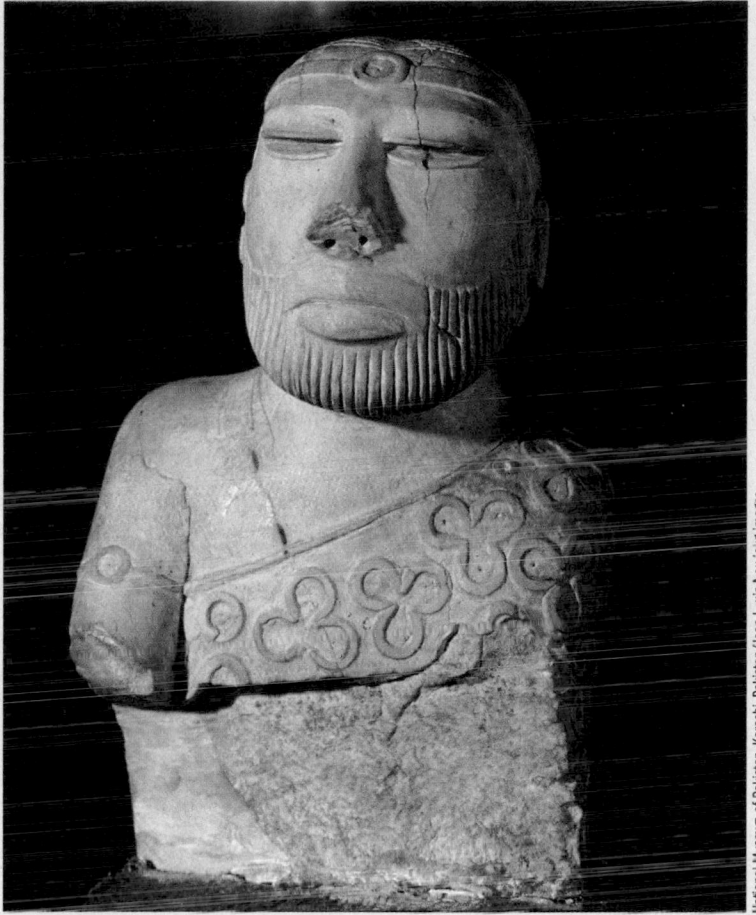

National Museum of Pakistan, Karachi, Pakistan/Jean-Louis Nou/akg-images

■ ■ ■

SOURCE 2.4 **Cart and Oxen from Mohenjo Daro** ▶

Indus Valley statuary can also provide insight into the everyday lives of commoners. Made over 3,500 years ago, this simple stone model of a cart being pulled by two oxen depicts what must have been a common sight in both major cities and the countryside. Such carvings may have served as children's toys, reminding us that some aspects of life, like the need to amuse and distract children, are shared by parents in all times and places.

■ What might an archeologist learn by carefully examining a statue like this? The driver of this cart appears to be female. If so, what does this cart suggest about gender roles in the Indus Valley civilization?

■ What do you think might be the purpose of such a toy beyond simple amusement?

Stone Model of a Cart Pulled by Two Oxen | ca. 2400 B.C.E.

National Museum of Pakistan, Karachi, Pakistan/Universal Images Group/Art Resource, NY

■ ■ ■

SOURCE 2.5 Dancing Girl ▶

Limited archeological evidence suggests that some urban women played important social and religious roles in Indus Valley civilization. Figurines of women or goddesses are more common than those of men. Women, apparently, were buried near their mothers and grandmothers, while men were not interred with their male relatives. The great variety of clothing, hairstyles, and decorations displayed on female figurines indicates considerable class, ethnic, and perhaps individual variation.

Among the most delightful discoveries in the Indus Valley cities is the evocative statue shown in Source 2.5. It is about four inches tall and dates to around 2500 B.C.E. This young female nude is known generally as the "dancing girl." Cast in bronze using a sophisticated "lost wax" method, this statue provides evidence for a well-developed copper/bronze industry. The figure herself was portrayed in a dancer's pose, her hair gathered in a bun and her left arm covered with bangles and holding a small bowl. Both her arms and legs seem disproportionately long. She has been described variously as a queen, a high-status woman, a sacred temple dancer, and a tribal girl. Although no one really knows her precise identity, she has evoked wide admiration and appreciation. Mortimer Wheeler, a famous British archeologist, described her as "a girl perfectly, for the moment, perfectly confident of herself and the world." American archeologist Gregory Possehl, also active in the archeology of the Indus Valley civilization, commented, "We may not be certain that she was a dancer, but she was good at what she did and she knew it."[25]

■ What features of this statue may have provoked such observations?

■ How do you react to this statue? What qualities does the figure evoke?

■ What does Source 2.5 suggest about views of women, images of female beauty, and attitudes about sexuality and the body?

An Indus Valley Girl │ ca. 2500 B.C.E.

National Museum of India, New Delhi, India/Bridgeman Images

DOING HISTORY

1. **Using art as evidence:** What can we learn about the Indus Valley civilization from these visual sources? How does our level of understanding of this civilization differ from that of Egypt and Mesopotamia, where plentiful written records are available?

2. **Considering accessibility:** Do you think that the art of civilizations, such as that of the Indus Valley, resonates more with modern people than artistic products of earlier eras? Is it possible to speak of artistic "progress" or "development," or should we be content with simply noticing differences?

3. **Comparing representations of people:** Notice the various ways that human figures were portrayed in the images shown in Chapters 1 and 2, both those in the chapter narrative and in the Working with Evidence features. How might you define those differences? Can you identify changes from the Paleolithic to the Neolithic eras and then to the age of First Civilizations? How are gender differences represented in these images?

4. **Seeking further evidence:** What additional kinds of archeological discoveries would further our understanding of the Indus Valley civilization?

The State . . . or Its Absence . . . in the Indus Valley

These two selections explore what we can learn about Indus Valley political life and the types of evidence that support these conclusions. In Voice 2.1 the archeologist Gregory Possehl discusses the Indus Valley in the context of other ancient civilizations. Voice 2.2, from the anthropologist and archeologist Jonathan Mark Kenoyer, examines what can be surmised about the political structure of Indus Valley civilization.

- What specific features of other First Civilizations are missing in the Indus Valley historical record?

- What types of sources do scholars use to piece together Indus political culture?

- Which arguments do you find convincing, and which ideas are more speculative?

- **Integrating Primary and Secondary Sources:** How might Source 2.3 support or counter the claims made by these scholars?

VOICE 2.1

Gregory Possehl on Indus Valley Civilization in Context | 2002

The Indus Civilization is something of a faceless sociocultural system. Individuals, even prominent ones, do not readily emerge from the archaeological record, as they do in Mesopotamia and Dynastic Egypt, for example. There are no clear signs of kingship in the form of sculpture or palaces. There is no evidence for a state bureaucracy or the other trappings of "stateness." Nor is there evidence for a state religion in the form of large temples or other monumental public works.

It is clear that the Indus Civilization is . . . just as complex in its own way as the archaic civilizations of Mesopotamia and Dynastic Egypt or the Maya and Inca of the New World. But the Indus Civilization was not organized as a state, if by *state* we adhere to the criteria previously outlined [royal sculptures/palaces and state bureaucracies/religions].

It is its marked deviance from the norm of ancient sociocultural complexity that makes the Indus civilization fascinating. . . . To my knowledge, there is, for example, no close parallel to it in either the archeological or ethnographic record. In that sense, the Indus

Civilization comes across as a kind of counterintuitive civilization, possibly "strange" because there are no existing examples that we can point to as comparative.

Source: Gregory L. Possehl, *The Indus Civilization: A Contemporary Perspective* (New York: AltaMira, 2002), 6.

VOICE 2.2

Jonathan Kenoyer on Political Life in the Indus Valley | 1998

The political organization of these cities was probably not a hereditary monarchy, where one would expect to see palaces and royal storehouses. On the contrary numerous large buildings and public spaces in the lower town at Mohenjo-daro and on Mound F at Harappa support the interpretation that several distinct elite groups were living in the [major] cities. . . .

Due to the long distances between the four major cities [400 miles between Harappa and Mohenjo Daro], it is highly unlikely that a single ruler ever dominated the entire Indus Valley. Each of the largest cities may have been organized as an independent city-state, with different communities competing for control. At times a single charismatic leader may have ruled the city, but most of the time it was probably controlled by a small group of elites, comprised of merchants, landowners and ritual specialists. . . .

The famous stone sculptures found at Mohenjo-daro may represent the rise and fall of one such community of the ruling elite. These stone sculptures were found on the surface of the site or in the topmost levels, buried under the fallen walls of the latest Indus structures. Because all of these sculptures were broken, many scholars feel that they were intentionally vandalized. However, they were made from relatively soft stone, and some may have been damaged [through natural weathering or building collapses]. . . .

If the distribution of the sculptures can be taken to indicate residence localities, then these communities were living on the citadel mound as well as in different neighborhoods of the lower city. . . . It is likely that the individuals depicted in these sculptures were influential citizens or even rulers at Mohenjo-daro.

Source: Jonathan Mark Kenoyer, *Ancient Cities of the Indus Valley Civilization* (Oxford: Oxford University Press, 1998), 100 and 102.

PART 2

Continuity and Change in the Second-Wave Era

600 B.C.E.–600 C.E.

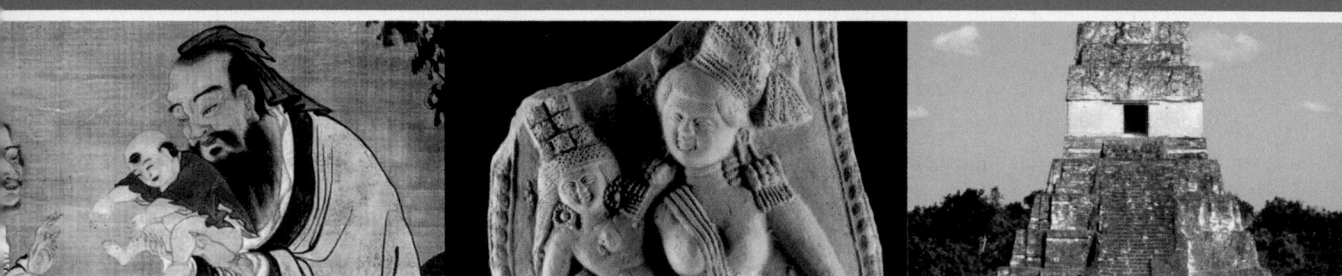

THE BIG PICTURE

The Globalization of Civilization

Studying world history has much in common with using the zoom lens of a camera. Sometimes, we pull the lens back to get a picture of the global panorama. At other times, we zoom in a bit for a middle-range shot of a particular region or civilization, or even farther for a close-up of some specific individual, event, or place. As we bid farewell to the First Civilizations, we look broadly, and briefly, at the entire age of agricultural civilizations, a period from about 3500 B.C.E., when the earliest of the First Civilizations arose, to about 1750 C.E., when the first Industrial Revolution launched a new and distinctively modern phase of

PHOTOS: left, The Art Archive/REX/Shutterstock; center, Musée des Arts Asiatiques–Guimet, Paris, France/ photo: Thierry Ollivier/© RMN–Grand Palais/Art Resource, NY; right, © Peter M. Wilson/Alamy world history. During these more than 5,000 years, the most prominent large-scale trend was the globalization of civilization as this new form of human community increasingly spread across the planet, encompassing more people and larger territories.

The first wave of that process, addressed in Chapter 2, was already global in scope, with expressions in Asia, Africa, and the Americas. But those First Civilizations, impressive as they were, also proved fragile. By the middle of the first millennium B.C.E., all of them had collapsed, fragmented, or been absorbed into new and larger empires. But there was no going back, for "civilization" as a form of social organization proved resilient as well. Thus, in the 1,200 years between 600 B.C.E. and 600 C.E., new or enlarged urban-centered and state-based societies emerged to replace the First Civilizations in the Mediterranean basin, the Middle East, India, China, Mesoamerica, and the Andes. In short, the development of civilization was becoming a global process.

Many of these second-wave civilizations likewise perished, as the collapse of the Roman Empire, Han dynasty China, and the Maya cities reminds us. They were followed by yet a third wave of civilizations, from roughly 600 to 1500 C.E., including those of China, Western Europe, West Africa, Russia, and the Islamic World (see Part 3). Furthermore, smaller expressions of civilization began to take shape elsewhere—in Ethiopia and West Africa, in Japan, Korea, Indonesia, Vietnam, and Cambodia. Thus the globalization of civilization continued apace. So too did the interaction of civilizations with one another and with the gathering and hunting peoples, agricultural village societies, and pastoral communities who were their neighbors.

But how did these second and third waves of civilization differ from the first ones? From a panoramic perspective, the answer is "not much." States and empires rose, expanded, and collapsed. But little fundamental change occurred amid these fluctuations. Monarchs continued to rule most of the new civilizations; women remained subordinate to men in all of them; a sharp divide between the elite and everyone else persisted almost everywhere, as did the practice of slavery. Furthermore, no technological or economic breakthrough occurred to create new kinds of human societies as the Agricultural Revolution had done earlier or as the Industrial Revolution would do much later.

But if we zoom in a bit more closely, significant changes emerge, even if they did not result in a thorough transformation of human life. Global population, for example, grew more rapidly, though with important fluctuations, as the Snapshot illustrates. This rate of growth, though rapid in comparison with Paleolithic times, was quite slow if measured against the explosive expansion of the past century. Another change lies in the growing size of the states or empires that structured civilizations. The Roman, Persian, Indian, and Chinese empires of second-wave civilizations, as well as the Arab, Mongol, and Inca empires of the third wave, all dwarfed the city-states of Mesopotamia and the Egypt of the pharaohs.

Second- and third-wave civilizations also generated important innovations in many spheres. Those in the cultural realm have been perhaps the most widespread and enduring.

SNAPSHOT World Population during the Age of Agricultural Civilization

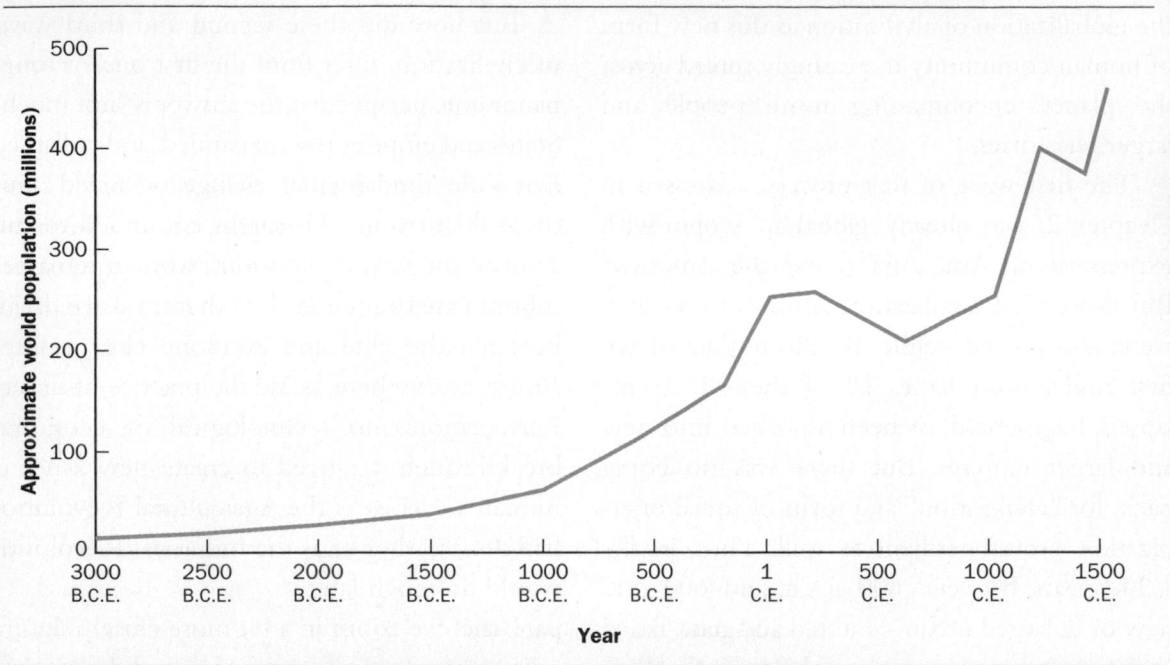

Data from Stephen K. Sanderson, *Social Transformation* (Oxford: Blackwell, 1995), 103.

The philosophical/religious systems of Confucianism and Daoism in China; Hinduism and Buddhism in India; Greek rationalism in the Mediterranean; and Judaism, Zoroastrianism, Christianity, and Islam in the Middle East — these traditions have provided the moral and spiritual framework within which most of the world's peoples have sought to order their lives.

Furthermore, technological innovations considerably enhanced human potential for manipulating the environment. "Chinese inventions and discoveries," wrote one prominent historian, "passed in a continuous flood from East to West for twenty centuries before the scientific revolution."[1] They included silk-handling machinery, the wheelbarrow, a better harness for draft animals, the crossbow, iron casting, gunpowder and firearms, the magnetic compass, paper, printing, porcelain, and more. India pioneered the crystallization of sugar and techniques for the manufacture of cotton textiles. Roman technological achievements were particularly apparent in construction and civil engineering — the building of roads, bridges, aqueducts, and fortifications — and in the art of glassblowing.

Nor were social hierarchies immune to change and challenge. India's caste system grew far more elaborate over time. Roman slaves and Chinese peasants on occasion rose in rebellion. Some Buddhist and Christian women found a measure of autonomy and opportunities for leadership and learning in the monastic communities of their respective traditions. Gender systems, too, fluctuated in the intensity with which women were subordinated to men.

A further process of change following the end of the First Civilizations lay in the emergence of far more elaborate, widespread, and dense networks of communication and exchange that connected many of the world's peoples to one another. Technologies diffused widely across large areas, as did religions and diseases, often borne by long-distance trade routes, such as the Silk Roads, that traversed Eurasia. In all of these ways, the world became quite different from what it had been in the age of the First Civilizations, even though economic and social patterns had not fundamentally changed.

The first three chapters of Part 2 focus in a thematic fashion on the Eurasian/North African civilizations of the second-wave era (600 B.C.E.–600 C.E.), which hosted the vast majority of the world's population, some 80 percent or more. Chapter 3 introduces them by examining and comparing their political frameworks and especially the empires that took shape in most of them. Far more enduring than their empires were the cultural or religious traditions that second-wave civilizations generated. These are examined, also comparatively, in Chapter 4. The social life of these civilizations, expressed in class, caste, slavery, and gender relationships, also varied considerably, as Chapter 5 spells out. In Chapter 6, the historical spotlight turns to inner Africa, the Americas, and Pacific Oceania, asking whether their histories paralleled Eurasian patterns or explored alternative possibilities.

In recalling this second-wave phase of the human journey, we will have occasion to compare the experiences of its various peoples, to note their remarkable achievements, to lament the tragedies that befell them and the suffering to which they gave rise, and to ponder their continuing power to fascinate us still.

Landmarks in World History (ca. 600 B.C.E.–ca. 600 C.E.)

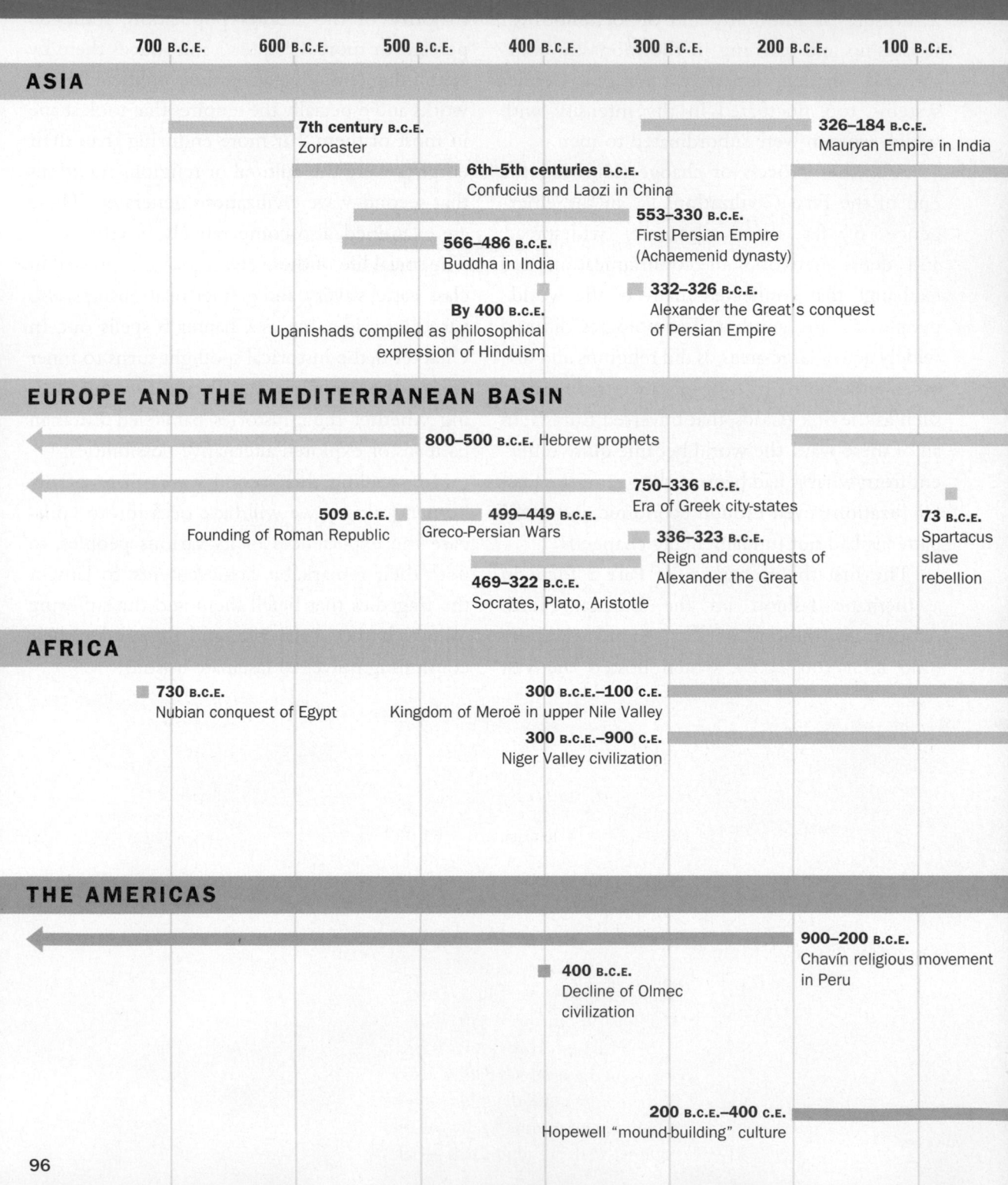

| | 700 B.C.E. | 600 B.C.E. | 500 B.C.E. | 400 B.C.E. | 300 B.C.E. | 200 B.C.E. | 100 B.C.E. |

ASIA

7th century B.C.E.
Zoroaster

326–184 B.C.E.
Mauryan Empire in India

6th–5th centuries B.C.E.
Confucius and Laozi in China

553–330 B.C.E.
First Persian Empire
(Achaemenid dynasty)

566–486 B.C.E.
Buddha in India

332–326 B.C.E.
Alexander the Great's conquest
of Persian Empire

By 400 B.C.E.
Upanishads compiled as philosophical
expression of Hinduism

EUROPE AND THE MEDITERRANEAN BASIN

800–500 B.C.E. Hebrew prophets

750–336 B.C.E.
Era of Greek city-states

509 B.C.E.
Founding of Roman Republic

499–449 B.C.E.
Greco-Persian Wars

73 B.C.E.
Spartacus
slave
rebellion

336–323 B.C.E.
Reign and conquests of
Alexander the Great

469–322 B.C.E.
Socrates, Plato, Aristotle

AFRICA

730 B.C.E.
Nubian conquest of Egypt

300 B.C.E.**–100** C.E.
Kingdom of Meroë in upper Nile Valley

300 B.C.E.**–900** C.E.
Niger Valley civilization

THE AMERICAS

900–200 B.C.E.
Chavín religious movement
in Peru

400 B.C.E.
Decline of Olmec
civilization

200 B.C.E.**–400** C.E.
Hopewell "mound-building" culture

96

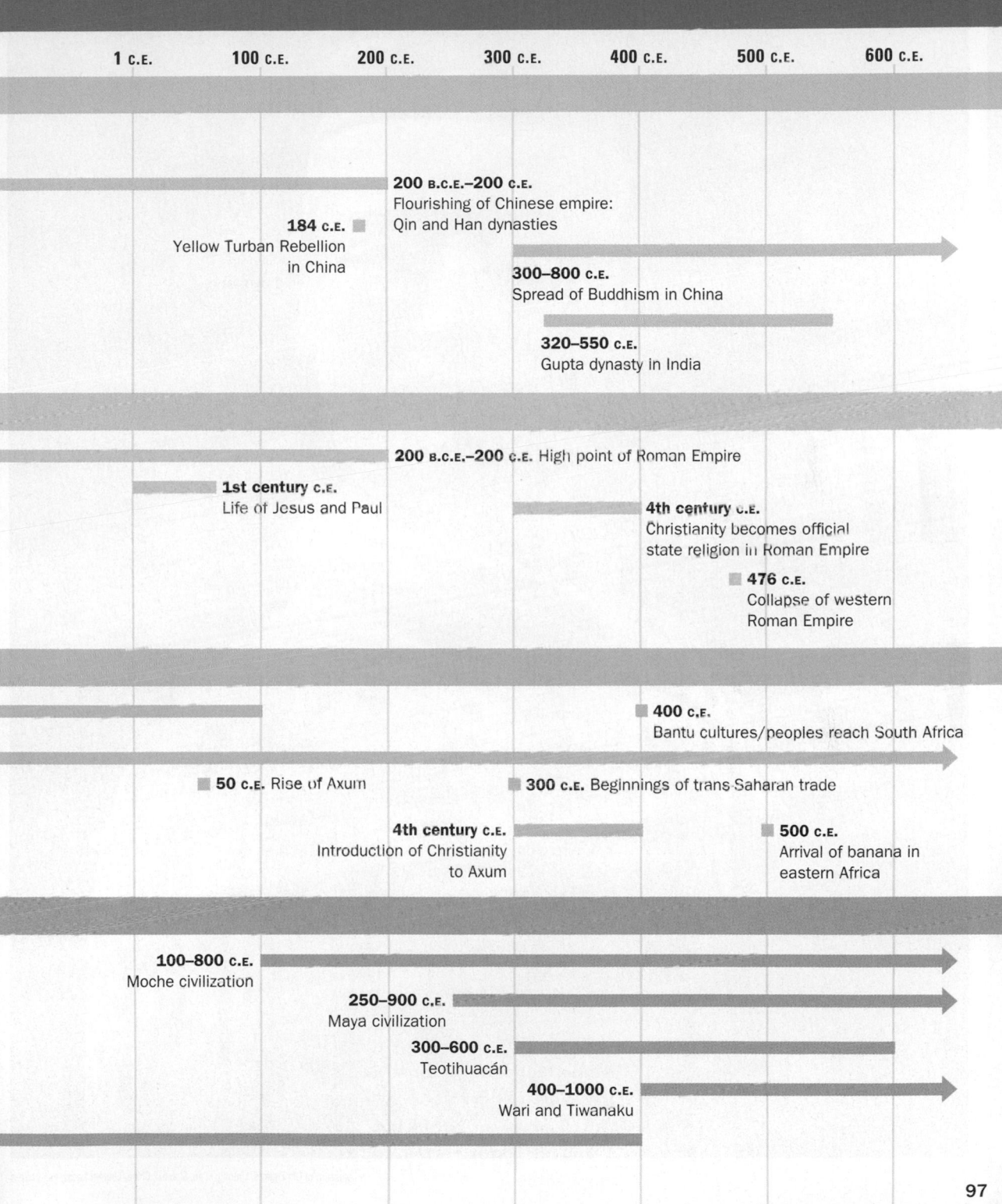

1 C.E.	100 C.E.	200 C.E.	300 C.E.	400 C.E.	500 C.E.	600 C.E.

200 B.C.E.–200 C.E.
Flourishing of Chinese empire:
Qin and Han dynasties

184 C.E.
Yellow Turban Rebellion
in China

300–800 C.E.
Spread of Buddhism in China

320–550 C.E.
Gupta dynasty in India

200 B.C.E.–200 C.E. High point of Roman Empire

1st century C.E.
Life of Jesus and Paul

4th century C.E.
Christianity becomes official
state religion in Roman Empire

476 C.E.
Collapse of western
Roman Empire

400 C.E.
Bantu cultures/peoples reach South Africa

50 C.E. Rise of Axum

300 C.E. Beginnings of trans-Saharan trade

4th century C.E.
Introduction of Christianity
to Axum

500 C.E.
Arrival of banana in
eastern Africa

100–800 C.E.
Moche civilization

250–900 C.E.
Maya civilization

300–600 C.E.
Teotihuacán

400–1000 C.E.
Wari and Tiwanaku

State and Empire in Eurasia / North Africa

600 B.C.E.–600 C.E.

Are We Rome? It was the title of a thoughtful book, published in 2007, asking what had become a familiar question in the early twenty-first century: "Is the United States the new Roman Empire?"[1] With the collapse of the Soviet Union by 1991 and the subsequent U.S. invasions of Afghanistan and Iraq, some commentators began to make the comparison. The United States' enormous multicultural society, its technological achievements, its economically draining and overstretched armed forces, its sense of itself as unique and endowed with a global mission, its concern about foreigners penetrating its borders, its apparent determination to maintain military superiority—all of this invited comparison with the Roman Empire.

Supporters of a dominant role for the United States argued that Americans must face up to their responsibilities as "the undisputed master of the world" as the Romans did in their time. Critics warned that the Roman Empire became overextended abroad and corrupt and dictatorial at home and then collapsed, suggesting that a similar fate may await the American empire. Either way, the point of reference was an empire that had passed into history some 1,500 years earlier, a continuing reminder of the significance of the distant past for our contemporary world. In fact, for at least several centuries, that empire has been a source of metaphors and "lessons" about personal morality, corruption, political life, military expansion, and much more.

Even in a world largely critical of empires, they still excite the imagination of historians and readers of history alike. The earliest empires show up in the era of the First Civilizations when Akkadian, Babylonian, and Assyrian empires encompassed the city-states of Mesopotamia and established an enduring imperial tradition in the Middle East. Egypt became an imperial state when it temporarily ruled Nubia and the lands of

≪ Terra-Cotta Warrior Part of the immense funerary complex of terra-cotta warriors constructed for the Chinese ruler Qin Shihuangdi, this crossbow marksman represents the military power that reunified a divided China under the Qin dynasty in 221 B.C.E.

the eastern Mediterranean. Following in their wake were many more empires, whose rise and fall have been central features of world history for the past 4,000 years. ■

But what exactly is an empire? At one level, empires are simply states, political systems that exercise coercive power. The term, however, is normally reserved for larger and more aggressive states, those that conquer, rule, and extract resources from other states and peoples. Thus empires have generally encompassed a considerable variety of peoples and cultures within a single political system, and they have often been associated with political or cultural oppression. Frequently, empires have given political expression to a civilization or culture, as in the Chinese and Persian empires. But civilizations have also flourished without a single all-encompassing state or empire, as in the competing city-states of Mesopotamia, Greece, and Mesoamerica or the many rival states of post-Roman Europe. In such cases, civilizations were expressed in elements of a common culture rather than in a unified political system.

The major Eurasian empires of the second-wave era—those of Persia, Greece under Alexander the Great, Rome, China during the Qin (chihn) and Han dynasties, and India during the Mauryan (MORE-yuhn) and Gupta dynasties—shared a set of common problems. Would they seek to impose the culture of the imperial heartland on their varied subjects? Would they rule conquered people directly or through established local authorities? How could they extract the wealth of empire in the form of taxes, tribute, and labor while maintaining order in conquered territories? And they also shared a common destiny, as they vanished into history.

Why have these and other empires been of such lasting fascination to both ancient and modern people? Perhaps part of the reason is that they were so big, creating a looming presence in their respective regions. Their armies and their tax collectors were hard to avoid. Perhaps they fascinate also because they were so bloody. The violence of conquest easily grabs our attention, and certainly all of these empires were founded and sustained at a great cost in human life. Many people have found the collapse of these once-powerful states likewise intriguing. But empires have also commanded attention simply because they were influential. Probably the majority of humankind before the twentieth century lived out their lives in empires, where they were often governed by rulers culturally different from themselves. These imperial states brought together people of quite different traditions and religions and so stimulated the exchange of ideas, cultures, and values. Despite their violence, exploitation, and oppression, empires also imposed substantial periods of peace and security, which fostered economic and artistic development, commercial exchange, and cultural mixing. In many places, empire also played an important role in defining masculinity, as conquest generated a warrior culture that gave particular prominence to the men who created and ruled those imperial states.

SEEKING THE MAIN POINT

How might you assess—both positively and negatively—the role of empires in the history of the second-wave era?

Landmarks for Chapter 3

600 B.C.E.	400 B.C.E.	200 B.C.E.	1 C.E.	200 C.E.	400 C.E.	600 C.E.

THE PERSIAN WORLD

550–330 B.C.E.
Persian Empire

522–486 B.C.E.
Reign of Darius

331 B.C.E. Defeat at the hands of Alexander

490 and 480 B.C.E.
Greeks defeat Persia in major battles

THE MEDITERRANEAN WORLD

750–336 B.C.E.
Era of the Greek city-states

509 B.C.E.
Founding of Rome

200 B.C.E.–200 C.E.
High point of Roman Empire

499–449 B.C.E.
Greco-Persian Wars

334–323 B.C.E.
Conquests of Alexander the
Great/beginning of Hellenistic era

ca. 476 C.E.
Collapse of western Roman Empire

431–404 B.C.E.
Peloponnesian War

THE CHINESE WORLD

500–221 B.C.E.
Age of warring states

221–210 B.C.E.
Reign of Qin Shihuangdi

581–618 C.E.
Reunification of China under Sui dynasty

THE SOUTH ASIAN WORLD

ca. 600 B.C.E.
Crystallization of a northern Indian civilization

326–184 B.C.E.
Mauryan dynasty empire

320–550 C.E.
Gupta dynasty empire

268–232 B.C.E.
Reign of Ashoka

Empires and Civilizations in Collision: The Persians and the Greeks

The centuries between 600 B.C.E. and 600 C.E. witnessed the flowering of second-wave civilizations in the Mediterranean world, the Middle East, India, and China. For the most part, these distant civilizations did not directly encounter one another, as each established its own political system, cultural values, and ways of organizing society. A great exception to that rule lay in the Mediterranean world and in the Middle East, where the emerging Persian Empire and Greek civilization, physically adjacent to each other, experienced a centuries-long interaction and clash. It was one of the most consequential cultural encounters of the ancient world.

The Persian Empire

By the mid-sixth century B.C.E., the largest and most impressive of the world's empires was that of the Persians, an Indo-European people whose homeland lay on the Iranian plateau just north of the Persian Gulf. Living on the margins of the earlier Mesopotamian civilization, the Persians under the Achaemenid (ah-KEE-muh-nid) dynasty (550–330 B.C.E.) constructed an imperial system that drew on previous examples, such as the Babylonian and Assyrian empires, but far surpassed them all in both size and splendor. Under the leadership of the famous monarchs Cyrus (r. 559–530 B.C.E.) and Darius (r. 522–486 B.C.E.), Persian conquests quickly reached from Egypt to India, encompassing in a single state some 35 to 50 million people, an immensely diverse realm containing dozens of peoples, states, languages, and cultural traditions (see Map 3.1).

Guided Reading Question

■ **COMPARISON**
How did Persian and Greek civilizations differ in their political organization and values?

The **Persian Empire** centered on an elaborate cult of kingship in which the monarch, secluded in royal magnificence, could be approached only through an elaborate ritual. When the king died, sacred fires all across the land were extinguished, Persians were expected to shave their hair in mourning, and the manes of horses were cut short. Ruling by the will of the great Persian god Ahura Mazda (uh-HOORE-uh MAHZ-duh), kings were absolute monarchs, more than willing to crush rebellious regions or officials. Interrupted on one occasion while engaged with his wife, Darius ordered the offender, a high-ranking nobleman, killed, along with his entire clan. In the eyes of many, Persian monarchs fully deserved their effusive title—"Great king, King of kings, King of countries containing all kinds of men, King in this great earth far and wide." Darius himself best expressed the authority of the Persian ruler when he observed, "What was said to them by me, night and day, it was done."[2]

But more than conquest and royal decree sustained the empire. An effective administrative system placed Persian governors, called *satraps* (SAY-traps), in each of the empire's twenty-three provinces, while lower-level officials were drawn from local authorities. A system of imperial spies, known as the "eyes and ears of the King," represented a further imperial presence in the far reaches of the empire.

Map 3.1 The Persian Empire

At its height, the Persian Empire was the largest in the world. It dominated the lands of the First Civilizations in the Middle East and was commercially connected to neighboring regions.

A general policy of respect for the empire's many non-Persian cultural traditions also cemented the state's authority. Cyrus won the gratitude of the Jews when in 539 B.C.E. he allowed those exiled in Babylon to return to their homeland and rebuild their temple in Jerusalem (see "Judaism" in Chapter 4). In Egypt and Babylon, Persian kings took care to uphold local religious cults in an effort to gain the support of their followers and officials. The Greek historian Herodotus commented that "there is no nation which so readily adopts foreign customs. They have taken the dress of the Medes and in war they wear the Egyptian breastplate. As soon as they hear of any luxury, they instantly make it their own."[3] (See more on Herodotus's perceptions of Persia in Working with Evidence, Source 3.1, page 130.) For the next 1,000 years or more, Persian imperial bureaucracy and court life, replete with administrators, tax collectors, record keepers, and translators, provided a model for all subsequent regimes in the region, including, later, those of the Islamic world.

The infrastructure of empire included a system of standardized coinage, predictable taxes levied on each province, and a newly dug canal linking the Nile

Persepolis The largest palace in Persepolis, the Persian Empire's ancient capital, was the Audience Hall. The emperor officially greeted visiting dignitaries at this palace, which was constructed around 500 B.C.E. This relief, which shows a lion attacking a bull and Persian guards at attention, adorns a staircase leading to the Audience Hall. (Bridgeman Images)

with the Red Sea, which greatly expanded commerce and enriched Egypt. A "royal road," some 1,700 miles in length, facilitated communication and commerce across this vast empire. Caravans of merchants could traverse this highway in three months, but agents of the imperial courier service, using a fresh supply of horses every twenty-five to thirty miles, could carry a message from one end of the road to another in a week or two. Herodotus was impressed. "Neither snow, nor rain, nor heat, nor darkness of night," he wrote, "prevents them from accomplishing the task proposed to them with utmost speed." And an elaborate underground irrigation system sustained a rich agricultural economy in the semi-arid conditions of the Iranian plateau and spread from there throughout the Middle East and beyond.

Elaborate imperial centers, particularly Susa and Persepolis (per-SEP-uh-lis), reflected the immense wealth and power of the Persian Empire. Palaces, audience halls, quarters for the harem, monuments, and carvings made these cities into powerful symbols of imperial authority. Materials and workers alike were drawn from all corners of the empire and beyond. Inscribed in the foundation of Persepolis was Darius's commentary on what he had set in motion: "And Ahura Mazda was of such a mind, together with all the other gods, that this fortress [should] be built. And [so] I built it. And I built it secure and beautiful and adequate, just as I was intending to."[4]

The Greeks

It would be hard to imagine a sharper contrast than that between the huge and centralized Persian Empire, governed by an absolute and almost unapproachable monarch, and the small competing city-states of classical Greece, which allowed varying degrees of popular participation in political life. Like the Persians, the Greeks were an Indo-European people whose early history drew on the legacy of the First Civilizations, especially Egypt. The classical Greece of historical fame emerged around 750 B.C.E. as a new civilization and flourished for about 400 years before it was incorporated into a succession of foreign empires. During that relatively short period, the civilization of Athens and Sparta, of Plato and Socrates, of Zeus and Apollo took shape and collided with its giant neighbor to the east.

Map 3.2 Classical Greece and Its Colonies

The classical civilization of Greece was centered on a small peninsula of southeastern Europe, but Greek settlers planted elements of that civilization along the coasts of the Mediterranean and Black seas.

Calling themselves Hellenes, the Greeks created a distinctive civilization, particularly in comparison with that of the Persians. The total population of Greece and the Aegean basin was just 2 million to 3 million, a fraction of that of the Persian Empire. Furthermore, Greek civilization took shape on a small peninsula, deeply divided by steep mountains and valleys. Its geography certainly contributed to its political organization, which found expression, not in a Persian-style empire, but in hundreds of city-states or small settlements (see Map 3.2). Most were quite modest in size, with between 500 and 5,000 male citizens or free men. But Greek

Guided Reading Question

■ **CHANGE**
How did semidemocratic governments emerge in some of the Greek city-states?

civilization, like its counterparts elsewhere, also left a decisive environmental mark on the lands it encompassed. Smelting metals such as silver, lead, copper, bronze, and iron required enormous supplies of wood, leading to deforestation and soil erosion. Plato declared that the area around Athens had become "a mere relic of the original country. . . . All the rich soil has melted away, leaving a country of skin and bone."[5]

Each of these city-states was fiercely independent and in frequent conflict with its neighbors, yet they had much in common, speaking the same language and worshipping the same gods. Every four years they temporarily suspended their continual conflicts to participate together in the Olympic Games, which began in 776 B.C.E. But this emerging sense of Greek cultural identity did little to overcome the endemic political rivalries of the larger city-states, including Athens, Sparta, Thebes, and Corinth, among many others.

Like the Persians, the Greeks were an expansive people, but their expansion took the form of settlement in distant places rather than conquest and empire. Pushed by a growing population, Greek traders in search of iron and impoverished Greek farmers in search of land undertook a remarkable emigration. Between 750 and 500 B.C.E., the Greeks established settlements all around the Mediterranean basin and the rim of the Black Sea. Settlers brought Greek culture, language, and building styles to these new lands, even as they fought, traded, and intermarried with their non-Greek neighbors.

The most distinctive feature of Greek civilization, and the greatest contrast with Persia, lay in the extent of popular participation in political life that occurred within at least some of the city-states. It was the idea of "citizenship," of free people managing the affairs of state and of equality for all citizens before the law, that was so unique. A foreign king, observing the operation of the public assembly in Athens, was amazed that male citizens as a whole actually voted on matters of policy: "I find it astonishing," he noted, "that here wise men speak on public affairs, while fools decide them."[6] Compared to the rigid hierarchies, inequalities, and absolute monarchies of Persia and other ancient civilizations, the Athenian experiment was remarkable. This is how one modern scholar defined it:

> Among the Greeks the question of who should reign arose in a new way. Previously the most that had been asked was whether one man or another should govern and whether one alone or several together. But now the question was whether all the citizens, including the poor, might govern and whether it would be possible for them to govern as citizens, without specializing in politics. In other words, should the governed themselves actively participate in politics on a regular basis?[7]

The extent of participation and the role of "citizens" varied considerably, both over time and from city to city. Early in Greek history, only wealthy and well-born men had the rights of full citizenship, such as speaking and voting in the assembly, holding public office, and fighting in the army. Gradually, men of the lower classes, mostly small-scale farmers, also obtained these rights as they gained the means to purchase the armor and weapons that would allow them to serve as hoplites, or infantrymen, in the armies of the city-states. In many places, strong but benevolent rulers known as tyrants emerged for a time, usually with the support of the poorer classes, to challenge the prerogatives of the wealthy. Sparta developed a distinctive political and social system, famous for its extreme military discipline and its large population of helots, conquered people who lived in slave-like conditions. Most political authority was vested in its Council of Elders, composed of twenty-eight men over the age of sixty, who came from the wealthier and more influential segment of society and served for life.

It was in Athens that the Greek experiment in political participation achieved its most distinctive expression. Early steps in this direction were the product of intense class conflict, leading almost to civil war. A reforming leader named Solon emerged in 594 B.C.E. to push Athenian politics in a more democratic direction, breaking the hold of a small group of aristocratic families. Debt slavery was abolished, access to public office was opened to a wider group of men, and all citizens were allowed to take part in the Assembly. Later reformers such as Cleisthenes (KLEYE-sthuh-nees) and Pericles extended the rights of citizens even further. By 450 B.C.E., all holders of public office were chosen by lot and were paid, so that even the poorest could serve. The Assembly, where all citizens could participate, became the center of political life.

Athenian democracy was direct rather than representative, and it was distinctly limited. Women, slaves, and foreigners, who together constituted far more than half of the population, were wholly excluded from political participation. Nonetheless, political life in Athens was a world away from that of the Persian Empire and even from that of many other Greek cities.

Collision: The Greco-Persian Wars

In recent centuries, many writers and scholars have claimed classical Greece as the foundation of Western or European civilization. But the ancient Greeks themselves looked primarily to the East—to Egypt and the Persian Empire. In Egypt, Greek scholars found impressive mathematical and astronomical traditions on which they built. And Persia represented both an immense threat and later, under Alexander the Great, an opportunity for Greek empire building.

If ever there was an unequal conflict between civilizations, surely it was the collision of the Greeks and the Persians during a half century of intermittent military conflict known to us as the **Greco-Persian Wars** (499–449 B.C.E.). The confrontation between the small and divided Greek cities and Persia, the world's largest empire, grew out of their respective patterns of expansion. A number of Greek settlements on the Anatolian seacoast, known to the Greeks as Ionia, came under Persian control as that empire extended its domination to the west. In 499 B.C.E., some of these Ionian Greek cities revolted against Persian domination and found support from Athens on the Greek mainland. Outraged by this assault from the

Guided Reading Question

■ **CONNECTION**
What were the consequences for both sides of the encounter between the Persians and the Greeks?

remote and upstart Greeks, the Persians, twice in ten years (490 and 480 B.C.E.), launched major military expeditions to punish the Greeks in general and Athens in particular. Against all odds and all expectations, the Greeks held them off, defeating the Persians on both land and sea.

Though no doubt embarrassing, their defeat on the far western fringes of the empire had little effect on the Persians. However, it had a profound impact on Greece and especially on Athens, whose forces had led the way to victory. Beating the Persians in battle was a source of enormous pride for Greeks. In their view, this victory was the product of Greek freedoms, which had motivated men to fight with extraordinary courage for what they valued so highly. It contributed to a European construction of the world as sharply divided between East and West in which Persia represented Asia and despotism, and Greece signified Europe and freedom. The Greek victory also radicalized Athenian democracy, for it had been men of the poorer classes who had rowed their ships to victory and who were now in a position to insist on full citizenship. The fifty years or so after the Greco-Persian Wars were not only the high point of Athenian democracy but also the Golden Age of Greek culture. During this period, the Parthenon, that marvelous temple to the Greek goddess Athena, was built; Greek theater was born from the work of Aeschylus, Sophocles, and Euripides; and Socrates was beginning his career as a philosopher and an irritant in Athens.

But Athens's Golden Age was also an era of incipient empire. In the Greco-Persian Wars, Athens had led a coalition of more than thirty Greek city-states on the basis of its naval power, but Athenian leadership in the struggle against Persian aggression had spawned an imperialism of its own. After the war, Athens's efforts to solidify its dominant position among the allies led to intense resentment and finally to a bitter civil war (431–404 B.C.E.), with Sparta taking the lead in defending the traditional independence of Greek city-states. In this bloody conflict, known as the **Peloponnesian War**, Athens was defeated, and the Greeks exhausted themselves and magnified their distrust of one another. Thus the way was open to their eventual takeover by the growing forces of Macedonia, a frontier kingdom on the northern fringes of the Greek world. The glory days of the Greek experiment were over, but the spread of Greek culture was just beginning.

Collision: Alexander and the Hellenistic Era

By 338 B.C.E. Philip II, king of Macedonia, had politically unified Greece under his rule—something the Greeks themselves had been unable to achieve—but this unification came at the cost of the prized independence of its various city-states. It also set in motion a second round in the collision of Greece and Persia as Philip's son, known later as **Alexander the Great**, prepared to lead a massive Greek expedition against the Persian Empire. Such a project appealed to those who sought vengeance for the earlier Persian assault on Greece, but it also served to unify the fractious Greeks in a war against their common enemy.

The story of this ten-year expedition (334–323 B.C.E.), accomplished while Alexander was still in his twenties, has become the stuff of legend (see Map 3.3). Surely it was among the greatest military feats of the ancient world in that it created a Greek empire from Egypt and Anatolia in the west to Afghanistan and India in the east. In the process, the great Persian Empire was thoroughly defeated; its capital, Persepolis, was looted and burned; and Alexander was hailed as the "king of Asia." In Egypt, Alexander, then just twenty-four years old, was celebrated as a liberator from Persian domination, was anointed as pharaoh, and

Guided Reading Question

....

■ **CONNECTION**

What changes did Alexander's conquests bring in their wake?

MAPPING HISTORY

Map 3.3 Alexander's Empire and Successor States

Alexander's conquests, though enormous, did not long remain within a single empire, for his generals divided those lands into three successor states shortly after Alexander's death. This was the Hellenistic world within which Greek culture spread.

READING THE MAP: During which stage of Alexander's empire-building enterprise did he establish the most new cities?

MAKING CONNECTIONS: Compare this map with Map 3.2, which shows an earlier period of Greek political and cultural expansion. How would you describe the differences between the two processes of expansion? Are they similar in any way?

was declared by Egyptian priests to be the "son of the gods." Arrian, a later Greek historian, described Alexander in this way:

> His passion was for glory only, and in that he was insatiable. . . . Noble indeed was his power of inspiring his men, of filling them with confidence, and in the moment of danger, of sweeping away their fear by the spectacle of his own fearlessness.[8]

Alexander died in 323 B.C.E., without returning to Greece, and his empire was soon divided into three kingdoms, ruled by leading Macedonian generals.

From the viewpoint of world history, the chief significance of Alexander's amazing conquests lay in the widespread dissemination of Greek culture during what historians call the **Hellenistic era** (323–30 B.C.E.). Elements of that culture, generated in a small and remote Mediterranean peninsula, now penetrated the lands of the First Civilizations—Egypt, Mesopotamia, and India—resulting in one of the great cultural encounters of the ancient world.

The major avenue for the spread of Greek culture lay in the many cities that Alexander and later Hellenistic rulers established throughout the empire. Complete with Greek monuments, sculptures, theaters, markets, councils, and assemblies, these cities attracted many thousands of Greek settlers serving as state officials, soldiers, or traders. **Alexandria** in Egypt—the largest of these cities, with half a million people—was an enormous cosmopolitan center where Egyptians, Greeks, Jews, Babylonians, Syrians, Persians, and many others rubbed elbows. A harbor with space for 1,200 ships facilitated long-distance commerce. Greek learning flourished thanks to a library of some 700,000 volumes and the Museum, which sponsored scholars and writers of all kinds.

From cities such as these, Greek culture spread. From the Mediterranean to India, Greek became the language of power and elite culture. The Indian monarch Ashoka published some of his decrees in Greek, while an independent Greek state was established in Bactria in what is now northern Afghanistan. The attraction of many young Jews to Greek culture prompted the Pharisees to develop their own school system, as this highly conservative Jewish sect feared for the very survival of Judaism.

Cities such as Alexandria were very different from the original city-states of Greece, both in their cultural diversity and in the absence of the

Alexander the Great This mosaic of Alexander on horseback comes from the Roman city of Pompeii. It depicts the Battle of Issus (333 B.C.E.), in which Greek forces, although considerably outnumbered, defeated the Persian army, led personally by Emperor Darius III.
(ullstein bild via Getty Images)

independence so valued by Athens and Sparta. Now they were part of large conquest states ruled by Greeks: the Ptolemaic (TOL-uh-MAY-ik) empire in Egypt and the Seleucid empire in Persia. These were imperial states, which, in their determination to preserve order, raise taxes, and maintain the authority of the monarch, resembled the much older empires of Mesopotamia, Egypt, Assyria, and Persia. Macedonians and Greeks, representing perhaps 10 percent of the population in these Hellenistic kingdoms, were clearly the elite and sought to keep themselves separate from non-Greeks.

In Egypt, for example, different legal systems for Greeks and native Egyptians maintained this separation. An Egyptian agricultural worker complained that because he was an Egyptian, his supervisors despised him and refused to pay him.[9] Periodic rebellions expressed resentment at Greek arrogance, condescension, and exploitation. But the separation between the Greeks and native populations was by no means complete, and a fair amount of cultural interaction and blending occurred. Alexander himself had taken several Persian princesses as his wives and actively encouraged intermarriage between his troops and Asian women. In both Egypt and Mesopotamia, Greek rulers patronized the building of temples to local gods and actively supported their priests. A growing number of native peoples were able to become Greek citizens by obtaining a Greek education, speaking the language, dressing appropriately, and assuming Greek names. In India, Greeks were assimilated into the hierarchy of the caste system as members of the Kshatriya (warrior) caste, while in Bactria a substantial number of Greeks converted to Buddhism, including one of the Bactrian kings, Menander. A school of Buddhist art that emerged in the early centuries of the Common Era depicted the Buddha in human form for the first time, but in Greek-like garb with a face resembling the god Apollo. Clearly, not all was conflict between the Greeks and the peoples of the East.

In the long run, much of this Greek cultural influence faded as the Hellenistic kingdoms that had promoted it weakened and vanished by the first century B.C.E. While it lasted, however, it represented a remarkable cultural encounter, born of the collision of two empires and two second-wave civilizations. In the western part of that Hellenistic world, Greek rule was replaced by that of the Romans, whose empire, like Alexander's, also served as a vehicle for the continued spread of Greek culture and ideas.

Comparing Empires: Roman and Chinese

While the adjacent civilizations of the Greeks and the Persians collided, two other empires were taking shape—the Roman Empire on the far western side of Eurasia and China's imperial state on the far eastern end. They flourished at roughly the same time (200 B.C.E.–200 C.E.); they occupied a similar area (about 1.5 million square miles); and they encompassed populations of a similar size (50 to 60 million). They were the giant empires of their time, shaping the lives of close to half of the world's population. Unlike the Greeks and the Persians, the

Romans and the Chinese were only dimly aware of each other and had almost no direct contact. Historians, however, have seen them as fascinating variations on an imperial theme and have long explored their similarities and differences.

Rome: From City-State to Empire

Like the Persian Empire, that of the Romans took shape initially on the margins of the civilized world and was an unlikely rags-to-riches story. Beginning as a small and impoverished city-state on the western side of central Italy in the eighth century B.C.E., Rome later became the center of an enormous imperial state that encompassed the Mediterranean basin and included parts of continental Europe, Britain, North Africa, and the Middle East.

Originally ruled by a king, around 509 B.C.E. Roman aristocrats threw off the monarchy and established a republic in which the men of a wealthy class, known as patricians, dominated. Executive authority was exercised by two consuls, who were advised by a patrician assembly, the Senate. Deepening conflict with the poorer classes, called plebeians (plih–BEE-uhns), led to important changes in Roman political life. A written code of law offered plebeians some protection from abuse; a system of public assemblies provided an opportunity for lower classes to shape public policy; and a new office of tribune, who represented plebeians, allowed them to block unfavorable legislation. Romans took great pride in this political system, believing that they enjoyed greater freedom than did many of their more autocratic neighbors. The values of the republic—rule of law, the rights of citizens, the absence of pretension, upright moral behavior, keeping one's word—were later idealized as "the way of the ancestors."

With this political system and these values, the Romans launched their empire-building enterprise, a prolonged process that took more than 500 years (see Map 3.4). That empire began in the 490s B.C.E. with the Romans gaining control first over their Latin neighbors in central Italy and then, during the next several hundred years, over most of the Italian peninsula. Between 264 and 146 B.C.E., victory in the Punic Wars with Carthage, a powerful empire with its capital in North Africa, extended Roman control over the western Mediterranean, including Spain, and made Rome a naval power. Subsequent expansion in the eastern Mediterranean brought the ancient civilizations of Greece, Egypt, and Mesopotamia under Roman domination. Rome also expanded into territories in Southern and Western Europe, including present-day France and Britain. By early in the second century C.E., the Roman Empire had reached its maximum extent.

No overall design or blueprint drove the building of empire, nor were there any precedents to guide the Romans. What they created was something wholly new—an empire that encompassed the entire Mediterranean basin and beyond. It was a piecemeal process, which the Romans invariably saw as defensive. Each addition of territory created new vulnerabilities, which could be relieved only by more conquests. For some, the growth of empire represented opportunity. Poor soldiers hoped for land, loot, or salaries that might lift their families out of poverty. The well-to-do

Guided Reading Question

■ **CHANGE**
How did Rome grow from a single city to the center of a huge empire?

MAPPING HISTORY

Map 3.4 The Roman Empire

At its height in the second century C.E., the Roman Empire incorporated the entire Mediterranean basin, including the lands of the Carthaginian Empire, the less developed region of Western Europe, the heartland of Greek civilization, and the ancient civilizations of Egypt and Mesopotamia.

READING THE MAP: Where were the imperial borders demarcated by geographical features like rivers, oceans, or deserts? Where were they not?

MAKING CONNECTIONS: Comparing Map 3.4 with Maps 3.3 and 3.1, which regions of the former Persian and Greek empires did the Roman Empire incorporate?

---

or well-connected gained great estates, earned promotions, and sometimes achieved public acclaim and high political office. The wealth of long-established societies in the eastern Mediterranean (Greece and Egypt, for example) beckoned, as did the resources and food supplies of the less developed regions, such as Western Europe. There was no shortage of motivation for the creation of the Roman Empire.

Although Rome's central location in the Mediterranean basin provided a convenient launching pad for empire, it was the army, "well-trained, well-fed, and well-rewarded," that built the empire.[10] Drawing on the growing population of Italy, that army was often brutal in war. Carthage, for example, was utterly destroyed; the city was razed to the ground, and its inhabitants were either killed or sold into slavery. Nonetheless, Roman authorities could be generous to former enemies. Some were granted Roman citizenship; others were treated as allies and allowed to maintain their local rulers. As the empire grew, so too did political forces in Rome that favored its continued expansion and were willing to commit the necessary manpower and resources.

Centuries of empire building and the warfare that made it possible had an impact on Roman society and values. That vast process, for example, shaped Roman understandings of gender and the appropriate roles of men and women. Rome was becoming a warrior society in which the masculinity of upper-class male citizens was defined in part by a man's role as a soldier and a property owner. In private life, this translated into absolute control over his wife, children, and slaves, including the theoretical right to kill them without interference from the state. This ability of a free man and a Roman citizen to act decisively in both public and private life lay at the heart of ideal male identity. A Roman woman could participate proudly in this warrior culture by bearing brave sons and inculcating these values in her offspring.

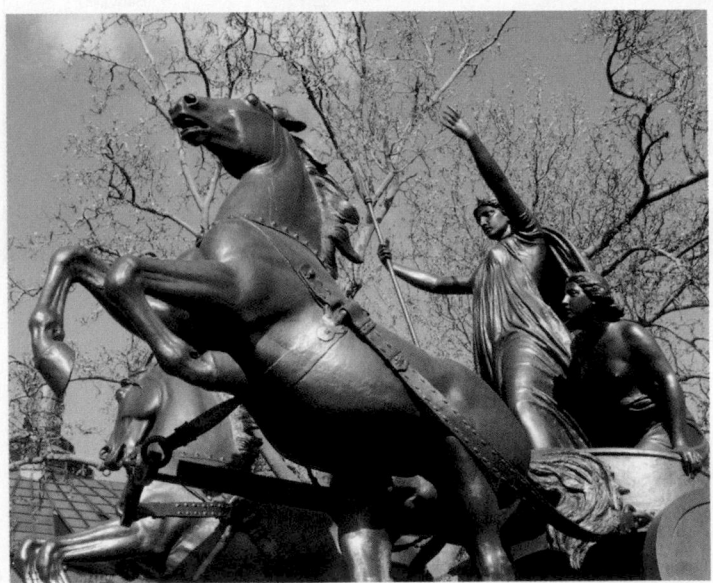

Queen Boudica This statue in London commemorates the resistance of the Celtic people of eastern Britain against Roman rule during a revolt in 60–61 C.E., led by Queen Boudica. A later Roman historian lamented that "all this ruin was brought upon the Romans by a woman, a fact which in itself caused them the greatest shame." (Daniel Boulet, photographer)

Strangely enough, by the early centuries of the Common Era the wealth of empire, the authority of the imperial state, and the breakdown of older Roman social patterns combined to offer women in the elite classes a less restricted life than they had known in the early centuries of the republic. Upper-class Roman women had never been as secluded in the home as were their Greek counterparts, and now the legal authority of their husbands was curtailed by the intrusion of the state into what had been private life. The head of household, or *pater familias*, lost his earlier power of life and death over his family. Furthermore, such women could now marry without transferring legal control to their husbands and were increasingly able to manage their own finances and take part in the growing commercial economy of the empire. According to one scholar, Roman women of the wealthier classes gained "almost complete liberty in matters of property and marriage."[11] At the other end of the social spectrum, Roman conquests brought many thousands of women as well as men into the empire as slaves, who were often brutally treated and subject to the whims of their masters (see "The Making of Roman Slavery" in Chapter 5).

The relentless expansion of empire raised yet another profound question for Rome: could republican government and values survive the acquisition of a huge empire? The wealth of empire enriched a few, enabling them to acquire large estates and many slaves, while pushing growing numbers of free farmers into the cities and poverty. Imperial riches also empowered a small group of military leaders — Marius, Sulla, Pompey, Julius Caesar — who recruited their troops directly from the ranks of the poor and whose fierce rivalries brought civil war to Rome during the first century B.C.E. Traditionalists lamented the apparent decline of republican values — simplicity, service, free farmers as the backbone of the army, the authority of the Senate — amid the self-seeking ambition of the newly rich and powerful. When the dust settled from the civil war, Rome was clearly changing, for authority was now vested primarily in an emperor, the first of whom was Octavian, later granted the title of **Augustus** (r. 27 B.C.E.–14 C.E.), which implied a divine status for the ruler. The republic was history; Rome had become an empire and its ruler an emperor.

But it was an empire with an uneasy conscience, for many felt that in acquiring an empire, Rome had betrayed and abandoned its republican origins. Augustus was careful to maintain the forms of the republic — the Senate, consuls, public assemblies — and referred to himself as "first man" rather than "king" or "emperor," even as he accumulated enormous personal power. And in a bow to republican values, he spoke of the empire's conquests as reflecting the "power of the Roman people" rather than of the Roman state. Despite this rhetoric, he was emperor in practice, if not in name, for he was able to exercise sole authority, backed up by his command of a professional army. Later emperors were less reluctant to flaunt their imperial prerogatives.

During the first two centuries C.E., this empire in disguise provided security, grandeur, and relative prosperity for the Mediterranean world. This was the *pax Romana*, the Roman peace, the era of imperial Rome's greatest extent and greatest authority.

China: From Warring States to Empire

About the same time, on the other side of Eurasia, another huge imperial state was in the making — China. Here, however, the task was understood differently. It was not a matter of creating something new, as in the case of the Roman Empire, but of restoring something old. As one of the First Civilizations, a Chinese state had emerged as early as 2200 B.C.E. and under the Xia, Shang, and Zhou dynasties had grown progressively larger. By 500 B.C.E., however, this Chinese state was in shambles. Any earlier unity vanished in an "age of warring states," featuring the endless rivalries of seven competing kingdoms.

Trung Trac: Resisting the Chinese Empire

Empires have long faced resistance from people they conquer, and never more fiercely than in Vietnam, which was incorporated into an expanding Chinese empire for over a thousand years (111 B.C.E.–939 C.E.). Among the earliest examples of Vietnamese resistance to this occupation was that led around 40 C.E. by Trung Trac and her younger sister Trung Nhi, daughters in an aristocratic, military family. Trung Trac married a prominent local lord, Thi Sach, who was a vocal opponent of offensive Chinese policies—high taxes, even on the right to fish in local rivers; required payoffs to Chinese officials; and the imposition of Chinese culture on the Vietnamese. In response to this opposition, the Chinese governor of the region ordered Thi Sach's execution.

This personal tragedy provoked Trung Trac to take up arms against the Chinese occupiers, and she quickly gained a substantial following among peasants and aristocrats alike. Famously addressing some 30,000 soldiers, while dressed in full military regalia rather than the expected mourning clothes, she declared to the assembled crowd:

> Foremost I will avenge my country.
> Second I will restore the Hung lineage.
> Third I will avenge the death of my husband.
> Lastly I vow that these goals will be accomplished.

Within months, her forces had captured sixty-five towns, and, for two years, they held the Chinese at bay, while Trung Trac and Trung Nhi ruled a briefly independent state as co-queens. Chinese sources referred to Trung Trac as a "ferocious warrior." During their rule, the sisters eliminated the hated tribute taxes imposed by the Chinese and sought to restore the authority of Vietnamese aristocrats. A large military force, said to number roughly 80,000, counted among its leaders thirty-six female "generals," including the Trung sisters' mother.

Soon, however, Chinese forces overwhelmed the rebellion, and Trung Trac's support faded. Later Vietnamese records explained the failure of the revolt as a consequence of its female leadership. In traditional Vietnamese accounts, the Trung sisters committed suicide, jumping into a nearby river, as did a number of their followers.

Trung Trac and Trung Nhi.

Although the revolt failed, it lived on in stories and legends to inspire later Vietnamese resistance to invaders—Chinese, French, Japanese, and American alike. Men were reminded that women had led this rebellion. "What a pity," wrote a thirteenth-century Vietnamese historian, "that for a thousand years after this, the men of our land bowed their heads, folded their arms, and served the northerners [Chinese]."[12] To this day, temples, streets, and neighborhoods bear the name of the Trung sisters, and a yearly celebration in their honor coincides with International Women's Day. Usually depicted riding on war elephants and wielding swords, these two women also represent the more fluid gender roles then available to some Vietnamese women in comparison to the stricter patriarchy prevalent in China.

QUESTION

How might you imagine the reactions to the Trung sisters' revolt from Chinese officials; Vietnamese aristocrats; Vietnamese peasants, both male and female; and later generations of Vietnamese men and women?

---

photo: CPA Media

To many Chinese, this was a wholly unnatural and unacceptable condition, and rulers in various states vied to reunify China. One of them, known to history as **Qin Shihuangdi** (chihn shee-HUANG-dee) (i.e., Shihuangdi from the state of Qin), succeeded brilliantly. The state of Qin had already developed an effective bureaucracy, subordinated its aristocracy, equipped its army with iron weapons, and enjoyed rapidly rising agricultural output and a growing population. It also had adopted a political philosophy called Legalism, which advocated clear rules and harsh punishments as a means of enforcing the authority of the state. With these resources, Shihuangdi (r. 221–210 B.C.E.) launched a military campaign to reunify China and in just ten years soundly defeated the other warring states. Believing that he had created a universal and eternal empire, he grandly named himself Shihuangdi, which means the "first emperor." Unlike Augustus, he showed little ambivalence about empire. Subsequent conquests extended China's boundaries far to the south into the northern part of Vietnam, to the northeast into Korea, and to the northwest, where the Chinese pushed back the nomadic pastoral people of the steppes. (See Zooming In: Trung Trac, page 116, for an example of resistance to Chinese expansion.) Although the boundaries fluctuated over time, Shihuangdi laid the foundations for a unified Chinese state, which has endured, with periodic interruptions, to the present (see Map 3.5).

Building on earlier precedents, the Chinese process of empire formation was far more compressed than the centuries-long Roman effort, but it was no less dependent on military force and no less brutal. Scholars who opposed Shihuangdi's policies were executed and their books burned. Aristocrats who resisted his centralizing policies were moved physically to the capital. Hundreds of thousands of laborers were recruited to construct the Great Wall of China, designed to keep out northern "barbarians," and to erect a monumental mausoleum as the emperor's final resting place. More positively, Shihuangdi imposed a uniform system of weights, measures, and currency and standardized the length of axles for carts and the written form of the Chinese language.

As in Rome, the creation of the Chinese empire had domestic repercussions, but they were brief and superficial compared to Rome's transition from republic to empire. The speed and brutality of Shihuangdi's policies ensured that his own Qin dynasty did not last long, and it collapsed unmourned in 206 B.C.E. The **Han dynasty** that followed (206 B.C.E.–220 C.E.) retained the centralized features of Shihuangdi's creation, although it moderated the harshness of his policies, adopting a milder and moralistic Confucianism in place of Legalism as the governing philosophy of the state. It was Han dynasty rulers who consolidated China's imperial state and established the political patterns that lasted into the twentieth century.

Guided Reading Question

■ **COMPARISON**
Why was the Chinese empire able to take shape so quickly, while that of the Romans took centuries?

Map 3.5 Classical China

The brief Qin dynasty brought unity to the heartland of Chinese civilization, and the much longer Han dynasty extended its territorial reach south toward Vietnam, east to Korea, and west into Central Asia. To the north lay the military confederacy of the nomadic Xiongnu.

Consolidating the Roman and Chinese Empires

Once established, these two huge imperial systems shared a number of common features. Both, for example, defined themselves in universal terms. The Roman writer Polybius spoke of bringing "almost the entire world" under the control of Rome, while the Chinese state was said to encompass "all under heaven." Both of them invested heavily in public works—roads, bridges, aqueducts, canals, protective walls—all designed to integrate their respective domains militarily and commercially.

Furthermore, Roman and Chinese authorities both invoked supernatural sanctions to support their rule. By the first century C.E., Romans began to regard their deceased emperors as gods and established a religious cult to bolster the authority of living rulers. It was the refusal of early Christians to take part in this cult that provoked their periodic persecution by Roman authorities.

In China, a much older tradition had long linked events on Earth with the invisible realm called "Heaven." Neither a place nor a supreme being, Heaven was an impersonal moral force that regulated the universe. Emperors were called the Son of Heaven and were said to govern by the Mandate of Heaven so long as they ruled morally and with benevolence. Peasant rebellions, "barbarian" invasions, or disastrous floods were viewed as signs that the emperor had ruled badly and had thus lost the Mandate of Heaven. Among the chief duties of the emperor was the performance of various rituals thought to maintain the appropriate relationship between Heaven and Earth.

Both of these second-wave civilizations also absorbed a foreign religious tradition—Christianity in the Roman world and Buddhism in China—although the process unfolded somewhat differently. In the case of Rome, Christianity was born as a small sect in a remote corner of the empire. Aided by the *pax Romana* and Roman roads, the new faith spread slowly for several centuries, particularly among the poor and lower classes. Women were prominent in the leadership of the early Church, as were a number of more well-to-do individuals from urban families. After suffering intermittent persecution, Christianity in the fourth century C.E. obtained state support from emperors who hoped to shore up a tottering empire with a common religion, and thereafter the religion spread quite rapidly. (See "Society and the Church" in Chapter 10.)

In the case of China, by contrast, Buddhism came from India, far beyond the Chinese world. It was introduced to China by Central Asian traders and received little support from Han dynasty rulers. In fact, the religion spread only modestly among Chinese until after the Han dynasty collapsed (220 C.E.), when it appealed to people who felt bewildered by the loss of a predictable and stable society. Not until the Sui (sway) dynasty emperor Wendi (r. 581–604 C.E.) reunified China did the new religion gain state support, and then only temporarily. Buddhism thus became one of several alternative cultural traditions in a complex Chinese mix, while Christianity, though divided internally, ultimately became the dominant religious tradition throughout Europe. (See "China and Buddhism" in Chapter 8.)

The Roman and Chinese empires also had a different relationship to the societies they governed. Rome's beginnings as a small city-state meant that Romans, and even Italians, were always a distinct minority within the empire. The Chinese empire, by contrast, grew out of a much larger cultural heartland, already ethnically Chinese. Furthermore, as the Chinese state expanded, especially to the south, it actively assimilated the non-Chinese, or "barbarian," people. In short, they became Chinese, culturally, linguistically, and through intermarriage in physical appearance as well. Many Chinese in modern times are in fact descended from people who at one point or another were not Chinese at all.

The Roman Empire offered a different kind of assimilation to its subject peoples. Gradually and somewhat reluctantly, the empire granted Roman citizenship to various individuals, families, or whole communities for their service to the empire or in recognition of their adoption of Roman culture. In 212 C.E., Roman

Guided Reading Question

■ **EXPLANATION**
Why were the Roman and Chinese empires able to enjoy long periods of relative stability and prosperity?

Roman Actors This mosaic from Pompeii, likely created during the first century c.e., depicts the staging of a theatrical production. (DEA Picture Library/A Dagli Orti/Getty Images)

citizenship was bestowed on almost all free men of the empire. Citizenship offered clear advantages—the right to hold public office, to serve in the Roman military units known as legions, to wear a toga, and more—but it conveyed a legal status, rather than cultural assimilation, and certainly did not erase other identities, such as being Greek, Egyptian, or a citizen of a particular city.

Various elements of Roman culture—its public buildings, its religious rituals, its Latin language, its style of city life—were attractive, especially in Western Europe, where urban civilization was something new. In the eastern half of the empire, however, things Greek retained tremendous prestige. Many elite Romans in fact regarded Greek culture—its literature, philosophy, and art—as superior to their own and proudly sent their sons to Athens for a Greek education. To some extent, the two blended into a mixed Greco-Roman tradition, which the empire disseminated throughout the realm. Other non-Roman cultural traditions—such as the cult of the Persian god Mithra or the compassionate Egyptian goddess Isis, and, most extensively, the Jewish-derived religion of Christianity—also spread throughout the empire. Nothing similar occurred in Han dynasty China, except for Buddhism, which established a modest presence, largely among foreigners. Chinese culture experienced little competition from older, venerated, or foreign traditions.

It was widely recognized across much of East Asia—in Japan, Korea, and Vietnam, for example—as the model to which others should conform.

Language served these two empires in important but contrasting ways. Latin, an alphabetic language depicting sounds, gave rise to various distinct languages—Spanish, Portuguese, French, Italian, Romanian—whereas Chinese did not. Chinese characters, which represented words or ideas more than sounds, were not easily transferable to other languages. Written Chinese, however, could be understood by all literate people, no matter which spoken dialect of the language they used. Thus Chinese, more than Latin, served as an instrument of elite assimilation. For all of these reasons, the various peoples of the Roman Empire were able to maintain their separate cultural identities far more than was the case in China.

Politically, both empires established effective centralized control over vast regions and huge populations, but the Chinese, far more than the Romans, developed an elaborate bureaucracy to hold the empire together. The Han emperor Wudi (r. 141–87 B.C.E.) established an imperial academy for training officials for an emerging bureaucracy with a curriculum based on the writings of Confucius. This was the beginning of a civil service system, complete with

A Chinese Musician This Chinese stone relief from the fifth century C.E. depicts a "celestial musician," a minor Buddhist deity, playing a *pipa*, a string instrument of Central Asian origin. (De Agostini Picture Library/G. Dagli Orti/Bridgeman Images)

examinations and selection by merit, which did much to integrate the Chinese empire and lasted into the early twentieth century. Roman administration was a somewhat ramshackle affair, relying more on regional aristocratic elites and the army to provide cohesion. Unlike the Chinese, however, the Romans developed an elaborate body of law, applicable equally to all people of the realm, that dealt with matters of justice, property, commerce, and family life. Chinese and Roman political development thus generated different answers to the question of what made for good government. For those who inherited the Roman tradition, it was good laws, whereas for those in the Chinese tradition, it was good men.

Finally, both Roman and Chinese civilizations had marked effects on the environment in various ways. The Roman poet Horace complained of the noise and smoke of the city and objected to the urban sprawl that extended into the adjacent fertile lands. Rome's mining operations, the smelting of metals, its large-scale agriculture, and its growing population—all of this led to extensive deforestation and consequent soil erosion. The shortage of wood in the heartland of the empire led to the relocation of some ceramic workshops to Gaul, where timber was more plentiful. Lead pollution, derived from the smelting of lead ores in open furnaces and from lead water pipes and cooking pots, shows up in the bones of Roman burials and as far away as Greenland, where studies of the ice cap indicate that lead in the atmosphere increased during Roman times. Here is perhaps the earliest example of international atmospheric pollution.

Large-scale Chinese ironworking during the Han dynasty likewise contributed to substantial urban air pollution, while a rapidly growing and dense population practicing intensive agriculture stripped the north China plain of its ancient forest cover, causing sufficient soil erosion to turn the Hwang-ho River its characteristic yellow-brown color. What had been known simply as "the River" now became the Yellow River, which frequently flooded with devastating results and over many centuries dramatically changed course. In addition, as China expanded north and west into the steppe lands of the pastoral peoples, military/agricultural colonies of Chinese farmers turned pasturelands into farmlands, plowing up long-established sod. When the Chinese state subsequently grew weaker or actually collapsed, such farms were abandoned, wind erosion took hold, and deserts emerged.

The Collapse of Empires

Empires rise, and then, with some apparent regularity, they fall, and in doing so, they provide historians with one of their most intriguing questions: what causes the collapse of these once-mighty structures? In China, the Han dynasty empire came to an end in 220 C.E.; the traditional date for the final disintegration of the Roman Empire is 476 C.E., although a process of decline had been under way for several centuries. In the Roman case, however, only the western half of the empire collapsed, while the eastern part, subsequently known as the Byzantine Empire, maintained the tradition of imperial Rome for another thousand years.

Despite these differences, a number of common factors have been associated with the end of these imperial states. At one level, they both simply got too big, too overextended, and too expensive to be sustained by the available resources, and no fundamental technological breakthrough was available to enlarge these resources. Furthermore, the growth of large landowning families with huge estates and political clout enabled them to avoid paying taxes, turned free peasants into impoverished tenant farmers, and diminished the authority of the central government. In China, such conditions led to a major peasant revolt, known as the Yellow Turban Rebellion, in 184 C.E. (see "Peasants" in Chapter 5).

Rivalry among elite factions created instability in both empires and eroded imperial authority. In China, persistent tension between castrated court officials (eunuchs) loyal to the emperor and Confucian-educated scholar-bureaucrats weakened the state. In the Roman Empire between 235 and 284 C.E., some twenty-six individuals claimed the title of Roman emperor, only one of whom died of natural causes. In addition, epidemic disease ravaged both societies, though more extensively in the Roman world. The population of the Roman Empire declined by 25 percent in the two centuries following 250 C.E., a demographic disaster that meant diminished production, less revenue for the state, and fewer men available to defend the empire's long frontiers.

Historians have often linked the collapse of empires with environmental factors as well, more often with reference to Rome than to Han dynasty China. Considerable fluctuations in the climate after about 250 C.E. led to drought in the third century, cold and wet conditions in the fourth, and increased rainfall and cooler temperatures in the fifth, all of which generated substantial soil erosion and declining agricultural productivity. The North African breadbasket of the empire suffered from serious salinization and increasingly desert-like conditions. The extent to which such factors contributed to the collapse of the Roman Empire remains a point of dispute among scholars.

To these mounting internal problems was added a growing threat from nomadic or semi-agricultural peoples occupying the frontier regions of both empires. The Chinese had long developed various ways of dealing with the Xiongnu and other nomadic people to the north—building the Great Wall to keep them out, offering them trading opportunities at border markets, buying them off with lavish gifts, contracting marriage alliances with nomadic leaders, and conducting periodic military campaigns against them. But as the Han dynasty weakened in the second and third centuries C.E., such peoples more easily breached the frontier defenses and set up a succession of "barbarian states" in north China. Culturally, however, many of these foreign rulers gradually became Chinese, encouraging intermarriage, adopting Chinese dress, and setting up their courts in Chinese fashion.

Guided Reading Question

■ **CHANGE**

What internal and external factors contributed to the collapse of the Roman and Chinese empires?

Anglo-Saxon Treasure This purse hinge recovered from the royal grave site at Sutton Hoo—one of the greatest hordes of Anglo-Saxon treasure ever found in England—is an exquisite piece of seventh-century barbarian art that combines intricate gold work inlaid with gemlike garnets and glass. The paired images in the center depict birds of prey hunting smaller birds—perhaps ducks. The outer pair comprise men standing between beasts. Above are three plaques decorated with elaborate geometric patterns, which are a hallmark of Germanic art from this period. (DEA Picture Library/Getty Images)

A weakening Roman Empire likewise faced serious problems from Germanic-speaking peoples living on its northern frontier. Growing numbers of these people began to enter the empire in the fourth century C.E.—some as mercenaries in Roman armies and others as refugees fleeing the invasions of the ferocious Huns, who were penetrating Europe from Central Asia. Once inside the declining empire, various Germanic groups established their own kingdoms, at first controlling Roman emperors and then displacing them altogether by 476 C.E. Unlike the nomadic groups in China, who largely assimilated Chinese culture, Germanic kingdoms in Western Europe developed their own ethnic identities—Visigoths, Franks, Anglo-Saxons, and others—even as they drew on Roman law and adopted Roman Christianity. Far more than in China, the fall of the western Roman Empire produced a new culture, blending Latin and Germanic elements, which provided the foundation for the hybrid civilization that would arise in Western Europe.

The collapse of empire meant more than the disappearance of centralized government and endemic conflict. In post-Han China and post-Roman Europe, it also meant the decline of urban life, a contracting population, less area under cultivation, diminishing international trade, and vast insecurity for ordinary people. It must have seemed that civilization itself was unraveling.

The most significant difference between the collapse of empire in China and that in the western Roman Empire lay in what happened next. In China, after about 350 years of disunion, disorder, frequent warfare, and political chaos, a Chinese imperial state, similar to that of the Han dynasty, was reassembled under the Sui (581–618 C.E.), Tang (618–907), and Song (960–1279) dynasties. Once again, a single emperor ruled; a bureaucracy selected by examinations governed; and the ideas of Confucius informed the political system. Such a Chinese empire persisted into the early twentieth century.

The story line of European history following the end of the western Roman Empire was very different indeed. No large-scale, centralized, imperial authority encompassing all of Western Europe has ever been successfully reestablished there for any length of time. The memory of Roman imperial unity certainly persisted, and many subsequently tried unsuccessfully to re-create it. But most of Western Europe dissolved into highly decentralized political systems involving nobles, knights and vassals, kings with little authority, various city-states in Italy, and small territories ruled by princes, bishops, or the pope. From this point on, Europe would be a civilization without an encompassing imperial state.

Why were Europeans unable to reconstruct something of the unity of their classical empire, while the Chinese clearly did? Surely the greater cultural homogeneity of Chinese civilization made that task easier than it was amid the vast ethnic and linguistic diversity of Europe. The absence in the Roman legacy of a strong bureaucratic tradition also contributed to European difficulties, whereas in China the bureaucracy provided some stability even as dynasties came and went. The Chinese also had in Confucianism a largely secular ideology that placed great value on political matters in the here and now. The Roman Catholic Church in

Europe, however, was frequently at odds with state authorities, and its "otherworldliness" did little to support the creation of large-scale empires. Finally, Chinese agriculture was much more productive than that of Europe, and for a long time its metallurgy was more advanced. These conditions gave Chinese state builders more resources to work with than were available to their European counterparts.

PRACTICING HISTORICAL THINKING

In comparing the Roman and Chinese empires, which do you find more striking—their similarities or their differences?

Intermittent Empire: The Case of India

Among the second-wave civilizations of Eurasia, empire loomed large in Persian, Mediterranean, and Chinese history, but it played a rather less prominent role in Indian history. The demise of the Indus Valley civilization by 1500 B.C.E. was followed over the next thousand years by the creation of a new civilization based farther east, along the Ganges River on India's northern plain.

By 600 B.C.E. what would become the second-wave civilization of South Asia had begun to take shape across northern India. Politically, that civilization emerged as a fragmented collection of towns and cities, some small republics governed by public assemblies, and a number of regional states ruled by kings. An astonishing range of ethnic, cultural, and linguistic diversity also characterized this civilization, as an endless variety of peoples migrated into India from Central Asia across the mountain passes in the northwest. These features of Indian civilization—political fragmentation and vast cultural diversity—have informed much of South Asian history throughout many centuries, offering a sharp contrast to the pattern of development in China. What gave Indian civilization a recognizable identity and character was neither an imperial tradition nor ethno-linguistic commonality, but rather a distinctive religious tradition,

Map 3.6 Empire in South Asia
Large-scale empires in the Indian subcontinent were less frequent and less enduring than those in China. Two of the largest efforts were those of the Mauryan and Gupta dynasties.

**Guided Reading
Question**

∎ **COMPARISON**

Why were centralized
empires so much less
prominent in India than
in China?

known later to outsiders as Hinduism, and a unique social organization, the caste
system. These features of Indian life are explored further in Chapters 4 and 5.

Nonetheless, empires and emperors were not entirely unknown in India's long
history. Northwestern India had been briefly ruled by the Persian Empire and then
conquered by Alexander the Great. These Persian and Greek influences helped stimulate the first and largest of India's short experiments with a large-scale political
system, the **Mauryan Empire** (326–184 B.C.E.), which encompassed all but the
southern tip of the subcontinent (see Map 3.6).

The Mauryan Empire was an impressive political structure, equivalent to the
Persian, Chinese, and Roman empires, though not nearly as long-lasting. With a
population of perhaps 50 million, the Mauryan Empire boasted a large military
force, a civilian bureaucracy with various ministries, and a large contingent of spies
to provide the rulers with local information. A famous treatise called the *Arthashastra* (*The Science of Worldly Wealth*) articulated a pragmatic, even amoral, political
philosophy for Mauryan rulers. It was, according to one scholar, "a book that frequently discloses to a king what calculating and sometimes brutal measures he must
carry out to preserve the state and the common good."[13] The state also operated
many industries—spinning, weaving, mining, shipbuilding, and armaments. This
complex apparatus was financed by taxes on trade, on herds of animals, and especially on land, from which the monarch claimed a quarter or more of the crop.

Mauryan India is perhaps best known for one of its emperors, **Ashoka**
(r. 268–232 B.C.E.), who left a record of his activities and his thinking in a series of
edicts carved on rocks and pillars throughout the kingdom. Ashoka's conversion to
Buddhism and his moralistic approach to governance gave his reign a different tone
than that of China's Shihuangdi or Greece's Alexander the Great, who, according to
legend, wept because he had no more worlds to conquer. Ashoka's legacy to modern India has been that of an enlightened ruler, who sought to govern in accord
with the religious values and moral teachings of Hinduism and Buddhism.

Despite his good intentions, these policies did not long preserve the empire, which
broke apart soon after Ashoka's death. About 600 years later, a second brief imperial experiment, known as the **Gupta Empire** (320–550 C.E.), took shape. Faxian, a
Chinese Buddhist traveler in India at the time, noted a generally peaceful, tolerant, and
prosperous land, commenting that the ruler "governs without decapitation or corporal punishment." Free hospitals, he reported, were available to "the destitute, crippled
and diseased," but he also noticed "untouchables" carrying bells to warn upper-caste
people of their polluting presence.[14] Culturally, the Gupta era witnessed a flourishing of art, literature, temple building, science, mathematics, and medicine, much of
it patronized by rulers. Indian trade with China also thrived, and Indian commerce
reached as far as the Roman world. When a Germanic leader named Alaric laid siege
to Rome in 410 C.E., he demanded 3,000 pounds of Indian pepper to spare the city.

Thus India's political history resembled that of Western Europe after the collapse of the Roman Empire far more than that of China or Persia. Neither imperial

The Great Stupa The Great Stupa of Sanchi, the oldest stone building in India, was commissioned by Ashoka in the third century B.C.E. to house precious relics of the Buddha.
(© Luca Tettoni/Bridgeman Images)

nor regional states commanded the kind of loyalty or exercised the degree of influence that they did in other second-wave civilizations. India's unparalleled cultural diversity surely was one reason, as were invasions from Central Asia, which repeatedly smashed emerging states that might have provided the nucleus for an all-India empire. Finally, India's social structure, embodied in a caste system linked to occupational groups, made for intensely local loyalties at the expense of wider identities.

Nonetheless, a frequently vibrant economy fostered a lively internal commerce and made India the focal point of an extensive network of trade in the Indian Ocean basin. In particular, its cotton textile industry long supplied cloth throughout the Afro-Eurasian world. Strong guilds of merchants and artisans provided political leadership in major towns and cities, and their wealth supported lavish temples, public buildings, and religious festivals. Great creativity in religious matters generated Hindu and Buddhist traditions that later penetrated much of Asia. Indian mathematics and science, especially astronomy, were also impressive; Indian scientists plotted the movements of stars and planets and recognized quite early that the earth was round. Clearly, the absence of consistent imperial unity did not prevent the evolution of a lasting civilization.

REFLECTIONS

Enduring Legacies of Second-Wave Empires

These second-wave empires have long ago passed into history, but their descendants have kept them alive in memory, for they have proved useful, even in the twentieth and early twenty-first centuries. Such ancient empires have provided legitimacy for contemporary states, inspiration for new imperial ventures, and abundant warnings and cautions for those seeking to criticize more recent empires. For example, in bringing communism to China in the twentieth century, the Chinese leader Mao Zedong compared himself to Shihuangdi, the unifier of China and the brutal founder of its Qin dynasty. Reflecting on his campaign against intellectuals in general and Confucianism in particular, Mao declared to a Communist Party conference: "Emperor Qin Shihuang was not that outstanding. He only buried alive 460 Confucian scholars. We buried 460 thousand Confucian scholars. . . . To the charge of being like Emperor Qin, of being a dictator, we plead guilty."[15]

In contrast, modern-day Indians, who have sought to present their country as a model of cultural tolerance and nonviolence, have been quick to link themselves to Ashoka and his policies of inclusiveness. When the country became independent from British colonial rule in 1947, India soon placed an image of Ashoka's Pillar on the new nation's currency.

In the West, it has been the Roman Empire that has provided a template for thinking about political life. Many in Great Britain celebrated their own global empire as a modern version of the Roman Empire. If the British had been civilized by Roman rule, then surely Africans and Asians would benefit from falling under the control of the "more civilized" British. Likewise, to the Italian fascist dictator Benito Mussolini, his country's territorial expansion during the 1930s and World War II represented the creation of a new Roman Empire. Most recently, the United States' dominant role in the world has prompted the question, are the Americans the new Romans?

Historians frequently cringe as politicians and students use (and perhaps misuse) historical analogies to make their case for particular points of view in the present. But we have little else to go on except history in making our way through the complexities of contemporary life, and historians themselves seldom agree on the "lessons" of the past. Lively debate about the continuing relevance of these ancient empires shows that although the past may be gone, it surely is not dead.

Second Thoughts

What's the Significance?

Persian Empire, 102

Athenian democracy, 107

Greco-Persian Wars, 107

Peloponnesian War, 108

Alexander the Great, 108

Hellenistic era, 110

Alexandria, 110

Augustus, 115

pax Romana, 115

Qin Shihuangdi, 117

Han dynasty, 117

Mauryan Empire, 126

Ashoka, 126

Gupta Empire, 126

Big Picture Questions

1. What common features can you identify in the empires described in this chapter? In what ways did they differ from one another? What accounts for those differences?

2. Are you more impressed with the "greatness" of empires or with their destructive and oppressive features? Why?

3. Do you think that these second-wave empires hold "lessons" for the present, or are contemporary circumstances sufficiently unique as to render the distant past irrelevant?

4. **Looking Back:** How do these empires of the second-wave civilizations differ from the political systems of the First Civilizations?

Next Steps: For Further Study

Jane Burbank and Frederick Cooper, *Empires in World History* (2010). A fascinating account by two major scholars of the imperial theme across the world. Chapter 2 compares the Roman and Chinese empires.

Stanley Burstein, *The World from 1000 B.C.E. to 300 C.E.* (2017). An up-to-date account of Afro-Eurasian civilizations and their relationships by a prominent historian of the ancient world.

Arthur Cotterell, *The First Emperor of China* (1988). A biography of Shihuangdi.

Sarah Pomeroy et al., *Ancient Greece* (1999). A highly readable survey of Greek history by a team of distinguished scholars.

Walter Scheidel, ed., *Rome and China: Comparative Perspectives on Ancient World Empires* (2009). Places the historical trajectory and various themes of Roman and Han dynasty empires in a comparative context.

Romila Thapar, *Ashoka and the Decline of the Mauryas* (1961). A classic study of India's early empire builder.

Illustrated History of the Roman Empire, http://www.roman-empire.net. An interactive website with maps, pictures, and much information about the Roman Empire.

BBC, "The Immortal Emperor. Qin Shi Huang," presented by Tony Spawforth, 1996, https://www.youtube.com/watch?v=_6zcd68h-hs. A documentary film about China's "first emperor" and his enormous funerary complex of terra-cotta warriors.

Perceptions of Outsiders in the Ancient World

The peoples of ancient Eurasia did not live in splendid isolation from one another. Nor did they inhabit the kind of deeply interconnected and globalized world that the past century has created. But through war, commerce, the migration of peoples, the spread of religions, and sheer geographic proximity, some of those peoples became sharply aware of one another and developed mental images of life beyond the familiar confines of their own culture. What distortions arose as they pondered those outside their circle? How did the "other" provide opportunities to question or critique their own society? How and in what contexts were outsiders depicted in ancient art and in writing? The sources that follow provide five examples of this process from the ancient world.

SOURCE 3.1 A Greek Historian on Persia

Born to a wealthy Greek family in Asia Minor, Herodotus (ca. 485–425 B.C.E.) came of age when the wars between the Greeks and Persians were still recent memories. He devoted much of his life to recording the history of that great conflict in a series of books known as *The Histories*. In doing so, he pretty much invented for the Western world the craft of history as a systematic and connected narrative based on research. As a man of means, he was able to travel widely in the Persian Empire, Egypt, Syria, Babylon, Sicily, and Italy, making notes of what he saw and collecting stories, myths, and oral recollections along the way. The selection that follows contains some of his personal impressions of Persia.

- What cultural differences does Herodotus notice between Greek ways of living and those of Persia?

- What posture does Herodotus take toward these differences? He does refer to Persians as "barbarians," but at the time that term may have meant simply "non-Greek," without the implication of "savage" or "uncivilized" that it later acquired. Does he express a critical view of the Persians or a more positive understanding?

- What parts of this account might be helpful to historians seeking to describe life in ancient Persia? What might a historian learn about the Greeks' views of themselves from this description?

HERODOTUS | *The Histories* | **mid-5th century** B.C.E.

The customs that I know the Persians follow are these. They have no images of the gods and no temples or altars; they consider the use of them a sign of foolishness. This comes, I think, from their not believing the gods to have the same nature as human beings, as the Greeks imagine. The Persians' practice is to climb to the tops of the highest mountains to offer sacrifices to Zeus, the Greek name for the chief god of the universe. The Persians use this god's name to refer to the whole extent of the sky. They also sacrifice to the sun and moon, to the earth, to fire, to water, and to the winds. . . .

Of all the days in the year, the one they celebrate the most is their birthday. It is customary to serve much more food on that day than usual. The richer Persians have an ox, a horse, a camel, and an ass roasted whole for the meal; poorer people cook smaller kinds of cattle. They eat relatively few main courses but many extra courses, which they serve a few dishes at a time. For this reason, the Persians say that the Greeks leave a meal hungry because they have nothing worth mentioning served to them as an extra after the meats and that if the Greeks did have extra courses served, they would never stop eating. The Persians love wine and drink large amounts of it. . . .

When they meet another person in the street, you can tell if the people meeting are of equal status by the following indication: If they are, instead of speaking, they kiss each other on the lips. In the case where one is a little inferior to the other, the kiss is given on the cheek. Where the difference of rank is great, the inferior lies down on the ground in front of the superior. . . . The farther away other peoples live, the less the Persians respect them. The reason is that they regard themselves as very greatly superior in all respects to the rest of humanity, believing that other peoples' excellence is directly proportional to how close they live to Persia. . . .

No one so readily adopts foreign customs as the Persians. For this reason, they wear clothing like that of the Medes, considering it superior to their own. In war, they wear Egyptian armor to protect their chests. As soon as they hear of any luxury from any country, they instantly make it their own. In particular, they learned from the Greeks to have sex with adolescent boys. Each man has several wives and an even greater number of concubines.

In terms of manliness, manly courage on the battlefield is the greatest proof, with fathering many sons the second greatest. . . . They carefully educate their sons from the age of five to the age of twenty in only three subjects: riding horses, shooting arrows, and speaking the truth. Until boys are five, they are not allowed to come into the sight of their fathers, but instead spend their time with the women. They do this so that if the child dies young, the father will not be saddened at losing him.

I praise this custom and the following one too. The king does not put anyone to death for a single instance of wrong-doing, and no Persian inflicts an extreme penalty on a slave for a single instance of wrong-doing.

I can say all these things about the Persians with complete certainty, relying on my own personal knowledge.

Source: Herodotus, *The Histories*, 1:131–37, 140, in *Herodotus and Sima Qian: The First Great Historians of Greece and China*, edited by Thomas R. Martin (Boston: Bedford/St. Martin's, 2010), 46–49.

■ ■ ■

SOURCE 3.2 A Greek Goldsmith Depicts the Scythians ▶

Nomadic Scythian pastoralists who grazed their animals on the vast grasslands north of the Black Sea traded extensively with Greek colonies along the coast. Skilled craftsmen in these settlements regularly created luxury items for nomadic elites like this magnificent gold beaker dating from the fourth century B.C.E. The beaker depicts scenes from the everyday life of pastoralists, including the stringing of a bow, the bandaging of a wound, and, in the scene depicted here, the pulling of a tooth—a common if painful procedure in the ancient world. Found in a Scythian grave on the Crimean Peninsula, the lifelike figures reflect Greek artistic sensibilities, but the hairstyles and clothing are distinctly Scythian.

■ An elite Scythian most likely commissioned this beaker. How does this information shape how you think about this Greek depiction of the Scythians?

■ Does the beaker offer any evidence that the Greek craftsman who made it had directly encountered Scythians?

■ Both the beaker and Herodotus present Greek views of other cultures. What does the beaker add to the insights offered by Herodotus?

Scythian Cup, Crimea │ **4th century** B.C.E.

State Hermitage Museum, St. Petersburg, Russia/Archives Charmet/Bridgeman Images

SOURCE 3.3 **A Roman Historian on the Germans**

Occupying much of Central Europe north of the Roman Empire, ancient Germanic-speaking peoples were never a single "nation" but rather a collection of tribes, clans, and chiefdoms. They were regarded by the Romans as barbarians, though admired and feared for their military skills. These Germanic peoples were famously described by Tacitus (56–117 C.E.), a Roman official and well-known historian. Tacitus himself had never visited the lands of the people he describes; rather, he relied on earlier written documents and interviews with merchants and soldiers who had traveled and lived in the region. Unlike Herodotus, he wrote about people who lived without the states and cities characteristic of civilizations.

■ What can we learn from Tacitus's account about the economy, politics, society, and culture of the Germanic peoples of the first century C.E.?

■ Which statements of Tacitus might you regard as reliable, and which are more suspect? Why?

■ Modern scholars have argued that Tacitus used the Germanic peoples to criticize aspects of his own Roman culture. What evidence might support this point of view?

■ What differences might you notice between Herodotus's description of Persian civilization and Tacitus's discussion of an agricultural village society?

TACITUS | *Germania* | 1st century C.E.

The tribes of Germany are free from all taint of intermarriages with foreign nations, and they appear as a distinct, unmixed race, like none but themselves. . . . All have fierce blue eyes, red hair, huge frames, fit only for a sudden exertion. They are less able to bear laborious work. Heat and thirst they cannot in the least endure; to cold and hunger their climate and their soil inure them. . . .

They choose their kings by birth, their generals by merit. These kings have not unlimited or arbitrary power, and the generals do more by example than by authority. . . . And what most stimulates their courage is that their squadrons or battalions, instead of being formed by chance or by a fortuitous gathering, are composed of families and clans. Close by them, too, are those dearest to them, so that they hear the shrieks of women, the cries of infants. . . .

Tradition says that armies already wavering and giving way have been rallied by women who, with earnest entreaties and bosoms laid bare, have vividly represented the horrors of captivity, which the Germans fear with such extreme dread on behalf of their women. . . . They even believe that the female sex has a certain sanctity and prescience, and they do not despise their counsels, or make light of their answers. . . .

Mercury is the deity whom they chiefly worship, and on certain days they deem it right to sacrifice to him even with human victims. . . . Augury and divination by lot no people practice more diligently. . . .

When they go into battle, it is a disgrace for the chief to be surpassed in valor, a disgrace for his followers not to equal the valor of the chief. . . . Feasts and entertainments, which though inelegant, are plentifully furnished, are their only pay. The means of this bounty come from war or rapine. Nor are they as easily persuaded to plough the earth and to wait for the year's produce as to challenge an enemy and earn the honor of wounds. Nay, they actually think it tame and stupid to acquire by the sweat of toil what they might win by their blood.

Whenever they are not fighting, they pass much of their time in hunting, and still more in idleness, giving themselves up to sleep and to feasting, the bravest and the most warlike doing nothing, and surrendering the management of the household of the home, and of the land, to the women, the old men, and all the weakest members of the family. . . . It is the custom of the states to bestow by voluntary and individual contribution on the chief a present of cattle or of grain, which, while accepted as a compliment, supplies their wants. They are particularly delighted by gifts from neighboring tribes . . . such as choice steeds, heavy armor, trappings, and neckchains. We have now taught them to accept money also.

It is well known that the nations of Germany have no cities, and that they do not even tolerate closely contiguous dwellings. They live scattered and apart. . . . No use is made by them of stone or tile; they employ timber for all purposes, rude masses without ornament or attractiveness. . . .

Their marriage code, however, is strict, and indeed no part of their manners is more praise-worthy. Almost alone among barbarians they are content with one wife, except a very few among them. . . .

Very rare for so numerous a population is adultery, the punishment of which is prompt, and in the husband's power. Having cut off the hair of the adulteress and stripped her naked, he expels her from the house in the presence of her kinfolk, and then flogs her through the whole village. The loss of chastity meets with no indulgence; neither beauty, youth, nor wealth will procure the culprit a husband.

To limit the number of their children or to destroy any of their subsequent offspring is accounted infamous, and good habits are here more effectual than good laws elsewhere. . . .

It is the duty among them to adopt the feuds as well as the friendships of a father or a kinsman. These feuds are not implacable; even homicide is expiated by the payment of a certain number of cattle and of sheep, and the satisfaction is accepted by the entire family, greatly to the advantage of the state, since feuds are dangerous in proportion to a people's freedom. . . .

[S]laves are not employed after our manner with distinct domestic duties assigned to them, but each one has the management of a house and home of his own. The master requires from the slave a certain quantity of grain, of cattle, and of clothing, as he would from a tenant, and this is the limit of subjection.

Source: Alfred John Church and William Jackson Brodribb, *The Agricola and Germania of Tacitus* (London: Macmillan, 1877), 87ff.

■ ■ ■

SOURCE 3.4 A Roman Depiction of Sarmatians ▶

Germans were not the only people to periodically threaten the borders of the Roman Empire. Various groups of pastoralists from north of the Black Sea regularly migrated west, raiding and sometimes invading Roman territory, especially along the Danube River. The Romans respected the military prowess of these nomadic horsemen, whom they frequently fought and sometimes absorbed into their armies. Dating from the second century C.E., this bas-relief sculpture of pastoralist Sarmatians battling Roman forces was one scene among dozens carved onto a nearly one-hundred-foot-tall triumphal column in Rome celebrating the victories of Emperor Trajan. It depicts the distinctly heavily armored Sarmatian cavalry fleeing from advancing Romans. Some Sarmatians were taken as prisoners to Rome by Trajan in 104 C.E. to participate in victory celebrations, which may explain why they were incorporated into the column.

■ Trajan's column was created to celebrate the emperor's victories. How might its purpose affect how you interpret and use this source?

■ Notice the detailed depiction of Sarmatian weapons and their distinctive scale-like armor, which protected both rider and horse. What can these elements of the sculpture tell us about Roman knowledge of their enemies?

■ What can the depiction of Scythians in Source 3.2 and Sarmatians here tell us about the pastoralists that lived on the northern fringes of the Greek and Roman civilizations?

Scene from Trajan's Column, Rome | **107–113** C.E.

Pictures from History/Bridgeman Images

■ ■ ■

SOURCE 3.5 A Chinese Historian on the Xiongnu

During the time of the Han dynasty, the Chinese historian and high official Sima Qian (ca. 145–86 B.C.E.), like his Roman counterpart Tacitus, had occasion to observe and describe neighboring "barbarian" peoples and their history. In Sima Qian's case, those people were the Xiongnu, pastoral nomads living to the north of China's Great Wall. China's relationship with these peoples fluctuated, involving war, trade, exchange of ambassadors, and periodic treaties (see "China and the

Northern Nomads" in Chapter 8). While the Chinese generally felt enormously superior to such "uncivilized" people, they were compelled on occasion to accommodate the military prowess of the Xiongnu. The following excerpts from Sima Qian's enormous history of ancient China illustrate his understanding of these people, who long represented a mirror through which the Chinese defined their image of themselves.

- Based on this document and what you know about Chinese life, what aspects of Xiongnu culture would likely appear most different or distasteful to Sima Qian?

- What can you infer about the relationship between China and the Xiongnu from the letter of Emperor Wen? How do you imagine he and Sima Qian felt about that letter?

- How might Sima Qian have reacted to the depictions of pastoralists in Sources 3.2 and 3.4?

SIMA QIAN | *Records of the Grand Historian* | ca. 100 B.C.E.

The ancestor of the Xiongnu descended from the ruler of the Xia dynasty, whose name was Qun Wei. From before the time of Emperors [of the third millennium B.C.E.], there have been barbarians . . . living in northern uncivilized areas and wandering around herding animals. They herd mainly horses, cattle, and sheep, but also some unusual animals, such as camels, donkeys, mules, and wild horses. . . . They move around looking for water and pasture and have no walled settlements or permanent housing. They do not farm, but they do divide their land into separate holdings under different leaders. They have no writing, and all contracts are verbal. When their children can ride a sheep, they begin to use bows and arrows to shoot birds and rodents. When they are older, they shoot foxes and rabbits for food. In this way, all the young men are easily able to become archers and serve as cavalry. It is their custom when times are easy to graze their animals and hunt with the bow for their living, but when hard times come, they take up weapons to plunder and raid. This is their innate nature. Their long-range weapons are bows and arrows; they use swords and spears in close combat. When they have the advantage in battle, they advance, but if not,

they retreat, since there is no shame in running away. They are only concerned with self-interest, knowing nothing of proper behavior or justice.

Everyone, including the chiefs, eats the meat of their domesticated animals and wears clothing of hides and coats of fur. The men who are in their prime eat the fattiest and best food, while the elderly eat what is left over, since the Xiongnu treasure the strong and healthy but place little value on the weak and old. When his father dies, a son marries his stepmother, and when brothers die, the surviving brothers marry their widows. . . .

Following a battle . . . they are allowed to keep the plunder that they have seized. They make slaves of any prisoners of war. Therefore, when they make war, each warrior works for his own profit. They are very skilled at using decoy soldiers to trick opponents to their destruction. As soon as they see the enemy, they go after their booty like a flock of birds hungry for prey, but when they are defeated they disperse and evaporate. . . .

[*In describing the fluctuating relationship between the Chinese and the Xiongnu, Sima Qian quotes a letter written by the Chinese emperor Wen in 162 B.C.E. to the Xiongnu.*]

"The emperor respectfully asks about the health of the chief of the Xiongnu. Your ambassadors . . . have brought us two horses. We accept them with respect.

In accordance with what the previous emperor decreed the chief of the Xiongnu was to command the region north of the Great Wall where men shoot arrows from their bows, while we were to rule the region south of the wall, where the people live in houses and wear hats and sashes. Under this arrangement, the multitudes of inhabitants of these areas would get their food and clothing by farming, weaving, or hunting, fathers and sons would live side by side, rulers and officials would both be safe, and no one would act violently or rebel. We have heard, however, that a number of evil and deluded men, whose greed for wealth has overcome them, have forsaken justice and broken our peace treaty, paying no heed to what will happen to the multitudes of inhabitants and destroying the harmony that has been in place between the rulers of our two lands.

This, however, is now past history. You said in your [earlier] letter to me that, since our two nations have been brought together again in peace and our two rulers are again in agreement, you want to rest your army and let your horses graze, so that there may be prosperity and happiness for generation upon generation, and so that we can begin again to exist peacefully and harmoniously. We enthusiastically agree with what you said. . . . As long as we and the chief of the Xiongnu join together to walk this path . . . then no one in the entire world will fail to benefit. . . . Since the Xiongnu live in the north, where the country is cold and the severe frosts arrive early in the year, we have ordered our imperial officials to send annually to the chief of the Xiongnu a specified amount of grain, yeast, gold, silk cloth, thread, fiber stuffing for clothing, and other items.

The world currently is experiencing a secure peace, and our peoples are undisturbed. We and the chief of the Xiongnu must be like their parents. When we look back at the past, we recognize that the plans of our officials came to nothing as a result of minor things and insignificant causes. Nothing of this sort deserves to overturn the concord existing between brothers."

Source: Sima Qian, *The Records of the Historian*, chap. 110 in *Herodotus and Sima Qian: The First Great Historians of Greece and China*, edited by Thomas R. Martin (Boston: Bedford/St. Martin's, 2010), 129–30, 133, 136–37.

DOING HISTORY

1. **Making comparisons:** How might you compare the perceptions of outsiders in Sources 3.1, 3.3, and 3.5? Did the authors notice the same features of these societies? Did they focus more on what was exotic or different rather than on what may have been familiar? Did they adopt a similar posture toward the peoples they were describing? Were they simply reporting what they observed, or were they making judgments as well?

2. **Describing the "uncivilized":** Sources 3.2, 3.3, 3.4, and 3.5 all describe or depict peoples living beyond the boundaries of "civilization." To what extent did they describe or depict these peoples in a similar fashion? How do their descriptions differ?

3. **Relating encounters and observations:** How might the political or military relationships among different peoples affect perceptions of those peoples?

Early Sources on Foreign Cultures

Descriptions of ancient societies, particularly by eyewitness observers from other cultures, provide a rich but problematic source for modern historians. In the passages that follow, two such historians grapple with some of the potential difficulties with using descriptions of cultures written by outsiders. In Voice 3.1, Stephen Gosch and Peter Stearns examine some of the common problems with travelers' accounts and their implications for how historians use them. In Voice 3.2, Jerry Bentley explores the emergence of the concept of "barbarian" in Greek and Chinese thinking.

- What key problems with travelers' accounts as historical sources do Gosch and Stearns identify?

- Compare and contrast the emergence and meaning of "barbarian" in Greece and China. Which elements are similar? Which are distinctive?

- **Integrating Primary and Secondary Sources:** From your reading of Herodotus's description of Persia (Source 3.1), do you agree with the argument in Voice 3.1 that Herodotus's account is only useful for understanding his own beliefs and the outlook of his audience, or do you think that his account also provides useful evidence about Persia?

- **Integrating Primary and Secondary Sources:** What aspects of Tacitus's account of the Germans (Source 3.3) and Sima Qian's description of the Xiongnu (Source 3.5) support Bentley's description of barbarians in Greek and Chinese thinking? What aspects contradict or question his assertions?

VOICE 3.1

Stephen Gosch and Peter Stearns on Travelers' Accounts as Historical Sources | 2008

But can premodern travelers be believed? Are the narratives that they produced credible sources of evidence for modern scholars? Strabo, a Greek traveler in the first century CE, once wrote, "Everybody who tells the story of his own travels is a braggart.". . .

Premodern travelers not only frequently bragged about their experiences, they also depicted some of the peoples they encountered en route as strange and weird, as "others" quite different from, and often inferior to, themselves. An aspect of much travel writing before 1500, to which all students must remain alert, is the contrast, often implied rather than explicit, between "we" who are "normal" and "they" who are "bizarre." Some of the travelers . . . went even further spicing up their narratives with fantastic stories of monstrous beings, usually said to inhabit the outer edges of the earth. . . .

The bragging, the "othering" and the fantasies about strange creatures and monsters in premodern travel narratives, have led some researchers to reject much of this writing as of not real value to the historian. Some scholars, mostly in the field of literary studies, have argued that premodern travel is useful, but only for understanding the beliefs of the traveler and the expectations of his or her audience at home. One of the most interesting recent books about Herodotus . . . makes precisely this claim.

Source: Stephen S. Gosch and Peter N. Stearns, *Premodern Travel in World History* (New York: Routledge, 2008), 4.

VOICE 3.2

Jerry Bentley on the Idea of "Barbarian" | 1993

In Greek usage, the term *barbarian* originally was a linguistic rather than a social or cultural category: it referred to an individual who did not speak Greek. After Greeks became prominent in Mediterranean trade and began to develop an increasingly sophisticated civilization, about the eighth century B.C.E., the term *barbarian* took on strong connotations of cultural inferiority. The presence in Greek city-states of increasing numbers of foreign slaves—barbarians by definition—reinforced this semantic shift. Over time, the association of barbarism with inferiority encouraged settled, civilized peoples to adopt an aggressive and sometimes violent policy toward their nomadic or less urbanized neighbors. . . . By no means, though, was the notion of barbarism an exclusively western concept. Owen Lattimore has shown how early Chinese agriculturalists and steppe nomads progressively differentiated themselves, largely as a result of the almost inexorable enlargement by Chinese of the zone dedicated to agriculture. . . . As they enlarged the agricultural zone, they encountered mixed agriculturalists and herding peoples, whom they either absorbed into their own ranks or pushed into steppe regions beyond the point where settled agriculture was a practical activity. . . . Political, social, and cultural differentiation followed naturally from the radically different economic and environmental conditions of agricultural and steppe societies. Chinese soon came to regard nomadic steppe peoples as barbarians and to place relations with them under close supervision.

Source: Jerry H. Bentley, *Old World Encounters: Cross-Cultural Contacts and Exchanges in Pre-Modern Times* (New York: Oxford University Press, 1993), 23–24.

CHAPTER

4

Culture and Religion in Eurasia / North Africa

600 B.C.E.–600 C.E.

In September of 2009, Kong Dejun returned to China from her home in Great Britain. The occasion was a birthday celebration for her ancient ancestor Kong Fuzi, or Confucius, born 2,560 years earlier. Together with some 10,000 other people—descendants, scholars, government officials, and foreign representatives—Kong Dejun attended ceremonies at the Confucian Temple in Qufu, the hometown of China's famous sage. "I was touched to see my ancestor being revered by people from different countries and nations," she said.[1] What made this celebration remarkable was that it took place in a country still ruled by the Communist Party, which had long devoted enormous efforts to discrediting Confucius and his teachings. In the view of communist China's revolutionary leader, Mao Zedong, Confucianism was associated with class inequality, patriarchy, feudalism, superstition, and all things old and backward. But the country's ancient teacher and philosopher had apparently outlasted its revolutionary hero, for now the Communist Party has claimed Confucius as a national treasure and has established over 300 Confucian Institutes to study his writings. He appears in TV shows and movies, even as many anxious parents offer prayers at Confucian temples when their children are taking the national college entrance exams.

Buddhism and Daoism (DOW-i'zm) have also experienced something of a revival in China, as thousands of temples, destroyed during the heyday of communism, have been repaired and reopened. Christianity too has grown rapidly since the death of Mao in 1976. Here are reminders, in a Chinese context, of the continuing appeal of cultural traditions forged long ago. Those traditions are among the most enduring legacies that second-wave civilizations have bequeathed to the modern world. ■

« China's Cultural Traditions   In this idealized painting, attributed to the Chinese artist Wang Shugu (1649–1730), the Chinese teacher Confucius presents a baby Buddha to the Daoist master Laozi. The image illustrates the assimilation of a major Indian religion into China as well as the generally peaceful coexistence of these three traditions.

141

While the states and empires of Eurasia and North Africa transformed the political framework of the civilizations in these areas, the cultural and religious dimension of life in this huge region also changed dramatically. In China, it was the time of Confucius and Laozi (low-ZUH), whose teachings gave rise to Confucianism and Daoism, respectively. In India, a series of religious writings known as the Upanishads gave expression to the classical philosophy of what we know as Hinduism, while a religious reformer, Siddhartha Gautama (sih-DHAR-tuh GOW-tau-mah), set in motion a separate religion known later as Buddhism. In the Middle East, a distinctively monotheistic religious tradition appeared, expressed in Persian Zoroastrianism and in Judaism. Later, this Jewish religious outlook became the foundation for both Christianity and Islam. Finally, in Greece, a rational and humanistic tradition found expression in the writings of Socrates, Plato, Aristotle, and many others.

But alongside these larger and more extensive cultural systems, a multitude of locally embedded and orally transmitted religious traditions also flourished. Within the major civilizations, these "little traditions" interacted constantly with the emerging "great traditions." Thus ancient Greek gods persisted even as classical Greek philosophy took shape; older practices of Chinese ancestor veneration came to be incorporated in the emerging tradition of Confucianism; and Jews continued to be attracted to foreign deities despite the growing prominence of the one God, Yahweh. Furthermore, in societies that lay beyond the zone of civilization, such as those in Aboriginal Australia, local traditions linked living human beings to the land, to the vegetable and animal worlds, to their ancestors, and to the gods or spirits that inhabited everything. In this chapter, however, the spotlight falls on those larger cultural or religious traditions that emerged from the civilizations of the second-wave era and that have persisted into the twenty-first century.

> **SEEKING THE MAIN POINT**
>
> Fundamentally, the religions of the second-wave era were similar. Does the material of this chapter support or challenge this idea?

China and the Search for Order

By the eighth century B.C.E., the authority of China's Zhou dynasty had substantially weakened, and by 500 B.C.E. any unity that China had earlier enjoyed was long gone and violence grew in its wake. It was during these dreadful centuries of disorder and turmoil, known as the era of warring states (ca. 500–221 B.C.E.), that a number of Chinese thinkers began to consider how order might be restored, how the apparent tranquility of an earlier time could be realized again (see "China: From Warring States to Empire" in Chapter 3). From their reflections emerged classical cultural traditions of Chinese civilization.

The Legalist Answer

One answer to the problem of disorder—though not the first to emerge—was a hardheaded and practical philosophy known as **Legalism**. To Legalist thinkers,

	600 B.C.E.	400 B.C.E.	200 B.C.E.	1 C.E.	200 C.E.	400 C.E.	600 C.E.

CHINA

ca. 551–479 B.C.E.
Life of Confucius

206 B.C.E.–220 C.E.
Confucianism prominent in Han dynasty

221–206 B.C.E.
Legalism prominent in Qin dynasty

184–204 C.E.
Yellow Turban Rebellion; informed by
Daoist beliefs

INDIA

ca. 800–400 B.C.E.
Upanishads compiled

ca. 300 C.E.
Bhagavad Gita compiled
in final form

ca. 566–486 B.C.E.
Life of Buddha

ca. 650 C.E.
Bhakti forms of Hinduism emerge

MIDDLE EAST

ca. 7th century B.C.E.(?)
Life of Zoroaster

4 B.C.E.–29 C.E.
Life of Jesus

ca. 45–65 C.E.
Paul's missionary journeys in eastern
Mediterranean region

586 B.C.E.
Jewish exile in Babylon

ca. 100–313 C.E.
Intermittent persecutions
of Christians in Roman Empire

310–380 C.E.
Christianity becomes state religion in
Armenia, Axum, and the Roman Empire

GREECE

ca. 600–300 B.C.E.
Greek rationalism

469–399 B.C.E.
Life of Socrates

429–348 B.C.E.
Life of Plato

384–322 B.C.E.
Life of Aristotle

the solution to China's problems lay in rules or laws, clearly spelled out and strictly enforced through a system of rewards and punishments. "If rewards are high," wrote Han Fei, one of the most prominent Legalist philosophers, "then what the ruler wants will be quickly effected; if punishments are heavy, what he does not want will be swiftly prevented."[2]

Legalists generally entertained a rather pessimistic view of human nature. Most people, they believed, were stupid and shortsighted. Only the state and its rulers could act in their long-term interests. Doing so meant promoting farmers and soldiers, the only two groups in society who performed essential functions, while suppressing merchants, aristocrats, scholars, and other classes regarded as useless.

Legalist thinking provided inspiration and methods for the harsh reunification of China under Shihuangdi and the Qin dynasty (221–206 B.C.E.), but the brutality of that short dynasty thoroughly discredited Legalism. Although its techniques and practices played a role in subsequent Chinese statecraft, few philosophers or rulers ever again openly advocated its ideas as the sole guide for Chinese political life. The Han dynasty (206 B.C.E.–220 C.E.) and all subsequent dynasties drew instead on the teachings of China's greatest sage — Confucius.

Guided Reading Question

■ **COMPARISON**

What different answers to the problem of disorder arose in classical China?

The Confucian Answer

Born to an aristocratic family in the state of Lu in northern China, Confucius (551–479 B.C.E.) was both learned and ambitious. Believing that he had found the key to solving China's problem of disorder, he spent much of his adult life seeking a political position from which he might put his ideas into action. But no such opportunity came his way. Perhaps it was just as well, for it was as a thinker and a teacher that Confucius left a profound imprint on Chinese history and culture and also on other East Asian societies, such as Korea and Japan. After his death, his students collected his teachings in a short book called the *Analects*, and later scholars elaborated and commented endlessly on his ideas, creating a body of thought known as **Confucianism**.

The Confucian answer to the problem of China's disorder was very different from that of the Legalists. Not laws and punishments, but the moral example of superiors was the Confucian key to a restored social harmony. For Confucius, human society consisted primarily of unequal relationships: the father was superior to the son; the husband to the wife; the older brother to the younger brother; and, of course, the ruler to the subject. If the superior party in each of these relationships behaved with sincerity, benevolence, and genuine concern for others, then the inferior party would be motivated to respond with deference and obedience. Harmony would then prevail. As Confucius put it, "The relation between superiors and inferiors is like that between the wind and the grass. The grass must bend when the wind blows across it." Thus, in both family life and in political life, the cultivation of *ren* — human-heartedness, benevolence, goodness — was the essential ingredient of a tranquil society.

Guided Reading Question

■ **DESCRIPTION**

Why has Confucianism been defined as a "humanistic philosophy" rather than a supernatural religion?

Filial Piety The long-enduring social order that Confucius advocated began at home with unquestioning obedience and the utmost respect for parents and other senior members of the family. This Qing dynasty woodcut illustrates the proper filial relationship between father and son in a variety of circumstances. (Private Collection/Roland and Sabrina Michaud/akg-images)

But how were these humane virtues to be nurtured? Because people have a capacity for improvement, the key to moral progress was education, particularly an immersion in language, literature, history, philosophy, and ethics, all applied to the practical problems of government. Ritual and ceremonies were also important, for they conveyed the rules of appropriate behavior in the many and varying circumstances of life. For the "superior person," or "gentleman" in Confucian terms, serious personal reflection and a willingness to strive continuously to perfect his moral character were essential.

Such ideas had a pervasive influence in Chinese life as Confucianism became almost synonymous with Chinese culture. As China's bureaucracy took shape during and after the Han dynasty, Confucianism became the central element of the educational system, which prepared students for the examinations required to gain official positions. Thus generation after generation of China's male elite was steeped in the ideas and values of Confucianism.

In Confucian thinking, the family became a model for political life, a kind of miniature state. Filial piety, the honoring of one's ancestors and parents, was both valuable in itself and a training ground for the reverence due to the emperor and state officials. Such views of the family were rigidly patriarchal and set the tone for defining the lives of women and men alike. They were linked to a hierarchical and gendered understanding of the cosmos in which an inferior and receptive Earth, associated with the feminine, was in balance with the superior and creative principle of Heaven, associated with the masculine. Thus the subordinate and deferential position of women in relation to men was rooted in the structure of the cosmos itself. What this meant for women was spelled out by a somewhat later woman writer, **Ban Zhao** (bahn jow) (45–116 C.E.), in a famous work called *Lessons for Women.* "Let a woman modestly yield to others. . . . Always let her seem to tremble and to fear. . . . Then she may be said to humble herself before others."[3] Ban Zhao called for greater attention to education for young girls, not because they were equal to boys, but so that a young woman might be better prepared to serve her husband. Education for boys, on the other hand, enabled them to more effectively control their wives.

Corresponding Confucian virtues for ideal men were contained in the paired concepts of *wen* and *wu*, both limited largely to males. The superior principle of wen referred to the refined qualities of rationality, scholarship, and literary and artistic abilities, while wu focused attention on physical and martial achievements. Thus men alone, and superior men at that, were eligible for the civil service exams that led to political office and high prestige, while military men and merchants occupied a distinctly lower position in a male social hierarchy.[4]

Beyond defining gender expectations, Confucianism also placed great importance on history, for the ideal good society lay in the past. Confucian ideas were reformist, perhaps even revolutionary, but they were consistently presented as an effort to restore a past golden age. Those ideas also injected a certain democratic element into Chinese elite culture, for the great sage had emphasized that "superior men" and potential government officials were those of outstanding moral character and intellectual achievement, not simply those of aristocratic background. Usually only young men from wealthy families could afford the education necessary for passing examinations, but on occasion villagers could find the resources to sponsor one of their bright sons, potentially propelling him into the stratosphere of the Chinese elite while bringing honor and benefit to the village itself.

Confucian ideas were clearly used to legitimate the many inequalities of Chinese society, but they also established certain expectations for the superior parties in China's social hierarchy. Thus emperors should keep taxes low, administer justice, and provide for the material needs of the people. Those who failed to govern by these moral norms forfeited the Mandate of Heaven and invited upheaval and their replacement by another dynasty. Likewise, husbands should deal kindly with their wives and children, lest they invite conflict and disharmony in the family.

Finally, Confucianism marked Chinese elite culture by its secular, or nonreligious, character. Confucius did not deny the reality of gods and spirits. In fact, he advised people to participate in family and state rituals "as if the spirits were present," and he believed that the universe had a moral character with which human beings should align themselves. But the thrust of Confucian teaching was distinctly this-worldly and practical, concerned with human relationships, effective government, and social harmony. Members of the Chinese elite generally acknowledged that magic, the gods, and spirits were perhaps necessary for the lower orders of society, but educated people, they argued, would find them of little help in striving for moral improvement and in establishing a harmonious society.

The Daoist Answer

No civilization has ever painted its cultural outlook in a single color. As Confucian thinking became generally known in China, a quite different school of thought also took shape. Known as **Daoism**, it was associated with the legendary figure Laozi, who, according to tradition, was a sixth-century-B.C.E. archivist. He is said to have penned a short poetic volume, the *Daodejing* (DOW-DAY-JIHNG) (*The Way and Its Power*), before vanishing in the wilderness to the west of China on his water buffalo.

In many ways, Daoist thinking ran counter to that of Confucius, who had emphasized the importance of education and earnest striving for moral improvement and good government. The Daoists ridiculed such efforts as artificial and useless, claiming that they generally made things worse. In the face of China's disorder and chaos, Daoists urged withdrawal into the world of nature and encouraged behavior that was spontaneous, individualistic, and natural. Whereas Confucius focused on the world of human relationships, the Daoists turned the spotlight on the immense realm of nature and its mysterious unfolding patterns in which the "ten thousand things" appeared, changed, and vanished. "Confucius roams within society," the Chinese have often said. "Laozi wanders beyond."

The central concept of Daoist thinking is *dao*, an elusive notion that refers to the way of nature, the underlying and unchanging principle that governs all natural phenomena. The dao "moves around and around, but does not on this account suffer," wrote Laozi in the *Daodejing*. "All life comes from it. It wraps everything with its love as in a garment, and yet it claims no honor, for it does not demand to be lord. I do not know its name and so I call it the Dao, the Way, and I rejoice in its power."[5]

Amid the world of civilization, so highly valued by Confucius, the Daoists yearned for an earlier time, "an age of perfect virtue" that had been disrupted by Confucian striving for something better. Then, according to one Daoist master, "there were no paths and ramps on the mountains and no boats upon the bridges. . . . There were vast numbers of animals and grasses, and trees reached their natural growth. Wild animals could be taken for walks on leashes, and one could climb up to the nests of magpies and other birds." Such a vision of human harmony with nature contrasted sharply with the Confucian outlook, which urged "the development of a world of culture from a nature experienced as hostile." To Confucians, humankind "disposes over the world of [wild] things, tames wild animals, and brings cowed vermin under his control."[6] In contrast,

Guided Reading Question

■ **COMPARISON**
How did the Daoist outlook differ from that of Confucianism?

Chinese Landscape Painting
Focused largely on mountains and water, Chinese landscape paintings were much influenced by the Daoist search for harmony with nature. Thus human figures and buildings were usually eclipsed by towering peaks, waterfalls, clouds, mists, and trees. This thirteenth-century ink-on-silk painting illustrates that sensibility. The poem at the top reads: "Night rains cleansed the capital's suburban farms, / Morning sun brightens the emperor's city; / People work happily in a good year, / Dancing and singing they cross a path in the field." (Art Collection 2/Alamy)

individual Daoists often fled to the mountains, where they might experience the dao in union with nature. (See Sources 8.3 and 8.4 in Working with Evidence, Chapter 8, pages 350–353.)

Applied to human life, Daoism invited people to withdraw from the world of political and social activism, to disengage from the public life so important to Confucius, and to align themselves with the way of nature. It meant simplicity in living, small self-sufficient communities, limited government, and the abandonment of education and active efforts at self-improvement. "Give up learning," declares the *Daodejing*, "and put an end to your troubles." The flavor of the Daoist approach to life is evident in this passage from the *Daodejing*, describing a small and simple society:

> Though there were individuals with the abilities of ten or a hundred men,
> there should be no employment of them . . . ;
> Though they had boats and carriages, they should have no occasion to ride in
> them;
> There should be a neighbouring state within sight . . . ,
> but I would make the people . . . not have any intercourse with it.[7]

Like Confucianism, the Daoist perspective viewed family life as central to Chinese society, though the element of male/female hierarchy was downplayed in favor of complementarity and balance between the sexes.

The Yin Yang Symbol

Despite its various differences with the ideas of Confucianism, the Daoist perspective was widely regarded by elite Chinese as complementing rather than contradicting Confucian values (see the opening image in this chapter). Such an outlook was facilitated by the ancient Chinese concept of *yin* and *yang*, which expressed a belief in the unity of opposites (see figure). Thus a scholar-official might pursue the Confucian project of "government by goodness" during the day, but upon returning home in the evening or following his retirement, he might well behave in a more Daoist fashion—pursuing the simple life, reading Daoist philosophy, practicing meditation and breathing exercises in mountain settings, or enjoying painting, poetry, or calligraphy.

Daoism also shaped the culture of ordinary people as it entered popular religion. This kind of Daoism sought to tap the power of the dao for practical uses and came to include magic, fortune-telling, and the search for immortality. It also on occasion provided an ideology for peasant uprisings, such as the Yellow Turban Rebellion (184–204 C.E.), which imagined a utopian society without the oppression of governments and landlords. In its many and varied forms, Daoism, like Confucianism, became an enduring element of the Chinese cultural tradition.

Cultural Traditions of Classical India

The cultural development of Indian civilization was far different from that of China. Whereas Confucianism paid little attention to the gods, spirits, and speculation about religious matters, Indian elite culture embraced the Divine and all things spiritual with enthusiasm and generated elaborate philosophical visions about the nature of ultimate reality. But the Indian religious tradition — later called Hinduism — differed from other world religions as well. Unlike Buddhism, Christianity, or Islam, Hinduism had no historical founder; rather, it grew up over many centuries along with Indian civilization. Although it later spread into Southeast Asia, Hinduism was not a missionary religion seeking converts, but was, like Judaism, associated with a particular people and territory.

In fact, "Hinduism" was never a single tradition at all, and the term itself derived from outsiders — Greeks, Muslims, and later the British — who sought to reduce the infinite variety of Indian cultural patterns into a recognizable system. From the inside, however, Hinduism dissolved into a vast diversity of gods, spirits, beliefs, practices, rituals, and philosophies. This endlessly variegated Hinduism served to incorporate into Indian civilization the many diverse peoples who migrated into or invaded the South Asian peninsula over many centuries and several millennia. Its ability to accommodate this diversity gave India's cultural development a distinctive quality.

South Asian Religion: From Ritual Sacrifice to Philosophical Speculation

Despite the fragmentation and variety of Indian cultural and religious patterns, an evolving set of widely recognized sacred texts provided some commonality. The earliest of these texts, known as the **Vedas** (VAY-duhs), were collections of poems, hymns, prayers, and rituals. Compiled by priests called Brahmins, the Vedas were for centuries transmitted orally and were reduced to writing in Sanskrit around 600 B.C.E. In the Vedas, historians have caught fleeting glimpses of Indian civilization in its formative centuries (1500–600 B.C.E.). Those sacred writings tell of small competing chiefdoms or kingdoms, of sacred sounds and fires, of numerous gods, rising and falling in importance over the centuries. They also suggest a clearly patriarchal society, but one that afforded upper-class women somewhat greater opportunities than they later enjoyed. Vedic women participated in religious sacrifices, sometimes engaged in scholarship and religious debate, were allowed to wear the sacred thread that symbolized ritual purity in the higher castes, and could on occasion marry a man of their own choosing. The Vedas described as well the elaborate ritual sacrifices that Brahmin priests performed and for which they received substantial payments, enabling them to acquire enormous power and wealth, sometimes exceeding even that of kings and warriors.

As ritual became mechanical, formal, and expensive, criticism of Brahmins also grew. From this dissatisfaction arose another body of sacred texts, the **Upanishads** (oo-PAHN-ee-shahds). Composed by largely anonymous thinkers between 800 and 400 B.C.E., these were mystical and highly philosophical works that sought to probe the inner meaning of the rituals prescribed in the Vedas. In the Upanishads, external ritual gave way to introspective thinking, which expressed in many and varied formulations the central concepts of philosophical Hinduism that have persisted into

Guided Reading Question

....

■ **CHANGE**

In what ways did the religious traditions of South Asia change over the centuries?

modern times. Chief among them was the idea of Brahman, the World Soul, the final and ultimate reality. Beyond the multiplicity of material objects and individual persons and beyond even the various gods themselves lay this primal unitary energy or divine reality infusing all things, similar in some ways to the Chinese notion of the dao. This alone was real; the immense diversity of existence that human beings perceived with their senses was but an illusion.

The fundamental assertion of philosophical Hinduism was that the individual human soul, or *atman*, was in fact a part of Brahman. Beyond the quest for pleasure, wealth, power, and social position, all of which were perfectly normal and quite legitimate, lay the effort to achieve the final goal of humankind — union with Brahman, an end to our illusory perception of a separate existence. This was *moksha* (MOHK-shuh), or liberation, compared sometimes to a bubble in a glass of water breaking through the surface and becoming one with the surrounding atmosphere.

Achieving this exalted state was held to involve many lifetimes, and the notion of *samsara*, or rebirth/reincarnation, became a central feature of Hindu thinking. Human souls migrated from body to body over many lifetimes, depending on the actions of individuals. This was the law of *karma*. Pure actions, appropriate to one's station in life, resulted in rebirth in a higher social position or caste. Thus the caste system of distinct and ranked groups, each with its own duties, became a register of spiritual progress.

If Hinduism underpinned caste, it also legitimated and expressed India's gender system. As South Asian civilization crystallized during the second-wave era, its patriarchal features tightened. Women were increasingly seen as "unclean below the navel," forbidden to learn the Vedas, and excluded from public religious rituals. The Laws of Manu, probably composed in the early centuries of the Common Era, advocated child marriage for girls to men far older than themselves and famously proclaimed: "In childhood a female must be subject to her father; in youth to her husband; when her lord [husband] is dead to her sons; a woman must never be independent."[8]

And yet some aspects of Hinduism served to empower women. Sexual pleasure was considered a legitimate goal for both men and women, and its many and varied techniques were detailed in the *Kamasutra*. Many Hindu deities were female, some life-giving and faithful and others, like Kali, fiercely destructive. Women were particularly prominent in the growing devotional cults dedicated to particular deities, where neither gender nor caste was an obstacle to spiritual fulfillment.

Hindu Ascetics Hinduism called for men in the final stage of life to leave ordinary ways of living and withdraw into the forests to seek spiritual liberation, or moksha. Here, in an illustration from an early thirteenth-century Indian manuscript, a holy man explores a text with three disciples in a secluded rural setting. (Musée des Arts Asiatiques-Guimet, Paris, France/© RMN–Grand Palais/Art Resource, NY)

A further feature of Hindu religious thought lay in its provision of different paths to the ultimate goal of liberation, or moksha. Various ways to this final release, appropriate to people of different temperaments, were spelled out in Hindu teachings. Some might achieve moksha through knowledge or study; others by means of detached action in the world, doing one's ordinary work without regard to consequences; still others through passionate devotion to some deity or through extended meditation practice. Such ideas—carried by Brahmin priests and wandering ascetics or holy men, who had withdrawn from ordinary life to pursue their spiritual development—became widely known throughout India.

The Buddhist Challenge

About the same time as philosophical Hinduism was emerging, another movement took shape that soon became a distinct and separate religious tradition—Buddhism. Unlike Hinduism, this new faith had a historical founder, **Siddhartha Gautama** (ca. 566–ca. 486 B.C.E.), a prince from a small north Indian state. According to Buddhist tradition, the prince had enjoyed a sheltered and delightful youth until he encountered human suffering in the form of an old man, a sick person, and a corpse. Shattered by these revelations of aging, illness, and death, Siddhartha determined to find the cause of such sufferings and a remedy for them. And so, at the age of twenty-nine, the young prince left his luxurious life as well as his wife and child, shed his royal jewels, cut off his hair, and set off on a quest for enlightenment. This act of severing his ties to the attachments of ordinary life is known in Buddhist teaching as the Great Renunciation.

What followed were six years of spiritual experimentation that finally led Siddhartha to an ancient fig tree in northern India, now known as the Bodhi (enlightenment) tree. There, Buddhist sources tell us, he began a forty-nine-day period of intensive meditation that ended with an indescribable experience of spiritual realization. Now he was the **Buddha**, the man who had awakened. For the next forty years, he taught what he had learned, setting in motion the cultural tradition of Buddhism.

"I teach but one thing," the Buddha said, "suffering and the end of suffering." To the Buddha, suffering or sorrow—experiencing life as imperfect, impermanent, and unsatisfactory—was the central and universal feature of human life. This kind of suffering derived from desire

The Buddha's Enlightenment Dating from the late eighth century in Korea, this monumental and beautifully proportioned sculpture portrays the Buddha at the moment of his enlightenment, symbolized by his right hand touching the earth. Seated on a lotus pedestal, this image of the Buddha also shows the *ushnisha*, the round oval at the top of his head, which represents his spiritual attainment, and the dot in the center of his forehead indicating wisdom. This sculpture is located in the Seokguram Grotto or cave, where it is surrounded by numerous supernatural figures and by two Indian gods. It is widely considered a masterpiece of Buddhist art and is a Korean National Treasure. (Copyright © Cultural Heritage Administration of Korea, Courtesy of the Academy of Korean Studies, South Korea)

**Guided Reading
Question**

■ **COMPARISON**
In what ways did
Buddhism reflect Hindu
traditions, and in what
ways did it challenge
them?

or craving for individual fulfillment, from attachment to that which inevitably changes, particularly to the notion of a core self or ego that is uniquely and solidly "me." The cure for this "dis-ease" lay in living a modest and moral life combined with meditation practice. Those who followed the Buddhist path most fully could expect to achieve enlightenment, or *nirvana*, a virtually indescribable state in which individual identity would be "extinguished" along with all greed, hatred, and delusion. With the pain of unnecessary suffering finally ended, the enlightened person would experience an overwhelming serenity, even in the midst of difficulty, as well as an immense loving-kindness, or compassion, for all beings. It was a simple message, elaborated endlessly and in various forms by those who followed the Buddha.

Much of the Buddha's teaching reflected the Hindu traditions from which it sprang. The idea that ordinary life is an illusion, the concepts of karma and rebirth, the goal of overcoming the incessant demands of the ego, the practice of meditation, the hope for final release from the cycle of rebirth—all of these Hindu elements found their way into Buddhist teaching. In this respect, Buddhism was a simplified and more accessible version of Hinduism.

Other elements of Buddhist teaching, however, sharply challenged prevailing Hindu thinking. Rejecting the religious authority of the Brahmins, the Buddha ridiculed their rituals and sacrifices as irrelevant to the hard work of dealing with one's suffering. Nor was he much interested in abstract speculation about the creation of the world or the existence of God, for such questions, he declared, "are not useful in the quest for holiness; they do not lead to peace and to the direct knowledge of *nirvana*." Individuals had to take responsibility for their own spiritual development with no help from human authorities or supernatural beings. It was a path of intense self-effort, based on personal experience. The Buddha also challenged the inequalities of a Hindu-based caste system, arguing that neither caste position nor gender was a barrier to enlightenment. The possibility of "awakening" was available to all.

But when it came to establishing a formal organization of the Buddha's most devoted followers, the prevailing patriarchy of Indian society made itself felt. Only after considerable resistance did the Buddha reluctantly allow women to join a newly created order of monks, and they could do so only in a separate order of nuns, who were subjected to a series of rules that clearly subordinated them to men. Male monks, for example, could officially admonish the nuns, but the reverse was forbidden. Such policies reflected a particular strain of Buddhist thinking that viewed women as a distracting obstacle to male enlightenment.

Nonetheless, thousands of women flocked to join the Buddhist order of nuns, where they found a degree of independence unavailable elsewhere in Indian society. Buddhist nuns delighted in the relative freedom of their order, where they largely ran their own affairs, were forbidden to do household chores, and devoted themselves wholly to the search for "awakening," which many apparently achieved. A nun named Mutta declared: "I am free from the three crooked things: mortar, pestle, and my crooked husband. I am free from birth and death and all that dragged me back."[9]

Gradually, Buddhist teachings found an audience in India. Buddhism's egalitarian message appealed especially to lower-caste groups and to women. The availability of its teaching in the local language of Pali, rather than the classical Sanskrit, made it accessible. Establishing monasteries and stupas (commemorative monuments containing relics of the Buddha) on the site of neighborhood shrines to earth spirits or near a sacred tree linked the new religion to local traditions. The most dedicated followers joined monasteries, devoting their lives to religious practice and spreading the message among nearby people. State support during the reign of Ashoka (r. 268–232 B.C.E.) likewise helped the new religion gain a foothold in India as a distinct tradition separate from Hinduism.

As Buddhism spread, both within and beyond India, differences in understanding soon emerged, particularly as to how nirvana could be achieved or, in a common Buddhist metaphor, how to "cross the river" to the far shore of enlightenment. The Buddha had taught a rather austere doctrine of intense self-effort, undertaken most actively by monks and nuns who withdrew from society to devote themselves fully to the quest. This early version of the new religion, known as **Theravada** (Teaching of the Elders), portrayed the Buddha as an immensely wise teacher and model, but certainly not divine. It was more psychological than religious, a set of practices rather than a set of beliefs. The gods, though never completely denied, played little role in assisting believers in crossing the river. Each person had to row his or her own boat. Clearly, this was not for everyone.

As the message of the Buddha gained a mass following and spread across much of Asia, some of its early features — rigorous and time-consuming meditation practice, a focus on monks and nuns withdrawn from ordinary life, the absence of accessible supernatural figures able to provide help and comfort — proved difficult for many converts. And so the religion adapted. A new form of the faith, **Mahayana Buddhism**, developed in the early centuries of the Common Era and offered greater accessibility, a spiritual path available to a much wider range of people beyond the monks and ascetics, who were the core group in early Buddhism.

In most expressions of Mahayana Buddhism, enlightenment (or becoming a Buddha) was available to everyone; it was possible within the context of ordinary life, rather than a monastery; and it might occur within a single lifetime rather than over the course of many lives. While Buddhism had originally put a premium on spiritual wisdom or insight, Mahayana expressions of the faith emphasized compassion — the ability to feel the sorrows of other people as if they were one's own. This compassionate religious ideal found expression in the notion of bodhisattvas, fully enlightened beings who postponed their own final liberation in order to assist a suffering humanity. They were spiritual beings on their way to "Buddhahood." Furthermore, the historical Buddha himself became something of a god, and both earlier and future Buddhas were available to offer help. Elaborate descriptions and artistic representations of these supernatural beings, together with various levels of Heavens and Hells, transformed Buddhism into a popular religion of salvation.

Guided Reading Question

■ **COMPARISON**

What is the difference between the Theravada and Mahayana expressions of Buddhism?

Furthermore, religious merit, leading to salvation, might now be earned by acts of piety and devotion, such as contributing to the support of a monastery, and that merit might be transferred to others. This was the Great Vehicle, providing spiritual assistance and allowing far more people to make the voyage across the river. In many forms and variations, Mahayana Buddhism took root in China, Japan, Korea, Southeast Asia, and elsewhere. (See Working with Evidence: Representations of the Buddha, page 176, for the evolution of Buddhism reflected in images and stories.)

Hinduism as a Religion of Duty and Devotion

Strangely enough, Buddhism as a distinct religious practice ultimately died out in the land of its birth as it was reincorporated into a broader Hindu tradition, but it spread widely and flourished, particularly in its Mahayana form, in other parts of Asia. Buddhism declined in India perhaps in part because the mounting wealth of monasteries and the economic interests of their leading figures separated them from ordinary people. Competition from Islam after 1000 C.E. also played a role. But the most important reason for the waning of Buddhism in India was the growth during the first millennium C.E. of a new kind of popular Hinduism that was more accessible than the elaborate sacrifices of the Brahmins or the philosophical speculations of intellectuals. Expressed in the widely known epic poems called the *Mahabharata* (mah-hah-BAH-rah-tah) and the *Ramayana*, this revived Hinduism indicated more clearly that action in the world and the detached performance of caste duties (as a priest, farmer, merchant, or sweeper, for example) might also provide a path to liberation. It was perhaps a response to the challenge of Buddhism.

A much-beloved Hindu text known as the **Bhagavad Gita** (BUH-guh-vahd GEE-tuh) (compiled in its final form by 300 C.E.) conveyed the message that ordinary people, not just Brahmins, could also find spiritual fulfillment by selflessly performing the ordinary duties of their lives: "The man who, casting off all desires, lives free from attachments, who is free from egoism, and from the feeling that this or that is mine, obtains tranquility." Withdrawal from the world and asceticism were not the only ways to moksha.

Also becoming increasingly prominent was yet another religious path—the way of devotion to one or another of India's many gods and goddesses. Beginning in south India and moving northward between 600 and 1000 C.E., this *bhakti* (BAHK-tee) (worship) **movement** involved the intense adoration of and identification with a particular deity through songs, prayers, and rituals. By far the most popular deities were Vishnu, the protector and preserver of creation who was associated with mercy and goodness, and Shiva, a god representing the Divine in its destructive aspect, but many others also had their followers. This form of Hindu expression sometimes pushed against the rigid caste and gender hierarchies of Indian society by inviting all to an adoration of the Divine. Krishna, an incarnation of Vishnu as portrayed in the Bhagavad Gita, had declared that "those who take

Guided Reading Question

■ CHANGE
What new emphases characterized Hinduism as it responded to the challenge of Buddhism?

shelter in Me, though they be of lower birth—women, vaishyas [merchants] and shudras [workers]—can attain the supreme destination."

The proliferation of gods and goddesses, and of their bhakti cults, occasioned very little friction or serious religious conflict. "Hinduism," writes a leading scholar, "is essentially tolerant, and would rather assimilate than rigidly exclude."[10] This capacity for assimilation extended to an already-declining Buddhism, which for many people had become yet another cult worshipping yet another god. The Buddha in fact was incorporated into the Hindu pantheon as the ninth incarnation of Vishnu. By 1000 C.E., Buddhism had largely disappeared as a separate religious tradition within India.

Thus a constantly evolving and enormously varied South Asian religious tradition had been substantially transformed. An early emphasis on ritual sacrifice had given way to that of philosophical speculation, devotional worship, and detached action in the world. In the process, that tradition had generated Buddhism, which became the first of the great universal religions of world history, and then had absorbed that new faith back into the fold of an emerging popular Hinduism.

> **PRACTICING HISTORICAL THINKING**
>
> How did the evolution of cultural traditions in India and China differ during the era of second-wave civilizations?

Toward Monotheism: The Search for God in the Middle East

Paralleling the evolution of Chinese and Indian cultural traditions was the movement toward a distinctive monotheistic religious outlook in the Middle East, which found expression in Persian Zoroastrianism and in Judaism. Neither of these religions themselves spread very widely, but the monotheism that they nurtured became the basis for both Christianity and Islam, which have shaped so much of world history over the past 2,000 years. Amid the proliferation of gods and spirits that had long characterized religious life throughout the ancient world, monotheism—the idea of a single supreme deity, the sole source of all life and being—was a radical cultural innovation. That conception created the possibility of a universal religion, open to all of humankind, but it could also mean an exclusive and intolerant faith.

Zoroastrianism

During the glory years of the powerful Persian Empire, a new religion arose to challenge the polytheism of earlier times. Tradition dates its Persian prophet, Zarathustra (Zoroaster to the Greeks), to the sixth or seventh century B.C.E., although some scholars place him centuries earlier. Whenever he actually lived, his ideas took hold in Persia and received a degree of state support during the

The Zoroastrian Tradition in Persia Dating to around 500 B.C.E., this cylinder seal impression depicts the winged disk, symbolizing the Zoroastrian creator god Ahura Mazda, watching over the Persian emperor Darius during a lion hunt. Persian emperors were powerful patrons of the Zoroastrian faith, and Ahura Mazda was often depicted protecting or guiding their activities. (Werner Forman Archive/Bridgeman Images)

Achaemenid dynasty (550–330 B.C.E.). Appalled by the endemic violence of recurring cattle raids, Zarathustra recast the traditional Persian polytheism into a vision of a single unique god, Ahura Mazda, who ruled the world and was the source of all truth, light, and goodness. This benevolent deity was engaged in a cosmic struggle with the forces of evil, embodied in an equivalent supernatural figure, Angra Mainyu. Ultimately this struggle would be decided in favor of Ahura Mazda, aided by the arrival of a final savior who would restore the world to its earlier purity and peace. At a day of judgment, those who had aligned with Ahura Mazda would be granted new resurrected bodies and rewarded with eternal life in Paradise. Those who had sided with evil and the "Lie" (which found expression as greed, anger, and envy) were condemned to everlasting punishment. **Zoroastrianism** (zohr-oh-ASS-tree-ahn-i'zm) thus placed great emphasis on the free will of humankind and the necessity for each individual to choose between good and evil.

The Zoroastrian faith achieved widespread support within the Persian heartland, although it also found adherents in other parts of the empire, such as Egypt, Mesopotamia, and Anatolia. But it never became an active missionary religion and did not spread widely beyond the region. Alexander the Great's invasion of the Persian Empire and the subsequent Greek-ruled Seleucid dynasty (330–155 B.C.E.) were disastrous for Zoroastrianism, as temples were plundered, priests slaughtered,

Guided Reading Question

••••••••••••••••••••••••

■ **CONNECTION**

What aspects of Zoroastrianism and Judaism later found a place in Christianity and Islam?

and sacred writings burned. But the new faith managed to survive this onslaught and flourished again during the Parthian (247 B.C.E.–224 C.E.) and Sassanid (224–651 C.E.) dynasties. It was the arrival of Islam and an Arab empire that occasioned the final decline of Zoroastrianism in Persia. Like Buddhism, the Zoroastrian faith vanished from its place of origin, but unlike Buddhism, it did not spread beyond Persia in a recognizable form. Some elements of the Zoroastrian belief system, however, did become incorporated into other religious traditions. The presence of many Jews in the Persian Empire meant that they surely became aware of Zoroastrian ideas. Many of those ideas—including the conflict of God and an evil counterpart (Satan); the notion of a last judgment and resurrected bodies; and a belief in the final defeat of evil, the arrival of a savior (Messiah), and the remaking of the world at the end of time—found a place in an evolving Judaism. Some of these teachings, especially the concepts of Heaven and Hell, later became prominent in those enormously influential successors to Judaism—Christianity and Islam. Thus the Persian tradition of Zoroastrianism continued to echo well beyond its disappearance in the land of its birth.

Judaism

While Zoroastrianism emerged in the greatest empire of its time, **Judaism**, the Middle East's other ancient monotheistic tradition, was born among one of the region's smaller and, at the time, less significant peoples—the Hebrews, also known as Jews. Their traditions, recorded in the Hebrew scriptures, tell of a dramatic history leading to the establishment around 1000 B.C.E. of a small state that soon split into two parts—a northern kingdom called Israel and a southern state called Judah.

In a region politically dominated by the large empires of Assyria, Babylon, and Persia, these tiny Hebrew communities lived a precarious existence. Israel was conquered by Assyria in 722 B.C.E., and many of its inhabitants were deported to distant regions, where they assimilated into the local culture. In 586 B.C.E., the kingdom of Judah likewise came under Babylonian control, and its elite class was shipped off to exile. "By the rivers of Babylon," wrote one of their poets, "there we sat down, yea, we wept, when we remembered Zion [Jerusalem]." In Babylonian exile these people, now calling themselves Jews, retained and renewed their cultural identity, and later a small number were able to return to their homeland. A large part of that identity lay in their unique religious ideas. It was in creating that religious tradition, rather than in building a powerful empire, that this small people cast a long shadow in world history.

From their unique historical memory of exodus from Egyptian slavery and exile in Babylon, the Hebrews evolved over many centuries a distinctive conception of God. Unlike the peoples of Mesopotamia, India, Greece, and elsewhere—all of whom populated the invisible realm with numerous gods and goddesses—Jews found in their God, whom they called Yahweh (YAH-way), a powerful and jealous

Guided Reading Question

■ **DESCRIPTION**
What was distinctive about the Jewish religious tradition?

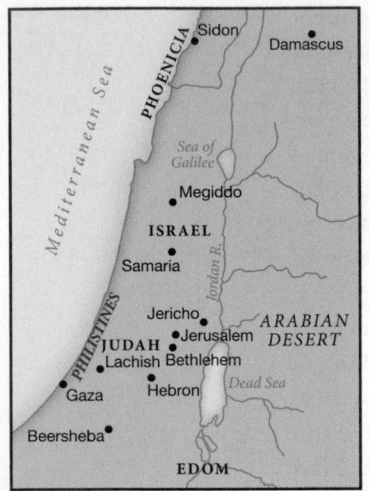

Ancient Israel

deity, who demanded their exclusive loyalty. "Thou shalt have no other gods before me"—this was the first of the Ten Commandments. It was a difficult requirement, for as the Hebrews turned from a pastoral life to agriculture, many of them were attracted by the fertility gods of neighboring peoples. Their neighbors' goddesses were also attractive, offering a kind of spiritual support that the primarily masculine Yahweh could not. Foreign deities also entered Hebrew culture through royal treaty obligations with nearby states. Thus the emerging Hebrew conception of the Divine was not quite monotheism, for the repeated demands of the Hebrew prophets to turn away from other gods show that those deities remained real for many Jews. Over time, however, the priesthood that supported the one-god theory triumphed. The Jews came to understand their relationship to Yahweh as a contract or a covenant. In return for their sole devotion and obedience to God's laws, Yahweh would consider the Jews his chosen people, favoring them in battle, causing them to grow in numbers, and bringing them prosperity and blessing.

Unlike the bickering, arbitrary, polytheistic gods of Mesopotamia or ancient Greece, who were associated with the forces of nature and behaved in quite human fashion, Yahweh was increasingly seen as a lofty, transcendent deity of utter holiness and purity. But unlike the impersonal conceptions of ultimate reality found in Daoism and Hinduism, Yahweh was encountered as a divine person with whom people could actively communicate. He also acted within the historical process, bringing the Jews out of Egypt or using foreign empires to punish them for their disobedience.

Furthermore, for some, Yahweh was transformed from a god of war, who ordered his people to "utterly destroy" the original inhabitants of the Promised Land, to a god of social justice and compassion for the poor and the marginalized, especially in the passionate pronouncements of Jewish prophets. One of them, Isaiah, describes Yahweh as rejecting the empty rituals of his chosen but sinful people: "What to me is the multitude of your sacrifices, says the Lord. . . . Wash yourselves, make yourselves clean, . . . cease to do evil, learn to do good; seek justice; correct oppression; defend the fatherless; plead for the widow."[11]

Here was a distinctive conception of the Divine—singular, transcendent, personal, ruling over the natural order, engaged in history, and demanding social justice and moral righteousness above sacrifices and rituals. This set of ideas sustained a separate Jewish identity in both ancient and modern times, and it was this understanding of God that provided the foundation on which those later Abrahamic faiths of Christianity and Islam were built.

Jewish understanding of the natural world likewise informed all three religious traditions. The Jewish scriptures pronounced the world of nature as real and positively valued, not simply an illusion or a distraction from spiritual concerns, as in some versions of Hindu or Buddhist thinking. The first chapter of Genesis ends with God's review of his creation: "And God saw everything that he had made, and behold it was very good." Moreover, the material world disclosed or revealed something of the divine mystery. The writer of the Psalms affirmed that "the heavens declare the glory of God and the firmament shows his handiwork." Finally, Jewish tradition gave humankind a distinct role within God's creation. They were to "have dominion . . . over all the earth," even as Adam and Eve in the Garden of Eden were instructed "to till it and keep it." For some, this has meant permission to exploit the world's resources and its other creatures for human purposes, while for others it has been a mandate to preserve and protect the natural order.

The Cultural Tradition of Classical Greece: The Search for a Rational Order

Unlike the Jews, the Persians, or the civilization of India, Greek thinkers of the second-wave era generated no lasting religious tradition of world historical importance. The religion of these city-states brought together the unpredictable, quarreling, and lustful gods of Mount Olympus, secret fertility cults, oracles predicting the future, and the ecstatic worship of Dionysus, the god of wine. The distinctive feature of the classical Greek cultural tradition was the willingness of many Greek intellectuals to abandon this mythological framework, to affirm that the world was a physical reality governed by natural laws, and to assert that human rationality could both understand these laws and work out a system of moral and ethical life. In separating science and philosophy from conventional religion, the Greeks developed a way of thinking that bore some similarity to the secularism of Confucian thought in China.

The Greek Way of Knowing

The foundations of this **Greek rationalism** emerged in the three centuries between 600 and 300 B.C.E., coinciding with the flourishing of Greek city-states, especially Athens, and with the growth of its artistic, literary, and theatrical traditions. The enduring significance of Greek thinking lay not so much in the answers it provided to life's great issues, for the Greeks seldom agreed with one another, but rather in their way of asking questions. Their emphasis on argument, logic, and the relentless questioning of received wisdom; their confidence in human reason; their enthusiasm for puzzling out the world without much reference to the gods — these were the defining characteristics of the major Greek thinkers.

The great exemplar of this approach to knowledge was **Socrates** (469–399 B.C.E.), an Athenian philosopher who walked about the city engaging others in conversation about the good life. He wrote nothing, and his preferred manner of teaching was not the lecture or exposition of his own ideas but rather a constant questioning of the assumptions and logic of his students' thinking. Concerned always to puncture the pretentious, he challenged conventional ideas about the importance of wealth and power in living well, urging instead the pursuit of wisdom and virtue. He was

Guided Reading Question

■ **DESCRIPTION**
What were the distinctive features of the Greek intellectual tradition?

critical of Athenian democracy and on occasion had positive things to say about Sparta, the great enemy of his own city. Such behavior brought him into conflict with city authorities, who accused him of corrupting the youth of Athens and sentenced him to death. At his trial, he defended himself as the "gadfly" of Athens, stinging its citizens into awareness. "I shall question, and examine and cross-examine him," he declared, "and if I find that he does not possess virtue, but says he does, I shall rebuke him for scorning the things that are most important and caring more for what is of less worth."[12]

The earliest of the classical Greek thinkers, many of them living on the Ionian coast of Anatolia, applied this rational and questioning way of knowing to the world of nature. For example, Thales, drawing on Babylonian astronomy, predicted an eclipse of the sun and argued that the moon simply reflected the sun's light. He was also one of the first Greeks to ask about the fundamental nature of the universe and came up with the idea that water was the basic stuff from which all else derived, for it existed as solid, liquid, and gas. Others argued in favor of air or fire or some combination. Democritus suggested that atoms, tiny "uncuttable" particles, collided in various configurations to form visible matter. Pythagoras believed that beneath the chaos and complexity of the visible world lay a simple, unchanging mathematical order. What these thinkers had in common was a commitment to a rational and nonreligious explanation for the material world.

Such thinking also served to explain the functioning of the human body and its diseases. Hippocrates and his followers came to believe that the body was composed of four fluids, or "humors," that caused various ailments when out of proper balance. He also traced the origins of epilepsy, known to the Greeks as "the sacred disease," to simple heredity, arguing that it "has a natural cause . . . like other afflictions."[13] A similar approach informed Greek thinking about the ways of humankind. Herodotus, who wrote about the Greco-Persian Wars, explained his project as an effort to discover "the reason why they fought one another." This assumption that

Plato in Conversation This first-century-B.C.E. Roman mosaic depicts Plato (second from left) seated among students and other philosophers in conversation. This image reflects the continued importance of Greek philosophy in the Roman world and illustrates the type of setting in which Plato taught. (World History Archive/Image Asset Management/AGE Fotostock)

human reasons lay behind the conflict, not simply the whims of the gods, was what made Herodotus a historian in the modern sense of that word. Ethics and government also figured importantly in Greek thinking. **Plato** (429–348 B.C.E.) famously sketched out in *The Republic* a design for a good society. It would be ruled by a class of highly educated "guardians" led by a "philosopher-king." Such people would be able to penetrate the many illusions of the material world and to grasp the "world of forms," in which ideas such as goodness, beauty, and justice lived a real and unchanging existence. Only such people, he argued, were fit to rule.

Aristotle (384–322 B.C.E.), a student of Plato and a teacher of Alexander the Great, represents the most complete expression of the Greek way of knowing, for he wrote or commented on practically everything. With an emphasis on empirical observation, he cataloged the constitutions of 158 Greek city-states, identified hundreds of species of animals, and wrote about logic, physics, astronomy, the weather, and much else besides. Famous for his reflections on ethics, he argued that "virtue" was a product of rational training and cultivated habit and could be learned. As to government, he urged a mixed system, combining the principles of monarchy, aristocracy, and democracy. (See Controversies: Debating Religion and the Axial Age, page 162, for a discussion of controversial issues surrounding the emergence of Greek rationalism and other philosophical and religious traditions of this period.)

The Greek Legacy

The rationalism of the Greek tradition was clearly not the whole of Greek culture. The gods of Mount Olympus continued to be a reality for many people, and the ecstatic songs and dances that celebrated Dionysus, the god of wine, were anything but rational and reflective. The death of Socrates at the hands of an Athenian jury showed that philosophy could be a threat as well as an engaging pastime. Nonetheless, Greek rationalism, together with Greek art, literature, and theater, persisted long after the glory days of Athens were over. Alexander's empire and that of the Romans facilitated the spread of Greek culture within the Mediterranean basin and beyond, and many leading Roman figures sent their children to be educated in Athens at the Academy, which Plato had founded. An emerging Christian theology was expressed in terms of Greek philosophical concepts, especially those of Plato. Even after the western Roman Empire collapsed, classical Greek texts were preserved in the eastern half, known as the Byzantine Empire or Byzantium.

In the West, however, direct access to Greek texts was far more difficult in the chaotic conditions of post-Roman Europe, and for centuries Greek scholarship was neglected in favor of distinctly Christian writers. Much of that legacy was subsequently rediscovered after the twelfth century C.E. as European scholars

Debating Religion and the Axial Age

In 1947 a German philosopher, Karl Jaspers, coined a new term—the Axial Age. It referred to a time of particular creativity that gave rise to new cultural traditions all across Eurasia, but particularly in China, India, the Middle East, and the eastern Mediterranean region between 800 to 200 B.C.E. Here was an "axis," a pivot, or a major turning point in human cultural history, as Buddhism, Hinduism, Judaism, Confucianism, Daoism, and Greek rationalism began to take shape.[14]

It has been a controversial idea. Why, for example, did groups or individuals willing to challenge established traditions emerge during these centuries? Historians have noted disruptions to established patterns of life that may have opened the way to new thinking, but they do not always agree on which disruptions to emphasize.[15] Were economic factors the cause—an emerging iron-age technology, which generated more productive economies and more deadly warfare; greater prosperity in urban centers; or increased trade and the use of money? Or perhaps political disruptions were more important, such as the breakdown of political order during China's "age of warring states" or the endemic rivalries of Greek city-states. Social factors, such as a growing resentment against the pretensions and privileges of Brahmin priests, were likely part of the appeal of an emerging Buddhist faith. All of these disruptions, occurring in already literate societies, perhaps led thinkers to question older outlooks and to come up with new solutions to fundamental questions.

But how much did these Axial Age traditions have in common? The most enthusiastic advocates of the Axial Age idea believed they shared a great deal. All these traditions sought an alternative to an earlier polytheism, in which the activities of various gods and spirits explained what happened in this world. These gods and spirits had generally been seen as similar to human beings, though much more powerful. Through ritual and sacrifice, men and women might placate the gods or persuade them to do human bidding. In contrast, the new cultural traditions of the Axial Age sought to define a single source of order and meaning in the universe, some moral or religious realm that was sharply different from and higher than the sphere of human life.

Axial Age thinkers also shared a skepticism about the ability of human language to capture this Absolute or Ultimate Reality. Laozi in China famously declared that "the Dao that can be named is not the eternal Dao." The task of humankind, according to these new ways of thinking, was not so much about seeking intellectual clarity or beseeching the gods for favors as it was about transforming oneself morally or spiritually by aligning with that higher order. Living morally, controlling desire, taming the ego, and developing compassion—these were the goals of Axial Age traditions.

Those traditions also meant that people might more easily question and criticize their rulers or their societies, for now there was a higher point of reference from which to judge all of human life. Thus Jewish prophets strongly denounced the injustices of their society, and the Buddha challenged India's ancient caste system. Religion was becoming more clearly ethical. And at least implicitly, the Axial Age traditions suggested the possibility of a universal spiritual outlook available to everyone.

gained access to classical Greek texts. From that point on, the Greek legacy has been viewed as a central element of an emerging "Western" civilization. It played a role in formulating an updated Christian theology, in fostering Europe's seventeenth-century Scientific Revolution, and in providing a point of departure for much of European philosophy.

But despite these broad similarities, many historians and other scholars have been sharply critical or entirely dismissive of the Axial Age idea. Some critics have argued that the concept of an Axial Age greatly overestimated the uniqueness of what occurred during those few centuries in the first millennium B.C.E. After all, ancient Egyptian religion had long emphasized the moral behavior of individuals and judgment after death. In addition, the fourteenth-century-B.C.E. pharaoh Akhenaten directly challenged traditional Egyptian religion as he vigorously promoted a quasi-monotheistic faith focused on worship of the sun god Aten. Furthermore, the major religious breakthroughs of both Christianity and Islam, the most prominent religions of the past 2,000 years, occurred well after the Axial Age had supposedly ended. Was it not somewhat arrogant or condescending to think that religious creativity was limited to those few centuries? Was it appropriate for Karl Jaspers, who first articulated the Axial Age idea, to declare that pre-Axial religion was "in some measure unawakened"?[16]

Furthermore, while advocates of the Axial Age concept found broad similarities among those emerging traditions, their critics noticed differences. Chinese and Greek thinkers focused more on the affairs of this world and credited human rationality with the power to understand that reality. Indian and Jewish thinkers, by contrast, explored the unseen realm of the Divine and the relationship of God or the gods to human life. While Jewish prophets located the transcendent realm in the activities of a highly personal deity actively involved in the world, Laozi, Confucius, and the Buddha largely avoided much discussion of the supernatural. This emphasis on sharp differences among cultural traditions undermined the idea of an Axial Age of common understandings.

Finally, critics of the Axial Age concept charge its proponents with "presentism," or reading the past through the lens of current values and problems. Karl Jaspers originally proposed the term in 1947, while the world was still reeling from the horrors of World War II. He, and many world historians after him, wanted desperately to find something that all of humankind might share, "a base for the unity of mankind" that was not specifically Christian or Western. And they found it in the Axial Age traditions, which, they believed, provided a foundation for moving toward a more unified and peaceful world. Critics maintain that although this may seem wonderful, in adopting the Axial Age idea as a solution for current problems, Jaspers and others gave it a solidity and coherence that it does not deserve.[17] The needs of the present do not provide a sound basis for uncovering the realities of the past.

Or do they? Would we have women's history without the demands of feminist movements? Would we have environmental history without an emerging awareness of environmental problems? Would we have world history without a growing recognition of global interdependence? Current realities always shape our understanding of the past, or at least the questions we pose about the past. Perhaps we have no choice but to conduct our historical inquiries with one eye firmly fixed on the present while the other gazes thoughtfully at the past. Navigating that tension is among the central tasks of all historical study. Both the advocates of the Axial Age idea and its critics are engaged in that enduring balancing act.

QUESTIONS TO CONSIDER

1. How might you summarize the benefits and limitations of the Axial Age idea?

2. Can you think of other examples of "presentism" in historical thinking?

Long before this European rediscovery, the Greek legacy had also entered the Islamic world. Systematic translations of Greek works of science and philosophy into Arabic, together with Indian and Persian learning, stimulated Muslim thinkers and scientists, especially in the fields of medicine, astronomy, mathematics, geography, and chemistry. It was in fact largely from Arabic translations of Greek writers that Europeans became reacquainted with the legacy of classical Greece, especially during the twelfth and thirteenth centuries. Despite the many centuries that have passed since the flourishing of ancient Greek culture, that tradition has remained, especially in the West, an inspiration for those who celebrate the powers of the human mind to probe the mysteries of the universe and to explore the equally challenging domain of human life.

The Birth of Christianity . . . with Buddhist Comparisons

About 500 years after the time of Confucius, the Buddha, and Socrates, a young Jewish peasant/carpenter in the remote province of Judaea in the Roman Empire began a brief three-year career of teaching and miracle working before he got in trouble with local authorities and was executed. In one of history's most unlikely stories, the life and teachings of that obscure man, barely noted in the historical records of the time, became the basis of the world's second great universal religion. This man, **Jesus of Nazareth** (ca. 4 B.C.E.–29 C.E.), and the religion of Christianity that grew out of his brief career had a dramatic impact on world history, often compared with that of India's Siddhartha Gautama, the Buddha.

The Lives of the Founders

The family background of the two teachers could hardly have been more different. Gautama was born to royalty and luxury, whereas Jesus was a rural or small-town worker from a distinctly lower-class family. But both became spiritual seekers, mystics in their respective traditions, who claimed to have personally experienced another and unseen level of reality. Those powerful religious experiences provided the motivation for their life's work and the personal authenticity that attracted their growing band of followers.

Both were "wisdom teachers," challenging the conventional values of their time, urging the renunciation of wealth, and emphasizing the supreme importance of love or compassion as the basis for a moral life. The Buddha had instructed his followers in the practice of *metta*, or loving-kindness, "cultivating a boundless heart toward all beings." In a similar vein during his famous Sermon on the Mount, Jesus told his followers "to love your enemies and pray for those who persecute you." Both Jesus and the Buddha called for the personal transformation of their followers, through "letting go" of the grasping that causes suffering, in the Buddha's teaching, or "losing one's life in order to save it," in the language of Jesus.

Despite these similarities, there were also some differences in their teachings and their life stories. Jesus inherited from his Jewish tradition an intense devotion to a single personal deity with whom he was on intimate terms, referring to him

Guided Reading Question

■ **COMPARISON**

How would you compare the lives and teachings of Jesus and the Buddha? In what different ways did the two religions evolve after the deaths of their founders?

as Abba ("papa"). And he gained a reputation as a miracle worker. The Buddha's original message, by contrast, largely ignored the supernatural, involved no miracles, and taught a path of intense self-effort aimed at ethical living and mindfulness as a means of ending suffering. Furthermore, Jesus' teachings had a sharper social and political edge than did those of the Buddha. Jesus spoke more clearly on behalf of the poor and the oppressed, directly criticized the hypocrisies of the powerful, and deliberately associated with lepers, adulterous women, and tax collectors, all of whom were regarded as "impure." These actions reflected his lower-class background, the Jewish tradition of social criticism, and the reality of Roman imperial rule over his people, none of which corresponded to the Buddha's experience. Finally, Jesus' public life was very brief, probably less than three years, compared to more than forty years for the Buddha. His teachings had so antagonized both Jewish and Roman authorities that he was crucified as a political rebel. The Buddha's message was apparently less threatening to the politically powerful, and he died a natural death at age eighty.

The Spread of New Religions

Neither Jesus nor the Buddha had any intention of founding a new religion; rather, they sought to revitalize the traditions from which they had come. Nonetheless, Christianity and Buddhism soon emerged as separate religions, distinct from Judaism and Hinduism, proclaiming their messages to a much wider and more inclusive audience. In the process, both teachers were transformed by their followers into gods. According to many scholars, Jesus never claimed divine status, seeing himself as a teacher or a prophet whose close relationship to God could be replicated by anyone. The Buddha likewise viewed himself as an enlightened but fully human person, an example of what was possible for all who followed the path. But in Mahayana Buddhism, the Buddha became a supernatural being who could be worshipped and prayed to and was spiritually available to his followers. Jesus also soon became divine in the eyes of his early followers, such as Saint Paul and Saint John. According to one of the first creeds of the Church, he was "the Son of God, Very God of Very God."

The transformation of Christianity from a small Jewish sect to a world religion began with **Saint Paul** (ca. 6–67 C.E.), an early convert whose missionary journeys in the eastern Roman Empire led to the founding of small Christian communities that included non-Jews. The Good News of Jesus, Paul argued, was for everyone, and Gentile (non-Jewish) converts need not follow Jewish laws or rituals such as circumcision. In one of his many letters to these new communities, later collected as part of the New Testament, Paul wrote, "There is neither Jew nor Greek . . . neither slave nor free . . . neither male nor female, for you are all one in Christ Jesus."[18] (See the Snapshot for Saint Paul's place in a long line of "wisdom teachers" during the second-wave era.)

Guided Reading Question

■ CHANGE

In what ways was Christianity transformed in the five centuries following the death of Jesus?

SNAPSHOT Thinkers and Philosophies of the Second-Wave Era

Person	Date	Location	Religion/Philosophy	Key Ideas
Zoroaster	7th century B.C.E.(?)	Persia (present-day Iran)	Zoroastrianism	Single High God; cosmic conflict of good and evil
Hebrew prophets (such as Isaiah, Amos, Jeremiah)	9th–6th centuries B.C.E.	Eastern Mediterranean/ Palestine/Israel	Judaism	Transcendent High God; covenant with chosen people; social justice
Anonymous writers of Upanishads	800–400 B.C.E.	India	Brahmanism/Hinduism	Brahman (the single impersonal divine reality); karma; rebirth; goal of liberation (moksha)
Confucius	6th–5th centuries B.C.E.	China	Confucianism	Social harmony through moral example; secular outlook; importance of education; family as model of the state
Mahavira	6th century B.C.E.	India	Jainism	All creatures have souls; purification through nonviolence; opposed to caste
Siddhartha Gautama	6th–5th centuries B.C.E.	India	Buddhism	Suffering caused by desire/ attachment; end of suffering through modest and moral living and meditation practice
Laozi, Zhuangzi	6th–3rd centuries B.C.E.	China	Daoism	Withdrawal from the world into contemplation of nature; simple living; end of striving
Socrates, Plato, Aristotle	5th–4th centuries B.C.E.	Greece	Greek rationalism	Style of persistent questioning; secular explanation of nature and human life
Jesus	Early 1st century C.E.	Palestine/Israel	Christianity	Supreme importance of love based on intimate relationship with God; at odds with established authorities
Saint Paul	1st century C.E.	Palestine/Israel/ eastern Roman Empire	Christianity	Christianity as a religion for all; salvation through faith in Jesus Christ

Despite Paul's egalitarian pronouncement, early Christianity, like Buddhism, offered a mix of opportunities and restrictions for women. Jesus himself had interacted easily with a wide range of women, and they had figured prominently among his followers. One of them, Mary Magdalene, was arguably a part of his inner circle. And women played leadership roles in the "house churches" of the first century C.E. Nonetheless, some New Testament writings counseled women to "be subject to your husbands" and declared that "it is shameful for a woman to speak in church." Men were identified with the role of Christ himself, for "the husband is head of the wife as Christ is head of the Church."[19] It was not long before male spokesmen for the faith had fully assimilated older and highly negative views of women. As daughters of Eve, they were responsible for the introduction of sin and evil into the world and were the source of temptation for men.

On the other hand, Jesus' mother, Mary, soon became the focus of a devotional cult, and women were among the martyrs of the early Church. Prominent among them was **Perpetua** (181–203 C.E.), a young North African woman of Roman background who wrote a famous account of trial and imprisonment before she was "condemned to the beasts" for her refusal to renounce her Christian faith (see Zooming In: Perpetua, Christian Martyr, page 168). Growing numbers of Christian women, like their Buddhist counterparts, found a more independent space in the monasteries, even as the official hierarchy of the Church became wholly male.

Nonetheless, the inclusive message of early Christianity was one of the attractions of the new faith as it spread very gradually within the Roman Empire during the several centuries after Jesus' death (see Map 4.1). The earliest converts were usually lower-stratum people — artisans, traders, and a considerable number of women — mostly from towns and cities, while a scattering of wealthier, more prominent, and better-educated people later joined their ranks. The spread of the faith was often accompanied by reports of miracles, healings, and the casting out of demons — all of which were impressive to people thoroughly accustomed to expecting supernatural intervention in the events of ordinary life. Christian communities also attracted converts by the way their members cared for one another. By 300 C.E., perhaps 10 percent of the Roman Empire's population (some 5 million people) identified themselves as Christians.

Although Christians in the West often think of their faith as a European-centered religion, during the first six centuries of the Christian era, most followers of Jesus lived in Southwest Asia and Africa. The first Christian communities formed along the eastern Mediterranean coast, mostly in the major towns of Syria and Anatolia. But the faith soon took root elsewhere as well. A distinctive **Church of the East** spread from Syria into Persia, where it developed a unique liturgy with strong Jewish influences and a musical tradition of chants and hymns, all in Syriac — a language closely related to the Aramaic that Jesus spoke. Its missionaries took Christianity even farther to the east. By the fourth century, and perhaps much earlier, a well-organized Church had taken root in southern India, which later gained tax privileges and special rights from local rulers. In the early seventh century, a Persian monk named Alopen initiated a small but remarkable Christian experiment in China (see "Asian Christianity" in Chapter 10). A modest Christian presence in Central Asia was also an outgrowth of this Church of the East. To the north on the slopes of the Caucasus Mountains, the Kingdom of Armenia around 310 C.E. became the first place where rulers adopted Christianity as a state religion, providing the environment for the flowering of an Armenian church. To the south, a number of Arabs had become Christian by the time of Muhammad's birth in 570, and one of them was among the first to affirm Muhammad as an authentic prophet.

Perpetua, Christian Martyr

"The blood of the martyrs," declared the Christian writer Tertullian, "is the seed of the church." Few of those martyrs, whose stories so inspired the persecuted converts of the early Christian centuries, could match that of Perpetua, a young woman whose prison diary provides a highly personal account of her arrest and trial.[20]

Born in 181 C.E. in the North African city of Carthage, Perpetua hailed from an upper-class Roman family and was quite well educated, literate in Latin and probably Greek, and acquainted with Roman philosophical

Perpetua.

writings. By the time she entered the historical record at age twenty-two, she had given birth to a son, had lost her husband to either death or abandonment, and had recently begun to study Christianity, becoming part of a small but growing group of educated people who were turning toward the new faith. Coinciding with her conversion was a wave of persecutions ordered by the Roman

emperor Septimus Severus, also of North African descent and a devotee of the Egyptian cult of Isis and Osiris. Severus sought to forbid new conversions rather than punish long-established Christians. In line with this policy, in 203 C.E., the hard-line governor of the region ordered the arrest of Perpetua along with four others—two slaves, one of them a woman named Felicitas who was eight months pregnant, and two free men. Before she was taken to the prison, however, Perpetua decisively confirmed her commitment to Christianity by accepting baptism.

Once in the "dark hole" of the prison, Perpetua was terrified. It was crowded and stiflingly hot, and she was consumed with anxiety for her child. Several fellow Christians managed to bribe the prison guards to permit Perpetua to nurse her baby son. Reunited with her child,

photo: Archbishop's Palace, Ravenna, Italy/Scala/Art Resource, NY

In Africa, a particularly vibrant center of Christianity developed in Egypt, where priests soon translated the Bible into the Egyptian language known as Coptic, and Egyptian Christians pioneered various forms of monasticism. By 400 C.E., hundreds of monasteries, cells, and caves dotted the desert, inhabited by reclusive monks dedicated to their spiritual practices. Increasingly, the language, theology, and practice of Egyptian Christianity diverged from that of Rome and Constantinople, giving expression to Egyptian resistance against Roman or Byzantine oppression. To the west of Egypt, a Church of North Africa furnished a number of the intellectuals of the early Church, including Saint Augustine, as well as many Christian martyrs to Roman persecution. (See Zooming In: Perpetua, Christian Martyr, above.) Here and elsewhere, the coming of Christianity provoked not only hostility from Roman political authorities but also tensions within families. The North African Carthaginian writer Tertullian (160–220 C.E.), known as the "father of Latin Christianity," described the kind of difficulties that might arise between a Christian wife and her "pagan" husband:

she found that "my prison had suddenly become a palace, so that I wanted to be there rather than anywhere else."

A few days later, Perpetua's deeply distressed non-Christian father arrived for a visit, hoping to persuade his only daughter to recant her faith and save her life and the family's honor. It was a heartbreaking encounter. "Daughter," he said, "have pity on my grey head. . . . Do not abandon me to be the reproach of men. Think of your brothers, think of your mother and your aunt, think of your child, who will not be able to live once you are gone. Give up your pride! You will destroy all of us!" Firm in her faith, Perpetua refused his entreaties, and she reported that "he left me in great sorrow."

On the day of her trial, with her distraught father in attendance, the governor Hilarianus also begged Perpetua to consider her family and renounce her faith by offering a sacrifice to the emperor. Again she refused and together with her four companions was "condemned to the beasts," a humiliating form of execution normally reserved for the lower classes. Although she was now permanently separated from her child, she wrote, "We returned to the prison in high spirits." During her last days in the prison, Perpetua and the others were treated "more humanely" and were allowed to visit with family and friends, as the head of the jail was himself a Christian.

But then, on the birthday of the emperor, this small band of Christians was marched to the amphitheater, "joyfully as though they were going to heaven," according to an eyewitness account. After the prisoners strenuously and successfully resisted dressing in the robes of pagan priests, the three men were sent into the arena to contend with a boar, a bear, and a leopard. Then it was the turn of the women, Perpetua and the slave Felicitas, who had given birth only two days earlier. When a mad cow failed to kill them, a soldier was sent to finish the work. As he approached Perpetua, he apparently hesitated, but as an eyewitness account put it, "she took the trembling hand of the young gladiator and guided it to her throat." Appended to her diary was this comment from an unknown observer: "It was as though so great a woman, feared as she was by the unclean spirit, could not be dispatched unless she herself were willing."

QUESTIONS

How might you understand the actions and attitudes of Perpetua? Is her experience accessible to people living in a largely secular modern society?

She is engaged in a fast; her husband has arranged a banquet. It is her Christian duty to visit the streets and the homes of the poor; her husband insists on family business. She celebrates the Easter Vigil throughout the night; her husband expects her in his bed. . . .[21]

Farther south in Africa, by 350 C.E. Christianity had become the state religion of Axum, an emerging kingdom in what is now Eritrea and Ethiopia (discussed further in Chapter 6). This occurred during the same century as both Armenia and the Roman Empire officially endorsed Christianity. In Axum, a distinctively African expression of Christianity took root, with open-air services, the use of drums and stringed instruments in worship, and colorful umbrellas covering priests and musicians from the elements. Linked theologically and organizationally to Coptic Christianity in Egypt, the Ethiopian Church used Ge'ez, a local Semitic language and script, for its liturgy and literature.

MAPPING HISTORY

Map 4.1 The Spread of Early Christianity and Buddhism

In the five centuries after the birth of Jesus, Christianity found converts from Spain to Northeast Africa, the Middle East, Central Asia, and India. In the Roman Empire, Axum, and Armenia, the new religion enjoyed state support as well. Subsequently, Christianity took root solidly in Europe and after 1000 C.E. in Russia. Meanwhile, Buddhism was spreading from its South Asian homeland to various parts of Asia, even as it was weakening in India itself.

READING THE MAP: From its start on the eastern shore of the Mediterranean Sea, in which direction did Christianity spread the farthest?

MAKING CONNECTIONS: Compare this map with Map 7.1: The Silk Roads and Map 7.2: The Sea Roads, and identify regions where Christianity and Buddhism spread along these long-distance trade routes.

In the Roman world, the strangest and most offensive feature of the new faith was its exclusive monotheism and its antagonism to all other supernatural powers, particularly the cult of the emperors. Christians' denial of these other gods caused them to be tagged as "atheists" and was one reason behind the empire's intermittent persecution of Christians during the first three centuries of the Common Era. All of that ended with Emperor Constantine's conversion in the early fourth century C.E. and the proclamation of Christianity as the state religion in 380 C.E.

Roman rulers sought to use an increasingly popular Christianity as glue to hold together a very diverse population in a weakening imperial state. Constantine and his successors thus provided Christians with newfound security and opportunities. The emperor Theodosius (r. 379–395 C.E.) enforced a ban on all polytheistic ritual sacrifices and ordered the temples that practiced them closed. Christians, by contrast, received patronage for their buildings, official approval for their doctrines, suppression of their rivals, and prestige from imperial recognition. All of this set in motion a process by which the Roman Empire, and later all of Europe, became overwhelmingly Christian. At the time, however, Christianity was expanding at least as rapidly to the east and south as it was to the west. In 500, few observers could have predicted that the future of Christianity would lie primarily in Europe.

The spread of Buddhism in India was quite different from that of Christianity in the Roman Empire. Even though Ashoka's support gave Buddhism a considerable boost, it was never promoted to the exclusion of other faiths. Ashoka sought harmony among India's diverse population through religious tolerance rather than religious uniformity. The kind of monotheistic intolerance that Christianity exhibited in the Roman world was quite foreign to Indian religious practice. Whereas Buddhism later died out in India as it was absorbed into a reviving Hinduism, no renewal of Roman polytheism occurred in the West, and Christianity became an enduring element of European civilization. Nonetheless, Christianity did adopt some elements of religious practice from the Roman world,

The First Christian Emperor Constantine Following Constantine's conversion, artists used both Roman imperial and Christian symbols to present him as a Christian emperor. In this circa fourth-century carving from what is now Croatia, Constantine is portrayed sitting on an imperial throne holding a Christian cross while a man lies prostrate before him. (DEA/A. DAGLI ORTI/Getty Images)

including, perhaps, the cult of saints and the dating of the birth of Jesus to the winter solstice. Finally, both of these new religions spread widely beyond their places of origin. Buddhism provided a network of cultural connections across much of Asia, while Christianity during its early centuries established an Afro-Eurasian presence.

Institutions, Controversies, and Divisions

As Christianity spread within the Roman Empire and beyond, it developed a hierarchical organization, with patriarchs, bishops, and priests—all men—replacing the house churches of the early years, in which women played a more prominent part. At least in some places, however, women continued to exercise leadership and even priestly roles, prompting Pope Gelasius in 494 to speak out sharply against those who encouraged women "to officiate at the sacred altars, and to take part in all matters imputed to the offices of the male sex, to which they do not belong."[22]

In general, though, the exclusion of women from the priesthood established a male-dominated clergy and a patriarchal church, which has lasted into the twenty-first century.

The emerging Christian movement was, however, anything but unified. Its immense geographic reach, accompanied by inevitable differences in language, culture, and political regime, ensured that a single focus for Christian belief and practice was difficult to achieve. Doctrinal differences also tore at the unity of Christianity and embroiled church authorities in frequent controversy about the nature of Jesus (was he human, divine, or both?), his relationship to God (equal or inferior?), and the always-perplexing concept of the Trinity (God as Father, Son, and Holy Spirit). There was debate as well about what writings belonged in the official New Testament, as dozens of letters, gospels, poems, and songs circulated among the early Christian communities. A series of church councils—at Nicaea (325 C.E.), Chalcedon (451 C.E.), and Constantinople (553 C.E.), for example—sought to define an orthodox, or correct, position on these and other issues, declaring those who disagreed as *anathema* and expelling them from the Church. The Church of the East, for example, adopted Nestorianism, which emphasized the human side of Jesus' nature, an idea rejected by the Roman Catholic and Eastern Orthodox Churches.

Beyond these theological debates, political and cultural differences generated division even among the orthodox. The bishop of Rome gradually emerged as the dominant leader, or pope, of the Church in the western half of the empire, but his authority was sharply contested in the East. This division contributed to the later split between the Latin, or Roman Catholic, and the Greek, or Eastern Orthodox, branches of Christendom, a division that continues to the present. Thus the Christian world of 500 C.E. was not only geographically extensive but also politically and theologically very diverse and highly fragmented.

Buddhists too clashed over various interpretations of the Buddha's teachings, and a series of councils failed to prevent the division between Theravada, Mahayana, and other approaches. A considerable proliferation of different sects, practices, teachings, and meditation techniques subsequently emerged within the Buddhist world, but these divisions generally lacked the "clear-cut distinction between 'right' and 'wrong' ideas" that characterized conflicts within the Christian world.[23] Although Buddhist states and warrior classes (such as the famous samurai of Japan) sometimes engaged in warfare, religious differences among Buddhists seldom provided the basis for the bitterness and violence that often accompanied religious conflict within Christendom. Nor did Buddhists develop the kind of overall religious hierarchy that characterized Christianity, although communities of monks and nuns, organized in monasteries, created elaborate rules to govern their internal affairs.

PRACTICING HISTORICAL THINKING

How might you understand the appeal of Buddhism and Christianity as opposed to the more rationalist approaches of Greek and Confucian philosophy?

REFLECTIONS

Religion and Historians

To put it mildly, religion has always been a sensitive subject, and no less so for historians than for anyone else. Seeking to understand the religious dimension of human life has generated various tensions and misunderstandings between scholars and believers.

One of these tensions involves the question of change. Most religions present themselves as timeless revelations from the beyond, partaking of eternity or at least reflecting ancient practice. In the eyes of historians, however, the religious aspect of human life changes as much as any other. The Hindu tradition changed from a religion of ritual and sacrifice to one of devotion and worship. Buddhism became more conventionally religious, with an emphasis on the supernatural, as it evolved from Theravada to Mahayana forms. A male-dominated hierarchical Christian Church, with its pope, bishops, priests, and state support, was very different from the small house churches that suffered persecution by imperial authorities in the early Christian centuries. The implication—that religions are largely a human phenomenon—has been troublesome to some believers.

Historians, on the other hand, have sometimes been uncomfortable in the face of claims by believers that they have actually experienced a divine reality. Certainly, modern scholars are in no position to validate or refute the spiritual claims of religious leaders and their many followers, but we need to take them seriously. Although we will never know precisely what happened to the Buddha as he sat in meditation in northern India or what transpired when Jesus spent forty days in the wilderness, clearly those experiences changed the two men and motivated their subsequent actions. Millions of their followers have also acted on the basis of what they perceived to be a compelling encounter with an unseen realm. This interior dimension of human experience, though difficult to grasp with any precision and impossible to verify, has been a significant mover and shaper of the historical process.

Yet a third problem arises from debates within particular religious traditions about which group most accurately represents the "real" or authentic version of the faith. Historians usually refuse to take sides in such disputes. They simply notice with interest that most human cultural traditions generate conflicting views, some of which become the basis for serious conflict in societies.

Reconciling personal religious convictions with the perspectives of modern historical scholarship is no easy task. At the very least, all of us can appreciate the immense human effort that has gone into the making of religious traditions, and we can acknowledge their enormous significance in the unfolding of the human story. They have shaped the meanings that billions of people over thousands of years have attached to the world they inhabit. These religious traditions have justified the vast social inequalities and oppressive states of human civilizations, but they have also enabled human beings to endure the multiple sufferings that attend human life, and on occasion they have stimulated reform and rebellion. And the religions born in second-wave civilizations have guided much of humankind in its endless efforts to penetrate the mysteries of the world beyond and of the world within.

Second Thoughts

What's the Significance?

Legalism, 142

Confucianism, 144

Ban Zhao, 145

Daoism, 147

Vedas, 149

Upanishads, 149

Siddhartha Gautama (the Buddha), 151

Theravada Buddhism, 153

Mahayana Buddhism, 153

Bhagavad Gita, 154

bhakti movement, 154

Zoroastrianism, 156

Judaism, 157

Greek rationalism, 159

Socrates, 159

Plato, 161

Aristotle, 161

Jesus of Nazareth, 164

Saint Paul, 165

Perpetua, 167

Church of the East, 167

Big Picture Questions

1. Is a secular outlook on the world an essentially modern phenomenon, or does it have precedents in the second-wave era?
2. "Religion is a double-edged sword, both supporting and undermining political authority and social elites." How would you support both sides of this statement?
3. How would you define the appeal of the religious/cultural traditions discussed in this chapter? To what groups were they attractive, and why?
4. Imagine that you were a Christian traveler in the Eurasian world of 500 C.E. writing home about your encounter with other religious traditions. What similarities and differences might you notice? What might you appreciate in those traditions? And what might you find distasteful or appalling?
5. **Looking Back:** What relationships can you see between the political dimensions of second-wave civilizations described in Chapter 3 and their cultural or religious aspects discussed in this chapter?

Next Steps: For Further Study

Karen Armstrong, *The Great Transformation* (2006). A comparative and historical study of the major religions by a well-known scholar.

Robert N. Bellah, *Religion in Human Evolution: From the Paleolithic to the Axial Age* (2011). An impressive but controversial account of the origins of religion in general and those of second-wave civilizations in particular.

Diarmaid MacCulloch, *Christianity: The First 3000 Years* (2009). A magisterial account of Jewish and Christian history.

Huston Smith, *An Illustrated World's Religions* (1994). A sympathetic account of major world religions, beautifully illustrated, by a prominent scholar of comparative religion.

Arthur Waley, *Three Ways of Thought in Ancient China* (1983). A classic work, first published more than half a century ago, about the major philosophies of old China.

Jonathan S. Walters, *Finding Buddhists in Global History* (1998). A brief account that situates Buddhism in a world history framework.

Annenberg Learner, "Early Belief Systems," http://www.learner.org/vod/vod_window.html?pid=2148. Explores the origins of the religious impulse and many of the traditions covered in this chapter.

Hinduism Today Videos, "The History of Hindu India, Part One: From Ancient Times," directed and produced by Sushma Khadepaun in collaboration with Professor Shiva Bajpai, https://www.youtube.com/watch?v=dBZRTzXARWM&vl=en. A thoughtful examination of the origins and development of the Hindu tradition.

Representations of the Buddha

Buddhism derived from a single individual, Siddhartha Gautama, born in northern India around the middle of the first millennium B.C.E. Over many centuries, the religion evolved as it spread within and beyond India, attracting growing numbers of followers and intersecting with various cultures throughout Asia, including those of China, Japan, Tibet, Korea, Thailand, Burma, and Vietnam. But the figure of the Buddha remained central to all versions and variations of the faith. Perceptions of the Buddha took on the flavor of the various cultures in which Buddhism took root. In China, for example, descriptions of the Buddha emphasized his "filial piety," citing the conversion of his father.

Understandings of the Buddha found expression in the titles and qualities attributed to him, such as "the teacher of gods and men," the Blessed One, the "great cosmic person," and many others. A proliferating body of written texts—sermons, biographies, stories, and myths—also featured various understandings of the Buddha. Over time, these descriptions increasingly emphasized the superhuman and transcendent elements of the Buddha, portrayed his actions as miraculous and magical, and invoked numerous past and future Buddhas. He was also represented artistically in sculptures and paintings. But for almost five centuries after his death, artists depicted the Buddha as an empty throne, a horse with no rider, a tree, a wheel, a set of footprints, or in some other symbolic way, while largely shunning any image of him in human form. All of these played a role in Buddhist worship, prayer, and meditation, allowing his followers to experience the Buddha as a living presence in their own lives.

SOURCE 4.1 A Greco-Indian Buddha ▶

By the first century C.E., the impulse to show the Buddha in human form had surfaced, with some of the earliest examples coming from the region of South Asia in what is now northern Pakistan and eastern Afghanistan (see Map 3.3, page 109). That area had been a part of the empire of Alexander the Great and his Hellenistic successors during the three centuries before the birth of Jesus and had developed commercial ties to the Roman Empire. These early images of the Buddha reflect this Greco-Roman influence, portraying him with a face similar to that of the Greek god Apollo, dressed in a Roman-style toga, and with curly hair characteristic of the Mediterranean region.

Greco-Roman influence is apparent in Source 4.1. Dating from the second or third century C.E., it comes from India and depicts a famous scene from the life of the Buddha—his temptation by the demon Mara and Mara's seductive daughters while he was meditating under the Bodhi tree.

■ How are Mara and his daughters, shown on the right, portrayed in this relief?

■ What attitude characterizes the Buddha, shown on the left and surrounded by attendants?

■ One scholar has recently argued that "statues of the Buddha started to appear only after the cult of Apollo became established [in the region]. Buddhists felt threatened by the success of the new religious practices and began to create their own visual images."[24] How might this possibility shape your understanding of Greco-Roman cultural influences on Buddhism? Can you imagine other possible explanations for the creation of the first physical representations of the Buddha?

■ Does the idea that competition from a Greek religious cult caused Buddhists to create early images of the Buddha affect your analysis of this image?

The Temptation of the Buddha

Siddhartha at the Bodhi Tree, 100–200 A.D. (stone)/Cleveland Museum of Art, Cleveland, Ohio, USA/Bridgeman Images

■ ■ ■

SOURCE 4.2 **A Classical Indian Buddha**

By the time of India's Gupta dynasty (320–550 C.E.), Greco-Roman influence in Buddhist art was fading, replaced by more completely Indian images of the Buddha. Such representations became the "classic" model illustrated in Source 4.2, which dates from the sixth century C.E. The Buddha's right hand with palm facing the viewer indicates reassurance, or "have no fear." The partially webbed fingers are among the *lakshanas*, or signs of a Buddha image, that denote the Buddha's unique status. So too is the hair knot on the top of his head, symbolizing enlightenment.

■   The elongated earlobes reflect the heavy, luxurious earrings that the Buddha wore earlier in his life before becoming the enlightened one. Why might the artist have included this detail in his depiction of the Buddha?

■   The creator of this statue intended to convey the Buddha's calm and detached posture toward the world. What features of the statue might illustrate this posture? What similarities and differences can you observe between this depiction of the Buddha and that in Source 4.1?

An Indian Buddha

The Metropolitan Museum of Art, New York, NY, USA/Purchase, Florance Waterbury Bequest, 1969 (69.222). Photo: Bruce White/Image copyright © The Metropolitan Museum of Art. Image source: Art Resource, NY

■ ■ ■

SOURCE 4.3 The Reputation of the Buddha in Ancient Buddhist Stories

Various perceptions of the Buddha found expression not only in artistic form, but also in the growing body of Buddhist texts, known as the Pali Canon, originally passed on orally and reduced to writing during the first century B.C.E. Source 4.3 recounts a conversation derived from one of these texts between the Buddha and a wandering holy man, Sakuludayin, about the qualities of various religious leaders in the area.

■ How might you summarize the perception of the Buddha reflected in this source?

■ To what extent are these qualities expressed in the artistic representations of the Buddha?

The Greater Discourse to Sakuludayin | ca. 1st century B.C.E.

[Sakuludayin reported:] And some said this: This recluse Gotama [the Buddha] is the head of an order, the head of a group, the teacher of a group, the well-known and famous founder of a sect regarded by many as a saint. He is honoured, respected, revered, and venerated by his disciples, and his disciples live in dependence on him. . . .

Once the recluse Gotama was teaching his Dhamma [truth, wisdom, teachings] to an assembly of several hundred followers and there a certain disciple of his cleared his throat. Thereupon one of his companions in the holy life nudged him with his knee. "Be quiet, venerable sir, make no noise; the Blessed One, the Teacher, is teaching us the Dhamma."

When the recluse Gotama is teaching the Dhamma to an assembly of several hundred followers, on that occasion there is no sound of his disciples' coughing or clearing their throats. For then that large assembly is poised in expectancy . . . just as though a man were at a crossroads pressing out pure honey and a large group of people were poised in expectancy. . . .

"But, [asked the Buddha] how many qualities do you see in me because of which my disciples honour, respect, revere, and venerate me?" [Sakuludayin replied] "Venerable sir, I see five qualities in the Blessed One: . . . First, venerable sir, the Blessed One eats little. . . . Again, the Blessed One is content with any kind of robe. . . . Again, the Blessed One is content with any kind of resting place. . . . Again, venerable sir, the Blessed One is secluded and commends seclusion."

Source: Bhikkhu Nanamola and Bhikkhu Bodhi, trans., *The Middle Length Discourses of the Buddha* (Boston: Wisdom Publications, 1995), 631–32.

■ ■ ■

SOURCE 4.4 **A Korean Bodhisattva of Compassion** ▶

Across the world of Asian Mahayana Buddhism, a popular artistic representation of Buddhist values found expression in numerous images of bodhisattvas, those spiritually developed beings who delayed their own entry into nirvana to assist others on the path. The historical Buddha had on occasion described himself as a bodhisattva. In sculpture or painting, bodhisattvas became objects of worship and sources of comfort and assistance to many Buddhists. The most widely popular of the many bodhisattva figures was that of Avalokitesvara, known in China as Guan-yin and in Japan as Kannon. This Bodhisattva of Compassion, often portrayed as a woman or with distinctly feminine characteristics, was known as "the one who hears the cries of the world."

Among the most striking of the many representations of this bodhisattva are those that portray him or her with numerous heads, with which to hear the many cries of a suffering humanity, or with multiple arms to aid them. Source 4.4 provides an illustration of such a figure, a gilded wooden statue from Korea dating to the tenth or eleventh century C.E.

■ What elements of Buddhist imagery can you identify in this statue?

■ To whom might such an image appeal? And why?

■ How does this image differ from the classical Indian Buddha shown in Source 4.2?

A Bodhisattva of Compassion: Avalokitesvara with a Thousand Arms

■ ■ ■

SOURCE 4.5 The Buddha and the Outcast

According to Buddhist sacred texts, the Buddha himself both taught and practiced compassion. Among the most widely known of his teachings are those about loving-kindness or compassion: "Like a caring mother holding and guarding the life of her only child, so with a boundless heart of lovingkindness, hold yourself and all beings as your beloved children." The story in Source 4.5, contained in the Buddhist scriptures, conveys this sensibility in action from the perspective of an untouchable cleaner named Sunita.

- How does this story convey the Buddhist ideal of compassion?

- In what ways was Sunita transformed by his encounter with the Buddha?

- How does the Buddha define a genuine Brahmin? How might Hindu Brahmins, with whom the Buddha was in frequent dispute, respond to this story?

Sunita the Outcast

In a lowly family I was born, poor, with next to no food. My work was degrading: I gathered the spoiled, the withered flowers from shrines and threw them away. People found me disgusting, despised me, disparaged me. Lowering my heart, I showed reverence to many.

Then I saw the One Self-awakened, arrayed with a squadron of monks, entering the city. . . . Throwing down my carrying pole, I approached him to do reverence. He—the supreme man—stood still out of sympathy just for me. After paying homage to the feet of the teacher [the Buddha], I stood to one side and requested the Going Forth [permission to enter the rank of monks] from him, supreme among all living beings. The compassionate Teacher, sympathetic to all the world, said: "Come, monk." That was my formal Acceptance.

Alone, I stayed in the wilds, untiring, I followed the Teacher's words, just as he, the Conqueror, had taught me. . . . Indra & Brahma [powerful Hindu/Buddhist deities] came to pay homage to me, hands palm-to-palm at their hearts: "Homage to you, O thoroughbred of men. . . . You, dear sir, are worthy of offerings."

Seeing me, arrayed with a squadron of devas [god-like spiritual beings], the Teacher smiled & said: "Through austerity, celibacy, restraint, and self-control: That's how one is a brahman. He is a brahman supreme."

Source: "Sunita the Outcaste" (Thag 12.2), translated from the Pali by Thanissaro Bhikkhu, *Access to Insight (BCBS Edition)*, November 30, 2013, http://www.accesstoinsight.org/tipitaka/kn/thag/thag.12.02.than.html.

■ ■ ■

SOURCE 4.6 A Chinese Buddha ▶

Mahayana Buddhism not only featured numerous bodhisattvas, but it also populated the spiritual universe with various Buddhas in addition to the historical Buddha. One of these is the Maitreya Buddha, or the Buddha of the Future, predicted to appear when the teachings of the historical Buddha have been lost or forgotten. In China, this Buddha of the future was sometimes portrayed as the "laughing Buddha," a fat, smiling, contented figure, said to be modeled on a tenth-century monk named Budai, who wandered the country merrily spreading happiness and good cheer while evoking contentment and abundance. Source 4.6 illustrates this Chinese Maitreya Buddha, together with some of his disciples, in a carving dating to the tenth through fourteenth centuries, in China's Feilai Feng caves.

- How does this Buddha image differ, both physically and in its religious implications, from the other Buddhas already discussed in this feature? Why might this image be appealing to some Buddhists, and why might others object to it?

- In what ways does this figure represent an adaptation of Buddhist imagery to Chinese culture? Consider what you know about Confucian and Daoist postures to the world.

The Chinese Maitreya Buddha

DOING HISTORY

1. **Tracing change:** What transformations in Buddhist belief and practice are disclosed in these sources?

2. **Identifying cultural adaptation:** What evidence do these sources provide about the blending of Buddhism into a variety of cultural settings?

3. **Understanding the growth of Buddhism:** What do these sources suggest about the appeal of Buddhism to growing numbers of people across Asia?

4. **Considering cultural boundaries:** To what extent are these sources meaningful to people outside the Buddhist tradition? In what ways might they speak to universal human needs or desires? What is specifically Buddhist or Asian about them?

On the Buddha

All of the preceding sources were the work of "insiders," reflecting the perceptions of the Buddha among those who operated within the Buddhist world at varying times and places in the distant past. Modern historians, particularly those from the Western world, are "outsiders," even if they are personally sympathetic with Buddhism. The following selections come to us from such historians, one American and the other British. Both John Strong (Voice 4.1) and Karen Armstrong (Voice 4.2) have written early-twenty-first-century biographies of the Buddha.

■ What features of the Buddha's life does John Strong (Voice 4.1) emphasize? Why does he largely omit the supernatural and miraculous elements that so often accompany "insider" understandings of the Buddha?

■ Why does Karen Armstrong in Voice 4.2 suggest that some Buddhists might be skeptical of any effort to create a modern biography of the Buddha? What aspects of the Buddha's life does she highlight?

■ **Integrating Primary and Secondary Sources:** How do these modern scholarly reflections on the Buddha differ from the much earlier insider accounts and images? Which do you find more useful in understanding the life of Siddhartha Gautama?

VOICE 4.1

John Strong on the Context of the Buddha's Life | 2001

Historically speaking, we know very little for certain about the life of Siddhartha Gautama, the man who came to be known as the Buddha. Although no one today seriously questions his actual existence, debates still rage over the dates of his life . . . the contents of his teaching, and the nature of the religious community he is said to have founded. . . .

We know that the India of his day was caught up in a period of ferment and religious questioning spawned by the rise of new urban centers and the breakdown of old political systems. As two contemporary religious scholars put it: "The historical Buddha responded to

this kind of situation. . . . He was a renouncer and an ascetic . . . although it seems mild by Indian standards. He shared with other renunciants an ultimately somber view of life and its pleasures, and he practiced and recommended a mode of religious life in which individual participation in a specifically religious community was of primary importance. He experimented with the practices of . . . begging, wandering, celibacy, . . . self-restraint (yoga) and the like, and he organized a community in which discipline played a central role. Judging from the movement he inspired, he was not only an innovator but also a charismatic personality. Through the course of his ministry, he gathered around him a group of wandering mendicants and nuns as well as men and women who continued to live the life of householders."

Source: John S. Strong, *The Buddha: A Short Biography* (Oxford: Oneworld Publications, 2001), 1–2. Quotation from Frank E. Reynolds and Charles Hallisey, "Buddha," in *Encyclopedia of Religion* (New York: Macmillan, 1987), 2:321.

VOICE 4.2

Karen Armstrong on the Buddha and Biography | 2001

Some Buddhists might say that to write a biography of Sidhatta Gotama is a very un-Buddhist thing to do. In their view no authority should be revered, however august; Buddhists must rely on their own efforts and motivate themselves, not on a charismatic leader. One ninth century master . . . even went so far as to command his disciples: "If you meet the Buddha, kill the Buddha!" to emphasize the importance of maintaining this independence from authority figures. . . . Throughout his life, he [the Buddha] fought against the cult of personality and endlessly deflected the attention of his disciples from himself. It was not his life and personality, but his teaching that was important. He believed he had woken up to a truth that was inscribed in the deepest structure of existence. It was a *dhamma*, . . . a fundamental law of life for gods, humans, and animals alike. By discovering this truth, he had become enlightened and had experienced a profound inner transformation; he had won peace and immunity in the midst of life's sufferings. Gotama has thus become a Buddha, an Enlightened or Awakened One. Any one of his disciples could achieve the same enlightenment if he or she followed this method. But if people start to revere Gotama the man, they would distract themselves from their task and the cult could become a prop, causing an unworthy dependence that could only impede spiritual progress.

Source: Karen Armstrong, *Buddha* (New York: Penguin Books, 2001), xi–xii.

Society and Inequality in Eurasia / North Africa

600 B.C.E.–600 C.E.

"Caste has no impact on life today," declared Chezi K. Ganesan in 2010.[1] Certainly, Mr. Ganesan's low caste background as a Nadar, ranking just above the "untouchables," has had little impact on the career of this prosperous high tech businessman, who shuttles between California's Silicon Valley and the city of Chennai in southern India. Yet his grandfather could not enter Hindu temples, and until the mid-nineteenth century, the women of his caste, as a sign of their low status, were forbidden to cover their breasts in the presence of Brahmin men. But if caste has proven no barrier to Mr. Ganesan, it remains significant for many others in contemporary India. Personal ads for those seeking a marriage partner in many online services often indicate an individual's caste as well as other personal data. Affirmative action programs benefiting low-caste Indians have provoked great controversy and resentment among some upper-caste groups. The brutal murder of an entire Dalit, or "untouchable," family in 2006 sparked much soul-searching in the Indian media. So while caste has changed in modern India, it has also persisted. ■

The past several centuries have called into question social patterns long assumed to be natural and permanent. The French, Russian, and Chinese revolutions challenged and destroyed ancient monarchies and class hierarchies; the abolitionist movement of the nineteenth century attacked slavery, largely unquestioned for millennia; the women's movement has confronted long and deeply held patriarchal assumptions about the proper relationship between the sexes; and during and after India's struggle for

《 Mother and Child Mothers and their children have been at the core of social life everywhere and a prominent theme of many artistic traditions. This lovely statue comes from the Sunga dynasty, which flourished in northeastern India from about 185 to 73 B.C.E., after the collapse of the Mauryan Empire.

187

independence from Great Britain in the twentieth century, some have challenged their country's ancient caste system. Nevertheless, caste, class, patriarchy, and even slavery have certainly not vanished from human society, even now. During the era of second-wave civilizations in Eurasia, such patterns of inequality prevailed widely and generated social tensions that endured well beyond that era.

As Chapter 3 pointed out, millions of individual men and women inhabiting the civilizations of Eurasia and North Africa lived within a political framework of states or empires. They also occupied a world of ideas, religions, and values that derived both from local folkways and from the teaching of the great religious or cultural traditions born in the second-wave era, as described in Chapter 4. In this chapter, the focus turns to the social arrangements of these civilizations— relationships between rich and poor, powerful and powerless, slaves and free people, and men and women. Those relationships shaped the daily lives and the life chances of everyone and provided the foundation for political authority as well as challenges to it.

Like the First Civilizations, those of the second-wave era were sharply divided along class lines, and they too were patriarchal, with women clearly subordinated to men in most domains of life. In constructing their societies, however, these second-wave civilizations differed substantially from one another. Chinese, Indian, and Mediterranean civilizations provide numerous illustrations of the many and varied ways in which these peoples organized their social lives. The assumptions, tensions, and conflicts accompanying these social patterns provided much of the distinctive character and texture that distinguished these diverse civilizations from one another.

SEEKING THE MAIN POINT

To what extent were the massive inequalities of second-wave civilizations generally accepted, and in what ways were they resisted or challenged?

Society and the State in China

Chinese society was unique in the ancient world in the extent to which it was shaped by the actions of the state. Nowhere was this more apparent than in the political power and immense social prestige of Chinese state officials, all of them male. For more than 2,000 years, these officials, bureaucrats acting in the name of the emperor both in the capital and in the provinces, represented the cultural and social elite of Chinese civilization. This class had its origins in the efforts of early Chinese rulers to find administrators loyal to the central state rather than to their own families or regions. Philosophers such as Confucius had long advocated selecting such officials on the basis of merit and personal morality rather than birth or wealth. As the Han dynasty established its authority in China around 200 B.C.E., its rulers required each province to send men of promise to the capital, where they were examined and chosen for official positions based on their performance.

Landmarks for Chapter 5

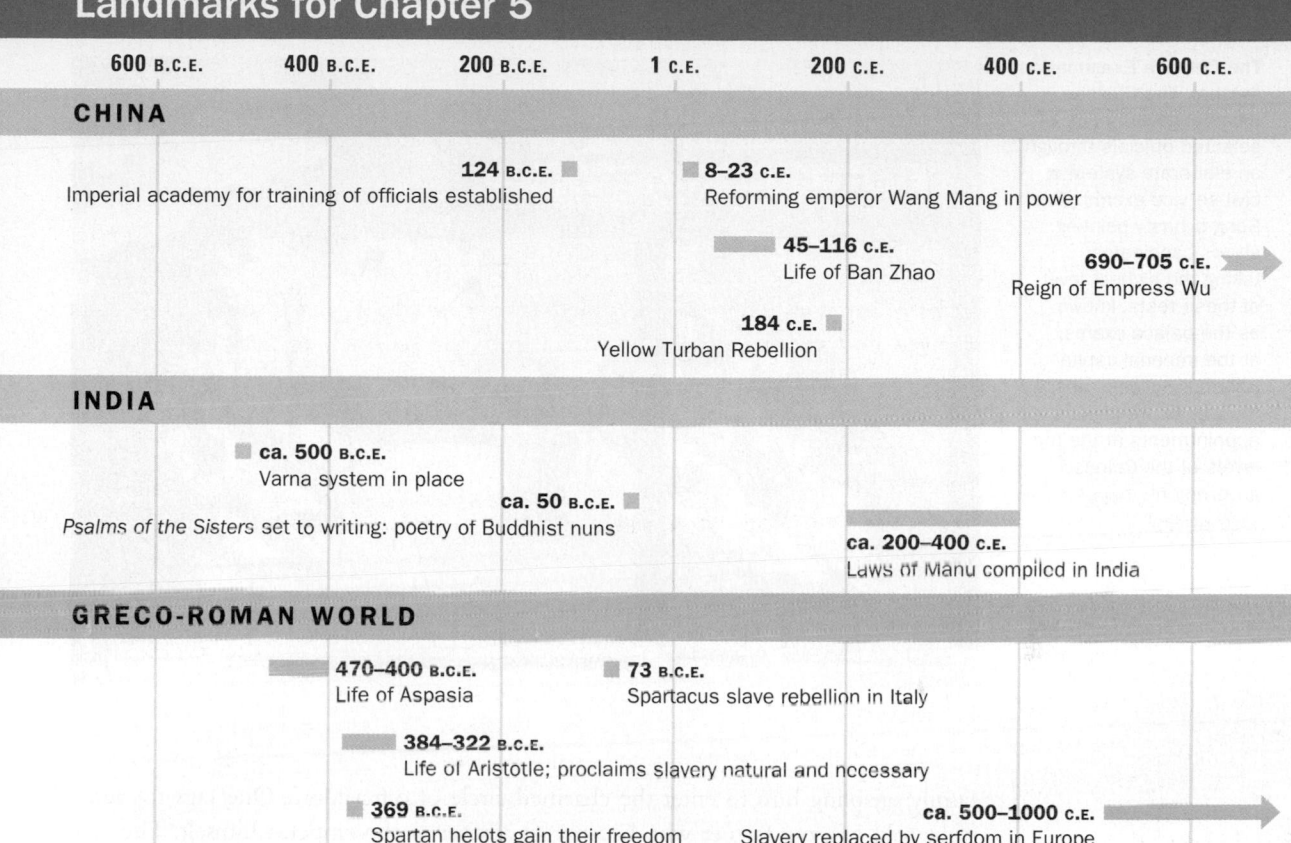

600 B.C.E.	400 B.C.E.	200 B.C.E.	1 C.E.	200 C.E.	400 C.E.	600 C.E.

CHINA

124 B.C.E. ■
Imperial academy for training of officials established

■ **8–23 C.E.**
Reforming emperor Wang Mang in power

45–116 C.E.
Life of Ban Zhao

690–705 C.E. ▶
Reign of Empress Wu

184 C.E. ■
Yellow Turban Rebellion

INDIA

■ **ca. 500 B.C.E.**
Varna system in place

ca. 50 B.C.E. ■
Psalms of the Sisters set to writing: poetry of Buddhist nuns

ca. 200–400 C.E.
Laws of Manu compiled in India

GRECO-ROMAN WORLD

470–400 B.C.E.
Life of Aspasia

■ **73 B.C.E.**
Spartacus slave rebellion in Italy

384–322 B.C.E.
Life of Aristotle; proclaims slavery natural and necessary

■ **369 B.C.E.**
Spartan helots gain their freedom

ca. 500–1000 C.E. ▶
Slavery replaced by serfdom in Europe

An Elite of Officials

Over time, this system of selecting administrators evolved into the world's first professional civil service. In 124 B.C.E., Emperor Wudi established an imperial academy where potential officials were trained as scholars and immersed in texts dealing with history, literature, art, and mathematics, with an emphasis on Confucian teachings. By the end of the Han dynasty, it enrolled some 30,000 students, who were by then subjected to a series of written examinations to select officials of various grades. Private schools in the provinces funneled still more aspiring candidates into this examination system, which persisted until the early twentieth century. In theory open to all men, this system in practice favored those whose families were wealthy enough to provide the years of education required to pass even the lower-level exams. Proximity to the capital and family connections to the imperial court also helped in gaining a position in this highest of Chinese elites. Nonetheless, village communities or a local landowner might sponsor the education of a bright young man from a commoner

Guided Reading Question

■ **DESCRIPTION**
How would you characterize the social hierarchy of China during the second-wave era?

189

The Chinese Examination System The Chinese imperial government selected officials through an elaborate system of civil service exams. This Song dynasty painting shows candidates taking the highest level of these tests, known as the palace exams, at the imperial capital Kaifeng. Success opened the way to prestigious appointments at the top levels of the Chinese government. (Pictures from History/Bridgeman Images)

family, enabling him to enter the charmed circle of officialdom. One rags-to-riches story told of a pig farmer who became an adviser to the emperor himself. Thus the examination system provided a modest measure of social mobility in an otherwise quite hierarchical society.

In later dynasties, that system grew even more elaborate and became an enduring and distinguishing feature of Chinese civilization. During the Tang dynasty, the famous poet and official Po Chu-I (772–846 C.E.) wrote a poem titled "After Passing the Examination," which shows something of the fame and fortune that awaited an accomplished student as well as the continuing loyalty to family and home that ideally marked those who succeeded:

> For ten years I never left my books, / I went up . . . and won unmerited praise.
> My high place I do not much prize; / The joy of my parents will first make me proud.
> Fellow students, six or seven men, / See me off as I leave the City gate.
> My covered coach is ready to drive away . . . / On a Spring day the road that leads to home.[2]

Those who made it into the bureaucracy entered a realm of high privilege and great prestige. Senior officials moved about in carriages and were bedecked with robes, ribbons, seals, and headdresses appropriate to their rank. Even lower officials who served in the provinces rather than the capital were distinguished by their polished speech, their cultural sophistication, and their urban manners as well as their political authority. Proud of their learning, they were the bearers, and often the makers, of Chinese culture. "Officials are the leaders of the populace," stated an imperial edict of 144 B.C.E., "and it is right and proper that the carriages they ride in and the robes that they wear should correspond to the degrees of their dignity."[3] Some of these men, particularly in times of political turmoil, experienced tension between their official duties and their personal inclination toward a more withdrawn life of reflective scholarship. (See Working with Evidence: China's Scholar-Officials in Chapter 8.)

The Landlord Class

Most officials came from wealthy families, and in China wealth meant land. When the Qin dynasty unified China by 210 B.C.E., most land was held by small-scale peasant farmers. But by the first century B.C.E., the pressures of population growth, taxation, and indebtedness had generated a class of large landowners as impoverished peasants found it necessary to sell their lands to more prosperous neighbors. This accumulation of land in sizable estates was a persistent theme in Chinese history and one that was frequently, though not very successfully, opposed by state authorities. Landlords of such large estates were often able to avoid paying taxes, thus decreasing state revenues and increasing the tax burden for the remaining peasants. In some cases, they could also raise their own military forces that might challenge the authority of the emperor.

One of the most dramatic state efforts to counteract the growing power of large landowners is associated with **Wang Mang**, a high court official of the Han dynasty who usurped the emperor's throne in 8 C.E. and immediately launched a series of startling reforms. A firm believer in Confucian good government, Wang Mang saw his reforms as re-creating a golden age of long ago in which small-scale peasant farmers represented the backbone of Chinese society. Accordingly, he ordered the great private estates to be nationalized and divided up among the landless. Government loans to peasant families, limits on the amount of land a family might own, and an end to private slavery were all part of his reform program, but these measures proved impossible to enforce. Opposition from wealthy landowners, nomadic invasions, poor harvests, floods, and famines led to the collapse of Wang Mang's reforms and his assassination in 23 C.E.

Large landowning families, therefore, remained a central feature of Chinese society, although the fate of individual families rose and fell as the wheel of fortune lifted them to great prominence or plunged them into poverty and disgrace. As a class, they benefited both from the wealth that their estates generated and from the power and prestige that accompanied their education and their membership in the official elite. The term "scholar-gentry" reflected their twin sources of privilege. With homes in both urban and rural areas, members of the scholar-gentry class lived luxuriously. Multi-storied houses, the finest of silk clothing, gleaming carriages, private orchestras, high-stakes gambling—all of this was part of the life of **China's scholar-gentry class**.

Peasants

Throughout the long course of China's civilization, the vast majority of its population consisted of peasants, living in small households representing two or three generations. Some owned enough land to support their families and perhaps even sell something on the local market. Many others could barely survive. Nature, the state, and landlords combined to make the life of most peasants extremely vulnerable. Famines, floods, droughts, hail, and pests could wreak havoc without warning. State authorities required the payment of taxes, demanded about a month's labor every year on various public projects, and conscripted young men for military service. During the Han dynasty, growing numbers of impoverished and desperate peasants had to sell out to large landlords and work as tenants or sharecroppers on their estates, where rents could run as high as one-half to two-thirds of the crop. Other peasants fled, taking to a life of begging or joining gangs of bandits in remote areas.

An eighth-century-C.E. Chinese poem by Li Shen reflects poignantly on the enduring hardships of peasant life:

> The cob of corn in springtime sown / In autumn yields a hundredfold.
> No fields are seen that fallow lie: / And yet of hunger peasants die.
> As at noontide they hoe their crops, / Sweat on the grain to earth down drops.
> How many tears, how many a groan, / Each morsel on thy dish did mould![4]

Guided Reading Question

·························

■ **CHANGE**
What class conflicts disrupted Chinese society?

Such conditions provoked periodic peasant rebellions, which have punctuated Chinese history for over 2,000 years. Toward the end of the second century C.E., wandering bands of peasants began to join together as floods along the Yellow River and resulting epidemics compounded the misery of landlessness and poverty. What emerged was a massive peasant uprising known as the **Yellow Turban Rebellion** because of the yellow scarves the peasants wore around their heads. That movement, which swelled to about 360,000 armed followers by 184 C.E., found leaders, organization, and a unifying ideology in a popular form of Daoism. Featuring supernatural healings, collective trances, and public confessions of sin, the Yellow Turban movement looked forward to the "Great Peace"—a golden age of equality, social harmony, and common ownership of property. Although the rebellion was suppressed by the military forces of the Han dynasty, the Yellow Turban and other peasant upheavals devastated the economy, weakened the state, and contributed to the overthrow of the dynasty a few decades later. Repeatedly in Chinese history, such peasant movements, often expressed in religious terms, registered the sharp class antagonisms of Chinese society and led to the collapse of more than one ruling dynasty.

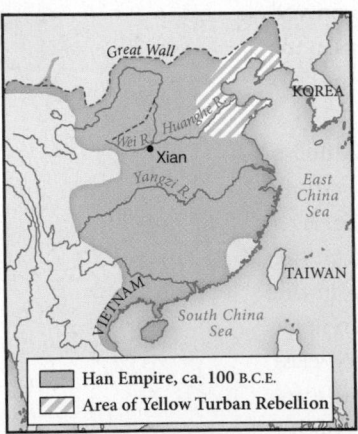

Han Empire, ca. 100 B.C.E.

Area of Yellow Turban Rebellion

The Yellow Turban Rebellion

Merchants

Peasants were oppressed in China and certainly exploited, but they were also honored and celebrated in the official ideology of the state. In the eyes of the scholar-gentry, peasants were the solid productive backbone of the country, and their hard work and endurance in the face of difficulties were worthy of praise. Merchants, however, did not enjoy such a favorable reputation in the eyes of China's cultural elite. They were widely viewed as unproductive, making a shameful profit from selling the work of others. Stereotyped as greedy, luxury loving, and materialistic, merchants stood in contrast to the presumed frugality, altruism, and cultured tastes of the scholar-gentry. They were also seen as a social threat, as their ill-gained wealth impoverished others, deprived the state of needed revenues, and fostered resentments.

Such views lay behind periodic efforts by state authorities to rein in merchant activity and to keep them under control. Early in the Han dynasty, merchants were forbidden to wear silk clothing, ride horses, or carry arms. Nor were they permitted to sit for civil service examinations or hold public office. State monopolies on profitable industries such as salt, iron, and alcohol limited merchant opportunities. Later dynasties sometimes forced merchants to loan large sums of money to the state. Despite this active discrimination, merchants frequently became quite wealthy. Some tried to achieve a more respectable elite status by purchasing landed estates or educating their sons for the civil service examinations. Many had backdoor relationships with state officials and landlords who found them useful and were not averse to profiting from business connections with merchants, despite their unsavory reputation.

Class and Caste in India

India's social organization shared certain broad features with that of China. In both civilizations, birth determined social status for most people; little social mobility was available for the vast majority; sharp distinctions and great inequalities characterized social life; and religious or cultural traditions defined these inequalities as natural, eternal, and ordained by the gods. Despite these similarities, the organization, flavor, and texture of ancient Indian society were distinctive compared to almost all other civilizations. These unique aspects of Indian society have long been embodied in what is now called the caste system, a term that comes from the Portuguese word *casta*, which means "race" or "purity of blood." That social organization emerged over thousands of years and in some respects has endured into modern times.

Caste as Varna

The origins of the caste system are at best hazy. Broadly speaking, however, the distinctive social system of India grew out of the interactions among South Asia's immensely varied cultures. Also contributing to the development of caste was the growth of economic and social differences among these peoples as the class inequalities common to "civilization" spread throughout the Ganges River valley and beyond.

Whatever the precise origins of the caste system, by around 500 B.C.E., the idea that society was forever divided into four ranked classes, or **varnas**, was deeply

Guided Reading Question

■ **DESCRIPTION**
What set of ideas was associated with India's caste-based society?

Caste in India This 1947 photograph from *Life* magazine illustrates the "purity and pollution" thinking that has long been central to the ideology of caste. It shows a high-caste landowner carefully dropping wages wrapped in a leaf into the outstretched hands of his low-caste workers. By avoiding direct physical contact with them, he escapes the ritual pollution that would otherwise ensue. (Margaret Bourke-White/The LIFE Picture Collection/Getty Images)

embedded in Indian thinking. Everyone was born into and remained within one of these classes for life. At the top of this hierarchical system were the Brahmins, priests whose rituals and sacrifices alone could ensure the proper functioning of the world. They were followed by the Kshatriya class, warriors and rulers charged with protecting and governing society. Next was the Vaisya class, originally commoners who cultivated the land. These three classes came to be regarded as possessing a distinctive nobility and purity, which was conveyed by the term "Aryan." They were also called the "twice-born," for they experienced not only a physical birth but also formal initiation into their respective varnas and status as people of prestigious Aryan descent. Far below these twice-born in the hierarchy of varna groups were the Sudras, native peoples incorporated into the margins of Aryan society in very subordinate positions. Regarded as servants of their social betters, they were not allowed to hear or repeat the Vedas, an early collection of religious texts, or to take part in Aryan rituals. So little were they valued that a Brahmin who killed a Sudra was penalized as if he had killed a cat or a dog.

According to varna theory, these four classes were formed from the body of the god Purusha and were therefore eternal and changeless. Although these divisions are widely recognized in India even today, historians have noted considerable social flux in ancient Indian history. Members of the Brahmin and Kshatriya groups, for example, were frequently in conflict over which ranked highest in the varna hierarchy, and only slowly did the Brahmins emerge clearly in the top position. Although theoretically purely Aryan, both groups absorbed various tribal peoples as Indian civilization expanded. Tribal medicine men or sorcerers found a place as Brahmins, while warrior groups entered the Kshatriya varna. The Vaisya varna, originally defined as cultivators, evolved into a business class with a prominent place for merchants, while the Sudra varna became the domain of peasant farmers. Finally a whole new category, ranking lower even than the Sudras, emerged in the "untouchables," men and women who did the work considered most unclean and polluting, such as cremating corpses, dealing with the skins of dead animals, and serving as executioners. (See Snapshot: Social Life and Duty in Classical India.")

SNAPSHOT Social Life and Duty in Classical India

Much personal behavior in classical India, at least ideally, was regulated according to caste. Each caste was associated with a particular color, with a part of the body of the god Purusha, and with a set of duties.

Caste (Varna)	Color/Symbolism	Part of Purusha	Duties
Brahmin	white/spirituality	head	priests, teachers
Kshatriya	red/courage	shoulders	warriors, rulers
Vaisya	yellow/wealth	thighs	farmers, merchants, artisans
Sudra	black/ignorance	feet	labor
Untouchables (outside of the varna system; thus no color and not associated with Purusha)	—	—	polluted labor

Beyond caste, behavior was ideally defined in terms of four stages of life, at least for the first three varna groups. Each new stage was marked by a *samskara*, a ritual initiating the person into this new phase of life.

Stage of Life	Duties
Student	Boys live with a teacher (guru); learn Sanskrit, rituals, Vedas; practice obedience, respect, celibacy, nonviolence.
Householder	Marriage and family; men practice caste-based career/occupation; women serve as wives and mothers, perform household rituals and sacrifices, actively support children and elders.
Retirement	Both husband and wife withdraw to the forests following birth of grandchildren; diminished household duties; greater focus on spiritual practice; sex permitted once a month.
Wandering ascetic	Only for men (women return to household); total rejection of ordinary existence; life as wandering hermit without shelter or possessions; caste becomes irrelevant; focus on achieving moksha and avoiding future rebirth.

Caste as Jati

As the varna system took shape in India, another set of social distinctions also arose, based largely on occupations. In India as elsewhere, urban-based civilization gave rise to specialized occupations, many organized in guilds that regulated their own affairs in a particular region. Over time, these occupationally based groups, known as *jatis*, blended with the varna system to create India's unique caste-based society.

Guided Reading Question

■ **COMPARISON**
What is the difference between varna and jati as expressions of caste?

The many thousands of jatis became the primary cells of India's social life beyond the family or household, but each of them was associated with one of the great classes (varnas). Thus Brahmins were divided into many separate jatis, or sub-castes, as were each of the other varnas as well as the untouchables. In a particular region or village, each jati was ranked in a hierarchy known to all, from the highest of the Brahmins to the lowest of the untouchables. Marriage and eating together were permitted only within an individual's own jati. Each jati was associated with a particular set of duties, rules, and obligations that defined its members' unique and separate place in the larger society. Brahmins, for example, were forbidden to eat meat, while Kshatriyas were permitted to do so. Upper-caste women covered their breasts, while some lower-caste women were forbidden this privilege as a sign of their subordination. "It is better to do one's own duty badly than another's well"—this frequently quoted saying summed up the underlying idea of Indian society. With its many separate, distinct, and hierarchically ranked social groups, Indian society was quite different from that of China or the Greco-Roman world.

It was also unique in the set of ideas that explained and justified that social system. Foremost among them was the notion of **ritual purity and pollution** applied to caste groups. Brahmins or other high-caste people who came in contact with members of lower castes, especially those who cleaned latrines, handled corpses, or butchered and skinned dead animals, were in great danger of being polluted, or made ritually unclean. Thus untouchables were forbidden to use the same wells or to enter the temples designated for higher-caste people. Sometimes they were required to wear a wooden clapper to warn others of their approach. A great body of Indian religious writing defined various forms of impurity and the ritual means of purification.

A further support for this idea of inherent inequality and permanent difference derived from emerging Hindu notions of *karma*, *dharma*, and rebirth. Being born into a particular caste was generally regarded as reflecting the good or bad deeds (karma) of a previous life. Thus an individual's prior actions were responsible for his or her current status. Any hope for rebirth in a higher caste rested on the faithful and selfless performance of one's present caste duties (dharma) in this life. Doing so contributed to spiritual progress by subduing the relentless demands of the ego. Such teachings, like that of permanent impurity, provided powerful sanctions for the inequalities of Indian society. So too did the threat of social ostracism, because each jati had the authority to expel members who violated its rules.

No greater catastrophe could befall a person than this, for it meant the end of any recognized social life and the loss of all social support.

As caste restrictions tightened, it became increasingly difficult—virtually impossible—for individuals to raise their social status during their lifetimes. However, another kind of upward mobility enabled entire jatis, over several generations, to raise their standing in the local hierarchy of caste groups. By acquiring land or wealth, by adopting the behaviors of higher-caste groups, by finding some previously overlooked "ancestor" of a higher caste, a particular jati might slowly be redefined in a higher category. India's caste system was in practice rather more fluid and changing than the theory of caste might suggest.

India's social system thus differed from that of China in several ways. It gave priority to religious status and ritual purity (the Brahmins), whereas China elevated political officials to the highest of elite positions. The caste system divided Indian society into vast numbers of distinct social groups; China had fewer, but broader, categories of society—scholar-gentry, landlords, peasants, merchants. Finally, India's caste society defined these social groups far more rigidly than in China and provided even less opportunity for social mobility.

The Functions of Caste

This caste-based social structure shaped India's emerging civilization in various ways. Because caste (jati) was a very local phenomenon, rooted in particular regions or villages, it focused the loyalties of most people on a quite restricted territory and weakened the appeal or authority of larger all-Indian states. This localization is one reason that India, unlike China, seldom experienced an empire that encompassed the entire subcontinent (see "Intermittent Empire: The Case of India" in Chapter 3). Caste, together with the shared culture of a diverse Hinduism, provided a substitute for the state as an integrative mechanism for Indian civilization. It offered a distinct and socially recognized place for almost everyone. In looking after widows, orphans, and the destitute, jatis also provided a modest measure of social security and support. Even the lowest-ranking jatis had the right to certain payments from the social superiors whom they served.

Furthermore, caste represented a means of accommodating the many migrating or invading peoples who entered the subcontinent. The cellular, or honeycomb, structure of caste society allowed various peoples, cultures, and traditions to find a place within a larger Indian civilization while retaining something of their unique identity. The process of assimilation was quite different in China, where it meant becoming Chinese ethnically, linguistically, and culturally. Finally, India's caste system facilitated the exploitation of the poor by the wealthy and powerful. The multitude of separate groups into which it divided the impoverished and oppressed majority of the population made class consciousness and organized resistance across caste lines much more difficult to achieve.

PRACTICING HISTORICAL THINKING

How did India's caste system differ from China's class system?

Slavery: The Case of the Roman Empire

Beyond the inequalities of class and caste lay those of slavery, a social institution with deep roots in human history, extending into the Paleolithic era of gathering and hunting peoples, but expanding greatly in agricultural civilizations. Some have suggested that the early domestication of animals provided a model for enslaving people. Certainly, slave owners have everywhere compared their slaves to tamed animals. Aristotle, for example, observed that the ox is "the poor man's slave." War, patriarchy, and the notion of private property, all of which accompanied the First Civilizations, also contributed to the growth of slavery. Large-scale warfare generated numerous prisoners, and everywhere in the ancient world capture in war meant the possibility of enslavement. Early records suggest that women captives were the first slaves, usually raped and then enslaved as concubines, whereas male captives were killed. Patriarchal societies, in which men sharply controlled and perhaps even "owned" women, may have suggested the possibility of using other people, men as well as women, as slaves. The class inequalities of early civilizations, which were based on great differences in privately owned property, also made it possible to imagine people owning other people.

Slavery and Civilization

Whatever its precise origins, slavery generally meant ownership by a master, the possibility of being sold, working without pay, and the status of an "outsider" at the bottom of the social hierarchy. For most, it was a kind of "social death,"[5] for slaves usually lacked any rights or independent personal identity recognized by the larger society. By the time Hammurabi's law code casually referred to Mesopotamian slavery (ca. 1750 B.C.E.), it was already a long-established tradition in the region and in all the First Civilizations. Likewise, virtually all subsequent civilizations—in the Americas, Africa, and Eurasia—practiced some form of slavery.

Slave systems throughout history have varied considerably. In some times and places, such as ancient Greece and Rome, a fair number of slaves might be emancipated in their own lifetimes, through their owners' generosity or religious convictions or the desire to avoid caring for them in old age, and sometimes slaves were allowed to purchase their freedom with their own funds. In some societies, the children of slaves inherited the status of their parents, while in others, such as the Aztec Empire, they were considered free people. Slaves likewise varied considerably in the labor they were required to do, with some working for the state in high positions, others performing domestic duties in their owner's household, and still others toiling in fields or mines in large work gangs.

The second-wave civilizations of Eurasia differed considerably in the prominence and extent of slavery in their societies. In China, it was a minor element, amounting to perhaps 1 percent of the population. Among the earliest slaves in Han dynasty China were convicted criminals and their families, confiscated by the government

Guided Reading Question

■ **COMPARISON**

How did the inequalities of slavery differ from those of caste?

and sometimes sold to wealthy private individuals. In desperate circumstances, impoverished or indebted peasants might sell their children into slavery. In southern China, teenage boys of poor families could be purchased by the wealthy, for whom they served as status symbols. Chinese slavery, however, was never very widespread and did not become a major source of labor for agriculture or manufacturing.

In India as well, people could fall into slavery as criminals, debtors, or prisoners of war and served their masters largely in domestic settings, but religious writings and secular law offered, at least in theory, some protection for slaves. Owners were required to provide adequately for their slaves and were forbidden to abandon them in old age. According to one ancient text, "A man may go short himself or stint his wife and children, but never his slave who does his dirty work for him."[6] Slaves in India could inherit and own property and earn money in their spare time. A master who raped a slave woman was required to set her free and pay compensation. The law encouraged owners to free their slaves and allowed slaves to buy their freedom. All of this suggests that Indian slavery was more restrained than that of other ancient civilizations. Nor did Indian civilization depend economically on slavery, for most work was performed by lower-caste, though free, men and women.

The Making of Roman Slavery

In sharp contrast to other second-wave civilizations, slavery played an immense role in the Mediterranean, or Western, world. Although slavery was practiced in Chinese, Indian, and Persian civilizations, **Greco-Roman slavery** was far more central to social life. By a conservative estimate, classical Athens alone was home to perhaps 60,000 slaves, or about one-third of the total population. In Athens, ironically, the growth of democracy and citizenship was accompanied by the simultaneous growth of slavery on a mass scale. During the fourth century B.C.E., the greatest of the Greek philosophers, Aristotle (384–322 B.C.E.), developed the notion that some people were "slaves by nature" and should be enslaved for their own good and for that of the larger society.

"The ancient Greek attitude toward slavery was simple," writes one modern scholar. "It was a terrible thing to become a slave, but a good thing to own a slave."[7] Even poor households usually had at least one or two female slaves, who provided domestic work and sexual services for their owners. Although substantial numbers of Greek slaves were granted freedom by their owners, they did not usually become citizens or gain political rights. Nor could they own land or marry citizens, and particularly in Athens they had to pay a special tax. Their status remained "halfway between slavery and freedom."[8]

Practiced on an even larger scale, slavery was a defining element of Roman society. By the time of Christ, the Italian heartland of the Roman Empire had some 2 to 3 million slaves, representing 33 to 40 percent of the population. Not until the modern slave societies of the Caribbean, Brazil, and the southern United States was slavery practiced again on such an enormous scale. Wealthy Romans could own

Guided Reading Question

■ **COMPARISON**

How did Greco-Roman slavery differ from that of other classical civilizations?

many hundreds or even thousands of slaves. One woman in the fifth century C.E. freed 8,000 slaves when she withdrew into a life of Christian monastic practice. Even people of modest means frequently owned two or three slaves. In doing so, they confirmed their own position as free people, demonstrated their social status, and expressed their ability to exercise power. Slaves and former slaves also might be slave owners. One freedman during the reign of Augustus owned 4,116 slaves at the time of his death. (For more on Roman society, see Working with Evidence: Pompeii as a Window on the Roman World, page 215.)

As the Roman Empire grew, social disruption and new wealth set loose forces that transformed it into a society in which slaves played a large role in the economy. In the early republic, landowning freemen, who both tilled the soil and served in the army, provided the backbone of this agrarian society. But as the empire expanded through constant warfare, many ordinary Roman families found it difficult to maintain their small farms when the head of the household was away serving in the military. Meanwhile, conquest brought Rome unthinkable wealth in the form of plunder, slaves, and later taxes and tribute, which flowed especially to the most well connected in society. These elites bought the small holdings of impoverished Roman freemen to create large estates and staffed those estates with slave labor, freely available from recent conquests. Displaced freemen abandoned farming and congregated in the growing cities of the empire, becoming buyers of the foodstuffs produced by slave estates. Thus a combination of economic and political disruption caused by war and wealth, together with slave labor derived from conquest, propelled Rome down the road toward becoming a slave society.

The vast majority of Roman slaves were prisoners captured in the many wars that accompanied the creation of the empire. In 146 B.C.E., following the destruction of the North African city of Carthage, some 55,000 people were enslaved en masse. From all over the Mediterranean basin, men and women were funneled into the major slave-owning regions of Italy and Sicily. Pirates also furnished slaves, kidnapping tens of thousands and selling them to Roman slave traders on the island of Delos. Roman merchants purchased still other slaves through networks of long-distance commerce extending to the Black Sea, the East African coast, and northwestern Europe. Slaves were also supplied through natural reproduction, as the children of slave mothers were regarded as slaves

Roman Slavery This Roman mosaic from the third century C.E. shows the slave Myro serving a drink to his master, Fructus. (Musée National du Bardo, Tunis, Tunisia/ G. Dagli Orti/De Agostini/REX/Shutterstock)

themselves. Such "home-born" slaves had a certain prestige and were thought to be less troublesome than those who had known freedom earlier in their lives. Finally, abandoned or exposed children could legally become the slave of anyone who rescued them.

Unlike American slavery of later times, Roman practice was not identified with a particular racial or ethnic group. Egyptians, Syrians, Jews, Greeks, Gauls, North Africans, and many other people found themselves enslaved. From within the empire and its adjacent regions, an enormous diversity of people were bought and sold at Roman slave markets.

Like slave owners everywhere, Romans regarded their slaves as "barbarians"— lazy, unreliable, immoral, prone to thieving—and came to think of certain peoples, such as Asiatic Greeks, Syrians, and Jews, as slaves by nature. Nor was there any serious criticism of slavery in principle, although on occasion owners were urged to treat their slaves in a more benevolent way. Even the triumph of Christianity within the Roman Empire did little to undermine slavery, for Christian teaching held that slaves should be "submissive to [their] masters with all fear, not only to the good and gentle, but also to the harsh."[9] In fact, the New Testament used the metaphor of slavery to describe the relationship of believers to God, styling them as "slaves of Christ," while Saint Augustine (354–430 c.e.) described slavery as God's punishment for sin. Thus slavery was deeply embedded in the religious thinking and social outlook of elite Romans.

Similarly, slavery was entrenched throughout the Roman economy. No occupation was off-limits to slaves except military service, and no distinction existed between jobs for slaves and those for free people. Frequently they labored side by side. In rural areas, slaves provided much of the labor force on the huge estates, or *latifundia*, that produced grain, olive oil, and wine, mostly for export, much like the later plantations in the Americas. There they often worked chained together. In the cities, slaves worked in their owners' households, but also as skilled artisans, teachers, doctors, business agents, entertainers, and actors. In the empire's many mines and quarries, slaves and criminals labored under brutal conditions. Slaves in the service of the emperor provided manpower for the state bureaucracy, maintained temples and shrines, and kept Rome's water supply system functioning. Trained in special schools, they also served as gladiators in the violent spectacles of Roman public life. Female slaves usually served as domestic servants but were also put to work in brothels, served as actresses and entertainers, and could be used sexually by their male owners. Thus slaves were represented among the highest and most prestigious occupations and in the lowest and most degraded.

Slave owners in the Roman Empire were supposed to provide the necessities of life to their slaves. When this occurred, slaves may have had a more secure life than was available to impoverished free people, who had to fend for themselves, but the price of this security was absolute subjection to the will of the master. Beatings, sexual abuse, and sale to another owner were constant possibilities. Lacking all rights in the law, slaves could not legally marry, although many contracted unofficial unions.

The Spartacus Slave Revolt

Despite the prominence of slavery in ancient civilizations, large-scale slave revolts were rare. One of the most impressive began in the Roman Empire during the summer of 73 B.C.E. when around seventy slaves escaped from a gladiator school at Capua, about 125 miles south of Rome. Grabbing knives and skewers from the kitchen on their way out, this small band of men, who had been trained to fight to the death for the entertainment of spectators, established a stronghold on nearby Mount Vesuvius and chose as their leader Spartacus, described by the historian Sallust as "a man of immense bodily strength and spirit."[10] The defeat of Roman forces sent to seize them encouraged other slaves and some free men to join the rebellion. Their numbers eventually swelled to as many as 120,000 men, women, and children at the height of the uprising, reflecting the large number of slaves employed on the great estates of southern Italy.

The death of Spartacus, 71 B.C.E.

Roman authorities became increasingly concerned when Spartacus and his followers began to manufacture their own weapons and to organize into a more coherent military force, which defeated in turn several hurriedly assembled Roman armies and plundered the rich farming region of Campania. The fortunes of the rebels peaked in 72 B.C.E. when they briefly threatened Rome itself. Both sides treated their opponents brutally. The Greek historian Appian reported that Spartacus ordered the sacrifice of 300 Roman prisoners in honor of the slain rebel leader Crixus, while another historian claimed that Spartacus staged gladiatorial games using 400 captives. When the revolt was finally suppressed, captured rebel slaves received similarly brutal treatment from the Roman authorities.

Slaves often accumulated money or possessions, but such property legally belonged to their masters and could be seized at any time. If a slave murdered his master, Roman law demanded the lives of all of the victim's slaves. When one Roman official was killed by a slave in 61 C.E., every one of his 400 slaves was condemned to death. For an individual slave, the quality of life depended almost entirely on the character of the master. Brutal owners made life a living hell. Benevolent owners made life tolerable and might even grant favored slaves their freedom or permit them to buy that freedom. As in Greece, manumission of slaves was a widespread practice, but in the Roman Empire, unlike in Greece, freedom was accompanied by citizenship.

Roman slaves, like their counterparts in other societies, responded to enslavement in many ways. Most, no doubt, did what was necessary to survive, but there are recorded cases of Roman prisoners of war who chose to commit mass suicide rather than face the horrors of slavery. Others, once enslaved, resorted to the "weapons of the weak"—small-scale theft, sabotage, pretending illness, working poorly, and placing curses on their masters. Slaves fleeing to the anonymous crowds of the city or to remote rural areas prompted owners to post notices in public places,

Fearful for the safety of the capital, the Roman authorities acted decisively. They appointed Marcus Licinius Crassus, a rich and ambitious Roman aristocrat and military commander, to lead eight Roman legions, totaling perhaps 40,000 troops, against Spartacus and his rebels. Crassus cornered the slave army in the far south of Italy, and Spartacus soon realized that his followers faced a fight to the death. According to the historian Appian, he advertised their precarious situation to his troops by crucifying a Roman soldier "as a visual reminder to his own men of what would happen to them if they did not win."[11] Rather than be captured, Spartacus and the slaves with him chose to make a last stand.

The Greek historian Plutarch reports that Spartacus killed his horse in front of his troops to show that he had no intention of fleeing and led his forces in a final desperate engagement with Crassus's army. Even the most hostile of later historians recounted that Spartacus died bravely during the battle, though some claimed that his body was never found. For those who survived, a terrible vengeance followed as some 6,000 captured rebel slaves were nailed to crosses along the Appian Way, between Capua, where the rebellion began, and Rome. These crucified prisoners, spaced some thirty-five to forty yards apart for over a hundred miles, provided a clear warning to all others who contemplated rebellion.

Spartacus's revolt had little lasting effect on the society in which he lived. No further large-scale revolts took place in the Roman Empire, and Rome continued its economic system based on slave labor. Moreover, the rebellion occasioned little historical comment until the eighteenth century. However, over the past two and a half centuries, a number of groups have embraced Spartacus, casting him as an inspirational leader of the downtrodden who resisted injustice and subjugation. Marxists, socialists, and nationalists have all found something to admire in Spartacus and his rebellion. In the United States, Spartacus entered the popular imagination due in no small part to the success of the 1960 epic film *Spartacus*, starring Kirk Douglas as the rebel leader fighting against the odds to free the oppressed. While there is no historical evidence that Spartacus ever intended to abolish slavery or fundamentally reform Roman society, in modern times his heroic, if ultimately failed, quest for freedom has been recovered from the past, becoming for many an inspirational symbol of just resistance to oppression. In such ways, the past continues to resonate in the present.

QUESTIONS

What can Spartacus's revolt tell us about the nature of the slave system in the Roman Empire? How might you account for the renewed interest in Spartacus over the past several centuries?

asking for information about their runaways. Catching runaway slaves became an organized private business. Occasional murders of slave owners made masters conscious of the dangers they faced. "Every slave we own is an enemy we harbor" ran one Roman saying.[12]

On several notable occasions, the slaves themselves rose in rebellion. The most famous uprising occurred in 73 B.C.E. when a slave gladiator named **Spartacus** led seventy other slaves from a school for gladiators in a desperate bid for freedom that mushroomed into a huge uprising. (See Zooming In: The Spartacus Slave Revolt, page 202, for a more detailed account.) Nothing on the scale of Spartacus's rebellion occurred again in the Western world of slavery until the Haitian Revolution of the 1790s. But Haitian rebels sought the creation of a new society free of slavery altogether. None of the Roman slave rebellions, including that of Spartacus, had any such overall plan or goal. The rebels simply wanted to escape Roman slavery. Although rebellions created a perpetual fear in the minds of slave owners, slavery itself was hardly affected.

The Rebellion of Spartacus

Comparing Patriarchies

Social inequality was embedded not only in the structures of class, caste, and slavery, but also in the gender systems of second-wave civilizations, as patterns of male dominance practiced in the patriarchy of the First Civilizations were replicated and elaborated in those that followed. (See "Hierarchies of Gender" in Chapter 2.) The basic idea of patriarchy, involving the sharp subordination of women to men, found expression in the Laws of Manu, an Indian compilation of prescriptions for a good society that developed around 200 to 400 C.E. It tied a woman irrevocably to the men in her life—father, husband, and son—declaring that "a woman must never be independent." Such patriarchal attitudes have been so widespread and pervasive that historians have been slow to recognize that gender systems had a history, changing over time. New agricultural technologies, the rise or decline of powerful states, the incorporation of world religions, interaction with culturally different peoples—all of these developments and more generated significant change in understandings of what was appropriate masculine and feminine behavior. Most often, patriarchies were lighter and less restrictive for women in the early years of a civilization's development and during times of upheaval, when established ways of living were disrupted.

Furthermore, women were often active agents in the histories of their societies, even while largely accepting their overall subordination. As the central figures in family life, they served as repositories and transmitters of their peoples' culture. Some were able to occupy unorthodox and occasionally prominent positions outside the home as scholars, religious functionaries, managers of property and participants in commerce, and even as rulers or military leaders. In Britain, Egypt, and Vietnam, for example, women led efforts to resist their countries' incorporation into the Roman or Chinese empires. (In Chapter 3, see Zooming In: Trung Trac, page 116, and the statue of Boudica, page 114.) Both Buddhist and Christian nuns carved out small domains of relative freedom from male control. In India, Buddhist nuns composed hundreds of poems that were brought together in a collection known as the *Psalms of the Sisters*, probably during the first century B.C.E. Those writings became part of the officially recognized Buddhist scriptures and represent the only early text in any of the world's major religions that was written by and about women. But these changes or challenges to male dominance occurred within a patriarchal framework, and nowhere did they evolve out of or beyond that framework. Thus a kind of "patriarchal equilibrium" ensured the long-term persistence of women's subordination despite fluctuations and various efforts to redefine gender roles or push against gendered expectations.[13]

Nor was patriarchy everywhere the same. Restrictions on women were far sharper in urban-based civilizations than in those pastoral or agricultural societies that lay beyond the reach of cities and empires. The degree and expression of patriarchy also varied from one civilization to another, as the discussion of Mesopotamia and Egypt in Chapter 2 illustrated. And within particular civilizations, elite women both enjoyed privileges and suffered the restrictions of seclusion in the home to a much greater extent than their lower-class counterparts, whose economic circumstances required them to operate in the larger social arena. China provides a fascinating example of how patriarchy changed over time, while the contrasting patriarchies of Athens and Sparta illustrate clear variations even within the much smaller world of Greek civilization.

A Changing Patriarchy: The Case of China

As Chinese civilization took shape during the Han dynasty, elite thinking about gender issues became more explicitly patriarchal, more clearly defined, and linked to an emerging Confucian ideology. Long-established patterns of thinking in terms of pairs of opposites were now described in gendered and unequal terms. The superior principle of *yang* was viewed as masculine and related to Heaven, rulers, strength, rationality, and light, whereas *yin*, the lower feminine principle, was associated with the Earth, subjects, weakness, emotion, and darkness. Thus female inferiority was seen as permanent and embedded in the workings of the universe.

What this view meant more practically was spelled out repeatedly over the centuries in various Confucian texts. Two notions in particular summarized the ideal position of women, at least in the eyes of elite male writers. The adage "Men go out, women stay in" emphasized the public and political roles of men in contrast to the domestic and private domain of women. A second idea, known as the **"three obediences,"** emphasized a woman's subordination first to her father, then to her husband, and finally to her son. "Why is it," asked one text, "that according to the rites the man takes his wife, whereas the woman leaves her house [to join her husband's family]? It is because the *yin* is lowly, and should not have the initiative; it proceeds to the *yang* in order to be completed."[14]

The Chinese woman writer and court official Ban Zhao (45–116 C.E.) observed that the ancients had practiced three customs when a baby girl was born. She was placed below the bed to show that she was "lowly and weak," required always to "humble herself before others." Then she was given a piece of broken pottery to play with, signifying that "her primary duty [was] to be industrious." Finally, her birth was announced to the ancestors with an offering to indicate that she was responsible for "the continuation of [ancestor] worship in the home."[15]

Yet such notions of passivity, inferiority, and subordination were not the whole story of women's lives in ancient China. A few women, particularly the wives, concubines, or widows of emperors, were able on occasion to exercise considerable political authority. Several others led peasant rebellions. In doing so, they provoked much antifemale hostility on the part of male officials, who understood governance as a masculine task and often blamed the collapse of a dynasty or natural disasters on the "unnatural" and "disruptive" influence of women in political affairs. Others, however, praised women of virtue as wise counselors to their fathers, husbands, and rulers and depicted them positively as active agents.

Guided Reading Question

■ **CHANGE**
In what ways did the expression of Chinese patriarchy change over time, and why did it change?

Elite Chinese Women at Leisure This Ming dynasty (1368–1644) painting shows elite Chinese women at leisure in the imperial palace known as the Forbidden City. In the center of the painting two women play a board game called *weiqi*, while two others look on and a servant attends them with a fan. Elite Chinese women were largely confined in their living quarters, where they socialized among themselves. (Pictures from History/Bridgeman Images)

Within her husband's family, a young woman was clearly subordinate as a wife and daughter-in-law, but as a mother of sons, she was accorded considerable honor for her role in producing the next generation of male heirs to carry on her husband's lineage. When her sons married, she was able to exercise the significant authority of a mother-in-law. Furthermore, a woman, at least in the upper classes, often brought with her a considerable dowry, which was regarded as her own property and gave her some leverage within her marriage. Women's roles in the production of textiles, often used to pay taxes or to sell commercially, made a woman's labor quite valuable to the family economy. And a man's wife was sharply distinguished from his concubines, for she was legally mother to all her husband's children. Furthermore, peasant women could hardly follow the Confucian ideal of seclusion in the home, as their labor was required in the fields. Thus women's lives were more complex and varied than the prescriptions of Confucian orthodoxy might suggest.

Much changed in China following the collapse of the Han dynasty in the third century C.E. Centralized government vanished amid much political fragmentation and conflict. Confucianism, the main ideology of Han China, was discredited, while Daoism and Buddhism attracted a growing following. Pastoral and nomadic peoples invaded northern China and ruled a number of the small states that had replaced the Han government. These new conditions resulted in some loosening of the strict patriarchy of Han dynasty China over the next five or six centuries.

The cultural influence of nomadic peoples, whose women were far less restricted than those of China, was noticed, and criticized, by more Confucian-minded male observers. One of them lamented the sad deterioration of gender roles under the influence of nomadic peoples:

> In the north of the Yellow river it is usually the wife who runs the household. She will not dispense with good clothing or expensive jewelry. The husband has to settle for old horses and sickly servants. The traditional niceties between husband and wife are seldom observed, and from time to time he even has to put up with her insults.[16]

Ordinary Chinese Women at Work For a long time, the spinning and weaving of cloth were part of women's domestic work in China. In this detail from a Ming dynasty vase, women are shown weaving silk. (Detail from a vase [ceramic], Ming Dynasty [1368–1644]/Golestan Palace, Tehran, Iran/ Bridgeman Images)

Others criticized the adoption of nomadic styles of dress, makeup, and music. By the time of the Tang dynasty (618–907), writers and artists depicted elite women as capable of handling legal and business affairs on their own and on occasion riding horses and playing polo, bareheaded and wearing men's clothing. Tang legal codes even recognized a married daughter's right to inherit property from her family of birth. Such images of women were quite different from those of Han dynasty China.

A further sign of a weakening patriarchy and the cause of great distress to advocates of Confucian orthodoxy lay in the unusual reign of **Empress Wu** (r. 690–705 C.E.), a former high-ranking concubine in the imperial court who came to power amid much palace intrigue and was the only woman ever to rule China with the title of emperor. With the support of China's growing Buddhist establishment, Empress Wu governed despotically, but she also consolidated China's civil service examination system for the selection of public officials and actively patronized scholarship and the arts. Some of her actions seem deliberately designed to elevate the position of women. She commissioned the biographies of famous women, decreed that the mourning period for mothers be made equal to that for fathers, and ordered the creation of a Chinese character for "human being" that suggested the process of birth flowing from one woman without a prominent male role. Her reign was brief and unrepeated.

The growing popularity of Daoism provided new images of the feminine and new roles for women. Daoist texts referred to the *dao* as "mother" and urged the traditionally feminine virtues of yielding and passive acceptance rather than the male-oriented striving of Confucianism. Daoist sects often featured women as priests, nuns, or reclusive meditators, able to receive cosmic truth and to use it for the benefit of others. A variety of female deities from Daoist or Buddhist traditions found a place in Chinese village religion, while growing numbers of women found an alternative to family life in Buddhist monasteries. None of this meant an end to patriarchy, but it does suggest some change in the tone and expression of that patriarchy. However, during the Song dynasty that followed, a more restrictive patriarchy reemerged.

Contrasting Patriarchies: Athens and Sparta

The patriarchies of second-wave civilizations not only fluctuated over time but also varied considerably from place to place. Nowhere is this variation more apparent than in the contrasting cases of Athens and Sparta, two of the leading city-states of Greek civilization (see Map 3.2, page 105). Even within this small area, the opportunities available to women and the restrictions imposed on them differed substantially. Although Athens has been celebrated as a major expression of democracy and rationalism, its posture toward women was far more restrictive than that of the highly militaristic and much less democratic Sparta.

In the several centuries between about 700 and 400 B.C.E., as the free male citizens of Athens moved toward unprecedented participation in political life, the city's women experienced growing limitations. They had no role whatsoever in the Assembly, the councils, or the juries of Athens, which were increasingly the focus of life for free men. In legal matters, women had to be represented by a guardian, and court proceedings did not even refer to them by name, but only as someone's wife or mother.

Greek thinkers, especially Aristotle, provided a set of ideas that justified women's exclusion from public life and their general subordination to men. According to Aristotle, "A woman is, as it were, an infertile male. She is female in fact on account of a kind of inadequacy." That inadequacy lay in her inability to generate sperm, which contained the "form" or the "soul" of a new human being. Her role in the reproductive process was passive, providing a receptacle for the vital male contribution. Compared often to children or domesticated animals, women were associated with instinct and passion and lacked the rationality to take part in public life. "It is the best for all tame animals to be ruled by human beings," wrote Aristotle. "In the same way, the relationship between the male and the female is by nature such that the male is higher, the female lower, that the male rules and the female is ruled."[17]

As in China, elite Athenian women were expected to remain inside the home, except perhaps for religious festivals or funerals. Even within the home, women's space was quite separate from that of men. Although poorer women, courtesans, and prostitutes had to leave their homes to earn money, collect water, or shop, ideal behavior for upper-class women meant assigning these tasks to slaves or to men and

Guided Reading Question

■ **COMPARISON**
How did the patriarchies of Athens and Sparta differ from each other?

involved a radical segregation of male and female space. "What causes women a bad reputation," declared Andromache, a female character in the Greek playwright Euripides' *The Trojan Women*, "is not remaining inside."

Within the domestic realm, Athenian women were generally married in their midteens to men ten to fifteen years older than themselves. Their main function was the management of domestic affairs and the production of sons who would become active citizens. These sons were expected to acquire a literate education, while their sisters were normally limited to learning spinning, weaving, and other household tasks. The Greek writer Menander exclaimed: "Teaching a woman to read and write? What a terrible thing to do! Like feeding a vile snake on more poison." Nor did women have much economic power. Although they could own personal property obtained through dowry, gifts, or inheritance, land was usually passed through male heirs. By law, women were forbidden to buy or sell land and could negotiate contracts only if the sum involved was valued at less than a bushel of barley.

There were exceptions, although rare, to the restricted lives of upper-class Athenian women, the most notable of which was **Aspasia** (ca. 470–400 B.C.E.). She was born in the Greek city of Miletus, on the western coast of Anatolia, to a wealthy family that believed in educating its daughters. As a young woman, Aspasia found her way to Athens,

A Woman of Athens This grave stele from about 400 B.C.E. marked the final resting place of Hegeso, a wealthy Athenian woman, shown in the women's quarter of a Greek home examining her jewelry, perhaps for the last time, while attended by her slave. The domestic setting of this grave marker contrasts with that common for men, which usually showed them as warriors in a public space. (Grave stele of Hegeso/National Archeological Museum, Athens, Greece/Marie Mauzy/Art Resource, NY)

where her foreign birth gave her somewhat more freedom than was normally available to the women of that city. She soon attracted the attention of Pericles, Athens's leading political figure. The two lived together as husband and wife until Pericles' death in 429 B.C.E., although they were not officially married. Treated as an equal partner by Pericles, Aspasia proved to be a learned and witty conversationalist who moved freely in the cultured circles of Athens. Her foreign birth and her apparent influence on Pericles provoked critics to suggest that she was a *hetaera*, a professional, educated, high-class entertainer and sexual companion, similar to a Japanese geisha. Although little is known about Aspasia, a number of major Athenian writers commented about her, both positively and negatively. She was, by all accounts, a rare and remarkable woman in a city that offered little opportunity for individuality or achievement to its female population.

A Girl of Sparta This figurine portrays a young female Spartan athlete or runner. Compare her clothing with that worn by Hegeso in the photo "A Woman of Athens." (The British Museum, London, UK/Bridgeman Images)

The evolution of Sparta differed in many ways from that of Athens. Early on, Sparta solved the problem of feeding a growing population not by creating overseas colonies as did many Greek city-states, but by conquering its immediate neighbors and reducing them to a status of permanent servitude, not far removed from slavery. Called **helots**, these dependents far outnumbered the free citizens of Sparta and represented a permanent threat of rebellion. Solving this problem shaped Spartan society decisively. Sparta's answer was a militaristic regime, constantly ready for war to keep the helots in their place. To maintain such a system, all boys were removed from their families at the age of seven to be trained by the state in military camps, where they learned the ways of war. There they remained until the age of thirty. The ideal Spartan male was a warrior, skilled in battle, able to endure hardship, and willing to die for his city. Mothers are said to have told their sons departing for battle to "come back with your shield . . . or on it." Although economic equality for men was the ideal, it was never completely realized in practice. And unlike Athens, political power was exercised primarily by a small group of wealthy men.

This militaristic and far-from-democratic system had implications for women that, strangely enough, offered them greater freedoms and fewer restrictions. As in many warrior societies, their central task was reproduction—bearing warrior sons for Sparta. To strengthen their bodies for childbearing, girls were encouraged to take part in sporting events—running, wrestling, throwing the discus and javelin, even driving chariots. At times, women and men alike competed in the nude before mixed audiences. Their education, like that of boys, was prescribed by the state, which also insisted that newly married women cut their hair short, unlike adult Greek women elsewhere. Thus Spartan women were not secluded or segregated, as were their Athenian counterparts.

Furthermore, Spartan young women, unlike those of Athens, usually married men of their own age, about eighteen years old, thus putting the new couple on a more equal basis. Marriage often began with a trial period to make sure the new couple could produce children, with divorce and remarriage readily available if they could not. Because men were so often away at war or preparing for it, women exercised much more authority in the household than was the case in Athens and actively managed family estates, some of which they controlled as their inheritance. Despite the intentions of the government, these busy women limited their fertility, sometimes through the use of various birth control practices. Over time they produced too few children to maintain the Spartan population, leading to a demographic crisis. According to the Roman orator Cicero, they preferred the active life to "barbarous fertility," a development experienced in many other societies where women have secured greater control over their lives and activities.[18]

It is little wonder that the freedom of Spartan women appalled other Greeks, who believed that it undermined good order and state authority. Aristotle complained that the more egalitarian inheritance practices of Spartans led to their women controlling some 40 percent of landed estates. In Sparta, he declared, women "live in every sort of intemperance and luxury" and "the [male] rulers are ruled by women." Plutarch, a Greek writer during the heyday of the Roman Empire, observed critically that "the men of Sparta always obeyed their wives." Moreover, the clothing worn by Spartan women to give them greater freedom of movement seemed immodest to other Greeks. However, the freedoms of Sparta's women did not endure. After the helots permanently overthrew Spartan rule in 369 B.C.E., it seems that the Spartan government increasingly restricted the rights and status of women, bringing Sparta's gender practices more in line with those of its neighbors. Thus freedom for the helots gradually brought restrictions for Spartan women.

Sparta clearly was a patriarchy, with women serving as breeding machines for its military system and lacking any formal role in public life, but it was a less restrictive patriarchy than that of Athens. The joint efforts of men and women seemed necessary to maintain a huge class of helots in permanent subjugation at least until 369 B.C.E. Death in childbirth was considered the equivalent of death in battle, for both contributed to the defense of Sparta, and both were honored alike. In Athens, on the other hand, growing freedom and democracy were associated with the strengthening of the male-dominated, property-owning household, and within that household, the cornerstone of Athenian society, men were expected to exercise authority. Doing so required increasingly severe limitations and restrictions on the lives of women. Together, the cases of Athens and Sparta illustrate how the historical record appears in a different light when viewed through the lens of gender. Athens, so celebrated for its democracy and philosophical rationalism, offered little to its women, whereas Sparta, often condemned for its militarism and virtual enslavement of the helots, provided a somewhat wider scope for the free women of the city-state.

If Athenian and Spartan patriarchies differed substantially in the opportunities they offered to women, they were more similar in their posture toward homoerotic relationships than other second-wave civilizations. Ancient Greeks generally approved of such relationships, and they were fairly common for both men and women, although this did not prevent their participants from entering heterosexual marriages as well. In Athens, the ideal homosexual relationship—between an older man and a young adolescent boy—was viewed as limited in time, for it was supposed to end when the boy's beard began to grow. Spartans possessed much the same attitudes, even if their homosexual relationships were shaped by a warrior society. Plato wrote that homosexual encounters in Sparta were the result of nudity in gymnasia and the custom of men dining together, while several historians refer to specific homosexual relationships between Spartan soldiers. One modern scholar noted that "records of Sparta from the classical period seem to refer to homosexual boyfriends at least as often as to wives."[19] Unlike contemporary Western societies, where sexuality is largely seen as an identity, in ancient Greece sexual choice was viewed more casually and as a matter of taste.

REFLECTIONS

What Changes? What Persists?

So what is more impressive in human history—the innovations and changes or the enduring patterns and lasting features? Our perception of change or continuity surely depends on when we are living. During the long Paleolithic and Neolithic eras, few people were aware of major changes in the larger patterns of life. Of course, change happened: nomadic peoples settled down in villages; agriculture developed; cities arose; states and empires took shape; class structures evolved; patriarchy emerged more sharply defined. But few of these changes occurred quickly enough to be noticeable in a single lifetime. It is among the great contributions of world history to call attention to transformations of which we might otherwise be unaware. In the modern era, and certainly in our own time, the pace of change has dramatically accelerated. We have come to value, celebrate, expect, and promote change in ways that many of our distant—and not so distant—ancestors would find unimaginable.

What might we say about the balance of change and persistence in the era of second-wave civilizations? Clearly, there was much that was new, even if those innovations had roots in earlier times. The Greek conquest of the Persian Empire under the leadership of Alexander the Great was both novel and unexpected. The Roman Empire encompassed the entire Mediterranean basin in a single political system for the first time. Buddhism and Christianity emerged as new, distinct, and universal religious traditions, although both bore the marks of their origin in Hindu and Jewish religious thinking, respectively. The collapse of dynasties, empires, and civilizations long thought to be solidly entrenched—the Chinese and Roman, for example—must surely have seemed to people of the time to be something fearfully new.

But much that was created in the second-wave era—particularly its social and cultural patterns—has demonstrated an impressive continuity throughout many centuries, even if it also changed in particular ways over time. China's scholar-gentry class retained its prominence throughout the ups and downs of changing dynasties into the twentieth century. India's caste-based social structure still endures as a way of thinking and behaving for hundreds of millions of men and women on the South Asian peninsula. Although slavery gave way to serfdom in post-Roman Europe (500–1000 C.E.), it was widely practiced in the Islamic world and massively extended in Europe's American colonies after 1500. Slavery remained an important and largely unquestioned feature of all civilizations until the nineteenth century, and in various forms it still exists. Patriarchy, with its assumptions of male superiority and dominance, has surely been the most fundamental, long-lasting, and taken-for-granted feature of all civilizations. Not until recent centuries have those assumptions effectively been challenged, and even so, patriarchy has continued to shape the lives and the thinking of the vast majority of humankind. And many hundreds of millions of people in the twenty-first century still honor or practice religious and cultural traditions begun during the second-wave era.

Persistence and change alike have long provided the inextricable warp and woof of both individual experience and historical study. Each of us no doubt ponders the tension between them in our own lives. Untangling their elusive relationship has figured prominently in the task of historians and has contributed much to the enduring fascination of historical study.

Second Thoughts

What's the Significance?

Wang Mang, 191
China's scholar-gentry class, 191
Yellow Turban Rebellion, 192
varnas, 193
jatis, 196
ritual purity and pollution, 196
Greco-Roman slavery, 199
Spartacus, 203
"three obediences," 205
Empress Wu, 207
Aspasia, 209
helots, 210

Big Picture Questions

1. What might an observant Chinese traveler from the Han dynasty era find surprising or offensive in India or the Greco-Roman world? What similarities might he or she notice?
2. Why do you think slavery was so much more prominent in Greco-Roman civilization than in India or China?
3. What philosophical, religious, or cultural ideas served to legitimate the class and gender inequalities of second-wave civilizations?
4. What changes in the patterns of social life in second-wave civilizations can you identify? What accounts for these changes?
5. **Looking Back:** The cultural and social patterns of civilizations seem to endure longer than the political framework of states and empires. What evidence from Chapters 3, 4, and 5 might support this statement? How might you account for this phenomenon? Is there evidence that could support a contrary position?

Next Steps: For Further Study

Jeannine Auboyer, *Daily Life in Ancient India* (2002). A social history of ancient India, with a focus on caste, ritual, religion, and art.

Sue Blundell, *Women in Ancient Greece* (1999). A well-written academic study, with occasional humorous stories and anecdotes.

Sandra R. Joshel, *Slavery in the Roman World* (2010). An overview of slave life in the Roman Empire by an established scholar in the field.

Michael Lowe, *Everyday Life in Early Imperial China* (1968). A vivid description of social life during the Han dynasty.

Peter Stearns, *Gender in World History* (2015). A prominent world historian explores the relationship between changing gender roles and cross-cultural interactions.

Merry Wiesner-Hanks, *Gender in History* (2011). A thoughtful overview by a leading scholar in both women's history and world history.

BBC, "The Indian Caste System: An Introduction," part of the series "The Story of India," written and presented by Michael Wood, 2009, www.youtube.com/watch?v=Oh_xvKLhZHg. An excerpt from a BBC documentary dealing with the beginnings of caste in India.

Roy Rosenzweig Center for History and New Media, George Mason University, "Women in World History," http://chnm.gmu.edu/wwh/. Documents, reviews, and lesson plans for learning and teaching about women's history in a global context.

Pompeii as a Window on the Roman World

You could hear the shrieks of women, the wailing of infants, and the shouting of men; some were calling their parents, others their children or their wives, trying to recognize them by their voices. People bewailed their own fate or that of their relatives, and there were some who prayed for death in their terror of dying. Many besought the aid of the gods, but still more imagined there were no gods left, and that the universe was plunged into eternal darkness for evermore.[20]

Written by a prominent Roman known as Pliny the Younger, this eyewitness account details reactions to the volcanic eruption of Mount Vesuvius, located on the southwestern side of the Italian peninsula, on August 24, 79 C.E. That eruption buried the nearby city of Pompeii and the smaller town of Herculaneum, located about 150 miles south of Rome, but it also preserved those cities, frozen in time, until archeologists began to uncover them in the mid-eighteenth century (see Map 3.4, page 113). Now substantially excavated, Pompeii is an archeological and historical treasure, offering a unique window into the life of a Roman city during the first century C.E.

As this city of some 12,000 to 15,000 people emerged from layers of ash, it stood revealed as a small but prosperous center of commerce and agriculture, serving as a point of entry for goods coming to southern Italy by sea. Pompeii also hosted numerous vineyards, production facilities for wine and olive oil, and a fisheries industry. Laid out in a grid pattern with straight streets, the city hosted numerous public facilities, including a central bathing/swimming pool, some twenty-five street fountains, various public bathhouses, and a large food market as well as many bars and small restaurants. More than thirty brothels, often featuring explicit erotic art, offered sexual services at relatively inexpensive prices. An inscription, apparently aimed at the many tourists visiting Pompeii, declared: "If anyone is looking for some tender love in this town, keep in mind that here all the girls are very friendly."

The houses of the wealthy were elegant structures, often built around a central courtyard, and were decorated with lovely murals displaying still-life images, landscapes, and scenes from Greek and Roman mythology. Carved on the threshold of one house was an expression of the entrepreneurial spirit of the town: "Gain is pure joy."

SOURCE 5.1 Terentius Neo and His Wife

The preserved art of Pompeii provides a glimpse into the city's social life, especially that of the more prosperous classes. Source 5.1 shows a portrait of Terentius Neo, a prominent businessman and magistrate (an elected public official), and his unnamed wife. He is wearing a toga and holding a papyrus scroll, while she wears a tunic and is holding a stylus, used for writing on the wax-covered wooden tablet that she carries. Her hair is styled in a fashion popular in the mid-first century.

■ What significance do you attribute to the lack of a name for the woman?

■ What is conveyed by highlighting the literacy of this couple?

■ How do you view these two people and their relationship to one another?

An Elite Couple of Pompeii | **1st century C.E.**

Museo Archeologico Nazionale, Naples, Italy/De Agostini Picture Library/Bridgeman Images

■ ■ ■

SOURCE 5.2 A Pompeii Banquet

Terentius Neo and his wife were no doubt served by slaves in their home, as slave owning was common in the Roman world, particularly among the upper classes. A wealthy household in Pompeii might own five to seven slaves. In the streets and homes of urban areas, slaves and free people mingled quite openly. Roman slavery was not distinguished by race, and the outward signs of urban slavery were few, especially for those practicing professions. Terentius Neo and his wife no doubt gave and attended banquets similar to the one depicted in Source 5.2, where well-to-do guests reclined on padded couches while slaves served them food and drink. Dancers, acrobats, and singers often provided entertainment at such events, which offered an occasion for elites to impress others with their lavish display of wealth and generosity.

- What signs of social status are evident in this painting? What conclusion might you draw from the gender balance at the banquet?

- How might you imagine the conversation at this event?

- What differences among the four slaves, shown in the foreground and second from the right at top, can you identify? Notice also the performing acrobat at the bottom right. What might these differences indicate about Roman slavery?

A Dinner with Friends | **1st century C.E.**

Museo Archeologico Nazionale, Naples, Italy/Roger-Viollet, Paris/Bridgeman Images

■ ■ ■

SOURCE 5.3 From a Pompeii Tavern

The lives of the less exalted appear infrequently in the art of Pompeii, but the images in Source 5.3 provide some entrée into their world. These frescoes, a style of mural painting, were found on the wall of a *caupona*, an inn or tavern catering to the lower classes. The first image shows Myrtale, a prostitute, kissing a man, while the caption above reads: "I don't want to, with Myrtale." In the second image, a female barmaid serves two customers with a large jug and a cup, while they compete for her attention. In the third image, two men playing dice are arguing.

■ Why do you think a tavern owner might have such paintings in his place of business?

■ What might we learn about tavern life from these images?

■ What roles did women play in the tavern?

■ What differences do you notice between these paintings and those depicting the lives of the upper classes?

An Evening Out at a Pompeii Bar | **1st century C.E.**

Museo Archeologico Nazionale, Naples, Italy/
Photos: Fotografia Foglia/Scala/Art Resource, NY

■ ■ ■

SOURCE 5.4 **The Graffiti of Pompeii**

The ordinary life of Pompeii is also revealed in some 11,000 inscriptions written, painted, or incised on the walls all over the city. They include public notices, advertisements, political endorsements, poetic reflections, . . . and graffiti galore. Even locals were impressed at the proliferation of these inscriptions. One of them wrote: "Oh walls, you have held up so much tedious graffiti that I am amazed that you have not already collapsed in ruin."

■ What might historians learn about everyday life in Pompeii from these inscriptions?

■ Do you recognize some similarity to modern life in these inscriptions, or do they seem to derive from a wholly different time and place?

The Graffiti of Pompeii | **1st century C.E.**

Politics and Advertising

- If modesty in life should be considered worth anything at all, then Lucretius Fronto is worthy of the office.

- The late night drinkers unanimously support Marcus Cerrinius Vatia for aedile [a city official].

- May all who refuse to vote for Quintius be turned into a donkey.

- Thirty pairs of gladiators . . . will fight at Pompeii on April 8th–13th. There will be a beast hunt and awnings [to provide shade]. Aemilius Celer wrote this alone by the light of the moon.

Commerce and Business

- What a lot of tricks you use to deceive, innkeeper. You sell water but privately drink unmixed wine.

- A copper pot went missing from my shop. Anyone who returns it to me will receive 65 bronze coins. Twenty more will be given for information leading to the capture of the thief.

- We have wet the bed, innkeeper. I confess we have done wrong. If you want to know why, there was no chamber pot in the room.

- The city block of Arrii Pollii . . . is available for rent from July 1. There are shops on the first floor, upper stories, high class rooms and a house. A person interested in renting this property should contact Primus, the slave of Gnaeus Alleius Nigidus Maius.

Love and Lovers

- Adimetus got me pregnant.

- Sarra, you are not being very nice, leaving me all alone like this.

- If anyone does not believe in Venus, they should gaze at my girlfriend.

- Successus, a weaver, loves the innkeeper's slave girl named Iris. She, however, does not love him. Still he begs her to have pity on him. His rival wrote this. Goodbye.

- Love dictates to me as I write and Cupid shows me the way, but may I die if I should prefer to be god without you.

Miscellaneous

- Anyone who wants to defecate in this place is advised to move along. If you act contrary to this warning, you will have to pay a penalty. Children must pay [?] silver coins. Slaves will be beaten on their behinds.

- Once you are dead, you are nothing.

- Chie, I hope your hemorrhoids hurt so much that they burn worse than they ever have before.

- Hey, Lucius Istacidius, I consider a man a barbarian who does not invite me to dinner at his house.

- Pyrrhus says hello to his friend Chius. I have a heavy heart because I heard that you died. And so, my friend, I bid you goodbye.

———————————

Source: Brian Harvey, *Daily Life in Ancient Rome: A Sourcebook* (Indianapolis: Hackett, 2016), 145–49, 292, 311–12. All translations of these inscriptions are by Professor Brian Harvey of Kent State University.

■ ■ ■

SOURCE 5.5 Household Religion in Pompeii ▶

The excavated ruins of Pompeii disclose the religious as well as the social life of the Roman world in the first century C.E., before Christianity had spread widely. Based on ritual observance rather than doctrine or theology, Roman religious practice sought to obtain the favor of the gods as a way of promoting success, prosperity, and good fortune. A core expression of the diverse and eclectic world of Roman religion was the imperial cult. In Pompeii, a number of temples were dedicated to one or another of the deified emperors, employing together a large cadre of priests and priestesses. Linked to the imperial cult were temples devoted to the traditional Greco-Roman gods such as Apollo, Venus, and Jupiter.

Probably more important to ordinary people were their *lararia* (household shrines), often a niche in the wall that housed paintings or sculptures of *lares* (guardian spirits or deities believed to provide protection within the home). Families offered gifts of fruit, cakes, and wine to these spirits, and the lararia were the focal point for various sacrifices and rituals associated with birth, marriage, and death. Source 5.5 shows one of these shrines, uncovered in the home of a well-to-do freedman (former slave) named Vetti. In the center was the *genius*, the spirit of the male head of household. Dressed in a toga and offering a sacrifice, this spirit embodied the character of the man, especially his procreative powers, and so guaranteed many children for the household. Protecting the family from external danger were two lares, standing on either side of the genius and holding their drinking horns. The snake at the bottom represented still other benevolent guardian spirits of the family.

■ Why might such a shrine and the spirits it accommodated be more meaningful for many people than the state-approved cults?

■ What significance might you find in the temple-like shape of the lararium?

A Household Shrine from Pompeii | 1st century c.e.

. . .

SOURCE 5.6 **Mystery Religion in Pompeii** ▶

In addition to the official cults and the veneration of household gods, by the first century C.E. a number of newer traditions, often called "mystery religions," were spreading widely in the Roman Empire. Deriving from the eastern realm of the empire and beyond (including Greece, Egypt, and Persia), they offered an alternative to the official cults, for they were more personal, emotional, and intimate, usually featuring a ritual initiation into sacred mysteries, codes of moral behavior, and the promise of an afterlife. Among the most popular of these mystery cults in Pompeii was that of Isis, an Egyptian goddess who restored her husband/brother, Osiris, to life and was worshipped as a compassionate protector of the downtrodden.

Another mystery cult, this one of Greek origin, was associated with Dionysus, a god of wine, ecstasy, and poetic inspiration, who was especially popular with women. Often associated with drunkenness, trance states, wild dancing, and unrestrained sexuality, the cult of Dionysus encouraged at least the temporary abandonment of conventional inhibitions and social restrictions as initiates sought union with Dionysus. A series of wall paintings on a Pompeii building known as the Villa of Mysteries depicts the process of initiation into the cult of Dionysus, perhaps in preparation for marriage.

Source 5.6 shows a particularly dramatic phase of that initiation in which a woman is ritually whipped, while a naked devotee dances ecstatically with a pair of cymbals above her head and a companion holds a rod of phallic symbolism sacred to Dionysus. In any such process of religious initiation, the initiate undergoes a series of trials or purifications in which he or she "dies" symbolically, achieves mystical union with the god, and is "reborn" into the new community of the cult.

■ How might you interpret the significance of the various aspects of the initiation process displayed here? Consider the role of whipping, the naked dancer, and the relationship of the initiate and the woman on whose lap she is resting her head.

■ Why might sexual union, symbolized by the rod, be significant in the initiation?

■ Why do you think Roman authorities took action against these mystery religions, even as they did against Christianity?

■ What did the mystery cults of Isis or Dionysus provide that neither the state cults nor household gods might offer?

An Initiation Ritual | **1st century** C.E.

Villa of the Mysteries, Pompeii, Italy/Werner Forman Archive/Bridgeman Images

DOING HISTORY

1. **Characterizing Pompeii:** What does the art and graffiti of Pompeii, as reflected in these sources, tell us about the social and religious life of this small Roman city in the first century C.E.?

2. **Analyzing class differences:** What class or social distinctions are apparent in these sources?

3. **Identifying gender roles:** What do these sources suggest about the varied lives and social roles of women and men in Pompeii?

On Pompeii

Historians have long delighted in the opportunities that an uncovered Pompeii has offered them and have argued vigorously about the meaning of what they found there. In Voice 5.1, Mary Beard, a prominent British classics scholar, muses on the unique insights that Pompeii presents to students of the ancient world. Voice 5.2, from a recent book on the economy of Pompeii by Andrew Wilson and Miko Flohr, uses evidence from Pompeii to challenge older views of Roman life that emphasized mass poverty, the absence of economic growth, and very limited entrepreneurial activity.

- What is it about the archeological evidence from Pompeii that so enchants Mary Beard in Voice 5.1?

- How would you summarize the view of Pompeii's economy presented in Voice 5.2? What kind of evidence supports this view?

- **Integrating Primary and Secondary Sources:** To what extent does the evidence in the visual and documentary sources presented here support or challenge the conclusions of these contemporary historians?

- **Integrating Primary and Secondary Sources:** Taking all of these sources together, which do you find more impressive — the similarities of life in Pompeii to that of the contemporary world or the notion that Pompeii was a "world apart" compared to modern life?

VOICE 5.1

Mary Beard on the Artifacts of Pompeii | 2017

[I]t is the sheer ordinariness of [Pompeii and Herculaneum] that makes them so *extraordinary* for us . . . , from a touching child's cradle to lavish jewellery. . . . It is not just the simple fact of the cities' preservation — though . . . hopping across an ancient street on the real ancient stepping stones gives most visitors a thrill, as does a peek into the very seedy brothel down one of the city's back alleys. It is also the fact that in Pompeii and Herculaneum we come face to face, not with the rich, larger-than-life Romans who fill the history books, but with the average men, women and children, both slaves and free — the ones who are otherwise largely *hidden* from history.

. . . [O]ccasional glimpses of luxury are enticing. But . . . even more fascinating [are] . . . the places where the ordinary city folk lived, worked, ate, drank, bathed, or simply hung out. . . . In one set of baths in Pompeii a store of 500 pottery lamps was found, showing that they did try to do something about the gloom. . . . Or take the little shops that lined the streets [of both cities]. . . .

Some of these remains of everyday Roman life seem reassuringly familiar. The mosaic "Beware of the Dog" sign . . . would look at home on the gate of any modern dog-owning household. . . . But other features seem bafflingly alien. No one, for example, has ever quite worked out how to explain the presence of so many phalluses all over the city, carved into the road surface, hanging over ovens, on jewellery around the necks of children, or made into novelty lamps.

Source: Mary Beard, "Pompeii Exhibition," *The Telegraph*, April 10, 2017, http://www.telegraph.co.uk/history/pompeii/9848596/Pompeii-exhibition-Mary-Beard-on-life-in-Pompeii-and-Herculaneum.html.

VOICE 5.2

Andrew Wilson and Miko Flohr on the Economy of Pompeii | 2017

To sum up, Pompeiians consumed a rather varied diet, lived reasonably long and healthy lives, and had relatively easy access to consumer goods and art. The city's economy was highly monetized. . . . Continuous investment in commercial facilities like shops and workshops testifies [to] the vibrant and stable character of the Pompeian economy. . . . Pompeii was performing rather well. . . .

This book does not offer a lot of support for the more pessimistic readings of Roman economic performance. . . . Pompeii and its surrounding countryside were connected, directly or indirectly, to the Mediterranean trade system. . . . Without these networks, Pompeii would have been a different, and probably a smaller and less wealthy, city. . . . Pompeii . . . and Herculaneum were able not only to support the consumption of luxuries by a small group of elite households but also by large parts of the rest of the population. . . . This means that, under the right circumstances, Roman urban economies were able to provide opportunities for non-poor, non-elite households to accumulate wealth.

In the end, Pompeii was far more prosperous and this prosperity did reach down to much lower strata than . . . once thought.

Source: Andrew Wilson and Miko Flohr, eds., *The Economy of Pompeii* (Oxford: Oxford University Press, 2017), 15, 425.

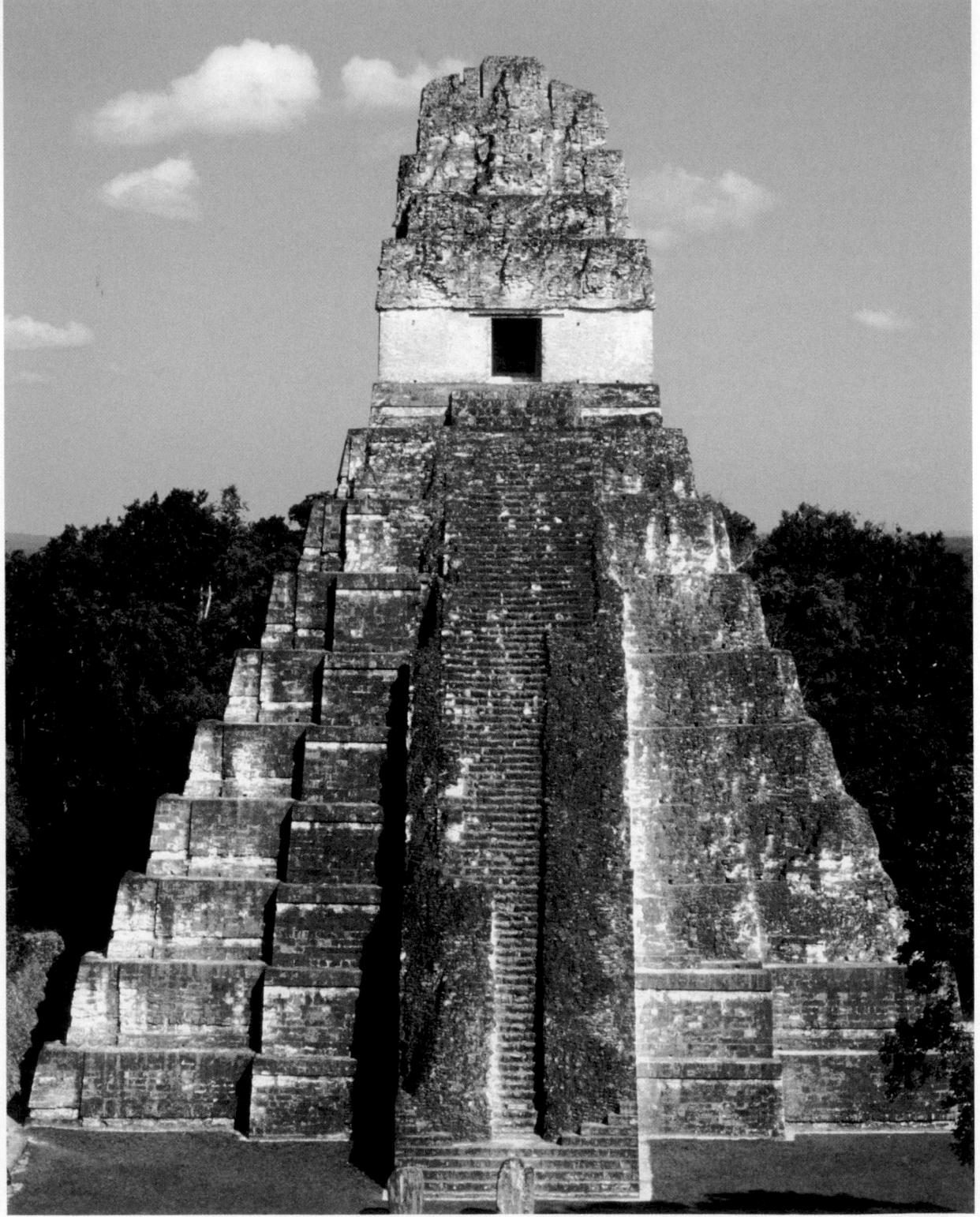

Commonalities and Variations

Africa, the Americas, and Pacific Oceania

600 B.C.E.–1200 C.E.

《 The Maya Temple of the Great Jaguar in Tikal Located in the Maya city of Tikal in present-day Guatemala, this temple was constructed in the eighth century C.E. and excavated by archeologists in the late nineteenth century. It served as the tomb of the Tikal ruler Jasaw Chan K'awiil I (682–734). Some 144 feet tall, it was topped by a three-room temple complex and a huge roofcomb showing the ruler on his throne.

In early 2010, Bolivian president Evo Morales was inaugurated for his second term in office, the only Native American ever elected to that post. Before his official inauguration, Morales traveled to Tiwanaku (tee-wah-NAH-coo), the center of an impressive empire that had flourished in the Andean highlands between 400 and 1000 C.E., long before either the Incas or the Spanish ruled the area. There he sought to link himself and his administration to this ancient culture, a symbol of Bolivian nationalism and indigenous pride. On his arrival, Morales was ritually cleansed, offerings were made to traditional deities, and he was invested with symbols of both kingship and spiritual leadership, thus joining political and religious sources of authority.[1] Thus memories of this American second-wave civilization remained alive and were available for mobilizing political support and legitimating political authority in the very different circumstances of the early twenty-first century. ∎

For many people, the second-wave era evokes most vividly the civilizations of Eurasia — the Greeks and the Romans, the Persians and the Chinese, and the Indians of South Asia — yet civilization also flourished elsewhere, both in the Americas and in sub-Saharan Africa. Furthermore, those peoples who did not organize themselves around cities or states likewise had histories of note and alternative ways of constructing their societies, although they are often neglected in favor of civilizations. This chapter explores the histories of the varied peoples of Africa, the Americas, and Pacific Oceania during

227

SEEKING THE MAIN POINT

To what extent did the histories of Africa, Oceania, and the Americas parallel those of Eurasia? In what ways did they forge new or different paths?

this phase of world history. On occasion, those histories will extend some centuries beyond the chronological boundaries of the second-wave era in Eurasia because patterns of historical development around the world did not always coincide precisely.

Continental Comparisons

At the broadest level, human cultures evolved in quite similar fashion around the world. All were part of that grand process of human migration that initially peopled the planet. Almost everywhere, gathering, hunting, and fishing long remained the sole basis for sustaining life and society. Then, in various parts of the three supercontinents—Eurasia, Africa, and the Americas—the momentous turn of the Agricultural Revolution took place independently, as noted in Chapter 1, and subsequently generated in all three regions those more complex societies that we know as civilizations, featuring cities, states, monumental architecture, and great social inequality, as described in Chapter 2. In these ways, the historical trajectory of the human journey has a certain unity and similarity across quite distinct continental regions. These commonalities provide the foundation for a genuinely global history of humankind.

Guided Reading Question

■ COMPARISON
What similarities and differences are noticeable in the historical development of the three major continents?

The world's human population was then distributed very unevenly across the three giant continents, as the Snapshot of population on page 230 indicates. Eurasia was then home to more than 85 percent of the world's people, Africa about 10 percent, the Americas around 5 percent, and Oceania less than 1 percent. That unevenness in population distribution, a pattern that has persisted to the present, is part of the reason that world historians focus more attention on Eurasia than on these other regions.

Another continental difference involved the absence in the Americas of most animals capable of domestication. This meant that few pastoral societies developed in the Western Hemisphere, and only in pockets of the Andes Mountains based on the herding of llamas and alpacas. No animals were available in the Americas to pull plows or carts or to be ridden into combat. Metallurgy in the Americas was likewise far less developed than in Eurasia and Africa, where iron tools and weapons played such an important role in economic and military life. In the Americas, writing was limited to the Mesoamerican region and was most highly developed among the Maya, whereas in Africa it was confined to the northern and northeastern parts of the continent. In Eurasia, by contrast, writing emerged elaborately in many regions. Furthermore, civilizations in Africa and the Americas were fewer in number and generally smaller than those of Eurasia, and larger numbers of people in those two continents lived outside the confines of any civilization in communities that did not feature cities and states.

A final continental comparison distinguishes the history of Africa from that of the Americas and Pacific Oceania. Geography placed Africa adjacent to Eurasia, while it separated the Americas and Oceania from both Africa and Eurasia. So parts of Africa were joined with Europe and Asia in a larger zone of Afro-Eurasian

1200 B.C.E.	800 B.C.E.	400 B.C.E.	1 C.E.	400 C.E.	800 C.E.	1200 C.E.

AFRICA

730 B.C.E.
Nubian conquest of Egypt

300 B.C.E.–100 C.E.
Kingdom of Meroë in upper Nile Valley

300 B.C.E.–900 C.E.
Niger Valley civilization in West Africa

4th century C.E.
Introduction of Christianity to Axum

ca. 400 C.E. Bantu-speaking peoples
established in southern Africa

NORTH AMERICA

200 B.C.E.–400 C.E.
Hopewell mound-building culture

ca. 860–1130 C.E.
Chaco Phenomenon

ca. 900–1250 C.E.
Cahokia

ca. 1200–1400 C.E.
Southeast Ceremonial Complex

CENTRAL AND SOUTH AMERICA

900–200 B.C.E.
Chavin movement

100–800 C.E.
Moche civilization in Peru

250–900 C.E.
Maya civilization

300–600 C.E.
Teotihuacán

400–1000 C.E.
Wari and Tiwanaku in the Andes

OCEANIA

1400–800 B.C.E.
Lapita culture

1100–1600 C.E.
Saudeleur dynasty on Pohnpei

ca. 1000 C.E.
Tongan trading network

1200 C.E.
Initial settlement of New Zealand

SNAPSHOT Continental Population in the Second-Wave Era and Beyond

(Note: Population figures for such early times are merely estimates and are often controversial among scholars. Percentages do not always total 100 percent due to rounding.)

	Eurasia	Africa	North America	Central/South America	Australia/ Oceania	Total World
Area (in square miles and as percentage of world total)						
	21,049,000 (41%)	11,608,000 (22%)	9,365,000 (18%)	6,880,000 (13%)	2,968,000 (6%)	51,870,000
Population (in millions and as percentage of world total)						
400 B.C.E.	127 (83%)	17 (11%)	1 (0.7%)	7 (5%)	1 (0.7%)	153
10 C.E.	213 (85%)	26 (10%)	2 (0.8%)	10 (4%)	1 (0.4%)	252
200 C.E.	215 (84%)	30 (12%)	2 (0.8%)	9 (4%)	1 (0.4%)	257
600 C.E.	167 (80%)	24 (12%)	2 (1%)	14 (7%)	1 (0.5%)	208
1000 C.E.	195 (77%)	39 (15%)	2 (0.8%)	16 (6%)	1 (0.4%)	253
1500	329 (69%)	113 (24%)	4.5 (0.9%)	53 (11%)	3 (0.6%)	477
1750	646 (83%)	104 (13%)	3 (0.4%)	15 (1.9%)	3 (0.4%)	771
2017	5,246 (69.5%)	1,256 (16.6%)	361 (4.8%)	646 (8.6%)	40 (0.5%)	7,549

Source: Population figures through 1750 are taken from Paul Adams et al., *Experiencing World History* (New York: New York University Press, 2000), 334; 2017 figures derive from "World Population by Region," Worldometers, http://www.worldometers.info/world-population/#region. Accessed December 8, 2017.

interaction. Early Christianity, for example, spread widely across North and Northeast Africa. Camels, probably originating in Arabia, enabled a trans-Saharan commerce that linked interior West Africa to the world of Mediterranean civilization. Bananas brought from Southeast Asia by Austronesian voyagers greatly enriched the diets of many African peoples. The Americas and Oceania, by contrast, developed almost wholly apart from this Afro-Eurasian network until that separation was breeched by the voyages of Columbus and later European explorers from 1492 on.

This chapter examines first the civilizations that emerged in sub-Saharan Africa and the Americas. Then our historical spotlight turns to those regions on both continents and Pacific Oceania that remained outside the zone of civilization. They remind us that the histories of many peoples unfolded without the cities, states, and empires that were so prominent within that zone.

Civilizations of Africa

When historians refer to Africa in premodern times, they are speaking generally of a geographic concept, a continental landmass, and not a cultural identity. Certainly few, if any, people living on the continent during the second-wave era thought of themselves as Africans. Like Eurasia or the Americas, Africa hosted numerous separate societies, cultures, and civilizations with vast differences among them as well as some interaction between them.

Many of these differences grew out of the continent's environmental variations. Small regions of Mediterranean climate in the northern and southern extremes, large deserts (the Sahara and the Kalahari), even larger regions of savanna grasslands, tropical rain forest in the continent's center, highlands and mountains in eastern Africa—all of these features, combined with the continent's enormous size, ensured endless variation among Africa's many peoples. Africa did, however, have one distinctive environmental feature: bisected by the equator, it was the most tropical of the world's three supercontinents. While some regions, such as highland Ethiopia, sustained very productive agriculture, elsewhere lower crop yields and diminished soil fertility prevailed, owing to heavy but sometimes erratic rainfall, long dry seasons, and the leaching of nutrients from ancient soils. Climatic conditions also spawned numerous disease-carrying insects and parasites that have long created serious health problems in many parts of the continent. It was within these environmental constraints that African peoples made their histories. In several distinct regions of the continent—the upper Nile Valley, northern Ethiopia/Eritrea, and the Niger River valley—small civilizations flourished during the second-wave era, while others followed later. A further African civilization falling partly within this time period grew up along the East African coast in conjunction with Indian Ocean commerce. Known as Swahili civilization, it is treated in greater detail in Chapter 7.

Meroë: Continuing a Nile Valley Civilization

In the Nile Valley south of Egypt lay the lands of Nubian civilization, almost as old as Egypt itself. Over many centuries, Nubians both traded and fought with Egypt, and on one occasion, in 730 B.C.E., the Nubian Kingdom of Kush conquered Egypt and ruled it for a century. While borrowing heavily from Egypt, Nubia remained a distinct and separate civilization. As Egypt fell increasingly under foreign control, Nubian civilization came to center on the southern city of **Meroë** (MER-oh-ee), where it flourished between 300 B.C.E. and 100 C.E. (see Map 6.1).

Politically, the Kingdom of Meroë was governed by an all-powerful and sacred monarch, a position held on at least ten occasions by women, governing alone or as co-rulers. Unlike the female pharaoh Hatshepsut in Egypt, who was portrayed in male clothing, Meroë queens appeared in sculptures as women and with a prominence and power equivalent to their male counterparts. In accordance with ancient traditions, such rulers were buried along with a number of human sacrificial victims.

Guided Reading Question

••••••••••••••••••••••••••••••••••

■ **CONNECTION**

How did the history of Meroë and Axum reflect interaction with neighboring civilizations?

MAPPING HISTORY

Map 6.1 Africa in the Second-Wave Era

During the second-wave era, older African civilizations such as Egypt and Nubia persisted and changed, while new civilizations emerged in Axum and the Niger River valley. South of the equator, the process of Bantu expansion created many new societies and identities.

READING THE MAP: What major pathways can you identify that linked regions of Africa south of the Sahara Desert with North Africa and Eurasia?

INTERPRETING THE MAP: Does this map support the idea that major cities in the Sahara Desert and sub-Saharan West Africa were located primarily along trade routes?

The city of Meroë and other urban centers housed a wide variety of economic specialties—merchants, weavers, potters, and masons, as well as servants, laborers, and slaves. The smelting of iron and the manufacture of iron tools and weapons were especially prominent industries. The rural areas surrounding Meroë were populated by peoples who practiced some combination of herding and farming and paid periodic tribute to the ruler. Rainfall-based agriculture was possible in Meroë, and consequently farmers were less dependent on irrigation. This meant that the rural population did not need to concentrate so heavily near the Nile as was the case in Egypt.

The wealth and military power of Meroë derived in part from extensive long-distance trading connections, to the north via the Nile and to the east and west by means of camel caravans. Its iron weapons and cotton cloth, as well as its access to gold, ivory, tortoiseshells, and ostrich feathers, gave Meroë a reputation for great riches in the world of northeastern Africa and the Mediterranean. The discovery in Meroë of a statue of the Roman emperor Augustus, probably seized during a raid on Roman Egypt, testifies to contact with the Mediterranean world. Culturally, Meroë seemed to move away from the heavy Egyptian influence of earlier times. A local lion god, Apedemek, grew more prominent than Egyptian deities such as Isis and Osiris, while the use of Egyptian-style writing declined as a new and still undeciphered Meroitic script took its place.

In the centuries following 100 C.E., the Kingdom of Meroë declined, in part because of deforestation caused by the need for wood to make charcoal for smelting iron. Furthermore, as Egyptian trade with the African interior switched from the Nile Valley route to the Red Sea, the resources available to Meroë's rulers diminished and the state weakened. The effective end of the Meroë phase of Nubian civilization came with the kingdom's conquest in the 340s C.E. by the neighboring and rising state of Axum. In the centuries that followed, three separate Nubian states emerged, and Coptic (Egyptian) Christianity penetrated the region. For almost a thousand years, Nubia was a Christian civilization, using Greek as a liturgical language and constructing churches in Coptic or Byzantine fashion. After 1300 or so, political division, Arab immigration, and the penetration of Islam eroded this Christian civilization, and Nubia became part of the growing world of Islam.

A Bracelet from Meroë This gold bracelet, dating to about 100 B.C.E., illustrates the skill of Meroë's craftsmen as well as the kingdom's reputation as one of the wealthiest states of the ancient world. The bracelet's depiction of a seated Hathor, a popular Egyptian goddess, shows the influence of Egyptian culture in Nubia. (Bracelet with image of Hathor, Nubian, Meroitic Period, 250–100 B.C. Findspot: Pyramid 8, Gebel Barkal, Nubia, Sudan. Gold and enamel. Overall: 1.8 x 5.7 x 5.1 cm. [¹¹/₁₆ x 2¼ x 2 in.]/ Photograph © 2018 Museum of Fine Arts, Boston/MFA Images/Harvard University–Boston Museum of Fine Arts Expedition, 20.333)

Axum: The Making of a Christian Kingdom

If Meroë represented the continuation of an old African/Nubian civilization, **Axum** marked the emergence of a new one. (For various accounts about or from Axum, see Working with Evidence: Axum and the World, page 260.) Axum lay in the Horn of Africa, in what is now Eritrea and northern Ethiopia (see Map 6.1). Its economic foundation was a highly productive agriculture that used a plow-based farming system, unlike most of the rest of Africa, which relied on the hoe or digging stick. Axum's agriculture generated substantial amounts of wheat, barley, millet, and teff, a highly nutritious grain unique to that region. By 50 C.E. or so, a substantial state had emerged, stimulated by its participation in the rapidly increasing Red Sea and Indian Ocean commerce, which was itself a product of growing Roman demand for Indian products, especially pepper. At Adulis, then the largest port on the East African coast, a wide range of merchants sought the products of the African interior — animal hides, rhinoceros horn, ivory, obsidian, tortoiseshells, and slaves. Taxes on this trade provided a major source of revenue for the Axumite state and the complex society that grew up within it. Thus the decline of Meroë and the rise of Axum were both connected to changing patterns of long-distance commerce.

The interior capital city, also known as Axum, was a center of monumental building and royal patronage for the arts. The most famous structures were huge stone obelisks, which most likely marked royal graves. Some of them were more than 100 feet tall and at the time were the largest structures in the world hewn from a single piece of rock. (See Source 6.2 in "Working with Evidence," page 261.) The language used at court, in the towns, and for commerce was Ge'ez, written in a script derived from South Arabia. The Axumite state exercised a measure of control over the mostly Agaw-speaking people of the country through a loose administrative structure focusing on the collection of tribute payments. To the Romans, Axum was the third major empire within the world they knew, following their own and the Persian Empire.

Through its connections to Red Sea trade and the Roman world, particularly Egypt, Axum was introduced to Christianity in the fourth century C.E. Its monarch at the time, King Ezana, adopted the new religion about the same time as Constantine did in the Roman Empire. Early in his reign, the kingdom's coins featured images of gods derived from southern Arabia, while by the end, they were inscribed with the Christian cross. Supported by royal authority, Christianity took root in Axum, linking that kingdom religiously to Egypt, where a distinctive Christian Church known as Coptic was already well established. Although Egypt later became largely Islamic, reducing its Christian community to a small minority, Christianity maintained a dominant position in the mountainous terrain of highland Ethiopia and in the early twenty-first century still represents the faith of perhaps 60 percent of the country's population.

During the fourth through the sixth centuries C.E., Axum mounted a campaign of imperial expansion that took its forces into the Kingdom of Meroë and across the Red Sea into Yemen in South Arabia. By 571, the traditional date for the birth of Muhammad, an Axumite army, including a number of African war elephants, had reached the gates of Mecca, but it was a fairly short-lived imperial venture.

The next several centuries were ones of decline for the Axumite state, owing partly to environmental changes, such as soil exhaustion, erosion, and deforestation, brought about by intensive farming. Equally important was the rise of Islam, which altered trade routes and diminished the revenue available to the Axumite state. Its last coins were struck in the early seventh century. When the state revived several centuries later, it was centered farther south on the Ethiopian plateau. In this new location, there emerged the Christian Church and the state that present-day Ethiopia has inherited, but the link to ancient Axum was long remembered and revered.

With their long-distance trading connections, urban centers, centralized states, complex societies, monumental architecture, written languages, and imperial ambitions, both Meroë and Axum paralleled on a smaller scale the major features of the second-wave civilizations of Eurasia. Furthermore, both were in direct contact with the world of Mediterranean civilizations. Across the continent in West Africa, a rather different civilization took shape.

Along the Niger River: Cities without States

The middle stretches of the Niger River in West Africa witnessed the emergence of a remarkable urbanization (see Map 6.1, page 232). A prolonged dry period during the five centuries after 500 B.C.E. brought growing numbers of people from the southern Sahara into the fertile floodplain of the middle Niger in search of more reliable access to water. Accompanying them were their domesticated cattle, sheep, and goats; their agricultural skills; and their ironworking technology. Over many centuries (roughly 300 B.C.E.–900 C.E.), the peoples of this region created a distinctive city-based civilization. The most fully studied of the urban clusters that grew up along the middle Niger was the city of Jenne-jeno (jihn-AY jihn-OH), which at its high point probably housed more than 40,000 people.

Among the most distinctive features of the **Niger Valley civilization** was the apparent absence of a corresponding state structure. Unlike the cities of Egypt, China, the Roman Empire, or Axum, these middle Niger urban centers were not

The Legacy of Axumite Christianity While the Axumite kingdom faded away, its assimilation of Christianity proved an enduring legacy for Ethiopia, as illustrated by this late-fourteenth- or early-fifteenth-century depiction of the ascension of Jesus, with his disciples pointing upwards. (The Metropolitan Museum of Art, New York, NY, USA/Rogers Fund, 1998 [1998.66]/Image copyright © The Metropolitan Museum of Art/Image source: Art Resource, NY)

Guided Reading Question

■ **DESCRIPTION**
How does the experience of the Niger Valley challenge conventional notions of "civilization"?

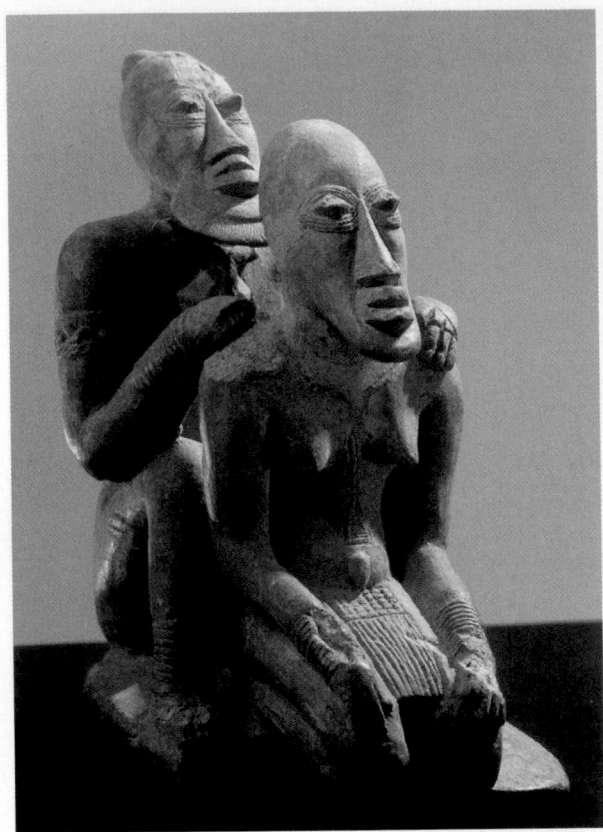

Terra-Cotta Statue from Jenne-jeno The artistic tradition of Niger Valley civilization includes a number of terra-cotta couples, reflecting perhaps the emphasis on the separate but complementary roles of men and women in much of African thought. This statue and others like it date to sometime after the twelfth century and may express the resistance of an indigenous tradition to the growing penetration of Islam. (Entwistle Gallery, London, UK/Werner Forman/Art Resource, NY)

encompassed within some larger imperial system. Nor were they like the city-states of ancient Mesopotamia, in which each city had its own centralized political structure, embodied in a monarch and his accompanying bureaucracy. According to a leading historian of the region, they were "cities without citadels," complex urban centers that apparently operated without the coercive authority of a state, for archeologists have found in their remains few signs of despotic power, widespread warfare, or deep social inequalities.[2] In this respect, these urban centers resemble the early cities of Norte Chico or the Indus Valley civilization, where likewise little archeological evidence of centralized state structures has been found.

In place of such hierarchical organization, Jenne-jeno and other cities of the region emerged as clusters of economically specialized settlements surrounding a larger central town. The earliest and most prestigious of these specialized occupations was iron smithing. Working with fire and earth (ore) to produce this highly useful metal, the smiths of the Niger Valley were both feared and revered. Archeologist Roderick McIntosh, a leading figure in the excavation of Jenne-jeno, argued that "their knowledge of the transforming arts—earth to metal, insubstantial fire to the mass of iron—was the key to a secret, occult realm of immense power and immense danger."[3]

Other specializations followed. Villages of cotton weavers, potters, leather workers, and griots (praise-singers who preserved and recited the oral traditions of their societies) grew up around the central towns. Gradually these urban artisan communities became occupational castes, whose members passed their jobs and skills to their children and could marry only within their own group. In the surrounding rural areas, as in all urban-based civilizations, farmers tilled the soil and raised their animals, but specialization also occurred in food production as various ethnic groups focused on fishing, rice cultivation, or some other agricultural pursuit. At least for a time, these middle Niger cities represented an African alternative to an oppressive state, which in many parts of the world accompanied an increasingly complex urban economy and society. A series of distinct and specialized economic groups shared authority and voluntarily used the services of one another, while maintaining their own identities through physical separation.

Accompanying this unique urbanization, and no doubt stimulating it, was a growing network of indigenous West African commerce. The middle Niger floodplain supported a rich agriculture and contained clay for pottery, but it lacked stone, iron ore, salt, and fuel. This scarcity of resources was the basis for a long-distance commerce that operated by boat along the Niger River and overland by donkey to the north and south. Jenne-jeno itself was an important transshipment point in this commerce, in which goods were transferred from boat to donkey or vice versa. By the 500s C.E., there is evidence of an even wider commerce, and at least indirect contact, from Mauritania in the west to present-day Mali and Burkina Faso in the east.

In the second millennium C.E., new historical patterns developed in West Africa (see "Gold, Salt, and Slaves" in Chapter 7). A number of large-scale states or empires emerged in the region—Ghana, Mali, and Songhay, among the most well known. At least partially responsible for this development was the flourishing of a camel-borne trans-Saharan commerce, previously but a trickle across the great desert. As West Africa became more firmly connected to North Africa and the Mediterranean, Islam penetrated the region, marking a gradual but major cultural transformation. All of this awaited West Africa in later centuries, submerging, but not completely eliminating, the decentralized city life of the Niger Valley.

Civilizations of Mesoamerica

Westward across the Atlantic Ocean lay an altogether separate world, later known as the Americas, which housed two major centers of civilization—Mesoamerica and the Andes. Together, they were home to the vast majority of the population of the Americas. But unlike the Egyptians and Mesopotamians or the Persians and the Greeks, these civilizations had little if any direct contact with each other. They shared, however, a rugged mountainous terrain with an enormous range of microclimates as well as great ecological and biological diversity. Arid coastal environments, steamy lowland rain forests, cold and windy highland plateaus cut by numerous mountains and valleys—all of this was often encompassed in a relatively small area. Such conditions contributed to substantial linguistic and ethnic diversity and to the development of many distinct and competing cities, chiefdoms, and states. It also meant that states, and sometimes individual families, sought "**vertical integration**," an effort to control a variety of ecological zones where a number of different crops and animals could flourish. The remarkable achievements of these early American civilizations occurred without the many large domesticated animals or ironworking technologies that were so important throughout the Eastern Hemisphere. In the Andes, an important exception to this generalization involved the domestication of the llama and alpaca, which offered food, fiber, and transport for the civilizations of that region and in a few places provided for a time the basis for largely pastoral communities.

Mesoamerican civilizations stretched from central Mexico to northern Central America. Despite its environmental and ethnic diversity, Mesoamerica was also a distinct region, bound together by elements of a common culture. Its many peoples shared an intensive agricultural technology devoted to raising maize, beans, chili peppers, and squash and based their economies on market exchange. They practiced religions featuring a similar pantheon of male and female deities, understood time as a cosmic cycle

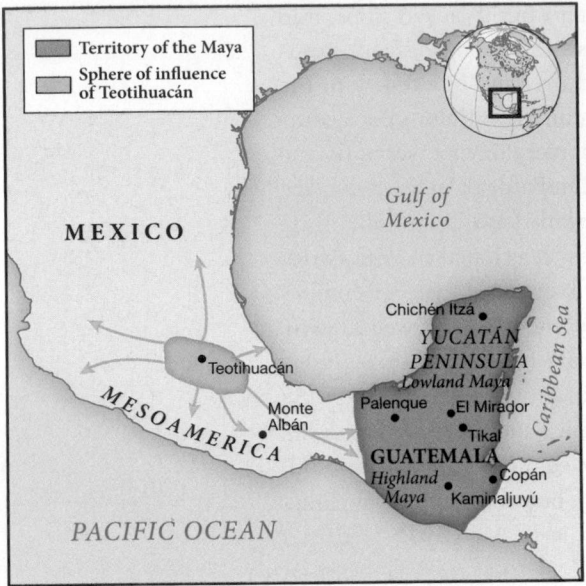

Map 6.2 Civilizations of Mesoamerica

During the second-wave era, Maya civilization and the large city of Teotihuacán represented the most prominent features of Mesoamerican civilization.

Guided Reading Question

■ **COMPARISON**

With what Eurasian civilizations might the Maya be compared?

of creation and destruction, practiced human sacrifice, and constructed monumental ceremonial centers. Furthermore, they employed a common ritual calendar of 260 days and hieroglyphic writing. During the first millennium B.C.E., the various small states and chiefdoms of the region, particularly the Olmec, exchanged various luxury goods used to display social status and for ritual purposes—jade, obsidian tools, ceramic pottery, shell ornaments, stingray spines, and turtle shells. As a result, aspects of Olmec culture, such as artistic styles, temple pyramids, the calendar system, and rituals involving human sacrifice, spread widely throughout Mesoamerica and influenced many of the civilizations that followed.

The Maya: Writing and Warfare

Among Mesoamerican civilizations, none has attracted more attention than that of the Maya. Scholars have traced the beginnings of the Maya people to ceremonial centers constructed as early as 2000 B.C.E. in present-day Guatemala and the Yucatán region of Mexico (see Map 6.2). During the first millennium B.C.E., a number of substantial urban centers with concentrated populations and monumental architecture had emerged in the region. But it was during a later phase of **Maya civilization**, between 250 and 900 C.E., that their most well-known cultural achievements emerged. Intellectuals, probably priests, developed a mathematical system that included the concept of zero and place notation and was capable of complex calculations. They combined this mathematical ability with careful observation of the night skies to plot the cycles of planets, to predict eclipses of the sun and the moon, to construct elaborate calendars, and to calculate accurately the length of the solar year. The distinctive art of the Maya elite was likewise impressive to later observers.

Accompanying these intellectual and artistic achievements was the creation of the most elaborate writing system in the Americas, which used both pictographs and phonetic or syllabic elements. Carved on stone and written on bark paper or deerskin books, Mayan writing recorded historical events, masses of astronomical data, and religious or mythological texts. Temples, pyramids, palaces, and public plazas abounded, graced with painted murals and endless stone carving.

The economic foundations for these cultural achievements were embedded in an "almost totally engineered landscape."[4] The Maya drained swamps, terraced hillsides, flattened ridgetops, and constructed an elaborate water-management system. Much of this underpinned a flourishing agriculture, which supported a very rapidly growing and dense population by 750 C.E. This agriculture sustained substantial elite classes of nobles, priests, merchants, architects, and sculptors, as well as specialized artisans producing pottery, tools, and cotton textiles. And it was sufficiently productive to free a large labor force for work on the many public structures that continue to amaze contemporary visitors.

Early scholars viewed Maya civilization somewhat romantically as a peaceful society led by gentle stargazing priest-kings devoted to temple building and intellectual pursuits. This view of Maya civilization changed as scholars realized that its many achievements took place within a highly fragmented political system of city-states, local lords, and regional kingdoms with no central authority, with frequent warfare, and with the extensive capture and sacrifice of prisoners. The larger political units of Maya civilization were densely populated urban and ceremonial centers, ruled by powerful kings and on a few occasions queens. They were divine rulers or "state shamans" able to mediate between humankind and the supernatural.

One of these cities, Tikal (tee-KAHL), contained perhaps 50,000 people, with another 50,000 or so in the surrounding countryside, by 750 C.E. (See this chapter's opening photo, of a temple from Tikal.) Some of these city-states had imperial ambitions, but none succeeded in creating a unified Maya empire. Various centers of Maya civilization rose and fell; fluctuating alliances among them alternated with periods of sporadic warfare; ruling families intermarried; the elite classes sought luxury goods from far away to bolster their authority and status. In its political dimensions, Maya civilization more closely resembled the competing city-states of ancient Mesopotamia or classical Greece than the imperial structures of Rome, Persia, or China.

But large parts of that imposing civilization collapsed with a completeness and finality rare in world history. Clearly, this was not a single or uniform phenomenon, as flourishing centers of Maya civilization persisted in the northern Yucatán, and many Maya survived to fight the Spanish in the sixteenth century. But in the southern regions where the collapse was most complete, its outcomes were devastating. In less than a century following the onset of a long-term drought in 840, the population of the low-lying southern heartland of the Maya dropped by 85 percent or more as famine, epidemics, and fratricidal warfare reaped a horrific toll. It was a catastrophe from which there was no recovery. Elements of Maya culture survived in scattered settlements, but the great cities were deserted, and large-scale construction and artistic work ceased. The last date inscribed in stone corresponds to 909–910 C.E. As a complex civilization, the Maya had passed into history.

Explaining this remarkable demise has long kept scholars guessing, with recent accounts focusing on ecological and political factors. Rapid population growth after 600 C.E. pushed total Maya numbers to perhaps 5 million or more and soon outstripped available resources, resulting in deforestation and the erosion of hillsides. Under such conditions, climate change in the form of prolonged droughts in the 800s may well have placed unbearable pressures on Maya society. Political disunity and endemic rivalries, long a prominent feature of Maya civilization, prevented a coordinated and effective response to the emerging catastrophe. Warfare in fact became more frequent as competition for increasingly scarce land for cultivation became sharper. Rulers dependent on ritual splendor for their legitimacy competed to mount ever more elaborate temples, palaces, and pageants, requiring more labor and taxes from their subjects and tribute from their enemies. Whatever the precise explanation, the Maya collapse, like that of the Romans and others, illustrates the fragility of civilizations, whether they are embodied in large empires or organized in a more decentralized fashion.

Teotihuacán: The Americas' Greatest City

At roughly the same time as the Maya flourished in the southern regions of Meso-america, the giant city of **Teotihuacán** (tay-uh-tee-wah-KAHN) was also emerging further north in the Valley of Mexico, where its control over important sources of green obsidian made it an increasingly important trading power in the region. Begun around 150 B.C.E. and apparently built to a plan rather than evolving haphazardly, the city by 550 C.E. had a population estimated at between 125,000 and 150,000. It was by far the largest urban complex in the Americas at the time and one of the six largest in the world. Physically, the city was enormously impressive, replete with broad avenues, spacious plazas, huge marketplaces, temples, palaces, apartment complexes, slums, waterways, reservoirs, drainage systems, and colorful murals. Along the main north/south boulevard, now known as the Avenue of the Dead, were the grand homes of the elite, the headquarters of state authorities, many temples, and two giant pyramids. At the Temple of the Feathered Serpent, archeologists have found the remains of some 200 people, their hands and arms tied behind them; they were the apparently unwilling sacrificial victims meant to accompany the high-ranking persons buried there into the afterlife.

Teotihuacán Taken from the summit of the Pyramid of the Moon, this photograph looks down the famous Avenue of the Dead to the Pyramid of the Sun in the upper left. (Alison Wright/Science Source)

Off the main avenues of Teotihuacán in a grid-like pattern of streets lay thousands of residential apartment compounds, home to the city's commoners. In these compounds, perhaps in groups of related families or lineages, lived many of the farmers who tilled the lands outside the city, as well as thousands of Maya specialists — masons, leather workers, potters, construction laborers, merchants, and civil servants. Here also lived skilled makers of obsidian blades, who plied their trade in hundreds of separate workshops, generating products that were in great demand throughout Mesoamerica. At least two small sections of the city were reserved exclusively for foreigners.

Guided Reading Questions

■ **CONNECTION**
In what ways did Teotihuacán shape the history of Mesoamerica?

Buildings, both public and private, were decorated with mural paintings, sculptures, and carvings. Many of these works of art display abstract geometric and stylized images. Others depict gods and goddesses, arrayed in various forms — feathered serpents, starfish, jaguars, flowers, and warriors. One set of murals shows happy people cavorting in a paradise of irrigated fields, playing games, singing, and chasing butterflies, which were thought to represent the souls of the dead. Another, however, portrays dancing warriors carrying elaborate curved knives, to which were attached bleeding human hearts.

The art of Teotihuacán, unlike that of the Maya, has revealed few images of self-glorifying rulers or individuals. Nor did the city have a tradition of written public inscriptions as the Maya did, although a number of glyphs or characters indicate at least a limited form of writing. Nonetheless, Teotihuacán cast a huge shadow over Mesoamerica, particularly from 300 to 600 c.e. A core region of perhaps 10,000 square miles was administered directly from the city itself, while tribute was no doubt exacted from other areas within its broader sphere of influence. At a greater distance, the power of Teotihuacán's armies gave it a presence in the Maya heartland more than 600 miles to the east. At least one Maya city, Kaminaljuyú in the southern highlands, was completely taken over by the Teotihuacán military and organized as a colony. In the year 378 c.e., agents of Teotihuacán apparently engineered a coup in the lowland Maya city of Tikal that placed a collaborator on the throne and turned the city for a time into an ally or a satellite. Elsewhere — in the Zapotec capital of Monte Albán, for example — murals show unarmed persons from Teotihuacán engaged in what seem to be more equal diplomatic relationships.

At least some of this political and military activity was no doubt designed to obtain, either by trade or by tribute, valued commodities from afar — food products, cacao beans, tropical bird feathers, honey, salt, and medicinal herbs. The presence in Teotihuacán of foreigners, perhaps merchants, from the Gulf Coast and Maya lowlands, as well as much pottery from those regions, provides further evidence of long-distance trade. Moreover, the sheer size and prestige of Teotihuacán surely persuaded many, all across Mesoamerica, to imitate the architectural and artistic styles of the city. Thus, according to a leading scholar, "Teotihuacán meant something of surpassing importance far beyond its core area."[5] Almost a thousand years after its still-mysterious collapse around 650 c.e., the great metropolis was dubbed Teotihuacán, the "city of the gods," by the peoples of the Aztec Empire.

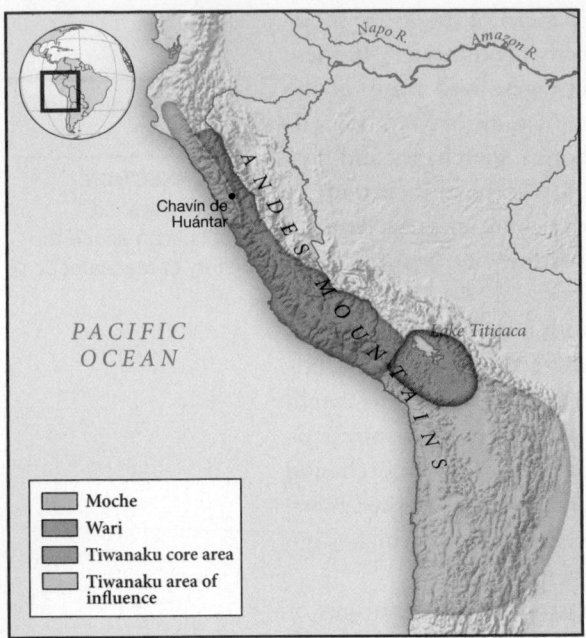

Map 6.3 Civilizations of the Andes

No single civilization dominated the Andes region during the second-wave era. Rather, a number of religious movements, states, and empires rose and fell before the entire region was encompassed by the Inca Empire in the fifteenth century.

Civilizations of the Andes

Yet another and quite separate center of civilization in the Americas lay in the dramatic landscape of the Andes. Bleak deserts along the coast supported human habitation only because they were cut by dozens of rivers flowing down from the mountains, offering the possibility of irrigation and cultivation. The offshore waters of the Pacific Ocean also provided an enormously rich marine environment with an endless supply of seabirds and fish. The Andes themselves, a towering mountain chain with many highland valleys, afforded numerous distinct ecological niches, depending on altitude. Andean societies generally sought access to the resources of these various environments through colonization, conquest, or trade—seafood from the coastal regions; maize and cotton from lower-altitude valleys; potatoes, quinoa, and pastureland for their llamas in the high plains; tropical fruits and coca leaves from the moist eastern slope of the Andes and the arid western slope as well (see Map 6.3).

The most well known of the civilizations to take shape in this environment was that of the Incas, which encompassed practically the entire region, some 2,500 miles in length, in the fifteenth century. Yet the Incas represented only the most recent and the largest in a long history of civilizations in the area. The coastal region of central Peru had in fact generated one of the world's First Civilizations, known as Norte Chico, dating back to around 3000 B.C.E. (see "Introducing the First Civilizations" in Chapter 2). During the two millennia between roughly 1000 B.C.E. and 1000 C.E., a number of Andean civilizations rose and passed away. Because none of them had developed writing, historians are largely dependent on archeology for an understanding of these civilizations.

Chavín: A Pan-Andean Religious Movement

In both the coastal and highland regions of Peru, archeologists have uncovered numerous local ceremonial centers or temple complexes, dating between 2000 and 1000 B.C.E. Then around 900 B.C.E., one such center, situated in the Andean highlands at a village called **Chavín** (cha-BEEN) de Huántar, became the focus of a religious movement that soon swept through both coastal and highland Peru, aided by its strategic location on trade routes to both the coastal region to the west and the Amazon rain forest to the east.

By perhaps 750 B.C.E., this small center had become a town of 2,000 to 3,000 people, with clear distinctions between an elite class, who lived in stone houses,

Guided Reading Question

••••••••••••••••••••••••••••

■ **CONNECTION**

What kind of influence did Chavín exert in the Andes region?

and ordinary people, with adobe dwellings. An elaborate temple complex included numerous galleries, hidden passageways, staircases, ventilation shafts, drainage canals, and distinctive carvings. Chavín artwork suggests influences from both the desert coastal region and the rain forests. Major deities were represented as jaguars, crocodiles, and snakes, all of them native to the Amazon basin. Shamans or priests likely made use of the San Pedro cactus, native to the Andes Mountains, employing its hallucinogenic properties to penetrate the supernatural world. Some of the fantastic artwork of this civilization—its jaguar-human images, for example—may well reflect the visions of these religious leaders.

Over the next several centuries, this blended religious movement proved attractive across much of Peru and beyond, as Chavín-style temple architecture, sculpture, pottery, religious images, and painted textiles were widely imitated within the region. Chavín itself became a pilgrimage site and perhaps a training center for initiates. Although some evidence suggests violence and warfare, no Chavín "empire" emerged. Instead, a widespread religious cult, erected on the back of a trading network, provided for the first time and for several centuries a measure of economic and cultural integration to much of the Peruvian Andes.

Moche: A Civilization of the Coast

By 200 B.C.E., the pan-Andes Chavín cult had faded, replaced by a number of regional civilizations. Among them, **Moche** (MOH-chee) civilization clearly stands out. Dominating a 250-mile stretch of Peru's northern coast and incorporating thirteen river valleys, the Moche people flourished between about 100 and 800 C.E. Their economy was rooted in a complex irrigation system, requiring constant maintenance, that funneled runoff from the Andes into fields of maize, beans, squash, and acres of cotton, all fertilized by rich bird droppings called guano. Moche fishermen also harvested millions of anchovies from the bountiful Pacific.

Politically, Moche was governed by warrior-priests, some of whom lived atop huge pyramids, the largest of which was constructed from 143 million sun-dried bricks. There shaman-rulers, often under the influence of hallucinogenic drugs, conducted ancient rituals that mediated between the world of humankind and that of the gods. They also presided over the ritual sacrifice of human victims, drawn from their many prisoners of war, which became central to the politico-religious life of the Moche. Images on Moche pottery show a ruler attired in a magnificent feather headdress and seated on a pyramid, while a parade of naked prisoners marches past him. Other scenes of decapitation and dismemberment indicate the fate that awaited those destined for sacrifice. For these rulers, the Moche world was apparently one of war, ceremony, and diplomacy.

The immense wealth of this warrior-priest elite and the exquisite artistry of Moche craftsmen are reflected in the elaborate burials accorded the rulers. (See Zooming In: The Lord of Sipan and the Lady of Cao, page 244.) In the absence of written texts, these artistic products are the most accessible aspect of Moche life, and much of what scholars know about the Moche world derives from the superb

Guided Reading Questions

■ **DESCRIPTION**
What features of Moche life characterize it as a civilization?

The Lord of Sipan and the Lady of Cao

In the mid- to late third century C.E., a prominent man of Moche society died in what is now Peru. We do not know his name, for a written language was not a part of Moche life. But since archeologists uncovered his final resting place in 1987, scholars have learned a great deal about him and about his culture. He was five feet four inches in height, relatively tall for his time and place, and was somewhere around forty years of age. The condition of his teeth and bones suggests that he ate a well-balanced diet and probably performed little physical labor during his life. The cause of his death is unclear, but scholars think that he may well have died of an epidemic disease during a severe famine.

The Moche ruler in the center of the grave, dating to about 250 C.E., was about forty years old when he died and, at five feet four inches, was quite tall for the time.

Much more obvious is his high social status, for which he has been dubbed the Lord of Sipan, named for the town in Peru where the archeological site is located. Laid to rest in the official and ceremonial finery he likely donned in life, the Lord of Sipan was bedecked in gold. He wore a huge gold crescent headdress, a gold face mask, two necklaces with gold and silver beads in the shape of oversized peanuts, and gold earspools exquisitely inlaid with turquoise; he had a gold warrior's shield on his back and a golden scepter in his hand. Hundreds of pots contained food and drink, while 451 ceremonial objects also accompanied the burial. Guarding the entrance to his tomb was the skeleton of a man with his feet cut off, presumably to prevent him from leaving his post. Buried with the Lord of Sipan were six other individuals: a young child (perhaps his own?); two robust men (perhaps ritually sacrificed warriors?); and three young women (perhaps his wives?). A dog, claimed by local traditions to guide the dead into the afterworld, and two llamas also attended the lord in death. In its archeological significance and its material splendor, this burial site (see the photo above) has been compared to that of Tutankhamen, the young pharaoh of Egypt.

Clearly, the Lord of Sipan was a very high-ranking member of Moche's highly stratified society. Such lords received food from their subjects, some of which they passed on to

photo: © Karl Heinz Raach/LAIF/Redux

skill of its craftspeople, such as metalworkers, potters, weavers, and painters. Face masks, figures of animals, small earrings, and other jewelry items, many plated in gold, display amazing technical abilities and a striking artistic sensibility. Decorating Moche ceramic pottery are naturalistic portraits of noble lords and rulers and images from the life of common people, including the blind and the sick. Battle scenes show warriors confronting their enemies with raised clubs. Erotic encounters between men and women and gods making love to humans likewise represent common themes, as do grotesque images of the many Moche gods and goddesses. Much of this, of course, reflects the culture of the Moche elite. We know much less about the daily life of the farmers, fishermen, weavers, traders, construction workers, and servants whose labor made that elite culture possible.

These cultural achievements, however, rested on fragile environmental foundations, for the region was subject to drought, earthquakes, and occasional torrential lesser lords, and they had access to the rare and prestigious objects created for them by Moche's immensely skillful artisans. Various objects in the tomb correspond closely to images on Moche pottery and temple walls of prisoners being slaughtered and a warrior-priest collecting and drinking their blood. Perhaps the Lord of Sipan was one such warrior-priest.

Object found in the tomb of the Lady of Cao.

At the time the Lord of Sipan came to light, it was widely assumed that the ruling elite of Moche society was all male. Then in 2005, another remarkable burial site was uncovered, containing the intact body of a young woman who had died in childbirth around 450 C.E. while still in her twenties. Now known as the Lady of Cao, she had been carefully wrapped in hundreds of yards of cotton strips, wore long braided hair, and bore numerous tattoos of snakes, crabs, and spiders on her arms and legs. Accompanying her was a huge collection of elaborate grave goods indicating great wealth: fifteen elaborate necklaces, gold sewing needles, weaving tools, beautiful jewelry, and a vessel depicting a nursing mother. But beyond these feminine objects were more surprising signs of real power. Her nose rings featured designs of men wielding war clubs and heads being pecked by condors. Two copper and wood staffs, symbols of authority, were entombed with her, as well as many weapons,

including two massive war clubs and twenty-three spear throwers. "The war clubs are clear symbols not only of combat but of power," declared one member of the archeological team.[6]

So was the Lady of Cao a local ruler in her own right or simply a woman from an elite family? The case for her political and religious role has been strengthened by the subsequent discovery of eight more burials of prominent Moche women. One of them contained a tall silver goblet, very similar to those depicted in Moche artistic scenes of ritual sacrifice and the consumption of blood. Some scholars suggest that Moche society was highly decentralized, with men in positions of authority in some communities and women in others. Thus the Lord of Sipan and the Lady of Cao, though living several hundred years apart, may have played equivalent roles in Moche society.

QUESTIONS

What do we learn about Moche society from these two figures? If you could interview these individuals, what would you want to ask them? What might be inferred from these burials about Moche understandings of the afterlife?

photo: © FFF/ZUMAPRESS.com

rains associated with El Niño episodes (dramatic changes in weather patterns caused by periodic warming of Pacific Ocean currents). During the sixth century C.E., some combination of these forces caused extended ecological disruption, which seriously undermined Moche civilization. In these circumstances, the Moche were vulnerable to aggressive neighbors and possibly to internal social tensions as well. By the end of the eighth century C.E., that civilization had passed into history.

Wari and Tiwanaku: Empires of the Interior

Far more than the Moche and other coastal civilizations, the interior empires of **Wari** (wah-ree) and **Tiwanaku** provided a measure of political integration and cultural commonality for the entire Andean region. Growing out of ancient settlements, these two states flourished between 400 and 1000 C.E., Wari in the northern highlands and Tiwanaku to the south. Both were centered in large urban capitals, marked by monumental architecture and stratified populations numbering in the tens of thousands. Both governments collected surplus food in warehouses as an insurance against times of drought and famine.

Guided Reading Question
....
■ DESCRIPTION
What was the significance of Wari and Tiwanaku in the history of Andean civilization?

But neither state controlled a continuous band of territory. Adapting to their vertical environment, both empires established colonies at lower elevations on the eastern and western slopes of the Andes as well as throughout the highlands, seeking access to resources such as seafood, maize, chili peppers, cocoa, hallucinogenic plants, obsidian, and feathers from tropical birds. Caravans of llamas linked distant centers, allowing the exchange and redistribution of goods, while the religious prestige and ceremonial power of the capital city provided further integration. Cultural influences from the center, such as styles of pottery and textiles, spread well beyond the regions of direct political control. Similar religious symbols and images prevailed in both places, including the ancient Andean Staff God, a deity portrayed with a staff in each hand. Versions of this image have been found in Norte Chico, Chavín, and Moche sites as well, suggesting a long-term continuity in the religious culture of the Andean region.

But Wari and Tiwanaku were hardly carbon copies of each other. Wari's agriculture employed an elaborate system of hillside terracing and irrigation, using snowmelt from the Andes. Tiwanaku's highly productive farming economy, by contrast, utilized a "raised field" system in which artificially elevated planting surfaces in swampy areas were separated by small irrigation canals. Tiwanaku, furthermore, has become famous for its elaborately fitted stone walls and buildings, while Wari's tombs and temples were built of fieldstone set in mud mortar and covered with smooth plaster. Cities in the Wari region seemed built to a common plan and linked to the capital by a network of highways, which suggests a political system more tightly controlled from the center than in Tiwanaku.[7]

Despite these differences and a 300-mile common border, little overt conflict or warfare occurred between Wari and Tiwanaku. In areas where the two peoples lived near one another, they apparently did not mingle much. They each spoke their own language, wore different clothing, furnished their homes with distinctive goods, and looked to their respective capital cities for inspiration.

In the several centuries following 1000 C.E., both civilizations collapsed, their impressive cities permanently abandoned. What followed was a series of smaller kingdoms, one of which evolved into the Inca Empire that gave to Andean civilization a final and spectacular expression before all of the Americas was swallowed up in European empires from across the sea. The Incas themselves clearly drew on the legacy of Wari and Tiwanaku, adopting aspects of their imperial models and systems of statecraft, building on the Wari highway system, and utilizing similar styles of dress and artistic expression. Such was the prestige of Tiwanaku centuries after its collapse that the Incas claimed it as their place of origin.

PRACTICING HISTORICAL THINKING

What features common to all civilizations can you identify in the civilizations of Africa and the Americas? What distinguishing features give each of them a distinctive identity?

Alternatives to Civilization

Since historians are frequently preoccupied with civilizations, it is useful to remind ourselves that other ways of organizing human communities evolved alongside civilizations, and they too made history. Two such regions were Africa south of the equator and North America. They shared environments that featured plenty of land and relatively few people compared to the greater population densities and pressure on the land that characterized many civilizations. And a third region was Pacific Oceania, where small numbers of people navigated a sea covering about one-third of the world's surface, settled the mostly tiny specks of land that rose above the surface of that ocean, and created there a remarkable range of human communities.

Bantu Africa: Cultural Encounters and Social Variation

In the vast region of Africa south of the equator, the most significant development during the second-wave era involved the accelerating movement of Bantu-speaking peoples, cultures, and technologies into the enormous subcontinent. That process had begun many centuries earlier, probably around 3000 B.C.E., from a homeland region in what are now southeastern Nigeria and the Cameroons. Over the long run, some 400 distinct but closely related languages emerged, known collectively as Bantu. By the first century C.E., agricultural peoples speaking Bantu languages and now bearing an ironworking technology had largely occupied the forest regions of equatorial Africa, and at least a few of them had probably reached the East African coast. In the several centuries that followed, they established themselves quite rapidly in most of eastern and southern Africa (see Map 6.1, page 232), introducing immense economic and cultural changes to a huge region of the continent.

Bantu migration was not a conquest or invasion such as that of Alexander the Great; nor was it a massive and self-conscious migration like that of Europeans to the Americas in more recent times. Rather, it was a slow movement of peoples, perhaps a few extended families at a time. And sometimes Bantu expansion was less a movement of people than the diffusion of new patterns of living involving language, root crops, grains, sheep and cattle, pottery styles, and ironworking technology. In this way, already established communities could "become Bantu" without the wholesale migration of outsiders. Taken as a whole, these processes brought to Africa south of the equator a measure of cultural and linguistic commonality, marking it as a distinct region of the continent.

That movement of individuals and cultural patterns also generated numerous interactions among culturally distinct peoples. Among those encounters, none was more significant than that between the agricultural Bantu and the gathering and hunting peoples who earlier occupied this region of Africa. Their interaction was part of a long-term global phenomenon in which farmers largely replaced foragers as the dominant people on the planet.

Guided Reading
Question
....

■ **CONNECTION**
In what ways did the pro-
cess of Bantu expansion
stimulate cross-cultural
interaction?

In these encounters, Bantu-speaking farmers had various advantages. One was numerical, as agriculture generated a more productive economy and larger populations. A second advantage was a greater immunity to animal-borne disease, acquired by prolonged exposure to both parasitic and infectious illnesses common to farming and herding societies. Foraging peoples lacked that immunity, and many quickly succumbed when they encountered the agricultural newcomers. A third advantage was iron, so useful for tools and weapons when interacting with peoples still operating with stone-age technology. Thus gathering and hunting peoples were displaced, absorbed, or largely eliminated in most parts of Africa south of the equator—but not everywhere.

In the rain forest region of Central Africa, the foraging Batwa (Pygmy) people, at least some of them, became "forest specialists" who produced honey, wild game, elephant products, animal skins, and medicinal barks and plants, all of which entered regional trading networks in exchange for the agricultural products of their Bantu neighbors. Some also adopted Bantu languages, thus becoming Bantu linguistically, while maintaining a gathering and hunting lifestyle and a separate identity.

Bantu-speaking peoples themselves also changed as they encountered different environments and peoples. In the drier climate of East Africa, the yam-based agriculture of the West African Bantu homeland was unable to support their growing numbers, so Bantu farmers increasingly adopted grains as well as domesticated sheep and cattle from the already established people of the region. They also enriched their agriculture by acquiring a variety of food crops from Southeast Asia—coconuts, sugarcane, and especially bananas—which were brought to East Africa by Indonesian Malay sailors and immigrants early in the first millennium C.E. This agricultural package and its associated ironworking technology then spread throughout the vast area of eastern and southern Africa, probably reaching present-day South Africa by 400 C.E. Some newly "Bantuized" areas incorporated musical traditions, linguistic patterns, and kinship systems derived from the earlier inhabitants. From these interactions a common set of cultural and social practices diffused widely across Bantu Africa. One prominent historian described these practices:

> [They encompassed] in religion, the centrality of ancestor observances; in
> philosophy, the problem of evil understood as the consequence of individual
> malice or of the failure to honor one's ancestors; in music, an emphasis on
> polyrhythmic performance with drums as the key instrument; in dance, a new
> form of expression in which a variety of prescribed body movements took
> preference over footwork; and in agriculture, the pre-eminence of women as
> the workers and innovators.[8]

All of this became part of the common culture of Bantu-speaking Africa.

As Bantu-derived patterns of living became established in Africa south of the equator during the thousand or so years between 500 and 1500 C.E., a wide variety of quite distinct societies and cultures took shape. Some societies—in present-day Kenya, for example—organized themselves without any formal political specialists at all. Instead, they made decisions, resolved conflicts, and maintained order by using kinship structures or lineage principles supplemented by age grades, which joined men of a particular generation together across various lineages. Elsewhere, lineage heads who acquired a measure of personal wealth, or who proved skillful at mediating between the local spirits and the people, might evolve into chiefs with a modest political authority. In several areas, such as the region around Lake Victoria or present-day Zimbabwe, larger and more substantial kingdoms evolved. Along the East African coast after 1000 C.E., dozens of rival city-states linked the African interior with the commerce of the Indian Ocean basin (see "Sea Roads as a Catalyst for Change," in Chapter 7).

Many societies in the Bantu-speaking world developed gender systems that were markedly less patriarchal than those of established urban-based civilizations. Male ironworkers in the Congo River basin, for example, sought to appropriate the power and prestige of female reproductive capacity by decorating their furnaces with clay breasts and speaking of their bellows as impregnating the furnaces. Among the Luba people of Central Africa, male rulers operated in alliance with powerful women, partic- ularly spirit mediums, who were thought to contain the spirit of the king. Only a woman's body was considered sufficiently strong to acquire this potent and dangerous presence. Luba art represented female ancestors as "keep- ers of secret royal knowledge." And across a wide area of south central Africa, a system of "gender parallelism" asso- ciated female roles with village life (child care, farming, food preparation, making pots, baskets, and mats), while masculine identity revolved around hunting and forest life (fishing, trapping, collecting building materials and medici- nal plants). It was a complementary or "separate but equal" definition of gender roles.[9]

In terms of religion, Bantu practice in general placed less emphasis on a High or Creator God, who was viewed as remote and largely uninvolved in ordinary life, and focused instead on ancestral or nature spirits. The power of dead ancestors might be accessed through rituals of sacrifice, espe- cially of cattle. Supernatural power deriving from ancient heroes, ancestors, or nature spirits also resided in charms, which could be activated by proper rituals and used to con- trol the rains, defend the village, achieve success in hunting, or identify witches. Belief in witches was widespread, reflecting the idea that evil or misfortune was the work of malicious people. Diviners, skilled in penetrating the unseen world, used dreams, visions, charms, or trances to identify the source of misfortune and to prescribe remedies. Was a particular ill- ness the product of broken taboos, a dishonored ancestor, an unhappy nature spirit, or a witch? Was a remedy to be found

A Female Luba Ancestral Statue Representations of powerful women, often ancestral figures, were frequent in the wood carvings of the Bantu speaking Luba people of Central Africa. Many of them showed women touching their breasts, a gesture signifying devotion, respect, and the holding of secret knowledge. (© Musée du Quai Branly – Jacques Chirac, Paris, France/Dist. RMN-Grand-Palais/Art Resource, NY)

Map 6.4 North America in the Second-Wave Era

A sparsely populated North America hosted a number of semi-sedentary agricultural societies as well as various gathering and hunting peoples rather than the "civilizations" characteristic of Mesoamerica and the Andes.

in a cleansing ceremony, a sacrifice to an ancestor, the activation of a charm, or the elimination of a witch?[10]

Unlike the major monotheistic religions, with their "once and for all" revelations from God through the Christian Bible or the Muslim Quran, Bantu religious practice was predicated on the notion of "continuous revelation"—the possibility of constantly receiving new messages from the world beyond through dreams, visions, or trance states. Moreover, unlike Buddhism, Christianity, or Islam, Bantu religions were geographically confined, intended to explain, predict, and control local affairs, with little missionary impulse or inclination toward universality.

North America: Ancestral Pueblo and Mound Builders

If the Americas hosted civilizations, cities, and empires in Mesoamerica and the Andes, they also housed various alternative forms of human community during the second-wave era and beyond. Arctic and subarctic cultures, the bison hunters of the Great Plains, the complex and settled communities of the Pacific coast of North America, nomadic bands living in the arid regions of southern South America—all of these represent the persistence of gathering and hunting ways of living.

Even more widespread—in the eastern woodlands of the United States, Central America, the Amazon basin, the Caribbean islands—were societies sustained by village-based agriculture. Owing to environmental or technological limitations, it was a less intensive and productive agriculture than in Mesoamerica or the Andes and supported usually much smaller populations (see Map 6.4 and Map 12.5, page 515). These peoples too made their own histories, changing in response to their unique environments, their interactions with outsiders, and their own visions of the world. The Anasazi of the southwestern United States, now called the Ancestral Pueblo, and the mound-building cultures of the eastern woodlands provide two illustrations from North America.

The southwestern region of North America, an arid land cut by mountain ranges and large basins, first acquired maize from its place of origin in Mesoamerica during the second millennium B.C.E., but it took roughly 2,000 years for that crop, later supplemented by beans and squash, to become the basis of a settled agricultural way of living. As maize was adapted to the local environment, permanent village life gradually took hold, with people initially living in pit houses below ground level. By 900 C.E., many of these villages also included kivas, much larger pit structures used for ceremonial purposes, which symbolized the widespread belief

Guided Reading Question

■ **COMPARISON**

How do the histories of these North American societies compare to that of African Bantu-speaking peoples?

that humankind emerged into this world from another world below. Individual settlements were linked to one another in local trading networks and sometimes in wider webs of exchange that brought them buffalo hides, copper, turquoise, seashells, macaw feathers, and coiled baskets from quite distant locations.

These processes of change—growing dependence on agriculture, increasing population, more intensive patterns of exchange—gave rise to larger settlements and adjacent aboveground structures known as pueblos. The most spectacular of these took shape in Chaco canyon in what is now northwestern New Mexico. There, between 860 and 1130 C.E., five major pueblos emerged. This **Chaco Phenomenon** encompassed 25,000 square miles and linked some seventy outlying settlements to the main centers. The largest of these towns, or "great houses," Pueblo Bonito, stood five stories high and contained more than 600 rooms and many kivas. Hundreds of miles of roads, up to forty feet wide, radiated out from Chaco, prompting much debate among scholars. Without wheeled carts or large domesticated animals, such an elaborate road system seems unnecessary for ordinary trade or travel. Did the roads represent, as some scholars speculate, a ceremonial or sacred landscape leading perhaps to an entrance to the underworld?

Among the Chaco elite were highly skilled astronomers who constructed an arrangement of three large rock slabs situated so as to throw a beam of light during the summer solstice across a spiral rock carving located behind this observatory. By the eleventh century, Chaco also had become a dominant center for the production of turquoise ornaments, which became a major item of regional commerce, extending as far south as Mesoamerica. Not all was sweetness and light, however. Warfare, internal conflict, and occasional cannibalism (a matter of much controversy among scholars) apparently increased in frequency as an extended period of drought in the half century following 1130 brought this flourishing culture to a rather abrupt end. By 1200, the great houses had been abandoned and their inhabitants scattered in small communities that later became the Pueblo peoples of more recent times.

Unlike the Chaco region in the southwest, the eastern woodlands of North America and especially the Mississippi River valley generated an independent Agricultural Revolution. By 2000 B.C.E., many of its peoples had domesticated local plant species, including sumpweed, goosefoot, some gourds and squashes, and a form of artichoke. Sunflowers, originally domesticated in Mesoamerica, also found a place in diets of eastern woodland peoples. These few plants, however, were not sufficient to support a fully settled agricultural village life; rather, they supplemented diets derived from gathering and hunting without fundamentally changing that ancient way of life. Such peoples created societies distinguished by arrays of large earthen mounds, found all over the United States east of the Mississippi, prompting archeologists to dub them the **Mound Builders**. The earliest of these mounds date to around 4000 B.C.E., but the most elaborate and widespread took shape between 200 B.C.E. and 400 C.E. The builders of these mounds created what is commonly called the **Hopewell culture**, after an archeological site in Ohio.

Several features of the Hopewell culture have intrigued archeologists. Particularly significant are the striking burial mounds and geometric earthworks, sometimes covering areas equivalent to several city blocks, and the wide variety of artifacts found within them—smoking pipes, human figurines, mica mirrors, flint blades, fabrics, and jewelry of all kinds. The mounds themselves were no doubt the focus of elaborate burial rituals, but some of them were aligned with the moon with such precision as to mark lunar eclipses. Developed most elaborately in the Ohio River valley, Hopewell-style earthworks, artifacts, and ceremonial pottery have also been found throughout the eastern woodlands region of North America. Hopewell centers in Ohio contained mica from the Appalachian Mountains, volcanic glass from Yellowstone, conch shells and a few sharks' teeth from the Gulf of Mexico, and copper from the Great Lakes. All of this suggests a large "Hopewell Interaction Sphere" linking this entire region in a loose network of exchange, as well as a measure of cultural borrowing of religious ideas and practices.[11]

The next and most spectacular phase in the history of these mound-building peoples took shape as corn-based agriculture, derived ultimately but indirectly from Mexico, gained ground in the Mississippi valley after 800 C.E., allowing larger populations and more complex societies to emerge. The dominant center was **Cahokia**, near present-day St. Louis, Missouri, which flourished from about 900 to 1250 C.E. Its central mound, a terraced pyramid of four levels, measured 1,000 feet long by 700 feet wide, rose more than 100 feet above the ground, and occupied fifteen acres. It was the largest structure north of Mexico, the focal point of a community numbering 10,000 or more people, and the center of a widespread trading network.

Evidence from burials and from later Spanish observers suggests that Cahokia and other centers of this Mississippi culture were stratified societies with a clear elite and with rulers able to mobilize the labor required to build such enormous structures. One high-status male was buried on a platform of 20,000 shell beads, accompanied by 800 arrowheads, sheets of copper and mica, and a number of sacrificed men and women nearby.[12] Well after Cahokia had declined and was abandoned, sixteenth-century Spanish and French explorers encountered another such chiefdom among the Natchez people, located in southwestern Mississippi. Paramount chiefs, known as Great Suns, dressed in knee-length fur coats and lived luxuriously in deerskin-covered homes. An elite class of "principal men" or "honored peoples" clearly occupied a different status from commoners, sometimes referred to as "stinkards." These sharp class distinctions were blunted by the requirement that upper-class people, including the Great Suns, had to marry "stinkards."

The military capacity of these Mississippi chiefdoms greatly impressed European observers, as this Spanish account indicates:

> The next day the cacique [paramount chief] arrived with 200 canoes filled with men, having weapons, . . . the warriors standing erect from bow to stern, holding bows and arrows. . . . [F]rom under the canopy where the chief man was, the course was directed and orders issued to the rest. . . . [W]hat with the awnings, the plumes, the shields, the pennons, and the number of people in the fleet, it appeared like a famous armada of galleys.[13]

Here then, in the eastern woodlands of North America, were peoples who independently generated a modest Agricultural Revolution, assimilated corn and beans from distant sources, developed increasingly complex chiefdoms, and created monumental structures, new technologies, and artistic traditions. Beyond the separate societies that emerged within this large area, scholars have noticed some similarities in artifacts, symbols, ceremonies, mythologies, and artistic styles, many of which seem related to marking the status of elites. A horned serpent, sometimes depicted with wings, and various animal-god representations were widely shared symbols, though the meaning of these symbols no doubt changed as they entered new cultural environments. Dubbed the Southeast Ceremonial Complex, the loose networks of connection that generated these similarities grew outward from Cahokia for several centuries after 1200 or so, continuing earlier patterns of interaction associated with the Hopewell cultural region. While no linguistic, cultural, or political unity emerged from these relationships, they testify to a measure of exchange, borrowing, and cultural adaptation across an enormous region of North America.

Pacific Oceania: Peoples of the Sea

The peoples of Pacific Oceania, like those of Bantu Africa and North America, created enduring human communities without the large cities, states, and empires so prominent in civilizations. But the ecological setting for these historical journeys was distinctive, for they took place on the islands of the immense Pacific: a few larger territories, such as New Guinea and New Zealand, as well as thousands of much smaller islands, many of them specks in the sea (see Map 6.5). New Guinea had been settled for perhaps 50,000 years, initially at a time when it was connected to Australia by a land bridge. But the rest of Oceania was the last part of the world to receive human settlers, who began arriving from Island Southeast Asia only about 3,500 years ago (see "Into the Pacific" in Chapter 1). By 1200 C.E., they had achieved a presence on every habitable piece of land throughout this enormous region. It was, as one historian summarized the process, "the greatest maritime expansion known to history."[14]

The settlers' arrival, however, produced an enormous and sometimes devastating environmental impact as humans entered and disrupted bountiful but fragile ecosystems, especially as their populations grew. Referring to some of the early settlers in Melanesia during the first millennium B.C.E., Pacific historian Ian Campbell wrote: "They hunted, gathered, and fished profligately, and burnt large tracts of previously undisturbed forests."[15] In New Zealand, initially settled much later, around 1200 C.E., human hunting largely eliminated the huge flightless *moa* bird within a century. Archeologists have discovered the remains of some 90,000 moa at a single butchery. A similar impact occurred in Hawaii and elsewhere as smaller birds fell victim to the rats, pigs, and dogs introduced by the settlers. Resource depletion, deforestation, and soil erosion followed, no doubt contributing to the abandonment of at least several dozen islands, as their inhabitants found themselves forced to flee or perish. Rapa Nui (Easter Island) in easternmost Polynesia had come almost to the point of

Guided Reading Question

■ **CHANGE**
What changes marked the history of Pacific Oceania?

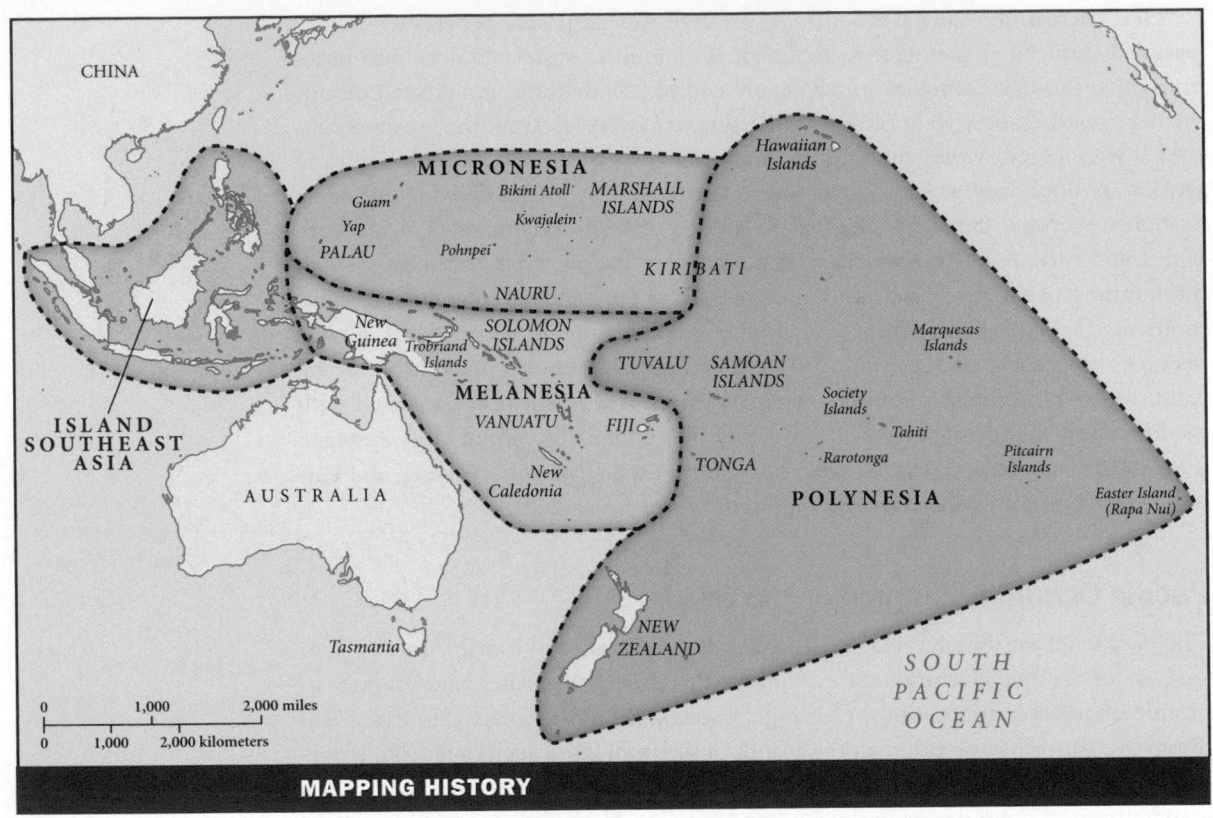

MAPPING HISTORY

Map 6.5 Pacific Oceania

Covering about one-third of the world's surface, the Pacific Ocean encompasses thousands of islands, which were home to many distinct societies but also constituted a cultural region that shared numerous commonalities and connections.

READING THE MAP: About how far is New Guinea from Easter Island (Rapa Nui)? Plot a course from New Guinea to Easter Island (Rapa Nui) using other islands as stopping-off points. How does an island-by-island approach change your impression of the journey?

MAKING CONNECTIONS: While reading "Pacific Oceania: Peoples of the Sea," trace on the map the chronological order in which the islands of the Pacific Ocean were settled. What patterns do you see? Which islands were settled last, and why?

---

ecological collapse by the time Europeans arrived in the eighteenth century, as much of its tree cover had vanished and many bird species had likewise disappeared. Human activity had surely contributed to this outcome with overhunting, overfishing, and the cutting down of forests. But Polynesian rats, whether introduced accidentally or intentionally by the original settlers to the island, were at least equally responsible, as their numbers exploded and they devoured the seeds of the palm trees.[16]

Growing populations also resulted in increased social complexity on some of the most densely populated islands. One example comes from the Microne-sian island of **Pohnpei**, where an urban complex, constructed from stone and coral, served as the ceremonial, administrative, and burial center of a powerful

Saudeleur dynasty that governed the island for several centuries after 1100 C.E. This impressive urban center, later dubbed by Europeans the "Venice of the Pacific," contained numerous seawalls and canals, over ninety small artificial islands, marketplaces, and a large tomb and funerary complex. However, local legends tell of increasingly despotic rulers whose oppressive policies triggered a revolt by lower-ranking chiefs.

The Polynesian **Tonga Islands** witnessed yet another example of growing social complexity. By the fourteenth century, powerful rulers, known as Tu'i Tonga, stood at the head of a royal court that included many wives and concubines, various relatives, ceremonial attendants, prisoners of war, and specialized craftsmen such as carvers, navigators, and fishermen. The court collected and redistributed food and various gifts to lesser chiefs, who then did the same for their followers. The widespread military and commercial influence of Tonga in the central Pacific has led some scholars to regard it as an incipient empire, while others view it as a tributary network or a system of economic interdependence.

Given the vast distances separating these island societies, considerable diversity among them is hardly surprising. And yet they also participated in the making of a single cultural region with numerous commonalities and connections. Many of their cultural and dietary similarities derive from their common origin in Island Southeast Asia and ultimately from southern China as well as from a common Pacific environment. Variations developed from the adaptation of this shared heritage to the distinctive environment of particular islands — large or small, tropical or semi-tropical, sea-level coastal terrain or mountainous interior, uninhabited or containing established societies as in New Guinea. The relative isolation of these societies, as well as periodic contact with near and more distant neighboring islands, also shaped their histories.

Linguistically, the peoples of Oceania, despite their small numbers, have spoken hundreds of different languages, over 100 on the small island chain of Melanesian Vanuatu alone. But almost all of them are members of the Austronesian family of languages, whose speakers also include those of Malaysia, Indonesia, and Madagascar. New Guinea, however, is a different story, with well over 1,000 languages, most of which are part of the Papuan language family, derived from its much earlier settlement. Similarly, Pacific islanders everywhere practiced the art of body decoration called *tatau* (which became "tattoo" in English), but particularly in Polynesia each archipelago developed distinctive designs, reflecting its unique identity.

This pattern of diversity and unity found other expression as well, both among the three major regions of Melanesia, Micronesia, and Polynesia and within them. In economic life, for example, these people of the sea drew heavily on the ocean as a major source of food, while its shells were used as currency and tools. But they were also farmers, raising pigs, dogs, and fowl, while everywhere cultivating taro, a starchy root vegetable. Other crops — yams, sweet potatoes, breadfruit, coconut palms — were also cultivated as availability and conditions allowed.

In political and social life, Oceanic societies were generally organized as chiefdoms, but with considerable variation. On small islands, chiefs and priests could hardly be distinguished from anyone else, while village councils, operating by consensus, made decisions. In parts of Melanesia, so-called "big men," or locally influential individuals, exercised authority through ceremony, feasts, and gift giving. Elsewhere, societies were more stratified and authority more centralized. In New Zealand, the Maori people distinguished among chiefly families, commoners, and slaves derived from prisoners of war. Frequent warfare among its chiefdoms prevented greater political unity. In Hawaii and Tonga, by contrast, elaborate social hierarchies emerged with powerful rulers who had hundreds or even thousands of warriors at their disposal.

Women everywhere in ancient Oceania were considered dangerous and polluting, especially during menstruation and childbirth, and were isolated at those times. However, gender roles differed substantially from place to place. In Melanesia, women were more actively involved in food production, but in Polynesia their labor was directed more toward the making of mats and cloth. Throughout Polynesia, women were accorded high status, and women of chiefly families could exercise considerable power through their male relatives. Melanesian women, by contrast, were more sharply subordinated to men than their counterparts in other regions of Oceania.

Religious life in Oceania was pragmatic, designed to protect against harm and to manipulate the spirits or gods in one's favor. It found expression in two pervasive concepts: **mana** and **tapu**. Mana was a spiritual energy or power, associated especially with chiefs and demonstrated by remarkable actions or great success. To maintain the purity of mana, ritual restriction or prohibitions known as tapu (which came into English as "taboo") served to make someone or something sacred or elevated far above the ordinary. Throughout Polynesia, only a particular official could handle the chief's food or his possessions. A Maori chief in New Zealand could not allow even his shadow to fall on food, for doing so made it forbidden to all others. Hawaiians prostrated themselves on the ground before their major chiefs. Since violating a tapu could result in death, religion provided supernatural sanctions for political authorities and social elites, as it has in so many other societies.

The Moai of Rapa Nui The most iconic artistic representations of Polynesian culture are these huge stone figures called *moai*. Carved from volcanic rock on the island of Rapa Nui sometime between 1200 and 1600, they are thought to depict sacred ancestors or clan chiefs. Around 1,000 of them were quarried and carved, and hundreds were somehow transported up to eight miles to stand on stone platforms near the coast. The largest were some thirty-three feet tall and weighed over eighty tons.
(© Ken Welsh/Bridgeman Images)

While much of this was common across all of Pacific Oceania, the gods, ghosts, ancestors, and spirits differed considerably, as did the role of priests or shamans as well as the associated rituals and artistic expression of religious life.

Despite the distances between these island societies, they were not wholly isolated from one another. Networks of exchange and communication — both regional and at a greater distance — allowed for some interaction among the various peoples of Oceania. Between roughly 1400 and 800 B.C.E., the spread of a distinctive pottery style known as Lapita throughout Melanesia and as far as Tonga and Samoa suggests a widespread pattern of exchange involving both commercial and ceremonial elements. During this time, obsidian from the island of New Britain off the northeastern coast of New Guinea had a distribution that extended over 4,000 miles from Borneo in Island Southeast Asia to Fiji in eastern Melanesia.

In western Micronesia, another system of exchange arose in the Caroline Island chain, with a particular focus on the island of **Yap**. It involved trade in commodities such as sea turtles, coconuts, and breadfruit; permission to fish near neighboring islands; and promises of refuge and shelter in times of famine. But it was also a set of tributary relationships in which the high-ranking island of Yap periodically received payments such as woven cloth, various coconut products, mats, and shells from islands of lesser rank up to 1,200 miles farther east. In return, the subordinates received gifts from Yap that exceeded the value of their tribute: wood for canoes, flint stone, food, and powdered turmeric, used as a skin paste and in coming-of-age rituals. Cast in terms of a parent-child relationship between Yap and the other islands, the whole system was supported by fears of powerful Yapese sorcery capable of generating great storms, should the required tribute not be forthcoming. Such trading circuits often contained an elaborate ceremonial element in which the exchange of noneconomic items — bracelets, necklaces, feathers, or shells — served to display status, to cement bonds of mutual assistance across great distances, and to confirm relationships of dominance and submission. Small island societies were invariably vulnerable and limited in resources; such networks of exchange provided insurance for their survival.

Polynesian networks of exchange also flourished in the centuries after 1000 C.E., with Tonga at the center of a system linked by trade with Samoa and Fiji. Finely woven Samoan mats were highly valued for displaying prestige, and large logs from Fiji were prized for the huge canoes that could be carved from them for Tonga's impressive warships. From the far eastern edge of Polynesia, sailors had apparently reached the coast of South America, from which they returned with sweet potatoes and bottle gourds. Taking hold in Rapa Nui, those domesticates from the Americas then entered Polynesian voyaging networks and found their way to Hawaii, New Zealand, and elsewhere, becoming a major food source.

Linked to Asia by their distant origins and to the Americas by the slender thread of the sweet potato, the peoples of Pacific Oceania lived largely, but not entirely, in a world apart from the rest of humankind.

REFLECTIONS

Deciding What's Important: Balance in the Writing of World History

Among the perennial problems that teachers and writers of world history confront is sorting through the vast record of times past and choosing what to include and what to leave out. A related issue involves the extent to which particular peoples or civilizations will be treated. Should the Persians get as much space as the Greeks? Does Africa merit equal treatment with Eurasia? Where do the Americas fit in the larger human story? What, in short, are the criteria for deciding what is important in recalling the history of the human venture?

One standard might be duration. Should ways of living that have endured for longer periods of time receive greater attention than those of lesser length? If historians followed only this criterion, then the Paleolithic era of gathering, hunting, and fishing societies should occupy 90 percent or more of any world history text. On the other hand, perhaps change is more important than continuity. If so, then something new merits more space than something old. Thus we pay attention to both agriculture and civilizations because they represent significant turning points in human experience.

Population provides yet another principle for determining inclusion. That, of course, is the reason that Eurasia / North Africa, with over 80 percent of the world's population, is addressed in three chapters of this section, whereas inner Africa, the Americas, and Pacific Oceania together receive just one chapter.

There is also the related issue of range of influence. Buddhism, Christianity, and Islam spread more widely and shaped the lives of more people than did the religions of the Maya or the Bantu-speaking peoples of Africa. Do they therefore deserve more extended treatment? Still another factor involves the availability of evidence. In this respect, Eurasia generated far more written records than either Africa or the Americas did, and therefore its history has been investigated far more thoroughly.

A final possible criterion involves the location of the historian and his or her audience. Those who have recently developed world history as a field of study have vigorously sought to counteract a Eurocentric telling of the human story. Still, is there anything inherently wrong with an account of world history that is centered on one's own people? Ethiopian high schools in the 1960s operated within an Afrocentric history curriculum, which focused first on Ethiopian history, then on Africa as a whole, and finally on the larger world. Might a world historian from the Middle East, for example, legitimately strike a somewhat different balance in the treatment of various civilizations than someone writing for a largely Western audience or for Chinese readers?

Any account of the world's past will mix and match these criteria in various and contested ways. Among historians, there exists neither a consensus about this question nor any formula to ensure a "proper" balance. You may want to consider whether the choices made in this chapter, and the book as a whole, are appropriate. What other choices might be possible?

Second Thoughts

What's the Significance?

Meroë, 231

Axum, 234

Niger Valley civilization, 235

vertical integration, 237

Maya civilization, 238

Teotihuacán, 240

Chavín, 242

Moche, 243

Wari and Tiwanaku, 245

Bantu migration, 247

Chaco Phenomenon, 251

Mound Builders, 251

Hopewell culture, 251

Cahokia, 252

Pohnpei, 254

Tonga Islands, 255

mana and *tapu*, 256

Yap, 257

Big Picture Questions

1. "The particular cultures and societies of Africa, the Americas, and Pacific Oceania discussed in this chapter developed largely in isolation." What evidence would support this statement, and what might challenge it?
2. How do you understand areas of the world, such as Bantu Africa, North America, and Pacific Oceania, that did not generate "civilizations"? Do you see them as "backward," as moving slowly toward civilization, or as simply different?
3. How did Africa's proximity to Eurasia shape its history? And how did America's separation from the Eastern Hemisphere affect its development?
4. **Looking Back:** "The histories of Africa and the Americas during the second-wave era largely resemble those of Eurasia." Do you agree with this statement? Explain why or why not.

Next Steps: For Further Study

Christopher Ehret, *The Civilizations of Africa* (2002). An overview of African history before 1800 by a prominent scholar.

Brian M. Fagan, *Ancient North America* (2005). A prominent archeologist's account of North American history.

Steven R. Fischer, *A History of the Pacific Islands* (2013). A recent account of the history of Pacific Oceania from ancient times to the present.

Eric Gilbert and Jonathan T. Reynolds, *Africa in World History* (2011). An accessible account of African history set in a global context.

Guy Gugliotta, "The Maya: Glory and Ruin," *National Geographic* (August 2007). A beautifully illustrated account of the rise and fall of Maya civilization.

Charles C. Mann, *1491: New Revelations of the Americas before Columbus* (2005). A journalist's thoughtful account, delightfully written, of the controversies surrounding the history of the Americas before 1492.

Annenberg Media, "Human Migration," 2004, https://www.learner.org/vod/vod_window.html?pid=2146. A video that demonstrates how historians trace migration patterns, including those of Bantu-speaking peoples in Africa.

National Geographic, "Lost Kingdom of the Maya," 1997, https://www.youtube.com/watch?v=bSd2P0guPFk. A lovely documentary on classical Maya civilization and its collapse.

Axum and the World

In the world of ancient African history, Axum has occupied a unique position in several ways (see Map 6.1 and "Axum: The Making of a Christian Kingdom" in this chapter). It is one of the few places in Africa, outside of Egypt, for which considerable documentary evidence exists. Some of the written sources—royal inscriptions and coins, for example—derive from within Axum itself, while others come from Greco-Roman and Christian visitors. Furthermore, after the rise of Islam, Axum—and its Ethiopian successor state—was the major surviving outpost of a Christian tradition that had earlier spread widely across northern and northeastern Africa. Finally, Axum has demonstrated an impressive cultural and religious continuity. Even after the decline of the Axumite Empire by the eighth century C.E., the city of Axum remained a major pilgrimage site for Christians, while Ethiopian kings into the twentieth century were crowned there. The sources that follow offer a series of windows into this African kingdom.

SOURCE 6.1 The Making of an Axumite Empire

At its high point in the mid-fourth century C.E., Axum ruled an empire stretching from Meroë in the upper Nile Valley, across much of what is now Eritrea and Ethiopia, and incorporating parts of southern Arabia on the opposite side of the Red Sea. Source 6.1 comes from an Axumite inscription written in Greek on a stone throne adorned with figures of the Greek gods Hercules and Mercury. Commissioned by an unknown Axumite monarch, the inscription dates probably from the second or third century C.E. It was copied and then published in the sixth century by Cosmas, a Greek merchant born in Alexandria, Egypt, who had become a monk. This text describes some of the conquests that generated the Axumite Empire.

- What evidence from the document itself dates it prior to Axum's acceptance of Christianity?

- How would you describe the point of view from which the document was written?

- What techniques of imperial control does the document reveal?

- How would you describe the religious or ideological underpinnings of this empire? Why might the Axumite ruler who commissioned this inscription single out Ares, Zeus, and Poseidon for special attention?

Inscription on a Stone Throne | **2nd or 3rd century** c.e.

Having after this with a strong hand compelled the nations bordering on my kingdom to live in peace, I made war upon the following nations, and by force of arms reduced them to subjection. I warred first with the nation of Gaze [Axum, probably in an internal struggle for power], then with Agame and Sigye, and having conquered them, I exacted the half of all that they possessed.... [There follows a long list of other peoples that this ruler conquered.]

All these nations, protected though they were by mountains all but impregnable, I conquered, after engagements in which I was myself present. Upon their submission I restored their territories to them, subject to the payment of tribute. Many other tribes besides these submitted of their own accord, and became likewise tributary. And I sent a fleet and land forces against the Arabitae and Cinaedocolpitae who dwelt on the other side of the Red Sea [southern Arabia], and having reduced the sovereigns of both,

I imposed on them a land tribute and charged them to make traveling safe both by sea and by land....

I first and alone of the kings of my race made these conquests. For this success I now offer my thanks to my mighty god, Ares [the Greek god of warfare and slaughter], who begat me, and by whose aid I reduced all the nations bordering on my own country.... Having thus brought all the world under my authority to peace, I came down to Adulis and offered sacrifice to Zeus [chief god of the Greek pantheon], and to Ares, and to Poseidon [Greek god of the sea], whom I entreated to befriend all who go down to the sea in ships. Here also I reunited all my forces, and setting down this Chair [throne] in this place, I consecrated it to Ares in the twenty-seventh year of my reign.

Source: J. W. McCrindle, trans. and ed., *The Christian Topography of Cosmas, an Egyptian Monk* (London: Hakluyt Society, 1897), 59, 63–66.

■ ■ ■

SOURCE 6.2 **The Columns of Axum** ▶

Dating from around 300 c.e. and standing 79 feet tall, this column was one of the largest raised on an artificial terrace in Axum's capital. Carved to depict a building, it includes two false doors on the ground level and window frame designs on nine upper stories. While no inscriptions accompany any of the monuments, they likely marked the tombs of royalty. Made from single blocks of stone, the largest, at nearly 100 feet, still lies where it fell. According to one authority, it "is probably the largest—but not the longest—single block of stone that people anywhere have ever attempted to set on end."[17] The conversion of the Axum kings to Christianity brought an abrupt end to the practice of erecting royal funeral columns.

■ Why do you think these columns were carved to resemble multistory houses? Archeologists note that few if any houses in Axum would have been taller than three stories, so what might this ten-story structure convey?

■ Why might conversion to Christianity have led rulers to stop constructing columns to commemorate their burials?

An Axumite Monument | late 3rd or early 4th century C.E.

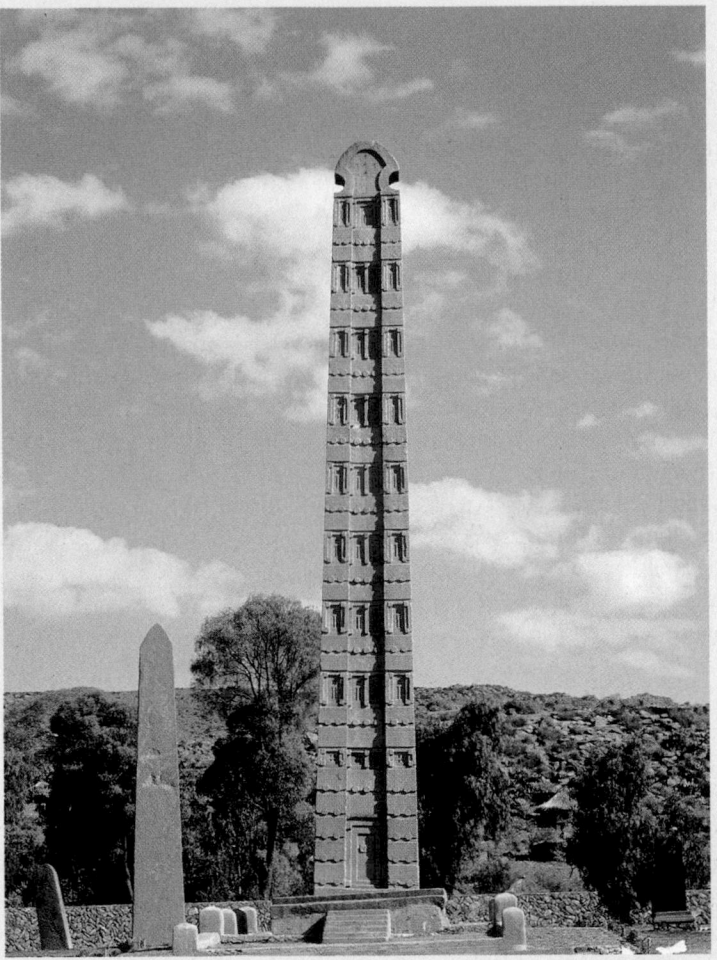

Werner Forman/Getty Images

■ ■ ■

SOURCE 6.3 The Coming of Christianity to Axum

The introduction of Christianity in the mid-fourth century C.E. represented a major change in the cultural history of Axum. It meant that Axum would be more closely aligned to Christian Egypt and Byzantium than to South Arabia, from which many of its earlier cultural traditions had derived. Source 6.3 relates the story of the coming of Christianity to Axum. It was written by Rufinus (345–410 C.E.), a Christian monk and writer who was born in Italy but spent much of his life in Jerusalem, where he heard this story from those who had taken part in it. Note that Greco-Roman writers of this time used "India" to refer vaguely to East Africa and southern Arabia as well as the South Asian peninsula.

■ According to this document, by what means was Christianity introduced to Axum? What do you think was the relative importance of Frumentius and Aedesius, as opposed to Roman merchants living in Axum?

■ Why do you think the Axumite royal family was so receptive to this foreign religion? How might the story differ if told from the ruling family's perspective?

■ How does the fact that this document was written by outsiders shape the emphasis of the story?

RUFINUS │ *On the Evangelization of Abyssinia* │ **late 4th century** c.e.

Meropius, a philosopher from Tyre [a Roman-controlled city in what is now Lebanon], . . . decided to go to India [to study their world and investigate their regions]. Two little boys went with him. He had been educating them in the liberal arts because they were his relatives. The younger boy was named Aedesius, the older Frumentius.

During the journey the things Meropius studied and learned nourished his mind. Then, while headed home, the philosopher's ship had to land because the travelers needed water or some other necessities. Where they landed the barbarians had a custom of cutting the throats of all Romans they found among them whenever neighboring nations announced that their treaties with the Romans were broken. The barbarians attacked the philosopher's ship. They killed him and all with him likewise. But the little boys they found studying and doing their reading under a tree. The barbarians spared the boys out of pity and led them to their king [the ruler of Axum].

The king made Aedesius his cup bearer. But he trusted Frumentius to be his accountant and scribe because he understood that the boy had a sharp mind and wisdom. From then on the king honored and loved them both. When the king died, he left as his successor his wife, who had a little son. He granted the boys, now young men, free opportunity to do whatever they wanted. And the queen, as if she trusted no one in the kingdom more,

humbly asked them to share in taking care of the kingdom with her until her son was a young man. She especially wanted Frumentius to help because he had enough wisdom to direct a kingdom. . . .

[D]uring the time Frumentius directed the government of the kingdom, he carefully began to inquire—for God moved his mind and spirit—whether there were any Christians among the Roman merchants. And he gave the greatest power to these Christians and advised them to make meeting places in every part of the country so that they could congregate in them for prayer in the Roman manner. Moreover, he himself did the same to a much greater degree, and so encouraged others, motivated them with favor and benefits, offered whatever might be useful, supplied land for buildings and other necessities, and acted in every way to grow the Christian seed in the kingdom.

When the royal child for whom Aedesius and Frumentius were taking care of the kingdom became a young man, their task was fulfilled and they faithfully handed over everything to him. Then they returned again to our world [the Roman Empire], even though the queen and her son delayed their journey and asked them to remain.

Source: *The Church History of Rufinus of Aquileia,* book 10, sections 9 and 10. Translation from Latin by Edward M. Gutting, Missouri State University.

■ ■ ■

SOURCE 6.4 **Axum and the Gold Trade**

The foundations of the Axumite state lay not only in its military conquests and its adoption of a new religion but also in its economic ties to the larger world. Among these ties was its reputation as a major source of gold for the Roman Empire. Source 6.4 describes the distinctive fashion in which Axumite traders obtained the gold from the African peoples living on the margins of the Axumite state. The author, Cosmas (see Source 6.1), was involved in this trade.

- How would you define the pattern of exchange described in this document? Was it state-directed trade, private enterprise, or both? To what problems of cross-cultural interaction was it a response?

- Who, if anyone, had the upper hand in this trade? Was it conducted between politically equal parties?

- What purposes did this trade serve for the people who mined and "sold" the gold?

COSMAS | *The Gold Trade of Axum* | **6th century** C.E.

The country known as that of Sasu is itself near the ocean . . . in which there are many gold mines. The King of the Axumites accordingly, every other year, through the governor of Agau, sends thither special agents to bargain for the gold, and these are accompanied by many other traders—upwards, say, of five hundred—bound on the same errand as themselves. They take along with them to the mining district oxen, lumps of salt, and iron, and when they reach its neighborhood, they make a halt at a certain spot and form an encampment, which they fence round with a great hedge of thorns. Within this they live, and having slaughtered the oxen, cut them in pieces, and lay the pieces on the top of the thorns, along with the lumps of salt and the iron. Then come the natives bringing gold in nuggets like peas, and lay one or two or more of these upon what pleases them—the pieces of flesh or the salt or the iron, and then they retire to some distance off. Then the owner of the meat approaches, and if he is satisfied he takes the gold away, and upon seeing this, its owner comes and takes the flesh or the salt or the iron. If, however, he is not satisfied, he leaves the gold, when the native, seeing that he has not taken it, comes and either puts down more gold, or takes up what he had laid down, and goes away. Such is the mode in which business is transacted with the people of that country, because their language is different and interpreters are hardly to be found.

The time they stay in that country is five days more or less, according as the natives, more or less readily coming forward, buy up all their wares. On the journey homeward they all agree to travel well-armed, since some of the tribes through whose country they must pass might threaten to attack them from a desire to rob them of their gold. The space of six months is taken up with this trading expedition, including both the going and the returning.

Source: J. W. McCrindle, trans. and ed., *The Christian Topography of Cosmas, an Egyptian Monk* (London: Hakluyt Society, 1897), 52–53.

■ ■ ■

SOURCE 6.5 Axum Gold Coin

Axum was the only kingdom in sub-Saharan Africa to mint coins in ancient times. This example from the first half of the fifth century depicts King Eon wearing his royal crown flanked by two grain stalks symbolizing abundance. Around the edge, his name and what may be his clan affiliation is inscribed in Greek, punctuated by four crosses advertising his Christian faith. Eon's predecessor and first Christian ruler of Axum, King Ezana (ca. 330–356), started this tradition and may have been the first ruler anywhere to mint coins with Christian crosses. Before Ezana, rulers had instead used a disk and crescent symbol representing sun and moon gods.

■ The only surviving evidence for many Axumite kings is their coins. What can we learn about individual kings from their coinage?

■ Some scholars have argued that Axumite coins may have been primarily intended to circulate beyond the borders of the kingdom. As evidence, they note that coins like this one used the same weight standards as Roman coins. What else about this coin supports the theory that it was intended to circulate outside of Axum? If true, what impression might King Eon have hoped to make on foreigners who came across his coin?

A "Christian Coin" from Axum

• • •

DOING HISTORY

1. **Assessing sources:** How does each of the written sources reflect the distinctive perspective of its author?

2. **Considering external influences:** Based on these sources, how would you describe Axum's various relationships with the world beyond its borders? How did its geographic location shape those relationships? (See Map 6.1, page 232.) In what ways did those external connections influence Axum's historical development?

3. **Explaining the rise and significance of Axum:** Based on these sources, how might you account for the flourishing of Axum? What was the economic, religious, and military significance of Axum within the region?

4. **Comparing civilizations:** In what ways might Axum be viewed as a smaller-scale version of the second-wave civilizations of Eurasia? In what ways was it different?

Christian Axum

The coming of Christianity to Axum was just one manifestation of a broader set of cross-cultural contacts and exchanges that tied Northeast Africa with Southwest Asia and the Mediterranean. In Voice 6.1, Erik Gilbert and Jonathan Reynolds, both specialists in African history, explore the transregional nature of early Christianity and the relationships between Axum, Egypt, and the eastern Mediterrenean that the new faith fostered. In Voice 6.2, Christopher Ehret, one of the leading scholars working in early African history, examines the role of trade in the gradual assimilation of Christianity into Axum society.

■ Drawing on these two passages, describe the forces that brought Christianity to Axum. What do the two accounts agree on, and what distinct contributions does each make to your own conclusions?

■ Beyond religious rewards, can you discern in these accounts any other benefits that a king of Axum might have hoped to secure through conversion to a religion that originated in the Roman world?

■ **Integrating Primary and Secondary Sources:** In what ways might the primary sources in this feature support or challenge the conclusions about the emergence of Christianity made by Gilbert/Reynolds and Ehert?

VOICE 6.1

Erik Gilbert and Jonathan Reynolds on the Transregional Nature of Early Christianity | 2004

It is notable that Ezana's conversion came very shortly after the conversion of the Roman Emperor Constantine. This fact represents a parallel example of Christianity's growing acceptance by political elites at the time. King Ezana's conversion not only fostered the spread of Christianity in the region of the upper Nile, but also helped forge trading links between Aksum and Christian communities of the Eastern Mediterranean. So deeply did Christianity become entrenched in the region that in the sixth century

[the Axumite ruler] King Kaleb invaded Yemen (in the southern Arabian Peninsula). The action was allegedly taken at the behest of the Byzantine Emperor Justinian and was ostensibly to protect Christian communities in Yemen from repression at the hands of the region's non-Christian population. Some scholars, however, discount the religious motivation of the two monarchs and stress that perhaps their goal was to weaken the Persian Empire and gain greater control over the lucrative trade that flowed through Arabia. Either way, the cooperation of Byzantine and Aksum monarchs says much about the transregional nature of early Christianity.

Source: Erik Gilbert and Jonathan Reynolds, *Africa in World History* (Boston: Pearson, 2004), 75.

VOICE 6.2

Christopher Ehret on the Role of Trade in the Coming of Christianity to Axum | 2002

Aksumite intellectual history in the fourth to sixth centuries illustrates a recurrent influence of trade on world history: trade routes are not only the conduit of goods from one part of the world to another but also the conduit of ideas. In particular the Levantine merchants who plied their commerce at Aksum's port city of Adulis included a number of Christians in the fourth century, and through these contacts Christianity was adopted by the fourth-century Aksumite king Ezana. At first a religion of limited outreach beyond the towns, Christianity in the late fifth and early sixth centuries began to be widely proselytized about the countryside by a number of Syrian monks. During this period . . . large numbers of Agaw [the native peoples of Axum] became Christian, and in many rural areas different dialects of Ge'ez, the written language of government and the towns, gradually became the first language of country folk too.

Source: Christopher Ehret, *The Civilizations of Africa* (Charlottesville: University of Virginia Press, 2002), 291.

Civilizations and Encounters during the Third-Wave Era

600–1450

THE BIG PICTURE

Patterns and Processes of the Third-Wave Era

In world history, the dates that define major periods of time are normally used symbolically rather than for denoting actual events. They point toward processes that mark major global transformations. In Part 3, the date 600 C.E. evokes the disruption, decline, or collapse of many second-wave states and civilizations between 200 and 800 C.E., including Han dynasty China, the western Roman Empire, Gupta India, Axum, Maya cities, Teotihuacán, and others. And 1450 highlights the start of European overseas expansion, which began to link the world's peoples together in new ways.

Third-Wave Civilizations

In the centuries between 600 and 1450, two large-scale processes occupied center stage in the unfolding drama of world history. First, a new phase in the continuing history of civilization took shape during these centuries. In some areas, wholly new civilizations arose where none had existed before: in Swahili city-states along the East African coast; in the West African kingdoms of Ghana, Mali, and Songhay; in Kievan Rus, located in what is now Ukraine and western Russia; in Japan, Korea, and Vietnam; in Srivijaya on the Indonesian island of Sumatra; and in the Angkor kingdom centered in present-day Cambodia. All of these represent a continuation of a long-established pattern in world history—the globalization of civilization. These newcomers to the growing number of civilizations borrowed heavily from larger or more established centers. So too did the new civilization that took shape in Western Europe following the collapse of the Roman Empire, combining Greco-Roman and Germanic elements in a distinctive blending.

The largest, most expansive, and most widely influential of the new third-wave civilizations was surely that of Islam. It began in Arabia in the seventh century C.E., projecting the Arab peoples into a prominent role as builders of an enormous empire while offering a new, vigorous, and attractive religion. As a new civilization defined by its religion, the world of Islam came to encompass many other centers of civilization, including Egypt, Mesopotamia, Persia, India, and Byzantium.

The persistence or reconstruction of already established civilizations represented yet another historical pattern during this third-wave era. The Byzantine Empire, embracing the eastern half of the old Roman Empire, continued the patterns of Mediterranean Christian civilization and persisted until 1453, when it was overrun by the Ottoman Turks. In China, following almost four centuries of fragmentation, the Sui, Tang, and Song dynasties (581–1279) restored China's imperial unity and reasserted its Confucian tradition. Indian civilization retained its ancient patterns of caste and religion amid vast cultural diversity, even as parts of India fell under the control of Muslim rulers.

Variations on this theme of continuing or renewing older traditions took shape in the Western Hemisphere. In Mesoamerica, the Mexica or Aztec people created a powerful and impressive state in the fifteenth century, drawing on earlier patterns of civilized life in that region. About the same time, on the western rim of South America, a Quechua-speaking people, now known as the Incas, incorporated various centers of Andean civilization into a huge bureaucratic empire. Both the Aztecs and the Incas gave a new expression to much older patterns of civilized life.

The Ties That Bind: Transregional Interaction in the Third-Wave Era

A second global pattern in the third-wave era involves heightened interaction among the world's various regions, cultures, and peoples. More than before, change in human societies was the product of contact with strangers, or at least with their ideas, armies, goods, or diseases. One vehicle for the interaction of culturally different peoples was long-distance trade, which grew considerably during the third-wave era: along the Silk Roads of Eurasia, within the Indian Ocean basin, across the Sahara, and along the Mississippi and other rivers. Everywhere it acted as an agent of change for all its participants. In places where such commerce was practiced extensively, it required that more people devote their energies to producing for a distant market rather than for consumption by their own communities. Those who controlled this kind of trade often became extremely wealthy, exciting envy or outrage among those less fortunate. Such exchange among distant lands also had political consequences, as many new states or empires were constructed on the basis of resources derived from long-distance commerce.

Yet another mechanism of cross-cultural interaction lay in large empires. Not only did they incorporate many distinct cultures within a single political system, but their size and stability also provided the security that encouraged travelers and traders to journey long distances from their homelands. Empires, of course, were nothing new in world history, but those of the third-wave era were larger. The Arab Empire, which accompanied the initial spread of Islam, stretched from Spain to India. Even more extensive was the Mongol Empire of the thirteenth and fourteenth centuries. In the Western Hemisphere, the Inca Empire encompassed dozens of distinct peoples in a huge state that ran some 2,500 miles along the spine of the Andes Mountains. Furthermore,

the largest of these empires were the creation of nomadic or pastoral peoples, while earlier empires in the Mediterranean basin, China, India, and Persia had been the work of settled farming societies.

Together, large-scale empires and long-distance trade gave rise to cosmopolitan urban centers such as Baghdad in what is now Iraq, Dunhuang in western China, Timbuktu in West Africa, and Malacca in Southeast Asia, where people of various backgrounds mixed and mingled. Conquest and commerce likewise facilitated the spread of ideas, technologies, food crops, and disease far beyond their points of origin. Thus Islam became an Afro-Eurasian phenomenon with an enormous reach. Chinese silk-making technology became available in Korea, Japan, the Middle East, and later in Europe. Corn gradually diffused from Mesoamerica to North America, where it stimulated population growth and the development of more complex societies. The plague, or Black Death, decimated many parts of Eurasia and North Africa as it made its deadly way from east to west in the fourteenth century.

Much of the readily visible "action" in the third-wave era, as in all earlier civilizations, featured male actors. The vast majority of rulers, traders, soldiers, religious officials, and long-distance travelers were men, as were most heads of households and families. The building of states and empires, so prominent in the third-wave era, meant war and conquest, fostering distinctly masculine warrior values and reinforcing the dominant position of men. Much of what follows in Part 3 is, frankly, men's history.

But behind all of this lay a vast realm of women's activity, long invisible to historians or simply assumed. Women sustained the family life that was the foundation of all human community; they were the repositories of language, religious ritual, group knowledge, and local history; their labor generated many of the products that entered long-distance trade routes as well as those that fed and clothed their communities. The changing roles and relationships of men and women and their understandings of gender also figure in the chapters that follow.

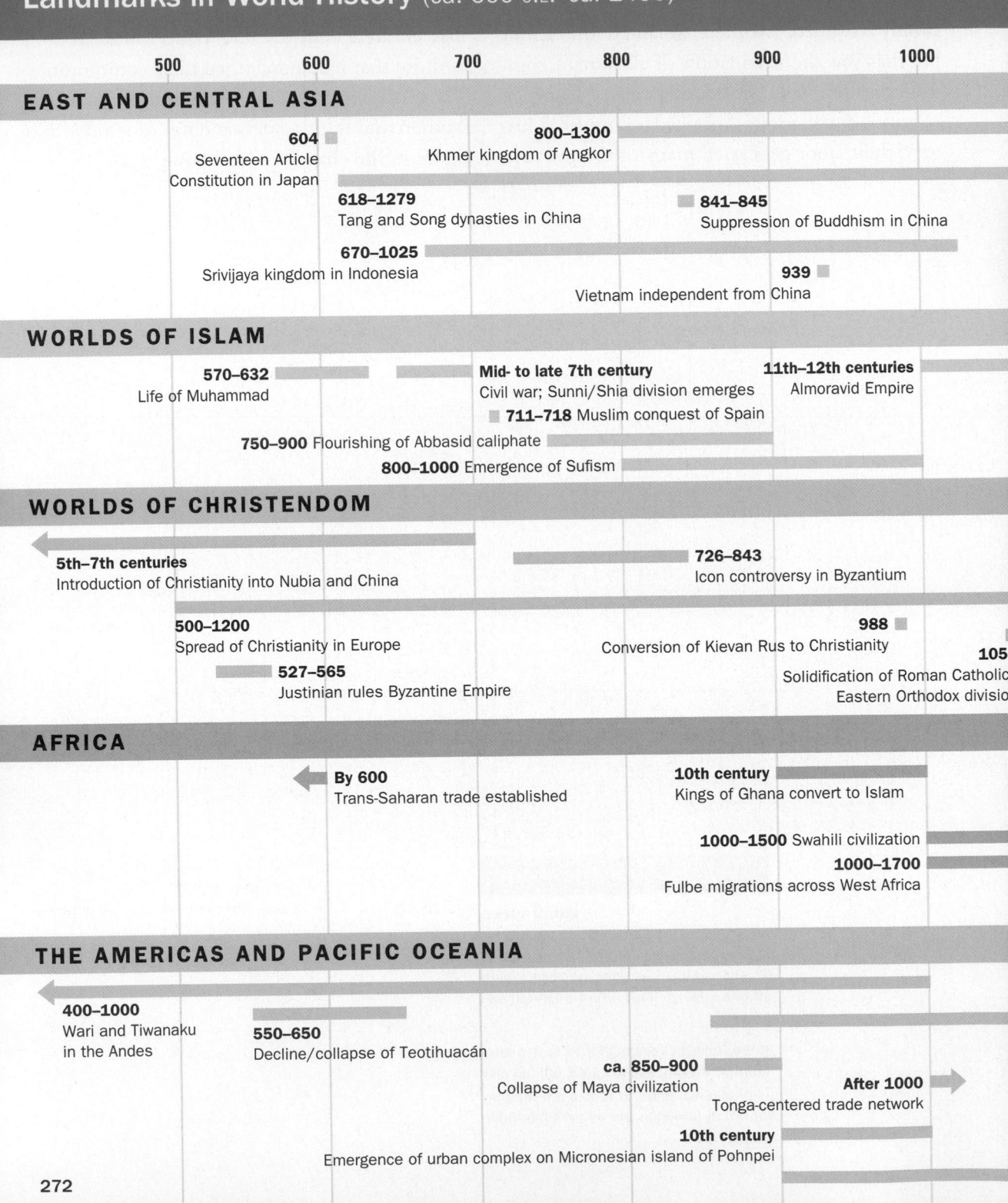

Landmarks in World History (ca. 600 C.E.–ca. 1450)

	500	600	700	800	900	1000

EAST AND CENTRAL ASIA

604
Seventeen Article
Constitution in Japan

800–1300
Khmer kingdom of Angkor

618–1279
Tang and Song dynasties in China

841–845
Suppression of Buddhism in China

670–1025
Srivijaya kingdom in Indonesia

939
Vietnam independent from China

WORLDS OF ISLAM

570–632
Life of Muhammad

Mid- to late 7th century
Civil war; Sunni/Shia division emerges

11th–12th centuries
Almoravid Empire

711–718 Muslim conquest of Spain

750–900 Flourishing of Abbasid caliphate

800–1000 Emergence of Sufism

WORLDS OF CHRISTENDOM

5th–7th centuries
Introduction of Christianity into Nubia and China

726–843
Icon controversy in Byzantium

500–1200
Spread of Christianity in Europe

988
Conversion of Kievan Rus to Christianity

1054

527–565
Justinian rules Byzantine Empire

Solidification of Roman Catholic/
Eastern Orthodox division

AFRICA

By 600
Trans-Saharan trade established

10th century
Kings of Ghana convert to Islam

1000–1500 Swahili civilization

1000–1700
Fulbe migrations across West Africa

THE AMERICAS AND PACIFIC OCEANIA

400–1000
Wari and Tiwanaku
in the Andes

550–650
Decline/collapse of Teotihuacán

ca. 850–900
Collapse of Maya civilization

After 1000
Tonga-centered trade network

10th century
Emergence of urban complex on Micronesian island of Pohnpei

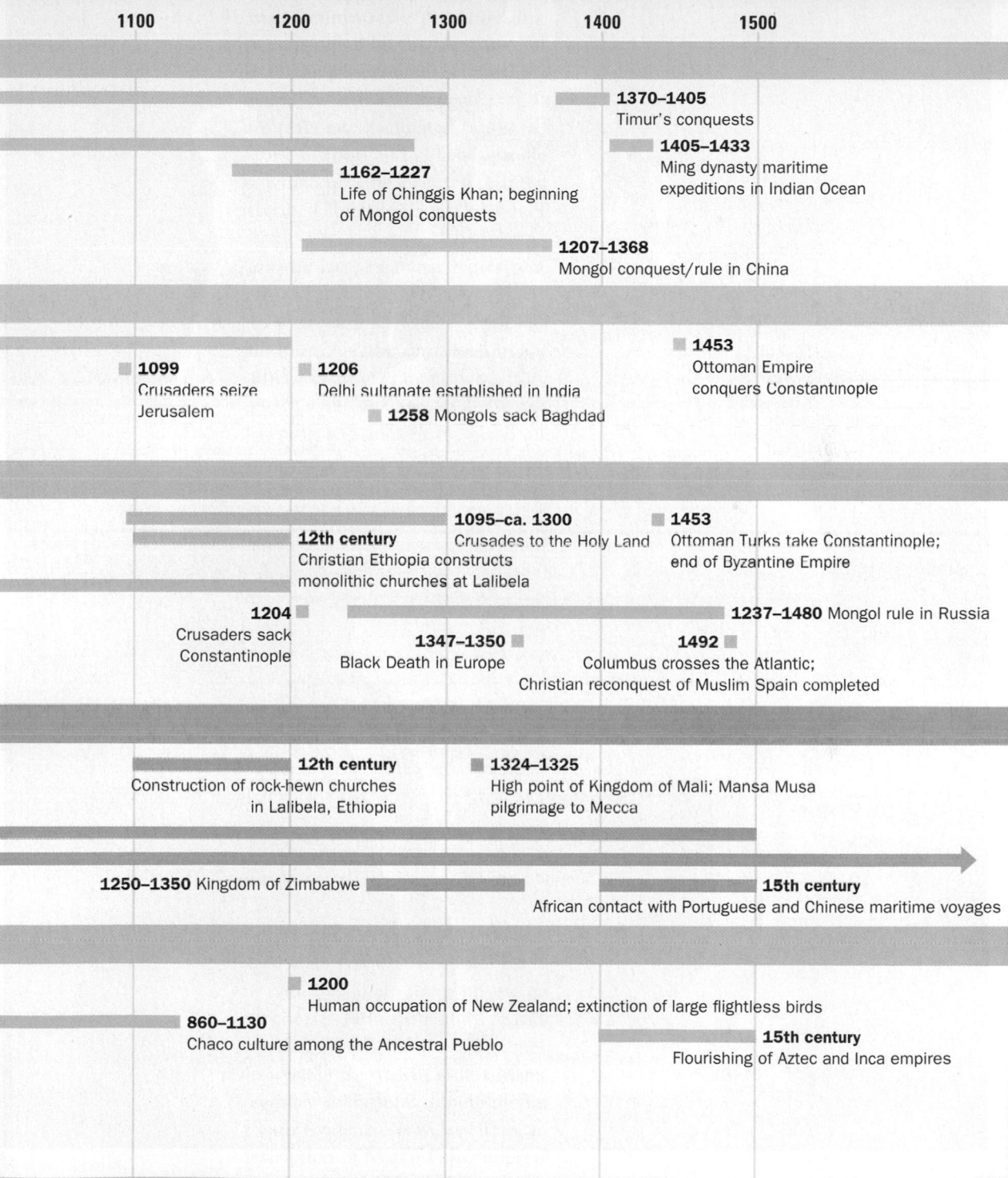

1100   1200   1300   1400   1500

1370–1405
Timur's conquests

1405–1433
Ming dynasty maritime
expeditions in Indian Ocean

1162–1227
Life of Chinggis Khan; beginning
of Mongol conquests

1207–1368
Mongol conquest/rule in China

1453
Ottoman Empire
conquers Constantinople

1099
Crusaders seize
Jerusalem

1206
Delhi sultanate established in India

1258 Mongols sack Baghdad

1095–ca. 1300
Crusades to the Holy Land

12th century
Christian Ethiopia constructs
monolithic churches at Lalibela

1453
Ottoman Turks take Constantinople;
end of Byzantine Empire

1204
Crusaders sack
Constantinople

1347–1350
Black Death in Europe

1237–1480 Mongol rule in Russia

1492
Columbus crosses the Atlantic;
Christian reconquest of Muslim Spain completed

12th century
Construction of rock-hewn churches
in Lalibela, Ethiopia

1324–1325
High point of Kingdom of Mali; Mansa Musa
pilgrimage to Mecca

1250–1350 Kingdom of Zimbabwe

15th century
African contact with Portuguese and Chinese maritime voyages

1200
Human occupation of New Zealand; extinction of large flightless birds

860–1130
Chaco culture among the Ancestral Pueblo

15th century
Flourishing of Aztec and Inca empires

900–1250 Flourishing of Cahokia chiefdom

273

CHAPTER 7

Commerce and Culture

600–1450

"In the spring of 2004, I was looking for an appropriate college graduation present for my son Ateesh and decided on an Apple iPod music player. . . . I placed my order online. . . . I was astonished by what followed. I received a confirmation e-mail within minutes . . . [and learned that] the product was being shipped . . . from Shanghai, China. . . . Ateesh's personalized iPod landed on our New Haven [Connecticut] doorstep barely 40 hours after I had clicked 'Buy.'"[1] To Nayan Chanda, a fifty-eight-year-old journalist, born and educated in India and at the time working at Yale University, this was an astonishing transaction. Probably it was less surprising to his son. But both of them, no doubt, understood this kind of commercial exchange as something quite recent in human history.

And in the speed of the transaction, it surely was. But from the perspective of world history, exchange among distant peoples is not altogether new, and the roots of economic globalization lie deep in the past. In fact, just three years after purchasing his son's iPod, Nayan Chanda wrote a well-received book titled *Bound Together*, describing how traders, preachers, adventurers, and warriors had long created links among peoples living in widely separated cultures and civilizations. Those early transregional interactions and their capacity for transforming human societies, for better and for worse, played an increasingly significant role in this era of third-wave civilizations. ■

« Travels on the Silk Roads This Chinese ceramic figurine from the Tang dynasty (618–907 C.E.) shows a group of musicians riding on a camel along the famous Silk Road commercial network that long linked the civilizations of western and eastern Eurasia. The bearded figures represent Central Asian merchants, while the others depict Chinese.

The exchange of goods among communities occupying different ecological zones has long been a prominent feature of human history. Coastlands and

275

highlands, steppes and farmlands, islands and mainlands, valleys and mountains, deserts and forests—each generates different products. Furthermore, some societies have been able to monopolize, at least temporarily, the production of particular goods—such as silk in China, certain spices in Southeast Asia, and incense in southern Arabia—that others have found valuable. This uneven distribution of goods and resources has long motivated exchange, not only within particular civilizations or regions but among them as well. In the world of 600 to 1450, long-distance trade became more important than ever before in linking and shaping distant societies and peoples. For the most part, it was indirect, a chain of separate transactions in which goods traveled farther than individual merchants. Nonetheless, a network of exchange and communication extending all across the Afro-Eurasian world, and separately in parts of the Americas as well, slowly came into being.

Such commerce shaped the daily life of many millions. It altered habits of consumption; for example, West Africans imported scarce salt, so necessary for seasoning and preserving food, from distant mines in the Sahara in exchange for the gold of their region. Incense grown in southern Arabia found eager consumers all across the ancient Eurasian world, where it was used for medicinal purposes, for religious ceremonies, and as an antidote to the odors of unsanitary cities. Incense also bore the "aroma of eros." "I have perfumed my bed with myrrh, aloes, and cinnamon," declared a harlot featured in the Old Testament book of Proverbs. "Come, let us take our fill of love till morning."[2]

Trade also affected the working lives of many people, encouraging them to specialize in producing particular products for sale in distant markets rather than for use in their own communities. Merchants often became a distinct social group, viewed with suspicion by others because of their impulse to accumulate wealth without actually producing anything themselves. In some societies, trade became a means of social mobility, as Chinese merchants, for example, were able to purchase landed estates and establish themselves within the gentry class. Long-distance trade also enabled elite groups in society to distinguish themselves from commoners by acquiring prestigious goods from a distance—silk, tortoiseshell, jade, rhinoceros horn, or particular feathers. Trade also had the capacity to transform political life. The wealth available from controlling and taxing trade motivated the creation of states in various parts of the world and sustained those states once they had been constructed. Furthermore, commerce posed a set of problems to governments everywhere. Should trade be left in private hands, as in the Aztec Empire, or should it be controlled by the state, as in the Inca Empire? How should state authorities deal with men of commerce, who were both economically useful and potentially disruptive?

Moreover, the saddlebags of camel caravans or the cargo holds of merchant vessels carried more than goods. Trade became a vehicle for the spread of religious ideas, technological innovations, disease-bearing germs, and plants and animals to regions far from their places of origin. In this fashion, Buddhism made its way from India

Landmarks for Chapter 7

	1 C.E.	300	600	900	1200	1500

THE SILK ROADS: EURASIAN COMMERCE

ca. 200 B.C.E.–200 C.E.
Initial flourishing of Silk Road commerce

200 B.C.E.–300 C.E.
Spread of Buddhism to Central Asian cities and northern China

500–600
Initial spread of silk-making technology beyond China

1200–1400
Mongol Empire revitalizes Silk Road commerce

1347
Black Death enters Europe via transcontinental trade routes

THE SEA ROADS: INDIAN OCEAN COMMERCE

1–300
Knowledge of monsoons enables Indian Ocean commerce

ca. 350
All-sea routes open between India and China

610–700
Rise and spread of Islam

670–1025
Srivijaya kingdom

ca. 1000–1500
Swahili civilization flourishes along East African coast

THE SAND ROADS: TRANS-SAHARAN COMMERCE

1–300
Introduction of camel to North Africa/Sahara

300–400
Beginning of trans-Saharan trade

1354
Ibn Battuta visits West Africa

ca. 500–1600
Flourishing of West African civilization (Ghana, Mali, Songhay)

AMERICAN COMMERCE

ca. 850–1250
Chaco culture in American southwest (New Mexico) trades with Mesoamerican societies

ca. 900–1250
Cahokia at the hub of North American commercial network

ca. 1000–1100
Diffusion of sweet potatoes from South America to Pacific Oceania

1400–1500
Aztec and Inca empires facilitate commercial exchange

SEEKING THE MAIN POINT

In what ways did long-distance commerce act as a motor of change in premodern world history?

to Central and East Asia, and Islam crossed the Sahara into West Africa. The pathogens that devastated much of Eurasia during the Black Death, as well as technologies of gunpowder, printing, and much more, also traversed the trade routes of the third-wave era.

Silk Roads: Exchange across Eurasia

The most famous of those networks of exchange, widely known now as the **Silk Roads** after their most famous product, linked the various peoples and civilizations of the Eurasian landmass (see Map 7.1). None of this network's numerous participants knew the full extent of its reach, for it was largely a "relay trade" in which goods were passed down the line, changing hands many times before reaching their final destination. Nonetheless, the Silk Roads provide a certain unity and coherence to Eurasian history alongside the distinct stories of its separate civilizations and peoples.

The Growth of the Silk Roads

The beginnings of the Silk Roads lay in both geography and history. As a geographic unit, Eurasia is often divided into inner and outer zones that represent quite different environments. Outer Eurasia consists of relatively warm, well-watered

Map 7.1 The Silk Roads
For 2,000 years, goods, ideas, technologies, and diseases made their way across Eurasia on the several routes of the Silk Roads.

areas, suitable for agriculture, which provided the setting for the great civilizations of China, India, the Middle East, and the Mediterranean. Inner Eurasia—the lands of eastern Russia and Central Asia—lies farther north and has a harsher and drier climate, much of it not conducive to agriculture. Herding their animals from horseback, the pastoral people of this region had for centuries traded with and raided their agricultural neighbors to the south. Products of the forest and of semi-arid northern grasslands known as the steppes—such as hides, furs, livestock, wool, and amber—were exchanged for the agricultural products and manufactured goods of adjacent civilizations. The movement of pastoral peoples for thousands of years also served to diffuse Indo-European languages, bronze metallurgy, horse-based technologies, and more all across Eurasia.

The construction of the second-wave civilizations and their imperial states during the last five centuries B.C.E. clearly enhanced these ancient patterns of exchange. From the south, the Persian Empire invaded the territory of pastoral peoples in present-day Turkmenistan and Uzbekistan. From the west, Alexander the Great's empire stretched well into Central Asia. From the east, China's Han dynasty extended its authority westward, seeking to control the nomadic Xiongnu and to gain access to their horses, a distinctive Central Asian breed known to the Chinese as "heavenly horses" that had become important to Chinese military forces. By the early centuries of the Common Era, indirect trading connections, often brokered by pastoral peoples, linked these Eurasian civilizations in a network of transcontinental commerce.

Guided Reading Question

■ **CHANGE**
What lay behind the emergence of Silk Road commerce, and what kept it going for so many centuries?

Silk Road trading networks prospered most when large and powerful states provided relative security for merchants and travelers across long distances. Such conditions prevailed during the second-wave era when the Roman and Chinese empires anchored long-distance commerce at the western and eastern ends of Eurasia. Silk Road trade flourished again during the seventh and eighth centuries C.E. as the Byzantine Empire, the Muslim Abbasid (ah-BAH-sihd) dynasty, and Tang dynasty China created an almost continuous belt of strong states across Eurasia. In the thirteenth and fourteenth centuries, the Mongol Empire briefly encompassed almost the entire route of the Silk Roads in a single state, giving a renewed vitality to long-distance trade. Over many centuries, various technological innovations, such as yokes, saddles, and stirrups, made the use of camels, horses, and oxen more effective means of transportation across the vast distances of the Silk Roads.

Goods in Transit

During prosperous times especially, a vast array of goods (detailed in the Snapshot on page 280) made its way across the Silk Roads, often carried in large camel caravans that traversed the harsh and dangerous steppes, deserts, and oases of Central Asia. Most of these goods were luxury products destined for an elite and wealthy market, rather than staple goods, for only readily moved commodities of great value could compensate for the high costs of transportation across such long and forbidding distances.

SNAPSHOT Economic Exchange Along the Silk Roads

Region	Products Contributed to Silk Road Commerce
China	silk, bamboo, mirrors, gunpowder, paper, rhubarb, ginger, lacquerware, chrysanthemums
Forest lands of Siberia and grasslands of Central Asia	furs, walrus tusks, amber, livestock, horses, falcons, hides, copper vessels, tents, saddles, slaves
India	cotton textiles, herbal medicine, precious stones, spices, pepper, pearls, ebony
Middle East	dates, nuts, dried fruit, dyes, lapis lazuli, swords
Mediterranean basin	gold coins, glassware, glazes, grapevines, jewelry, artworks, perfume, wool and linen textiles, olive oil

It was silk that came to symbolize this Eurasian network of exchange. From the time of silk's origin in China, by 3000 B.C.E. or earlier, that civilization long held a monopoly on its production. After 300 B.C.E. or so, the precious fabric increasingly found a growing market all across the linked commercial network of the Afro-Eurasian world. Although the silk trade itself was largely in the hands of men, women figured hugely in the process in terms of both supply and demand. For many centuries, Chinese women, mostly in rural areas, were responsible for every step of the ingenious and laborious enterprise of silk production. They tended the mulberry trees on whose leaves silkworms fed; they unwound the cocoons in very hot water to extract the long silk fibers; they turned these fibers into thread and wove them into textiles. Thus Chinese homes became the primary site of textile production, with rural women as its main labor force. By the time of the Tang dynasty (618–907 C.E.), women were making a large contribution to the household economy, to technological innovation in the silk industry, and to the state, which depended heavily on peasant taxes, often paid in cloth. Nonetheless, many rural families persisted in poverty, as the thirteenth-century writer Wen-hsiang indicated:

> The silkworms have finished their third sleep and are famished. The family is poor, without cash to buy the mulberry leaves to feed them. What can they do? Hungry silkworms do not produce silk. . . . The daughter is twenty but does not have wedding clothes. Those the government sends to collect taxes are like tigers. If they have no clothes to dress their daughter, they can put the [wedding] off. If they have no silk to turn over to the government, they will go bankrupt.[3]

Elite Chinese women, and their men as well, also furnished part of the demand for these luxurious fabrics, which marked their high status. So too did Chinese officials, who required huge quantities of silk to exchange for much-needed

Guided Reading Question

■ **SIGNIFICANCE**

What made silk such a highly desired commodity across Eurasia?

horses and to buy off "barbarian" invaders from the north. Beyond China, women in many cultures ardently sought Chinese silk for its comfort and its value as a fashion statement. The demand for silk, as well as for cotton textiles from India, was so great in the Roman Empire that various Roman writers were appalled at the drain of resources that it represented. They also were outraged at the moral impact of wearing revealing silk garments. "I can see clothes of silk," lamented Seneca the Younger in the first century C.E., "if materials that do not hide the body, nor even one's decency, can be called clothes. . . . Wretched flocks of maids labour so that the adulteress may be visible through her thin dress, so that her husband has no more acquaintance than any outsider or foreigner with his wife's body."[4]

By the sixth century C.E., the knowledge and technology for producing raw silk had spread beyond China. An old Chinese story attributes it to a Chinese princess who smuggled out silkworms in her turban when she was married off to a Central Asian ruler. However it happened, artisans in Korea, Japan, India, Persia, and the Byzantine Empire likewise learned how to produce this precious fabric.

As the supply of silk increased, its many varieties circulated even more extensively across Afro-Eurasian trade routes. In Central Asia, silk was used as currency and as a means of accumulating wealth. In both China and the Byzantine Empire, silk became a symbol of high status, and governments passed laws that restricted silk clothing to members of the elite. Furthermore, silk became associated with the sacred in the expanding world religions of Buddhism and Christianity. Chinese Buddhist pilgrims who made their way to India seeking religious texts and relics took with them large quantities of silk as gifts to the monasteries they visited. Buddhist monks in China received purple silk robes from Tang dynasty emperors as a sign of high honor. In the world of Christendom, silk wall hangings, altar covers, and vestments became highly prestigious signs of devotion and piety. Because no independent silk industry developed in Western Europe until the twelfth century C.E., a considerable market developed for silks imported from the Islamic world. Ironically, the splendor of Christian churches depended in part on Islamic trading networks and on silks manufactured in the Muslim world. Some of those silks were even inscribed with passages in Arabic from the Quran, unbeknownst to their European buyers.[5] By the twelfth century, the West African king of Ghana was wearing silk, and that fabric circulated in Egypt, Ethiopia, and along the East African coast as well.

A Muslim Silk Hanging in a Christian Cathedral This thirteenth-century silk hanging, created in the Islamic world, found a home in the Christian cathedral of Barcelona in Spain, illustrating that this precious fabric moved between civilizations. Around the seated figures is the text of the essential Muslim affirmation: "There is no God but God." (Werner Forman/Getty Images)

**Guided Reading
Question**

■ **CONNECTION**

What were the major
economic, social, and
cultural consequences
of Silk Road commerce?

Compared to contemporary global commerce, the volume of trade on the Silk Roads was modest, and its focus on luxury goods limited its direct impact on most people. Nonetheless, it had important economic and social consequences. Peasants in the Yangzi River delta of southern China sometimes gave up the cultivation of food crops, choosing to focus instead on producing silk, paper, porcelain, lacquerware, or iron tools, many of which were destined for the markets of the Silk Roads. In this way, the impact of long-distance trade trickled down to affect the lives of ordinary farmers. Furthermore, merchants could benefit immensely from their involvement in long-distance trade. One such individual, a twelfth-century Persian trader named Ramisht whose ships traversed the Indian Ocean and Red Sea, made a personal fortune with which he commissioned an enormously expensive covering made of Chinese silk for the Kaaba, the central shrine of Islam in Mecca.

Cultures in Transit

More important even than the economic impact of the Silk Roads was their role as a conduit of culture. Buddhism in particular, a cultural product of Indian civilization, spread widely throughout Central and East Asia, owing much to the activities of merchants along the Silk Roads. From its beginnings in India during the sixth century B.C.E., Buddhism had appealed to merchants, who preferred its universal message to that of a Brahmin-dominated Hinduism that privileged the higher castes. Indian traders and Buddhist monks, sometimes supported by rulers such as Ashoka, brought the new religion to the trans-Eurasian trade routes. To the west, Persian Zoroastrianism largely blocked the spread of Buddhism, but in the oasis cities of Central Asia, such as Merv, Samarkand, Khotan, and Dunhuang, Buddhism quickly took hold. By the first century B.C.E., many of the inhabitants of these towns had converted to Buddhism, and foreign merchant communities soon introduced it to northern China as well.

**Guided Reading
Question**

■ **CHANGE**

What accounted for the
spread of Buddhism
along the Silk Roads?

Particularly important in this process were the Sogdians, a Central Asian people whose merchants established an enduring network of exchange with China. Two such Sogdians living in China during the second century C.E. were instrumental in translating Sanskrit Buddhist texts into Chinese. Sogdians dominated Silk Road trade for much of the first millennium C.E., and their language became a medium of communication all along that commercial network.

Conversion to Buddhism in the oasis cities was a voluntary process, without the pressure of conquest or foreign rule. Dependent on long-distance trade, the inhabitants and rulers of those sophisticated and prosperous cities found in Buddhism a link to the larger, wealthy, and prestigious civilization of India. Well-to-do Buddhist merchants could earn religious merit by building monasteries and supporting monks. The monasteries in turn provided convenient and culturally familiar places of rest and resupply for merchants making the long and arduous trek across Central Asia. Many of these cities became cosmopolitan centers of learning and commerce.

Dunhuang Located in western China at a critical junction of the Silk Road trading network, Dunhuang was also a center of Buddhist learning, painting, and sculpture as that religion made its way from India to China and beyond. In some 492 caves, carved out of the rock between about 400 and 1400 C.E., a remarkable gallery of Buddhist art has been preserved. In this image the Buddha is surrounded by other enlightened beings or bodhisattvas. (Steve Vidler/Prisma by Dukas Presseagentur GmbH/Alamy)

Thousands of Buddhist texts, together with hundreds of cave temples lavishly decorated with murals and statues, have been discovered in the city of Dunhuang, where several branches of the Silk Roads joined to enter western China.

Outside of the oasis communities, Buddhism progressed only slowly among pastoral peoples of Central Asia. The absence of a written language was an obstacle to the penetration of a highly literate religion, and pastoralists' nomadic ways made the founding of monasteries, so important to Buddhism, quite difficult. But as pastoralists became involved in long-distance trade or came to rule settled agricultural peoples, Buddhism seemed more attractive. The nomadic Jie people, who controlled much of northern China after the collapse of the Han dynasty, are a case in point. Their ruler in the early fourth century C.E., Shi Le, became acquainted with a Central Asian Buddhist monk called Fotudeng who had traveled widely on the Silk Roads. The monk's reputation as a miracle worker, a rainmaker, and a fortune-teller and his skills as a military strategist cemented a personal relationship with Shi Le and led to the conversions of thousands and the construction of hundreds of Buddhist temples. In China itself, Buddhism remained for many centuries a religion of foreign merchants or foreign rulers. Only slowly did it become popular among the Chinese themselves, a process examined more closely in Chapter 8.

As Buddhism spread across the Silk Roads from India to Central Asia, China, and beyond, it also changed. The original faith had shunned the material world, but Buddhist monasteries in the rich oasis towns of the Silk Roads found themselves very much involved in secular affairs. Some of them became quite prosperous, receiving gifts from well-to-do merchants, artisans, and local rulers. The begging bowls of the monks became a symbol rather than a daily activity. Sculptures and murals in the monasteries depicted musicians and acrobats, women applying makeup, and even drinking parties, all of which suggested a more wealthy and worldly style of living, far removed from traditions of Buddhist asceticism.

Doctrines changed as well. It was the more devotional Mahayana form of Buddhism (see Chapter 4)—featuring the Buddha as a deity, numerous bodhisattvas, an emphasis on compassion, and the possibility of earning merit—that flourished on the Silk Roads, rather than the more austere psychological teachings of the historical Buddha. Moreover, Buddhism picked up elements of other cultures while in transit on the Silk Roads. In the Sogdian city of Samarkand, the use of Zoroastrian fire rituals apparently became a part of Buddhist practice. And in the area northwest of India that had been influenced by the invasions of Alexander the Great, statues of the Buddha reveal distinctly Greek and Roman influences in dress and physical features. In a similar way, the gods of many peoples along the Silk Roads were incorporated into Buddhist practice as bodhisattvas.

Disease in Transit

Beyond goods and cultures, diseases too traveled the trade routes of Eurasia, and with devastating consequences. Each of the major population centers of the Afro-Eurasian world had developed characteristic disease patterns, mechanisms for dealing with them, and in some cases immunity to them. But when contact among previously isolated human communities occurred, people were exposed to unfamiliar diseases for which they had little immunity or few effective methods of coping. The epidemics that followed often brought suffering and death on an enormous scale to rich and poor alike. An early example involved the Greek city-state of Athens, which in 430–429 B.C.E. was suddenly afflicted by a new and still-unidentified infectious disease that had entered Greece via seaborne trade from Egypt, killing perhaps 25 percent of its army and permanently weakening the city-state.

Even more widespread diseases affected the Roman Empire and Han dynasty China as the Silk Roads promoted contact all across Eurasia, particularly from the second century C.E. on. Smallpox, measles, various forms of plague, and perhaps malaria devastated the populations of both empires, contributing to their political collapse. Paradoxically, such disasters may well have strengthened the appeal of Christianity in Europe and Buddhism in China, for both of them offered compassion in the face of immense suffering.

Again in the period between 534 and 750 C.E., intermittent outbreaks of bubonic plague ravaged the coastal areas of the Mediterranean Sea. One leading theory suggests

Guided Reading
Question
....
■ CONNECTION
What was the impact of
disease along the Silk
Roads?

that black rats and the infected fleas they bore carried the disease via the seaborne trade with India, Ethiopia, and Egypt. What followed was catastrophic. Constantinople, the capital city of the Byzantine Empire, lost thousands of people per day during a forty-day period in 534 C.E., according to a contemporary historian. The repeated recurrence of the disease over the next several centuries also weakened the ability of Christendom to resist Muslim armies from Arabia in the seventh century C.E.

The most well-known dissemination of disease was associated with the Mongol Empire, which briefly unified much of the Eurasian landmass during the thirteenth and fourteenth centuries C.E. (see "The Plague: An Afro-Eurasian Pandemic" in Chapter 11). That era of intensified interaction facilitated the spread of the **Black Death**—identified variously with the bubonic plague, anthrax, or a package of epidemic diseases—from China to Europe. Its consequences were enormous. Between 1346 and 1348, up to half of the population of Europe perished from the plague. "A dead man," wrote the Italian writer Boccaccio, "was then of no more account than a dead goat."[6] A similar death toll afflicted China and parts of the Islamic world. The Central Asian steppes, home to many nomadic peoples, including the Mongols, also suffered terribly, undermining Mongol rule and permanently altering the balance between pastoral and agricultural peoples to the advantage of settled farmers. In these and many other ways, disease carried by long-distance trade shaped the lives of millions and altered the historical development of entire civilizations.

In the long run of world history, the exchange of diseases gave Europeans a certain advantage when they confronted the peoples of the Western Hemisphere after 1500. Exposure over time had provided them with some degree of immunity to Eurasian diseases. In the Americas, however, the absence of domesticated animals, the less intense interaction among major centers of population, and isolation from the Eastern Hemisphere ensured that native peoples had little defense against the diseases of Europe and Africa. Thus, when their societies were suddenly confronted by Europeans and Africans from across the Atlantic, they perished in appalling numbers. Such was the long term outcome of the very different histories of the two hemispheres.

Sea Roads: Exchange across the Indian Ocean

If the Silk Roads linked Eurasian societies by land, sea-based trade routes likewise connected distant peoples all across the Eastern Hemisphere. Since the days of the Phoenicians, Greeks, and Romans, the Mediterranean Sea had been an avenue of maritime commerce throughout the region, a pattern that continued during the third-wave era. The Italian city of Venice emerged by 1000 C.E. as a major center of that commercial network, with its ships and merchants active in the Mediterranean and Black seas as well as on the Atlantic coast. Much of its wealth derived from control of expensive and profitable imported goods from Asia, many of which came up the Red Sea through the Egyptian port of Alexandria. There Venetian merchants picked up those goods and resold them throughout the Mediterranean basin. This type of transregional exchange linked the maritime commerce of the

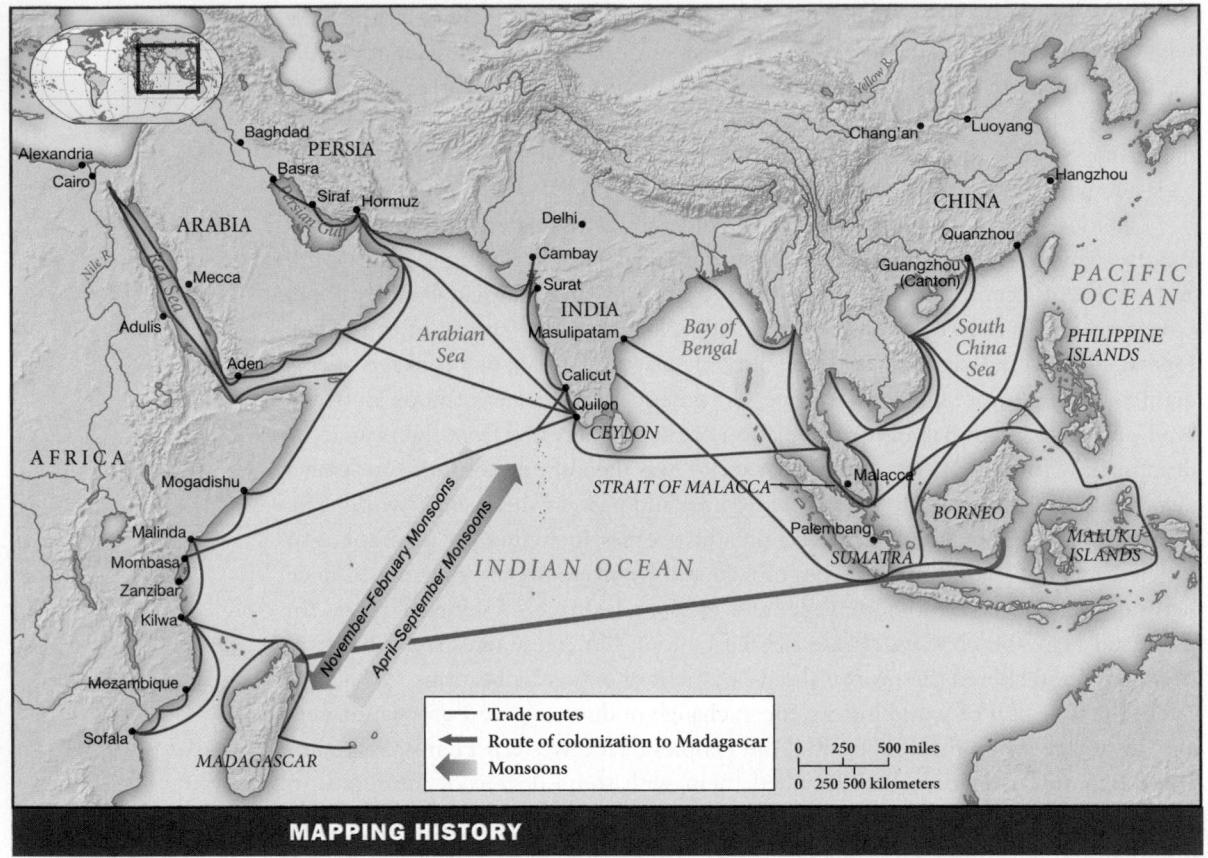

Map 7.2 The Sea Roads

Paralleling the Silk Road trading network, a sea-based commerce in the Indian Ocean basin connected the many peoples between China and East Africa.

READING THE MAP: If a captain wanted to sail from Malindi on the east coast of Africa to Calicut in southern India, what months in the monsoon season would give favorable winds?

MAKING CONNECTIONS: Compare this map with Map 7.1: The Silk Roads. Where do the Silk and Sea Roads intersect? What different geographical obstacles might travelers or traders confront on these two routes?

Mediterranean Sea to the much larger and more extensive network of seaborne trade in the Indian Ocean basin.

Until the creation of a genuinely global oceanic system of trade after 1500, the Indian Ocean represented the world's largest sea-based system of communication and exchange, stretching from southern China to eastern Africa (see Map 7.2). Like the Silk Roads, these transoceanic trade routes—the **Sea Roads**—grew out of the vast environmental and cultural diversities of the region. The desire for various goods not available at home—such as porcelain from China, spices from the islands of Southeast Asia (present-day Indonesia), cotton goods and pepper from India, ivory and gold from the East African coast, incense from southern

Arabia—provided incentives for Indian Ocean commerce. Transportation costs were lower on the Sea Roads than on the Silk Roads because ships could accommodate larger and heavier cargoes than camels. Thus the Sea Roads could eventually carry more bulk goods and products destined for a mass market—textiles, pepper, timber, rice, sugar, wheat—whereas the Silk Roads were limited largely to luxury goods for the few.

What made Indian Ocean commerce possible were the monsoons, alternating wind currents that blew predictably northeast during the summer months and southwest during the winter (see Map 7.2). An understanding of monsoons and a gradually accumulating technology of shipbuilding and oceanic navigation drew on the ingenuity of many peoples—Chinese, Malays, Indians, Arabs, Swahilis, and others. Collectively they made "an interlocked human world joined by the common highway of the Indian Ocean."[7]

But this world of Indian Ocean commerce did not involve exchanges between entire regions and certainly not between "countries," even though historians sometimes write about India, Indonesia, Southeast Asia, or East Africa as a matter of convenience. It operated rather across a network of towns and cities whose merchants often had more in common with one another than with the people of their own hinterlands.[8] These urban centers, strung out around the entire Indian Ocean basin, provided the nodes of this widespread commercial network.

Weaving the Web of an Indian Ocean World

The world of Indian Ocean commerce was long in the making, dating back to the time of the First Civilizations. Archeological finds in both Mesopotamia and India have disclosed seaborne trade via the Persian Gulf between ancient Mesopotamia and the Indus Valley civilization. The ancient Egyptians, and later the Phoenicians, likewise traded down the Red Sea, exchanging their manufactured goods for gold, ivory, frankincense, and slaves from the coasts of Ethiopia, Somalia, and southern Arabia. These ventures mostly hugged the coast and took place over short distances. Malay sailors, however, jumped off from the islands of present-day Indonesia during the first millennium B.C.E. and made their way in double-outrigger canoes across thousands of miles of open ocean to the East African island of Madagascar. There they introduced their Austronesian language and their crops—bananas, coconuts, and taro—which soon spread to the mainland, where they greatly enriched the diets of African peoples.

An Arab Dhow Painted by the thirteenth-century Arab artist Al-Wasiti, this image shows an oceangoing vessel of Indian or Arab origin known as a *dhow*, which was central to the commerce of the Sea Roads. In use in the Red Sea and Indian Ocean since at least the early centuries of the Common Era, dhows used triangular sails and were constructed by sewing or stitching the boards of the hull together with fibers, cords, or thongs without nails. (Miniature from the "Maqam" or "Assembly" illustrated by Yahya ibn Mahmud al-Wasiti, 1237/Pictures from History/Bridgeman Images)

SNAPSHOT Economic Exchange in the Indian Ocean Basin

Region	Products Contributed to Indian Ocean Commerce
Mediterranean basin	ceramics, glassware, wine, gold, olive oil
East Africa	ivory, gold, iron goods, slaves, tortoiseshells, quartz, leopard skins
Arabia	frankincense, myrrh, perfumes
India	grain, ivory, precious stones, cotton textiles, spices, timber, tortoiseshells
Southeast Asia	tin, sandalwood, cloves, nutmeg, mace
China	silks, porcelain, tea

The tempo of Indian Ocean commerce picked up during the early centuries of the Common Era, as mariners learned how to ride the monsoons. Various technological innovations also facilitated Indian Ocean trade — improvements in sails, new kinds of ships such as Chinese *junks* and Indian or Arab *dhows*, new means of calculating latitude such as the astrolabe, and evolving versions of the magnetic needle or compass. Merchants from the Roman world, mostly Greeks, Syrians, and Jews, established settlements in southern India and along the East African coast. The introduction of Christianity into both Axum and Kerala (in southern India) testifies to the long-term cultural impact of that trade. In the eastern Indian Ocean and the South China Sea, Chinese and Southeast Asian merchants likewise generated a growing commerce, and by 100 c.e. Chinese traders had reached India.

The fulcrum of this growing commercial network lay in India itself. Its ports bulged with goods from both west and east, as illustrated in the Snapshot above. Its merchants were in touch with Southeast Asia by the first century c.e., and settled communities of Indian traders appeared throughout the Indian Ocean basin and as far away as Alexandria in Egypt. Indian cultural practices such as Hinduism and Buddhism, as well as South Asian political ideas, began to take root in Southeast Asia.

In the era of third-wave civilizations between 600 and 1450, two major processes changed the landscape of the Afro-Eurasian world and wove the web of Indian Ocean exchange even more densely than before. One was the economic and political revival of China, some four centuries after the collapse of the Han dynasty (see Chapter 8). Especially during the Tang and Song dynasties (618–1279), China reestablished an effective and unified state, which actively encouraged maritime trade. China's population shifted southward along with many of the most productive parts of the commercial economy, which grew impressively during this period. This geographic shift led to the expansion of Chinese maritime trade as Chinese products poured out of southern port towns into the circuits of Indian Ocean commerce, even as the thriving Chinese economy attracted goods from India and

Guided Reading Question

....

■ **CHANGE**

What lay behind the flourishing of Indian Ocean commerce in the postclassical millennium?

Southeast Asia. Chinese technological innovations, such as larger ships and the magnetic compass, likewise added to the momentum of commercial growth.

A second transformation in the world of Indian Ocean commerce involved the sudden rise of Islam in the seventh century C.E. and its subsequent spread across much of the Afro-Eurasian world (see Chapter 9). Unlike Confucian culture, which was quite suspicious of merchants, Islam was friendly to commercial life; the Prophet Muhammad himself had been a trader. The creation of an Arab Empire, stretching from the Atlantic Ocean through the Mediterranean basin and all the way to India, brought together in a single political system an immense range of economies and cultural traditions and provided a vast arena for the energies of Muslim traders.

Those energies greatly intensified commercial activity in the Indian Ocean basin. Middle Eastern gold and silver flowed into southern India to purchase pepper, pearls, textiles, and gemstones. Muslim merchants and sailors, as well as Jews and Christians living within the Islamic world, established communities of traders from East Africa to the south China coast. Efforts to reclaim wasteland in Mesopotamia to produce sugar and dates for export stimulated a slave trade from East Africa, which landed thousands of Africans in southern Iraq to work on plantations and in salt mines under horrendous conditions. A massive fifteen-year revolt (868–883) among these slaves badly disrupted the Islamic Abbasid Empire before that rebellion was brutally crushed.

Beyond these specific outcomes, the expansion of Islam gave rise to an international maritime culture by 1000, shared by individuals living in the widely separated port cities around the Indian Ocean. The immense prestige, power, and prosperity of the Islamic world stimulated widespread conversion, which in turn facilitated commercial transactions. Even those who did not convert to Islam, such as Buddhist rulers in Burma, nonetheless regarded it as commercially useful to assume Muslim names. Thus was created "a maritime Silk Road . . . a commercial and informational network of unparalleled proportions."[9] After 1000, the culture of this network was increasingly Islamic.

Sea Roads as a Catalyst for Change: Southeast Asia

Oceanic commerce transformed all of its participants in one way or another, but nowhere more so than in Southeast Asia and East Africa, at opposite ends of the Indian Ocean network. In both regions, trade stimulated political change as ambitious or aspiring rulers used the wealth derived from commerce to construct larger and more centrally governed states or cities. Both areas likewise experienced cultural change as local people were attracted to foreign religious ideas from Confucian, Hindu, Buddhist, or Islamic sources. As on the Silk Roads, trade was a conduit for culture.

Located between the major civilizations of China and India, Southeast Asia was situated by geography to play an important role in the evolving world of Indian Ocean commerce. During the third-wave era, a series of cities and states or kingdoms

Guided Reading Question

■ **CONNECTION**
In what ways did Indian influence register in Southeast Asia?

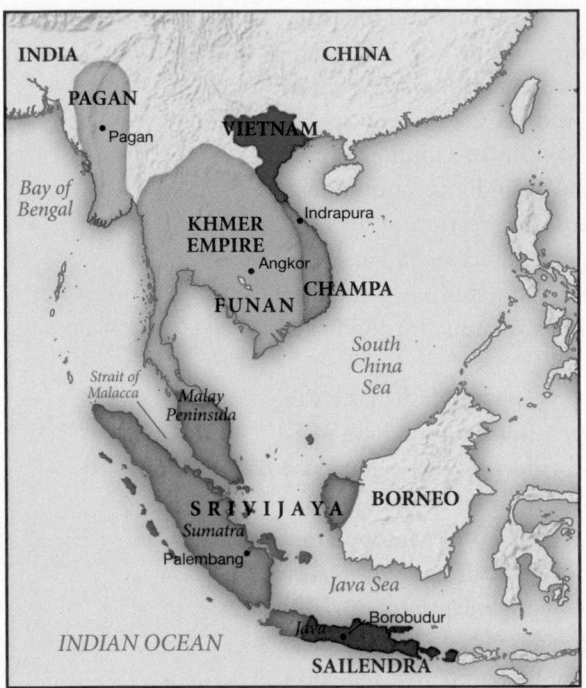

Map 7.3 Southeast Asia, ca. 1200 c.e.
Both mainland and island Southeast Asia were centrally involved in the commerce of the Indian Ocean basin, and both were transformed by that experience.

emerged on both the islands and mainland of Southeast Asia that represented new civilizations in this vast region (see Map 7.3). That process paralleled a similar development of new civilizations in East and West Africa, Japan, Russia, and Western Europe in what was an Afro-Eurasian phenomenon. In Southeast Asia, many of those new societies were stimulated and decisively shaped by their interaction with the sea-based trade of the Indian Ocean.[10]

The case of **Srivijaya** (SREE-vih-juh-yuh) illustrates the connection between commerce and state building. When Malay sailors, long active in the waters around Southeast Asia, opened an all-sea route between India and China through the Straits of Malacca around 350 c.e., the many small ports along the Malay Peninsula and the coast of Sumatra began to compete intensely to attract the growing number of traders and travelers making their way through the straits. From this competition emerged the Malay kingdom of Srivijaya, which dominated this critical choke point of Indian Ocean trade from 670 to 1025. A number of factors—Srivijaya's plentiful supply of gold; its access to the source of highly sought-after spices, such as cloves, nutmeg, and mace; and the taxes levied on passing ships—provided resources to attract supporters, to fund an embryonic bureaucracy, and to create the military and naval forces that brought some security to the area.

The inland states on the mainland of Southeast Asia, whose economies were based more on domestically produced rice than on international trade, nonetheless participated in the commerce of the region. The state of Funan, which flourished during the first six centuries of the Common Era in what is now southern Vietnam and eastern Cambodia, hosted merchants from both India and China. Archeologists have found Roman coins as well as trade goods from Persia, Central Asia, and Arabia in the ruins of its ancient cities. The Khmer kingdom of Angkor (flourished 800–1300) exported exotic forest products, receiving in return Chinese and Indian handicrafts, while welcoming a considerable community of Chinese merchants. Traders from Champa in what is now central and southern Vietnam operated in China, Java, and elsewhere, practicing piracy when trade dried up.

Beyond the exchange of goods, commercial connections served to spread elements of Indian culture across much of Southeast Asia, even as Vietnam was incorporated into the Chinese sphere of influence. (See "Vietnam and China" in Chapter 8.) Indian alphabets such as Sanskrit and Pallava were used to write a number of Southeast Asian languages. Indian artistic forms provided models for Southeast Asian sculpture and architecture, while the Indian epic *Ramayana* became widely popular across the region.

Borobudur This huge Buddhist monument in Java, constructed probably in the ninth century c.e., was later abandoned and covered with layers of volcanic ash and vegetation as Java came under Islamic influence. It was rediscovered by British colonial authorities in the early nineteenth century and has undergone several restorations over the past two centuries. Although Indonesia is a largely Muslim country, its small Buddhist minority still celebrates the Buddha's birthday at Borobudur. (Luca Tettoni/robertharding/Alamy)

Politically, Southeast Asian rulers and elites found attractive the Indian belief that leaders were god-kings, perhaps reincarnations of a Buddha or the Hindu deity Shiva. Srivijayan monarchs, for example, employed Indians as advisers, clerks, or officials and assigned Sanskrit titles to their subordinates. The capital city of Palembang was a cosmopolitan place, where even the parrots were said to speak four languages. While these rulers drew on indigenous beliefs that chiefs possessed magical powers and were responsible for the prosperity of their people, they also made use of imported Indian political ideas and Buddhist religious concepts, which provided a "higher level of magic" for rulers as well as the prestige of association with Indian civilization.[11] They also sponsored the creation of images of the Buddha and various bodhisattvas whose faces resembled those of deceased kings and were inscribed with traditional curses against anyone who would destroy them. Srivijaya grew into a major center of Buddhist observance and teaching, attracting thousands of monks and students from throughout the Buddhist world. The seventh-century Chinese monk Yi Jing was so impressed that he advised Buddhist monks headed for India to study first in Srivijaya for several years.

Elsewhere as well, elements of Indian culture took hold in Southeast Asia. The Sailendra kingdom in central Java, an agriculturally rich region closely allied with Srivijaya, mounted a massive building program between the eighth and tenth

Angkor Wat Constructed in the early twelfth century, the Angkor Wat complex was designed as a state temple dedicated to the Hindu god Vishnu and was lavishly decorated with carved bas-reliefs depicting scenes from Hindu mythology. By the late thirteenth century, it was in use by Buddhists, as it is to this day. This photo shows a small section of the temple and three Buddhist monks in their saffron robes. (Jose Fuste Raga/ Getty Images)

centuries featuring Hindu temples and Buddhist monuments. The most famous, known as Borobudur, is an enormous mountain-shaped structure of ten levels, with a three-mile walkway and elaborate carvings illustrating the spiritual journey from ignorance and illusion to full enlightenment. The largest Buddhist monument anywhere in the world, it is nonetheless a distinctly Javanese creation, whose carved figures have Javanese features and whose scenes are clearly set in Java, not India. Its shape resonated with an ancient Southeast Asian veneration of mountains as sacred places and the abode of ancestral spirits. Borobudur represents the process of Buddhism becoming culturally grounded in a new place.

Hinduism too, though not an explicitly missionary religion, found a place in Southeast Asia. It was well established in the Champa kingdom, for example, where Shiva was worshipped, cows were honored, and phallic imagery was prominent. But the prosperous and powerful Angkor kingdom of the twelfth century C.E. hosted the most stunning architectural expression of Hinduism in the temple complex known as **Angkor Wat**. The largest religious structure in the premodern world, it sought to express a Hindu understanding of the cosmos centered on a mythical Mount Meru, the home of the gods. Later, it was used by Buddhists as well, with little sense of contradiction. To the west of Angkor, the state of Pagan likewise devoted enormous resources to shrines, temples, and libraries inspired by both Hindu and Buddhist faiths.

This extensive Indian influence in Southeast Asia has led some scholars to speak of the "Indianization" of the region, similar perhaps to the earlier spread of Greek culture within the empires of Alexander the Great and Rome. In the case of Southeast Asia, however, no imperial control accompanied Indian cultural influence. It was a matter of voluntary borrowing by independent societies that found Indian traditions and practices useful and were free to adapt those ideas to their own needs and cultures. Traditional religious practices mixed with the imported faiths or existed alongside them with little conflict. And much that was distinctively Southeast Asian persisted despite influences from afar. In family life, for example, most Southeast Asian societies traced an individual's ancestry from both the mother's and father's line, in contrast to India and China, where patrilineal descent was practiced. Furthermore, Southeast Asian women had fewer restrictions and a greater role in public life than women in the more patriarchal civilizations of China and India. They were generally able to own property together with their husbands and to initiate divorce. A Chinese visitor to Angkor observed, "It is the women who are concerned with commerce." Women in Angkor also served as gladiators, warriors, and members of the palace staff, and as poets, artists, and religious teachers. Almost 1,800 realistically carved images of women decorate the temple complex of Angkor Wat. In neighboring Pagan, a thirteenth-century queen, Pwa Saw, exercised extensive political and religious influence for some forty years amid internal intrigue and external threats, while donating some of her lands and property to a Buddhist temple. Somewhat later, but also via Indian Ocean commerce, Islam too began to penetrate Southeast Asia as the world of seaborne trade brought yet another cultural tradition to the region.

Sea Roads as a Catalyst for Change: East Africa

On the other side of the Indian Ocean, the transformative processes of long-distance trade were likewise at work, giving rise to **Swahili civilization**. Emerging in the eighth century C.E., this civilization took shape as a set of commercial city-states stretching all along the East African coast, from present-day Somalia to Mozambique.

The earlier ancestors of the Swahili lived in small farming and fishing communities, spoke Bantu languages, and traded with the Arabian, Greek, and Roman merchants who occasionally visited the coast during the second-wave era. But what stimulated the growth of Swahili cities was the far more extensive commercial life of the western Indian Ocean following the rise of Islam. As in Southeast Asia, local people and aspiring rulers found opportunity for wealth and power in the growing demand for East African products associated with an expanding Indian Ocean commerce. Gold, ivory, quartz, leopard skins, and sometimes slaves acquired from interior societies, as well as iron and processed timber manufactured along the coast, found a ready market in Arabia, Persia, India, and beyond. At least one East African giraffe found its way to Bengal in northeastern India, and from there was sent on

Guided Reading Question

······················

■ **CONNECTION**
What was the role of Swahili civilization in the world of Indian Ocean commerce?

to China. In response to such commercial opportunities, an African merchant class developed, villages turned into sizable towns, and clan chiefs became kings. A new civilization was in the making.

Between 1000 and 1500, that civilization flourished along the coast, and it was a very different kind of society from the farming and pastoral cultures of the East African interior. It was thoroughly urban, centered in cities of 15,000 to 18,000 people, such as Lamu, Mombasa, Kilwa, Sofala, and many others. Like the city-states of ancient Greece, each Swahili city was politically independent, was generally governed by its own king, and was in sharp competition with other cities. No imperial system or larger territorial states unified the world of Swahili civilization. Nor did any of these city-states control a critical choke point of trade, as Srivijaya did for the Straits of Malacca. Swahili cities were commercial centers that accumulated goods from the interior and exchanged them for the products of distant civilizations, such as Chinese porcelain and silk, Persian rugs, and Indian cottons. While the transoceanic journeys occurred largely in Arab vessels, Swahili craft navigated the coastal waterways, concentrating goods for shipment abroad. This long-distance trade generated class-stratified urban societies with sharp distinctions between a mercantile elite and commoners.

Culturally as well as economically, Swahili civilization participated in the larger Indian Ocean world. Arab, Indian, and Persian merchants were welcome visitors, and some settled permanently. Many ruling families of Swahili cities claimed Arab or Persian origins as a way of bolstering their prestige, even while they dined from Chinese porcelain and dressed in Indian cottons. The Swahili language, widely spoken in East Africa today, was grammatically an African tongue within the larger Bantu family of languages, but it was written in Arabic script and contained a number of Arabic loan words. A small bronze lion found in the Swahili city of Shanga and dating to about 1100 illustrates the distinctly cosmopolitan character of Swahili culture. It depicted a clearly African lion, but it was created in a distinctly Indian artistic style and was made from melted-down Chinese copper coins.[12]

Furthermore, Swahili civilization rapidly became Islamic. Introduced by Arab traders, Islam was voluntarily and widely adopted within the Swahili world. Like Buddhism in Southeast Asia, Islam linked Swahili cities to the larger Indian Ocean world, and these East African cities were soon dotted with substantial mosques. When Ibn Battuta (IH-buhn ba-TOO-tuh), a widely traveled Arab scholar, merchant, and public official, visited the Swahili coast in the early fourteenth century, he found altogether Muslim societies in which religious leaders often spoke Arabic, and all were eager to welcome a learned Islamic visitor. But these were African Muslims, not colonies of transplanted Arabs. A prominent historian of Ibn Battuta's travels commented on Swahili society: "The rulers, scholars, officials, and big merchants as well as the port workers, farmers, craftsmen, and slaves, were dark-skinned people speaking African tongues in everyday life."[13]

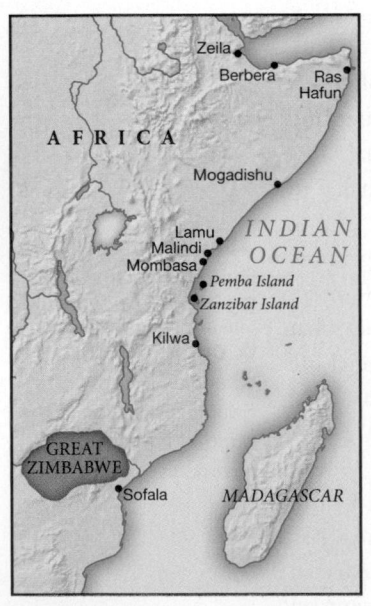

The Swahili Coast of East Africa

Islam sharply divided the Swahili cities from their African neighbors to the west, for neither the new religion nor Swahili culture penetrated much beyond the coast until the nineteenth century. Economically, however, the coastal cities acted as intermediaries between the interior producers of valued goods and the Arab merchants who carried them to distant markets. Particularly in the southern reaches of the Swahili world, this relationship extended the impact of Indian Ocean trade well into the African interior. Hundreds of miles inland, between the Zambezi and Limpopo rivers, lay rich sources of gold, much in demand on the Swahili coast. The emergence of a powerful state, known as **Great Zimbabwe**, seems clearly connected to the growing trade in gold to the coast as well as to the wealth embodied in its large herds of cattle. At its peak between 1250 and 1350, Great Zimbabwe had the resources and the labor power to construct huge stone enclosures entirely without mortar, with walls sixteen feet thick and thirty-two feet tall. "[It] must have been an astonishing sight," writes a recent historian, "for the subordinate chiefs and kings who would have come there to seek favors at court."[14] Here in the interior of southeastern Africa lay yet another example of the reach and transforming power of Indian Ocean commerce.

PRACTICING HISTORICAL THINKING

To what extent did the Silk Roads and the Sea Roads operate in a similar fashion? How did they differ?

Sand Roads: Exchange across the Sahara

In addition to the Silk Roads and the Sea Roads, another important pattern of long-distance trade—this one across the vast reaches of the Sahara in a series of **Sand Roads**—linked North Africa and the Mediterranean world with the land and peoples of interior West Africa. Like the others, these Sand Road commercial networks had a transforming impact, stimulating and enriching West African civilization and connecting it to larger patterns of world history during the third-wave era.

Commercial Beginnings in West Africa

Trans-African trade, like the commerce of the Silk Roads and the Sea Roads, was rooted in environmental variation. The North African coastal regions, long part of Roman or later Arab empires, generated cloth, glassware, weapons, books, and other manufactured goods. The great Sahara held deposits of copper and especially salt, and its oases produced sweet and nutritious dates. While the sparse populations of the desert were largely pastoral and nomadic, farther south lived agricultural peoples who grew a variety of crops, produced their own textiles and metal products, and mined a considerable amount of gold. These agricultural regions of sub-Saharan Africa are normally divided into two ecological zones: the savanna grasslands immediately south of the Sahara, which produced grain crops such as millet and sorghum, and the forest areas farther south, where root and tree crops such as yams and kola nuts predominated. These quite varied environments provided the economic incentive for the exchange of goods.

The Arabian Camel

Animals have their own histories, and they have long played a large role in human history as well. Consider the single-humped Arabian camel, for thousands of years an important means of transport and a beast of burden on the Silk and Sand Roads. Even today, the Arabian camel is a common sight across northern Africa and the Middle East. But it took millennia for this breed of camel to spread beyond its native Arabian Peninsula, where it had been domesticated by 3000 B.C.E. Camels were initially valued by Arab tribesmen for their milk; however, over time their endurance and ability to carry heavy loads resulted in their adoption as pack animals along the caravan routes between the frankincense- and myrrh-producing regions of southern Arabia and cities on the northern edges of the peninsula.

Part of a camel caravan.

This trade slowly introduced Arabian camels to the rest of the Middle East, where they were well established by 500 B.C.E. But the invention of a new saddle that allowed each animal to carry a heavier load transformed the camel into the most versatile and efficient form of transport in the region by 100 B.C.E. Ultimately the camel displaced the ox and cart, which for millennia had been a mainstay for moving goods. The advantages of the camel were significant. Camels ate desert plants that thrived on lands unsuitable to agriculture, while oxen required fodder grown on arable land. Moreover, camels carried loads on their backs rather than pulling carts made of wood, a scarce resource in the Middle East. In many parts of the region, the camel's triumph was complete. By 500 C.E., wheeled vehicles had

photo: BnF, Dist. RMN–Grand Palais/Art Resource, NY

The earliest long-distance trade within this huge region was not across the Sahara at all, but largely among the agricultural peoples themselves in the area later known to Arabs as the Sudan, or "the land of black people." On the basis of this trade, a number of independent urban clusters emerged by the early centuries of the Common Era, giving rise to the Niger Valley civilization, described in Chapter 6.

Gold, Salt, and Slaves: Trade and Empire in West Africa

A major turning point in African commercial life occurred with the introduction of the **Arabian camel** to North Africa and the Sahara in the early centuries of the Common Era. (See Zooming In: The Arabian Camel, above.) This remarkable animal, which could go for ten days without water, finally made possible the long trek across the Sahara. It was camel-owning dwellers of desert oases who initiated regular trans-Saharan commerce by 300 to 400 C.E. Several centuries later, North African Arabs, now bearing the new religion of Islam, also organized caravans across the desert.

What these Arab merchants sought, above all else, was gold, which was found in some abundance in the border areas straddling the grasslands and the forests of disappeared entirely from most of the Middle East, and the camel maintained its dominance for fifteen hundred years. In the 1780s, a French traveler in Syria commented, "It is noteworthy that in all of Syria no wagon or cart is seen."[15] Only with the emergence of the automobile in the twentieth century did the camel decisively lose its advantage over wheeled vehicles. From the Middle East, Arabian camels and related hybrid species moved along the Silk Roads, becoming a major means of transport as far away as modern Afghanistan. Only the cold climatic conditions of Central Asia halted their spread. In the frigid Gobi Desert, it was the Arabian camel's cousin—the two-humped Bactrian camel—that traders relied upon to carry their loads.

The Arabian camel had perhaps an even more profound impact on long-distance trade across the Sahara. Before the arrival of the camel, the western Sahara proved an imposing barrier to trade. Just a trickle of goods flowed across the vast arid region, often through indirect exchange. The first camels most likely filtered into western Africa from the Middle East along the southern borders of the Sahara around 200 B.C.E., and they probably arrived after 100 C.E. in Roman North Africa, where they were used for a variety of purposes, including the plowing of fields. From the time of their arrival, camels stimulated trade and contact across the Sahara, but these exchanges really took off when the Arab conquerors of North Africa brought their expertise in camel caravan trading to the region in the sixth century C.E. At their height, caravans of up to 5,000 camels regularly crossed the Sahara on several established routes, traveling mostly at night because of the heat. Covering 15 to 25 miles per day, it could take seventy days to traverse the desert, but profits from trade in gold, ivory, salt, and slaves made the journey worthwhile. These trade routes facilitated the emergence of empires in West Africa and the spread of Islam into the region. The Arabian camel remained the chief source of transport between sub-Saharan West Africa and the Mediterranean for over a thousand years, until European ships sailing along the Atlantic coast challenged their dominance in the fifteenth century.

QUESTIONS

Was the disappearance of the wheel an advance in terms of transport in the Middle East? What impact did the Arabian camel have on long-distance trade in Eurasia and Africa? How might reliance on the camel rather than the wheel affect human settlements?

West Africa. From its source, it was transported by donkey to transshipment points on the southern edge of the Sahara and then transferred to camels for the long journey north across the desert. African ivory, kola nuts, and slaves were likewise in considerable demand in the desert, the Mediterranean basin, and beyond. In return, the peoples of the Sudan received horses, cloth, dates, various manufactured goods, and especially salt from the rich deposits in the Sahara.

Thus the Sahara was no longer simply a barrier to commerce and cross-cultural interaction; for a thousand years, it was a major international trade route that fostered new relationships among distant peoples. As in Southeast Asia and East Africa, this trans-Saharan trade provided both incentives and resources for the construction of new and larger political structures. The West African peoples living in the savannah grasslands between the forests and the desert were in the best position to take advantage of these new opportunities. Between roughly 500 and 1600, a new **West African civilization** took shape in the region, stretching from the Atlantic coast to Lake Chad. It included the states of Ghana, Mali, Songhay, and Kanem, as well as numerous towns and cities such as Kumbi Saleh, Jenne, Timbuktu, Gao, Gobir, Kano, and others (see Map 7.4).

Guided Reading Question

....

■ **CONNECTION**
What changes did trans-Saharan trade bring to West Africa?

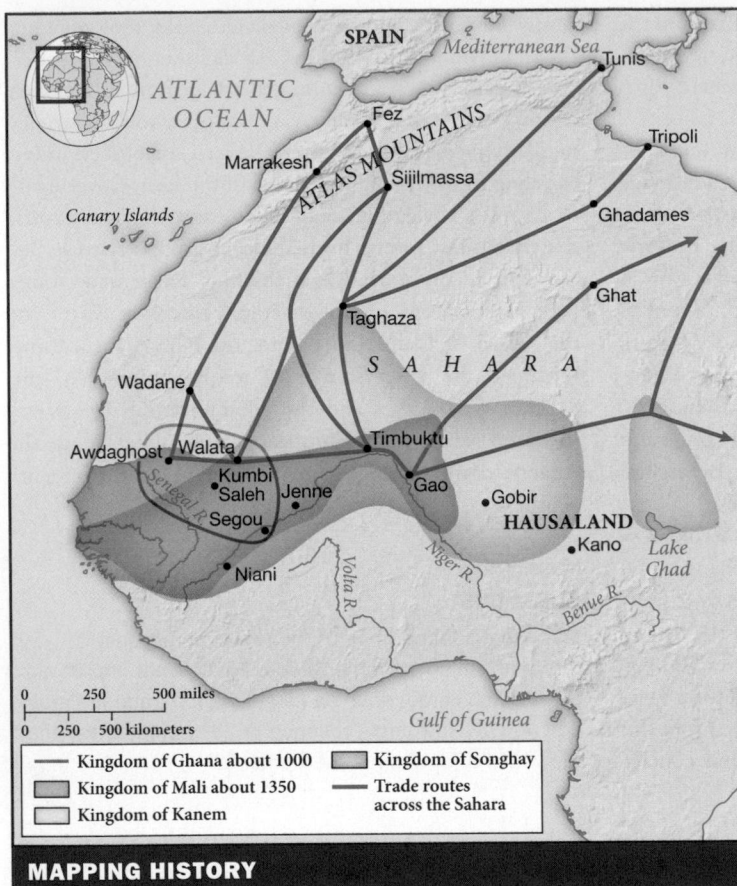

ATLANTIC OCEAN

SPAIN

Mediterranean Sea

Tunis

Fez

Tripoli

Marrakesh

Sijilmassa

Ghadames

Canary Islands

ATLAS MOUNTAINS

Ghat

Taghaza

S A H A R A

Wadane

Awdaghost

Walata

Timbuktu

Kumbi
Saleh

Jenne

Gao

Gobir

Segou

HAUSALAND

Niani

Kano

Lake
Chad

Senegal R.

Volta R.

Niger R.

Benue R.

Gulf of Guinea

0   250   500 miles

0   250   500 kilometers

— Kingdom of Ghana about 1000

▨ Kingdom of Mali about 1350

▨ Kingdom of Kanem

▨ Kingdom of Songhay

— Trade routes
across the Sahara

MAPPING HISTORY

Map 7.4 The Sand Roads

For a thousand years or more, the Sahara was an ocean of sand that linked the interior of West Africa with the world of North Africa and the Mediterranean but separated them as well.

READING THE MAP: Which cities were built at points where the Sand Roads trade routes arrived at the Niger River?

INTERPRETING THE MAP: The Kingdom of Mali was much larger than the earlier Kingdom of Ghana. What might you infer from the map about the motives for Mali's westward expansion?

All of these states were monarchies with elaborate court life and varying degrees of administrative complexity and military forces at their disposal. All drew on the wealth of trans-Saharan trade, taxing the merchants who conducted it. In the wider world, these states soon acquired a reputation for great riches. An Arab traveler in the tenth century C.E. described the ruler of **Ghana** as "the wealthiest king on the face of the earth because of his treasures and stocks of gold."[16] At its high point in the fourteenth century, the rulers of **Mali** monopolized the import of strategic goods such as horses and metals; levied duties on salt, copper, and other merchandise; and reserved large nuggets of gold for themselves while permitting the free export of gold dust. (See Working with Evidence, Source 7.4, for an early sixteenth-century account of this West African civilization.)

This growing integration with the world of international commerce generated the social complexity and hierarchy characteristic of all civilizations. Royal families and elite classes, mercantile and artisan groups, military and religious officials, free peasants and slaves—all of these were represented in this emerging West African civilization. So too were gender hierarchies, although without the rigidity of more established Eurasian civilizations. Rulers, merchants, and public officials were almost always male, and by 1200 earlier matrilineal descent patterns had been largely replaced by those tracing descent through the male line. Male bards, the repositories for their communities' history, often viewed powerful women as dangerous, not to be trusted, and a seductive distraction for men. But ordinary women were central to agricultural production and weaving; royal women played important political roles in many places; and oral traditions and mythologies frequently portrayed a complementary rather than hierarchal relationship between the sexes. According to a recent scholar:

> Men [in West African civilization] derive[d] their power and authority by releasing and accumulating *nyama* [a pervasive vital power] through acts of transforming one thing into another—making a living animal dead in hunting, making a lump of metal into a fine bracelet at the smithy. Women derive[d] their power from similar acts of transformation—turning clay into pots or turning the bodily fluids of sex into a baby.[17]

Certainly, the famous Muslim traveler Ibn Battuta, visiting Mali in the mid-fourteenth century, was surprised, and appalled, at the casual intimacy of unmarried men and women, despite their evident commitment to Islam.

As in all civilizations, slavery found a place in West Africa. Early on, most slaves had been women, working as domestic servants and concubines. As West African civilization crystallized, however, male slaves were put to work as state officials, porters, craftsmen, miners harvesting salt from desert deposits, and especially agricultural laborers producing for the royal granaries on large estates or plantations. Most came from non-Islamic and stateless societies farther south, which were raided during the dry season by cavalry-based forces of West African states. A song in honor of one eleventh-century ruler of Kanem boasted of his slave-raiding achievements:

> The best you took (and sent home) as the first fruits of battle. The children crying on their mothers you snatched away from their mothers. You took the slave wife from a slave, and set them in lands far removed from one another.[18]

Most of these slaves were used within this emerging West African civilization, but a **trans-Saharan slave trade** also developed. Between 1100 and 1400, perhaps 5,500 slaves per year made the perilous trek across the desert, where most were put to work in the homes of the wealthy in Islamic North Africa.

The states of this West African civilization developed substantial urban and commercial centers—such as Kumbi Saleh, Jenne, Timbuktu, Gao, Gobir, and Kano—where traders congregated and goods were exchanged. Some of these cities also became centers of manufacturing, creating finely wrought beads, iron tools, or cotton textiles, some of which entered the circuits of commerce. Visitors described them as cosmopolitan places where court officials, artisans, scholars, students, and local and

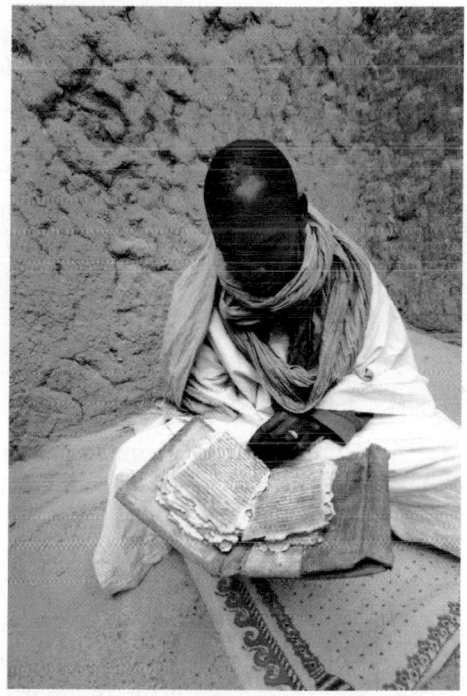

Manuscripts of Timbuktu The West African city of Timbuktu, a terminus of the Sand Road commercial network, became an intellectual center of Islamic learning—both scientific and religious. Its libraries were stocked with books and manuscripts, often transported across the Sahara from the heartland of Islam. Many of these have been preserved and are now being studied once again. (Alex Dissanayake/Getty Images)

foreign merchants all rubbed elbows. As in East Africa, Islam accompanied trade and became an important element in the urban culture of West Africa. Thus the growth of long-distance trade had stimulated the development of a West African civilization, which was linked to the wider networks of exchange in the Eastern Hemisphere.

An American Network: Commerce and Connection in the Western Hemisphere

Before the voyages of Columbus, the world of the Americas developed quite separately from that of Afro-Eurasia. But if the Silk, Sea, and Sand Roads linked the diverse peoples of the Eastern Hemisphere, did a similar network of interaction join and transform the various societies of the Western Hemisphere?

Clearly, direct connections among the various civilizations and cultures of the Americas were less densely woven than in the Afro-Eurasian region. The llama and the potato, both domesticated in the Andes, never reached Mesoamerica; nor did the writing system of the Maya diffuse to Andean civilizations. The Aztecs and the Incas, contemporary civilizations in the fifteenth century, had little if any direct contact with each other. The limits of these interactions owed something to the absence of horses, donkeys, camels, wheeled vehicles, and large oceangoing vessels, all of which facilitated long-distance trade and travel in Afro-Eurasia.

Geographic or environmental differences added further obstacles. The narrow bottleneck of Panama, largely covered by dense rain forests, surely inhibited contact between South and North America. Furthermore, the north/south orientation of the Americas—which required agricultural practices to move through, and adapt to, quite distinct climatic and vegetation zones—slowed the spread of agricultural products. By contrast, the east/west axis of Eurasia meant that agricultural innovations could diffuse more rapidly because they were entering roughly similar environments. Thus nothing equivalent to the long-distance trade of the Silk, Sea, or Sand Roads of the Eastern Hemisphere arose in the Americas, even though local and regional commerce flourished in many places. Nor did distinct cultural traditions spread widely to integrate distant peoples, as Buddhism, Christianity, and Islam did in the Afro-Eurasian world.

Nonetheless, scholars have discerned "a loosely interactive web stretching from the North American Great Lakes and upper Mississippi south to the Andes."[19] (See Map 7.5.) Partly, it was a matter of slowly spreading cultural elements, such as the gradual diffusion of maize from its Mesoamerican place of origin to the southwestern United States and then on to eastern North America as well as to much of South America in the other direction. A game played with rubber balls on an outdoor court has left traces in the Caribbean, Mexico, and northern South America. The spread of particular pottery styles and architectural conventions likewise suggests at least indirect contact over wide distances.

Commerce too played an important role in the making of this "**American web**." A major North American chiefdom at Cahokia, near present-day St. Louis, lay at the center of a widespread trading network. Those linkages brought to Cahokia shells from the Atlantic coast, copper from the Lake Superior region, buffalo hides from the Great Plains, obsidian from the Rocky Mountains, and mica from the southern Appalachian Mountains. Sturdy dugout canoes plied the rivers of the eastern woodlands, loosely connecting their diverse societies.

Early European explorers and travelers along the Amazon and Orinoco rivers of South America reported active networks of exchange that may well have operated for many centuries among densely populated settlements of agricultural peoples. Caribbean peoples using large oceangoing canoes had long conducted an inter-island trade, and the Chincha people of southern coastal Peru undertook a privately organized ocean-based exchange in copper, beads, and shells along the Pacific coasts of Peru and Ecuador in large seagoing rafts. Another regional commercial network, centered in Mesoamerica, extended north to what is now the southwestern United States

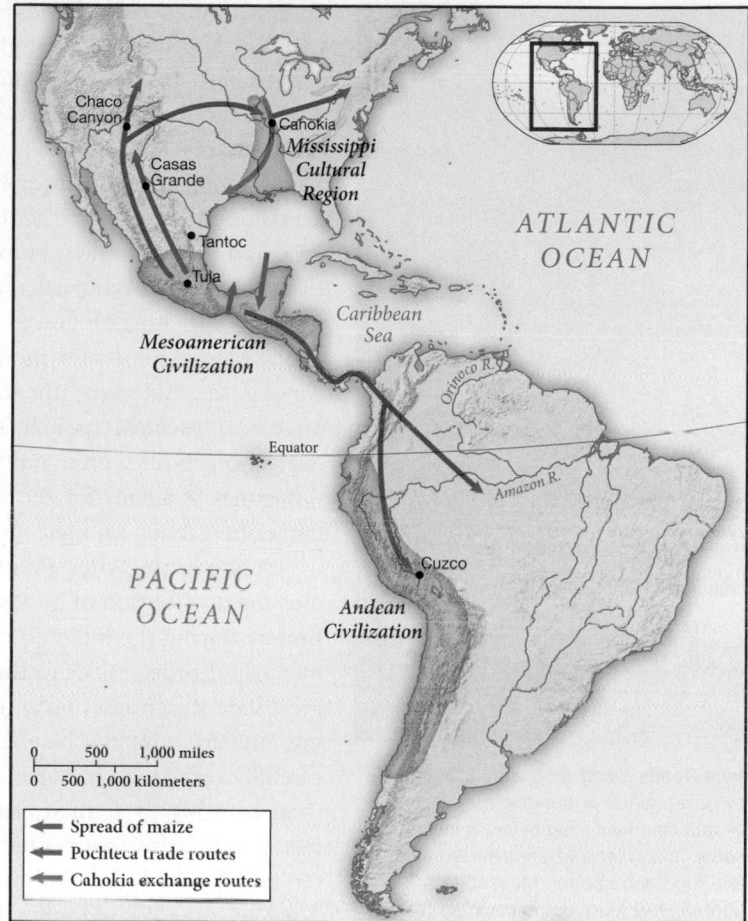

Map 7.5 The American Web

Transcontinental interactions within the American web were more modest than those of the Afro-Eurasian hemisphere. The most intense areas of exchange and communication occurred within the Mississippi valley, Mesoamerican, and Andean regions.

and south to Ecuador and Colombia. Many items from Mesoamerica—copper bells, macaw feathers, tons of shells—have been found in the Chaco region of New Mexico. Residents of Chaco also drank liquid chocolate, using jars of Maya origin and cacao beans imported from Mesoamerica, where the practice began. Turquoise, mined and worked by the people of Chaco (see "North America: Ancestral Pueblo and Mound Builders" in Chapter 6), flowed in the other direction.

But the most active and dense networks of communication and exchange in the Americas lay within, rather than between, the regions that housed the two great civilizations of the Western Hemisphere—Mesoamerica and the Andes. During the flourishing of Mesoamerican civilization (200–900 C.E.), both the Maya cities in the Yucatán area of Mexico and Guatemala and the huge city-state of

Inca Roads Used for transporting goods by pack animal or sending messages by foot, the Inca road network included some 2,000 inns where travelers might find food and shelter. Messengers, operating in relay, could cover as many as 150 miles a day. Here contemporary hikers still make use of an old Inca trail road. (William H. Mullins/Science Source)

Teotihuacán in central Mexico maintained commercial relationships with one another and throughout the region. In addition to this land-based trade, the Maya conducted a seaborne commerce, using large dugout canoes holding forty to fifty people, along both the Atlantic and Pacific coasts.

Although most of this trade was in luxury goods rather than basic necessities, it was critical to upholding the position and privileges of royal and noble families. Items such as cotton clothing, precious jewels, and feathers from particular birds marked the status of elite groups and served to attract followers. Controlling access to such high-prestige goods was an important motive for war among Mesoamerican states. Among the Aztecs of the fifteenth century, professional merchants known as *pochteca* (pohch-TEH-cah) undertook large-scale trading expeditions both within and well beyond the borders of their empire, sometimes as agents for the state or for members of the nobility, but more often acting on their own as private businessmen.

Unlike in the Aztec Empire, in which private traders largely handled the distribution of goods, economic exchange in the Andean Inca Empire during the fifteenth century was a state-run operation, and no merchant group similar to the Aztec pochteca emerged there. Instead, great state storehouses bulged with immense quantities of food, clothing, military supplies, blankets, construction materials, and more, all carefully recorded on *quipus* (knotted cords used to record numerical data) by a highly trained class of accountants. From these state centers, goods were transported as needed by caravans of human porters and llamas across the numerous roads and bridges of the empire. Totaling some 20,000 miles, Inca roads traversed the coastal plain and the high Andes in a north/south direction, while lateral roads linked these diverse environments and extended into the eastern rain forests and plains as well. Despite the general absence of private trade, local exchange took place at highland fairs and along the borders of the empire with groups outside the Inca state.

REFLECTIONS

Economic Globalization—Ancient and Modern

The densely connected world of the modern era, linked by ties of commerce and culture around the planet, has paralleled much earlier patterns. Particularly in the era of third-wave civilizations, the Silk, Sea, and Sand Roads of the Afro-Eurasian world and the looser networks of the American web linked distant peoples both economically and culturally, prompted the emergence of new states, and sustained elite privileges in many ancient civilizations. In those ways, they resembled the globalized world of modern times.

In other respects, though, the networks and webs of the premodern millennium differed sharply from those of more recent centuries. Most people still produced primarily for their own consumption rather than for the market, and a much smaller range of goods was exchanged in the marketplaces of the world. Far fewer people then were required to sell their own labor for wages, an almost universal practice in modern economies. Because of transportation costs and technological limitations, most trade was in luxury goods rather than in necessities. In addition, the circuits of commerce were rather more limited than the truly global patterns of exchange that emerged after 1500.

Furthermore, the world economy of the modern era increasingly had a single center—industrialized Western European countries—which came to dominate much of the world both economically and politically during the nineteenth century. Though never completely equal, the economic relationships of earlier times occurred among much more equivalent units. For example, no one region dominated the complex pattern of Indian Ocean exchange, although India and China generally offered manufactured goods, while Southeast Asia and East Africa mostly contributed agricultural products or raw materials. And with the exception of the brief Mongol control of the Silk Roads and the Inca domination of the Andes for a century, no single power exercised political control over the major networks of world commerce.

Economic relationships among third-wave civilizations, in short, were more balanced and multicentered than those of the modern era. Although massive inequalities occurred within particular regions or societies, interaction among the major civilizations operated on a rather more equal basis than in the globalized world of the past several centuries. With the rise of China, India, Turkey, and Brazil as major players in the world economy of the twenty-first century, are we perhaps witnessing a return to that earlier pattern?

Second Thoughts

What's the Significance?

Big Picture Questions

1. What motivated and sustained the long-distance commerce of the Silk Roads, Sea Roads, and Sand Roads?
2. Why did the peoples of the Eastern Hemisphere develop long-distance trade more extensively than did those of the Western Hemisphere?
3. "Cultural change often derived from commercial exchange in the third-wave era." What evidence from this chapter supports this observation?
4. In what ways was Afro-Eurasia a single interacting zone, and in what respects was it a vast region of separate cultures and civilizations?
5. **Looking Back:** Compared to the cross-cultural interactions of earlier times, what was different about those of the third-wave era?

Next Steps: For Further Study

Jerry Bentley, *Old World Encounters* (1993). A wonderfully succinct and engaging history of cross-cultural interaction all across Afro-Eurasia before 1500.

William J. Bernstein, *A Splendid Exchange* (2008). A global account of "how trade shaped the world."

E. W. Bovill, *The Golden Trade of the Moors* (1970). A classic account of the trans-Saharan trade.

K. N. Chaudhuri, *Trade and Civilization in the Indian Ocean* (1985). A well-regarded study that treats the Indian Ocean basin as a single region linked by both commerce and culture during the third-wave era.

Barry Cunliffe, *By Steppe, Desert, and Ocean: The Birth of Eurasia* (2015). Examines all of Eurasia over 10,000 years, with special focus on the Silk and Sea Roads that bound it together.

Philip Curtin, *Cross-Cultural Trade in World History* (1984). Explores long-distance trade as a generator of social change on a global level.

Xinru Liu, *The Silk Road in World History* (2010). A brief, accessible, and up-to-date account by a leading scholar.

J. R. McNeill and William H. McNeill, *The Human Web* (2003). A highly regarded survey of the evolving networks of human interaction by two leading world historians.

Marion Mayer-Hohdahl, "The Last Salt Caravan," Journeyman.tv, 2013, http://www.youtube.com/watch?v=yNwQeLFk74o. A ten-minute trailer for a documentary showing an early twenty-first-century camel caravan crossing the Sahara, reminiscent of much earlier caravans of the Sand Roads network.

Daniel Waugh, University of Washington, "Silk Road Seattle," 2007, http://depts.washington.edu/silkroad/. A wonderful website about the Silk Roads with many artistic images, primary sources, and maps as well as extensive narrative descriptions of that vast network of exchange.

Travelers' Tales and Observations

During the third-wave era, as long-distance trade flourished and large trans-regional empires grew, opportunities increased for individuals to travel far beyond their homelands. Their accounts have provided historians with invaluable information about particular regions and cultures, as well as about interactions among disparate peoples. The authors of these accounts, perhaps inadvertently, also reveal much about themselves and about the perceptions and misperceptions generated by cross-cultural encounters. The sources that follow offer examples of how intrepid long-distance travelers described distant lands and how artists and mapmakers depicted faraway regions for those who stayed at home.

SOURCE 7.1 A Chinese Buddhist in India

In 629, Xuanzang (SCHWEN-ZAHNG) (600–664 C.E.), a highly educated Buddhist monk from China, made a long and difficult journey to India through some of the world's most daunting deserts and mountain ranges, returning home in 645 C.E. after sixteen years abroad. His motives, like those of many other Buddhist travelers to India, were essentially religious. He wrote, "I regretted that the teachings of [Buddhism] were not complete and the scriptures deficient in my own country. . . . That was why I decided to travel to the West."[20] In India, the homeland of Buddhism, he hoped to find the teachers and the sacred texts that would answer his questions and resolve the many disputes that had created serious divisions within the Buddhist community of his own country.

During a ten-year stay in India, Xuanzang visited many of the holy sites associated with the Buddha's life and studied with leading Buddhist teachers, particularly those at Nalanda, a huge monastic complex dedicated to Buddhist scholarship (see Map 7.1, page 278). He traveled widely within India and established a personal relationship with Harsha, the ruler of the state that then encompassed much of northern India. On his return journey to China, he carried hundreds of manuscripts, at least seven statues of the Buddha, and even some relics. Warmly greeted by the Chinese emperor, Xuanzang spent the last two decades of his life translating the texts he had collected into Chinese. He also wrote an account of his travels, known as the *Record of the Western Regions,* from which this selection is drawn. It conveys something of Xuanzang's impressions of Indian civilization in the seventh century C.E.

- What surprised or impressed Xuanzang on his visit to India? What features of Indian life might seem most strange to a Chinese visitor?

- How might this selection illustrate or contradict the descriptions of Indian civilization found in Chapters 3–5?

- What can this document contribute to our understanding of Buddhist practice in India?

XUANZANG | *Record of the Western Regions* | 7th century C.E.

On Towns and Villages

The towns and villages have inner gates; the walls are wide and high; the streets and lanes are tortuous, and the roads winding. The thoroughfares are dirty and the stalls arranged on both sides of the road with appropriate signs. Butchers, fishers, dancers, executioners, and scavengers, and so on [untouchables], have their abodes without [outside] the city. In coming and going these persons are bound to keep on the left side of the road till they arrive at their homes. Their houses are surrounded by low walls and form the suburbs. . . .

On Buddhist Studies

The different schools are constantly at variance, and their contending utterances rise like the angry waves of the sea. The different sects have their separate masters. . . . There are eighteen schools, each claiming pre-eminence. . . . According to their fraternity, they are governed by distinctive rules and regulations. . . . When a man's renown has reached to a high distinction, then at different times he convokes an assembly for discussion. He judges of the superior or inferior talent of those who take part in it; he distinguishes their good or bad points; he praises the clever and reproves the faulty; if one of the assembly distinguishes himself by refined language, subtle investigation, deep penetration, and severe logic, then he is mounted on an elephant covered with precious ornaments, and conducted by a numerous suite to the gates of the convent.

If, on the contrary, one of the members breaks down in his argument, or uses poor and inelegant phrases, or if he violates a rule in logic and adapts his words accordingly, they proceed to disfigure his face with red and white, and cover his body with dirt and dust, and then carry him off to some deserted spot or leave him in a ditch. Thus they distinguish between the meritorious and the worthless, between the wise and the foolish.

On Caste and Marriage

With respect to the division of families, there are four classifications. The first is called the Brâhman, men of pure conduct. They guard themselves in religion, live purely, and observe the most correct principles. The second is called Kshattriya, the royal caste. For ages they have been the governing class: they apply themselves to virtue and kindness. The third is called Vaiśyas, the merchant class: they engage in commercial exchange, and they follow profit at home and abroad. The fourth is called Sûdra, the agricultural class: they labor in plowing and tillage. In these four classes purity or impurity of caste assigns to every one his place. When they marry they rise or fall in position according to their new relationship. They do not allow promiscuous marriages between relations. A woman once married can never take another husband. Besides these there are other classes of many kinds that intermarry according to their several callings.

On Manners and Justice

With respect to the ordinary people, although they are naturally light-minded, yet they are upright and honorable. In money matters they are without craft, and in administering justice they are considerate. They dread the retribution of another state of existence, and make light of the things of the present world. They are not deceitful or treacherous in their conduct, and are faithful to their oaths and promises. In their rules of government there is remarkable rectitude, whilst in their behavior there is much gentleness and sweetness. With respect to criminals or rebels, these are few in number, and only occasionally troublesome. When the laws are broken or the power of the ruler violated, then the matter is clearly sifted and the offenders imprisoned. There is no infliction of corporal punishment; they are simply left to live or die, and are not counted among men. When the rules of propriety or justice are violated, or when a man fails in fidelity or filial piety, then they cut his nose or his ears off, or his hands and feet, or expel him from the country or drive him out into the desert wilds. For other faults, except these, a small payment of money will redeem the punishment. In the investigation of criminal cases there is no use of rod or staff to obtain proofs (*of guilt*).

Source: Samuel Beal, trans., *Su-Yu-Ki: Buddhist Records of the Western World* (London: K. Paul, Trench, Trubner, 1906), vol. 1, bk. 2, 73–74, 80–84.

■ ■ ■

SOURCE 7.2 A European Christian in China

Of all the travelers along the Silk Road network, the best known and most celebrated, at least in the West, was Marco Polo (1254–1324). Born and raised in the prosperous commercial city-state of Venice in northern Italy, he was a member of a family engaged in the long-distance trade of the Mediterranean and Black Sea regions. At the age of seventeen, Marco accompanied his father and an uncle on an epic journey across Eurasia that, by 1275, brought the Polos to China, recently conquered by the Mongols. It was, in fact, the relative peace that the Mongols had created in their huge transcontinental empire that facilitated the Polos' journey (see Map 11.1, page 458). For the next seventeen years, they lived in China, where they were employed in minor administrative positions by Khubilai Khan, the country's Mongol ruler. During these years, Marco Polo apparently traveled widely within China, where he gathered material for a book about his travels, which he dictated to a friend after returning home in 1295. The selection that follows conveys Marco Polo's description of Hangzhou—one of the largest cities in the world at the time—which he refers to as Kinsay. Polo tells his reader that he constructed this description from both his visit to Hangzhou and a written account of the city sent to the Mongol khan in the hopes of sparing the city from destruction following its conquest.

■ How would you describe Marco Polo's impressions of the city? What did he notice? What surprised him?

■ Why did Marco Polo describe the city as "the finest and the noblest in the world"?

■ What marks his account of the city as that of a foreigner and a Christian?

■ What evidence of China's engagement with a wider world does this account offer?

MARCO POLO | *The Travels of Marco Polo* | 1299

The city is beyond dispute the finest and the noblest in the world.... First and foremost, then, the document stated the city of Kinsay to be so great that it hath an hundred miles of compass. And there are in it 12,000 bridges of stone.... [Most scholars consider these figures a considerable exaggeration.]

[T]here were in this city twelve guilds of the different crafts, and that each guild had 12,000 houses in the occupation of its workmen. Each of these houses contains at least twelve men, whilst some contain twenty and some forty. . . . And yet all these craftsmen had full occupation, for many other cities of the kingdom are supplied from this city with what they require.

[T]he number and wealth of the merchants, and the amount of goods that passed through their hands, were so enormous that no man could form a just estimate thereof. . . [T]hose masters of the different crafts . . . neither they nor their wives ever touch a piece of work with their own hands, but live as nicely and delicately as if they were kings and queens. . . .

Inside the city there is a Lake . . . and all round it are erected beautiful palaces and mansions, of the richest and most exquisite structure that you can imagine, belonging to the nobles of the city. There are also on its shores many abbeys and churches of the Idolaters [Buddhists]. In the middle of the Lake are two Islands, on each of which stands a rich, beautiful, and spacious edifice, furnished in such style as to seem fit for the palace of an Emperor. And when any one of the citizens desired to hold a marriage feast, or to give any other entertainment, it used to be done at one of these palaces. And everything would be found there ready to order, such as silver plate, trenchers, and dishes, napkins and table-cloths, and whatever else was needful. . . .

Both men and women are fair and comely, and for the most part clothe themselves in silk, so vast is the supply of that material, both from the whole district of Kinsay, and from the imports by traders from other provinces. And you must know they eat every kind of flesh, even that of dogs and other unclean beasts, which nothing would induce a Christian to eat. . . .

You must know also that the city of Kinsay has some 3,000 baths, the water of which is supplied by springs. They are hot baths, and the people take great delight in them, frequenting them several times a month, for they are very cleanly in their persons. They are the finest and largest baths in the world. . . .

And the Ocean Sea comes within twenty-five miles of the city at a place called Ganfu, where there is a town and an excellent haven, with a vast amount of shipping which is engaged in the traffic to and from India and other foreign parts, exporting and importing many kinds of wares, by which the city benefits. . . .

I repeat that everything appertaining to this city is on so vast a scale, and the Great [Khan's] yearly revenues therefrom are so immense, that it is not easy even to put it in writing. . . .

In this part are the ten principal markets, though besides these there are a vast number of others in the different parts of the town. . . . [T]oward the [market] squares are built great houses of stone, in which the merchants from India and other foreign parts store their wares, to be handy for the markets. In each of the squares is held a market three days in the week, frequented by 40,000 or 50,000 persons, who bring thither for sale every possible necessary of life, so that there is always an ample supply of every kind of meat and game. . . .

Other streets are occupied by the Physicians, and by the Astrologers, who are also teachers of reading and writing; and an infinity of other professions have their places round about those squares. In each of the squares there are two great palaces facing one another, in which are established the officers appointed by the King to decide differences arising between merchants, or other inhabitants of the quarter. . . .

The natives of the city are men of peaceful character, both from education and from the example of their kings, whose disposition was the same. They know nothing of handling arms, and keep none in their houses. You hear of no feuds or noisy quarrels or dissensions of any kind among them. Both in their commercial dealings and in their manufactures they are thoroughly honest and truthful, and there is such a degree of good will and neighborly attachment among both men and women that you would take the people who live in the same street to be all one family.

Source: *The Book of Ser Marco Polo, the Venetian, Concerning the Kingdoms and Marvels of the East,* translated and edited by Henry Yule (London: John Murray, 1871), 2:145–50, 158, 160–61.

■ ■ ■

SOURCE 7.3 **A European Artist Depicts Asia**

While Marco Polo's account is largely devoid of the wondrous monsters and races of humans that peopled many earlier European accounts of the East, his book did not immediately overturn these more fanciful ideas about distant lands. Source 7.3, an image that was created to illustrate an elaborate manuscript copy of Polo's book, provides a revealing window into the persistence of older ideas. Drawn around 1400, it depicts three mythical creatures—a blemmyae or headless man, a sciopod or single-footed man, and a cyclops or one-eyed monster—none of which are mentioned in Polo's text.

- What about the three figures and the landscape in which they are placed might evoke ideas of wilderness or barbarity in the viewer?

- Why might an artist commissioned to decorate Polo's book of travels choose to incorporate these mythical creatures despite their absence in the accompanying text?

- What does this source add to our understanding of how Europeans viewed East Asia in the early fifteenth century?

The Marvelous Races of the East | ca. 1410

From the "Livre des Merveilles du Monde," ca. 1410–1412 (tempera on vellum)/Boucicaut Master (fl. 1390–1430) (and workshop)/Bibliothèque Nationale de France, Paris, France/Bridgeman Images

■ ■ ■

SOURCE 7.4 A Moroccan Diplomat in West Africa

Known to the world by his European-derived nickname of Leo Africanus, this widely traveled Arabic-speaking Muslim was actually born as al-Hassan Ibn Muhammad al Wazzan in Granada, Spain, during the late fifteenth century, just as Islam was being pushed out of that country. His family moved to Fez in Morocco, where he was educated in Islamic law. Later, he served the sultan of Morocco as a diplomat and commercial agent, traveling widely in North Africa, the Middle East, Italy, and West Africa. On one of these journeys, he was captured by pirates and wound up in Rome, where he came to the attention of Pope Leo X. There he apparently converted to Christianity, at least for a time, though he later chose to live in Muslim North Africa and likely returned to his original Muslim faith. It was during his stay in Italy that he completed in 1526 the book for which he is most clearly remembered, *The History and Description of Africa*, based on observations and knowledge picked up during his travels. Later published in many languages, it became a major source of European knowledge of the African Islamic world, much as Marco Polo's writings introduced Europeans to China. In the following excerpts from that book, Leo Africanus describes several of the major kingdoms and cities of West African civilization.

■ Based on these accounts, how does Leo Africanus characterize West African civilization? What can you infer about his own attitude toward this civilization?

■ What connections between West Africa and a wider world are evident in these passages?

■ What can you learn about the role of slavery in West Africa at a time before the Atlantic slave trade had become big business?

■ Why do you think these passages say so little about the practice of Islam, focusing instead on political and economic matters? (Keep in mind that the book was first published in Italy and in Italian.) Despite this omission, what can you infer about variations in Islamic observance in West African civilization at this time?

LEO AFRICANUS │ *The History and Description of Africa* │ **1526**

The City of Timbuktu

All its houses are . . . cottages, built of mud and covered with thatch. However, there is a most stately mosque to be seen, whose walls are made of stone and lime, and a princely palace also constructed by the highly skilled craftsmen of Granada. Here there are many shops of artisans and merchants, especially of those who weave linen and cotton, and here Barbary [Muslim North African] merchants bring European cloth. The inhabitants, and especially resident aliens, are exceedingly rich, since the present king married both of his daughters to rich merchants. Here are many wells, containing sweet water. Whenever the Niger River overflows, they carry the water into town by means of sluices. This region yields great quantities of grain, cattle, milk, and butter, but salt is very scarce here, for it is brought here by land from Tegaza, which is five hundred miles away.

The rich king of Timbuktu has many plates and scepters of gold, some of which weigh 1,300 pounds, and he keeps a magnificent and well-furnished court. When he travels anywhere, he rides upon a camel, which is led by some of his noblemen. He does so likewise when going to war, and all his soldiers ride upon horses. Whoever wishes to speak to this king must first of all fall down before his feet and then taking up earth must sprinkle it on his own head and shoulders. . . . [The king] always has under arms 3,000 horsemen and a great number of foot soldiers who shoot poisoned arrows. They often skirmish with those who refuse to pay tribute and whomever they capture they sell to the merchants of Timbuktu. Here very few horses are bred. . . . Their best horses are brought out of North Africa. As soon as the king learns that any merchants have come to the town with horses, he commands that a certain number be brought before him. Choosing the best horse for himself, he pays a most liberal price for it. . . .

Here are great numbers of [Islamic] religious teachers, judges, scholars and other learned persons, who are bountifully maintained at the king's expense. Here too are brought various [Arabic] manuscripts or written books from Barbary, which are sold for more money than any other merchandise.

The coin of Timbuktu is gold, without any stamp or inscription, but in matters of small value they use certain shells from the kingdom of Persia.

The inhabitants are gentle and cheerful and spend a great part of the night in singing and dancing throughout the city streets. They keep large numbers of male and female slaves, and their town is greatly vulnerable to fire. At the time of my second visit, almost half the town burned down in the space of five hours.

The Kingdom of Borno

They embrace no religion at all, being neither Christian, Muhametans [Muslims], nor Jews, nor any other profession, but living after a brutish manner, having wives and children in common. . . . They have a most powerful prince. . . . He has in readiness as many as three thousand horsemen and a huge number of foot soldiers; for all his subjects are so serviceable and obedient to him, that whenever he commands them, they will arm themselves and will follow him wherever he leads them. They pay him no tribute except tithes on their grain; neither does the king have any revenues to support his state except the spoils he gets from his enemies by frequent invasions and assaults. He is in a state of perpetual hostility with a certain people who live beyond the desert of Seu, who in times past marching with a huge army of footsoldiers over the said desert, devastated a great part of the Kingdom of Borno. Whereupon the king sent for the merchants of Barbary and ordered them to bring him a great store of horses: for in this country they exchange horses for slaves, and sometimes give fifteen or twenty slaves for a horse. And by this means there were a great many horses bought although the merchants were forced to stay for their slaves until the king returned home as a conqueror with a great number of captives, and satisfied his creditors for his horses. Frequently it happens that the merchants must stay three months before the king returned from the wars. . . . Sometimes he does not bring home enough slaves to satisfy the merchants and sometimes they are forced to wait a whole year. . . . And yet the king seems marvelously rich, because his spurs, bridles, platters, dishes, pots, and other vessels are made of gold. The king is extremely covetous and would rather pay his debts in slaves rather than gold.

Source: Leo Africanus, *The History and Description of Africa*, edited by Robert Brown (London: The Hakluyt Society, 1896), 3:824–25, 833–34.

■ ■ ■

SOURCE 7.5 **A Korean World Map** ▶

Created in Korea in 1402, the Kangnido map by the Confucian scholar Kwŏn Kŭn is the oldest world map from East Asia of which copies survive. It provides an East Asian perspective on the world in the early fifteenth century, a period immediately following the collapse of the Mongol Empire, which had put distant regions of the Afro-Eurasia world into more sustained contact than ever before. The Kangnido map drew upon earlier maps from China, Korea, Japan, and the Islamic world. While Korea features prominently, appearing larger than Africa, China is understood as the center of the world, as Kwŏn Kŭn makes clear in the preface: "The world is very wide. We do not know how many tens of thousands of *li* there are from China in the center to the four seas in the outer limits." (A *li* is a Chinese unit of distance, about a third of a mile.) The map includes hundreds of place names for even the most remote regions of Eurasia. Most of those for North Africa and Europe incorporate Arabic or Persian roots, revealing the influence of Islamic maps and mapmakers brought to East Asia by the Mongols. Regional labels not original to the map have been added to help you orient yourself. Note that the Mediterranean Sea is clearly outlined between Africa and Europe but is not colored in. Also note that much of the center of Africa is shaded in, indicating either a large body of water or perhaps the Sahara Desert.

■ Compare this map with a modern map of Africa and Eurasia. Which regions does the map depict most accurately? Which are least accurate? Why might this be the case?

■ What can a map like this tell us about East Asian knowledge of Eurasia and Africa around 1400?

■ How does this map reflect a China-centered view of the world?

■ What types of questions might this map help historians to answer?

The Honkōji Copy of the Kangnido Map, Korea | 15th century

Pictures from History/Bridgeman Images

DOING HISTORY

1. **Describing a foreign culture:** All of these sources were created by outsiders to the peoples or societies they described. What different postures toward these foreign cultures are evident in the sources? How did the travelers' various religions shape their perception of the places they visited?

2. **Defining the self-perception of authors:** What can we learn from Sources 7.1, 7.2, and 7.4 about the men who wrote them? What motivated them to travel so far from home? How did they define themselves in relationship to the societies they observed?

3. **Assessing the credibility of sources:** What information in these sources would be most valuable for historians? What about these sources might be viewed with the most skepticism? You will want to consider the creators' purposes and their intended audiences.

4. **Considering outsiders' accounts:** What are the advantages and limitations for historians in drawing on the observations of foreign observers?

On Travel Writers

Travel accounts provide rich and often unique sources for historians, but they must be handled with care. The two selections that follow consider issues that historians confront when studying travelers' accounts. In Voice 7.1, John Larner, an expert on Marco Polo, examines the suspicion put forward by some that Polo never traveled to China. In Voice 7.2, Natalie Zemon Davis, a prominent historian of the early modern period, explores the audiences for which Leo Africanus wrote his book.

■ Why have scholars questioned whether Marco Polo actually traveled to China?

■ How might Leo Africanus have altered his account for a North African rather than Italian audience?

■ **Integrating Primary and Secondary Sources:** How do these two voices influence your reading of the Polo and Africanus selections in the source feature?

VOICE 7.1

John Larner on Whether Polo Really Traveled to China | 1999

From the eighteenth century, as a result above all of Marco's silence about many things in the China of his own time, the suspicion has been aroused in some readers that we are faced here with a fiction, the nagging doubt that the whole of Marco's story of having been to China is untrue. Why does he never mention the Great Wall? Why is there nothing about what, in the fourteenth century, Odoric da Pordenone [another traveler] was to notice: fishing with cormorants, or the binding up of young girls' feet? Why nothing on printing, Chinese script, acupuncture, tea or tea-houses? Why no mention of Confucianism or Taoism? Had he actually *seen* China . . . ? It is not too difficult to offer answers to most of these points. The myth of the Great Wall, for instance, obscures . . . the fact that much of it had fallen down by the thirteenth century. Almost everything the tourist is normally shown today was built in the sixteenth century. Referred to as the "sensi" or "sensin," Taoist monks are in fact briefly mentioned in

chapter LXXV. Foot binding was at this period limited to upper class ladies who were confined to their houses, and would be rarely observed by anyone outside their family. Tea-culture at that time had not reached North and Central China where Marco mostly resided. . . . [I]t can also easily be thought that Marco identified himself so strongly with Mongol rulers that he was indifferent to the mass of the population over whom they rule.

Source: John Larner, *Marco Polo and the Discovery of the World* (New Haven, CT: Yale University Press, 1999), 59.

VOICE 7.2

Natalie Zemon Davis on Leo Africanus's Audiences | 2006

He [Leo Africanus] was keeping notes throughout his travels and consulting manuscripts whenever he could; he may have had an initial plan for a book and partial drafts of some sections in Arabic on his person when he was kidnapped. However that may be, it was in Italy that he became an author, and the final version [of his book] bears the stamp of his stay there. . . .

In a sense, though, [Leo Africanus] wrote his book with two audiences in mind. His primary audience was in Italy. For his Italian readers he searched for equivalents in weights, measures, coinages, foods, and material objects. For them, he sought Italian translations for words with no perfect equivalent. . . . For them, he struggled valiantly to transcribe Arabic words, names, and place names. . . . For Italian readers, too, he included only those animals "not found in Europe or that were in some ways different from those in Europe."

Yet [he] also had African or at least North African readers and listeners in part of his mind as he composed. He must have imagined at least a few of them as possible readers of this Italian manuscript, and many of them as potential readers of a much revised Arabic version.

Source: Natalie Zemon Davis, *Trickster Travels: A Sixteenth-Century Muslim between Worlds* (New York: Hill and Wang, 2006), 105–7.

China and the World

East Asian Connections

600–1300

《 Chinese Astronomy The impressive achievements of Chinese astronomy included the observation of sunspots, supernovae, and solar and lunar eclipses as well as the construction of elaborate star maps and astronomical devices such as those shown here. The print itself is of Japanese origin and depicts a figure wearing the dragon robes of a Chinese official. It illustrates the immense cultural influence of China on its smaller Japanese neighbor.

"There is only one Earth in the universe and we mankind have only one homeland," observed the Chinese president Xi Jinping during his address before the United Nations in January 2017. "The Paris agreement is a milestone in the history of climate governance. We must ensure that this endeavor is not derailed."[1] With these words, the leader of China signaled his country's willingness to take a global leadership role in limiting climate change even as the United States was poised to withdraw from the Paris Accords under its new president Donald Trump. China's remarkable economic development since the 1980s had transformed it by the early twenty-first century into a major global power and one of the largest consumers of fossil fuels on the planet. Its decision to embrace the Paris Accords mattered to peoples and nations around the globe.

From the viewpoint of world history, China's recent prominence on the world stage was hardly something new, and its nineteenth- and twentieth-century position as a "backward," weak, or "developing" country was distinctly at odds with its long history. Its leadership on climate change provided another example of China resuming in recent years a much older and more powerful role in world affairs. ■

I n the world of third–wave civilizations, even more than in earlier times, China cast a long shadow. Its massive and powerful civilization, widely imitated by adjacent peoples, gave rise to a China-centered set of relationships encompassing Tibet, Korea, Japan, and Vietnam. China extended its borders deep into Central Asia, while its wealthy and cosmopolitan culture attracted visitors from all over Eurasia. Far beyond its near neighbors, China's booming economy and many technological innovations had ripple effects all across the Afro-Eurasian world.

Even as China so often influenced the world, it too was changed by its many interactions with non-Chinese peoples. Northern nomads—"barbarians" to the Chinese—frequently posed a military threat and on occasion even conquered and ruled parts of China. The country's growing involvement in international trade stimulated important social, cultural, and economic changes within China itself. Buddhism, a religion of Indian origin, took root in China, and, to a much lesser extent, so did Christianity and Islam. In short, China's engagement with the wider world became a very significant element in the global interactions of the third-wave era.

> ### SEEKING THE MAIN POINT
>
> Chinese history has often been viewed in the West as impressive perhaps, but largely static or changeless and self-contained or isolated. In what ways might the material in this chapter counteract such impressions?

Together Again: The Reemergence of a Unified China

The collapse of the Han dynasty around 220 C.E. ushered in more than three centuries of political fragmentation in China and signaled the rise of powerful and locally entrenched aristocratic families. It also meant the incursion of northern nomads, many of whom learned Chinese, dressed like Chinese, married into Chinese families, and governed northern regions of the country in a Chinese fashion. Such conditions of disunity, unnatural in the eyes of many thoughtful Chinese, discredited Confucianism and opened the door to a greater acceptance of Buddhism and Daoism among the elite. Those centuries also witnessed substantial Chinese migration southward toward the Yangzi River valley, a movement of people that gave southern China some 60 percent of the country's population by 1000. That movement of Chinese people, accompanied by their intensive agriculture, set in motion a vast environmental transformation marked by the destruction of the old-growth forests that once covered much of the country and the retreat of the elephants that had inhabited those lands. Around 800 C.E., the Chinese official and writer Liu Zongyuan lamented what was happening:

> A tumbled confusion of lumber as flames on the hillside crackle
> Not even the last remaining shrubs are safeguarded from destruction
> Where once mountain torrents leapt—nothing but rutted gullies.[2]

A "Golden Age" of Chinese Achievement

While the collapse of the western Roman Empire led to permanent political fragmentation, the fall of China's Han dynasty did not, for China regained its earlier political unity under the **Sui dynasty** (581–618). Its emperors solidified that unity by vastly extending the country's canal system, which stretched some 1,200 miles

Landmarks for Chapter 8

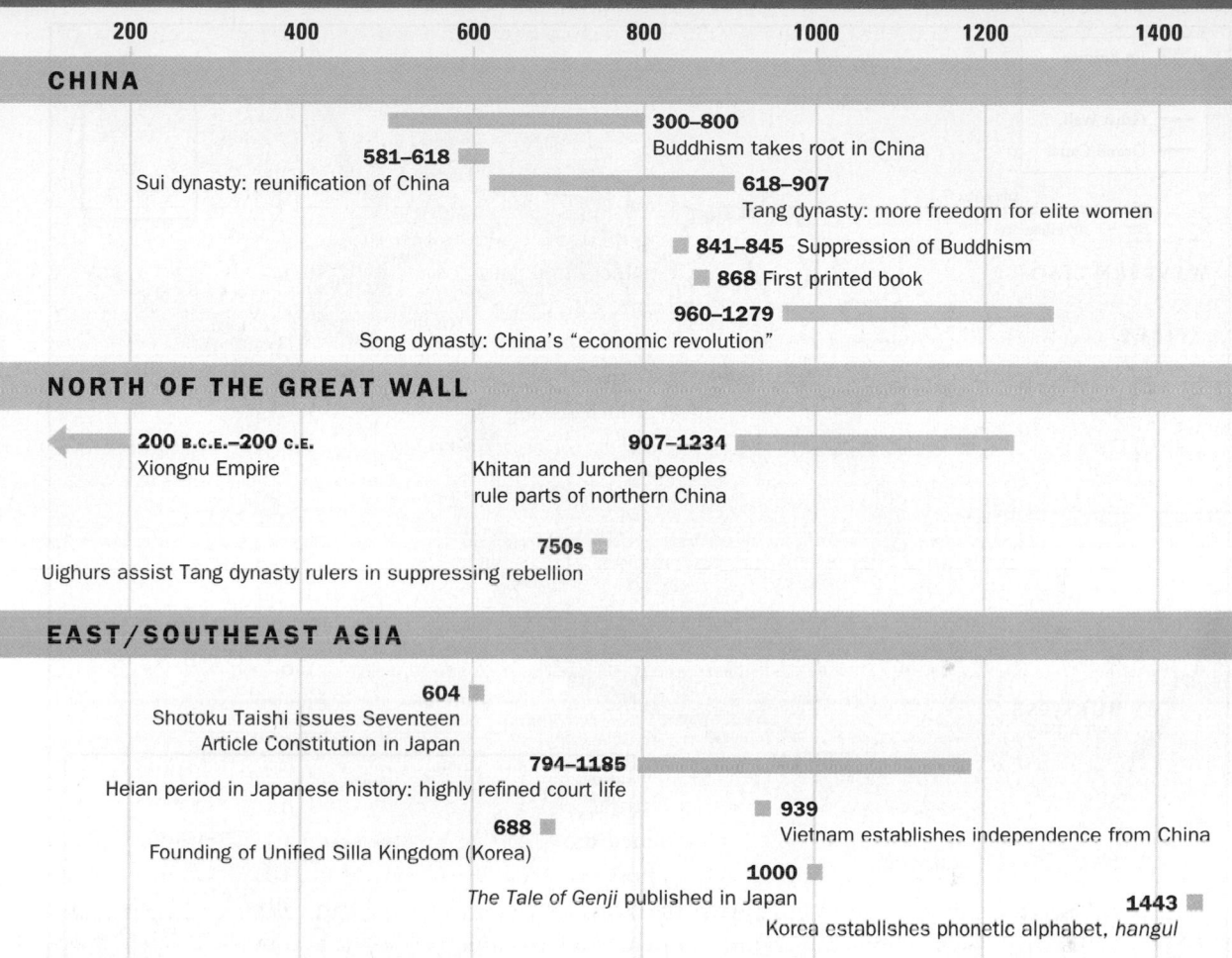

200   400   600   800   1000   1200   1400

CHINA

300–800
Buddhism takes root in China

581–618
Sui dynasty: reunification of China

618–907
Tang dynasty: more freedom for elite women

841–845 Suppression of Buddhism

868 First printed book

960–1279
Song dynasty: China's "economic revolution"

NORTH OF THE GREAT WALL

200 B.C.E.–200 C.E.
Xiongnu Empire

907–1234
Khitan and Jurchen peoples
rule parts of northern China

750s
Uighurs assist Tang dynasty rulers in suppressing rebellion

EAST/SOUTHEAST ASIA

604
Shotoku Taishi issues Seventeen
Article Constitution in Japan

794–1185
Heian period in Japanese history: highly refined court life

688
Founding of Unified Silla Kingdom (Korea)

939
Vietnam establishes independence from China

1000
The Tale of Genji published in Japan

1443
Korea establishes phonetic alphabet, *hangul*

---

in length and is described by one scholar as "an engineering feat without parallel in the world of its time."[3] Those canals linked northern and southern China economically and contributed much to the prosperity that followed. But the ruthlessness of Sui emperors and a futile military campaign to conquer Korea exhausted the state's resources, alienated many people, and prompted the overthrow of the dynasty.

This dynastic collapse, however, witnessed no prolonged disintegration of the Chinese state. The two dynasties that followed — the **Tang dynasty** (618–907) and the **Song dynasty** (960–1279) — built on the Sui foundations of renewed unity (see Map 8.1). Together they established patterns of Chinese life that endured into the twentieth century. Culturally, this era has long been regarded as a "golden age" of arts and literature, setting standards of excellence in poetry, landscape painting, and ceramics. Particularly during the Song dynasty, an explosion of scholarship gave rise to Neo-Confucianism, an effort to revive Confucian thinking while incorporating some of the insights of Buddhism and Daoism.

Guided Reading Question

■ CHANGE
Why are the centuries of the Tang and Song dynasties in China sometimes referred to as a "golden age"?

319

MAPPING HISTORY

Map 8.1 Tang and Song Dynasty China

During the third-wave era, China interacted extensively with its neighbors. The Tang dynasty extended Chinese control deep into Central Asia. Under the Song dynasty, nomadic Jurchen peoples conquered much of northern China, creating two states—the Song in the south and the Jin in the north. Both claimed to be the heirs to the Tang dynasty and thus the true emperors of China.

READING THE MAP: Compare the extent of Tang dynasty China to that of Southern Song dynasty China. Which major regions did the Tang control that the Southern Song did not?

MAPPING COMPARISONS: Compare the extent of Song dynasty China on Map 8.1 with that of Han dynasty China on Map 3.5. What differences are apparent in the relationship between China and the northern "barbarians"?

Politically, the Tang and Song dynasties built a state structure that endured for a thousand years. Six major ministries—personnel, finance, rites, army, justice, and public works—were accompanied by the Censorate, an agency that exercised surveillance over the rest of the government, checking on the character and competence of public officials. To staff this bureaucracy, the examination system was revived and made more elaborate, facilitated by the ability to print books for the first time in world history. Schools and colleges proliferated to prepare candidates for the rigorous exams, which became a central feature of upper-class life. A leading world historian has described Tang dynasty China as "the best ordered state in the world."[4]

Selecting officials on the basis of merit represented a challenge to established aristocratic families' hold on public office. Still, a substantial percentage of official positions went to the sons of the privileged, even if they had not passed the exams. Moreover, because education and the examination system grew far more rapidly than the number of official positions, many who passed lower-level exams could not be accommodated with a bureaucratic appointment. Often, however, they were able to combine landowning and success in the examination system to maintain an immense cultural prestige and prominence in their local areas. (See Working with Evidence: China's Scholar-Officials, page 348, for more on the life of the "scholar-official" class.)

Underlying these cultural and political achievements was **China's economic revolution**, which made Song dynasty China "by far the richest, most skilled, and most populous country on earth."[5] The most obvious sign of China's prosperity was its rapid growth in population, which jumped from about 50 million or 60 million during the Tang dynasty to 120 million by 1200. Behind this doubling of the population were remarkable achievements in agricultural production, particularly the adoption of a fast-ripening and drought-resistant strain of rice from Vietnam.

Many people found their way to the cities, making China the most urbanized country in the world. Dozens of Chinese cities numbered over 100,000, while the Song dynasty capital of **Hangzhou** was home to more than a million people. A Chinese observer in 1235 provided a vivid description of that city.[6] Specialized markets abounded for meat, herbs, vegetables, books, rice, and much more, with troupes of actors performing for the crowds. Restaurants advertised their unique offerings, including pickled dates, juicy lungs, and pigs' feet. "Luxuriant inns," marked by red lanterns, featured prostitutes and "wine chambers equipped with beds." Specialized agencies managed elaborate dinner parties for the wealthy, complete with a Perfume and Medicine Office to "help sober up the guests." Schools for musicians offered thirteen different courses. Numerous clubs provided companionship for poets, fishermen, Buddhists, physical fitness enthusiasts, antiques collectors, horse lovers, and many other groups. No wonder the Italian visitor Marco Polo described Hangzhou later in the thirteenth century as "beyond dispute the finest and noblest [city] in the world."[7] (See Working with Evidence: Travelers' Tales and Observations, Source 7.2, page 307, for a fuller description of Marco Polo's impressions of Hangzhou.)

Gunpowder

The Chinese Tang and Song dynasties (618–1279) witnessed a golden age of technological innovation in China. Both woodblock and movable type generated the world's first printed books, while Chinese innovations in navigational and shipbuilding technologies led the world. Among these many developments, the invention of gunpowder stands out because it spawned a permanent revolution in military affairs that had global dimensions. But gunpowder, a mixture of saltpeter, sulfur, and charcoal, was not originally developed for use in war. Instead, it was an accidental byproduct of the search by Daoist alchemists for an elixir of immortality. Indeed, the first reference to gunpowder appeared in a mid-ninth-century

A tenth-century Chinese Buddhist painting depicting demons armed with a fire lance and grenade.

Daoist text that warns alchemists not to mix together its component parts because "smoke and flames result, so that [the alchemists'] hands and faces have been burnt, and even the whole house where they were working burned down."[8] This association with alchemy may explain why the Chinese referred to gunpowder as *huo yao*, or "fire

photo: akg-images/Pictures from History

drug." The same properties that made gunpowder so dangerous in an alchemist's lab attracted the interest of those seeking to entertain and amaze audiences through fireworks and pyrotechnic displays, especially at the Chinese imperial court.

Military authorities also noticed its potential as a weapon, and its uses in war developed rapidly during the Song dynasty. At first, military engineers drew on the incendiary rather than the explosive possibilities of gunpowder. In 1044, an imperial official wrote a tract for the emperor on military technologies that included two recipes for gunpowder, both for weapons designed to set fire to their targets. Decades later, Song engineers borrowed techniques from fireworks makers to produce "Thunderclap Bombs" designed to scare and disorient opposing troops through noise and light. While these bombs were not yet powerful

Industrial production likewise soared. In both large-scale enterprises employing hundreds of workers and in smaller backyard furnaces, China's iron industry increased its output dramatically. By the eleventh century, it was providing the government with 32,000 suits of armor and 16 million iron arrowheads annually, in addition to supplying metal for coins, tools, construction, and bells in Buddhist monasteries. This industrial growth was fueled almost entirely by coal, which also came to provide most of the energy for heating homes and cooking and no doubt generated considerable air pollution. Technological innovation in other fields also flourished. Inventions in printing, both woodblock and movable type, generated the world's first printed books, and by 1000 relatively cheap books on religious, agricultural, mathematical, and medical topics became widely available in China. Its navigational and shipbuilding technologies led the world. The Chinese invention enough to kill large numbers of the enemy, a chronicler of a siege of the Song capital in 1127 described them as "hitting the lines of the enemy well and throwing them into great confusion."

Through the twelfth and early thirteenth centuries, both the Song dynasty, which controlled southern China, and the Jin, which controlled much of the north, continued to develop ever more powerful gunpowder weapons. Engineers experimented with gunpowder blends that included larger quantities of saltpeter, the nitrate-rich substance that gives gunpowder its explosiveness. When the Mongols invaded northern China in 1231, the defenders of the capital, Kaifeng, were able to deploy what they called the "Heaven-Shaking Thunder Crash Bomb" against Mongol forces. An eyewitness recorded that "the attacking soldiers were blown to bits, not even a trace being left behind."

The Mongols recognized the effectiveness of gunpowder, and following their conquest of China, encouraged engineers to continue to develop new weapons. During the thirteenth and fourteenth centuries, powerful bombs were produced with such names as "Match for Ten Thousand Enemies Bomb" and the "Bone-Burning and Bruising Fire Oil Magic Bomb." At the same time, Chinese technicians developed the first rockets, which were employed in battle from the middle of the thirteenth century. These experiments with more powerful forms of gunpowder culminated in the emergence of weapons designed to fire projectiles. The first of these evolved from earlier fire lances, bamboo or metal tubes filled with gunpowder that spewed flames and sparks. However, unlike the fire lance, which used the incendiary properties of gunpowder to attack the enemy, these new guns used its explosive power as a propellant to fire projectiles. Handheld guns were in regular use by the second half of the thirteenth century; cannons were common on the battlefield by 1350.

Gunpowder and gunpowder-based weapons spread rapidly across Eurasia from the thirteenth century on, changing the nature of warfare wherever they were adopted. While there is some debate as to exactly when gunpowder arrived in India, the Middle East, and Europe, it is clear that the Mongols' use of gunpowder weapons in their conquests spurred its spread and use. Its rapid adoption ensured that by the sixteenth century the "fire drug" developed by Daoist alchemists in search of immortality had sparked what scholars have labeled the gunpowder revolution in warfare, transforming military conflict across the globe. Gunpowder remained the dominant explosive used in war until the advent of nitroglycerin in the mid-nineteenth century.

It is more than a little ironic that a substance originally derived from a search for happiness and immortality would result in unimaginable human suffering and an untold number of deaths. Such are the unintended outcomes of human effort.

QUESTION

What can the development of gunpowder-based weapons tell us about technological innovation in China?

----

of **gunpowder** created within a few centuries a revolution in military affairs that had global dimensions. (See Zooming In: Gunpowder, page 322.) But China's remarkable industrial revolution stalled, perhaps because the country was repeatedly invaded and devastated by nomadic peoples from the north, culminating in the Mongol conquests of the thirteenth century.

These innovations occurred within the world's most highly commercialized society, in which producing for the market, rather than for local consumption, became a very widespread phenomenon. An immense network of internal waterways stretching perhaps 30,000 miles—canals, rivers, and lakes—facilitated the cheap movement of goods, allowing peasants to grow specialized crops for sale while they purchased rice or other staples on the market. In addition, government demands for taxes paid in cash rather than in kind required peasants to sell

Kaifeng This detail comes from a huge watercolor scroll, titled *Upper River during Qing Ming Festival*, originally painted during the Song dynasty. It illustrates the urban sophistication of Kaifeng and other Chinese cities at that time and has been frequently imitated and copied since then. (© VIEW STOCK RF/age-fotostock)

something—their products or their labor—in order to meet their obligations. The growing use of paper money, as well as financial instruments such as letters of credit and promissory notes, further contributed to the commercialization of Chinese society. Two prominent scholars have described the outcome: "Output increased, population grew, skills multiplied, and a burst of inventiveness made Song China far wealthier than ever before—or than any of its contemporaries."[9] (See Snapshot, page 339.)

Women in the Song Dynasty

The "golden age" of Song dynasty China was perhaps less than "golden" for many of its women, for that era marked yet another turning point in the history of Chinese patriarchy. Under the influence of steppe nomads, whose women led less restricted lives, elite Chinese women of the Tang dynasty era, at least in the north, had participated in social life with greater freedom than in earlier times. Paintings and statues show aristocratic women riding horses, while the Queen Mother of the West, a Daoist deity, was widely worshipped by female Daoist priests and practitioners. By the Song dynasty, however, a reviving Confucianism and rapid economic growth seemed to tighten patriarchal restrictions on women and to restore some of the earlier Han dynasty notions of female submission and passivity.

Once again, Confucian writers emphasized the subordination of women to men and the need to keep males and females separate in every domain of life. The Song dynasty historian and scholar Sima Guang (1019–1086) summed up the prevailing view: "The boy leads the girl, the girl follows the boy; the duty of husbands to be resolute and wives to be docile begins with this."[10] For men, masculinity came to be defined less in terms of horseback riding, athleticism, and the warrior values of northern nomads and more in terms of the refined pursuits of calligraphy, scholarship, painting, and poetry. Corresponding views of feminine qualities emphasized women's weakness, reticence, and delicacy. Women were also frequently viewed as a distraction to men's pursuit of a contemplative and introspective life. The remarriage of widows, though legally permissible, was increasingly condemned, for "to walk through two courtyards is a source of shame for a woman."[11]

The most compelling expression of a tightening patriarchy lay in **foot binding**. Apparently beginning among dancers and courtesans in the tenth or eleventh century c.e., this practice involved the tight wrapping of young girls' feet, usually breaking the bones of the foot and causing intense pain. During and after the Song dynasty, foot binding found general acceptance among elite families and later became even more widespread in Chinese society. It was associated with new images of female beauty and eroticism that emphasized small size, frailty, and deference and served to keep women restricted to the "inner quarters," where Confucian tradition asserted that they belonged. Many mothers imposed this painful procedure on their daughters, perhaps to enhance their marriage prospects and to assist them in competing with concubines for the attention of their husbands.[12] For many women, it became a rite of passage, and their tiny feet and the beautiful slippers that encased them became a source of some pride, even a topic of poetry for some literate women. Foot binding also served to distinguish Chinese women from their "barbarian" counterparts and elite women from commoners and peasants.

Furthermore, a rapidly commercializing economy undermined the position of women in the textile industry. Urban workshops and state factories, run by men, increasingly took over the skilled tasks of weaving textiles, especially silk, which had previously been the work of rural women in their homes. Although these women continued to tend silkworms and spin silk thread, they had lost the more lucrative income-generating work of weaving silk fabrics. But as their economic role in textile production declined, other opportunities beckoned in an increasingly prosperous Song China. In the cities, women operated restaurants, sold fish and vegetables, and worked as maids, cooks, and dressmakers. The growing prosperity of elite families funneled increasing numbers of women into roles as concubines, entertainers, courtesans, and prostitutes. Their ready availability surely reduced the

Guided Reading Question

■ **CHANGE**

In what ways did women's lives change during the Tang and Song dynasties?

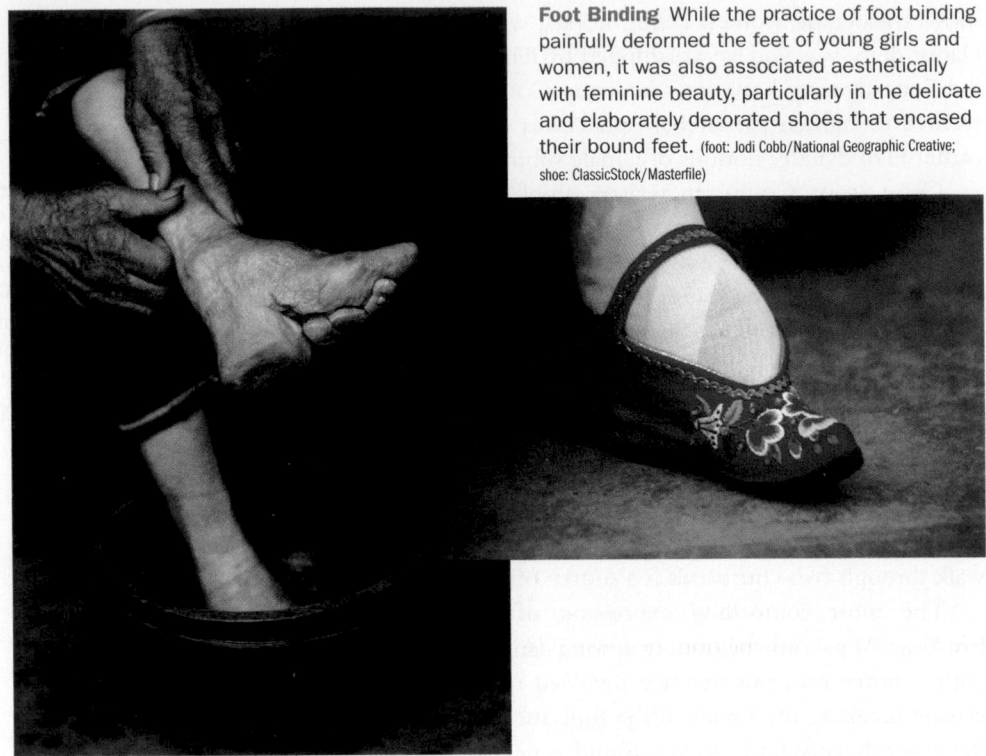

Foot Binding While the practice of foot binding painfully deformed the feet of young girls and women, it was also associated aesthetically with feminine beauty, particularly in the delicate and elaborately decorated shoes that encased their bound feet. (foot: Jodi Cobb/National Geographic Creative; shoe: ClassicStock/Masterfile)

ability of wives to negotiate as equals with their husbands, setting women against one another and creating endless household jealousies.

In other ways, the Song dynasty witnessed more positive trends in the lives of women. Their property rights expanded, allowing women to control their own dowries and to inherit property from their families. "Neither in earlier nor in later periods," writes one scholar, "did as much property pass through women's hands" as during the Song dynasty.[13] Furthermore, lower-ranking but ambitious officials strongly urged the education of women, so that they might more effectively raise their sons and increase the family's fortune. Song dynasty China, in short, offered a mixture of tightening restrictions and new opportunities to its women.

China and the Northern Nomads: A Chinese World Order in the Making

Among China's various interactions with a larger Eurasian world, the most enduring and intense involved the many nomadic pastoral or semi-agricultural peoples of the steppes north of the Great Wall. Living in areas unable to sustain Chinese-style farming, these northern nomads had long focused their economies around the raising of livestock (sheep, cattle, goats) and the mastery of horse riding. Organized locally in small, mobile, kinship-based groups, these peoples also periodically created much larger and powerful states or confederations that could draw on the impressive horsemanship and military skills of virtually the entire male population of their societies. Such specialized pastoral societies needed grain and other agricultural products from China, and their leaders developed a taste for Chinese manufactured and luxury goods—wine and silk, for example—with which they could attract and reward followers. Thus the nomads were drawn like a magnet toward China, trading, raiding, and extorting to obtain the resources so vital to their way of life. For 2,000 years or more, pressure from the steppes and the intrusion of nomadic peoples were constant factors in China's historical development.

From the nomads' point of view, the threat often came from the Chinese, who periodically directed their own military forces deep into the steppes, built the Great Wall to keep the nomads out, and often proved unwilling to allow pastoral peoples easy access to trading opportunities within China. And yet the Chinese needed the nomads and especially their horses, which were essential for the Chinese military. Other products of the steppes and the forests beyond, such as skins, furs, hides, and amber, were also of value in China. Furthermore, pastoral nomads controlled much of the Silk Road trading network, which funneled goods from the West into China. The continuing interaction between China and the northern nomads brought together peoples occupying different environments, practicing different economies, governing themselves with different institutions, and thinking about the world in quite different ways.

Guided Reading Question

■ **CONNECTION**
How did the Chinese and their nomadic neighbors to the north view each other?

The Tribute System in Theory

An enduring outcome of this cross-cultural encounter was a particular view the Chinese held of themselves and of their neighbors, fully articulated by the time of the Han dynasty (ca. 200 B.C.E. 200 C.E.) and lasting for more than two millennia. That understanding cast China as the "middle kingdom," the center of the world, infinitely superior to the "barbarian" peoples beyond its borders. With its long history, great cities, refined tastes, sophisticated intellectual and artistic achievements, bureaucratic state, literate elite, and prosperous economy, China represented "civilization." All of this, in Chinese thinking, was in sharp contrast to the rude cultures and primitive life of the northern nomads, who continually moved about "like beasts and birds," lived in tents, ate mostly meat and milk, and practically lived on their horses, while making war on everyone within reach. Educated Chinese saw their own society as self-sufficient, requiring little from the outside world, while barbarians, quite understandably, sought access to China's wealth and wisdom. Furthermore, China was willing to permit that access under controlled conditions, for its sense of superiority did not preclude the possibility that barbarians could become civilized Chinese. China was a "radiating civilization," graciously shedding its light most fully to nearby barbarians and with diminished intensity to those farther away.

The Tribute System This eighteenth-century Korean painting depicts a Korean diplomatic mission to Qing China approaching the city of Sanhaegwan on its way to offer tribute to the emperor in Beijing, 190 miles away. Such tribute missions offered opportunities for the Korean delegation to see something of China. According to diaries of Korean envoys, they categorized sites along the route to Beijing under such titles as historical, curiosity, or spectacle. (© Copyright The Korean Christian Museum at Soongsil University, Courtesy of the Academy of Korean Studies, South Korea)

Guided Reading Question

....

■ **CONNECTION**

What assumptions underlay the tribute system?

That worldview also took shape as a practical system for managing China's relationship with these people. Known as the **tribute system**, it was a set of practices that required non-Chinese authorities to acknowledge Chinese superiority and their own subordinate place in a Chinese-centered world order. Foreigners seeking access to China had to send a delegation to the Chinese court, where they would perform the kowtow, a series of ritual bowings and prostrations, and present their tribute—products of value from their countries—to the Chinese emperor. In return for these expressions of submission, he would grant permission for foreigners to trade in China's rich markets and would provide them with gifts or "bestowals," often worth far more than the tribute they had offered. This was the mechanism by which successive Chinese dynasties attempted to regulate their relationships with northern nomads; with neighboring states such as Korea, Vietnam, Tibet, and Japan; and, after 1500, with those European barbarians from across the sea.

Often, this system seemed to work. Over the centuries, countless foreign delegations proved willing to present their tribute, say the required words, and perform the rituals necessary for gaining access to the material goods of China. Aspiring non-Chinese rulers also gained prestige as they basked in the reflected glory of even this subordinate association with the great Chinese civilization. The official titles, seals of office, and ceremonial robes they received from China proved useful in their local struggles for power.

The Tribute System in Practice

But the tribute system also disguised some realities that contradicted its assumptions. On occasion, China was confronting not separate and small-scale barbarian societies, but large and powerful nomadic empires able to deal with China on at least equal terms. An early nomadic confederacy was the **Xiongnu Empire**, established about the same time as the Han dynasty (ca. 200 B.C.E.) and eventually reaching from Manchuria to Central Asia (see Map 3.5, page 118). Devastating Xiongnu raids into northern China persuaded the Chinese emperor to negotiate an arrangement that recognized the nomadic state as a political equal, promised its leader a princess in marriage, and, most important, agreed to supply him annually with large quantities of grain, wine, and silk. In return for these goods, so critical for the functioning of the nomadic state, the Xiongnu agreed to refrain from military incursions into China. The basic realities of the situation were summed up in this warning to the Han dynasty in the first century B.C.E.:

> Just make sure that the silks and grain stuffs you bring the Xiongnu are the right measure and quality, that's all. What's the need for talking? If the goods you deliver are up to measure and good quality, all right. But if there is any deficiency or the quality is no good, then when the autumn harvest comes, we will take our horses and trample all over your crops.[14]

Something similar occurred during the Tang dynasty as a series of Turkic empires arose in Mongolia. Like the Xiongnu, they too extorted large "gifts" from the Chinese. One of these peoples, the Uighurs, actually rescued the Tang dynasty from a serious internal revolt in the 750s. In return, the Uighur leader gained one of the Chinese emperor's daughters as a wife and arranged a highly favorable exchange of poor-quality horses for high-quality silk, which brought half a million rolls of the precious fabric annually into the Uighur lands. Despite the rhetoric of the tribute system, the Chinese were not always able to dictate the terms of their relationship with the northern nomads.

Steppe nomads were generally not much interested in actually conquering and ruling China. It was easier and more profitable to extort goods from a functioning Chinese state. On occasion, however, that state broke down and various nomadic groups moved in to "pick up the pieces," conquering and governing parts of China. Such a process took place following the fall of the Han dynasty and again after the collapse of the Tang dynasty, when the Khitan (kee-THAN) (907–1125) and then the Jin, or Jurchen (JER-chihn) (1115–1234), peoples established states that encompassed parts of China as well as major areas of the steppes to the north. Both of them required the Chinese Song dynasty, located farther south, to deliver annually huge quantities of silk, silver, and tea, some of which found its way into the Silk Road trading network. The practice of "bestowing gifts on barbarians," long a part of the tribute system, allowed the proud Chinese to imagine that they were still in control of the situation even as they were paying heavily for protection from nomadic incursion. Those gifts, in turn, provided vital economic resources to nomadic states.

Cultural Influence across an Ecological Frontier

When nomadic peoples actually ruled parts of China, some of them adopted Chinese ways, employing Chinese advisers, governing according to Chinese practice, and, at least for the elite, immersing themselves in Chinese culture and learning. This process of "becoming Chinese" went furthest among the Jurchen, many of whom lived in northern China and learned to speak Chinese, wore Chinese clothing, married Chinese husbands and wives, and practiced Buddhism or Daoism.

On the whole, however, Chinese culture had only a modest impact on the nomadic people of the northern steppes. Unlike the native peoples of southern China, who were gradually absorbed into Chinese culture, the pastoral societies north of the Great Wall generally retained their own cultural patterns. Few of them were incorporated, at least not for long, within a Chinese state, and most lived in areas where Chinese-style agriculture was simply impossible. Under these conditions, there were few incentives for adopting Chinese culture wholesale. But various modes of interaction — peaceful trade, military conflict, political negotiations, economic extortion, some cultural influence — continued across the ecological frontier that divided two quite distinct and separate ways of life. Each was necessary for the other.

On the Chinese side, elements of steppe culture had some influence in those parts of northern China that were periodically conquered and ruled by nomadic peoples. The founders of the Sui and Tang dynasties were in fact of mixed nomad and Chinese ancestry and came from the borderland region where a blended Chinese/Turkic culture had evolved. High-ranking members of the imperial family personally led their troops in battle in the style of Turkic warriors. Furthermore, Tang dynasty China was awash with foreign visitors from all over Asia — delegations bearing tribute, merchants carrying exotic goods, and bands of clerics or religious pilgrims bringing new religions such as Christianity, Islam, Buddhism, and Manichaeism. For a time in the Tang dynasty, almost anything associated with "Western barbarians" — Central Asians, Persians, Indians, Arabs — had great appeal among northern Chinese elites. Their music, dancing, clothing, foods, games, and artistic styles found favor among the upper classes. The more traditional southern Chinese, feeling themselves heir to the legacy of the Han dynasty, were sharply critical of their northern counterparts for allowing women too much freedom, for drinking yogurt rather than tea, and for listening to "Western" music, all of which they attributed to barbarian influence. Around 800 C.E., the poet Yuan Chen gave voice to a growing backlash against this too-easy acceptance of things "Western":

> Ever since the Western horsemen began raising smut and dust,
> Fur and fleece, rank and rancid, have filled Hsien and Lo [two Chinese cities].
> Women make themselves Western matrons by the study of Western makeup.
> Entertainers present Western tunes, in their devotion to Western music.[15]

Guided Reading Question

■ **CONNECTION**

In what ways did China and the nomads influence each other?

Coping with China: Comparing Korea, Vietnam, and Japan

Also involved in tributary relationships with China were the newly emerging states and civilizations of Korea, Vietnam, and Japan. Unlike the northern nomads, these societies were thoroughly agricultural and sedentary. During the first millennium C.E., they were part of a larger process—the globalization of civilization—that produced new city- and state-based societies in various parts of the world. Proximity to their giant Chinese neighbor decisively shaped the histories of these new East Asian civilizations, for all of them borrowed major elements of Chinese culture. But unlike the native peoples of southern China, who largely became Chinese, the peoples of Korea, Vietnam, and Japan did not. They retained distinctive identities, which have lasted into modern times. While resisting Chinese political domination, they also appreciated Chinese culture and sought the source of Chinese wealth and power. Korea, Vietnam, and Japan, however, encountered China and responded to it in quite different ways.

Korea and China

Immediately adjacent to northeastern China, the Korean peninsula and its people have long lived in the shadow of their imposing neighbor (see Map 8.2). Temporary Chinese conquest of northern Korea during the Han dynasty and some colonization by Chinese settlers provided an initial channel for Chinese cultural influence, particularly in the form of Buddhism. Emerging in the first century B.C.E. and reaching their most powerful and sophisticated forms between the fourth and seventh century C.E., early Korean states all referred to their rulers with the Chinese term *wang* (king). Bitter rivals with one another, they also strenuously resisted Chinese political control, except when they found it advantageous to join with China against a local enemy. In the seventh century, one of these states—the **Silla** (SHEE-lah) **kingdom**—allied with Tang dynasty China to bring some political unity to the peninsula for the first time, founding what is known as the Unified Silla Kingdom. But Chinese efforts to set up puppet regimes and to assimilate Koreans to Chinese culture provoked sharp military resistance, persuading the Chinese to withdraw their military forces in 688 and to establish a tributary relationship with a largely independent Korea.

Under a succession of dynasties—the Unified Silla (688–900), Koryo (918–1392), and Joseon (1392–1910)—Korea generally maintained its political independence while participating in China's tribute system. Its leaders actively embraced the connection with China and, especially during the Silla dynasty, sought to turn their small state into a miniature version of Tang China.

Tribute missions to China provided legitimacy for Korean rulers and models of court life and administrative techniques, which they sought to replicate back home. A new capital city of Kumsong was modeled directly on the Chinese capital

Guided Reading Question

■ **CONNECTION**

In what ways did China have an influence in Korea, Vietnam, and Japan? In what ways was that influence resisted?

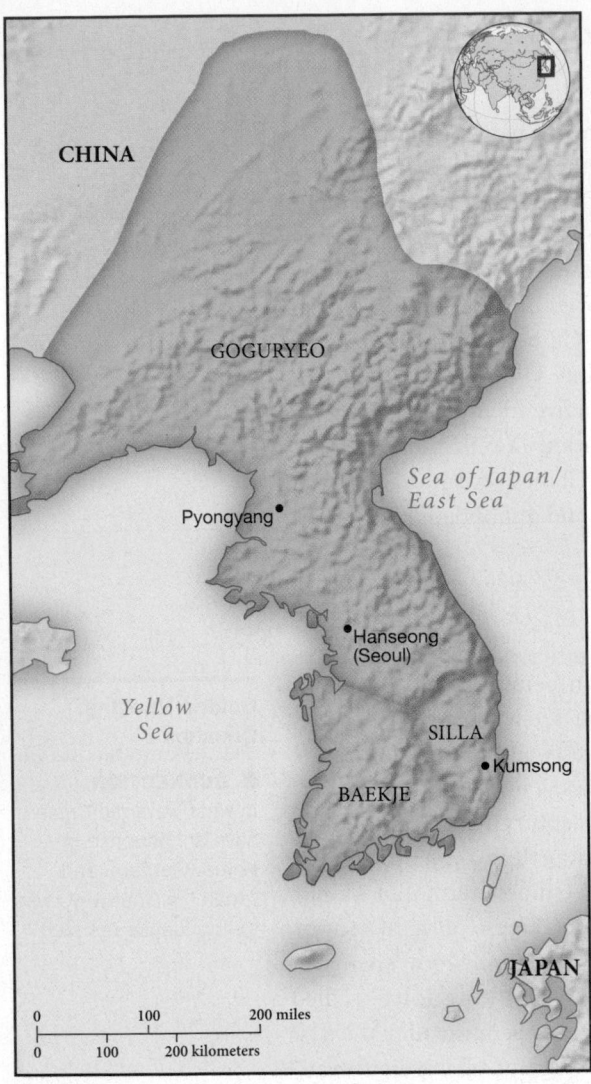

Map 8.2 Korean Kingdoms, ca. 500 C.E.
The three early kingdoms of Korea were brought together by the seventh century in a unified state, which was later governed by a series of dynastic regimes.

of Chang'an (chahng-ahn). Tribute missions also enabled both official and private trade, mostly in luxury goods such as ceremonial clothing, silks, fancy teas, Confucian and Buddhist texts, and artwork. All of this enriched the lives of a Korean aristocracy that was becoming increasingly Chinese in culture. Thousands of Korean students were sent to China, where they studied primarily Confucianism but also the sciences and the arts. Buddhist monks visited centers of learning and pilgrimage in China and brought back popular forms of Chinese Buddhism, which quickly took root in Korea. Schools for the study of Confucianism, using texts in the Chinese language, were established in Korea. In these ways, Korea became a part of the expanding world of Chinese culture, and refugees from the peninsula's many wars carried Chinese culture to Japan as well.

These efforts to plant Confucian values and Chinese culture in Korea had what one scholar has called an "overwhelmingly negative" impact on Korean women, particularly after 1300.[16] Early Chinese observers noticed, and strongly disapproved of, free-choice marriages in Korea as well as the practice of women singing and dancing together late at night. With the support of the Korean court, Chinese models of family life and female behavior, especially among the elite, gradually replaced the more flexible Korean patterns. Earlier, a Korean woman had generally given birth and raised her young children in her parents' home, where she was often joined by her husband. This was now strongly discouraged, for Confucian orthodoxy demanded that a married woman belonged to her husband's family. Other Korean customs—funeral rites in which a husband was buried in the sacred plot of his wife's family, the remarriage of widowed or divorced women, and female inheritance of property—also eroded under the pressure of Confucian orthodoxy. So too did the practice of plural marriages for men. In 1413, a legal distinction between primary and secondary wives required men to identify one of their wives as primary. Because she and her children now had special privileges and status, sharp new tensions emerged within families. Korean restrictions on elite women, especially widows, came to exceed even those in China itself.

Still, Korea remained Korean. After 688, the country's political independence, though periodically threatened, was largely intact. Chinese cultural influence, except for Buddhism, had little impact beyond the aristocracy and certainly did not penetrate the lives of Korea's serf-like peasants. Nor did it register among Korea's many slaves, amounting to about one-third of the country's population by 1100. In fact, Korean Buddhist monasteries used slaves to cultivate their lands. A Chinese-style examination system to recruit government officials, though encouraged by some Korean rulers, never assumed the prominence that it gained in Tang and Song dynasty China. Korea's aristocratic class was able to maintain an even stronger monopoly on bureaucratic office than its Chinese counterpart did. And in the mid-1400s, Korea moved toward greater cultural independence by developing a phonetic alphabet, known as **hangul** (HAHN-gool), for writing the Korean language. Although resisted by conservative male elites, who were long accustomed to using the more prestigious Chinese characters to write Korean, this new form of writing gradually took hold, especially in private correspondence, in popular fiction, and among women. Clearly part of the Chinese world order, Korea nonetheless retained a distinctive culture as well as a separate political existence.

Vietnam and China

At the southern fringe of the Chinese cultural world, the people who eventually came to be called Vietnamese had a broadly similar historical encounter with China (see Map 8.3). As in Korea, the elite culture of Vietnam borrowed heavily from China—adopting Confucianism, Daoism, Buddhism, administrative techniques, the examination system, and artistic and literary styles—even as its popular culture remained distinctive. And, like Korea, Vietnam achieved political independence while participating fully in the tribute system as a vassal state.

Unlike Korea, however, the cultural heartland of Vietnam in the Red River valley was fully incorporated into the Chinese state for more than a thousand years (111 B.C.E.–939 C.E.). Regarded by the Chinese as "southern barbarians," the Vietnamese were ruled by Chinese officials who expected to fully assimilate this rich rice-growing region into China culturally as well as politically. To these officials, it was simply a further

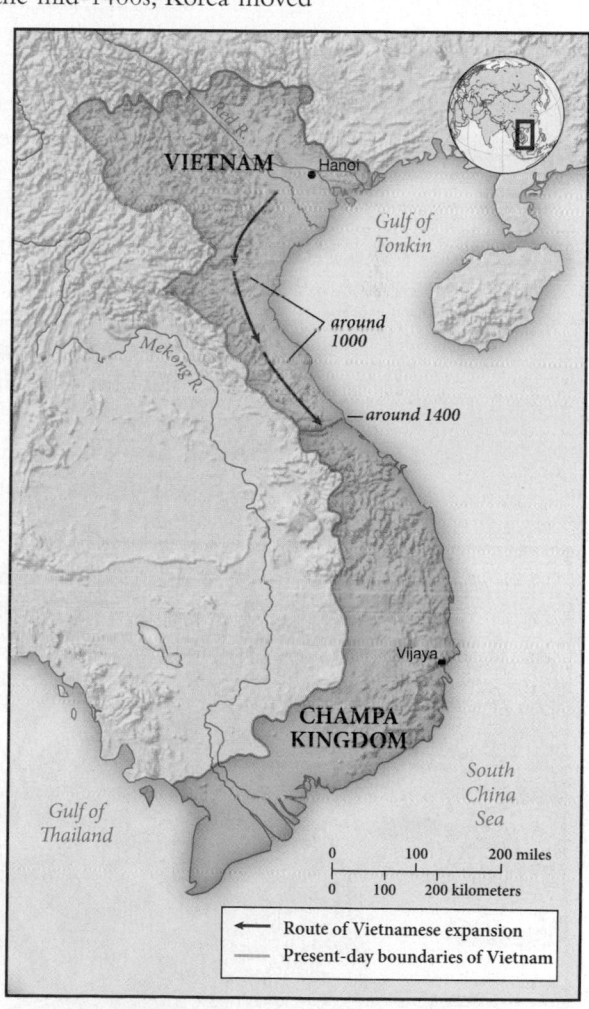

Map 8.3 Vietnam

As Vietnam threw off Chinese control, it also expanded to the south, while remaining wary of its larger Chinese neighbor to the north.

extension of the southward movement of Chinese civilization. Thus Chinese-style irrigated agriculture was introduced; Vietnamese elites were brought into the local bureaucracy and educated in Confucian-based schools; Chinese replaced the local language in official business; Chinese clothing and hairstyles became mandatory; and large numbers of Chinese, some fleeing internal conflicts at home, flooded into the relative security of what they referred to as "the pacified south," while often despising the local people. The heavy pressure of the Chinese presence generated not only a Vietnamese elite thoroughly schooled in Chinese culture but also periodic rebellions, on several occasions led by women. (See Zooming In: Trung Trac, Chapter 3, page 116.)

The weakening of the Tang dynasty in the early tenth century C.E. finally enabled a particularly large rebellion to establish Vietnam as a separate state, though one that carefully maintained its tributary role, sending repeated missions to do homage at the Chinese court. Nonetheless, successive Vietnamese dynasties found the Chinese approach to government useful, styling their rulers as emperors, claiming the Mandate of Heaven, and making use of Chinese court rituals, while expanding their state steadily southward. More so than in Korea, a Chinese-based examination system in Vietnam functioned to undermine an established aristocracy, to provide some measure of social mobility for commoners, and to create a merit-based scholar-gentry class to staff the bureaucracy. Furthermore, members of the Vietnamese elite class remained deeply committed to Chinese culture, viewing their own country less as a separate nation than as a southern extension of a universal civilization, the only one they knew.

Beyond the elite, however, there remained much that was uniquely Vietnamese, such as a distinctive language, a fondness for cockfighting, and the habit of chewing betel nuts. More importantly, Vietnam long retained a greater role for women in social and economic life, despite heavy Chinese influence. In the third century C.E., a woman leader of an anti-Chinese resistance movement declared: "I want to drive away the enemy to save our people. I will not resign myself to the usual lot of women who bow their heads and become concubines." Female nature deities and a "female Buddha" continued to be part of Vietnamese popular religion, even as Confucian-based ideas took root among the elite. In the centuries following independence from China, as Vietnam expanded to the south, northern officials tried in vain to impose more orthodox Confucian

Independence for Vietnam In 938, Vietnamese forces under the leadership of General Ngo Quyen defeated the Chinese in the Battle of Bach Dang River, thus ending a thousand years of direct Chinese rule. This image is one of many that celebrate that victory. (Pictures from History/CPA Media)

gender practices in place of local customs that allowed women to choose their own husbands and married men to live in the households of their wives. So persistent were these practices that a seventeenth-century Chinese visitor opined, with disgust, that Vietnamese preferred the birth of a girl to that of a boy. These features of Vietnamese life reflected larger patterns of Southeast Asian culture that distinguished it from China. And like Koreans, the Vietnamese developed a variation of Chinese writing called ***chu nom*** ("southern script"), which provided the basis for an independent national literature and a vehicle for the writing of most educated women.

Japan and China

Unlike Korea and Vietnam, the Japanese islands were physically separated from China by 100 miles or more of ocean and were never successfully invaded or conquered by their giant mainland neighbor (see Map 8.4). Thus Japan's very extensive borrowing from Chinese civilization was wholly voluntary, rather than occurring under conditions of direct military threat or outright occupation. The high point of that borrowing took place during the seventh to the ninth centuries C.E., as the first more or less unified Japanese state began to emerge from dozens of small clan-based aristocratic chiefdoms. That state found much that was useful in Tang dynasty China and set out, deliberately and systematically, to transform Japan into a centralized bureaucratic state on the Chinese model.

The initial leader of this effort was **Shotoku Taishi** (572–622), a prominent aristocrat from one of the major clans. He launched a series of large-scale missions to China that took hundreds of Japanese monks, scholars, artists, and students to the mainland. In 604 C.E. Shotoku issued the Seventeen Article Constitution, proclaiming the Japanese ruler a Chinese-style emperor and encouraging both Buddhism and Confucianism. In good Confucian fashion, that document emphasized the moral quality of rulers as a foundation for social harmony. In the decades that followed, Japanese authorities adopted Chinese-style court rituals as well as the Chinese calendar. Later, they likewise established Chinese-based taxation systems, law codes, government ministries, and a provincial administration, at least on paper. Two capital cities, first Nara and then Heian-kyo (Kyoto), were both modeled on the Chinese capital of Chang'an.

Map 8.4 Japan

Japan's distance from China enabled it to maintain its political independence and to draw selectively from Chinese culture.

Chinese culture, no less than its political practices, also found favor in Japan. Various schools of Chinese Buddhism took root, first among the educated and literate classes and later more broadly in Japanese society. Buddhism deeply affected Japanese art, architecture, education, medicine, views of the afterlife, and attitudes toward suffering and the impermanence of life. The Chinese writing system—and with it an interest in historical writing, calligraphy, and poetry—likewise proved attractive among the elite.

The absence of any compelling threat from China made it possible for the Japanese to be selective in their borrowing. By the tenth century, deliberate efforts to absorb additional elements of Chinese culture diminished, and formal tribute missions to China stopped, although private traders and Buddhist monks continued to make the difficult journey to the mainland. Over many centuries, the Japanese combined what they had assimilated from China with elements of their own tradition into a distinctive Japanese civilization.

In the political realm, for example, the Japanese never succeeded in creating an effective centralized and bureaucratic state to match that of China. Although the court and the emperor retained an important ceremonial and cultural role, their real political authority over the country gradually diminished in favor of competing aristocratic families, both at court and in the provinces. As political power became increasingly decentralized, local authorities developed their own military forces, the famous *samurai* warrior class of Japanese society. Bearing their exquisite curved swords, the samurai developed a distinctive set of values featuring bravery, loyalty, endurance, honor, great skill in martial arts, and a preference for death over surrender. This was **bushido** (boo-shee-doh), the way of the warrior. Japan's celebration of the samurai and of military virtues contrasted sharply with China's emphasis on intellectual achievements and political office holding, which were accorded higher prestige than bearing arms. "The educated men of the land," wrote a Chinese minister in the eleventh century, "regard the carrying of arms as a disgrace."[17] The Japanese, clearly, did not agree.

Religiously as well, Japan remained distinctive. Although Buddhism in many forms took hold in the country, it never completely replaced the native

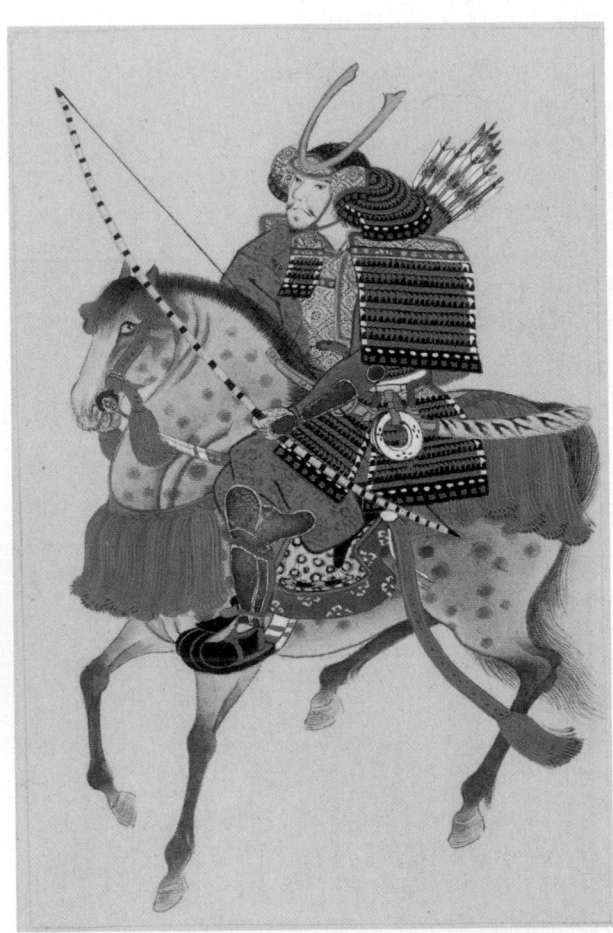

The Samurai of Japan This late nineteenth-century image shows a samurai warrior on horseback clad in armor and a horned helmet while carrying a sword as well as a bow and arrows. The prominence of martial values in Japanese culture was one of the ways in which Japan differed from its Chinese neighbor, despite much borrowing. (Library of Congress, Prints and Photographs Division, LC-DIG-jpd-01046)

beliefs and practices, which focused attention on numerous *kami*, sacred spirits associated with human ancestors and various natural phenomena. Much later referred to as Shinto, this tradition provided legitimacy to the imperial family, based on claims of descent from the sun goddess. Because veneration of the kami lacked an elaborate philosophy or ritual, it conflicted very little with Buddhism. In fact, numerous kami were assimilated into Japanese Buddhism as local expressions of Buddhist deities or principles.

Japanese literary and artistic culture likewise evolved in distinctive ways, despite much borrowing from China. As in Korea and Vietnam, there emerged a unique writing system that combined Chinese characters with a series of phonetic symbols. A highly stylized Japanese poetic form, known as tanka, developed early and has remained a favored means of expression ever since. Particularly during the Heian period of Japanese history (794–1185), a highly refined aesthetic culture found expression at the imperial court, even as the court's real political authority melted away. Court aristocrats and their ladies lived in splendor, composed poems, arranged flowers, and conducted their love affairs. "What counted," wrote one scholar, "was the proper costume, the right ceremonial act, the successful turn of phrase in a poem, and the appropriate expression of refined taste."[18] Much of our knowledge of this courtly culture comes from the work of women writers, who composed their diaries and novels in the vernacular Japanese script rather than in the classical Chinese used by elite men. *The Tale of Genji*, a Japanese novel written by the woman author Murasaki Shikibu around 1000, provides an intimate picture of the intrigues and romances of court life.

At this level of society, Japan's women, unlike those in Korea, largely escaped the more oppressive features of Chinese Confucian culture, such as the prohibition of remarriage for widows and seclusion within the home. Perhaps this is because the most powerful Chinese influence on Japan occurred during the Tang dynasty, when Chinese elite women enjoyed considerable freedom. Japanese women continued to inherit property; Japanese married couples often lived apart or with the wife's family; and marriages were made and broken easily. None of this corresponded to Confucian values. When Japanese women did begin to lose status in the twelfth century and later, it had less to do with Confucian pressures than with the rise of a warrior culture. As the personal relationships of samurai warriors to their lords replaced marriage alliances as a political strategy, the influence of women in political life was reduced, but this was an internal Japanese phenomenon, not a reflection of Chinese influence.

Guided Reading Question

■ **COMPARISON**
In what different ways did Japanese and Korean women experience the pressures of Confucian orthodoxy?

Lady Murasaki Shikibu Lady Murasaki Shikibu drew on her experience as a lady-in-waiting at the imperial court to craft her famous novel, *The Tale of Genji*. She allegedly began to write the novel in 1004 at the Buddhist temple of Ishiyama-dera under the inspiration of a full moon, as depicted in this eighteenth-century woodblock print. (Ukiyo-e [Japanese woodblock print] by Harunobu Suzuki, ca. 1767/Pictures from History/Bridgeman Images)

PRACTICING HISTORICAL THINKING

In what different ways did Korea, Vietnam, Japan, and northern nomads experience and respond to Chinese influence?

Japan's ability to borrow extensively from China while developing its own distinctive civilization perhaps provided a model for its encounter with the West in the nineteenth century. Then, as before, Japan borrowed selectively from a foreign culture without losing either its political independence or its cultural uniqueness.

China and the Eurasian World Economy

Beyond China's central role in East Asia was its economic interaction with the wider world of Eurasia generally. On the one hand, China's remarkable economic growth, taking place during the Tang and Song dynasties, could hardly be contained within China's borders and clearly had a major impact throughout Eurasia. On the other hand, China was recipient as well as donor in the economic interactions of the third-wave era, and its own economic achievements owed something to the stimulus of contact with the larger world.

Spillovers: China's Impact on Eurasia

One of the outcomes of China's economic revolution lay in the diffusion of its many technological innovations to peoples and places far from East Asia. (See Snapshot, page 339, for a wider view of Chinese technological achievements.) Papermaking, known in China since the Han dynasty, spread to Korea and Vietnam by the fourth century C.E., to Japan and India by the seventh, to the Islamic world by the eighth, to Muslim Spain by 1150, to France and Germany in the 1300s, and to England in the 1490s. Printing, likewise a Chinese invention, rapidly reached Korea, where movable type became a highly developed technique, and Japan as well. Both technologies were heavily influenced by Buddhism, which accorded religious merit to the reproduction of sacred texts. The Islamic world, however, highly valued handwritten calligraphy and generally resisted printing as impious until the nineteenth century. The adoption of printing in Europe was likewise delayed because of the absence of paper until the twelfth century. Then movable type was reinvented by Johannes Gutenberg in the fifteenth century, although it is unclear whether he was aware of Chinese and Korean precedents. With implications for mass literacy, bureaucracy, scholarship, the spread of religion, and the exchange of information, papermaking and printing were Chinese innovations of revolutionary and global dimensions.

Chinese technologies were seldom simply transferred from one place to another. More often, a particular Chinese technique or product stimulated innovations in more distant lands in accordance with local needs.[19] For example, as the Chinese formula for gunpowder, invented in the ninth century, became available in Europe, together with some early and simple firearms, these innovations triggered the development of cannons in the early fourteenth century. Soon cannons appeared in the Islamic world, and by the 1350s they were in common use in China itself,

Guided Reading Question

■ **CONNECTION**
In what ways did China participate in the world of Eurasian commerce and exchange, and with what outcomes?

SNAPSHOT Chinese Technological Achievements

Before the technological explosion of the European Industrial Revolution during the eighteenth and nineteenth centuries, China had long been the major center of global technological innovation. Many of those inventions spread to other civilizations, where they stimulated imitation or modification. Since Europe was located at the opposite end of the Eurasian continent from China, it often took considerable time for those innovations to give rise to something similar in the West. That lag is also a measure of the relative technological development of the two civilizations in premodern times.

Innovation	First Used in China (approximate)	Adoption/Recognition in the West: Time Lag in Years (approximate)
Iron plow	6th–4th century B.C.E.	2,000+
Cast iron	4th century B.C.E.	1,000–1,200
Efficient horse collar	3rd–1st century B.C.E.	1,000
Paper	2nd century B.C.E.	1,000
Wheelbarrow	1st century B.C.E.	900–1,000
Rudder for steering ships	1st century C.E.	1,100
Iron chain suspension bridge	1st century C.E.	1,000–1,300
Porcelain	3rd century C.E.	1,500
Magnetic compass for navigation	9th–11th century C.E.	400
Gunpowder	9th century C.E.	400
Chain drive for transmission of power	976 C.E.	800
Movable type printing	1045 C.E.	400

Source: Compiled from Joseph Needham, *Science and Civilization in China* (Cambridge: Cambridge University Press, 1965), 1:242; and Robert Temple, *The Genius of China* (New York: Simon and Schuster, 1986).

which first used cast iron rather than bronze in their construction. But the highly competitive European state system drove the "gunpowder revolution" much further and more rapidly than in China's imperial state. Chinese textile, metallurgical, and naval technologies such as the magnetic compass likewise stimulated imitation and innovation all across Eurasia.

In addition to its technological influence, China's prosperity during the Song dynasty greatly stimulated commercial life and market-based behavior all across the Afro-Eurasian trading world. China's products—silk, porcelain, lacquerware—found eager buyers from Japan to East Africa, and everywhere in between. The immense size and wealth of China's domestic economy also provided a ready market for hundreds of commodities from afar. For example, the lives of many thousands of people in the spice-producing islands of what is now Indonesia were transformed as they came to depend on Chinese consumers' demand for their products. "[O]ne hundred million [Chinese] people," wrote historian William McNeill, "increasingly caught up within a commercial network, buying and selling to supplement every day's livelihood, made a significant difference to the way other human beings made their livings throughout a large part of the civilized world."[20] Such was the ripple effect of China's economic revolution.

On the Receiving End: China as Economic Beneficiary

But Chinese interaction with the wider world was not a one-way street, for China too was changed by its engagement with other parts of Eurasia. During the third-wave era, for example, China had learned about the cultivation and processing of both cotton and sugar from India. From Vietnam, around 1000, China gained access to the new, fast-ripening, and drought-resistant strains of rice that made a highly productive rice-based agriculture possible in the drier and more rugged regions of southern China. This marked a major turning point in Chinese history, as the frontier region south of the Yangzi River grew rapidly in population, overtaking the traditional centers of Chinese civilization in the north. In the process, the many non-Chinese peoples of the area were painfully overwhelmed by Chinese military forces and by the migration of at least a million Han Chinese farmers by 1400.

Technologically as well, China's extraordinary burst of creativity owed something to the stimulus of cross-cultural contact. Awareness of Persian windmills, for example, spurred the development of a distinct but related device in China. Printing arose from China's growing involvement with the world of Buddhism, which put a spiritual premium on the reproduction of the Buddha's image and of short religious texts that were carried as charms. It was in Buddhist monasteries during the Tang dynasty that the long-established practice of printing with seals was elaborated by Chinese monks into woodblock printing. The first printed book, in 868 C.E., was a famous Buddhist text, the *Diamond Sutra*.

A further transforming impact of China's involvement with a wider world derived from its growing participation in Indian Ocean trade. By the Tang dynasty, thousands of ships annually visited the ports of southern China, and settled communities of foreign merchants—Arabs, Persians, Indians, Southeast Asians—turned some of these cities into cosmopolitan centers. Buddhist temples, Muslim mosques and cemeteries, and Hindu phallic sculptures graced the skyline of Quanzhou, a coastal city in southern China. Occasionally the

The *Diamond Sutra* The world's earliest dated printed book was produced in China in 868. It was a scroll of the *Diamond Sutra*, a classical text of Mahayana Buddhism measuring fifteen feet in length and printed from carved woodblocks. This image shows the frontispiece of that text, depicting the Buddha teaching while surrounded by a collection of monks and bodhisattvas. This copy of the *Diamond Sutra* dates to the first half of the tenth century. (Frontispiece to "The Diamond Sutra" painted in ink and colors on paper, ca. 901-950/© The Trustees of the British Museum/Art Resource, NY)

tensions of cultural diversity erupted in violence, such as the massacre of tens of thousands of foreigners in Canton during the 870s when Chinese rebel forces sacked the city. Indian Ocean commerce also contributed much to the transformation of southern China from a subsistence economy to one more heavily based on producing for export. In the process, merchants achieved a degree of social acceptance not known before, including their frequent appointment to high-ranking bureaucratic positions. Finally, much-beloved stories of the monkey god, widely popular even in contemporary China, derived from Indian sources transmitted by Indian Ocean commerce.

China and Buddhism

By far the most important gift that China received from India was neither cotton nor sugar, but a religion, Buddhism. Until the adoption of Marxism in the twentieth century, Buddhism was the only large-scale cultural borrowing in Chinese history. It also made China into a launching pad for Buddhism's dispersion to Korea and from there to Japan as well (see Map 8.5).

Making Buddhism Chinese

Buddhism initially entered China via the Silk Road trading network during the first and second centuries C.E. The stability and prosperity of the Han dynasty, then at its height, ensured that the new "barbarian" religion held little appeal for native Chinese. Furthermore, the Indian culture from which Buddhism sprang was at odds with Chinese understandings of the world in many ways. Buddhism's commitment to a secluded and monastic life for monks and nuns seemed to dishonor Chinese family values, and its concern for individual salvation or enlightenment appeared selfish, contradicting the social orientation of Confucian thinking. Furthermore, the Buddhist concept of infinite eons of time, endlessly repeating themselves, was quite a stretch for the Chinese, who normally thought in terms of finite family generations or dynastic cycles. No wonder that for the first several centuries C.E., Buddhism was largely the preserve of foreign merchants and monks living in China.

In the half millennium between roughly 300 and 800 C.E., however, Buddhism took solid root in China within both elite and popular culture, becoming a permanent, though fluctuating, presence in Chinese life. It began, arguably, with the collapse of the Han dynasty around 200 C.E. The chaotic, violent, and politically fragmented centuries that followed seriously discredited Confucianism and opened the door to alternative understandings of the world. Nomadic rulers, now governing much of northern China, found Buddhism useful in part because it was foreign. "We were born out of the marches [beyond the realm of Chinese culture]," declared one of them, "and though we are unworthy, we have complied with our appointed destiny and govern the Chinese as their prince. . . . Buddha being a barbarian god is the very one we should worship."[21] Rulers and elite families provided

Guided Reading Question

....

■ **CHANGE**

What facilitated the rooting of Buddhism within China?

Origin, 5th century B.C.E.
5th century B.C.E. to 2nd century B.C.E.
2nd century B.C.E. to 3rd century C.E.
3rd century C.E. to 8th century C.E.
→ Spread of Buddhism

MAPPING HISTORY

Map 8.5 The World of Asian Buddhism

Originating in India, Buddhism later spread widely throughout much of Asia to provide a measure of cultural or religious commonality across this vast region.

READING THE MAP: Trace the routes and speed with which Buddhism spread from its heartland along the Ganges River. How quickly did it reach China, Korea, Japan, and Tibet? Why might it have taken longer to become established in Korea, Japan, and Tibet?

MAKING CONNECTIONS: Comparing Map 8.5 with Map 7.1: The Silk Roads, identify regions where Buddhism spread along this long-distance trade route. How quickly did Buddhism establish itself along the Silk Roads?

patronage for Buddhist monasteries, temples, and works of art. In southern China, where many northern aristocrats had fled following the disastrous decline of the Han dynasty, Buddhism provided some comfort in the face of a collapsing society. Its emphasis on ritual, morality, and contemplation represented an intellectually and aesthetically satisfying response to times that were so clearly out of joint.

Meanwhile, Buddhist monasteries increasingly provided an array of services for ordinary people. In them, travelers found accommodation; those fleeing from China's many upheavals discovered a place of refuge; desperate people received charity; farmers borrowed seed for the next planting; the sick were treated; and children learned to read. And for many, Buddhism was associated with access to magical powers as reports of miracles abounded. Battles were won, rain descended on drought-ridden areas, diseases were cured, and guilt was relieved—all through the magical ministrations of charismatic monks.

Accompanying all of this was a serious effort by monks, scholars, and translators to present this Indian religion in terms that Chinese could more readily grasp. Thus the Buddhist term *dharma*, referring to the Buddha's teaching, was translated as *dao*, or "the way," a notion long familiar in both Daoist and Confucian thinking. The Buddhist notion of "morality" was rendered with the Confucian term that referred to "filial submission and obedience." Some Indian concepts were modified in the process of translation. For example, the idea that "husband supports wife," which reflected a considerable respect for women and mothers in early Indian Buddhism, became in translation "husband controls wife."[22]

As Buddhism took hold in China, it was primarily in its broader Mahayana form—complete with numerous deities, the veneration of relics, many heavens and hells, and bodhisattvas to aid the believer—rather than its more psychological and individualistic Theravada form (see "The Buddhist Challenge" in Chapter 4). One of the most popular expressions of Buddhism in China was the Pure Land School, in which faithfully repeating the name of an earlier Buddha, the Amitabha, was sufficient to ensure rebirth in a beautifully described heavenly realm, the Pure Land. In its emphasis on salvation by faith, without arduous study or intensive meditation, Pure Land Buddhism became a highly popular and authentically Chinese version of the Indian faith.

China's reunification under the Sui and early Tang dynasties witnessed growing state support for Buddhism. The Sui emperor Wendi (r. 581–604 C.E.) had monasteries constructed at the base of China's five sacred mountains, further identifying the imported religion with traditional Chinese culture. He even used Buddhism to justify his military campaigns. "With a hundred victories in a hundred battles," he declared, "we promote the practice of the ten Buddhist virtues."[23] By 600 C.E., some 4,000 monasteries had been established. With state support and growing popular acceptance, they became centers of great wealth. They were largely exempt from taxation and owned large estates; ran businesses such as oil presses, water mills, and pawn shops; collected gems, gold, and lavish works of art; and employed millions of slaves, serfs, and other unfree and dependent workers. But Buddhism never achieved the independence from state authorities that the Christian Church acquired in Europe. The examinations for becoming a monk were supervised by the state, and education in the monasteries included the required study of the Confucian classics. In the mid-ninth century, the state showed quite dramatically just how much control it could exercise over the Buddhist establishment.

Losing State Support: The Crisis of Chinese Buddhism

The impressive growth of **Chinese Buddhism** was accompanied by a persistent undercurrent of resistance and criticism. Some saw the Buddhist establishment, at least potentially, as a "state within a state" and a challenge to imperial authority. More important was a deepening resentment of its enormous wealth. One fifth-century critic, referring to monks, put the issue squarely: "Why is it that their ideals are noble and far-reaching and their activities still are base and common? [They] become merchants and engage in barter, wrangling with the masses for profit."[24] Nor did the environmental impact of Buddhist monasteries escape the notice of state officials. In 707 c.e., one such official wrote: "Extensive construction of monasteries are undertaken and large mansions are built. Even though for such works trees are felled to the point of stripping the mountains, it does not suffice. . . . Though earth is moved to the point of obstructing roads, it does not suffice."[25] When state treasuries were short of funds, government officials cast a covetous eye on these wealthy and tax-exempt monasteries. Furthermore, Buddhism was clearly of foreign origin and offensive for that reason to some Confucian and Daoist thinkers. The celibacy of the monks and their withdrawal from society, the critics argued, undermined the Confucian-based family system of Chinese tradition.

Such criticisms took on new meaning in the changed environment of China after about 800 c.e. Following centuries of considerable foreign influence in China, a growing resentment against foreign culture, particularly among the literate classes, increasingly took hold. The turning point may well have been the An Lushan rebellion (755–763), in which a general of foreign origin led a major revolt against the Tang dynasty. Whatever its origin, an increasingly xenophobic reaction set in among the upper classes, reflected in a desire to return to an imagined "purity" of earlier times. In this setting, the old criticisms of Buddhism became more sharply focused. In 819, Han Yu, a leading figure in the Confucian counterattack on Buddhism, wrote a scathing memorial to the emperor criticizing his willingness to honor a relic of the Buddha's finger.

> Now the Buddha was of barbarian origin. His language differed from Chinese speech; his clothes were of a different cut; his mouth did not pronounce the prescribed words of the Former Kings. . . . He did not recognize the relationship between prince and subject, nor the sentiments of father and son. . . . I pray that Your Majesty will turn this bone over to the officials that it may be cast into water or fire.[26]

Guided Reading Question

■ **CHANGE**
What were the major sources of opposition to Buddhism within China?

Several decades later, the Chinese state took direct action against the Buddhist establishment as well as against other foreign religions. A series of imperial decrees between 841 and 845 ordered some 260,000 monks and nuns to return to normal life as tax-paying citizens. Thousands of monasteries, temples, and shrines were either destroyed or turned to public use, while the state confiscated the lands, money, metals, and serfs belonging to monasteries. Buddhists were now forbidden to use gold, silver, copper, iron, and gems in constructing their images. These actions dealt a serious blow to Chinese Buddhism. Its scholars and monks were scattered, its creativity was diminished, and its institutions came even more firmly under state control.

Despite this persecution, Buddhism did not vanish from China. At the level of elite culture, its philosophical ideas played a role in the reformulation of Confucian thinking that took place during the Song dynasty. At the village level, Buddhism became one element of Chinese popular religion, which also included the veneration of ancestors, the honoring of Confucius, and Daoist shrines and rituals. Temples frequently included statues of Confucius, Laozi, and the Buddha, with little sense of any incompatibility among them. "Every black-haired son of Han," the Chinese have long said, "wears a Confucian thinking cap, a Daoist robe, and Buddhist sandals." (See the opening photo for Chapter 4.) Unlike in Europe, where an immigrant religion triumphed over and excluded all other faiths, Buddhism in China became assimilated into Chinese culture alongside its other traditions.

REFLECTIONS

Why Do Things Change?

Explaining how and why human societies change is perhaps the central issue that historians confront, no matter which societies or periods of time they study. Those who specialize in the history of some particular culture or civilization often emphasize sources of change operating within those societies, although there is intense disagreement as to which are most significant. The ideas of great thinkers, the policies of leaders, struggles for power, the conflict of classes, the invention of new technologies, the growth or decline in population, variations in climate or weather—all of these and more have their advocates as the primary motor of historical transformation.

Of course, it is not necessary to choose among them. The history of China illustrates the range of internal factors that have driven change in that civilization. The political conflicts of the "era of warring states" provided the setting and the motivation for the emergence of Confucianism and Daoism, which in turn have certainly shaped the character and texture of Chinese civilization over many centuries.

The personal qualities and brutal policies of China's "first emperor" Shihuangdi surely played a role in China's unification and in the brief duration of the Qin dynasty. The subsequent creation of a widespread network of canals and waterways, as well as the country's technological achievements, maintained that unity over very long periods of time. But the massive inequalities of Chinese society generated the peasant upheavals that periodically shattered that unity and led to new ruling dynasties. Sometimes natural events, such as droughts and floods, triggered those rebellions.

World historians, more than those who study particular civilizations or nations, have been inclined to find the primary source of change in contact with strangers, in external connections and interactions, whether direct or indirect. The history of China and East Asia provides plenty of examples for this point of view. Conceptions of China as the "middle kingdom," infinitely superior to all surrounding societies, grew out of centuries of involvement with its "barbarian" neighbors. Some of those neighbors became Chinese as China's imperial reach grew, especially to the south. Even those that did not, such as Koreans, Vietnamese, and Japanese, were decisively transformed by proximity to the "radiating civilization" of China. China's own cuisine, so distinctive in recent centuries, may well be a quite recent invention, drawing heavily on Indian and Southeast Asian cooking. Buddhism, of course, is an obvious borrowing from abroad, although its incorporation into Chinese civilization and its ups and downs within China owed much to internal cultural and political realities.

In the end, clear distinctions between internal and external sources of change in China's history—or that of any other society—are perhaps misleading. The boundary between "inside" and "outside" is itself a constantly changing line. Should the borderlands of northern China, where Chinese and Turkic peoples met and mingled, be regarded as internal or external to China itself? And, as the histories of Chinese Buddhism and of Japanese culture so clearly indicate, what comes from beyond is always transformed by what it encounters within.

Second Thoughts

What's the Significance?

Sui dynasty, 318

Tang dynasty, 319

Song dynasty, 319

China's economic revolution, 321

Hangzhou, 321

gunpowder, 323

foot binding, 325

tribute system, 328

Xiongnu Empire, 329

Silla kingdom, 331

hangul, 333

chu nom, 335

Shotoku Taishi, 335

bushido, 336

Chinese Buddhism, 344

Big Picture Questions

1. How can you explain the changing reception of Buddhism in China?
2. How did China influence the world of the third-wave era? How was China itself transformed by its encounters with the wider world?
3. How might China's position in the world during the Tang and Song dynasty era compare to its emerging role in global affairs in the twenty-first century?
4. **Looking Back:** In what ways did Tang and Song dynasty China resemble the earlier Han dynasty period, and in what ways had China changed?

Next Steps: For Further Study

Samuel Adshead, *Tang China: The Rise of the East in World History* (2004). Explores the role of China within the larger world.

Patricia Buckley Ebrey, *The Inner Quarters* (1993). A balanced account of the gains and losses experienced by Chinese women during the changes of the Song dynasty.

Mark Elvin, *The Retreat of the Elephants: An Environmental History of China* (2004). Explores the environmental cost of civilization in a Chinese setting.

James L. Huffman, *Japan in World History* (2010). The first three chapters of this recent work place Japan's early history in the framework of world history.

Paul S. Ropp, *China in World History* (2010). An up-to-date telling of China's historical development, cast in a global context.

Arthur F. Wright, *Buddhism in Chinese History* (1959). An older account filled with wonderful stories and anecdotes.

Ben Hedges and Christy Sammett (producers), "Discovering China: The Song Dynasty," NTD Television, https://www.youtube.com/watch?v=QO7NHZJ-eE4. A brief documentary with lovely visuals that highlights the achievements of Song dynasty China.

Karin Yuen, "Early Heian Period: Japanese Art History," Little Art Talks, 2015, https://www.youtube.com/watch?v=5WEvKtaj0cQ. A short documentary on the cultural history of Japan during the early centuries of the Heian period (794–1185), when Chinese influence was at its height.

China's Scholar-Officials

China's elite class—those men who had passed the highest-level examinations and held important offices in the state bureaucracy—represented only a tiny fraction of their country's huge population, but they established the tone and set the standards of elite behavior for Chinese civilization (see "An Elite of Officials" in Chapter 5). Active in political affairs and social life, they also honored leisure, contemplation, poetry, painting, and calligraphy. In the images and documents that follow, we catch a glimpse of how these scholar-officials lived and what they valued.

SOURCE 8.1 Scholar-Officials and the Emperor ▶

The close association of China's scholar class with the country's political life is reflected in Source 8.1, which shows a group of scholar-officials drinking tea and wine together with the emperor, who is presiding at the left. The painting is usually attributed to the emperor Huizong (1082–1135), who was himself a noted painter, poet, calligrapher, and collector. This emperor's great attention to the arts rather than to affairs of state gained him a reputation as a negligent and dissolute ruler. His reign ended in disgrace as China suffered a humiliating defeat at the hands of the northern nomadic Jin people, who took the emperor captive.

- How would you describe this event to someone who had not attended it?
- What might you say about the relationship of the emperor and the scholar-officials?
- How might you imagine the conversation around this table?
- In painting this picture, what do you think the emperor was trying to convey?

Scholars Gathering in a Bamboo Garden | **12th century**

Ink and color on silk, 15th century/Private Collection/Photo © Christie's Images/Bridgeman Images

■ ■ ■

SOURCE 8.2 A Gathering of Scholars ▶

Confucian cultural ideals gave great prominence to literature, poetry, and scholarly pursuits as activities appropriate for "gentlemen." Confucius himself had declared that "gentlemen make friends through literature, and through friendship increase their benevolence." For some, a more reclusive life devoted to study, painting, poetry, and conversation with friends represented an honorable alternative to government service. Thus literary gatherings of scholars and officials were common themes in Tang and Song dynasty paintings. Source 8.2 provides an illustration of such an event. It portrays the eighth-century poet-official Wang Changling, shown in his red scholar-official's robe seated by the table, talking with three friends.

■ What marks these figures as cultivated men of literary or scholarly inclination?

■ Notice the various gazes of the four figures. What do they suggest about the character of this gathering and the relationships among its participants?

■ Do you think the artist was seeking to convey an idealized image of what a gathering of "gentlemen" ought to be or a realistic portrayal of an actual event? What elements of the painting support your answer?

Scholars of the Liuli Hall | **late 13th century**

© age-fotostock/Art Collection/age-fotostock

■ ■ ■

SOURCE 8.3 A Solitary Scholar ▶

Chinese scholar-officials are often shown as solitary contemplatives, immersing themselves in nature. The famous Song dynasty painter Ma Yuan (1160–1225) depicted such an image in his masterpiece entitled *On a Mountain Path in Spring*, showing a scholar walking in the countryside watching several birds, while his servant trails behind carrying his master's *qin* (lute). A short poem in the upper right, composed by the reigning emperor Ningzong, reads: "The wild flowers dance when brushed by my sleeves. Reclusive birds make no sound as they shun the presence of people."[27]

■ How would you define the mood of this painting? What posture toward the natural environment does it suggest? What techniques did Ma Yuan use to convey this mood or posture?

■ How might this painting reflect the perspectives of Daoism (see "The Daoist Answer" in Chapter 4)? In what respects does it differ from the more Confucian tone of Source 8.2?

■ During Ma Yuan's lifetime, the northern part of China was coming under the control of the feared Mongols. How might an awareness of this situation affect our understanding of this painting?

MA YUAN | *On a Mountain Path in Spring* | early 13th century

Petal Foam/Alamy

■ ■ ■

SOURCE 8.4 Tang Dynasty Poetry

The sensibility evoked in Ma Yuan's painting also found expression in much of Chinese poetry, which was a central feature in the lives of almost everyone in the educated classes, scholar-officials and emperors alike. They studied poetry, wrote poetry, and shared their creations with one another both privately and on social occasions. At first poems were hand-copied on calligraphic scrolls, but after printing became widely available during the ninth century C.E., they appeared in printed books as well. Friendship, wine, war, loss and parting, aging and death, social criticism — all of these found a place in classical Chinese poetry. But it was nature — rivers, fields, gardens, clouds, seasons, and, above all, mountains — that most fundamentally animated the classical poetry of China. "Artist-intellectuals found their spiritual home in mountains,"[28] wrote David Hinton, a prominent

American translator of Chinese poetry. The poems that follow offer a brief glimpse into the intellectual and spiritual life of Chinese scholar-officials, through the writings of three of the greatest Tang dynasty poets: Li Po, Wang Wei, and Du Fu. Each of them served in official positions or aspired to do so, while yearning for immersion in the wilderness and in their poetry.

■ How might you characterize the sensibility reflected in these poems?

■ What relationship between poet and nature can you discern? Is the poet a detached observer, an interested witness, or an active participant in the natural order? To what relationship with nature do the poets aspire?

■ What elements of Daoist or Buddhist feeling can you identify in these poems? Notice the reference to "the Way" in Selection C.

SOURCE 8.4A

LI PO │ *The Mountain and Me* │ 8th century

The birds have vanished into the sky
And now the last cloud drains away.
We sit together, the mountain and me
   until only the mountain remains.

Source: "Zazen on Ching-t'ing Mountain" in *Crossing the Yellow River: Three Hundred Poems from the Chinese,* trans. Sam Hamill (Buffalo, NY: Tiger Bark Press, 2000).

SOURCE 8.4B

LI PO │ *Drinking Alone with the Moon* │ 8th century

From a pot of wine among the flowers
I drank alone. There was no one with me—
Till, raising my cup, I asked the bright
   moon
To bring me my shadow and make us three.
Alas, the moon was unable to drink
And my shadow tagged me vacantly;
But still for a while I had these friends
To cheer me through the end of spring. . . .
I sang. The moon encouraged me.
I danced. My shadow tumbled after.

As long as I knew, we were boon companions.
And then I was drunk, and we lost one
   another. . . .
Shall goodwill ever be secure?
I watch the long road of the River of Stars
   [the Milky Way].

Source: *Tang Shi—300 Tang Poems,* translated by Witter Bynner, 1929, http://wengu.tartarie.com/wg/wengu.php?l=Tangshi&no=6. Also in Witter Bynner, *The Jade Mountain: A Chinese Anthology* (New York: Alfred A. Knopf, 1929).

SOURCE 8.4C

WANG WEI │ *My Retreat at Mount Zhongnan* │ 8th century

My heart in middle age found the Way.
And I came to dwell at the foot of this
   mountain.

When the spirit moves, I wander alone
Amid beauty that is all for me. . . .
I will walk till the water checks my path,

Then sit and watch the rising clouds —
And some day meet an old wood-cutter
And talk and laugh and never return.

Source: *Tang Shi—300 Tang Poems,* translated by Witter Bynner, 1929, http://wengu.tartarie.com/wg/wengu.php?l=Tangshi&no=123. Also in Witter Bynner, *The Jade Mountain: A Chinese Anthology* (New York: Alfred A. Knopf, 1929).

SOURCE 8.4D

DU FU | *A View of Taishan* | 8th century

What shall I say of the Great Peak? —
The ancient dukedoms are everywhere green,
Inspired and stirred by the breath of creation,
With the Twin Forces balancing day and
   night. . . .
I bare my breast toward opening clouds,
I strain my sight after birds flying home.
When shall I reach the top and hold
All mountains in a single glance?

Source: *Tang Shi—300 Tang Poems,* translated by Witter Bynner, 1929, http://wengu.tartarie.com/wg/wengu.php?l=Tangshi&no=8. Also in Witter Bynner, *The Jade Mountain: A Chinese Anthology* (New York: Alfred A. Knopf, 1929).

■ ■ ■

SOURCE 8.5 Scholar-Officials at Play ▶

Not all was poetry and contemplation of nature in the lives of China's scholar-officials. Nor were men and women always so strictly segregated as the preceding sources may suggest. Source 8.5 illustrates another side of Chinese elite life. These images are part of a long tenth-century scroll painting titled *The Night Revels of Han Xizai.* Apparently, the Tang dynasty emperor Li Yu became concerned that one of his ministers, Han Xizai, was overindulging in suspicious nightlong parties in his own home. He therefore commissioned the artist Gu Hongzhong to attend these parties secretly and to record the events in a painting, which he hoped would shame his wayward but talented official into more appropriate and dignified behavior. The entire scroll shows men and women together, sometimes in flirtatious situations, while open sleeping areas suggest sexual activity.

■ What kinds of entertainment were featured at this gathering?

■ What aspects of these parties shown in the scroll paintings might have caused the emperor some concern? In what respects might these kinds of gatherings run counter to Confucian values?

■ How are women portrayed in this image? In what ways are they relating to the men in the paintings?

GU HONGZHONG | *The Night Revels of Han Xizai* | 10th century

---

DOING HISTORY

1. **Describing elite society:** Based on these sources, write a brief description of the activities and outlook of China's scholar-officials during the Tang and Song dynasties.

2. **Defining the self-image of scholar-officials:** What do these sources suggest about how members of this elite class ideally viewed themselves?

3. **Identifying cultural influences:** In what ways did Confucian, Daoist, or Buddhist teachings shape the lives and values of the scholar-official class?

4. **Seeking additional sources:** What other kinds of sources might provide further insight into the lives of Chinese elites?

Assessing China's Scholar-Officials

Contemporary scholars have both criticized and celebrated China's official elite, as the following sources indicate. Voice 8.1 is that of Jacques Garnet, a prominent French historian of China, while Voice 8.2 comes from David Hinton, who is the premier American translator of Chinese philosophical and poetic texts.

- How do these two selections differ in their assessment of China's scholar-official class? On what might they agree?

- With which of these sources do you feel more sympathetic?

- **Integrating Primary and Secondary Sources:** In what ways might the images and documents above support or challenge the conclusions of these two accounts?

VOICE 8.1

Jacques Garnet on the "Learned Culture" of Song Dynasty China | 1996

. . . [T]he governing class of the eleventh to thirteenth centuries, consisting of rich, educated families usually living in an urban environment on the income from their estates, despised physical effort and wished to stand aloof from traditions of the steppe and from popular amusements. The profession of arms . . . had lost its prestige ever since the armies had consisted of mercenaries recruited from the dregs of society. The intellectual, contemplative, learned . . . aspects of the arts and letters among the Chinese upper classes asserted itself in the Sung period and was to remain dominant under the Ming and Ch'ing dynasties. . . . Henceforth, the lettered Chinese . . . was to be a pure intellectual who thought that games of skill and athletic competitions were things

for the lower classes. This deeply rooted contempt in the governing classes for physical effort and aptitude was to persist down to our own day. . . . [O]nly learned literature, calligraphy, the collection of books and works of art, and the designing of gardens found favor with the educated classes.

Source: Jacques Garnet, *A History of Chinese Civilization* (Cambridge: Cambridge University Press, 1996), 331.

VOICE 8.2

David Hinton on "Public Service" and "Mountain Seclusion" | 2005

The deep commitment felt by intellectuals in ancient China to both the Confucian realm of social responsibility and the Taoist realm of spiritual self-cultivation gave rise to a recluse ideal that answered both of these commitments. In the most mythic version of this ideal, a sage recluse living contentedly in the mountains recognizes that the nation is in crisis and needs his wisdom—so he reluctantly joins the government; resolves the crisis; and then, having no interest in the wealth and renown associated with that life, returns to cultivate his simple life of spiritual depth in the mountains. This ideal was enacted by countless intellectuals in ancient China, though in a bit more realistic form. They devoted themselves to public service, always watching for a chance to spend time in mountain seclusion (often at monasteries) and at some point retired permanently from government service to live as recluses.

Source: David Hinton, *Mountain Home: The Wilderness Poetry of Ancient China* (New York: New Directions Books, 2005), 210.

The Worlds of Islam

CHAPTER 9

Afro-Eurasian Connections

600–1450

Hassan Kargbo, a citizen of the small West African country of Sierra Leone, is a "ChrisMus," which in local parlance is a person who identifies with both Christianity and Islam. "I see it as the same religion," he stated. Interviewed in early 2014, he acknowledged going to church every Sunday, wearing a Jesus bracelet, and praying at a mosque every day. Kelfala Conteh, the caretaker of an ancient mosque in Sierra Leone's capital of Freetown, reported, "Of course [Christians] come here. We have both Christians and Muslims praying side by side." Wurle Bah, another Muslim from Freetown, said, "We all believe in God. If my friends invite me to church, of course I will go." On one of the colorfully decorated minibuses that carry passengers around the city is the declaration that "God loves Allah."[1]

In the world of the early twenty-first century, where headlines often highlight bitter struggles among Muslims and violent conflict with Christians, Jews, or Hindus, it is perhaps useful to recall places such as Sierra Leone where religious tolerance is both practiced and celebrated. Nor is it alone. Indonesia, the most heavily populated Muslim country in the world, has inscribed freedom of religion in its constitution; has officially recognized Christian, Hindu, and Buddhist holidays as well as those of Islam; and has generally maintained peace among its various religious communities. And millions of ordinary Muslims all around the world have long lived in peaceful proximity to neighbors belonging to different religious communities.

The vast diversity of contemporary Islam echoes the earlier history of this newest of humankind's major religions. During the first Muslim millennium (600–1600), the Islamic world found expression in various forms—Sunni, Shia, Sufi, Arab, Persian, Turkic, West African—some displaying a

« **The Hajj** The pilgrimage to Mecca, known as the *hajj*, has long been a central religious ritual in Islamic practice. It also embodies the cosmopolitan character of Islam as pilgrims from all over the vast Islamic realm assemble in the city where the faith was born. This painting, dating to 1237, shows a group of joyful pilgrims, led by a band, on their way to Mecca.

broad acceptance of diversity and others engaged in serious and at times violent conflict with those of a different religious outlook.

Furthermore, both then and now, the world of Islam occupied a central position in the larger global arena. During its first millennium, peoples claiming allegiance to Islam represented a highly successful, prosperous, and expansive civilization encompassing parts of Africa, Europe, the Middle East, and Asia. In our own times, the relationship of the Islamic world to the wider world has been shaped by the many, varying, and continuing efforts of Muslim societies to overcome several centuries of humiliating European intrusion and to find their place in modern international life. ■

The significance of a burgeoning Islamic world during the third-wave era was enormous. It thrust the previously marginal and largely nomadic Arabs into a central role in world history, for it was among them and in their language that the newest of the world's major religions was born. The sudden emergence and rapid spread of that religion in the seventh century C.E. was accompanied by the creation of a huge empire that stretched from Spain to India. Both within that empire and beyond it, a new and innovative civilization took shape, drawing on Arab, Persian, Turkic, Greco-Roman, South Asian, and African cultures. It was clearly the largest and most influential of the new third-wave civilizations. Finally, the broad reach of Islam generated many of the great cultural encounters of this era as Islamic civilization challenged and provoked Christendom, penetrated and was transformed by African cultures, and also took root in India, Central Asia, and Southeast Asia.

SEEKING THE MAIN POINT

In what ways did the civilization of Islam draw on other civilizations in the Afro-Eurasian world? And in what respects did it shape or transform those civilizations?

The Birth of a New Religion

Most of the major religious or cultural traditions of the second-wave era had emerged from the core of established civilizations—Confucianism and Daoism from China, Hinduism and Buddhism from India, and Zoroastrianism from Persia. Christianity and Islam, by contrast, emerged more from the margins of Mediterranean and Middle Eastern civilizations. Christianity appeared among a small Middle Eastern people, the Jews, in a remote province of the Roman Empire, while Islam took hold in the cities and deserts of the Arabian Peninsula.

The Homeland of Islam

The central region of the Arabian Peninsula had long been inhabited by nomadic Arabs, known as Bedouins, who herded their sheep and camels in seasonal migrations. These peoples lived in fiercely independent clans and tribes that often engaged

Landmarks for Chapter 9

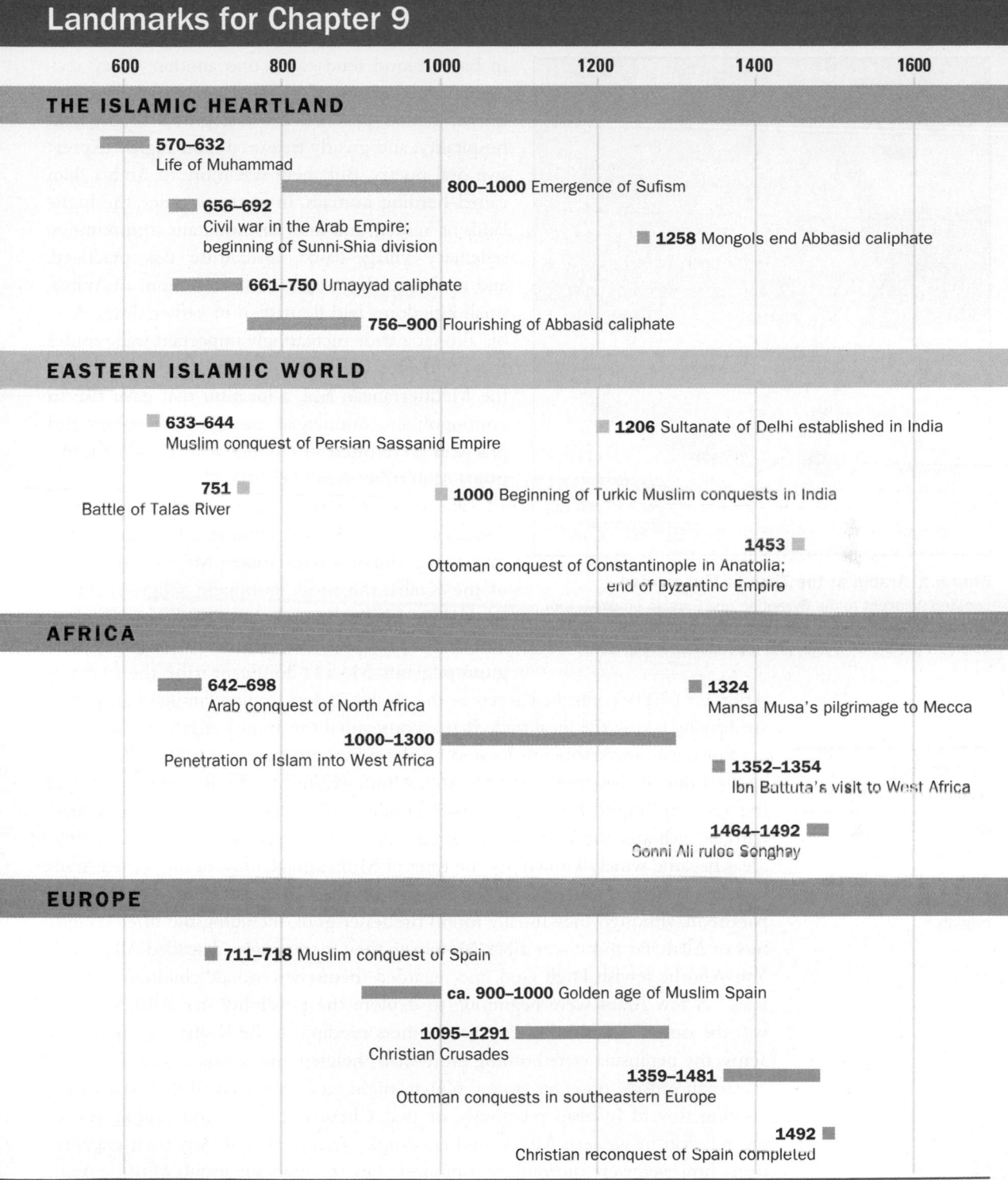

	600	800	1000	1200	1400	1600

THE ISLAMIC HEARTLAND

570–632 Life of Muhammad

800–1000 Emergence of Sufism

656–692 Civil war in the Arab Empire; beginning of Sunni-Shia division

1258 Mongols end Abbasid caliphate

661–750 Umayyad caliphate

756–900 Flourishing of Abbasid caliphate

EASTERN ISLAMIC WORLD

633–644 Muslim conquest of Persian Sassanid Empire

1206 Sultanate of Delhi established in India

751 Battle of Talas River

1000 Beginning of Turkic Muslim conquests in India

1453 Ottoman conquest of Constantinople in Anatolia; end of Byzantine Empire

AFRICA

642–698 Arab conquest of North Africa

1324 Mansa Musa's pilgrimage to Mecca

1000–1300 Penetration of Islam into West Africa

1352–1354 Ibn Battuta's visit to West Africa

1464–1492 Sonni Ali rules Songhay

EUROPE

711–718 Muslim conquest of Spain

ca. 900–1000 Golden age of Muslim Spain

1095–1291 Christian Crusades

1359–1481 Ottoman conquests in southeastern Europe

1492 Christian reconquest of Spain completed

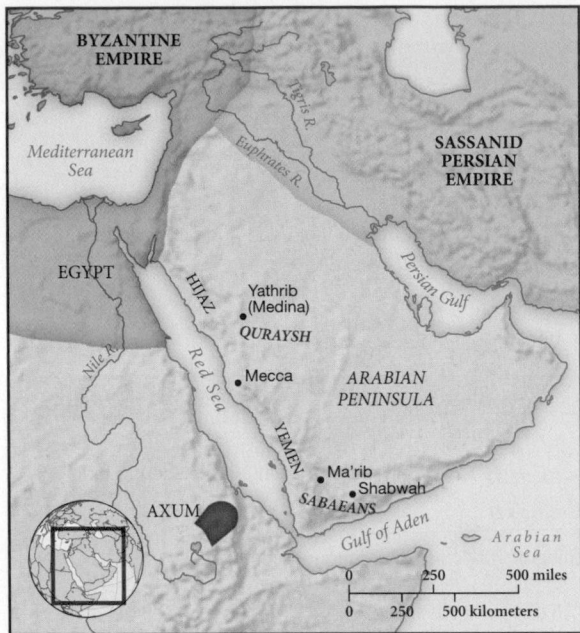

Map 9.1 Arabia at the Time of Muhammad
Located adjacent to the Byzantine and Persian empires, the eastern coast of Arabia was the site of a major trade route between the Indian Ocean and the Mediterranean Sea.

Guided Reading Question
....

■ **DESCRIPTION**
In what ways did the early history of Islam reflect its Arabian origins?

in bitter blood feuds with one another. They recognized a variety of gods, ancestors, and nature spirits; valued personal bravery, group loyalty, and hospitality; and greatly treasured their highly expressive oral poetry. But there was more to Arabia than camel-herding nomads. In scattered oases, the highlands of Yemen, and interior mountain communities, sedentary village-based agriculture was practiced, and in the northern and southern regions of Arabia, small kingdoms had flourished in earlier times. Arabia also sat astride increasingly important trade routes that connected the Indian Ocean world with that of the Mediterranean Sea, a location that gave rise to cosmopolitan commercial cities, whose values and practices were often in conflict with those of traditional Arab tribes (see Map 9.1).

One of those cities, Mecca, came to occupy a distinctive role in Arabia. Though somewhat off the major long-distance trade routes, Mecca was the site of the Kaaba, the most prominent religious shrine in Arabia, which housed representations of some 360 deities and was the destination for many religious pilgrims. Mecca's dominant tribe, the Quraysh (koor-EYE'SH), controlled access to the Kaaba, and its leading families had grown wealthy by taxing the local trade that accompanied the annual pilgrimage season.

Furthermore, Arabia was located on the periphery of two established and rival civilizations of that time — the Byzantine Empire, heir to the Roman world, and the Sassanid Empire, heir to the imperial traditions of Persia. Many Jews and Christians, as well as some Zoroastrians, lived among the Arabs, and their monotheistic ideas became widely known. By the time of Muhammad, most of the settled Arabs had acknowledged the preeminent position of Allah, the supreme god of the Arab pantheon, although they usually found the lesser gods, including the three daughters of Allah, far more accessible. Moreover, they increasingly identified Allah with Yahweh, the Jewish High God, and regarded themselves too as "children of Abraham." A few Arabs were beginning to explore the possibility that Allah/Yahweh was the only God and that the many others residing in the Kaaba and in shrines across the peninsula were nothing more than "helpless and harmless idols."[2]

To an outside observer around 600, it might well have seemed that Arabs were moving toward Judaism religiously or that Christianity, the most rapidly growing religion in western Asia, would encompass Arabia as well. Any such expectations, however, were thoroughly confounded by the dramatic events of the seventh century.

The Messenger and the Message

The catalyst for those events and for the birth of this new religion was a single individual, **Muhammad** Ibn Abdullah (570–632 C.E.), who was born in Mecca to a Quraysh family. As a young boy, Muhammad lost his parents, came under the care of an uncle, and worked as a shepherd to pay his keep. Later he became a trader and traveled as far north as Syria. At the age of twenty-five, he married a wealthy widow, Khadija, herself a prosperous merchant, with whom he fathered six children. A highly reflective man deeply troubled by the religious corruption and social inequalities of Mecca, he often undertook periods of withdrawal and meditation in the arid mountains outside the city. There, like the Buddha and Jesus, Muhammad had a powerful, overwhelming religious experience that left him convinced, albeit reluctantly, that he was Allah's messenger to the Arabs, commissioned to bring to them a scripture in their own language. (See Working with Evidence, Sources 9.1 to 9.3, pages 391–396, for three images from the life of Muhammad.)

According to Muslim tradition, the revelations began in 610 and continued periodically over the next twenty-two years. Those revelations, recorded in the **Quran**, became the sacred scriptures of Islam, which to this day most Muslims regard as the very words of God and the core of their faith. Intended to be recited rather than simply read for information, the Quran, Muslims claim, when heard in its original Arabic, conveys nothing less than the very presence of the Divine. Its unmatched poetic beauty, miraculous to Arabic-speaking Muslims, convinced many that it was indeed a revelation from God. One of the earliest converts testified to its power: "When I heard the Quran, my heart was softened and I wept and Islam entered into me."[3]

In its Arabian setting, the Quran's message, delivered through Muhammad, was revolutionary. Religiously, it was radically monotheistic, presenting Allah as the only God, the all-powerful Creator, the "Lord sustainer of the worlds, the Compassionate, the Caring, master of the day of reckoning" and known to human beings "on the farthest horizon and within their own selves."[4] Here was an exalted conception of Deity that drew heavily on traditions of Jewish and Christian monotheism. As "the Messenger of God," Muhammad presented himself in the line of earlier prophets—Abraham, Moses, Jesus, and many others. He was the last, "the seal of the prophets," bearing God's final revelation to humankind. It was not so much a call to a new faith as an invitation to return to the old and pure religion of Abraham from which Jews, Christians, and Arabs alike had deviated. Jews had wrongly conceived of themselves as a uniquely "chosen people"; Christians had made their prophet into a god; and Arabs had become wildly polytheistic. To all of this, the message of the Quran was a corrective.

Submission to Allah ("Muslim" means "one who submits") was the primary obligation of believers and the means of achieving a God-conscious life in this world and a place in Paradise after death. According to the Quran, however, submission

Guided Reading Question

■ **DESCRIPTION**
What did the Quran expect from those who followed its teachings?

Muslims, Jews, and Christians The close relationship of three Middle Eastern monotheistic traditions is illustrated in this fifteenth-century Persian painting, which portrays Muhammad leading Moses, Abraham, Jesus, and other prophets in prayer. The fire surrounding the Prophet's head represents his religious fervor. The painting reflects the Islamic belief that the revelations granted to Muhammad built on and completed those given earlier to Jews and Christians. (Bibliothèque Nationale de France, Paris, France/© BnF, Dist. RMN-Grand Palais/Art Resource, NY)

was not merely an individual or a spiritual act, for it involved the creation of a whole new society. Over and again, the Quran denounced the prevailing social practices of an increasingly prosperous Mecca: the hoarding of wealth, the exploitation of the poor, the charging of high rates of interest on loans, corrupt business deals, the abuse of women, and the neglect of widows and orphans. Like the Jewish prophets of the Old Testament, the Quran demanded social justice and laid out a prescription for its implementation. It sought a return to the older values of Arab tribal life — solidarity, equality, concern for the poor — which had been undermined, particularly in Mecca, by growing wealth and commercialism.

The message of the Quran challenged not only the ancient polytheism of Arab religion and the social injustices of Mecca but also the entire tribal and clan structure of Arab society, which was so prone to war, feuding, and violence. The just and moral society of Islam was the *umma* (OOM-mah), the community of all believers, replacing tribal, ethnic, or racial identities. In this community, women too had an honored and spiritually equal place. "The believers, men and women, are protectors of one another," declared the Quran.[5] The umma, then, was to be a new and just community, bound by common belief rather than by territory, language, or tribe.

The core message of the Quran — the remembrance of God — was effectively summarized as a set of five requirements for believers known as the **Pillars of Islam**. The first pillar expressed the heart of the Islamic message: "There is no god but God, and Muhammad is the messenger of God." The second pillar was ritual prayer, performed five times a day, which reminded believers that they were living in the presence of God. The third pillar, almsgiving, reflected the Quran's repeated demands for social justice by requiring believers to give generously to support the poor and needy of the community. The fourth pillar established a month of fasting during Ramadan, which meant abstaining from food, drink, and sexual relations from the first light of dawn to sundown. It provided an occasion for self-purification and a reminder of the needs of the hungry. The fifth pillar encouraged a pilgrimage to Mecca, known as the *hajj* (HAHJ), during which believers from all over the Islamic world assembled once a year and put on identical simple white clothing as they rehearsed key events in Islamic history. For at least the few days of the hajj, the many worlds of Islam must surely have seemed a single realm.

A further requirement for believers, sometimes called the sixth pillar, was "struggle," or *jihad* in Arabic. Its more general meaning, which Muhammad referred to as the "greater jihad," was an interior personal effort of each believer against greed and selfishness, a spiritual striving toward living a God-conscious life. In its "lesser" form, the "jihad of the sword," the Quran authorized armed struggle against the forces of unbelief and evil as a means of establishing Muslim rule and of defending the umma from the threats of infidel aggressors. The understanding and use of the jihad concept have varied widely over the many centuries of Islamic history and remain a matter of much controversy among Muslims in the twenty-first century.

The Transformation of Arabia

As the revelations granted to Muhammad became known in Mecca, they attracted a small following of some close relatives, a few prominent Meccan leaders, and an assortment of lower-class dependents, freed slaves, and members of poorer clans. Those teachings also soon attracted the vociferous opposition of Mecca's elite families, particularly those of Muhammad's own tribe, the Quraysh. Muhammad's claim to be a "messenger of Allah," his unyielding monotheism, his call for social reform, his condemnation of Mecca's business practices, and his apparent disloyalty to his own tribe enraged the wealthy and ruling families of Mecca. So great had this opposition become that in 622 Muhammad and his small band of followers emigrated to the more welcoming town of Yathrib, soon to be called Medina, the city of the Prophet. This agricultural settlement of mixed Arab and Jewish population had invited Muhammad to serve as an arbitrator of their intractable conflicts. The emigration to Yathrib, known in Arabic as the **hijra** (HIJJ-ruh) ("the journey"), was a momentous turning point in the early history of Islam and thereafter marked the beginning of a new Islamic calendar.

The new community, or umma, that took shape in Medina was a kind of "supertribe," but very different from the traditional tribes of Arab society. Membership was a matter of belief rather than birth, allowing the community to expand rapidly. Furthermore, all authority, both political and religious, was concentrated in the hands of Muhammad, who proceeded to introduce radical changes. Charging interest on loans was outlawed as exploitative, tax-free marketplaces were established, and a mandatory payment to support the poor was imposed.

In Medina, Muhammad not only began to create a new society but also declared his movement's independence from its earlier affiliation with Judaism. In the early years, he had anticipated a warm response from Jews and Christians, based on a common monotheism and prophetic tradition, and had directed his followers to pray facing Jerusalem. But when some Jewish groups allied with his enemies, Muhammad acted harshly to suppress them, exiling some and enslaving or killing others. This was not, however, a general suppression of Jews, since others among them remained loyal to Muhammad's new state. But the Prophet now redirected his followers' prayer toward Mecca, essentially declaring Islam an Arab religion, though one with a universal message.

Guided Reading Question

■ **CHANGE**
How was Arabia transformed by the rise of Islam?

Islamic Scholars at Work As the umma—the community of all believers—grew and developed, mosques and their libraries became a focus for the faithful's study of Islam. In this twelfth-century miniature, scholars are listening intently to the figure reading from a book, while numerous texts lie stacked on shelves in the background. With a written text as the core of their religion, Muslims were a "people of the book." (Arabic miniature, 12th Century/De Agostini Picture Library/Bridgeman Images)

From its base in Medina, the Islamic community rapidly extended its reach throughout Arabia. Early military successes against Muhammad's Meccan opponents convinced other Arab tribes that the Muslims and their God were on the rise, and they sought to negotiate alliances with the new power. The religious appeal of the new faith, the end of incessant warfare among feuding tribes, periodic military actions skillfully led by Muhammad, and the Prophet's willingness to enter into marriage alliances with leading tribes—all of this contributed to the consolidation of Islamic control throughout Arabia. In 630, Muhammad triumphantly and peacefully entered Mecca itself, purging the Kaaba of its idols and declaring it a shrine to the one God, Allah. By the time Muhammad died in 632, most of Arabia had come under the control of this new Islamic state, and many had embraced the new faith.

Thus the birth of Islam differed sharply from that of Christianity. Jesus' teaching about "giving to Caesar what is Caesar's and to God what is God's" reflected the minority and subordinate status of the Jews within the Roman Empire. Early Christians found themselves periodically persecuted by Roman authorities for more than three centuries, requiring them to work out some means of dealing with an often-hostile state. The answer lay in the development of a separate church hierarchy and the concept of two coexisting authorities, one religious and one political, an arrangement that persisted even after the state became Christian.

The young Islamic community, by contrast, constituted a state, and soon a huge empire, at the very beginning of its history. Muhammad was not only a religious figure but also, unlike Jesus or the Buddha, a political and military leader able to implement his vision of an ideal Islamic society. Nor did Islam give rise to a separate religious organization. No professional clergy mediating between God and humankind emerged within Islam. Teachers, religious scholars, prayer leaders, and judges within an Islamic legal system did not have the religious role that priests held in the Christian world. No distinction between religious law and civil law, so important within Christendom, existed within the realm of Islam. One law, known as the *sharia* (shah-REE-ah), regulated, at least in theory, political, economic, social, and religious life. The sharia (literally, "a path to water," which is the source of life) evolved over the several centuries following the birth of this new religion and found expression in a number of separate schools of Islamic legal practice.

In little more than twenty years (610–632), a profound transformation had occurred in the Arabian Peninsula. What would subsequently become a new religion had been born, though it was one with roots in earlier Jewish, Christian, and Zoroastrian traditions. A new and vigorous state had emerged, bringing peace to the warring tribes of Arabia. Within that state, a distinctive society had begun to take shape, one that served ever after as a model for Islamic communities everywhere. In his farewell sermon, Muhammad described the outlines of this community:

> All mankind is from Adam and Eve, an Arab has no superiority over a non-Arab nor a non-Arab has any superiority over an Arab; also a white has no superiority over a black nor a black has any superiority over a white—except by piety and good action. Learn that every Muslim is a brother to every Muslim and that the Muslims constitute one brotherhood.[6]

The Making of an Arab Empire

In the centuries that followed the Prophet's death, the energies born of those vast changes in Arabia profoundly transformed much of the Afro-Eurasian world. The new Arab state became a huge empire, encompassing all or part of Egyptian, Roman/Byzantine, Persian, Mesopotamian, and Indian civilizations. The Islamic faith spread widely within and outside that empire. So too did the culture and language of Arabia, as many Arabs migrated far beyond their original homeland and many others found it advantageous to learn Arabic. From the mixing and blending of these many peoples emerged the new and distinctive third-wave civilization of Islam, bound by the ties of a common faith but divided by differences of culture, class, politics, gender, and religious understanding. These enormously consequential processes—the making of a new religion, a new empire, and a new civilization—were central to world history during the third-wave era.

War, Conquest, and Tolerance

Within a few years of Muhammad's death in 632, Arab armies engaged the Byzantine and Persian Sassanid empires, the great powers of the region, and within a century an Arab empire stretched from Spain to India (see Map 9.2). Weakened by periodic bouts of plague and their endemic rivalries, the Persian Sassanid Empire had been defeated by Arab forces by 644, while Byzantium, the remaining eastern regions of the old Roman Empire, soon lost the southern half of its territories. Beyond these victories, Muslim forces, operating on both land and sea, swept westward across North Africa (642–698), conquered Spain in the early 700s, and attacked southern France. To the east, Arab armies reached the Indus River and seized some of the major oasis towns of Central Asia. In 751, they inflicted a crushing defeat on Chinese forces in the Battle of Talas River, which checked the further expansion of China to the west and made possible the conversion to Islam of Central Asia's Turkic-speaking people. Most of the violence of conquest involved imperial armies, though on occasion civilians too were caught up in the fighting

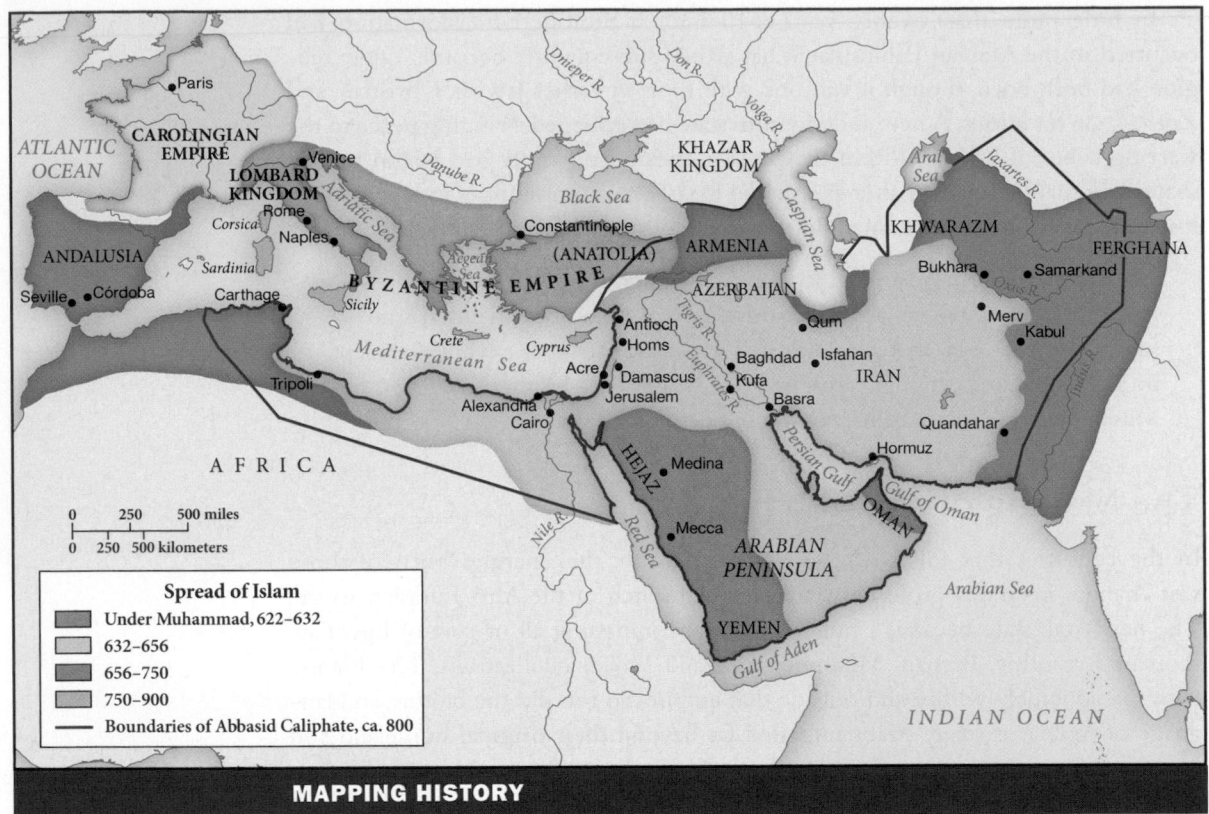

MAPPING HISTORY

Map 9.2 The Arab Empire and the Initial Expansion of Islam, 622–900 C.E.

Far more so than with Buddhism or Christianity, the initial spread of Islam was both rapid and extensive. And unlike the other two world religions, Islam quickly gave rise to a huge empire, ruled by Muslim Arabs, that encompassed many of the older civilizations of the region.

READING THE MAP: During what period of time did the Arab Empire expand most rapidly?

MAKING CONNECTIONS: By comparing Map 9.2 with Maps 7.1 and 7.2, answer the following: At what places might the Abbasid caliphate have been able to control the flow of goods along the Silk and Sea roads between Western Europe and China/India around 800 C.E.?

and suffered terribly. (See Working with Evidence, Source 9.5A, page 398, for an eyewitness account of the conquest in Palestine.)

The motives driving the creation of the Arab Empire were broadly similar to those of other empires. The merchant leaders of the new Islamic community wanted to capture profitable trade routes and wealthy agricultural regions. Individual Arabs found in military expansion a route to wealth and social promotion. The need to harness the immense energies of the Arabian transformation was also important. The fragile unity of the umma threatened to come apart after Muhammad's death, and external expansion provided a common task for the community.

Guided Reading Question

··

■ **CHANGE**

Why were Arabs able to construct such a huge empire so quickly?

While many among the new conquerors viewed the mission of empire in terms of jihad, bringing righteous government to the peoples they conquered, this did not mean imposing a new religion. In fact, for the better part of a century after Muhammad's death, his followers usually referred to themselves as "believers," a term that appears in the Quran far more often than "Muslims" and one that included pious Jews and Christians as well as newly monotheistic Arabs. Such a posture eased the acceptance of the new political order, for many people recently incorporated in the emerging Arab Empire were already monotheists and familiar with the core ideas and practices of the "believers' movement"—prayer, fasting, pilgrimage, revelation, and prophets. Furthermore, the new rulers were remarkably tolerant of established Jewish and Christian faiths. The first governor of Arab-ruled Jerusalem was a Jew. Many old Christian churches continued to operate and new ones were constructed. A Christian patriarch in Iraq wrote to one of his bishops around 647 C.E., observing that the new rulers "not only do not fight Christianity, they even commend our religion, show honor to the priests and monasteries and saints of the Lord, and make gifts to the monasteries and churches."[7] Formal agreements or treaties recognized Jews, Christians, and Zoroastrians as "people of the book," giving them the status of *dhimmis* (dihm-mees), protected but second-class subjects. Such people were permitted to freely practice their own religion, so long as they paid a special tax known as the *jizya*. (See Working with Evidence, Source 9.5B, page 398, for an agreement between invading Arab forces and the Christian people of Tiflis in the Caucasus region.) Theoretically the tax was a substitute for military service, supposedly forbidden to non-Muslims. In practice, many dhimmis served in the highest offices within Muslim kingdoms and in their armies as well.

In other ways too, the Arab rulers of an expanding empire sought to limit the disruptive impact of conquest. To prevent indiscriminate destruction and exploitation of conquered peoples, occupying Arab armies were restricted to garrison towns, segregated from the native population. Local elites and bureaucratic structures were incorporated into the new Arab Empire. Nonetheless, the empire worked many changes on its subjects, the most enduring of which was the mass conversion of Middle Eastern peoples to what became by the eighth century the new and separate religion of Islam.

Conversion

For some people, no doubt, converting to Islam was or subsequently became a matter of profound spiritual or psychological transformation, but far more often, at least initially, it was "social conversion," motivated more by convenience than conviction.[8] It happened at various rates and in different ways, but in the four centuries or so after the death of Muhammad, millions of individuals and many whole societies within the Arab Empire found their cultural identity bound up with a belief in Allah and the message of his prophet. They had become Muslims.

In some ways, perhaps, the change was not so dramatic, as major elements of Islam—monotheism; ritual prayer and cleansing ceremonies; fasting; divine revelation;

Guided Reading Question

■ **EXPLANATION**

What accounts for the widespread conversion to Islam?

the ideas of Heaven, Hell, and final judgment—were quite familiar to Jews, Christians, and Zoroastrians. Furthermore, Islam was from the beginning associated with the sponsorship of a powerful state, quite unlike the experience of early Buddhism or Christianity. Conquest called into question the power of old gods, while the growing prestige of the Arab Empire attracted many to Islam. Although deliberately forced conversion was rare and explicitly forbidden in the Quran, living in an Islamic-governed state provided a variety of incentives for claiming Muslim identity. Slaves and prisoners of war were among the early converts, particularly in Persia. Converts could also avoid the jizya, the tax imposed on non-Muslims. People aspiring to official positions found conversion to Islam an aid to social mobility. In Islam, merchants found a religion friendly to commerce. The Prophet himself had been a trader, acting as a commercial agent for his wife Khadija. As Islamic law developed over several centuries, it defined what merchants might expect from one another and so reduced the uncertainty of long-distance commerce. And in the expansive Arab Empire, merchants enjoyed a huge and secure arena for trade.

Conversion was not an automatic or easy process. Vigorous resistance delayed conversion for centuries among the Berbers of North Africa; a small group of zealous Spanish Christians in the ninth century provoked their own martyrdom by publicly insulting the Prophet; and some Persian Zoroastrians fled to avoid Muslim rule. More generally, though, a remarkable and lasting religious transformation occurred throughout the Arab Empire.

In Persia, for example, between 750 and 900, about 80 percent of the population made the transition to a Muslim religious identity. But they did so in a manner quite distinct from the people of Iraq, Syria, Egypt, and North Africa. In these regions, converts to Islam gradually abandoned their native languages, adopted Arabic, and came to see themselves as Arabs. In Iran or Persia, by contrast, Arab conquest did not involve cultural Arabization, despite some initial efforts to impose the Arabic language. By the tenth century, the vast majority of Persians had become Muslims, but the Persian language (called Farsi in Iran) flourished, enriched now by a number of Arabic loan words and written in an Arabic script. In 1010, that language received its classic literary expression when the Persian poet Ferdowsi completed his epic work, the *Shahnama* (*The Book of Kings*). A huge text of some 60,000 rhyming couplets, it recorded the mythical and pre-Islamic history of Iran and gave an enduring expression to a distinctly Persian cultural identity. Thus, in places where large-scale Arab migration had occurred, such as Egypt, North Africa, and Iraq, Arabic culture and language, as well as the religion of Islam, took hold. Such areas are today both Muslim and Arab, while the peoples of Iran, Turkey, Pakistan, Indonesia, and West Africa, for example, have "Islamized" without "Arabizing."

The preservation of Persian language and culture had enormous implications for the world of Islam. In Iran, Central Asia, India, and later in the Ottoman Empire, Islam was accompanied by pervasive Persian influences. Persian administrative and bureaucratic techniques; Persian court practices with their palaces, gardens, and splendid garments; Persian architecture, poetry, music, and painting—all of this decisively shaped the high culture of these eastern Islamic lands. One of the Abbasid caliphs, himself an Arab, observed: "The Persians ruled for a thousand years and did not need us Arabs even for a day. We have been ruling them for one or two centuries and cannot do without them for an hour."[9]

Divisions and Controversies

The ideal of a unified believer's community, so important to Muhammad, proved difficult to realize as conquest and conversion vastly enlarged the Islamic umma. A central problem involved leadership and authority in the absence of Muhammad's towering presence. Who should hold the role of caliph (KAY-lihf), the successor to Muhammad as the political leader of the umma, the protector and defender of the faith? That issue crystallized a variety of emerging conflicts within the Islamic world—between early and later converts, among various Arab tribes and factions, between Arabs and non-Arabs, and between privileged and wealthy rulers and their far less fortunate subjects. Many of these political and social conflicts found expression in religious terms as various understandings of the Quran and of Muhammad's life and teachings took shape within the growing Islamic community.

The first four caliphs, known among most Muslims as the Rightly Guided Caliphs (632–661), were close "companions of the Prophet," selected by the Muslim elders of Medina. Division surfaced almost immediately as a series of Arab tribal rebellions and new "prophets" persuaded the first caliph, Abu Bakr, to suppress them forcibly. The third and fourth caliphs, Uthman and Ali, were both assassinated, and from 656 to 661, less than twenty-five years after Muhammad's death, civil war pitted Muslim against Muslim. A second civil war (680–692) continued that bitter and often savage family feud among the leaders of the "believers movement."

Out of that conflict emerged one of the deepest and most enduring rifts within the Islamic world. On one side were the Sunni (SOON-nee) Muslims, who held that the caliphs were rightful political and military leaders, selected by the Islamic community. On the other side of this sharp divide was the Shia (SHEE-ah) (an Arabic word meaning "party" or "faction") branch of Islam. Its adherents felt strongly that leadership in the Islamic world should derive from the line of Ali and his son Husayn, blood relatives of Muhammad, both of whom died at the hands of their political or religious enemies. If the caliph was the idealized communal leader for Sunnis, *imams* (leaders) served this purpose for most of the Shia Muslims. They were widely thought to have some special charisma based on descent from the Prophet, giving them a religious authority that the caliphs lacked and allowing them to infallibly interpret divine revelation and law.

Thus what began as a purely political conflict acquired over time a deeper significance. For much of early Islamic history, Shia Muslims saw themselves as the minority opposition within Islam. They felt that history had taken a wrong turn and that they were "the defenders of the oppressed, the critics and opponents of privilege and power," while the Sunnis were the advocates of the established

Guided Reading Question

■ **COMPARISON**

What is the difference between Sunni and Shia Islam?

The Kaaba Located in Mecca, this stone structure, covered with a black cloth and known as the Kaaba, was originally home to the numerous deities of pre-Islamic Arabia. Cleansed by Muhammad, it became the sacred shrine of Islam and the destination of countless pilgrims undertaking the hajj. This photograph from 2015 shows worshippers praying around the Kaaba at the end of Ramadan, the holy month devoted to fasting. (AFP/Getty Images)

order.[10] Various armed revolts by Shias over the centuries, most of which failed, led to a distinctive conception of martyrdom and to the expectation that their defeated leaders were merely in hiding and not really dead and that they would return in the fullness of time. Thus a messianic element entered Shia Islam. The Sunni/Shia schism became a lasting division in the Islamic world, reflected in conflicts among various Islamic states, and was exacerbated by further splits among the Shia. Those divisions echo still in the twenty-first century.

As the Arab Empire grew, its caliphs were transformed from modest Arab chiefs into absolute monarchs, "the shadow of God on earth," of the Byzantine or Persian variety, complete with elaborate court rituals, a complex bureaucracy, a standing army, and centralized systems of taxation and coinage. They were also subject to the dynastic rivalries and succession disputes common to other empires. The first dynasty, following the era of the Rightly Guided Caliphs, came from the Umayyad (oo-MEYE-ahd) family (r. 661–750). Under the leadership of the **Umayyad caliphate**, the Arab Empire expanded greatly, caliphs became hereditary rulers, and the capital moved from Medina to the cosmopolitan Roman/Byzantine city of Damascus in Syria. Its ruling class was an Arab military aristocracy, drawn from various tribes. But Umayyad rule provoked growing criticism and unrest. The emerging Shia faction viewed the Umayyad caliphs as illegitimate usurpers, and non-Arab

Muslims resented their second-class citizenship in the empire. Many Arabs protested the luxurious living and impiety of their rulers. The Umayyads, they charged, "made God's servants slaves, God's property something to be taken by turns among the rich, and God's religion a cause of corruption."[11]

Such grievances lay behind the overthrow of the Umayyads in 750 and their replacement by a new Arab dynasty, the Abbasids. With a splendid new capital in Baghdad, the **Abbasid caliphate** presided over a flourishing and prosperous Islamic civilization in which non-Arabs, especially Persians, now played a prominent role. But the political unity of the Abbasid Empire did not last long. Beginning in the mid-ninth century, many local governors or military commanders effectively asserted the autonomy of their regions, while still giving formal allegiance to the caliph in Baghdad. Long before Mongol conquest put an official end to the Abbasid Empire in 1258, the Islamic world had fractured politically into a series of "sultanates," many ruled by Persian or Turkish military dynasties.

A further tension within the world of Islam, though one that seldom produced violent conflict, lay in different answers to one central question: what does it mean to be a Muslim, to submit wholly to Allah? One answer lay in the development of the sharia, the body of Islamic law developed primarily in the eighth and ninth centuries by religious scholars, Sunni and Shia alike, who were known as the *ulama*. Based on the Quran, the life and teachings of Muhammad, deductive reasoning, and the consensus of scholars, the emerging sharia addressed in great detail practically every aspect of life. It was a blueprint for an authentic Islamic society, providing meticulous guidance for prayer and ritual cleansing; marriage, divorce, and inheritance; business and commercial relationships; the treatment of slaves; political life; personal hygiene; dietary requirements; and much more. Debates among the ulama led to the creation of four schools of law among Sunni Muslims and still others in the lands of Shia Islam. To the ulama and their followers, living as a Muslim meant following the sharia and thus participating in the creation of an Islamic society.

A second and quite different understanding of the faith emerged between 800 and 1000 C.E. among those who saw the worldly success of Islamic civilization as a distraction and deviation from the purer spirituality of Muhammad's time. Known as Sufis (SOO-fees), they represented Islam's mystical dimension, in that they sought a direct and personal experience of the Divine. Through renunciation of the material world, meditation on the words of the Quran, the chanting of the names of God, the use of music and dance, and the veneration of

Guided Reading Question

■ COMPARISON
In what ways were Sufi Muslims critical of mainstream Islam?

Sufis and Worldly Power This early seventeenth-century painting from India illustrates the tension between Sufis and worldly authorities. Here the Muslim Mughal emperor Jahangir, seated on an hourglass throne, gives his attention to the white-bearded Sufi holy man rather than to the prominent men, including a European figure, shown in the bottom left. (bpk Bildagentur/Museum für Islamische Kunst, Staatliche Museen, Berlin, Germany/Photo: Georg Niedermeiser/Art Resource, NY)

Mullah Nasruddin, the Wise Fool of Islam

In the Islamic world, a mullah was a man of some learning, often a local cleric or leader of a village mosque. Far and away the most famous and beloved of mullahs is Nasruddin, considered both a wise man and a fool, both a sage and a simpleton. Stories about him have circulated for centuries and were well known long before the earliest written references to him appeared in the thirteenth century. Many peoples have claimed him, some have sought to find a historical figure on which he is based, and in the Turkish city of Akšehir there is even a tomb and an annual Nasruddin festival, where people dress in costumes to reenact his jokes and stories.

In fact, Mullah Nasruddin has long been an imaginary folk character within the world of Islam and especially among Sufis, gently expressing a skeptical attitude toward the rational mind, sanctimonious posturing, human vanity, and the many faces of the ego. His tales usually take place in a village setting and highlight the limitations of the intellect; the role of humor and intuition in spiritual life; the importance of generosity,

Mullah Nasruddin.

tolerance, and humility; and the many mysteries of existence. The only way to get acquainted with Mullah Nasruddin is to reflect on some of his tales. Here are just a few of the thousands:[12]

- The Mullah was in Mecca for the pilgrimage and had fallen asleep with his feet pointing toward the Kaaba, the large black cube that is the central shrine of Islam. He was awakened and rebuked by some pious Muslims, who told him it was offensive to have his dirty feet pointing at the Kaaba, where God himself resided. The Mullah apologized profusely and then added, "Perhaps you could move my feet to some place where God is *not* present."

- Mullah Nasruddin was invited to a formal reception and upon entering took the seat of greatest honor. Approached by the chief of the guard, he was asked if he was a diplomat, a minister of the king, or perhaps

photo: akg-images/The Image Works

Muhammad and various "saints," adherents of **Sufism** pursued an interior life, seeking to tame the ego and achieve spiritual union with Allah. To describe that inexpressible experience, they often resorted to metaphors of drunkenness or the embrace of lovers. "Stain your prayer rug with wine," urged the famous Sufi poet Hafiz, referring to the intoxication of the believer with the Divine Presence. (See the Zooming In feature on Mullah Nasruddin, above, for an expression of popular or folk Sufism.)

This mystical tendency in Islamic practice, which became widely popular by the ninth and tenth centuries, was at times sharply critical of the more scholarly and legalistic practitioners of the sharia. To Sufis, establishment teachings about the law and correct behavior, while useful for daily living, did little to bring the believer into the presence of God. Furthermore, Sufis felt that many of the ulama had been compromised by their association with worldly and corrupt governments. Sufis therefore the king himself in disguise. To each of these queries, he replied, "No, I am more than that." "Then who are you?" demanded the guard. His answer: "I am nobody."

- A villager rushed to tell the Mullah about visions of God he had been having. He asked if this meant he had become enlightened. The Mullah replied by asking him about his goats and servants. The man was enraged at this apparent dismissal of his visions. Then the Mullah explained, "If you are becoming more tender and kind toward your goats and servants, then you are on the way to enlightenment. If not, your visions are an illusion of your ego."

- Mullah Nasruddin was asked to present a lecture on "the nature of Allah" in the local mosque together with many highly learned scholars. When the scholars had finished their eloquent and wise expositions, the humble Mullah arose and hesitantly began his talk by declaring "Allah is an eggplant," while holding one of the vegetables aloft. An uproar followed at this blasphemy. When he was finally given a chance to explain himself, the Mullah declared, "Everyone before me has spoken of what they do not know or have never seen. But we can all see this eggplant. Can anyone deny that Allah is manifest in all things?" When no one was willing to dispute the point, the Mullah concluded, "Well, then Allah is an eggplant."

- One evening, after spending many hours in the local tavern, a thoroughly intoxicated Mullah was stumbling along the streets. A local police official approached him and asked, "Who are you? Where did you come from? Where are you going? Why are you out so late?" The Mullah replied, "If I had answers to all those questions, I'd be home already." [Note: To Sufis, taverns and drunkenness often symbolized spiritual insight or mystical "intoxication" with the Divine.]

- When some neighbors told Nasruddin that his donkey was lost, the Mullah exclaimed, "Thank goodness I was not on the donkey or I'd be lost as well." [Note: In Sufi circles, the donkey has long symbolized the unruly human ego.]

The Mullah's tales have been understood on several levels. Most obviously, they are jokes. But they also convey moral teachings about individual behavior as well as social commentary. And especially for Sufis, they have become a spiritual resource, gradually dissolving limited and culturally conditioned thinking, while opening the way to more fully realizing humanity's divine potential.

QUESTIONS

Pick several of these tales and explain in your own words the lessons they might convey for Muslims. In what ways might these tales be considered subversive of established authorities? Might they strike a chord with contemporary sensibilities of our own time?

often charted their own course to God, implicitly challenging the religious authority of the ulama. For these orthodox religious scholars, Sufi ideas and practice sometimes verged on heresy, as Sufis on occasion claimed unity with God, received new revelations, or incorporated novel religious practices from outside the Islamic world.

Despite their differences, adherents of the legalistic emphasis of the sharia and practitioners of Sufi spirituality coexisted, mostly peacefully, mixing and mingling, collaborating and disagreeing, in various combinations. For many centuries, roughly 1100 to 1800, Sufism was central to mainstream Islam, and many, perhaps most, Muslims affiliated with one or another Sufi organization, making use of its spiritual practices. Nonetheless, differences in emphasis about the essential meaning of Islam remained an element of tension and sometimes discord within the Muslim world.

Women and Men in Early Islam

What did the rise of Islam and the making of the Arab Empire mean for the daily lives of women and their relationship with men? Virtually every aspect of this question has been and remains highly controversial. The debates begin with the Quran itself. Did its teachings release women from earlier restrictions, or did they impose new limitations? At the level of spiritual life, the Quran was quite clear and explicit: men and women were equal. Numerous passages in the Quran use gender-inclusive language, referring to "believers, both men and women."

Guided Reading
Question
• • • • • • • • • • • • • • • • • • • •
■ CHANGE
How did the rise of Islam
change the lives of
women?

But in social terms, and especially within marriage, the Quran, like the written texts of almost all civilizations, viewed women as inferior and subordinate: "Men have authority over women because Allah has made the one superior to the other, and because they spend their wealth to maintain them. Good women are obedient."[13] More specifically, the Quran provided a mix of rights, restrictions, and protections for women. Female infanticide, for example, widely practiced in many cultures as a means of gender selection, was now forbidden for Muslims. Women were given control over their own property, particularly their dowries, and were granted rights of inheritance, but at half the rate of their male counterparts. Marriage was considered a contract between consenting parties, thus making marriage by capture illegitimate. Divorce was possible for both parties, although it was far more readily available for men. The practice of taking multiple husbands, which operated in some pre-Islamic Arab tribes, was prohibited, while polygyny (the practice of having multiple wives) was permitted, though more clearly regulated than before. Men were limited to four wives and required to treat each of them equally. (The difficulty of doing so has been interpreted by some as virtually requiring monogamy.) Men were, however, permitted to have sexual relations with female slaves, but any children born of those unions were free, as was the mother once her owner died. Furthermore, men were strongly encouraged to marry orphans, widows, and slaves.

Such Quranic prescriptions were but one factor shaping the lives of women and men. At least as important were the long-established practices of the societies into which Islam spread and the growing sophistication, prosperity, and urbanization of Islamic civilization. As had been the case in Athens and China during their "golden ages," Muslim women, particularly in the upper classes, experienced growing restrictions as Islamic civilization flourished culturally and economically in the Abbasid era. In early Islamic times, a number of women played visible public roles, particularly Muhammad's youngest wife, Aisha. Women prayed in the mosques, although separately, standing beside the men. Nor were women generally veiled or secluded. As the Arab Empire grew in size and splendor, however, the position of women became more restricted. The second caliph, Umar, asked women to offer prayers at home. Now veiling and the seclusion of women became standard practice among the upper and ruling classes, removing them from public life. Separate quarters within the homes of the wealthy were the domain of women, from which they could emerge only completely veiled. The caliph Mansur (r. 754–775) carried this separation of the sexes even further when he ordered a separate bridge for women to be built over the

Euphrates River in the new capital of Baghdad. Such seclusion was less possible for lower-class women, who lacked the servants of the rich and had to leave the home for shopping or work.

Such practices derived far more from established traditions of Middle Eastern cultures than from the Quran itself, but they soon gained an Islamic rationale in the writings of Muslim thinkers. The famous philosopher and religious scholar al-Ghazali clearly saw a relationship between Muslim piety and the separation of the sexes:

> It is not permissible for a stranger to hear the sound of a pestle being pounded by a woman he does not know. If he knocks at the door, it is not proper for the woman to answer him softly and easily because men's hearts can be drawn to [women] for the most trifling [reason]. . . . However, if the woman has to answer the knock, she should stick her finger in her mouth so that her voice sounds like that of an old woman.[14]

Other signs of a tightening patriarchy—such as "honor killing" of women by their male relatives for violating sexual taboos and, in some places, clitoridectomy (female genital cutting)—likewise derived from local cultures, with no sanction in the Quran or Islamic law. Where they were practiced, such customs often

Women and Worship This thirteenth-century painting by the well-known Arab artist/illustrator al-Wasiti, born in southern Iraq, depicts women sitting separately on an upstairs balcony of a mosque while listening to a sermon. The Quran defined both male and female believers as equal before God, but long-established social customs in many Muslim societies prescribed the separation of men and women in public and especially during times of worship. (Miniature from the "Maqam" or "Assembly" of Yahya ibn Mahmud al-Wasiti, 1237/Pictures from History/Bridgeman Images)

came to be seen as Islamic, but they were certainly not limited to the Islamic world. In many cultures, concern with family honor linked to women's sexuality dictated harsh punishments for women who violated sexual taboos. Negative views of women, presenting them variously as weak, deficient, and a sexually charged threat to men and social stability, emerged in the *hadiths* (hah-DEETHS), traditions about the sayings or actions of Muhammad that became an important source of Islamic law.

Even as women faced growing restrictions in society generally, Islam, like Buddhism and Christianity, also offered new outlets for them in religious life. While Sunni Islam prohibited women from studying in madrassas (religious schools or colleges), it did allow them to become transmitters of the hadiths by studying with prominent scholars. Aisha, a fourteenth-century woman from Damascus, attracted students of her own after studying under some of the most renowned teachers of her generation and gained such a reputation for her learning that a seventeenth-century historian described her as her generation's most reliable transmitter of the hadith. Within the world of Shia Islam, women teachers of the faith were called mullahs, the same as their male counterparts. Islamic education, either in the home or in Quranic schools, allowed some to become literate and a few to achieve higher levels of learning. Visits to the tombs of major Islamic figures, as well as the ritual of the public bath, likewise provided some opportunity for women to interact with other women beyond their own family circle.

Sufi mystical practice allowed a greater role for women than did mainstream Islam, for the spiritual equality that the Quran accorded to male and female alike allowed women also to aspire to union with God. Among the earliest of well-known Sufi practitioners was Rabia, an eighth-century woman from Basra in southern Iraq who renounced numerous proposals of marriage and engaged, apparently successfully, in repeated religious debates with men. But for some male Sufi scholars, such as the twelfth-century mystical poet Attar, Rabia's spiritual attainments meant that "she is a man and one cannot any more call her a woman."[15]

Islam and Cultural Encounter: A Four-Way Comparison

In its earliest centuries, the rapid spread of Islam had been accompanied by the creation of an immense Arab Empire, very much in the tradition of earlier Mediterranean and Middle Eastern empires. By the tenth century, however, little political unity remained, and in 1258 even the powerless symbol of that earlier unity vanished as Mongol forces sacked Baghdad and killed the last Abbasid caliph. But even as the empire disintegrated, the civilization that was born within it grew and flourished. Perhaps the most significant sign of a flourishing Islamic civilization was the continued spread of the religion both within and beyond the boundaries of a vanishing Arab Empire (see Map 9.3), although that process differed considerably from place to place. The examples of India, Anatolia, West Africa, and Spain illustrate the various ways that Islam penetrated these societies as well as the rather different outcomes of these epic cultural encounters.

The Case of India

In South Asia, Islam found a permanent place in a long-established civilization when invasions by Turkic-speaking warrior groups from Central Asia, recently converted to Islam, brought the faith to northern India. Thus Turkic peoples became the third major carrier of Islam, after the Arabs and Persians, as their conquests initiated an enduring encounter between Islam and a Hindu-based Indian civilization. Beginning around 1000, those conquests gave rise to a series of Turkic and Muslim regimes that governed much of India until the British takeover in the eighteenth and nineteenth centuries. The early centuries of this encounter were violent indeed, as the invaders smashed Hindu and Buddhist temples and carried off vast quantities

MAPPING HISTORY

Map 9.3 The Growing World of Islam, 900–1500

Islam as a religion, a civilization, and an arena of commerce continued to grow even as the Arab Empire fragmented.

READING THE MAP: Where did Ibn Battuta's travels take him outside the worlds of Islam?

INTERPRETING THE MAP: Between 900 and 1500 Islam primarily spread along the Silk, Sea, and Sand Roads. To what extent does the map support this statement?

of Indian treasure. With the establishment of the Sultanate of Delhi in 1206 (see Map 9.4), Turkic rule became more systematic, although the Turks' small numbers and internal conflicts allowed only a very modest penetration of Indian society.

In the centuries that followed, substantial Muslim communities emerged in India, particularly in regions less tightly integrated into the dominant Hindu culture. Disillusioned Buddhists as well as low-caste Hindus and untouchables found the more egalitarian Islam attractive. So did peoples just beginning to make the transition to settled agriculture. Others benefited from converting to Islam by avoiding

Guided Reading Question

....

■ **COMPARISON**

What similarities and differences can you identify in the spread of Islam to India, Anatolia, West Africa, and Spain?

Map 9.4 The Sultanate of Delhi

Between 1206 and 1526 a number of Muslim dynasties ruled northern India as the Delhi sultanate, while an explicitly Hindu kingdom of Vijayanagar arose in the south after 1340. It drew on north Indian Muslim architectural features and made use of Muslim mercenaries for its military forces.

the tax imposed on non-Muslims. Sufis were particularly important in facilitating conversion, for India had always valued "god-filled men" who were detached from worldly affairs. Sufi holy men, willing to accommodate local gods and religious festivals, helped to develop a "popular Islam" that was not always so sharply distinguished from the more devotional (*bhakti*) forms of Hinduism.

Unlike the earlier experience of Islam in the Middle East, North Africa, and Persia, where Islam rapidly became the dominant faith, in India it was never able to claim more than 20 to 25 percent of the total population. Furthermore, Muslim communities were especially concentrated in the Punjab and Sind regions of northwestern India and in Bengal to the east. The core regions of Hindu culture in the northern Indian plain were not seriously challenged by the new faith, despite centuries of Muslim rule. One reason perhaps lay in the sharpness of the cultural divide between Islam and Hinduism. Islam was the most radically monotheistic of the world's religions, largely forbidding any representation of Allah, while Hinduism was surely among the most prolifically polytheistic, generating endless statues and images of the Divine in many forms. The Muslim notion of the equality of all believers contrasted sharply with the hierarchical assumptions of the caste system. Believing in sexual modesty, Muslims were deeply offended by the open eroticism of some Hindu religious art.

Although such differences may have limited the appeal of Islam in India, they also may have prevented it from being absorbed into the tolerant and inclusive embrace of Hinduism, as so many other religious ideas, practices, and communities had been. The religious exclusivity of Islam, born of its firm monotheistic belief and the idea of a unique revelation, set a boundary that the great sponge of Hinduism could not completely absorb.

Certainly, not all was conflict across that boundary. Many prominent Hindus willingly served in the political and military structures of a Muslim-ruled India. Mystical seekers after the Divine blurred the distinction between Hindu and Muslim, suggesting that God was to be found "neither in temple nor in mosque." "Look within your heart," wrote the great fifteenth-century mystic poet Kabir, "for there you will find both [Allah] and Ram [a famous Hindu deity]."[16] During the early sixteenth century, a new and distinct religious tradition emerged in India known as **Sikhism** (SIHK-iz'm), which blended elements of Islam, such as devotion to one universal

God, with Hindu concepts, such as karma and rebirth. "There is no Hindu and no Muslim. All are children of God," declared Guru Nanak (1469–1539), the founder of Sikhism.

Nonetheless, Muslims usually lived quite separately, remaining a distinctive minority within an ancient Indian civilization, which they now largely governed but which they proved unable to completely transform.

The Case of Anatolia

At the same time as India was being subjected to Turkic invasion, so too was Anatolia (now modern Turkey), where the largely Christian and Greek-speaking population was then governed by the Byzantine Empire (see Map 9.2 and Map 9.5). Here, as in India, the invaders initially wreaked havoc as Byzantine authority melted away beginning in the eleventh century. Sufi practitioners likewise played a major role in the process of conversion. The outcome, however, was a far more profound cultural transformation than in India. By 1500, the population was 90 percent Muslim and largely Turkic-speaking, and Anatolia was the heartland of the powerful Turkic Ottoman Empire that had overrun Christian Byzantium and captured Constantinople in 1453. Why did the Turkic intrusion into Anatolia generate a much more thorough Islamization than in India?

One factor clearly lies in a very different demographic balance. The population of Anatolia—perhaps 8 million—was far smaller than India's roughly 48 million people, but far more Turkic-speaking peoples settled in Anatolia, giving them a much greater cultural weight than the smaller colonizing force in India. Furthermore, the disruption of Anatolian society was much more extensive. Massacres, enslavement, famine, and flight led to a sharp drop in the native population. The Byzantine state had been fatally weakened. Church properties were confiscated, and monasteries were destroyed or deserted. Priests and bishops were sometimes unable to serve their congregations. Christians, though seldom forced to convert, suffered many discriminations. They had to wear special clothing and pay special taxes, and they were forbidden to ride saddled horses or carry swords. Not a few Christians came to believe that these disasters represented proof that Islam was the true religion. Thus Byzantine civilization in Anatolia, previously focused on the

Map 9.5 The Ottoman Empire by the Mid-Fifteenth Century
As Turkic-speaking migrants bearing the religion of Islam penetrated Anatolia, the Ottoman Empire took shape, reaching into southeastern Europe and finally displacing the Christian Byzantine Empire. Subsequently, it came to control much of the Middle East and North Africa as well.

Guided Reading Question

■ CHANGE
In what ways was Anatolia changed by its incorporation into the Islamic world?

centralized institutions of church and state, was rendered leaderless and dispirited, whereas India's decentralized civilization, lacking a unified political or religious establishment, was better able to absorb the shock of external invasion while retaining its core values and identity.

The Turkic rulers of Anatolia built a new society that welcomed converts and granted them material rewards and opportunity for high office. Moreover, the cultural barriers to conversion were arguably less severe than in India. The common monotheism of Islam and Christianity, and Muslim respect for Jesus and the Christian scriptures, made conversion easier than crossing the great gulf between Islam and Hinduism. Such similarities lent support to the suggestion of some Sufi teachers that the two religions were but different versions of the same faith. Sufis also established schools, mills, orchards, hospices, and rest places for travelers and thus replaced the destroyed or decaying institutions of Christian Anatolia. All of this contributed to the thorough religious transformation of Anatolia and laid a foundation for the Ottoman Empire, which by 1500 had become the most impressive and powerful state within the Islamic world. It reached across Anatolia and the Black Sea, encompassed parts of Greece and southeastern Europe, and in the sixteenth century extended into the Arab lands of the Middle East and North Africa.

But the Islamization of Anatolia occurred within a distinctly Turkic context. A Turkic language, not Arabic, predominated. Some Sufi religious practices, such as ecstatic turning dances, actually derived from Central Asian Turkic shamanism. And Turkic tradition, common among pastoral peoples, offered a freer, more gender-equal life for women. This practice caught the attention of the Arab Moroccan visitor Ibn Battuta (1304–1368) during his travels among the Turks. He commented, "A remarkable thing that I saw . . . was the respect shown to women by the Turks, for they hold a more dignified position than the men. . . . The windows of the tent are open and her face is visible, for the Turkish women do not veil themselves."[17] He was not pleased.

The Case of West Africa

Still another pattern of Islamic expansion prevailed in West Africa. Here Islam accompanied Muslim traders across the Sahara rather than being brought by invading Arab or Turkic armies. Its gradual acceptance in the emerging civilization of West African states in the centuries after 1000 was largely peaceful and voluntary, lacking the incentives associated elsewhere with foreign conquest. Introduced by Muslim merchants from an already Islamized North Africa, the new faith was accepted primarily in the urban centers of the West African empires—Ghana, Mali, Songhay, Kanem-Bornu, and others (see Map 9.6). For African merchant communities, Islam provided an important link to Muslim trading partners, much as Buddhism had done in Southeast Asia. For the monarchs and their courts, it offered a source of literate officials to assist in state administration as well as religious legitimacy, particularly for those who gained the prestige conferred by a pilgrimage to Mecca. The most prominent such pilgrim was Mansa Musa, the ruler of Mali, who

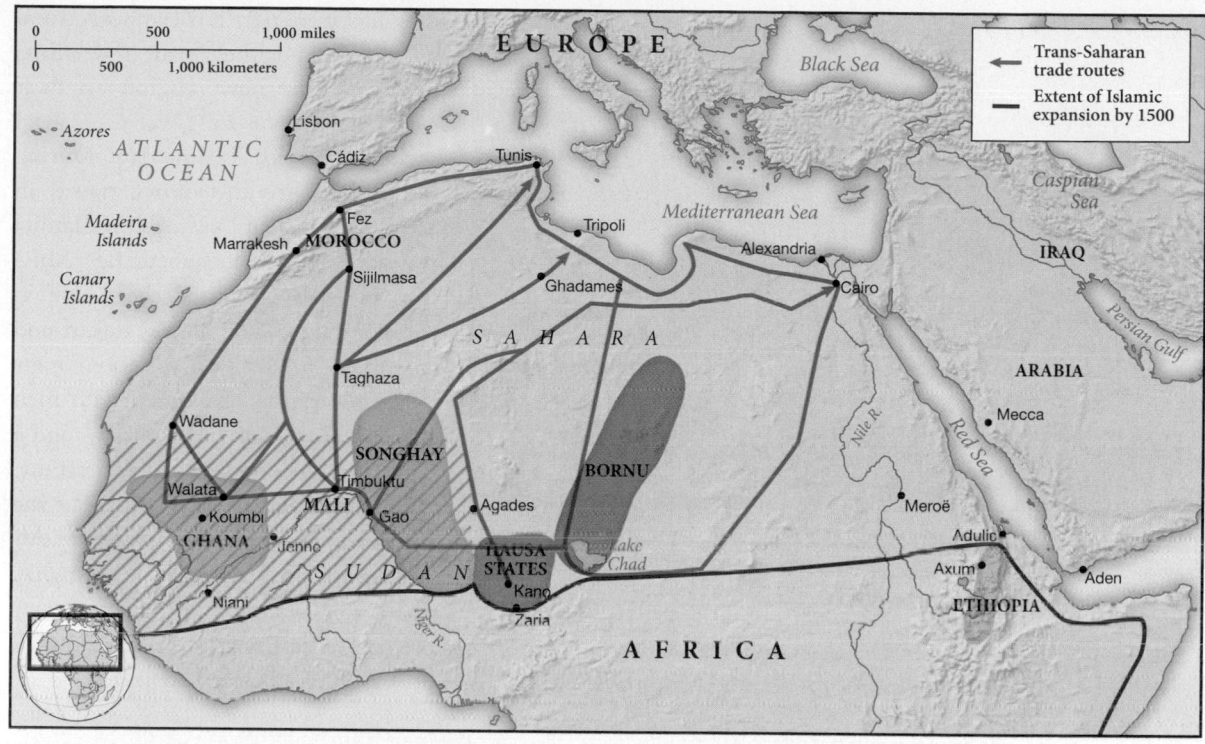

Map 9.6 West Africa and the World of Islam
Both trans-Saharan commerce and Islam linked the civilization of West Africa to the larger Muslim world.

in 1324 undertook the hajj accompanied by a huge entourage and enormous quantities of gold. As a world religion with a single universal Creator-God, Islam had a religious appeal for societies that were now participating in a wider world.

By the sixteenth century, a number of West African cities had become major centers of Islamic religious and intellectual life, attracting scholars from throughout the Muslim world. **Timbuktu** boasted more than 150 lower-level Quranic schools and several major centers of higher education, with thousands of students from all over West Africa and beyond. Libraries held tens of thousands of books and scholarly manuscripts (see the "Manuscripts of Timbuktu" photo on page 299). Monarchs subsidized the construction of mosques as West Africa became an integral part of a larger Islamic world. Arabic became an important language of religion, education, administration, and trade, but it did not become the dominant language of daily life. Nor did West Africa experience the massive migration of Arab peoples that had promoted the Arabization of North Africa and the Middle East.

Islam remained the culture of urban elites and spread little into the rural areas of West Africa until the nineteenth century. No thorough religious transformation occurred in West Africa as it had in Anatolia. Although many rulers adopted Islam, they governed people who steadfastly practiced African religions and whose sensibilities

The Great Mosque at Jenne This mosque in the city of Jenne, initially constructed in the thirteenth century, illustrates the assimilation of Islam into West African civilization. (Antonello Lanzellotto/age-fotostock)

they had to respect if social peace were to prevail. Thus they made few efforts to impose the new religion on their rural subjects or to govern in strict accordance with Islamic law. During his mid-fourteenth-century travels in West Africa, Arab visitor Ibn Battuta was appalled that practicing Muslims in Mali permitted their women to appear in public almost naked and to mingle freely with unrelated men. "The association of women with men is agreeable to us," he was told, "and a part of good conduct to which no suspicion attaches. They are not like the women of your country."[18] Sonni Ali, a fifteenth-century ruler of Songhay, observed Ramadan and built mosques, but he also consulted traditional diviners and performed customary sacrifices. In such ways, Islam became Africanized even as parts of West Africa became Islamized.

The Case of Spain

The chief site of Islamic encounter with Christian Europe occurred in Spain, called **al-Andalus** by Muslims, which was conquered by Arab and Berber forces in the early eighth century during the first wave of Islamic expansion. By the tenth century, Muslim Spain was a vibrant civilization, often portrayed as a place of harmony and tolerance between its Muslim rulers and its Christian and Jewish subjects.

Certainly, Spain's agricultural economy was the most prosperous in Europe during this time, and its capital of Córdoba was among the largest and most splendid cities in the world. Muslims, Christians, and Jews alike contributed to a brilliant high culture in which astronomy, medicine, the arts, architecture, and literature flourished. Furthermore, social relationships among upper-class members of different faiths were easy and frequent. By 1000, perhaps 75 percent of the population had converted to Islam. Many of the remaining Christians learned Arabic, veiled their women, stopped eating pork, appreciated Arabic music and poetry, and sometimes married Muslims. One Christian bishop complained that Spanish Christians knew the rules of Arabic grammar better than those of Latin. During the reign of Abd al-Rahman III (r. 912–961), freedom of worship was declared as well as the opportunity for all to rise in the bureaucracy of the state.

But this so-called golden age of Muslim Spain was both limited and brief. Even assimilated or Arabized Christians remained religious infidels and second-class citizens in the eyes of their Muslim counterparts, and by the late tenth century toleration began to erode. The Córdoba-based regime fragmented into numerous rival states. Warfare with the remaining Christian kingdoms in northern Spain picked up in the tenth and eleventh centuries, and more puritanical and rigid forms of Islam entered Spain from North Africa. Under the rule of al-Mansur (r. 981–1002), an official policy of tolerance turned to one of overt persecution against Christians, which now included the plundering of churches and the seizure of their wealth, although he employed many Christian mercenaries in his armies. Social life also changed. Devout Muslims avoided contact with Christians; Christian homes had to be built lower than those of Muslims; priests were forbidden to carry a cross or a Bible, lest they offend Muslim sensibilities; and Arabized Christians were permitted to live only in particular places. Thus, writes one scholar, "the era of harmonious interaction between Muslim and Christian in Spain came to an end, replaced by intolerance, prejudice, and mutual suspicion."[19]

That intolerance intensified as the Christian reconquest of Spain gained ground after 1200. The end came in 1492, when Ferdinand and Isabella, the Catholic monarchs of a unified Spain, took Granada, the last Muslim stronghold on the Iberian Peninsula. Despite initial promises to maintain the freedom of Muslims to worship, in the opening decades of the sixteenth century the Spanish monarchy issued a series of edicts outlawing Islam in its various territories, forcing Muslims to choose between conversion or exile. Many Muslims were thus required to emigrate, often to North Africa or the Ottoman Empire, along with some 200,000 Jews expelled from Spain because they too refused to convert. In the early seventeenth century, even Muslim converts to Christianity were likewise banished from Spain. And yet cultural interchange persisted for a time. The translation of Arab texts into Latin continued under Christian rule, while Christian churches and palaces were constructed on the sites of older mosques and incorporated Islamic artistic and architectural features.

Thus Spain, unlike most other regions incorporated into the Islamic world, experienced a religious reversal as Christian rule was reestablished and Islam was painfully eradicated from the Iberian Peninsula. In world historical terms, perhaps the chief significance of Muslim Spain was its role in making the rich heritage of Islamic learning available to Christian Europe. As a cross-cultural encounter, it was largely a one-way street. European scholars wanted the secular knowledge—Greek as well as Arab—that had accumulated in the Islamic world, and they flocked to Spain to acquire it. That knowledge of philosophy, mathematics, medicine, optics, astronomy, botany, and more played a major role in the making of a new European civilization in the thirteenth century and beyond. Muslim Spain remained only as a memory.

> **PRACTICING HISTORICAL THINKING**
>
> "Islam had a revolutionary impact on every society that it touched." What evidence might support this statement, and what might challenge it?

The World of Islam as a New Civilization

As the religion spread and the Abbasid dynasty declined, the civilization of Islam, unlike that of China but similar to Western Christendom, operated without a dominant political center, bound more by a shared religious culture than by a shared state.

Twice that civilization was threatened from outside. The most serious intrusion came during the thirteenth century from the Mongols, whose conquest of Central Asia and Persia proved devastating while incorporating many Muslims within the huge Mongol domains. Less serious but more well known, at least in the West, were the Christian Crusades (1095–1291), which seized Jerusalem and established several small and temporary outposts along the eastern Mediterranean (see "Europe Outward Bound" in Chapter 10).

Despite these external threats and its various internal conflicts, Islamic civilization flourished and often prospered, embracing at least parts of virtually every other civilization in the Afro-Eurasian hemisphere. It was in that sense "history's first truly global civilization," although the Americas, of course, were not involved.[20] What held this Islamic world together? What enabled many people to feel themselves part of a single civilization despite its political fragmentation, religious controversies, and cultural and regional diversity?

Networks of Faith

At the core of that vast civilization was a common commitment to Islam. No group was more important in the transmission of those beliefs and practices than the ulama. These learned scholars were not "priests" in the Christian sense, for in Islam, at least theoretically, no person could stand between the believer and Allah. Rather, they served as judges, interpreters, administrators, prayer leaders, and reciters of the Quran, but especially as preservers and teachers of the sharia. Supported mostly by their local communities, some also received the patronage of sultans, or rulers, and were therefore subject to criticism for corruption and undue submission to state authority. In their homes, mosques, shrines, and Quranic schools, the ulama passed on the core teachings of the faith. Beginning in the eleventh century, formal colleges called **madrassas** offered more advanced instruction in the Quran and the sayings of Muhammad; grammar and rhetoric; sometimes philosophy, theology, mathematics, and medicine; and, above all else, law. Teaching was informal, mostly oral, and involved much memorization of texts. It was also largely conservative, seeking to preserve an established body of Islamic learning.

The ulama were an "international elite," and the system of education they created served to bind together an immense and diverse civilization. Common texts were shared widely across the world of Islam. Students and teachers alike traveled great distances in search of the most learned scholars. From Indonesia to West Africa, educated Muslims inhabited a "shared world of debate and reference."[21]

Paralleling the educational network of the ulama were the emerging religious orders of the Sufis. By the tenth century, particular Sufi *shaykhs* (shakes), or teachers, began to attract groups of disciples who were eager to learn their unique devotional practices and techniques of personal transformation. The disciples usually swore allegiance to their teacher and valued highly the chain of transmission by which those teachings and practices had come down from earlier masters. In the

---

Guided Reading Question

■ **DESCRIPTION**

What makes it possible to speak of the Islamic world as a distinct and coherent civilization?

twelfth and thirteenth centuries, Sufis began to organize in a variety of larger associations, some limited to particular regions and others with chapters throughout the Islamic world. The Qadiriya order, for example, began in Baghdad but spread widely throughout the Arab world and into sub-Saharan Africa.

Sufi orders were especially significant in the frontier regions of Islam because they followed conquering armies or traders into Central and Southeast Asia, India, Anatolia, parts of Africa, and elsewhere. Their devotional teachings, modest ways of living, and reputation for supernatural powers gained a hearing for the new faith. Their emphasis on personal experience of the Divine, rather than on the law, allowed the Sufis to accommodate elements of local belief and practice and encouraged the growth of a popular or blended Islam. The veneration of deceased Sufi "saints," or "friends of God," particularly at their tombs, created sacred spaces that enabled Islam to take root in many places despite its foreign origins. But that flexibility also often earned Sufi practitioners the enmity of the ulama, who were sharply critical of any deviations from the sharia.

Like the madrassas and the sharia, Sufi religious ideas and institutions spanned the Islamic world and were yet another thread in the cosmopolitan web of Islamic civilization. Particular devotional teachings and practices spread widely, as did the writings of such famous Sufi poets as Hafiz and Rumi. Devotees made pilgrimages to the distant tombs of famous teachers, who, they often believed, might intercede with God on their behalf. Wandering Sufis, in search of the wisdom of renowned shaykhs, found fellow seekers and welcome shelter in the compounds of Sufi religious orders.

In addition to the networks of the Sufis and the ulama, many thousands of people, from kings to peasants, made the grand pilgrimage to Mecca—the hajj—no doubt gaining some sense of the umma. There men and women together, hailing from all over the Islamic world, joined as one people to rehearse the central elements of their faith. The claims of local identities based on family, clan, tribe, ethnicity, or state never disappeared, but now overarching them all was the inclusive unity of the Muslim community.

Networks of Exchange

The world of Islamic civilization cohered not only as a network of faith but also as an immense arena of exchange in which goods, technologies, food products, and ideas circulated widely. By 1000, large areas of the Afro-Eurasian world operated within a single cultural realm, practicing Islam or speaking Arabic. This huge region rapidly became a vast trading zone of hemispheric dimensions. In part, this was due to its central location in the Afro-Eurasian world and the breaking down of earlier political barriers between the Byzantine and Persian empires. Furthermore, commerce was valued positively within Islamic teaching, and laws regulating it figured prominently in the sharia, creating a predictable framework for exchange across many cultures. The pilgrimage to Mecca, as well as the urbanization that accompanied the growth of Islamic civilization, likewise fostered commerce. Baghdad, established in 756 as the capital of the Abbasid Empire, soon grew into a magnificent city of half a million people. The appetite of urban elites for luxury goods stimulated both craft production and the desire for foreign products.

Thus Muslim merchants, Arabs and Persians in particular, quickly became prominent and sometimes dominant players in all the major Afro-Eurasian trade routes of the third-wave era—in the Mediterranean Sea, along the revived Silk Roads, across the Sahara, and throughout the Indian Ocean basin. By the eighth century, Arab and Persian traders had established a commercial colony in Canton in southern China, thus linking the Islamic heartland with Asia's other giant and flourishing economy. Various forms of banking, partnerships, business contracts, and instruments for granting credit facilitated these long-distance economic relationships and generated a prosperous, sophisticated, and highly commercialized economy that spanned the Old World.

The vast expanse of Islamic civilization also contributed to ecological change as agricultural products and practices spread from one region to another, a process already under way in the earlier Roman and Persian empires. Among the food crops that circulated within and beyond the Islamic world were different varieties of sugarcane, rice, apricots, artichokes, eggplants, lemons, oranges, almonds, figs, and bananas. Equally significant were water-management practices, so important to the arid or semi-arid environments of many parts of the Islamic world. Persian-style reservoirs and irrigation technologies spread as far as Tunisia and Morocco, the northern fringes of the Sahara, Spain, and Yemen. All of this contributed to an "Islamic Green Revolution" of increased food production, as well as to population growth, urbanization, and industrial development across the Islamic world.

Technology too diffused widely within the realm of Islam. Muslim technicians made improvements on rockets, first developed in China, by developing one that carried a small warhead and another that was used to attack ships. Papermaking techniques entered the Abbasid Empire from China in the eighth century or earlier, with paper mills soon operating in Persia, Iraq, and Egypt. This revolutionary technology, which everywhere served to strengthen bureaucratic governments, passed from the Middle East into India and Europe over the following centuries. Everywhere it spurred the emergence of books and written culture at the expense of earlier orally based cultural expressions.

Ideas likewise circulated across the Islamic world. The religion itself drew heavily and quite openly on Jewish

Guided Reading Question

....

■ **CONNECTION**

In what ways was the world of Islam a "cosmopolitan civilization"?

A Muslim Astronomical Observatory Drawing initially on Greek, Indian, and Persian astronomy, the Islamic world after 1000 developed its own distinctive tradition of astronomical observation and prediction, reflected in this Turkish observatory constructed in 1557. Muslim astronomy later exercised considerable influence in both China and Europe. (From the "Sehinsahname of Murad III," ca. 1581/ Istanbul University Library, Istanbul, Turkey/Bridgeman Images)

and Christian precedents. Persia also contributed much in the way of bureaucratic practice, court ritual, and poetry, with Persian becoming a major literary language in elite circles. Scientific, medical, and philosophical texts, especially from ancient Greece, the Hellenistic world, and India, were systematically translated into Arabic, providing an enormous boost to Islamic scholarship and science for several centuries. In 830, the Abbasid caliph al-Mamun, himself a poet and scholar with a passion for foreign learning, established the **House of Wisdom** in Baghdad as an academic center for this research and translation. Stimulated by Greek texts, a school of Islamic thinkers known as Mutazalites ("those who stand apart") argued that reason, rather than revelation, was the "surest way to truth."[22] In the long run, however, the philosophers' emphasis on logic, rationality, and the laws of nature was subject to increasing criticism by those who held that only the Quran, the sayings of the Prophet, or mystical experience represented a genuine path to God.

But the realm of Islam was much more than a museum of ancient achievements from the civilizations that it encompassed. Those traditions mixed and blended to generate a distinctive Islamic civilization with many new contributions to the world of learning. (See Snapshot: Key Achievements in Islamic

SNAPSHOT Key Achievements in Islamic Science and Scholarship

Person/Dates	Achievement
al-Khwarazim (790–840)	Mathematician; spread use of Arabic numerals in Islamic world; wrote first book on algebra
al-Razi (865–925)	Discovered sulfuric acid; wrote a vast encyclopedia of medicine, drawing on Greek, Syrian, Indian, and Persian work and his own clinical observation
al-Biruni (973–1048)	Mathematician, astronomer, cartographer; calculated the radius of the earth with great accuracy; worked out numerous mathematical innovations; developed a technique for displaying a hemisphere on a plane
Ibn Sina (Avicenna) (980–1037)	Prolific writer in almost all fields of science and philosophy; especially known for *Canon of Medicine*, a fourteen-volume work that set standards for medical practice in Islamic and Christian worlds for centuries
Omar Khayyam (1048–1131)	Mathematician; critic of Euclid's geometry; measured the solar year with great accuracy; Sufi poet; author of *The Rubaiyat*
Ibn Rushd (Averroës) (1126–1198)	Translated and commented widely on Aristotle; rationalist philosopher; made major contributions in law, mathematics, and medicine
Nasir al-Din Tusi (1201–1274)	Founder of the famous Maragha observatory in Persia (data from Maragha probably influenced Copernicus); mapped the motion of stars and planets
Ibn Khaldun (1332–1406)	Greatest Arab historian; identified trends and structures in world history over long periods of time

Science and Scholarship, page 387.) Using Indian numerical notation, for example, Arab scholars developed algebra as a novel mathematical discipline. They also undertook much original work in astronomy and optics. They built on earlier Greek and Indian practice to create a remarkable tradition in medicine and pharmacology. Arab physicians such as al-Razi and Ibn Sina accurately diagnosed many diseases, such as hay fever, measles, smallpox, diphtheria, rabies, and diabetes. In addition, treatments such as using a mercury ointment for scabies, cataract and hernia operations, and filling teeth with gold emerged from Arab doctors. The first hospitals, traveling clinics, and examinations for physicians and pharmacologists were also developed within the Islamic world. In the eleventh and twelfth centuries, this enormous body of Arab medical scholarship entered Europe via Spain, and it remained at the core of European medical practice for many centuries.

REFLECTIONS

Past and Present: Choosing Our History

Prominent among the many uses of history is the perspective it provides on the present. Although historians sometimes worry that an excessive "present-mindedness" may distort our perception of the past, all of us look to history, almost instinctively, to comprehend the world we now inhabit. Given the obvious importance of the Islamic world in the international arena of the twenty-first century, how might some grasp of the early development of Islamic civilization assist us in understanding our present circumstances?

Certainly, that history reminds us of the central role that Islam played in the Afro-Eurasian world for a thousand years or more. From 600 to 1600 or later, it was a proud, cosmopolitan, often prosperous, and frequently powerful civilization that spanned Africa, Europe, the Middle East, and Asia. What followed were several centuries of European or Western imperialism that many Muslims found humiliating, even if some were attracted by elements of modern Western culture. In their recent efforts to overcome those centuries of subordination and exploitation, Muslims have found encouragement and inspiration in reflecting on the more distant and perhaps more glorious past. But they have not all chosen to emphasize the same past. Those labeled as "fundamentalists" have often viewed the early Islamic community associated with Medina, Mecca, and Muhammad as a model for Islamic renewal in the present. Others, often known as Islamic modernizers, have looked to the somewhat later achievements of Islamic science and scholarship as a foundation for a more open engagement with the West and the modern world.

The history of Islam also reveals a world of great diversity and debate. Sharp religious differences between Sunni and Shia understandings of the faith; differences in emphasis between advocates of the sharia and of Sufi spirituality; political conflicts among various groups and regions within the larger Islamic world; different postures toward women—all of this and more divided the umma and divide it still. Recalling that diversity is a useful reminder for any who would tag all Muslims with a single label.

A further dimension of that diversity lies in the many cultural encounters that the spread of Islam has spawned. Sometimes great conflict and violence have accompanied those encounters, as in the Crusades and in Turkic invasions of India and Anatolia. At other times and places, Muslims and non-Muslims have lived together in relative tranquillity and tolerance—in Spain, in West Africa, in India, and in the Ottoman Empire. Some commentaries on the current interaction of Islam and the West seem to assume an eternal hostility or an inevitable clash of civilizations. The record of the past, however, shows considerable variation in the interaction of Muslims and others. While the past certainly shapes and conditions what happens next, the future, as always, remains open. Within limits, we can choose the history on which we seek to build.

Second Thoughts

What's the Significance?

Muhammad, 361

Quran, 361

umma, 362

Pillars of Islam, 362

hijra, 363

sharia, 364

jizya, 367

Umayyad caliphate, 370

Abbasid caliphate, 371

ulama, 371

Sufism, 372

Sikhism, 378

Timbuktu, 381

al-Andalus, 382

madrassas, 384

House of Wisdom, 387

Big Picture Questions

1. How might you account for the immense religious and political/military success of Islam in its early centuries?
2. In what ways might Islamic civilization be described as cosmopolitan, international, or global?
3. "Islam was simultaneously a single world of shared meaning and interaction and a series of separate, distinct, and conflicting communities." What evidence could you provide to support both parts of this statement?
4. What changes did Islamic expansion generate in those societies that encountered it, and how was Islam itself transformed by those encounters?
5. **Looking Back:** What distinguished the early centuries of Islamic history from a similar phase in the history of Christianity and Buddhism?

Next Steps: For Further Study

Reza Aslan, *No God but God* (2005). A well-written and popular history of Islam by an Iranian immigrant to the United States.

G. W. Bowerstock, *The Crucible of Islam* (2017). Highlights the significance of Arab history and culture in the emergence of Islam.

Fred M. Donner, *Muhammad and the Believers* (2010). An innovative account of the first century of Islam by a leading scholar of that era.

John Esposito, ed., *The Oxford History of Islam* (1999). Up-to-date essays on various periods and themes in Islamic history. Beautifully illustrated.

Francis Robinson, ed., *Cambridge Illustrated History of the Islamic World* (1996). A series of essays by major scholars, with lovely pictures and maps.

Judith Tucker, *Gender and Islamic History* (1994). A brief overview of the changing lives of Islamic women.

Tim Mackintosh Smith, *The Man Who Walked across the World*, BBC FOUR, http://topdocumentaryfilms.com/man-who-walked-across-world/. A documentary travelogue tracing the many journeys of Ibn Battuta.

"Religions: Islam," http://www.bbc.co.uk/religion/religions/islam/. A BBC website providing information about all aspects of Islamic life and culture.

The Islamic World in the Seventh Century

The first seventy years of the Islamic era—roughly 610 to 680 C.E.—witnessed three major developments of enduring world historical significance: the emergence of a new religious tradition, a sharp and lasting division within the Islamic world, and the beginnings of a growing Arab Empire. The sources that follow provide a glimpse—both visual and documentary—into those processes.

SOURCE 9.1 Depicting Muhammad with the Angel Gabriel ▶

The three images that follow portray major events in the life of Muhammad. They are etched into the memory of Muslims everywhere, for they mark the beginnings of what became Islam. Representing these events artistically, and especially the figure of Muhammad, has long been controversial within Islamic societies. While not prohibited in the Quran, visual depictions of the Prophet have often been discouraged or even forbidden as a way of preventing idolatry. Nonetheless, Muhammad was on occasion portrayed in Persian and Turkish miniature painting, sometimes in full face, but often with his face obscured.

According to all Muslims, the central and defining experience in Muhammad's life occurred in the year 610 C.E. when he encountered for the first time an angel, usually identified as Gabriel, an event that marked the beginning of his revelations. While meditating in a cave outside Mecca, a towering and overpowering presence of the angel appeared to him, filling the entire horizon, squeezing the very breath from his body, and commanding him to "recite" or to "read." After repeated protests that "I am not a reciter/reader," Muhammad found himself speaking what became the first revelation of the Quran. Source 9.1, an early fourteenth-century Persian miniature painting, depicts this encounter between Muhammad and Gabriel.

■ What impression of this encounter does the artist seek to convey?

■ Traditional accounts of Muhammad's encounter with the angel stress the mysterious and overpowering "otherness" of the Divine Presence, which prompted Muhammad's initial fear and terror. What is the religious significance of such a depiction of the Divine? To what extent does this image convey that impression?

■ Muslims have traditionally stressed that their prophet was illiterate, based in part on his response to the angel: "I am not a reader." Why might it be important to Muslims to believe that Muhammad was illiterate?

Muhammad and the Angel Gabriel | ca. 1307

■ ■ ■

SOURCE 9.2 **Muhammad in Jerusalem** ▶

By far the most frequently portrayed event in the life of Muhammad was the *miraj*, the Prophet's Night Journey, said to have taken place in 619 or 620. The Quran refers briefly to God taking the Prophet "from the sacred place of worship to the far distant place of worship." This passage became the basis for a story, much embellished over the centuries, of deep meaning for Muslims. In this religious narrative, Muhammad was led one night by the angel Gabriel from Mecca to Jerusalem. For the journey he was given a *buraq*, a mythical winged creature with the body of a mule or donkey and the face of a woman. Upon arriving in Jerusalem, Muhammad led prayers for an assembly of earlier prophets including Abraham, Moses, and Jesus. (See the image "Muslims, Jews, and Christians" on page 362 for a fifteenth-century Persian painting illustrating this event.) Then, accompanied by many angels, Muhammad made his way through seven heavens, coming almost into the presence of God, where, according to the Quran, "he saw some of the greatest signs of his Lord."

Some believers have interpreted this literally as a miraculous event, while others have considered it a dream or vision. Source 9.2, dating from the early sixteenth century, is one of many representations of the Night Journey that emerged within Persian miniature painting.

■ Looking closely at the image, what significance might one attach to the female head of the buraq, to the accompanying angels and their gifts, to the fiery halo around Muhammad's head, and to the image of the world below and slightly to the right of the buraq?

■ What meaning might be derived from Muhammad's encounter with earlier prophets such as Abraham, Moses, and Jesus?

■ How might the destination of the Night Journey (Jerusalem) have affected Muslim views of that city?

■ How might Sufis have understood the Night Journey?

AQA MIRAK | *The Night Journey of Muhammad* | 16th century

SOURCE 9.3 **Victory in Mecca** ▶

Widespread opposition to Muhammad's revolutionary message required almost a decade of struggle, military action, and negotiation before he was able to establish his control over most of Arabia. But finally in 630, Muhammad and some 10,000 soldiers triumphantly entered Mecca, almost completely without violence, and in a posture of reconciliation rather than revenge. In sharp contrast to traditional Arab practice, Muhammad issued a general amnesty for those who had opposed him. Then he turned his attention to the religious rationale of his entire movement. Riding his favorite camel, Muhammad circled the Kaaba seven times, shouting "Allahu Akbar" (God is greater), thus declaring the triumph of the believer's movement. Refusing to enter the Kaaba until it had been purified from its idolatry, Muhammad ordered its 360 idols and paintings removed. He then smashed each one, reciting a Quranic verse: "The truth has come and falsehood has vanished away." Muslim sources record that the Prophet invited his cousin and son-in-law Ali, the first male convert to the new faith, to stand on his shoulders to strike down the highest idols. Thus the Kaaba was cleansed and, in Muslim thinking, restored to its original purpose as a focal point for the worship of Allah alone.

Source 9.3, a fifteenth century Persian image, portrays this dramatic event, showing Muhammad with Ali on his shoulders, both enveloped in holy fire, smashing the offensive idols while their followers look on.

- What understanding of pre-Islamic Arab religion does this image reflect?

- What fundamental Muslim teachings does this painting seek to convey? How do you understand the Muslim concern with idolatry?

- Some traditions suggest that Muhammad ordered pictures of Mary and Jesus within the Kaaba to be left intact. What purpose might this tradition serve?

MIR HAVAND | *The Cleansing of the Kaaba* | ca. 1590

SOURCE 9.4 Conflict and Division: The Emergence of Shia Islam

Less than twenty-five years after Muhammad died, his beloved community, the umma, had descended into civil war, largely over the political issue of leadership. From this violent struggle emerged the lasting division of the Islamic world into Sunni and Shia versions of the faith. (See "Divisions and Controversies" in this chapter.) The Shia perspective on this conflict is reflected in a bitter poem attributed to Ali ibn Husayn, who was in the line of direct descent from the Prophet Muhammad. It was written as he went into battle against the dominant forces of the Umayyad dynasty in 680.

- The Shia outlook placed great emphasis on retaining the leadership of the Islamic community in the family line descending from Muhammad and his cousin and son-in-law Ali. How is this sensibility reflected in this poem?

- Another Shia ideal was that "the righteous should wage struggle against tyrants, even in the face of hopeless odds."[23] What evidence of this stance do you find in the poem?

ALI IBN HUSAYN | *Poem* | ca. 680

I am Ali, son of Husayn son of Ali; / We and the household of God are closer to the prophet

Than Shabath and Shamir the vile [military leaders of the opposing forces]. I strike you with the sword until it bends / the blows of a Hasimite [family of the prophet] youth, an 'Alid [in the family line of Ali, the fourth caliph and cousin and son-in-law of the Prophet] / And today I will not stop defending my father [Husayn, the great Shia martyr] / By God the son of the bastard [the local Umayyad governor] shall not rule over us.

Source: Quoted in Fred M. Donner, *Muhammad and the Believers* (Cambridge, MA: Harvard University Press, 2010), 179.

■ ■ ■

SOURCE 9.5 Conquest

Even as the Arab/Islamic world splintered internally, it was expanding externally. That expansion involved both military force and political agreements, as the two brief documents in Source 9.5 indicate. The first, from a Syrian Christian eyewitness known as Thomas the Presbyter, illustrates the violence of conquest in what is now Palestine in 634 C.E., just two years after the Prophet Muhammad's death. The second records an agreement between the invading Arab forces and the Christian people of Tiflis in the Caucasus region in 642–643.

■ Arab empire building has been described variously as extremely violent, generally tolerant, and motivated by the desire to convert people to Islam. In what ways might these documents support or challenge such characterizations?

■ What advantages and disadvantages does Source 9.5B hold for the people of Tiflis?

SOURCE 9.5A

Text of Thomas the Presbyter | 640

On Friday, 4 February [634 C.E.], at the ninth hour, there was a battle between the Romans [forces of the Byzantine Empire] and the Arabs of Muhammad in Palestine twelve miles east of Gaza. The Romans fled, leaving behind the patriarch Bryrdn, whom the Arabs killed. Some 4,000 poor villagers of Palestine were killed there, Christians, Jews and Samaritans. The Arabs ravaged the whole region. . . .

Source: Andrew Palmer (with contributions from Sebastian P. Brock and Robert G. Hoyland), *The Seventh Century in the West-Syrian Chronicles Including Two Seventh-Century Syriac Apocalyptic Texts* (Liverpool: Liverpool University Press, 1993), 18–19.

SOURCE 9.5B

Pact of Ibn Muslama and the People of Tiflis | 653

This is a statement from Habib ibn Muslama [commander of the invading Arab forces] to the inhabitants of Tiflis, . . . securing them safety for their lives, churches, convents, religious services, and faith, provided they acknowledge and pay tax to the amount of one *dinar* on every household. You are not to combine more than one household into one in order to reduce the tax and we are not to divide the same household into more than one in order to increase it. You owe us counsel and support against the enemies of Allah and his Prophet to the utmost of your ability, and are bound to entertain the needy Muslim for one night and provide him with food used by the "people of the book" and which it is legal for us to partake of. If a Muslim is cut off from his companions and falls into your hands, you are bound to deliver him to the nearest body of the "Believers." . . . If you return to the obedience of Allah and observe prayer, you are our brethren in faith; otherwise poll-tax is incumbent on you. In case an enemy of yours attacks and subjugates you while Muslims are too busy to come to your aid, the Muslims are not held responsible, nor is it a violation of the covenant with you.

Source: Al-Baladhuri, *The Origins of the Islamic State*, translated by P. K. Hitti (New York: Columbia University, 1916), 316–17.

SOURCE 9.6   Governing an Empire

Conquering an empire was one thing; governing it was another. In 658 C.E. the fourth caliph Ali sent a letter to Malik Ashtar, the newly appointed governor of Egypt, which was now part of a growing Arab Empire, outlining the principles of governance that he should follow. The high-minded nature of this letter provided a model for benevolent political leadership of an increasingly pluralistic empire, although few Arab or other rulers lived up to that high standard. In fact, Malik Ashtar was poisoned by a rival before he could take up his duties. Nonetheless, the letter has long stood, both in the Islamic world and beyond, as a charter for a moral approach to government.

■ How might you define the principles of governance outlined in Ali's letter?

■ To what extent does his letter reflect Islamic values?

■ In what ways might it be seen as a response to a growing empire?

CALIPH ALI │ *Letter to Malik Ashtar* │ 658

Develop in your heart the feeling of love for your people. . . . Do not behave with them like a barbarian, and do not appropriate to yourself that which belongs to them. . . . Do not say: "I am your overlord and dictator, and that you should, therefore, bow to my commands," as that will corrupt your heart, weaken your faith in religion and create disorder in the state. . . .

Maintain justice in administration and impose it on your own self and seek the consent of the people, for the discontent of the masses sterilizes the contentment of the privileged few. . . . It is the common man who is the strength of the State and Religion. It is he who fights the enemy. So live in close contact with the masses and be mindful of their welfare. . . .

Never let men who have been companions of tyrants or shared their crimes be your counsellors. Keep close to you the upright, and the God fearing, and make clear to them that they are never to flatter you and never to give you credit for any good that you may not have done. . . .

Never select men for responsible posts either out of any regard for personal connections or under any influence, for that might lead to injustice and corruption. . . .

You should regard the proper upkeep of the land in cultivation as of greater importance than the collection of revenue, for revenue cannot be derived except by making the land productive. He who demands revenue without helping the cultivator to improve his land, inflicts unmerited hardship on the cultivator and ruins the state. . . .

Treat businessmen and artisans well. . . . Trade and industry are the real sources of profit to the state and the suppliers of consumer goods. . . . Visit every part of the country and establish personal contact with this class, and inquire into their condition. But bear in mind that a good many of them are intensely greedy. . . . They hoard grain and try to sell it at a high price and this is most harmful to the public. . . . Prevent them from hoarding, for the prophet of God had prohibited it . . .

Fear God when dealing with the problem of the poor. . . . For God's sake, safeguard their rights, for on you rests the responsibility of protecting their interests. Assign for their uplift a portion of the state exchequer. . . . Meet the oppressed and the lowly periodically in an open conference and conscious of the divine presence there, have a heart-to-heart talk with them, . . . so that the representatives of the poor might state their grievances fearlessly and without reserve. . . .

Do not forget to set apart the best of your time for communion with God.

Source: Paul Salahuddin Armstrong, ed., "Caliph Ali's Letter to Malik Ashtar," https://paulsarmstrong.com/articles/caliph-ali-letter-to-malik-ashtar/.

DOING HISTORY

1. **Noticing visual sources:** Consider the first three visual sources together with the other images within the chapter. What general impression of the Islamic world emerges? What point of view, if any, is reflected in this selection of visual sources? Do they convey a positive, negative, or neutral impression of Islamic civilization?

2. **Considering Islamic unity and division:** What do these sources suggest about the factors that enhanced the unity of the Islamic world and those that divided it?

3. **Analyzing the usefulness of sources:** To what extent do these sources provide useful information about what really happened? And in what ways do they help us rather to understand the evolving Muslim view of Islam's history?

4. **Comparing narrative text and primary sources:** What do these sources add to the understanding of Islam you derived from the narrative text of this chapter?

Assessing the Prophet Muhammad

Clearly the Prophet Muhammad has been one of world history's outsized actors, whose life has resonated across many domains of human activity around the world for many centuries. In Voice 9.1, Francis Robinson, a prominent historian of Islam, reviews the evolving image of Muhammad in the Western world, while Voice 9.2 by Karen Armstrong, who has written a biography of the prophet, explores the meaning of Muhammad for Muslims.

- According to Robinson in Voice 9.1, in what different ways has Muhammed been understood in the Western world?

- How does Armstrong in Voice 9.2 understand Muhammad's personal significance for millions of ordinary Muslims?

- **Integrating Primary and Secondary Sources:** In what ways might the primary sources in this feature be used to support Muslim understandings of Muhammad as described in Voice 9.2?

VOICE 9.1

Francis Robinson on Western Attitudes to Muhammad | 1996

The changing image of the Prophet Muhammad is a touchstone of the changing western attitudes to Islam. For a thousand years he was the false prophet, the imposter. Hence the terrible fate which Dante contrived for him in the *Inferno* . . . consigned to the ninth of ten gloomy ditches surrounding Satan's stronghold [hell], where, branded a spreader of scandal and discord, he was doomed to being split in twain continuously. From the eighteenth century a more complex picture begins to emerge. The historian Edward Gibbon in his *Decline and Fall of the Roman Empire* was able to admire the original genius of the Muhammad of Mecca, the moral leader, while questioning the motives of the Muhammad of Medina, the calculating politician. Some fifty years later, the historian Thomas Carlyle was able to make Muhammad his prophetic hero. . . . "He is by no means the truest of the Prophets, . . . but I do esteem

him a true one . . . a great soul." . . . [A] half century later the Victorian entrepreneur Thomas Holloway had little difficulty in having the Prophet's image affixed to the Chapel of his university college for women alongside other great teachers of humankind. In the twentieth century, attitudes range from the secular that would dismiss Muhammad along with Jesus as the misguided catalyst of religious enthusiasm to some recent Christian Roman Catholic scholars who have gone so far as to regard him as a religious genius and have wondered if he might not be a true prophet.

Source: Francis Robinson, ed., *Cambridge Illustrated History: Islamic World* (Cambridge: Cambridge University Press, 1996), xv.

VOICE 9.2

Karen Armstrong on Muslim Devotion to the Prophet | 1992

Muslims have continued to emphasize that Muhammad is merely an ordinary man like themselves, but over the centuries they have added a qualification. Yes, Muhammad is a man like other men, but he is "like a precious gem among stones." . . . Muhammad's life has become a "sign," like other signs that the Quran urges Muslims to see in the natural world. His prophetic career was a symbol, a theophany, which not only shows God's activity in the world, but illustrates the perfect human surrender to God. The development of the ideal of Muhammadan sanctity [holy behavior worthy of respect and imitation] has been an imaginative attempt to penetrate the meaning of his life and apply it to the circumstances of daily life. . . . Muhammad is therefore seen symbolically as the Perfect Man, the human archetype and the image of a perfect receptivity to God. . . . Muslims seek to imitate Muhammad in their daily lives in order to approximate as closely as possible to this perfection and so to come as close as they can to God himself.

Source: Karen Armstrong, *Muhammad: A Biography of the Prophet* (New York: Harper Collins, 1992), 262.

From "Grandes Chroniques de France," 1375–1379/Bibliothèque Municipale, Castres, France/Bridgeman Images

The Worlds of Christendom

Contraction, Expansion, and Division

600–1450

« Charlemagne This fourteenth-century manuscript painting depicts Charlemagne, king of the Franks, being crowned emperor by Pope Leo III surrounded by other churchmen. His coronation in 800 C.E. illustrates the close and sometimes-conflicted relationship of political and religious authorities in an emerging European civilization. His crowning also represents the futile desire of many in Western Europe to revive the old Roman Empire, even as a substantially new civilization was taking shape in the aftermath of the Roman collapse several centuries earlier.

Yao Hong, a Chinese woman, was about twenty years of age around 1990, when, distraught at discovering that her husband was having an affair, she became a Christian. As a migrant from a rural village to the huge city of Shanghai, Yao Hong found support and a sense of family in a Christian community. Interviewed in 2010, she observed, "Whether they know you or not, they treat you as a brother or sister. . . . [T]hey help out with money or material assistance or spiritual aid." Nor did she find the Christian faith alien to her Chinese culture. To the contrary, she felt conversion to Christianity as a patriotic act, even a way of becoming more fully modern. "God is rising here in China," she declared. "If you look at the United States or England, . . . [t]heir churches are rich, because God blesses them."[1] ■

Yao Hong is but one of many millions who have made Christianity a very rapidly growing faith in China over the past thirty years or so. In neighboring South Korea, practicing Christians now outnumber Buddhists. Even more impressively, the non-Muslim regions of Africa witnessed an explosive advance of Christianity during the twentieth century. By the early twenty-first century, over 60 percent of the world's Christians lived in Asia, Africa, or Latin America.

Interestingly enough, the sixth- and seventh-century world of Christendom revealed a broadly similar pattern. Christianity then enjoyed an Afro-Eurasian reach with flourishing communities in Anatolia, Arabia, Egypt, North Africa, Ethiopia,

Nubia, Syria, Armenia, Persia, India, and China, as well as Europe. But during the third-wave era, radical changes reshaped that Christian world. Its African and Asian outposts largely vanished, declined, or were marginalized as Christianity became primarily a European phenomenon for the next thousand years or more. Furthermore, this European Christian world became deeply divided. Its eastern half, known as the Byzantine Empire or Byzantium (bihz-ANN-tee-uhm), continued the traditions of the Greco-Roman world in the eastern Mediterranean basin until its conquest by the Muslim Ottoman Empire in 1453. Centered on the magnificent city of Constantinople, Byzantium gradually developed a particular form of Christianity known as Eastern Orthodoxy and a distinctive third-wave civilization.

In Western, or Latin, Christendom, encompassing what we now know as Western Europe, the setting was far different. There the Roman imperial order had largely vanished by 500 C.E., replaced by highly localized societies—fragmented, decentralized, and competitive—in sharp contrast to the unified state of Byzantium. In Western Europe, a Roman Catholic version of the faith gradually emerged, increasingly centered on the pope and with an independence from political authorities that the Eastern Orthodox Church did not possess. Moreover, the Western Church in particular and its society in general were far more rural than Byzantium and certainly had nothing to compare to the imperial splendor of Constantinople. However, slowly at first and then with increasing speed after 1000, Western Europe emerged as an especially dynamic, expansive, and innovative third-wave civilization, combining elements of its Greco-Roman-Christian past with the culture of Germanic and Celtic peoples to produce a distinctive hybrid, or blended, civilization.

Thus the story of global Christendom in the era of third-wave civilizations is one of contractions and expansions. As a religion, Christianity contracted sharply in Asia and Africa even as it expanded in Western Europe and Russia. As a civilization, Christian Byzantium flourished for a time, then gradually contracted and finally disappeared. The trajectory of civilization in the West traced an opposite path, at first contracting as the Roman Empire collapsed and later expanding as a new and blended civilization took hold in Western Europe.

SEEKING THE MAIN POINT

In what different ways did the history of Christianity and Christian civilizations unfold in various parts of the Afro-Eurasian world during the third-wave era?

Christian Contraction in Asia and Africa

It was the wholly unforeseen birth of Islam, an expanding Arab Empire, and a sophisticated transcontinental Muslim civilization that led to the contraction of Christendom in Asia and Africa. As a result, European civilization emerged as the principal center of the Christian faith.[2]

Landmarks for Chapter 10

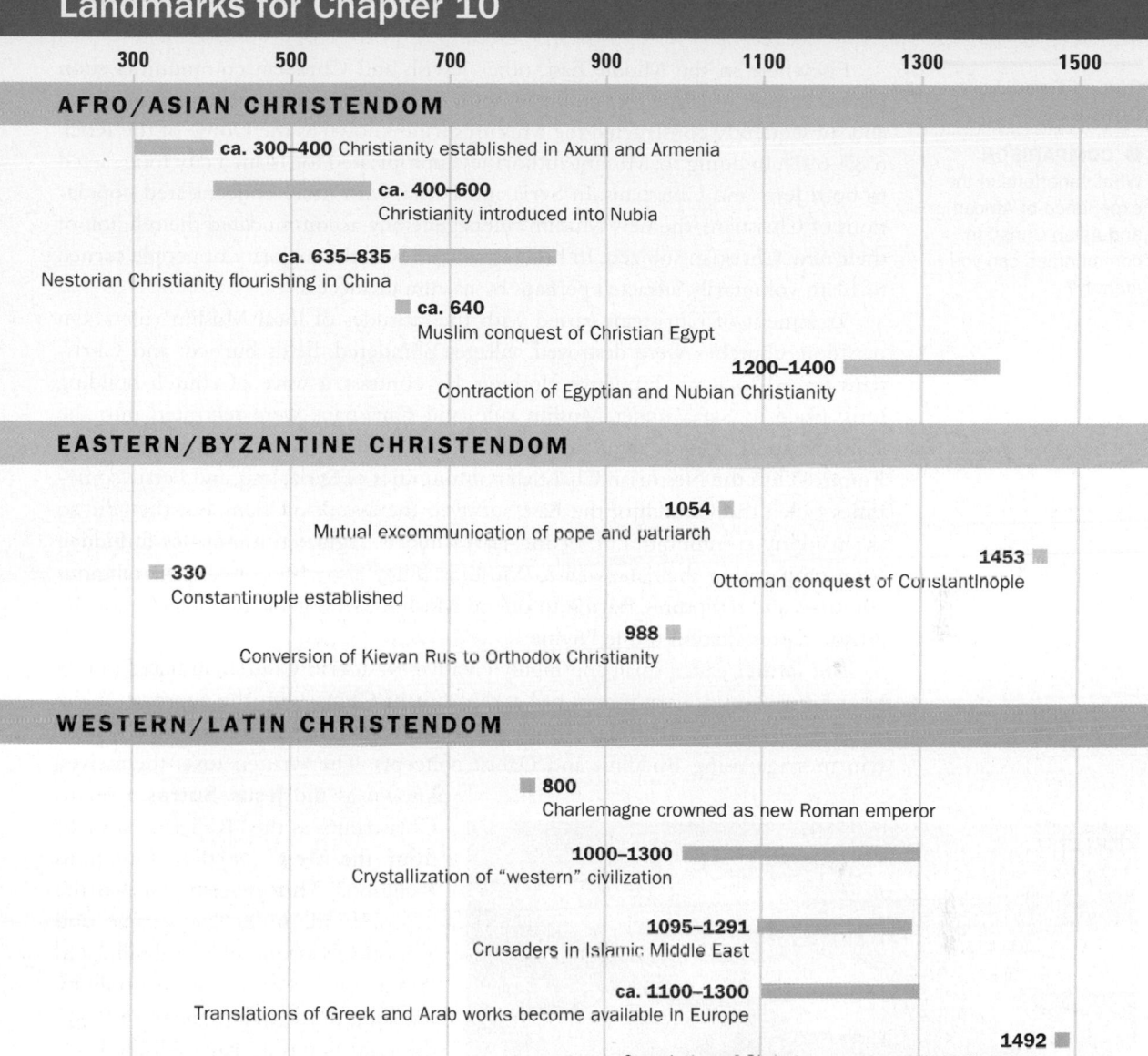

| | 300 | 500 | 700 | 900 | 1100 | 1300 | 1500 |

AFRO/ASIAN CHRISTENDOM

ca. 300–400 Christianity established in Axum and Armenia

ca. 400–600 Christianity introduced into Nubia

ca. 635–835 Nestorian Christianity flourishing in China

ca. 640 Muslim conquest of Christian Egypt

1200–1400 Contraction of Egyptian and Nubian Christianity

EASTERN/BYZANTINE CHRISTENDOM

1054 Mutual excommunication of pope and patriarch

330 Constantinople established

1453 Ottoman conquest of Constantinople

988 Conversion of Kievan Rus to Orthodox Christianity

WESTERN/LATIN CHRISTENDOM

800 Charlemagne crowned as new Roman emperor

1000–1300 Crystallization of "western" civilization

1095–1291 Crusaders in Islamic Middle East

ca. 1100–1300 Translations of Greek and Arab works become available in Europe

1492 Completion of Christian conquest of Muslim Spain

Asian Christianity

In Arabia, the homeland of Islam, the decimation of earlier Christian communities occurred most completely and most quickly, for within a century or so of Muhammad's death in 632, only a few Christian groups remained. During the eighth century, triumphant Muslims marked the replacement of the old religion by using pillars of a demolished Christian cathedral to construct the Grand Mosque of Sana'a in southern Arabia.

**Guided Reading
Question**

■ **COMPARISON**
What variations in the
experience of African
and Asian Christian
communities can you
identify?

Elsewhere in the Middle East, other Jewish and Christian communities soon felt the impact of Islam. Expanding Muslim forces took control of Jerusalem in 638 and subsequently constructed the Muslim shrine known as the Dome of the Rock (687–691). In doing so, Muslim authorities appropriated for Islam a city long sacred to both Jews and Christians. In Syria and Persia, with more concentrated populations of Christians, the new Muslim rulers generally accommodated the religion of their new Christian subjects. In both areas, however, the majority of people turned to Islam voluntarily, attracted perhaps by its aura of success.

Treatment of Christians varied with the attitudes of local Muslim rulers. On occasion, churches were destroyed, villages plundered, fields burned, and Christians forced to wear distinctive clothing. By contrast, a wave of church building took place in Syria under Muslim rule, and Christians were recruited into the administration, schools, translation services, and even the armed forces of the Arab Empire. Thus the Nestorian Christian communities of Syria, Iraq, and Persia, sometimes called the Church of the East, survived the assault of Islam, but they did so as shrinking communities of second-class subjects, regulated minorities forbidden from propagating their message to Muslims. They also abandoned their religious paintings and sculptures, fearing to offend Muslims, who generally objected to any artistic representation of the Divine.

But farther east, a small and highly creative Nestorian Church, initiated in 635 by a Persian missionary monk, had taken root in China with the approval of the country's Tang dynasty rulers. Both its art and literature articulated the Christian message using Buddhist and Daoist concepts. The written texts themselves, known as the **Jesus Sutras**, refer to Christianity as the "Religion of Light from the West" or the "Luminous Religion." They describe God as the "Cool Wind," sin as "bad karma," and a good life as one of "no desire" and "no action." "People can live only by dwelling in the living breath of God," the Jesus Sutras declare. "All the Buddhas are moved by this wind, which blows everywhere in the world."[3] By the end of the Tang dynasty (907 C.E.), the Nestorian Church had substantially faded away. The contraction of this remarkable experiment owed little to Islam and more to the vagaries of Chinese politics. In the mid-ninth century, the Chinese state turned against all religions of foreign origin, Islam and Buddhism as well as Christianity (see "Losing State Support:

The Dome of the Rock, Jerusalem To Muslims, the Dome of the Rock was constructed on the site from which Muhammad ascended into the presence of Allah during his Night Journey. It was the first large-scale building in the Islamic world and drew heavily on Roman, Byzantine, and Persian precedents. Its location in Jerusalem marked the arrival of a competing faith to Jews and Christians, who had long considered the city sacred. (Aaron Horowitz/Getty Images)

The Crisis of Chinese Buddhism" in Chapter 8). Wholly dependent on the goodwill of Chinese authorities, this small outpost of Christianity withered.

African Christianity

The churches of Africa, like those of the Middle East and Asia, also found themselves on the defensive and declining in the face of an expanding Islam. Across coastal North Africa, widespread conversion to Islam over several centuries reduced to virtual extinction Christian communities that had earlier provided many of the martyrs and intellectuals of the early Church.

In Egypt, however, Christianity had become the religion of the majority by the time of the Muslim conquest around 640, and for the next 500 years or so, large numbers continued to speak Coptic and practice their religion as *dhimmis*, legally inferior but protected people paying a spe-

Nestorian Christianity in China This wall painting from western China, dating to the seventh or eighth century C.E., shows Nestorian priests in a procession on Palm Sunday. It provides visual evidence of a meaningful Christian presence in Tang dynasty China. (7th- or 8th-century wall painting from Gaochang [Khocho], Xinjiang, China/Pictures from History/Bridgeman Images)

cial tax, under relatively tolerant Muslim rulers. Many found Arab government less oppressive than that of their former Byzantine overlords, who considered Egyptian Christians heretics. By the thirteenth century, things changed dramatically as Christian Crusaders from Europe and Mongol invaders from the east threatened Egypt. In these circumstances, the country's Muslim rulers came to suspect the political loyalty of their Christian subjects. The mid-fourteenth century witnessed violent anti-Christian pogroms, destruction of churches, and the forced removal of Christians from the best land. Many felt like "exiles in their own country." As a result, most rural Egyptians converted to Islam and moved toward the use of Arabic rather than Coptic, which largely died out. But although Egypt was becoming an Arab and Muslim country, a substantial Christian minority persisted, especially among the literate in urban areas and in monasteries located in remote regions. In the early twenty-first century, Egyptian Christians still numbered about 10 percent of the population.

Even as Egyptian Christianity was contracting, a new center of African Christianity was taking shape during the fifth and sixth centuries in the several kingdoms of Nubia to the south of Egypt, where the faith had been introduced by Egyptian traders and missionaries. Parts of the Bible were translated into the Nubian language, while other writings appeared in Greek, Arabic, and the Ethiopian language of Ge'ez. A great cathedral in the Nubian city of Faras was decorated with magnificent murals, and the earlier practice of burying servants to provide for rulers in the afterlife stopped abruptly. At times, kings served as priests, and Christian bishops held state offices. By the mid-seventh century, both the ruling class and many commoners had become Christian. At the same time, Nubian armies twice defeated Arab incursions, and following these defeats an agreement with Muslim Egypt protected this outpost of Christianity for some 600 years. But pressures mounted in the thirteenth and fourteenth centuries as Egypt adopted a more hostile stance toward Christians, while Islamized peoples from the desert and Arab migrants pushed against Nubia. By 1500, **Nubian Christianity**, like its counterparts in coastal North Africa, had largely disappeared.

An important exception to these various contractions of Asian and African Christianity lay in Ethiopia. There the rulers of Axum had adopted Christianity in the fourth century, and it later took root among the general population as well. Over the centuries of Islamic expansion, Ethiopia became a Christian island in a Muslim sea, protected by its mountainous geography and its distance from major centers of Islamic power. Nonetheless, the spread of Islam largely cut Ethiopia off from other parts of Christendom and rendered its position in Northeast Africa precarious.

In its isolated location, **Ethiopian Christianity** developed some of its most distinctive features. One of these was a fascination with Judaism and Jerusalem, reflected in a much-told story about the visit of an Ethiopian Queen of Sheba to King Solomon. The story includes an episode in which Solomon seduces the queen, producing a child who becomes the founding monarch of the Ethiopian state. Since Solomon figures in the line of descent to Jesus, it meant that Ethiopia's Christian rulers could legitimate their position by tracing their ancestry to Jesus himself. Furthermore, Ethiopian monks long maintained a presence in Jerusalem's Church of the Holy Sepulcher, said to mark the site where Jesus was crucified and buried. Then, in the twelfth century, the rulers of a new Ethiopian dynasty constructed a remarkable cluster of about a dozen linked underground churches and buildings, apparently attempting to create a New Jerusalem on Christian Ethiopian soil, as the original city lay under Muslim control. Those churches are in use to this day in modern Ethiopia, where over 60 percent of the country's population retains an affiliation with this ancient Christian church.

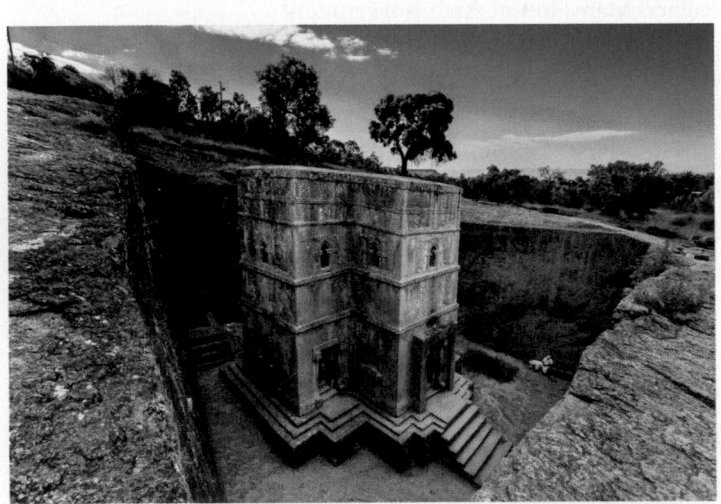

The Church of St. George, Lalibela, Ethiopia Excavated from solid rock in the twelfth century, the churches of Lalibela were distinctive Christian structures, invisible from a distance and apparent only when looking down on them from ground level. Local legend has it that their construction was aided by angels. This one in the shape of a cross is named for Saint George, the patron saint of Ethiopia. (WtR/Shutterstock)

Byzantine Christendom: Building on the Roman Past

The contraction of the Christian faith and Christian societies in Asia and Africa left the two civilizations of western Eurasia, the **Byzantine Empire** and Western Europe, largely by default, as the centers of Christendom. At the end of the third century, the Roman Empire was divided into eastern and western halves in an effort to provide more effective governance in the face of mounting political instability. But this action launched a division of Christendom that has lasted into the twenty-first century.

Unlike most empires, Byzantium has no clear starting point. Its own leaders, as well as its neighbors and enemies, viewed it as simply a continuation of the Roman Empire, and it lasted for a thousand years after the collapse of Roman rule in the West. Housing the ancient civilizations of Egypt, Greece, Syria, and Anatolia, the eastern Roman Empire (Byzantium) was far wealthier, more urbanized, and more cosmopolitan than its western counterpart; it possessed a much more defensible capital in the heavily walled city of **Constantinople**; and it had a shorter frontier to guard. Byzantium also enjoyed access to the Black Sea and command of the eastern Mediterranean. With a stronger army, navy, and merchant marine as well as clever diplomacy, its leaders were able to deflect the Germanic and Hun invaders who had overwhelmed the western Roman Empire.

Much that was late Roman—its roads, taxation system, military structures, centralized administration, imperial court, laws, Christian Church—persisted in the East for many centuries. Like Tang dynasty China seeking to restore the glory of the Han era, Byzantium consciously sought to preserve the legacy of classical Greco-Roman civilization. Constantinople, established in 330 C.E., was to be a "New Rome," and people referred to themselves as "Romans." Fearing contamination by "barbarian" (non-Roman) customs, emperors forbade the residents of Constantinople to wear boots, trousers, clothing made from animal skins, and long hairstyles, all of which were associated with Germanic peoples, and insisted instead on Roman-style robes and sandals. But much changed as well over the centuries, marking the Byzantine Empire as the home of a distinctive civilization.

Guided Reading Question

■ **CONTINUITY AND CHANGE**

In what respects did Byzantium continue the patterns of the classical Roman Empire? In what ways did it diverge from those patterns?

The Byzantine State

Perhaps the most obvious change was one of scale, as the Byzantine Empire never approximated the size of its Roman predecessor (see Map 10.1). The western Roman Empire was permanently lost to Byzantium, despite Emperor Justinian's (r. 527–565) impressive but short-lived attempt to reconquer the Mediterranean basin. The rapid Arab/Islamic expansion in the seventh century resulted in the loss of Syria/Palestine, Egypt, and North Africa. Nonetheless, until roughly 1200, a more compact Byzantine Empire remained a major force in the eastern Mediterranean, controlling Greece, much of the Balkans (southeastern Europe), and Anatolia.

Map 10.1 The Byzantine Empire

The Byzantine Empire reached its greatest extent under Emperor Justinian in the mid-sixth century C.E. It later lost considerable territory to various Christian European powers as well as to Muslim Arab and Turkic invaders.

From that territorial base, the empire's naval and merchant vessels were active in both the Mediterranean and Black seas.

In its heyday, the Byzantine state was an impressive creation. Political authority remained tightly centralized in Constantinople, where the emperor claimed to govern all creation as God's worldly representative, styling himself the "peer of the Apostles" and the "sole ruler of the world." The imperial court tried to imitate the awesome grandeur of what it thought was God's heavenly court, but in fact it resembled ancient Persian imperial splendor. Aristocrats trained in Greek rhetoric and literature occupied high positions in the administration, participating in court ceremonies that maintained their elite status. But this centralized state touched only lightly on the lives of most people, as it focused primarily on collecting taxes, maintaining order, and suppressing revolts. The Byzantine central authorities proved quite adaptable in their efforts to give local elites the autonomy necessary to reduce tensions within the empire and to mount an effective defense of its borders.

Nonetheless, the ongoing inability of the empire to develop an orderly system for selecting new rulers sparked civil wars several times. Furthermore, periodic invasions by powerful neighbors—Huns, Persians, Arabs, Western Europeans, and Turks—weakened and diminished the empire even as it showed remarkable resilience and capacity for revival. After 1085 the empire entered a period of slow and ultimately terminal decline. Byzantine territory shrank, owing to incursions by aggressive Western European powers, by Catholic Crusaders, and by Turkic Muslim invaders. The end came in 1453 when the Turkic Ottoman Empire, then known as the "sword of Islam," finally took Constantinople. One eyewitness to the event wrote a moving lament to his fallen city:

> And the entire city was to be seen in the tents of the [Turkish] camp, the city deserted, lying lifeless, naked, soundless, without either form or beauty. O city, head of all cities, center of the four corners of the world, pride of the Romans, civilizer of the barbarians. . . . Where is your beauty, O paradise . . . ? Where are the bodies of the Apostle of my Lord . . . ? Where are the relics of the saints, those of the martyrs? Where are the remains of Constantine the Great and the other emperors? . . . Oh, what a loss![4]

The Byzantine Church and Christian Divergence

Intimately tied to the Byzantine state was the Eastern Orthodox Church, a relationship that became known as **caesaropapism**. Unlike in Western Europe, where the Roman Catholic Church maintained some degree of independence from political authorities, in Byzantium the emperor assumed something of the role of both "Caesar," as head of state, and the pope, as head of the Church. Thus he appointed the patriarch, or leader, of the Orthodox Church; sometimes made decisions about doctrine; called church councils into session; and generally treated the Church as a government department. "The [Empire] and the church have a great unity and community," declared a twelfth-century patriarch. "Indeed they cannot be separated."[5] A dense network of bishops and priests brought the message of the Church to every corner of the empire, while numerous monasteries accommodated holy men, whose piety, self-denial, and good works made them highly influential among both elite and ordinary people.

Eastern Orthodox Christianity had a pervasive influence on every aspect of Byzantine life. It legitimated the supreme and absolute authority of the emperor, for he was a God-anointed ruler, a reflection of the glory of God on earth. It also provided a cultural identity for the empire's subjects. Even more than being "Roman," they were orthodox, or "right-thinking," Christians for whom the empire and the Church were equally essential to achieving eternal salvation. Constantinople was filled with churches and the relics of numerous saints. And the churches were filled with icons—religious paintings, some of them artistic masterpieces, of Jesus, Mary, and numerous saints—that many believed conveyed the Divine Presence to the faithful.

Guided Reading Question

■ COMPARISON

How did Eastern Orthodox Christianity differ from Roman Catholicism?

St. Mark's Basilica Consecrated in 1094, this ornate cathedral, although located in Venice, Italy, is a classic example of Byzantine architecture. Such churches represented perhaps the greatest achievement of Byzantine art and were certainly the most monumental expressions of Byzantine culture. (Erich Lessing/Art Resource, NY)

Complex theological issues about the Trinity and especially about the relationship of God and Jesus engaged the attention of ordinary people. For example, partisans of competing chariot-racing teams, known as the Greens and the Blues, vigorously debated theological issues as well as the merits of their favorite drivers.

In its early centuries and beyond, the Christian movement was rent by theological controversy and political division. But the most lasting and deepest division within the Christian world occurred as Eastern Orthodoxy came to define itself against an emerging Latin Christianity centered on papal Rome. Both had derived, of course, from the growth of Christianity in the Roman Empire and therefore had much in common—the teachings of Jesus; the Bible; the sacraments; a church hierarchy of patriarchs, bishops, and priests; a missionary impulse; and intolerance toward other religions. Despite these shared features, any sense of a single widespread Christian community was increasingly replaced by an awareness of difference, competition, and outright hostility that even a common fear of Islam could not overcome. In part, this growing religious divergence reflected the political separation and rivalry between the Byzantine Empire and the emerging kingdoms of Western Europe. As the growth of Islam in the seventh century submerged earlier centers of Christianity in the Middle East and North Africa, Constantinople and Rome alone remained as alternative hubs of the Church. But they were now in different states that competed with each other for territory and for the right to claim the legacy of imperial Rome.

Beyond such political differences were those of language and culture. Although Latin remained the language of the Church and of elite communication in the West, it was abandoned in the Byzantine Empire in favor of Greek, which remained the basis for Byzantine education. More than in the West, Byzantine thinkers sought to formulate Christian doctrine in terms of Greek philosophical concepts.

Differences in theology and church practice likewise widened the gulf between Orthodoxy and Catholicism. Disagreements about the nature of the Trinity, the source of the Holy Spirit, original sin, and the relative importance of faith and reason gave rise to much controversy. So too, for a time, did the Byzantine efforts to prohibit the use of icons, popular paintings of saints and biblical scenes that were usually painted on small wooden panels. Other more modest differences also occasioned mutual misunderstanding and disdain. Priests in the West shaved and, after 1050 or so, were supposed to remain celibate, while those in Byzantium allowed their beards to grow long and were permitted to marry. Orthodox ritual called for using bread leavened with yeast in the Communion, but Catholics used unleavened bread. Far more significant was the question of authority. Eastern Orthodox leaders sharply rejected the growing claims of Roman popes to be the sole and final authority for all Christians everywhere.

This rift in the world of Christendom grew gradually from the seventh century on, punctuated by various efforts to bridge the mounting divide between the Western and Eastern branches of the Church. A sign of this continuing deterioration occurred in 1054 when representatives of both churches mutually excommunicated each other, declaring in effect that those in the opposing tradition were not genuine Christians. The **Crusades**, launched in 1095 by the Catholic pope against the forces of Islam, made things worse. Western Crusaders, passing through the Byzantine Empire on their way to the Middle East, engaged in frequent conflict with Eastern Orthodox Christians, whom they regarded as "blasphemous, even heretical." During the Fourth Crusade in 1204, Western forces seized and looted Constantinople, and they ruled Byzantium for the next half century. According to one Byzantine account, "They sacked the sacred places and trampled on divine things . . . they tore children from their mothers . . . and they defiled virgins in the holy chapels, fearing neither God's anger nor man's vengeance."[6] After this, the rupture in the world of Christendom proved irreparable.

Byzantium and the World

Beyond its tense relationship with Western Europe, the Byzantine Empire, located astride Europe and Asia, also interacted intensively with its other neighbors. On a political and military level, Byzantium continued the long-term Roman struggle with the Persian Empire. That persisting conflict weakened both of them and was one factor in the remarkable success of Arab armies as they marched out of Arabia in the seventh century. Although Persia quickly became part of the Islamic world, Byzantium held out, even as it lost considerable territory to the Arabs. A Byzantine military innovation known as "Greek fire"—a potent and flammable combination of oil, sulfur, and lime that was launched from bronze tubes—helped hold off the Arabs. It operated as something like a flamethrower and subsequently passed into Arab and Chinese arsenals as well. Byzantium's ability to defend its core regions delayed for many centuries the Islamic advance into southeastern

Europe, which finally occurred at the hands of the Turkish Ottoman Empire in the fifteenth and sixteenth centuries.

Economically, the Byzantine Empire was a central player in the long-distance trade of Eurasia, with commercial links to Western Europe, Russia, Central Asia, the Islamic world, and China. Its gold coin, the bezant, was a widely used currency in the Mediterranean basin for more than 500 years, and wearing such coins as pendants was a high-status symbol in the less developed kingdoms of Western Europe. The luxurious products of Byzantine craftspeople—jewelry, gemstones, silver and gold work, linen and woolen textiles, purple dyes—were much in demand. Byzantium's silk industry, based on Chinese technology, supplied much of the Mediterranean basin with this precious fabric.

Guided Reading Question

■ **CONNECTION**
In what ways was the Byzantine Empire linked to a wider world?

The cultural influence of Byzantium was likewise significant. Preserving much of ancient Greek learning, the Byzantine Empire transmitted this classical heritage to the Islamic world as well as to the Christian West. In both places, it had an immensely stimulating impact among scientists, philosophers, theologians, and other intellectuals. Some saw it as an aid to faith and to an understanding of the world, while others feared it as impious and distracting. Byzantine religious culture also spread widely among Slavic-speaking peoples in the Balkans and Russia. As lands to the south and the east were overtaken by Islam, Byzantium looked to the north. By the early eleventh century, steady military pressure had brought many of the Balkan Slavic peoples and the Turkic-speaking Bulgars under Byzantine control. Christianity and literacy accompanied this Byzantine offensive. Already in the ninth century, two Byzantine missionaries, Cyril and Methodius, had developed an alphabet, based on Greek letters, with which Slavic languages could be written. This Cyrillic script made it possible to translate the Bible and other religious literature into these languages and greatly aided the process of conversion.

The Conversion of Russia

The most significant expansion of Orthodox Christianity occurred among the Slavic peoples of what is now Ukraine and western Russia. In this culturally diverse region, which also included Finnic and Baltic peoples as well as Viking traders, a modest state known as **Kievan Rus** (KEE-yehv-ihn ROOS)—named after the most prominent city, Kiev—emerged in the ninth century. (See Map 10.3, page 420.) As in many of the new third-wave civilizations, the development of Rus was stimulated by trade, in this case along the Dnieper River, which linked Scandinavia and Byzantium. Loosely led by various princes, especially the prince of Kiev, Rus was a society of slaves and freemen, privileged people and commoners, dominant men and subordinate women. This stratification marked it as a third-wave civilization in the making.

Religion reflected the region's cultural diversity, as ancestral spirits, household deities, and various gods related to the forces of nature were worshipped. Small numbers of Christians, Muslims, and Jews were likewise part of the mix. Then, in 988, a decisive turning point occurred. The growing interaction of Rus with the larger world prompted **Prince Vladimir of Kiev** to affiliate with the Eastern Orthodox faith of the Byzantine Empire. The prince was searching for a religion that would unify the diverse peoples of his region while linking Rus into wider networks of communication and exchange.

As elsewhere in Europe, the coming of Christianity to Rus was a top-down process in which ordinary people followed their rulers into the Church. It was also a slow process, and elements of traditional religious sensibility long lingered among those who defined themselves as Christian. Perun, the god of thunder, continued to speak to some, and "magicians" sometimes led people astray in the eyes of church authorities. But building churches on the site where images of Perun and other gods once stood helped to anchor the new faith in its new land.

It was a fateful choice with long-term implications for Russian history, for it brought this fledgling civilization firmly into the world of Orthodox Christianity, separating it from both the realm of Islam and the Roman Catholic West. Like many new civilizations, Rus borrowed extensively from its older and more sophisticated Byzantine neighbor. Among these borrowings were Byzantine architectural styles, the Cyrillic alphabet, the extensive use of icons, a monastic tradition stressing prayer and service, and political ideals of imperial control of the Church, all of which became part of a transformed Rus. Orthodoxy also provided a more unified identity for this emerging civilization and religious legitimacy for its rulers. Centuries later, when Byzantium had fallen to the Turks, a few Russian church leaders proclaimed the doctrine of a "third Rome." The original Rome had abandoned the true Orthodox faith for Roman Catholicism, and the second Rome, Constantinople, had succumbed to Muslim infidels. Moscow was now the third Rome, the final protector and defender of Orthodox Christianity. Though not widely proclaimed in Russia itself, such a notion reflected the "Russification" of Eastern Orthodoxy and its growing role as an element of Russian national identity. It was also a reminder of the enduring legacy of a thousand years of Byzantine history, long after the empire itself had vanished.

Guided Reading Question

■ **CONNECTION**

How did links to Byzantium transform the new civilization of Kievan Rus?

Western Christendom: Rebuilding in the Wake of Roman Collapse

The western half of the European Christian world followed a rather different path than that of the Byzantine Empire. For much of the third-wave era, **Western Christendom** was distinctly on the margins of world history, partly because of its geographic location at the far western end of the Eurasian landmass. Thus it was at a distance from the growing routes of world trade — by sea in the Indian Ocean and by land across the Silk Roads to China and the Sand Roads to West Africa. Internally, Europe's geography made political unity difficult, for population centers were divided by mountain ranges and dense forests as well as by five major peninsulas and two large islands (Britain and Ireland). However, Europe's extensive coastlines and interior river systems facilitated exchange, while a moderate climate, plentiful rainfall, and fertile soils enabled a productive agriculture that could support a growing population.

Political Life in Western Europe

In the early centuries of this era, history must have seemed more significant than geography, for the Roman Empire was gone. Much that had characterized Roman civilization also weakened, declined, or disappeared in the several centuries before and after 476, the traditional date marking the collapse of Roman rule in the West when German general Odoacer overthrew the last Roman emperor. Any semblance of large-scale centralized rule vanished. Disease and warfare reduced Western Europe's population by more than 25 percent. Land under cultivation contracted, while forests, marshland, and wasteland expanded. Urban life too diminished sharply, as Europe reverted to a largely rural existence. Rome at its height was a city of 1 million people, but by the tenth century it numbered perhaps 10,000. Public buildings crumbled from lack of care. Outside Italy, long-distance trade dried up as Roman roads deteriorated, and money exchange gave way to barter in many places. Literacy lost ground as well. Germanic peoples, whom the Romans had viewed as barbarians—Goths, Visigoths, Franks, Lombards, Angles, Saxons—now emerged as the dominant peoples of Western Europe. In the process, Europe's center of gravity moved away from the Mediterranean toward the north and west.

Yet much that was classical or Roman persisted, even as a new order emerged in Europe. On the political front, a series of regional kingdoms—led by Visigoths in Spain, Franks in France, Lombards in Italy, and Angles and Saxons in England—arose to replace Roman authority. As these Germanic peoples migrated into or invaded Roman lands, many were deeply influenced by Roman culture, especially if they had served in the Roman army. On the funeral monument of one such person was a telling inscription: "I am a Frank by nationality, but a Roman soldier under arms."[7]

The prestige of things Roman remained high, even after the empire itself had collapsed. Now as leaders of their own kingdoms, the Germanic rulers actively embraced written Roman law, using fines and penalties to provide order and justice in place of feuds and vendettas. One Visigoth ruler named Athaulf (r. 410–415), who had married a Roman noblewoman, gave voice to the continuing attraction of Roman culture and its empire:

> At first I wanted to erase the Roman name and convert all Roman territory into a Gothic empire. . . . But long experience has taught me that . . . without law a state is not a state. Therefore I have more prudently chosen the different glory of reviving the Roman name with Gothic vigour, and I hope to be acknowledged by posterity as the initiator of a Roman restoration.[8]

Guided Reading Question

....

■ **CHANGE**
What replaced the Roman order in Western Europe?

Several of the larger, though relatively short-lived, Germanic kingdoms also had aspirations to re-create something of the unity of the Roman Empire. **Charlemagne** (SHAHR-leh-mane) (r. 768–814), ruler of the Carolingian Empire, occupying what is now France, Belgium, the Netherlands, and parts of Germany and Italy, erected an embryonic imperial bureaucracy, standardized weights and measures, and began to act like an imperial ruler. On Christmas Day of the year 800, he was crowned as a new Roman emperor by the pope, although his realm splintered shortly after his death (see Map 10.2). Later Otto I of Saxony (r. 936–973) gathered much of Germany under his control, saw himself as renewing Roman rule, and was likewise invested with the title of emperor by the pope. Otto's realm, later known as the **Holy Roman Empire**, was largely limited to Germany and soon proved little more than a collection of quarreling principalities. Though unsuccessful in reviving anything approaching Roman imperial authority, these efforts testify to the continuing appeal of the classical world, even as a new political system of rival kingdoms blended Roman and Germanic elements.

Map 10.2 Western Europe in the Ninth Century

Charlemagne's Carolingian Empire brought a temporary political unity to parts of Western Europe, but it was subsequently divided among his three sons, who then waged war on one another.

Society and the Church

Within these new kingdoms, a highly fragmented and decentralized society, widely known as **feudalism**, emerged with great local variation. In thousands of independent, self-sufficient, and largely isolated landed estates or manors, power—political, economic, and social—was exercised by a warrior elite of landowning lords. In the constant competition of these centuries, lesser lords and knights swore allegiance to greater lords or kings and thus became their vassals, frequently receiving lands and plunder in return for military service.

Such reciprocal ties between superior and subordinate were also apparent at the bottom of the social hierarchy, as Roman-style slavery gradually gave way to serfdom.

Unlike slaves, serfs were not the personal property of their masters, could not be arbitrarily thrown off their land, and were allowed to live in families. However, they were bound to their masters' estates as peasant laborers and owed various payments and services to the lord of the manor. One family on a manor near Paris in the ninth century owed four silver coins, wine, wood, three hens, and fifteen eggs per year. Women generally were required to weave cloth and make clothing for the lord, while men labored in the lord's fields. In return, the serf family received a small farm and such protection as the lord could provide. In a violent and insecure world adjusting to the absence of Roman authority, the only security available to many individuals or families lay in these communities, where the ties to kin, manor, and lord constituted the primary human loyalties. It was a world apart from the stability of life in imperial Rome or its continuation in Byzantium.

Also filling the vacuum left by the collapse of empire was the Church, later known as Roman Catholic, yet another link to the now-defunct Roman world. Its hierarchical organization of popes, bishops, priests, and monasteries was modeled on that of the Roman Empire and took over some of the empire's political, administrative, educational, and welfare functions. Latin continued as the language of the Church even as it gave way to various vernacular languages in common speech. In fact, literacy in the classical languages of Greek and Latin long remained the hallmark of educated people in the West.

Like the Buddhist establishment in China, the Church subsequently became quite wealthy, with reformers often accusing it of forgetting its central spiritual mission. It also provided a springboard for the conversion of Europe's many "pagan" peoples. Numerous missionaries, commissioned by the pope, monasteries, or already converted rulers, fanned out across Europe, generally pursuing a "top-down" strategy. Frequently it worked, as local kings and warlords found status and legitimacy in association with a literate and "civilized" religion that still bore something of the grandeur that was Rome. With "the wealth and protection of the powerful," ordinary people followed their rulers into the fold of the Church.[9] Christianity, like Buddhism in China, also bore the promise of superior supernatural powers, and its spread was frequently associated with reported miracles of healing, rainfall, fertility, and victory in battle.

But it was not an easy sell. Outright coercion was sometimes part of the process. More often, however, softer methods prevailed. The Church proved willing to accommodate a considerable range of earlier cultural practices, absorbing them into an emerging Christian tradition. For example, amulets and charms to ward off evil became medals with the image of Jesus or the Virgin Mary; traditionally sacred wells and springs became the sites of churches; and festivals honoring ancient gods became Christian holy days. December 25 was selected as the birthday of Jesus, for it was associated with the winter solstice, the coming of more light, and the birth or rebirth of various deities in pre-Christian European traditions. By 1100, most of Europe had embraced Christianity. Even so, for centuries priests and bishops had to warn their congregations against the worship of rivers, trees, and mountains, and for many people, ancient gods, monsters, trolls, and spirits still inhabited the land. The spreading Christian faith, like the new political framework of European civilization, was a blend of many elements. (For more on the rooting of Christianity in Western Europe, see Working with Evidence: The Remaking of Western Europe, page 438.)

Church authorities and the nobles/warriors who exercised political influence reinforced each other. Rulers provided protection for the papacy and strong encouragement for the faith. In return, the Church offered religious legitimacy for the powerful and the prosperous. "It is the will of the Creator," declared the teaching of the Church, "that the higher shall always rule over the lower. Each individual and class should stay in its place [and] perform its tasks."[10] But church and political authorities competed as well as cooperated, for they were rival centers of power in post-Roman Europe. Particularly controversial was the right to appoint bishops and the pope himself; this issue, known as the investiture conflict, was especially prominent in the eleventh and twelfth centuries. Was the right to make such appointments the responsibility of the Church alone, or did kings and emperors also have a role? In the compromise that ended the conflict, the Church won the right to appoint its own officials, while secular rulers retained an informal and symbolic role in the process.

Accelerating Change in the West

After various invaders—Huns, Magyars (Hungarians), and Vikings (see Map 10.3)—had been absorbed into settled society and in some cases had converted to Christianity, the pace of change in this emerging European civilization picked up considerably. In the several centuries after 1000, the greater security and stability that came with relative peace arguably opened the way to an accelerating tempo of change. The climate also seemed to cooperate. A generally warming trend after 750 reached its peak in the eleventh and twelfth centuries, enhancing agricultural production, especially in northern and highland regions.

During this new phase of European civilization, commonly called the High Middle Ages (1000–1300), the signs of expansion and growth were widely evident. The population of Europe grew from perhaps 35 million in 1000 to about 80 million in 1340. Many new lands were opened for cultivation in a process paralleling China's expansion to the south at the same time. Great lords, bishops, and religious orders organized new villages on what had recently been forest, marshes, or wasteland. Warmer weather during the summer months allowed farmers and pastoralists to herd their flocks into previously wild highland regions. Everywhere trees were felled at tremendous rates to clear agricultural land and to use as fuel or building material. By 1300, the forest cover of Europe had been reduced to about 20 percent of the land area. "I believe that the forest . . . covers the land to no purpose," declared a German abbot, "and hold this to be an unbearable harm."[11] These developments took a heavy toll on both the terrestrial and aquatic environments. Deforestation, overfishing, human waste, and the proliferation of new water mills and their associated ponds damaged freshwater ecosystems in many places. Lamenting the declining availability of fish, the French king Philip IV declared in 1289: "Today each and every river and waterside of our realm, large and small, yields nothing."[12]

Guided Reading Question

■ **CHANGE**
In what ways was European civilization changing after 1000?

Viking invasions
Muslim invasions
Magyar invasions
Muslim lands

0   200   400 miles
0   200   400 kilometers

MAPPING HISTORY

Map 10.3 Europe in the Middle Ages

By the eleventh century, the national monarchies that would organize European political life—France, Spain, England, Poland, and Germany—had begun to take shape. The earlier external attacks on Europe from Vikings, Magyars, and Muslims had largely ceased, although it was clear that European civilization was developing in the shadow of the Islamic world.

READING THE MAP: Trace the routes taken by the Vikings of Sweden to establish contact with the Byzantine Empire. What major waterways did they use?

MAKING CONNECTIONS: Comparing Maps 8.1 and 10.3, what differences do you notice between Chinese and European civilizations and their relationship with their neighbors?

A European Urban Market This image from a fourteenth-century Italian illuminated manuscript depicts a market scene in an urban setting. It illustrates two major elements of an emerging Western European civilization—urbanization and commercialization. (Biblioteca Nazionale, Turin, Italy/Mondadori Fortfolio/Electa/Paolo Manusardi/ Bridgeman Images)

The increased production associated with this agricultural expansion stimulated a considerable growth in long-distance trade, much of which had dried up in the aftermath of the Roman collapse. One center of commercial activity lay in Northern Europe from England to the Baltic coast. The other major trading network centered on northern Italian towns such as Florence, Genoa, and Venice. Their trading partners were the more established civilizations of Islam and Byzantium, and the primary objects of trade included silks, drugs, precious stones, and spices from Asia. At great trading fairs, particularly those in the Champagne area of France near Paris, merchants from Northern and Southern Europe met to exchange the products of their respective areas, such as northern woolens for Mediterranean spices. Thus the self-sufficient communities of earlier centuries increasingly forged commercial bonds among themselves and with more distant peoples.

The population of towns and cities likewise grew on the sites of older Roman towns, at trading crossroads and fortifications, and around cathedrals all over Europe. In the early 1300s, London had about 40,000 people, Paris had approximately 80,000, and Venice by the end of the fourteenth century could boast perhaps 150,000. To keep these figures in perspective, Constantinople housed some 400,000 people in 1000, Córdoba in Muslim Spain about 500,000, and the Song dynasty capital of Hangzhou more than 1 million in the thirteenth century. These towns gave rise

Cecilia Penifader, an English Peasant and Unmarried Woman

Born in 1297 in a small English village, Cecilia Penifader was an illiterate peasant woman who seldom if ever traveled more than twenty miles beyond her birthplace. She was of no particular historical importance outside of her family and community. Nonetheless, her life, reconstructed from court records by historian Judith Bennett, provides a window into the conditions of ordinary rural people as a new European civilization was taking shape.[13]

From birth to death, Cecilia lived in Brigstock, a royal manor owned by the king of England or a member of the royal family. Free tenants such as Cecilia owed rents and various dues to the lord of the manor. Thus Cecilia occupied a social position above the serfs, unfree people who owed labor service to the lord, but infinitely below the clergy and nobility, to whom the lower orders of society owed constant deference.

But within the class of "those who work"—the peasantry—Cecilia was fortunate. She was born the seventh of eight children, six of whom survived to adulthood,

A European peasant woman such as Cecilia Penifader.

an unusual occurrence at a time when roughly half of village children died. Her family had substantially larger landholdings than most of their neighbors and no doubt lived in a somewhat larger house. Still, it was probably a single-room dwelling measuring about thirty by fifteen feet, with a dirt floor, and surely it was smoky, for chimneys were not a part of peasant homes.

Between 1315 and 1322, as Cecilia entered early adulthood, England and much of the rest of Europe experienced an immense famine, caused by several years of especially cold and wet weather that marked the end of centuries of favorable climatic conditions. During those years, Cecilia first entered the court records of Brigstock. In 1316, another peasant lodged a complaint against Cecilia and her father for ignoring his boundary stones and taking hay from his fields. Such petty quarrels and minor crimes proliferated as neighborliness broke down in the face of bad harvests and desperate circumstances. Furthermore, both of Cecilia's parents died during the famine years.

to and attracted new groups of people, particularly merchants, bankers, artisans, and university-trained professionals such as lawyers, doctors, and scholars. Many of these groups, including university professors and students, organized themselves into guilds (associations of people pursuing the same line of work) to regulate their respective professions. Thus, from the rural social order of lord and peasant, a new more productive and complex division of labor was reshaping European society.

A further sign of accelerating change in the West lay in the growth of territorial states with more effective institutions of government commanding the loyalty, or at least the obedience, of their subjects. Since the disintegration of the Roman Empire, Europeans' loyalties had focused on the family, the manor, or the religious community, but seldom on the state. But in the eleventh through the thirteenth centuries, the nominal monarchs of Europe gradually and painfully began to consolidate their authority, and the outlines of French, English, Spanish, Scandinavian, and other states began to appear, each with its own distinct language and culture

Thus Cecilia was left a single woman in her early twenties, but the relative prosperity of her family allowed her to lead a rather independent life. In 1317, she acquired her first piece of land, probably with financial assistance from her father and her own earnings as a day laborer. In fact, Cecilia benefited from the famine because it forced desperate peasants to sell their land at reduced prices. As a result, Cecilia was able to accumulate additional land. By the time of her death in 1344, she was a fairly prosperous woman with a house and farmyard, seventy acres of pasture, and two acres of good farming land. She hired servants or day laborers to work her lands and depended considerably on her brothers, who lived nearby.

If class and family shaped Cecilia's life, so did gender. As a woman, she was unable to hold office in the manor; she was paid about one-third less than men when she worked as an unskilled day laborer; and she could not serve as an official ale-taster, responsible for the quality of the beverage, although women brewed the ale. Like all women, she suffered under a sexual double standard. Two of her brothers, one of whom was a priest, produced children out of wedlock, with no apparent damage to their reputations. But should Cecilia have done so, scandal would surely have ensued.

Unlike most women of her time, Cecilia never married. Did her intended perhaps die during the famine? Did she have a socially inappropriate lover? Did she have an intimate relationship with Robert Malin, a man to whom she left one-third of her estate? Or did she consider marriage a disadvantage? Married women and their property were legally under the control of their husbands, but as a free tenant and head of household, Cecilia bought and sold land on her own and participated as a full member in the deliberations of the local court, which regulated the legal affairs of the manor.

For a woman, the pros and cons of marriage depended very much on whom she married. As a medieval poem put it: "The good and bad happenstances that some women have had / Stands in the choice of a good husband or bad." So while Cecilia missed out on the social approval and support that marriage offered as well as the pleasures of intimacy and children, she also avoided the potential abuse and certain dependency that married life carried for women.

Cecilia's death in 1344 provoked sharp controversy within her family network over the familiar issues of inheritance, kinship, and land. She left her considerable property to the illegitimate son of her brother, to the daughter of her sister Agnes, and to the mysterious Robert Malin. Aggrieved parties, particularly her sister Christina and a nephew Martin, succeeded in having her will overturned.

QUESTION

In what ways did class, family, gender, and natural catastrophe shape Cecilia's life?

(see Map 10.3, page 420). Royal courts and fledgling bureaucracies were established, and groups of professional administrators appeared. In Italy, city-states flourished as urban areas grew wealthy and powerful, while the Germans remained divided among a large number of small principalities within the Holy Roman Empire.

These changes, which together represented the making of a new civilization, had implications for the lives of countless women and men. (See Zooming In: Cecilia Penifader, page 422.) Economic growth and urbanization initially offered European women substantial new opportunities. Women were active in a number of urban professions, such as weaving, brewing, milling grain, midwifery, small-scale retailing, laundering, spinning, and prostitution. In twelfth-century Paris, for example, a list of 100 occupations identified 86 as involving women workers, of which 6 were exclusively female. In England, women worked as silk weavers, hatmakers, tailors, brewers, and leather processors and were entitled to train female apprentices in some of these trades. However, much as economic and technological change in

China had eroded female silk production, by the fifteenth century artisan opportunities were declining for European women as well. Most women's guilds were gone, and women were restricted or banned from many others. Even brothels were run by men. In England, guild regulations now outlawed women's participation in manufacturing particular fabrics and forbade their being trained on new and larger weaving machines. Women might still spin thread, but the more lucrative and skilled task of weaving fell increasingly to men. Technological progress may have been one reason for this change. Water- and animal-powered grain mills replaced the hand-grinding previously undertaken by women, and larger looms making heavier cloth replaced the lighter looms that women had worked. Men increasingly took over these professions and trained their sons as apprentices, making it more difficult for women to remain active in these fields.

The Church had long offered some women an alternative to home, marriage, family, and rural life. As in Buddhist lands, substantial numbers of women, particularly from aristocratic families, were attracted to the secluded monastic life of poverty, chastity, and obedience within a convent, in part for the relative freedom from male control that it offered. Here was one of the few places where women might exercise authority as abbesses of their orders and obtain a measure of education. The twelfth-century abbess Hildegard of Bingen, for example, won wide acclaim for her writings on theology, medicine, botany, and music.

But by 1300, much of the independence that such abbesses and their nuns had enjoyed was curtailed and male control tightened, even as veneration of the Virgin Mary swept across Western Christendom. Restrictions on women hearing confessions, preaching, and chanting the Gospel were now more strictly enforced. The educational activities of monastic centers, where men and women could both participate, now gave way to the new universities, where only ordained men could study and teach. Furthermore, older ideas of women's intellectual inferiority, the impurity of menstruation, and their role as sexual temptresses were mobilized to explain why women could never be priests and must operate under male control.

Thus tightening male control of women took place in Europe as it did in Song dynasty China at about the same time. Accompanying this change was a new understanding of masculinity, at least in the growing towns and cities. No longer able to function as warriors protecting their women, men increasingly defined themselves as "providers"; a man's role was to brave the new marketplaces "to win wealth for himself and his children." In one popular tale, a woman praised her husband: "He was a good provider; he knew how to rake in the money and how to save it." By 1450, the English word "husband" had become a verb meaning "to keep" or "to save."[14]

Europe Outward Bound: The Crusading Tradition

Accompanying the growth of a new European civilization after 1000 were efforts to engage more actively with both near and more distant neighbors. This "medieval expansion" of Western Christendom took place as the Byzantine world was contracting under pressure from the West, from Arab invasion, and later from

Turkish conquest (see Map 10.1, page 410). The western half of Christendom was on the rise, while the eastern part was in decline. It was a sharp reversal of their earlier trajectories.

As Western Europe's population mounted, settlers cleared new land, much of it on the eastern fringes of Europe. The Vikings of Scandinavia, having raided much of Europe, set off on a maritime transatlantic venture around 1000 that briefly established a colony in Newfoundland in North America, and more durably in Greenland and Iceland. As Western economics grew, merchants, travelers, diplomats, and missionaries brought European society into more intensive contact with more distant peoples and with Eurasian commercial networks. By the thirteenth and fourteenth centuries, Europeans had direct, though limited, contact with India, China, and Mongolia. Europe clearly was outward bound.

The Crusades This fourteenth-century painting illustrates the Christian seizure of Jerusalem during the First Crusade in 1099. The crowned figure in the center is Godefroi de Bouillon, a French knight and nobleman who played a prominent role in the attack and was briefly known as the king of Jerusalem. (From "Le Roman de Godefroi de Bouillon" [vellum], 14th century/Bibliothèque Nationale de France, Paris, France/Bridgeman Images)

Nothing more dramatically revealed European expansiveness and the religious passions that informed it than the Crusades, a series of "holy wars" that captured the imagination of Western Christendom for several centuries, beginning in 1095. In European thinking and practice, the Crusades were wars undertaken at God's command and authorized by the pope as Christ's representative on earth. Crusaders were required to swear a vow and in return received an indulgence, which removed the penalties for any confessed sins, and were also granted various material benefits, such as immunity from lawsuits and a moratorium on the repayment of debts. Any number of political, economic, and social motives underlay the Crusades, but at their core they were religious wars. Within Europe, the amazing support for the Crusades reflected an understanding of them "as providing security against mortal enemies threatening the spiritual health of all Christendom and all Christians."[15] Crusading drew on both Christian piety and the warrior values of the elite, with little sense of contradiction between these impulses.

The most famous Crusades were those aimed at wresting Jerusalem and the holy places associated with the life of Jesus from Islamic control and returning them to Christendom (see Map 10.4). Beginning in 1095, wave after wave of Crusaders from all walks of life and many countries flocked to the eastern Mediterranean,

Guided Reading Question

■ **CHANGE**

What was the impact of the Crusades in world history?

MAPPING HISTORY

Map 10.4 The Crusades

Western Europe's crusading tradition reflected the expansive energy and religious impulses of an emerging civilization. It was directed against Muslims in the Middle East, Sicily, and Spain as well as the Eastern Orthodox Christians of the Byzantine Empire. The Crusades also involved attacks on Jewish communities, probably the first organized mass pogroms against Jews in Europe's history.

READING THE MAP: Which of the Crusades were directed against other Christian peoples and which against Muslim lands?

INTERPRETING THE MAP: From the information provided by this map, how would you describe the role of Constantinople in the four Crusades to the eastern Mediterranean?

where they temporarily carved out four small Christian states, the last of which was recaptured by Muslim forces in 1291. Led or supported by an assortment of kings, popes, bishops, monks, lords, nobles, and merchants, the Crusades demonstrated a growing European capacity for organization, finance, transportation, and recruitment, made all the more impressive by the absence of any centralized direction for the project. They also demonstrated considerable cruelty. The seizure of Jerusalem in 1099 was accompanied by the slaughter of many Muslims and Jews as the Crusaders made their way to the tomb of Christ through streets littered with corpses and ankle deep in blood, according to no doubt exaggerated reports.

Crusading was not limited to targets in the Islamic Middle East, however. Those Christians who waged war for centuries to reclaim the Iberian Peninsula from Muslim hands were likewise declared "crusaders," with a similar set of spiritual and material benefits. So too were Scandinavian and German warriors who took part in wars to conquer, settle, and convert lands along the Baltic Sea. The Byzantine Empire and Russia, both of which followed Eastern Orthodox Christianity, were also on the receiving end of Western crusading, as were Christian heretics, Jews, and various enemies of the pope in Europe itself. Crusading, in short, was a pervasive feature of European expansion, which persisted as Europeans began their oceanic voyages in the fifteenth century and beyond.

Surprisingly perhaps, the Crusades had little lasting impact, either politically or religiously, in the Middle East. European power was not sufficiently strong or long-lasting to induce much conversion, and the small European footholds there had come under Muslim control by 1300. The penetration of Turkic-speaking peoples from Central Asia and the devastating Mongol invasions of the thirteenth century were far more significant in Islamic history than were the temporary incursions of European Christians. In Europe, however, crusading in general and interaction with the Islamic world in particular had very significant long-term consequences. Spain, Sicily, and the Baltic region were brought permanently into the world of Western Christendom, while a declining Byzantium was further weakened by the Crusader sacking of Constantinople in 1204 and left even more vulnerable to Muslim Turkish conquest. In Europe itself, popes strengthened their position, at least for a time, in their continuing struggles with secular authorities. Tens of thousands of Europeans came into personal contact with the Islamic world, from which they picked up a taste for the many luxury goods available there, stimulating a demand for Asian goods. They also learned techniques for producing sugar on large plantations using slave labor, a process that had incalculable consequences in later centuries as Europeans transferred the plantation system to the Americas. Muslim scholarship, together with the Greek learning that it incorporated, also flowed into Europe, largely through Spain and Sicily.

If cross-cultural contacts born of crusading opened channels of trade, technology transfer, and intellectual exchange, they also hardened cultural barriers between peoples. The rift between Eastern Orthodoxy and Roman Catholicism deepened further and remains to this day a fundamental divide in the Christian world. Christian anti-Semitism was both expressed and exacerbated as Crusaders on their way to Jerusalem found time to massacre Jews, regarded as "Christ-killers," in a number of European cities, particularly in Germany. Such pogroms, however, were not sanctioned by the Church. A leading figure in the Second Crusade, Bernard of Clairvaux, declared, "It is good that you march against the Muslims, but anyone who touches a Jew to take his life, is as touching Jesus himself."[16] The Crusades also had other long-term influences. European empire building, especially in the Americas, continued the crusading notion that "God wills it." And more recently, over the past two centuries, as the world of the Christian West and that of Islam have collided, both sides have found many occasions

PRACTICING HISTORICAL THINKING

How did the historical development of the European West differ from that of Byzantium in the third-wave era?

for which images of the Crusades, however distorted, have proved politically popular or ideologically useful.

The West in Comparative Perspective

At one level, the making of Western civilization was unremarkable. Civilizations had
risen, fallen, renewed themselves, and evolved at many times and in many places. The
European case has received extraordinary scrutiny, not so much because of its special
significance at the time, but because of its later role as a globally dominant region.
However we might explain Europe's subsequent rise to prominence on the world stage,
its development in the several centuries after 1000 made only modest ripples beyond
its own region. Europe was surely distinctive, as are all civilizations, but it was not yet a
major player in the global arena. Comparisons, particularly with China and the Islamic
world, help to place these European developments in a world history context.

Catching Up

As the civilization of the West evolved, it was clearly less developed in comparison
to Byzantium, China, India, and the Islamic world. Europe's cities were smaller, its
political authorities weaker, its economy less commercialized, and its technology
inferior. Muslim observers who encountered Europeans saw them as barbarians. An
Arab geographer of the tenth century commented: "Their bodies are large, their
manners harsh, their understanding dull, and their tongues heavy. . . . Those of them
who are farthest to the north are the most subject to stupidity, grossness and brut-
ishness."[17] Muslim travelers over the next several centuries saw more to be praised
in West African kingdoms, where Islam was practiced and gold was plentiful.

Furthermore, thoughtful Europeans who directly encountered other peoples
often acknowledged their own comparative backwardness. "In our time," wrote a
twelfth-century European scholar, "it is in Toledo [a Spanish city long under Muslim
rule] that the teaching of the Arabs . . . is offered to the crowds. I hastened there to
listen to the teaching of the wisest philosophers of this world."[18] The Italian traveler
Marco Polo in the thirteenth century proclaimed Hangzhou in China "the finest
and noblest [city] in the world." In the early sixteenth century, Spanish invaders of
Mexico were stunned at the size and wealth of the Aztec capital, especially its huge
market, claiming that they "had never seen such a thing before."[19]

Curious about the rest of the world, Europeans proved quite willing to engage
with and borrow from the more advanced civilizations to the east. Growing European
economies, especially in the northwest, reconnected with the Eurasian trading system,
with which they had lost contact after the fall of Rome. Now European elites eagerly
sought spices, silks, porcelain, and sugar from afar even as they assimilated various technological, intellectual, and cultural innovations, as the Snapshot demonstrates. When
the road to China opened in the thirteenth and fourteenth centuries, many Europeans,
including the merchant-traveler Marco Polo, were more than willing to make the
long and difficult journey, returning with amazing tales of splendor and abundance far

**Guided Reading
Question**
....
■ **CHANGE**
In what ways did borrow-
ing from abroad shape
European civilization
after 1000?

SNAPSHOT   European Borrowing

Like people in other emerging civilizations of the third-wave era, Europeans borrowed extensively from their near and more distant counterparts. They adapted these imports, both technological and cultural, to their own circumstances and generated distinctive innovations as well.

Borrowing	Source	Significance
Horse collar	China / Central Asia via Tunisia	Enabled heavy plowing and contributed to European agricultural development
Stirrup	India/Afghanistan	Revolutionized warfare by enhancing cavalry forces
Gunpowder	China	Enhanced the destructiveness of warfare
Paper	China	Enabled bureaucracy; fostered literacy; prerequisite for printing
Spinning wheel	India	Sped up production of yarn, usually by women at home
Wheelbarrow	China	Laborsaving device for farm and construction work
Aristotle	Byzantium / Islamic Spain	Recovery of classical Greek thought
Medical knowledge/ treatments	Islamic world	Sedatives, antiseptics, surgical techniques, optics, and knowledge of contagious diseases enriched European medicine
Christian mysticism	Muslim Spain	Mutual influence of Sufi, Jewish, and Christian mysticism
Music/poetry	Muslim Spain	Contributed to tradition of troubadour poetry about chivalry and courtly love
Mathematics	India / Islamic world	Foundation for European algebra
Chess	India/Persia	A game of prestige associated with European nobility

beyond what was available in Europe. When Europeans took to the oceans in the fifteenth and sixteenth centuries, they were seeking out the sources of African and Asian wealth. Thus the accelerating growth of European civilization was accompanied by its reintegration into the larger Afro-Eurasian networks of exchange and communication.

In this willingness to borrow, Europe resembled several other third-wave civilizations of the time. Japan, for example, took much from China; West Africa drew heavily on Islamic civilization; and Russia actively imitated Byzantium. All of them were then developing civilizations, in a position analogous perhaps to the developing countries of recent times.

Technological borrowing required adaptation to the unique conditions of Europe and was accompanied by considerable independent invention as well. Together these processes generated a significant tradition of technological innovation that allowed Europe by 1500 to catch up with, and in some areas perhaps to surpass, China and the Islamic

European Technology Europeans' fascination with technology and their religious motivation for investigating the world are apparent in this thirteenth-century portrayal of God as a divine engineer, laying out the world with a huge compass. (Oesterreichische Nationalbibliothek, Vienna, Austria/Erich Lessing/Art Resource, NY)

world. That achievement bears comparison with the economic revolution of Song dynasty China (960–1279), although Europe began at a lower level and depended more on borrowing than did its Chinese counterpart. But in the several centuries surrounding 1000, at both ends of Eurasia, major processes of technological innovation were under way.

In Europe, technological breakthroughs first became apparent in agriculture as Europeans adapted to the very different environmental conditions north of the Alps in the several centuries following 500 C.E. They developed a heavy wheeled plow that could handle the dense soils of Northern Europe far better than the light, or "scratch," plow used in Mediterranean agriculture. To pull the plow, Europeans began to rely increasingly on horses rather than oxen and to use iron horseshoes and a more efficient collar, which probably originated in China or Central Asia and could support much heavier loads. In addition, Europeans developed a new three-field system of crop rotation, which allowed considerably more land to be planted at any one time. These were the technological foundations for a more productive agriculture that could support the growing population of European civilization, especially in its urban centers, far more securely than before.

Beyond agriculture, Europeans began to tap non-animal sources of energy in a major way, particularly after 1000. A new type of windmill, very different from an earlier Persian version, was widely used in Europe by the twelfth and thirteenth centuries. The water-driven mill was even more important. By the ninth century water mills were rapidly becoming more evident in Europe. In the early fourteenth century, a concentration of sixty-eight mills dotted a one-mile stretch of the Seine River near Paris. In addition to grinding grain, these mills provided power for sieving flour, tanning hides, making beer, sawing wood, manufacturing iron, and making paper. Devices such as cranks, flywheels, camshafts, and complex gearing mechanisms, when combined with water or wind power, enabled Europeans of the High Middle Ages to revolutionize production in a number of industries and to break with the ancient tradition of depending almost wholly on animal or human muscle as sources of energy. So intense was the interest of European artisans and engineers in tapping mechanical sources of energy that a number of them experimented with perpetual-motion machines, an idea borrowed from Indian philosophers.

Technological borrowing was also evident in the arts of war. Gunpowder was invented in China, but Europeans were probably the first to use it in cannons, in the early fourteenth century, and by 1500 they had the most advanced arsenals in the world. In 1517, one Chinese official, on first encountering European ships and weapons, remarked with surprise, "The westerns are extremely dangerous because of their artillery. No weapon ever made since memorable antiquity is superior to their cannon."[20] Advances in shipbuilding and navigational techniques—including the magnetic compass and sternpost rudder from China and adaptations of the Mediterranean or Arab lateen sail, which enabled vessels to sail against the wind—provided the foundation for European mastery of the seas.

Europe's passion for technology was reflected in its culture and ideas as well as in its machines. About 1260, the English scholar and Franciscan friar Roger Bacon wrote of the possibilities he foresaw, and in doing so, he expressed the confident spirit of the age:

> Machines of navigation can be constructed, without rowers . . . which are borne under the guidance of one man at a greater speed than if they were full of men. Also a chariot can be constructed, that will move with incalculable speed without any draught animal. . . . Also flying machines may be constructed so that a man may sit in the midst of the machine turning a certain instrument by means of which wings artificially constructed would beat the air after the manner of a bird flying . . . and there are countless other things that can be constructed.[21]

Pluralism in Politics

Unlike the large centralized states of Byzantium, the Islamic world, and China, this third-wave European civilization never regained the earlier unity it had under Roman rule. Rather, political life gradually crystallized into a system of competing states (France, Spain, England, Sweden, Prussia, the Netherlands, and Poland, among others) that has persisted into the twenty-first century and that the European Union still confronts. Geographic barriers, ethnic and linguistic diversity, and the shifting balances of power among its many states prevented the emergence of a single European empire, despite periodic efforts to re-create something resembling the still-remembered unity of the Roman Empire.

This multicentered political system shaped the emerging civilization of the West in many ways. It gave rise to frequent wars, enhanced the role and status of military men, and drove the "gunpowder revolution." Thus European society and values were militarized far more than in China, which gave greater prominence to scholars and bureaucrats. Intense interstate rivalry, combined with a willingness to borrow, also stimulated European technological development. By 1500, Europeans had gone a long way toward catching up with their more advanced Asian counterparts in agriculture, industry, war, and sailing.

The states within this emerging European civilization also differed from those to the east. Their rulers generally were weaker and had to contend with competing sources of power. Unlike the Orthodox Church in Byzantium, with its practice of caesaropapism, the **Roman Catholic Church** in the West maintained a degree

Guided Reading Question

■ **COMPARISON**
Why was Europe unable to achieve the kind of political unity that China experienced? What impact did this have on the subsequent history of Europe?

of independence from state authority that served to check the power of kings and lords. Moreover, European vassals had certain rights in return for loyalty to their lords and kings. By the thirteenth century, this meant that high-ranking nobles, acting through formal councils, had the right to advise their rulers and to approve new taxes.

This three-way struggle for power among kings, warrior aristocrats, and church leaders, all of them from the nobility, enabled urban-based merchants in Europe to achieve an unusual independence from political authority. Many cities where wealthy merchants exercised local power won the right to make and enforce their own laws and appoint their own officials. Some of them—Venice, Genoa, Pisa, and Milan, for example—became almost completely independent city-states. Elsewhere, kings granted charters that allowed cities to have their own courts, laws, and governments, while paying their own kind of taxes to the king instead of feudal dues. Powerful, independent cities were a distinctive feature of European life after 1100 or so. By contrast, Chinese cities, which were far larger than those of Europe, were simply part of the empire and enjoyed few special privileges. Although commerce was far more extensive in China than in the emerging European civilization, the powerful Chinese state favored the landowners over merchants, monopolized the salt and iron industries, and actively controlled and limited merchant activity far more than the new and weaker royal authorities of Europe were able to do.

The relative weakness of Europe's rulers allowed urban merchants more leeway and, according to some historians, opened the way to a more thorough development of capitalism in later centuries. It also led to the development of representative institutions or parliaments through which the views and interests of these contending forces could be expressed and accommodated. Intended to strengthen royal authority by consulting with major social groups, these embryonic parliaments did not represent the "people" or the "nation" but instead embodied the three great "estates of the realm"—the clergy (the first estate), the landowning nobility (the second estate), and urban merchants (the third estate).

Reason and Faith

A further feature of this emerging European civilization was a distinctive intellectual tension between the claims of human reason and those of faith. Christianity had developed in a world suffused with Greek rationalism. Some early Christian thinkers sought to maintain a clear separation between the new religion and the ideas of Plato and Aristotle. "What indeed has Athens to do with Jerusalem?" asked Tertullian (150–225 C.E.), an early church leader from North Africa. More common was the notion that Greek philosophy could serve as a "handmaiden" to faith, more fully disclosing the truths of Christianity. In the reduced circumstances of Western Europe after the collapse of the Roman Empire, however, the Church had little direct access to the writings of the Greeks, although some Latin translations and commentaries provided a continuing link to the world of classical thought.

But intellectual life in Europe changed dramatically in the several centuries after 1000, amid a rising population, a quickening commercial life, emerging towns and cities, and the Church's growing independence from royal or noble authorities. Moreover, the West was developing a legal system that provided a measure of independence for a variety of institutions—towns and cities, guilds, professional associations, and especially universities. An outgrowth of earlier cathedral schools, these European universities—in Paris, Bologna, Oxford, Cambridge, Salamanca—became "zones of intellectual autonomy" in which scholars could pursue their studies with some freedom from the dictates of religious or political authorities, although that freedom was never complete and was frequently contested.[22]

This was the setting in which a small group of literate churchmen began to emphasize, quite self-consciously, the ability of human reason to penetrate divine mysteries and to grasp the operation of the natural order. In the late eleventh century students in a monastic school in France asked their teacher, Anselm, to provide a proof for the existence of God based solely on reason, without using the Bible or other sources of divine revelation.

The new interest in rational thought was applied first and foremost to theology, the "queen of the sciences" to European thinkers. Logic, philosophy, and rationality would operate in service to Christ. Of course, some opposed this new emphasis on human reason. Bernard of Clairvaux, a twelfth-century French abbot, declared, "Faith believes. It does not dispute."[23] His contemporary and intellectual opponent, the French scholar William of Conches, lashed out: "You poor fools. God can make a cow out of a tree, but has he ever done so? Therefore show some reason why a thing is so or cease to hold that it is so."[24]

European intellectuals also applied their newly discovered confidence in human reason to law, medicine, and the world of nature, exploring optics, magnetism, astronomy, and alchemy. Slowly and never completely, the scientific study of nature, known as "natural philosophy," began to separate itself from theology. This mounting enthusiasm for rational inquiry stimulated European scholars to seek out original Greek texts, particularly those of Aristotle. They found them in the Greek-speaking world of Byzantium and in the Islamic world, where they had long ago been translated into Arabic. In the twelfth and thirteenth centuries, an explosion of translations from Greek and Arabic into Latin, many of them undertaken in Spain, gave European scholars direct access to the works of ancient Greeks and to the remarkable results of Arab scholarship in astronomy, optics, medicine, pharmacology, and more. One of these translators, Adelard of Bath (1080–1142), remarked that he had learned, "under the guidance of reason from Arabic teachers," not to trust established authority.[25]

It was the works of the prolific Aristotle, with his logical approach and "scientific temperament," that made the deepest impression. His writings became the basis for university education and largely dominated the thought of Western Europe in the five centuries after 1200. In the work of the thirteenth-century theologian Thomas Aquinas, Aristotle's ideas were thoroughly integrated into a logical and systematic

Guided Reading Question

■ **COMPARISON**
In what different ways did classical Greek philosophy and science have an impact in the West, in Byzantium, and in the Islamic world?

European University Life in the Middle Ages This fourteenth-century manuscript painting shows a classroom scene from the University of Bologna in Italy. Note the sleeping and disruptive students. Some things apparently never change. (bpk Bildagentur/Kupferstichkabinett, Staatliche Museen, Berlin, Germany/Photo: Joerg P. Anders/Art Resource, NY)

presentation of Christian doctrine. In this growing emphasis on human rationality, which some considered to be at least partially separate from divine revelation, lay one of the foundations of the later Scientific Revolution and the secularization of European intellectual life.

Surprisingly, nothing comparable occurred in the Byzantine Empire, where knowledge of the Greek language was widespread and access to Greek texts was easy. Although Byzantine scholars kept the classical tradition alive, their primary interest lay in the humanities (literature, philosophy, history) and theology rather than in the natural sciences or medicine. Furthermore, both state and church had serious reservations about Greek learning. In 529, the emperor Justinian closed Plato's Academy in Athens, claiming that it was an outpost of paganism. Its scholars dispersed into lands that soon became Islamic, carrying Greek learning into the Islamic world. Church authorities as well were suspicious of Greek thought, sometimes persecuting scholars who were too enamored with the ancients. Even those who did study the Greek writers did so in a conservative spirit, concerned with preserving and transmitting the classical heritage rather than with using it as a springboard for creating new knowledge. "The great men of the past," declared the fourteenth-century Byzantine scholar and statesman Theodore Metochites, "have said everything so perfectly that they have left nothing for us to say."[26]

In the Islamic world, Greek thought was embraced "with far more enthusiasm and creativity" than in Byzantium.[27] A massive translation project in the ninth and tenth centuries made Aristotle and many other Greek writers available in Arabic. That work contributed to a flowering of Arab scholarship, especially in the sciences and natural philosophy, between roughly 800 and 1200, but it also stimulated a debate about faith and reason among Muslim thinkers, many of whom greatly admired Greek philosophical, scientific, and medical texts. As in the Christian world, the issue was whether secular Greek thought was an aid or a threat to the faith. Western European church authorities after the thirteenth century had come to regard natural philosophy as a wholly legitimate enterprise and had thoroughly incorporated Aristotle into university education, but learned opinion in the Islamic world swung the other way. Though never completely disappearing from Islamic scholarship, the ideas of Plato and Aristotle receded after the thirteenth century in favor of teachings that drew more directly from the Quran or from mystical experience. Nor was natural philosophy a central concern of Islamic higher education, as it was in the West. The integration of political and religious life in the Islamic world, as in Byzantium, contrasted with their separation in the West, where there was more space for the independent pursuit of scientific subjects.

REFLECTIONS

Remembering and Forgetting: Continuity and Surprise in the Worlds of Christendom

Many of the characteristic features of Christendom that emerged during the era of third-wave civilizations have had a long life, extending well into the modern era. The crusading element of European expansion was prominent among the motives of Spanish and Portuguese explorers. Europe's grudging freedom for merchant activity and its eagerness to borrow foreign technology arguably contributed to the growth of capitalism and industrialization in later centuries. The endemic military conflicts of European states, unable to recover the unity of the Roman Empire, found terrible expression in the world wars of the twentieth century. The controversy about reason and faith resonates still, at least in the United States, in debates about the authority of the Bible in secular and scientific matters. The rift between Eastern Orthodoxy and Roman Catholicism remains one of the major divides in the Christian world. Modern universities and the separation of religious and political authority likewise have their origins in the European Middle Ages. Such a perspective, linking the past with what came later, represents one of the great contributions that the study of history makes to human understanding. We are limited and shaped by our histories.

Yet that very strength of historical study can be misleading, particularly if it suggests a kind of inevitability, in which the past determines the future. Knowing the outcome of the stories we tell can be a serious disadvantage, for it may rob the people we study of the freedom and uncertainty that they surely experienced. In 500 C.E., few people would have predicted that Europe would become the primary center of Christianity, while the African and Asian expressions of that faith withered away. As late as 1000, the startling reversal of roles between the Eastern and Western wings of Christendom that the next several centuries witnessed was hardly on the horizon. At that time, the many small, rural, unsophisticated, and endlessly quarreling warrior-based societies of Western Europe would hardly have borne comparison with the powerful Byzantine Empire and its magnificent capital of Constantinople. Even in 1500, when Europe had begun to catch up with China and the Islamic world in various ways, there was little to predict its remarkable transformation over the next several centuries and the dramatic change in the global balance of power that this transformation produced.

Usually students of history are asked to remember. But forgetting can also be an aid to historical understanding. To recapture the unexpectedness of the historical process and to allow ourselves to be surprised, it may be useful on occasion to forget—or at least set aside—what we know about what happened next and to see the world as contemporaries viewed it.

Second Thoughts

What's the Significance?

Big Picture Questions

1. What accounts for the different historical trajectories of the Byzantine and West European expressions of Christendom?

2. How did Byzantium and Western Europe interact with each other and with the larger world of the third-wave era?

3. In what respects was the civilization of the Latin West distinctive and unique, and in what ways was it broadly comparable to other third-wave civilizations?

4. **Looking Back:** How does the evolution of the Christian world in the third-wave era compare with that of Tang and Song dynasty China and of the Islamic world?

Next Steps: For Further Study

Bonnie S. Anderson and Judith P. Zinsser, *A History of Their Own* (2000). An overview of European women's history by two prominent scholars.

Edward Grant, *Science and Religion from Aristotle to Copernicus* (2004). Demonstrates the impact of Greek philosophy and science in Europe, with comparisons to Byzantium and the Islamic world.

Barbara A. Hanawalt, *The Middle Ages: An Illustrated History* (1999). A brief and beautifully illustrated introduction to the Middle Ages in European history.

Rowena Loverance, *Byzantium* (2004). A lavishly illustrated history of the Byzantine Empire, drawing on the rich collection of artifacts in the British Museum.

Diarmaid MacCulloch, *Christianity: The First Three Thousand Years* (2010). A recent and much-praised overview of the history of Christendom.

Christopher Tyerman, *Fighting for Christendom: Holy Wars and the Crusades* (2005). A very well-written, up-to-date history of the Crusades designed for nonspecialists.

"Byzantine Empire," http://www.history.com/topics/ancient-history/byzantine-empire. A History channel website that features a number of short, thoughtful videos about Byzantium.

"Middle Ages," http://www.learner.org/interactives/middleages/. An interactive website with text and images relating to life in Europe after the collapse of the Roman Empire.

The Remaking of Western Europe

Following the final collapse of the western part of the Roman Empire in the fifth century C.E., would-be kings and church leaders alike sought to maintain links with the older Greco-Roman-Christian traditions of classical Mediterranean civilization. In the absence of empire, however, new and far more decentralized societies emerged, led now by Germanic peoples and centered in Northern and Western Europe, considerably removed from the older centers of Rome and Athens. It was a hybrid civilization, combining Greco-Roman, Christian, and Germanic/Celtic elements, in a distinctive blending. The sources that follow illustrate how this blending created a new civilization at the western edge of Eurasia.

SOURCE 10.1 The Conversion of Clovis

Among the Germanic peoples of post-Roman Western Europe, none were of greater significance than the Franks, who occupied the region of present-day France (see Map 10.1, page 410). By the early sixth century, a loosely unified Frankish kingdom had emerged under the leadership of Clovis (r. 485–511), whose Merovingian dynasty ruled the area until 751. Clovis's conversion to Christianity, an important step in the mixing of German and Christian culture, was described about a century later by a well-known bishop and writer, Gregory of Tours (538–594).

■ What issues are evident in the religious discussions of Clovis and his wife, Clotilda?

■ Notice how Gregory modeled his picture of Clovis on that of Constantine, the famous Roman emperor whose conversion to Christianity in the fourth century gave official legitimacy and state support to the faith. What message did Gregory seek to convey in making this implied comparison?

GREGORY OF TOURS | *History of the Franks* | late 6th century

---

[Clovis] had a first-born son by queen Clotilda, and as his wife wished to consecrate him in baptism, she tried unceasingly to persuade her husband, saying: "The gods you worship are nothing, and they will be unable to help themselves or anyone else. For they are graven out of stone or wood or some metal. . . . They are endowed rather with the magic arts than with the power of the divine name. But he [God] ought rather to be worshipped who created by his word heaven and earth, the sea and all that is in them out of a state of nothingness . . . [and] by whose hand mankind was created. . . ."

But though the queen said this, the spirit of the king was by no means moved to belief, and he said: "It was at the command of our gods that all things were created and came forth, and it is plain that your God has no power and, what is more, he is proven not to belong to the family of the gods." Meantime the faithful queen made her son ready for baptism; [but], the boy, whom they named Ingomer, died after being baptized. . . . At this the king was violently angry, and reproached the queen harshly, saying: "If the boy had been dedicated in the name of my gods he would certainly have lived. . . ." To this the queen said: "I give thanks to the omnipotent God, creator of all, who has judged me not wholly unworthy, that he should deign to take to his kingdom one born from my womb . . . he will be fed by the vision of God. . . ."

The queen did not cease to urge him to recognize the true God and cease worshipping idols. But he could not be influenced in any way to this belief, until at last a war arose with the Alamanni [another Germanic people], in which he was driven by necessity to confess what before he had of his free will denied. It came about that as the two armies were fighting fiercely, there was much slaughter, and Clovis's army began to be in danger of destruction. He saw it and raised his eyes to heaven, and with remorse in his heart he burst into tears and cried: "Jesus Christ, whom Clotilda asserts to be the son of the living God . . . , if thou wilt grant me victory over these enemies . . . , I will believe in thee and be baptized. . . . I believe that they [my own gods] possess no power, since they do not help those who obey them. . . ." And when he said thus, the Alamanni turned their backs, and began to disperse in flight. And when they saw that their king was killed, they submitted to the dominion of Clovis, saying: "Let not the people perish further, we pray; we are yours now." And he stopped the fighting, and after encouraging his men, retired in peace and told the queen how he had had merit to win the victory by calling on the name of Christ. . . .

And so the king confessed all-powerful God in the Trinity, and was baptized in the name of the Father, Son and Holy Spirit, and was anointed with the holy ointment with the sign of the cross of Christ. And of his army more than 3,000 were baptized.

Source: Gregory Bishop of Tours, *History of the Franks*, translated by Ernest Brehaut (New York: Columbia University Press, 1916; copyright renewed 1944), bk. 2, selections from secs. 29, 30, 31.

■ ■ ■

SOURCE 10.2 Advice on Dealing with "Pagans"

In their dealings with the "pagan," or non-Christian, peoples and kings of Western Europe, church authorities such as missionaries, bishops, and the pope himself sometimes advocated compromise with existing cultural traditions rather than overt hostility to them. For example, Pope Gregory (r. 590–604) urged the bishop of England to adopt a strategy of accommodation with the prevailing religious practices of the Anglo-Saxon peoples of the island. Gregory's advice was included in a famous work about the early Christian history of England composed by a Benedictine monk known as the Venerable Bede and completed about 731.

■ What can we learn about the religious practices of the Anglo-Saxons from Bede's account?

■ In what specific ways did the pope urge toleration? Why did he advocate accommodation or compromise with existing religious practices? Keep in mind that the political authorities in England at the time had not yet become thoroughly Christian.

■ How might such an approach to conversion contribute to the emerging hybrid civilization in Western Europe?

POPE GREGORY | *Advice to the English Church* | 601

The temples of the idols in that nation [England] ought not to be destroyed; but let the idols that are in them be destroyed; let holy water be made and sprinkled in the said temples, let altars be erected, and relics placed. For if those temples are well built, it is requisite that they be converted from the worship of devils to the service of the true God; that the nation, seeing that their temples are not destroyed, may remove error from their hearts, and knowing and adoring the true God, may the more familiarly resort to the places to which they have been accustomed.

And because they have been used to slaughter many oxen in the sacrifices to devils, some solemnity must be exchanged for them on this account, as that on the day of the dedication, or the nativities of the holy martyrs, whose relics are there deposited, they may build themselves huts of the boughs of trees, about those churches which have been turned to that use from temples, and celebrate the solemnity with religious feasting, and no more offer beasts to the Devil, but kill cattle to the praise of God in their eating, and return thanks to the Giver of all things for their sustenance; to the end that, while some gratifications are outwardly permitted them, they may the more easily consent to the inward consolations of the grace of God. For there is no doubt that it is impossible to efface everything at once from their obdurate minds; because he who endeavors to ascend to the highest place, rises by degrees or steps, and not by leaps.

Source: The Venerable Bede, *The Ecclesiastical History of the English Nation*, edited by Ernest Rhys (London: J. M. Dent and Sons; New York: E. P. Dutton, 1910), 52–53.

■ ■ ■

SOURCE 10.3 Pagan Art and Christian Texts ▶

The mixing of Christian and pre-Christian cultural traditions during the conversion of Europe spawned remarkable hybrid works of art. Source 10.3 provides one example of the use of long-established Celtic and Anglo-Saxon artistic styles to decorate a copy of the Christian gospels in Latin. While most illuminated manuscripts were created by teams of artists and scribes, this one was the work of a single man named Eadfrith, Bishop of Lindisfarne. Over several decades between 698 and 721, he produced this manuscript at a monastery on remote Holy Island off the coast of northern England. Nowhere are Eadfrith's artistic skills more apparent than on the "incipit" pages, those containing the opening words of each gospel. Note the repeating designs, made up of elaborate patterns, swirls, birds, and animals, long used in Celtic and Germanic artistic expression.

- What reaction to the Christian scriptures might Eadfrith hope to engender through this book?

- In what ways does the Lindisfarne gospel reflect the new hybrid civilization that emerged in Western Europe after the fall of Rome?

- Monks viewed the copying of holy works as acts of faith and piety. With this in mind, why might Eadfrith have so elaborately decorated his manuscript?

■ Compare this image to the Anglo-Saxon purse hinge from the pre-Christian Sutton Hoo burial site in southern England shown in the "Anglo-Saxon Treasure" photo in Chapter 3. What similarities can you identify between these two pieces of art?

Lindisfarne Gospel | **698–721**

■ ■ ■

SOURCE 10.4 **Germanic Law**

As Germanic tribes conquered and then settled in regions of the former Roman Empire, they faced the practical challenge of ruling over kingdoms that incorporated both their followers and Romans. King Gundobad (r. 473–516), whose Germanic tribe, known as the Burgundians, had established a kingdom in what is now central France, sought to address this problem by creating two law codes—one for his own people based on their unwritten laws grounded in ancient customs, and a second for his conquered peoples or "Romans" based on Roman law. Germanic law prevailed in cases between "barbarians" and "Romans." While Gundobad's law code for his Germanic subjects sought to preserve Burgundian culture, the recording of customary law also represented a major shift because it embraced the Roman idea of written codified law and the role of rulers as lawmakers and judges. The selections that follow are drawn from Gundobad's law code for his Germanic subjects and give a sense of the values and organization of Burgundian society during this transitional period.

■   What does this law code tell us about the customs of the Germanic peoples who settled in Western Europe?

■   What social classes can you identify in Burgundian society?

■   How would you describe the status of women in Burgundian society?

■   To what extent is Gundobad the creator or enforcer of the law? To what extent is he constrained by the traditions and customs of his people? Why might Gundobad have opted for a written law code rather than maintaining unwritten traditions?

Burgundian Code | ca. 474 C.E.

II. Of Murders

1. If anyone presumes with boldness or rashness bent on injury to kill a native freeman of people of any nation or a servant of the king, in any case a man of barbarian tribe, let him make restitution for the committed crime not otherwise than by the shedding of his own blood.

2. [I]f violence shall have been done by anyone to any person so that he is injured by blows of lashes or by wounds and if he pursues his persecutor and overcome by grief and indignation kills him, proof of the deed shall be afforded by the act itself or by suitable witnesses who can be believed. Then the guilty party shall be compelled to pay to the relatives of the person killed half his wergeld [an amount paid as compensation to the family of someone who is slain based on that person's social rank] . . .

3. If a slave unknown to his master presumes to kill a native freeman, let the slave be handed over to death, and let the master not be made liable for damages.

4. If the master knows of the deed, let both be handed over for death.

VIII. Crimes Charged Against Freemen

1. If a native freeman either barbarian or Roman, is accused of a crime through suspicion let him render oath, and let him swear with his wife and sons and twelve relatives; if indeed he does not have wife and sons and he has mother or father, let him complete the designated number with father and mother. But if he has neither father nor mother, let him complete the oath with twelve relatives.

XXXIV. Of Divorces

1. If any woman leaves (puts aside) her husband to whom she is legally married, let her be smothered in mire.

2. If anyone wishes to put away his wife without cause, let him give her another payment such as he gave for her marriage price, and let the amount of the fine be 12 solidi [a form of currency].

3. If by chance a man wishes to put away his wife, and is able to prove one of these three crimes against her, that of adultery, witchcraft, or violation of graves, let him have full rights to put her away; and let the judge pronounce the sentence of law against her, just as should be done against criminals.

4. But if she admits to none of these three crimes, let no man be permitted to put away his wife for any other crime. But if he chooses, he may go away from the home, leaving all household property behind, and his wife with their children may possess the property of her husband.

XLV. [Of Trial by Combat]

We know that many of our people are corrupted through inability to establish a case and because of instinct of greed, so that they do not hesitate frequently to offer oaths about uncertain matters and likewise to perjure themselves about known matters. To break up this criminal practice, we decree by the present law that . . . [if the parties cannot agree] let the right of combat not be refused; . . . God being the judge.

Source: *The Burgundian Code*, translated by Katherine Fischer, in *Translations and Reprints from the Original Sources of History* (Philadelphia: University of Pennsylvania Press, 1949), 5:23, 29, 45–46, 52.

■ ■ ■

SOURCE 10.5 **Charlemagne's Palace Chapel** ▶

During the late eighth and early ninth centuries C.E., Charlemagne (r. 768–814) turned his powerful Frankish kingdom into a Christian empire that briefly incorporated much of continental Western Europe. Crowned Holy Roman Emperor on Christmas day 800 C.E. by Pope Leo III, Charlemagne was seemingly on the brink of reuniting the western portion of the Roman Empire under his rule. Instead, his empire quickly fragmented after his death. Nonetheless, during its height his empire was perhaps the fullest expression of the new hybrid Western European culture to that time.

Nowhere did Charlemagne display his understanding of his imperial status more clearly than in the chapel at his palace at Aachen. Several elements of the building were designed to evoke the majesty of previous Roman emperors, and particularly the first Christian emperor Constantine. The chapel was decorated with imported marble shipped in from Rome and elsewhere and was designed to echo two important Roman imperial churches—the Holy Sepulcher in Jerusalem and San Vitale in Ravenna. Moreover, Aachen itself was a former Roman site. Beyond these links to imperial Rome, Charlemagne also intended for the chapel to represent heavenly Jerusalem. Its octagonal design decorated in expensive marbles "heightened the celestial atmosphere," as did a fresco on the domed ceiling depicting the twenty-four elders adoring the throne of God, mentioned in the Bible's Book of Revelation (4:1–4). While most visitors hailed from the elite strata of society, even the most powerful nobles and churchmen of Charlemagne's realm were normally restricted to the lower floor, where religious ceremonies took place. Charlemagne observed proceedings from his throne on the second floor overlooking the main altar—visible in the center of Source 10.5. Positioned between Heaven and Earth in this holy setting, Charlemagne reminded all visitors of his unique status in society as God's anointed ruler on Earth. In the centuries that followed, Charlemagne's burial in the chapel and later coronations of Holy Roman Emperors in this space ensured that it became one of the most influential buildings in Western Europe.

■ What specific elements of the chapel's structure and decoration might have evoked holy or otherworldly feelings in the viewer?

■ What does the placement of Charlemagne's throne tell us about how he viewed his power and authority as emperor? Why do you think his throne is set back from the balcony edge? What might Charlemagne seek to convey from such a position?

■ How might Charlemagne describe his chapel to a visitor?

Aachen Palace Chapel | completed 805 C.E.

DOING HISTORY

1. **Describing cultural encounters:** What elements of cultural mixing do these sources highlight? What specific elements of ancient Roman, Christian, and Germanic/Celtic culture can you identify in each source?

2. **Thinking about legitimacy:** What strategies did Clovis, Gundobad, and Charlemagne use to bolster their legitimacy? How do their actions reflect or react to the evolving societies over which they ruled?

3. **Noticing point of view and assessing credibility:** From what point of view is each of the written sources created? Which elements of each source might historians find unreliable, and which would they find most useful?

The Legacy of Rome

The legacy of Rome in the hybrid Western European society that emerged from the fifth century has been the subject of much scholarly debate over the past thirty years. These two voices consider questions of survival and revival of the Roman past in the fifth to ninth centuries. In Voice 10.1, Wim Blockmans and Peter Hoppenbrouwers, both professors of medieval history at the University of Leiden, assess whether Roman civilization in Western Europe disappeared with the collapse of the empire. In Voice 10.2, Barry Cunliffe, a leading archeologist, looks at the controversy surrounding Charlemagne's effort to revive the title of "Roman Emperor."

■ What major shifts in society do Blockmans and Hoppenbrouwers identify with the fall of the Roman Empire?

■ What can Cunliffe's description of the dispute over Charlemagne's crowning as emperor tell us about the importance of the title "Roman Emperor" centuries after Rome's collapse in the West?

■ **Integrating Primary and Secondary Sources:** How do these voices help you to better understand the primary sources in this feature?

VOICE 10.1

Blockmans and Hoppenbrouwers on the End of Roman Civilization | 2014

Did the fall of the Roman Empire in the West also mark the end of Roman civilization in the West? One is easily inclined to think it did because archaeology does not lie. What could better illustrate the end of a civilization than the astounding impoverishment of its material culture? Nothing crafted in the sixth and seventh centuries could equal the superb urban planning and construction of roads, harbours, aqueducts and drains of the Roman age, nothing compares to the magnificent public and private building of that time, to their refined house design, their decorations, their utensils, their tableware. . . .

Yet, there are three asides to be made here. The first is that this impoverishment of material culture cannot have been caused by barbarian invasions alone. . . . [T]here were other factors at stake. We have already pointed out two: the disappearance of classical city councils, responsible for public infrastructure and building, and the penetration of world-averse Christian ethics. . . .

The second aside is prompted by the consideration that loss of luxury and monumentality does not say all about average human well-being on a more elementary level. It was not all roses in the Roman world, and indeed proportionally more people may have been better fed in the early Middle Ages than they had during the later Roman Empire. And thirdly, neither did the demise of conveniences and comfort imply the death of Roman civilization in terms of ideals and ideas. On the contrary, in a sense, Rome's appeal proved to be eternal. Throughout the Middle Ages, and long after, Roman ideas on government and law, on science and literature continued to exert a compelling force on the imagination and activities of the upper strata of society in Western Europe.

Source: Wim Blockmans and Peter Hoppenbrouwers, *Introduction to Medieval Europe 300–1500,* 2nd ed. (London: Routledge, 2014), 40.

VOICE 10.2

Cunliffe on Charlemagne | 2008

On Christmas Day AD 800 in Rome, Charlemagne, king of the Franks and Lombards, was crowned *imperator et augustus* [a title given to Roman emperors] by Pope Leo III. It was an act of great symbolism designed to legitimize Charlemagne's claim to be the natural heir of old Rome—of the Latin-speaking, Christian West—an act not without its political dangers since it was done without the approval of the Byzantine emperor, who might have been expected to have views on the matter. The Byzantine rulers regarded themselves as the legitimate emperors of the Roman Empire and now the Frankish usurper was challenging their authority. It took twelve years of confrontation and bargaining before a compromise could be reached. Charlemagne was recognized as "emperor" by Constantinople but not as *Roman* emperor. Henceforth it was publicly accepted that there were two empires which could work together against common enemies, but only one—Byzantium—was "Roman."

Source: Barry Cunliffe, *Europe between the Oceans, 9000 BC–AD 1000* (New Haven, CT: Yale University Press, 2008), 445.

Moghul court painting, ca.1596/Pictures from History/Bridgeman Images

Pastoral Peoples on the Global Stage

The Mongol Moment

1200–1450

In late 2012, the Central Asian nation of Mongolia celebrated a "Day of Mongolian Pride," marking the birth of the country's epic hero Chinggis Khan 850 years earlier. Officials laid wreaths at a giant monument to the warrior leader; wrestlers and archers tested their skills in competition; dancers performed; over 100 scholars made presentations; traditional costumes abounded. For this small and somewhat remote country, seeking to navigate between its two giant neighbors, China and Russia, it was an occasion to express its own distinctive identity. And Chinggis Khan is central to that identity.

The 2012 celebrations marked a shift in Mongolian thinking about Chinggis Khan that has been under way since the 1990s. Under the country's earlier Soviet-backed communist government, the great Mongol leader had been regarded in very negative terms. After all, his forces had decimated Russia in the thirteenth century, and resentment lingered. But as communism faded in both Russia and Mongolia at the end of the twentieth century, the memory of Chinggis Khan made a remarkable comeback in the land of his birth. "He is like a god to us," said Bat-Erdene Batbayar, a Mongolian historian and political figure. "He is the founder of our state, the root of our history. The communists very brutally cut us off from our traditions and history. . . . Now we are becoming Mongols again."[1]

Increasingly, his bloody conquests were played down, and he was celebrated as a unifier of the Mongolian peoples, the creator of an empire tolerant of various faiths, and a promoter of economic and cultural ties among distant peoples. Vodka, cigarettes, a chocolate bar, two brands of beer, the country's most prominent rock band, and the central square of the capital city all bore his name, while his picture appeared on Mongolia's stamps and money. Rural young

« **Chinggis Khan and His Family** This late sixteenth-century Indian painting shows Chinggis Khan, the founder of the Mongol Empire, seated next to his primary wife, Borte Ujin, with his four sons seated to his left. At his death each of these sons inherited a portion of his vast empire, while his five daughters were strategically married to politically prominent men.

449

people on horseback sang songs in his honor, and their counterparts in urban Internet cafés constructed websites to celebrate his achievements. ■

All of this is a reminder of the enormous and surprising role that the Mongols played in the Eurasian world of the thirteenth and fourteenth centuries and of the continuing echoes of that long-vanished empire. More generally, the story of the Mongols serves as a useful corrective to the almost-exclusive focus that historians often devote to agricultural peoples and their civilizations, for the Mongols, and many other such peoples, were pastoralists who disdained farming while centering their economic lives around their herds of animals. Normally they did not construct elaborate cities, enduring empires, or monumental works of art, architecture, and written literature. Nonetheless, they left an indelible mark on the historical development of the entire Afro-Eurasian hemisphere, and particularly on the agricultural civilizations with which they so often interacted.

SEEKING THE MAIN POINT

What has been the role in world history of pastoral peoples in general and the Mongols in particular?

The Long History of Pastoral Peoples

On the arid margins of agricultural lands, where productive farming was difficult or impossible, an alternative kind of food-producing economy emerged around 4000 B.C.E., focused on the raising of livestock. Horses, camels, goats, sheep, cattle, yaks, and reindeer were the primary animals that separately, or in some combination, enabled the construction of herding or **pastoral societies**. Such societies took shape in the vast grasslands of inner Eurasia and sub-Saharan Africa, in the Arabian and Saharan deserts, in the subarctic regions of the Northern Hemisphere, and in the high plateau of Tibet. (See Snapshot: Varieties of Pastoral Societies, page 452.)

The World of Pastoral Societies

Guided Reading Question
····························
■ **COMPARISON**
In what ways did pastoral societies differ from their agricultural counterparts?

Despite their many differences, pastoral societies shared several important features that distinguished them from settled agricultural communities and civilizations. Their generally less productive economies and their need for large grazing areas meant that they supported far smaller populations than did agricultural societies. People generally lived in small and widely scattered encampments or seasonal settlements made up of related kinfolk rather than in the villages, towns, and cities characteristic of agrarian civilizations. Beyond the family unit, pastoral peoples organized themselves in kinship-based groups or clans that claimed a common ancestry, usually through the male line. Related clans might on occasion come together as a tribe, which could also absorb unrelated people into the community. Although their values stressed equality and individual achievement, in some pastoral societies clans were ranked as noble or commoner, and considerable differences

Landmarks for Chapter 11

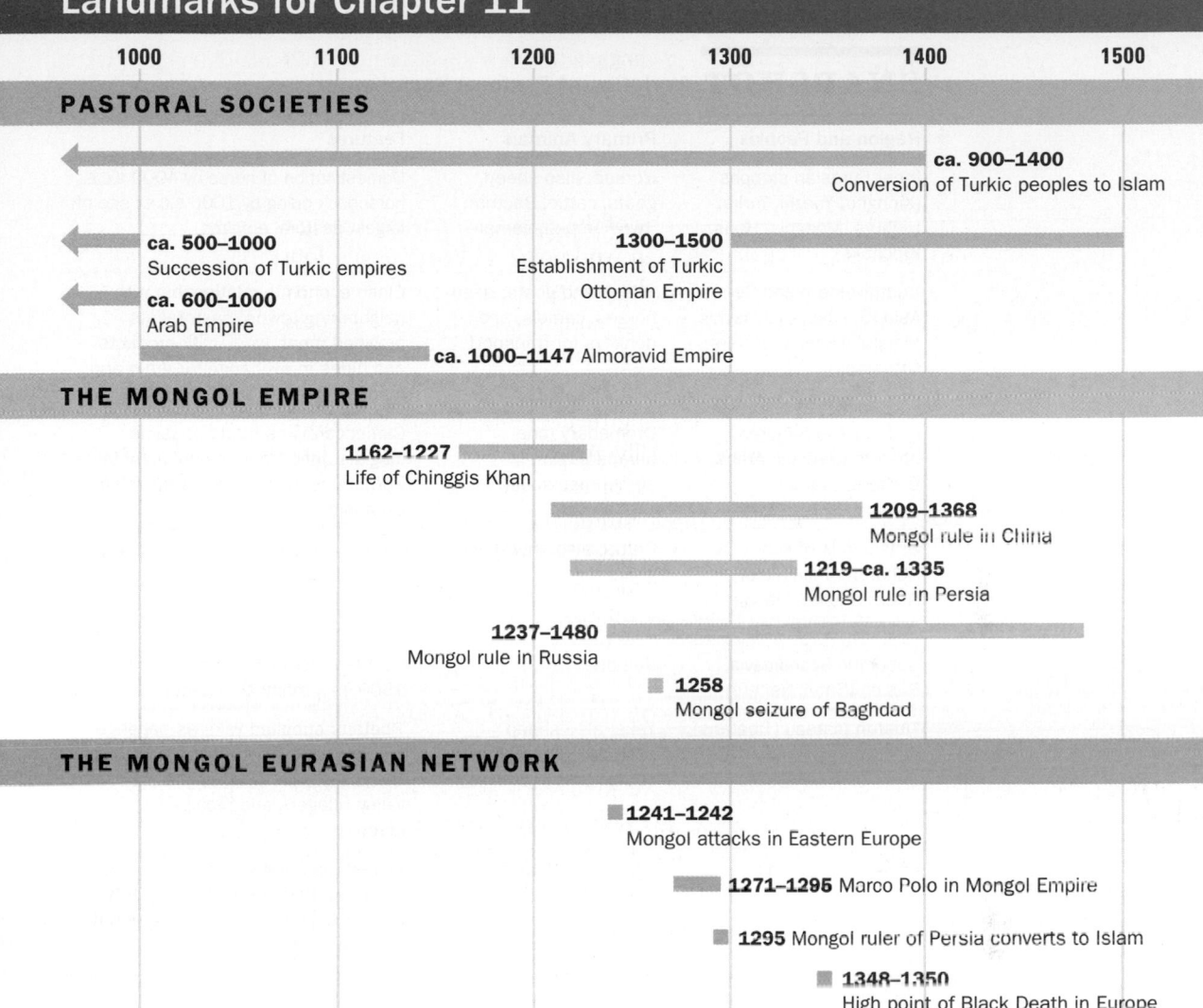

1000   1100   1200   1300   1400   1500

PASTORAL SOCIETIES

ca. 900–1400
Conversion of Turkic peoples to Islam

ca. 500–1000
Succession of Turkic empires

1300–1500
Establishment of Turkic
Ottoman Empire

ca. 600–1000
Arab Empire

ca. 1000–1147 Almoravid Empire

THE MONGOL EMPIRE

1162–1227
Life of Chinggis Khan

1209–1368
Mongol rule in China

1219–ca. 1335
Mongol rule in Persia

1237–1480
Mongol rule in Russia

1258
Mongol seizure of Baghdad

THE MONGOL EURASIAN NETWORK

1241–1242
Mongol attacks in Eastern Europe

1271–1295 Marco Polo in Mongol Empire

1295 Mongol ruler of Persia converts to Islam

1348–1350
High point of Black Death in Europe

emerged between wealthy aristocrats owning large flocks of animals and poor herders. Many pastoral societies held slaves as well.

Furthermore, pastoral peoples generally offered women a higher status, fewer restrictions, and a greater role in public life than their counterparts in agricultural civilizations. Everywhere pastoral women were involved in productive labor as well as having domestic responsibility for food and children. The care of smaller animals such as sheep and goats usually fell to women, although only rarely did women own or control their own livestock. Among the Mongols, the remarriage of a widow, often to a male relative of her husband, carried none of the negative connotations that it did among the Chinese, and women could initiate divorce. Mongol women frequently served as political advisers and were active in military

SNAPSHOT   Varieties of Pastoral Societies

Region and Peoples	Primary Animals	Features
Inner Eurasian steppes (Xiongnu, Yuezhi, Turks, Uighurs, Mongols, Huns, Kipchaks)	Horses; also sheep, goats, cattle, Bactrian (two-humped) camel	Domestication of horse by 4000 B.C.E.; horseback riding by 1000 B.C.E.; site of largest pastoral empires
Southwestern and Central Asia (Seljuks, Ghaznavids, Mongol il-khans, Uzbeks, Ottomans)	Sheep and goats; used horses, camels, and donkeys for transport	Close economic relationship with neighboring towns; pastoralists provided meat, wool, milk products, and hides in exchange for grain and manufactured goods
Arabian and Saharan deserts (Bedouin Arabs, Berbers, Tuareg)	Dromedary (one-humped) camel; sometimes sheep	Camel caravans made possible long-distance trade; camel-mounted warriors central to early Arab/Islamic expansion
Grasslands of sub-Saharan Africa (Fulbe, Nuer, Turkana, Masai)	Cattle; also sheep and goats	Cattle were a chief form of wealth and central to ritual life; little interaction with wider world until nineteenth century
Subarctic Scandinavia, Russia (Sami, Nenets)	Reindeer	Reindeer domesticated only since 1500 C.E.; many also fished
Tibetan plateau (Tibetans)	Yaks; also sheep, cashmere goats, some cattle	Tibetans supplied yaks as baggage animals for overland caravan trade; exchanged wool, skins, and milk with valley villagers and received barley in return
Andean Mountains	Llamas and alpacas	Andean pastoralists in a few places relied on their herds for a majority of their subsistence, supplemented with horticulture and hunting

All data derived from Thomas J. Barfield, "Pastoral Nomadic Societies," in *Berkshire Encyclopedia of World History* (Great Barrington, MA: Berkshire, 2005), 4:1432–37.

affairs as well. A thirteenth-century European visitor, the Franciscan friar Giovanni DiPlano Carpini, recorded his impressions of Mongol women:

> Girls and women ride and gallop as skillfully as men. We even saw them carrying quivers and bows, and the women can ride horses for as long as the men; they have shorter stirrups, handle horses very well, and mind all the property. . . . They all wear trousers, and some of them shoot just like men.[2]

Certainly, literate observers from adjacent civilizations noticed and clearly disapproved of the freedom granted to pastoral women. Ancient Greek writers thought that the pastoralists with whom they were familiar were "women governed." To Han Kuan, a Chinese Confucian scholar in the first century B.C.E., China's northern pastoral neighbors "[made] no distinction between men and women."[3]

The most characteristic feature of pastoral societies was their mobility, as local environmental conditions largely dictated their patterns of movement. In some favorable regions, pastoralists maintained seasonal settlements, migrating, for instance, between highland pastures in the summer and less harsh lowland environments in the winter. Others lived more nomadic lives, moving their herds frequently in regular patterns to systematically follow the seasonal changes in vegetation and water supply. But even the most nomadic pastoralists were not homeless; they took their homes, often elaborate felt tents, with them. Whatever their patterns of movement, pastoralists shared a life based on turning grass, which people cannot eat, into usable food and energy through their animals.

Although pastoralists represented an alternative to the agricultural way of life that they disdained, they were almost always deeply connected to, and often dependent on, their farming neighbors. Few of these peoples could live solely from the products of their animals, and most of them actively sought access to the foodstuffs, manufactured goods, and luxury items available from nearby farming communities. Particularly among the pastoral peoples of inner Eurasia, this desire for the fruits of civilization periodically stimulated the creation of tribal confederations or states that could more effectively deal with the powerful agricultural societies on their borders.

Constructing a large state among pastoralists was no easy task. Such societies generally lacked the surplus wealth needed to pay for the professional armies and bureaucracies that everywhere sustained the states and empires of agricultural civilizations. And the fierce independence of widely dispersed pastoral clans and tribes as well as their internal rivalries made any enduring political unity difficult to achieve. Nonetheless, charismatic leaders, such as Chinggis Khan, were periodically able

Guided Reading Question

■ **CONNECTION**

In what ways did pastoral societies interact with their agricultural neighbors?

The Scythians An ancient horse-riding pastoral people during the second-wave era, the Scythians occupied a region in present-day Kazakhstan and southern Russia. Their pastoral way of life is apparent in this detail from an exquisite gold necklace from the fourth century B.C.E. (Historical Museum, Kiev, Ukraine/photo © Boltin Picture Library/Bridgeman Images)

to weld together a series of tribal alliances that for a time became powerful states. Despite their limited populations, such states had certain military advantages in confronting larger and more densely populated civilizations. They could draw on the horseback-riding and hunting skills of virtually the entire male population and some women as well. But what sustained these states was their ability to extract wealth, through raiding, trading, or extortion, from agricultural civilizations such as China, Persia, and Byzantium. Pastoralists interacted with their agricultural neighbors not only economically and militarily but also culturally, as they "became acquainted with and tried on for size all the world and universal religions."[4] At one time or another, Judaism, Buddhism, Islam, and several forms of Christianity all found a home somewhere among the pastoral peoples of inner Eurasia. So did Manichaeism, a religious tradition born in third-century Persia and combining elements of Zoroastrian, Christian, and Buddhist practice. Usually conversion was a top-down process as pastoral elites and rulers adopted a foreign religion for political purposes, sometimes changing religious allegiance as circumstances altered. Pastoral peoples, in short, did not inhabit a world totally apart from their agricultural and civilized neighbors.

As the pastoral peoples of the Inner Asian steppes learned the art of horseback riding, by roughly 1000 B.C.E., their societies changed dramatically. Now they could accumulate and tend larger herds of horses, sheep, and goats and move more rapidly over a much wider territory. New technologies, invented or adapted by pastoral societies, added to the mastery of their environment and spread widely across the Eurasian steppes, creating something of a common culture in this vast region. These innovations included complex horse harnesses, saddles with iron stirrups, a small compound bow that could be fired from horseback, various forms of armor, and new kinds of swords. Agricultural peoples were amazed at the centrality of the horse in pastoral life. As a Roman historian noted about the Huns, "From their horses, by day and night every one of that nation buys and sells, eats and drinks, and bowed over the narrow neck of the animal relaxes in a sleep so deep as to be accompanied by many dreams."[5]

Before the Mongols: Pastoralists in History

What enabled pastoral peoples to make their most visible entry onto the stage of world history was the military potential of horseback riding, and of camel riding somewhat later. Their mastery of mounted warfare made possible a long but intermittent series of pastoral empires across the steppes of inner Eurasia and parts of Africa. For 2,000 years, those states played a major role in Afro-Eurasian history and represented a standing challenge to and influence upon the agrarian civilizations on their borders.

One early large-scale pastoral empire was associated with the people known as the Xiongnu, who lived in the Mongolian steppes north of China. Provoked by Chinese penetration of their territory, the Xiongnu in the third and second centuries B.C.E. created a huge military confederacy that stretched from Manchuria deep into Central Asia (see map of Xiongnu Empire). "All the people who draw the bow have now become one family," declared **Modun** (r. 210–174 B.C.E.), the charismatic founder of the **Xiongnu Empire**. Tribute, exacted from other pastoral peoples and from China itself, sustained the Xiongnu Empire and forced the Han dynasty emperor Wen to acknowledge, unhappily, the equality of people he regarded as barbarians. "Our two great nations," he declared, "the Han and the Xiongnu, stand side by side."[6] Although it subsequently disintegrated under sustained Chinese counterattacks, the Xiongnu Empire provided a model and inspiration for later Turkic and Mongol empires.

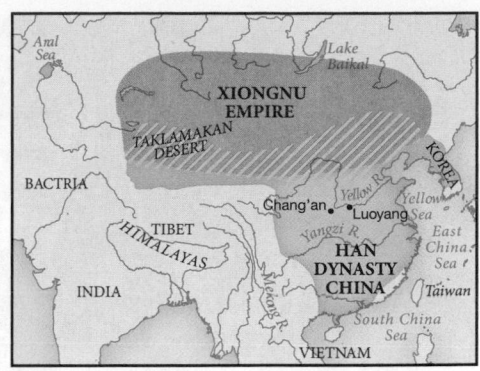

The Xiongnu Empire

It was during the era of third-wave civilizations that pastoral peoples made their most significant mark on the larger canvas of world history. Arabs, Berbers, Turks, and Mongols—all of them of pastoral origin—created the largest and most influential empires of that era. The most expansive religious tradition of that time, Islam, derived from a largely pastoral people, the Arabs, and was carried to new regions by another pastoral people, the Turks. Most of the great civilizations of outer Eurasia—Byzantium, Persia, India, and China—had come under the control of previously pastoral people, at least for a time. But as pastoralists entered and shaped the arena of world history, they too were transformed by the experience.

The first and most dramatic of these incursions came from Arabs. In the Arabian Peninsula, the development of a reliable camel saddle somewhere between 500 and 100 B.C.E. enabled pastoral Bedouin (desert-dwelling) Arabs to fight effectively from atop their enormous beasts. With this new military advantage, they came to control the rich trade routes in incense running through Arabia. Even more important, these camel pastoralists served as the shock troops of Islamic expansion, providing many of the new religion's earliest followers and much of the military force that carved out the Arab Empire. Although intellectual and political leadership came from urban merchants and settled farming communities, the Arab Empire was in some respects a pastoralist creation that subsequently became the foundation of a new and distinctive civilization.

Even as the pastoral Arabs encroached on the world of Eurasian civilizations from the south, Turkic-speaking pastoralists were making inroads from the north. Never a single people, various Turkic-speaking clans and tribes migrated from their homeland in Mongolia and southern Siberia generally westward and entered the historical record as creators of a series of empires between 552 and 965 C.E., most of them lasting little more than a century. Like the Xiongnu Empire, they were fragile alliances of various tribes headed by a supreme ruler known as a *kaghan*, who was supported by a faithful corps of soldiers called "wolves," for the wolf was the mythical ancestor of **Turkic peoples**. From their base in the steppes, these Turkic states confronted the great civilizations to their south—China, Persia, Byzantium—alternately raiding them, allying with them against common enemies, trading with them, and extorting tribute payments from them. Turkic language and culture spread widely over much of Inner Asia, and elements of that culture entered

Guided Reading Question

■ **SIGNIFICANCE**
In what ways did the Xiongnu, Arabs, Turks, and Berbers make an impact on world history?

Seljuk Tiles Among the artistic achievements of Turkic Muslims were lovely ceramic tiles used to decorate mosques, minarets, palaces, and other public spaces. They contained intricate geometric designs, images of trees and birds, and inscriptions from the Quran. This one, dating from the thirteenth century, was used in a Seljuk palace, built as a summer residence for the sultan in the city of Konya in what is now central Turkey. (© Images & Stories/Alamy)

the agrarian civilizations. In the courts of northern China, for example, yogurt thinned with water, a drink derived from the Turks, replaced for a time the traditional beverage of tea, and at least one Chinese poet wrote joyfully about the delights of snowy evenings in a felt tent.[7]

A major turning point in the history of the Turks occurred with their conversion to Islam between the tenth and fourteenth centuries. This extended process represented a major expansion of the faith and launched the Turks into a new role as the third major carrier of Islam, following the Arabs and the Persians. It also brought the Turks into an increasingly important position within the heartland of an established Islamic civilization as they migrated southward into the Middle East. There they served first as slave soldiers within the Abbasid caliphate, and then, as the caliphate declined, they increasingly took political and military power themselves. In the **Seljuk Turkic Empire** of the eleventh and twelfth centuries, centered in Persia and present-day Iraq, Turkic rulers began to claim the Muslim title of *sultan* (ruler) rather than the Turkic *kaghan*. Although the Abbasid caliph remained the formal ruler, real power was exercised by Turkic sultans.

Not only did Turkic peoples become Muslims themselves, but they carried Islam to new areas as well. Their invasions of northern India solidly planted Islam in that ancient civilization. In Anatolia, formerly ruled by Christian Byzantium, they brought both Islam and a massive infusion of Turkic culture, language, and people, even as they created the Ottoman Empire, which by 1500 became one of the great powers of Eurasia. In both places, Turkic dynasties governed and would continue to do so well into the modern era. Thus Turkic people, many of them at least, had transformed themselves from pastoralists to sedentary farmers, from creators of steppe empires to rulers of agrarian civilizations, and from polytheistic worshippers of their ancestors and various gods to followers and carriers of a monotheistic Islam.

Broadly similar patterns prevailed in Africa as well. All across northern Africa and the Sahara, the introduction of the

The Seljuk Empire

camel, probably during the first millennium B.C.E., gave rise to pastoral societies. Much like the Turkic-speaking pastoralists of Central Asia, many of these peoples later adopted Islam, but at least initially had little formal instruction in the religion. In the eleventh century C.E., a reform movement arose among the Sanhaja Berber pastoralists living in the western Sahara; they had only recently converted to Islam and were practicing it rather superficially. The movement was sparked by a scholar, Ibn Yasin, who returned from a pilgrimage to Mecca around 1039 seeking to purify the practice of the faith among his own people in line with orthodox principles. That religious movement soon became an expansive state, the **Almoravid Empire**, which incorporated a large part of northwestern Africa and in 1086 crossed into southern Spain, where it offered vigorous opposition to Christian efforts to conquer the region.

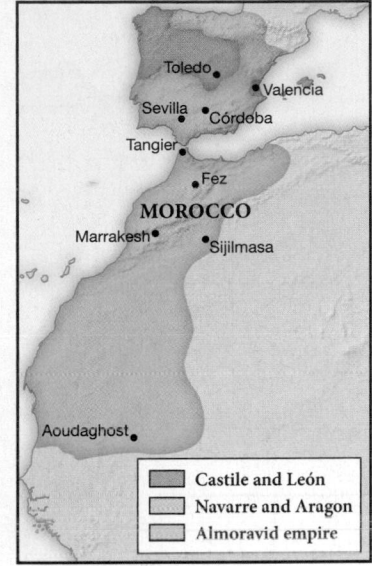

The Almoravid Empire

For a time, the Almoravid state enjoyed considerable prosperity, based on its control of much of the West African gold trade and the grain-producing Atlantic plains of Morocco. The Almoravids also brought to Morocco the sophisticated Islamic culture of southern Spain, still visible in the splendid architecture of the city of Marrakesh, for a time the capital of the Almoravid Empire. By the mid-twelfth century, that empire had been overrun by its longtime enemies, Berber farming people from the Atlas Mountains. But for roughly a century, the Almoravid movement represented an African pastoral people who had converted to Islam, had come into conflict with their agricultural neighbors and built a short-lived empire, and had a considerable impact on neighboring civilizations in both North Africa and Europe.

Breakout: The Mongol Empire

Of all the pastoral peoples who took a turn on the stage of world history, the Mongols made the most stunning entry. Their thirteenth-century breakout from Mongolia gave rise to the largest land-based empire in all of human history, stretching from the Pacific coast of Asia to Eastern Europe (see Map 11.1). This empire joined the pastoral peoples of the inner Eurasian steppes with the settled agricultural civilizations of outer Eurasia more extensively and more intimately than ever before. It also brought the major civilizations of Eurasia—Europe, China, and the Islamic world—into far more direct contact than in earlier times. Both the enormous destructiveness of the process and the networks of exchange and communication that it spawned were the work of the Mongols, numbering only about 700,000 people. It was another of history's unlikely twists.

For all of its size and fearsome reputation, the Mongol Empire left a surprisingly modest cultural imprint on the world it had briefly governed. Unlike the Arabs, the Mongols bequeathed to the world no new language, religion, or civilization. Mongol religion centered on rituals invoking the ancestors that were performed around the family hearth. Rulers sometimes consulted religious specialists, known

MAPPING HISTORY

Map 11.1 The Mongol Empire

Encompassing much of Eurasia, the Mongol Empire was divided into four khanates after the death of Chinggis Khan.

READING THE MAP: Which of the four khanates included the traditional Mongol homeland?

MAKING CONNECTIONS: What does a comparison of this map with Map 7.1: The Silk Roads suggest about the limits of Mongol expansion?

as shamans, who might predict the future, offer sacrifices, and communicate with the spirit world, particularly with Tengri, the supreme sky god of the Mongols. There was little in this tradition to attract outsiders, and in any event the Mongols proved uninterested in spreading their own faith among subject peoples.

Although people with skills were put to work in ways useful to Mongol authorities, Mongols offered the majority of their conquered people little more than the status of defeated, subordinate, and exploited subjects. Unlike the Turks, whose languages and culture flourish today in many places far from the Turkic homeland in Central Asia, Mongol culture remains confined largely to Mongolia. The Mongol Empire proved to be "the last, spectacular bloom of pastoral power in Inner Eurasia."[8] After the decline and disintegration of the Mongol Empire, the tide turned against the pastoralists of inner Eurasia, who were increasingly swallowed up in the expanding Russian or Chinese empire. Nonetheless, while it lasted and for a few centuries thereafter, the Mongol Empire made an enormous impact throughout the entire Eurasian world.

From Temujin to Chinggis Khan: The Rise of the Mongol Empire

World historians are prone to focus attention on large-scale and long-term processes of change in explaining "what happened in history," but in understanding the rise of the Mongol Empire, most scholars have found themselves forced to look closely at the role of a single individual — **Temujin** (TEM-oo-chin) (1162–1227), later known as **Chinggis Khan** (universal ruler). The twelfth-century world into which he was born found the Mongols an unstable and fractious collection of tribes and clans, much reduced from a somewhat earlier and more powerful position in the shifting alliances in what is now Mongolia. "Everyone was feuding," declared a leading Mongol shaman. "Rather than sleep, they robbed each other of their possessions. . . . There was no respite, only battle. There was no affection, only mutual slaughter."[9]

The early life of Temujin showed few signs of a prominent future. The boy's father had been a minor chieftain of a noble clan, but he was murdered by tribal rivals before Temujin turned ten, and the family was soon deserted by other members of the clan. As social outcasts without livestock, Temujin's small family, headed by his resourceful mother, was forced to abandon pastoralism, living instead by hunting, fishing, and gathering wild foods. It was an enormous and humiliating drop in their social status. In these desperate circumstances, Temujin's remarkable character came into play. His personal magnetism and courage and his inclination to rely on trusted friends rather than ties of kinship allowed him to build up a small following and to ally with a more powerful tribal leader. This alliance received a boost from Chinese patrons, always eager to keep the pastoralists divided. Soon Temujin was recognized as a chief in his own right with a growing band of followers.

Temujin's rise to power within the complex tribal politics of Mongolia was a surprise to everyone, as it took place amid shifting alliances and betrayals. Temujin achieved a mounting string of military victories, aided by the indecisiveness of his enemies, a reputation as a leader generous to friends and ruthless to enemies, and the incorporation of warriors from defeated tribes into his own forces. In 1206, a Mongol tribal assembly recognized Temujin as Chinggis Khan, supreme leader of a now unified Great Mongol Nation. It was a remarkable achievement, but one little noticed beyond the highland steppes of Mongolia. That would soon change.

The unification of the Mongol tribes raised an obvious question: what was Chinggis Khan to do with the powerful army he had assembled? Without a common

Guided Reading Question

■ **DESCRIPTION**
Identify the major steps in the rise of the Mongol Empire.

A Mongol Failure: The Invasion of Japan

The Mongols are best known for the remarkable military victories that gave them one of the largest empires in history, but they experienced stunning defeats as well.[10] None was more dramatic than the failed invasion of Japan in 1281. The armada assembled by the Mongols for

Japanese samurai attacking a Mongol warship.

this campaign was one of the largest in history, comprising thousands of ships and as many as 140,000 sailors and soldiers. With little experience in naval warfare, the Mongols built their armada by drawing on the resources of their vassal state in Korea and their recently conquered subjects in China. But even with the aid of these seafaring peoples, this huge invasion fleet stretched the resources of the Mongols, who resorted to commuting the death sentences of criminals willing to serve in the fleet.

The invasion was the culmination of a deteriorating relationship between Japanese authorities and the Mongol ruler Khubilai Khan, grandson of Chinggis Khan and founder of the Chinese Yuan dynasty. In the 1260s,

Japan's government ignored the khan's demands that it become a vassal state of the Mongol Empire. In 1274, the khan dispatched a raiding force against Japan that briefly landed on the main Japanese island of Kyushu. This force both scouted a suitable invasion route and put pressure on the Japanese to accept Mongol demands. In the years that followed, tensions increased, especially when the Japanese summarily beheaded Mongol envoys sent to demand their submission.

Following the final conquest of China in 1279, the khan shifted his attention to subjugating Japan. The massive invasion fleet sailed from ports in Korea and southern China with plans to combine off the shores of Japan. The fleet from Korea arrived first and attacked the mainland without waiting for the Chinese fleet. The Mongols sought to establish a beachhead at the site where Mongol

task, the new and fragile unity of the Mongols would surely dissolve into quarrels and chaos; and without external resources to reward his followers, Chinggis Khan would be hard-pressed to maintain his supreme position. Both considerations pointed in a single direction—expansion, particularly toward China, long a source of great wealth for pastoral peoples.

In 1209, the first major attack on the settled agricultural societies south of Mongolia set in motion half a century of a **Mongol world war**, a series of military campaigns, massive killing, and empire building without precedent in world history. In the process, Chinggis Khan, followed by his sons and grandsons (Ogodei, Mongke, and Khubilai), constructed an empire that contained China, Central Asia, Russia, much of the Islamic Middle East, and parts of Eastern Europe (see Map 11.1, page 458). "In a flash," wrote a recent scholar, "the Mongol warriors would defeat every army, capture every fort, and bring down the walls of every city they encountered. Christians, Muslims, Buddhists, and Hindus would soon kneel before the dusty boots of illiterate young Mongol horsemen."[11]

forces had briefly come ashore in 1274, but the heavily outnumbered Japanese forces were waiting for them behind recently constructed defensive walls. Unable to establish a beachhead, the Mongol fleet anchored in the harbor, where it was attacked by groups of Japanese warriors, known as samurai, in small open boats, like the one depicted in a contemporary scroll recounting the battle (see photo). In daring raids, often at night, the samurai boarded the much larger Mongol ships and engaged their crews in deadly close-quarters combat.

Under pressure, the Korean fleet withdrew and made its rendezvous with the Chinese fleet, which had arrived in the waters off Japan. The combined forces then moved against another Japanese island, where they engaged in a fierce all-night sea battle that once again pitted the large seagoing ships of the Mongol armada against heavily outnumbered groups of samurai in small raiding boats. It was at this moment that a typhoon, named the *kamikaze*, or "divine wind," by the Japanese defenders, struck, destroying perhaps 30 percent of the Korean fleet and between 60 and 90 percent of the Chinese flotilla. In the aftermath, the Mongol commanders abandoned the invasion, leaving behind thousands of shipwrecked soldiers and sailors on the beaches. Such was the role of natural events in confounding human plans.

The defeat had little impact on Khubilai Khan, whose empire recovered quickly from the setback. But the khan never again turned his attentions to Japan, instead seeking to expand his empire elsewhere, including the islands of Southeast Asia, the target of another ambitious but unsuccessful naval expedition in the 1290s. In Japan, the Mongol invasion had a much greater long-term impact. The destruction of the Mongol fleet through what was perceived as divine intervention strengthened Japanese conceptions of their island nation as the *shinkoku*, or "land of the gods." Memories of triumph over the Mongols continued to resonate into the twentieth century. At the end of World War II, when Japan was again faced with foreign invasion, Japanese suicide pilots who sought to stop the Allied advance took the name *kamikazes*, evoking the memory of the typhoon that had turned back the Mongol invasion centuries earlier.

QUESTION

How does the Mongols' military defeat at the hands of the Japanese shape your understanding of the Mongols and their empire?

Various setbacks marked the outer limits of the Mongol Empire—the Mongols' withdrawal from Eastern Europe (1242), their defeat at Ain Jalut in Palestine at the hands of Egyptian forces (1260), the failure of their invasion of Japan owing to typhoons, and the difficulty of penetrating the tropical jungles of Southeast Asia. (See Zooming In: A Mongol Failure, page 460.) But what an empire it was! How could a Mongol confederation, with a total population of less than 1 million people and few resources beyond their livestock, assemble an imperial structure of such staggering transcontinental dimensions?

Explaining the Mongol Moment

Like the Roman Empire but far more rapidly, the Mongol realm grew of its own momentum without any grand scheme or blueprint for world conquest. Each fresh victory brought new resources for making war and new threats or insecurities that seemed to require further expansion. As the empire took shape and certainly by the

A Mongol Warrior Horseback-riding skills, honed in herding animals and adapted to military purposes, were central to Mongol conquests, as illustrated in this Ming dynasty Chinese painting of a mounted Mongol archer. (Victoria & Albert Museum, London, UK/Bridgeman Images)

end of his life, Chinggis Khan had come to see his career in terms of a universal mission. "I have accomplished a great work," he declared, "uniting the whole world in one empire."[12] Thus the Mongol Empire acquired an ideology in the course of its construction.

What made this "great work" possible? The odds seemed overwhelming, for China alone outnumbered the Mongols 100 to 1 and possessed incomparably greater resources. Furthermore, the Mongols did not enjoy any technological superiority over their many adversaries. They did, however, enjoy the luck of good timing, for China was divided, with the Song dynasty having already lost control of its northern territory to the pastoral Jurchen people, while the decrepit Abbasid caliphate, once the center of the Islamic world, had shrunk to a fraction of its earlier size. But clearly, the key to the Mongols' success lay in their army. According to one scholar, "Mongol armies were simply better led, organized, and disciplined than those of their opponents."[13] In an effort to diminish a divisive tribalism, Chinggis Khan reorganized the entire social structure of the Mongols into military units of 10, 100, 1,000, and 10,000 warriors, an arrangement that allowed for effective command and control. Conquered tribes, especially, were broken up, and their members were scattered among these new units, which enrolled virtually all men and supplied the cavalry forces of Mongol armies. A highly prestigious imperial guard also recruited members across tribal lines.

An impressive discipline and loyalty to their leaders characterized Mongol military forces, and discipline was reinforced by the provision that should any members of a unit desert in battle, all were subject to the death penalty. More positively, loyalty was cemented by the leaders' willingness to share the hardships of their men. "I eat the same food and am dressed in the same rags as my humble herdsmen," wrote Chinggis Khan. "I am always in the forefront, and in battle I am never at the rear."[14] Such discipline and loyalty made possible the elaborate tactics of encirclement, retreat, and deception that proved decisive in many a battle. Furthermore, the enormous flow of wealth from conquered civilizations benefited all Mongols, though not equally. Even ordinary Mongols could now dress in linens and silks rather than hides and felt, could own slaves derived from the many prisoners of war, and had far greater opportunities to improve their social position in a constantly expanding empire.

To compensate for their own small population, the Mongols incorporated huge numbers of conquered peoples into their military forces. "People who lived in felt tents"—mostly Mongol and Turkic pastoralists—were conscripted en masse into the cavalry units of the Mongol army, while settled agricultural peoples supplied the infantry and artillery forces. As the Mongols penetrated major civilizations, with their walled cities and elaborate fortifications, they quickly acquired Chinese techniques and technology of siege warfare. Some 1,000 Chinese artillery crews, for example, took part in the Mongol invasion of distant Persia. Beyond military recruitment, Mongols demanded that their conquered people serve as laborers, building roads and bridges and ferrying supplies over long distances. Artisans, craftsmen, and skilled people generally were carefully identified, spared from massacre, and often sent to distant regions of the empire where their services were required. A French goldsmith captured by Mongol forces in Hungary wound up as a slave in the Mongol capital of Karakorum (kah-rah-KOR-um), where he constructed an elaborate silver fountain that dispensed wine and other intoxicating drinks.

A further element in the military effectiveness of Mongol forces lay in a growing reputation for a ruthless brutality and utter destructiveness. City after city was utterly destroyed. Chinggis Khan's policy was clear: "Whoever submits shall be spared, but those who resist, they shall be destroyed with their wives, children and dependents . . . so that the others who hear and see should fear and not act the same."[15] (See Working with Evidence, Source 11.3, page 487.) One scholar explained such policies in this way: "Extremely conscious of their small numbers and fearful of rebellion, Chinggis often chose to annihilate a region's entire population, if it appeared too troublesome to govern."[16] These policies also served as a form of psychological warfare, a practical inducement to surrender for those who knew of the Mongol terror. Historians continue to debate the extent and uniqueness of the Mongols' brutality, but their reputation for unwavering harshness proved a military asset.

Underlying the purely military dimensions of the Mongols' success was an impressive ability to mobilize both the human and material resources of their growing empire. Elaborate census-taking allowed Mongol leaders to know what was available to them and made possible the systematic taxation of conquered people. An effective system of relay stations, about a day's ride apart, provided rapid communication across the empire and fostered trade as well. The beginnings of a centralized bureaucracy with various specialized offices took shape in the new capital of Karakorum. There scribes translated official decrees into the various languages of the empire, such as Persian, Uighur, Chinese, and Tibetan.

Other policies appealed to various groups among the conquered peoples of the empire. Interested in fostering commerce, Mongol rulers often offered merchants 10 percent or more above their asking price and allowed them the free use of the relay stations for transporting their goods. In administering the conquered regions, Mongols held the highest decision-making posts, but Chinese and Muslim officials held many advisory and lower-level positions in China and Persia, respectively. In religious matters, the Mongols welcomed and supported many religious traditions—Buddhist, Christian, Muslim, Daoist—as long as they did not become the focus of political opposition. This policy of religious toleration allowed Muslims to seek converts among Mongol troops and afforded Christians much greater freedom than they had enjoyed under Muslim rule. One of Chinggis Khan's successors, Mongke, arranged a debate among representatives of several religious faiths, after which he concluded: "Just as God gave different fingers to the hand, so has He given different ways to men."[17] Such economic, administrative, and religious policies provided some benefits and a place within the empire—albeit subordinate—for many of its conquered peoples.

PRACTICING HISTORICAL THINKING

What accounts for the political and military success of the Mongols?

Encountering the Mongols in China, Persia, and Russia

The Mongol moment in world history represented an enormous cultural encounter between pastoralists and the settled civilizations of Eurasia. The process of conquest, the length and nature of Mongol rule, the impact on local people, and the extent of Mongol assimilation into the cultures of the conquered—all this and more varied considerably across the Eurasian domains of the empire. The experiences of China, Persia, and Russia provide brief glimpses into several expressions of this massive encounter of cultures.

China and the Mongols

Long the primary target for pastoral steppe dwellers in search of agrarian wealth, China proved the most difficult and extended of the Mongols' many conquests, lasting some seventy years, from 1209 to 1279. The invasion began in northern China, which had been ruled for several centuries by various dynasties of pastoral origin, and was characterized by destruction and plunder on a massive scale. Southern China, under the control of the native Song dynasty, was a different story, for there the Mongols were far less violent and more concerned with accommodating the local population. Landowners, for example, were guaranteed their estates in exchange for their support or at least their neutrality. By whatever methods, the outcome was the unification of a divided China, a treasured ideal among educated Chinese. This achievement persuaded some of them that the Mongols had indeed been granted the Mandate of Heaven and, despite their foreign origins, were legitimate rulers. One highly educated Chinese scholar wrote a short biography of a recently deceased Mongol official, praising him for curtailing the violence of Mongol soldiers, offering leniency to rebels, and providing tax relief and food during a famine. In short, he was behaving like a good Confucian Chinese official.

Having acquired China, what were the Mongols to do with it? One possibility, apparently considered by the Great Khan Ogodei (ERG-uh-day) in the 1230s, was to exterminate everyone in northern China and turn the country into pastureland for Mongol herds. That suggestion, fortunately, was rejected in favor of extracting as much wealth as possible from the country's advanced civilization. Doing so meant some accommodation to Chinese culture and ways of governing, for the Mongols had no experience with the operation of a complex agrarian society.

That accommodation took many forms. The Mongols made use of Chinese administrative practices and techniques of taxation as well as their postal system. They gave themselves a Chinese dynastic title, the Yuan, suggesting a new beginning in Chinese history. They transferred their capital from Karakorum in Mongolia to what is now Beijing, building a wholly new capital city there known as Khanbalik, the "city of the khan." Thus the Mongols were now rooting themselves solidly on the soil of a highly sophisticated civilization, well removed from their homeland on the steppes. **Khubilai Khan** (koo-buh-l'eye kahn), the grandson of Chinggis Khan and China's Mongol ruler from 1271 to 1294 who initiated the **Yuan dynasty**, ordered a set of Chinese-style ancestral tablets to honor his ancestors and posthumously awarded them Chinese names. Many of his policies evoked the values of a benevolent Confucian-inspired Chinese emperor, as he improved roads, built canals, lowered some taxes, patronized scholars and artists, limited the death penalty and torture, supported peasant agriculture, and prohibited Mongols from grazing their animals on peasants' farmland. (See Working with Evidence, Source 11.2, page 483, for various impressions of Khubilai Khan.) Mongol khans also made use of traditional Confucian rituals, supported the building of some Daoist temples, and were particularly attracted to a Tibetan form of Buddhism, which returned the favor with strong political support for the invaders.

Guided Reading Question

■ **CHANGE**
How did Mongol rule change China? In what ways were the Mongols changed by China?

Despite these accommodations, Mongol rule was still harsh, exploitative, foreign, and resented. Marco Polo, who was in China at the time, reported that some Mongol officials or their Muslim intermediaries treated Chinese "just like slaves," demanding bribes for services, ordering arbitrary executions, and seizing women at will—all of which generated outrage and hostility. The Mongols did not become Chinese, nor did they accommodate every aspect of Chinese culture. Deep inside the new capital, the royal family and court could continue to experience something of steppe life as their animals roamed freely in large open areas, planted with steppe grass. Many of the Mongol elite much preferred to live, eat, sleep, and give birth in the traditional tents that sprouted everywhere. In administering the country, the Mongols largely ignored the traditional Chinese examination system and relied heavily on foreigners, particularly Muslims from Central Asia and the Middle East, to serve as officials, while keeping the top decision-making posts for

Khubilai Khan This famous portrait of Khubilai Khan was probably painted by Aniko (1244–1306), a Nepalese artist and architect who designed a number of buildings for China's Mongol ruler. (Science History Images/Alamy)

themselves. Few Mongols learned Chinese, and Mongol law discriminated against the Chinese, reserving for them the most severe punishments. Furthermore, the Mongols honored and supported merchants and artisans far more than Confucian bureaucrats had been inclined to do.

In social life, the Mongols forbade intermarriage and prohibited Chinese scholars from learning the Mongol script. Mongol women never adopted foot binding and scandalized the Chinese by mixing freely with men at official gatherings and riding to the hunt with their husbands. The Mongol ruler Khubilai Khan retained the Mongol tradition of relying heavily on female advisers, the chief of which was his favorite wife, Chabi. Ironically, she urged him to accommodate his Chinese subjects, forcefully and successfully opposing an early plan to turn Chinese farmland into pastureland. Unlike many Mongols, biased as they were against farming, Chabi recognized the advantages of agriculture and its ability to generate tax revenue. With a vision of turning Mongol rule into a lasting dynasty that might rank with the splendor of the Tang, she urged her husband to emulate the best practices of that earlier era of Chinese history.

However one assesses Mongol rule in China, it was relatively brief, lasting little more than a century. By the mid-fourteenth century, intense factionalism among the Mongols, rapidly rising prices, furious epidemics of the plague, and growing peasant rebellions combined to force the Mongols out of China. By 1368, rebel forces had triumphed, and thousands of Mongols returned to their homeland in the steppes. For several centuries, they remained a periodic threat to China, but during the Ming dynasty that followed, the memory of their often-brutal and alien rule stimulated a renewed commitment to Confucian values and restrictive gender practices and an effort to wipe out all traces of the Mongols' impact.

Persia and the Mongols

A second great civilization conquered by the Mongols was Islamic Persia. There the Mongol takeover was far more abrupt than the extended process of conquest in China. A first invasion (1219–1221), led by Chinggis Khan himself, was followed thirty years later by a second assault (1251–1258) under his grandson **Hulegu** (HE-luh-gee), who became the first il-khan (subordinate khan) of Persia. Although Persia had been repeatedly attacked, from the invasion of Alexander the Great to that of the Arabs and Turkic peoples, nothing prepared it for the Mongols. In the eyes of Persian Muslims, the Mongols were infidels, and their stunning victory was a profound shock to people accustomed to viewing history as the progressive expansion of Islamic rule. Furthermore, Mongol military victory brought in its wake a degree of ferocity and slaughter that had no parallel in Persian experience. (See Working with Evidence, Source 11.3, page 487, for an account of the Mongol seizure of Bukhara.) The Persian historian Juvaini described it in fearful terms:

> Every town and every village has been several times subjected to pillage and massacre and has suffered this confusion for years so that even though there

be generation and increase until the Resurrection the population will not attain to a tenth part of what it was before.[18]

The sacking of Baghdad in 1258, which put an end to the Abbasid caliphate, was accompanied by the massacre of more than 200,000 people, according to Hulegu himself.

Beyond this human catastrophe lay the damage to Persian and Iraqi agriculture and to those who tilled the soil. Heavy taxes, sometimes collected twenty or thirty times a year and often under torture or whipping, pushed large numbers of peasants off their land. Furthermore, the in-migration of pastoral Mongols, together with their immense herds of sheep and goats, turned much agricultural land into pasture and sometimes into desert. As a result, a fragile system of underground water channels that provided irrigation to the fields was neglected, and much good agricultural land was reduced to waste. Some sectors of the Persian economy gained, however. Wine production increased because the Mongols were fond of alcohol, and the Persian silk industry benefited from close contact with a Mongol-ruled China. In general, though, even more so than in China, Mongol rule in Persia represented "disaster on a grand and unparalleled scale."[19]

Nonetheless, the Mongols in Persia were themselves transformed far more than their counterparts in China. They made extensive use of the sophisticated Persian bureaucracy, leaving the greater part of government operations in Persian hands. During the reign of Ghazan (haz-ZAHN) (1295–1304), they made some efforts to repair the damage caused by earlier policies of ruthless exploitation by rebuilding damaged cities and repairing neglected irrigation works. Most important, the Mongols who conquered Persia became Muslims, following the lead of Ghazan, who converted to Islam in 1295. No such widespread conversion to the culture of the conquered occurred in China or in Christian Russia. Members of the court and Mongol elites learned at least some Persian, unlike most of their counterparts in China. A number of Mongols also turned to farming, abandoning their pastoral ways, while some married local people.

When the Mongol dynasty of Hulegu's descendants collapsed in the 1330s for lack of a suitable heir, the Mongols were not driven out of Persia as they had been from China. Rather,

Guided Reading Question

■ **COMPARISON**

How was Mongol rule in Persia different from that in China?

The Mongols and Islam in Persia This image from the first half of the fourteenth century depicts a Mongol prince studying the Quran in what is likely a mosque tent. The arch at the left marks the *mihrab,* which points toward Mecca and indicates the direction that worshippers should face during ritual prayers. Above it is an inscription reading "Allah is the Ruler." The conversion of the Mongols in Persia to Islam was a crucial development in their rule over the region. (bpk Bildagentur/Staatsbibliothek zu Berlin, Stiflung Preussicher Kulturbesitz/Photo: Ellwardt/Art Resource, NY)

Mongol Rulers and Their Women The wives of Mongol rulers exercised considerable influence at court. This fourteenth-century painting shows Chinggis Khan's fourth son, Tului, the ruler of the Mongol heartland after his father's death, with his Christian wife Sorgaqtani. After her husband's early death from alcoholism, she maneuvered her children, including Khubilai Khan, into powerful positions and strongly encouraged them in the direction of religious toleration. (Bibliothèque Nationale de France, Paris, France/akg-images)

they and their Turkic allies simply disappeared, assimilated into Persian society. From a Persian point of view, the barbarians had been civilized, and Persians had successfully resisted cultural influence from their uncivilized conquerors. When the great Persian historian Rashid al-Din wrote his famous history of the Mongols, he apologized for providing information about women, generally unmentioned in Islamic writing, explaining that Mongols treated their women equally and included them in decisions of the court.[20] Now Persian rulers could return to their more patriarchal ways.

Russia and the Mongols

When the Mongol military machine rolled over Russia between 1237 and 1240, it encountered a relatively new third-wave civilization located on the far eastern fringe of Christendom. Whatever political unity this new civilization of Kievan Rus had earlier enjoyed was now gone, and various independent princes proved unable to unite even in the face of the Mongol onslaught. Although they had interacted extensively with pastoral people of the steppes north of the Black Sea, Mongol ferocity was stunning. City after city fell to Mongol forces, which were now armed with the catapults and battering rams adopted from Chinese or Muslim sources. What followed was described in horrific terms by Russian chroniclers, who reported mass slaughter of "men, women, and children, monks, nuns and priests" and the violation of "good women and girls in the presence of their mothers and sisters." From the survivors and the cities that surrendered early, laborers and skilled craftsmen were deported to other Mongol lands or sold into slavery. A number of Russian crafts were so depleted of their workers that they did not recover for a century or more.

If the violence of initial conquest bore similarities to the experiences of Persia, Russia's incorporation into the Mongol Empire was very different. To the Mongols, it was the Kipchak (KIP-chahk) Khanate, named after the Kipchak Turkic-speaking peoples north of the Caspian and Black seas, among whom the Mongols had settled. To the Russians, it was the "**Khanate of the Golden Horde**." By whatever name, the Mongols had conquered Russia, but they did not occupy it as they had China and Persia. Thus in Russia there were no garrisoned cities, permanently stationed administrators, or Mongol settlers. From the Mongol point of view, Russia had little to offer. Its economy was not nearly so sophisticated or productive as that of more established civilizations; nor was it located on major international trade routes. It was simply not worth the expense of occupying. Furthermore, the availability of extensive steppe lands for pasturing their flocks north of the Black and Caspian seas meant that the Mongols could maintain their preferred pastoral way of life, while remaining in easy reach of Russian cities when the need arose to send further military expeditions. They could dominate and exploit Russia from the steppes.

And exploit they certainly did. Russian princes received appointment from the khan and were required to send substantial tribute to the Mongol capital at Sarai, located on the lower Volga River. A variety of additional taxes created a heavy burden, especially on the peasantry, while continuing border raids sent tens of thousands of Russians into slavery. The Mongol impact was highly uneven, however. The Russian Orthodox Church flourished under the Mongol policy of religious toleration, for it received exemption from many taxes. Russian nobles who participated in Mongol raids earned a share of the loot. Some cities, such as Kiev, resisted the Mongols and were devastated, while others surrendered and collaborated and were left undamaged. Moscow in particular emerged as the primary collector of tribute for the Mongols, with one of its rulers, Ivan I, earning the nickname Ivan the Moneybags because of the riches that flowed to him from this position. Moscow's princes parlayed this position into a leading role as the nucleus of a renewed Russian state when Mongol domination receded in the fifteenth century.

The absence of direct Mongol rule had implications for the Mongols themselves, for they were far less influenced by or assimilated within Russian cultures than their counterparts in China and Persia had been. The Mongols in China had turned themselves into a Chinese dynasty, with the khan as a Chinese emperor. Some learned calligraphy, and a few came to appreciate Chinese poetry. In Persia, the

Guided Reading Question

■ **COMPARISON**

What was distinctive about the Russian experience of Mongol rule?

Mongol Russia This sixteenth-century painting depicts the Mongol burning of the Russian city of Ryazan in 1237. Similar destruction awaited many Russian towns that resisted the invaders. (Universal Images Group/Sovfoto/akg-images)

Mongols had converted to Islam, with some becoming farmers. Not so in Russia. There "the Mongols of the Golden Horde were still spending their days in the saddle and their nights in tents."[21] They could dominate Russia from the adjacent steppes without in any way adopting Russian culture. Even though they remained culturally separate from Christian Russians, eventually the Mongols assimilated to the culture and the Islamic faith of the Kipchak people of the steppes, and in the process they lost their distinct identity and became Kipchaks.

Despite this domination from a distance, "the impact of the Mongols on Russia was, if anything, greater than on China and Iran [Persia]," according to a leading scholar.[22] Russian princes, who were more or less left alone if they paid the required tribute and taxes, found it useful to adopt the Mongols' weapons, diplomatic rituals, court practices, taxation system, and military draft. Mongol policies facilitated, although not intentionally, the rise of Moscow as the core of a new Russian state, and that state made good use of the famous Mongol mounted courier service. Mongol policies also strengthened the hold of the Russian Orthodox Church and enabled it to penetrate the rural areas more fully than before. Some Russians, seeking to explain their country's economic backwardness and political autocracy in modern times, have held the Mongols responsible for both conditions, though most historians consider such views vastly exaggerated.

Divisions among the Mongols, the disruptive influence of plague, and the growing strength of the Russian state—centered now on the city of Moscow—enabled the Russians to break the Mongols' hold by the end of the fifteenth century. With the earlier demise of Mongol rule in China and Persia, and now in Russia, the Mongols had retreated from their brief but spectacular incursion into the civilizations of outer Eurasia. Nonetheless, they continued to periodically threaten these civilizations for several centuries, until their homelands were absorbed into the expanding Russian and Chinese empires. But the Mongol moment in world history was over.

The Mongol Empire as a Eurasian Network

During the third-wave era, Chinese culture and Buddhism provided a measure of integration among the peoples of East Asia; Christianity did the same for Europe, while the realm of Islam connected most of the lands in between. But it was the

Mongol Empire, during the thirteenth and fourteenth centuries, that brought all of these regions into a single interacting network, enabling the circulation of goods, information, disease, and styles of warfare all across Eurasia and parts of Africa.

Toward a World Economy

The Mongols themselves did not produce much of value for distant markets, nor were they active traders. Nonetheless, they consistently promoted international commerce, largely so that they could tax it and thus extract wealth from more developed civilizations. The Great Khan Ogodei, for example, often paid well over the asking price to attract merchants to his capital of Karakorum. The Mongols also provided financial backing for caravans, introduced standardized weights and measures, and gave tax breaks to merchants.

In providing a relatively secure environment for merchants making the long and arduous journey across Central Asia between Europe and China, the Mongol Empire brought the two ends of the Eurasian world into closer contact than ever before and launched a new phase in the history of the Silk Roads. Marco Polo was only the most famous of many European merchants, mostly from Italian cities, who made their way to China through the Mongol Empire. So many traders attempted the journey that guidebooks circulated with much useful advice about the trip. Merchants returned with tales of rich lands and prosperous commercial opportunities, but what they described were long-established trading networks of which Europeans had been largely ignorant.

The Mongol trading circuit was a central element in an even larger commercial network that linked much of the Afro-Eurasian world in the thirteenth century (see Map 11.2). Mongol-ruled China was the fulcrum of this vast system, connecting the overland route through the Mongol Empire with the oceanic routes through the South China Sea and Indian Ocean.

Guided Reading Question

■ **CONNECTION**
What kinds of cross-cultural interactions did the Mongol Empire generate?

Diplomacy on a Eurasian Scale

Not only did the Mongol Empire facilitate long-distance commerce, but it also prompted diplomatic relationships from one end of Eurasia to the other. As their invasion of Russia spilled over into Eastern Europe, Mongol armies destroyed Polish, German, and Hungarian forces in 1241–1242 and seemed poised to march on Central and Western Europe. But the death of the Great Khan Ogodei required Mongol leaders to return to Mongolia, and Western Europe lacked adequate pasture for Mongol herds. Thus Western Europe was spared the trauma of conquest, but fearing the possible return of the Mongols, both the pope and European rulers dispatched delegations to the Mongol capital, mostly led by Franciscan friars. They hoped to learn something about Mongol intentions, to secure Mongol aid in the Christian crusade against Islam, and, if possible, to convert Mongols to Christianity. These efforts were largely in vain, for no alliance or widespread conversion occurred. In fact, one of these missions came back with a letter for the pope from the Great Khan Guyuk, demanding that Europeans submit to him.

MAPPING HISTORY

Map 11.2 Trade and Disease in the Fourteenth Century

The Mongol Empire played a major role in the commercial integration of the Eurasian world as well as in the spread of the plague across this vast area.

READING THE MAP: Which circuits of trade played the greatest role in the spread of the plague?

INTERPRETING THE MAP: What does the map suggest about the regions—temperate, tropical (along the equator), subarctic—in which the plague spread most widely?

Perhaps the most important outcome of these diplomatic probings was the useful information about lands to the east that European missions brought back. Those reports contributed to a dawning European awareness of a wider world, and they have certainly provided later historians with much useful information about the Mongols. Somewhat later, in 1287, the il-khanate of Persia sought an alliance with European powers to take Jerusalem and crush the forces of Islam, but the

Persian Mongols' conversion to Islam soon put an end to any such anti-Muslim coalition.

Within the Mongol Empire itself, close relationships developed between the courts of Persia and China. They regularly exchanged ambassadors, shared intelligence information, fostered trade between their regions, and sent skilled workers back and forth. Thus political authorities all across Eurasia engaged in diplomatic relationships with one another to an unprecedented degree.

Cultural Exchange in the Mongol Realm

Accompanying these transcontinental economic and political relationships was a substantial exchange of peoples and cultures. Mongol policy forcibly transferred many thousands of skilled craftsmen and educated people from their homelands to distant parts of the empire, while the Mongols' religious tolerance and support of merchants drew missionaries and traders from afar. The Mongol capital at Karakorum was a cosmopolitan city with places of worship for Buddhists, Daoists, Muslims, and Christians. Chinggis Khan and several other Mongol rulers married Christian women. This relatively open Mongol outlook facilitated the exchange and blending of religious ideas. In Persia, for example, images of the Prophet Muhammad appeared, drawing on Chinese painting techniques and using Buddhist and Christian traditions as models. One such painting even portayed the birth of the Prophet in a distinctly Christian nativity scene. Actors and musicians from China, wrestlers from Persia, and a jester from Byzantium provided entertainment for the Mongol court. Persian and Arab doctors and administrators were sent to China, while Chinese physicians and engineers found their skills in demand in the Islamic world.

This movement of people facilitated the exchange of ideas and techniques, a process actively encouraged by Mongol authorities. A great deal of Chinese technology and artistic conventions—such as painting, printing, gunpowder weapons, compass navigation, high-temperature furnaces, and medical techniques—flowed westward. Acupuncture, for example, was poorly received in the Middle East because it required too much bodily contact for Muslim taste, even as Chinese techniques for diagnosing illness by taking the pulse of patients proved quite popular, as they involved minimal body contact. Muslim astronomers brought their skills and knowledge to China because Mongol authorities wanted "second opinions on the reading of heavenly signs and portents" and assistance in constructing the accurate calendars needed for ritual purposes.[23] Plants and crops likewise circulated within the Mongol domain. Lemons and carrots from the Middle East found a welcome reception in China, while the Persian il-khan Ghazan sent envoys to India, China, and elsewhere to seek "seeds of things which are unique in that land."[24] Europeans arguably gained more than most from these exchanges, for they had long been cut off from the fruitful interchange with Asia, and in comparison to the Islamic and Chinese worlds, they were less technologically developed. Now they could reap the benefits of new technology, new crops, and new knowledge of a wider world.

Debating Empire

The empires of the third-wave era—Chinese, Byzantine, Arab, and Mongol—have attracted considerable attention from historians, as have both earlier and later empires. And no wonder. Over the past 2,500 years, more people have lived in empires, where multiple distinct ethnic communities were ruled and often exploited by a dominant group, than in any other type of state or society.

Historians have long been intrigued by the various ways in which empires were born. The early Chinese and Egyptian empires, for example, took root in the heartland of already settled agricultural regions. The Persian, Greek, and Roman empires, by contrast, expanded from the edges of established agriculture civilizations, while the pastoralist empires of the Arabs, Mongols, and Turks found their origins in regions without much settled agriculture. More recently, European powers conquered and colonized regions thousands of miles from their home countries, creating the first overseas empires. But some civilizations developed for centuries without generating empires, such as those in ancient Sumer, in post-Roman Europe, and among the cities of the Maya and the Niger River valley. Was it because the rivalry of many small states or cities confounded efforts to develop larger imperial systems?

Other variations on the imperial theme have likewise surfaced in the work of historians. Empires were most frequently constructed through violence and conquest, but with important exceptions. The Athenian empire, for instance, started as a voluntary league. The European domains of the Habsburg Empire were largely brought together through family marriage strategies and inheritance. Some empires were constructed deliberately, like those of the Greek ruler Alexander the Great, the first Chinese emperor Qin Shihuangdi, and the Mongol leader Chinggis Khan. Others, like the Roman and Arab empires, grew more slowly in reaction to frontier insecurity or internal pressures. Autocrats frequently ruled over imperial enterprises, but democracies and republics have also created empires, including two of the largest, the ancient Roman and nineteenth-century British empires. Scholars have emphasized the durability of empires like that of Byzantium, which persisted for over a millennium, or its Ottoman successor, which survived for six centuries. But abortive or short-lived imperial adventures are also common, including that of the Mauryan dynasty in India, Axum in Northeast Africa, and Japan's East Asian empire in the early twentieth century. Explaining these variations provides grist for the mill of historical controversy.

So too does the collapse of empires. Historians have discovered that few imperial regimes have been toppled by internal rebellions of the oppressed. Even the largest rebellions, like the Yellow Turban in Han China or Spartacus's slaves in ancient Rome, were ultimately crushed. More commonly, empires fell or fragmented due to external invasion, as happened to the Aztec and Inca empires, or when the ruling elite split, as was the case following the deaths of Alexander the Great, Charlemagne, and Chinggis Khan. The end of the western Roman Empire has fostered endless controversy, with scholars emphasizing various factors: economic decline owing to war, corruption, and overreliance on slavery; penetration of the empire and its military forces by Germanic peoples; frequent turnover of emperors, often by murder; the invasion of the Huns; the coming of Christianity and the erosion of traditional values; environmental degradation; and many others. Scholars even disagree about when or if the empire ended. Was it in 476 C.E. when Emperor Romulus was overthrown by a German warlord? Or had the empire ceased to function as a state decades before Romulus was deposed? Still others date its demise to the

And almost alone among the peoples of Eurasia, they could do so without having suffered the devastating consequences of Mongol conquest. In these circumstances, some historians have argued, lay the roots of Europe's remarkable rise to global prominence in the centuries that followed. (See Controversies: Debating Empire, above, for a look at how historians think about empires.)

fall of Constantinople nearly 1,000 years later in 1453, arguing that the Roman Empire lived on in Byzantium.

Historians have also differed in their assessments of empire, in part reflecting the cultural attitudes of the times in which they wrote. The rapid expansion of European imperial enterprises in Africa and parts of Asia in the late nineteenth century coincided with the emergence of university history departments and professional historians in Europe and the United States. In this context, many Western historians produced studies of the remarkable accomplishments of empires through history, focusing on their military and administrative successes and exploring how imperial projects brought "civilization" to "traditional" societies. Historians identified the freer spread of ideas, goods, and people; the standardization of laws and currency; and the building of infrastructure and establishment of peace as advances for humankind as a whole—or, as Lord Curzon, a prominent imperial official and writer about empire, put it in 1894: "the British Empire is under Providence the greatest instrument for good that the world has seen."[25]

However, an increasingly negative assessment of empire gained influence among historians as the twentieth century progressed. Already in the nineteenth century some historians had emphasized the exploitative and oppressive aspects of modern European empires, which were built to feed the capitalist world's insatiable appetite for raw materials and markets. But the global spread of anticolonial ideologies and the breakup of European empires in the aftermath of World War II sparked a reassessment of imperial rule by historians and the emergence of the new fields of colonial and postcolonial studies in which the experiences of colonized peoples found voice. These historians put new emphasis on the massive bloodshed and oppression—enslavement, impoverishment, forced tribute and taxes, deportation—that frequently accompanied imperial conquest and rule. They also questioned the alleged "civilizing" missions of empires,

instead highlighting the repression or destruction of the cultures and societies of conquered peoples. Commenting on this more negative assessment of empire, one scholar has recently noted that "in our time 'imperialist' ranks second only to 'fascist' in the lexicon of political swear words."[26]

Over the past century, empires have been largely replaced by nation-states organized around the very different idea that sovereign countries should be composed of a single people or ethnic group. This transformation of the political landscape has sparked some nostalgic reflections on empires, perhaps none so influential or controversial as that of Niall Ferguson, a historian of the British Empire who recently argued that European empires were often better for their subjects than the local regimes they replaced. "It's hard to make the case . . . ," he declared, "that somehow the world would have been better off if the Europeans had stayed home. . . . Imperial guilt can lead to self-flagellation . . . [and] very simplistic judgements."[27] Other scholars, when comparing empires to modern nation-states, have found advantages to empires, especially their tolerance toward ethnic minorities within their boundaries.

The theme of empire resonates still among historians and the general public in the early twenty-first century. Is contemporary Russia seeking to re-create the old Russian Empire? Does Turkey want to replicate something of the Ottoman Empire? Does the global reach of the United States represent a new kind of empire, even if a declining one? The debates continue.

QUESTIONS TO CONSIDER

1. What variations in the experience of empires have historians noticed?

2. How might you account for their differing assessments of empire?

The Plague: An Afro-Eurasian Pandemic

Any benefits derived from participation in Mongol networks of communication and exchange must be measured alongside the hemispheric catastrophe known as the "**plague**" or the "pestilence" and later called the **Black Death**. Originating most likely in China, the bacteria responsible for the disease, known as *Yersinia pestis*, spread across the trade routes of the vast Mongol Empire in the early fourteenth century (see Map 11.2, page 472). Carried by rodents and transmitted by fleas to humans, the plague erupted initially in 1331 in northeastern China and had reached the Middle East and Western Europe by 1347. In 1409, the plague reached East Africa, probably by way of the famous Chinese maritime expeditions that encompassed the Indian Ocean basin.

Guided Reading Question

■ **CHANGE**
Disease changes societies. How might this argument apply to the plague?

The disease itself was associated with swelling of the lymph nodes, terrible headaches, high fever, and internal bleeding just below the skin. Infected people generally died within a few days. In the densely populated civilizations of China, the Islamic world, and Europe as well as in the steppe lands of the pastoralists, the plague claimed enormous numbers of human victims, causing a sharp contraction in Eurasian population for a century or more. Chroniclers reported rates of death that ranged from 50 to 90 percent of the affected population, depending on the time and place. A recent study suggests that about half of Europe's people perished during the initial outbreak of 1348–1350.[28] A fifteenth-century Egyptian historian wrote that within a month of the plague's arrival in 1349, "Cairo had become an abandoned desert. . . . Everywhere one heard lamentations and one could not pass by any house without being overwhelmed by the howling."[29] The Middle East generally had lost perhaps one-third of its population by the early fifteenth century.[30] The intense first wave of the plague was followed by periodic visitations over the next several centuries. However, other regions of the Eastern Hemisphere, especially India and sub-Saharan Africa, were much less affected.

In those places where it struck hardest, the plague left thoughtful people grasping for language with which to describe a horror of such unprecedented dimensions. One Italian man, who had buried all five of his children with his own hands, wrote in 1348 that "so many have died that everyone believes it is the end of the world."[31] Another Italian, the Renaissance scholar Francesco Petrarch, was equally stunned by the impact of the Black Death; he wrote to a friend in 1349:

> When at any time has such a thing been seen or spoken of? Has what happened in these years ever been read about: empty houses, derelict cities, ruined estates, fields strewn with cadavers, a horrible and vast solitude encompassing the whole world? Consult historians, they are silent; ask physicians, they are stupefied; seek the answers from philosophers, they shrug their shoulders, furrow their brows, and with fingers pressed against their lips, bid you be silent. Will posterity believe these things, when we who have seen it can scarcely believe it?[32]

In the Islamic world, the famous historian Ibn Khaldun, who had lost both of his parents to the plague, also wrote about it in apocalyptic terms:

> Civilization in both the East and the West was visited by a destructive plague which devastated nations and caused populations to vanish. It swallowed up many of the good things of civilization and wiped them out. . . . It was as if the voice of existence had called out for oblivion and restriction, and the world responded to its call.[33]

Beyond its immediate devastation, the Black Death worked longer-term social changes in Europe, the region where the plague's impact has been most thoroughly studied. Labor shortages following the initial outburst provoked sharp conflict between scarce workers, who sought higher wages or better conditions, and the rich, who resisted those demands. A series of peasant revolts in the fourteenth century reflected this tension, which also undermined the practice of serfdom. That labor shortage also may have fostered a greater interest in technological innovation and created, at least for a time, more employment opportunities for women. Thus a resilient European civilization survived a cataclysm that had the power to destroy it. In a strange way, that catastrophe may have actually fostered its future growth.

Whatever its impact in particular places, the plague also had larger consequences. Ironically, that human disaster, born of the Mongol network, was a primary reason for the demise of that network in the fourteenth and fifteenth centuries. Population contracted, cities declined, and the volume of trade diminished all across the Mongol world. By 1350, the Mongol Empire itself was in disarray, and within a century the Mongols had lost control of Chinese, Persian, and Russian civilizations. The Central Asian trade route, so critical to the entire Afro-Eurasian world economy, largely closed.

This disruption of the Mongol-based land routes to the East, coupled with a desire to avoid Muslim

The Plague This illustration depicts a European doctor visiting a patient with the plague. Notice that the doctor and others around the bedside cover their noses to prevent infection. During the Black Death, doctors were often criticized for refusing to treat dying patients, as they feared for their own lives.

intermediaries, provided incentives for Europeans to take to the sea in their continuing efforts to reach the riches of Asia. Their naval technology gave them military advantages on the seas, much as the Mongols' skill with the bow and their mobility on horseback gave these pastoralists a decisive edge in land battles. As Europeans penetrated Asian and Atlantic waters in the sixteenth century, they took on, in some ways, the role of the Mongols in organizing and fostering world trade and in creating a network of communication and exchange over an even larger area. Like the Mongols, Europeans were people on the periphery of the major established civilizations; they too were economically less developed in comparison to Chinese and Islamic civilizations. Both Mongols and Europeans were apt to forcibly plunder the wealthier civilizations they encountered, and European empire building in the Americas, like that of the Mongols in Eurasia, brought devastating disease and catastrophic population decline in its wake.[34] Europeans, of course, brought far more of their own culture and many more of their own people to the societies they conquered, as Christianity, European languages, settler societies, and Western science and technology took root within their empires. Although their imperial presence lasted far longer and operated on a much larger scale, European actions at the beginning of their global expansion bore some resemblance to those of their Mongol predecessors. Perhaps they were, as one historian put it, "the Mongols of the seas."[35]

REFLECTIONS

Changing Images of Pastoral Peoples

Historians frequently change their minds, and long-term consensus on most important matters has been difficult to achieve. For example, until recently, pastoralists generally received bad press in history books. Normally they entered the story only when they were threatening or destroying established civilizations. In presenting a largely negative image of pastoral peoples, historians were reflecting the long-held attitudes of literate elites in the civilizations of Eurasia. Fearing and usually despising such peoples, educated observers in China, the Middle East, and Europe often described them as bloodthirsty savages or barbarians, bringing only chaos and destruction in their wake. Han Kuan, a Chinese scholar of the first century B.C.E., described the Xiongnu people as "abandoned by Heaven . . . in foodless desert wastes, without proper houses, clothed in animal hides, eating their meat uncooked and drinking blood."[36] To the Christian Saint Jerome (340–420 C.E.), the Huns "filled the whole earth with slaughter and panic alike as they flitted hither and thither on their swift horses."[37] Almost a thousand years later, the famous Arab historian Ibn Khaldun described pastoralists in a very similar fashion: "It is their nature to plunder whatever other people possess."[38]

Because pastoral peoples generally did not have written languages, the sources available to historians came from less-than-unbiased observers in adjacent agricultural civilizations. Furthermore, in the long-running conflict across the farming/pastoral frontier, agricultural civilizations ultimately triumphed. Over the centuries, some pastoralist or semi-agricultural peoples, such as the Germanic tribes of Europe and the Arabs, created new civilizations. Others, such as the Turkic and Mongol peoples, took over existing civilizations or were encompassed within established agrarian empires. By the early twentieth century, and in most places much earlier, pastoral peoples everywhere had lost their former independence and had often shed their pastoral life as well. Since "winners" usually write history, the negative views of pastoralists held by agrarian civilizations normally prevailed.

Reflecting more inclusive contemporary values, historians in recent decades have sought to present a more balanced picture of pastoralists' role in world history, emphasizing what they created as well as what they destroyed. These historians have highlighted the achievements of herding peoples, such as their adaptation to inhospitable environments; their technological innovations; their development of horse-, camel-, or cattle-based cultures; their role in fostering cross-cultural exchange; and their state-building efforts.

A less critical or judgmental posture toward the Mongols may also owe something to the "total wars" and genocides of the twentieth century, in which the mass slaughter of civilians became a strategy to induce enemy surrender. During the cold war, the United States and the Soviet Union were prepared, apparently, to obliterate each other's entire population with nuclear weapons in response to an attack. In light of this recent history, Mongol massacres may appear a little less unique. Historians living in the glass houses of contemporary societies are perhaps more reluctant to cast stones at the Mongols. In understanding the Mongols, as in so much else, historians are shaped by the times and circumstances of their own lives as much as by "what really happened" in the past.

Second Thoughts

What's the Significance?

Big Picture Questions

1. What accounts for the often-negative attitudes of settled societies toward the pastoral peoples living on their borders?
2. Why have historians often neglected pastoral peoples' role in world history? How would you assess the perspective of this chapter toward the Mongols? Does the chapter strike you as negative and critical of the Mongols, as bending over backward to portray them in a positive light, or as a balanced presentation?

3. In what different ways did Mongol rule affect the Islamic world, Russia, China, and Europe? In what respects did it foster Eurasian integration?

4. Why did the Mongol Empire last only a relatively short time?

5. **Looking Back:** In what ways did the Mongol Empire resemble previous empires (Arab, Roman, Chinese, or the Greek empire of Alexander, for example), and in what ways did it differ from them?

Next Steps: For Further Study

John Aberth, *The First Horseman: Disease in Human History* (2007). A global study of the history of disease, with a fine chapter on the Black Death.

Thomas Allsen, *Culture and Conquest in Mongol Eurasia* (2001). A history of cultural exchange within the Mongol realm, particularly between China and the Islamic world.

Thomas J. Barfield, *The Nomadic Alternative* (1993). An anthropological and historical survey of pastoral peoples on a global basis.

Carter Finley, *The Turks in World History* (2005). The evolution of Turkic-speaking people, from their nomadic origins to the twentieth century.

Carl Fredrik Sverdrup, *The Mongol Conquests* (2017). A thorough analysis of the military dimension of the Mongol experience.

Jack Weatherford, *Genghis Khan and the Making of the Modern World* (2010). A lively, well-written, and balanced account of the world the Mongols made and the legacy they left for the future.

"Horseback Riding and Bronze Age Pastoralism in the Eurasian Steppes," http://www .youtube.com/watch?v=QapUGZOObjA. An illustrated lecture on the origins of pastoralism by David W. Anthony, a prominent scholar.

"The Mongols in World History," http://afe.easia.columbia.edu/mongols. A wonderful resource on the Mongols generally, with a particular focus on their impact in China.

Perceptions of the Mongols

Questions about perception across the boundaries of culture, class, or gender loom large in any study of world history. Such issues certainly arise as historians seek to understand the Mongol phenomenon. How did the Mongols, and especially their rulers, understand themselves and the huge empire they had created? And how were the Mongols perceived by others, especially those they conquered or threatened? The sources that follow provide some raw material for reflecting on those questions.

SOURCE 11.1 The Self-Perception of Mongol Rulers

Both Chinggis Khan and his son and successor Ogodei engaged in some thoughtful self-reflection about their achievements as well as their mistakes, limitations, and needs. Source 11.1A derives from a personally revealing letter that Chinggis Khan wrote to an elderly Chinese Daoist master named Changchun seeking guidance on the "means of preserving life" and requesting a personal meeting with the teacher. Changchun did arrive at Chinggis Khan's camp, but confessed that "no medicine for immortality" existed. And in Source 11.1B, Ogodei ponders his own successes and failures toward the end of his reign. His reflections are contained in the major literary work that emerged among the Mongols themselves, known as *The Secret History of the Mongols*. Its unknown author was likely a member of the royal household.

■ How does Chinggis Khan define his life's work? What is his image of himself? What does his request for a meeting with Changchun reveal about his own anxieties and his view of China?

■ What does Ogodei regard as his greatest achievements and his most notable mistakes?

■ What do these documents disclose about Mongol values and Mongol exercise of political authority?

SOURCE 11.1A
CHINGGIS KHAN │ *Letter to Changchun* │ 1219

Heaven has abandoned China owing to its haughtiness and extravagant luxury. But I, living in the northern wilderness, have not inordinate passions. I hate luxury and exercise moderation. I have only one coat and one food. I eat the same food and am dressed in the same tatters as my humble herdsmen. I consider the people my children, and take an interest in talented men as if they were my brothers. . . . At military exercises I am always in the front, and in time of battle am never behind. In the space of seven years I have succeeded in accomplishing a great work, and uniting the whole world into one empire. I have not myself distinguished qualities. But the government of the [Chinese] is inconstant, and therefore Heaven assists me to obtain the throne. . . .

All together have acknowledged my supremacy. It seems to me that since the remote time . . . such an empire has not been seen. . . . Since the time I came to the throne I have always taken to heart the ruling of my people; but I could not find worthy men to occupy [high offices]. . . . With respect to these circumstances I inquired, and heard that thou, master, hast penetrated the truth. . . . For a long time thou hast lived in the caverns of the rocks, and hast retired from the world; . . . [H]ave pity upon me, and communicate to me the means of preserving life. I shall serve thee myself. I hope that at least thou wilt leave me a trifle of thy wisdom.

Source: E. Bretschneider, *Medieval Researches for Eastern Asiatic Sources* (London, 1875), 1:37–39.

SOURCE 11.1B
The Secret History of the Mongols │ ca. 1240

Then Ogodei Khan spoke these words: "Since my father the Khan passed away and I came to sit on his great throne, what have I done? I went to war against the people of Cathay [China] and I destroyed them. For my second accomplishment I established a network of post stations so that my words are carried across the land with great speed. Another of my accomplishments has been to have my commanders dig wells in the desert so that there would be pasture and water for the people there. Lastly I placed spies and agents among all the people of the cities. In all directions I've brought peace to the Nation and the people. . . .

"But also since my father passed away . . . , I allowed myself to be conquered by wine. This was one of my mistakes. Another of my mistakes was to listen to a woman with no principles and because of her take away the daughters who belonged to my Uncle Odchigin. Even though I'm the Khan, the Lord of the Nation, I have no right to go against established principle, so this was my mistake.

"Another mistake was to secretly harm Dokholkhu. If you ask, 'Why was this wrong?' I would say that to secretly harm Dokholkhu, a man who had served his proper lord, my father the Khan, performing heroic deeds in his service, was a mistake. Now that I've done this, who'll perform heroic deeds in my service? Then my last mistake was to desire too much, to say to myself, 'I'm afraid that all the wild game born under Heaven will run off toward the land of my brothers.' So I ordered earthen walls to be built to keep the wild game from running away, but even as these walls were being built I heard my brothers speaking badly of me. I admit that I was wrong to do this. Since the time of my father the Khan I've added four accomplishments to all that he'd done and I've done four things which I admit were wrong."

Source: Paul Kahn, *The Secret History of the Mongols: The Origin of Chingis Khan* (San Francisco: North Point Press, 1984), 192–93.

■ ■ ■

SOURCE 11.2 **Picturing Khubilai Khan**

After Chinggis Khan, the most well known of the Mongol emperors was his grand-son, Khubilai Khan, whose main base lay in China, where he established the Yuan dynasty during the second half of the thirteenth century. He has been perceived and portrayed in various ways among the many peoples who encountered the Mongols. Three such images illustrate those different understandings of Khubilai Khan.

SOURCE 11.2A

LIU GUANDAO │ *Khubilai on a Hunt* │ **1280**

The first, showing Khubilai Khan on a Mongol hunt accompanied by his wife and various attendants, was painted by the Chinese artist Liu Guandao under a commission from Khubilai himself. It portrays Khubilai dressed in a traditional red imperial robe and white lambskin coat.

- What marks this as a hunting scene?

- Why might Khubilai order this painting to show him on a hunt, though he was clearly aged and obese?

- What do the other people in the image contribute to the overall impression it makes?

- Does this image represent a Chinese or a Mongol perception of Khubilai Khan?

SOURCE 11.2B

Marco Polo and Khubilai Khan | 15th century

A second image derives from a European artist who provided illustrations for Marco Polo's *Book of the Marvels of the World*, in which he describes his close to twenty years in Mongol-ruled China. It shows Marco Polo and his father Nicolai presenting letters and gifts from the pope to Khubilai Khan upon their arrival in the early 1270s.

■ What relationship between the Polos and the Mongol ruler is suggested in this image? What do the postures of the khan and his attendants imply about how the pope's gifts were received?

■ Why did the artist depict the khan with European features and dress and seated on a European-style throne?

■ How does this portrayal differ from that of Liu Guandao? Which artist provides a more authentic depiction of the khan and his retainers? What factors might explain the differences?

From the *Livre des Merveilles du Monde*, ca. 1410–1412 (tempera on vellum)/Boucicaut Master (fl. 1390–1430), and workshop/Bibliothèque Nationale de France, Paris, France/Bridgeman Images

SOURCE 11.2C

Khubilai Khan in Council with His Courtiers and Scribes | 1590

A third image of Khubilai Khan derives from India, which the Mongols attacked but never conquered. Over the centuries, a number of Turkic/Mongol groups invaded India, the most successful of which were the Mughals, who claimed descent from the Mongols and Chinggis Khan. During the sixteenth century, these Turkic warriors constructed the Mughal Empire over much of India, which boasted a magnificent court and a sophisticated Islamic Persian culture. It was from artists at that court that this painting emerged, showing Khubilai Khan, in a black robe at the top of the image, in council with his courtiers and officials.

Werner Forman/Getty Images

- What is distinctive about the setting in which Khubilai Khan is placed in this image?

- Why might an artist at the Mughal court present Khubilai Khan in this elaborate imperial setting? How might you compare this painting with the other two images of Khubilai Khan?

- In what specific ways do these images reflect the expectations of the cultures that produced them?

■ ■ ■

SOURCE 11.3 A Persian View of the Conquest of Bukhara

Literate members of societies conquered by the Mongols sometimes expressed their understanding of these dramatic events in writing. Among the most well known was the thirteenth-century Persian historian Juvaini, himself a high official in the Mongol government ruling his Persian homeland. He composed an account of the creation of the Mongol Empire titled *The History of the World Conqueror*. In this excerpt from that work, he describes the Mongol conquest of the city of Bukhara, a major commercial and intellectual center of the Persian Islamic world located in what is now Uzbekistan.

- How might you describe Juvaini's posture toward the Mongols? What factors might have influenced his portrayal of them?

- What can we learn about the policies and strategies of the Mongols from Juvaini's account? What parts of this account seem most reliable?

- What aspects of Mongol behavior would be most offensive to Muslims?

- How did Chinggis Khan justify his conquest of Bukhara?

JUVAINI | *The History of the World Conqueror* | **1219**

[Chinggis Khan's] troops were more numerous than ants or locusts, being in their multitude beyond estimation or computation. . . . When [our] forces reached the banks of the Oxus, the patrols and advance parties of the Mongol army fell upon them and left no trace of them.

On the following day . . . Chingis-Khan . . . entered to inspect the town and citadel. He rode into the Juma Mosque. . . . Chingis-Khan asked those present whether this was the palace of the Sultan; they replied it was the house of God. Then he too got down from his horse, and mounting two or three steps of the pulpit he exclaimed: "The countryside is empty of fodder, fill our horses' bellies." Whereupon they opened all the magazines in the town and began carrying off the grain. And they brought the cases in which the Qurans were kept out in the courtyard of the mosque, where they cast the Qurans right and left and turned the cases into mangers for their horses. After which they circulated cups and sent for the singing-girls of the town to sing and dance for them; while the Mongols raised their voices to the tunes of their own songs. . . . [T]he leaves of the Quran were trampled beneath the dirt beneath their own feet and their horses' hooves.

When Chingis-Khan left the town, he went to the festival muhalla and mounted the pulpit. . . . He then began a speech, in which, after describing the resistance and treachery of the Sultan, he addressed them as follows: "O People! know that you have committed great sins, and that the great ones among you have committed these sins. If you ask me what proof I have for these words, I say it is because I am the punishment of God. If you had not committed these great sins, God would not have sent a punishment like me upon you." When he had finished speaking in this strain, he continued his discourse with words of admonition, saying, "There is no need to declare your property that is on the face of the earth; tell me of that which is in the belly of the earth." . . . [A]lthough not subjecting them to disgrace or humiliation, they began to exact money from these men; and when they delivered it up they did not torment them by excessive punishment or demanding what was beyond their power to pay.

Chingis-Khan had given orders for the Sultan's troops to be driven out of the interior of the town and the citadel. . . . [H]e now gave orders for all quarters of the town to be set on fire; and since the houses were built entirely out of wood, within several days the greater part of the town had been consumed. . . . Then the people of Bukhara were driven against the citadel. And on either side the furnace of battle was heated. On the outside, mangonels [catapults] were erected, bows bent, and stones and arrows discharged, and, on the inside . . . pots of naphtha [a flammable liquid] were set in motion. It was like a red hot furnace. . . . For days they fought in this manner. . . . But finally . . . resistance was no longer in their power. . . . The moat had been filled with animate and inanimate and raised up with [the bodies of] levies [soldiers] and Bukharans. . . . [T]heir khans, leaders and notables . . . now became captives of abasement and were drowned in the sea of annihilation. . . . Of the Qanqli [Turkic defenders of the city] no male was spared who stood higher than the butt of a whip and more than thirty thousand were counted amongst the slain; whilst their small children, the children of their nobles and their womenfolk, slender as the cypress, were sold to slavery.

When the town and the citadel had been purged of rebels and the walls and outworks levelled with the dust, the inhabitants of the town, men and women, ugly and beautiful, were driven out onto the field of the *musalla* [an open space outside of a mosque]. Chingis-Khan spared their lives, but the youths and full-grown men that were fit for such service were pressed into a levy [body of soldiers] for the attack on Samarqand and Dabusiya.

Source: Juvaini, *The History of the World Conqueror*, translated by John Boyle (Manchester: Manchester University Press, 1958), 103–6.

■ ■ ■

SOURCE 11.4　A European View of Mongol Life

Although Western Europe was never conquered by the Mongols, European traders such as Marco Polo and various envoys from church or state authorities had contact with the Mongol Empire, especially in China. The accounts of these visitors provided Europeans with impressions of Mongol society. One of them, a Flemish Franciscan friar named William of Rubruck (1220–1293), left a detailed account of Mongol life in the mid-thirteenth century, which included observations about the domestic roles of men and women.

■　How does William of Rubruck portray the lives of Mongol women? What was the class background of the Mongol women he describes?

■　What do you think he would have found most upsetting about the position of women in Mongol society?

■ Based on this account, how might you compare the life of Mongol women to
   that of women in more established civilizations, such as China, Europe, or the
   Islamic world?

WILLIAM OF RUBRUCK | *Journey to the Land of the Mongols* | ca. 1255

The matrons [married women] make for themselves most beautiful [luggage] carts.... A single rich Mo'al or Tartar [Mongol] has quite one hundred or two hundred such carts with coffers. ... And when they set up their houses, the first wife places her dwelling on the extreme west side, and after her the others according to their rank, so that the last wife will be in the extreme east; ... The *ordu* [residence] of a rich Mo'al seems like a large town, though there will be very few men in it.

It is the duty of the women to drive the carts, get the dwellings on and off them, milk the cows, make butter and *gruit* [sour curd], and to dress and sew skins, which they do with a thread made of tendons. They divide the tendons into fine shreds, and then twist them into one long thread. They also sew the boots, the socks, and the clothing. They never wash clothes, for they say that God would be angered, and that it would thunder if they hung them up to dry. They will even beat those they find washing [their clothes]. Thunder they fear extraordinarily; and when it thunders they will turn out of their dwellings all strangers, wrap themselves in black felt, and thus hide themselves till it has passed away. Furthermore, they never wash their bowls, but when the meat is cooked they rinse out the dish in which they are about to put it with some of the boiling broth from the kettle, which they pour back into it. They [the women] also make the felt and cover the houses.

The men make bows and arrows, manufacture stirrups and bits, make saddles, do the carpentering on their dwellings and the carts; they take care of the horses, milk the mares, churn the *cosmos* or

mare's milk, make the skins in which it is put; they also look after the camels and load them. Both sexes look after the sheep and goats, sometimes the men, other times the women, milking them.

As to their marriages, you must know that no one among them has a wife unless he buys her; so it sometimes happens that girls are well past marriageable age before they marry, for their parents always keep them until they sell them.... Among them no widow marries, for the following reason: they believe that all who serve them in this life shall serve them in the next, so as regards a widow they believe that she will always return to her first husband after death. Hence this shameful custom prevails among them, that sometimes a son takes to wife all his father's wives, except his own mother; for the *ordu* of the father and mother always belongs to the youngest son, so it is he who must provide for all his father's wives ... and if he wishes it, he uses them as wives, for he esteems not himself injured if they return to his father after death. When then anyone has made a bargain with another to take his daughter, the father of the girl gives a feast, and the girl flees to her relatives and hides there. Then the father says: "Here, my daughter is yours: take her wheresoever you find her." Then he searches for her with his friends till he finds her, and he must take her by force and carry her off with a semblance of violence to his house.

Source: *The Journey of William of Rubruck* . . . , translated from the Latin and edited, with an introductory notice, by William Woodville Rockhill (London: Hakluyt Society, 1900), 56–57, 75–78.

DOING HISTORY

1. **Assessing sources:** What are the strengths and limitations of these sources for understanding the Mongols? Taking the positions of their authors or artists into account, what exaggerations, biases, or misunderstandings can you identify in these sources? What information seems credible, and what should be viewed more skeptically?

2. **Characterizing the Mongols:** Based on these sources and on the text of Chapter 11, write an essay arguing that the Mongols were more than destructive barbarians. How do your own values affect your understanding of the Mongol moment?

3. **Considering values and practice:** How would you describe the core values of Mongol culture? (Consider the leaders' goals, their attitudes toward conquered peoples, the duties of rulers, the views of political authority, and the role of women.) To what extent were these values put into practice in acquiring and ruling the Mongols' huge empire? And in what ways were these values undermined or eroded as that empire took shape?

4. **Assessing perceptions:** In what ways do the sources deriving from outside the Mongol world affirm or challenge the Mongols' own view of themselves?

Assessing the Mongol Impact

What has been the impact of the Mongol Empire? It is a question with which many historians have struggled. The answer, of course, is "it depends." It depends on whether historians are looking at the extraordinarily brutal process by which the empire was constructed or the later period of settled administration and adaptation to the cultures of conquered peoples. It also depends on whether they are interested in particular societies, such as China, or the larger interacting network of the Afro-Eurasian world. And finally, it depends on what aspect of Mongol life engages their attention—political, economic, or cultural, for example. In Voice 11.1, historian Jack Weatherford takes a global and quite positive view of the Mongol era, while Voice 11.2 by Paul S. Ropp focuses more explicitly on China and with a more critical posture.

- What does Voice 11.1 praise about the Mongols? What might he be leaving out of this account?

- What does Voice 11.2 criticize about Mongol rule in China? What might he be omitting?

- The author of Voice 11.1 has focused his research on the Mongols, while Voice 11.2 was written by a historian of China. How might these scholarly commitments have shaped their outlook on the Mongols?

- **Integrating Primary and Secondary Sources:** How might one or more of the primary sources support or challenge the conclusions of these historians?

VOICE 11.1

Jack Weatherford on the Mongols in World History | 2004

Genghis [Chinggis] Khan's empire connected and amalgamated the many civilizations around him into a new world order. . . . By the time of his death in 1227, he had connected them with diplomatic and commercial contacts that still remain unbroken.

As he smashed the feudal system of aristocratic privilege and birth, he built a new and unique system based on individual merit, loyalty, and achievement. He took the disjointed and languorous trading towns along the Silk Route and organized them into the world's largest free trade zone. He lowered taxes for everyone, and abolished them altogether for doctors, teachers, priests, and educational institutions. He established a regular census and created the first international postal system. . . . He widely distributed the goods he acquired in combat, so that they could make their way back into commercial circulation. He created an international law. . . . Genghis Khan insisted on laws holding rulers as equally accountable as the lowest herder. He granted religious freedom in his realms, though he demanded total loyalty from conquered subjects of all religions. He insisted on the rule of law and abolished torture. . . . He refused to hold hostages and, instead, instituted the novel practice of granting diplomatic immunity for all ambassadors and envoys. . . .

Source: Jack Weatherford, *Genghis Khan and the Making of the Modern World* (New York: Broadway Books, 2004), xix.

VOICE 11.2

Paul S. Ropp on the Mongol Impact on China's Economy | 2010

The Mongol conquest of China took a terrible economic toll. The Song [dynasty] iron industry was devastated and never fully regained Song levels of productivity. Intense warfare greatly reduced the population, and the spread of infectious diseases, such as bubonic plague, from Central Asia to China produced several terrible epidemics that killed millions in the fourteenth century (and eliminated one-fourth of Europe's population soon thereafter). The wars destroyed farmlands and irrigation works, and in places Mongol princes and generals turned rice-producing land into parks and pastures. The combined effect of war and disease greatly reduced the tax base. The Yuan government responded by printing more money, which only fueled inflation and undermined the economic health of the dynasty. . . .

The Mongols ambitiously undertook naval expeditions of conquest against Japan . . . and against the kingdom of Java. They also launched attacks on Vietnam and Burma. . . . These wars were a serious drain on the state's resources and only served to delay the economic recovery of the Yuan from the dislocation of their early years.

Source: Paul S. Ropp, *China in World History* (Oxford: Oxford University Press, 2010), 81–82.

The Worlds of the Fifteenth Century

« The Meeting of Two Worlds This nineteenth-century painting shows Columbus on his first voyage to the New World. He is reassuring his anxious sailors by pointing to the first sight of land. In light of its long-range consequences, this voyage represents a major turning point in world history.

By 2016, a number of American cities and the state of Vermont had transformed October 12 from a celebration of Columbus Day to a commemoration of Indigenous Peoples Day. Opposed in many places, such transformations of the holiday reflected a growing debate about the significance and legacy of Columbus. Was he "a perpetrator of genocide . . . , a slave trader, a thief, a pirate, and most certainly not a hero,"[1] as Winona LaDuke, president of the Indigenous Women's Network, declared in 1992, which marked the 500th anniversary of Columbus's arrival in the Americas? Or should Americans celebrate Columbus, as the Latino novelist and publisher Jonathan Marcantoni recommended in 2015, remembering "his achievement of connecting the Europeans with the Americas . . . because without it, the societies we love would not exist"?[2] ■

This sharp debate about Columbus reminds us that the past is endlessly contested and that it continues to resonate in the present. But it also reflects a broad agreement that the voyages of Columbus marked a decisive turning point, for better or worse, in world history and represent arguably the most important event of the fifteenth century.

It was not, however, the only globally significant departure of that century. If Columbus launched a European empire-building process in the Americas, other empires were also in the making during the fifteenth century. In 1383, a Central Asian Turkic warrior named Timur launched the last major pastoral invasion of adjacent civilizations. Then in 1405, an enormous Chinese fleet set out across the entire Indian Ocean basin, only to voluntarily withdraw twenty-eight years later, thus forgoing an empire in Asia. Four new empires gave the Islamic world a distinct political and cultural shape. One of them, the Ottoman Empire, put a final end to Christian Byzantium with the conquest of Constantinople in 1453, even as Spanish Christians completed the "reconquest" of the Iberian Peninsula from the Muslims in 1492. And in the Americas, the Aztec and Inca empires gave a final and spectacular expression to Mesoamerican and Andean civilizations before they were both swallowed up in the burst of European imperialism that followed the arrival of Columbus.

Because the fifteenth century was a hinge of major historical change on many fronts, it provides an occasion for a bird's-eye view of the world through an imaginary global tour. This excursion around the world will serve to briefly review the human saga thus far and to establish a baseline from which the enormous transformations of the centuries that followed might be measured. How, then, might we describe the world, and the worlds, of the fifteenth century?

SEEKING THE MAIN POINT

What predictions about the future might a global traveler in the fifteenth century have reasonably made?

Societies and Cultures of the Fifteenth Century

One way to describe the world of the fifteenth century is to identify the various types of human communities that it contained. Bands of gatherers and hunters, villages of agricultural peoples, newly emerging chiefdoms or small states, pastoral communities, established civilizations and empires—all of these social or political forms would have been apparent to a widely traveled visitor in the fifteenth century. Representing alternative ways of organizing human life, all of them were long established by the fifteenth century, but the balance among them in 1500 was quite different than it had been a thousand years earlier.

Paleolithic Persistence: Australia and North America

Despite millennia of agricultural advance, substantial areas of the world still hosted gathering and hunting societies, known to historians as Paleolithic (Old Stone Age) peoples. All of Australia, much of Siberia, the arctic coastlands, and parts of Africa and the Americas fell into this category. These peoples were not simply relics of a bygone age, for they too had a history, although most history books largely ignore them after the age of agriculture arrived. Nonetheless, this most ancient way of life still had a sizable and variable presence in the world of the fifteenth century.

Consider, for example, Australia. That continent's many separate groups, some 250 of them, still practiced a gathering and hunting way of life in the fifteenth century, a pattern that continued well after Europeans arrived in the late eighteenth century. Over many thousands of years, these people had assimilated various material items or cultural practices from outsiders—outrigger canoes, fishhooks, complex netting techniques, artistic styles, rituals, and mythological ideas—but despite the presence of farmers in nearby New Guinea, no agricultural practices penetrated the Australian mainland. Was it because large areas of Australia were unsuited for

Guided Reading Question

■ COMPARISON

In what ways did the gathering and hunting people of Australia differ from those of the northwest coast of North America?

Landmarks for Chapter 12

	1375	1400	1425	1450	1475	1500	1525

CHINA

1368–1644
Ming dynasty

1402–1424
Emperor Yongle relocates capital to Beijing;
Forbidden City constructed

1405–1433 Chinese maritime voyages

EUROPE

1337–1453
Hundred Years' War

ca. 1350–1500
European Renaissance

1415–1497
Portuguese exploration
of West African coast

1492–1498
Columbus's voyage to the Americas;
da Gama's voyage to India

1492
Christian reconquest of
Muslim Spain completed

ISLAMIC WORLD

1453
Ottoman seizure of Constantinople

1464
Founding of Songhay Empire in West Africa

1501
Founding of Safavid
Empire in Persia

1526
Founding of Mughal Empire in India

THE AMERICAS

1345–1528
Aztec Empire

ca. 1400–1450
Iroquois League established

1438–1533
Inca Empire

495

the kind of agriculture practiced in New Guinea? Or did the peoples of Australia, enjoying an environment of sufficient resources, simply see no need to change their way of life?

Despite the absence of agriculture, Australia's peoples had mastered and manipulated their environment, in part through "firestick farming," the practice of deliberately setting fires, which they described as "cleaning up the country." These controlled burns cleared the underbrush, thus making hunting easier and encouraging the growth of certain plant and animal species. In addition, native Australians exchanged goods among themselves over distances of hundreds of miles, created elaborate mythologies and ritual practices, and developed sophisticated traditions of sculpture and rock painting. They accomplished all of this on the basis of an economy and technology rooted in the distant Paleolithic past.

A very different kind of gathering and hunting society flourished in the fifteenth century along the northwest coast of North America among the Chinookan, Tulalip, Skagit, and other peoples. With some 300 edible animal species and an abundance of salmon and other fish, this extraordinarily bounteous environment provided the foundation for what scholars sometimes call "complex" or "affluent" gathering and hunting cultures. What distinguished the northwest coast peoples from those of Australia were permanent village settlements with large and sturdy houses, considerable economic specialization, ranked societies that sometimes included slavery, chiefdoms dominated by powerful clan leaders or "big men," and extensive storage of food.

Although these and other gathering and hunting peoples persisted in the fifteenth century, both their numbers (an estimated 1 percent of the world's population by 1500) and the area they inhabited had contracted greatly as the Agricultural Revolution unfolded across the planet. That relentless advance of the farming frontier continued in the centuries ahead as the Russian, Chinese, and European empires encompassed the lands of the remaining Paleolithic peoples.

Agricultural Village Societies: The Igbo and the Iroquois

Far more numerous than gatherers and hunters but still a small percentage of the total world population were those many peoples who, though fully agricultural, had avoided incorporation into larger empires or civilizations and had not developed their own city- or state-based societies. Living usually in small village-based communities and organized in terms of kinship relations, such people predominated during the fifteenth century in much of North America; in most of the tropical lowlands of South America and the Caribbean; in parts of the Amazon River basin, Southeast Asia, and Africa south of the equator; and throughout Pacific Oceania. Historians have often treated them as marginal to the cities, states, and large-scale civilizations that predominate in most accounts of the global past. Viewed from within their own circles, though, these societies were at the center of things, each with its own history of migration, cultural transformation, social conflict, incorporation of new people, political rise and fall, and interaction with strangers.

East of the Niger River in the heavily forested region of West Africa lay the lands of the **Igbo** (EE-boh) peoples. By the fifteenth century, their neighbors, the Yoruba and Bini, had begun to develop small states and urban centers. But the Igbo, whose dense population and extensive trading networks might well have given rise to states, declined to follow suit. The deliberate Igbo preference was to reject the kingship and state-building efforts of their neighbors. They boasted on occasion that "the Igbo have no kings." Instead, they relied on other institutions to maintain social cohesion beyond the level of the village: title societies in which wealthy men received a series of prestigious ranks, women's associations, hereditary ritual experts serving as mediators, and a balance of power among kinship groups. It was a "stateless society," famously described in Chinua Achebe's *Things Fall Apart*, the most widely read novel to emerge from twentieth-century Africa.

But the Igbo peoples and their neighbors did not live in isolated, self-contained societies. They traded actively among themselves and with more distant peoples, such as the large African kingdom of Songhay (sahn-GEYE) far to the north. Cotton cloth, fish, copper and iron goods, decorative objects, and more drew neighboring peoples into networks of exchange. Common artistic traditions reflected a measure of cultural unity in a politically fragmented region, and all of these peoples seem to have changed from a matrilineal to a patrilineal system of tracing their descent. Little of this registered in the larger civilizations of the Afro-Eurasian world, but to the peoples of the West African forest during the fifteenth century, these processes were central to their history and their daily lives. Soon, however, all of them would be caught up in the transatlantic slave trade and would be changed substantially in the process.

Across the Atlantic in what is now central New York State, other agricultural village societies were also undergoing major change during the several centuries preceding their incorporation into European trading networks and empires. The Iroquois-speaking peoples of that region had only recently become fully agricultural, adopting maize- and bean-farming techniques that had originated centuries earlier in Mesoamerica. As this productive agriculture took hold by 1300 or so, the population grew, the size of settlements increased, and distinct peoples emerged. Frequent warfare also erupted among them. Some scholars have speculated that as agriculture, largely seen as women's work, became the primary economic activity, "warfare replaced successful food getting as the avenue to male prestige."[3]

Whatever caused it, this increased level of conflict among **Iroquois** peoples triggered a remarkable political innovation around the fifteenth century: a loose alliance or confederation among five Iroquois-speaking peoples—the Mohawk, Oneida, Onondaga, Cayuga, and Seneca (see Map 12.5, page 515). Based on an agreement known as the Great Law of Peace, the Five Nations, as they called themselves, agreed to settle their differences peacefully through a confederation council of clan leaders, some fifty of them altogether, who had the authority to adjudicate

Guided Reading Question

■ **CHANGE**
What kinds of changes were transforming the societies of the West African Igbo and the North American Iroquois as the fifteenth century unfolded?

Iroquois Women This seventeenth-century French engraving depicts two Iroquois women preparing a meal. Among the Iroquois, women controlled both agriculture and property and had a significant voice in public affairs. (From "Historiae Canadensis" by Father Francisco Creuxio, 1664/De Agostini Picture Library/Bridgeman Images)

disputes and set reparation payments. Operating by consensus, the Iroquois League of Five Nations effectively suppressed the blood feuds and tribal conflicts that had only recently been so widespread. It also coordinated its peoples' relationship with outsiders, including the Europeans, who arrived in growing numbers in the centuries after 1500.

The Iroquois League gave expression to values of limited government, social equality, and personal freedom, concepts that some European colonists found highly attractive. One British colonial administrator declared in 1749 that the Iroquois had "such absolute Notions of Liberty that they allow no Kind of Superiority of one over another, and banish all Servitude from their Territories."[4] Such equality extended to gender relationships, for among the Iroquois, descent was matrilineal (reckoned through the woman's line), married couples lived with the wife's family, and women controlled agriculture and property. While men were hunters, warriors, and the primary political officeholders, women selected and could depose those leaders.

Wherever they lived in 1500, over the next several centuries independent agricultural peoples such as the Iroquois and Igbo were increasingly encompassed in expanding economic networks and conquest empires based in Western Europe, Russia, China, or India, as had many other such peoples before them.

Pastoral Peoples: Central Asia and West Africa

Pastoral peoples had long impinged more directly and dramatically on civilizations than did gathering and hunting or agricultural village societies. The Mongol incursion, along with the enormous empire to which it gave rise, was one in a long series of challenges from the steppes, but it was not quite the last. As the Mongol Empire disintegrated, a brief attempt to restore it occurred in the late fourteenth and early fifteenth centuries under the leadership of a Turkic warrior named **Timur**, born in what is now Uzbekistan and known in the West as Tamerlane (see Map 12.1, page 501).

With a ferocity that matched or exceeded that of his model, Chinggis Khan, Timur's army of pastoralists brought immense devastation yet again to Russia and Persia, and also to India. Timur himself died in 1405, while preparing for an invasion of China. Conflicts among his successors prevented any lasting empire, although his

Guided Reading Question

■ **SIGNIFICANCE**
What role did Central Asian and West African pastoralists play in their respective regions?

descendants retained control of the area between Persia and Afghanistan for the rest of the fifteenth century. That state hosted a sophisticated elite culture combining Turkic and Persian elements, particularly at its splendid capital of Samarkand, as its rulers patronized artists, poets, traders, and craftsmen. Timur's conquest proved to be the last great military success of pastoral peoples from Central Asia. In the centuries that followed, their homelands were swallowed up in the expanding Russian and Chinese empires, as the balance of power between steppe pastoralists of inner Eurasia and the civilizations of outer Eurasia turned decisively in favor of the latter.

Modern Fulbe Herdsmen This photo shows modern Fulbe herdsmen from Nigeria tending to perhaps their most distinctive animal, long-horned cattle. Wealth in many pastoralist groups is reckoned through the size of cattle herds. (Eye Ubiquitous/ Newscom)

In Africa, pastoral peoples stayed independent of established empires several centuries longer than those of Inner Asia, for not until the late nineteenth century were they incorporated into European colonial states. The experience of the **Fulbe** (FULB), West Africa's largest pastoral society, provides an example of an African herding people with a highly significant role in the fifteenth century and beyond. From their homeland in the western fringe of the Sahara along the upper Senegal River, the Fulbe had migrated gradually eastward in the centuries after 1000 C.E. (see Map 12.3, page 506). Unlike the pastoral peoples of Inner Asia, they generally lived in small communities among agricultural peoples and paid various grazing fees and taxes for the privilege of pasturing their cattle. Relations with their farming hosts often were tense because the Fulbe resented their subordination to agricultural peoples, whose way of life they despised. That sense of cultural superiority became even more pronounced as the Fulbe, in the course of their eastward movement, slowly adopted Islam. Some of them in fact dropped out of a pastoral life and settled in towns, where they became highly respected religious leaders. In the eighteenth and nineteenth centuries, the Fulbe were at the center of a wave of religiously based uprisings, or jihads, that greatly expanded the practice of Islam and gave rise to a series of new states ruled by the Fulbe themselves.

Civilizations of the Fifteenth Century: Comparing China and Europe

Beyond the foraging, farming, and pastoral societies of the fifteenth-century world were its civilizations, those city-centered and state-based societies that were far larger and more densely populated, more powerful and innovative, and much more unequal in terms of class and gender than other forms of human community. Since the First Civilizations had emerged between 3500 and 1000 B.C.E., both the geographic space they encompassed and the number of people they embraced had grown substantially. By the fifteenth century, about 30 percent of the world's land was controlled by states and a considerable majority of the world's population lived within one or another of these civilizations. But most of these people, no doubt, identified more with local communities than with a larger civilization. What might an imaginary global traveler notice about the world's major civilizations in the fifteenth century?

Ming Dynasty China

Such a traveler might well begin his or her journey in China. That civilization had been greatly disrupted by a century of Mongol rule, and its population had been sharply reduced by the plague. During the **Ming dynasty** (1368–1644), however, China recovered (see Map 12.1). In the early decades of that dynasty, the Chinese attempted to eliminate all signs of foreign rule, discouraging the use of Mongol names and dress while promoting Confucian learning and orthodox gender roles based on earlier models from the Han, Tang, and Song dynasties. Emperor Yongle (YAHNG-leh) (r. 1402–1424) sponsored an enormous *Encyclopedia* of some 11,000 volumes. With contributions from more than 2,000 scholars, this work sought to summarize or compile all previous writing on history, geography, philosophy, ethics, government, and more. Yongle also relocated the capital to Beijing, ordered the building of a magnificent imperial residence known as the Forbidden City, and constructed the Temple of Heaven, where subsequent rulers performed Confucian-based rituals to ensure the well-being of Chinese society. Two empresses wrote instructions for female behavior, emphasizing traditional expectations after the disruptions of the previous century. Culturally speaking, China was looking to its past.

Politically, the Ming dynasty reestablished the civil service examination system that had been neglected under Mongol rule and went on to create a highly centralized government. Power was concentrated in the hands of the emperor himself, while a cadre of eunuchs (castrated men) personally loyal to the emperor exercised great authority, much to the dismay of the official bureaucrats. The state acted vigorously to repair the damage of the Mongol years by restoring millions of acres to cultivation; rebuilding canals, reservoirs, and irrigation works; and planting, according to some estimates, a billion trees in an effort to reforest China. As a result, the economy rebounded, both international and domestic trade flourished, and the population grew. During the fifteenth century, China had recovered and was perhaps the best governed and most prosperous of the world's major civilizations.

China also undertook the largest and most impressive maritime expeditions the world had ever seen. Since the eleventh century, Chinese sailors and traders

Guided Reading Question
....

■ **DESCRIPTION**
How would you define the major achievements of Ming dynasty China?

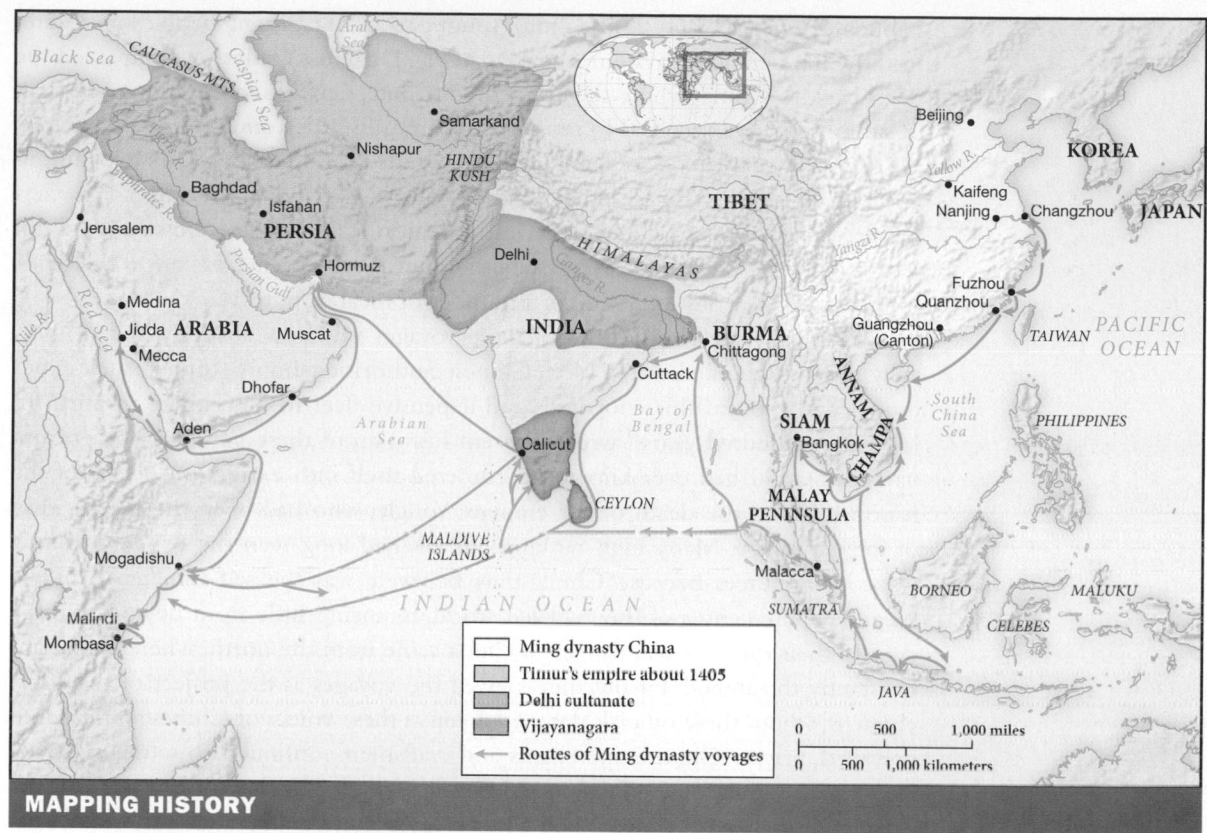

MAPPING HISTORY

Map 12.1 Asia in the Fifteenth Century

The fifteenth century in Asia witnessed the massive Ming dynasty voyages into the Indian Ocean, the last major eruption of pastoral power in Timur's empire, and the flourishing of the maritime city of Malacca.

READING THE MAP: Which major cities did the Ming dynasty voyages visit?

MAKING CONNECTIONS: Compare Map 12.1 with Map 11.1. Which part of the Mongol Empire did Timur's empire most closely resemble? OR Compare Map 12.1 with Map 13.3. How did the Chinese empire evolve after the Qing dynasty replaced the Ming?

had been a major presence in the South China Sea and in Southeast Asian port cities, with much of this activity in private hands. But now, after decades of preparation, an enormous fleet, commissioned by Emperor Yongle himself, was launched in 1405, followed over the next twenty-eight years by six more such expeditions. On board more than 300 ships of the first voyage was a crew of some 27,000, including 180 physicians, hundreds of government officials, 5 astrologers, 7 high-ranking or grand eunuchs, carpenters, tailors, accountants, merchants, translators, cooks, and thousands of soldiers and sailors. Visiting many ports in Southeast Asia, Indonesia, India, Arabia, and East Africa, these fleets, captained by the Muslim eunuch **Zheng He** (JUHNG-huh), sought to enroll distant peoples and states in the Chinese tribute system (see Map 12.1). Dozens of rulers accompanied the fleets back to China, where they presented tribute, performed the required rituals of submission, and received in return abundant gifts, titles, and trading opportunities. Officially described as "bringing order to the world," Zheng He's expeditions served to establish Chinese power and prestige in the Indian Ocean and to exert Chinese control over foreign trade in the region. The Chinese, however, did not seek to conquer new territories, establish Chinese settlements, or spread their culture, though they did intervene in a number of local disputes.

The most surprising feature of these voyages was how abruptly and deliberately they were ended. After 1433, Chinese authorities simply stopped such expeditions and allowed this enormous and expensive fleet to deteriorate in port. "In less than a hundred years," wrote a recent historian of these voyages, "the greatest navy the world had ever known had ordered itself into extinction."[5] Part of the reason involved the death of the emperor Yongle, who had been the chief patron of the enterprise. Many high-ranking officials had long seen the expeditions as a waste of resources because China, they believed, was the self-sufficient "middle kingdom," the center of the civilized world, requiring little from beyond its borders. In their eyes, the real danger to China came from the north, where barbarians constantly threatened. Finally, they viewed the voyages as the project of the court eunuchs, whom these officials despised. Even as these voices of Chinese officialdom prevailed, private Chinese merchants and craftsmen continued to settle and trade in Japan, the Philippines, Taiwan, and Southeast Asia, but they did so without the support of their government. The Chinese state quite deliberately turned its back on what was surely within its reach—a large-scale maritime empire in the Indian Ocean basin.

European Comparisons: State Building and Cultural Renewal

At the other end of the Eurasian continent, similar processes of demographic recovery, political consolidation, cultural flowering, and overseas expansion were under way. Western Europe, having escaped Mongol conquest but devastated by the plague, began to regrow its population during the second half of the fifteenth century. As in China, the infrastructure of civilization proved a durable foundation for demographic and economic revival.

Politically too, Europe joined China in continuing earlier patterns of state building. In China, however, this meant a unitary and centralized government that encompassed almost the whole of its civilization, while in Europe a decidedly fragmented system of many separate, independent, and highly competitive states made for a sharply divided Western civilization (see Map 12.2). Many of these states—Spain, Portugal, France, England, the city-states of Italy (Milan, Venice, and Florence), various German principalities—learned to tax their citizens more

Map 12.2 Europe in 1500

By the end of the fifteenth century, Christian Europe had assumed its early modern political shape as a system of competing states threatened by an expanding Muslim Ottoman Empire.

efficiently, to create more effective administrative structures, and to raise standing armies. A small Russian state centered on the city of Moscow also emerged in the fifteenth century as Mongol rule faded away. Much of this state building was driven by the needs of war, a frequent occurrence in such a fragmented and competitive political environment. England and France, for example, fought intermittently for more than a century in the Hundred Years' War (1337–1453) over rival claims to territory in France. Nothing remotely similar disturbed the internal life of Ming dynasty China.

**Guided Reading
Question**

....

■ **COMPARISON**
What political and cultural differences stand out in the histories of fifteenth-century China and Western Europe? What similarities are apparent?

A renewed cultural blossoming, the **European Renaissance**, likewise paralleled the revival of all things Confucian in Ming dynasty China. In Europe, however, that blossoming celebrated and reclaimed a classical Greco-Roman tradition that earlier had been lost or obscured. Beginning in the vibrant commercial cities of Italy between roughly 1350 and 1500, the Renaissance reflected the belief of the wealthy male elite that they were living in a wholly new era, far removed from the confined religious world of feudal Europe. Educated citizens of these cities sought inspiration in the art and literature of ancient Greece and Rome; they were "returning to the sources," as they put it. Their purpose was not so much to reconcile these works with the ideas of Christianity, as the twelfth- and thirteenth-century university scholars had done, but to use them as a cultural standard to imitate and then to surpass. The elite patronized great Renaissance artists such as Leonardo da Vinci, Michelangelo, and Raphael, whose paintings and sculptures were far more naturalistic, particularly in portraying the human body, than those of their medieval counterparts. Some of these artists looked to the Islamic world for standards of excellence, sophistication, and abundance. (See Working with Evidence: Islam and Renaissance Europe, page 527.)

Although religious themes remained prominent, Renaissance artists now included portraits and busts of well-known contemporary figures and scenes from ancient mythology. In the work of those scholars known as humanists, reflections on secular topics such as grammar, history, politics, poetry, rhetoric, and ethics complemented more religious matters. For example, Niccolò Machiavelli's (1469–1527) famous work *The Prince* was a prescription for political success based on the way politics actually operated in a highly competitive Italy of rival city-states rather than on idealistic and religiously based principles. His slim volume was filled with ruthless advice, including the observation that "the ends justify the means" when ruling a state and that it was safer for a sovereign to be feared than loved by his subjects. But the teachings in *The Prince* were controversial, with many critics at the time rejecting its amoral analysis of political life and its assertion that rulers should—indeed must—set aside moral concerns to rule effectively.

While the great majority of Renaissance writers and artists were men, among the remarkable exceptions to that rule was Christine de Pizan (1363–1430), the daughter of a Venetian official who lived mostly in Paris. Her writings pushed against the misogyny of many European thinkers of the time. In her *City of Ladies*, she mobilized numerous women from history, Christian and pagan alike, to demonstrate that women too could be active members of society and deserved an education equal to that of men. "No matter which way I looked at it," she wrote, "I could find no evidence from my own experience to bear out such a negative view of female nature and habits. Even so . . . I could scarcely find a moral work by any author which didn't devote some chapter or paragraph to attacking the female sex."[6]

Heavily influenced by classical models, Renaissance figures were more interested in capturing the unique qualities of particular individuals and in describing the world as it was than in portraying or exploring eternal religious truths. In its

The Waldseemüller Map of 1507 Just fifteen years after Columbus landed in the Western Hemisphere, this map, which was created by the German cartographer Martin Waldseemüller, reflected a dawning European awareness of the planet's global dimensions and the location of the world's major landmasses. (bpk, Bildagentur/Staatsbibliothek zu Berlin, Stiftung Preussicher Kulturbesitz/Photo: Ruth Schacht/ Art Resource, NY)

focus on the affairs of this world, Renaissance culture reflected the urban bustle and commercial preoccupations of Italian cities. Its secular elements challenged the otherworldliness of Christian culture, and its individualism signaled the dawning of a more capitalist economy of private entrepreneurs. A new Europe was in the making, one more different from its own recent past than Ming dynasty China was from its pre-Mongol glory.

European Comparisons: Maritime Voyaging

A global traveler during the fifteenth century might be surprised to find that Europeans, like the Chinese, were also launching outward-bound maritime expeditions. Initiated in 1415 by the small country of Portugal, those voyages sailed ever farther down the west coast of Africa, supported by the state and blessed by the pope (see Map 12.3). As the century ended, two expeditions marked major breakthroughs, although few suspected it at the time. In 1492, Christopher Columbus, funded by Spain, Portugal's neighbor and rival, made his way west across the Atlantic hoping to arrive in the East and, in one of history's most consequential mistakes, ran into the Americas. Five years later, in 1497, Vasco da Gama launched a voyage

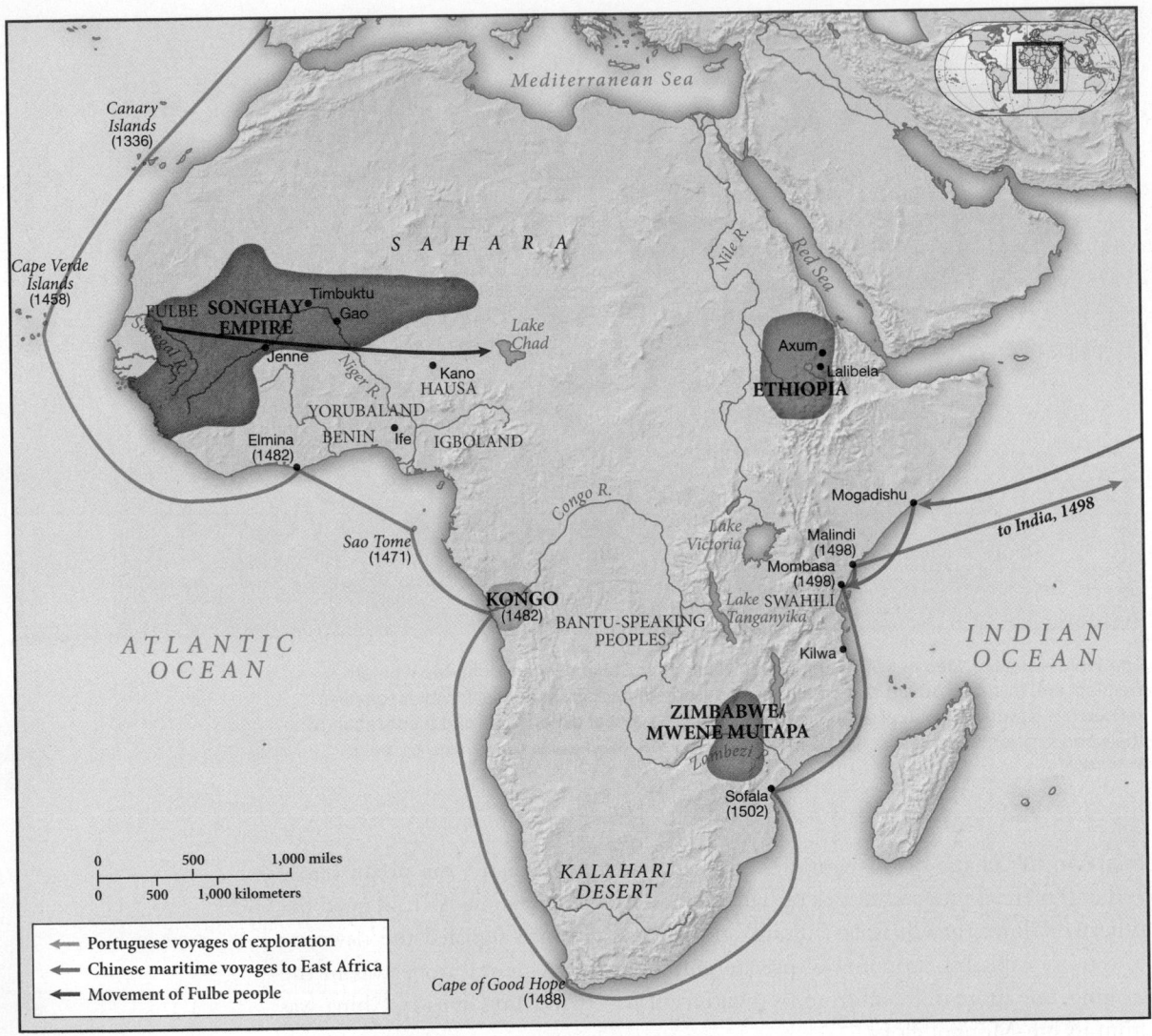

Map 12.3 Africa in the Fifteenth Century

By the fifteenth century, Africa was a panorama of political and cultural diversity, encompassing large empires, such as Songhay; smaller kingdoms, such as Kongo; city-states among the Yoruba, Hausa, and Swahili peoples; village-based societies without states at all, as among the Igbo; and pastoral peoples, such as the Fulbe. Both European and Chinese maritime expeditions touched on Africa during that century, even as Islam continued to find acceptance in the northern half of the continent.

that took him around the tip of South Africa, along the East African coast, and, with the help of a Muslim pilot, across the Indian Ocean to Calicut in southern India.

The differences between the Chinese and European oceangoing ventures were striking, most notably perhaps in terms of size. Columbus captained three ships and a crew of about 90, while da Gama had four ships, manned by perhaps 170 sailors. These were minuscule fleets compared to Zheng He's hundreds of ships and a crew in the many thousands. "All the ships of Columbus and da Gama combined," according to a recent account, "could have been stored on a single deck of a single vessel in the fleet that set sail under Zheng He."[7]

Motivation as well as size differentiated the two ventures. Europeans were seeking the wealth of Africa and Asia—gold, spices, silk, and more. They also were in search of Christian converts and of possible Christian allies with whom to continue their long crusading struggle against threatening Muslim powers. China, by contrast, faced no similar threat in the Indian Ocean basin, needed no military allies, and required little that these regions produced. Nor did China possess an impulse to convert foreigners to its culture or religion, as the Europeans surely did. Furthermore, the confident and overwhelmingly powerful Chinese fleet sought neither conquests nor colonies, while the Europeans soon tried to monopolize by force the commerce of the Indian Ocean and violently carved out huge empires in the Americas.

The most striking difference in these two cases lay in the sharp contrast between China's decisive ending of its voyages and the continuing, indeed escalating, European effort, which soon brought the world's oceans and growing numbers of the world's people under its control. This is why Zheng He's voyages were so long neglected in China's historical memory. They led nowhere, whereas the initial European expeditions, so much smaller and less promising, were but the first steps on a journey to world power. But why did the Europeans continue a process that the Chinese had deliberately abandoned?

In the first place, Europe had no unified political authority with the power to order an end to its maritime outreach. Its system of competing states, so unlike China's single state, ensured that once begun, rivalry alone would drive the Europeans to the ends of the earth. Beyond this, much of Europe's elite had an interest in overseas expansion. Its budding merchant communities saw opportunity for profit; its competing monarchs eyed the revenue from taxing overseas trade or from seizing overseas resources; the Church foresaw the possibility of widespread conversion; impoverished nobles might imagine fame and fortune abroad. In China, by contrast, support for Zheng He's voyages was very shallow in official circles, and when the emperor Yongle passed from the scene, those opposed to the voyages prevailed within the politics of the court.

Finally, the Chinese were very much aware of their own antiquity, believed strongly in the absolute superiority of their culture, and felt with good reason that, should they desire something from abroad, others would bring it to them. Europeans too believed themselves unique, particularly in religious terms as the possessors of Christianity, the "one true religion." In material terms, though, they were seeking out the greater riches of the East, and they were highly conscious that Muslim power blocked easy access to these treasures and posed a military and religious threat to Europe itself. All of this propelled continuing European expansion in the centuries that followed.

Guided Reading Question

■ **COMPARISON**
In what ways did European maritime voyaging in the fifteenth century differ from that of China? What accounts for these differences?

The Chinese withdrawal from the Indian Ocean actually facilitated the European entry. It cleared the way for the Portuguese to penetrate the region, where they faced only the eventual naval power of the Ottomans. Had Vasco da Gama encountered Zheng He's massive fleet as his four small ships sailed into Asian waters in 1498, world history may well have taken quite a different turn. As it was, however, China's abandonment of oceanic voyaging and Europe's embrace of the seas marked different responses to a common problem that both civilizations shared—growing populations and land shortage. In the centuries that followed, China's rice-based agriculture was able to expand production internally by more intensive use of the land, while the country's territorial expansion was inland toward Central Asia. By contrast, Europe's agriculture, based on wheat and livestock, expanded primarily by acquiring new lands in overseas possessions, which were gained as a consequence of a commitment to oceanic expansion.

Civilizations of the Fifteenth Century: The Islamic World

Beyond the domains of Chinese and European civilization, our fifteenth-century global traveler would surely have been impressed with the transformations of the Islamic world. Stretching across much of Afro-Eurasia, the enormous realm of Islam experienced a set of remarkable changes during the fifteenth and early sixteenth centuries, as well as the continuation of earlier patterns. The most notable change lay in the political realm, for an Islamic civilization that had been severely fragmented since at least 900 now crystallized into four major states or empires (see Map 12.4). At the same time, a long-term process of conversion to Islam continued the cultural transformation of Afro-Eurasian societies both within and beyond these new states.

In the Islamic Heartland: The Ottoman and Safavid Empires

The most impressive and enduring of the new Islamic states was the **Ottoman Empire**, which lasted in one form or another from the fourteenth to the early twentieth century. It was the creation of one of the many Turkic warrior groups that had migrated into Anatolia, slowly and sporadically, in the several centuries following 1000 C.E. By the mid-fifteenth century, these Ottoman Turks had already carved out a state that encompassed much of the Anatolian peninsula and had pushed deep into southeastern Europe (the Balkans), acquiring in the process a substantial Christian population. During the sixteenth century, the Ottoman Empire extended its control to much of the Middle East, coastal North Africa, the lands surrounding the Black Sea, and even farther into Eastern Europe.

Map 12.4 Empires of the Islamic World

The most prominent political features of the vast Islamic world in the fifteenth and sixteenth centuries were four large states: the Songhay, Ottoman, Safavid, and Mughal empires.

The Ottoman Empire was a state of enormous significance in the world of the fifteenth century and beyond. In its huge territory, long duration, incorporation of many diverse peoples, and economic and cultural sophistication, it was one of the great empires of world history. In the fifteenth century, only Ming dynasty China and the Incas matched it in terms of wealth, power, and splendor. The empire represented the emergence of the Turks as the dominant people of the Islamic world, ruling now over many Arabs, who had initiated this new faith more than 800 years before. In adding "caliph" (successor to the Prophet) to their other titles, Ottoman sultans claimed the legacy of the earlier Abbasid Empire. They sought to bring a renewed unity to the Islamic world, while also serving as protector of the faith, the "strong sword of Islam."

The Ottoman Empire also represented a new phase in the long encounter between Christendom and the world of Islam. In the Crusades, Europeans had

Guided Reading Question

■ **COMPARISON**

What differences can you identify among the four major empires in the Islamic world of the fifteenth and sixteenth centuries?

1453 in Constantinople

On May 29, 1453, forces of the Muslim Ottoman sultan Mehmed II seized control of the great Christian city of Constantinople, an event that marked the final end of the Roman/Byzantine Empire and the ascendency of the Ottoman Empire. In retrospect, this event acquired a certain air of inevitability about it, for the Byzantine Empire had been retreating for almost two centuries before the steady advance of the Ottomans. By 1453, that once-great empire, heir to all things Roman, had shrunk to little more than the city

Ottoman Turks storm the walls of Constantinople in 1453.

itself, with only some 50,000 inhabitants and 8,000 active defenders compared to a vast Ottoman army of 60,000 soldiers. And little was left of the fabled wealth of the city. But what later observers see as inevitable generally occurs only with great human effort and amid vast uncertainty about the outcome. So it was in Constantinople in 1453.

Constantine XI, the last Byzantine emperor, was well aware of the odds he faced. Yet his great city, protected by water on two sides and a great wall on a third, had repeatedly withstood many attacks and sieges. Further-

more, until the very end, he had hoped for assistance from Western Christians, even promising union with the Roman Church to obtain it. But no such help arrived, at least not in sufficient quantities to make a difference, though rumors of a fleet from Venice persisted. The internal problems of the Western powers as well as the long-standing hostility between Eastern Orthodoxy and Roman Catholicism ensured that Constantinople would meet its end alone.

On the Ottoman side, enormous effort was expended with no assurance of success. In 1451, a new sultan came to the throne of the Ottoman Empire, Mehmed II, only nineteen years old and widely regarded as not very promising. Furthermore, some among the court officials had reservations about an attack on Constantinople. But the young sultan seemed determined to gain the honor promised in Islamic prophesies, going back to Muhammad himself, to the one who conquered the city. Doing so

photo: © ullstein bild/The Image Works

taken the aggressive initiative in that encounter, but the rise of the Ottoman Empire reversed their roles. The **Ottoman seizure of Constantinople** in 1453 marked the final demise of Christian Byzantium and allowed Ottoman rulers to see themselves as successors to the Roman Empire. (See Zooming In: 1453 in Constantinople, above.) It also opened the way to further expansion, and in 1529 a rapidly expanding Ottoman Empire laid siege to Vienna in the heart of Central Europe. The political and military expansion of Islam, at the expense of Christendom, seemed clearly under way. Many Europeans spoke fearfully of the "terror of the Turk."

In the neighboring Persian lands to the east of the Ottoman Empire, another Islamic state was also taking shape in the late fifteenth and early sixteenth could also rid him of a potential rival to the Ottoman throne, who had taken refuge in Constantinople.

And so preparations began for an assault on the once-great city. The Ottomans assembled a huge fleet, gathered men and materials, and constructed a fortress to control access to Constantinople by water. In late 1452, Mehmed secured the services of a Hungarian master cannon builder named Orban, who constructed a number of huge cannons, one of which could hurl a 600-pound stone ball over a mile. These weapons later had a devastating effect on the walls surrounding Constantinople. Interestingly enough, Orban had first offered his services to the Byzantine emperor, who simply could not afford to pay for this very expensive project.

In early April of 1453, the siege began, and it lasted for fifty-seven days. As required by Islamic law, Mehmed offered three times to spare the emperor and his people if they surrendered. Constantine apparently considered the offer seriously, but he finally refused, declaring, "We have all decided to die with our own free will." After weeks of furious bombardment, an ominous silence descended on May 28. Mehmed had declared a day of rest and prayer before the final assault the next day. That evening, the Byzantine emperor ordered a procession of icons and relics about the city and then entered the ancient Christian church of Hagia Sophia, seeking forgiveness for his sins and receiving Holy Communion.

And then, early the next day, the final assault began as Ottoman forces breached the walls of Constantinople and took the city. The Christians bravely defended their city, and Constantine discarded his royal regalia and died fighting like a common soldier. A later legend suggested that angels turned Constantine into marble and buried him in a nearby cave from which he would eventually reappear to retake the city for Christendom.

Islamic law required that soldiers be permitted three days of plundering the spoils, but Mehmed was reluctant, eager to spare the city he longed for as his capital. So he limited plundering to one day. Even so, the aftermath was terrible. According to a Christian eyewitness, "The enraged Turkish soldiers . . . gave no quarter. When they had massacred and there was no longer any resistance, they were intent on pillage and roamed through the town stealing, disrobing, pillaging, killing, raping, taking captive men, women, children, monks, priests."[8] When Mehmed himself entered the city, praying at the Christian altar of Hagia Sophia, he reportedly wept at seeing the destruction that had occurred.

Constantinople was now a Muslim city, capital of the Ottoman Empire, and Hagia Sophia became a mosque. A momentous change had occurred in the relationship between the world of Islam and that of Christendom.

QUESTIONS

What factors contributed to Mehmed's victory? Under what circumstances might a different outcome have been possible?

centuries—the Safavid (SAH-fah-vihd) Empire. Its leadership was also Turkic, but in this case it had emerged from a Sufi religious order founded several centuries earlier by Safi al-Din (1252–1334). The long-term significance of the **Safavid Empire**, which was established in the decade following 1500, was its decision to forcibly impose a Shia version of Islam as the official religion of the state. Over time, this form of Islam gained popular support and came to define the unique identity of Persian (Iranian) culture.

This Shia empire also introduced a sharp divide into the political and religious life of heartland Islam, for almost all of Persia's neighbors practiced a Sunni form of the faith. For a century (1534–1639), periodic military conflict erupted between the Ottoman and Safavid empires, reflecting both territorial rivalry and sharp religious differences. In 1514, the Ottoman sultan wrote to the Safavid ruler in the most bitter of terms:

> You have denied the sanctity of divine law . . . you have deserted the path of salvation and the sacred commandments . . . you have opened to Muslims the gates of tyranny and oppression . . . you have raised the standard of irreligion and heresy. . . . [Therefore] the *ulama* and our doctors have pronounced a sentence of death against you, perjurer and blasphemer.[9]

This Sunni/Shia hostility has continued to divide the Islamic world into the twenty-first century.

On the Frontiers of Islam: The Songhay and Mughal Empires

While the Ottoman and Safavid empires brought both a new political unity and a sharp division to the heartland of Islam, two other states performed a similar role on the expanding African and Asian frontiers of the faith. In the West African savannas, the **Songhay Empire** rose in the second half of the fifteenth century. It was the most recent and the largest in a series of impressive states that operated at a crucial intersection of the trans-Saharan trade routes and that derived much of their revenue from taxing that commerce. Islam was a growing faith in Songhay but was limited largely to urban elites. This cultural divide within Songhay largely accounts for the religious behavior of its fifteenth-century monarch Sonni Ali (r. 1465–1492), who gave alms and fasted during Ramadan in proper Islamic style but also enjoyed a reputation as a magician and possessed a charm thought to render his soldiers invisible to their enemies. Nonetheless, Songhay had become a major center of Islamic learning and commerce by the early sixteenth century. A North African traveler known as Leo Africanus remarked on the city of **Timbuktu**:

> Here are great numbers of [Muslim] religious teachers, judges, scholars, and other learned persons who are bountifully maintained at the king's expense. Here too are brought various manuscripts or written books from Barbary [North Africa] which are sold for more money than any other merchandise. . . . Here are very rich merchants and to here journey continually large numbers of negroes who purchase here cloth from Barbary and Europe. . . . It is a wonder to see the quality of merchandise that is daily brought here and how costly and sumptuous everything is.[10]

The Mughal (MOO-guhl) Empire in India bore similarities to Songhay, for both governed largely non-Muslim populations. Much as the Ottoman Empire initiated a new phase in the interaction of Islam and Christendom, so too did the **Mughal Empire** continue an ongoing encounter between Islamic and Hindu civilizations. Established in the early sixteenth century, the Mughal Empire was the

Ottoman Janissaries Originating in the fourteenth century, the Janissaries became the elite infantry force of the Ottoman Empire. Complete with uniforms, cash salaries, and marching music, they were the first standing army in the region since the days of the Roman Empire. When gunpowder technology became available, Janissary forces soon were armed with muskets, grenades, and handheld cannons. This Turkish miniature painting dates from the sixteenth century. (Topkapi Palace Museum, Istanbul, Turkey/Album/Art Resource, NY)

creation of yet another Islamized Turkic group that invaded India in 1526. Over the next century, the Mughals (a Persian term for Mongols) established unified control over most of the Indian peninsula, giving it a rare period of political unity and laying the foundation for subsequent British colonial rule. During its first 150 years, the Mughal Empire, a land of great wealth and imperial splendor, undertook a remarkable effort to blend many Hindu groups and a variety of Muslims into an effective partnership. The inclusive policies of the early Mughal emperors showed that Muslim rulers could accommodate their overwhelmingly Hindu subjects in somewhat the same fashion as Ottoman authorities provided religious autonomy for their Christian minority.

Together these four Muslim empires—Ottoman, Safavid, Songhay, and Mughal—brought to the Islamic world a greater measure of political coherence, military power, economic prosperity, and cultural brilliance than it had known since the early centuries of Islam. This new energy, sometimes called a "second flowering of Islam," impelled the continuing spread of the faith to yet new regions.

The most prominent of these was oceanic Southeast Asia, which for centuries had been intimately bound up in the world of Indian Ocean commerce, while borrowing elements of both Hindu and Buddhist traditions. By the fifteenth century, that trading network was largely in Muslim hands, and the demand for Southeast Asian spices was mounting as the Eurasian world recovered from the devastation of Mongol conquest and the plague. Growing numbers of Muslim traders, many of them from India, settled in Java and Sumatra, bringing their faith with them. Eager to attract those traders to their port cities, a number of Hindu or Buddhist rulers along the Malay Peninsula and in Indonesia converted to Islam, while transforming themselves into Muslim sultans and imposing Islamic law. Thus, unlike in the Middle East and India, where Islam was established in the wake of Arab or Turkic conquest, in Southeast Asia, as in West Africa, it was introduced by traveling merchants and solidified through the activities of Sufi holy men.

The rise of **Malacca**, strategically located on the waterway between Sumatra and Malaya, was a sign of the times (see Map 12.1, page 501). During the fifteenth century, it was transformed from a small fishing village to a major Muslim port city. A Portuguese visitor in 1512 observed that Malacca had "no equal in the world. . . . Commerce between different nations for a thousand leagues on every hand must come to Malacca."[11] That city also became a springboard for the spread of Islam throughout the region. In the eclectic style of Southeast Asian religious history, the Islam of Malacca demonstrated much blending with local and Hindu/Buddhist traditions, while the city itself, like many port towns, had a reputation for "rough behavior." An Arab Muslim pilot in the 1480s commented critically: "They have no culture at all. . . . You do not know whether they are Muslim or not."[12] Nonetheless, Malacca, like Timbuktu on the West African frontier of an expanding Islamic world, became a center for Islamic learning, and students from elsewhere in Southeast Asia were studying there in the fifteenth century. As the core regions of Islam were consolidating politically, the frontier of the faith continued to move steadily outward.

PRACTICING HISTORICAL THINKING

In what ways did the civilizations of China, Europe, and the Islamic world in the fifteenth century seem to be moving in the same direction, and in what respects were they diverging from one another?

Civilizations of the Fifteenth Century: The Americas

Across the Atlantic, centers of civilization had long flourished in Mesoamerica and in the Andes. The fifteenth century witnessed new, larger, and more politically unified expressions of those civilizations, embodied in the Aztec and Inca empires. Both were the work of previously marginal peoples who had forcibly taken over and absorbed older cultures, giving them new energy, and both were decimated in the sixteenth century at the hands of Spanish conquistadores and their diseases (see Map 12.5).

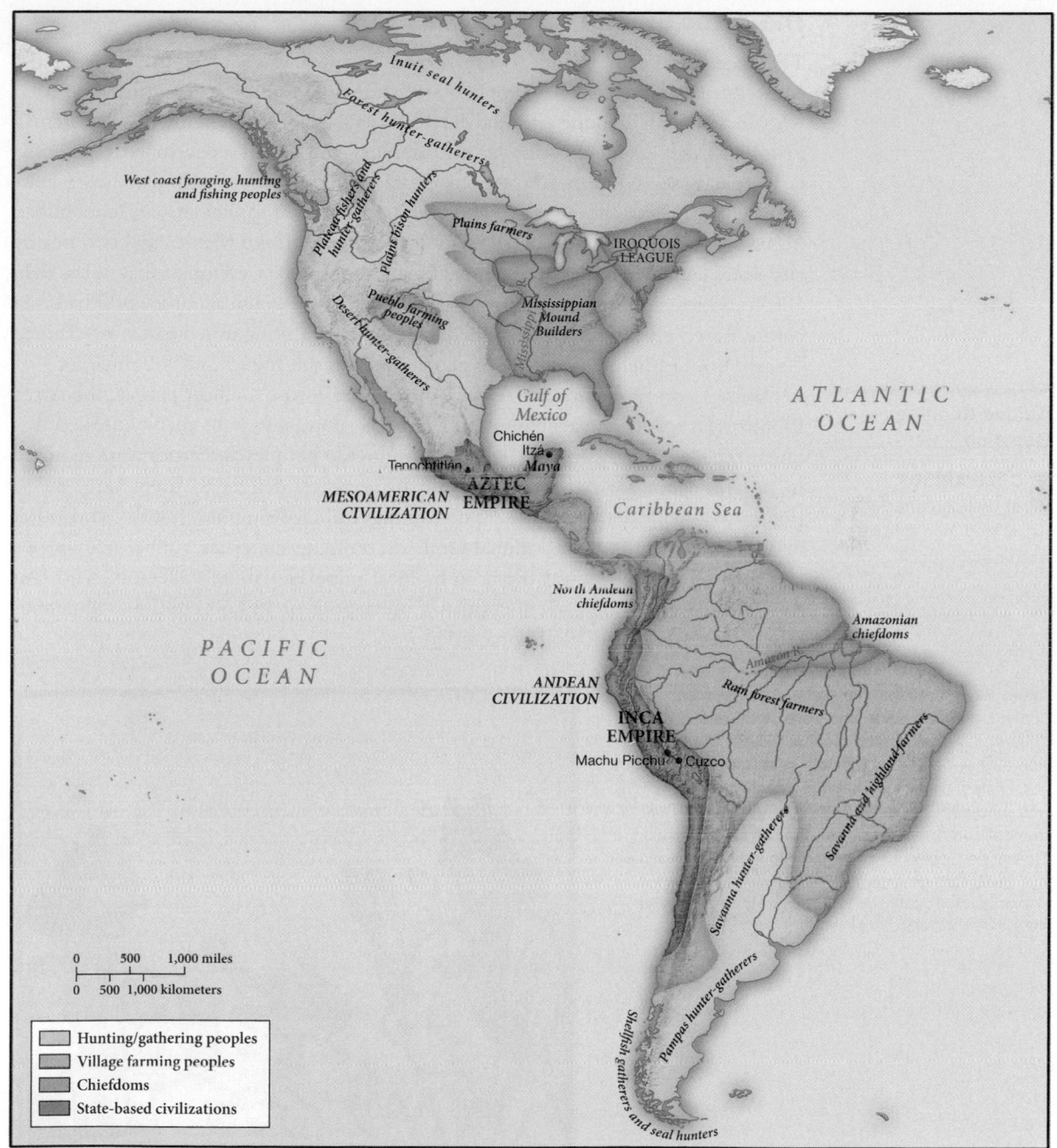

Map 12.5 The Americas in the Fifteenth Century

The Americas before Columbus represented a world almost completely separate from Afro-Eurasia. It featured similar kinds of societies, though with a different balance among them, but it largely lacked the pastoral economies that were so important in the Eastern Hemisphere.

The Aztec Empire

The state known to history as the **Aztec Empire** was largely the work of the Mexica (meh-SHEEH-kah) people, a semi-nomadic group from northern Mexico who had migrated southward and by 1325 had established themselves on a small island in Lake Texcoco. Over the next century, the Mexica developed their military capacity, served as mercenaries for more powerful people, negotiated elite marriage alliances with those people, and built up their own capital city of Tenochtitlán (te-nawch-tee-tlahn). In 1428, a Triple Alliance between the Mexica and two nearby city-states launched a highly aggressive program of military conquest that in less than 100 years brought more of Mesoamerica within a single political framework than ever before. Aztec authorities, eager to shed their rather undistinguished past, now claimed descent from earlier Mesoamerican peoples such as the Toltecs and Teotihuacán.

With a core population recently estimated at 5 to 6 million people, the Aztec Empire was a loosely structured and unstable conquest state that witnessed frequent rebellions by its subject peoples. Conquered peoples and cities were required to provide labor for Aztec projects and to regularly deliver to their Aztec rulers impressive quantities of textiles and clothing, military supplies, jewelry and other luxuries, various foodstuffs, animal products, building materials, rubber balls, paper, and more. The process was overseen by local imperial tribute collectors, who sent the required goods on to Tenochtitlán, a metropolis of 150,000 to 200,000 people, where they were meticulously recorded.

Guided Reading Question

■ **COMPARISON**

What distinguished the Aztec and Inca empires from each other?

Aztec Women Within the home, Aztec women cooked, cleaned, spun and wove cloth, raised their children, and undertook ritual activities. Outside the home, they served as officials in palaces, priestesses in temples, traders in markets, teachers in schools, and members of craftworkers' organizations. This domestic image comes from the sixteenth-century Florentine Codex, which was compiled by the Spanish but illustrated by Aztec artists. (Facsimile detail from Book IV of Florentine Codex, "General History of the Things of New Spain"/Museo del Templo Mayor, Mexico City, Mexico/De Agostini Picture Library/Bridgeman Images)

That city featured numerous canals, dikes, causeways, and bridges. A central walled area of palaces and temples included a pyramid almost 200 feet high. Surrounding the city were "floating gardens," artificial islands created from swamplands that supported a highly productive agriculture. Vast marketplaces reflected the commercialization of the economy. A young Spanish soldier who beheld the city in 1519 declared, "Gazing on such wonderful sights, we did not know what to say, or whether what appeared before us was real."[13]

Beyond tribute from conquered peoples, ordinary trade, both local and long-distance, permeated Aztec domains. The extent of empire and rapid population growth stimulated the development of markets and the production of craft goods, particularly in the fifteenth century. Virtually every settlement, from the capital city to the smallest village, had a marketplace that hummed with activity during weekly market days. The largest was that of Tlatelolco, near the capital city, which stunned the Spanish with its huge size, its good order, and the immense range of goods available. Hernán Cortés, the Spanish conquistador who defeated the Aztecs, wrote that "every kind of merchandise such as can be met with in every land is for sale there, whether of food and victuals, or ornaments of gold and silver, or lead, brass, copper, tin, precious stones, bones, shells, snails and feathers."[14] Professional merchants, known as *pochteca*, were legally commoners, but their wealth, often exceeding that of the nobility, allowed them to rise in society and become "magnates of the land."

Among the "goods" that the pochteca obtained were slaves, many of whom were destined for sacrifice in the bloody rituals so central to Aztec religious life. Long a part of Mesoamerican and many other world cultures, human sacrifice assumed an unusually prominent role in Aztec public life and thought during the fifteenth century. Tlacaelel (1398–1480), who was for more than half a century a prominent official of the Aztec Empire, is often credited with crystallizing the ideology of state that gave human sacrifice such great importance.

In that cyclical understanding of the world, the sun, central to all life and identified with the Aztec patron deity Huitzilopochtli (wee-tsee-loh-pockt-lee), tended to lose its energy in a constant battle against encroaching darkness. Thus the Aztec world hovered always on the edge of catastrophe. To replenish its energy and thus postpone the descent into endless darkness, the sun required the life-giving force found in human blood. Because the gods had shed their blood ages ago in creating humankind, it was wholly proper for people to offer their own blood to nourish the gods in the present. The high calling of the Aztec state was to supply this blood, largely through its wars of expansion and from prisoners of war, who were destined for sacrifice. The victims were "those who have died for the god." The growth of the Aztec Empire therefore became the means for maintaining cosmic order and avoiding utter catastrophe. This ideology also shaped the techniques of Aztec warfare, which put a premium on capturing prisoners rather than on killing the enemy. As the empire grew, priests and rulers became mutually dependent, and "human sacrifices were carried out in the service of politics."[15] Massive sacrificial

Guided Reading Question

■ **DESCRIPTION**
How did Aztec religious thinking support the empire?

rituals, together with a display of great wealth, served to impress enemies, allies, and subjects alike with the immense power of the Aztecs and their gods.

Alongside these sacrificial rituals was a philosophical and poetic tradition of great beauty, much of which mused on the fragility and brevity of human life. Such an outlook characterized the work of Nezahualcoyotl (1402–1472), a poet and king of the city-state of Texcoco, which was part of the Aztec Empire:

> Truly do we live on Earth?
> Not forever on earth; only a little while here.
> Although it be jade, it will be broken.
> Although it be gold, it is crushed.
> Although it be a quetzal feather, it is torn asunder.
> Not forever on earth; only a little while here.[16]

The Inca Empire

While the Mexica were constructing an empire in Mesoamerica, a relatively small community of Quechua-speaking people, known to us as the Incas, was building the Western Hemisphere's largest imperial state along the entire spine of the Andes Mountains. Much as the Aztecs drew on the traditions of the Toltecs and Teoti-huacán, the Incas incorporated the lands and cultures of earlier Andean civilizations: Chavín, Moche, Wari, and Tiwanaku. The **Inca Empire**, however, was much larger than the Aztec state; it stretched some 2,500 miles along the Andes and contained perhaps 10 million subjects. Whereas the Aztec Empire controlled only part of the Mesoamerican cultural region, the Inca state encompassed practically the whole of Andean civilization during its short life in the fifteenth and early sixteenth centuries. In the speed of its creation and the extent of its territory, the Inca Empire bears some similarity to that of the Mongols.

Both the Aztec and Inca empires represent rags-to-riches stories in which quite modest and remotely located people very quickly created by military conquest the largest states ever witnessed in their respective regions, but the empires themselves were quite different. In the Aztec realm, the Mexica rulers largely left their con-quered people alone, if the required tribute was forthcoming. No elaborate admin-istrative system arose to integrate the conquered territories or to assimilate their people to Aztec culture.

The Incas, on the other hand, erected a rather more bureaucratic empire. At the top reigned the emperor, an absolute ruler regarded as divine, a descendant of the creator god Viracocha and the son of the sun god Inti. Each of the some eighty provinces in the empire had an Inca governor. In theory, the state owned all land and resources, though in practice state lands, known as "lands of the sun," existed alongside properties owned by temples, elites, and traditional communities. At least in the central regions of the empire, subjects were grouped into hierarchi-cal units of 10, 50, 100, 500, 1,000, 5,000, and 10,000 people, each headed by local officials, who were appointed and supervised by an Inca governor or the emperor.

Guided Reading Question

■ **DESCRIPTION**
In what ways did Inca authorities seek to integrate their vast domains?

A separate set of "inspectors" provided the imperial center with an independent check on provincial officials.

Births, deaths, marriages, and other population data were carefully recorded on *quipus*, the knotted cords that served as an accounting device. A resettlement program moved one-quarter or more of the population to new locations, in part to disperse conquered and no doubt resentful people and sometimes to reward loyal followers with promising opportunities. Efforts at cultural integration required the leaders of conquered peoples to learn Quechua (keh-choo-wah). Their sons were removed to the capital of Cuzco for instruction in Inca culture and language. Even now, millions of people from Ecuador to Chile still speak Quechua, and it is the official second language of Peru after Spanish.

But the sheer human variety of the Incas' enormous empire required great flexibility. In some places Inca rulers encountered bitter resistance; in others local elites were willing to accommodate Incas and thus benefit from their inclusion in the empire. Where centralized political systems already existed, Inca overlords could delegate control to native authorities. Elsewhere they had to construct an administrative system from scratch. Everywhere they sought to incorporate local people into the lower levels of the administrative hierarchy. While the Incas required their subject peoples to acknowledge major Inca deities, these peoples were then largely

Machu Picchu Machu Picchu, high in the Andes Mountains, was constructed by the Incas in the fifteenth century on a spot long held sacred by local people. Its 200 buildings stand at some 8,000 feet above sea level, making it a "city in the sky." It was probably a royal retreat or religious center, rather than a location serving administrative, commercial, or military purposes. The outside world became aware of Machu Picchu only in 1911, when it was popularized by a Yale University archeologist. (fStop/Superstock)

free to carry on their own religious traditions. The Inca Empire was a fluid system that varied greatly from place to place and over time. It depended as much on the posture of conquered peoples as on the demands and desires of Inca authorities.

Like the Aztec Empire, the Inca state represented an especially dense and extended network of economic relationships within the "American web," but these relationships took shape in quite a different fashion. Inca demands on their conquered people were expressed, not so much in terms of tribute, but as labor service, known as *mita*, which was required periodically of every household. What people produced at home usually stayed at home, but almost everyone also had to work for the state. Some labored on large state farms or on "sun farms," which supported temples and religious institutions; others herded, mined, served in the military, or toiled on state-directed construction projects.

Those with particular skills were put to work manufacturing textiles, metal goods, ceramics, and stonework. The most well known of these specialists were the "chosen women," who were removed from their homes as young girls, trained in Inca ideology, and set to producing corn beer and cloth at state centers. Later they were given as wives to men of distinction or sent to serve as priestesses in various temples, where they were known as "wives of the Sun." In return for such labor services, Inca ideology, expressed in terms of family relationships, required the state to arrange elaborate feasts at which large quantities of food and drink were consumed and to provide food and other necessities when disaster struck. Thus the authority of the state penetrated and directed Inca society and economy far more than did that of the Aztecs.

If the Inca and Aztec civilizations differed sharply in their political and economic arrangements, they resembled each other more closely in their gender systems. Both societies practiced what scholars call "gender parallelism," in which "women and men operate in two separate but equivalent spheres, each gender enjoying autonomy in its own sphere."[17] In both Mesoamerican and Andean societies, such systems had emerged long before their incorporation into the Aztec and Inca empires. In the Andes, men reckoned their descent from their fathers and women from their mothers, while Mesoamericans had long viewed children as belonging equally to their mothers and fathers. Parallel religious cults for women and men likewise flourished in both societies. Inca men venerated the sun, while women worshipped the moon, with matching religious officials. In Aztec temples, both male and female priests presided over rituals dedicated to deities of both sexes. Particularly among the Incas, parallel hierarchies of male and female political officials governed the empire, while in Aztec society, women officials exercised local authority under a title that meant "female person in charge of people." Social roles were clearly defined and different for men and women, but the domestic concerns of women—childbirth, cooking, weaving, cleaning—were not regarded as inferior to the activities of men. Among the Aztecs, for example, sweeping was a powerful and sacred act with symbolic significance as "an act of purification and a preventative against evil elements penetrating the center of the Aztec universe, the home."[18]

In the Andes, men broke the ground, women sowed, and both took part in the harvest.

This was gender complementarity, not gender equality. Men occupied the top positions in both political and religious life, and male infidelity was treated more lightly than was women's unfaithfulness. As the Inca and Aztec empires expanded, military life, limited to men, grew in prestige, perhaps skewing an earlier gender parallelism. The Incas in particular imposed a more rigidly patriarchal order on their subject peoples. In other ways, the new Aztec and Inca rulers adapted to the gender systems of the people they had conquered. Among the Aztecs, the tools of women's work, the broom and the weaving spindle, were ritualized as weapons; sweeping the home was believed to assist men at war; and childbirth was regarded by women as "our kind of war."[19] Inca rulers replicated the gender parallelism of their subjects at a higher level, as the *sapay Inca* (the Inca ruler) and the *coya* (his female consort) governed jointly, claiming descent respectively from the sun and the moon.

Webs of Connection

Few people in the fifteenth century lived in entirely separate and self-contained communities. Almost all were caught up, to one degree or another, in various and overlapping webs of influence, communication, and exchange.[20] Perhaps most obvious were the webs of empire, large-scale political systems that brought together a variety of culturally different people. Christians and Muslims encountered each other directly in the Ottoman Empire, as did Hindus and Muslims in the Mughal Empire. And no empire tried more diligently to integrate its diverse peoples than the fifteenth-century Incas.

Inca Agricultural Practice This sixteenth-century drawing by Felipe Guaman Poma, an Inca nobleman, illustrates the cooperation of Inca men and women in agriculture. The men are loosening the soil with a "foot-plow," while the women plant the seeds. (Werner Forman/Getty Images)

Religion too linked far-flung peoples, and divided them as well. Christianity provided a common religious culture for peoples from England to Russia, although the great divide between Roman Catholicism and Eastern Orthodoxy endured, and in the sixteenth century the Protestant Reformation would shatter permanently the Christian unity of the Latin West. Although Buddhism had largely vanished from its South Asian homeland, it remained a link among China, Korea, Tibet, Japan, and parts of Southeast Asia, even as it splintered into a variety of sects and practices. More than either of these, Islam actively brought together its many peoples. In the hajj, the pilgrimage to Mecca, Africans, Arabs, Persians, Turks, Indians, and many others joined as one people as they rehearsed together the events that gave birth to their common faith. And yet divisions and conflicts persisted within the vast realm of Islam, as the violent hostility between the Sunni Ottoman Empire and the Shia Safavid Empire so vividly illustrates.

Guided Reading Question

■ **CONNECTION**
In what different ways did the peoples of the fifteenth century interact with one another?

Long-established patterns of trade among peoples occupying different environments and producing different goods were certainly much in evidence during the fifteenth century, as they had been for millennia. Hunting societies of Siberia funneled furs and other products of the forest into the Silk Road trading network traversing the civilizations of Eurasia. In the fifteenth century, some of the agricultural peoples in southern Nigeria were receiving horses brought overland from the drier regions of Africa to the north, where those animals flourished better. The Mississippi River in North America and the Orinoco and Amazon rivers in South America facilitated a canoe-borne commerce along those waterways. Coastal shipping in large seagoing canoes operated in the Caribbean and along the Pacific coast between Mexico and Peru. In Pacific Polynesia, the great voyaging networks across vast oceanic distances that had flourished especially since 1000 were in decline by 1500 or earlier, leading to the abandonment of a number of islands.

The great long-distance trading patterns of the Afro-Eurasian world, in operation for a thousand years or more, continued in the fifteenth century, although the balance among them was changing (see Map 12.6). The Silk Road overland network, which had flourished under Mongol control in the thirteenth and fourteenth centuries, contracted in the fifteenth century as the Mongol Empire broke up and the devastation of the plague reduced demand for its products. The rise of the Ottoman Empire also blocked direct commercial contact between Europe and China, but oceanic trade from Japan, Korea, and China through the islands of Southeast Asia and across the Indian Ocean picked up considerably. Larger ships made it possible to trade in bulk goods such as grain as well as luxury products, while more sophisticated partnerships and credit mechanisms greased the wheels of commerce. A common Islamic culture over much of this vast region likewise smoothed the passage of goods among very different peoples, as it also did for the trans-Saharan trade.

After 1500: Looking Ahead to the Modern Era

While ties of empire, culture, commerce, and disease surely linked many of the peoples in the world of the fifteenth century, none of those connections operated on a genuinely global scale. Although the densest webs of connection had been woven within the Afro-Eurasian zone of interaction, this huge region had no enduring ties with the Americas, and neither of them had sustained contact with the peoples of Pacific Oceania. That situation was about to change as Europeans in the sixteenth century and beyond forged a set of genuinely global relationships that generated sustained interaction among all of these regions. That huge process and the many outcomes that flowed from it marked the beginning of what world historians

MAPPING HISTORY

Map 12.6 Religion and Commerce in the Afro-Eurasian World

By the fifteenth century, the many distinct peoples and societies of the Eastern Hemisphere were linked to one another by ties of religion and commerce. Of course, most people were not directly involved in long-distance trade, and many people in areas shown as Buddhist or Islamic on the map practiced other religions. While much of India, for example, was ruled by Muslims, the majority of its people followed some form of Hinduism. And although Islam had spread to West Africa, that religion had not penetrated much beyond the urban centers of the region.

READING THE MAP: Where were Buddhists concentrated in the Indian Ocean region? In which areas were Muslims most prominent?

INTERPRETING THE MAP: What does this map suggest about the places where cross-cultural contacts and interactions among the three major faiths during the fifteenth century might most likely occur?

commonly call the modern age—the more than five centuries that followed the voyages of Columbus starting in 1492.

Over those five centuries, the previously separate worlds of Afro-Eurasia, the Americas, and Pacific Oceania became inextricably linked, with enormous consequences for everyone involved. Global empires, a global economy, global cultural exchanges, global migrations, global disease, global wars, and global environmental changes have made the past 500 years a unique phase in the human journey. Those webs of communication and exchange—the first defining feature of the modern era—have progressively deepened, so much so that by the end of the twentieth century few if any people lived beyond the cultural influences, economic ties, or political relationships of a globalized world.

Several centuries after the Columbian voyages, and clearly connected to them, a second distinctive feature of the modern era took shape: the emergence of a radically new kind of human society, first in Europe during the nineteenth century and then in various forms elsewhere in the world. The core feature of such societies was industrialization. That revolutionary economic process was accompanied by a host of other transformations: accelerating technological innovation; the massive consumption of energy and raw materials; a scientific outlook on the world; an unprecedented increase in human population (see the Snapshot); rapid urbanization; widespread commercialization; more powerful and intrusive states; the growing prominence and dominance of Europeans on the world stage; and a very different balance of global power.

This was the revolution of modernity, comparable in its pervasive consequences only to the Agricultural Revolution of some 10,000 years ago. It usually meant a self-conscious and often uneasy awareness of living and thinking in new ways that deliberately departed from tradition. Sorting out what was gained and what was lost during the modern transformation has been a persistent and highly controversial thread of human thought over the past several centuries. And it is a central concern of historians who trace the contours of the human journey in the centuries after 1500.

SNAPSHOT World Population Growth, 1000–2000

Data from David Christian, *Map of Time* (Berkeley: University of California Press, 2004), 343.

REFLECTIONS

What If? Chance and Contingency in World History

Seeking meaning in the stories they tell, historians are inclined to look for deeply rooted or underlying causes for the events they recount. And yet, is it possible that, at least on occasion, historical change derives less from profound and long-term sources than from coincidence, chance, or the decisions of a few that might well have gone another way?

Consider, for example, the problem of explaining the rise of Europe to a position of global power in the modern era. What if the Great Khan Ogodei had not died in 1241, requiring the Mongol forces then poised for an assault on Germany to return to Mongolia? It is surely possible that Central and Western Europe might have been overrun by Mongol armies as so many other civilizations had been, a prospect that could have drastically altered the trajectory of European history. Or what if the Chinese had decided in 1433 to continue their huge maritime expeditions, creating an empire in the Indian Ocean basin and perhaps moving on to "discover" the Americas and Europe? Such a scenario suggests a wholly different future for world history than the one that in fact occurred. Or what if the forces of the Ottoman Empire had taken the besieged city of Vienna in 1529? Might they then have incorporated even larger parts of Europe into their expanding domain, requiring a halt to Europe's overseas empire-building enterprise?

None of this necessarily means that the rise of Europe was merely a fluke or an accident of history, but it does raise the issue of "contingency," the role of unforeseen or small events in the unfolding of the human story. An occasional "what if" approach to history reminds us that alternative possibilities existed in the past and that the only certainty about the future is that we will be surprised.

Second Thoughts

What's the Significance?

Big Picture Questions

1. Assume for the moment that the Chinese had not ended their maritime voyages in 1433. How might the subsequent development of world history have been differ-ent? What value is there in asking this kind of "what if" or counterfactual question?

2. How does this chapter distinguish among the various kinds of societies contained in the world of the fifteenth century? What other ways of categorizing the world's peoples might work as well or better?

3. What common patterns might you notice across the world of the fifteenth century? And what variations in the historical trajectories of various regions can you identify?

4. **Looking Back:** What would surprise a knowledgeable observer from 500 or 1000 C.E., were he or she to make a global tour in the fifteenth century? What features of that earlier world might still be recognizable?

Next Steps: For Further Study

Terence N. D'Altroy, *The Incas* (2002). A history of the Inca Empire that draws on recent archeological and historical research.

Alan Covey, *How the Incas Built their Heartland* (2006). An interdisciplinary examination of the processes and strategies that allowed the Inca to create their empire.

Edward L. Dreyer, *Zheng He: China and the Oceans in the Early Ming Dynasty* (2006). The most recent scholarly account of the Ming dynasty voyages.

Halil Inalcik and Donald Quataert, *An Economic and Social History of the Ottoman Empire, 1300–1914* (1994). A classic study of the Ottoman Empire.

Robin Kirkpatrick, *The European Renaissance, 1400–1600* (2002). A beautifully illus-trated history of Renaissance culture as well as the social and economic life of the period.

Charles C. Mann, *1491: New Revelations of the Americas before Columbus* (2005). A review of Western Hemisphere societies and academic debates about their pre-Columbian history.

J. R. McNeill and William H. McNeill, *The Human Web* (2003). A succinct account of the evolving webs or relationships among human societies in world history.

Michael Smith, *The Aztecs* (2003). A history of the Aztec Empire, with an emphasis on the lives of ordinary people.

Khan Academy, "An Introduction to the Ming Dynasty (1368–1644)," https://www .khanacademy.org/humanities/art-asia/imperial-china/ming-dynasty/a/an -introduction-to-the-ming-dynasty-13681644. A collection of brief essays, images, and videos about Ming dynasty China.

Joel Westerbrook, Executive Producer, "Inca: Secrets of the Ancestors," Time-Life, Lost Civilizations, 1995, https://www.youtube.com/watch?v=3GrcN24PqmE. A thoughtful video exploring this largest of pre-Columbian states.

Islam and Renaissance Europe

The Renaissance era in Europe, roughly 1350 to 1500, represented the crystallization of a new third-wave civilization at the western end of Eurasia. In cultural terms, its writers and artists sought to link themselves to the legacy of the pre-Christian Greeks and Romans. But if Europeans were reaching back to their classical past, they were also reaching out—westward to the wholly new world of the Americas, southward to Africa, and eastward to Asia generally and the Islamic world in particular. The European Renaissance, in short, was shaped not only from within but also by its encounters with a wider world.

Interaction with the world of Islam was, of course, nothing new. Centuries of Muslim rule in Spain, the Crusades, and the expansion of the Ottoman Empire were markers in the long relationship of conflict, cooperation, and mutual influence between Christendom and the realm of Islam. Politically, that relationship was changing in the fifteenth century. The Christian reconquest of Spain from Muslim rule was completed by 1492. At the other end of the Mediterranean Sea, the Turkish Ottoman Empire was expanding into the previously Christian regions of the Balkans (southeastern Europe), seizing the ancient capital of the Byzantine Empire, Constantinople, in 1453, while becoming a major player in European international politics.

Despite such conflicts, commerce flourished across political and religious divides. European bulk goods such as wool, timber, and glassware, along with silver and gold, were exchanged for high-value luxury goods from the Islamic world or funneled through it from farther east. These included spices, silks, carpets, tapestries, brocades, art objects, precious stones, gold, dyes, and pigments. In 1384, a Christian pilgrim from the Italian city of Florence wrote: "Really all of Christendom could be supplied for a year with the merchandise of Damascus."[21] Along with goods, Arab and Muslim learning—in medicine, astronomy, philosophy, architecture, mathematics, business practices, and more—also flowed into the Christian West. These various engagements with the Islamic world all found expression in Renaissance Italy, as the sources that follow illustrate.

SOURCE 12.1 **Portrait of Mehmed II** ▶

The year 1453 marked a watershed in the long relationship between Christendom and the Islamic world, for it was in that year that the Ottoman sultan Mehmed II decisively conquered the great Christian city of Constantinople, bringing the thousand-year history of Byzantium to an inglorious end. To many Europeans, that event was a catastrophe and Mehmed was the "terror of the world." Others, however, saw opportunity. Less than a year after that event, the northern Italian city of Venice signed a peace treaty with the Ottoman sultan, declaring, "It is our intention to live in peace and friendship with the Turkish emperor."[22] Some even expressed admiration for the conquering Muslim ruler. George of Trebizond, a Greek-speaking Renaissance scholar, described Mehmed as "a wise king and one who philosophizes about the greatest matters."[23]

For his part, Mehmed admired both classical and contemporary European culture, even as his armies threatened European powers. This cosmopolitan emperor stocked his library with Western texts and decorated the walls of his palace with Renaissance-style frescoes. Seeing himself as heir to Roman imperial authority, he now added "Caesar" to his other titles. And in 1480, he had his portrait painted by the leading artist of Venice, Gentile Bellini, who had been sent to the Ottoman court as a cultural ambassador of his city.

Source 12.1 shows Bellini's portrait of the emperor sitting under a marble arch, a symbol of triumph that evokes his dramatic conquest of Constantinople. The three golden crowns on the upper left and right likely represent the lands recently acquired for the Ottoman Empire, and the inscription at the bottom describes Mehmed as "Conqueror of the World."

- What overall impression of the sultan does this portrait convey?

- Why might this Muslim ruler want his portrait painted by a Christian artist from Venice?

- Why might Bellini and the city government of Venice be willing—even eager—to undertake the assignment, less than thirty years after the Muslim conquest of Constantinople?

GENTILE BELLINI | *Portrait of Mehmed II* | 1480

National Gallery, London, UK/Bridgeman Images

• • •

SOURCE 12.2 Machiavelli on the Turkish State

The increasing power of the Ottoman Empire inspired fear and admiration among Christian observers, along with a growing interest in how the Turkish sultan governed his state. Niccolò Machiavelli (1469–1527), the diplomat, historian, and political theorist from Florence, offered his assessment of Ottoman government in his most famous treatise, *The Prince*, when he compared the Turkish state to that of France, one of the most powerful kingdoms in Western Europe.

■ How would you characterize Machiavelli's view of the Ottoman state? Does he see it clearly as superior or inferior to that of France, or just different?

■ Does religion enter into Machiavelli's analysis?

■ Many at the time criticized Machiavelli's *Prince* for its amoral analysis of political life and its assertion that rulers must set aside concerns about morality to rule effectively. Is there anything in this passage that supports this interpretation of Machiavelli's thought?

NICCOLÒ MACHIAVELLI | *The Prince* | 1513

Examples of these two kinds of government in our own time are the Turk and the King of France. All the Turkish monarchy is governed by one ruler, the others are his servants, and dividing his kingdom into "sangiascates" [administrative units], he sends to them various administrators, and charges or recalls them at his pleasure. But the King of France is surrounded by a large number of ancient nobles, recognized as such by their subjects, and loved by them; they have their prerogatives, which the king cannot deprive them of without danger to himself. Whoever now considers these two states will see that it would be difficult to acquire the state of the Turk; but having conquered it, it would be very easy to hold it.

The causes of the difficulty of occupying the Turkish kingdom are, that the invader could not be invited by princes of that kingdom, nor hope to facilitate his enterprise by the rebellion of those around [the Turkish sultan], as will be evident from reasons given above. Because, being all slaves, and bound, it will be more difficult to corrupt them, and even if they were corrupted, little effect could be hoped for, as they would not be able to carry the people with them for the reasons mentioned. Therefore, whoever assaults the Turk must be prepared to meet his united forces, and must rely more on his own strength than on the disorders of others [i.e., rebellious subjects of the Turkish ruler]; but having once conquered him, and beaten him in battle so that he can no longer raise armies, nothing else is to be feared except the family of the prince, and if this is extinguished [i.e., if all members of the Turkish ruler's family are killed], there is no longer any one to be feared, the others having no credit with the people; and as the victor before the victory could place no hope in them, so he need not fear them afterwards. The contrary is the case in the kingdoms governed like that of France, because it is easy to enter them by winning over some baron of the kingdom, there being always some malcontents, and those desiring innovations. These can, for the reasons stated, open the way to you and facilitate victory; but afterwards, if you wish to keep possession, infinite difficulties arise, both from those who have aided you and from those you have oppressed. Nor is it sufficient to extinguish the family of the prince, for there remain those nobles who will make themselves the head of new changes, and being neither able to content them nor exterminate them, you will lose the state whenever an occasion arises.

Source: Niccolò Machiavelli, *The Prince*, translated by Luigi Ricci (London: Grant Richards, 1903), 15–16.

■ ■ ■

SOURCE 12.3 **Venetian Trade in the Middle East** ▶

Venice had long been the primary point of commercial contact between Europe and the East and the source of the much-desired luxury goods that its merchants obtained from Alexandria in Egypt. At that time, Muslim Egypt was ruled by the Mamluks, a warrior caste of slave origins who had checked the westward advance of the Mongols in 1260 and had driven the last of the European Crusaders out of the Middle East in 1291. Venetian traders, however, were more interested in commerce than in religion, and by the fifteenth century they enjoyed a highly profitable relationship with the Mamluk rulers of Egypt and Syria, despite the periodic opposition of the pope and threats of excommunication. Thus it is not surprising that the Renaissance artists of Venice were prominent among those who reflected the influence of the Islamic world in their work. By the late fifteenth century, something of a fad for oriental themes surfaced in Venetian pictorial art.

Source 12.3, painted by an anonymous Venetian artist in 1511, expresses this intense interest in the Islamic world. The setting is Damascus in Syria, then ruled by the Egyptian Mamluk regime. The local Mamluk governor of the city, seated on a low platform with an elaborate headdress, is receiving an ambassador from Venice, shown in a red robe and standing in front of the governor. Behind him in black robes are other members of the Venetian delegation, while in the foreground various members of Damascus society—both officials and merchants—are distinguished from one another by variations in their turbans. Behind the wall lies the city of Damascus with its famous Umayyad mosque, formerly a Roman temple to Jupiter and later a Christian church, together with its three minarets. The city's lush gardens and its homes with wooden balconies and rooftop terraces complete the picture of urban Islam.

- What impressions of the city and its relationship with Venice does the artist seek to convey?

- How are the various social groups of Damascus distinguished from one another in this painting? What does the very precise visual description of these differences suggest about Venetian understanding of urban Mamluk society?

- What does the total absence of women suggest about their role in the public life of Damascus?

- How would you know that this is a Muslim city? What role, if any, does religion play in this depiction of the relationship between Christian Venice and Islamic Damascus?

The Venetian Ambassador Visits Damascus | 1511

Musée du Louvre, Paris, France/Bridgeman Images

■ ■ ■

SOURCE 12.4 Greek and Islamic Philosophers in Renaissance Art ▶

Beyond political and commercial relationships, Europeans had long engaged with the Islamic world intellectually as well. Source 12.4 illustrates that engagement in a work by Girolamo da Cremona, a fifteenth-century Italian painter known for his "illuminations" of early printed books. Created in 1483 (only some forty years after the invention of the printing press in Europe), it served as the frontispiece for one of the first printed versions of Aristotle's writings, translated into Latin, along with commentaries by the twelfth-century Muslim scholar Ibn Rushd (1126–1198), better known in the West as Averroes.

Aristotle, of course, was the great Greek philosopher of the fourth century B.C.E. whose writings presented a systematic and rational view of the world, while commenting on practically every branch of knowledge. The legacy of Greek thought in general and Aristotle in particular passed into both the Christian and Islamic worlds. Ibn Rushd, who wrote voluminous commentaries on Aristotle's works and much else as well, lived in Muslim Spain, where he argued for the compatibility of Aristotelian philosophy and the religious perspectives of Islam. While that outlook faced growing opposition in the Islamic world, Aristotle's writings found more fertile ground among European scholars in the new universities of the twelfth and thirteenth centuries, where they became the foundation of university curricula and nourished the growth of "natural philosophy." In large measure it was through translations of Ibn Rushd's Arabic commentaries on Aristotle that Europeans regained access to the thinking of that ancient philosopher. A long line of European scholars defined themselves as "Averroists."

The painting in Source 12.4 is presented as a parchment leaf, torn to disclose two worlds behind Aristotle's text. At the top in a rural setting, Aristotle, dressed in a blue robe, is speaking to Ibn Rushd, clad in a yellow robe with a round white turban. The bottom of the painting depicts the world of classical Greek mythology. The painted jewels, gems, and pearls testify to the great value placed on such illuminated and printed texts.

- What overall impression of Renaissance thinking about the classical world and the world of Islam does this painting convey?

- Notice the gestures of the two men at the top as well as the pen in Ibn Rushd's hand and the book at his feet. How might you describe the relationship between the men?

- What made it possible for at least some European Christians of the Renaissance era to embrace both the pagan Aristotle and the Islamic Ibn Rushd?

Aristotle and Averroes | 1483

■ ■ ■

SOURCE 12.5 A Papal Call for Crusade

Violent conflict was also a feature of Christian/Muslim relations during the Renaissance, particularly on the Iberian Peninsula, where Christian forces had triumphed by the 1490s. In the eastern Mediterranean, the growing power of the Turks led to several less successful military campaigns or Crusades by Christian powers, several of which were organized by the papacy. In this selection dating from 1343, Pope Clement VI seeks support to send a fleet to counter Turkish navel raids against Christian communities in what are now Greece and the Aegean Islands.

- What specific strategies does Clement pursue to recruit the faithful to his cause?

- How might you describe Clement's posture toward Islam?

- How does this call to crusade compare to earlier Crusader movements to seize the Holy Lands?

POPE CLEMENT VI | *Call for Crusade* | **September 30, 1343**

Those who launch themselves against the Catholic faith and strive to destroy the Christian religion must be resisted by the faithful with valour and steadfastness. The faithful themselves, fired by ardour for the orthodox faith, and armed to the fullest extent by its virtues, must oppose their hateful design with a rampart of determination, and forbid their evil undertakings with a firm defence. In this way, arrayed in mental and bodily armour, and directed by the light of faith, they may, with the assistance of God for whom they fight, cast down the insurgents, who lack [such] spiritual protection and are blinded by the shadows of unbelief.

To our sorrow, recent proof has confirmed what we have been hearing for some time now about groups of those unbelieving pagans, called . . . the Turks, who thirst for blood of Christian people and seek the destruction of the Catholic faith. For some time past they have mobilised the strength of their nation and used a great number of armed vessels to invade by sea Christian territories in the region of *Romania* [Greece and the Aegean Islands], and other neighbouring places in the hands of the faithful. Raging atrociously against the Christians and their lands and islands, they have taken to roaming the seas, as they are doing at present, despoiling and depopulating the settlements . . . and what is worse, seizing the Christians themselves as booty and subjecting them to horrible and perpetual slavery, selling them like animals and forcing them to deny their Catholic faith.

[The pope then declares his plan to create a fleet to counter the Turks.]

And so that the faithful may respond the more willingly, in so far as they know that they will receive the greater grace for their labours . . . we grant to those faithful who proceed with the flotilla or in another fashion in support of the Christians . . . and who remain on campaign for a year . . . and also those who die while engaged on this matter, or receive wounds in the field . . . forgiveness of their sins, for which they are truthfully contrite and which they have confessed orally. . . .

We grant the same indulgence of their sins to those who do not take part in person, but who send suitable soldiers at their own expense in accordance with their means and standing . . . and also to those who offer as much from their own goods for the matter, as they would have spent going there, staying there for a year, and coming back. . . .

Source: Norman Housley, *Documents on the Later Crusades 1274–1580* (New York: St. Martin's Press, 1996), 79–81.

DOING HISTORY

1. **Making comparisons:** What range of postures toward the Islamic world do these sources convey? How might you account for the differences among them?

2. **Imagining reactions:** How might Clement VI in Source 12.5 react to the other four sources in this feature?

3. **Analyzing sources:** While all of these sources deal with the Islamic world, with what different aspects of that world are they concerned?

4. **Considering European identity:** What role did the Islamic world play in the emerging identity of European civilization?

Christian/Muslim Relations during the Renaissance

The relationship between Christian and Islamic civilizations during the Middle Ages and Renaissance has been the subject of considerable attention from historians, who have emphasized both hostility and competition and peaceful cross-cultural contacts and exchanges between the two faiths. In Voice 12.1, Jerry Brotton, a specialist on the Renaissance, explores how trade and cultural exchange between Christians and Muslims profoundly shaped the European Renaissance. In Voice 12.2, Bernard Lewis, an expert in Islamic history, examines the reasons behind Christians' and Muslims' hostility toward one another during their first millennium of interaction.

- What reasons do these two sources identify for the intense cultural interaction between Christian and Islamic societies during the Renaissance?

- What do Brotton and Lewis agree on? And on what matters do they disagree?

- **Integrating Primary and Secondary Sources:** Which sources in this collection might Brotton and Lewis draw upon to support their assertions?

VOICE 12.1

Jerry Brotton on the Role of Cross-cultural Exchange in the European Renaissance | 2002

The Renaissance Bazaar [Brotton's book] describes the historical period starting in the early 15th century when eastern and western societies vigorously traded art, ideas, and luxury goods in a competitive but amicable exchange that shaped what we now call the European Renaissance. The eastern bazaar is a fitting metaphor for the fluid transactions that occurred throughout the 15th and 16th centuries, when Europe began to define itself by purchasing and emulating the opulence and cultured sophistication of the cities, merchants, scholars and empires of the Ottomans, the Persians, and the Egyptian Mamluks. The flow of spices, silks, carpets, porcelain, majolica, porphyry, glassware, lacquer, dyes, and pigments from the eastern bazaars of Muslim Spain, Mamluk Egypt, Ottoman Turkey, Persia, and the Silk Road between China and Europe provided the inspiration and materials for the [Renaissance] art and architecture

of Bellini, van Eyck, Dürer, and Alberti. The transmission of Arabic understanding of astronomy, philosophy, and medicine also profoundly influenced thinkers and scientists like Leonardo da Vinci, Copernicus, Vesalius, and Montaigne, whose insights into the workings of the human mind and body, as well as the individual's relationship to the wider world, are often still seen as the foundation of modern science and philosophy. It was the complex impact of these exchanges between east and west that created the culture, art, and scholarship that have been popularly associated with the Renaissance.

Source: Jerry Brotton, *The Renaissance Bazaar: From the Silk Road to Michelangelo* (Oxford: Oxford University Press, 2002), 1.

VOICE 12.2

Bernard Lewis on Hostility between Christians and Muslims | 1995

Between Islam and Christendom there was inevitably great and continuing hostility, but it was not due, in accordance with currently fashionable notions, to misperception and misunderstanding. On the contrary, the two understood each other very well, far better than either of them, in their other encounters could understand the more remote civilizations of Asia and, later, pre-Columbian America. As well as a shared or, rather, disputed mission and domain, Islam and Christendom had a great shared inheritance, which drew on common sources: the science and philosophy of Greece, the law and government of Rome, the ethical monotheism of Judaea, and beyond all of them, the deeply rooted cultures of the ancient Middle East. Christians and Muslims around the Mediterranean could find a common language in both the figurative and the literal senses. They could communicate, they could argue, if only to disagree; they could translate, as they did, both ways. All of this would have been difficult, if not impossible, between Christians or Muslims, on the one hand, and exponents of the civilizations of India or China, on the other.

Source: Bernard Lewis, *Cultures in Conflict: Christians, Muslims and Jews in the Age of Discovery* (Oxford: Oxford University Press, 1995), 14.

PART 4

The Early Modern World

1450–1750

THE BIG PICTURE

Toward Modernity . . . or Not?

For the sake of clarity and coherence, historians often characterize a particular period of time in a brief phrase such as "the age of First Civilizations" or "the era of revolutions." Though useful and even necessary, such capsule descriptions vastly oversimplify what actually happened. Historical reality is always more messy, more complicated, and more uncertain than any shorthand label can convey. Such is surely the case when we examine the three centuries spanning the years from roughly 1450 to 1750, commonly labeled the "early modern era."

Sprouts of Modernity?

In defining those centuries as "the early modern era," historians are suggesting that during this period of time we can find some initial signs, markers, or sprouts of what became the modern world. Such indicators of a new era in human history include the beginnings of genuine globalization; new demographic, economic, and intellectual patterns; and a growing European presence in world affairs.

The most obvious expression of globalization lay in the oceanic journeys of European explorers, the European conquest and colonial settlement of the Americas, and all that followed from these events. The Atlantic slave trade linked Africa permanently to Europe and the Western Hemisphere, while the global silver trade allowed Europeans to buy their way into ancient Asian markets. The massive exchange of plants, animals, diseases, and people, known to historians as the Columbian Exchange, created wholly new networks of interaction across both the Atlantic and Pacific Oceans, with enormous global implications. Furthermore, missionaries carried Christianity far beyond Europe, making it a genuinely global religion with a presence in the Americas, China, Japan, the Philippine Islands, Siberia, and south central Africa.

But Western Europeans were not alone in weaving this emerging global web. Russians marched across Siberia to the Pacific, creating the world's largest territorial state. China expanded deep into Inner Asia, bringing Mongolia, Xinjiang, and Tibet into a much enlarged Chinese empire. The Turkish Ottoman Empire brought much of the Middle East, North Africa, and southeastern Europe into the Islamic world's largest and most powerful state. Japanese merchants moved aggressively to open up commercial opportunities in Southeast Asia even as Indian traders penetrated the markets of Central Asia, Persia, and Russia.

Scattered signs of what later generations thought of as "modern life" likewise appeared in various places around the world. The obviously modern cultural development took place in Europe, where the Scientific Revolution transformed, at least for a few people, their view of the world, their approach to seeking knowledge, and their understanding of traditional Christianity. Subsequently, a scientific outlook spread globally, becoming perhaps the most potent marker of modern life.

Demographically, China, Japan, India, and Europe experienced the beginnings of modern population growth. Human numbers more than doubled between 1400 and 1800 (from about 374 million to 968 million), even as the globalization of disease produced a demographic catastrophe in the Americas and the slave trade limited African population growth.

Yet another indication of modern life lay in more highly commercialized economies centered in large cities that developed in various parts of Eurasia and the Americas. By the early eighteenth century, for example, Japan was one of the most urbanized societies in the world. In China, Southeast Asia, India, and across the Atlantic basin, more and more people found themselves, sometimes willingly and at other times involuntarily, producing for distant markets rather than for the use of their local communities.

Stronger and more cohesive states represented yet another modern global pattern as they incorporated various local societies into larger units while actively promoting trade, manufacturing, and a common culture within their borders. France, the Dutch Republic, Russia, Morocco, the Mughal Empire, Vietnam, Burma, Siam, and Japan all represent this kind of state. Their military power likewise soared as the "gunpowder revolution" kicked in around the world. Thus large-scale empires proliferated across Asia and the Middle East, while various European powers carved out new domains in the Americas. Within these empires, human pressures on the land intensified as forests were felled, marshes were drained, and the hunting grounds of foragers and the grazing lands of pastoralists were confiscated for farming or ranching.

Continuing Older Patterns?

But all of this may be misleading if it suggests that European world domination and more fully modern societies were a sure thing, an inevitable outgrowth of early modern developments. In fact, that future was far from clear in 1750. Although Europeans ruled the Americas and controlled the world's sea routes, their political and military power in mainland Asia and Africa was very limited, and they certainly did not hold all the leading roles in the global drama of these three centuries.

Furthermore, Islam, not Christianity, was the most rapidly spreading faith in much of Asia and Africa. And in 1750 Europe, India, and China were roughly comparable in their manufacturing output. It was not obvious that Europeans

would soon dominate the planet. Moreover, populations and economies had surged at various points in the past, only to fall back again in a cyclical pattern. Nothing guaranteed that the early modern surge would be any more lasting than the others.

Nor was there much to suggest that anything approaching modern industrial society was on the horizon. Animal and human muscles, wind, wood, and water still provided almost all of the energy that powered human economies. Handicraft techniques of manufacturing had nowhere been displaced by factory-based production, steam power, or electricity. Long-established elites, not middle-class upstarts, everywhere provided leadership and enjoyed the greatest privileges, while rural peasants, not urban workers, represented the primary social group in the lower classes. Kings and nobles, not parliaments and parties, governed. Female subordination was assumed to be natural almost everywhere, for nowhere had ideas of gender equality taken root.

Thus modern society, with its promise of liberation from ancient inequalities and from mass poverty, hardly seemed around the corner. Kings ruled most of Europe, and male landowning aristocrats remained at the top of the social hierarchy. Another change in ruling dynasties occurred in China, where that huge country affirmed Confucian values and a social structure that privileged landowning and office-holding elites, all of them men. Most Indians practiced some form of Hinduism and owed their most fundamental loyalty to local castes. The realm of Islam maintained its central role in the Eastern Hemisphere as the Ottoman Empire revived the political fortunes of Islam, and the religion sustained its long-term expansion into Africa and Southeast Asia. In short, for the majority of people, the three centuries between 1450 and 1750 marked less an entry into the modern era than the continuation of older patterns.

From this mixture of what was new and what was old during the early modern era, the three chapters that follow highlight the changes. Chapter 13 turns the spotlight on the new empires of those three centuries—European, Middle Eastern, and Asian. New global patterns of long-distance commerce in spices, sugar, silver, fur, and slaves represent the themes of Chapter 14. New cultural trends—both within the major religious traditions of the world and in the emergence of modern science—come together in Chapter 15. With the benefit of hindsight, we may see various "sprouts of modernity" as harbingers of things to come, but from the viewpoint of 1700 or so, the future was open and uncertain, as it almost always is.

Landmarks in World History (ca. 1450–ca. 1750)

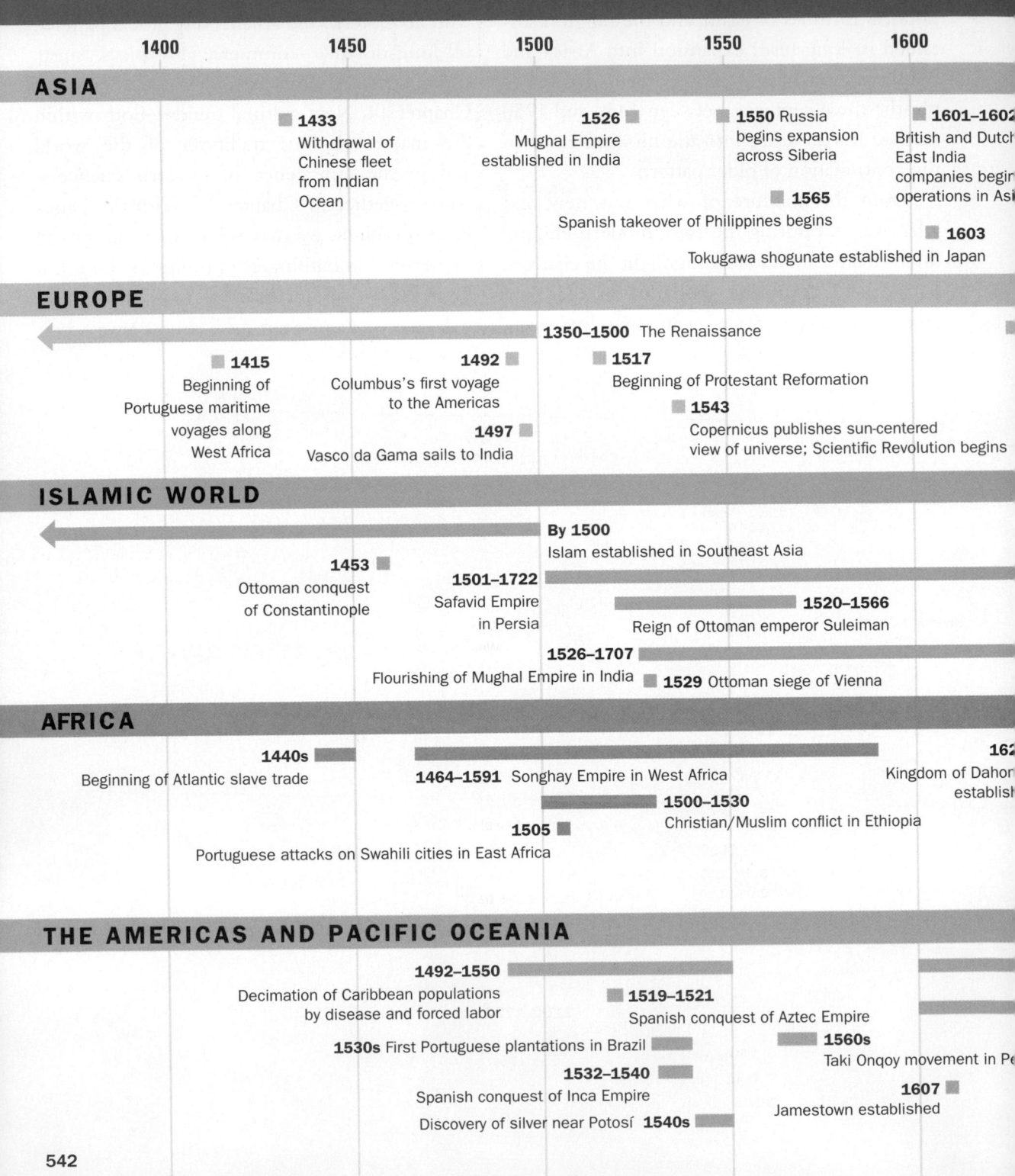

	1400	1450	1500	1550	1600

ASIA

1433 Withdrawal of Chinese fleet from Indian Ocean

1526 Mughal Empire established in India

1550 Russia begins expansion across Siberia

1601–1602 British and Dutch East India companies begin operations in Asia

1565 Spanish takeover of Philippines begins

1603 Tokugawa shogunate established in Japan

EUROPE

1350–1500 The Renaissance

1415 Beginning of Portuguese maritime voyages along West Africa

1492 Columbus's first voyage to the Americas

1497 Vasco da Gama sails to India

1517 Beginning of Protestant Reformation

1543 Copernicus publishes sun-centered view of universe; Scientific Revolution begins

ISLAMIC WORLD

By 1500 Islam established in Southeast Asia

1453 Ottoman conquest of Constantinople

1501–1722 Safavid Empire in Persia

1520–1566 Reign of Ottoman emperor Suleiman

1526–1707 Flourishing of Mughal Empire in India

1529 Ottoman siege of Vienna

AFRICA

1440s Beginning of Atlantic slave trade

1464–1591 Songhay Empire in West Africa

1621 Kingdom of Dahomey established

1500–1530 Christian/Muslim conflict in Ethiopia

1505 Portuguese attacks on Swahili cities in East Africa

THE AMERICAS AND PACIFIC OCEANIA

1492–1550 Decimation of Caribbean populations by disease and forced labor

1519–1521 Spanish conquest of Aztec Empire

1530s First Portuguese plantations in Brazil

1560s Taki Onqoy movement in Peru

1532–1540 Spanish conquest of Inca Empire

Discovery of silver near Potosí **1540s**

1607 Jamestown established

542

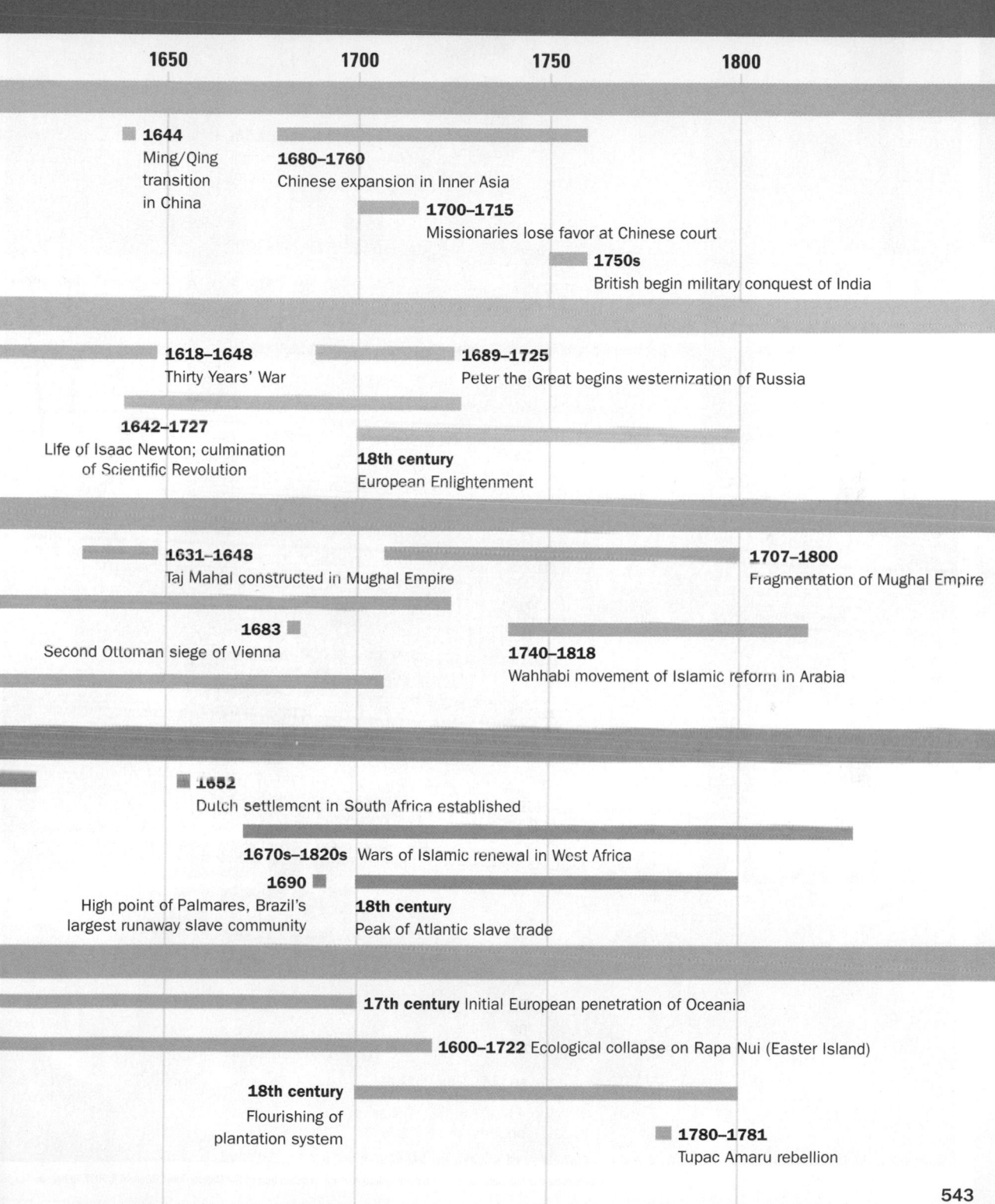

1650 1700 1750 1800

1644
Ming/Qing
transition
in China

1680–1760
Chinese expansion in Inner Asia

1700–1715
Missionaries lose favor at Chinese court

1750s
British begin military conquest of India

1618–1648
Thirty Years' War

1689–1725
Peter the Great begins westernization of Russia

1642–1727
Life of Isaac Newton; culmination
of Scientific Revolution

18th century
European Enlightenment

1631–1648
Taj Mahal constructed in Mughal Empire

1707–1800
Fragmentation of Mughal Empire

1683
Second Ottoman siege of Vienna

1740–1818
Wahhabi movement of Islamic reform in Arabia

1652
Dutch settlement in South Africa established

1670s–1820s Wars of Islamic renewal in West Africa

1690
High point of Palmares, Brazil's
largest runaway slave community

18th century
Peak of Atlantic slave trade

17th century Initial European penetration of Oceania

1600–1722 Ecological collapse on Rapa Nui (Easter Island)

18th century
Flourishing of
plantation system

1780–1781
Tupac Amaru rebellion

Illustration from the Padshahnama, ca. 1630–40/Royal Collection/Royal Collection Trust © Her Majesty Queen Elizabeth II, 2017/Bridgeman Images

Political Transformations

Empires and Encounters

1450–1750

In early 2017, a U.S. newspaper writer, L. Todd Wood, stated, "Mr. Putin . . . does want a return of the Russian Empire." Such sentiments have become commonplace following the Russian president's actions in seizing Crimea and in pressuring Ukraine to remain within a Russian sphere of influence. In reflecting on this very current political situation, Mr. Wood and many others have invoked the Russian Empire, which had taken shape during the early modern era. In the same vein, commentators on the economic and political resurgence of twenty-first-century Turkey often refer to it as an effort "to rebuild the Ottoman Empire," likewise a creation of the early modern era.[1] In such ways, the memories of these earlier empires continue to shape understanding of current events and perhaps to inspire actions in the present as well. ■

Underlying these comments is a sharply critical posture toward any revival of these earlier empires. Indeed, empire building has been largely discredited during the twentieth and twenty-first centuries, and "imperialist" has become a term of insult rather than a source of pride. How very different were the three centuries (1450–1750) of the early modern era, when empire building was a global process! In the Americas, the Aztec and Inca empires flourished before they were incorporated into the rival empires of the Spanish, Portuguese, British, French, and Dutch, constructed all across the Western Hemisphere. Within those European imperial systems, vast transformations took place:

« **The Mughal Empire** Among the most magnificent of the early modern empires was that of the Mughals in India. In this painting by an unknown Mughal artist, the seventeenth-century emperor Shah Jahan is holding a *durbar*, or ceremonial assembly, in the audience hall of his palace. The material splendor of the setting shows the immense wealth of the court, while the halo around Shah Jahan's head indicates the special spiritual grace or enlightenment associated with emperors.

old societies were destroyed, and new societies arose as Native Americans, Europeans, and Africans came into sustained contact with one another for the first time in world history. It was a revolutionary encounter with implications that extended far beyond the Americas themselves.

But European empires in the Americas were not alone on the imperial stage of the early modern era. Across the immense expanse of Siberia, the Russians constructed what was then the world's largest territorial empire, making Russia an Asian as well as a European power. Qing (chihng) dynasty China penetrated deep into Inner Asia, doubling the size of the country while incorporating millions of non-Chinese people who practiced Islam, Buddhism, or animistic religions. On the South Asian peninsula, the Islamic Mughal Empire brought Hindus and Muslims into a closer relationship than ever before, sometimes quite peacefully and at other times with great conflict. In the Middle East, the Turkish Ottoman Empire reestablished something of the earlier political unity of heartland Islam and posed a serious military and religious threat to European Christendom. Thus the early modern era was an age of empire.

SEEKING THE MAIN POINT

In what ways did European empires in the Americas resemble their Russian, Chinese, Mughal, and Ottoman counterparts, and in what respects were they different? Do you find the similarities or the differences more striking?

European Empires in the Americas

Among the early modern empires, those of Western Europe were distinctive because the conquered territories lay an ocean away from the imperial heartland, rather than adjacent to it. Following the breakthrough voyages of Columbus, the Spanish focused their empire-building efforts in the Caribbean and then, in the early sixteenth century, turned to the mainland, making stunning conquests of the powerful but fragile Aztec and Inca empires. Meanwhile, the Portuguese established themselves along the coast of present-day Brazil. In the early seventeenth century, the British, French, and Dutch launched colonial settlements along the eastern coast of North America. From these beginnings, Europeans extended their empires to encompass most of the Americas, at least nominally, by the mid-eighteenth century (see Map 13.1). It was a remarkable achievement. What had made it possible?

The European Advantage

Guided Reading Question

■ **CONNECTION**
What enabled Europeans to carve out huge empires an ocean away from their homelands?

Geography provides a starting point for explaining Europe's American empires. Countries on the Atlantic rim of Europe (Portugal, Spain, Britain, and France) were simply closer to the Americas than were any potential Asian competitors. Furthermore, the complex current system and the fixed winds of the Atlantic that blew steadily in the same direction provided a far different maritime environment than the alternating monsoon winds of the Indian Ocean, one that forced Western mariners to innovate in ways that made their ships among the most maneuverable in the world.

The enormously rich markets of the Indian Ocean world provided little incentive for its Chinese, Indian, or Muslim participants to venture much beyond

Landmarks for Chapter 13

1450   1500   1550   1600   1650   1700   1750

EUROPEAN EMPIRES

1519–1540 Spanish conquest of Aztec and Inca empires

ca. 1530s First Portuguese plantations in Brazil

1565 Spanish takeover of Philippines begins

1492–1502 Voyages of Columbus to Americas

1607–1608
English colony at Jamestown; French colony in Quebec

RUSSIAN EMPIRE

1480 Russia emerges from Mongol rule

ca. 1550–1795
Russian expansion across Siberia

1648–1709
Russian incorporation of Ukraine

1689–1725
Peter the Great; "westernization" policies

CHINESE EMPIRE

1433 Chinese withdrawal from Indian Ocean

1644 Qing/Manchu dynasty established

1680–1760
Chinese expansion into Central Asia

1689
Treaty of Nerchinsk resolves border between Chinese and Russian empires

OTTOMAN EMPIRE

1453 Ottoman conquest of Constantinople

1517 Ottoman conquest of Egypt

1529 Siege of Vienna

1534–1639
Ottoman military conflict with
Persian Safavid Empire

MUGHAL EMPIRE

1526 Mughal Empire established

1683
Second Ottoman siege
of Vienna

1556–1605 Reign of Akbar

1658–1707
Fragmentation of Mughal Empire

Map 13.1 European Colonial Empires in the Americas

By the beginning of the eighteenth century, European powers had laid claim to most of the Western Hemisphere. Their wars and rivalries during that century led to an expansion of Spanish and English claims, at the expense of the French.

READING THE MAP: Which European power controlled the most territory in the Americas? Which controlled the least?

MAKING CONNECTIONS: Compare Map 13.1 with Map 16.3. Which European powers lost control of their Central and South American colonies by the 1830s? Which retained theirs? Which did both?

Legend:
- Dutch territories
- English territories
- French territories
- Portuguese territories
- Spanish territories

their own waters. Europeans, however, were powerfully motivated to do so. After 1200 or so, European elites were increasingly aware of their region's marginal position in the rich world of Eurasian commerce and were determined to gain access to that world. Once the Americas were discovered, windfalls of natural resources, including highly productive agricultural lands, drove further expansion, ultimately underpinning the long-term growth of the European economy into the nineteenth and twentieth centuries. The drive to expand beyond Europe was also motivated by the enduring rivalries of competing European states. At the same time, the growing and relatively independent merchant class sought direct access to Asian wealth to avoid the reliance on Muslim intermediaries that they found so distasteful. Impoverished nobles and commoners alike found opportunity for gaining wealth and status in the colonies. Missionaries and others were inspired by crusading zeal to enlarge the realm of Christendom. Persecuted minorities were in search of a new start in life. All of these compelling motives drove the relentlessly expanding imperial frontier in the Americas. Summarizing their intentions, one Spanish conquistador declared: "We came here to serve God and the King, and also to get rich."[2]

In carving out these empires, often against great odds and with great difficulty, Europeans nonetheless had certain advantages, despite their distance from home. Their states and trading companies effectively mobilized both human and material resources. European innovations in mapmaking, navigation, sailing techniques, and ship design — building on earlier models from the Mediterranean, Indian Ocean, and Chinese regions — likewise enabled Europeans to penetrate the Atlantic Ocean. Their ironworking technology, gunpowder weapons, and horses initially had no parallel in the Americas, although many peoples later acquired them.

Divisions within and between local societies provided allies for the determined European invaders. Various subject peoples of the Aztec Empire, for example, resented Mexica domination and willingly joined conquistador **Hernán Cortés** in the Spanish assault on that empire. In the final attack on the Aztec capital of Tenochtitlán, Cortés's forces contained fewer than 1,000 Spaniards and many times that number of Tlaxcalans, former subjects of the Aztecs. After their defeat, tens of thousands of Aztecs themselves joined Cortés as he carved out a Spanish Mesoamerican empire far larger than that of the Aztecs. (See Zooming In: Doña Marina, page 550.) Much of the Inca elite, according to a recent study, "actually welcomed the Spanish invaders as liberators and willingly settled down with them to share rule of Andean farmers and miners."[3] A violent dispute between two rival contenders for the Inca throne, the brothers Atahualpa and Huáscar, certainly helped the European invaders recruit allies to augment their own minimal forces. In short, Spanish military victories were not solely of their own making, but the product of alliances with local peoples, who supplied the bulk of the Europeans' conquering armies.

Perhaps the most significant of European advantages lay in their germs and diseases, with which Native Americans had no familiarity. Those diseases decimated society after society, sometimes in advance of the Europeans' actual arrival.

Doña Marina: Between Two Worlds

In her brief life, she was known variously as Malinal, Doña Marina, and La Malinche. By whatever name, she was a woman who experienced the encounter of the Old World and the New in particularly intimate ways, even as she became a bridge between them. Born around 1505, Malinal was the daughter of an elite and cultured family in the borderlands between the Maya and Aztec cultures in what is now southern Mexico. Two dramatic events decisively shaped her life. The first occurred when her father died and her mother remarried, bearing a son to her new husband. To protect this boy's inheritance, Malinal's family sold her into slavery. Eventually, she came into the possession of a Maya chieftain in Tabasco on the Gulf of Mexico.

Here her second life-changing event took place in March 1519, when the Spanish conquistador Hernán Cortés landed his troops and inflicted a sharp military defeat on Tabasco. In the negotiations that followed, Tabasco authorities gave lavish gifts to the Spanish, including twenty women, one of whom was Malinal.

Doña Marina (left) translating for Cortés.

Described by Bernal Díaz, one of Cortés's associates, as "good-looking, intelligent, and self-assured," the teenage Malinal soon found herself in service to Cortés himself. Since Spanish men were not supposed to touch non-Christian women, these newcomers were distributed among his officers, quickly baptized, and given Christian names. Thus Malinal became Doña Marina.

With a ready ear for languages and already fluent in Mayan and Nahuatl, the language of the Aztecs, Doña Marina soon picked up Spanish and quickly became indispensable to Cortés as an interpreter, cross-cultural broker, and strategist. She accompanied him on his march inland to the Aztec capital, Tenochtitlán, and on several occasions her language skills and cultural awareness allowed her to uncover spies and plots that might well have seriously impeded Cortés's defeat of the Aztec Empire. Díaz reported that "Doña Marina, who understood full well

photo: Biblioteca Nacional, Madrid, Spain/Bridgeman Images

In particular regions such as the Caribbean, Virginia, and New England, the rapid buildup of immigrant populations, coupled with the sharply diminished native numbers, allowed Europeans to actually outnumber local peoples within a few decades.

The Great Dying and the Little Ice Age

However Europeans acquired American empires, their global significance is apparent. Chief among the consequences was the demographic collapse of Native American societies. Although precise figures remain the subject of much debate, scholars generally agree that the pre-Columbian population of the Western Hemisphere was substantial, perhaps 60 to 80 million. The greatest concentrations of what was happening, told [Cortés] what was going on." In the Aztec capital, where Cortés took the emperor Moctezuma captive, it fell to Doña Marina to persuade him to accept this humiliating position and surrender his wealth to the Spanish. Even Cortés, who was never very gracious with his praise for her, acknowledged that "after God, we owe this conquest of New Spain to Doña Marina." Aztecs soon came to see this young woman as the voice of Cortés, referring to her as La Malinche, a Spanish approximation of her original name. So paired did Cortés and La Malinche become in Aztec thinking that Cortés himself was often called Malinche.

More than an interpreter for Cortés, Doña Marina also became his mistress and bore him a son. But after the initial conquest of Mexico was complete and he no longer needed her skills, Cortés married Doña Marina off to another Spanish conquistador, Juan Jaramillo, with whom she lived until her death, probably around 1530. Cortés did provide her with several pieces of land, one of which, ironically, had belonged to Moctezuma. Her son, however, was taken from her and raised in Spain.

In 1523, Doña Marina performed one final service for Cortés, accompanying him on a mission to Honduras to suppress a rebellion. There her personal life seemed to come full circle, for near her hometown she encountered her mother, who had sold her into slavery, and her half-brother. Díaz reported that they "were very much afraid of Doña Marina," thinking that they would surely be put to death by their now-powerful and well-connected relative. But in a replay of the biblical story of Joseph and his brothers, Doña Marina quickly reassured and forgave them, while granting them "many golden jewels and some clothes."

In the centuries since her death, Doña Marina has been highly controversial. For much of the colonial era, she was viewed positively as an ally of the Spanish. But after independence, some came to see her as a traitor to her own people, shunning her heritage and siding with the invaders. Still others have considered her as the mother of Mexico's mixed-race, or mestizo, culture. Should she be understood primarily as a victim or as a skillful survivor negotiating hard choices under difficult circumstances?

Whatever the judgments of later generations, Doña Marina herself seems to have made a clear choice to cast her lot with the Europeans. Even when Cortés had given her to another man, Doña Marina expressed no regret. According to Díaz, she declared, "Even if they were to make me mistress of all the provinces of New Spain, I would refuse the honor, for I would rather serve my husband and Cortés than anything else in the world."

QUESTIONS

How might you define the significance of Doña Marina's life? In what larger contexts might her life find a place?

people lived in the Mesoamerican and Andean zones, which were dominated by the Aztec and Inca empires. Long isolation from the Afro-Eurasian world and the lack of most domesticated animals meant the absence of acquired immunities to Old World diseases such as smallpox, measles, typhus, influenza, malaria, and, later, yellow fever.

Therefore, when Native American peoples came into contact with these European and African diseases, they died in appalling numbers, in many cases losing up to 90 percent of the population. The densely settled peoples of Caribbean islands virtually vanished within fifty years of Columbus's arrival. Central Mexico, with a population estimated at some 10 to 20 million before the Spanish conquest, declined to about 1 million by 1650. A native Nahuatl (nah-watl) account depicted the social breakdown that accompanied the smallpox pandemic: "A great many died from this plague, and many others died of hunger. They could not get up to search for food, and everyone else was too sick to care for them, so they starved to death in their beds."[4]

The situation was similar in Dutch and British territories of North America. A Dutch observer in New Netherland (later New York) reported in 1656 that "the Indians . . . affirm that before the arrival of the Christians, and before the small pox broke out amongst them, they were ten times as numerous as they are now, and that their population had been melted down by this disease, whereof nine-tenths of them have died."[5] To Governor Bradford of Plymouth colony (in present-day Massachusetts), such conditions represented the "good hand of God" at work, "sweeping away great multitudes of the natives . . . that he might make room for us."[6] Not until the late seventeenth century did native numbers begin to recuperate somewhat from this catastrophe, and even then, not everywhere.

As the **Great Dying** took hold in the Americas, it interacted with another natural phenomenon, this time one of genuinely global proportions. Known as the **Little Ice Age**, it was a period from the thirteenth to nineteenth century of unusually cool temperatures that spanned much of the early modern period, most prominently in the Northern Hemisphere. Scholars continue to debate its causes. Some have suggested a low point in sunspot activity, while others cite volcanic eruptions, whose ash and gases blocked the sun's warming energy. More recently, some scientists have linked the Little Ice Age to the demographic collapse in the Americas. The Great Dying, they argue, resulted in the desertion of large areas of Native American farmland and ended the traditional practices of forest management through burning in many regions. These changes sparked a resurgence of plant life, which in turn took large amounts of carbon dioxide, a greenhouse gas, out of the atmosphere, contributing to global cooling. Whatever the causes, shorter growing seasons and less hospitable weather conditions adversely affected food production in regions across the globe.

While the onset, duration, and effects of the Little Ice Age varied from region to region, the impact of a cooler climate reached its peak in many regions in the mid-seventeenth century, helping to spark what scholars term the **General Crisis**. Much of China, Europe, and North America experienced record or near-record cold winters during this period. Regions near the equator in the tropics and Southern Hemisphere also experienced extreme conditions and irregular rainfall, resulting, for instance, in the growth of the Sahara Desert. Wet, cold summers reduced harvests dramatically in Europe, while severe droughts ruined crops in many other regions, especially China, which suffered terrible drought between 1637 and 1641. Difficult weather conditions accentuated other stresses in societies, leading to widespread famines, epidemics, uprisings, and wars in which millions perished. Eurasia did not escape lightly from these stresses: the collapse of the Ming dynasty in China, nearly constant warfare in Europe, and civil war in Mughal India all occurred in the context of the General Crisis, which only fully subsided when more favorable weather patterns took hold starting in the eighteenth century.

Nor were the Americas, already devastated by the Great Dying, spared the suffering that accompanied the Little Ice Age and the General Crisis of the seventeenth century. In central Mexico, heartland of the Aztec Empire and the center of Spanish colonial rule in the area, severe drought in the five years after 1639 sent the price of maize skyrocketing, left granaries empty and many people without water, and prompted an unsuccessful plot to declare Mexico's independence from Spain. Continuing drought years in the decades that followed witnessed repeated public processions of the statue of Our Lady of Guadalupe, who had gained a reputation for producing rain. The Caribbean region during the 1640s experienced the opposite condition — torrential rains that accompanied more frequent El Niño weather patterns — which provided ideal conditions for the breeding of mosquitoes that carried both yellow fever and malaria. A Maya chronicle for 1648 noted, "There was bloody vomit and we began to die."[7]

Like the Great Dying, the General Crisis reminds us that climate often plays an important role in shaping human history. But it also reminds us that human activity — the importation of deadly diseases to the Americas, in this case — may also help shape the climate, and that this has been true long before our current climate crisis.

The Columbian Exchange

In sharply diminishing the population of the Americas, the Great Dying, together with the impact of the Little Ice Age, created an acute labor shortage and certainly did make room for immigrant newcomers, both colonizing Europeans and enslaved Africans. Over the several centuries of the colonial era and beyond, various combinations of indigenous, European, and African peoples created entirely new societies in the Americas, largely replacing the many and varied cultures that had flourished before 1492. To those colonial societies, Europeans and Africans brought not only their germs and their people but also their plants and animals. Wheat, rice, sugarcane, grapes, and many garden vegetables and fruits, as well as numerous weeds, took hold in the Americas, where they transformed the landscape and made possible a recognizably European diet and way of life. In what is now the continental United States, for example, the centuries since 1600 have witnessed the destruction of some 90 percent of the old-growth forests as the land has been burned, logged, and turned into fields and pastures. Even more revolutionary were the newcomers' animals — horses, pigs, cattle, goats, sheep — all of which were new to the Americas and multiplied spectacularly in an environment largely free of natural predators. These domesticated animals made possible the ranching economies and cowboy cultures of both North and South America. Horses also transformed many Native American societies, particularly in the North American West, as settled farming peoples such as the Pawnee abandoned their fields to hunt bison from horseback. As a male-dominated hunting and warrior culture emerged, women lost much of their earlier role as food producers. Both environmentally and socially, these changes were revolutionary.

Disease and Death among the Aztecs Smallpox, which accompanied the Spanish to the Americas, devastated native populations. This image, drawn by an Aztec artist and contained in the sixteenth-century Florentine Codex, illustrates the impact of the disease in Mesoamerica. (Private Collection/Peter Newark American Pictures/Bridgeman Images)

Guided Reading Question
....
■ **CHANGE**
What large-scale transformations did European empires generate?

In the other direction, American food crops such as corn, potatoes, and cassava spread widely in the Eastern Hemisphere, where they provided the nutritional foundation for the population growth that became everywhere a hallmark of the modern era. In Europe, calories derived from corn and potatoes helped push human numbers from some 60 million in 1400 to 390 million in 1900. Those Amerindian crops later provided cheap and reasonably nutritious food for millions of industrial workers. Potatoes, especially, allowed Ireland's population to grow enormously and then condemned many of the Irish to starvation or emigration when an airborne fungus, also from the Americas, destroyed the crop in the mid-nineteenth century. In China, corn, peanuts, and especially sweet potatoes supplemented the traditional rice and wheat to sustain China's modern population explosion. By the early twentieth century, food plants of American origin represented about 20 percent of total Chinese food production. In Africa, corn took hold quickly and was used as a cheap food for the human cargoes of the transatlantic trade. Beyond food crops, American stimulants such as tobacco and chocolate were soon used around the world. By the seventeenth century, how-to manuals instructed Chinese users on smoking techniques, and tobacco had become, in the words of one enamored Chinese poet, "the gentleman's companion, it warms my heart and leaves my mouth feeling like a divine furnace."[8] Tea from China and coffee from the Islamic world also spread globally, contributing to this worldwide biological exchange. Never before in human history had such a large-scale and consequential diffusion of plants and animals operated to remake the biological environment of the planet.

This enormous network of communication, migration, trade, disease, and the transfer of plants and animals, all generated by European colonial empires in the Americas, has been dubbed the "**Columbian exchange**." It gave rise to something wholly new in world history: an interacting Atlantic world that permanently connected Europe, Africa, and North and South America. But the long-term benefits of this Atlantic network were very unequally distributed. The peoples of Africa and the Americas experienced social disruption, slavery, disease, and death on an almost unimaginable scale, while Western Europeans reaped the greatest rewards. Mountains of new information flooded into Europe, shaking up conventional understandings of the world and contributing to a revolutionary new way of thinking known as the Scientific Revolution. The wealth of the colonies — precious metals, natural resources, new food crops, slave labor, financial profits, colonial markets — provided one of the foundations on which Europe's Industrial Revolution was built. The colonies also provided an outlet for the rapidly growing population of European societies and represented an enormous extension of European civilization. In short, the colonial empires of the Americas greatly facilitated a changing global balance of power, which now thrust the previously marginal Western Europeans into an increasingly central and commanding role on the world stage. "Without a New World to deliver economic balance in the Old," concluded a prominent world historian, "Europe would have remained inferior, as ever, in wealth and power, to the great civilizations of Asia."[9]

Comparing Colonial Societies in the Americas

European colonial empires — Spanish, Portuguese, British, and French alike — did not simply conquer and govern established societies, but rather generated wholly new societies, born of the decimation of Native American populations and the introduction of European and African peoples, cultures, plants, and animals. European colonial strategies were based on an economic theory known as **mercantilism**, which held that governments served their countries' economic interests best by encouraging exports and accumulating bullion (precious metals such as silver and gold). In this scheme of things, colonies provided closed markets for the manufactured goods of the "mother country" and, if they were lucky, supplied great quantities of bullion as well. Such an outlook fueled European wars and colonial rivalries around the world in the early modern era.

Meanwhile, in the colonies themselves, empire took shape in various ways. Some differences derived from the contrasting societies of the colonizing powers, such as a semi-feudal and Catholic Spain and a more rapidly changing Protestant England. The kind of economy established in particular regions — settler-dominated agriculture, slave-based plantations, ranching, or mining — likewise influenced the colonies' development. So too did the character of the Native American cultures — the more densely populated and urbanized Mesoamerican and Andean civilizations differed greatly from the more sparsely populated rural villages of North America.

Furthermore, women and men often experienced colonial intrusion in quite distinct ways. Beyond the common burdens of violent conquest, epidemic disease, and coerced labor, both Native American and enslaved African women had to cope with the additional demands made on them as females. Conquest was often accompanied by the transfer of women to the new colonial rulers. Cortés, for example, marked his alliance with the city of Tlaxcala (tlah-SKAH-lah) against the Aztecs by an exchange of gifts in which he received hundreds of female slaves and eight daughters of elite Tlaxcalan families, whom he distributed to his soldiers. And he commanded the Aztec ruler: "You are to deliver women with light skins, corn, chicken, eggs, and tortillas."[10]

Soon after conquest, many Spanish men married elite native women. It was a long-standing practice in Amerindian societies and was encouraged by both Spanish and indigenous male authorities as a means of cementing their new relationship. It was also advantageous for some of the women involved. One of Aztec emperor Moctezuma's daughters, who was mistress to Cortés and eventually married several other Spaniards, wound up with the largest landed estate in the Valley of Mexico. Below this elite level of interaction, however, far more women experienced sexual violence and abuse. Rape accompanied conquest in many places, and dependent or enslaved women working under the control of European men frequently found themselves required to perform sexual services. This was a tragedy and humiliation for native and enslaved men as well, for they were unable to protect their women from such abuse.

Such variations in culture, policy, economy, and gender generated quite different colonial societies in several major regions of the Americas.

In the Lands of the Aztecs and the Incas

The Spanish conquest of the Aztec and Inca empires in the early sixteenth century gave Spain access to the most wealthy, urbanized, and densely populated regions of the Western Hemisphere. Within a century and well before the British had even begun their colonizing efforts in North America, the Spanish in Mexico and Peru had established nearly a dozen major cities; several impressive universities; hundreds of cathedrals, churches, and missions; an elaborate administrative bureaucracy; and a network of regulated international commerce.

The economic foundation for this emerging colonial society lay in commercial agriculture, much of it on large rural estates, and in silver and gold mining. In both cases, native peoples, rather than African slaves or European workers, provided most of the labor, despite their much-diminished numbers. Almost everywhere that labor was coerced, often directly required by colonial authorities under a legal regime known as *encomienda*. It was, in fact, a forced labor system not far removed from slavery. By the seventeenth century, the *hacienda* system had taken shape, by which the private owners of large estates directly employed native workers. With low wages, high taxes, and large debts to the landowners, the *peons* who worked these estates enjoyed little control over their lives or their livelihood.

On this economic base, a distinctive social order grew up, replicating something of the Spanish class and gender hierarchy while accommodating the racially and culturally different Indians and Africans as well as growing numbers of racially mixed people. At the top of this colonial society were the male Spanish settlers, who were politically and economically dominant and seeking to become a landed aristocracy.

Guided Reading Question

■ **CHANGE**
What was the economic foundation of colonial rule in Mexico and Peru? How did it shape the kinds of societies that arose there?

One Spanish official commented in 1619: "The Spaniards, from the able and rich to the humble and poor, all hold themselves to be lords and will not serve [do manual labor]."[11] Politically, they increasingly saw themselves not as colonials, but as residents of a Spanish kingdom, subject to the Spanish monarch yet separate and distinct from Spain itself and deserving of a large measure of self-government. Therefore, they chafed under the heavy bureaucratic restrictions imposed by the Crown. "I obey but I do not enforce" was a slogan that reflected local authorities' resistance to orders from Spain. But the Spanish minority, never more than 20 percent of the population, was itself a divided community. Descendants of the original conquistadores sought to protect their privileges against immigrant newcomers; Spaniards born in the Americas (*creoles*) resented the pretensions to superiority of those born in Spain (*peninsulares*); landown-ing Spaniards felt threatened by the growing wealth of commercial and mercantile groups practicing less prestigious occupations. Span-ish missionaries and church authorities were often sharply critical of how these settlers treated native peoples. While Spanish women shared the racial privileges of their husbands, they were clearly subordinate in gender terms, unable to hold public office and viewed as weak and in need of male protection. But they were also regarded as the "bearers of civiliza-tion," and through their capacity to produce legitimate children, they were the essential link for transmitting male wealth, honor, and status to future generations. This required strict control of their sexuality and a contin-uation of the Iberian obsession with "purity of blood." In Spain, that concern had focused on potential liaisons with Jews and Muslims; in the colonies, the alleged threat to female vir-tue derived from Native American and Afri-can men.

From a male viewpoint, the problem with Spanish women was that there were very few of them. This demographic fact led to the most distinctive feature of these new colonial societies in Mexico and Peru—the emergence of a *mestizo* (mehs-TEE-zoh), or mixed-race, population, initially the product of unions between Spanish men and Indian women. Rooted in the sexual imbalance

Racial Mixing in Colonial Mexico This eighteenth-century painting by the famous Zapotec artist Miguel Cabrera shows a Spanish man, a *mestiza* woman, and their child, who was labeled as *castiza*. By the twentieth century, such mixed-race people represented the majority of the population of Mexico, and cultural blending had become a central feature of the country's identity. (Museo de América, Madrid, Spain/Bridgeman Images)

among Spanish immigrants (seven men to one woman in early colonial Peru, for example), the emergence of a mestizo population was facilitated by the desire of many surviving Indian women for the relative security of life in a Spanish household, where they and their children would not be subject to the abuse and harsh demands made on native peoples. Over the 300 years of the colonial era, mestizo numbers grew substantially, becoming the majority of the population in Mexico sometime during the nineteenth century. Such mixed-race people were divided into dozens of separate groups known as *castas* (castes), based on their precise racial heritage and skin color.

Mestizos were largely Hispanic in culture, but Spaniards looked down on them during much of the colonial era, regarding them as illegitimate, for many were not born of "proper" marriages. Despite this attitude, their growing numbers and the economic usefulness of their men as artisans, clerks, supervisors of labor gangs, and lower-level officials in both church and state bureaucracies led to their recognition as a distinct social group. *Mestizas*, women of mixed racial background, worked as domestic servants or in their husbands' shops, wove cloth, and manufactured candles and cigars, in addition to performing domestic duties. A few became quite wealthy. An illiterate mestiza named Mencia Perez married successively two reasonably well-to-do Spanish men and upon their deaths took over their businesses, becoming in her own right a very rich woman by the 1590s. At that point, no one would have referred to her as a mestiza. Particularly in Mexico, mestizo identity blurred the sense of sharp racial difference between Spanish and Indian peoples and became a major element in the identity of modern Mexico.

At the bottom of Mexican and Peruvian colonial societies were the indigenous peoples, known to Europeans as "Indians." Traumatized by the Great Dying, they were subject to gross abuse and exploitation as the primary labor force for the mines and estates of the Spanish Empire and were required to render tribute payments to their Spanish overlords. Their empires dismantled by Spanish conquest, their religions attacked by Spanish missionaries, and their diminished numbers forcibly relocated into larger settlements, many Indians gravitated toward the world of their conquerors. Many learned Spanish; converted to Christianity; moved to cities to work for wages; ate the meat of cows, chickens, and pigs; used plows and draft animals rather than traditional digging sticks; and took their many grievances to Spanish courts. Indian women endured some distinctive conditions because Spanish legal codes generally defined them as minors rather than responsible adults. As those codes took hold, Indian women were increasingly excluded from the courts or represented by their menfolk. This made it more difficult to maintain female property rights. In 1804, for example, a Maya legal petition identified eight men and ten women from a particular family as owners of a piece of land, but the Spanish translation omitted the women's names altogether.

But much that was indigenous persisted. At the local level, Indian male authorities retained a measure of autonomy, and traditional markets operated regularly. Both Andean and Maya women continued to leave personal property to their female descendants. Maize, beans, and squash persisted as the major elements of Indian diets in Mexico. Christian saints in many places blended easily with specialized indigenous gods, while belief in magic, folk medicine, and communion with the dead remained strong. Memories of the past also endured. The Tupac Amaru revolt in Peru during 1780–1781 was made in the name of the last independent Inca emperor. In that revolt, the wife of the leader, Micaela Bastidas, was referred to as La Coya, the female Inca, evoking the parallel hierarchies of male and female officials who had earlier governed the Inca Empire (see "The Inca Empire" in Chapter 12).

Thus Spaniards, mestizos, and Indians represented the major social categories in the colonial lands of what had been the Inca and Aztec empires, while African slaves and freemen were less numerous than elsewhere in the Americas. Despite the sharp divisions among these groups, some movement was possible. Indians who acquired an education, wealth, and some European culture might "pass" as mestizo. Likewise, more fortunate mestizo families might be accepted as Spaniards over time. Colonial Spanish America was a vast laboratory of ethnic mixing and cultural change. It was dominated by Europeans, to be sure, but with a rather more fluid and culturally blended society than in the racially rigid colonies of British North America.

Colonies of Sugar

Another and quite different kind of colonial society emerged in the lowland areas of Brazil, ruled by Portugal, and in the Spanish, British, French, and Dutch colonies in the Caribbean. These regions lacked the great civilizations of Mexico and Peru. Nor did they provide much mineral wealth until the Brazilian gold rush of the 1690s and the discovery of diamonds a little later. Still, Europeans found a very profitable substitute in sugar, which was much in demand in Europe, where it was used as a medicine, a spice, a sweetener, a preservative, and in sculptured forms as a decoration that indicated high status. Whereas commercial agriculture in the Spanish Empire served a domestic market in its towns and mining camps, these sugar-based colonies produced almost exclusively for export, while importing their food and other necessities.

Large-scale sugar production had been pioneered by Arabs, who had introduced it in the Mediterranean. Europeans learned the technique and transferred it to their Atlantic island possessions and then to the Americas. For a century (1570–1670), Portuguese planters along the northeast coast of Brazil dominated the world market for sugar. Then the British, French, and Dutch turned their Caribbean territories into highly productive sugar-producing colonies, breaking the Portuguese and Brazilian monopoly.

Guided Reading Question

■ **COMPARISON**

How did the plantation societies of Brazil and the Caribbean differ from those of southern colonies in British North America?

Sugar decisively transformed Brazil and the Caribbean. Its production, which involved both growing the sugarcane and processing it into usable sugar, was very labor-intensive and could most profitably occur in a large-scale, almost industrial setting. It was perhaps the first modern industry in that it produced for an international and mass market, using capital and expertise from Europe, with production facilities located in the Americas. However, its most characteristic feature—the massive use of slave labor—was an ancient practice. In the absence of a Native American population, which had been almost totally wiped out in the Caribbean or had fled inland in Brazil, European sugarcane planters turned to Africa and the Atlantic slave trade for an alternative workforce. The vast majority of the African captives transported across the Atlantic, some 80 percent or more, ended up in Brazil and the Caribbean. (See "Commerce in People" in Chapter 14).

Plantation Life in the Caribbean This painting from 1823 shows the use of slave labor on a plantation in Antigua, a British-ruled island in the Caribbean. Notice the overseer with a whip supervising the tilling and planting of the field. (From *Ten Views in the Island of Antigua*, 1823, colored engraving by William Clark [fl. 1823]/The British Library, London, UK/© British Library Board. All Rights Reserved/Bridgeman Images)

Slaves worked on sugar-producing estates in horrendous conditions. The heat and fire from the cauldrons, which turned raw sugarcane into crystallized sugar, reminded many visitors of scenes from Hell. These conditions, combined with disease, generated a high death rate, perhaps 5 to 10 percent per year, which required plantation owners to constantly import fresh slaves. A Jesuit observer in 1580 aptly summarized the situation: "The work is great and many die."[12]

More male slaves than female slaves were imported from Africa into the sugar economies of the Americas, leading to major and persistent gender imbalances. Nonetheless, female slaves did play distinctive roles in these societies. Women made up about half of the field gangs that did the heavy work of planting and harvesting sugarcane. They were subject to the same brutal punishments and received the same rations as their male counterparts, though they were seldom permitted to undertake the more skilled labor inside the sugar mills. Women who worked in urban areas, mostly for white female owners, did domestic chores and were often hired out as laborers in various homes, shops, laundries, inns, and brothels. Discouraged from establishing stable families, women had to endure, often alone, the wrenching separation from their children that occurred when they were sold. Mary Prince, a Caribbean slave who wrote a brief account of her life, recalled the pain of families torn apart: "The great God above alone knows the thoughts of the poor slave's heart, and the bitter pains which follow such separations as these. All that we love taken away from us—oh, it is sad, sad! and sore to be borne!"[13]

The extensive use of African slave labor gave these plantation colonies a very different ethnic and racial makeup than that of highland Spanish America, as the Snapshot: Ethnic Composition of Colonial Societies in Latin America, below, indicates. Thus, after three centuries of colonial rule, a substantial majority of Brazil's population was either partially or wholly of African descent. In the French Caribbean colony of Haiti in 1790, the corresponding figure was 93 percent.

SNAPSHOT Ethnic Composition of Colonial Societies in Latin America (1825)

	Highland Spanish America	Portuguese America (Brazil)
Europeans	18.2 percent	23.4 percent
Mixed-race	28.3 percent	17.8 percent
Africans	11.9 percent	49.8 percent
Native Americans	41.7 percent	9.1 percent

Data from Thomas E. Skidmore and Peter H. Smith, *Modern Latin America* (New York: Oxford University Press, 2001), 25.

As in Spanish America, a considerable amount of racial mixing took place in colonial Brazil. Cross-racial unions accounted for only about 10 percent of all marriages, but the use of concubines and informal liaisons among Indians, Africans, and Portuguese produced a substantial mixed-race population. From their ranks derived much of the urban skilled workforce and many of the supervisors in the sugar industry. *Mulattoes*, the product of European-African unions, predominated, but as many as forty separate and named groups, each indicating a different racial mixture, emerged in colonial Brazil.

The plantation complex of the Americas, based on African slavery, extended beyond the Caribbean and Brazil to encompass the southern colonies of British North America, where tobacco, cotton, rice, and indigo were major crops, but the social outcomes of these plantation colonies were quite different from those farther south. Because European women had joined the colonial migration to North America at an early date, these colonies experienced less racial mixing and certainly demonstrated less willingness to recognize the offspring of such unions and accord them a place in society. A sharply defined racial system (with black Africans, "red" Native Americans, and white Europeans) evolved in North America, whereas both Portuguese and Spanish colonies acknowledged a wide variety of mixed-race groups.

Slavery too was different in North America than in the sugar colonies. By 1750 or so, slaves in what became the United States proved able to reproduce themselves, and by the time of the Civil War almost all North American slaves had been born in the New World. That was never the case in Latin America, where large-scale importation of new slaves continued well into the nineteenth century. Nonetheless, many more slaves were voluntarily set free by their owners in Brazil than in North America, and free blacks and mulattoes in Brazil had more economic opportunities than did their counterparts in the United States. At least a few among them found positions as political leaders, scholars, musicians, writers, and artists. Some were even hired as slave catchers.

Does this mean, then, that racism was absent in colonial Brazil? Certainly not, but it was different from racism in North America. For one thing, in North America, any African ancestry, no matter how small or distant, made a person "black"; in Brazil, a person of African and non-African ancestry was considered not black, but some other mixed-race category. Racial prejudice surely persisted, for European characteristics were prized more highly than African features, and people regarded as white had enormously greater privileges and opportunities than others. Nevertheless, skin color in Brazil, and in Latin America generally, was only one criterion of class status, and the perception of color changed with the educational or economic standing of individuals. A light-skinned mulatto who had acquired some wealth or education might well pass as a white. One curious visitor to Brazil was surprised to find a darker-skinned man serving as a local official. "Isn't the governor a mulatto?" inquired the visitor. "He was, but he isn't any more," was the reply. "How can a governor be a mulatto?"[14]

Settler Colonies in North America

Yet another distinctive type of colonial society emerged in the northern British colonies of New England, New York, and Pennsylvania. The lands they acquired were widely regarded in Europe as the unpromising leftovers of the New World, lacking the obvious wealth and sophisticated cultures of the Spanish possessions. Until at least the eighteenth century, these British colonies remained far less prominent on the world stage than those of Spain or Portugal.

The British settlers came from a more rapidly changing society than did those from an ardently Catholic, semi-feudal, authoritarian Spain. When Britain launched its colonial ventures in the seventeenth century, it had already experienced considerable conflict between Catholics and Protestants, the rise of a merchant capitalist class distinct from the nobility, and the emergence of Parliament as a check on the authority of kings. Although they brought much of their English culture with them, many of the British settlers—Puritans in Massachusetts and Quakers in Pennsylvania, for example—sought to escape aspects of an old European society rather than to re-create it, as was the case for most Spanish and Portuguese colonists. The easy availability of land and the outsider status of many British settlers made it even more difficult to follow the Spanish or Portuguese colonial pattern of sharp class hierarchies, large rural estates, and dependent laborers.

Thus men in Puritan New England became independent heads of family farms, a world away from Old England, where most land was owned by nobles and gentry and worked by servants, tenants, and paid laborers. But if men escaped the class restrictions of the old country, women were less able to avoid its gender limitations. While Puritan Christianity extolled the family and a woman's role as wife and mother, it reinforced largely unlimited male authority. "Since he is thy Husband," declared Boston minister Benjamin Wadsworth in 1712 to the colony's women, "God has made him the Head and set him above thee."[15] Few girls attended school; and while women were the majority of church members, they could never become ministers.

Furthermore, British settlers were far more numerous than their Spanish counterparts, outnumbering them five to one by 1750. By the time of the American Revolution, some 90 percent or more of the population in the New England and middle Atlantic colonies were Europeans. Devastating diseases and a highly aggressive military policy had largely cleared the colonies of Native Americans, and their numbers, which were far smaller to start with, did not rebound in subsequent centuries as they did in the lands of the Aztecs and the Incas. Moreover, slaves were not needed in an agricultural economy dominated by numerous small-scale independent farmers working their own land, although elite families, especially in urban areas, sometimes employed household slaves. These were almost pure European **settler colonies**, for they lacked the substantial presence of indigenous, African, and mixed-race people who were so prominent in Spanish and Portuguese territories.

Guided Reading Question

■ **COMPARISON**
What distinguished the British settler colonies of North America from their counterparts in Latin America?

Settler Farms In this eighteenth-century engraving, men work clearing the land for agriculture while a woman in the foreground collects water from a well. Unlike other regions of the Americas, the New England and middle Atlantic colonies were dominated by European immigrants who created small family farms. (Sarin Images/Granger, NYC – All rights reserved)

Other differences likewise emerged. A largely Protestant England was far less interested in spreading Christianity among the remaining native peoples than were the large and well-funded missionary societies of Catholic Spain. Although religion loomed large in the North American colonies, the church and colonial state were not so intimately connected as they were in Latin America. The Protestant emphasis on reading the Bible for oneself led to a much greater mass literacy than in Latin America, where three centuries of church education still left some 95 percent of the population illiterate at independence. By contrast, well over 75 percent of white males in British North America were literate by the 1770s, although women's literacy rates were somewhat lower. Furthermore, British settler colonies evolved traditions of local self-government more extensively than in Latin America. Preferring to rely on joint stock companies or wealthy individuals operating under a royal charter, Britain had nothing resembling the elaborate imperial bureaucracy that governed Spanish colonies. For much of the seventeenth century, a prolonged power struggle between the English king and Parliament meant that the British government paid little attention to the internal affairs of the colonies. Therefore, elected colonial assemblies, seeing themselves as little parliaments defending "the rights of Englishmen," vigorously contested the prerogatives of royal governors sent to administer their affairs.

The grand irony of the modern history of the Americas lay in the reversal of long-established relationships between the northern and southern continents. For thousands of years, the major centers of wealth, power, commerce, and innovation lay in Mesoamerica and the Andes. That pattern continued for much of the colonial era, as the Spanish and Portuguese colonies seemed far more prosperous and successful than their British or French counterparts in North America. In the nineteenth and twentieth centuries, however, the balance shifted. What had once been the "dregs" of the colonial world became the United States, more politically stable, more democratic, more economically successful, and more internationally powerful than a divided, unstable, and much less prosperous Latin America.

PRACTICING HISTORICAL THINKING

In what ways might European empire building in the Americas be understood as a single phenomenon? And in what respects should it be viewed as a set of distinct and separate processes?

The Steppes and Siberia: The Making of a Russian Empire

At the same time that Western Europeans were building their empires in the Americas, the **Russian Empire**, which subsequently became the world's largest state, was taking shape. By 1480, a small Russian state centered on the city of Moscow was emerging from two centuries of Mongol rule. That state soon conquered a number of neighboring Russian-speaking cities and incorporated them into its expanding territory. Located on the remote, cold, and heavily forested eastern fringe of Christendom, it was perhaps an unlikely candidate for constructing one of the great empires of the modern era. And yet, over the next three centuries, it did precisely that, extending Russian domination over the vast tundra, forests, and grasslands of northern Asia that lay to the south and east of Moscow, all the way to the Pacific Ocean. Russians also expanded westward, bringing numerous Poles, Germans, Ukrainians, Belorussians, and Baltic peoples into the Russian Empire.

It was security concerns that drew Russian attention to the grasslands south and east of the Russian heartland, where pastoral peoples, like the Mongols before them, frequently raided their agricultural Russian neighbors and sold many into slavery. To the east, across the vast expanse of Siberia, Russian motives were quite different, for the scattered peoples of its endless forests and tundra posed no threat to Russia. Numbering only some 220,000 in the seventeenth century and speaking more than 100 languages, they were mostly hunting, gathering, and herding people, living in small-scale societies and largely without access to gunpowder weapons. What drew the Russians across Siberia was opportunity—primarily the "soft gold" of fur-bearing animals, whose pelts were in great demand on the world market, especially as the world cooled during the Little Ice Age.

Whatever motives drove it, this enormous Russian Empire took shape in the three centuries between 1500 and 1800 (see Map 13.2). A growing line of wooden forts offered protection to frontier towns and trading centers as well

Guided Reading Question

■ **DESCRIPTION**
What motivated Russian empire building?

Map 13.2 The Russian Empire

From its beginnings as a small principality under Mongol control, Moscow became the center of a vast Russian Empire during the early modern era.

as to mounting numbers of Russian farmers. Empire building was an extended process, involving the Russian state and its officials as well as a variety of private interests — merchants, hunters, peasants, churchmen, exiles, criminals, and adventurers. For the Russian migrants to these new eastern lands, the empire offered "economic and social improvements over what they had known at home — from more and better land to fewer lords and officials."[16] Political leaders and educated Russians generally defined the empire in grander terms: defending Russian frontiers; enhancing the power of the Russian state; and bringing Christianity, civilization, and enlightenment to savages. But what did that empire mean to those on its receiving end?

Experiencing the Russian Empire

First, of course, empire meant conquest. Although resistance was frequent, in the long run Russian military might, based in modern weaponry and the organizational capacity of a state, brought both the steppes and Siberia under Russian control. Everywhere Russian authorities demanded an oath of allegiance by which native peoples swore "eternal submission to the grand tsar," the monarch of the Russian Empire. They also demanded *yasak*, or "tribute," paid in cash or in kind. In Siberia, this meant enormous quantities of furs, especially the extremely valuable sable, which Siberian peoples were compelled to produce. As in the Americas, devastating epidemics accompanied conquest, particularly in the more remote regions of Siberia, where local people had little immunity to smallpox or measles. Also accompanying conquest was an intermittent pressure to convert to Christianity. Tax breaks, exemptions from paying tribute, and the promise of land or cash provided incentives for conversion, while the destruction of many mosques and the forced resettlement of Muslims added to the pressures. Yet the Russian state did not pursue conversion with the single-minded intensity that Spanish authorities exercised in Latin America, particularly if missionary activity threatened political and social stability. The empress Catherine the Great, for example, established religious tolerance for Muslims in the late eighteenth century and created a state agency to oversee Muslim affairs.

The Cossacks In the vanguard of Russian expansion across Siberia were the Cossacks, bands of fiercely independent warriors consisting of peasants who had escaped serfdom as well as criminals and other adventurers. Here the sixteenth-century Cossack warrior Yermak is shown leading his troops. (De Agostini Picture Library/akg-images)

Guided Reading Question

■ **CHANGE**

How did the Russian Empire transform the life of its conquered people and of the Russian homeland itself?

The most profoundly transforming feature of the Russian Empire was the influx of Russian settlers, whose numbers by the end of the eighteenth century had overwhelmed native peoples, giving their lands a distinctively Russian character. By 1720, some 700,000 Russians lived in Siberia, thus reducing the native Siberians to 30 percent of the total population, a proportion that dropped to 14 percent in the nineteenth century. The loss of hunting grounds and pasturelands to Russian agricultural settlers undermined long-standing economies and rendered local people dependent on Russian markets for grain, sugar, tea, tobacco, and alcohol. Pressures to encourage pastoralists to abandon their nomadic ways included the requirement to pay fees and to obtain permission to cross agricultural lands. Kazakh herders responded with outrage: "The grass and the water belong to Heaven, and why should we pay any fees?"[17] Intermarriage, prostitution, and sexual abuse resulted in some mixed-race offspring, but these were generally absorbed as Russians rather than identified as distinctive communities, as in Latin America.

Over the course of three centuries, both Siberia and the steppes were incorporated into the Russian state. Their native peoples were not driven into reservations or eradicated as in the Americas. Many of them, though, were Russified, adopting the Russian language and converting to Christianity, even as their traditional ways of life—hunting and herding—were much disrupted. The Russian Empire represented the final triumph of an agrarian civilization over the hunting societies of Siberia and over the pastoral peoples of the grasslands.

Russians and Empire

If the empire transformed the conquered peoples, it also fundamentally changed Russia itself. Within an increasingly multiethnic empire, Russians diminished as a proportion of the overall population, although they remained politically dominant. Among the growing number of non-Russians in the empire, Slavic-speaking Ukrainians and Belorussians predominated, while the vast territories of Siberia and the steppes housed numerous separate peoples, but with quite small populations. The wealth of empire—rich agricultural lands, valuable furs, mineral deposits—played a major role in making Russia one of the great powers of Europe by the eighteenth century, and it has enjoyed that position ever since.

Unlike its expansion to the east, Russia's westward movement occurred in the context of military rivalries with the major powers of the region—the Ottoman Empire, Poland, Sweden, Lithuania, Prussia, and Austria. During the late seventeenth and eighteenth centuries, Russia acquired substantial territories in the Baltic region, Poland, and Ukraine. This contact with Europe also fostered an awareness of Russia's backwardness relative to Europe and prompted an extensive program of westernization, particularly under the leadership of Peter the Great (r. 1689–1725). His massive efforts included vast administrative changes, the enlargement and modernization of Russian military forces, a new educational system for the sons of noblemen, and dozens of manufacturing enterprises. Russian nobles were instructed to dress in European styles and to shave their sacred and much-revered beards. The newly created capital city of St. Petersburg was to be Russia's "window on the West." One of Peter's successors, Catherine the Great (r. 1762–1796), followed up with further efforts to Europeanize Russian cultural and intellectual life, viewing herself as part of the European Enlightenment. Thus Russians were the first of many peoples to measure themselves against the West and to mount major "catch-up" efforts.

But this European-oriented and Christian state had also become an Asian power, bumping up against China, India, Persia, and the Ottoman Empire. It was on the front lines of the encounter between Christendom and the world of Islam. This straddling of Asia and Europe was the source of a long-standing identity problem that has troubled educated Russians for 300 years. Was Russia a backward European country, destined to follow the lead of more highly developed Western European societies? Or was it different, uniquely Slavic or even Asian, shaped by its Mongol legacy and its status as an Asian power? It is a question that Russians have not completely answered even in the twenty-first century. Either way, the very size of that empire, bordering on virtually all of the great agrarian civilizations of outer Eurasia, turned Russia, like many empires before it, into a highly militarized state, "a society organized for continuous war," according to one scholar.[18] It also reinforced the highly autocratic character of the Russian Empire because such a huge state arguably required a powerful monarchy to hold its vast domains and highly diverse peoples together.

Clearly, the Russians had created an empire, similar to those of Western Europe in terms of conquest, settlement, exploitation, religious conversion, and feelings of superiority. Nonetheless, the Russians had acquired their empire under different circumstances than did the Western Europeans. The Spanish and the British had conquered and colonized the New World, an ocean away and wholly unknown to them before 1492. They acquired those empires only after establishing themselves as distinct European states. The Russians, on the other hand, absorbed adjacent territories, and they did so at the same time that a modern Russian state was taking shape. "The British had an empire," wrote historian Geoffrey Hosking. "Russia *was* an empire."[19] Perhaps this helps explain the unique longevity of the Russian Empire. Whereas the Spanish, Portuguese, and British colonies in the Americas long ago achieved independence, the Russian Empire remained intact until the collapse of the Soviet Union in 1991. So thorough was Russian colonization that Siberia and much of the steppes remain still an integral part of the Russian state.

Asian Empires

Even as West Europeans were building their empires in the Americas and the Russians were expanding across Siberia, other imperial projects were likewise under way. The Chinese pushed deep into central Eurasia; Turko-Mongol invaders from Central Asia created the Mughal Empire, bringing much of Hindu South Asia within a single Muslim-ruled political system; and the Ottoman Empire brought Muslim rule to a largely Christian population in southeastern Europe and Turkish rule to largely Arab populations in North Africa and the Middle East. None of these empires had the global reach or worldwide impact of Europe's American colonies; they were regional rather than global in scope. Nor did they have the same devastating and transforming impact on their conquered peoples, for those peoples were not being exposed to new diseases. Nothing remotely approaching the catastrophic population collapse of Native American peoples occurred in these Asian empires. Moreover, the process of building these empires did not transform the imperial homeland as fundamentally as did the wealth of the Americas and to a lesser extent Siberia for European imperial powers. Nonetheless, these expanding Asian empires reflected the energies and vitality of their respective civilizations in the early modern era, and they gave rise to profoundly important cross-cultural encounters, with legacies that echoed for many centuries.

Making China an Empire

In the fifteenth century, China had declined an opportunity to construct a maritime empire in the Indian Ocean, as Zheng He's massive fleet was withdrawn after 1433 and left to wither away (see "Ming Dynasty China" in Chapter 12). In the seventeenth and eighteenth centuries, however, China built another kind of empire on its northern and western frontiers that vastly enlarged the territorial size of the country and incorporated a number of non-Chinese peoples. Undertaking this enormous project of imperial expansion was China's Qing, or Manchu, dynasty (1644–1912). Strangely enough, the Qing dynasty was itself of foreign and nomadic origin, hailing from Manchuria, north of the Great Wall. The violent Manchu takeover of China, part of the General Crisis of the seventeenth century, was facilitated by a widespread famine and peasant rebellions associated with the Little Ice Age. But having conquered China, the Qing rulers sought to maintain their ethnic distinctiveness by forbidding intermarriage between themselves and the Chinese. Nonetheless, their ruling elites also mastered the Chinese language and Confucian teachings and used Chinese bureaucratic techniques to govern the empire.

Guided Reading Question

■ **DESCRIPTION**
What were the distinctive features of Qing empire building in the early modern era?

For many centuries, the Chinese had interacted with the nomadic peoples who inhabited the dry and lightly populated regions now known as Mongolia, Xinjiang, and Tibet. Trade, tribute, and warfare ensured that these ecologically and culturally different worlds were well known to the Chinese, quite unlike the New World "discoveries" of the Europeans. Chinese authority in the area had been intermittent and actively resisted. Then, in the early modern era, the Qing dynasty undertook an eighty-year military effort (1680–1760) that brought these huge regions solidly under its control. It was largely security concerns, rather than economic need, that motivated this aggressive posture. During the late seventeenth century, the creation of a substantial state among the western Mongols, known as the Zunghars, revived Chinese memories of an earlier Mongol conquest. As in so many other cases, expansion was viewed as a defensive necessity. The eastward movement of the Russian Empire likewise appeared potentially threatening, but after increasing tensions and a number of skirmishes and battles, this danger was resolved diplomatically, rather than militarily, in the Treaty of Nerchinsk (1689), which marked the boundary between Russia and China.

Although undertaken by the non-Chinese Manchus, the Qing dynasty campaigns against the Zunghar Mongols marked the evolution of China into a Central Asian empire. The Chinese, however, have seldom thought of themselves as an imperial power. Rather, they spoke of the "unification" of the peoples of central Eurasia within a Chinese state. Nonetheless, historians have seen many similarities between **Qing expansion** and other cases of early modern empire building, while noting some clear differences as well.

Clearly the Qing dynasty takeover of central Eurasia was a conquest, making use of China's more powerful military technology and greater resources. Furthermore, the area was ruled separately from the rest of China through a new office called the Court of Colonial Affairs. Like other colonial powers, the Qing made active use of local notables—Mongol aristocrats, Muslim officials, Buddhist leaders—as they attempted to govern the region as inexpensively as possible. Sometimes these native officials abused their authority, demanding extra taxes or labor service from local people and thus earning their hostility. In places, those officials imitated Chinese ways by wearing peacock feathers, decorating their hats with gold buttons, or adopting a Manchu hairstyle that was much resented by many Chinese who were forced to wear it.

Qing Conquests in Central Asia Painted by the Chinese artist Jin Tingbiao in the mid-eighteenth century, this image portrays Machang, a leading warrior involved in the westward extension of the Qing Empire. The painting was commissioned by the emperor himself and served to honor the bravery of Machang. (Pictures from History/CPA Media)

Map 13.3 China's Qing Dynasty Empire
After many centuries of intermittent expansion into Central Asia, the Qing dynasty brought this vast region firmly under its control.

More generally, however, Qing officials did not seek to assimilate local people into Chinese culture and showed considerable respect for the Mongolian, Tibetan, and Muslim cultures of the region. People of noble rank, Buddhist monks, and those associated with monasteries were excused from the taxes and labor service required of ordinary people. Nor was the area flooded with Chinese settlers. In parts of Mongolia, for example, Qing authorities sharply restricted the entry of Chinese merchants and other immigrants in an effort to preserve the area as a source of recruitment for the Chinese military. They feared that the "soft" and civilized Chinese ways might erode the fighting spirit of the Mongols.

The long-term significance of this new Qing imperial state was tremendous. It greatly expanded the territory of China and added a small but important minority of non-Chinese people to the empire's vast population (see Map 13.3). The borders of contemporary China are essentially those created during the Qing dynasty. Some of those peoples, particularly those in Tibet and Xinjiang, have retained their older identities and in recent decades have actively sought greater autonomy or even independence from China.

Even more important, Qing conquests, together with the expansion of the Russian Empire, utterly transformed Central Asia. For centuries, that region had been the cosmopolitan crossroads of Eurasia, hosting the Silk Road trading network, welcoming all the major world religions, and generating an enduring encounter between the nomads of the steppes and the farmers of settled agricultural regions. Now under Russian or Qing rule, it became the backward and impoverished region known to nineteenth- and twentieth-century observers. Land-based commerce across Eurasia increasingly took a backseat to oceanic trade. Indebted Mongolian nobles lost their land to Chinese merchants, while nomads, no longer able to herd their animals freely, fled to urban areas, where many were reduced to begging. The incorporation of inner Eurasia into the Russian and Qing empires "eliminated permanently as a major actor on the historical stage the nomadic pastoralists, who had been the strongest alternative to settled agricultural society since the second millennium."[20] It was the end of a long era.

Muslims and Hindus in the Mughal Empire

If the creation of a Qing imperial state in the early modern era provoked a final clash of nomadic pastoralists and settled farmers, India's **Mughal Empire** hosted a different kind of encounter—a further phase in the long interaction of Islamic and

Hindu cultures in South Asia. That empire was the product of Central Asian warriors who were Muslims in religion and Turkic in culture and who claimed descent from Chinggis Khan and Timur. Their brutal conquests in the sixteenth century provided India with a rare period of relative political unity (1526–1707), as Mughal emperors exercised a fragile control over a diverse and fragmented subcontinent that had long been divided into a bewildering variety of small states, principalities, tribes, castes, sects, and ethno-linguistic groups.

The central division within Mughal India was religious. The ruling dynasty and perhaps 20 percent of the population were Muslims; most of the rest practiced some form of Hinduism. Mughal India's most famous emperor, **Akbar** (r. 1556–1605), clearly recognized this fundamental reality and acted deliberately to accommodate the Hindu majority. After conquering the warrior-based and Hindu Rajputs of northwestern India, Akbar married several of their princesses but did not require them to convert to Islam. He incorporated a substantial number of Hindus into the political-military elite of the empire and supported the building of Hindu temples as well as mosques, palaces, and forts. (See Working with Evidence, Source 13.1, page 581.) But Akbar also acted to soften some Hindu restrictions on women, encouraging the remarriage of widows and discouraging child marriages and *sati* (the practice in which a widow followed her husband to death by throwing herself on his funeral pyre). A few elite women were also able to exercise political power, including Nur Jahan, the twentieth and favorite wife of Akbar's successor Emperor Jahangir (r. 1605–1627). She was widely regarded as the power behind the throne of her alcohol- and opium-addicted husband, giving audiences to visiting dignitaries, consulting with ministers, and even having a coin issued in her name.

In directly religious matters, Akbar imposed a policy of toleration, deliberately restraining the more militantly Islamic *ulama* (religious scholars) and removing the special tax (*jizya*) on non-Muslims. He constructed a special House of Worship where he presided over intellectual discussion with representatives of many religions—Muslim, Hindu, Christian, Buddhist, Jewish, Jain, and Zoroastrian. Akbar went so far as to create his own state cult, a religious faith aimed at the Mughal elite that drew on Islam, Hinduism, and Zoroastrianism and emphasized loyalty to the emperor himself. The overall style of the Mughal Empire was that of a blended elite culture in which both Hindus and various Muslim groups could feel comfortable. Thus Persian artists and writers were welcomed into the empire, and the Hindu epic *Ramayana* was translated into Persian, while various Persian classics appeared in Hindi and Sanskrit. In short, Akbar and his immediate successors downplayed a distinctly Islamic identity for the Mughal Empire in favor of a cosmopolitan and hybrid Indian-Persian-Turkic culture.

Such policies fostered sharp opposition among some Muslims. The philosopher Shaykh Ahmad Sirhindi (1564–1624), claiming to be a "renewer" of authentic Islam in his time, strongly objected to this cultural synthesis. The worship of saints, the sacrifice of animals, and support for

Guided Reading Question

■ **CHANGE**

How did Mughal attitudes and policies toward Hindus change from the time of Akbar to that of Aurangzeb?

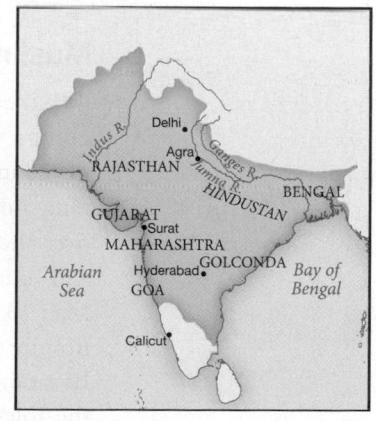

The Mughal Empire

Hindu religious festivals all represented impure intrusions of Sufi Islam or Hindu-ism that needed to be rooted out. In Sirhindi's view, it was primarily women who had introduced these deviations: "Because of their utter stupidity [Muslim] women pray to stones and idols and ask for their help. . . . Women participate in the holidays of Hindus and Jews. They celebrate Diwali [a major Hindu festival] and send their sisters and daughters presents similar to those exchanged by the infidels."[21] It was therefore the duty of Muslim rulers to impose the sharia (Islamic law), to enforce the jizya, and to remove non-Muslims from high office.

This strain of Muslim thinking found a champion in the emperor **Aurangzeb** (ow-rang-ZEHB) (r. 1658–1707), who reversed Akbar's policy of accommodation and sought to impose Islamic supremacy. While Akbar had discouraged the Hindu practice of sati, Aurangzeb forbade it outright. Music and dance were now banned at court, and previously tolerated vices such as gambling, drinking, prostitution, and narcotics were actively suppressed. Dancing girls were ordered to get married or leave the empire altogether. Some Hindu temples were destroyed, and the jizya was reimposed. "Censors of public morals," posted to large cities, enforced Islamic law.

Aurangzeb's religious policies, combined with intolerable demands for taxes to support his many wars of expansion, antagonized Hindus and prompted various movements of opposition to the Mughals. "Your subjects are trampled underfoot," wrote one anonymous protester. "Every province of your empire is impoverished. . . . God is the God of all mankind, not the God of Mussalmans [Muslims] alone."[22] These opposition movements, some of them self-consciously Hindu, fatally fractured the Mughal Empire, especially after Aurangzeb's death in 1707, and opened the way for a British takeover in the second half of the eighteenth century.

Thus the Mughal Empire was the site of a highly significant encounter between two of the world's great religious traditions. It began with an experiment in multicultural empire building and ended in growing antagonism between Hindus and Muslims. In the centuries that followed, both elements of the Mughal experience would be repeated.

Muslims and Christians in the Ottoman Empire

Like the Mughal state, the **Ottoman Empire** was also the creation of Turkic warrior groups, whose aggressive raiding of agricultural civilizations was sometimes legitimized in Islamic terms as *jihad*, religiously sanctioned warfare against infidels. Beginning around 1300 from a base area in northwestern Anatolia, these Ottoman Turks over the next three centuries swept over much of the Middle East, North Africa, and southeastern Europe to create the Islamic world's most significant empire (see Map 13.4). During those centuries, the Ottoman state was transformed from a small frontier principality to a prosperous, powerful, cosmopolitan empire, heir both to the Byzantine Empire and to leadership within the Islamic world. Its sultan combined the roles of a Turkic warrior prince, a Muslim caliph, and a conquering emperor, bearing the "strong sword of Islam" and serving as chief defender of the faith.

Map 13.4 The Ottoman Empire

At its high point in the mid-sixteenth century, the Ottoman Empire encompassed a vast diversity of peoples; straddled Europe, Africa, and Asia; and battled both the Austrian and Safavid empires.

READING THE MAP: What geographical features and political realities were barriers to further expansion of the Ottoman Empire?

MAKING CONNECTIONS: Compare this map with Map 13.2: The Russian Empire. What happened to the Ottoman Empire's tributary states north of the Black Sea after 1689? Where were the likely points of tension or conflict between the Ottoman and Russian empires during the early modern period?

Gaining such an empire transformed Turkish social life as well. The relative independence of Central Asian pastoral women, their open association with men, and their political influence in society all diminished as the Turks adopted Islam, beginning in the tenth century, and later acquired an empire in the heartland of ancient and patriarchal Mediterranean civilizations. Now elite Turkish women found themselves secluded and often veiled; slave women from the Caucasus Mountains and the Sudan grew more numerous; official imperial censuses did not count women; and orthodox Muslim reformers sought to restrict women's religious gatherings.

And yet within the new constraints of a settled Islamic empire, Turkish women retained something of the social power they had enjoyed in pastoral societies. From around 1550 to 1650, women of the royal court had such an influence in political matters that their critics referred to the "sultanate of women." Islamic law permitted women important property rights, which enabled some to become quite wealthy, endowing religious and charitable institutions. Many women actively used the Ottoman courts to protect their legal rights in matters of marriage, divorce, and inheritance, sometimes representing themselves or acting as agents for female relatives. In 1717, the wife of an English ambassador to the Ottoman Empire compared the lives of Turkish and European women, declaring, "'Tis very easy to see that they have more liberty than we have."[23]

Guided Reading Question

■ **SIGNIFICANCE**

In what ways was the Ottoman Empire important for Europe in the early modern era?

Within the Islamic world, the Ottoman Empire represented the growing prominence of Turkic people, for their empire now incorporated a large number of Arabs, among whom the religion had been born. The responsibility and the prestige of protecting Mecca, Medina, and Jerusalem—the holy cities of Islam—now fell to the Ottoman Empire. A century-long conflict (1534–1639) between the Ottoman Empire, espousing the Sunni version of Islam, and the Persian Safavid Empire, holding fast to the Shia form of the faith, expressed a deep and enduring division within the Islamic world. Nonetheless, Persian culture, especially its poetry, painting, and traditions of imperial splendor, occupied a prominent position among the Ottoman elite.

The Ottoman Empire, like its Mughal counterpart, was the site of a highly significant cross-cultural encounter in the early modern era, adding yet another chapter to the long-running story of interaction between the Islamic world and Christendom. As the Ottoman Empire expanded across Anatolia, and as the Byzantine state visibly weakened and large numbers of Turks settled in the region, the empire's mostly Christian population converted in large numbers to Islam. By 1500, some 90 percent of Anatolia's inhabitants were Muslims and Turkic speakers. The climax of this Turkic assault on the Christian world of Byzantium occurred in the 1453 conquest of Constantinople, when the city fell to Muslim invaders. Renamed Istanbul, that splendid Christian city became the capital of the Ottoman Empire. Byzantium, heir to the glory of Rome and the guardian of Orthodox Christianity, was no more.

The Ottoman Siege of Vienna, 1683 In this late seventeenth-century painting by the Flemish artist Frans Geffels, the last Ottoman incursion into the Austrian Empire is pushed back with French and Polish help, marking the end of a serious Muslim threat to Christian Europe. (Wien Museum Karlsplatz, Vienna, Austria/Erich Lessing/Art Resource, NY)

In the empire's southeastern European domains, known as the Balkans, the Ottoman encounter with Christian peoples unfolded quite differently than it had in Anatolia. In the Balkans, Muslims ruled over a large Christian population, but the scarcity of Turkish settlers and the willingness of the Ottoman authorities to accommodate the region's Christian churches led to far fewer conversions. By the early sixteenth century, only about 19 percent of the area's people were Muslims, and 81 percent were Christians.

Many of these Christians had welcomed Ottoman conquest because taxes were lighter and oppression less pronounced than under their former Christian rulers. Christian communities such as the Eastern Orthodox and Armenian Churches were granted considerable autonomy in regulating their internal social, religious, educational, and charitable affairs. Nonetheless, many Christian and Jewish women appealed legal cases dealing with marriage and inheritance to Muslim courts, where their property rights were greater. A substantial number of Christian men—Balkan landlords, Greek merchants, government officials, and high-ranking clergy—became part of the Ottoman elite, sometimes without converting to Islam. Jewish refugees fleeing Christian persecution in a Spain recently "liberated" from Islamic rule likewise found greater opportunity in the Ottoman Empire, where they became prominent in trade and banking circles. In these ways, Ottoman dealings with the Christian and Jewish populations of the empire broadly resembled Akbar's policies toward the Hindu majority of Mughal India. In another way, however, Turkish rule bore heavily on Christians. Through a process known as the ***devshirme*** (devv-shirr-MEH) (the collecting or gathering), Ottoman authorities siphoned off many thousands of young boys from Christian families into the service of the state. Removed from their families and required to learn Turkish, these boys usually converted to Islam and were trained for either the civil administration or military service in elite Janissary units. Although it was a terrible blow for families who lost their children, the *devshirme* also represented a means of upward mobility within the Ottoman Empire, but this social gain occurred at a high price.

Even though Ottoman authorities were relatively tolerant toward Christians within their borders, the empire itself represented an enormous threat to Christendom generally. The seizure of Constantinople, the conquest of the Balkans, Ottoman naval power in the Mediterranean, and the siege of Vienna in 1529 and again in 1683 raised anew "the specter of a Muslim takeover of all of Europe."[24] One European ambassador reported fearfully in 1555 from the court of the Turkish ruler Suleiman:

> He tramples the soil of Hungary with 200,000 horses, he is at the very gates of Austria, threatens the rest of Germany, and brings in his train all the nations that extend from our borders to those of Persia.[25]

Indeed, the "terror of the Turk" inspired fear across much of Europe and placed Christendom on the defensive, even as Europeans were expanding aggressively across the Atlantic and into the Indian Ocean.

But the Ottoman encounter with Christian Europe spawned admiration and cooperation as well as fear and trembling. Italian Renaissance artists portrayed the splendor of the Islamic world. (See Working with Evidence, Chapter 12.) The sixteenth-century French philosopher Jean Bodin praised the religious tolerance of the Ottoman sultan in contrast to Christian intolerance: "The King of the Turks who rules over a great part of Europe safeguards the rites of religion as well as any prince in this world. Yet he constrains no-one, but on the contrary permits everyone to live as his conscience dictates."[26] The French government on occasion found it useful to ally with the Ottoman Empire against its common enemy of Habsburg Austria, while European merchants willingly violated a papal ban on selling firearms to the Turks. Cultural encounter involved more than conflict.

REFLECTIONS

The Centrality of Context in World History

World history is, to put it mildly, a big subject. To teachers and students alike, it can easily seem overwhelming in its detail. And yet the central task of world history is *not* the inclusion of endless facts or particular cases. It is rather to establish contexts or frameworks within which carefully selected facts and cases take on new meaning. In world history, every event, every process, every historical figure, and every culture, society, or civilization gains significance from its incorporation into some larger context or framework. Contextual thinking is central to world history.

The broad outlines of European colonization in the Americas are familiar to most American and European students. And yet, when that story is set in the context of other empire-building projects of the early modern era, it takes on new and different meanings. Such a context helps to counter any remaining Eurocentrism in our thinking about the past by reminding us that Western Europe was not the only center of vitality and expansion and that the interaction of culturally different peoples, so characteristic of the modern age, derived from multiple sources. How often do we notice that a European Christendom creating empires across the Atlantic was also the victim of Ottoman imperial expansion in the Balkans?

This kind of contextualizing also allows us to see more clearly the distinctive features of European empires as we view them in the mirror of other imperial creations. The Chinese, Mughal, and Ottoman empires continued older patterns of historical development, while those of Europe represented something wholly new in human history—an interacting Atlantic world of Europe, Africa, and the Americas. Furthermore, the European empires had a far greater impact on the peoples they incorporated than did other empires. Nowhere else did empire building generate such a catastrophic population collapse as in the Americas. Nor did Asian empires foster the kind of slave-based societies and transcontinental trade in slaves that were among the chief outcomes of Europe's American colonies. Finally, Europe was enriched and transformed by its American possessions far more than China and the Ottomans were by their territorial acquisitions. Europeans gained enormous new biological resources from their empires—corn, potatoes, tomatoes, chocolate, tobacco, timber, and much more—as well as enormous wealth in the form of gold, silver, and land.

Should we need a motto for world history, consider this one: in world history, nothing stands alone; context is everything.

Second Thoughts

What's the Significance?

Hernán Cortés, 549

Great Dying, 552

Little Ice Age, 552

General Crisis, 552

Columbian exchange, 555

mercantilism, 555

mestizo, 557

mulattoes, 562

settler colonies, 563

Russian Empire, 565

yasak, 567

Qing expansion, 571

Mughal Empire, 572

Akbar, 573

Aurangzeb, 574

Ottoman Empire, 574

devshirme, 578

Big Picture Questions

1. The experience of empire for conquered peoples was broadly similar whoever their rulers were. Does the material in this chapter support or challenge this idea?
2. In thinking about the similarities and differences among the empires of the early modern era, what categories of comparison might be most useful to consider?
3. In the chapter maps, notice areas of the world not included in a major empire. Pick an area and research what was happening there in the early modern era.
4. **Looking Back:** Compared to the world of the fifteenth century, what new patterns of development are visible in the empire-building projects of the following centuries?

Next Steps: For Further Study

Jane Burbank and Frederick Cooper, *Empires in World History* (2010). Chapters 5 to 7 of this recent work describe and compare the empires of the early modern world.

Jorge Canizares-Esguerra and Erik R. Seeman, eds., *The Atlantic in Global History* (2007). A collection of essays that treats the Atlantic basin as a single interacting region.

Alfred W. Crosby, *The Columbian Voyages, the Columbian Exchange, and Their Historians* (1987). A classic account of changing understandings of Columbus and his global impact.

John Kicza, *Resilient Cultures: America's Native Peoples Confront European Colonization, 1500–1800* (2003). An account of European colonization in the Americas that casts the native peoples as active agents rather than passive victims.

Charles C. Mann, *1493: Uncovering the New World Columbus Created* (2011). A global account of the Columbian exchange that presents contemporary scholarship in a very accessible fashion.

Peter Perdue, *China Marches West: The Qing Conquest of Central Eurasia* (2005). Tells how China became an empire as it incorporated the non-Chinese people of Central Asia.

Willard Sutherland, *Taming the Wild Fields: Colonization and Empire on the Russian Steppe* (2004). An up-to-date account of Russian expansion in the steppes.

"Discover the Ottomans," http://www.theottomans.org. A series of essays and images that traces the history of the Ottoman Empire over six centuries.

"1492: An Ongoing Voyage," http://www.ibiblio.org/expo/1492.exhibit/Intro.html. An interactive website based on an exhibit from the Library of Congress that provides a rich context for exploring the meaning of Columbus and his voyages.

WORKING WITH EVIDENCE

State Building in the Early Modern Era

The empires of the early modern era were the projects of states, though these states often made use of various private groups—missionaries, settlers, merchants, mercenaries—to achieve the goals of empire. Such imperial states—Mughal India, the Ottoman Empire, France, the Inca Empire, and Ming dynasty China, for example—were invariably headed by kings or emperors who were the source of ultimate political authority in their lands. Each of those rulers sought to govern societies divided by religion, region, ethnicity, or class. During the three centuries between 1450 and 1750, all of these states, and a number of non-imperial states as well, moved toward greater political integration through more assertive monarchs and more effective central bureaucracies, which curtailed, though never eliminated, entrenched local interests. The growth of empire accompanied this process of political integration, and perhaps helped cause it. The sources that follow allow us to catch a glimpse of this state-building effort in several distinct settings.

SOURCE 13.1 The Memoirs of Emperor Jahangir

The diverse peoples of India had seldom experienced a political system that encompassed most of the subcontinent. But in the early modern era, the Mughal Empire gave to South Asia a rare period of substantial political unity. Source 13.1 offers excerpts from the memoirs of Jahangir, who ruled the Mughal state from 1605 to 1627, following the reign of his more famous father Akbar. Written in Persian, the literary language of the eastern Islamic world, Jahangir's account reflects on the events of his coronation and of the policies that he subsequently put in place.

- Why do you think Jahangir mounted such an elaborate coronation celebration for himself?

- In what ways did Jahangir seek to ensure the effective authority of the state he led?

- In what ways was Jahangir a distinctly Muslim ruler? In what respects did he and his father depart from Islamic principles?

- Based on these selections, what concrete problems of governance can you infer were facing Jahangir?

JAHANGIR | *Memoirs* | 1605–1627

At the age of thirty-eight, I became Emperor.... Hence I assumed the titles of . . . the world-subduing emperor, the world-subduing king.

On this occasion I made use of the throne prepared by my father, and enriched at an expense without parallel for the celebration of the festival of the new year.... Having thus seated myself on the throne of my expectations and wishes, I caused also the imperial crown, which my father had caused to be made after the manner of that which was worn by the great kings of Persia, to be brought before me, and then, in the presence of the whole assembled Emirs, having placed it on my brows, as an omen auspicious to the stability and happiness of my reign, kept it there for the space of a full astronomical hour....

For forty days and forty nights I caused the . . . great imperial state drum, to strike up, without ceasing, the strains of joy and triumph; and . . . around my throne, the ground was spread by my directions with the most costly brocades and gold embroidered carpets. Censers [containers for burning incense] of gold and silver were disposed in different directions for the purpose of burning odoriferous drugs, and nearly three thousand camphorated wax lights . . . illuminated the scene from night till morning. Numbers of blooming youths, beautiful as young Joseph in the pavilions of Egypt, clad in dresses of the most costly materials . . . awaited my commands. . . . And finally, the Emirs of the empire . . . covered from head to foot in gold and jewels, and shoulder to shoulder, stood round in brilliant array, also waiting for the commands of their sovereign....

I instituted . . . special regulations . . . as rules of conduct, never to be deviated from in their respective stations.

1. I remitted [canceled] altogether to my subjects three sources of revenue taxes or duties....

2. I directed, when the district lay waste or destitute of inhabitants, that towns should be built.

3. Merchants traveling through the country were not to have their bales or packages of any kind opened without their consent....

5. No person was permitted either to make or sell either wine or any other kind of intoxicating liquor. I undertook to institute this regulation, although it is sufficiently notorious that I have myself the strongest inclination for wine, in which from the age of sixteen I have liberally indulged. . . .

7. No person was to suffer, for any offense, the loss of a nose or ear. If the crime were theft, the offender was to be scourged with thorns, or deterred from further transgression by an attestation on the Koran.

8. [High officials] were prohibited from possessing themselves by violence of the lands of the subject, or from cultivating them on their own account....

10. The governors in all the principal cities were directed to establish infirmaries or hospitals, with competent medical aid for the relief of the sick....

[H]aving on one occasion asked my father [Akbar] the reason why he had forbidden any one to prevent or interfere with the building of these haunts of idolatry [Hindu temples], his reply was in the following terms: "My dear child," said he, "I find myself a powerful monarch, the shadow of God upon earth. I have seen that he bestows the blessings of his gracious providence upon all his creatures without distinction. Ill should I discharge the duties of my exalted station, were I to withhold my compassion and indulgence from any of those entrusted to my charge. With all of the human race, with all of God's creatures, I am at peace: why then should I permit myself, under any consideration, to be the cause of molestation or aggression to any one? Besides, are not five parts in six of mankind either Hindus or aliens to the faith; and were I to be governed by motives of the kind suggested in your inquiry, what alternative can I have but to put them all to death! I have thought it therefore my wisest plan to let these men alone. Neither is it to be forgotten, that the class of whom we are speaking . . . are usefully engaged, either in the pursuits of science or the arts, or of improvements for the benefit of mankind, and have in numerous instances arrived at the highest distinctions in the state, there being, indeed, to be found in this city men of every description, and of every religion on the face of the earth."

Source: *The Memoirs of the Emperor Jahangir,* translated from the Persian by Major David Price (London: Oriental Translation Committee, 1829), 1–3, 5–8, 15.

■ ■ ■

SOURCE 13.2 The Palace of an Ottoman Emperor ▶

Begun in 1465 and finished in 1478, the Topkapi Palace in Constantinople served for centuries as the main residence of the Ottoman emperors in their capital city. The palace, which was organized around a series of courtyards, housed government offices and a mint, an educational establishment, and the living quarters of the emperor and his harem. At the height of Ottoman power, around 4,000 family members, servants, eunuchs, officials, and soldiers of the imperial entourage resided in the complex.

Topkapi also served as a ceremonial space where important state occasions and religious celebrations took place. This late eighteenth-century painting depicts the second courtyard and the Felicity Gate, which guarded the entrance to the inner court, where no one aside from the ruler's relatives and closest advisers was granted access. Here, at the principal ceremonial site in the palace, emperors observed religious ceremonies, received foreign ambassadors, celebrated accessions to the throne, and at times of war handed the banner of the Prophet Muhammad to their military leaders. In this image, Sultan Selim III (r. 1789–1807) sits on his throne with his chief advisers around him. Ottoman officials and court dignitaries pay homage to their ruler. Participants are arrayed in hierarchical order according to their relative social or political importance, signaled by their clothing — note their increasingly tall and elaborate headgear — and their proximity to the sultan.

■ What can this image tell us about the size and form of Ottoman imperial ceremonies? What types of people are missing from this image, and what can their absence tell us about Ottoman imperial life?

■ Why might Ottoman rulers have chosen this space to stage important ceremonies?

■ How might ceremonies like the one depicted here help to strengthen the sultan's rule over his empire?

A Reception at the Court of Selim III | late 18th century

Topkapi Palace Museum, Istanbul, Turkey/Bridgeman Images

■ ■ ■

SOURCE 13.3 French State Building and Louis XIV

Like their counterparts in the Middle East and Asia, a number of European states in the early modern era also pursued the twin projects of imperial expansion abroad and political integration at home. Perhaps the most well-known example of such European state-building efforts is that of France under the rule of Louis XIV (r. 1643–1715). Louis and other European monarchs, such as those in Spain and Russia, operated under a set of assumptions known as absolutism, which held that kings ruled by "divine right" and could legitimately claim sole and uncontested authority in their realms. Louis's famous dictum *"L'état, c'est moi"* ("I am the state") summed up the absolutist ideal.

Source 13.3A illustrates one way in which Louis attempted to realize this ideal. Written by Louis himself, this document focuses on the importance of "spectacle" and public display in solidifying the exalted role of the monarch. The "carousel" described here was an extravagant pageant held in Paris in June 1662. It featured various exotic animals, slaves, princes, and nobles arrayed in fantastic costumes representing distant lands, as well as many equestrian competitions. Unifying this disparate assembly was King Louis himself, dressed as a Roman emperor, while on the shields of the nobles was that grand symbol of the monarchy, the sun.

Source 13.3B is a depiction of Louis XIV's costume for a 1653 ballet entitled *La Nuit* (The Night) in which he played the rising sun. Louis represents Apollo, the god of light and the sun, a deity that viewers of the opera would have associated with the Roman emperor Augustus, who considered Apollo his patron. Note the elaborate costume, which includes a magnificent gold wig and sun imagery on his chest and footwear. The images of the sun on this costume were similar to those that he adopted as his personal symbol at the 1662 carousel.

- What posture does Louis take toward his subjects in Source 13.3A?

- What does the image of Louis as Apollo in Source 13.3B tell us about the nature of royal spectacle? How does this image shape how you envision the carousel described in Source 13.3A?

- How does Louis understand the role of spectacle in general and the carousel in particular?

- What does the choice of the sun as a royal symbol suggest about Louis's conception of his role in the French state and empire?

SOURCE 13.3A
LOUIS XIV | *Memoirs* | 1670

It was necessary to conserve and cultivate with care all that which, without diminishing the authority and the respect due to me, linked me by bonds of affection to my peoples and above all to the people of rank. . . . The common people, on the other hand, are delighted by shows in which, at bottom, we always have the aim of pleasing them. . . . By this means we hold on to their hearts and their minds, sometimes more strongly perhaps than by recompenses and gifts; and with regard to foreigners, in a state they see flourishing and well ordered, that which is spent on expenses and which could be called superfluous, makes a very favorable impression on them, of magnificence, of power, of grandeur. . . .

The carousel . . . had only been conceived at first as a light amusement; but little by little . . . it became a spectacle that was fairly grand and magnificent, both in the number of exercises, and by the novelty of the costumes and the variety of the [heraldic] devices. [He then explains why the sun was chosen as the symbol of the monarchy] . . . For the device they chose the sun, which . . . is the most noble of all, and which, by its quality of being unique, by the brilliance that surrounds it, by the light that it communicates to the other stars which form for it a kind of court, by the just and equal share that the different climates of the world receive of this light, by the good it does in all places, ceaselessly producing as it does, in every sphere of life, joy and activity, by its unhindered movement, in which it nevertheless always appears calm, by its constant and invariable course, from which it never departs nor wavers, is the most striking and beautiful image of a great monarch.

Those who saw me governing with a good deal of ease and without being confused by anything, in all the numerous attentions that royalty demands, persuaded me to add the earth's globe, and for motto, *nec pluribus impar* (not unequal to many things): by which they meant something that flattered the aspirations of a young king, namely that, . . . I would doubtless be capable of governing other empires, just as the sun was capable of lighting up other worlds if they were exposed to its rays.

Source: Robert Campbell, *Louis XIV* (London: Longmans, 1993), 117–18.

SOURCE 13.3B
Louis XIV in Costume | 1653

PVDE/Bridgeman Images

■ ■ ■

SOURCE 13.4 An Outsider's View of the Inca Empire

Pedro de Cieza de León (1520–1554), a Spanish chronicler of the Inca Empire of the early sixteenth century, came to the Americas as a boy at the age of thirteen. For the next seventeen years, Cieza took part as a soldier in a number of expeditions that established Spanish rule in various parts of South America. Along the way, he collected a great deal of information, especially about the Inca Empire, which he began to publish on his return to Spain in 1550. Despite a very limited education, Cieza wrote a series of works that have become a major source for historians about the workings of the Inca Empire and about the Spanish conquest of that land. The selection that follows focuses on the techniques that the Incas used to govern their huge empire.

■ How would you describe Cieza's posture toward the Inca Empire? What in particular did he seem to appreciate about it?

■ Based on this account, what difficulties did the Inca rulers face in governing their realm?

■ What policies or practices did the Inca authorities follow in seeking to integrate their empire?

PEDRO DE CIEZA DE LEÓN | *Chronicles of the Incas* | ca. 1550

The Incas had the seat of their empire in the city of Cuzco, where the laws were given and the captains set out to make war. . . . As soon as one of these large provinces was conquered, ten or twelve thousand of the men and their wives, or six thousand, or the number decided upon were ordered to leave and remove themselves from it. These were transferred to another town or province of the same climate and nature as that which they left. . . .

One of the things most to be envied in these rulers is how well they knew to conquer such vast lands. . . .

[T]hey entered many lands without war, and the soldiers who accompanied the Inca were ordered to do no damage or harm, robbery or violence. If there was a shortage of food in the province, he ordered supplies brought in from other regions so that those newly won to his service would not find his rule and acquaintance irksome. . . .

In many others, where they entered by war and force of arms, they ordered that the crops and houses of the enemy be spared. . . . But in the end the Incas always came out victorious, and when they had vanquished the others, they did not do them further harm, but released those they had taken prisoner, if there were any, and restored the booty, and put them back in possession of their property and rule, exhorting them not to be foolish and try to compete with his royal majesty nor abandon his friendship, but to be his friends as their neighbors were. And saying this, he gave them a number of beautiful women and fine pieces of wool or gold. . . .

They never deprived the native chieftains of their rule. They were all ordered to worship the sun as God, but they were not prohibited from observing their own religions and customs. . . .

It is told for a fact of the rulers of this kingdom that in the days of their rule they [the Incas] had their representatives in the capitals of all the provinces.... They served as head of the provinces or regions, and from every so many leagues around the tributes were brought to one of these capitals. . . . [W]hen they came from the city of Cuzco to go over the accounts, or they were ordered to go to Cuzco to give an accounting . . . everything had to come out right. Few years went by in which an accounting of all these things was not made.. . .

When the Incas set out to visit their kingdom, it is told that they traveled with great pomp, riding in rich litters set upon smooth, long poles of the finest wood and adorned with gold and silver.. . .

So many people came to see his passing that all the hills and slopes seemed covered with them, and all called down blessings upon him.. . .

He [the Inca] traveled four leagues each day, or as much as he wished; he stopped wherever he liked to inquire into the state of his kingdom; he willingly listened to those who came to him with complaints, righting wrongs and punishing those who had committed an injustice.. . .

[T]hese rulers, as the best measure, ordered and decreed, with severe punishment for failure to obey, that all the natives of their empire should know and understand the language of Cuzco, both they and their women. . . .

[The Inca] appointed those whose duty it was to punish wrongdoers, and to this end they were always traveling about the country. The Incas took such care to see that justice was meted out that nobody ventured to commit a felony or theft.. . .

[I]n each of the many provinces there were many storehouses filled with supplies and other needful things; thus, in times of war, wherever the armies went they draw upon the contents of these storehouses, without ever touching the supplies of their confederates or laying a finger on what they had in their settlements. And when there was no war, all this stock of supplies and food was divided up among the poor and the widows.. . . If there came a lean year, the storehouses were opened and the provinces were lent what they needed in the way of supplies; then, in a year of abundance, they paid back all they had received.

Source: *The Incas of Pedro de Cieza de León*, translated by Harriet de Onis (Norman: University of Oklahoma Press, 1959), 56–57, 158–60, 165–73, 177–78.

■ ■ ■

SOURCE 13.5 **The Temple of Heaven: Beijing, China** ▶

The largest sacred site in the world in the fifteenth century lay in China. Known as the Temple of Heaven, it was constructed early in the century in the Ming dynasty capital of Beijing by the ambitious emperor Yongle (r. 1402–1424), who likewise ordered the building of the Forbidden City, a magnificent imperial residence.

Set in a forest of more than 650 acres, the Temple of Heaven was in Chinese thinking the primary place where Heaven and Earth met. From their residence in the Forbidden City, Chinese emperors of the Ming and Qing dynasties led a procession of thousands twice a year to this sacred site, where they offered sacrifices, implored the gods for a good harvest, and performed those rituals that maintained the cosmic balance. These sacred ceremonies, which commoners were barred even from watching, demonstrated the emperor's respect for the age-old source of his imperial authority, the Mandate of Heaven, from which Chinese emperors derived their legitimate right to rule. As the emperor bowed to Heaven, he was modeling in good Confucian fashion the respect required of all subordinates to their social superiors and especially to the emperor himself.

The temple complex and its various buildings were laced with ancient symbolism. The southern part of the wall that enclosed the complex was square, symbolizing the Earth, while the northern wall was rounded or semi-circular, suggesting Heaven in Daoist thinking. Major buildings were likewise built in the round while being situated within a square enclosure, also symbolizing the intersection of Heaven and Earth. The most prominent building was the Hall of Prayer for Good Harvest (Source 13.5), constructed by 1420. There the emperor prayed and conducted rituals to ensure a successful agricultural season on which the country's well-being and his own legitimacy depended. The emperor and others approached the hall from the south on a gradually ascending 360-meter walkway symbolizing progression from Earth to Heaven. The walkway divides into three parallel paths: the center one for the gods; the left for the emperor; and the right for the empress and court officials.

■ Which of these symbolic features can you identify in Source 13.5?

■ What impressions or understandings might those who observed the ceremonies or learned about them take away from the experience?

■ What does this ceremonial space have in common with that of the Felicity Gate in Topkapi Palace (Source 13.2)? What differentiates the two?

The Hall of Prayer for Good Harvest | ca. 1420

Doring Kindersley/UIG/Bridgeman Images

DOING HISTORY

1. **Making comparisons:** To what extent did these five early modern states face similar problems and devise similar solutions? How did they differ? In particular, how did the rulers of these states deal with subordinates?

2. **Assessing spectacle:** In what different ways was spectacle, royal splendor, or public display evident in the sources? How would you define the purpose of such display? How effective has spectacle been in consolidating state authority?

3. **Distinguishing power and authority:** Some scholars have made a distinction between "power," the ability of a state to coerce its subjects into some required behavior, and "authority," the ability of a state to persuade its subjects to do its bidding voluntarily by convincing them that it is proper, right, or natural to do so. What examples of power and authority can you find in these sources? How were power and authority related?

4. **Comparing past and present:** Early modern states differed in many ways from states today. How would you define those differences? Consider the personal role of the ruler, the use of violence, the means of establishing authority, and the extent to which the state could shape the lives of its citizens.

Early Modern Rulers

The following two voices provide recent descriptions of how early modern rulers defined and displayed their authority and power. In Voice 13.1, Charles Parker compares Emperor Kangxi of China and Louis XIV of France and finds them "cut from the same cloth." In Voice 13.2, John Darwin examines the many cultural influences that shaped the royal government of the Mughal emperor Akbar.

- According to Parker, what attributes of a powerful ruler did Kangxi and Louis XIV share?

- According to Darwin, what cultural and political traditions did Akbar draw upon to rule over the Mughal Empire? Which did he reject, abandon, or modify?

- **Integrating Primary and Secondary Sources:** What elements of kingship described by Parker and Darwin are evident in the primary sources preceding this feature? To what extent are these elements specific to certain rulers or states?

VOICE 13.1

Charles Parker on Emperor Kangxi of China and Louis XIV of France | 2010

For Europe's most powerful monarch [Louis XIV], the Qing dynasty under Kangxi emperor (r. 1661–1722) represented an ideal political order. The emperor wielded absolute power and enjoyed divine blessing; he employed an army of civil servants to govern his dominions; he possessed authority over a vast domain stretching from the eastern coastline to Outer Mongolia and Tibet; and he resided in a magnificent palace that exuded majestic order and power. In many respects Louis's reign (1643–1715) also embodied these characteristics, though on a less grand scale. Casting himself in the image of Apollo (the Greek god of light and sun), Louis promoted himself as the Sun King and he professed to rule by divine right; he dominated Europe and pushed France's borders to the farthest point; and he too presided over an elaborate court life at Versailles that reflected his prestige and authority. The Kangxi emperor and the Sun King, on opposite ends of Eurasia, were cut from the same cloth.

Source: Charles H. Parker, *Global Interactions in the Early Modern Age, 1400–1800* (Cambridge: Cambridge University Press, 2010), 13–14.

VOICE 13.2

John Darwin on Emperor Akbar's Public Image | 2008

Akbar projected himself not as a Muslim warrior-king, but as the absolute monarch of a diverse subject population. His official genealogy laid claim to descent from both Tamerlane and Genghis Khan, and thus to their legacy as "world conquerors." Mughal court ritual—especially Akbar's daily appearance on an elevated platform emphasized the *padshah*'s [an elevated Persian royal title referring to the monarch] supreme authority over even the greatest and wealthiest of his subjects. The court was the centre of lavish literary patronage. It promoted the study of the Muslim "rational sciences" and the writing of poetry, the main literary medium of the Islamic world. But Mughal court culture looked to Persian or Central Asian models for its art and literature. Persian was the language of intellectual life as well as of government. The life and landscape of Iran (not that of India) inspired the Mughal poets, who evoked a world far away "from the polluting influences of the subject peoples." . . . Akbar embarked upon a great building programme, of which the short-lived imperial capital at Fatehpur Sikri was the most astonishing product. Akbar's regime was cosmopolitan and eclectic, a tribute to Central Asia's influence as a great cultural entrepôt. It is even possible that his abortive attempt to impose a more centralized government in the 1570s and '80s (which led to the great revolt of 1580–82) was remotely inspired by the Chinese system of meritocratic bureaucracy. . . . Famously, Akbar rejected the classic Islamic distinction between the Muslim faithful (the *umma*) and the unbelievers. He abolished the *jizya* (poll-tax on non-Muslims) in 1579, and flirted with propagating a new religious synthesis of Islam and Hinduism.

Source: John Darwin, *After Tamerlane: The Rise and Fall of Global Empires 1400–2000* (London: Bloomsbury, 2008), 85–86.

Slave Merchant in Gorée Island, Senegal, from *Encyclopédie des Voyages*, engraved by L. F. Labrousse, 1796/Bibliothèque des Arts Decoratifs, Paris, France/Archives Charmet/Bridgeman Images

CHAPTER 14

Economic Transformations

Commerce and Consequence

1450–1750

"I have come full circle back to my destiny: from Africa to America and back to Africa. I could hear the cries and wails of my ancestors. I weep with them and for them."[1] This is what an African American woman from Atlanta wrote in 2002 in the guest book of the Cape Coast Castle, one of the many ports of embarkation for enslaved Africans located along the coast of Ghana in West Africa. There she no doubt saw the whips and leg irons used to discipline the captured Africans as well as the windowless dungeons in which hundreds were crammed while waiting for the ships that would carry them across the Atlantic to the Americas. Almost certainly she also caught sight of the infamous "gate of no return," through which the captives departed to their new life as slaves. ∎

This visitor's emotional encounter with the legacy of the transatlantic slave system reminds us of the enormous significance of this commerce in human beings for the early modern world and of its continuing resonance even in the twenty-first century. Commerce in enslaved people, however, was only one component of those international networks of exchange that shaped human interactions during the centuries between 1450 and 1750. Europeans now smashed their way into the ancient spice trade of the Indian Ocean, developing new relationships with Asian societies. Silver, obtained from mines in Spanish America, enriched Western Europe, even as much of it made its way to China, where it allowed Europeans to participate more fully in the rich commerce of East Asia. Furs from North America and Siberia found a ready

« **The Atlantic Slave Trade** This eighteenth-century French engraving shows the sale of enslaved Africans at Gorée, a major slave-trading port in what is now Dakar in Senegal. A European merchant and an African authority figure negotiate the arrangement, while the shackled victims themselves wait for their fate to be decided.

market in Europe and China, while the hunting and trapping of those fur-bearing animals transformed both natural environments and human societies. And despite their growing prominence in long-distance exchange, Europeans were far from the only actors in early modern commerce. Southeast Asians, Chinese, Indians, Armenians, Arabs, Africans, and Native Americans likewise played major roles in the making of the world economy during the early modern era.

SEEKING THE MAIN POINT

In what different ways did global commerce transform human societies and the lives of individuals during the early modern era?

Thus commerce joined empire as the twin creators of a global network during these centuries. Together they gave rise to new relationships, disrupted old patterns, brought distant peoples into contact with one another, enriched some, and impoverished or enslaved others. What was gained and what was lost in the transformations born of global commerce have been the subject of great controversy ever since.

Europeans and Asian Commerce

European empires in the Western Hemisphere grew out of an accident—Columbus's unknowing encounter with the Americas. In Asia, it was a very different story. The voyage (1497–1499) of the Portuguese mariner Vasco da Gama, in which Europeans sailed to India for the first time, was certainly no accident. It was the outcome of a deliberate, systematic, century-long Portuguese effort to explore a sea route to the East, by creeping slowly down the West African coast, around the tip of South Africa, up the East African coast, and finally across the Indian Ocean to India. There Europeans encountered an ancient and rich network of commerce that stretched from East Africa to China. They were certainly aware of the wealth of that commercial network, but largely ignorant of its workings.

Guided Reading Question

■ **CAUSATION**
What drove European involvement in the world of Asian commerce?

The most immediate motivation for this massive effort was the desire for tropical spices—cinnamon, nutmeg, mace, cloves, and, above all, pepper—which were widely used as condiments, preservatives, medicines, and aphrodisiacs. A fifteenth-century English book declared: "Pepper [from Java] is black and has a good smack, And every man doth buy it."[2] Other products of the East, such as Chinese silk, Indian cottons, rhubarb for medicinal purposes, emeralds, rubies, and sapphires, were also in great demand.

Underlying this growing interest in Asia was the more general recovery of European civilization following the disaster of the Black Death in the early fourteenth century. During the fifteenth century, Europe's population was growing again, and its national monarchies—in Spain, Portugal, England, and France—were learning how to tax their subjects more effectively and to build substantial military forces equipped with gunpowder weapons. Its cities were growing too. Some of them—in England, the Netherlands, and northern Italy, for example—were becoming centers of international commerce, giving birth to economies based on market exchange, private ownership, and the accumulation of capital for further investment.

Landmarks for Chapter 14

1450	1500	1550	1600	1650	1700	1750

EUROPEAN AND ASIAN COMMERCE

1498 Portuguese explorer Vasco da Gama reaches India

1505 Portuguese assault on Mombasa in East Africa

ca. 1565–ca. 1665
Spanish takeover of Philippine Islands

1601–1602
British and Dutch East India companies established

1635
Japanese seclusion from the West begins;
persecution of Christians

SILVER TRADE

ca. 1550 Silver discoveries in Bolivia and Japan

1570s Silver shipments from Mexico to Manila begin

1570s Chinese require tax payment in silver

ca. 1750
Decline of Spain as an imperial power

FUR TRADE

1600–1700
Growing European demand for furs; Little Ice Age at its peak

1600–1700
Peak of Russian fur trade in Siberia

1630s–1640s
Hurons decimated by European diseases

1664–1763
British-French rivalry for North America

ATLANTIC SLAVE TRADE

1440s First European export of slaves from West Africa

1526 King Afonso of Kongo protests impact of slave trade

1605–1694
Palmares: community of escaped slaves in Brazil

1700–1850
Peak of transatlantic slave system

1700–1800
Rise of Dahomey kingdom, based on slave trade

For many centuries, Eastern goods had trickled into the Mediterranean through the Middle East from the Indian Ocean commercial network. From the viewpoint of an increasingly dynamic Europe, several major problems accompanied this pattern of trade. First, of course, the source of supply for these much-desired goods lay solidly in Muslim hands, most immediately in Egypt. The Italian commercial city of Venice largely monopolized the European trade in Eastern goods, annually sending convoys of ships to Alexandria in Egypt. Venetians resented the Muslim monopoly on Indian Ocean trade, and other European powers disliked relying on Venice as well as on Muslims. Circumventing these monopolies provided both religious and political motivations for the Portuguese to attempt a sea route to India that bypassed both Venetian and Muslim intermediaries. In addition, many Europeans of the time were persuaded that a mysterious Christian monarch, known as Prester John, ruled somewhere in Asia or Africa. Joining with his mythical kingdom to continue the Crusades and combat a common Islamic enemy was likewise a goal of the Portuguese voyages.

A further problem for Europeans lay in paying for Eastern goods. Few products of an economically less developed Europe were attractive in Eastern markets. Thus Europeans were required to pay cash—gold or silver—for Asian spices or textiles. This persistent trade deficit contributed much to the intense desire for precious metals that attracted early modern European explorers, traders, and conquerors. Portuguese voyages along the West African coast, for example, were seeking direct access to African goldfields. The enormously rich silver deposits of Mexico and Bolivia provided at least a temporary solution to this persistent European problem.

First the Portuguese and then the Spanish, French, Dutch, and British found their way into the ancient Asian world of Indian Ocean commerce (see Map 14.1). How they behaved in that world and what they created there differed considerably among the various European countries, but collectively they contributed much to the new regime of globalized trade.

A Portuguese Empire of Commerce

The **Indian Ocean commercial network** into which Vasco da Gama and his Portuguese successors sailed was a world away from anything they had known. It was vast, both in geographic extent and in the diversity of those who participated in it. East Africans, Arabs, Persians, Indians, Malays, Chinese, and others traded freely. Most of them were Muslims, though hailing from many separate communities, but Hindus, Buddhists, Christians, Jews, and Chinese likewise had a role in this commercial network. Had the Portuguese sought simply to participate in peaceful trading, they certainly could have done so, but it was quickly apparent that European trade goods were crude and unattractive in Asian markets and that Europeans would be unable to compete effectively. Moreover, the Portuguese soon learned that most Indian Ocean merchant ships were not heavily armed and certainly lacked the onboard cannons that Portuguese ships carried. Since the withdrawal of

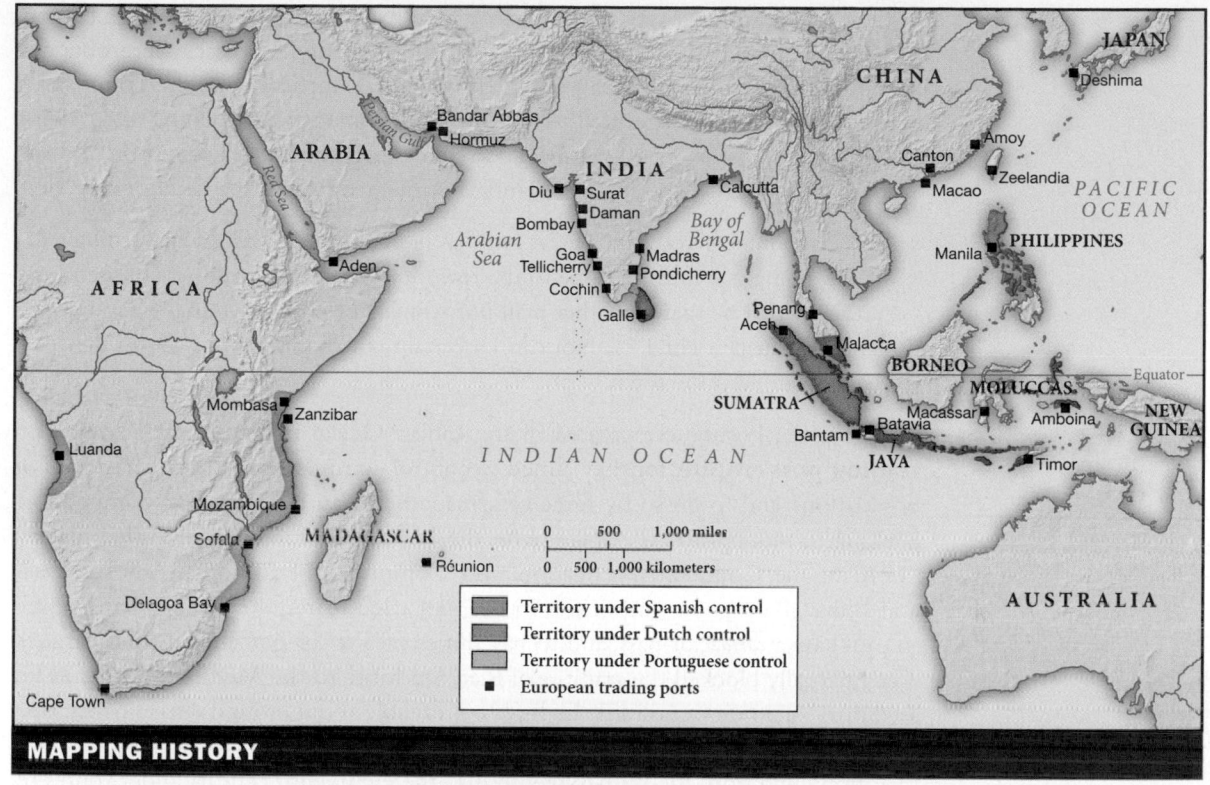

MAPPING HISTORY

Map 14.1 Europeans in Asia in the Early Modern Era

The early modern era witnessed only very limited territorial control by Europeans in Asia. Trade, rather than empire, was the chief concern of the Western newcomers, who were not, in any event, a serious military threat to major Asian states.

READING THE MAP: Where were Dutch-controlled territories concentrated? Where were Portuguese territories concentrated?

MAKING CONNECTIONS: Compare this map with Map 18.1: Colonial Asia in the Early Twentieth Century. What distinguished the European empires of the early modern period from those of the early twentieth century? What remained similar?

the Chinese fleet from the Indian Ocean early in the fifteenth century, no major power was in a position to dominate the sea lanes, and many smaller-scale merchants generally traded openly, although piracy was sometimes a problem.

Given these conditions, the Portuguese saw an opening, for their ships could outgun and outmaneuver competing naval forces, while their onboard cannons could devastate coastal fortifications. Although their overall economy lagged behind that of Asian producers, this military advantage enabled the Portuguese to quickly establish fortified bases at several key locations within the Indian Ocean world—Mombasa in East Africa, Hormuz at the entrance to the Persian Gulf, Goa on the west coast of India, Malacca in Southeast Asia, and Macao on the south coast

Guided Reading Question

■ **CONNECTION**
To what extent did the Portuguese realize their own goals in the Indian Ocean?

of China. With the exception of Macao, which had been obtained through bribery and negotiations with Chinese authorities, these Portuguese bases were obtained forcibly against small and weak states. In Mombasa, for example, the commander of a Portuguese fleet responded to local resistance in 1505 by burning and sacking the city, killing some 1,500 people, and seizing large quantities of cotton and silk textiles and carpets. The king of Mombasa wrote a warning to a neighboring city:

> This is to inform you that a great lord has passed through the town, burning it and laying it waste. He came to the town in such strength and was of such a cruelty that he spared neither man nor woman, or old nor young—nay, not even the smallest child. . . . Nor can I ascertain nor estimate what wealth they have taken from the town.[3]

What the Portuguese created in the Indian Ocean is commonly known as a **trading post empire**, for they aimed to control commerce, not large territories or populations, and to do so by force of arms rather than by economic competition. Seeking to monopolize the spice trade, the Portuguese king grandly titled himself "Lord of the Conquest, Navigation, and Commerce of Ethiopia, Arabia, Persia, and India." Portuguese authorities in the East tried to require all merchant vessels to purchase a *cartaz*, or pass, and to pay duties of 6 to 10 percent on their cargoes. They partially blocked the traditional Red Sea route to the Mediterranean and for a century or so monopolized the highly profitable route around Africa to Europe. Even so, they never succeeded in controlling much more than half of the spice trade to Europe, and from the mid-sixteenth into the eighteenth century older routes by both land and sea through the Ottoman Empire into the Mediterranean revived and even prospered.

The Spice Trade For thousands of years, spices were a major trade item in the Indian Ocean commercial network, as this fifteenth-century French depiction of the gathering of pepper in southern India illustrates. In the early modern era, Europeans gained direct access to this ancient network for the first time. (From the *Livres des Merveilles du Monde*, ca. 1410-1412, by Master Boucicaut [fl. 1390-1430] and workshop/Bibliothèque Nationale, Paris, France /Archives Charmet/ Bridgeman Images)

Failing to dominate Indian Ocean commerce as they had hoped, the Portuguese gradually assimilated themselves to its ancient patterns. They became heavily involved in the "carrying trade," transporting Asian goods to Asian ports, thus selling their shipping services because they were largely unable to sell their goods. Even in their major settlements, the Portuguese were outnumbered by Asian traders, and many married Asian women. Hundreds of Portuguese escaped the control of their government altogether and settled in Asian or African ports, where they learned local languages, sometimes converted to Islam, and became simply one more group in the diverse trading culture of the East.

By 1600, the Portuguese trading post empire was in steep decline. This small European country was overextended, and rising Asian states such as Japan, Burma, Mughal India, Persia, and the sultanate of Oman actively resisted Portuguese commercial control. Unwilling to accept a dominant Portuguese role in the Indian Ocean, other European countries also gradually contested Portugal's efforts to monopolize the rich spice trade to Europe.

Spain and the Philippines

The Spanish were the first to challenge Portugal's position as they established themselves on what became the Philippine Islands, named after the Spanish king Philip II. There they found an archipelago of islands, thousands of them, occupied by culturally diverse peoples and organized in small and highly competitive chiefdoms. One of the local chiefs later told the Spanish: "There is no king and no sole authority in this land; but everyone holds his own view and opinion, and does as he prefers."[4] Some of these chiefdoms were involved in tribute trade with China, and a small number of Chinese settlers lived in the port towns. Nonetheless, the region was of little interest to the governments of China and Japan, the major powers in the area.

These conditions—proximity to China and the Spice Islands, small and militarily weak societies, the absence of competing claims—encouraged the Spanish to establish outright colonial rule on the islands of the **Philippines**, rather than to imitate a Portuguese-style trading post empire. Accomplished largely from Spanish Mexico, conquest and colonization involved small-scale military operations, gunpowder weapons, local alliances, gifts and favors to chiefs, and the pageantry of Catholic ritual, all of which contributed to a relatively easy and often-bloodless Spanish takeover of the islands in the century or so after 1565. Accompanying Spanish rule was a major missionary effort that turned Filipino society into the only major outpost of Christianity in Asia. That effort also opened up a new front in the long encounter of Christendom and Islam, for on the southern island of Mindanao, Islam was gaining strength and provided an ideology of resistance to Spanish encroachment for 300 years. Indeed, Mindanao remains a contested part of the Philippines into the twenty-first century.

Beyond the missionary enterprise, other features of Spanish colonial practice in the Americas found expression in the Philippines. People living in scattered settlements were persuaded or forced to relocate into more concentrated Christian

Guided Reading Question

■ **COMPARISON**
How did the Portuguese, Spanish, Dutch, and British initiatives in Asia differ from one another?

communities. Tribute, taxes, and unpaid labor became part of ordinary life. Large landed estates emerged, owned by Spanish settlers, Catholic religious orders, or prominent Filipinos. Women who had played major roles as ritual specialists, healers, and midwives were now displaced by male Spanish priests, and the ceremonial instruments of these women were deliberately defiled and disgraced. Short-lived revolts and flight to interior mountains were among the Filipino responses to colonial oppression.

Yet others fled to **Manila**, the new capital of the colonial Philippines. By 1600, it had become a flourishing and culturally diverse city of more than 40,000 inhabitants and was home to many Spanish settlers and officials and growing numbers of Filipino migrants. Its rising prosperity also attracted some 3,000 Japanese and more than 20,000 Chinese. Serving as traders, artisans, and sailors, the Chinese in particular became an essential element in the Spanish colony's growing economic relationship with China; however, their economic prominence and their resistance to conversion earned them Spanish hostility and clearly discriminatory treatment. Periodic Chinese revolts, followed by expulsions and massacres, were the result. On one occasion in 1603, the Spanish killed about 20,000 people, nearly the entire Chinese population of the island.

The East India Companies

Far more important than the Spanish as European competitors for the spice trade were the Dutch and English, both of whom entered Indian Ocean commerce in the early seventeenth century. Together these rising North European powers quickly overtook and displaced the Portuguese, often by force, even as they competed vigorously with each other as well. During the sixteenth century, the Dutch had become a highly commercialized and urbanized society, and their business skills and maritime shipping operations were the envy of Europe. Around 1600, both the British and the Dutch, unlike the Portuguese, organized their Indian Ocean ventures through private companies, which were able to raise money and share risks among a substantial number of merchant investors. Both the **British East India Company** and the **Dutch East India Company** received charters from their respective governments granting them trading monopolies and the power to make war and to govern conquered peoples. Thus they established their own parallel and competing trading post empires, with the Dutch focused on the islands of Indonesia and the English on India. A similar French company also established a presence in the Indian Ocean basin, beginning in 1664.

Operating in a region of fragmented and weak political authority, the Dutch acted to control not only the shipping of cloves, cinnamon, nutmeg, and mace but also their production. With much bloodshed, the Dutch seized control of a number of small spice-producing islands, forcing their people to sell only to the Dutch and destroying the crops of those who refused. On the Banda Islands, famous for their nutmeg, the Dutch killed, enslaved, or left to starve virtually the entire population

Guided Reading Question

■ **CHANGE**

To what extent did the British and Dutch trading companies change the societies they encountered in Asia?

of some 15,000 people and then replaced them with Dutch planters, using a slave labor force, mostly from other parts of Asia, to produce the nutmeg crop. One Indonesian sultan asked a Dutch commander, "Do you believe that God has preserved for your trade alone islands which lie so far from your homeland?"[5] Apparently the Dutch did. And for a time in the seventeenth century, they were able to monopolize the trade in nutmeg, mace, and cloves and to sell these spices in Europe and India at fourteen to seventeen times the price they paid in Indonesia.[6] While Dutch profits soared, the local economy of the Spice Islands was shattered, and their people were impoverished.

The British East India Company operated differently than its Dutch counterpart. Less well financed and less commercially sophisticated, the British were largely excluded from the rich Spice Islands by the Dutch monopoly. Thus they fell back on India, where they established three major trading settlements during the seventeenth century: Bombay (now Mumbai), on India's west coast, and Calcutta and Madras, on the east coast. Although British naval forces soon gained control of the Arabian Sea and the Persian Gulf, largely replacing the Portuguese, on land they were no match for the powerful Mughal Empire, which ruled most of the Indian subcontinent. Therefore, the British were unable to practice "trade by warfare," as the Dutch did in Indonesia.[7] Rather, they secured their trading bases with the permission of Mughal authorities or local rulers, with substantial payments and bribes as the price of admission to the Indian market. When some independent English traders plundered a Mughal ship in 1636, local authorities detained British East India Company officials for two months and forced them to pay a whopping fine. Although pepper and other spices remained important in British trade, British merchants came to focus much more heavily on Indian cotton textiles, which were becoming widely popular in England and its American colonies. Hundreds of villages in the interior of southern India became specialized producers for this British market.

Like the Portuguese before them, both the Dutch and English became heavily involved in trade within Asia. The profits from this "carrying trade" enabled them to purchase Asian goods without

A European View of Asian Commerce The various East India companies (British, French, and Dutch) represented the major vehicle for European commerce in Asia during the early modern era. This wall painting, dating from 1778 and titled *The East Offering Its Riches to Britannia*, hung in the main offices of the British East India Company. (Oil on canvas by Roma Spiridione [d. 1787]/The British Library, London, UK/© British Library Board. All Rights Reserved/ Bridgeman Images) paying for them in gold or silver from Europe. Dutch and English traders also began to deal in bulk goods for a mass market—pepper, textiles, and later, tea and coffee—rather than just luxury goods for an elite market. In the second half of the eighteenth century, both the Dutch and British trading post empires slowly evolved into a more conventional form of colonial domination, in which the British came to rule India and the Dutch controlled Indonesia.

Asians and Asian Commerce

Guided Reading
Question
....
■ DESCRIPTION
In what ways did Asian
political authorities and
economic activities
persist in the face of
European intrusion?

The European presence was far less significant in Asia than it was in the Americas or Africa during these centuries. European political control was limited to the Philippines, parts of Java, and a few of the Spice Islands. The small Southeast Asian state of Siam was able to expel the French in 1688, outraged by their aggressive religious efforts at conversion and their plotting to extend French influence. To the great powers of Asia—Mughal India, China, and Japan—Europeans represented no real military threat and played minor roles in their large and prosperous economies. Japan provides a fascinating case study in the ability of major Asian powers to control the European intruders.

When Portuguese traders and missionaries first arrived in that island nation in the mid-sixteenth century, soon followed by Spanish, Dutch, and English merchants, Japan was plagued by endemic conflict among numerous feudal lords, known as *daimyo*, each with his own cadre of *samurai* warriors. In these circumstances, the European newcomers found a hospitable welcome; their military technology, shipbuilding skills, geographic knowledge, commercial opportunities, and even religious ideas proved useful or attractive to various elements in Japan's fractious and competitive society. The second half of the sixteenth century, for example, witnessed the growth of a substantial Christian movement, with some 300,000 converts and a Japanese-led church organization.

By the early seventeenth century, however, a series of remarkable military figures had unified Japan politically, under the leadership of a supreme military commander known as the *shogun*, who hailed from the Tokugawa clan. With the end of Japan's civil wars, successive shoguns came to view Europeans as a threat to the country's newly established unity rather than as an opportunity. They therefore expelled Christian missionaries and violently suppressed the practice of Christianity. This policy included the execution, often under torture, of some sixty-two missionaries and thousands of Japanese converts. Shogunate authorities also forbade Japanese from traveling abroad and banned most European traders altogether, permitting only the Dutch, who appeared less interested in spreading Christianity, to trade at a single site. Thus, for two centuries (1650–1850), Japanese authorities of the Tokugawa shogunate largely closed their country off from the emerging world of European commerce, although they maintained their trading ties to China, Korea, and Southeast Asia.

In the early seventeenth century, a large number of Japanese traders began to operate in Southeast Asia, where they behaved much like the newly arriving Europeans, frequently using force in support of their commercial interests. But unlike European states, the Japanese government of the Tokugawa shogunate explicitly disavowed any responsibility for or connection with these Japanese merchants. In one of many letters to rulers of Southeast Asian states, the Tokugawa shogun wrote to officials in Cambodia in 1610: "Merchants from my country [Japan] go to several places in your country [Cambodia] as well as Cochinchina and Champa [Vietnam]. There they become cruel and ferocious. . . . These men cause terrible damage. . . . They commit crimes and cause suffering. . . . Their offenses are extremely serious. Please punish them immediately according to the laws of your country. It is not necessary to have any reservations in this regard."[8] Thus Japanese merchants lacked the kind of support from their government that European merchants consistently received, but they did not refrain from trading in Southeast Asia.

Nor did other Asian merchants disappear from the Indian Ocean, despite European naval dominance. Arab, Indian, Chinese, Javanese, Malay, Vietnamese, and other traders benefited from the upsurge in seaborne commerce. A long-term movement of Chinese merchants into Southeast Asian port cities continued in the early modern era, enabling the Chinese to dominate the growing spice trade between that region and China. Southeast Asian merchants, many of them women, continued a long tradition of involvement in international trade. Malay proverbs from the sixteenth century, for example, encouraged "teaching daughters how to calculate and make a profit."[9] Overland trade within Asia remained wholly in Asian hands and grew considerably. Based in New Julfa near the capital of the Safavid Empire, Christian merchants originally from Armenia were particularly active in the commerce linking Europe, the Middle East, Central Asia, and India, with a few traveling as far as the Philippines and Mexico in pursuit of trading opportunities. Tens of thousands of Indian merchants and moneylenders, mostly Hindus representing sophisticated family firms, lived throughout Central Asia, Persia, and Russia, thus connecting this vast region to markets in India. These international Asian commercial networks, equivalent in their commercial sophistication to those of Europe, continued to operate successfully even as Europeans militarized the seaborne commerce of the Indian Ocean.

Within India, large and wealthy family firms, such as the one headed by Virji Vora during the seventeenth century, were able to monopolize the buying and selling of particular products, such as pepper or coral, and thus dictate terms and prices to the European trading companies. "He knoweth that wee must sell," complained one English trader about Vora, "and so beats us downe till we come to his owne rates." Furthermore, Vora was often the only source of loans for the cash-strapped Europeans, forcing them to pay interest rates as high as 12 to 18 percent annually. Despite their resentments, Europeans had little choice, because "none but Virji Vora hath moneye to lend or will lend."[10]

Silver and Global Commerce

Even more than the spice trade of Eurasia, it was the silver trade that gave birth to a genuinely global network of exchange (see Map 14.2). As one historian put it, silver "went round the world and made the world go round."[11] The mid-sixteenth-century discovery of enormously rich silver deposits in Bolivia, and simultaneously in Japan, suddenly provided a vastly increased supply of that precious metal. Spanish America alone produced perhaps 85 percent of the world's silver during the early modern era. Spain's sole Asian colony, the Philippines, provided a critical link in this emerging network of global commerce. Manila, the colonial capital of the Philippines, was the destination of annual Spanish shipments of silver, which were drawn from the rich mines of Bolivia, transported initially to Acapulco in Mexico, and from there shipped across the Pacific to the Philippines. This trade was the first direct and sustained link between the Americas and Asia, and it initiated a web of Pacific commerce that grew steadily over the centuries.

At the heart of that Pacific web, and of early modern global commerce generally, was China's huge economy, especially its growing demand for silver. In the 1570s, Chinese authorities consolidated a variety of tax levies into a single tax, which its huge population was now required to pay in silver. This sudden new demand for the white metal caused its value to skyrocket. It meant that foreigners with silver could now purchase far more of China's silks and porcelains than before.

Map 14.2 The Global Silver Trade

Silver was one of the first major commodities to be exchanged on a genuinely global scale.

This demand set silver in motion around the world, with the bulk of the world's silver supply winding up in China and much of the rest elsewhere in Asia. The routes by which this **"silver drain"** operated were numerous. Chinese, Portuguese, and Dutch traders flocked to Manila to sell Chinese goods in exchange for silver. European ships carried Japanese silver to China. Much of the silver shipped across the Atlantic to Spain was spent in Europe generally and then used to pay for the Asian goods that the French, British, and Dutch so greatly desired. Silver paid for some African slaves and for spices in Southeast Asia. The standard Spanish silver coin, known as a **piece of eight**, was used by merchants in North America, Europe, India, Russia, and West Africa as a medium of exchange. By 1600, it circulated widely in southern China. A Portuguese merchant in 1621 noted that silver "wanders throughout all the world . . . before flocking to China, where it remains as if at its natural center."[12]

In its global journeys, silver transformed much that it touched. At the world's largest silver mine in what is now Bolivia, the city of **Potosí** arose from a barren landscape high in the Andes, ten-weeks' journey by mule from Lima. "New people arrive by the hour, attracted by the smell of silver," commented a Spanish observer

Guided Reading Question

■ **CONNECTION**

What was the significance of the silver trade in the early modern era of world history?

A Silver Mine of Potosí This colonial-era painting shows the enormously rich silver mines of Potosí, then a major global source of the precious metal and the largest city in the Americas. Brutally hard work and poisonous exposure to mercury used in the refining process led to the deaths of many thousands of workers, even as the silver transformed the world economy in the early modern era.

in the 1570s.[13] With 160,000 people, Potosí became the largest city in the Americas and equivalent in size to London, Amsterdam, or Seville. Its wealthy European elite lived in luxury, with all the goods of Europe and Asia at their disposal. Meanwhile, the city's Native American miners worked in conditions so horrendous that some families held funeral services for men drafted to work in the mines. A Spanish priest observed, "Once inside they spend the whole week in there without emerging. . . . If 20 healthy Indians enter on Monday, half may emerge crippled on Saturday."[14] The environment too suffered, as highly intensive mining techniques caused severe deforestation, soil erosion, and flooding.

But the silver-fueled economy of Potosí also offered opportunity, not least to women. Spanish women might rent out buildings they owned for commercial purposes or send their slaves into the streets as small-scale traders, earning a few pesos for the household. Those less-well-to-do often ran stores, pawnshops, bakeries, and taverns. Indian and *mestiza* women likewise opened businesses that provided the city with beverages, food, clothing, and credit.

In Spain itself, which was the initial destination for much of Latin America's silver, the precious metal vastly enriched the Crown, making Spain the envy of its European rivals during the sixteenth century. Spanish rulers could now pursue military and political ambitions in both Europe and the Americas far beyond the country's own resource base. "New World mines," concluded several prominent historians, "supported the Spanish empire."[15] Nonetheless, this vast infusion of wealth did not fundamentally transform the Spanish economy, because it generated inflation of prices more than real economic growth. A rigid economy laced with monopolies and regulations, an aristocratic class that preferred leisure to enterprise, and a crusading insistence on religious uniformity all prevented the Spanish from using their silver windfall in a productive fashion. When the value of silver dropped in the early seventeenth century, Spain lost its earlier position as the dominant Western European power. More generally, the flood of American silver that circulated in Europe drove prices higher, further impoverished many, stimulated uprisings across the continent, and, together with the Little Ice Age of global cooling, contributed to what historians sometimes call a General Crisis of upheaval and instability in the seventeenth century. (See "The Great Dying and the Little Ice Age" in Chapter 13.)

Japan, another major source of silver production in the sixteenth century, did better. Its military rulers, the Tokugawa shoguns, used silver-generated profits to defeat hundreds of rival feudal lords and unify the country. Unlike their Spanish counterparts, the shoguns allied with the country's vigorous domestic merchant class to develop a market-based economy and to invest heavily in agricultural and industrial enterprises. Japanese state and local authorities alike acted vigorously to protect and renew Japan's dwindling forests, while millions of families in the eighteenth century took steps to have fewer children by practicing late marriages, contraception, abortion, and infanticide. The outcome was the dramatic slowing of Japan's population growth, the easing of an impending ecological crisis, and a flourishing, highly commercialized economy. These were the foundations for Japan's remarkable nineteenth-century Industrial Revolution.

In China, silver deepened the already substantial commercialization of the country's economy. To obtain the silver needed to pay their taxes, more and more people had to sell something—either their labor or their products. Communities that devoted themselves to growing mulberry trees, on which silkworms fed, had to buy their rice from other regions. Thus the Chinese economy became more regionally specialized. Particularly in southern China, this surging economic growth resulted in the loss of about half the area's forest cover as more and more land was devoted to cash crops. No Japanese-style conservation program emerged to address this growing problem. An eighteenth-century Chinese poet, Wang Dayue, gave voice to the fears that this ecological transformation generated:

> Rarer, too, their timber grew, and rarer still and rarer
> As the hills resembled heads now shaven clean of hair.
> For the first time, too, moreover, they felt an anxious mood
> That all their daily logging might not furnish them with fuel.[16]

China's role in the silver trade is a useful reminder of Asian centrality in the world economy of the early modern era. Its large and prosperous population, increasingly operating within a silver-based economy, fueled global commerce, vastly increasing the quantity of goods exchanged and the geographic range of world trade. Despite their obvious physical presence in the Americas, Africa, and Asia, economically speaking Europeans were essentially middlemen, funneling American silver to Asia and competing with one another for a place in the rich markets of the East. The productivity of the Chinese economy was evident in Spanish America, where cheap and well-made Chinese goods easily outsold those of Spain. In 1594, the Spanish viceroy of Peru observed that "a man can clothe his wife in Chinese silks for [25 pesos], whereas he could not provide her with clothing of Spanish silks with 200 pesos."[17] Indian cotton textiles likewise outsold European woolen or linen textiles in the seventeenth century to such an extent that French laws in 1717 prohibited the wearing of Indian cotton or Chinese silk clothing as a means of protecting French industry.

"The World Hunt": Fur in Global Commerce

In the early modern era, furs joined silver, textiles, and spices as major items of global commerce.[18] Their harvesting had an important environmental impact as well as serious implications for the human societies that generated and consumed them. Furs, of course, had long provided warmth and conveyed status in colder regions of the world, but the integration of North America and of northern Asia (Siberia) into a larger world economy vastly increased their significance in global trade.

By 1500, European population growth and agricultural expansion had sharply diminished the supply of fur-bearing animals, such as beaver, rabbits, sable, marten, and deer. Furthermore, much of the early modern era witnessed a period of cooling temperatures and harsh winters, known as the Little Ice Age, which may well have increased the demand for furs. "The weather is bitterly cold and everyone is in furs

Guided Reading Question

■ **CHANGE**
Describe the impact of the fur trade on North American native societies.

although we are almost in July," observed a surprised visitor from Venice while in London in 1604.[19] These conditions pushed prices higher, providing strong economic incentives for European traders to tap the immense wealth of fur-bearing animals found in North America.

The **fur trade** was a highly competitive enterprise. The French were most prominent in the St. Lawrence valley, around the Great Lakes, and later along the Mississippi River; British traders pushed into the Hudson Bay region; and the Dutch focused their attention along the Hudson River in what is now New York. They were frequently rivals for the great prize of North American furs. In the southern colonies of British North America, deerskins by the hundreds of thousands found a ready market in England's leather industry (see Map 14.3).

Only a few Europeans directly engaged in commercial trapping or hunting. They usually waited for Native Americans to bring the furs or skins initially to their coastal settlements and later to their fortified trading posts in the interior of North America. European merchants paid for the furs with a variety of trade goods, including guns, blankets, metal tools, rum, and brandy, amid much ceremony, haggling over prices, and ritualized gift giving. Native Americans represented a cheap labor force in this international commercial effort, but they were not a directly coerced labor force.

Over the three centuries of the early modern era, enormous quantities of furs and deerskins found their way to Europe, where they considerably enhanced the standard of living in those cold climates. The environmental price was paid in the Americas, and it was high. A consistent demand for beaver hats led to the near extinction of that industrious animal in much of North America by the early nineteenth century and with it the degradation or loss of many wetland habitats. By the 1760s, hunters in southeastern British colonies took about 500,000 deer every year, seriously diminishing the deer population of the region. As early as 1642, Miantonomo, a chief of the New England Narragansett people, spoke of the environmental consequences of English colonialism:

> You know our fathers had plenty of deer and skins and our plains were full
> of game and turkeys, and our coves and rivers were full of fish. But, brothers,
> since these Englishmen have seized our country, they have cut down the grass
> with scythes, and the trees with axes. Their cows and horses eat up the grass,
> and their hogs spoil our bed of clams; and finally we shall all starve to death.[20]

For the Native American peoples who hunted, trapped, processed, and transported these products, the fur trade bore various benefits, particularly at the beginning. One Native American trapper told a French missionary, "The beaver does everything perfectly well. It makes kettles, hatchets, swords, knives, bread; and, in short, it makes everything."[21] The Hurons, who lived on the northern shores of Lakes Erie and Ontario in the early seventeenth century, annually exchanged some 20,000 to 30,000 pelts, mostly beaver, for trade items, some of which they used to strengthen their relationships with neighboring peoples. These goods also

MAPPING HISTORY

Map 14.3 The North American Fur Trade

North America, as well as Russian Siberia, funneled an apparently endless supply of furs into the circuits of global trade during the early modern era.

READING THE MAP: Which overseas markets were American furs shipped to?

INTERPRETING THE MAP: How might waterways have facilitated the movement of furs from the interior of the Americas to overseas markets?

enhanced the authority of Huron chiefs by providing them with gifts to distribute among their followers. At least initially, competition among Europeans ensured that Native American leaders could negotiate reasonable prices for their goods. Furthermore, their important role in the lucrative fur trade protected them for a time from the kind of extermination, enslavement, or displacement that was the fate of native peoples in Portuguese Brazil.

Nothing, however, protected them against the diseases carried by Europeans. In the 1630s and 1640s, to cite only one example of many, about half of the Hurons perished from influenza, smallpox, and other European-borne diseases. Furthermore, the fur trade generated warfare beyond anything previously known. Competition among Native American societies became more intense as the economic stakes grew higher. Catastrophic population declines owing to disease stimulated "mourning wars," designed to capture people who could be assimilated into much-diminished societies. A century of French-British rivalry for North America (1664–1763) forced Native American societies to take sides, to fight, and to die in these European imperial conflicts. Firearms, of course, made warfare far more deadly than before.

Beyond the fur trade, many Native American peoples sought actively to take advantage of the new commercial economy now impinging upon them. The Iroquois, for example, began to sell new products such as ginseng root, much in demand in China as a medicine. They also rented land to Europeans, worked for wages in various European enterprises, and started to use currency, when barter was ineffective. But as they became enmeshed in these commercial relationships, Native Americans grew dependent on European trade goods. Among the Algonquians, for example, iron tools and cooking pots replaced those of stone, wood, or bone; gunpowder weapons took the place of bows and arrows; European textiles proved more attractive than traditional beaver and deerskin clothing; and flint and steel were found to be more effective for starting fires than wooden drills. A wide range of traditional crafts were thus lost, while the native peoples did not gain a corresponding ability to manufacture the new items for themselves. Enthusiasm for these imported goods and continued European demands for furs and skins frequently eroded the customary restraint that characterized traditional hunting practices, resulting in the depletion of many species. One European observer wrote of the Creek Indians: "[They] wage eternal war against deer and bear . . . which is indeed carried to an unreasonable and perhaps criminal excess, since the white people have dazzled their senses with foreign superfluities."[22]

Alongside germs and guns, yet another highly destructive European import was alcohol—rum and brandy, in particular. Whiskey, a locally produced grain-based alcohol, only added to the problem. With no prior experience of alcohol and little time to adjust to its easy availability, these drinks "hit Indian societies with explosive force."[23] Binge drinking, violence among young men, promiscuity, and addiction followed in many places. In 1753, Iroquois leaders complained bitterly to European authorities in Pennsylvania: "These wicked Whiskey Sellers, when they have once got the Indians in liquor, make them sell their very clothes from their backs. . . . If this practice be continued, we must be inevitably ruined."[24] In short, it was not so much the fur trade itself that decimated Native American societies, but all that accompanied it—disease, dependence, guns, alcohol, and the growing encroachment of European colonial empires.

All of this had particular implications for women. A substantial number of native women married European traders according to the "custom of the country"—with no sanction from civil or church authorities. Such marriages eased the difficulties of this cross-cultural exchange, providing traders with guides, interpreters, and negotiators. But sometimes these women were left abandoned when their husbands returned to Europe. More generally, the fur trade enhanced the position of men in their societies because hunting or trapping animals was normally a male occupation. Among the Ojibwa, a gathering and hunting people in the northern Great Lakes region, women had traditionally acquired economic power by creating food, utensils, clothing, and decorations from the hides and flesh of the animals that their husbands caught. With the fur trade in full operation, women spent more time processing those furs for sale than in producing household items, some of which were now available for purchase from Europeans. And so, as one scholar put it, "women lost authority and prestige." At the same time, however, women generated and controlled the trade in wild rice and maple syrup, both essential to the livelihood of European traders.[25] Thus the fur trade offered women a mix of opportunities and liabilities.

Paralleling the North American fur trade was the one simultaneously taking shape within a rapidly expanding Russian Empire, which became a major source of furs for Western Europe, China, and the Ottoman Empire. The profitability of that trade in furs was the chief incentive for Russia's rapid expansion during the sixteenth and seventeenth centuries across Siberia, where the **"soft gold"** of fur-bearing animals was abundant. The international sale of furs greatly enriched the Russian state as well as

Fur and the Russians This colored engraving shows a sixteenth-century Russian ambassador and his contingent arriving at the court of the Holy Roman Emperor and bearing gifts of animal pelts, the richest fruit of the expanding Russian Empire. (Color line engraving, 1576/Granger, NYC—All rights reserved)

many private merchants, trappers, and hunters. Here the silver trade and the fur trade intersected, as Europeans paid for Russian furs largely with American gold and silver.

The consequences for native Siberians were similar to those in North America as disease took its toll, as indigenous people became dependent on Russian goods, as the settler frontier encroached on native lands, and as many species of fur-bearing mammals were seriously depleted. In several ways, however, the Russian fur trade was unique. Whereas several European nations competed in North America and generally obtained their furs through commercial negotiations with Indian societies, no such competition accompanied Russian expansion across Siberia. Russian authorities imposed a tax or tribute, payable in furs, on every able-bodied Siberian male between eighteen and fifty years of age. To enforce the payment, they took hostages from Siberian societies, with death as a possible outcome if the required furs were not forthcoming. A further difference lay in the large-scale presence of private Russian hunters and trappers, who competed directly with their Siberian counterparts.

Guided Reading Question

■ **COMPARISON**
How did the North American and Siberian fur trades differ from each other? What did they have in common?

PRACTICING HISTORICAL THINKING

What differences can you identify in the operation and impact of the spice, silver, and fur trades?

Commerce in People: The Transatlantic Slave System

Of all the commercial ties that linked the early modern world into a global network of exchange, none had more profound or enduring human consequences than the **transatlantic slave system**. (See Controversies: Debating the Atlantic World, page 614.) Between 1500 and 1866, this trade in human beings took an estimated 12.5 million people from African societies, shipped them across the Atlantic in the infamous Middle Passage, and deposited some 10.7 million of them in the Americas, where they lived out their often-brief lives as slaves. About 1.8 million (14.4 percent) died during the transatlantic crossing, while countless others perished in the process of capture and transport to the African coast.[26] (See Map 14.4.) Despite the language of commerce and exchange with which it is often described, this transatlantic slave system was steeped in violence, coercion, and brutality. It involved forcible capture and repeated sale, beatings and brandings, chains and imprisonment, rebellions and escapes, lives of enforced and unpaid labor, broken families, and humans treated as property.

Beyond the multitude of individual tragedies that it spawned, the transatlantic slave system transformed entire societies. Within Africa itself, that commerce thoroughly disrupted some societies, strengthened others, and corrupted many. Elites often enriched themselves, while the enslaved Africans, of course, were victimized almost beyond imagination.

In the Americas, this transatlantic network added a substantial African presence to the mix of European and Native American peoples. This **African diaspora** (the global spread of African peoples) injected into these new societies issues of race that endure still in the twenty-first century. It also introduced elements of African

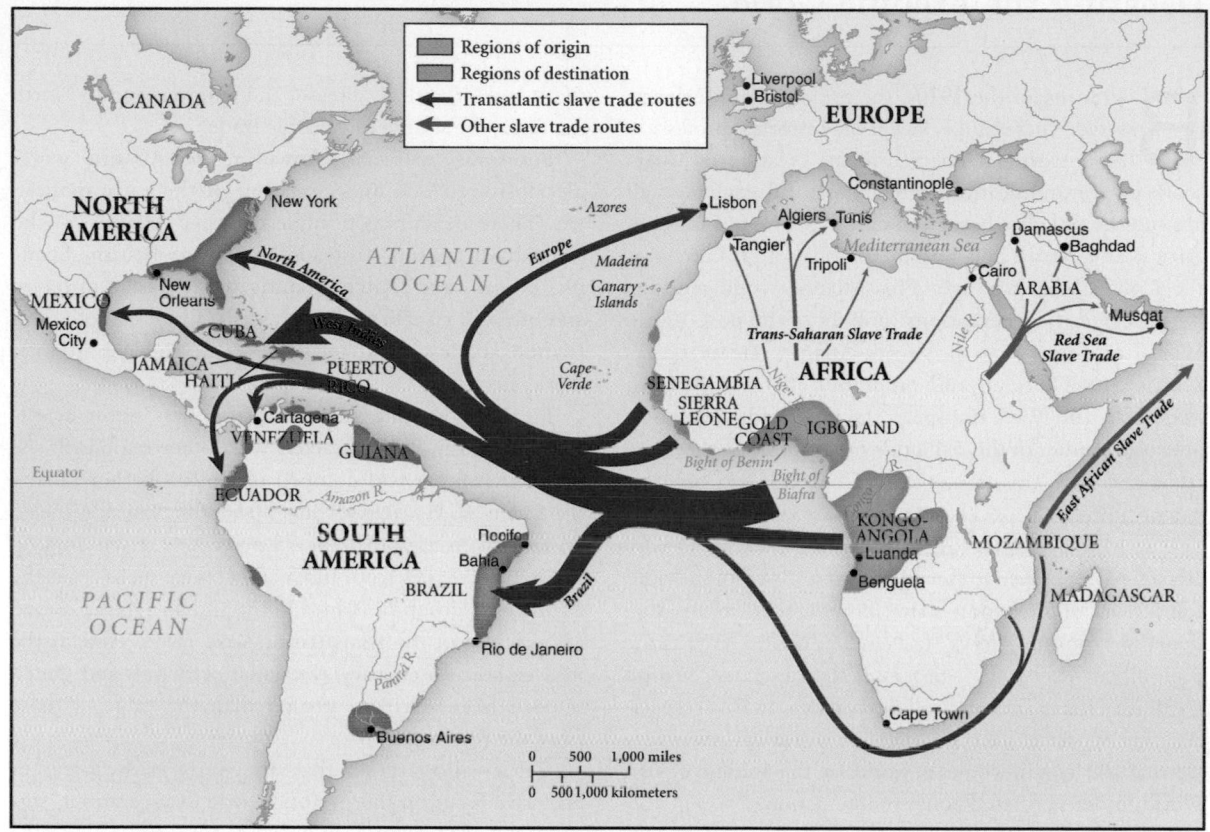

Map 14.4 The Transatlantic Slave System
Stimulated by the plantation complex of the Americas, the transatlantic slave system represented an enormous extension of the ancient practice of people owning and selling other people.

culture, such as religious ideas, musical and artistic traditions, and cuisine, into the making of American cultures. The profits from the slave trade and the labor of enslaved Africans certainly enriched European and Euro-American societies, even as the practice of slavery contributed much to the racial stereotypes of European peoples. Finally, slavery became a metaphor for many kinds of social oppression, quite different from plantation slavery, in the centuries that followed. Workers protested the slavery of wage labor, colonized people rejected the slavery of imperial domination, and feminists sometimes defined patriarchy as a form of slavery.

The Slave Trade in Context

The transatlantic slave system represented the most recent large-scale expression of a very widespread human practice—the owning and exchange of human beings. Before 1500, the Mediterranean and Indian Ocean basins were the major arenas of Old World slave systems, and southern Russia was a major source of its victims.

Debating the Atlantic World

Beginning in the 1970s, the notion of an "Atlantic world" increasingly swept the historical profession like a storm. It referred to the creation of a network of communication, interaction, and exchange all around the Atlantic basin among the peoples of Europe, Africa, and North and South America, often known as the Columbian exchange. This Atlantic world sensibility reflected the international politics of the post–World War II era, in which the North Atlantic Treaty Organization (NATO), an anticommunist alliance of North American and West European states, played an important role. Studies of the Atlantic world in earlier centuries resonated with this transatlantic Cold War–era political partnership.

For historians, the "Atlantic world" idea held many attractions. It helped to free historical study from the rigid framework of the nation-state, allowing scholars and students to examine "flows" or "circulations"—such as the Columbian exchange—processes that operated beyond particular states and within larger spaces. In this respect, Atlantic world thinking paralleled historical investigation of the Mediterranean world or the Indian Ocean world, other sea-based zones of interaction.

The "Atlantic world" idea also encouraged comparison, particularly attractive to world historians. How similar or different were the various European empires—Spanish, Portuguese, British, French, Dutch—constructed in the Americas? Students in the United States are often surprised to learn that fewer than 5 percent of the enslaved Africans transported across the Atlantic wound up in North America and that the vast majority landed in Brazil or the Caribbean region.

Moreover, the Atlantic world provided a larger context in which to situate the history of particular societies or nations. The modern history of the Caribbean region, for example, is inexplicable without some grasp of its connection to Africa, the source of slaves; to Europe, the source of settlers, disease, and empires; and to North America, the source of valuable trade.

For some historians, however, the Atlantic world idea distorted our understanding of the early modern era. There never was a single cohesive Atlantic world, some have argued. Instead there were British, Spanish, French, and Dutch Atlantic worlds, each different and often in conflict. There were Catholic, Protestant, Islamic, and Jewish Atlantic worlds, and a black Atlantic world as well.

Furthermore, the Atlantic region was never a self-contained unit, but interacted with other regions of the world. Asian tea was dumped in Boston harbor during the American "tea party." Silver from the Americas fueled trade with Asia, with some 75 percent of it winding up in China. Textiles from India and cowrie shells from the Maldives, a group of islands in the Indian Ocean, served as currency in the transatlantic slave trade. And in the mid-eighteenth century, the value of British and Dutch imports from Asia was greater than the value of those from the Americas.

Critics also argued that an overly enthusiastic or exclusive focus on the Atlantic world exaggerates its significance in early modern world history. But placing the Atlantic world in a larger global framework corrects any such exaggeration and raises many fascinating questions. Why were Europeans able to construct major empires in the Americas but not in Africa or Asia? Why did European empires in the Americas feature large-scale European settlement, while the Chinese and Ottoman empires in Asia and the Middle East did not involve much Chinese or Turkish migration? How does the transatlantic slave system look when it is compared to the trans-Saharan and Indian Ocean slave trades, both of which were much older? And how does the transatlantic commerce in the early modern era compare with earlier Afro-Eurasian patterns of long-distance trade that

Many African societies likewise both practiced slavery themselves and sold slaves into these international commercial networks. A trans-Saharan slave trade had long funneled African captives into Mediterranean slavery, and an East African slave trade from at least the seventh century C.E. brought Africans into the Middle East and the had a much longer history? In short, the Atlantic world becomes a more meaningful concept when it is framed in genuinely global contexts.

Beyond these controversies about the usefulness and limitations of the Atlantic world concept, historians have also debated the operation of this transoceanic network, with particular focus on questions of "agency" and "impact." "Agency" refers to the ability of individuals or groups to take action, to make things happen, and to affect the outcome of historical processes. So who created the Atlantic world? The earliest and most obvious answer to this question claimed that the Atlantic world was the product of European rulers, explorers, armies, settlers, merchants, and missionaries. But taking a closer look, historians have discovered agency in other places as well. Unknown to their European carriers, pathogens "acted" independently to generate the Great Dying in the Americas, largely beyond the intention or control of any human agent. Many indigenous rulers, acting in their own interests, joined their larger military forces to the small armies of the Spanish conquistadores to defeat the powerful Aztec and Inca empires. African rulers and commercial elites violently procured the human cargoes of the slave trade and sold them to European merchants waiting on Africa's western coast.

Agency was also expressed in numerous acts of resistance against Europeans, such as the Great Pueblo Rebellion of 1680, the creation of runaway slave communities in Brazil, and the Haitian Revolution, all of which shaped the contours of the Atlantic world. Culturally too, conquered and enslaved people retained their human capacity to act and create, even in enormously repressive conditions. For example, they adapted Christianity to their own needs, often blending it with elements of traditional beliefs and practices. A famous book about slavery in the American south by Eugene Genovese bore the pointed subtitle *The World the Slaves Made*. Agency, in short, was not limited to Europeans, and the Atlantic world was not wholly a European creation.

The multiple interactions of the Atlantic world have also stimulated debate about "impact" or the consequences of inclusion in this transoceanic network. For millions of enslaved individuals and millions more who perished in the Great Dying, the impact was tragic and painful almost beyond description. About this there is little debate. More controversial questions arise about the impact of Atlantic world encounters on broader regions and their peoples. Were indigenous societies of the Western Hemisphere destroyed or decimated by conquest, disease, labor demands, and loss of land? Or were they, as historian John Kicze describes them, remarkably "resilient cultures"? How did the demand for enslaved people affect African population growth, economic development, the role of women, and state formation? Did the wealth derived from the Atlantic world of empire, commerce, and slavery enable Britain's Industrial Revolution, or was it only a minor factor?

Finally, the intersection of questions about agency and impact in the Atlantic world has raised contentious issues about moral responsibility. If Europeans or Euro-Americans were the primary agents of the slave trade, the Great Dying, and the exploitation of native peoples, do they owe an apology and compensation to the descendants of their victims? Are such claims weakened if some joint responsibility for these tragedies is recognized?

About all of this, debate continues.

QUESTIONS TO CONSIDER

1. With what questions about the Atlantic world do you feel most engaged? Why?

2. What makes the Atlantic world a compelling concept for historians?

3. How does the treatment of early modern empires in Chapter 13 and commerce in Chapter 14 respond to the questions raised in this essay?

Indian Ocean basin. Both operated largely within the Islamic world and initiated the movement of African peoples beyond the continent itself.

Furthermore, slavery came in many forms. In the Indian Ocean world, for example, African slaves were often assimilated into the societies of their owners

Guided Reading
Question
••••••••••••••••••••••••••••••••••••

■ COMPARISON
What was distinctive
about the Atlantic slave
trade? What did it share
with other patterns of
slave owning and slave
trading?

and lost the sense of a distinctive identity that was so prominent in North America. In some places, children inherited the slave status of their parents; elsewhere those children were free persons. Within the Islamic world, where most slaves worked in domestic settings, the preference was for female slaves by a two-to-one margin, while the later transatlantic slave system, which funneled captives into plantation labor, favored males by a similar margin. Not all enslaved people, however, occupied degraded positions. Some in the Islamic world acquired prominent military or political status. Most slaves in the premodern world worked in their owners' households, farms, or shops, with smaller numbers laboring in large-scale agricultural or industrial enterprises.

The slave system that emerged in the Americas was distinctive in several ways. One was simply the immense size of that system and its centrality to the economies of colonial America, which featured a great deal of plantation agriculture. Furthermore, slave status throughout the Americas was inherited across generations, and there was little hope of eventual freedom for the vast majority. Nowhere else, with the possible exception of ancient Greece, was the contradiction beween slavery and social values affirming human freedom and equality quite so sharp. Perhaps most distinctive was the racial dimension: Atlantic slavery came to be identified wholly with Africa and with "blackness."

The origins of Atlantic slavery clearly lie in the Mediterranean world and with that now-common sweetener known as sugar. Until the Crusades, Europeans knew nothing of sugar and relied on honey and fruits to sweeten their bland diets. However, as they learned from the Arabs about sugarcane and the laborious techniques for producing usable sugar, Europeans established sugar-producing plantations within the Mediterranean and later on various islands off the coast of West Africa. It was a "modern" industry, perhaps the first one, in that it required huge capital investment, substantial technology, an almost factory-like discipline among workers, and a mass market of consumers. The immense difficulty and danger of the work, the limitations attached to serf labor, and the general absence of wageworkers all pointed to slavery as a source of labor for sugar plantations.

Initially, Slavic-speaking peoples from the Black Sea region furnished the bulk of the slaves for Mediterranean plantations, so much so that "Slav" became the basis for the word "slave" in many European languages. In 1453, however, when the Ottoman Turks seized Constantinople,

Slavery in the Islamic World This eighteenth-century image of a slave accompanying her upper-class Turkish owner to the public baths highlights the slave trade in the Ottoman and Indian Ocean worlds and serves as a reminder that slavery was not limited to the Atlantic world in the early modern era. Unlike in the Americas, most slaves in North Africa and Southwest Asia served as domestic servants, with female slaves generally preferred to males. (Oil on canvas by Francis Smith (fl. 1763–80)/Yale Center for British Art, Paul Mellon Collection, USA/Bridgeman Images)

the supply of Slavic slaves was effectively cut off. At the same time, Portuguese mariners were exploring the coast of West Africa; they were looking primarily for gold, but they also found there an alternative source of enslaved people available for sale. Thus, when sugar, and later tobacco and cotton, plantations took hold in the Americas, Europeans had already established links to a West African source of supply. They also now had religious justification for their actions, for in 1452 the pope formally granted to the kings of Spain and Portugal "full and free permission to invade, search out, capture, and subjugate the Saracens [Muslims] and pagans and any other unbelievers . . . and to reduce their persons into perpetual slavery."[27] Largely through a process of elimination, Africa became the primary source of slave labor for the plantation economies of the Americas. Slavic peoples were no longer available; Native Americans quickly perished from European diseases; even marginal Europeans such as the poor and criminals were Christians and therefore supposedly exempt from slavery; and European indentured servants, who agreed to work for a fixed period in return for transportation, food, and shelter, were expensive and temporary. Africans, on the other hand, were skilled farmers; they had some immunity to both tropical and European diseases; they were not Christians; they were, relatively speaking, close at hand; and they were readily available in substantial numbers through African-operated commercial networks.

Moreover, Africans were black. The precise relationship between slavery and European racism has long been a much-debated subject. Historian David Brion Davis has suggested the controversial view that "racial stereotypes were transmitted, along with black slavery itself, from Muslims to Christians."[28] For many centuries, Muslims had drawn on sub-Saharan Africa as one source of slaves and in the process had developed a form of racism. The fourteenth-century Tunisian scholar Ibn Khaldun wrote that black people were "submissive to slavery, because Negroes have little that is essentially human and have attributes that are quite similar to those of dumb animals."[29]

Other scholars find the origins of racism within European culture itself. For the English, argues historian Audrey Smedley, the process of conquering Ireland had generated by the sixteenth century a view of the Irish as "rude, beastly, ignorant, cruel, and unruly infidels," perceptions that were then transferred to Africans enslaved on English sugar plantations of the West Indies.[30] Whether Europeans borrowed such images of Africans from their Muslim neighbors or developed them independently, slavery and racism soon went hand in hand. "Europeans were better able to tolerate their brutal exploitation of Africans," writes a prominent world historian, "by imagining that these Africans were an inferior race, or better still, not even human."[31]

The Slave Trade in Practice

The European demand for slaves was clearly the chief cause of this tragic commerce, and from the point of sale on the African coast to the massive use of slave labor on American plantations, the entire enterprise was in European hands. Within Africa itself, however, a different picture emerges, for over the four centuries of the

Guided Reading Question

····································

■ **CAUSATION**

What explains the rise of the Atlantic slave trade?

Atlantic slave trade, European demand elicited an African supply. The slave trade quickly came to operate largely with Europeans waiting on the coast, either on their ships or in fortified settlements, to purchase slaves from African merchants and political elites. Certainly, Europeans tried to exploit African rivalries to obtain slaves at the lowest possible cost, and the firearms they funneled into West Africa may well have increased the warfare from which so many slaves were derived. But from the point of initial capture to sale on the coast, the entire enterprise was normally in African hands. Almost nowhere did Europeans attempt outright military conquest; instead they generally dealt as equals with local African authorities.

An arrogant agent of the British Royal Africa Company in the 1680s learned the hard way who was in control when he spoke improperly to the king of Niumi, a small state in what is now Gambia. The company's records describe what happened next:

> [O]ne of the grandees [of the king], by name Sambalama, taught him better manners by reaching him a box on the ears, which beat off his hat, and a few thumps on the back, and seizing him . . . and several others, who together with the agent were taken and put into the king's pound and stayed there three or four days till their ransom was brought, value five hundred bars.[32]

In exchange for slaves, African sellers sought both European and Indian textiles, cowrie shells (widely used as money in West Africa), European metal goods, firearms and gunpowder, tobacco and alcohol, and various decorative items such as beads. Europeans purchased some of these items—cowrie shells and Indian textiles, for example—with silver mined in the Americas. Thus the transatlantic slave system connected with commerce in silver and textiles as it became part of an emerging worldwide network of exchange. Issues about the precise mix of goods African authorities desired, about the number and quality of slaves to be purchased, and always about the price of everything were settled in endless negotiation. Most of the time, a leading historian concluded, the slave trade took place "not unlike international trade anywhere in the world of the period."[33]

For the slaves themselves—seized in the interior, often sold several times on the harrowing journey to the coast, sometimes branded, and held in squalid slave dungeons while awaiting transportation to the New World—it was anything but a normal commercial transaction. One European engaged in the trade noted that "the negroes are so willful and loath to leave their own country, that they have often leap'd out of the canoes, boat, and ship, into the sea, and kept under water till they were drowned, to avoid being taken up and saved by our boats."[34]

Over the four centuries of the slave trade, millions of Africans underwent such experiences, but their numbers varied considerably over time. During the sixteenth century, slave exports from Africa averaged fewer than 3,000 annually. In those years, the Portuguese were at least as much interested in African gold, spices, and textiles. Furthermore, as in Asia, they became involved in transporting African goods, including slaves, from one African port to another, thus becoming the "truck drivers" of coastal West African commerce.[35] In the seventeenth century, the pace

Guided Reading Question

■ **CONNECTION**

What roles did Europeans and Africans play in the unfolding of the Atlantic slave trade?

picked up as the slave trade became highly competitive, with the British, Dutch, and French contesting the earlier Portuguese monopoly. The century and a half between 1700 and 1850 marked the high point of the slave trade as the plantation economies of the Americas boomed. (See Snapshot: The Slave Trade in Numbers.)

Geographically, the slave system drew mainly on the societies of West and South-Central Africa, from present-day Mauritania in the north to Angola in the south. Initially focused on the coastal regions, the slave raiding progressively penetrated into the interior as the demand for slaves picked up. Socially, these enslaved people were mostly drawn from various marginal groups in African societies—prisoners of war, criminals, debtors, people who had been "pawned" during times of difficulty. Thus Africans did not generally sell "their own people" into slavery. Divided into hundreds of separate,

The Middle Passage This mid-nineteenth-century painting of slaves held below decks on a Spanish slave ship illustrates the horrendous conditions of the transatlantic voyage, a journey experienced by many millions of captured Africans. (Watercolor by Lt. Francis Meinell, British Royal Navy, 1846/Granger, NYC—All rights reserved)

usually small-scale, and often rival communities—cities, kingdoms, microstates, clans, and villages—the various peoples of West Africa had no concept of an "African" identity. Those whom they captured and sold were normally outsiders, vulnerable people who lacked the protection of membership in an established community. When short-term economic or political advantage could be gained, such people were sold. In this respect, the transatlantic slave system was little different from the experience of enslavement elsewhere in the world.

The destination of enslaved Africans, half a world away in the Americas, however, made the transatlantic system very different. The vast majority wound up in Brazil or the Caribbean, where the labor demands of the plantation economy were most intense. Smaller numbers found themselves in North America, mainland Spanish America, or in Europe. Their journey across the Atlantic was horrendous, with the Middle Passage having an overall mortality rate of more than 14 percent.

Enslaved Africans frequently resisted their fates in a variety of ways. About 10 percent of the transatlantic voyages experienced a major rebellion by desperate captives, and resistance continued in the Americas, taking a range of forms from surreptitious slowdowns of work to outright rebellion. One common act was

SNAPSHOT The Slave Trade in Numbers (1501–1866)

The Rise and Decline of the Slave Trade

The Destination of Slaves

Figures indicate numbers of slaves disembarked

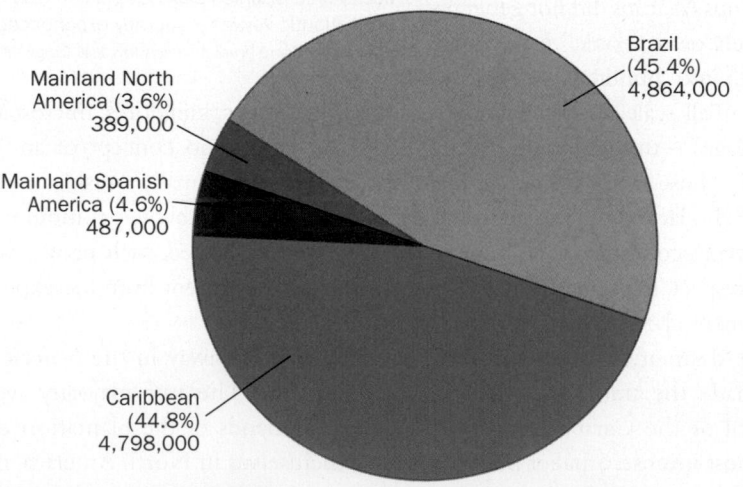

Mainland North America (3.6%) 389,000

Mainland Spanish America (4.6%) 487,000

Brazil (45.4%) 4,864,000

Caribbean (44.8%) 4,798,000

Data from Trans-Atlantic Slave Trade Database, accessed December 26, 2017, http://www.slavevoyages.org/assessment/estimates.

to flee. Many who escaped joined free communities of former slaves known as **maroon societies**, which were founded in remote regions, especially in South America and the Caribbean. The largest such settlement was **Palmares** in Brazil, which endured for most of the seventeenth century, housing 10,000 or more people, mostly of African descent but also including Native Americans, mestizos, and renegade whites. While slave owners feared wide-scale slave rebellions, these were rare, and even small-scale rebellions were usually crushed with great brutality. It was only with the Haitian Revolution of the 1790s that a full-scale slave revolt brought lasting freedom for its participants.

Consequences: The Impact of the Slave Trade in Africa

From the viewpoint of world history, the chief outcome of the transatlantic slave system lay in the new global linkages that it generated as Africa became a permanent part of an interacting Atlantic world. Millions of its people were now compelled to make their lives in the Americas, where they made an enormous impact both demographically and economically. Until the nineteenth century, they outnumbered European immigrants to the Americas by three or four to one, and West African societies were increasingly connected to an emerging European-centered world economy. These vast processes set in motion a chain of consequences that have transformed the lives and societies of people on both sides of the Atlantic.

Although the slave trade did not produce in Africa the kind of population collapse that occurred in the Americas, it certainly slowed Africa's growth at a time when Europe, China, and other regions were expanding demographically. Beyond the loss of millions of people over four centuries, the demand for African slaves produced economic stagnation and social disruption. Economically, the slave trade stimulated little positive change in Africa because those Africans who benefited most from the traffic in people were not investing in the productive capacities of their societies. Although European imports generally did not displace traditional artisan manufacturing, no technological breakthroughs in agriculture or industry increased the wealth available to these societies. Maize and manioc (cassava), introduced from the Americas, added a new source of calories to African diets, but the international demand was for Africa's people, not its agricultural products.

Socially too, the slave trade shaped African societies. It surely fostered moral corruption, particularly as judicial proceedings were manipulated to generate victims for export. A West African legend tells of cowrie shells, a major currency of the slave trade, growing on corpses of decomposing slaves, a symbolic recognition of the corrupting effects of this commerce in human beings.

African women felt the impact of the slave trade in various ways, beyond those who numbered among its transatlantic victims. Since far more men than women were shipped to the Americas, the labor demands on those women who remained increased substantially, compounded by the growing use of cassava, a labor-intensive

Guided Reading Question

■ **CHANGE**
In what different ways did the Atlantic slave trade transform African societies?

A *Signare* of Senegal While many women suffered greatly because of the Atlantic slave trade, a few grew quite wealthy and powerful. Known as *signares*, they married European merchants and built their own trading networks employing female slaves. The woman in this eighteenth-century French image was likely a signare. Depicted at the European slave port of St. Louis Island in Senegal, she is dressed in fashionable and expensive imported textiles and is accompanied by her slave. (Colored engraving from *Encyclopédie des Voyages*, 1796/Bibliothèque des Arts Decoratifs, Paris, France/Archives Charmet/Bridgeman Images)

import from the New World. Unbalanced sex ratios also meant that far more men than before could marry multiple women. Furthermore, the use of female slaves within West African societies grew as the export trade in male slaves expanded. Retaining female slaves for their own use allowed warriors and nobles in the Senegambia region to distinguish themselves more clearly from ordinary peasants. In the Kongo, female slaves provided a source of dependent laborers for the plantations that sustained the lifestyle of urban elites. A European merchant on the Gold Coast in the late eighteenth century observed that every free man had at least one or two slaves.

For much smaller numbers of women, the slave trade provided an opportunity to exercise power and accumulate wealth. In the Senegambia region, where women had long been involved in politics and commerce, marriage to European traders offered advantage to both partners. For European male merchants, as for fur traders in North America, such marriages afforded access to African-operated commercial networks as well as the comforts of domestic life. Some of the women involved in these cross-cultural marriages, known as ***signares***, became quite wealthy, operating their own trading empires, employing large numbers of female slaves, and acquiring elaborate houses, jewelry, and fashionable clothing.

Furthermore, the state-building enterprises that often accompanied the sale of slaves in West Africa offered yet other opportunities to a few women. As the Kingdom of Dahomey (deh-HOH-mee) expanded during the eighteenth century, the royal palace, housing thousands of women and presided over by a powerful Queen Mother, served to integrate the diverse regions of the state. Each lineage was required to send a daughter to the palace even as well-to-do families sent additional girls to increase their influence at court. In the Kingdom of Kongo, women held lower-level administrative positions, the head wife of a nobleman exercised authority over hundreds of junior wives and slaves, and women served on the council that advised the monarch. The neighboring region of Matamba was known for its female rulers, most notably the powerful Queen Nzinga (1626–1663), who guided the state amid the complexities and intrigues of various European and African rivalries and gained a reputation for her resistance to Portuguese imperialism.

Within particular African societies, the impact of the transatlantic slave system differed considerably from place to place and over time. Many small-scale kinship-based societies, lacking the protection of a strong state, were thoroughly disrupted by raids from more powerful neighbors, and insecurity was pervasive. Oral traditions in southern Ghana, for example, reported that "there was no rest in the land," that people went about in groups rather than alone, and that mothers kept their children inside when European ships appeared.[36] Some larger kingdoms such as Kongo and Oyo slowly disintegrated as access to trading opportunities and firearms enabled outlying regions to establish their independence. (For an account of one young man's journey to slavery and back, see Zooming In: Ayuba Suleiman Diallo, page 624.)

However, African authorities also sought to take advantage of the new commercial opportunities and to manage the slave trade in their own interests. The kingdom of **Benin**, in the forest area of present-day Nigeria, successfully avoided a deep involvement in the trade while diversifying the exports with which it purchased European firearms and other goods. As early as 1516, its ruler began to restrict the slave trade and soon forbade the export of male slaves altogether, a ban that lasted until the early eighteenth century. By then, the ruler's authority over outlying areas had declined, and the country's major exports of pepper and cotton cloth had lost out to Asian and then European competition. In these circumstances, Benin felt compelled to resume limited participation in the slave trade. The neighboring kingdom of **Dahomey**, on the other hand, turned to a vigorous involvement in the slave trade in the early eighteenth century under strict royal control. The army conducted annual slave raids, and the government soon came to depend on the trade for its essential revenues. The slave trade in Dahomey became the chief business of the state and remained so until well into the nineteenth century.

REFLECTIONS

Economic Globalization—Then and Now

The study of history reminds us of two quite contradictory truths. One is that our lives in the present bear remarkable similarities to those of people long ago. We are perhaps not so unique as we might think. The other is that our lives are very different from theirs and that things have changed substantially. This chapter about global commerce—long-distance trade in spices and textiles, silver and gold, beaver pelts and deerskins, slaves and sugar—provides both perspectives.

If we are accustomed to thinking about globalization as a product of the late twentieth century, early modern world history provides a corrective. Those three centuries reveal much that is familiar to people of the twenty-first century—the global circulation of goods; an international currency; production for a world market; the growing economic role of the West on the global stage; private enterprise, such as the British and Dutch East India companies, operating on a world scale; and national governments eager to support their merchants in a highly competitive environment.

Ayuba Suleiman Diallo: To Slavery and Back

February 1730 found Ayuba Suleiman Diallo, less than thirty years of age, living between the Gambia and Senegal rivers in West Africa among the Fulbe-speaking people.[37] Like his father, a prominent Islamic scholar and teacher, Ayuba was a Muslim who was literate in Arabic, a prayer leader in the local mosque, and a *hafiz*, someone who had memorized the entire Quran. He was also husband to two wives and father to four children. Now his father sent the young man on an errand. He was to take several of their many slaves to a location some 200 miles away, where an English trading ship had anchored, and exchange them for paper and other

Ayuba Suleiman Diallo.

goods. The paper was especially important, for his father's income depended on inscribing passages from the Quran on small slips of paper and selling them as protective charms.

To put it mildly, things did not go as planned. Unable to reach an agreement with the English merchant Captain Stephen Pike, Ayuba traveled farther south and traded his

slaves for a number of cows in the land of the Mandinka people. Well beyond the safety of his own country, he was in dangerous territory. As he and his companions stopped to rest on the journey home, they were seized, their heads were shaved, and they were sold as slaves to the very same Captain Pike. Although Ayuba was able to send a message to his father asking to be ransomed in exchange for some of their slaves, the ship sailed before a reply was received. And so Ayuba, along with 168 other slaves, both men and women, headed for the British American colony of Maryland, where 150 of them arrived alive.

Sold to a local planter, Ayuba was immediately sent to the tobacco fields, but when he became ill from this heavy and unaccustomed work, his owner assigned him the less

photo: Oil on canvas by William Hoare, of Bath (1707–1792)/Private Collection/Photo © Christie's Images/Bridgeman Images)

By the eighteenth century, many Europeans dined from Chinese porcelain dishes called china, wore Indian-made cotton textiles, and drank chocolate from Mexico, tea from China, and coffee from Yemen while sweetening these beverages with sugar from the Caribbean or Brazil. The millions who worked to produce these goods, whether slave or free, were operating in a world economy. Some industries were thoroughly international. New England rum producers, for example, depended on molasses imported from the Caribbean, where the West Indian sugar industry used African labor and European equipment to produce for a global market.

Nonetheless, early modern economic globalization was a far cry from that of the twentieth century. The most obvious differences, perhaps, were scale and speed. By 2000, immensely more goods circulated internationally, and far more people produced for and depended on the world market than was the case even in 1750. Back-and-forth communications between England and India that took eighteen months in the eighteenth century could be accomplished in an hour by telegraph in the late nineteenth century and almost instantaneously via the Internet in the late twentieth century. Moreover, by 1900 globalization was firmly centered in arduous and more familiar task of tending cattle. Alone with the cattle, Ayuba was able to withdraw into a nearby forest to pray, but he was spotted by a young white boy who mocked him and threw dirt in his face. Sometime later, no doubt in despair, Ayuba ran away, but he was soon captured and housed in the county jail, located in the back room of a tavern. There he became something of a local curiosity and attracted the attention of a lawyer named Thomas Bluett. When Ayuba refused wine, wrote a few lines in Arabic, and mentioned "Allah" and "Muhammad," Bluett realized that he was "no common slave." After locating an old slave who could translate for him, Bluett became fascinated by Ayuba's story, and he initiated a process that took both of them to England in 1733, where philanthropists purchased Ayuba's freedom.

Ayuba's reception in England was amazing. Now fluent in English, Ayuba was received by the English royal family and various members of the nobility, hosted by leading scholars, and entertained by wealthy merchants, eager to tap his knowledge of economic conditions in West Africa. The prominent artist William Hoare painted his portrait, complete with a small Quran hanging from his neck.

In 1734, he finally set off for home, loaded with gifts from his English friends. There he encountered, quite by chance, the same Mandinka men who had sold him only a few years before. Francis Moore, a European trader accompanying Ayuba, wrote that he "fell into a most terrible passion and was for killing them" and was restrained from doing so only with difficulty. He arrived in his hometown to find that his father had recently died. His wives and children, however, were all alive and welcomed him warmly. One of his wives had remarried, believing him gone forever, but her new husband readily gave way, and Ayuba resumed his place of prominence in his own community until his death in 1773.

He also resumed his life as a slave owner. Selling some of the gifts he had acquired in England, he purchased a woman slave and two horses soon after his arrival back in West Africa. According to Moore, he "spoke always very handsomely of the English," and he continued his association with the Royal African Company, the primary English trading firm in West Africa, in their rivalry with French traders.[38] The last mention of Ayuba in the records of that company noted that he was seeking compensation for the loss of two slaves and a watch, probably the one given him in England by Queen Caroline.

QUESTIONS

What might you infer about Ayuba's own view of slavery and the slave trade? What insights or questions about the slave trade does his remarkable story suggest?

---

the economics of Europe and North America. In the early modern era, by contrast, Asia in general and China in particular remained major engines of the world economy, despite the emerging presence of Europeans around the world. By the end of the twentieth century, the booming economies of Turkey, Brazil, India, and China suggested at least a partial return to that earlier pattern.

Early modern globalization differed in still other ways from that of the contemporary world. Economic life then was primarily preindustrial: it was still powered by human and animal muscles, wind, and water and lacked the enormous productive capacity that accompanied the later technological breakthroughs of the steam engine and the Industrial Revolution. Finally, the dawning of a genuinely global economy in the early modern era was tied unapologetically to empire building and to slavery, both of which had been discredited by the late twentieth century. Slavery lost its legitimacy during the nineteenth century, and formal territorial empires largely disappeared in the twentieth. Most people during the early modern era would have been surprised to learn that a global economy, as it turned out, could function effectively without either of these long-standing practices.

Second Thoughts

What's the Significance?

Indian Ocean commercial network, 596

trading post empire, 598

Philippines (Spanish), 599

Manila, 600

British East India Company, 600

Dutch East India Company, 600

"silver drain," 605

piece of eight, 605

Potosí, 605

fur trade, 608

"soft gold," 611

transatlantic slave system, 612

African diaspora, 612

maroon societies / Palmares, 621

signares, 622

Benin, 623

Dahomey, 623

Big Picture Questions

1. To what extent did Europeans transform earlier patterns of commerce, and in what ways did they assimilate into those older patterns?
2. How should we distribute the moral responsibility for the transatlantic slave system? Is this an appropriate task for historians?
3. What lasting legacies of early modern globalization are evident today?
4. **Looking Back:** Asians, Africans, and Native Americans experienced early modern European expansion in quite different ways. Based on Chapters 13 and 14, how might you describe and explain those differences? How were they active agents in the historical process rather than simply victims of European actions?

Next Steps: For Further Study

Glenn J. Ames, *The Globe Encompassed: The Age of European Discovery, 1500–1700* (2007). An up-to-date survey of European expansion in the early modern era.

Andre Gunder Frank, *ReOrient: Global Economy in the Asian Age* (1998). An account of the early modern world economy that highlights the centrality of Asia.

Erik Gilbert and Jonathan Reynolds, *Trading Tastes: Commodity and Cultural Exchange to 1750* (2006). A world historical perspective on transcontinental commerce.

David Northrup, ed., *The Atlantic Slave Trade* (2002). A fine collection of essays about the origins, practice, impact, and abolition of Atlantic slavery.

John Richards, *The Endless Frontier* (2003). Explores the ecological consequences of early modern commerce.

John K. Thornton, *A Cultural History of the Atlantic World, 1250–1820* (2012). A recent account of the intersection of European, African, and Native American people.

"Voyages: The Trans-Atlantic Slave Trade Database," http://www.slavevoyages.org. An enormous and searchable collection of information, maps, charts, and graphs on the Atlantic slave system.

"Pepper: the Master Spice," *The Spice of Life*, British Broadcasting Corporation, 1983, https://www.youtube.com/watch?v=NuZujx-LMfg. A BBC film that presents the history of pepper, so central to the spice trade of the early modern era.

Exchange and Status in the Early Modern World

As global commerce expanded in the early modern era, so too did the exchange of foods, fashions, finery, and more. In the centuries that followed, growing numbers of people all across the world, particularly in elite social circles, had access to luxury goods from far away with which they could display, and perhaps enhance, their status. Some of these goods—sugar, pepper, tobacco, tea, and Indian cotton textiles, for example—gradually dropped in price, becoming more widely available. The sources that follow illustrate this relationship between global trade and the display of status during the several centuries after 1500, using clothing, coffee, and tobacco as examples.

SOURCE 14.1 Clothing and Status in the Americas ▶

Imported fabrics and garments offered an important means of displaying one's status in public settings. Source 14.1 shows a woman of Native American ancestry (*India*) and a man of African/Indian descent (*Chino combujo*) as well as their child, who is categorized as a *loba*, or "wolf." The image comes from a series of paintings created in eighteenth-century Mexico by the well-known Zapotec artist Miguel Cabrera to depict some eighteen or more mixed-race couples and their children, each with a distinct designation. The woman in this image is wearing a *huipil*, a traditional Maya tunic or blouse, while the man is dressed in a European-style waistcoat, vest, and lace shirt, while holding a black tricorne hat, widely popular in Europe during the seventeenth and eighteenth centuries. While this system slotted people into a hierarchical social order defined by race and heritage, it did allow for some social mobility. If individuals managed to acquire some education, land, or money, they might gain in social prestige and even pass as members of a more highly favored category. Adopting the dress and lifestyle of higher-ranking groups could facilitate this process.

- What indications of status ambition or upward mobility can you identify in Source 14.1? Keep in mind that status here is associated with race and gender as well as the possession of foreign products.

- Why do you think the woman is shown in more traditional costume, while the man is portrayed in European dress?

- In what cultural traditions do you think this couple raised their daughter? What problems might they have experienced in the process?

MIGUEL CABRERA | *Detail from a Series on Mixed-Race Marriages in Mexico* | 1763

De Chino·cambuyo·ydlndia; Loba.

SOURCE 14.2 **Clothing and Status in Europe** ▶

In Europe as well, clothing was used to display wealth and status, and the arrival of rare, exotic fabrics and garments during the early modern period provided new opportunities for the display of social sophistication. Source 14.2, a portrait of the German princess Sophie of the Palatinate in southwest Germany (1630–1714), is remarkable for the period because she is wearing an elaborate red feather headdress and cape originally made by indigenous peoples from Brazil. Such featherworks were worn by their indigenous creators at important rituals, such as those associated with the killing of captives, where feathers symbolically transformed both the killer and victim into birds. But in Europe these rare and beautiful items were integrated into court pageants, entertainments, and ballets, where they were employed as the identifying symbol of Amerindians. By the seventeenth century, Europeans were associating Amerindians with Amazons—a mythical society of warrior women described by the ancient Greeks—and portraying Amazons in their pageants and entertainments with American featherworks as well.

■   How are European and Brazilian elements mixed in this painting? Note the various garments of clothing that Sophie is wearing. What do you make of the European clasp securing her Brazilian feather cloak and the background scenery?

■   How is Sophie demonstrating her status in this portrait? What specific messages might she hope to convey by donning the headdress and cape?

■   To what extent did featherworks like that worn by Sophie lose their original cultural context and meaning when they were taken to Europe? To what extent did their Brazilian origins shape their uses in Europe?

■   What can Sources 14.1 and 14.2 tell us about the relationship between clothing and status in the early modern world?

Portrait of Sophie of the Palatinate | 1645

Oil on canvas by Louise Hollandine of the Palatinate (1622–1709)/Museum Wasserburg Anholt, Isselburg, Germany/akg-images

■ ■ ■

SOURCE 14.3 A Critical View of Coffeehouses in the Ottoman Empire

As coffee entered the Ottoman Empire in the sixteenth century from its place of origin in Ethiopia and Yemen, it encountered considerable opposition, partly because it was consumed in the new social arena of the coffeehouse. Authorities suspected, sometimes quite rightly, that coffeehouses were places of moral decadence and political intrigue. Moralists in the Islamic world labeled the coffeehouse a "refuge of Satan" that drew people away from the mosques even as it brought together all different classes. In Source 14.3, Mustafa bin Ahmed (1541–1600), an

Ottoman official and writer better known by his pen name Mustafa Ali, offers a largely negative assessment of Cairo's coffeehouses in his description of a visit to the city in 1599.

- What is it about coffeehouses that Ali criticizes? Does he see any positive role for coffeehouses in society?

- How might Ali's role as an Ottoman official shape his view of coffeehouses?

- How might one of the "veteran soldiers" or "aged officers" that he identifies react to his description?

MUSTAFA ALI | *Description of Cairo* | 1599

Also [remarkable] is the multitude of coffee-houses in the city of Cairo, the concentration of coffee-houses at every step, and of perfect places where people can assemble. Early rising worshippers and pious men get up and go [there], drink a cup of coffee adding life to their life. They feel, in a way, that its slight exhilaration strengthens them for their religious observance and worship. From that point of view their coffee-houses are commended and praised. But if one considers the ignorant people that assemble in them it is questionable whether they deserve praise....

To make it short, the coffee-houses of Egypt are filled mostly with dissolute persons and opium-eaters.

Many are occupied by veteran soldiers, aged officers. When they arrive early in the morning rags and rush mats are spread out, and they stay until evening.... [These former military men] are a bunch of parasites... whose work consists of presiding over the coffeehouse, of drinking coffee on credit, talking of frugality, when the matter comes up, and, having told certain matters with all sorts of distortions.... In other words, their talk is mostly lies, their nonsensical speeches are either gossip and backbiting or slander and calumny....

Source: Mustafa Ali, *Mustafa Ali's Description of Cairo of 1599*, translated by Andreas Tietze (Vienna: Verlag der Österreichischen Akademie Der Wissenschaften, 1975), 37.

■ ■ ■

SOURCE 14.4 An Ottoman Coffeehouse ▶

Critics like Ali failed to stop the spread of coffee in the Ottoman Empire, where it came to embody a new "public culture of fun" as it wore away at earlier religious restrictions on the enjoyment of life.[39] Source 14.4 depicts the new social space of the Turkish coffeehouse, including the numerous activities that accompanied coffee drinking.

- What specific activities can you identify in this painting?

- Would you read this painting as critical of the coffeehouse, as celebrating it, or as a neutral description? Note that the musicians and those playing board games at the bottom are engaged in activities that were considered rather disreputable. How would you describe the general demeanor of the men in the coffeehouse?

- How do you think that Ali in Source 14.3 might react to this image?

A Gathering of Turkish Men at an Ottoman Coffeehouse │ 16th century

• • •

SOURCE 14.5 Coffeehouse Culture in England

Coffee spread from the Ottoman Empire to Europe, where authorities worried that coffee and coffeehouses encouraged both laziness and disorder, as King Charles II proclaimed in a short-lived effort to ban coffeehouses in his kingdom: "Many Tradesmen and others, do herein misspend much of their time, which might and probably would be employed in and about their Lawful Calling and Affairs; but also, for that in such Houses . . . divers false, malitious and scandalous reports are devised and spread abroad to the Defamation of His Majestie's Government, and to the Disturbance of the Peace and Quiet of the Realm."[40] But European authorities had even less success than their Ottoman counterparts in restraining coffee use. "News from the Coffee-house," a song published in 1667 by the actor and poet Thomas Jordan, conveys the types of conversation that one might expect at a coffeehouse in seventeenth-century London.

- What impression does this song give you of the type of atmosphere one would find in a seventeenth-century English coffeehouse? What sorts of topics were discussed at a coffeehouse?

- Does "News from the Coffee-house" support the case made by Charles II when he issued his ban just a few years after Jordan penned this song?

- How might Jordan respond to the criticism leveled against coffeehouses by Ali in Source 14.3 or by Charles II?

THOMAS JORDAN | *News from the Coffee-house* | 1667

You that delight in Wit and Mirth,
And long to hear such News,
As comes from all parts of the Earth,
Dutch, Danes, and Turks and Jews,
I'll send you a Rendezvous,
Where it is smoking new;
Go hear it at a *Coffee-house*;
It cannot but be true.

There battles and sea-fights are fought,
And bloody plots displayed;
They know more things that ere was thought,
Or ever was betrayed:
No money in the Minting-house
Is half so bright and new;
And coming from the coffee-house,
It cannot but be true. . . .

The drinking there of chocolate
Can make a fool a Sophy [wise man];

'Tis thought the Turkish Mahomet
  [Muhammad]
Was first inspired with coffee,
By which his powers did overflow
The land of Palestine;
Then let us to the coffee-house go,
'Tis cheaper far than wine.

You shall know there what fashions are,
How periwiggs are curl'd,
And for a penny you shall heare
All novells in the world;
Both old and young, and great and small,
And rich and poore, you'll see;
Therefore let's to the coffee all,
Come all away with me.

Source: R. Chambers, ed., *The Book of Days: A Miscellany of Popular Antiquities in Connection with the Calendar* (London: W. & R. Chambers, 1879), 1:172–73.

■ ■ ■

SOURCE 14.6 Tobacco Smoking in Eurasia

Tobacco, like coffee, soon found a growing range of consumers all across Eurasia in the sixteenth and seventeenth centuries. Originating in the Americas, tobacco smoking spread quickly to Europe and Asia. Typically "lower sorts"—sailors, soldiers, laborers—brought tobacco to new regions, and almost everywhere elites criticized smoking upon its first arrival. In the Ottoman Empire, for instance, it provoked strenuous opposition on the grounds that it was an intoxicant, like wine, and was associated with unwholesome and promiscuous behavior. The rulers of England, China, the Ottoman Empire—and with greater effect Russia—published promulgations or laws against the production and consumption of tobacco. In Source 14.6, King James I of England offers his reasons for opposing tobacco in his treatise *A Counterblaste to Tobacco*, published in 1604. His arguments were designed to counter common reasons for using tobacco at the opening of the seventeenth century, providing a window into the debate raging in Europe just as tobacco was becoming increasingly available.

■ What arguments against smoking does James I put forward?

■ What can we learn about why people took up smoking from James's critique of the practice?

■ How do James's criticisms of smoking compare to those advanced by opponents of smoking in the twenty-first century?

KING JAMES I │ *A Counterblaste to Tobacco* │ 1604

For *Tobacco* being a common herb, which . . . grows almost every where, was first found out by some of the barbarous Indians, to be a Preservative, or Antidote against the Pox. . . . [S]o from them likewise was brought this use of *Tobacco*. . . . Why do we not as well imitate them in walking naked as they do? In preferring glasses, feathers and such toys, to gold and precious stones, as they do? yea why do we not deny God and adore the Devil as they do? [James then rejects arguments that smoking offers health benefits]

. . . And so from hand to hand it spreads until it be practiced by all; not for any commodity [usefulness] that is in it, but only because it is come to be the fashion. . . .

Now how you are by this custom disabled in your goods [made poorer], let the Gentry of this land bear witness. Some of them bestowing three, some four hundred pounds [English currency] a year upon this precious stink, which I am sure might be bestowed upon many far better uses. . . .

[H]erein is not only a great vanity but a great contempt for God's good gifts, that the sweetness of man's breath, being a good gift of God, should be willfully corrupted by this stinking smoke. . . . A custom loathsome to the eye, hateful to the Nose, harmful to the brain, dangerous to the Lungs. . . .

Source: King James I, *A Counterblaste to Tobacco* (London: R. B., 1604), not paginated. Spelling modernized. Whole text available at https://books.google.com/books?id=EasUAAAAYAAJ&printsec=frontcover&dq=james+I+counterblaste+to+tobacco&hl=en&sa=X&ved=0ahUKEwiU3Iatx7vUAhVE3WMKHSCdCD0Q6AEIJDAA#v=onepage&q=spreads&f=false.

■ ■ ■

SOURCE 14.7 Chinese Poems about Smoking

Laws against the production and consumption of tobacco were largely ineffective, and tobacco use quickly spread to all levels of society across Eurasia. As one seventeenth-century observer in China put it: "Among those throughout the realm who enjoy smoking there is no distinction of high and low, or of male and female."[41] This enthusiasm for tobacco was expressed in the verses in Source 14.7, written by elite Chinese poets and compiled in Cheng Cong's *Tobacco Manual* in 1805.

■ When reading the first selection of Source 14.7, keep in mind that elite Chinese smokers often linked exhaled smoke to the clouds associated with the realm of the immortals or to rituals associated with the summoning of spirits. What spiritual imagery is incorporated into this poem?

■ Smokers established their status both by possessing ornate or expensive tools for smoking, like the "elephant's tusk"—a carved ivory pipe—described in the second selection of Source 14.7, and by showing awareness of social customs associated with smoking. How do the final two poems reflect these aspects of elite smoking culture?

Poems from Cheng Cong's Tobacco Manual | **17th and 18th centuries**

---

[1]

Soul-summoning fragrance rises from the
  tobacco
All over the country all the time the plant is
  being picked.
I laugh to think that in days of yore people
  had only ordinary leaves
As I watch a world of smoke and cloud pour
  out of you.

[2]

Through my pipe I draw the fiery vapour,
From out of my chest I spew white clouds.
The attendant takes away the ash.
Brings wine to amplify the intoxication.

I apply the flame to know the taste,
Letting it burn in the elephant's tusk.

[3]

The tobacco box is casually produced for my
  arriving guest,
A gentleman who has known all the matters of
  my heart for a decade.
Poetic blossoms have sprung from his brush
  since childhood,
And now *The Tobacco Manual* emerges from
  our clouds of smoke.

Source: Timothy Brook, *Vermeer's Hat: The Seventeenth Century and the Dawn of the Global World* (London: Bloomsbury, 2008), 144 [1], 143 [2], 144–45 [3].

DOING HISTORY

1. **Analyzing the display of status:** In what different ways did the possession of foreign objects convey status in the early modern world?

2. **Thinking about the social implications of consumption:** How did consumption of new products create new social environments?

3. **Raising questions about cultural borrowing:** What do these sources suggest about the problems and opportunities caused by cross-cultural borrowing?

4. **Making connections:** In our own time objects continue to be traded and exchanged between cultures. What examples of goods taken from one country and used in another to display high status can you identify in the highly globalized world of the twenty-first century?

Coffee and Coffeeshops

Coffee's spread across Eurasia sparked debates and controversies over its use even as it created new spaces for consumption and social interaction. In Voice 14.1, journalist and historian Tom Standage explores the Muslim debate surrounding the consumption of coffee in the early modern period. In Voice 14.2, independent scholar and author Mark Pendergrast offers a description of coffeehouse culture in seventeenth-century London and its relationship with tavern culture organized around drinking alcohol.

- According to Standage, what issues were at stake in the Muslim debate over coffee?
- According to Pendergrast, how did the arrival of coffee impact the drinking of alcohol in England?
- **Integrating Primary and Secondary Sources:** How do these voices enhance your understanding of coffeehouse culture beyond what is contained in Sources 14.3–14.5? How might you integrate the sources and voices together to create a more complete picture of coffee culture in the early modern period?

VOICE 14.1

Tom Standage on Muslim Debates over Coffee's Intoxicating Effects | 2005

As coffee percolated throughout the Arab world . . . the exact nature of its physical effects became the subject of much controversy. . . . It was embraced as a legal alternative to alcohol by many Muslims. Coffeehouses, unlike the illicit taverns that sold alcohol, were places where respectable people could afford to be seen. But coffee's legal state was ambiguous. Some Muslim scholars objected that it was intoxicating and therefore subject to the same religious prohibition as wine . . . which the prophet Muhammad had prohibited. . . .

But was coffee really an intoxicant? Muslim scholars had already spent much effort debating whether the prophet had meant to ban intoxicating drinks altogether or merely the act of drinking to intoxication. Everyone agreed on the need for a legal definition of intoxication, and several such definitions were duly devised. An intoxicated person was variously defined as someone who "becomes absent-minded and confused," "departs from whatever he has in the way of mild virtue and tranquility

into foolishness and ignorance," or "comprehends absolutely nothing at all, and who does not know a man from a woman, or the earth from the heavens." . . .

Yet coffee clearly failed to produce any such effects in the drinker, even when consumed in large quantities. In fact it did quite the opposite. . . .

Source: Tom Standage, *A History of the World in 6 Glasses* (London: Bloomsbury, 2005), 137–39.

VOICE 14.2

Mark Pendergrast on London's Coffeehouses | 2010

Before the advent of coffee, the British imbibed alcohol, often in Falstaffian proportions [Falstaff was a character in Shakespeare's plays who regularly drank to excess]. "What immoderate drinking every place!" complained a British commentator in 1624. "How they flock to the tavern! [Here they] drown their wits, seeth their brains in ale." Fifty years later another observed that "coffee-drinking hath caused a greater sobriety among the nations; for whereas formerly Apprentices and Clerks with others, used to take their mornings' draught In Ale, Beer or Wine, which by the dizziness they cause in the Brain, make many unfit for business, they use now to play the Good-fellows In this wakeful and civill [sic] drink."

Not that most coffeehouses were universally uplifting places; rather, they were chaotic, smelly, wildly energetic, and capitalistic. "There was a rabble going hither and thither, reminding me of a swarm of rats in a ruinous cheese-store," one contemporary noted. "Some came, others went; some were scribbling, others were talking; some were drinking, some smoking, and some arguing; the whole place stank of tobacco like the cabin of a barge." . . .

The *Women's Petition* [a pamphlet published in 1674] revealed that a typical male day involved spending the morning in a tavern "till every one of them is as Drunk as a Drum, and then back again to the Coffee-house to drink themselves sober." Then they were off to the tavern again, only to "stager back to *Soberize* themselves with Coffee." . . .

Source: Mark Pendergrast, *Uncommon Grounds: The History of Coffee and How It Transformed Our World*, rev. ed. (New York: Basic Books, 2010), 13.

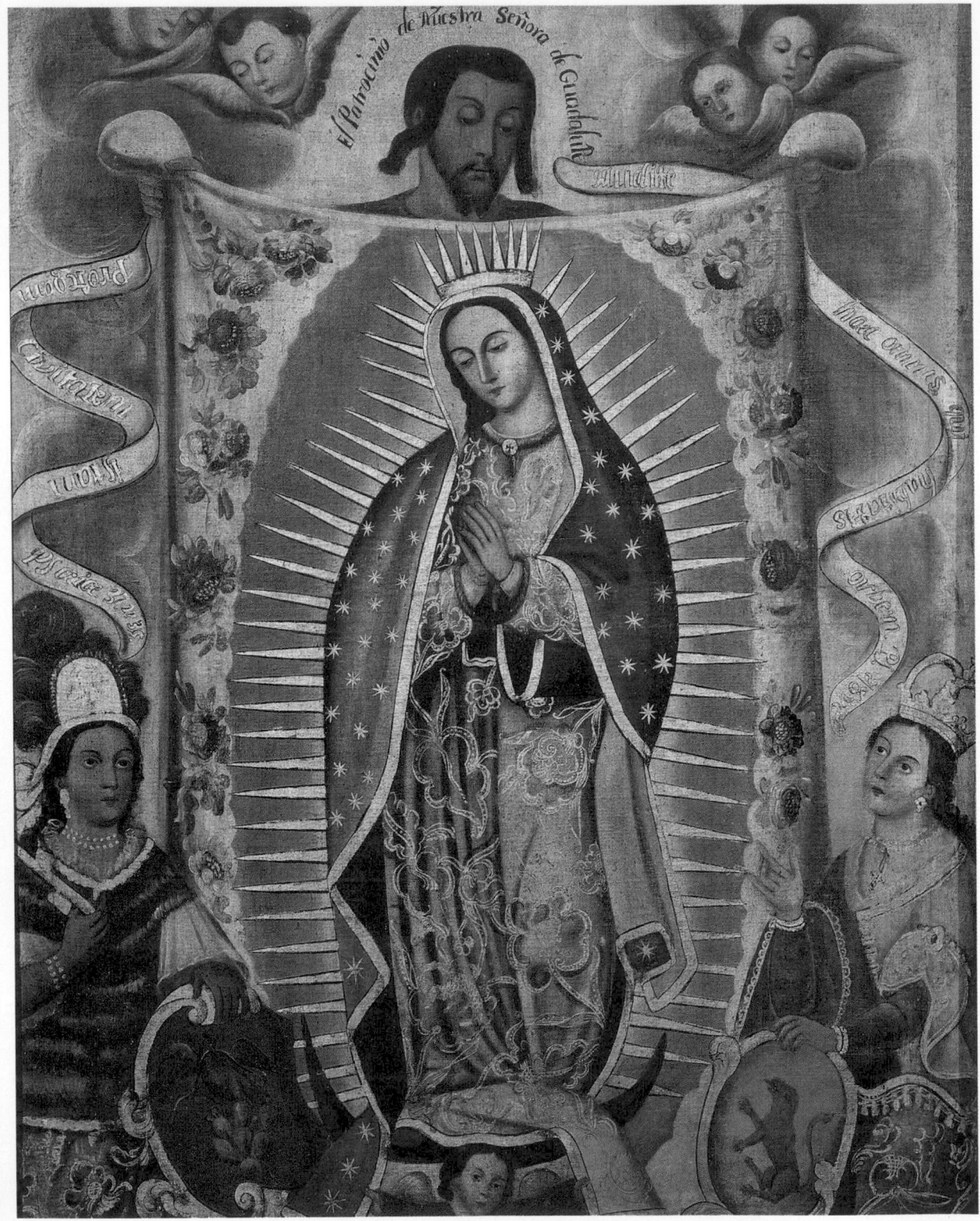

CHAPTER 15

Cultural Transformations

Religion and Science

1450–1750

《 The Virgin of Guadalupe According to Mexican tradition, a dark-skinned Virgin Mary appeared to an indigenous peasant named Juan Diego in 1531, an apparition reflected in this Mexican painting from 1720. Belief in the Virgin of Guadalupe represented the incorporation of European Catholicism into the emerging culture and identity of Mexico.

"We couldn't just throw up our hands and see these churches turned into nightclubs or mosques."[1] this was the view expressed in 2006 by Tokunboh Adeyemo, a Nigerian church leader and scholar, referring to a growing movement among African Christian organizations to bring the Gospel back to an "increasingly godless West." It represented a remarkable shift from earlier efforts by European and North American missionaries to bring Christianity to Africa and Asia, beginning in the early modern era. One reason for the discarded churches in the West lay in another cultural change—the spread of modern scientific and secular thinking, which for some people rendered religion irrelevant. That enormous transformation likewise took shape in the early modern era. ■

And so, alongside new empires and new patterns of commerce, the early modern centuries also witnessed novel cultural and religious transformations that likewise connected distant peoples. Riding the currents of European empire building and commercial expansion, Christianity was established solidly in the Americas and the Philippines and, though far more modestly, in Siberia, China, Japan, and India. A cultural tradition largely limited to Europe in 1500 now became a genuine world religion, spawning a multitude of cultural encounters—though it spread hardly at all within the vast and still-growing domains of Islam. While Christianity was spreading, a new understanding of the universe and a new approach to knowledge were taking shape among European thinkers of the Scientific Revolution, giving rise to

639

another kind of cultural encounter—that between science and religion. Science was a new and competing worldview, and for some it became almost a new religion. In time, it grew into a defining feature of global modernity, achieving a worldwide acceptance that exceeded that of Christianity or any other religious tradition.

Although Europeans were central players in the globalization of Christianity and the emergence of modern science, they were not alone in shaping the cultural transformations of the early modern era. Asian, African, and Native American peoples largely determined how Christianity would be accepted, rejected, or transformed as it entered new cultural environments. Science emerged within an international and not simply a European context, and it met varying receptions in different parts of

SEEKING THE MAIN POINT

To what extent did the cultural changes of the early modern world derive from cross-cultural interaction? And to what extent did they grow from within particular societies or civilizations?

the world. Islam continued a long pattern of religious expansion and renewal, even as Christianity began to compete with it as a world religion. Buddhism maintained its hold in much of East Asia, as did Hinduism in South Asia and numerous smaller-scale religious traditions in Africa. And Europeans themselves were certainly affected by the many "new worlds" that they now encountered. The cultural interactions of the early modern era, in short, did not take place on a one-way street.

The Globalization of Christianity

Despite its Middle Eastern origins and its earlier presence in many parts of the Afro-Asian world, Christianity was largely limited to Europe at the beginning of the early modern era. In 1500, the world of Christendom stretched from the Iberian Peninsula and British Isles in the west to Russia in the east, with small and beleaguered communities of various kinds in Egypt, Ethiopia, southern India, and Central Asia. Internally, the Christian world was seriously divided between the Roman Catholics of Western and Central Europe and the Eastern Orthodox of Eastern Europe and Russia. Externally, it was very much on the defensive against an expansive Islam. Muslims had ousted Christian Crusaders from their toeholds in the Holy Land by 1300, and with the Ottoman seizure of Constantinople in 1453, they had captured the prestigious capital of Eastern Orthodoxy. The Ottoman siege of Vienna in 1529, and again in 1683, marked a Muslim advance into the heart of Central Europe. Except in Spain and Sicily, which had recently been reclaimed for Christendom after centuries of Muslim rule, the future, it must have seemed, lay with Islam rather than Christianity.

Western Christendom Fragmented: The Protestant Reformation

As if these were not troubles enough, in the early sixteenth century the **Protestant Reformation** shattered the unity of Roman Catholic Christianity, which for the previous 1,000 years had provided the cultural and organizational foundation of an emerging Western European civilization. The Reformation began in 1517 when a

Landmarks for Chapter 15

	1450	1500	1550	1600	1650	1700	1750

EUROPE

1517 ■
Martin Luther posts 95 Theses;
beginning of Protestant
Reformation

■ **1543**
Copernicus, *On the Revolutions of the Heavenly Spheres*

1543–1727
Scientific Revolution

■ **1609** Galileo develops improved telescope

1545–1563
Council of Trent

1618–1648
Thirty Years' War

1642–1727
Life of Isaac Newton

1694–1778
Life of Voltaire

18th century
European Enlightenment

LATIN AMERICA

■ **1531** Juan Diego's vision of Virgin of Guadalupe

1560s
Taki Onqoy in Peru

1530s–1700
Widespread conversion to Christianity

■ **1535**
Bishop of Mexico destroys
traditional shrines and "idols"

ASIA

1469–1539 Life of Guru Nanak, founder of Sikhism

1498–1547 Life of Mirabai, bhakti poet

■ **1580** Muslim astronomical observatory dismantled

1582–1610 Jesuit missionary Matteo Ricci in China

■ **1636** Beginning of Japan's closure to the West

1715 ■
Jesuits lose favor at Chinese court

1740–1818
Wahhabi Islam in Arabia

German priest, **Martin Luther** (1483–1546), publicly invited debate about various abuses within the Roman Catholic Church by issuing a document, known as the Ninety-Five Theses, allegedly nailing it to the door of a church in Wittenberg. In itself, this was nothing new, for many had long been critical of the luxurious life of the popes,

The Protestant Reformation An engraving of Martin Luther nailing his Ninety-Five Theses to the door of the Wittenberg castle church in 1517, thus launching the Protestant Reformation. (Photo © Tarker/Bridgeman Images)

the corruption and immorality of some clergy, the Church's selling of indulgences (said to remove the penalties for sin), and other aspects of church life and practice.

What made Luther's protest potentially revolutionary, however, was its theological basis. A troubled and brooding man anxious about his relationship with God, Luther had recently come to a new understanding of salvation, which, he believed, came through faith alone. Neither the good works of the sinner nor the sacraments of the Church had any bearing on the eternal destiny of the soul. To Luther, the source of these beliefs, and of religious authority in general, was not the teaching of the Church, but the Bible alone, interpreted according to the individual's conscience. All of this challenged the authority of the Church and called into question the special position of the clerical hierarchy and of the pope in particular. In sixteenth-century Europe, this was the stuff of revolution. (See the Snapshot: Catholic/Protestant Differences in the Sixteenth Century, page 643.)

Contrary to Luther's original intentions, his ideas provoked a massive schism within the world of Catholic Christendom, for they came to express a variety of political, economic, and social tensions as well as religious differences. Some kings and princes, many of whom had long disputed the political authority of the pope, found in these ideas a justification for their own independence and an opportunity to gain the lands and taxes previously held by the Church. In the Protestant idea that all vocations were of equal merit, middle-class urban dwellers found a new religious legitimacy for their growing role in society, since the Roman Catholic

Guided Reading Question

▪ **CHANGE**

In what ways did the Protestant Reformation transform European society, culture, and politics?

SNAPSHOT Catholic/Protestant Differences in the Sixteenth Century

	Catholic	Protestant
Religious authority	Pope and church hierarchy	The Bible, as interpreted by individual Christians
Role of the pope	Ultimate authority in faith and doctrine	Authority of the pope denied
Ordination of clergy	Apostolic succession: direct line between original apostles and all subsequently ordained clergy	Apostolic succession denied; ordination by individual congregations or denominations
Salvation	Importance of church sacraments as channels of God's grace	Importance of faith alone; God's grace is freely and directly granted to believers
Status of Mary	Highly prominent, ranking just below Jesus; provides constant intercession for believers	Less prominent; Mary's intercession on behalf of the faithful denied
Prayer	To God, but often through or with Mary and saints	To God alone; no role for Mary and saints
Holy Communion	Transubstantiation: bread and wine become the actual body and blood of Christ	Transubstantiation denied; bread and wine have a spiritual or symbolic significance
Role of clergy	Priests are generally celibate; sharp distinction between priests and laypeople; priests are mediators between God and humankind	Ministers may marry; priesthood of all believers; clergy have different functions (to preach, administer sacraments) but no distinct spiritual status
Role of saints	Prominent spiritual exemplars and intermediaries between God and humankind	Generally disdained as a source of idolatry; saints refer to all Christians

Church was associated in their eyes with the rural and feudal world of aristocratic privilege. For common people, who were offended by the corruption and luxurious living of some bishops, abbots, and popes, the new religious ideas served to express their opposition to the entire social order, particularly in a series of German peasant revolts in the 1520s.

Although large numbers of women were attracted to Protestantism, Reformation teachings and practices did not offer them a substantially greater role in the Church or society. In Protestant-dominated areas, the veneration of Mary and female saints ended, leaving the male Christ figure as the sole object of worship. Protestant opposition to celibacy and monastic life closed the convents, which had offered some women an alternative to marriage. Nor were Protestants (except the Quakers) any more willing than Catholics to offer women an official role within their churches. The importance that Protestants gave to reading the Bible for oneself stimulated education and literacy for women, but given the emphasis on women as wives and mothers subject to male supervision, they had little opportunity to use that education outside of the family.

Reformation thinking spread quickly both within and beyond Germany, thanks in large measure to the recent invention of the printing press. Luther's many pamphlets and his translation of the New Testament into German were soon widely available. "God has appointed the [printing] Press to preach, whose voice the pope is never able to stop," declared the English Protestant writer John Foxe in 1563.[2] As the movement spread to France, Switzerland, England, and elsewhere, it also divided, amoeba-like, into a variety of competing Protestant churches—Lutheran, Calvinist, Anglican, Quaker, Anabaptist—many of which subsequently subdivided, producing a bewildering array of Protestant denominations. Each was distinctive, but none gave allegiance to Rome or the pope.

Thus to the sharp class divisions and the fractured political system of Europe was now added the potent brew of religious difference, operating both within and between states (see Map 15.1). For more than thirty years (1562–1598), French society was torn by violence between Catholics and the Protestant minority known as Huguenots (HYOO-guh-naht). The culmination of European religious conflict took shape in the **Thirty Years' War** (1618–1648), a Catholic–Protestant struggle that began in the Holy Roman Empire but eventually engulfed most of Europe. It was a horrendously destructive war, during which, scholars estimate, between 15 and 30 percent of the German population perished from violence, famine, or disease. Finally, the Peace of Westphalia (1648) brought the conflict to an end, with some reshuffling of boundaries and an agreement that each state was sovereign, authorized to control religious affairs within its own territory. Whatever religious unity Catholic Europe had once enjoyed was now permanently splintered.

The Protestant breakaway, combined with reformist tendencies within the Catholic Church itself, provoked a Catholic Reformation, or **Counter-Reformation**. In the Council of Trent (1545–1563), Catholics clarified and reaffirmed their unique doctrines, sacraments, and practices, such as the authority of the pope, priestly celibacy, the veneration of saints and relics, and the importance of church tradition and good works, all of which Protestants had rejected. Moreover, they set about correcting the abuses and corruption that had stimulated the Protestant movement by placing a new emphasis on the education of priests and their supervision by bishops. A crackdown on dissidents included the censorship of books, fines, exile, penitence, and sometimes the burning of heretics. Renewed attention was given to individual spirituality and personal piety. New religious orders, such as the Society of Jesus (Jesuits), provided a dedicated brotherhood of priests committed to the renewal of the Catholic Church and its extension abroad.

Although the Reformation was profoundly religious, it encouraged a skeptical attitude toward authority and tradition, for it had, after all, successfully challenged the immense prestige and power of the pope and the established Church. Protestant reformers fostered religious individualism, as people now read and interpreted the scriptures for themselves and sought salvation without the mediation of the Church. In the centuries that followed, some people turned that skepticism and the habit of

Protestant dominant
Some Protestant influence
Catholic
Eastern Orthodox Christian
— Boundary of the Holy Roman Empire

MAPPING HISTORY

Map 15.1 Reformation Europe in the Sixteenth Century

The rise of Protestantism added yet another set of religious divisions, both within and between states, to the world of Christendom, which was already sharply divided between the Roman Catholic Church and the Eastern Orthodox Church.

READING THE MAP: What parts of Western Europe were predominantly Protestant by the end of the sixteenth century? Which regions remained predominantly Catholic?

MAKING CONNECTIONS: Compare this map with Map 13.1: European Colonial Empires in the Americas. Did Catholic or Protestant states control the largest American colonies?

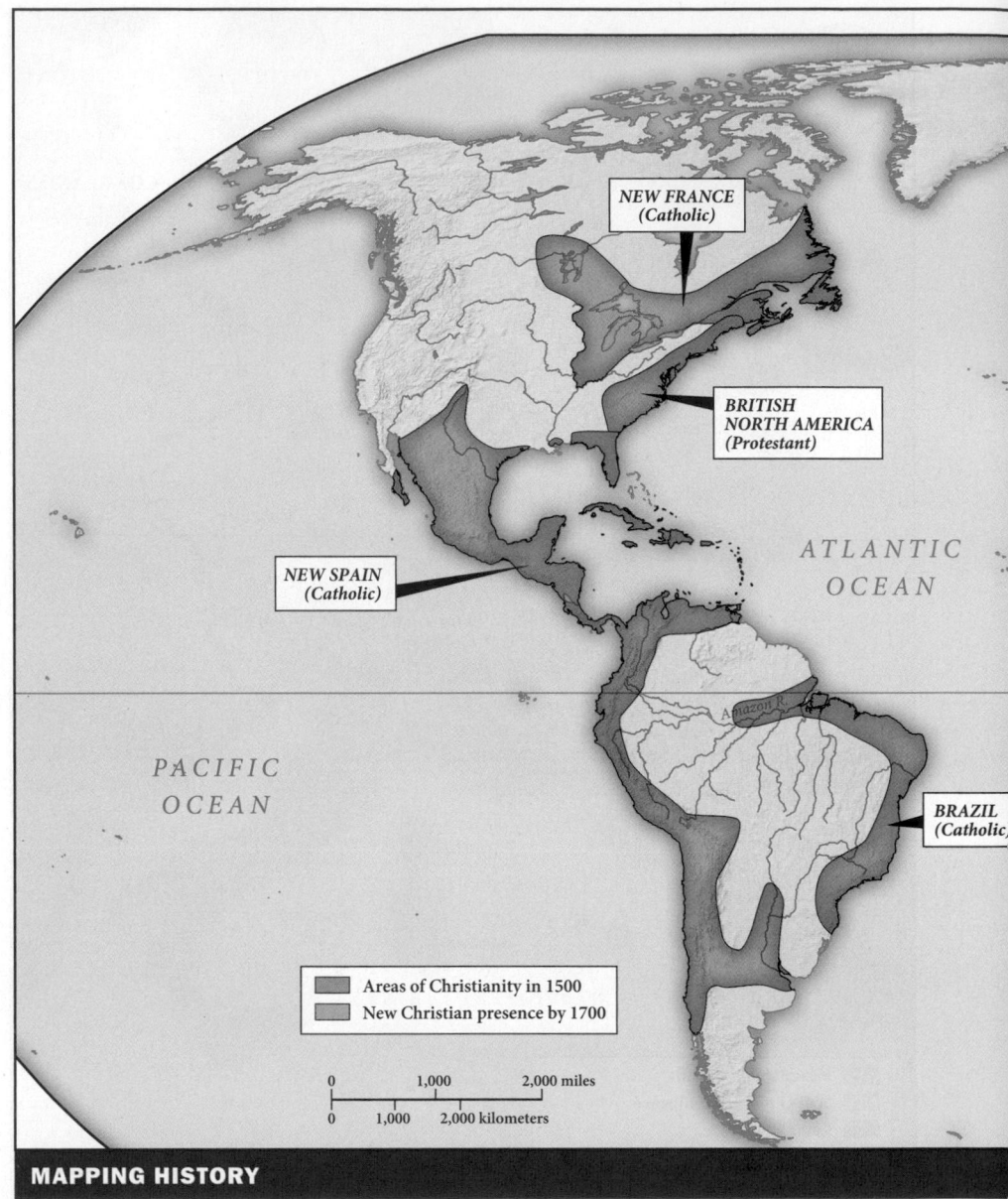

NEW FRANCE
(Catholic)

BRITISH
NORTH AMERICA
(Protestant)

NEW SPAIN
(Catholic)

ATLANTIC
OCEAN

BRAZIL
(Catholic)

PACIFIC
OCEAN

Amazon R.

☐ Areas of Christianity in 1500
☐ New Christian presence by 1700

0   1,000   2,000 miles

0   1,000   2,000 kilometers

MAPPING HISTORY

Map 15.2 The Globalization of Christianity

The growing Christian presence in Asia, Africa, and especially the Americas, combined with older centers of that faith, gave the religion derived from Jesus a global dimension during the early modern era.

thinking independently against all conventional religion. Thus the Protestant Reformation opened some space for new directions in European intellectual life.

In short, it was a more highly fragmented but also a renewed and revitalized Christianity that established itself around the world in the several centuries after 1500 (see Map 15.2).

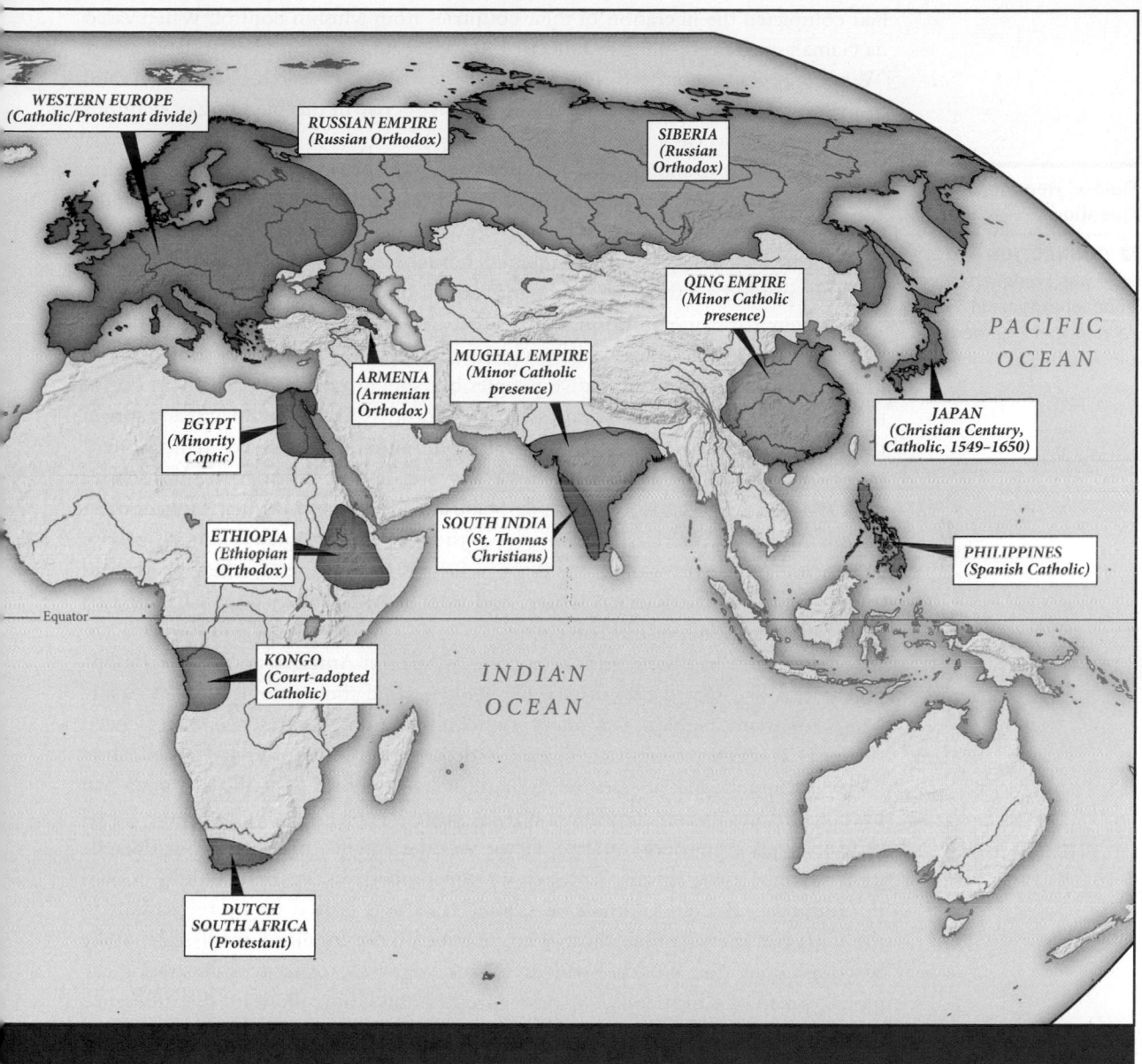

WESTERN EUROPE
(Catholic/Protestant divide)

RUSSIAN EMPIRE
(Russian Orthodox)

SIBERIA
(Russian Orthodox)

QING EMPIRE
(Minor Catholic presence)

PACIFIC OCEAN

ARMENIA
(Armenian Orthodox)

MUGHAL EMPIRE
(Minor Catholic presence)

EGYPT
(Minority Coptic)

JAPAN
(Christian Century, Catholic, 1549–1650)

ETHIOPIA
(Ethiopian Orthodox)

SOUTH INDIA
(St. Thomas Christians)

PHILIPPINES
(Spanish Catholic)

Equator

KONGO
(Court-adopted Catholic)

INDIAN OCEAN

DUTCH SOUTH AFRICA
(Protestant)

READING THE MAP: Where did Protestants establish overseas colonies?

INTERPRETING THE MAP: Did the Catholic, Protestant, or Russian Orthodox Church have the most success in establishing itself as a global faith during the early modern period? How might you explain the variations among them?

Christianity Outward Bound

Christianity motivated European political and economic expansion and also benefited from it. The resolutely Catholic Spanish and Portuguese both viewed their movement overseas as a continuation of a long crusading tradition that only recently had completed the liberation of their countries from Muslim control. When Vasco da Gama's small fleet landed in India in 1498, local authorities understandably asked, "What brought you hither?" The reply: they had come "in search of Christians and of spices."[3] No sense of any contradiction or hypocrisy in this blending of religious and material concerns attended the reply.

Guided Reading Question

■ **CONNECTION**

How was European imperial expansion related to the spread of Christianity?

If religion drove and justified European ventures abroad, it is difficult to imagine the globalization of Christianity (see Map 15.2) without the support of empire. Colonial settlers and traders, of course, brought their faith with them and sought to replicate it in their newly conquered homelands. New England Puritans, for example, planted a distinctive Protestant version of Christianity in North America, with an emphasis on education, moral purity, personal conversion, civic responsibility, and little tolerance for competing expressions of the faith. They did not show much interest in converting native peoples but sought rather to push them out of their ancestral territories. It was missionaries, mostly Catholic, who actively spread the Christian message beyond European communities. Organized in missionary orders such as the Dominicans, Franciscans, and Jesuits, Portuguese missionaries took the lead in Africa and Asia, while Spanish and French missionaries were most prominent in the Americas. Missionaries of the Russian Orthodox Church likewise accompanied the expansion of the Russian Empire across Siberia, where priests and monks ministered to Russian settlers and trappers, who often donated their first sable furs to a church or monastery.

Missionaries had their greatest success in Spanish America and in the Philippines, areas that shared two critical elements beyond their colonization by Spain. Most important, perhaps, was an overwhelming European presence, experienced variously as military conquest, colonial settlement, missionary activity, forced labor, social disruption, and disease. Surely it must have seemed as if the old gods had been bested and that any possible future lay with the powerful religion of the European invaders. A second common factor was the absence of a literate world religion in these two regions. Throughout the modern era, peoples solidly rooted in Confucian, Buddhist, Hindu, or Islamic traditions proved far more resistant to the Christian message than those who practiced more localized, small-scale, orally based religions. (See Working with Evidence, page 673, for sources illustrating the global spread of Christianity.) Spanish America and China illustrate the difference between those societies in which Christianity became widely practiced and those that largely rejected it.

Guided Reading Question

■ **CONNECTION**

In what ways was European Christianity assimilated into the Native American cultures of Spanish America?

Conversion and Adaptation in Spanish America

The decisive conquest of the Aztec and Inca empires and all that followed from it—disease, population collapse, loss of land to Europeans, forced labor, resettlement—created a setting in which the religion of the victors took hold in Spanish American colonies. Europeans saw their political and military success as a demonstration of the power of the Christian God. Native American peoples generally agreed, and by 1700 or earlier the vast majority had been baptized and saw themselves in some respects as Christians. After all, other conquerors such as the Aztecs and the Incas had always imposed their gods in some fashion on defeated peoples. So it made sense, both practically and spiritually, to affiliate with the Europeans' god, saints, rites, and rituals. Many millions accepted baptism, contributed to the construction of village churches, attended services, and embraced images of saints. Despite the prominence of the Virgin Mary as a religious figure across Latin America, the cost of conversion was high, especially for women. Many women who had long served as priests, shamans, or ritual specialists had no corresponding role in a Catholic church, led by an all-male clergy. And, with a few exceptions, convent life, which had provided some outlet for female authority and education in Catholic Europe, was reserved largely for Spanish women in the Americas.

Earlier conquerors had made no attempt to eradicate local deities and religious practices. The flexibility and inclusiveness of Mesoamerican and Andean religions had made it possible for subject people to accommodate the gods of their new rulers while maintaining their own traditions. But Europeans were different. They claimed an exclusive religious truth and sought the utter destruction of local gods and everything associated with them. Operating within a Spanish colonial regime that actively encouraged conversion, missionaries often proceeded by persuasion and patient teaching. At times, though, their frustration with the persistence of "idolatry, superstition, and error" boiled over into violent campaigns designed to uproot old religions once and for all. In 1535, the bishop of Mexico proudly claimed that he had destroyed 500 pagan shrines and 20,000 idols. During the seventeenth and early eighteenth centuries, church authorities in the Andean region periodically launched movements of "extirpation," designed to fatally undermine native religion. They destroyed religious images and ritual objects, publicly urinated on native "idols," desecrated the remains of ancestors, flogged "idolaters," and held religious trials and "processions of shame" aimed at humiliating offenders.

It is hardly surprising that such aggressive action generated resistance. Writing around 1600, the native Peruvian nobleman Guaman Poma de Ayala commented on the posture of native women toward Christianity: "They do not confess; they do not attend catechism classes . . . nor do they go to mass. . . . And resuming their ancient customs and idolatry, they do not want to serve God or

Andean Christianity Religious syncretism in the Andes emerged during the early modern era but continues to play an important role in the religious life of the region today. This 2016 image shows Peruvians participating in a religious procession that combines Incan mountain worship with Catholic traditions in a vibrant festival that attracts thousands of celebrants each year. (Barcroft Images/Getty Images)

the crown."[4] Occasionally, overt resistance erupted. One such example was the religious revivalist movement in central Peru in the 1560s, known as **Taki Onqoy** (dancing sickness). Possessed by the spirits of local gods, or *huacas*, traveling dancers and teachers predicted that an alliance of Andean deities would soon overcome the Christian God, inflict the intruding Europeans with the same diseases that they had brought to the Americas, and restore the world of the Andes to an imagined earlier harmony. "The world has turned about," one member declared, "and this time God and the Spaniards [will be] defeated and all the Spaniards killed and their cities drowned; and the sea will rise and overwhelm them, so that there will remain no memory of them."[5]

More common than such frontal attacks on Christianity, which colonial authorities quickly smashed, were efforts at blending two religious traditions, reinterpreting Christian practices within an Andean framework, and incorporating local elements into an emerging Andean Christianity. Even female dancers in the Taki Onqoy movement sometimes took the names of Christian saints, seeking to appropriate for themselves the religious power of Christian figures. Within Andean Christian communities, women might offer the blood of a llama to strengthen a village church or make a cloth covering for the Virgin Mary and a shirt for an image of a huaca with the same material. Although the state cults of the Incas faded away, missionary attacks did not succeed in eliminating the influence of local huacas. Images and holy sites might be destroyed, but the souls of the huacas remained, and their representatives gained prestige. One resilient Andean resident inquired of a Jesuit missionary: "Father, are you tired of taking our idols from us? Take away that mountain if you can, since that is the God I worship."[6]

In Mexico as well, an immigrant Christianity was assimilated into patterns of local culture. Churches built on or near the sites of old temples became the focus of community identity. *Cofradias*, church-based associations of laypeople, organized community processions and festivals and made provisions for proper funerals and burials for their members. Central to an emerging Mexican Christianity were the saints who closely paralleled the functions of precolonial gods. Saints were imagined as parents of the local community and the true owners of its land, and their images were paraded through the streets on the occasion of great feasts and were collected by individual households. Mexico's Virgin of Guadalupe neatly combined both Mesoamerican and Spanish notions of Divine Motherhood (see the chapter-opening photo and Historians' Voice 15.1, page 682). Although parish priests were almost always Spanish, the *fiscal*, or leader of the church staff, was a native Christian of great local prestige who carried on the traditions and role of earlier religious specialists.

Throughout the colonial period and beyond, many Mexican Christians also took part in rituals derived from the past, with little sense of incompatibility with Christian practice. Incantations to various gods for good fortune in hunting, farming, or healing; sacrifices of self-bleeding; offerings to the sun; divination; the use of hallucinogenic drugs—all of these practices provided spiritual assistance in those areas of everyday life not directly addressed by Christian rites. Conversely, these practices also showed signs of Christian influence. Wax candles, normally used in Christian services, might now appear in front of a stone image of a precolonial god. The anger of a neglected saint, rather than that of a traditional god, might explain someone's illness and require offerings, celebration, or a new covering to regain his or her favor. In such ways did Christianity take root in the new cultural environments of Spanish America, but it was a distinctly Andean or Mexican Christianity, not merely a copy of the Spanish version.

An Asian Comparison: China and the Jesuits

The Chinese encounter with Christianity was very different from that of Native Americans in Spain's New World empire. The most obvious difference was the political context. The peoples of Spanish America had been defeated, their societies thoroughly disrupted, and their cultural confidence sorely shaken. China, on the other hand, encountered European Christianity between the sixteenth and eighteenth centuries during the powerful and prosperous Ming (1368–1644) and Qing (1644–1912) dynasties. Although the transition between these two dynasties occasioned several decades of internal conflict, at no point was China's political independence or cultural integrity threatened by the handful of European missionaries and traders working there.

The reality of a strong, independent, confident China required a different missionary strategy, for Europeans needed the permission of Chinese authorities to operate in the country. Whereas Spanish missionaries working in a colonial setting sought primarily to convert the masses, the **Jesuits in China**, the leading missionary order there, took deliberate aim at the official Chinese elite. Following the example of their most famous missionary, Matteo Ricci (in China 1582–1610), many Jesuits learned Chinese, became thoroughly acquainted with classical Confucian texts, and dressed like Chinese scholars. Initially, they downplayed their mission to convert and instead emphasized their interest in exchanging ideas and learning from China's ancient culture. As highly educated men, the Jesuits carried the recent secular knowledge of Europe—science, technology, geography, mapmaking—to an audience of curious Chinese scholars. In presenting Christian teachings, Jesuits were at pains to be respectful of Chinese culture, pointing out parallels between Confucianism and Christianity rather than portraying Christianity as something new and foreign. They chose to define Chinese rituals honoring the emperor or venerating ancestors as secular or civil observances rather than as religious practices that had to be abandoned. Such efforts to accommodate Chinese culture contrast sharply with the frontal attacks on Native American religions in the Spanish Empire.

The religious and cultural outcomes of the missionary enterprise likewise differed greatly in the two regions. Nothing approaching mass conversion to Christianity took place in China, as it had in Latin America. During the sixteenth and seventeenth centuries, a modest number of Chinese scholars and officials did become Christians, attracted by the personal lives of the missionaries, by their interest in Western

Guided Reading Question

■ **COMPARISON**
Why were missionary efforts to spread Christianity so much less successful in China than in Spanish America?

Jesuits in China In this seventeenth-century Dutch engraving, two Jesuit missionaries hold a map of China. Their mapmaking skills were among the reasons that the Jesuits were initially welcomed among the educated elite of that country. (Frontispiece to *China Monumentis* by Athanasius Kircher, 1667/Private Collection/Bridgeman Images)

science, and by the moral certainty that Christianity offered. Jesuit missionaries found favor for a time at the Chinese imperial court, where their mathematical, astronomical, technological, and mapmaking skills rendered them useful. For more than a century, they were appointed to head the Chinese Bureau of Astronomy. Among ordinary people, Christianity spread very modestly amid tales of miracles attributed to the Christian God, while missionary teachings about "eternal life" sounded to some like Daoist prescriptions for immortality. At most, though, missionary efforts over the course of some 250 years (1550–1800) resulted in 200,000 to 300,000 converts, a minuscule number in a Chinese population approaching 300 million by 1800. What explains the very limited acceptance of Christianity in early modern China?

Fundamentally, the missionaries offered little that the Chinese really wanted. Confucianism for the elites and Buddhism, Daoism, and a multitude of Chinese gods and spirits at the local level adequately supplied the spiritual needs of most Chinese. Furthermore, it became increasingly clear that Christianity was an all-or-nothing faith that required converts to abandon much of traditional Chinese culture. Christian monogamy, for example, seemed to require Chinese men to put away their concubines. What would happen to these deserted women?

By the early eighteenth century, the papacy and competing missionary orders came to oppose the Jesuit policy of accommodation. The pope claimed authority over Chinese Christians and declared that sacrifices to Confucius and the veneration of ancestors were "idolatry" and thus forbidden to Christians. The pope's pronouncements represented an unacceptable challenge to the authority of the emperor and an affront to Chinese culture. In 1715, an outraged Emperor Kangxi prohibited Westerners from spreading Christian doctrine in his kingdom (see Working with Evidence, Source 15.4B, page 679). This represented a major turning point in the relationship between Christian missionaries and Chinese society. Many were subsequently expelled, and missionaries lost favor at court.

In other ways as well, missionaries played into the hands of their Chinese opponents. Their willingness to work under the Manchurian Qing dynasty, which came to power in 1644, discredited them with those Chinese scholars who viewed the Qing as uncivilized foreigners and their rule in China as disgraceful and illegitimate. Missionaries' reputation as miracle workers further damaged their standing as men of science and rationality, for elite Chinese often regarded miracles and supernatural religion as superstitions, fit only for the uneducated masses. Some viewed the Christian ritual of Holy Communion as a kind of cannibalism. Others came to see missionaries as potentially subversive, for various Christian groups met in secret, and such religious sects had often provided the basis for peasant rebellion. Nor did it escape Chinese notice that European Christians had taken over the Philippines and that their warships were active in the Indian Ocean. Perhaps the missionaries, with their great interest in maps, were spies for these aggressive foreigners. All of this contributed to the general failure of Christianity to secure a prominent presence in China.

Persistence and Change in Afro-Asian Cultural Traditions

Although Europeans were central players in the globalization of Christianity, theirs was not the only expanding or transformed culture of the early modern era. African religious ideas and practices, for example, accompanied slaves to the Americas. Common African forms of religious revelation—divination, dream interpretation, visions, spirit possession—found a place in the Africanized versions of Christianity that emerged in the New World. Europeans frequently perceived these practices as evidence of sorcery, witchcraft, or even devil worship and tried to suppress them. Nonetheless, syncretic (blended) religions such as Vodou in Haiti, Santeria in Cuba, and Candomblé and Macumba in Brazil persisted. They derived from various West African traditions and featured drumming, ritual dancing, animal sacrifice, and spirit possession. Over time, they incorporated Christian beliefs and practices such as church attendance, the search for salvation, and the use of candles and crucifixes and often identified their various spirits or deities with Catholic saints.

Expansion and Renewal in the Islamic World

The early modern era likewise witnessed the continuation of the "long march of Islam" across the Afro-Asian world. In sub-Saharan Africa, in the eastern and western wings of India, and in Central and Southeast Asia, the expansion of the Islamic frontier, a process already a thousand years in the making, extended farther still. Conversion to Islam generally did not mean a sudden abandonment of old religious practices in favor of the new. Rather, it was more often a matter of "assimilating Islamic rituals, cosmologies, and literatures into . . . local religious systems."[7]

Continued Islamization was not usually the product of conquering armies and expanding empires. It depended instead on wandering Muslim holy men or Sufis, Islamic scholars, and itinerant traders, none of whom posed a threat to local rulers. In fact, such people often were useful to those rulers and their village communities.

Guided Reading Question

■ **EXPLANATION**
What accounts for the continued spread of Islam in the early modern era and for the emergence of reform or renewal movements within the Islamic world?

They offered literacy in Arabic, established informal schools, provided protective charms containing passages from the Quran, served as advisers to local authorities and healers to the sick, often intermarried with local people, and generally did not insist that new converts give up their older practices. What they offered, in short, was connection to the wider, prestigious, prosperous world of Islam. Islamization extended modestly even to the Americas, particularly in Brazil, where Muslims led a number of slave revolts in the early nineteenth century.

The islands of Southeast Asia illustrate the diversity of belief and practice that accompanied the spread of Islam in the early modern era. During the seventeenth century in Aceh, a Muslim sultanate on the northern tip of Sumatra, authorities sought to enforce the dietary codes and almsgiving practices of Islamic law. After four successive women ruled the area in the late seventeenth century, women were forbidden from exercising political power. On Muslim Java, however, numerous women served in royal courts, and women throughout Indonesia continued their longtime role as buyers and sellers in local markets. Among ordinary Javanese, traditional animistic practices of spirit worship coexisted easily with a tolerant and accommodating Islam, while merchants often embraced a more orthodox version of the religion in line with Middle Eastern traditions.

To such orthodox Muslims, religious syncretism, which accompanied Islamization almost everywhere, became increasingly offensive, even heretical. Such sentiments played an important role in movements of religious renewal and reform that emerged throughout the vast Islamic world of the eighteenth century. The leaders of such movements sharply criticized those practices that departed from earlier patterns established by Muhammad and from the authority of the Quran. For example, in India, governed by the Muslim Mughal Empire, religious resistance to official policies that accommodated Hindus found concrete expression during the reign of the emperor Aurangzeb (r. 1658–1707) (see "Muslims and Hindus in the Mughal Empire" in Chapter 13). A series of religious wars in West Africa during the eighteenth and early nineteenth centuries took aim at corrupt Islamic practices and the rulers, Muslim and non-Muslim alike, who permitted them. In Southeast and Central Asia, tension grew between practitioners of localized and blended versions of Islam and those who sought to purify such practices in the name of a more authentic and universal faith.

The most well known and widely visible of these Islamic renewal movements took place during the mid-eighteenth century in Arabia itself, where they found expression in the teachings of the Islamic scholar Muhammad Ibn Abd al-Wahhab (1703–1792). The growing difficulties of the Islamic world, such as the weakening of the Ottoman Empire, were directly related, he argued, to deviations from the pure faith of early Islam. Al-Wahhab was particularly upset by common religious practices in central Arabia that seemed to him idolatry—the widespread veneration of Sufi saints and their tombs, the adoration of natural sites, and even the respect paid to Muhammad's tomb at Medina. All of this was a dilution of the absolute monotheism of authentic Islam.

The Wahhabi movement took a new turn in the 1740s when it received the political backing of Muhammad Ibn Saud, a local ruler who found al-Wahhab's ideas compelling. With Ibn Saud's support, the religious movement became an expansive state in central Arabia. Within that state, offending tombs were razed; "idols" were eliminated; books on logic were destroyed; the use of tobacco, hashish, and musical instruments was forbidden; and certain taxes not authorized by religious teaching were abolished.

Although **Wahhabi Islam** has long been identified with sharp restrictions on women, Al-Wahhab himself generally emphasized the rights of women within a patriarchal Islamic framework. These included the right to consent to and stipulate conditions for a marriage, to control her dowry, to divorce, and to engage in commerce. Such rights, long embedded in Islamic law, had apparently been forgotten or ignored in eighteenth-century Arabia. Furthermore, he did not insist on head-to toe covering of women in public and allowed for the mixing of unrelated men and women for business or medical purposes.

By the early nineteenth century, this new reformist state encompassed much of central Arabia, with Mecca itself coming under Wahhabi control in 1803 (see Map 15.3). Although an Egyptian army broke the power of the Wahhabis in 1818, the movement's influence continued to spread across the Islamic world. Together with the ongoing expansion of the religion, these movements of reform and renewal signaled the continuing cultural vitality of the Islamic world even as the European presence on the world stage assumed larger dimensions.

Map 15.3 The Expansion of Wahhabi Islam
From its base in central Arabia, the Wahhabi movement represented a challenge to the Ottoman Empire, while its ideas subsequently spread widely within the Islamic world.

China: New Directions in an Old Tradition

Neither China nor India experienced cultural or religious change as dramatic as that of the Reformation in Europe or the Wahhabi movement in Arabia. Nor did Confucian or Hindu cultures during the early modern era spread widely, as did Christianity and Islam. Nonetheless, neither of these traditions remained static. As in Christian Europe, challenges to established orthodoxies in China and India emerged as commercial and urban life, as well as political change, fostered new thinking.

China during the Ming and Qing dynasties continued to operate broadly within a Confucian framework, enriched now by the insights of Buddhism and Daoism to generate a system of thought called Neo-Confucianism. Chinese Ming dynasty rulers, in their aversion to the despised Mongols, embraced and actively supported

Guided Reading Question

■ **CHANGE**
What kinds of cultural changes occurred in China and India during the early modern era?

this native Confucian tradition, whereas the foreign Manchu or Qing rulers did so to woo Chinese intellectuals to support the new dynasty. Within this context, a considerable amount of controversy, debate, and new thinking emerged during the early modern era.

During late Ming times, for example, the influential thinker **Wang Yangming** (1472–1529) argued that "intuitive moral knowledge exists in people . . . even robbers know that they should not rob."[8] Thus anyone could achieve a virtuous life by introspection and contemplation, without the extended education, study of classical texts, and constant striving for improvement that traditional Confucianism prescribed for an elite class of "gentlemen." Such ideas figured prominently among Confucian scholars of the sixteenth century, although critics contended that such thinking promoted an excessive individualism. They also argued that Wang Yangming's ideas had undermined the Ming dynasty and contributed to China's conquest by the foreign Manchus. Some Chinese Buddhists as well sought to make their religion more accessible to ordinary people by suggesting that laypeople at home could undertake practices similar to those performed by monks in monasteries. Withdrawal from the world was not necessary for enlightenment. This kind of moral or religious individualism bore some similarity to the thinking of Martin Luther, who argued that individuals could seek salvation by "faith alone," without the assistance of a priestly hierarchy.

Another new direction in Chinese elite culture took shape in a movement known as **kaozheng**, or "research based on evidence." Intended to "seek truth from facts," kaozheng was critical of the unfounded speculation of conventional Confucian philosophy and instead emphasized the importance of verification, precision, accuracy, and rigorous analysis in all fields of inquiry. During the late Ming years, this emphasis generated works dealing with agriculture, medicine, pharmacology, botany, craft techniques, and more. In the Qing era, kaozheng was associated with the recovery and critical analysis of ancient historical documents, which sometimes led to sharp criticism of Neo-Confucian orthodoxy. It was a genuinely scientific approach to knowledge, but it was applied more to the study of the past than to the natural world of astronomy, physics, or anatomy, which was the focus in the West.

Dream of the Red Chamber This mid-eighteenth-century image depicts a garden scene from *Dream of the Red Chamber*, a wildly popular epic novel that found a wide readership in Qing China and is now considered one of China's "Four Great Classical Novels." (Pictures from History/Bridgeman Images)

While such matters occupied the intellectual elite of China, in the cities a lively popular culture emerged among the less educated. For city-dwellers, plays, paintings, short stories, and especially novels provided diversion and entertainment that were a step up from what could be found in teahouses and wine-shops. Numerous "how-to" painting manuals allowed a larger public to participate in this favorite Chinese art form. Even though Confucian scholars disdained popular fiction, a vigorous printing industry responded to the growing demand for exciting novels. The most famous was Cao Xueqin's mid-eighteenth-century novel ***The Dream of the Red Chamber***, a huge book that contained 120 chapters and some 400 characters, most of them women. It explored the social life of an eighteenth-century elite family with connections to the Chinese court.

India: Bridging the Hindu/Muslim Divide

In a largely Hindu India, ruled by the Muslim Mughal Empire, several significant cultural departures took shape in the early modern era that brought Hindus and Muslims together in new forms of religious expression. At the level of elite culture, the Mughal ruler Akbar formulated a state cult that combined elements of Islam, Hinduism, and Zoroastrianism (see Chapter 13, "Muslims and Hindus in the Mughal Empire"). The Mughal court also embraced Renaissance Christian art, and soon murals featuring Jesus, Mary, and Christian saints appeared on the walls of palaces, garden pavilions, and harems. The court also commissioned a prominent Sufi spiritual master to compose an illustrated book describing various Hindu yoga postures. Intended to bring this Hindu tradition into Islamic Sufi practice, the book, known as the *Ocean of Life*, portrayed some of the yogis in a Christ-like fashion.

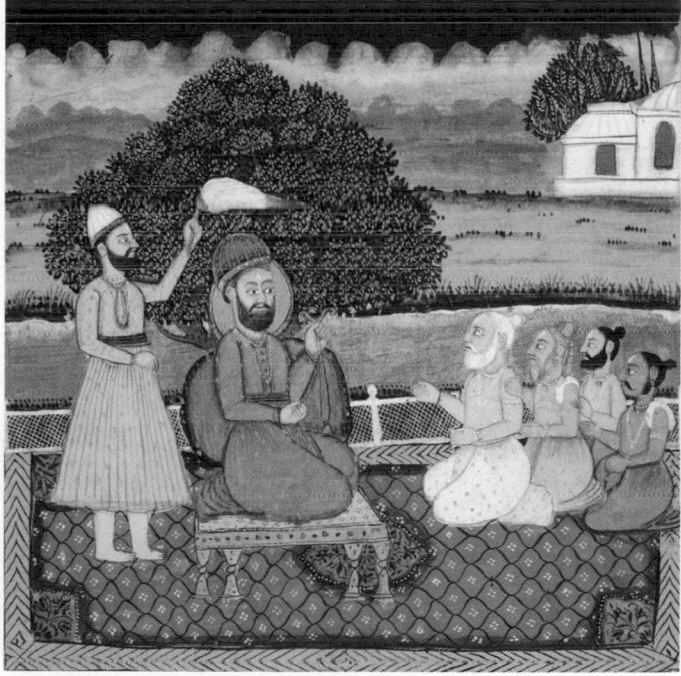

Within popular culture, the flourishing of a devotional form of Hinduism known as *bhakti* also bridged the gulf separating Hindu and Muslim. Through songs, prayers, dances, poetry, and rituals, devotees sought to achieve union with one or another of India's many deities. Appealing especially to women, the bhakti movement provided an avenue for social criticism. Its practitioners often set aside caste distinctions and disregarded the detailed rituals of the Brahmin priests in favor of personal religious experience. The mystical dimension of the bhakti movement had much in common with Sufi forms of Islam, which also emphasized direct experience of the Divine. Such similarities helped blur the distinction between Hinduism and Islam in India, as both *bhaktis* and Sufis honored spiritual sages and all those seeking after God.

Guru Nanak This painting shows a seated Guru Nanak, the founder of Sikhism, disputing with four kneeling Hindu holy men. (The British Library, London, UK/© British Library Board. All Rights Reserved/Bridgeman Images)

Among the most beloved of bhakti poets was **Mirabai** (1498–1547), a high-caste woman from northern India who abandoned her upper-class family and conventional Hindu practice. Upon her husband's death, tradition asserts, she declined to burn herself on his funeral pyre (a practice known as *sati*). She further offended caste restrictions by taking as her guru (religious teacher) an old untouchable shoemaker. To visit him, she apparently tied her saris together and climbed down the castle walls at night. Then she would wash his aged feet and drink the water from these ablutions. Much of her poetry deals with her yearning for union with Krishna, a Hindu deity she regarded as her husband, lover, and lord. She wrote:

> What I paid was my social body, my town body, my family body, and all my inherited jewels. Mirabai says: The Dark One [Krishna] is my husband now.[9]

Yet another major cultural change that blended Islam and Hinduism emerged with the growth of **Sikhism** as a new and distinctive religious tradition in the Punjab region of northern India. Its founder, Guru Nanak (1469–1539), had been involved in the bhakti movement but came to believe that "there is no Hindu; there is no Muslim; only God." His teachings and those of subsequent gurus also generally ignored caste distinctions and untouchability and ended the seclusion of women, while proclaiming the "brotherhood of all mankind" as well as the essential equality of men and women. Drawing converts from Punjabi peasants and merchants, both Muslim and Hindu, the Sikhs gradually became a separate religious community. They developed their own sacred book, known as the Guru Granth (teacher book); created a central place of worship and pilgrimage in the Golden Temple of Amritsar; and prescribed certain dress requirements for men, including keeping hair and beards uncut, wearing a turban, and carrying a short sword. During the seventeenth century, Sikhs encountered hostility from both the Mughal Empire and some of their Hindu neighbors. In response, Sikhism evolved from a peaceful religious movement, blending Hindu and Muslim elements, into a militant community whose military skills were highly valued by the British when they took over India in the late eighteenth century.

PRACTICING HISTORICAL THINKING

In what ways did religious changes in Asia and the Middle East parallel those in Europe, and in what ways were they different?

A New Way of Thinking: The Birth of Modern Science

While some Europeans were actively attempting to spread the Christian faith to distant corners of the world, others were nurturing an understanding of the cosmos at least partially at odds with traditional Christian teaching. These were the makers of Europe's **Scientific Revolution**, a vast intellectual and cultural transformation that took place between the mid-sixteenth and early eighteenth centuries. These men of science no longer relied on the external authority of the Bible, the Church, the speculations of ancient philosophers, or the received wisdom of cultural tradition.

For them, knowledge was acquired through rational inquiry based on evidence, the product of human minds alone. Those who created this revolution—Copernicus from Poland, Galileo from Italy, Descartes from France, Newton from England, and many others—saw themselves as departing radically from older ways of thinking. "The old rubbish must be thrown away," wrote a seventeenth-century English scientist. "These are the days that must lay a new Foundation of a more magnificent Philosophy."[10]

The long-term significance of the Scientific Revolution can hardly be overestimated. Within early modern Europe, it fundamentally altered ideas about the place of humankind within the cosmos and sharply challenged both the teachings and the authority of the Church. Over the past several centuries, it has substantially eroded religious belief and practice in the West, particularly among the well educated. When applied to the affairs of human society, scientific ways of thinking challenged ancient social hierarchies and political systems and played a role in the revolutionary upheavals of the modern era. But science was also used to legitimize gender and racial inequalities, giving new support to old ideas about the natural inferiority of women and enslaved people. When married to the technological innovations of the Industrial Revolution, science fostered both the marvels of modern production and the horrors of modern means of destruction. By the twentieth century, science had become so widespread that it largely lost its association with European culture and became the chief marker of global modernity. Like Buddhism, Christianity, and Islam, modern science became a universal worldview, open to all who could accept its premises and its techniques.

The Question of Origins: Why Europe?

Why did the breakthrough of the Scientific Revolution occur first in Europe and during the early modern era? The realm of Islam, after all, had generated the most advanced science in the world during the centuries between 800 and 1400. Arab scholars could boast of remarkable achievements in mathematics, astronomy, optics, and medicine, and their libraries far exceeded those of Europe.[11] And China's elite culture of Confucianism was both sophisticated and secular, less burdened by religious dogma than that of the Christian or Islamic worlds; its technological accomplishments and economic growth were unmatched anywhere in the several centuries after 1000. In neither civilization, however, did these achievements lead to the kind of intellectual innovation that occurred in Europe.

Europe's historical development as a reinvigorated and fragmented civilization arguably gave rise to conditions particularly favorable to the scientific enterprise. By the twelfth and thirteenth centuries, Europeans had evolved a legal system that guaranteed a measure of independence for a variety of institutions—the Church, towns and cities, guilds, professional associations, and universities. This legal revolution was based on the idea of a "corporation," a collective group of people that was treated as a unit, a legal person, with certain rights to regulate and control its own members.

Guided Reading Question

■ **COMPARISON**

Why did the Scientific Revolution occur in Europe rather than in China or the Islamic world?

Most important for the development of science in the West was the autonomy of its emerging universities. By 1215, the University of Paris was recognized as a "corporation of masters and scholars," which could admit and expel students, establish courses of instruction, and grant a "license to teach" to its faculty. Such universities—for example, in Paris, Bologna, Oxford, Cambridge, and Salamanca—became "neutral zones of intellectual autonomy" in which scholars could pursue their studies in relative freedom from the dictates of church or state authorities. Within them, the study of the natural order began to slowly separate itself from philosophy and theology and to gain a distinct identity. Their curricula featured "a core of readings and lectures that were basically scientific," drawing heavily on the writings of the Greek thinker Aristotle, which had only recently become available to Western Europeans.[12] Most of the major figures in the Scientific Revolution had been trained in and were affiliated with these universities.

By contrast, in Islamic colleges known as madrassas, Quranic studies and religious law held the central place, whereas philosophy and natural science were viewed with considerable suspicion. To religious scholars, the Quran held all wisdom, and scientific thinking might well challenge it. An earlier openness to free inquiry and religious toleration was increasingly replaced by a disdain for scientific and philosophical inquiry, for it seemed to lead only to uncertainty and confusion. "May God protect us from useless knowledge" was a saying that reflected this outlook. Nor did Chinese authorities permit independent institutions of higher learning in which scholars could conduct their studies in relative freedom. Instead, Chinese education focused on preparing for a rigidly defined set of civil service examinations and emphasized the humanistic and moral texts of classical Confucianism. "The pursuit of scientific subjects," one recent historian concluded, "was thereby relegated to the margins of Chinese society."[13]

Beyond its distinctive institutional development, Western Europe was in a position to draw extensively on the knowledge of other cultures, especially that of the Islamic world. Arab medical texts, astronomical research, and translations of Greek classics played a major role in the birth of European natural philosophy (as science was then called) between 1000 and 1500. Then, in the sixteenth through the eighteenth centuries, Europeans found themselves at the center of a massive new exchange of information as they became aware of lands, peoples, plants, animals, societies, and religions from around the world. This tidal wave of new knowledge, uniquely available to Europeans, shook up older ways of thinking and opened the way to new conceptions of the world. The sixteenth-century Italian doctor, mathematician, and writer Girolamo Cardano (1501–1576) clearly expressed this sense of wonderment: "The most unusual [circumstance of my life] is that I was born in this century in which the whole world became known; whereas the ancients were familiar with but a little more than a third part of it." He worried, however, that amid this explosion of knowledge, "certainties will be exchanged for uncertainties."[14] It was precisely those uncertainties—skepticism about established views—that provided such a fertile cultural ground for the emergence of modern science. The

Reformation too contributed to that cultural climate in its challenge to authority, its encouragement of mass literacy, and its affirmation of secular professions.

Science as Cultural Revolution

Before the Scientific Revolution, educated Europeans held to an ancient view of the world in which the earth was stationary and at the center of the universe, and around it revolved the sun, moon, and stars embedded in ten spheres of transparent crystal. This understanding coincided well with the religious outlook of the Catholic Church because the attention of the entire universe was centered on the earth and its human inhabitants, among whom God's plan for salvation unfolded. It was a universe of divine purpose, with angels guiding the hierarchically arranged heavenly bodies along their way while God watched over the whole from his realm beyond the spheres. The Scientific Revolution was revolutionary because it fundamentally challenged this understanding of the universe.

The initial breakthrough in the Scientific Revolution came from the Polish mathematician and astronomer Nicolaus **Copernicus**, whose famous book *On the Revolutions of the Heavenly Spheres* was published in the year of his death, 1543. Its essential argument was that "at the middle of all things lies the sun" and that the earth, like the other planets, revolved around it. Thus the earth was no longer unique or at the obvious center of God's attention.

Other European scientists built on Copernicus's central insight. In the early seventeenth century Johannes Kepler, a German mathematician, showed that the planets followed elliptical orbits, undermining the ancient belief that they moved in perfect circles. In 1609 the Italian **Galileo** (gal-uh-LAY-oh) developed an improved telescope, with which he made many observations that undermined established understandings of the cosmos. (See Zooming In: Galileo and the Telescope, page 662.) Some thinkers began to discuss the notion of an unlimited universe in which humankind occupied a mere speck of dust in an unimaginable vastness. The seventeenth-century French mathematician and philosopher Blaise Pascal perhaps spoke for many when he wrote, "The eternal silence of infinite space frightens me."[15]

The culmination of the Scientific Revolution came in the work of Sir Isaac **Newton** (1642–1727), the Englishman who formulated the modern laws of motion and mechanics, which remained unchallenged until the twentieth century. At the core of Newton's thinking was the concept of universal gravitation. "All bodies whatsoever," Newton declared, "are endowed with a principle of mutual gravitation."[16] Here was the grand unifying idea of early modern science. The radical implication of this view was that the heavens and the earth, long regarded as separate and distinct spheres, were not so different after all, for the motion of a cannonball or the falling of an apple obeyed the same natural laws that governed the orbiting planets.

By the time Newton died, a revolutionary new understanding of the physical universe had emerged among educated Europeans: the universe was no longer

Guided Reading Question

■ **CHANGE**
What was revolutionary about the Scientific Revolution?

Galileo and the Telescope: Reflecting on Science and Religion

Galileo on trial.

The Scientific Revolution was predicated on the idea that knowledge of how the universe worked was acquired through a combination of careful observations, controlled experiments, and the formulation of general laws, expressed in mathematical terms. New scientific instruments capable of making precise empirical observations underpinned some of the most important breakthroughs of the period. Perhaps no single invention produced more dramatic discoveries than the telescope, the first of which were produced in the early seventeenth century by Dutch eyeglass makers.

The impact of new instruments depended on how scientists employed them. In the case of the telescope, it was the brilliant Italian mathematician and astronomer Galileo Galilei (1564–1642) who unlocked its potential when he used it to observe the night sky. Within months of creating his own telescope, which improved on earlier designs, Galileo made a series of discoveries that called into question well-established understandings of the cosmos. He observed craters on the moon and sunspots, or blemishes, moving across the face of the sun, which challenged the traditional notion that no imperfection or change marred the heavenly bodies. Moreover, his discovery of the moons of Jupiter and many new stars suggested a cosmos far larger than the finite universe of traditional astronomy. In 1610, Galileo published his remarkable findings in a book titled *The Starry Messenger*, where he emphasized time and again that his precise observations provided irrefutable evidence of a cosmos unlike that described by traditional authorities. "With the aid of the telescope," he argued, "this has been scrutinized so directly and with such ocular certainty that all the disputes which have vexed the philosophers through so many ages have been resolved, and we are at last freed from wordy debates about it."[17]

Galileo's empirical evidence transformed the debate over the nature of the cosmos. His dramatic and unexpected discoveries were readily grasped, and with the aid of a telescope anyone could confirm their veracity. His initial findings were heralded by many in the scientific community, including Christoph Clavius, the Church's

photo: Detail, from *Trial of Galileo*, 1633/Private Collection/Bridgeman Images

propelled by supernatural forces but functioned on its own according to scientific principles that could be described mathematically. Articulating this view, Kepler wrote, "The machine of the universe is not similar to a divine animated being but similar to a clock."[18] Furthermore, it was a machine that regulated itself, requiring neither God nor angels to account for its normal operation. Knowledge of that universe could be obtained through human reason alone—by observation, deduction, and experimentation—without the aid of ancient authorities or divine revelation. The French philosopher René Descartes (day-KAHRT) resolved "to seek no other knowledge than that which I might find within myself, or perhaps in the book of nature."[19]

Like the physical universe, the human body also lost some of its mystery. The careful dissections of cadavers and animals enabled doctors and scientists to describe leading astronomer in Rome. Galileo's findings led him to conclude that Copernicus (1473–1543), an earlier astronomer and mathematician, had been correct when he had advanced the theory that the sun rather than the earth was at the center of the solar system. But Galileo's evidence could not definitively prove Copernicus's theory to the satisfaction of critics, leading Galileo to study other phenomena, such as the tides, that could provide further evidence that the earth was in motion.

When the Church condemned Copernicus's theory in 1616, it remained silent on Galileo's astronomical observations, instead warning him to refrain from teaching or promoting Copernicus's ideas. Ultimately, though, Galileo came into conflict with church authorities when in 1629 he published, with what he thought was the consent of the Church, the *Dialogue Concerning the Two Chief World Systems*, a work sympathetic to Copernicus's sun-centric system. In 1632, Galileo was tried by the Roman Inquisition, an ecclesiastical court charged with maintaining orthodoxy, and convicted of teaching doctrines against the express orders of the Church. He recanted his beliefs and at the age of sixty-nine was sentenced to house arrest.

Although Galileo was formally convicted of disobeying the Church's order to remain silent on the issue of Copernicus's theory, the question most fundamentally at stake in the trial was "What does it mean, 'to know something'?"[20] This question of the relationship between scientific knowledge, primarily concerned with how the universe works, and other forms of "knowledge,"

derived from divine revelation or mystical experience, has persisted in the West. Over 350 years after the trial, Pope John Paul II spoke of Galileo's conviction in a public speech in 1992, declaring it a "sad misunderstanding" that belongs to the past, but one with ongoing resonance because "the underlying problems of this case concern both the nature of science and the message of faith." Then the pope declared scientific and religious knowledge to be compatible: "There exist two realms of knowledge, one which has its source in Revelation and one which reason can discover by its own power. . . . The distinction between the two realms of knowledge ought not to be understood as opposition. . . . The methodologies proper to each make it possible to bring out different aspects of reality."[21]

Strangely enough, Galileo himself had expressed something similar centuries earlier. "Nor is God," he wrote, "any less excellently revealed in Nature's actions than in the sacred statements of the Bible."[22] Finding the place of new scientific knowledge in a constellation of older wisdom traditions proved a fraught but highly significant development in the emergence of the modern world.

QUESTION

What can Galileo's discoveries with his telescope and his conviction by the Inquisition tell us about the Scientific Revolution?

---

the human body with much greater accuracy and to understand the circulation of the blood throughout the body. The heart was no longer the mysterious center of the body's heat and the seat of its passions; instead it was just another machine, a complex muscle that functioned as a pump.

The movers and shakers of this enormous cultural transformation were almost entirely male. European women, after all, had been largely excluded from the universities where much of the new science was discussed. A few aristocratic women, however, had the leisure and connections to participate informally in the scientific networks of their male relatives. Through her marriage to the Duke of Newcastle, Margaret Cavendish (1623–1673) joined in conversations with a circle of "natural philosophers," wrote six scientific texts, and was the only seventeenth-century Englishwoman to attend a session of the Royal Society of London, created

The Telescope Johannes Hevelius, an astronomer of German Lutheran background living in what is now Poland, constructed extraordinarily long telescopes in the mid-seventeenth century with which he observed sunspots, charted the surface of the moon, and discovered several comets. Such telescopes played a central role in transforming understandings of the universe during the Scientific Revolution. (World History Archive/Alamy)

to foster scientific learning. In Germany, a number of women took part in astronomical work as assistants to their husbands or brothers. Maria Winkelman, for example, discovered a previously unknown comet, though her husband took credit for it. After his death, she sought to continue his work in the Berlin Academy of Sciences but was refused on the grounds that "mouths would gape" if a woman held such a position.

Much of this scientific thinking developed in the face of strenuous opposition from the Catholic Church, for both its teachings and its authority were under attack. The Italian philosopher Giordano Bruno, proclaiming an infinite universe and many worlds, was burned at the stake in 1600, and Galileo was compelled by the Church to publicly renounce his belief that the earth moved around an orbit and rotated on its axis.

But scholars have sometimes exaggerated the conflict of science and religion, casting it in military terms as an almost unbroken war. None of the early scientists, however, rejected Christianity. Copernicus, in fact, published his famous book with the support of several leading Catholic churchmen and dedicated it to the pope. Galileo himself proclaimed the compatibility of science and faith, and his lack of diplomacy in dealing with church leaders was at least in part responsible for his quarrel with the Church.[23]

Newton was a serious biblical scholar and saw no inherent contradiction between his ideas and belief in God. "This most beautiful system of the sun, planets, and comets," he declared, "could only proceed from the counsel and dominion of an intelligent Being."[24] In such ways the scientists sought to accommodate religion. Over time, scientists and Church leaders learned to coexist through a kind of compartmentalization. Science might prevail in its limited sphere of describing the physical universe, but religion was still the arbiter of truth about those ultimate questions concerning human salvation, righteous behavior, and the larger purposes of life.

Science and Enlightenment

Initially limited to a small handful of scholars, the ideas of the Scientific Revolution spread to a wider European public during the eighteenth century, aided by novel techniques of printing and bookmaking, by a popular press, by growing literacy, and by a host of scientific societies. Moreover, the new approach to knowledge—rooted in human reason, skeptical of authority, expressed in natural laws—was now applied to human affairs, not just to the physical universe. The Scottish professor Adam Smith (1723–1790), for example, formulated laws that accounted for the operation of the economy and that, if followed, he believed, would generate inevitably favorable results for society. Growing numbers of people believed that the long-term outcome of scientific development would be "enlightenment," a term that has come to define the eighteenth century in European history. If human reason could discover the laws that governed the universe, surely it could uncover ways in which humankind might govern itself more effectively.

"What is Enlightenment?" asked the prominent German intellectual Immanuel Kant (1724–1804). "It is man's emergence from his self-imposed . . . inability to use one's own understanding without another's guidance. . . . Dare to know! 'Have the courage to use your own understanding' is therefore the motto of the enlightenment."[25] Although they often disagreed sharply with one another, **European Enlightenment** thinkers shared this belief in the power of knowledge to transform human society. They also shared a satirical, critical style, a commitment to open-mindedness and inquiry, and in various degrees a hostility to established political and religious authority. Many took aim at arbitrary governments, the "divine right of kings," and the aristocratic privileges of European society. The English philosopher John Locke (1632–1704) offered principles for constructing a constitutional government, a contract between rulers and ruled that was created by human ingenuity rather than divinely prescribed. Much of Enlightenment thinking was directed against the superstition, ignorance, and corruption of established religion. In his *Treatise on Toleration*, the French writer **Voltaire** (1694–1778) reflected the outlook of the Scientific Revolution as he commented sarcastically on religious intolerance:

> This little globe, nothing more than a point, rolls in space like so many other globes; we are lost in its immensity. Man, some five feet tall, is surely a very small part of the universe. One of these imperceptible beings says to some of his neighbors in Arabia or Africa: "Listen to me, for the God of all these worlds has enlightened me; there are nine hundred million little ants like us on the earth, but only my anthill is beloved of God; He will hold all others in horror through all eternity; only mine will be blessed, the others will be eternally wretched."[26]

Voltaire's own faith, like that of many others among the "enlightened," was deism. Deists believed in a rather abstract and remote Deity, sometimes compared to a clockmaker, who had created the world, but not in a personal God who intervened in history or tampered with natural law. Others became *pantheists*, who believed that God and nature were identical. Here were conceptions of religion shaped by the outlook of science. Sometimes called "natural religion," it was devoid of mystery, revelation, ritual, and spiritual practice, while proclaiming a God that could be "proven" by human rationality, logic, and the techniques of scientific

Guided Reading Question

■ **CHANGE**
In what ways did the Enlightenment challenge older patterns of European thinking?

The Philosophers of the Enlightenment This painting shows the French philosopher Voltaire with a group of intellectual luminaries at the summer palace of the Prussian king Frederick II. Such literary gatherings, sometimes called salons, were places of lively conversation among mostly male participants and came to be seen as emblematic of the European Enlightenment. (akg-images/ The Image Works)

inquiry. In this view, all else was superstition. Among the most radical of such thinkers were the several Dutchmen who wrote the *Treatise of Three Imposters*, which claimed that Moses, Jesus, and Muhammad were fraudulent deceivers who based their teachings on "the ignorance of Peoples [and] resolved to keep them in it."[27]

Prominent among the debates spawned by the Enlightenment was the question of women's nature, their role in society, and the education most appropriate for them. Although well-to-do Parisian women hosted in their elegant salons many gatherings of the largely male Enlightenment figures, most of those men were anything but ardent feminists. The male editors of the famous *Encyclopédie*, a vast compendium of Enlightenment thought, included very few essays by women. One of the male authors expressed a common view: "[Women] constitute the principal ornament of the world. . . . May they, through submissive discretion and . . . artless cleverness, spur us [men] on to virtue." In his treatise *Emile*, Jean-Jacques Rousseau described women as fundamentally different from and inferior to men and urged that "the whole education of women ought to be relative to men."

Such views were sharply contested by any number of other Enlightenment figures—men and women alike. The *Journal des Dames* (Ladies Journal), founded in Paris in 1759, aggressively defended women. "If we have not been raised up in the sciences as you have," declared Madame Beaulmer, the *Journal's* first editor, "it is you [men] who are the guilty ones; for have you not always abused . . . the bodily strength that nature has given you?"[28] The philosopher Marquis de **Condorcet** (1743–1794) looked forward to the "complete destruction of those prejudices that have established an inequality of rights between the sexes." And in 1792, the British writer Mary Wollstonecraft directly confronted Rousseau's view of women and their education: "What nonsense! . . . Til women are more rationally educated, the progress of human virtue and improvement in knowledge must receive continual checks." Thus was initiated a debate that echoed throughout the centuries that followed.

Though solidly rooted in Europe, Enlightenment thought was influenced by the growing global awareness of its major thinkers. Voltaire, for example, idealized China as an empire governed by an elite of secular scholars selected for their talent, which stood in sharp contrast to continental Europe, where aristocratic birth and military prowess were far more important. The example of Confucianism—supposedly secular, moral, rational, and tolerant—encouraged Enlightenment thinkers to imagine a future for European civilization without the kind of supernatural religion that they found so offensive in the Christian West.

The central theme of the Enlightenment—and what made it potentially revolutionary—was the idea of progress. Human society was not fixed by tradition or divine command but could be changed, and improved, by human action guided by reason. No one expressed this soaring confidence in human possibility more clearly than the French thinker Condorcet, who boldly declared that "the perfectibility of humanity is indefinite." Belief in progress was a sharp departure from much of pre-modern social thinking, and it inspired those who later made the great revolutions of the modern era in the Americas, France, Russia, China, and elsewhere. Born of the Scientific Revolution, that was the faith of the Enlightenment. For some, it was virtually a new religion.

The age of the Enlightenment, however, also witnessed a reaction against too much reliance on human reason. Jean-Jacques Rousseau (1712–1778) minimized the importance of book learning for the education of children and prescribed instead an immersion in nature, which taught self-reliance and generosity rather than the greed and envy fostered by "civilization." The Romantic movement in art and literature appealed to emotion, intuition, passion, and imagination rather than cold reason and scientific learning. Religious awakenings—complete with fiery sermons, public repentance, and intense personal experience of sin and redemption—shook Protestant Europe and North America in the eighteenth and early nineteenth centuries. The Methodist movement—with its emphasis on Bible study, confession of sins, fasting, enthusiastic preaching, and resistance to worldly pleasures—was a case in point.

Various forms of "enlightened religion" also arose in the early modern centuries, reflecting the influence of Enlightenment thinking. Quakers, for example, emphasized tolerance, an absence of hierarchy and ostentation, a benevolent God, and an "inner light" available to all people. Unitarians denied the Trinity, original sin, predestination, and the divinity of Jesus, but honored him as a great teacher and a moral prophet. Later, in the nineteenth century, proponents of the "social gospel" saw the essence of Christianity not in personal salvation but in ethical behavior. Science and the Enlightenment surely challenged religion, and for some they eroded religious belief and practice. Just as surely, though, religion persisted, adapted, and revived for many others.

European Science beyond the West

In the long run, the achievements of the Scientific Revolution spread globally, becoming the most widely sought-after product of European culture and far more desired than Christianity, democracy, socialism, or Western literature. In the early modern era, however, interest in European scientific thinking within major Asian societies was both modest and selective. The telescope provides an example. Invented in early seventeenth-century Europe and endlessly improved in the centuries that followed, the telescope provoked enormous excitement in European scientific circles. "We are here . . . on fire with these things," wrote an English astronomer in 1610.[29] Soon the telescope was available in China, Mughal India, and the Ottoman Empire. But in none of these places did it evoke much interest or evolve into the kind of "discovery machine" that it was rapidly becoming in Europe.

In China, Qing dynasty emperors and scholars were most interested in European techniques for predicting eclipses, reforming the calendar, and making accurate maps of the empire. European mathematics was also of particular interest to Chinese scholars who were exploring the history of Chinese mathematics. To convince their skeptical colleagues that the barbarian Europeans had something to offer in this field, some Chinese scholars argued that European mathematics had in fact grown out of much earlier Chinese ideas and could therefore be adopted with comfort.[30] European medicine, however, was of little importance for Chinese physicians before the nineteenth century. In such ways, early modern Chinese thinkers selectively assimilated Western science very much on their own terms.[31]

Although Japanese authorities largely closed their country off from the West in the early seventeenth century (see Chapter 14), one window remained open. Alone among Europeans, the Dutch were permitted to trade in Japan at a single location near Nagasaki, but not until 1720 did the Japanese lift the ban on importing Western books. Then a number of European texts in medicine, astronomy, geography, mathematics, and other disciplines were translated and studied by a small group of Japanese scholars. They were especially impressed with Western anatomical studies, for in Japan dissection was work fit only for outcasts. Returning from an autopsy conducted by Dutch physicians in the mid-eighteenth century, several Japanese observers reflected on their experience: "We remarked to each other how amazing the autopsy had been, and how inexcusable it had been for us to be ignorant of the anatomical structure

Guided Reading Question

■ **CONNECTION**

In what ways was European science received in the major civilizations of Asia in the early modern era?

of the human body."[32] Nonetheless, this small center of "Dutch learning," as it was called, remained isolated amid a pervasive Confucian-based culture. Not until the mid-nineteenth century, when Japan was forcibly opened to Western penetration, would European-style science assume a prominent place in Japanese culture.

Like China and Japan, the Ottoman Empire in the sixteenth and seventeenth centuries was an independent, powerful, successful society whose intellectual elites saw no need for a wholesale embrace of things European. Ottoman scholars were conscious of the rich tradition of Muslim astronomy and chose not to translate the works of major European scientists such as Copernicus, Kepler, or Newton, although they were broadly aware of European scientific achievements by 1650. Insofar as they were interested in these developments, it was for their practical usefulness in making maps and calendars rather than for their larger philosophical implications. In any event, the notion of a sun-centered solar system did not cause the kind of upset that it did in Europe.

More broadly, theoretical science of any kind—Muslim or European—faced an uphill struggle in the face of a conservative Islamic educational system. In 1580, for example, a highly sophisticated astronomical observatory in Constantinople was dismantled under pressure from conservative religious scholars and teachers, who interpreted an outbreak of the plague as God's disapproval of those who sought to understand his secrets. As in Japan, the systematic embrace of Western science would have to await the nineteenth century, when the Ottoman Empire was under far more intense European pressure and reform seemed more necessary.

Looking Ahead: Science in the Nineteenth Century and Beyond

In Europe itself, the impetus of the Scientific Revolution continued to unfold. Modern science, it turned out, was a cumulative and self-critical enterprise, which in the nineteenth century and later was applied to new domains of human inquiry in ways that undermined some of the assumptions of the Enlightenment. This remarkable phenomenon justifies a brief look ahead at several scientific developments in the nineteenth and twentieth centuries.

In the realm of biology, for example, Charles Darwin (1809–1882) laid out a complex argument that all life was in constant change, that an endless and competitive struggle for survival over millions of years constantly generated new species of plants and animals, while casting others into extinction. Human beings were not excluded from this vast process, for they too were the work of evolution operating through natural selection. Darwin's famous books *The Origin of Species* (1859) and *The Descent of Man* (1871) were threatening to many traditional Christian believers, perhaps more so than Copernicus's ideas about a sun-centered universe had been several centuries earlier.

At the same time, Karl Marx (1818–1883) articulated a view of human history that likewise emphasized change and struggle. Conflicting social classes—slave

Guided Reading Question

....

■ **CHANGE**
How did nineteenth-century developments in the sciences challenge Enlightenment ideas and principles?

owners and slaves, nobles and peasants, capitalists and workers—successively drove the process of historical transformation. Although he was describing the evolution of human civilization, Marx saw himself as a scientist. He based his theories on extensive historical research; like Newton and Darwin, he sought to formulate general laws that would explain events in a rational way. Nor did he believe in heavenly intervention, chance, or the divinely endowed powers of kings. In Marx's view the coming of socialism—a society without classes or class conflict—was not simply a good idea; it was inevitable, inscribed in the laws of historical development. (See "Social Protest" in Chapter 17.) Like the intellectuals of the Enlightenment, Darwin and Marx believed strongly in progress, but in their thinking, conflict and struggle rather than reason and education were the motors of progress. The Enlightenment image of the thoughtful, rational, and independent individual was fading. Individuals—plant, animal, and human alike—were now viewed as enmeshed in vast systems of biological, economic, or social conflict.

The work of the Viennese doctor Sigmund Freud (1856–1939) applied scientific techniques to the operation of the human mind and emotions and in doing so cast further doubt on Enlightenment conceptions of human rationality. At the core of each person, Freud argued, lay primal impulses toward sexuality and aggression, which were only barely held in check by the thin veneer of social conscience derived from civilization. Our neuroses arose from the ceaseless struggle between our irrational drives and the claims of conscience and society. This too was a far cry from the Enlightenment conception of the human condition.

And in the twentieth century, developments in physics, such as relativity and quantum theory, called into question some of the established verities of the Newtonian view of the world, particularly at the subatomic level and at speeds approaching that of light. In this new physics, time is relative to the position of the observer; space can warp and light can bend; matter and energy are equivalent; black holes and dark matter abound; and probability, not certain prediction, is the best that scientists can hope for. None of this was even on the horizon of those who made the original Scientific Revolution in the early modern era.

REFLECTIONS

Cultural Borrowing and Its Hazards

Accompanying the cultural transformations of the early modern era was a great deal of cultural borrowing. Filipinos, Siberians, and many Native American peoples borrowed elements of Christianity from Europeans. Numerous Asian and African peoples borrowed Islam from the Arabs. North Indian Sikhs drew on both Hindu and Muslim teachings. Europeans borrowed scientific and medical ideas from the Islamic world and subsequently contributed their own rich scientific thinking to the entire planet.

In virtually every case, though, borrowing was selective rather than wholesale, even when it took place under conditions of foreign domination or colonial rule. Many peoples who appropriated Christianity or Islam certainly did not accept the rigid exclusivity and ardent monotheism of more orthodox versions of those faiths. Elite Chinese were far more interested in European mapmaking and mathematics than in Western medicine, while Japanese scholars became fascinated with the anatomical work of the Dutch. Neither, however, adopted Christianity in a widespread manner.

Borrowing was frequently the occasion for serious conflict. Some objected to much borrowing at all, particularly when it occurred under conditions of foreign domination or foreign threat. Thus members of the Taki Onqoy movement in Peru sought to wipe out Spanish influence and control, while Chinese and Japanese authorities clamped down firmly on European missionaries, even as they maintained some interest in European technological and scientific skills. Another kind of conflict derived from the efforts to control the terms of cultural borrowing. For example, European missionaries and Muslim reformers alike sought to root out "idolatry" among native converts.

To ease the tensions of cultural borrowing, efforts to "domesticate" foreign ideas and practices proliferated. Thus the Jesuits in China tried to point out similarities between Christianity and Confucianism, and Native American converts identified Christian saints with their own gods and spirits. By the late seventeenth century, some local churches in central Mexico had come to associate Catholicism less with the Spanish than with ancient pre-Aztec communities and beliefs that were now, supposedly, restored to their rightful position.

The pace of global cultural borrowing and its associated tensions stepped up even more as Europe's modern transformation unfolded in the nineteenth century and as its imperial reach extended and deepened around the world.

Second Thoughts

What's the Significance?

Big Picture Questions

1. Why did Christianity take hold in some places more than in others?
2. In what ways was the missionary message of Christianity reshaped by the cultures of Asian and American peoples?
3. In what ways did the spread of Christianity, Islam, and modern science give rise to culturally based conflicts?
4. **Looking Back:** Based on Chapters 13 through 15, how might you challenge a Eurocentric understanding of the early modern era while acknowledging the growing role of Europeans on the global stage?

Next Steps: For Further Study

Natana J. Delong-Bas, *Wahhabi Islam: From Revival and Reform to Global Jihad* (2004). A careful study of the origins of Wahhabi Islam and its subsequent development.

Patricia Buckley Ebrey et al., *East Asia: A Cultural, Social, and Political History* (2005). A broad survey by major scholars in the field.

Geoffrey C. Gunn, *First Globalization: The Eurasian Exchange, 1500–1800* (2003). Explores the two-way exchange of ideas between Europe and Asia in the early modern era.

Toby E. Huff, *The Rise of Early Modern Science* (2003). A fascinating and controversial explanation as to why modern science arose in the West rather than in China or the Islamic world.

Diarmaid MacCulloch, *The Reformation: A History* (2005). A readable and wide-ranging survey of the European Reformation and Counter-Reformation.

Deva Sobel, *A More Perfect Heaven: How Copernicus Revolutionized the Cosmos* (2011). A fascinating account of a major breakthrough in the Scientific Revolution.

Mari Aguayo Tabor, "The Scientific Revolution in Europe," created for the Liberal Arts and Science Academy, Austin, Texas, 2014, https://www.youtube.com/watch?v=HhlX-17p4VEs. A brief and well-illustrated video with a focus on astronomy and anatomy in the early modern era.

"Sikhism, Religion of the Sikh People," Sikhs.org, 2011, https://www.sikhs.org/topics.htm. A highly informative website that covers the history, philosophy, and ways of life of the Sikh people.

Christianity: Becoming a Global Religion

During the early modern centuries, missionaries—mostly Roman Catholic—rode the tide of European expansion to establish Christianity in the Americas and parts of Africa and Asia. In those places, native converts sometimes imitated European patterns and at other times adapted the new religion to their own cultural traditions. Thus the Christian world of the early modern era was far more globalized than before 1500. The sources that follow illustrate the variety of receptions that Christianity received in different places and the cultural blending or mixing that occurred when new peoples embraced the faith.

SOURCE 15.1 Cultural Blending in Andean Christianity ▶

Throughout Latin America, Christianity was established in the context of European conquest and colonial rule. As the new faith took hold across the region, it incorporated much that was of European origin, as the construction of many large and ornate churches illustrates. But local communities also sought to blend this European Catholic Christianity with religious symbols and concepts drawn from their own traditions in a process that historians call syncretism. In the Andes, for example, Inca religion featured a supreme creator god (Viracocha); a sun god (Inti), regarded as the creator of the Inca people; a moon goddess (Killa), who was the wife of Inti and was attended by an order of priestesses; and an earth mother goddess (Pachamama), associated with mountain peaks and fertility. Those religious figures found their way into Andean understanding of Christianity, as Source 15.1 illustrates.

Painted around 1740 by an unknown artist, this striking image shows the Virgin Mary placed within the "rich mountain" of Potosí in Bolivia, from which the Spanish had extracted so much silver (see "Silver and Global Commerce" in Chapter 14). Thus Christianity was visually expressed in an Andean tradition that viewed mountains as the embodiment of the gods. A number of smaller figures within the mountain represent the native miners whose labor had enriched their colonial rulers. A somewhat larger figure at the bottom of the mountain is an Inca ruler dressed in royal garb receiving tribute from his people. At the bottom left are the pope and a cardinal, while on the right stand the Habsburg emperor Charles V and perhaps his wife.

■ What is Mary's relationship to the heavenly beings standing above her (God the Father on the right; the dove, symbolizing the Holy Spirit, in the center; and Jesus on the left) as well as to the miners at work in the mountain? What is the significance of the crown above her head and her outstretched arms?

■ The European figures at the bottom are shown in a posture of prayer or thanksgiving. What might the artist have been trying to convey? How would you interpret the relative size of the European and Andean figures?

■ Why do you think the artist placed Mary actually inside the mountain rather than on it, while depicting her dress in a mountain-like form?

■ What marks this painting as an example of syncretism?

■ Do you read this image as subversive of the colonial order or as supportive of it? Do you think the artist who painted Source 15.1 was a European or a Native American Christian?

La Virgen del Cerro (Virgin Mary of the Mountains) | ca. 1740

Museo de la Casa de la Moneda, Potosi, Bolivia/Gilles Mermet/akg-images

■ ■ ■

SOURCE 15.2 **Christianity through Maya Eyes**

European missionaries, clergy, inquisitors, and government officials wrote most of the surviving sources about the conversion of Mesoamerica, but the *Books of the Chilam Balam* offer a rare indigenous perspective. Written in the seventeenth and eighteenth centuries, their Maya authors recorded local rituals, medical knowledge, history, myths, prophecies, and Christian instruction in the Yucatec Mayan language using the European Latin alphabet. The passages that follow come from the *Chilam Balam of Chumayel*, a town on the Yucatán Peninsula of modern Mexico. They reveal how Christian concepts were integrated into an existing Maya worldview and cosmology.

■ How is the exploitation of the Maya in the Spanish colonial system reflected in these passages? How do these conditions affect Maya understandings of Christianity and the relationship of indigenous people to the Christian God?

■ In what specific ways have Christian beliefs and practices been blended with their Maya counterparts? In the passage concerned with Christ's life and crucifixion, the four cardinal directions and arrow-stones are ritual elements drawn from pre-Christian Maya ceremonial practices, especially the arrow sacrifice, which involved the ritual slaying of a human being. How does this information shape your understanding of this Maya description of the crucifixion and resurrection of Christ?

■ Compare the elements of religious blending or syncretism in these passages and those in Source 15.1. What similarities and differences can you identify?

The Chilam Balam of Chumayel | **18th century**

[On the Fate of the Maya Gods]

Nevertheless, the first gods were perishable gods. Their worship came to its inevitable end. They lost their efficacy by the benediction of the Lord of Heaven, after the redemption of the world was accomplished, after the resurrection of the true God, the true Dios, when he blessed heaven and earth. Then was your worship abolished, Maya men. Turn away your hearts from your [old] religion.

[A Maya Account of Jesus' Birth, Crucifixion, and Resurrection]

In the middle of the town of Tihoo [Mérida] is the cathedral, the fiery house, the mountainous house, the dark house, for the benefit of God the Father, God the Son and God the Holy Spirit.

Who enters into the house of God? Father, it is the one named Ix-Kalem [the Holy One].

What day did the Virgin conceive? Father, 4 Oc [a specific day in the Maya calendar] . . . when she conceived.

What day did he come forth [from the womb]? On 3 Oc [a specific day in the Maya calendar] he came forth.

What day did he die? On 1 Cimi [a specific day in the Maya calendar] he died. Then he entered the tomb on 1 Cimi.

What entered his tomb? Father, a coffer of stone entered his tomb.

What entered into his thigh? Father, it was the red arrow-stone. It entered into the precious stone of the world, there in heaven.

And his arm? Father, the arrow-stone; and that it might be commemorated it entered into the red living rock in the east. Then it came to the north and entered into the white living rock. After that it entered the black living rock in the west. Thus also [it entered] the yellow living rock in the south. . . .

[On the Coming of Christianity and Prophecy for Future Divine Intervention]

Then with the true God, the true Dios [God], came the beginning of our misery. It was the beginning of tribute, the beginning of church dues, the beginning of strife with purse-snatching, the beginning of strife with blow-guns, the beginning of strife by trampling on the people, the beginning of robbery with violence, the beginning of forced debts. . . . This was the origin of service to the Spaniards and priests, of service to the local chiefs. . . . It was by Antichrist on earth, the kinkajous [a small rainforest mammal] of the towns, the foxes of the towns, the blood-sucking insects of the town, those who drained the poverty of the working people [who made working people poor]. But it shall still come to pass that tears shall come to the eyes of our Lord God. The justice of our Lord God shall descend upon every part of the world, straight from God upon . . . the avaricious hagglers of the world.

[Prophecy on the End Times]

Then, I tell you, justice shall descend to the end that Christianity and salvation may arise. Then the rulers of the towns shall be asked for their proofs and titles of ownership, if they know of them. Then they shall come forth from the forests and from among the rocks and live like men; then towns shall be established [again]. There shall be no fox to bite them. . . . Five years shall run until the end of my prophecy, and then shall come the time for the tribute to come down. Then there shall be an end to the paying for the wars which our fathers raised [against the Spaniards]. You shall not call the *katun* [a twenty-year period] which is to come a hostile one, when Jesus Christ, the guardian of our souls shall come. Just as [we are saved] here on earth, so shall he bear our souls to his holy heaven also. You are sons of the true God. Amen.

Source: *The Book of Chilam Balam of Chumayel*, translated by Ralph L. Roys (Norman: University of Oklahoma Press, 1967), 79, 98, 124–27.

■ ■ ■

SOURCE 15.3 Making Christianity Chinese ▶

In China, unlike in Latin America, Christian missionaries operated in a setting wholly outside of European political control and with far fewer converts. Nonetheless, in China too the tendency toward syncretism was evident. Jesuit missionaries themselves sought to present the Christian message within a Chinese cultural context to the intellectual and political elites who were their primary target audience. And Chinese Christians often transposed the new religion into more familiar cultural concepts.

Source 15.3 provides an example of Christianity becoming Chinese.[33] In the early seventeenth century, the Jesuits published several books in the Chinese language describing the life of Christ and illustrated them with a series of woodblock prints created by Chinese artists affiliated with the Jesuits. Although they were clearly modeled on European images, those prints cast Christian figures into an altogether Chinese setting. The print in Source 15.3 portrays the familiar biblical story of the Annunciation, when an angel informs Mary that she will be the mother of Jesus. The house and furniture shown in the print suggest the dwelling of a wealthy Chinese scholar. The reading table in front of Mary was a common item in the homes of the literary elite of the time. The view from the window shows a seascape, mountains in the distance, a lone tree, and a "scholar's rock"—all of which were common features in Chinese landscape painting. The clouds that appear at the angel's feet and around the shaft of light shining on Mary are identical to those associated with sacred Buddhist and Daoist figures. To Chinese eyes, the angel might well appear as a Buddhist bodhisattva, while Mary may resemble a Ming dynasty noblewoman or perhaps Kuanyin, the Chinese Buddhist goddess of mercy and compassion.

Illustration of the Annunciation | ca. 17th century

- What specifically Chinese elements can you identify in this image?

- To whom might this image have been directed?

- How might educated Chinese have responded to this image?

- The European engraving on which this Chinese print was modeled included in the background the scene of Jesus' crucifixion. Why might the Chinese artist have chosen to omit that scene from his image?

- How would European critics of the Jesuits' approach to missionary work have reacted to this image? To what extent has the basic message of Catholic Christianity been retained or altered in this Chinese cultural setting?

■ ■ ■

SOURCE 15.4 The Chinese Rites Controversy

Religious syncretism on occasion provoked heated debate, as the Chinese Rites Controversy illustrates. European opponents of the Jesuits—especially among the Dominicans, a rival missionary religious order—raised objections to Jesuit acceptance of some Chinese customs, including the honoring of ancestors (what their critics called ancestor worship) and devotion to Confucius. The Jesuits viewed ancestor reverence as compatible with Christianity and Confucian ceremonies as civil rites rather than religious observances, but many European opponents understood these Chinese practices as religious in nature and therefore incompatible with orthodox Christian teachings. Ultimately the Jesuits lost this debate when Pope Clement XI issued a decree banning these "Chinese rites" in 1715. Source 15.4A is the pope's decree, and Source 15.4B records the Chinese emperor's response to the pope's pronouncement.

- What specific practices did Clement prohibit, and what reasons did he offer for his ban? How would the pope's prohibitions make it more difficult for a Chinese convert to Christianity to maintain his or her place in Chinese society?

- Why did the emperor ban the teaching of Christianity in his realm? What can his reaction tell us about the Jesuit approach to conversion in China?

- Do you think that Source 15.3 contravenes Clement's decree, or would the pope approve of the continued dissemination of such images in China?

SOURCE 15.4A
Papal Decree Banning Chinese Rites | 1715

I. The West calls *Deus* [God] the creator of Heaven, Earth, and everything in the universe. Since the word *Deus* does not sound right in the Chinese language, the Westerners in China and Chinese converts to Catholicism have used the term "Heavenly Lord" for many years. From now on such terms as "Heaven" and "Shangti" should not be used: *Deus* should be addressed as the Lord of Heaven, Earth, and everything in the universe. The tablet that bears the Chinese words "Reverence for Heaven" should not be allowed to hang inside a Catholic church and should be immediately taken down if already there.

II. The spring and autumn worship of Confucius, together with the worship of ancestors, is not allowed among Catholic converts. It is not allowed even though the converts appear in the ritual as bystanders, because to be a bystander in this ritual is as pagan as to participate in it actively.

III. Chinese officials and successful candidates in the metropolitan, provincial, or prefectural examinations, if they have been converted to Roman Catholicism, are not allowed to worship in Confucian temples on the first and fifteenth days of each month....

IV. No Chinese Catholics are allowed to worship ancestors in their familial temples.

V. Whether at home, in the cemetery, or during the time of a funeral, a Chinese Catholic is not allowed to perform the ritual of ancestor worship....

Despite the above decisions, I have made it clear that other Chinese customs and traditions that can in no way be interpreted as heathen in nature should be allowed to continue among Chinese converts. The way the Chinese manage their households or govern their country should by no means be interfered with.

Source: Dun J. Li, *China in Transition, 1517–1911* (New York: Van Nostrand Reinhold, 1969), 22–24.

SOURCE 15.4B
Decree of Emperor Kangxi | 1721

Reading this proclamation, I have concluded that the Westerners are petty indeed. It is impossible to reason with them because they do not understand larger issues as we understand them in China. There is not a single Westerner versed in Chinese works, and their remarks are often incredible and ridiculous. To judge from this proclamation, their religion is no different from other small, bigoted sects of Buddhism or Taoism. I have never seen a document which contains so much nonsense. From now on, Westerners should not be allowed to preach in China, to avoid further trouble.

Source: Dun J. Li, *China in Transition, 1517–1911* (New York: Van Nostrand Reinhold, 1969), 22.

■ ■ ■

SOURCE 15.5 Christian Art in the Mughal Empire ▶

The rulers of Mughal India during the time of Akbar (r. 1556–1605) and Jahangir (r. 1605–1627) also invited Jesuit missionaries to their court. But while Chinese elite circles received the Jesuits for their scientific skills, especially in astronomy, the Mughal court seemed more interested in the religious and artistic achievements of European civilization. Akbar invited the Jesuits to take part in cross-religious discussions that included Muslim, Hindu, Jain, and Zoroastrian scholars. Furthermore, the Mughal emperors eagerly embraced the art of late Renaissance Europe, which the Jesuits provided to them, much of it devotional and distinctly Christian. Mughal artists quickly learned to paint in the European style, and soon murals featuring Jesus, Mary, and Christian saints appeared on the walls of palaces, garden pavilions, and harems of the Mughal court, while miniature paintings adorned books, albums, and jewelry.

In religious terms, however, the Jesuit efforts were "a fantastic and extravagant failure,"[34] for these Muslim rulers of India were not in the least interested in abandoning Islam for the Christian faith, and few conversions of any kind occurred. Akbar and Jahangir, however, were cosmopolitan connoisseurs of art, which they collected, reproduced, and displayed. European religious art also had propaganda value in enhancing their status. Jesus and Mary, after all, had a prominent place within Islam. Jesus was seen both as an earlier prophet and as a mystical figure, similar to the Sufi masters who were so important in Indian Islam. Mughal paintings pairing the adult Jesus and Mary side by side were placed above the imperial throne as well as on the emperor's jewelry and his official seal, suggesting an identification of Jesus and a semi-divine emperor. That the mothers of both Akbar and Jahangir were named Mary only added to the appeal. Thus Akbar and Jahangir sought to incorporate European-style Christian art into their efforts to create a blended and tolerant religious culture for the elites of their vast and diverse realm that drew on Islam, Hinduism, Zoroastrianism, and Christianity.

But as Catholic devotional art was reworked by Mughal artists, it was also subtly changed. Source 15.5 shows an early seventeenth-century depiction of the Holy Family painted by an Indian artist.

- Why do you think that this Mughal painter portrayed Mary and Joseph as rather distinguished and educated persons rather than as the humble carpenter and his peasant wife, as in so many European images? Why might he have placed the family in rather palatial surroundings instead of a stable?

- How do you imagine European missionaries responded to this representation of the Holy Family?

- How might more orthodox Muslims have reacted to the larger project of creating a blended religion making use of elements from many traditions?

- What similarities can you identify between this Indian image and the Chinese print in Source 15.3? Pay attention to the setting, the clothing, the class status of the human figures, and the scenes outside the windows.

The Holy Family | **early 17th century**

Free Library of Philadelphia/Bridgeman Images

DOING HISTORY

1. **Making comparisons:** What common Christian elements do you find in these sources? What differences in the expression of Christianity can you define?

2. **Considering Mary:** The Catholic Christian tradition as it developed in Latin America, China, and India as well as Europe assigned a very important role to representations of the Virgin Mary. Why might such images of Mary have been so widely appealing? In what ways does the image of the Holy Mother differ in Sources 15.1, 15.3, and 15.5? In what ways were those images adapted to the distinctive cultures in which they were created?

3. **Pondering syncretism:** From a missionary viewpoint, develop arguments for and against religious syncretism using these sources as points of reference.

4. **Considering visual sources as evidence:** What are the strengths and limitations of the visual sources in this collection, as opposed to the texts, for seeking to understand the globalization of Christianity in the early modern era?

Missions in Mesoamerica and China

Missionary efforts to win new converts and strengthen the devotion of new Christians took many different forms during the early modern period. These voices examine specific missionary efforts in sixteenth-century Mesoamerica and seventeenth- and eighteenth-century China. In Voice 15.1, Merry Wiesner-Hanks explores two alternative foundation narratives for the Virgin of Guadalupe shrine in Mexico (see the image at the beginning of this chapter). In Voice 15.2, Diarmaid MacCulloch describes Jesuit missionary strategies in China.

- How does your understanding of the Virgin of Guadalupe shrine and the way that Mexico was Christianized change depending on which interpretation of its foundation you accept?

- What challenges did the Jesuit mission in China face, and how did the Jesuits seek to overcome them?

- What strategies for strengthening the devotion of new converts are highlighted in these two voices?

- **Integrating Primary and Secondary Sources:** How do these voices help you to better understand the Working with Evidence sources?

VOICE 15.1

Merry Wiesner-Hanks on the Virgin of Guadalupe │ 2015

[T]he Virgin of Guadalupe can serve as a good example [of syncretism]. . . . In the seventeenth century, published texts in Spanish and Nahuatl [an indigenous Mexican language] told of the appearance of the Virgin Mary in 1531 to Juan Diego Cuauhtlatoatzin, an indigenous farmer and Christian convert, on a hill near Tenochtitlan (now within Mexico City). Speaking in Nahuatl, the apparition told Juan Diego that a church should be built at the site, and her image miraculously appeared on his cloak. Shortly afterward a church dedicated to the Virgin of Guadalupe was begun. . . . Preachers and teachers interpreted her appearance as a sign of the Virgin's special protection of indigenous people and those of mixed ancestry . . . , and pilgrims from all over Mexico began to make the trek to her shrine. . . .

In the twentieth century, however, many scholars, including some members of the Mexican clergy, came to doubt whether the apparition had ever happened or Juan Diego himself had even existed. They pointed out that written accounts were not published until over a century later, and that church officials and missionaries active in central Mexico in 1531 made no mention of the event. . . . Specialists in Nahuatl culture note that the hill where the apparition was reported was originally the site of a shrine to Coatlicue, the mother of the most powerful Aztec God Huitzilopochtli, and that aspects of the veneration of the Virgin of Guadalupe were also part of honoring Coatlicue or other Aztec mother goddesses. In their view, the colonial Catholic Church had simply invented the story as part of its efforts to strip Aztec Holy sites of their original meaning.

Source: Merry E. Wiesner-Hanks, *A Concise History of the World* (Cambridge: Cambridge University Press, 2015), 267.

VOICE 15.2

Diarmaid MacCulloch on Jesuit Missionary Strategies in China │ 2009

The Jesuits quickly decided that missionaries must adapt themselves to Chinese customs. This involved much rapid self-education. Their first great missionary, the Italian Matteo Ricci, on his arrival in 1582 adopted the dress of a Buddhist monk (*bonze*), without realizing that *bonzes* were despised by the people who mattered. When his mistake was pointed out, he and his fellow Jesuits began dressing as Confucian scholars, complete with long beards; they were determined to show that their learning was worthy of respect in a culture with a deep reverence for scholarship. . . . The Chinese upper class was indeed impressed by the Jesuits' knowledge of mathematics, astronomy and geography, and the Society gained an honoured place at the emperor's court through its specialist use of these skills. . . .

The Jesuit emphasis on their honoured place at Court was always something of a diversion from the real reasons for the growth of adherents, who were very different in their social profile from the exalted figures around the emperor. At the peak of the Chinese mission's success at the end of the seventeenth century, it was serving perhaps around a quarter of a million people. . . . Yet at that time there were only seventy-five priests to serve this number, laboring under enormous difficulties with language. . . . What the Jesuits did very effectively in this situation was to inspire a local leadership which was not clerical, both catechists [teachers of the basic tenets of the faith] and a particular Chinese phenomenon . . . , "Chinese virgins": laywomen consecrated to singleness but still living with their families, teaching women and children.

Source: Diarmaid MacCulloch, *Christianity: The First Three Thousand Years* (New York: Penguin, 2009), 706–7.

The European Moment in World History

1750–1900

THE BIG PICTURE

European Centrality and the Problem of Eurocentrism

During the century and a half between 1750 and 1900, sometimes referred to as the "long nineteenth century," two new and related phenomena held center stage in the global history of humankind and represent the major themes of the four chapters that follow. The first of these, explored in Chapters 16 and 17, was the creation of a new kind of human society, commonly called "modern," emerging from the intersection of the Scientific, French, and Industrial Revolutions, all of which took shape initially in

Western Europe. The second theme of this long nineteenth century, which is addressed in Chapters 18 and 19, was the growing ability of these modern societies to exercise enormous power and influence over the rest of humankind through their empires, economic penetration, military intervention, diplomatic pressure, and missionary activity.

These developments marked a major turning point in world history in several ways. Western Europeans and their North American offspring now assumed a new and far more prominent role in the world than ever before. Furthermore, this "European moment" in world history established a new phase of human connectedness or entanglement that later generations labeled as "globalization." Finally, Europeans were also leading a human intervention in the natural order of unprecedented dimensions, largely the product of industrialization. Thus the long nineteenth century represents the starting point of the Anthropocene era, or the "age of man," a concept that points to the many ways in which humankind itself has become an active agent of change in the physical and biological evolution of the planet. It marks an epic transformation in the relationship of humanity to the earth, equivalent perhaps to the early stages of the Agricultural Revolution.

Europe's global centrality during the nineteenth century generated understandings of both geography and history that centered the entire human story on Europe. Thus flat maps placed Europe at the center of the world, while dividing Asia in half. Europe was granted continental status, even though it was more accurately only the western peninsula of Asia, much as India was its southern peninsula. Other regions of the world, such as the Far East or the Near (Middle) East, were defined in terms of their distance from Europe. History textbooks often portrayed people of European extraction at the center of human progress. Other peoples and civilizations, by contrast, were long believed to be static or stagnant, thus largely lacking any real history. Most Europeans assumed that these "backward" peoples and regions must either imitate the Western model or face further decline and possible extinction. Until the mid-twentieth century, such ideas went largely unchallenged in the Western world.

The rise of the academic discipline of world history in the decades following World War II represented a sharp challenge to such Eurocentric understandings of the human past. But in dealing with recent centuries, historians have confronted a distinct problem: how to avoid Eurocentrism when dealing with a phase of world history in which Europeans were in fact central.

At least five responses to this dilemma are reflected in the chapters that follow. First, the "European moment" has been recent and perhaps brief. Other peoples too had times of "cultural flowering" that granted them a period of primacy or influence—for example, the Arabs (600–1000), Chinese (1000–1500), Mongols (1200–1350), and Incas and Aztecs (fifteenth century)—but all of these were limited to particular regions of Afro-Eurasia or the Americas.[1] Even though the European moment operated on a genuinely global scale, Western peoples enjoyed their worldwide primacy for two centuries at most. The events of the late twentieth and early twenty-first centuries—the dissolution of colonial empires, the rise of India and especially

China, and the assertion of Islam—suggest the end, or at least the erosion, of the age of European predominance.

Second, we need to remember that the rise of Europe occurred within an international context. It was the withdrawal of the Chinese naval fleet that allowed Europeans to enter the Indian Ocean in the sixteenth century, while Native Americans' lack of immunity to European diseases and their own divisions and conflicts greatly assisted the European takeover of the Western Hemisphere. The Industrial Revolution, explored in Chapter 17, benefited from New World resources and markets and from the stimulus of superior Asian textile and pottery production. Chapters 18 and 19 make clear that European control of other regions everywhere depended on the cooperation of local elites. Europeans, like everyone else, were embedded in a web of relationships that shaped their own histories.

A third reminder is that the rise of Europe to a position of global dominance was not an easy or automatic process. Frequently it occurred in the face of ferocious resistance and rebellion, which often required Europeans to modify their policies and practices. The so-called Indian mutiny in mid-nineteenth-century South Asia, a massive uprising against British colonial rule, did not end British control, but it substantially transformed the character of the colonial experience. Even when Europeans exercised political power, they could not do precisely as they pleased. Empire, formal and informal alike, was always in some ways a negotiated arrangement.

Fourth, peoples the world over made active use of Europeans and European ideas for their own purposes, seeking to gain advantage over local rivals or to benefit themselves in light of new conditions. During the Haitian Revolution, examined in Chapter 16, enslaved Africans made use of radical French ideas about "the rights of man" in ways that most Europeans never intended. Later in Southeast Asia, a number of highland minority groups, long oppressed by the dominant lowland Vietnamese, viewed the French invaders as liberators and assisted in their takeover of Vietnam. Recognizing that Asian and African peoples remained active agents, pursuing their own interests even in oppressive conditions, is another way of countering residual Eurocentrism.

Moreover, what was borrowed from Europe was always adapted to local circumstances. Thus Japanese or Russian industrial development did not wholly follow the pattern of England's Industrial Revolution. The Christianity that took root in the Americas or later in Africa evolved in culturally distinctive ways. Ideas of nationalism, born in Europe, were used to oppose European imperialism throughout Asia and Africa. The most interesting stories of modern world history are not simply those of European triumph or the imposition of Western ideas and practices but those of encounters, though highly unequal, among culturally different peoples.

Finally, despite Europeans' unprecedented prominence on the world stage, they were not the only game in town, nor were they the sole preoccupation of Asian, African, and Middle Eastern peoples. While China confronted Western aggression in the nineteenth century, it was also absorbing a huge population increase and experiencing massive peasant rebellions that grew out of distinctly Chinese conditions.

Furthermore, cultural influence moved in many directions as European and American intellectuals began to absorb the spiritual traditions of India and as Japanese art became highly fashionable in the West.

None of this diminishes the significance of the European moment in world history, but it sets that moment in a larger context of continuing patterns of historical development and of interaction and exchange with other peoples.

Landmarks in World History (ca. 1750–ca. 1900)

1750   **1775**   **1800**   **1825**

EUROPE

1780s Beginnings of abolitionist movement

1825
Decembrist revolt
in Russia

1789–1799
French Revolution

1799–1814
Reign of Napoleon Bonaparte

1750–1850
Beginnings of
Industrial
Revolution

1754–1763 Seven Years' War among European Great Powers

THE AMERICAS AND PACIFIC OCEANIA

1775–1787 Revolution in North America

1791–1804 Haitian Revolution

1788
Ratification of U.S. Constitution

1803 Louisiana Purchase

1808–1825
Latin American wars of independence

ASIA

1740–1818
Wahhabi movement of
Islamic renewal in Arabia

1788
Initial British settlement of Australia

1750s British takeover of India begins

1793 Chinese reject British requests for expanded trade

1707–1750 Fragmentation of Mughal Empire

AFRICA

1798 Napoleon's invasion of Egypt

1750–1800 High point of the Atlantic slave trade

1815–1840
Mfecane; rise of Zulu kingdom in South Africa

1804–1817
Islamic revolutions in West Africa

1830–1847
Initial French conquest of Algeria

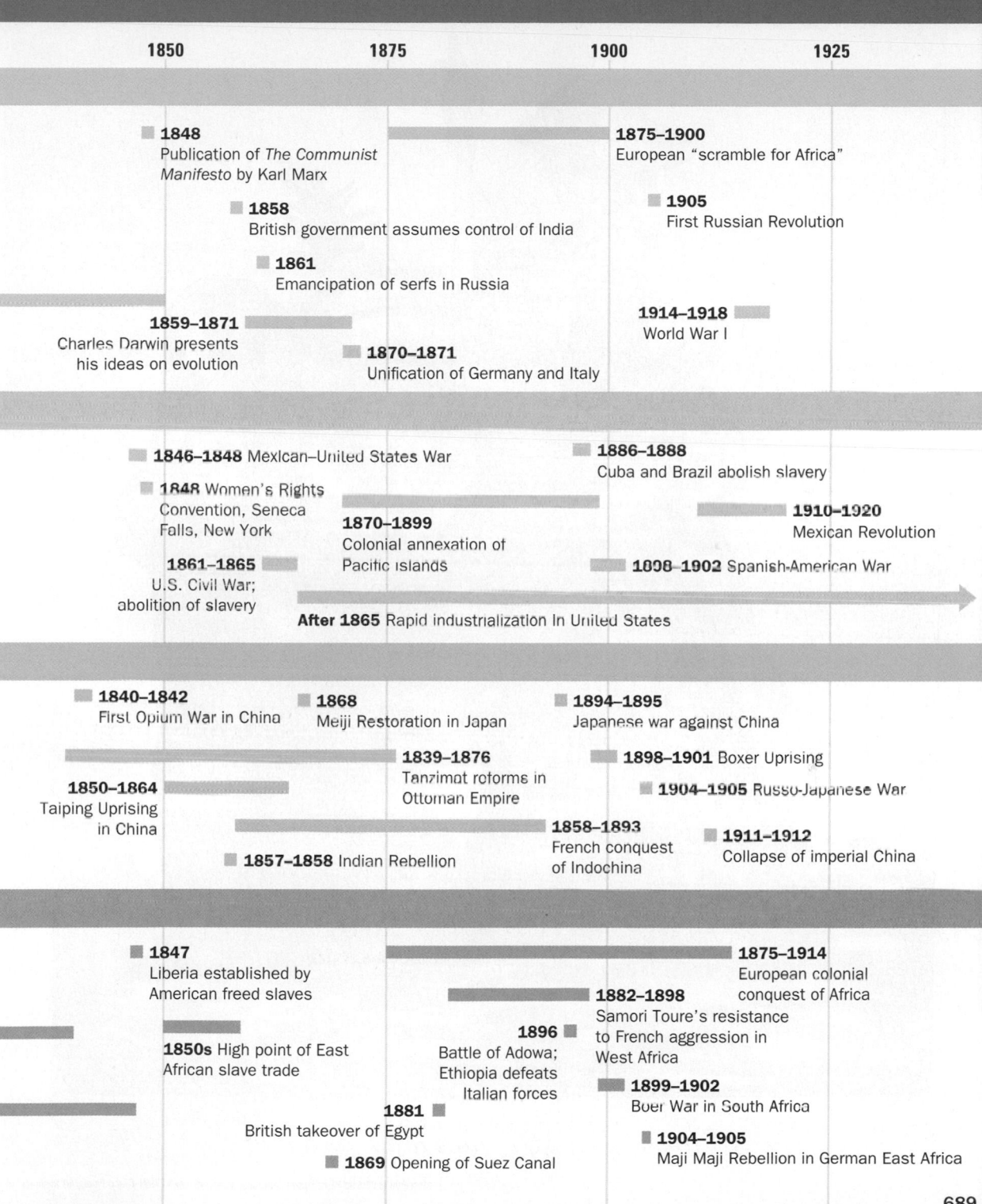

1850   1875   1900   1925

1848
Publication of *The Communist Manifesto* by Karl Marx

1858
British government assumes control of India

1861
Emancipation of serfs in Russia

1859–1871
Charles Darwin presents his ideas on evolution

1870–1871
Unification of Germany and Italy

1875–1900
European "scramble for Africa"

1905
First Russian Revolution

1914–1918
World War I

1846–1848 Mexican–United States War

1848 Women's Rights Convention, Seneca Falls, New York

1870–1899
Colonial annexation of Pacific islands

1861–1865
U.S. Civil War; abolition of slavery

After 1865 Rapid industrialization in United States

1886–1888
Cuba and Brazil abolish slavery

1910–1920
Mexican Revolution

1898–1902 Spanish-American War

1840–1842
First Opium War in China

1868
Meiji Restoration in Japan

1839–1876
Tanzimat reforms in Ottoman Empire

1850–1864
Taiping Uprising in China

1857–1858 Indian Rebellion

1858–1893
French conquest of Indochina

1894–1895
Japanese war against China

1898–1901 Boxer Uprising

1904–1905 Russo-Japanese War

1911–1912
Collapse of imperial China

1847
Liberia established by American freed slaves

1850s High point of East African slave trade

1881
British takeover of Egypt

1869 Opening of Suez Canal

1875–1914
European colonial conquest of Africa

1882–1898
Samori Toure's resistance to French aggression in West Africa

1896
Battle of Adowa; Ethiopia defeats Italian forces

1899–1902
Boer War in South Africa

1904–1905
Maji Maji Rebellion in German East Africa

Vive le Roi, Vive la Nation.

J'savois ben Qu'jaurions not tour.

CHAPTER 16

Atlantic Revolutions, Global Echoes

1750–1900

The Haitian earthquake of January 2010 not only devastated an already impoverished country but also reawakened issues deriving from that country's revolution against slavery and French colonial rule, which finally succeeded in 1804. Twenty-one years after its independence, the French government demanded from Haiti a payment of 150 million gold francs in compensation for the loss of its richest colony and its "property" in slaves. With French warships hovering offshore, Haitian authorities agreed. To make the heavy payments, even after they were somewhat reduced, Haiti took out major loans from French, German, and North American banks. Repaying those loans, finally accomplished only in 1947, represented a huge drain on the country's budget. In 2010, with the country in ruins, an international petition signed by over 100 prominent people called on the French government to repay some $17 billion, effectively returning the "independence debt" extorted from Haiti 185 years earlier. While the French government dismissed those claims, the issue provided a reminder of the continuing echoes of events from an earlier age of revolution. ■

T he Haitian Revolution was part of and linked to a much larger set of upheavals that shook both sides of the Atlantic world between 1775 and 1825. Haitians had drawn inspiration from the earlier North American and French revolutions, even as their successful overthrow of French rule helped shape the Latin American independence struggles that followed. These four closely related upheavals reflect the

« **Revolution and the Reversal of Class Roles** Three French female figures, representing from right to left the clergy, nobility, and commoners (Third Estate), show the reversal of class roles that the revolution generated. Now the commoner rides on the back of the noblewoman and is shown in a dominant position over the nun.

SEEKING THE MAIN POINT

What were the most important outcomes of the Atlantic revolutions, both immediately and in the century that followed?

new connections among Europe, Africa, North America, and South America that took shape in the wake of Columbus's voyages and the subsequent European conquests. Together, they launched a new chapter in the history of the Atlantic world, while the echoes of those revolutions reverberated in the larger world.

Atlantic Revolutions in a Global Context

Writing to a friend in 1772, before any of the Atlantic revolutions had occurred, the French intellectual Voltaire asked, "My dear philosopher, doesn't this appear to you to be the century of revolutions?"[1] He was certainly on target, and not only for Europe. From the early eighteenth century to the mid-nineteenth, many parts of the world witnessed political and social upheaval, leading some historians to think in terms of a "world crisis" or "converging revolutions." By the 1730s, the Safavid dynasty that had ruled Persia (now Iran) for several centuries had completely collapsed, even as the powerful Mughal Empire governing India also fragmented. About the same time, the Wahhabi movement in Arabia seriously threatened the Ottoman Empire, and its religious ideals informed major political upheavals in Central Asia and elsewhere (see "Expansion and Renewal in the Islamic World" in Chapter 15). The Russian Empire under Catherine the Great experienced a series of peasant uprisings, most notably one led by the Cossack commander Pugachev in 1773–1774 that briefly proclaimed the end of serfdom before that rebellion was crushed. China too in the late eighteenth and early nineteenth centuries hosted a number of popular though unsuccessful rebellions, a prelude perhaps to the huge Taiping revolution of 1850–1864. Beginning in the early nineteenth century, a new wave of Islamic revolutions shook West Africa, while in southern Africa a series of wars and migrations known as the *mfecane* (the breaking or crushing) involved widespread and violent disruptions as well as the creation of new states and societies.

Thus the Atlantic revolutions in North America, France, Haiti, and Latin America took place within a larger global framework. Like many of the other upheavals, they too occurred in the context of expensive wars, weakening states, and destabilizing processes of commercialization. But compared to upheavals elsewhere, the Atlantic revolutions were distinctive in various ways. The costly wars that strained European imperial states—Britain, France, and Spain in particular—were global rather than regional. In the so-called Seven Years' War (1754–1763), Britain and France joined battle in North America, the Caribbean, West Africa, and South Asia. The expenses of those conflicts prompted the British to levy additional taxes on their North American colonies and the French monarchy to seek new revenue from its landowners. These actions contributed to the launching of the North American and French revolutions, respectively.

Furthermore, the Atlantic revolutions were distinctive in that they were closely connected to one another. The American revolutionary leader Thomas Jefferson

Landmarks for Chapter 16

1775   1800   1825   1850   1875   1900   1925

EUROPE

1754–1763 Seven Years' War among European Great Powers

1789–1815 French Revolution and reign of Napoleon

1825 Anti-tsarist uprising in Russia

1833 Slavery prohibited in British Empire

1861 Emancipation of serfs in Russia

1870 Unification of Italy

1871 Unification of Germany

NORTH AMERICA

1775–1787 American Revolution

1848 Women's Rights Convention, Seneca Falls, NY

1861–1865 U.S. Civil War and abolition of slavery

1920
Women's suffrage in the United States

LATIN AMERICA

1780–1782 Tupac Amaru rebellion in Peru

1791–1804 Haitian Revolution

1808–1825 Latin American wars of independence

1810–1811 Hidalgo-Morales rebellion in Mexico

1852 Feminist newspaper established in Brazil

1888 End of slavery in Brazil

THE WORLD

1787 Establishment of Freetown, a freed slave colony in West Africa

1798–1801 Napoleon's invasion of Egypt

1815–1840
Mfecane; rise of Zulu
kingdom in South Africa

1870s
"Egypt for the Egyptians"
movement

1885
Indian National Congress
established

1893 Women's suffrage in New Zealand

was the U.S. ambassador to France on the eve of the French Revolution, providing advice and encouragement to French reformers and revolutionaries. Simón Bolívar, a leading figure in Spanish American struggles for independence, twice visited Haiti, where he received military aid from the first black government in the Americas.

Beyond such direct connections, the various Atlantic revolutionaries shared a set of common ideas, as the Atlantic basin became a world of intellectual and cultural exchange. The ideas that animated the Atlantic revolutions derived from the European Enlightenment and were shared across the ocean in newspapers, books, and pamphlets. At the heart of these ideas was the radical notion that human political and social arrangements could be engineered, and improved, by human action. Thus conventional and long-established ways of living and thinking—the divine right of kings, state control of trade, aristocratic privilege, the authority of a single church—were no longer sacrosanct and came under repeated attack. New ideas of liberty, equality, free trade, religious tolerance, republicanism, and human rationality were in the air. Politically, the core notion was "popular sovereignty," which meant that the authority to govern derived from the people rather than from God or from established tradition. As the Englishman John Locke (1632–1704) had argued, the "social contract" between ruler and ruled should last only as long as it served the people well. In short, it was both possible and desirable to start over in the construction of human communities. In the late eighteenth and early nineteenth centuries, these ideas were largely limited to the Atlantic world. While all of the Atlantic revolutions involved the elimination of monarchs, at least temporarily, across Asia and the Middle East such republican political systems (those operating with elected representatives of the people rather than a monarch) were virtually inconceivable until much later. There the only solution to a bad monarch was a new and better one.

In the world of the Atlantic revolutions, ideas born of the Enlightenment generated endless controversy. Were liberty and equality compatible? What kind of government—unitary and centralized or federal and decentralized—best ensured freedom? And how far should liberty be extended? Except in Haiti, the chief beneficiaries of these revolutions were propertied white men of the "middling classes." Although women, slaves, Native Americans, and men without property did not gain much from these revolutions, the ideas that accompanied those upheavals gave them ammunition for the future. Because their overall thrust was to extend political rights further than ever before, these Atlantic movements have often been referred to as "democratic revolutions."

A final distinctive feature of the Atlantic revolutions lies in their immense global impact, extending well beyond the Atlantic world. The armies of revolutionary France, for example, invaded Egypt, Germany, Poland, and Russia, carrying seeds of change. The ideals that animated these Atlantic revolutions inspired efforts in many countries to abolish slavery, to extend the right to vote, to develop constitutions, and to secure greater equality for women. Nationalism, perhaps the most potent ideology of the modern era, was nurtured in the Atlantic revolutions and shaped

Guided Reading Question

■ **CAUSATION**
In what ways did the ideas of the Enlightenment contribute to the Atlantic revolutions?

much of nineteenth- and twentieth-century world history. The ideas of human equality articulated in these revolutions later found expression in feminist, socialist, and communist movements. The Universal Declaration of Human Rights, adopted by the United Nations in 1948, echoed and amplified those principles while providing the basis for any number of subsequent protests against oppression, tyranny, and deprivation. In 1989, a number of Chinese students, fleeing the suppression of a democracy movement in their own country, marched at the head of a huge parade in Paris, celebrating the bicentennial of the French Revolution. And in 2011, the Middle Eastern uprisings known as the Arab Spring initially prompted numerous comparisons with the French Revolution. The Atlantic revolutions had a long reach.

Comparing Atlantic Revolutions

Despite their common political vocabulary and a broadly democratic character, the Atlantic revolutions differed substantially from one another. They were triggered by different circumstances, expressed quite different social and political tensions, and varied considerably in their outcomes. Liberty, noted Simón Bolívar, "is a succulent morsel, but one difficult to digest."[2] "Digesting liberty" occurred in quite distinct ways in the various sites of the Atlantic revolutions.

The North American Revolution, 1775–1787

Every schoolchild in the United States learns early that the **American Revolution** was a struggle for independence from oppressive British rule. That struggle was launched with the Declaration of Independence in 1776, resulted in an unlikely military victory by 1781, and generated a federal constitution in 1787, joining thirteen formerly separate colonies into a new nation (see Map 16.1). It was the first in a series of upheavals that rocked the Atlantic world and beyond in the century that followed. But was it a genuine revolution? What, precisely, did it change?

By effecting a break with Britain, the American Revolution marked a decisive political change, but in other ways it was, strangely enough, a conservative movement because it originated in an effort to preserve the existing liberties of the colonies rather than to create new ones. For much of the seventeenth and eighteenth centuries, the British colonies in North America enjoyed a considerable degree of local autonomy, as the British government was embroiled in its own internal conflicts and various European wars. Furthermore, Britain's West Indian colonies seemed more profitable and of greater significance than those of North America. In these circumstances, local elected assemblies in North America, dominated by the wealthier property-owning settlers, achieved something close to self-government. Colonists came to regard such autonomy as a birthright and part of their English heritage. Thus, until the mid-eighteenth century, almost no one in the colonies thought of breaking away from England because participation in the British Empire provided many

Guided Reading Question
....
■ **CHANGE**
What was revolutionary about the American Revolution, and what was not?

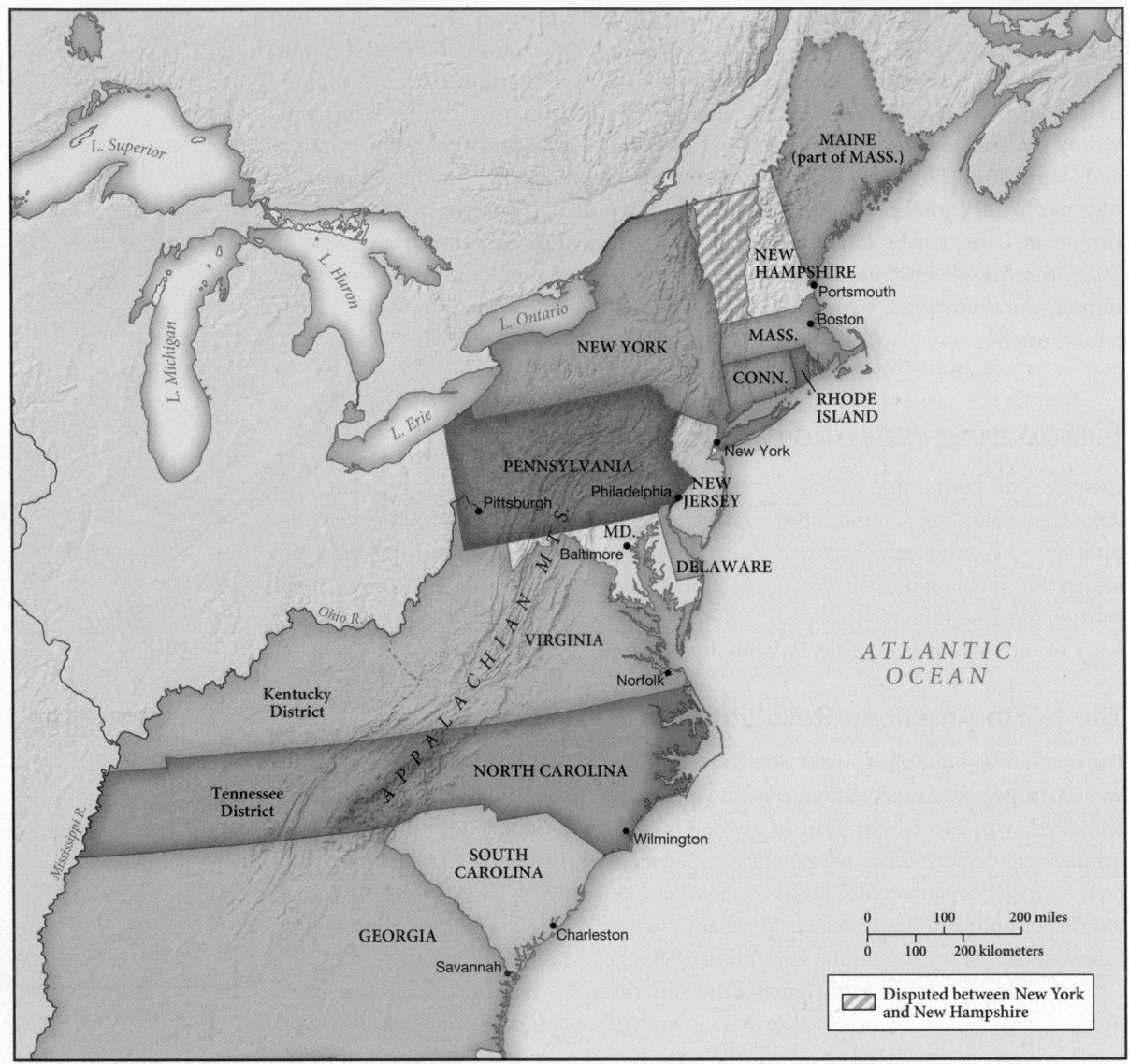

Map 16.1 The United States after the American Revolution

The union of the thirteen British colonies in North America created the embryonic United States, shown here in 1788. Over the past two centuries and more of anticolonial struggles, it was the only example of separate colonies joining together after independence to form a larger and enduring nation.

advantages—protection in war, access to British markets, and confirmation of the settlers' identity as "Englishmen"—and few drawbacks.

There were, however, real differences between Englishmen in England and those in the North American colonies. Within the colonies, English settlers had developed societies described by a leading historian as "the most radical in the contemporary Western world." Certainly class distinctions were real and visible, and a small class of wealthy "gentlemen"—the Adamses, Washingtons, Jeffersons, and Hancocks—wore powdered wigs, imitated the latest European styles, were prominent in political life, and were generally accorded deference by ordinary people. But the ready availability of land following the dispossession of Native Americans, the scarcity of people, and the absence of both a titled nobility and a single established church meant that social life was far more open than in Europe. No legal distinctions differentiated clergy, aristocracy, and commoners, as they did in France. All free men enjoyed the same status before the law, a situation that excluded black slaves and, in some ways, white women as well. These conditions made for less poverty, more economic opportunity, fewer social differences, and easier relationships among the classes than in Europe. The famous economist Adam Smith observed that British colonists were "republican in their manners . . . and their government" well before their independence from England.[3]

Thus the American Revolution grew not from social tensions within the colonies, but from a rather sudden and unexpected effort by the British government to tighten its control over the colonies and to extract more revenue from them. As Britain's global struggle with France drained its treasury and ran up its national debt, British authorities, beginning in the 1760s, looked to America to make good

Patriots and Loyalists This English engraving dating from 1776 depicts a club-wielding mob of "Liberty Men" forcing a Virginian loyalist [someone committed to continued British rule] to sign a document, probably endorsing independence for the colonies. The threat of violence toward the loyalist is apparent in the armed crowd, the barrel of tar being used as a table in the foreground, and the sack of feathers hanging from the gallows in the background. Patriots frequently tarred and feathered recalcitrant loyalists during the lead-up to the American Revolution. (Granger, NYC—All rights reserved)

these losses. Abandoning its neglectful oversight of the colonies, Britain began to act like a genuine imperial power, imposing a variety of new taxes and tariffs on the colonies without their consent, for they were not represented in the British Parliament. Many of the colonists were infuriated, because such measures challenged their economic interests, their established traditions of local autonomy, and their identity as true Englishmen. Armed with the ideas of the Enlightenment—popular sovereignty, natural rights, the consent of the governed—they went to war, and by 1781 they had prevailed, with considerable aid from the French, who were only too pleased to harm the interests of their British rivals.

What was revolutionary about the American experience was not so much the revolution itself but the kind of society that had already emerged within the colonies. Independence from Britain was not accompanied by any wholesale social transformation. Rather, the revolution accelerated the established democratic tendencies of the colonial societies. Political authority remained largely in the hands of the existing elites who had led the revolution, although property requirements for voting were lowered and more white men of modest means, such as small farmers and urban artisans, were elected to state legislatures.

This widening of political participation gradually eroded the power of traditional gentlemen, but no women or people of color shared in these gains. Land was not seized from its owners, except in the case of pro-British loyalists who had fled the country. Although slavery was gradually abolished in the northern states, where it counted for little, it remained firmly entrenched in the southern states, where it counted for much. Chief Justice John Marshall later gave voice to this conservative understanding of the American Revolution: "All contracts and rights, respecting property, remained unchanged by the Revolution."[4] In the century that followed independence, the United States did become the world's most democratic country, but this development was less the direct product of the revolution and more the gradual working out in a reformist fashion of earlier practices and the principles of equality announced in the Declaration of Independence.

Nonetheless, many American patriots felt passionately that they were creating "a new order for the ages." James Madison in the *Federalist Papers* made the point clearly: "We pursued a new and more noble course . . . and accomplished a revolution that has no parallel in the annals of human society." Supporters abroad agreed. On the eve of the French Revolution, a Paris newspaper proclaimed that the United States was "the hope and model of the human race."[5] In both cases, they were referring primarily to the political ideas and practices of the new country. The American Revolution, after all, initiated the political dismantling of Europe's New World empires. The "right to revolution," proclaimed in the Declaration of Independence and made effective only in a great struggle, inspired revolutionaries and nationalists from Simón Bolívar in nineteenth-century Latin America to Ho Chi Minh in twentieth-century Vietnam. Moreover, the new U.S. Constitution — with its Bill of Rights, checks and balances, separation of church and state, and federalism — was one of the first sustained efforts to put the political ideas of the Enlightenment into practice. That document, and the ideas that it embraced, echoed repeatedly in the political upheavals of the century that followed.

The French Revolution, 1789–1815

Act Two in the drama of the Atlantic revolutions took place in France, beginning in 1789, although it was closely connected to Act One in North America. Thousands of French soldiers had provided assistance to the American colonists and now returned home full of republican enthusiasm. Thomas Jefferson, the U.S. ambassador in Paris, reported that France "has been awakened by our revolution."[6] More immediately, the French government, which had generously aided the Americans in an effort to undermine its British rivals, was teetering on the brink of bankruptcy and had long sought reforms that would modernize the tax system and make it more equitable. In a desperate effort to raise taxes against the opposition of the privileged classes, the French king, Louis XVI, had called into session an ancient representative body, the Estates General. It consisted of male representatives of the three "estates," or legal orders, of prerevolutionary France: the clergy, the nobility, and the commoners. The first two estates comprised about 2 percent of the population, and the Third Estate included everyone else. When that body convened in 1789, representatives of the Third Estate soon organized themselves as the National Assembly, claiming the sole authority to make laws for the country. A few weeks later, they forthrightly claimed in the **Declaration of the Rights of Man and Citizen** that "men are born and remain free and equal in rights," and this declaration later became the preamble of the 1791 French Constitution. These actions, unprecedented and illegal in the *ancien régime* (the old regime), launched the **French Revolution** and radicalized many of the participants in the National Assembly.

The French Revolution was quite different from its North American predecessor. Whereas the American Revolution expressed the tensions of a colonial relationship with a distant imperial power, the French insurrection was driven by sharp conflicts within French society. Members of the titled nobility—privileged, prestigious, and wealthy—resented and resisted the monarchy's efforts to subject them to new taxes. Educated middle-class men such as doctors, lawyers, lower-level officials, and merchants were growing in numbers and sometimes in wealth and were offended by the remaining privileges of the aristocracy, from which they were excluded. Ordinary urban men and women, many of whose incomes had declined for a generation, were hit particularly hard in the late 1780s by the rapidly rising price of bread and widespread unemployment. Peasants in the countryside, though largely free of serfdom, were subject to hated dues imposed by their landlords, taxes from the state, obligations to the Church, and the requirement to work without pay on public roads. As Enlightenment ideas penetrated French society, more and more people, mostly in the Third Estate but also including some priests and nobles, found a language with which to articulate these grievances. The famous French writer Jean-Jacques Rousseau had told them that it was "manifestly contrary to the law of nature . . . that a handful of people should gorge themselves with superfluities while the hungry multitude goes in want of necessities."[7]

These social conflicts gave the French Revolution, especially during its first five years, a much more violent, far-reaching, and radical character than its American counterpart. It was a profound social upheaval, more comparable to the revolutions of Russia and China in the twentieth century than to the earlier American Revolution. Initial efforts to establish a constitutional monarchy and promote harmony among the classes gave way to more radical measures, as internal resistance and foreign opposition produced a fear that the revolution might be overturned. In the process, urban crowds organized insurrections. Some peasants attacked the residences of their lords, burning the documents that recorded their dues and payments.

Guided Reading Question

■ **COMPARISON**

How did the French Revolution differ from the American Revolution?

The National Assembly decreed the end of all legal privileges and eliminated what remained of feudalism in France. Even slavery was abolished, albeit briefly. Church lands were sold to raise revenue, and priests were put under government authority.

In 1793, King Louis XVI and his queen, Marie Antoinette, were executed, an act of regicide that shocked traditionalists all across Europe and marked a new stage in revolutionary violence. What followed was the Terror of 1793–1794. Under the leadership of Maximilien **Robespierre** (ROHBS-pee-air) and his Committee of Public Safety, tens of thousands deemed enemies of the revolution lost their lives on the guillotine. Shortly thereafter, Robespierre himself was arrested and guillotined, accused of leading France into tyranny and dictatorship. "The revolution," remarked one of its victims, "was devouring its own children."

Accompanying attacks on the old order were efforts to create a wholly new society, symbolized by a new calendar with the Year 1 in 1792, marking a fresh start for France. Unlike the Americans, who sought to restore or build on earlier freedoms, French revolutionaries perceived themselves to be starting from scratch and looked to the future. For the first time in its history, the country became a republic and briefly passed universal male suffrage, although it was never implemented. The old administrative system was rationalized into eighty-three territorial departments, each with a new name. As revolutionary France prepared for war against its threatened and threatening neighbors, it created the world's largest army, with some 800,000 men, and all adult males were required to serve. Led by officers from the middle and even lower classes, this was an army of citizens representing the nation.

In terms of gender roles, the French Revolution did not create a new society, but it did raise the question of female political equality far more explicitly than the American Revolution had done. Partly this was because French women were active in the major events of the revolution. In July 1789, they took part in the famous storming of the Bastille, a large fortress, prison, and armory that had come to symbolize the oppressive old regime. In October of that year, some 7,000 Parisian women, desperate about the shortage of bread, marched on the palace at Versailles, stormed through the royal apartments searching for the despised Queen Marie Antoinette, and forced the royal family to return with them to Paris.

Backed by a few male supporters, women also made serious political demands. They signed

The Execution of Robespierre The beheading of the radical leader Robespierre, who had himself brought thousands of others to the guillotine, marked a decisive turning point in the unfolding of the French Revolution and the end of its most violent phase. (Musée de la Ville de Paris, Musée Carnavalet, Paris, France/Bridgeman Images) petitions detailing their complaints: lack of education, male competition in female trades, the prevalence of prostitution, the rapidly rising price of bread and soap. One petition, reflecting the intersection of class and gender, referred to women as the "Third Estate of the Third Estate." Another demanded the right to bear arms in defense of the revolution. Over sixty women's clubs were established throughout the country. A small group called the Cercle Social (Social Circle) campaigned for women's rights, noting that "the laws favor men at the expense of women, because everywhere power is in your hands."[8] The French playwright and journalist Olympe de Gouges appropriated the language of the Declaration of Rights to insist that "woman is born free and lives equal to man in her rights."

But the assertion of French women in the early years of the revolution seemed wildly inappropriate and threatening to most men, uniting conservatives and revolutionaries alike in defense of male privileges. And so in late 1793, the country's all-male legislative body voted to ban all women's clubs. "Women are ill-suited for elevated thoughts and serious meditation," declared one of the male representatives. "A woman should not leave her family to meddle in affairs of government." Here was a conception of gender that defined masculinity in terms of exercising political power. Women who aspired to do so were, in the words of one revolutionary orator, "denatured *viragos*" (unnatural domineering women), in short, not really women at all.[9] Thus French revolutionaries were distinctly unwilling to offer any political rights to women, even though they had eliminated class restrictions, at least in theory; granted religious freedom to Jews and Protestants; and abolished slavery. Nonetheless, according to a leading historian, "the French Revolution, more than any other event of its time, opened up the question of women's rights for consideration" and thus laid the foundations for modern feminism.[10]

If not in terms of gender, the immediate impact of the revolution was felt in many other ways. Streets got new names, monuments to the royal family were destroyed; titles vanished; people referred to one another as "citizen so-and-so." Real politics in the public sphere emerged for the first time as many people joined political clubs, took part in marches and demonstrations, served on local committees, and ran for public office. Ordinary men and women, who had identified primarily with their local communities, now began to think of themselves as belonging to a nation. The state replaced the Catholic Church as the place for registering births, marriages, and deaths, and revolutionary festivals substituted for church holidays.

More radical revolutionary leaders deliberately sought to convey a sense of new beginnings and endless possibilities. At a Festival of Unity held in 1793 to mark the first anniversary of the end of monarchy, participants burned the crowns and scepters of the royal family in a huge bonfire while releasing a cloud of 3,000 white doves. The Cathedral of Notre Dame was temporarily turned into the Temple of Reason, while a "Hymn to Liberty" combined traditional church music with the explicit message of the Enlightenment:

Oh Liberty, sacred Liberty / Goddess of an enlightened people
Rule today within these walls. / Through you this temple is purified.

Map 16.2 Napoleon's European Empire
The French Revolution spawned a French Empire, under Napoleon's leadership, that encompassed most of Europe and served to spread the principles of the revolution.

Liberty! Before you reason chases out deception, / Error flees, fanaticism is
   beaten down.
Our gospel is nature / And our cult is virtue.
To love one's country and one's brothers, / To serve the Sovereign People
These are the sacred tenets / And pledge of a Republican.[11]

Elsewhere too the French Revolution evoked images of starting over. Witnessing that revolution in 1790, the young William Wordsworth, later a famous British Romantic poet, imagined "human nature seeming born again." "Bliss it was in that dawn to be alive," he wrote. "But to be young was very heaven."

The French Revolution also differed from the American Revolution in the way its influence spread. At least until the United States became a world power at the end of the nineteenth century, what inspired others was primarily the example of its revolution and its constitution. French influence, by contrast, spread through conquest, largely under the leadership of **Napoleon Bonaparte** (r. 1799–1815). A highly successful general who seized power in 1799, Napoleon is often credited with taming the revolution in the face of growing disenchantment with its more radical features and with the social conflicts it generated. He preserved many of its more moderate elements, such as civil equality, a secular law code, religious freedom, and promotion by merit, while reconciling with the Catholic Church and suppressing the revolution's more democratic elements in a military dictatorship. In short, Napoleon kept the revolution's emphasis on social equality for men but dispensed with liberty.

Like many of the revolution's ardent supporters, Napoleon was intent on spreading its benefits far and wide. In a series of brilliant military campaigns, his forces subdued most of Europe, thus creating the continent's largest empire since the days of the Romans (see Map 16.2). Within that empire, Napoleon imposed such revolutionary practices as ending feudalism, proclaiming equality of rights, insisting on religious toleration, codifying the laws, and rationalizing government administration. In many places, these reforms were welcomed, and seeds of further change were planted. But French domination was also resented and resisted, stimulating national consciousness throughout Europe. That too was a seed that bore fruit in the century that followed. More immediately, national resistance, particularly from Russia and Britain, brought down Napoleon and his amazing empire by 1815 and marked an end to the era of the French Revolution, though not to the potency of its ideas.

The Haitian Revolution, 1791–1804

Nowhere did the example of the French Revolution echo more loudly than in the French Caribbean colony of Saint Domingue, later renamed Haiti (see Map 16.3, page 706). Widely regarded as the richest colony in the world, Saint Domingue boasted 8,000 plantations, which in the late eighteenth century produced some 40 percent of the world's sugar and perhaps half of its coffee. A slave labor force of about 500,000 people made up the vast majority of the colony's population. Whites numbered about 40,000, sharply divided between very well-to-do plantation owners, merchants, and lawyers and those known as *petits blancs* (peh-TEE blahnk), or poor whites. A third social group consisted of some 30,000 *gens de couleur libres* (free people of color), many of them of mixed-race background. Given its enormous inequalities and its rampant exploitation, this Caribbean colony was primed for explosion.

In such a volatile setting, the ideas and example of the French Revolution lit several fuses and set in motion a spiral of violence that engulfed the colony for more than a decade. The principles of the revolution, however, meant different things to different people. To the *grands blancs*—the rich white landowners—it suggested greater autonomy for the colony and fewer economic restrictions on trade, but they resented the demands of the *petits blancs*, who sought equality of citizenship for all whites. Both white groups were adamantly opposed to the insistence of free people of color that the "rights of man" meant equal treatment for all free people regardless of race. To the slaves, the promise of the French Revolution was a personal freedom that challenged the entire slave labor system. In a massive revolt beginning in 1791, triggered by rumors that the French king had already declared an end to slavery, slaves burned 1,000 plantations and killed hundreds of whites as well as mixed-race people.

Soon warring factions of slaves, whites, and free people of color battled one another. Spanish and British forces, seeking to enlarge their own empires at the expense of the French, only added to the turmoil. Amid the confusion, brutality, and massacres of the 1790s, power gravitated toward the slaves, now led by the astute Toussaint Louverture, himself a former slave. He and his successor overcame internal resistance, outmaneuvered the foreign powers, and even defeated an attempt by Napoleon to reestablish French control.

When the dust settled in the early years of the nineteenth century, it was clear that something remarkable and unprecedented had taken place, a revolution unique in the Atlantic world and in world history. Socially, the last had become first. In the only completely successful slave revolt in world history, "the lowest order of the society—slaves—became equal, free, and independent citizens."[12] Politically, they had thrown off French colonial rule, creating the second independent republic in the Americas and the first non-European state to emerge from Western colonialism. They renamed their country "Haiti," a term meaning "mountainous" or "rugged" in the language of the original Taino people. It was a symbolic break with Europe and represented an effort to connect with the long-deceased native inhabitants of the land. Some, in fact, referred to themselves as "Incas." At the formal declaration of Haiti's independence on January 1, 1804, Jean-Jacques Dessalines, the new country's first head of state, declared: "I have given the French cannibals blood for blood; I have avenged America."[13] In defining all Haitian citizens as "black" and legally equal regardless of color or class, Haiti directly confronted elite preferences for lighter skin even as it disallowed citizenship for most whites. Economically, the country's plantation system, oriented wholly toward the export of sugar and coffee, had been largely destroyed. As whites fled or were killed, both private and state lands were redistributed among former slaves and free blacks, and Haiti became a nation of small-scale farmers producing mostly for their own needs, with a much smaller export sector.

The destructiveness of the **Haitian Revolution**, its bitter internal divisions of race and class, and continuing external opposition contributed much to Haiti's abiding poverty as well as to its authoritarian and unstable politics. So too did the enormous "independence debt" that the French forced on the fledgling republic in

Guided Reading Question

■ **COMPARISON**

What was distinctive about the Haitian Revolution, both in world history generally and in the history of Atlantic revolutions?

1825, a financial burden that endured for well over a century. "Freedom" in Haiti came to mean primarily the end of slavery rather than the establishment of political rights for all. In the early nineteenth century, however, Haiti was a source of enormous hope and of great fear. Within weeks of the Haitian slave uprising in 1791, Jamaican slaves had composed songs in its honor, and it was not long before slave owners in the Caribbean and North America observed a new "insolence" in their slaves. Certainly, its example inspired other slave rebellions, gave a boost to the dawning abolitionist movement, and has been a source of pride for people of African descent ever since.

To whites throughout the hemisphere, the cautionary saying "Remember Haiti" reflected a sense of horror at what had occurred there and a determination not to allow political change to reproduce that fearful outcome again. Particularly in Latin America, the events in Haiti injected a deep caution and social conservatism in the elites who led their countries to independence in the early nineteenth century. Ironically, though, the Haitian Revolution also led to a temporary expansion of slavery elsewhere. Cuban plantations and their slave workers considerably increased their production

The Haitian Revolution This early nineteenth-century engraving, titled *Revenge Taken by the Black Army*, shows black Haitian soldiers hanging a large number of French soldiers, thus illustrating both the violence and the racial dimension of the upheaval in Haiti. (From "An Historic Account of the Black Empire of Haiti," 1805, engraving by Marcus Rainsford [ca. 1750–1805]/Private Collection/Bridgeman Images)

of sugar as that of Haiti declined. Moreover, Napoleon's defeat in Haiti persuaded him to sell to the United States the French territories known as the Louisiana Purchase, from which a number of "slave states" were carved out. Nor did the example of Haiti lead to successful independence struggles in the rest of the thirty or so Caribbean colonies. Unlike mainland North and South America, Caribbean decolonization had to await the twentieth century. In such contradictory ways did the echoes of the Haitian Revolution reverberate in the Atlantic world.

Latin American Revolutions, 1808–1825

The final act in a half century of Atlantic revolutionary upheaval took place in the Spanish and Portuguese colonies of mainland Latin America (see Map 16.3). These **Latin American revolutions** were shaped by preceding events in North America, France, and Haiti as well as by their own distinctive societies and historical experiences. As in British North America, native-born elites (known as *creoles*) in the Spanish colonies were

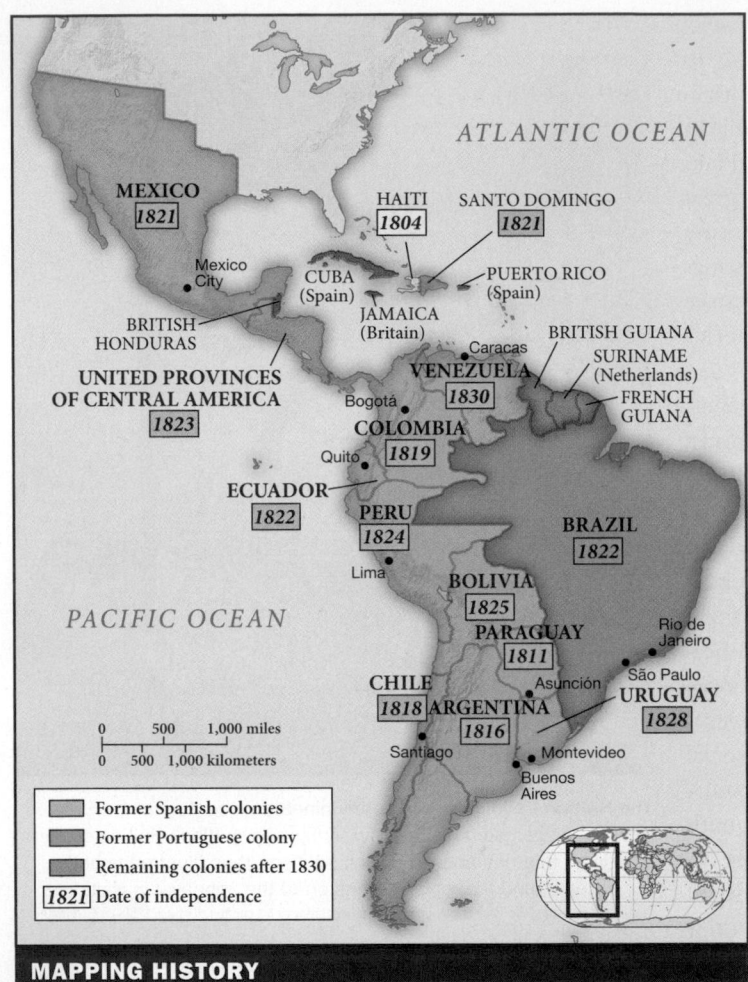

MAPPING HISTORY

Map 16.3 Latin American Independence

With the exception of Haiti, Latin American revolutions brought independence to new states but offered little social change or political opportunity for the vast majority of people.

READING THE MAP: Which regions remained colonies after 1830?

INTERPRETING THE MAP: Compare the political boundaries of South American states on this map and on Map 17.5: Latin America and the World, 1825–1935. What changes can you identify? Have the political boundaries remained relatively stable, or do the alterations to borders indicate significant political change?

offended and insulted by the Spanish monarchy's efforts during the eighteenth century to exercise greater power over its colonies and to subject them to heavier taxes and tariffs. Creole intellectuals had also become familiar with ideas of popular sovereignty, republican government, and personal liberty derived from the European Enlightenment. But these conditions, similar to those in North America, led initially only to scattered and uncoordinated protests rather than to outrage, declarations of independence, war, and unity, as had occurred in the British colonies. Why did Spanish colonies win their independence almost fifty years later than those of British North America?

Spanish colonies had long been governed in a rather more authoritarian fashion than their British counterparts and were more sharply divided by class. In addition, whites throughout Latin America were vastly outnumbered by Native Americans, people of African ancestry, and those of mixed race. All of this inhibited the growth of a movement for independence, notwithstanding the example of North America and similar provocations.

Despite their growing disenchantment with Spanish rule, creole elites did not so much generate a revolution as have one thrust upon them by events in Europe. In 1808, Napoleon invaded Spain and Portugal, deposing the Spanish king Ferdinand VII and forcing the Portuguese royal family into exile in Brazil. With legitimate royal authority now in disarray, Latin Americans were forced to take action. The outcome, ultimately, was independence for the various states of Latin America, established almost everywhere by 1826. But the way in which independence occurred and the kind of societies it generated differed greatly from the experience of both North America and Haiti.

The process lasted more than twice as long as it did in North America, partly because Latin American societies were so divided by class, race, and region. In North America, violence was directed almost entirely against the British and seldom spilled over into domestic disputes, except for some bloody skirmishes with loyalists. In Mexico, by contrast, the move toward independence began in 1810–1811 in a peasant insurrection, driven by hunger for land and by high food prices and led successively by two priests, Miguel Hidalgo and José Morelos. Alarmed by the social radicalism of the **Hidalgo–Morelos rebellion**, creole landowners, with the support of the Church, raised an army and crushed the insurgency. Later that alliance of clergy and creole elites brought Mexico to a more socially controlled independence in 1821. Such violent conflict among Latin Americans, along lines of race, class, and ideology, accompanied the struggle against Spain in many places.

The entire independence movement in Latin America took place under the shadow of a great fear—the dread of social rebellion from below—that had little counterpart in North America. The extensive violence of the French and Haitian revolutions was a lesson to Latin American elites that political change could easily get out of hand and was fraught with danger to themselves. An abortive rebellion of Native Americans in Peru in the early 1780s, led by **Tupac Amaru**, a man who claimed direct descent from the last Inca emperor, reminded whites that they sat atop a potentially explosive society, most of whose members were exploited and oppressed people of color. So too did the Hidalgo–Morelos rebellion in Mexico.

And yet the creole sponsors of independence movements, both regional military leaders such as Simón Bolívar and José de San Martín and their civilian counterparts, required the support of "the people," or at least some of them, if they were to prevail against Spanish forces. The answer to this dilemma was found in nativism, which cast all of those born in the Americas—creoles, Indians, mixed-race people, free blacks—as Americanos, while the enemy was defined as those born in Spain or Portugal.[14] This was no easy task, because many creole whites and mestizos saw themselves as Spanish and because great differences of race, culture, and wealth divided the Americanos. Nonetheless, nationalist leaders made efforts to mobilize people of color into the struggle with promises of freedom, the end of legal restrictions, and social advancement. Many of these leaders were genuine liberals who had been influenced by the ideals of the Enlightenment, the French Revolution, and Spanish liberalism. In the long run, however, few of those promises were kept. Certainly, the lower classes, Native Americans, and slaves benefited little from independence. "The imperial state was destroyed in Spanish America," concluded one historian, "but colonial society was preserved."[15]

Nor did women as a group gain much from the independence struggle, though they had participated in it in various ways. Upper-class or wealthy women gave and raised money for the cause and provided safe havens for revolutionary meetings. In Mexico, some women disguised themselves as men to join the struggle, while numerous working-class and peasant women served as cooks and carriers of supplies in a "women's brigade." A considerable number of women were severely

Simón Bolívar Among the heroic figures of Spanish American independence movements, none was more significant than Simón Bolívar, shown here in a moment of triumph entering his hometown of Caracas in present-day Venezuela. But Bolívar was immensely disappointed in the outcomes of independence, as his dream of a unified South America perished amid the rivalries of separate countries. (Chalk lithograph by R. Weibezahl, 1829/Sammlung Archiv für Kunst und Geschichte, Berlin, Germany/akg-images)

punished for their disloyalty to the Crown, with some forty-eight executed in Colombia. Yet, after independence, few social gains rewarded these efforts. General San Martín of Argentina accorded national recognition to a number of women, and modest improvement in educational opportunities for women appeared. But Latin American women continued to be wholly excluded from political life and remained under firm legal control of the men in their families.

A further difference in the Latin American situation lay in the apparent impossibility of uniting the various Spanish colonies, so much larger than the small British territories of North America, despite several failed efforts to do so. Thus no United States of Latin America emerged. Distances among the colonies and geographic obstacles to effective communication were certainly greater than in the Eastern Seaboard colonies of North America, and their longer colonial experience had given rise to distinct and deeply rooted regional identities. Shortly before his death in 1830, the prominent independence leader Simón Bolívar, who so admired George Washington and had so ardently hoped for greater unity, wrote in despair to a friend: "[Latin] America is ungovernable. Those who serve the revolution plough the sea."[16]

The aftermath of independence in Latin America marked a reversal in the earlier relationship of the two American continents. The United States, which began its history as the leftover "dregs" of the New World, grew increasingly wealthy, industrialized, democratic, internationally influential, and generally stable, with the major exception of the Civil War. The Spanish colonies, which took shape in the wealthiest areas and among the most sophisticated cultures of the Americas, were widely regarded as the more promising region compared to England's North American territories, which had a backwater reputation. But in the nineteenth century, as newly independent countries in both regions launched a new phase of their histories, those in Latin America became relatively underdeveloped, impoverished, undemocratic, politically unstable, and dependent on foreign technology and investment. Begun in broadly similar circumstances, the Latin American and North American revolutions occurred in very different societies and gave rise to very different historical trajectories.

Echoes of Revolution

The repercussions of the Atlantic revolutions reverberated far beyond their places of origin and persisted long after those upheavals had been concluded. Britain's loss of its North American colonies, for example, fueled its growing interest and interventions in Asia, contributing to British colonial rule in India and the Opium Wars in China. Napoleon's brief conquest of Egypt (1798–1801) opened the way for a modernizing regime to emerge in that ancient land and stimulated westernizing reforms in the Ottoman Empire (see "The Ottoman Empire and the West in the Nineteenth Century" in Chapter 19). During the nineteenth century, the idea of a "constitution" found advocates in Poland, Russia, the Spanish-ruled Philippines, China, the Ottoman Empire, and British-governed India.

Within Europe, which was generally dominated by conservative governments following Napoleon's final defeat, smaller revolutionary eruptions occurred in 1830, more widely in 1848, and in Paris in 1870. They reflected ideas of republicanism, greater social equality, and national liberation from foreign rule. Such ideas and social pressures pushed the major states of Western Europe, the United States, and Argentina to enlarge their voting publics, generally granting universal male suffrage by 1914. An abortive attempt to establish a constitutional regime even broke out in autocratic Russia in 1825, led by aristocratic military officers influenced by French revolutionary ideas. While it quickly failed, it marked the beginning of a revolutionary tradition in Russia, which came to fruition only in 1917. More generally, the American and French revolutions led sympathetic elites in Central Europe and elsewhere to feel that they had fallen behind, that their countries were "sleeping." As early as 1791, a Hungarian poet gave voice to such sentiments: "O you still in the slave's collar . . . And you too! Holy consecrated kings . . . turn your eyes to Paris! Let France set out the fate of both king and shackled slave."[17]

Beyond these echoes of the Atlantic revolutions, three major movements arose to challenge continuing patterns of oppression or exclusion. Abolitionists sought the end of slavery; nationalists hoped to foster unity and independence from foreign rule; and feminists challenged male dominance. Each of these movements bore the marks of the Atlantic revolutions, and although they took root first in Europe and the Americas, each came to have a global significance in the centuries that followed.

The Abolition of Slavery

In little more than a century, from roughly 1780 to 1890, a remarkable transformation occurred in human affairs as slavery, widely practiced and little condemned since at least the beginning of civilization, lost its legitimacy and was largely ended.

In this amazing process, the ideas and practices of the Atlantic revolutions played an important role.

Enlightenment thinkers in eighteenth-century Europe had become increasingly critical of slavery as a violation of the natural rights of every person, and the public pronouncements of the American and French revolutions about liberty and equality likewise focused attention on this obvious breach of those principles. To this secular antislavery thinking was added an increasingly vociferous religious voice, expressed first by Quakers and then by Protestant evangelicals in Britain and the United States. To them, slavery was "repugnant to our religion" and a "crime in the sight of God."[18] What made these moral arguments more widely acceptable was the growing belief that, contrary to much earlier thinking, slavery was not essential for economic progress. After all, England and New England were among the most prosperous regions of the Western world in the early nineteenth century, and both were based on free labor. Slavery in this view was out of date, unnecessary in the new era of industrial technology and capitalism. Thus moral virtue and economic success were joined. It was an attractive argument. The actions of slaves themselves likewise hastened the end of slavery. The dramatically successful Haitian Revolution was followed by three major rebellions in the British West Indies, all of which were harshly crushed, in the early nineteenth century. The **Great Jamaica Revolt** of 1831–1832, in which perhaps 60,000 slaves attacked several hundred plantations, was particularly important in prompting Britain to abolish slavery throughout its empire in 1833. These revolts demonstrated clearly that slaves were hardly "contented," and the brutality with which they were suppressed appalled British public opinion. Growing numbers of the British public came to believe that slavery was "not only morally wrong and economically inefficient, but also politically unwise."[19]

Abolitionism This unusual late eighteenth-century abolitionist image depicts an enslaved African in chains on the deck of a ship holding a knife. Unlike most abolitionist representations of Africans, which show their subjects kneeling, praying, or pleading, the subject of this engraving strikes a defiant pose as he seemingly contemplates suicide, or perhaps resistance, rather than captivity. (National Maritime Museum, London. UK/The Image Works)

These various strands of thinking—secular, religious, economic, and political—came together in an **abolitionist movement**, most powerfully in Britain, which brought growing pressure on governments to close down the trade in slaves and then to ban slavery itself. In the late eighteenth century, such a movement gained wide support among middle- and working-class people in Britain. Its techniques included pamphlets with heartrending descriptions of slavery, numerous petitions to Parliament, lawsuits, and boycotts of slave-produced sugar. Frequent public meetings dramatically featured the testimony of Africans who had experienced the horrors of slavery firsthand. In 1807, Britain forbade the sale of slaves within its empire and in 1834 emancipated those who remained enslaved. Over the next half century, other nations followed suit, responding to growing international pressure, particularly from Britain, then the world's leading economic and military power. British naval vessels patrolled the Atlantic, intercepted illegal slave ships, and freed their human cargoes in a small West African settlement called Freetown, in present-day Sierra Leone. Following their independence, most Latin American countries abolished slavery by the 1850s. Brazil, in 1888, was the last to do so, bringing more than four centuries of Atlantic slavery to an end. A roughly similar set of conditions—fear of rebellion, economic inefficiency, and moral concerns—persuaded the Russian tsar (zahr) to free the many serfs of that huge country in 1861, although there it occurred by fiat from above rather than from growing public pressure.

None of this happened easily. Slave economies continued to flourish well into the nineteenth century, and plantation owners vigorously resisted the onslaught of abolitionists. So did slave traders, both European and African, who together shipped millions of additional captives, mostly to Cuba and Brazil, long after the British had declared the trade illegal. Osei Bonsu, the powerful king of the West African state of Asante, was puzzled as to why the British would no longer buy his slaves. "If they think it bad now," he asked a local British representative in 1820, "why did they think it good before?"[20] Nowhere was the persistence of slavery more evident and resistance to abolition more intense than in the southern states of the United States. It was the only slaveholding society in which the end of slavery occurred through a bitter, prolonged, and highly destructive civil war (1861–1865).

The end of Atlantic slavery during the nineteenth century surely marked a major and quite rapid turn in the world's social history and in the moral thinking of humankind. Nonetheless, the outcomes of that process were often surprising and far from the expectations of abolitionists or the newly freed slaves. In most cases, the economic lives of the former slaves did not improve dramatically. Nowhere in the Atlantic world, except Haiti, did a redistribution of land follow the end of slavery. But freedmen everywhere desperately sought economic autonomy on their own land, and in parts of the Caribbean such as Jamaica, where unoccupied land was available, independent peasant agriculture proved possible for some. Elsewhere, as in the southern United States, various forms of legally free but highly dependent labor, such as sharecropping, emerged to replace slavery and to provide low-paid and often-indebted workers for planters. The understandable reluctance of former slaves to continue working in plantation agriculture created labor shortages and set in motion a huge new wave of global migration. Large numbers of indentured servants from India and China were imported into the Caribbean, Peru, South Africa, Hawaii, Malaya, and elsewhere to work in mines, on plantations, and in construction projects. There they often toiled in conditions not far removed from slavery itself.

Newly freed people did not achieve anything close to political equality, except in Haiti. White planters, farmers, and mine owners retained local authority in the Caribbean, where colonial rule persisted until well into the twentieth century. In the southern United States, a brief period of "radical reconstruction," during which

Guided Reading Question

■ CHANGE

What accounts for the end of Atlantic slavery during the nineteenth century?

Guided Reading Question

■ CHANGE

How did the end of slavery affect the lives of the former slaves?

newly freed blacks did enjoy full political rights and some power, was followed by harsh segregation laws, denial of voting rights, a wave of lynchings, and a virulent racism that lasted well into the twentieth century. For most former slaves, emancipation usually meant "nothing but freedom."[21] Unlike the situation in the Americas, the end of serfdom in Russia transferred to the peasants a considerable portion of the nobles' land, but the need to pay for this land with "redemption dues" and the rapid growth of Russia's rural population ensured that most peasants remained impoverished and politically volatile.

In both West and East Africa, the closing of the external slave trade decreased the price of slaves and increased their use within African societies to produce the export crops that the world economy now sought. Thus, as Europeans imposed colonial rule on Africa in the late nineteenth century, they loudly proclaimed their commitment to ending slavery in a continent from which they had extracted slaves for more than four centuries. This was surely among the more ironic outcomes of the abolitionist process.

In the Islamic world, where slavery had long been practiced and elaborately regulated, the freeing of slaves, though not required, was strongly recommended as a mark of piety. Some nineteenth-century Muslim authorities opposed slavery altogether on the grounds that it violated the Quran's ideals of freedom and equality. But unlike Europe and North America, the Islamic world generated no popular grassroots antislavery movements. There slavery was outlawed gradually only in the twentieth century under the pressure of international opinion.

Nations and Nationalism

In addition to contributing to the end of slavery, the Atlantic revolutions also gave new prominence to a relatively recent kind of human community—the nation. By the end of the twentieth century, the idea that humankind was divided into separate nations, each with a distinct culture and territory and deserving an independent political life, was so widespread as to seem natural and timeless. And yet for most of human experience, states did not usually coincide with the culture of a particular people, for all the great empires and many smaller states governed culturally diverse societies. Few people considered rule by foreigners itself a terrible offense because the most important identities and loyalties were local, limited to clan, village, or region, with only modest connection to the larger state or empire that governed them. People might on occasion consider themselves part of larger religious communities (such as Christians or Muslims) or ethno-linguistic groupings such as Greek, Arab, or Maya, but such identities rarely provided the basis for enduring states.

All of that began to change during the era of Atlantic revolutions. Independence movements in both North and South America were made in the name of new nations. The French Revolution declared that sovereignty lay with "the people," and its leaders mobilized this people to defend the "French nation" against its

Guided Reading Question

■ **EXPLANATION**

What accounts for the growth of nationalism as a powerful political and personal identity in the nineteenth century?

external enemies. In 1793, the revolutionary government of France declared a mass conscription (*levée en masse*) with a stirring call to service:

> Henceforth, until the enemies have been driven from the territory of the Republic, all the French are in permanent requisition for army service. The young men shall go to battle; the married men shall forge arms and transport provisions; the women shall make tents and clothes, and shall serve in the hospitals; the children shall turn old linen into lint; the old men shall repair to the public places, to stimulate the courage of the warriors and preach the unity of the Republic and the hatred of kings.[22]

Napoleon's conquests likewise stimulated national resistance in many parts of Europe. European states had long competed and fought with one another, but increasingly in the nineteenth century, those states were inhabited by people who felt themselves to be citizens of a nation, deeply bound to their fellows by ties of blood, culture, or common experience, not simply common subjects of a ruling dynasty. It was a novel form of political loyalty.

The rise of **nationalism** was also facilitated by Europe's modern transformation, as older identities and loyalties eroded. Science weakened the hold of religion on some. Migration to industrial cities or abroad diminished allegiance to local communities. At the same time, printing and the publishing industry standardized a variety of dialects into a smaller number of European languages, a process that allowed a growing reading public to think of themselves as members of a common linguistic group or nation. All of this encouraged political and cultural leaders to articulate an appealing idea of their particular nations and ensured a growing circle of people receptive to such ideas. Thus the idea of the "nation" was constructed or even invented, but it was often imagined and presented as a reawakening of older linguistic or cultural identities, and it certainly drew on the songs, dances, folktales, historical experiences, and collective memories of earlier cultures (see Map 16.4).

Whatever its precise origins, nationalism proved to be an infinitely flexible and enormously powerful idea in nineteenth-century Europe and beyond. It inspired the political unification of both Italy (1870) and Germany (1871), gathering their previously fragmented peoples into new states. It encouraged Greeks and Serbs to assert their independence from the Ottoman Empire; Czechs and Hungarians to demand more autonomy within the Austrian Empire; Poles and Ukrainians to become more aware of their oppression within the Russian Empire; and the Irish to seek "home rule" and separation from Great Britain. By the end of the nineteenth century, a small Zionist movement, seeking a homeland in Palestine, had emerged among Europe's frequently persecuted Jews.

Popular nationalism made the normal rivalry among European states even more acute and fueled a highly competitive drive for colonies in Asia and Africa. The immensity of the suffering and sacrifice that nationalism generated in Europe was vividly disclosed during the horrors of World War I. Furthermore, nationalism fueled rivalries among the various European-derived states in the Americas,

MAPPING HISTORY

Map 16.4 The Nations and Empires of Europe, ca. 1880

By the end of the nineteenth century, the national principle had substantially reshaped the map of Europe, especially in the unification of Germany and Italy. However, several major empires remained, each with numerous subject peoples who likewise sought national independence.

READING THE MAP: In which regions of Europe were empires most prominent? Where were nation-states most prominent?

INTERPRETING THE MAP: Compare this map with Map 16.2: Napoleon's European Empire. What changed on the political map of Europe after the collapse of Napoleon's empire? What stayed the same?

reflected, for example, in the Mexican–United States War of 1846–1848 and the devastating conflict between Paraguay and the Triple Alliance of Argentina, Brazil, and Uruguay between 1864 and 1870, in which about half of Paraguay's population perished.

Governments throughout the Western world now claimed to act on behalf of their nations and deliberately sought to instill national loyalties in their citizens through schools, public rituals, the mass media, and military service. Russian authorities, for example, imposed the use of the Russian language, even in parts of the country where it was not widely spoken. They succeeded, however, only in producing a greater awareness of Ukrainian, Polish, and Finnish nationalism.

As it became more prominent in the nineteenth century, nationalism took on a variety of political ideologies. Some supporters of liberal democracy and representative government, as in France or the United States, saw nationalism, with its

Nationalism in Poland In the eighteenth century, Poland had been divided among Prussia, Austria, and Russia and disappeared as a separate and independent state. Polish nationalism found expression in the nineteenth century in a series of revolts against Poland's Russian occupiers. This painting shows Russian officers surrendering their standards to Polish insurgents during the November Uprising of 1830. The revolt was subsequently crushed, and Poland regained its independence as a nation-state only in 1918 at the end of World War I.

emphasis on "the people," as an aid to their aspirations toward wider involvement in political life. Often called civic nationalism, such a view identified the nation with a particular territory and maintained that people of various cultural backgrounds could assimilate into the dominant culture, as in the process of "becoming American." Other versions of nationalism, in Germany, for example, sometimes defined the nation in racial terms that excluded those who did not share an imagined common ancestry, such as Jews. In the hands of conservatives, nationalism could be used to combat socialism and feminism, for those movements allegedly divided the nation along class or gender lines. Thus nationalism generated endless controversy because it provided no clear answer to the questions of who belonged to the nation or who should speak for it.

Nor was nationalism limited to the Euro-American world in the nineteenth century. An "Egypt for the Egyptians" movement arose in the 1870s as British and French intervention in Egyptian affairs deepened. When Japan likewise confronted European aggression in the second half of the nineteenth century, its long sense of itself as a distinct culture was readily transformed into an assertive modern nationalism. In British-ruled India, small groups of Western-educated men began to think of their enormously diverse country as a single nation. The Indian National Congress, established in 1885, gave expression to this idea. The notion of the Ottoman Empire as a Turkish national state rather than a Muslim or dynastic empire took hold among a few people. By the end of the nineteenth century, some Chinese intellectuals began to think in terms of a Chinese nation beset both by a foreign ruling dynasty and by predatory Europeans. Along the West African coast, the idea of an "African nation" stirred among a handful of freed slaves and missionary-educated men. Although Egyptian and Japanese nationalism gained broad support, elsewhere in Asia and Africa such movements would have to wait until the twentieth century, when they exploded with enormous power on the stage of world history.

Feminist Beginnings

A third echo of the Atlantic revolutions lay in the emergence of a feminist movement. Although scattered voices had earlier challenged patriarchy, never before had an organized and substantial group of women called into question this most fundamental and accepted feature of all preindustrial civilizations—the subordination of women to men. But in the century following the French Revolution, such a challenge took shape, especially in Europe and North America. Then, in the twentieth century, feminist thinking transformed "the way in which women and men work, play, think, dress, worship, vote, reproduce, make love and make war."[23] How did this extraordinary process get launched in the nineteenth century?

Thinkers of the European Enlightenment had challenged many ancient traditions, including on occasion that of women's intrinsic inferiority (see "Science and Enlightenment" in Chapter 15). The French writer Condorcet, for example, called for "the complete destruction of those prejudices that have established an inequality of rights between the sexes." The French Revolution then raised the possibility of re-creating human societies on new foundations. Many women participated in these events, and a few insisted, unsuccessfully, that the revolutionary ideals of liberty and equality must include women. In neighboring England, the French Revolution stimulated the writer Mary Wollstonecraft to pen her famous ***Vindication of the Rights of Woman***, one of the earliest expressions of a feminist consciousness. "Who made man the exclusive judge," she asked, "if woman partake with him of the gift of reason?"

Within the growing middle classes of industrializing societies, more women found both educational opportunities and some freedom from household drudgery. Such women increasingly took part in temperance movements, charities, abolitionism, and missionary work, as well as socialist and pacifist organizations. Some of their working-class sisters became active trade unionists. On both sides of the Atlantic, small numbers of these women began to develop a feminist consciousness that viewed women as individuals with rights equal to those of men. The first organized expression of this new feminism took place at the Women's Rights Convention in Seneca Falls, New York, in 1848. At that meeting, **Elizabeth Cady Stanton** drafted a statement that began by paraphrasing the Declaration of Independence: "We hold these truths to be self-evident, that all men and women are created equal."

Guided Reading Question

■ **SIGNIFICANCE**
What were the achievements and limitations of nineteenth-century feminism?

From the beginning, feminism became a transatlantic movement in which European and American women attended the same conferences, corresponded regularly, and read one another's work. Access to schools, universities, and the professions were among their major concerns as growing numbers of women sought these previously unavailable opportunities. The more radical among them refused to take their husbands' surname or wore trousers under their skirts. Elizabeth Cady Stanton published a Women's Bible, excising the parts she found offensive. As heirs to the French Revolution, feminists ardently believed in progress and insisted that it must now include a radical transformation of the position of women.

By the 1870s, feminist movements in the West were focusing primarily on the issue of suffrage and were gaining a growing constituency. Now many ordinary middle-class housewives and working-class mothers joined their better-educated sisters in the movement. By 1914, some 100,000 women took part in French feminist organizations, while the National American Woman Suffrage Association claimed 2 million members. Most operated through peaceful protest and persuasion, but the British Women's Social and Political Union organized a campaign of violence that included blowing up railroad stations, slashing works of art, and smashing department store windows. One British activist, Emily Davison, threw herself in front of the king's horse during a race in Britain in 1913 and was trampled to death. By the beginning of the twentieth century in the most highly industrialized countries of the West, the women's movement had become a mass movement.

That movement had some effect. By 1900, upper- and middle-class women had gained entrance to universities, though in small numbers, and women's literacy rates were growing steadily. In the United States, a number of states passed legislation allowing women to manage and control their own property and wages, separate from their husbands. Divorce laws were liberalized in some places. Professions such as medicine opened to a few, and teaching beckoned to many more. In Britain, Florence Nightingale professionalized nursing and attracted thousands of women into it, while Jane Addams in the United States virtually invented "social work," which also became a female-dominated profession. Progress was slower in the political domain. In 1893, New Zealand became the first country to give the vote to all adult women; Finland followed in 1906. Elsewhere widespread voting rights for women in national elections were not achieved until after World War I, in 1920 in the United States, and in France not until 1945.

Beyond these concrete accomplishments, the movement prompted an unprecedented discussion about the role of women in modern society. In Henrik Ibsen's play

Women's Suffrage What began as a few isolated voices of feminist protest in the early nineteenth century had become by the end of the century a mass movement in the United States and Western Europe. Here, in a photograph of an American suffrage parade in 1912, is an illustration of that movement in action. (Sarin Images/Granger, NYC—All rights reserved)

A Doll's House (1879), the heroine, Nora, finding herself in a loveless and oppressive marriage, leaves both her husband and her children. European audiences were riveted, and many were outraged. Writers, doctors, and journalists addressed previously taboo sexual topics, including homosexuality and birth control. Socialists too found themselves divided about women's issues. Did the women's movement distract from the class solidarity that Marxism proclaimed, or did it provide added energy to the workers' cause? Feminists themselves disagreed about the proper basis for women's rights. Some took their stand on the modern idea of human equality: "Whatever is right for a man is right for a woman." Others, particularly in France, based their claims more on the distinctive role of women as mothers. "It is above all this holy function of motherhood," wrote one advocate of **maternal feminism**, "which requires that women watch over the futures of their children and gives women the right to intervene not only in all acts of civil life, but also in all acts of political life."[24]

Not surprisingly, feminism provoked bitter opposition. Some academic and medical experts argued that the strains of education and life outside the home would cause serious reproductive damage and as a consequence depopulate the nation. Thus feminists were viewed as selfish, willing to sacrifice the family or even the nation while pursuing their individual goals. Some saw suffragists, like Jews and socialists, as "a foreign body in our national life." Never before in any society had such a passionate and public debate about the position of women erupted. It was a novel feature of Western historical experience in the aftermath of the Atlantic revolutions.

Like nationalism, a concern with women's rights spread beyond Western Europe and North America, though less widely. An overtly feminist newspaper was established in Brazil in 1852, and an independent school for girls was founded in Mexico in 1869. A handful of Japanese women and men, including the empress Haruko, raised issues about marriage, family planning, and especially education as the country began its modernizing process after 1868, but the state soon cracked down firmly, forbidding women from joining political parties or even attending political meetings. In Russia, the most radical feminist activists operated within socialist or anarchist circles, targeting the oppressive tsarist regime. Within the Islamic world and in China, some modernists came to believe that education and a higher status for women strengthened the nation in its struggles for development and independence and therefore deserved support. (See Zooming In: Kartini, page 720, for an example from the Dutch East Indies.) Huda Sharawi, founder of the first feminist organization in Egypt, returned to Cairo in 1923 from an international conference in Italy and threw her veil into the sea. Many upper-class Egyptian women soon followed her example.

Nowhere did nineteenth-century feminism have thoroughly revolutionary consequences. But as an outgrowth of the French and Industrial Revolutions, it raised issues that echoed repeatedly and more loudly in the century that followed.

Kartini: Feminism and Nationalism in Java

The ideas of the European Enlightenment and the Atlantic revolutions resonated deeply in the life of a remarkable young Javanese woman named Kartini during the late nineteenth century, when her country was part of the Dutch East Indies (now Indonesia).[25] Born in 1879 into a large aristocratic Javanese family, young Kartini attended a Dutch elementary school, where she learned the Dutch language and observed the relative freedom of her European classmates, in sharp contrast to the constraints and ritualized interactions of her own family. At the age of twelve, in keeping with Javanese Muslim custom, Kartini was abruptly removed from her school. For the next four years, she never left her home.

Through her father, a high official in the Dutch colonial administration who much admired Western education, Kartini still had access to Dutch books, and later she was tutored by several Europeans, including one woman with strong socialist and feminist leanings. She also read widely on her own and began an extensive correspondence, largely with Dutch friends in the Netherlands, that

Kartini.

photo: Royal Tropical Institute

lasted until her death. By the time she was twenty, Kartini had acquired an impressive Western education and a network of relationships with prominent Europeans both in the Netherlands and in Java.

From her letters, we learn something of Kartini's thinking. In light of her exposure to Europeans and European thought, she found the absolute subordination of Javanese women completely unacceptable. The seclusion of girls, the total separation of the sexes, the absence of educational opportunities—all of this drove her almost to despair. "Are fine women of no use to civilization?" she asked. But it was the prospect of a traditional high-class Javanese marriage that she found most appalling. Her husband would be "a stranger, an unknown man, whom my parents would choose for me . . . without my knowledge." During the wedding ceremony, she would be expected to prostrate herself before the bridegroom and kiss his feet as a sign of her future

---

REFLECTIONS

Revolutions: Pro and Con

Long after the dust had settled from the Atlantic upheavals, their legacies have continued to provoke controversy. Were these revolutions necessary? Did they really promote the freedoms that they advertised? Did their benefits outweigh their costs in blood and treasure?

To the people who made these revolutions, benefited from them, or subsequently supported them, they represented an opening to new worlds of human possibility, while sweeping away old worlds of oppression, exploitation, and privilege. Modern revolutionaries acted on the basis of Enlightenment ideas, believing submission. Even then, she would be only one of several wives. "Do you understand now," she wrote to a Dutch confidant, "the deep aversion I have for marriage?"

Kartini was equally outraged by particular features of Dutch colonial rule, especially its racism. Conscious of her membership in a "despised brown race," she deplored the need for "creeping in the dust" before Europeans. Javanese generally were not supposed to speak Dutch with their colonial masters, as if "Dutch is too beautiful to be spoken by a brown mouth." And yet, for Kartini, it was Dutch education and its universal Enlightenment values—"freedom, equality, fraternity," as she put it, echoing the slogan of the French Revolution—that would lead to Javanese emancipation from both Dutch and Javanese oppression. "Europe will teach us to be truly free," she wrote.

Nonetheless, Kartini openly embraced much of her own culture—its art, music, and poetry, its regard for the dead; its hospitality to the poor; its spiritual depth—and she certainly did not seek to transform Javanese into "half-Europeans." But she did believe that "contact with another civilization" and modern European education in particular would enable Javanese "to develop the fine qualities that are peculiar to their race." "Emancipation is in the air," she declared in early 1901.

Kartini's fondest hope was to contribute to that emancipation by studying in the Netherlands and then opening a school for girls in Java. But these grand dreams were thwarted by opposition from her own family, from Javanese officials, and from much of the Dutch colonial bureaucracy. Java's leading newspaper denounced her intentions as "outrageous," and local gossip had it that she simply wanted to marry a European and become a Europeanized woman. A backup plan to study in the colonial capital of Batavia likewise came to naught with a sudden announcement in mid-1903 that her father had arranged for her to be married to a much older and polygamous man of her social class. Kartini was devastated. "My crown has fallen from my head. My golden illusions of purity and chastity lie shattered in the dust. . . . Now I am nothing more than all the rest."[26]

Although Kartini felt that she was "done with all personal happiness," she determined to make her marriage a model for the future, actually meeting her husband before the wedding and extracting from him a written promise that she could continue with her plans to create a school for girls. But she soon became pregnant, and four days after the birth of her son in 1904, she died at the age of twenty-five. As her writings subsequently became known in Indonesia, Kartini came to be regarded as a pioneer of both feminist and nationalist thinking, and a number of "Kartini schools" were established in her memory.

QUESTION

In what ways was Kartini's life shaped by living at the intersection of Javanese and European worlds?

that the structure of human societies was not forever ordained by God or tradition and that it was both possible and necessary to reconstruct those societies. They saw themselves as correcting ancient and enduring injustices. To those who complained about the violence of revolutions, supporters pointed to the violence that maintained the status quo and the unwillingness of favored classes to accommodate changes that threatened those unjust privileges. It was persistent injustice that made revolution necessary and perhaps inevitable.

To their victims, critics, and opponents, revolutions appeared in a quite different light. Conservatives generally viewed human societies not as machines whose parts could be easily rearranged but as organisms that evolved slowly. Efforts at radical and sudden change only invited disaster, as the unrestrained violence of the French Revolution at its height demonstrated. The brutality and bitterness of the Haitian

Revolution arguably contributed to the unhappy future of that country. Furthermore, critics charged that revolutions were largely unnecessary since societies were in fact changing. France was becoming a modern society, and feudalism was largely gone well before the revolution exploded. Slavery was ended peacefully in many places, and democratic reform proceeded gradually throughout the nineteenth century. Was this not a preferable alternative to revolutionary upheaval?

Historians too struggle with the passions of revolution—both pro and con—as they seek to understand the origins and consequences of these momentous events. Were revolutions the product of misery, injustice, and oppression? Or did they reflect the growing weakness of established authorities, the arrival of new ideas, or the presence of small groups of radical activists able to fan the little fires of ordinary discontent into revolutionary conflagrations? The outcomes of revolutions have been as contentious as their beginnings. Did the American Revolution enable the growth of the United States as an economic and political Great Power? Did the Haitian Revolution stimulate the later end of slavery elsewhere in the Atlantic world? Did the French Revolution and the threat of subsequent revolutions encourage the democratic reforms that followed in the nineteenth century? Such questions have been central to an understanding of the Atlantic revolutions as well as to those that followed in Russia, China, and elsewhere in the twentieth century.

Second Thoughts

What's the Significance?

Big Picture Questions

1. Do revolutions originate in oppression and injustice, in the weakening of political authorities, in new ideas, or in the activities of small groups of determined activists?
2. "The influence of revolutions endured long after they ended and far beyond where they started." To what extent does this chapter support or undermine this idea?
3. Did the Atlantic revolutions fulfill or betray the goals of those who made them? Consider this question in both short- and long-term perspectives.
4. **Looking Back:** To what extent did the Atlantic revolutions reflect the influence of early modern historical developments (1450–1750)?

Next Steps: For Further Study

Benedict Anderson, *Imagined Communities: Reflections on the Origins and Spread of Nationalism* (1991). A now-classic though controversial examination of the process by which national identities were created.

Bonnie S. Anderson, *Joyous Greetings: The First International Women's Movement, 1830–1860* (2000). Describes the beginnings of transatlantic feminism.

David Armitage and Sanjay Subrahmanyam, eds., *The Age of Revolutions in Global Context, c. 1760–1840* (2010). A recent collection of scholarly essays that seeks to explore revolutions within a global framework.

Laurent Dubois and John Garrigus, *Slave Revolution in the Caribbean, 1789–1804* (2017). A brief and up-to-date summary of the Haitian Revolution, combined with a number of documents.

Eric Hobsbawm, *The Age of Revolution, 1789–1848* (1999). A highly respected survey by a well-known British historian.

Lynn Hunt, ed., *The French Revolution and Human Rights* (1996). A collection of documents, with a fine introduction by a prominent scholar.

Noland Walker (director), *Égalité for All: Toussaint Louverture and the Haitian Revolution,* 2009, http://www.youtube.com/watch?v=lOGVgQYX6SU. A thoughtful PBS documentary on the Haitian Revolution, focusing on its principal leader.

George Mason University and City University of New York, "Liberty, Equality, Fraternity: Exploring the French Revolution," http://chnm.gmu.edu/revolution/. A collection of essays, images, documents, songs, and maps illustrating the French Revolution.

Opponents of the Atlantic Revolutions

The radical notions that authority to govern derived from the people and that human societies could and should be improved through political and social engineering inspired many in the Atlantic world to overthrow their rulers during the late eighteenth and early nineteenth centuries. But others voiced their opposition to revolution. In doing so they raised concerns about the violence and disorder that often accompanied the overthrow of governments, the disruptive pace of change, the rejection of long-established traditions and institutions, and the social and cultural implications of new conceptions of liberty, equality, and religious freedom. Moreover, once in power, some revolutionaries denied or limited "universal rights" for slaves, women, and other groups. The sources that follow give voice to these opponents of the Atlantic revolutions.

SOURCE 16.1 A New York Clergyman's Criticism of the Continental Congress

Samuel Seabury (1729–1796), an Anglican minister and resident of Westchester, New York, was a vocal critic of the American Revolution who published a series of letters under the pseudonym "a Westchester Farmer." In his letters, Seabury frequently criticized the Continental Congress—the convention of delegates that became the governing body for the American revolutionaries—for infringing on the same personal freedoms that it accused the British government of disregarding. In this passage, Seabury expresses his opposition to the Non-Consumption agreement—a boycott established in late 1774 barring American colonists from engaging in direct trade with Britain.

- Which personal freedoms does Seabury accuse the Continental Congress of infringing upon?

- In what specific ways does Seabury draw on the language of rights and liberties to oppose the Continental Congress?

- Is Seabury a loyalist supporter of British colonial government, a supporter of the American Revolution, or a critic of both? Why?

SAMUEL SEABURY | *Letter of a Westchester Farmer* | 1774

My Friends and Countrymen,

Permit me to address you upon a subject, which … demands your most serious and dispassionate consideration. The American Colonies are unhappily involved in a scene of confusion and discord. The bands of civil society are broken; the authority of government weakened, and in some instances taken away: Individuals are deprived of their liberty; their property is frequently invaded by violence. From this distressed situation it was hoped, that the wisdom and prudence of the [Continental] Congress lately assembled at Philadelphia, would have delivered us.… We ardently expected that some prudent scheme of accommodating our unhappy disputes with the Mother-Country, would have been adopted and pursued. But alas! they are broken up without ever attempting it: they have taken no [sic] one step that tended to peace … and have either ignorantly misunderstood, carelessly neglected, or basely betrayed the interests of all the Colonies.…

Let us now attend a little to the Non-Consumption Agreement, which the Congress, in their Association, have imposed upon us.… [W]e are not to purchase or use any East-India Tea whatsoever; nor any goods, wares, or [newly imported] merchandise from Great-Britain or Ireland … nor any molasses, syrups, &c. from the British plantations in the West-Indies … nor wine from Madeira.…

Will you submit to this slavish regulation?—You must.—Our sovereign Lords and Masters, the High and Mighty Delegates, in Grand Continental Congress assembled, have ordered and directed it. They have directed the [Revolutionary] Committees in the respective colonies, to establish such further regulations as they may think proper, for carrying their association, of which this Non-consumption agreement is a part, into execution.… The Committee of New York … [will] inspect the conduct of the inhabitants.… Among other things, Whether they drink any Tea or wine in their families … or wear any British or Irish manufactures; or use any English molasses, &c.… If they do, their names are to be published in the Gazette, that they might be *publicly known*, and *universally condemned, as foes to the Rights of British America*, and *enemies of American Liberty.*—And then *the parties of the said Association will respectively break off all dealings with him or her.*—In plain English,—They shall be considered as Out-laws, unworthy of the protection of civil society, and delivered over to the vengeance of a lawless, outrageous mob, to be *tarred, feathered, hanged, drawn, quartered, and burnt.*—O rare American Freedom! …

Will you be instrumental in bringing the most abject slavery on yourselves? Will you choose such Committees? Will you submit to them, should they be chosen by the weak, foolish, turbulent part of the country people?—Do as you please: but, by HIM that made me, I will not.—No, if I must be enslaved, let it be by a KING at least, and not by a parcel of upstart lawless Committee-men. If I must be devoured, let me be devoured by the jaws of a lion, and not *gnawed* to death by rats and vermin.

Did you choose your supervisors for the purpose of enslaving you? … You ought, my friends, to assert your own freedom. Should such another attempt be made upon you, assemble yourselves together: tell your supervisor, that he has exceeded his commission:—That you will have no such Committees:—that you are Englishmen, and will maintain your rights and privileges, and will eat, and drink, and wear, whatever the public laws of your country permit, without asking leave of any illegal, tyrannical Congress or Committee on earth.…

… If you like it better, choose your Committee, or suffer it to be chosen by half a dozen Fools in your neighbourhood.—open your doors to them,—let them examine your tea-cannisters, and molasses-jugs, and your wives and daughters petty-coats,—bow, and cringe, and tremble, and quake,—fall down and worship our sovereign Lord the Mob.—But I repeat it, by H—n, I will not.—No my house is my castle.… Before *I* submit, I will die: live *you*, and be slaves.…

November 16, 1774.

A. W. Farmer

Source: Samuel Seabury, *Free Thoughts, on the Proceedings of the Continental Congress, Held at Philadelphia Sept. 5 1774* (New York: James Rivington, 1774), 3, 17–19. Spelling of some words has been modernized.

■ ■ ■

SOURCE 16.2 A British Conservative's Critique of the Universal Rights of Man

Edmund Burke (1729–1797), a member of the British Parliament and statesman from Ireland, was one of the first and most influential critics of the principles on which the French Revolution was based. In his *Reflections on the Revolution in France*, first published in 1790, Burke accepts that political change can and should occur but argues that successful political reform must happen incrementally and be based on existing political structures and traditions. Political systems founded on statements of universal rights were fatally flawed in Burke's view because they encouraged excessive individualism, selfishness, and personal ambition. At the root of all political communities, Burke identified the sacrifice of natural or universal rights as a positive trade-off that allowed individuals to live in peaceful civil societies. In some ways, Burke's more cautious approach reflected the experiences of his native Britain, which in the previous century had experienced two revolutionary upheavals, one of which included a prolonged and violent civil war that culminated in the execution of the king. Burke, however, was not an opponent of all revolutions. He had supported the American revolutionaries, whom he saw as working within British political traditions rather than abandoning them.

In Source 16.2, Burke rejects the idea that French revolutionaries could found a successful new state based on the principles espoused in the Declaration of the Rights of Man and Citizen. Burke published these objections before war, violence, and the Terror radicalized the French Revolution, so his arguments focus on those principles on which the Atlantic revolutions were based rather than on revulsion with the disorder and violence that often accompanied the overthrow of political regimes.

■ What is Burke's understanding of universal human rights and their place in government?

■ Which rights does Burke grant to individuals in a civil state?

■ How might Burke have reacted to Seabury's objections to revolutionary committees in Source 16.1?

EDMUND BURKE | *Reflections on the Revolution in France* | 1790

[I]t is in vain to talk to them [revolutionaries] of the practice of their ancestors, the fundamental laws of their country, the fixed form of a constitution, whose merits are confirmed by the solid test of long experience, and an increasing public strength and national prosperity. They despise experience as the wisdom of unlettered men; and as for the rest, they have wrought underground a mine that will blow up at one grand explosion all examples of antiquity, all precedents, charters, and acts of parliament. They have "the rights of men." Against these there can be no prescription; against these no agreement is binding: these admit no temperament, and no compromise: any thing withheld from their full demand is so much of fraud and injustice. Against these their rights of men let no government look for security in the length of its continuance, or in the justice and lenity of its administration. The objections of these specialists, if its forms do not quadrate [conform] with their theories, are as valid against such an old and beneficent government as against the most violent tyranny, or the greenest usurpation. . . .

In denying their false claims of right, I do not mean to injure those [rights] which are real, and are such as their pretended rights would totally destroy. If civil society be made for the advantage of man, all the advantages for which it is made become his right. It is an institution of beneficence; and law itself is only beneficence acting by a rule. Men have a right to live by that rule; they have a right to justice. . . . They have a right to the fruits of their industry, and to the means of making their industry fruitful. They have a right to the acquisitions of their parents; to the nourishment and improvement of their offspring; to instruction in life, and to consolation in death. Whatever each man can separately do, without trespassing upon others, he has a right to do for himself; and he has a right to a fair portion of all which society, with all its combinations of skill and force, can do in his favour. But as to the share of power, authority, and direction which each individual ought to have in the management of the state, that I must deny to be amongst the direct original rights of man in civil society; for I have in my contemplation the civil social man, and no other. . . .

Government is not made in virtue of natural rights, which may and do exist in total independence of it. . . . By having a right to every thing, they want every thing. Government is a contrivance of human wisdom to provide for human wants [desires]. Men have a right that these wants should be provided for by this wisdom. Among these wants is to be reckoned the want . . . of a sufficient restraint upon their passions. Society requires not only that the passions of individuals should be subjected, but that even in the mass and body, as well as in the individuals, the inclinations of men should frequently be thwarted, their will controlled, and their passions brought into subjection. This can only be done by a power out[side] of themselves; and not . . . subject to that will and to those passions which is its office to bridle and subdue. In this sense the restraints on men, as well as their liberties, are to be reckoned among their rights. But as the liberties and the restrictions vary with times and circumstances, and admit of infinite modifications, they cannot be settled upon any abstract rule; and nothing is so foolish as to discuss them upon that principle.

Source: Edmund Burke, *Reflections on the Revolution in France* (London: John Sharpe, 1820), 1:80–84.

■ ■ ■

SOURCE 16.3 An English Cartoon's Reaction to Revolutionary Violence

Over time, the French Revolution became more radical and violent, culminating in the Reign of Terror (1793–1794), during which thousands of political opponents of the revolutionary regime were executed. An important step in this descent into violence was the execution of Louis XVI in January 1793. Source 16.3, a British political cartoon, conveys a highly critical, indeed horrified, outlook on the violence that accompanied the French Revolution. Captioned "Hell Broke Loose," it depicts the execution of Louis XVI and was printed shortly after his death. The flying demonic figures in the image are repeating popular slogans of the revolution: "*Vive la nation*" ("Long live the nation") and "*Ça ira*" ("That will go well," or more loosely, "We will win").

■ What is the significance of the demons and dragons in the cartoon? How are the soldiers at the bottom of the image portrayed?

■ What meaning would you attribute to the caption, "Hell Broke Loose"? What disasters might critics of the revolution have imagined coming in its wake?

■ How do you understand the beam of light from heaven that falls on Louis XVI?

■ How might Burke (Source 16.2) react to this cartoon and the execution of Louis XVI?

Hell Broke Loose, or, The Murder of Louis | 1793

HELL BROKE LOOSE, OR, THE MURDER OF LOUIS.

■ ■ ■

SOURCE 16.4 The French National Assembly and Slavery

Victory in 1789 left revolutionaries in control of France and faced with the task of reconciling their idealistic slogans and principles with the competing demands of government. Few debates were more contentious than that surrounding the status of free men of color and slaves in the French colonies and especially the sugar islands of the Caribbean. Some revolutionary voices pressed for the outlawing of slavery as incompatible with a new state based on universal rights and liberties. Others pressed for free men of color to be embraced as full citizens while maintaining slavery, which, they argued, was too important for the colonial and French economies to be abandoned. Meanwhile, many white plantation owners and people in France whose livelihoods depended on colonial trade argued forcefully against granting any rights to peoples of color because this could lead to the emancipation of slaves in the future. In 1791 the lawmaking body in France known as the National Assembly opted for a compromise, rejecting freedom for slaves while granting citizenship to free men of color. Source 16.4 reproduces the text of this decree and an explanation offered by the Assembly for its decision. The law of 1791 set the stage for the Haitian Revolution. Only after the successful uprising of slaves in Haiti did the French revolutionary government finally pass a law abolishing slavery in 1794. But this law was short-lived; Napoleon rescinded it in 1802.

- How did the National Assembly justify its decision to maintain slavery in French colonies?

- What does the decision to grant the rights of citizenship to free men of color but not to slaves tell us about the reasoning of the Assembly?

- What does this source reveal about the thinking of French revolutionaries concerning race, property rights, and personal freedom?

Decree and Explanation of the French National Assembly | May 15 and 29, 1791

Decree of May 15

The National Assembly decrees that the legislature will never deliberate on the political status of people of color who were not born of free fathers and mothers without the previous free, and unprompted request of the colonies; that the presently existing Colonial Assemblies will admit the people of color born of free fathers and mothers if they otherwise have the required status.

Explanation of May 29

The National Assembly, attentive to all means of assuring prosperity in the colonies, to ensure that the citizens living there enjoy the advantages of the constitution . . . , recognizes that local circumstances and the kind of agriculture that brings colonial prosperity appear to require introducing into the colonial constitution several exceptions to the [French Revolution's] general principles.

. . . [On March 28, 1790] The National Assembly declared that the legislature would discuss the status of nonfree persons only on the unprompted request of the Colonial Assemblies.

The National Assembly was able to make this commitment because it only involved individuals [this paragraph refers to slaves] of a foreign land who, by their profound ignorance, the misfortune of their exile, the consideration of their own interest, and the urgent law of necessity, can only hope that in time the progress of public opinion and enlightenment will produce a change of conditions that, in the present state of things, would be contrary to the general good and might become equally dangerous for them.

Source: Laurent Dubois and John D. Garrigus, *Slave Revolution in the Caribbean 1789–1804: A Brief History with Documents*, 2nd ed. (Boston: Bedford/St. Martin's, 2017), 70–71.

■ ■ ■

SOURCE 16.5 Imagining Women's Suffrage ▶

Echoes of the Atlantic revolutions, including abolitionism and feminism, also had their opponents. Critics frequently made their cases against these movements by imagining a world that might be created if groups like the suffragettes won the rights that they sought. In this 1897 cartoon entitled "An Inauguration of the Future," the artist offers a vision of what America would become if women were granted the right to vote. It depicts the inauguration of a female president, who is surrounded on the stage by other women in positions of power. To the bottom right on the sidelines of the inauguration, a man is depicted in a distinctly domestic role holding a crying baby.

■ Note the women in military uniforms on the stage and in the crowd. Why do you think that the artist included these figures in the image?

■ What potential implications of granting women the right to vote does this artist want the viewer to consider?

■ While not so far-fetched today, how might this image have been viewed during the late nineteenth century?

An Inauguration of the Future | 1897

Stock Montage/Getty Images

DOING HISTORY

1. **Considering universal rights:** In what ways do these sources criticize the idea of universal human rights as the basis for government? Do they reject the concept of human rights altogether?

2. **Making comparisons:** In what different ways do opponents argue against the Atlantic revolutions and their echoes? Consider issues of rights, social stability, race, and gender.

3. **Identifying opponents of the revolution:** Based on these sources and the text narrative, which groups of people opposed the Atlantic revolutions? Why?

How the French Revolution Went Wrong

Criticism of the French Revolution continued into the nineteenth century as historians and others in France sought to explain why a movement based on universal rights and democratic principles became one defined by terror and later dictatorship. Voice 16.1 is from Alexis de Tocqueville (1805–1859), a nobleman, diplomat, historian, and social critic who is best known for his books *Democracy in America* (1830) and *The Old Regime and the French Revolution* (1856). Sympathetic to republican forms of government, he wrote about the French Revolution in the mid-nineteenth century during a period of political turmoil that saw a French republican government replaced by the monarchical rule of Napoleon III. In the passage reproduced here, Tocqueville lays out the broad contours of a proposed future book about the revolution. The historian and literary critic Hippolyte Taine (1828–1893) provides our second voice. Writing in the 1870s when the collapse of Napoleon III's government once again shook the French polity, Taine was an outspoken critic of the Jacobins, who led France during the most radical phase of the French Revolution. But in the passage reproduced here he also takes aim at the failures of leadership during the early years of the revolution, which he sees as opening the door to the Jacobins.

■ What do Tocqueville and Taine agree on? Where do they disagree?

■ Do Tocqueville and Taine offer any sense as to how the outcome of the revolution might have been different?

■ To what extent should a historian today take into account the historical contexts in which Tocqueville and Taine wrote when assessing their interpretations of the revolution?

■ **Integrating Primary and Secondary Sources:** To what extent do Tocqueville's and Taine's assessments agree with the criticisms of the French Revolution found in Sources 16.2 and 16.3?

VOICE 16.1

Tocqueville on the Course of the French Revolution | 1856

I shall first go over the period of 1789, when their affections were divided between the love of freedom and the love of equality; when they desired to establish free as well as democratic institutions, and to acknowledge and confirm rights as well as to destroy privileges. This was an era of youth, enthusiasm, of pride, of generous and heartfelt passions; despite its errors, men will remember it long, and for many a day to come it will disturb the slumbers of those who seek to corrupt or enslave the French.

In the course of a hasty sketch of the Revolution, I shall endeavour to show what errors, what faults, what disappointments led the French to abandon their first aim, to forget liberty, and to aspire to become the equal servants of the master of the world [Napoleon]; how a far stronger and more absolute government than the one the Revolution overthrew then seized and monopolized all political power, suppressed all the liberties which had been so dearly bought, and set up in their stead empty shams; deprived electors of all means of obtaining information, of the right of assemblage, and of the faculty of exercising a choice, yet talked of popular sovereignty; . . . and while stripping the nation of every vestige of self-government, of constitutional guarantees, and of liberty of thought, speech, and the press—that is to say, of the most precious and the noblest conquests of 1789—still dared to claim descent from that great era.

Source: Alexis de Tocqueville, *The Old Regime and the Revolution*, translated by John Bonner (New York: Harper and Brothers, 1856), v–vi.

VOICE 16.2

Hippolyte Taine on the Failure of the Early Years of the Revolution and the Rise of the Radical Revolution | 1881

So far, the weakness of the legal government is extreme. For four years [from the start of the revolution in 1789 to the beginning of the Terror in 1793], whatever its kind, everywhere and constantly, it [the revolutionary government] has been disobeyed, for four years, whatever its kind, it has never dared enforce obedience. Recruited among the cultivated and refined class, the rulers of the country have brought with them into power the prejudices and sensibilities of the epoch; . . . they have deferred to the will of the multitude and, with too much faith in the rights of man, they have had too little in the rights of the magistrate; moreover, through humanity, they have abhorred bloodshed and, unwilling to repress, they have allowed themselves to be repressed. Thus . . . they have carried on the administration, or legislated, athwart innumerable insurrections, almost all of them going unpunished; while their constitutions . . . have done no more than transform spontaneous anarchy into legal anarchy. Willfully and through distrust of authority they have undermined the principle of command, reduced the King to the post of a decorative puppet, and almost annihilated the central power: from the top to the bottom of the hierarchy the superior has lost his hold on the inferior. . . . [T]he Declaration of Rights [of Man and the Citizen], proclaiming "the jurisdiction of constituents over their clerks," has invited the assistants to make the assault. . . . [O]n the first attack, often at the first summons, all have surrendered, and now the citadel, with every other public fortress is in the hands of the Jacobins [the radicals who brought forth the Terror in France].

Source: Hippolyte Taine, *The French Revolution*, translated by John Durand (New York: Peter Smith, 1931), 3:2–4.

Revolutions of Industrialization

1750–1900

In mid-2017, Erik Solheim, the Norwegian head of the UN Environment Program, stated that "humanity's advancement in science, technology and industrialization [is] harming the planet, hence the need to reverse course."[1] At the same time, Dr. Lloyd G. Adu Amoah, a prominent professor at the University of Ghana in West Africa, declared: "We need to industrialize, because if we don't, we are not adding value to what the African continent has."[2] ∎

These two statements represent perhaps the most compelling dilemma facing humankind in the twenty-first century. How can we embrace the wealth and improvement in human life universally associated with industrialization, while preserving and protecting this fragile planet that sustains us all? That profound dilemma has its origins in the enormously transformative process of the Industrial Revolution, which took place initially in Europe during the century and a half between 1750 and 1900. Not since the Agricultural Revolution some 12,000 years ago have our ways of living and our relationship to the natural world been so fundamentally altered.

In any long-term reckoning, the history of industrialization is very much an unfinished story. Are we at the beginning of a movement leading to worldwide industrialization, stuck in the middle of a world permanently divided into rich and poor countries, or approaching the end of an environmentally unsustainable industrial era? Whatever the future holds, this chapter focuses on the early stages of an immense transformation in the global condition of humankind.

« Industrial Britain To the modern eye this engraving of one of the first and largest copper works in Wales vividly conveys a sense of the dirt, smoke, and pollution of early industrial societies. However, at the time of its publication in 1862, many viewers would have seen in this image a celebration of modern industry and humankind's growing productivity centered on factory production.

In what ways did the Industrial Revolution mark a sharp break with the past? In what ways did it continue earlier patterns?

Industrialization: The Global Context

The epic economic transformation of the Industrial Revolution took shape as a very substantial increase in human numbers unfolded—from about 375 million people in 1400 to about 1 billion in the early nineteenth century. Accompanying this growth in population was an emerging energy crisis, most pronounced in Western Europe, China, and Japan, as wood and charcoal, the major industrial fuels, became more scarce and more costly. In short, "global energy demands began to push against the existing local and regional ecological limits."[3] In broad terms, the Industrial Revolution marked a human response to that dilemma. It was a twofold revolution—drawing on new sources of energy and new technologies—that combined to utterly transform economic and social life on the planet.

In terms of energy, the Industrial Revolution came to rely on fossil fuels such as coal, oil, and natural gas, which supplemented and largely replaced the earlier energy sources of wind, water, wood, and the muscle power of people and animals that had long sustained humankind. It was a breakthrough of unprecedented proportions that made available for human use, at least temporarily, immensely greater quantities of energy. During the nineteenth century, yet another fuel became widely available as Europeans learned to exploit guano, or seabird excrement, found on the islands off the coast of Peru. Used as a potent fertilizer, guano enabled highly productive input-intensive farming practices. In much of Western Europe, North America, Australia, and New Zealand, it sustained the production of crops that fed both the draft animals and the growing human populations of the industrializing world.[4]

Guided Reading Question

■ CONTEXT
What is the significance of the Industrial Revolution in the larger context of human history?

The technological dimension of the Industrial Revolution has been equally significant. Early signs of the technological creativity that spawned the Industrial Revolution appeared in eighteenth-century Britain, where a variety of innovations transformed cotton textile production. It was only in the nineteenth century, though, that Europeans in general and the British in particular more clearly forged ahead of the rest of the world. (See Controversies: Debating "Why Europe?") The great breakthrough was the coal-fired **steam engine**, which provided an inanimate and almost limitless source of power beyond that of wind, water, or muscle and could be used to drive any number of machines as well as locomotives and oceangoing ships. Soon the Industrial Revolution spread beyond the textile industry to iron and steel production, railroads and steamships, food processing, and construction. Later in the nineteenth century, a so-called second Industrial Revolution focused on chemicals, electricity, precision machinery, the telegraph and telephone, rubber, printing, and much more. Agriculture too was affected as mechanical reapers, chemical fertilizers, pesticides, and refrigeration transformed this most ancient of industries. Sustaining this explosion of technological innovation was a "culture of innovation," a widespread and almost obsessive belief that things could be endlessly improved.

Together, these new sources of energy and new technologies gave rise to an enormously increased output of goods and services. In Britain, where the Industrial

Landmarks for Chapter 17

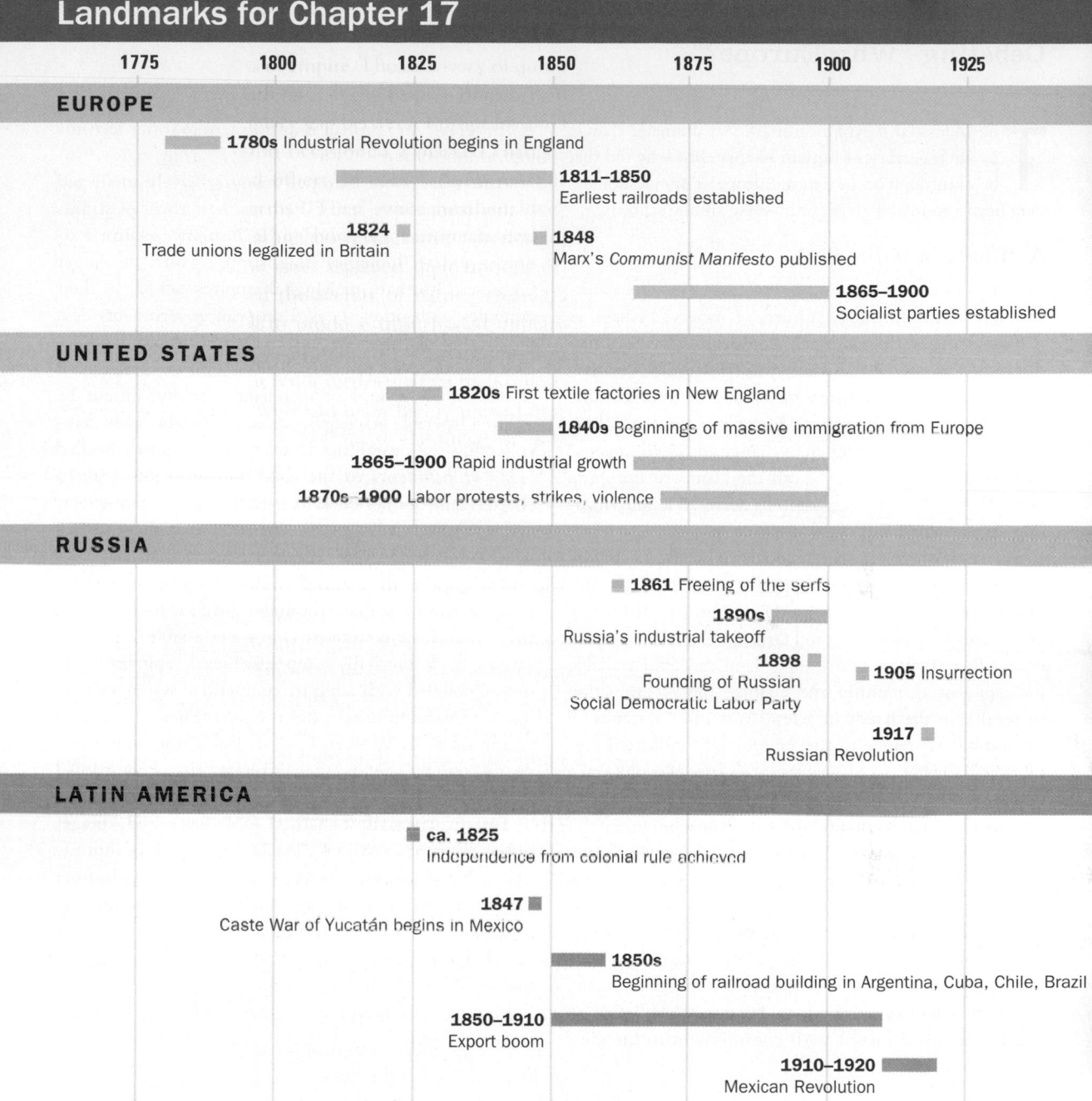

| | 1775 | 1800 | 1825 | 1850 | 1875 | 1900 | 1925 |

EUROPE

1780s Industrial Revolution begins in England

1811–1850
Earliest railroads established

1824
Trade unions legalized in Britain

1848
Marx's *Communist Manifesto* published

1865–1900
Socialist parties established

UNITED STATES

1820s First textile factories in New England

1840s Beginnings of massive immigration from Europe

1865–1900 Rapid industrial growth

1870s–1900 Labor protests, strikes, violence

RUSSIA

1861 Freeing of the serfs

1890s
Russia's industrial takeoff

1898
Founding of Russian
Social Democratic Labor Party

1905 Insurrection

1917
Russian Revolution

LATIN AMERICA

ca. 1825
Independence from colonial rule achieved

1847
Caste War of Yucatán begins in Mexico

1850s
Beginning of railroad building in Argentina, Cuba, Chile, Brazil

1850–1910
Export boom

1910–1920
Mexican Revolution

Revolution began, industrial output increased some fiftyfold between 1750 and 1900. It was a wholly unprecedented and previously unimaginable jump in the capacity of human societies to produce wealth, to extend life expectancies, and to increase human numbers. Furthermore, industrialization soon spread beyond Britain to continental Western Europe and then in the second half of the nineteenth

737

Debating "Why Europe?"

The Industrial Revolution marked a dramatic change in the trajectory of human history. But why did that breakthrough occur first in Europe? This question has long been a source of great controversy among scholars.

A "European Miracle"

Does the answer lie in some unique or "miraculous" feature of European history, culture, or society? Perhaps, as one scholar recently suggested, Europeans have been distinguished for several thousand years by a restless, creative, and freedom-loving culture with its roots in the aristocratic warlike societies of early Indo-European invaders, which rendered them uniquely open to change and development.[5] But critics have questioned both the claims to European cultural uniqueness and causal links between industrialization and developments of the distant past.

Or should we focus more narrowly on the period between about 1400 and 1800 for the origins of this "European miracle"?[6] During those centuries distinctive new forms of landowning and farming practices emerged, especially in Britain, which made land and labor available for capitalist agriculture and enabled the accumulation of wealth in the hands of a few. Was this "agricultural revolution" a prelude to the subsequent "industrial revolution"? Or perhaps it was the Scientific Revolution, a distinctly European event that generated a new view of the cosmos, that stimulated industrialization.

It turns out, however, that industrial technologies derived from the workshops of artisans and craftsmen rather than from the laboratories of scientists. And so by the early twenty-first century, many historians were thinking in terms of a broader cultural pattern, an eighteenth-century "Industrial Enlightenment" in which scientific methods and a general belief in an ordered universe mixed with commitment to the ideas of "progress" and human improvement to foster technological innovation.

And what about Europe's many relatively small and highly competitive states? Perhaps their rivalries stimulated innovation and provided an "insurance against economic and technological stagnation," which the larger Chinese, Ottoman, or Mughal empires lacked. In their struggles with other states, European governments desperately needed revenue, and to get it, European authorities developed an unusual alliance with their merchant classes. Small groups of merchant capitalists might be granted special privileges, monopolies, or even tax-collecting responsibilities in exchange for much-needed loans or payments to the state. Governments granted charters and monopolies to private trading companies, and states founded scientific societies and offered prizes to promote innovation. European merchants and other innovators after the fifteenth century became more independent from state control and enjoyed a higher social status than their counterparts in more established civilizations. Such internally competitive semi-capitalist economies, coupled with a highly competitive system of rival states, arguably fostered innovation in the new civilization taking shape in Western Europe. But at the same time, nearly constant war and the destruction that accompanied it also served as a long-term drain on European resources.

Britain especially benefited from several advantages of the "European Miracle," including a spirit of innovation, a lot of easily accessible coal, a growing consumer market, plentiful cheap capital accumulated in agriculture and trade, and its island geography, which frequently shielded it from the worst effects of Europe's wars. It also had a relatively high-wage workforce, which gave British businesses an extraordinary incentive to invent laborsaving technologies.

century to the United States, Russia, and Japan. In the twentieth century it became a genuinely global process. More than anything else, industrialization marks the past 250 years as a distinct phase of human history.

In the long run, the Industrial Revolution unarguably improved the material conditions of life for much of humankind. But it also unarguably wrought a mounting impact

The "Great Divergence"

But was Europe alone destined to lead the way to modern economic life? To many world historians, such views are both Eurocentric and deterministic; they also fly in the face of much recent research. Historians now know that India, the Islamic world, and especially China had experienced times of great technological and scientific flourishing. For reasons much debated, all of these flowerings of creativity had slowed down considerably or stagnated by the early modern era, when the pace of technological change in Europe began to pick up. But these earlier achievements certainly suggest that Europe was not alone in its capacity for technological innovation.

Nor did Europe enjoy any overall economic advantage as late as 1750. Recent scholars have found rather "a world of surprising resemblances" among major Eurasian societies during the eighteenth century. Economic indicators such as life expectancies, patterns of consumption and nutrition, wage levels, general living standards, widespread free markets, and prosperous merchant communities suggest "a global economic parity" across the major civilizations of Europe and Asia.[7] Thus Europe had no obvious economic lead, even on the eve of the Industrial Revolution. So much for the "European miracle"!

Trade and Empire

But if there was little that was economically distinctive within Europe itself, perhaps it was the spoils of empire and the benefits of global trade after 1500 that allowed Europeans to accumulate the wealth that funded industrial enterprises back home. European empires provided access to an abundance of raw materials—timber, fish, maize, potatoes, slave-produced sugar and cotton—far more than that of other early modern empires. Moreover, these empires generated a global economy that funneled the trade of the world through Europe, offering access to the raw materials and markets of the planet. Demand for Asian goods, including

porcelain and especially cotton cloth, also spurred manufacturers in Europe to produce similar items, while production for overseas markets further sparked industry in Europe. The new wealth spawned a growing middle class in Europe whose members bought the products of the Industrial Revolution. As one scholar has put it, "The industrial revolution . . . emerged from the exploitive advantages Europe was already gaining in the world's markets."[8] So rather than something distinctive about European society, perhaps it was Europe's increasing engagement with the wider world that sparked industrialization.

Many or most of these factors likely played some role in Europe's industrialization. But in considering the "Why Europe?" question, historians confront the relative importance of internal and external factors in explaining historical change. Was industrialization primarily spurred by some special combination of elements peculiar to Western Europe, or were broader global relationships of greater significance? Arguments giving great weight to internal features of European life seem to congratulate Europeans on their good fortune or wisdom, while those that contextualize it globally and point to the unique character of European imperial trade and exploitation are rather more critical. Furthermore, the former seem to imply a certain long-term inevitability to European prominence, while the latter see the Industrial Revolution as more of a surprise, the outcome of a unique conjuncture of events . . . in short, luck.

QUESTIONS TO CONSIDER

1. How might your understanding of the Industrial Revolution change if you subscribed to the "European Miracle," the "Great Divergence," or the "Trade and Empire" school of thought?

2. How does this overview of the "Why Europe?" debate shape your understanding of the Industrial Revolution?

on the environment. The massive extraction of nonrenewable raw materials to feed and to fuel industrial machinery—coal, iron ore, petroleum, and much more—altered the landscape in many places. Sewers and industrial waste emptied into rivers, turning them into poisonous cesspools. In 1858, the Thames River running through London smelled so bad that the British House of Commons had to suspend its session. Smoke

Producing Gas from Coal Coal was central to the Industrial Revolution. An early industrial process in Britain involved the burning of coal to produce "coal gas," used for public lighting. This image from 1822 shows that process in action at one such production facility in London. Those who stoked the furnaces often developed various lung diseases and died early. (Print Collector/Getty Images)

from coal-fired industries and domestic use polluted the air in urban areas and sharply increased the incidence of respiratory illness. (See the opening image to this chapter.) For many historians, the Industrial Revolution marked a new era in both human history and the history of the planet that scientists increasingly call the Anthropocene, or the "age of man." More and more, human industrial activity left a mark not only on human society but also on the ecological, atmospheric, and geological history of the earth.

The First Industrial Society

Wherever it took hold, the Industrial Revolution generated, within a century or less, an economic miracle, at least in comparison with earlier technologies. The **British textile industry**, which used 52 million pounds of cotton in 1800, consumed 588 million pounds in 1850, as multiple technological innovations and factory-based production vastly increased output. Britain's production of coal likewise soared from 5.23 million tons in 1750 to 68.4 million tons a century later.[9] Railroads crisscrossed Britain and much of Europe like a giant spider web (see Map 17.1). Most of this dramatic increase in production occurred in mining, manufacturing, and services. Thus agriculture, for millennia the overwhelmingly dominant economic sector in every civilization, shrank in relative importance. In Britain, for example, agriculture generated only 8 percent of national income in 1891 and employed fewer than 8 percent of working Britons in 1914. Accompanying this vast economic change was an epic transformation of social life. "In two centuries," wrote one prominent historian, "daily life changed more than it had in the 7,000 years before."[10] Nowhere were the revolutionary dimensions of industrialization more apparent than in Great Britain, the world's first industrial society.

The social transformation of the Industrial Revolution both destroyed and created. Referring to the impact of the Industrial Revolution on British society, historian Eric Hobsbawm wrote: "In its initial stages it destroyed their old ways of living and left them free to discover or make for themselves new ones, if they could and knew how. But it rarely told them how to set about it."[11] For many people, it was an enormously painful, even traumatic process, full of social conflict, insecurity, and false starts even as it offered new opportunities, an eventually higher standard of living, and greater participation in public life. The human gains and losses associated

Map 17.1 The Early Phase of Europe's Industrial Revolution

From its beginning in Great Britain, industrialization had spread by 1850 across Western Europe to include parts of France, Germany, Belgium, Bohemia, and Italy.

READING THE MAP: Which industrialized regions are most far removed from sources of coal and iron?

INTERPRETING THE MAP: Note the relationship between sources of coal and iron, railways, and industrialized regions. Then identify regions where the addition of further railway lines might facilitate industrialization.

Railroads The popularity of railroads, long a symbol of the Industrial Revolution, is illustrated in this early nineteenth-century watercolor that shows a miniature train offered as a paid amusement for enthusiasts in London's Euston Square. (*Richard Trevithick's Railroad, Euston Square in 1809*, by Thomas Rowlandson [1756–1827]/Science Museum, London, UK/Bridgeman Images)

with the Industrial Revolution have been debated ever since. Amid the arguments, however, one thing is clear: not everyone was affected in the same way.

The British Aristocracy

Individual landowning aristocrats, long the dominant class in Britain, suffered little in material terms from the Industrial Revolution. In the mid-nineteenth century, a few thousand families still owned more than half of the cultivated land in Britain, most of it leased to tenant farmers, who in turn employed agricultural wage laborers to work it. Rapidly growing population and urbanization sustained a demand for food products grown on that land. For most of the nineteenth century, landowners continued to dominate the British Parliament.

As a class, however, the British aristocracy declined as a result of the Industrial Revolution, as have large landowners in every industrial society. As urban wealth became more important, landed aristocrats had to make way for the up-and-coming businessmen, manufacturers, and bankers, newly enriched by the Industrial Revolution. By the end of the century, landownership had largely ceased to be the basis of great wealth, and businessmen, rather than aristocrats, led the major political parties. Even so, the titled nobility of dukes, earls, viscounts, and barons retained great social prestige and considerable personal wealth. Many among them found an outlet for their energies and opportunities for status and enrichment in the vast domains of the British Empire, where they went as colonial administrators or settlers. Famously described as a "system of outdoor relief for the aristocracy," the empire provided a cushion for a declining class.

The Middle Classes

Those who benefited most conspicuously from industrialization were members of that amorphous group known as the middle class. At its upper levels, this middle class contained extremely wealthy factory and mine owners, bankers, and merchants. Such rising businessmen readily assimilated into aristocratic life, buying country houses, obtaining seats in Parliament, sending their sons to Oxford or Cambridge University, and gratefully accepting titles of nobility from Queen Victoria.

Guided Reading Question

■ **CHANGE**
How did the Industrial Revolution transform British society?

Far more numerous were the smaller businessmen, doctors, lawyers, engineers, teachers, journalists, scientists, and other professionals required in any industrial society. Such people set the tone for a distinctly **middle-class society** with its own values and outlooks. Politically they were liberals, favoring constitutional government, private property, free trade, and social reform within limits. Their agitation resulted in the Reform Bill of 1832, which broadened the right to vote to many men of the middle class, but not to middle-class women. Ideas of thrift and hard work, a rigid morality, "respectability," and cleanliness characterized middle-class culture. According to Samuel Smiles's famous book *Self-Help*, an enterprising spirit was what distinguished the prosperous middle class from Britain's poor. The misery of the poorer classes was "voluntary and self-imposed—the results of idleness, thriftlessness, intemperance, and misconduct."[12]

Women in such middle-class families were increasingly cast as homemakers, wives, and mothers, charged with creating an emotional haven for their men and a refuge

Guided Reading Question

■ **CHANGE**
How did Britain's middle classes change during the nineteenth century?

The Industrial Middle Class This late nineteenth-century painting shows a prosperous French middle-class family, attended by a servant. (*Family Reunion at the Home of Madame Adolphe Brisson, 1893*, by Marcel André Baschet [1862–1941]/Château de Versailles, France/Bridgeman Images)

from a heartless and cutthroat capitalist world. They were also expected to be the moral centers of family life, the educators of "respectability," and the managers of household consumption as "shopping"—a new concept in eighteenth-century Britain— became a central activity for the middle classes. An **ideology of domesticity** defined homemaking, child rearing, charitable endeavors, and "refined" activities such as embroidery, music, and drawing as the proper sphere for women, while paid employment and the public sphere of life outside the home beckoned to men.

Male elites in many civilizations had long established their status by detaching women from productive labor. The new wealth of the Industrial Revolution now allowed larger numbers of families to aspire to that kind of status. With her husband as "provider," such a woman was now a "lady." "She must not work for profit," wrote the Englishwoman Margaretta Greg in 1853, "or engage in any occupation that money can command."[13] Employing even one servant became a proud marker of such middle-class status. But the withdrawal of middle-class women from the labor force turned out to be only a temporary phenomenon. By the late nineteenth century, some middle-class women began to enter the teaching, clerical, and nursing professions, and in the second half of the twentieth century, many more flooded into the labor force. By contrast, the withdrawal of children from productive labor into schools has proved a more enduring phenomenon as industrial economies increasingly required a more educated workforce.

As Britain's industrial economy matured, it also gave rise to a sizable **lower middle class**, which included people employed in the growing service sector as clerks, salespeople, bank tellers, hotel staff, secretaries, telephone operators, police officers, and the like. By the end of the nineteenth century, this growing segment of the middle class represented about 20 percent of Britain's population and provided new employment opportunities for women as well as men. In just twenty years (1881–1901), the number of female secretaries in Britain rose from 7,000 to 90,000. Almost all were single and expected to return to the home after marriage. For both men and women, such employment represented a claim on membership in the larger middle class and a means of distinguishing themselves clearly from a working class tainted by manual labor. The mounting ability of these middle classes to consume all manner of material goods—and their appetite for doing so—were among the factors that sustained the continuing growth of the industrializing process.

The Laboring Classes

The overwhelming majority of Britain's nineteenth-century population—some 70 percent or more—were neither aristocrats nor members of the middle classes. They were manual workers in the mines, ports, factories, construction sites, workshops, and farms of an industrializing Britain. Although their conditions varied considerably and changed over time, it was the **laboring classes** who suffered most and benefited least from the epic transformations of the Industrial Revolution. Their efforts to accommodate, resist, protest, and change those conditions contributed much to the texture of the first industrial society.

The lives of the laboring classes were shaped primarily by the rapid urbanization of the industrial era. Liverpool's population alone grew from 77,000 to 400,000 in the first half of the nineteenth century. By 1851, a majority of Britain's population lived in towns and cities, an enormous change from the overwhelmingly rural life of almost all previous civilizations. By the end of the century, London was the world's largest city, with more than 6 million inhabitants.

These cities were vastly overcrowded and smoky, with wholly insufficient sanitation, periodic epidemics, endless row houses and warehouses, few public services or open spaces, and inadequate and often-polluted water supplies. This was the environment in which most urban workers lived in the first half of the nineteenth century. By 1850, the average life expectancy in England was only 39.5 years, less than it had been some three centuries earlier. Nor was there much personal contact between the rich and the poor of industrial cities. Benjamin Disraeli's novel *Sybil*, published in 1845, described these two ends of the social spectrum as "two nations between whom there is no intercourse and no sympathy; who are ignorant of each other's habits, thoughts and feelings, as if they were dwellers in different zones or inhabitants of different planets."

The industrial factories to which growing numbers of desperate people looked for employment offered a work environment far different from the artisan's shop or the tenant's farm. Long hours, low wages, and child labor were nothing new for the poor, but the routine and monotony of work, dictated by the factory whistle and the needs of machines, imposed novel and highly unwelcome conditions of labor. Also objectionable were the direct and constant supervision and the rules and fines aimed at enforcing work discipline. In addition, the ups and downs of a capitalist economy made industrial work insecure as well as onerous.

In the early decades of the nineteenth century, Britain's industrialists favored girls and young unmarried women as employees in the textile mills, for they were often willing to accept lower wages, while male owners believed them to be both docile and more suitable for repetitive tasks such as tending machines. A gendered hierarchy of labor emerged in these factories, with men in supervisory and more skilled positions, while women occupied the less skilled and

DEATH'S DISPENSARY.
OPEN TO THE POOR, GRATIS, BY PERMISSION OF THE PARISH.

The Urban Poor of Industrial Britain This 1866 political cartoon shows an impoverished urban family forced to draw its drinking water from a polluted public well, while a figure of Death operates the pump. (Sarin Images/Granger, NYC — All rights reserved)

The English Luddites and Machine Breaking

If you do Not Cause those Dressing Machines to be Remov'd Within the Bounds of Seven Days . . . your factory and all that it Contains Will and Shall Surely Be Set on fire . . . it is Not our Desire to Do you the Least Injury, But We are fully Determin'd to Destroy Both Dressing Machines and Steam Looms.[14]

Luddites smashing a loom.

Between 1811 and 1813, this kind of warning was sent to hundreds of English workshops in the woolen and cotton industry, where more efficient machines, some of them steam-powered, threatened the jobs and livelihoods of workers. Over and over, that threat was carried out as well-organized bands of skilled artisans destroyed the offending machines, burned buildings, and on occasion attacked employers. These were the Luddites, taking their name from a mythical Robin Hood–like figure, Ned Ludd. A song called "General Ludd's Triumph" expressed their sentiments: "These Engines of mischief were sentenced to die / By unanimous vote of the Trade / And Ludd who can all opposition defy / Was the Grand executioner made."

So widespread and serious was this Luddite uprising that the British government sent 12,000 troops to suppress it, more than it was then devoting to the struggle against Napoleon in continental Europe. And a new law, rushed through Parliament as an "emergency measure" in 1812, made those who destroyed mechanized looms subject to the death penalty. Some sixty to seventy alleged Luddites were in fact hanged, and sometimes beheaded as well, for machine breaking.

In the governing circles of England, Luddism was widely regarded as blind protest, an outrageous, unthinking, and futile resistance to progress. It has remained in more recent times a term of insult applied to those who resist or reject technological innovation. And yet, a closer look suggests that the Luddites deserve some sympathy as an understandable response to a painful transformation of social life when few alternatives for expressing grievances were available.

At the time of the Luddite uprising, England was involved in an increasingly unpopular war with Napoleon's

"lighter" jobs that offered little opportunity for advancement. Nor were women welcome in the unions that eventually offered men some ability to shape the conditions under which they labored.

Thus, unlike their middle-class counterparts, many girls and young women of the laboring classes engaged in industrial work or found jobs as domestic servants for upper- and middle-class families to supplement meager family incomes. But after marriage, they too usually left outside paid employment because a man who could not support his wife was widely considered a failure. Within the home, however, many working-class women continued to earn money by taking in boarders, doing laundry, or sewing clothes in addition to the domestic and child-rearing responsibilities long assigned to women.

France, and mutual blockades substantially reduced trade and hurt the textile industry. The country was also in the early phase of an Industrial Revolution in which mechanized production was replacing skilled artisan labor. All of this, plus some bad weather and poor harvests, combined to generate real economic hardship, unemployment, and hunger. Bread riots and various protests against high prices proliferated.

Furthermore, English elites were embracing new laissez-faire, or free market, economic principles, which eroded customary protections for the poor and working classes. Over the previous several decades, many laws that had regulated wages and apprenticeships and prohibited certain laborsaving machines had been repealed, despite repeated workers' appeals to Parliament to maintain some minimal protections for their older way of life. A further act of Parliament in 1799 had forbidden trade unions and collective bargaining. In these circumstances, some form of direct action is hardly surprising.

At one level, the Luddite machine-breaking movement represented "collective bargaining by riot," a way of pressuring employers when legal negotiations with them had been outlawed. And the issues involved more than laborsaving machines. Luddites also argued for price reductions, minimum wages, and prohibitions on the flooding of their industry by unapprenticed workers. They wanted to return to a time when "full fashioned work at the old fashioned price is established by custom and law," according to one of their songs. More generally, Luddites sought to preserve elements of an older way of life in which industry existed to provide a livelihood for workers, in which indus-

men could take pride in their craft, in which government and employers felt some paternalistic responsibility to the lower classes, and in which journeymen workers felt some bonds of attachment to a larger social and moral order. All of this was rapidly eroding in the new era of capitalist industrialization. In these ways, the Luddite movement looked backward to idealized memories of an earlier time.

And yet in other ways, the rebels anticipated the future with their demands for a minimum wage and an end to child labor, their concern about inferior-quality products produced by machines, and their desire to organize trade unions. At the height of the Luddite movement, some among them began to move beyond local industrial action toward a "general insurrection" that might bring real political change to the entire country. In one letter from a Luddite in 1812, the writer expressed "hope for assistance from the French emperor [Napoleon] in shaking off the yoke of the rottenest, wickedest, and most tyrannous government that ever existed." He continued, "Then we will be governed by a just republic."

After 1813, the organized Luddite movement faded away. But it serves as a cautionary reminder that what is hailed as progress claims victims as well as beneficiaries.

QUESTIONS

To what extent did the concerns of the Luddites come to pass as the Industrial Revolution unfolded? How does your understanding of the Luddites affect your posture toward technological change in our time?

Social Protest

For workers of the laboring classes, industrial life "was a stony desert, which they had to make habitable by their own efforts."[15] Such efforts took many forms. By 1815, about 1 million workers, mostly artisans, had created a variety of "friendly societies." With dues contributed by members, these working-class self-help groups provided insurance against sickness, a decent funeral, and an opportunity for social life in an otherwise-bleak environment. Other skilled artisans who had been displaced by machine-produced goods and forbidden to organize in legal unions sometimes wrecked the offending machinery and burned the mills that had taken their jobs. (See Zooming In: The English Luddites and Machine Breaking, page 746.) The class consciousness of working people was such that one police informer reported that "most every creature of the lower order both in town and country are on their side."[16] Others acted within the political arena by joining movements aimed at obtaining the vote for working-class men, a goal that was gradually achieved in the second half of the nineteenth century. When trade unions were legalized in 1824, growing numbers of factory workers joined these associations in their efforts to achieve better wages and working conditions. Initially their strikes, attempts at nationwide organization, and threat of violence made them fearful indeed to the upper classes. One British newspaper in 1834 described unions as "the most dangerous institutions that were ever permitted to take root, under shelter of law, in any country,"[17] although they later became rather more "respectable" organizations.

Socialist ideas of various kinds gradually spread within the working class, challenging the assumptions of a capitalist society. Robert Owen (1771–1858), a wealthy British cotton textile manufacturer, urged the creation of small industrial communities where workers and their families would be well treated. He established one such community, with a ten-hour workday, spacious housing, decent wages, and education for children, at his mill in New Lanark in Scotland.

Of more lasting significance was the socialism of **Karl Marx** (1818–1883). German by birth, Marx spent much of his life in England, where he witnessed the brutal conditions of Britain's Industrial Revolution and wrote voluminously about history and economics. His probing analysis led him to conclude that industrial capitalism was an inherently unstable system, doomed to collapse in a revolutionary upheaval that would give birth to a classless socialist society, thus ending forever the ancient conflict between rich and poor. (See Working with Evidence, page 769, for the various expressions of a socialist tradition inspired by Marx.)

In Marx's writings, the combined impact of Europe's industrial, political, and scientific revolutions found expression. Industrialization created both the social conditions against which Marx protested so bitterly and the enormous wealth he felt would make socialism possible. The French Revolution, still a living memory in Marx's youth, provided evidence that grand upheavals, giving rise to new societies, had in fact taken place and could do so again. Moreover, Marx regarded himself as a scientist, discovering the laws of social development in much the same fashion as Newton discovered the laws of motion. His was therefore a "scientific socialism," embedded in these laws of historical change; revolution was a certainty and the socialist future was inevitable.

It was a grand, compelling, prophetic, utopian vision of human freedom and community—and it inspired socialist movements of workers and intellectuals amid the grim harshness of Europe's industrialization in the second half of the nineteenth century. Socialists established political parties in most European states and linked them together in international organizations as well. These parties recruited members, contested elections as they gained the right to vote, agitated for reforms, and in some cases plotted revolution.

Guided Reading Question

•••••••••••••••••••••••••••••••

■ **CHANGE**

How did Karl Marx understand the Industrial Revolution? In what ways did his ideas have an impact in the industrializing world of the nineteenth century?

In the later decades of the nineteenth century, such ideas echoed among more radical trade unionists and some middle-class intellectuals in Britain, and even more so in a rapidly industrializing Germany and elsewhere. By then, however, the British working-class movement was not overtly revolutionary. When a working-class political party, the **Labour Party**, was established in the 1890s, it advocated a reformist program and a peaceful democratic transition to socialism, largely rejecting the class struggle and revolutionary emphasis of classical Marxism. Generally known as "social democracy," this approach to socialism was especially prominent in Germany during the late nineteenth century and spread more widely in the twentieth century, when it came into conflict with the more violent and revolutionary movements calling themselves "communist."

Improving material conditions during the second half of the nineteenth century helped move the working-class movement in Britain, Germany, and elsewhere away from a revolutionary posture. Marx had expected industrial capitalist societies to polarize into a small wealthy class and a huge and increasingly impoverished proletariat. However, standing between "the captains of industry" and the workers was a sizable middle and lower middle class, constituting perhaps 30 percent of the population, most of whom were not really wealthy but were immensely proud that they were not manual laborers. Marx had not foreseen the development of this intermediate social group, nor had he imagined that workers could better their standard of living within a capitalist framework. But they did. Wages rose under

The Socialist Threat The growth of a socialist movement was immensely threatening to many elements of the established order in Europe. This image from a British Conservative Party poster in 1909 shows a demonic socialist figure strangling a pure female image of Great Britain, wearing a belt labeled "prosperity." (Pictorial Press LTD/Alamy)

pressure from unions; cheap imported food improved working-class diets; infant mortality rates fell; and shops and chain stores catering to working-class families multiplied. As English male workers gradually obtained the right to vote, politicians had an incentive to legislate in their favor, by abolishing child labor, regulating factory conditions, and even, in 1911, inaugurating a system of relief for the unemployed. Sanitary reform considerably cleaned up the "filth and stink" of early nineteenth-century cities, and urban parks made a modest appearance. Contrary to Marx's expectations, capitalist societies demonstrated some capacity for reform.

Further eroding working-class radicalism was a growing sense of nationalism, which bound workers in particular countries to their middle-class employers and compatriots, offsetting to some extent the economic and social antagonism between them. When World War I broke out, the "workers of the world," far from uniting against their bourgeois enemies as Marx had urged them, instead set off to slaughter one another in enormous numbers on the battlefields of Europe. National loyalty had trumped class loyalty.

Nonetheless, as the twentieth century dawned, industrial Britain was hardly a stable or contented society. Immense inequalities still separated the classes. Some 40 percent of the working class continued to live in conditions then described as "poverty." A mounting wave of strikes from 1910 to 1913 testified to the intensity of class conflict. The Labour Party was becoming a major force in Parliament. Some socialists and some feminists were becoming radicalized. "Wisps of violence hung in the English air," wrote Eric Hobsbawm, "symptoms of a crisis in economy and society, which the [country's] self-confident opulence . . . could not quite conceal."[18] The world's first industrial society remained dissatisfied and conflicted.

It was also a society in economic decline relative to industrial newcomers such as Germany and the United States. Britain paid a price for its early lead, for its businessmen became committed to machinery that became obsolete as the century progressed. Latecomers invested in more modern equipment and in various ways had surpassed the British by the early twentieth century.

Europeans in Motion

Europe's Industrial Revolution prompted a massive migratory process that uprooted many millions, setting them in motion both internally and around the globe. Within Europe itself, the movement of men, women, and families from the countryside to the cities involved half or more of the region's people by the mid-nineteenth century. More significant for world history was the exodus between 1815 and 1939 of fully 20 percent of Europe's population, some 50 to 55 million people, who left home for the Americas, Australia, New Zealand, South Africa, and elsewhere (see Map 17.2). They were pushed by poverty, a rapidly growing population, and the displacement of peasant farming and artisan manufacturing. And they were pulled abroad by the enormous demand for labor overseas, the ready availability of land in some places, and the relatively cheap transportation of railroads and steamships. But not all found a satisfactory life in their new homes, and perhaps 7 million returned to Europe.[19]

This huge process had a transformative global impact, temporarily increasing Europe's share of the world's population and scattering Europeans around the world. In 1800, less than 1 percent of the total world population consisted of overseas Europeans and their descendants; by 1930, they represented 11 percent.[20] In particular regions, the impact was profound. Australia and New Zealand became settler colonies, outposts of European civilization in the South Pacific that overwhelmed their native populations through conquest, acquisition of their lands, and disease. By the end of the nineteenth century, New Zealand's European population,

United States, 32,300,000	New Zealand, 650,000
Asian Russia, 13,000,000	Uruguay, 600,000
Argentina, 6,600,000	Cuba, 600,000
Brazil, 4,700,000	South Africa, 250,000
Canada, 4,300,000	Mexico, 250,000
Australia, 2,900,000	

MAPPING HISTORY

Map 17.2 European Migration in the Industrial Age

The Industrial Revolution not only transformed European society but also scattered millions of Europeans to the far corners of the world.

READING THE MAP: Which continent received the fewest European migrants?

INTERPRETING THE MAP: Which regions of the world were most affected by European emigration? Which regions were little affected? How might you explain the variations?

based on immigration of free people, outnumbered the native Maori by 700,000 to 40,000. Smaller numbers of Europeans found their way to South Africa, Kenya, Rhodesia, Algeria, and elsewhere, where they injected a sharp racial divide into those colonized territories.

But it was the Americas that felt the brunt of this huge movement of people. Latin America received about 20 percent of the European migratory stream, mostly from Italy, Spain, and Portugal, with Argentina and Brazil accounting for some 80 percent of those immigrants. Considered "white," they enhanced the social weight of the European element in those countries and thus enjoyed economic advantages over the mixed-race, Indian, and African populations.

In several ways the immigrant experience in the United States was distinctive. It was far larger and more diverse than elsewhere, with some 32 million newcomers arriving from all over Europe between 1820 and 1930. Furthermore, the United States offered affordable land to many and industrial jobs to many more, neither of which was widely available in Latin America. And the United States was unique in turning the immigrant experience into a national myth—that of the melting pot. Despite this ideology of assimilation, the earlier immigrants, mostly Protestants from Britain and Germany, were anything but welcoming to Catholics and Jews from Southern and Eastern Europe who arrived later. The newcomers were seen as distinctly inferior, even "un-American," and blamed for crime, labor unrest, and socialist ideas. Nonetheless, this surge of immigration contributed much to the westward expansion of the United States, to the establishment of a European-derived culture in a vast area of North America, and to the displacement of the native peoples of the region.

In the vast domains of the Russian Empire, a parallel process of European migration likewise unfolded. After the freeing of the serfs in 1861, some 13 million Russians and Ukrainians migrated to Siberia, where they overwhelmed the native population of the region, while millions more settled in Central Asia. The availability of land, the prospect of greater freedom from tsarist restrictions and from the exploitation of aristocratic landowners, and the construction of the trans-Siberian railroad—all of this facilitated the continued Europeanization of Siberia. As in the United States, the Russian government encouraged and aided this process, hoping to forestall Chinese pressures in the region and relieve growing population pressures in the more densely settled western lands of the empire.

Variations on a Theme: Industrialization in the United States and Russia

Not for long was the Industrial Revolution confined to Britain. It soon spread to continental Western Europe, and by the end of the nineteenth century it was well under way in the United States, Russia, and Japan. The globalization of industrialization had begun. Everywhere it took hold, industrialization bore a range of broadly similar outcomes. New technologies and sources of energy generated vast increases in production and spawned an unprecedented urbanization as well. Class structures changed as aristocrats, artisans, and peasants declined as classes, while the middle classes and a factory working class grew in numbers and social prominence. Middle-class women generally withdrew from paid labor altogether, and their working-class counterparts sought to do so after marriage. Working women usually received lower wages than their male counterparts, had difficulty joining unions, and were accused of taking jobs from men. Working-class frustration and anger gave rise to trade unions and socialist movements, injecting a new element of social conflict into industrial societies.

Nevertheless, different histories, cultures, and societies ensured that the Industrial Revolution unfolded variously in the diverse countries in which it became established. Differences in the pace and timing of industrialization, the size and shape of major industries, the role of the state, the political expression of social conflict, and many other factors have made this process rich in comparative possibilities. French industrialization, for example, occurred more slowly and perhaps less disruptively than did that of Britain. Germany focused initially on heavy industry—iron, steel, and coal—rather than on the textile industry with which Britain had begun. Moreover, German industrialization was far more highly concentrated in huge companies called cartels, and it generated a rather more militant and Marxist-oriented labor movement than in Britain.

Nowhere were the variations in the industrializing process more apparent than in those two vast countries that lay on the periphery of Europe. To the west across the Atlantic Ocean was the United States, a young, vigorous, democratic, expanding country, populated largely by people of European descent, along with a substantial number of slaves of African origin. To the east was Russia, with its Eastern Orthodox Christianity, an autocratic tsar, a huge population of serfs, and an empire stretching across all of northern Asia. By the early twentieth century, industrialization had turned the United States into a major global power and had spawned in Russia an enormous revolutionary upheaval that made that country the first outpost of global communism.

The United States: Industrialization without Socialism

American industrialization began in the textile factories of New England during the 1820s but grew explosively in the half century following the Civil War (1861–1865) (see Map 17.3). The country's huge size, the ready availability of natural resources, its expanding domestic market, and its relative political stability combined to make the United States the world's leading industrial power by 1914. At that time, it produced 36 percent of the world's manufactured goods, compared to 16 percent for Germany, 14 percent for Great Britain, and 6 percent for France. Furthermore, U.S. industrialization was closely linked to that of Europe. About one-third of the capital investment that financed its remarkable growth came from British, French, and German capitalists. But unlike Latin America, which also received much foreign investment, the United States was able to use those funds to generate an independent Industrial Revolution of its own.

As in other later industrializing countries, the U.S. government played an important role, though less directly than in Germany or Japan. Tax breaks, huge grants of public land to the railroad companies, laws enabling the easy formation of corporations, and the absence of much overt regulation of industry all fostered the rise of very large business enterprises. The U.S. Steel Corporation, for example, by 1901 had an annual budget three times the size of the federal government's budget. In this respect, the United States followed the pattern of Germany but differed from that of France and Britain, where family businesses still predominated.

The United States also pioneered techniques of mass production, using interchangeable parts, the assembly line, and "scientific management" to produce for a

Guided Reading Question
....
■ **COMPARISON**
What were the differences between industrialization in the United States and that in Russia?

Map 17.3   The Industrial United States in 1900
By the early twentieth century, manufacturing industries were largely in the Northeast and Midwest, whereas mining operations were more widely scattered across the country.

mass market. The nation's advertising agencies, Sears Roebuck's and Montgomery Ward's mail-order catalogs, and urban department stores generated a middle-class "culture of consumption." When the industrialist Henry Ford in the early twentieth century began producing the Model T at a price that many ordinary people could afford, he famously declared: "I am going to democratize the automobile." More so than in Europe, with its aristocratic traditions, self-made American industrialists of fabulous wealth such as Henry Ford, Andrew Carnegie, and John D. Rockefeller became cultural heroes, widely admired as models of what anyone could achieve with daring and hard work in a land of endless opportunity.

Nevertheless, well before the first Model T rolled off the assembly line, serious social divisions of a kind common to European industrial societies mounted. Preindustrial America had boasted of a relative social equality, quite unlike that of Europe, but by the end of the nineteenth century a widening gap separated the classes. In Carnegie's Homestead steel plant near Pittsburgh, employees worked every day except Christmas and the Fourth of July, often for twelve hours a day. In

Guided Reading Question

■ **EXPLANATION**

Why did Marxist socialism not take root in the United States?

Manhattan, where millions of European immigrants disembarked, many lived in five- or six-story buildings with four families and two toilets on each floor. In every large city, such conditions prevailed close by the mansions of elite neighborhoods. To some, the contrast was a betrayal of American ideals, while others saw it as a natural outcome of competition and "the survival of the fittest."

As elsewhere, such conditions generated much labor protest, the formation of unions, strikes, and sometimes violence. In 1877, when the eastern railroads announced a 10 percent wage cut for their workers, strikers disrupted rail service across the eastern half of the country, smashed equipment, and rioted. Both state militias and federal troops were called out to put down the movement. Class consciousness and class conflict were intense in the industrial America of the late nineteenth and early twentieth centuries.

Unlike in many European countries, however, no major political party emerged in the United States to represent the interests of the working class. Nor did the ideas of socialism, especially those of Marxism, appeal to American workers nearly as much as they did to European laborers. At its high point, the Socialist Party of America garnered just 6 percent of the vote for its presidential candidate in the 1912 election, whereas socialists at the time held more seats in Germany's Parliament than any other party. Even in the depths of the Great Depression of the 1930s, no major socialist movement emerged to champion American workers. How might we explain the relative weakness of **socialism in the United States**?

One answer lies in the relative conservatism of major American union organizations, especially the American Federation of Labor. Its focus on skilled workers excluded the more radical unskilled laborers, and its refusal to align with any party limited its influence in the political arena. Furthermore, massive immigration from Europe, beginning in the 1840s, created a very diverse industrial labor force on top of the country's sharp racial divide. This diversity contrasted sharply with the more homogeneous populations of many European countries. Catholics and Protestants; whites and blacks; English, Irish, Germans, Slavs, Jews, and Italians—such differences undermined the class solidarity of American workers, making it far more difficult to sustain class-oriented political parties and a socialist labor movement. Moreover, the country's remarkable economic growth generated on average a higher standard of living for American workers than their European counterparts experienced. Land was cheaper, and home ownership was more available. Workers with property generally found socialism less attractive than those without. By 1910, a particularly large group of white-collar workers in sales, services, and offices outnumbered factory laborers. Their middle-class aspirations further diluted impulses toward radicalism.

But political challenges to the abuses of capitalist industrialization did arise. In the 1890s, among small farmers in the U.S. South, West, and Midwest, "populists" railed against banks, industrialists, monopolies, the existing money system, and both major political parties, all of which they thought were dominated by the corporate interests of the eastern elites. More successful, especially in the early twentieth century, were the **Progressives**, who pushed for specific reforms, such as wages-and-hours legislation, better sanitation standards, antitrust laws, and greater governmental intervention in the economy. Socialism, however, came to be defined as fundamentally "un-American" in a country that so valued individualism and so feared "big government." It was a distinctive feature of the American response to industrialization.

Russia: Industrialization and Revolution

As a setting for the Industrial Revolution, it would be hard to imagine two more different environments than the United States and Russia. If the United States was the Western world's most exuberant democracy during the nineteenth century, Russia remained the sole outpost of absolute monarchy, in which the state exercised far greater control over individuals and society than anywhere in the Western world.

At the beginning of the twentieth century, Russia still had no national parliament, no legal political parties, and no nationwide elections. The tsar, answerable to God alone, ruled unchecked. Furthermore, Russian society was dominated by a titled nobility of various ranks. Its upper levels included great landowners, who furnished the state with military officers and leading government officials. Until 1861, most Russians were peasant serfs, bound to the estates of their masters, subject to sale, greatly exploited, and largely at the mercy of their owners. A vast cultural gulf separated these two classes. Many nobles were highly westernized, some

Russian Serfs This 1872 photograph shows a wealthy Russian landowner and his wife being pulled in a cart by serfs, who had been legally freed just eleven years earlier but continued to serve their master. They are attending a high-society wedding of another local estate owner. (© SZ Photo/Bridgeman Images)

speaking French better than Russian, whereas their serfs were steeped in a back-woods Orthodox Christianity that incorporated pre-Christian spirits, spells, curses, and magic.

A further difference between Russia and the United States lay in the source of social and economic change. In the United States, such change bubbled up from society as free farmers, workers, and businessmen sought new opportunities and operated in a political system that gave them varying degrees of expression. In autocratic Russia, change was far more often initiated by the state itself, in its continuing efforts to catch up with the more powerful and innovative states of Europe. This kind of "transformation from above" found an early expression in the reign of Peter the Great (r. 1689–1725). (See "Russians and Empire" in Chapter 13.) Such state-directed change continued in the nineteenth century with the freeing of the serfs in 1861, an action stimulated by military defeat at the hands of British and French forces in the Crimean War (1854–1856). To many thoughtful Russians, serfdom seemed incompatible with modern civilization and held back the country's overall development, as did its economic and industrial backwardness. Thus, beginning in the 1860s, Russia began a program of industrial development that was more heavily directed by the state than was the case in Western Europe or the United States.

By the 1890s, Russia's Industrial Revolution was launched and growing rapidly. It focused particularly on railroads and heavy industry and was fueled by a substantial amount of foreign investment. By 1900, Russia ranked fourth in the world in steel production and had major industries in coal, textiles, and oil. Its industrial enterprises, still modest in comparison to those of Europe, were concentrated in a few major cities—Moscow, St. Petersburg, and Kiev, for example—and took place in factories far larger than in most of Western Europe.

All of this contributed to the explosive social outcomes of Russian industrialization. A growing middle class of businessmen and professionals increasingly took shape. As modern and educated people, many in the middle class objected strongly to the deep conservatism of tsarist Russia and sought a greater role in political life, but they were also dependent on the state for contracts and jobs and for suppressing the growing radicalism of the workers, which they greatly feared. Although factory workers constituted only about 5 percent of Russia's total population, they quickly developed a radical class consciousness, based on harsh conditions and the absence of any legal outlet for their grievances. As in Western Europe, millions flocked to the new centers of industrial development. By 1897, over 70 percent of the population in Moscow and St. Petersburg were recent migrants from the rural areas. Their conditions of life resembled those of industrial migrants in New York or Berlin. One observer wrote: "People live in impossible conditions: filth, stench, suffocating heat. They lie down together barely a few feet apart; there is no division between the sexes and adults sleep with children."[21] Until 1897, a thirteen-hour working day was common, while ruthless discipline and overt disrespect from supervisors created resentment. In the absence of legal unions or political parties, these grievances often erupted in the form of large-scale strikes.

Guided Reading Question

■ **CHANGE**
What factors contributed to the making of a revolutionary situation in Russia by the beginning of the twentieth century?

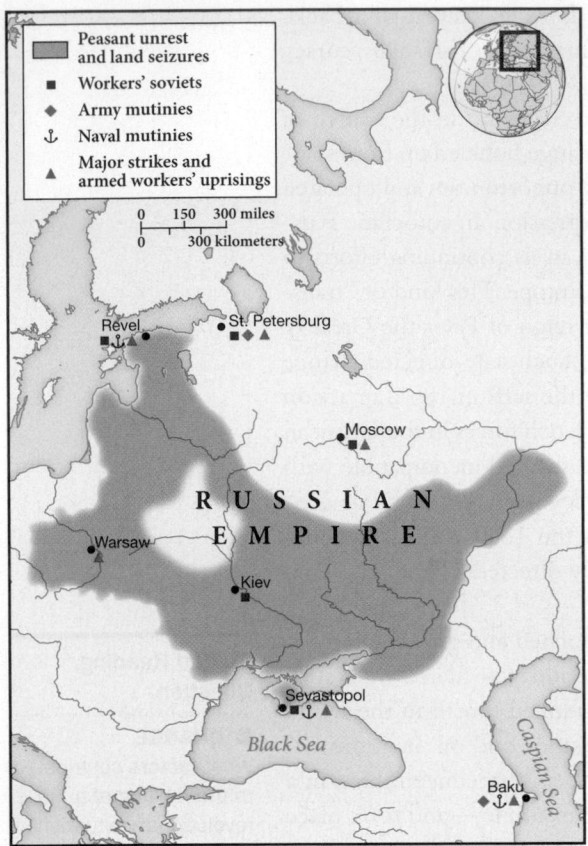

Map 17.4 Industrialization and Revolution in Russia, 1905

Only in Russia did industrialization lead to violent revolutionary upheavals, both in 1905 and more successfully in 1917.

In these conditions, a small but growing number of educated Russians found in Marxist socialism a way of understanding the changes they witnessed daily as well as hope for the future in a revolutionary upheaval of workers. In 1898, they created an illegal Russian Social Democratic Labor Party and quickly became involved in workers' education, union organizing, and, eventually, revolutionary action. By the early twentieth century, the strains of rapid change and the state's continued intransigence had reached the bursting point, and in 1905, following its defeat in a naval war with Japan, Russia erupted in spontaneous insurrection (see Map 17.4). Workers in Moscow and St. Petersburg went on strike and created their own representative councils, called soviets. Peasant uprisings, student demonstrations, revolts of non-Russian nationalities, and mutinies in the military all contributed to the upheaval. Recently formed political parties, representing intellectuals of various persuasions, came out into the open.

The **Russian Revolution of 1905**, though brutally suppressed, forced the tsar's regime to make more substantial reforms than it had ever contemplated. It granted a constitution, legalized both trade unions and political parties, and permitted the election of a national assembly, called the Duma. Censorship was eased, and plans were under way for universal primary education. Industrial development likewise continued at a rapid rate, so that by 1914 Russia stood fifth in the world in terms of overall output. But in the first half of that year, some 1,250,000 workers, representing about 40 percent of the entire industrial workforce, went out on strike.

Thus the tsar's limited political reforms, which had been granted with great reluctance and were often reversed in practice, failed to tame working-class radicalism or to bring social stability to Russia. In Russian political life, the people generally, and even the middle class, had only a very limited voice. Representatives of even the privileged classes had become so alienated by the government's intransigence that many felt revolution was inevitable. Various revolutionary groups, many of them socialist, published pamphlets and newspapers, organized trade unions, and spread their messages among workers and peasants. Particularly in the cities, these revolutionary parties had an impact. They provided a language through which workers could express their grievances; they created links among workers from different factories; and they furnished leaders who were able to act when the revolutionary moment arrived.

World War I provided that moment. The enormous hardships of that war, coupled with the immense social tensions of industrialization within a still-autocratic political system, sparked the Russian Revolution of 1917 (see Chapter 20). That massive upheaval quickly brought to power the most radical of the socialist groups operating in the country—the Bolsheviks, led by the charismatic Vladimir Ilyich Ulyanov, better known as Lenin. Only in Russia was industrialization associated with violent social revolution. This was the most distinctive feature of Russia's modern historical development. And only in Russia was a socialist political party, inspired by the teachings of Karl Marx, able to seize power, thus launching the modern world's first socialist society, with enormous implications for the twentieth century.

PRACTICING HISTORICAL THINKING

What was common to industrialization everywhere, and in what ways did it vary from place to place?

The Industrial Revolution and Latin America in the Nineteenth Century

Beyond the world of Europe and North America, only Japan underwent a major industrial transformation during the nineteenth century, part of that country's overall response to the threat of European aggression. (See "The Japanese Difference: The Rise of a New East Asian Power" in Chapter 19.) Elsewhere—in colonial India, Egypt, the Ottoman Empire, China, and Latin America—very modest experiments in modern industry were undertaken, but nowhere did they drive the kind of major social transformation that had taken place in Britain, Europe, North America, and Japan. However, even in societies that did not experience their own Industrial Revolution, the profound impact of European and North American industrialization was hard to avoid. Such was the case in Latin America during the nineteenth century. (See Snapshot: The Industrial Revolution and the Global Divide.)

After Independence in Latin America

The struggle for independence in Latin America had lasted far longer and proved far more destructive than in North America. Decimated populations, diminished herds of livestock, flooded or closed silver mines, abandoned farms, shrinking international trade and investment capital, and empty national treasuries—these were the conditions that greeted Latin Americans upon independence. Furthermore, the four major administrative units (viceroyalties) of Spanish America ultimately dissolved into eighteen separate countries, and regional revolts wracked Brazil in the early decades of its independent life. A number of international wars in the post-independence century likewise shook these new nations. Peru and Bolivia briefly united and then broke apart in a bitter conflict (1836–1839); Mexico lost huge territories to the United States (1846–1848); and an alliance of Argentina, Brazil, and Uruguay went to war with Paraguay (1864–1870) in a conflict that devastated Paraguay's small population.

SNAPSHOT   The Industrial Revolution and the Global Divide

During the nineteenth century, the Industrial Revolution generated an enormous and unprecedented economic division in the world, as measured by the share of manufacturing output. What patterns can you see in this table?

SHARE OF TOTAL WORLD MANUFACTURING OUTPUT (percentage)

	1750	1800	1860	1880	1900
EUROPE AS A WHOLE	23.2	28.1	53.2	61.3	62.0
United Kingdom	1.9	4.3	19.9	22.9	18.5
France	4.0	4.2	7.9	7.8	6.8
Germany	2.9	3.5	4.9	8.5	13.2
Russia	5.0	5.6	7.0	7.6	8.8
UNITED STATES	0.1	0.8	7.2	14.7	23.6
JAPAN	3.8	3.5	2.6	2.4	2.4
THE REST OF THE WORLD	73.0	67.7	36.6	20.9	11.0
China	32.8	33.3	19.7	12.5	6.2
South Asia (India/Pakistan)	24.5	19.7	8.6	2.8	1.7

Data from Paul Kennedy, *The Rise and Fall of the Great Powers* (New York: Random House, 1987), 149.

Within these new countries, political life was turbulent and unstable. Conservatives favored centralized authority and sought to maintain the social status quo of the colonial era in alliance with the Catholic Church, which at independence owned perhaps half of all productive land. Their often-bitter opponents were liberals, who attacked the Church in the name of Enlightenment values, sought at least modest social reforms, and preferred federalism. In many countries, conflicts between these factions, often violent, enabled military strongmen known as *caudillos* (kaw-DEE-yos) to achieve power as defenders of order and property, although they too succeeded one another with great frequency. One of them, Antonio López de Santa Anna of Mexico, was president of his country at least nine separate times between 1833 and 1855. Constitutions too replaced one another with bewildering speed. Bolivia had ten constitutions during the nineteenth century, while Ecuador and Peru each had eight.

Social life did not change fundamentally in the aftermath of independence. As in Europe and North America, women remained disenfranchised and wholly outside of formal political life. Slavery was abolished in most of Latin America by midcentury, although it persisted in both Brazil and Cuba until the late 1880s. Most of the legal distinctions among various racial categories also disappeared, and all free people were considered, at least officially, equal citizens. Nevertheless, productive economic resources such as businesses, ranches, and plantations remained overwhelmingly in the hands of creole white men, who were culturally oriented toward

Europe. The military provided an avenue of mobility for a few skilled and ambitious mestizo men, some of whom subsequently became caudillos. Other mixed-race men and women found a place in a small middle class as teachers, shopkeepers, or artisans. The vast majority—blacks, Indians, and many mixed-race people of both sexes—remained impoverished, working small subsistence farms or laboring in the mines or on the *haciendas* (ah-see-EHN-duhz) (plantations) of the well-to-do. Only rarely did the poor and dispossessed actively rebel against their social betters. One such case was the Caste War of Yucatán (1847–1901), a prolonged struggle of the Maya people of Mexico aimed at cleansing their land of European and mestizo intruders.

Facing the World Economy

During the second half of the nineteenth century, a measure of political consolidation took hold in Latin America, and countries such as Mexico, Peru, and Argentina entered periods of greater stability. At the same time, Latin America as a whole became more closely integrated into a world economy driven by the industrialization of Western Europe and North America. The new technology of the steamship cut the sailing time between Britain and Argentina almost in half, while the underwater telegraph instantly brought the latest news and fashions of Europe to Latin America.

The most significant economic outcome of this growing integration was a rapid growth of Latin American exports to the industrializing countries, which now needed the food products, raw materials, and markets of these new nations. Latin American landowners, businessmen, and governments proved eager to supply those needs, and in the sixty years or so after 1850, a **Latin American export boom** increased the value of goods sold abroad by a factor of ten.

Mexico continued to produce large amounts of silver, providing more than half the world's new supply until 1860. Now added to the list of raw materials flowing out of Latin America were copper from Chile, a metal that the growing electrical industry required; tin from Bolivia, which met the mounting demand for tin cans; and nitrates from Chile and guano (bird droppings) from Peru, both of which were used for fertilizer. Wild rubber from the Amazon rain forest was in great demand for bicycle and automobile tires, as was sisal from Mexico, used to make binder twine for the proliferating mechanical harvesters of North America. Bananas from Central America, beef from Argentina, cacao from Ecuador, coffee from Brazil and Guatemala, and sugar from Cuba also found eager markets in the rapidly growing and increasingly prosperous world of industrializing countries. In return for these primary products, Latin Americans imported the textiles, machinery, tools, weapons, and luxury goods of Europe and the United States (see Map 17.5).

Accompanying this burgeoning commerce was large-scale investment of European capital in Latin America, $10 billion alone between 1870 and 1919. Most of this capital came from Great Britain, which invested more in Argentina in the late

Guided Reading Question

■ **CONNECTION**

In what ways was Latin America linked to the global economy of the nineteenth century, and what was the impact of these links?

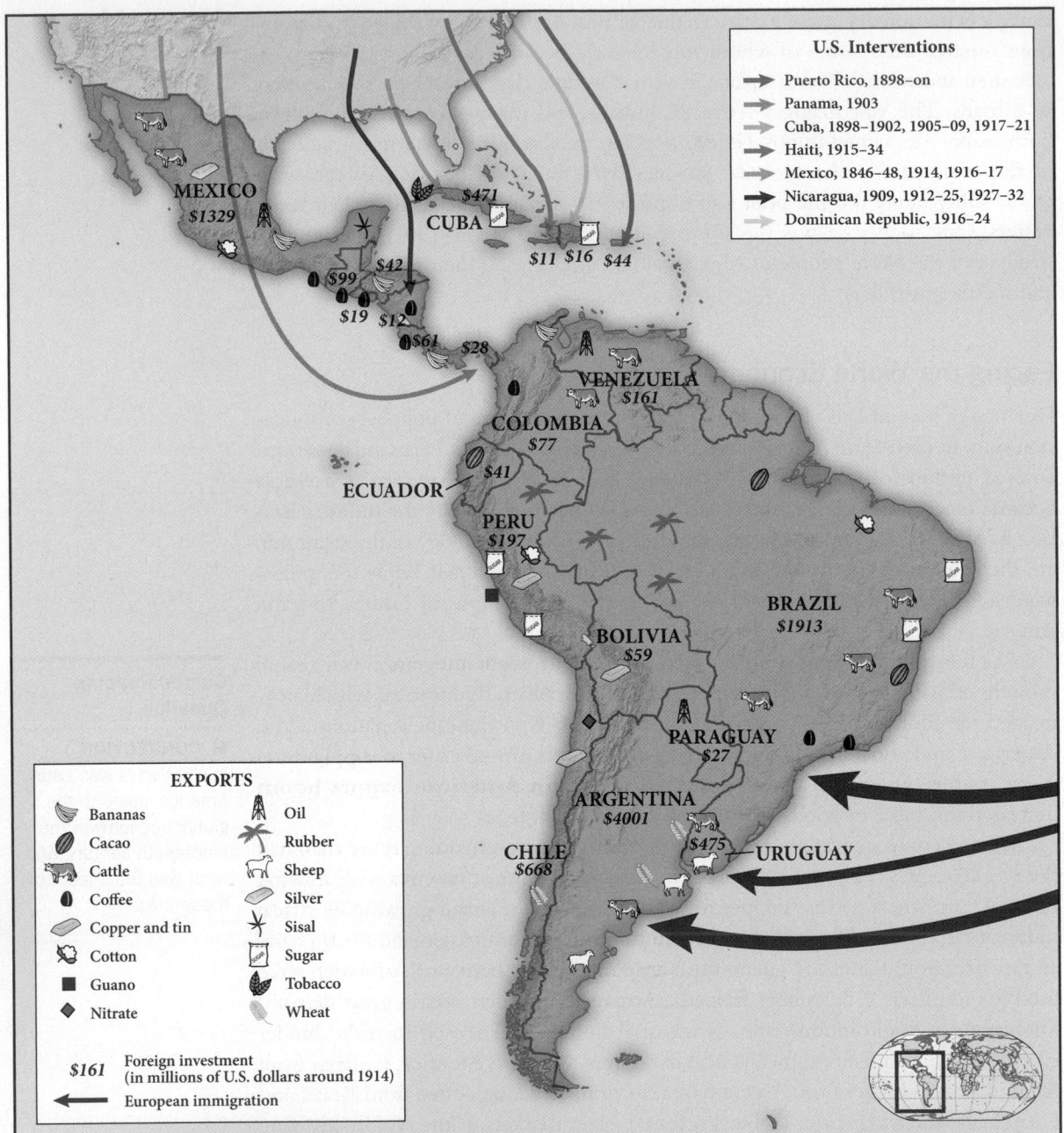

Map 17.5 Latin America and the World, 1825–1935

During the nineteenth and early twentieth centuries, Latin American countries interacted with the industrializing world via investment, trade, immigration, and military intervention from the United States.

nineteenth century than in its colony of India, although France, Germany, Italy, and the United States also contributed to this substantial financial transfer. By 1910, U.S. business interests controlled 40 percent of Mexican property and produced half of its oil. Much of this capital was used to build railroads, largely to funnel Latin American exports to the coast, where they were shipped to overseas markets. Mexico had only 390 miles of railroad in 1876; it had 15,000 miles in 1910. By 1915, Argentina, with 22,000 miles of railroad, had more track per person than the United States had.

Becoming like Europe?

To the economic elites of Latin America, intent on making their countries resemble Europe or the United States, all of this was progress. In some respects, they were surely right. Economies were growing, producing more than ever before. The population was also burgeoning; it increased from about 30 million in 1850 to more than 77 million in 1912 as public health measures (such as safe drinking water, inoculations, sewers, and campaigns to eliminate mosquitoes that carried yellow fever) brought down death rates.

Urbanization also proceeded rapidly. By the early twentieth century, wrote one scholar, "Latin American cities lost their colonial cobblestones, white-plastered walls, and red-tiled roofs. They became modern metropolises, comparable to urban giants anywhere. Streetcars swayed, telephones jangled, and silent movies flickered from Montevideo and Santiago to Mexico City and Havana."[22] Buenos Aires, Argentina's metropolitan center, boasted 750,000 people in 1900 and billed itself as the "Paris of South America." There the educated elite, just like the English, drank tea in the afternoon, while discussing European literature, philosophy, and fashion, usually in French.

To become more like Europe, Latin America sought to attract more Europeans. Because civilization, progress, and modernity apparently derived from Europe, many Latin American countries actively sought to increase their "white" populations by deliberately recruiting impoverished Europeans with the promise, mostly unfulfilled, of a new and prosperous life in the New World. Argentina received the largest wave of European immigrants (some 2.5 million between 1870 and 1915), mostly from Spain and Italy. Brazil and Uruguay likewise attracted substantial numbers of European newcomers.

Only a quite modest segment of Latin American society saw any great benefits from the export boom and all that followed from it. Upper-class landowners certainly gained as exports flourished and their property values soared. Middle-class urban dwellers—merchants, office workers, lawyers, and other professionals—also grew in numbers and prosperity as their skills proved valuable in a modernizing society. As a percentage of the total population, however, these were small elites. In Mexico in the mid-1890s, for example, the landowning upper class made up no more than 1 percent and the middle classes perhaps 8 percent of the population. Everyone else was lower class, and most of them were impoverished.[23]

Guided Reading Question

....

■ **COMPARISON**

Did Latin America follow or diverge from the historical path of Europe during the nineteenth century?

A new but quite small segment of this vast lower class emerged among urban workers who labored in the railroads, ports, mines, and a few factories. They initially organized themselves in a variety of mutual aid societies, but by the end of the nineteenth century they were creating unions and engaging in strikes. To authoritarian governments interested in stability and progress, such activity was highly provocative and threatening, and they acted harshly to crush or repress unions and strikes. In 1906, the Mexican dictator Porfirio Díaz invited the Arizona Rangers to suppress a strike at Cananea, near the U.S. border, an action that resulted in dozens of deaths. The following year in the Chilean city of Iquique, more than 1,000 men, women, and children were slaughtered by police when nitrate miners protested their wages and working conditions.

The vast majority of the lower class lived in rural areas, where they suffered the most and benefited the least from the export boom. Government attacks on communal landholding and peasant indebtedness to wealthy landowners combined to push many farmers off their land or into remote and poor areas where they could barely make a living. Many wound up as dependent laborers or peons on the haciendas of the wealthy, where their wages were often too meager to support a family. Thus women and children, who had earlier remained at home to tend the family plot, were required to join their menfolk as field laborers. Many immigrant Italian farmworkers in Argentina and Brazil were unable to acquire their own farms, as they had expected, and so drifted into the growing cities or returned to Italy.

Although local protests and violence were frequent, only in Mexico did these vast inequalities erupt into a nationwide revolution. There, in the early twentieth century, middle-class reformers joined with workers and peasants to overthrow the long dictatorship of Porfirio Díaz (r. 1876–1911). What followed was a decade of bloody conflict (1910–1920) that cost Mexico some 1 million lives, or roughly 10 percent of the population. Huge peasant armies under charismatic leaders such as Pancho Villa and Emiliano Zapata helped oust Díaz. Intent on seizing land and redistributing it to the peasants, they then went on to attack many of Mexico's large haciendas. But unlike the leaders of the later Russian and Chinese revolutions, whose most radical elements seized state power, Villa and Zapata proved unable to do so on any long-term basis, in part because they were hobbled by factionalism and focused on local or regional issues. Despite this limitation and its own internal conflicts, the **Mexican Revolution** transformed the country. When the dust settled, Mexico had a new constitution (1917) that proclaimed universal male suffrage; provided for the redistribution of land; stripped the Catholic Church of any role in public education and forbade it to own land; announced unheard-of rights for workers, such as a minimum wage and an eight-hour workday; and placed restrictions on foreign ownership of property. Much of Mexico's history in the twentieth century involved working out the implications of these nationalist and reformist changes. The revolution's direct influence, however, was largely limited to Mexico itself and a few places in Central America and the Andes; the upheaval did not have the wider international impact of the Russian and Chinese revolutions.

Perhaps the most significant outcome of the export boom lay in what did *not* happen, for nowhere in Latin America did it jump-start a thorough Industrial Revolution, despite a few factories that processed foods or manufactured textiles, clothing, and building materials. The reasons are many. A social structure that relegated some 90 percent of its population to an impoverished lower class generated only a very small market for manufactured goods. Moreover, economically powerful groups such as landowners and cattlemen benefited greatly from exporting agricultural products and had little incentive to invest in manufacturing. Domestic manufacturing enterprises could only have competed with cheaper and higher-quality foreign goods if they had been protected for a time by high tariffs. But Latin American political leaders had thoroughly embraced the popular European doctrine of prosperity through free trade, and many governments depended on taxing imports to fill their treasuries.

Instead of their own Industrial Revolutions, Latin Americans developed a form of economic growth that was largely financed by capital from abroad and

The Mexican Revolution Women were active participants in the Mexican Revolution. They prepared food, nursed the wounded, washed clothes, and at times served as soldiers on the battlefield, as illustrated in this cover image from a French magazine in 1913. (Apic/Getty Images)

dependent on European and North American prosperity and decisions. Brazil experienced this kind of dependence when its booming rubber industry suddenly collapsed in 1910–1911, after seeds from the wild rubber tree had been illegally exported to Britain and were used to start competing and cheaper rubber plantations in Malaysia.

Later critics saw this **dependent development** as a new form of colonialism, expressed in the power exercised by foreign investors. The influence of the U.S.-owned United Fruit Company in Central America was a case in point. Allied with large landowners and compliant politicians, the company pressured the governments of these "banana republics" to maintain conditions favorable to U.S. business. This indirect or behind-the-scenes imperialism was supplemented by repeated U.S. military intervention in support of American corporate interests in Cuba, Haiti, the Dominican Republic, Nicaragua, and Mexico. The United States also controlled the Panama Canal and acquired Puerto Rico as a territory in the aftermath of the Spanish-American War (see Map 17.5, page 762).

Thus, despite Latin America's domination by people of European descent and its close ties to the industrializing countries of the Atlantic world, that region's historical trajectory in the nineteenth century diverged considerably from that of Europe and North America.

REFLECTIONS

History and Horse Races

Historians and students of history seem endlessly fascinated by "firsts"—the first breakthrough to agriculture, the first domestication of horses, the first civilization, the first use of gunpowder, the first printing press, and so on. Each of these firsts presents a problem of explanation: why did it occur in some particular time and place rather than somewhere else or at some other time? Such questions have assumed historical significance because "first achievements" represent something new in the human journey and because many of them conveyed unusual power, wealth, status, or influence on their creators.

Nonetheless, the focus on firsts can be misleading as well. Those who accomplished something first may see themselves as generally superior to those who embraced that innovation later. Historians too can sometimes adopt a winners-and-losers mentality, inviting a view of history as a horse race toward some finish line of accomplishment. Most first achievements in history, however, were not the result of intentional efforts but rather the unexpected outcome of converging circumstances.

The Industrial Revolution is a case in point. Efforts to understand the European beginnings of this immense breakthrough are certainly justified by its pervasive global consequences and its global spread over the past several centuries. In terms of human ability to dominate the natural environment and to extract wealth from it, the Industrial Revolution marks a decisive turning point in the history of our species. But Europeans' attempts to explain their Industrial Revolution have at times stated or implied their own unique genius. In the nineteenth century, many Europeans saw their technological mastery as a sure sign of their cultural and racial superiority as they came to use "machines as the measure of men."[24] In pondering the European origins of the Industrial Revolution, historians too have sometimes sought an answer in some distinct or even superior feature of European civilization.

In emphasizing the unexpectedness of the first Industrial Revolution, and the global context within which it occurred, world historians have attempted to avoid a "history as horse race" outlook. Clearly, the first industrial breakthrough in Britain was not a self-conscious effort to win a race; it was the surprising outcome of countless decisions by many people to further their own interests. Subsequently, however, other societies and their governments quite deliberately tried to catch up, seeking the wealth and power that the Industrial Revolution promised.

The rapid spread of industrialization across the planet, though highly uneven, may diminish the importance of its Europeans beginnings. Just as no one views agriculture as a Middle Eastern phenomenon even though it occurred first in that region, it seems likely that industrialization will be seen increasingly as a global process rather than one uniquely associated with Europe. If industrial society proves to be a sustainable future for humankind—presently a very open question—historians of the future may well be more interested in the pattern of its global spread and in efforts to cope with its social and environmental consequences than in its origins in Western Europe.

Second Thoughts

What's the Significance?

steam engine, 736
British textile industry, 740
middle-class society, 743
idcology of domesticity, 744
lower middle class, 744
laboring classes, 744
Karl Marx, 748
Labour Party, 749
socialism in the United States, 755
Progressives, 755
Russian Revolution of 1905, 758
caudillos, 760
Latin American export boom, 761
Mexican Revolution, 764
dependent development, 765

Big Picture Questions

1. What did humankind gain from the Industrial Revolution, and what did it lose?
2. In what ways might the Industrial Revolution be understood as a global rather than simply a European phenomenon?
3. The Industrial Revolution transformed social as well as economic life. What evidence might support this statement?
4. How do you think the Industrial Revolution will be viewed 50, 100, or 200 years into the future?
5. **Looking Back:** How did the Industrial Revolution interact with the Scientific Revolution and the French Revolution to generate Europe's modern transformation?

Next Steps: For Further Study

Robert C. Allen, *The Industrial Revolution: A Very Short Introduction* (2017). A concise, accessible, and up-to-date summary by a leading scholar in the field.

John Charles Chasteen, *Born in Blood and Fire* (2006). A lively and well-written account of Latin America's turbulent history since the sixteenth century.

Jack Goldstone, *Why Europe? The Rise of the West in World History, 1500–1850* (2009). An original synthesis of recent research provided by a leading world historian.

David S. Landes, *The Wealth and Poverty of Nations* (1998). An argument that culture largely shapes the possibilities for industrialization and economic growth.

Robert B. Marks, *The Origins of the Modern World* (2007). An effective summary of new thinking about the origins of European industrialization.

Peter Stearns, *The Industrial Revolution in World History* (2012). A global and comparative perspective on the Industrial Revolution.

"Global Industrialization," Annenberg Learner, Bridging World History, http://www.learner .org/courses/worldhistory/unit_main_19.html. An innovative world history website that provides text and videos casting industrialization in a global context.

"The American Industrial Revolution." Rich Hawksworth (producer and director), United Learning, https://www.youtube.com/watch?v=7CvofeajOyO. A site that uses archival footage and period photography to tell a balanced story of the American Industrial Revolution during the late nineteenth century.

The Socialist Vision

The most compelling alternative to capitalist industrialization took shape during the nineteenth century in Europe under the banner of socialism. There it became enormously influential, generating great hopes and equally great fears. Then in the twentieth century socialism spread globally, providing inspiration for communist revolutions in Russia, China, Cuba, Vietnam, and elsewhere, serving as a critique of modern capitalism, and playing a prominent role in the cold war.

SOURCE 17.1 Socialism According to Marx

Almost everywhere, modern socialism has been linked to the life and work of Karl Marx (1818–1883). This German-born intellectual lived during the harshest phase of European industrialization, before the benefits of this new and highly productive system were widely shared. But in this brutal process, Marx discerned the inevitable approach of a new socialist world. In his voluminous writings, he exuberantly praised the productive capacity of the Industrial Revolution while providing devastating criticism of the social inequalities, the economic instability, and the blatant exploitation that accompanied this process. In short, Marx distinguished sharply between the technological achievements of industrialization and the capitalist socioeconomic system in which it occurred.

Source 17.1 presents excerpts from the most famous of Marx's writings, *The Communist Manifesto*, first published in 1848. In this effort and throughout much of his life, Marx was assisted by another German thinker, Friedrich Engels (1820–1895), the son of a successful textile manufacturer. Engels became radicalized as he witnessed the devastating social results of capitalist industrialization. Their *Manifesto* begins with a summary description of the historical process. Much of the document then analyzes what the authors call the "bourgeoisie" or the "bourgeois epoch," terms that refer to the age of industrial capitalism.

■ How do Marx and Engels understand the motor of change in human history? What are their criticisms of the existing social system? What do they see as its major achievements?

■ Why do they believe that the capitalist system is doomed? On what basis do Marx and Engels argue that only a revolution, "the forcible overthrow of all existing social conditions," will enable the creation of a socialist society? What kind of society do they envisage after the collapse of capitalism?

■ Which of Marx and Engels's descriptions and predictions ring true even now? In what respects was their analysis disproved by later developments?

KARL MARX AND FRIEDRICH ENGELS | *The Communist Manifesto* | 1848

The history of all hitherto existing society is the history of class struggles. . . . Our epoch, the epoch of the bourgeoisie, possesses, however, this distinct feature: it has simplified class antagonisms. Society as a whole is more and more splitting up into two great hostile camps, into two great classes directly facing each other—bourgeoisie and proletariat.

Modern industry has established the world market, for which the discovery of America paved the way. This market has given an immense development to commerce, to navigation, to communication by land. . . .

[T]he bourgeoisie has at last, since the establishment of Modern Industry and of the world market, conquered for itself, in the modern representative state, exclusive political sway. The executive of the modern state is but a committee for managing the common affairs of the whole bourgeoisie. . . .

The bourgeoisie, wherever it has got the upper hand, has put an end to all feudal, patriarchal, idyllic relations. It has . . . left no other nexus between people than naked self-interest, than callous "cash payment.". . . It has resolved personal worth into exchange value, and in place of the numberless indefeasible chartered freedoms, has set up that single, unconscionable freedom—Free Trade. In one word, for exploitation, veiled by religious and political illusions, it has substituted naked, shameless, direct, brutal exploitation.

The bourgeoisie has stripped of its halo every occupation hitherto honored and looked up to with reverent awe. It has converted the physician, the lawyer, the priest, the poet, the man of science, into its paid wage laborers.

The bourgeoisie has torn away from the family its sentimental veil, and has reduced the family relation into a mere money relation. . . .

It has been the first to show what man's activity can bring about. It has accomplished wonders far surpassing Egyptian pyramids, Roman aqueducts, and Gothic cathedrals. . . .

The need of a constantly expanding market for its products chases the bourgeoisie over the entire surface of the globe. It must nestle everywhere, settle everywhere, establish connections everywhere. . . .

All old-established national industries have been destroyed or are daily being destroyed. They are dislodged by new industries . . . , that [use] raw material drawn from the remotest zones; industries whose products are consumed, not only at home, but in every quarter of the globe. In place of the old wants, satisfied by the production of the country, we find new wants, requiring for their satisfaction the products of distant lands and climes. In place of the old local and national seclusion and self-sufficiency, we have intercourse in every direction, universal interdependence of nations. . . .

The bourgeoisie . . . has created enormous cities, has greatly increased the urban population as compared with the rural, and has thus rescued a considerable part of the population from the idiocy of rural life. Just as it has made the country dependent on the towns, so it has made barbarian and semibarbarian countries dependent on the civilized ones, nations of peasants on nations of bourgeois, the East on the West. . . .

The bourgeoisie, during its rule of scarce one hundred years, has created more massive and more colossal productive forces than have all preceding generations together. Subjection of nature's forces to man, machinery, application of chemistry to industry and agriculture, steam navigation, railways, electric telegraphs, clearing of whole continents for cultivation, canalization of rivers, whole populations conjured out of the ground—what earlier century had even a presentiment that such productive forces slumbered in the lap of social labor? . . .

It is enough to mention the commercial crises that, by their periodical return, put the existence of the entire bourgeois society on its trial, each time more threateningly. . . . In these crises, there breaks out an epidemic that, in all earlier epochs, would have seemed an absurdity—the epidemic of overproduction. . . .

But not only has the bourgeoisie forged the weapons that bring death to itself; it has also called into existence the men who are to wield those weapons—the modern working class—the proletarians. . . .

These laborers, who must sell themselves piecemeal, are a commodity, like every other article of commerce, and are consequently exposed to all the vicissitudes of competition, to all the fluctuations of the market.

Owing to the extensive use of machinery, and to the division of labor, the work of the proletarians has lost all individual character, and, consequently, all charm for the workman. He becomes an appendage of the machine, and it is only the most simple, most monotonous, and most easily acquired knack, that is required of him. . . .

Masses of laborers, crowded into the factory . . . they are daily and hourly enslaved by the machine, by the overlooker, and, above all, by the individual bourgeois manufacturer himself. . . .

The lower strata of the middle class—the small tradespeople, shopkeepers, and retired tradesmen generally, the handicraftsmen and peasants— all these sink gradually into the proletariat. . . . Thus, the proletariat is recruited from all classes of the population. . . .

What the bourgeoisie therefore produces, above all, are its own grave-diggers. Its fall and the victory of the proletariat are equally inevitable. . . .

[T]he first step in the revolution by the working class is to raise the proletariat to the position of ruling class, to win the battle of democracy. The proletariat will use its political supremacy to wrest, by degree, all capital from the bourgeoisie, to centralize all instruments of production in the hands of the state. . . . When, in the course of development, class distinctions have disappeared, and all production has been concentrated in the hands of a vast association of the whole nation, the public power will lose its political character. . . . In place of the old bourgeois society, with its classes and class antagonisms, we shall have an association in which the free development of each is the condition for the free development of all. . . .

The Communists disdain to conceal their views and aims. They openly declare that their ends can be attained only by the forcible overthrow of all existing social conditions. Let the ruling classes tremble at a communist revolution. The proletarians have nothing to lose but their chains. They have a world to win.

Source: John E. Toews, ed., *The Communist Manifesto by Karl Marx and Frederick Engels with Related Documents* (Boston: Bedford/St. Martin's, 2018), 64–95.

■ ■ ■

SOURCE 17.2 Socialism in Song

While socialist intellectuals like Marx developed a particular understanding of history and of capitalism, ordinary workers, many animated by socialist ideals, gave voice to their experience and aspirations in song. The hymn of the socialist movement was *The Internationale,* composed in 1871 by Eugène Pottier, a French working-class activist, poet, and songwriter. Source 17.2 offers an English translation made in 1900 by Charles Kerr, an American publisher of radical books. The song gave expression to both the oppression and the hopes of ordinary people as they worked for a socialist future.

■ What evidence of class consciousness is apparent in the song? What particular grievances are expressed in it?

■ How does *The Internationale* portray the struggle and the future?

■ What evidence of Marxist thinking can you find in its lyrics?

EUGÈNE POTTIER | *The Internationale* | 1871

Arise, ye prisoners of starvation!
Arise, ye wretched of the earth!
For justice thunders condemnation,
A better world's in birth!
No more tradition's chains shall bind us,
Arise ye slaves, no more in thrall!
The earth shall rise on new foundations,
We have been nought, we shall be all. (Chorus)

Chorus
'Tis the final conflict,
Let each stand in his place.
The international working class
Shall be the human race.

We want no condescending saviors
To rule us from a judgment hall;
We workers ask not for their favors;
Let us consult for all.
To make the thief disgorge his booty
To free the spirit from its cell,
We must ourselves decide our duty,
We must decide, and do it well. (Chorus)

The law oppresses us and tricks us,
Wage slav'ry drains the workers' blood;
The rich are free from obligations,

The laws the poor delude.
Too long we've languished in subjection,
Equality has other laws;
"No rights," says she, "without their duties,
No claims on equals without cause."
    (Chorus)

Behold them seated in their glory
The kings of mine and rail and soil!
What have you read in all their story,
But how they plundered toil?
Fruits of the workers' toil are buried
In the strong coffers of a few;
In working for their restitution
The men will only ask their due. (Chorus)

Toilers from shops and fields united,
The union we of all who work;
The earth belongs to us, the workers,
No room here for the shirk.
How many on our flesh have fattened;
But if the noisome birds of prey
Shall vanish from the sky some morning,
The blessed sunlight still will stay. (Chorus)

Source: Charles H. Kerr (compiler and translator), *Socialist Songs with Music* (Chicago: Charles H. Kerr, 1901), No. 2.

■ ■ ■

SOURCE 17.3 Socialist Perspectives in Art: The Present and the Future ▶

Socialists expressed in art both their understanding of existing capitalist society and a vision of what a socialist future might look like. Source 17.3A represents the former and Source 17.3B the latter.

■ What elements of Source 17.3A express Marx's understanding of "bourgeois society"?

■ Which of Marx's predictions about the socialist future is evoked in Source 17.3B? How does the artist deal with tension between nation and class?

■ Contrast these two images with "The Socialist Threat" poster on page 749. How might the artists who created Sources 17.3A and 17.3B react to "The Socialist Threat" image?

SOURCE 17.3A

INDUSTRIAL WORKERS OF THE WORLD | *A Pyramid of Capitalist Society* | 1911

SOURCE 17.3B

Manifest of International Trade Union Congress | 1896

PHAS/Universal Images Group/REX/Shutterstock

■ ■ ■

SOURCE 17.4 Socialist Variations: The Woman Question

Marxist socialism coincided with the emergence of feminism, giving rise to what many socialists called "the woman question." Should socialists treat women as members of an oppressed class or as members of an oppressed sex? Since most socialists believed that the lack of economic independence was the root cause of women's subordination, how should socialist parties relate to middle-class feminists in addressing uniquely female issues such as suffrage, equal pay, education, and maternity insurance? Among the leading figures addressing such issues was Clara Zetkin (1857–1933), a prominent member of the German Social Democratic Party and an ardent feminist. In Source 17.4, Zetkin describes the party's posture on "the woman question."

- How would you describe Zetkin's view of the relationship between socialism and feminism? Which one has priority in her thinking?

- Why is she so insistent that the Social Democratic Party of Germany address the concerns of women?

- Why does she believe that women's issues will be better served within a socialist framework than in a bourgeois women's rights movement?

- How might critics—both feminist and socialist—argue with Zetkin?

CLARA ZETKIN | *The German Socialist Women's Movement* | 1909

Socialist women have continued their propaganda in favor of the full political emancipation of their sex. The struggle for universal suffrage . . . was a struggle for adult suffrage for both sexes, vindicated in meetings and leaflets. . . . The work of our trade unions to enlighten, train, and organize wage-earning women is not smaller nor less important than what the S.D.P. has done to induce women to join in political struggles of the working class. . . .

The most prominent feature of the Socialist women's movement in Germany is its clearness and revolutionary spirit as to Socialist theories and principles. The women who head it are fully conscious that the social fate of their sex is indissolubly connected with the general evolution of society. . . . The integral human emancipation of all women depends in consequence on the social emancipation of labor; that can only be realized by the class-war of the exploited majority. Therefore, our Socialist women oppose strongly the bourgeois women righters' credo that the women of all classes must gather into an unpolitical, neutral movement striving exclusively for women's rights. In theory and practice they maintain the conviction that the class antagonisms are much more powerful, effective, and decisive than the social antagonisms between the sexes. . . . [T]hus the working-class women will [only] win their full emancipation . . . in the class war of all the exploited, without difference of sex, against all who exploit, without difference of sex. That does not mean at all that they undervalue the importance of the political emancipation of the female sex. On the contrary, they employ much more energy than the German women-righters to conquer the suffrage. But the vote is, according to their views, not the last word and term of their aspirations, but only a weapon—a means in [the] struggle for a revolutionary aim—the Socialistic order.

The Socialist women's movement in Germany . . . strives to help change the world by awakening the consciousness and the will of working-class women to join in performing the most Titanic deed that history will know: the emancipation of labor by the laboring class themselves.

Source: Clara Zetkin, *The German Socialist Women's Movement* (1909; Marxists Internet Archive, 2007), http://www.marxists.org/archive/zetkin/1909/10/09.htm.

■ ■ ■

SOURCE 17.5 Socialist Variations: The Case of Russia

By the late nineteenth century, most West European socialist parties were operating in a more or less democratic environment in which they could organize legally, contest elections, and serve in parliament. Some of them had largely abandoned any thoughts of violent revolution in favor of a peaceful and democratic path to socialism. But for others, this "revisionist" path amounted to a betrayal of the Marxist vision. That was certainly the case for Vladimir Ilyich Ulyanov, better known as Lenin, then a prominent figure in the small Russian Social Democratic Labor Party, established in 1898. Lenin was particularly hostile to what he called "economism" or "trade-unionism," which focused on immediate reforms such as higher wages, shorter hours, and better working conditions. He was operating in a still-autocratic Russian state, where neither political parties nor trade unions were legal and where no national parliament or elections allowed for the expression of popular grievances. How were socialists to act in such a situation? In a famous pamphlet titled *What Is to Be Done?* (1902), Lenin addressed this issue, well before he became the leader of the world's first successful socialist revolution in 1917.

■ What were Lenin's objections to economism?

■ What kind of party organization did he favor?

■ Why did Lenin believe that workers were unlikely to come to a revolutionary consciousness on their own? What was necessary to move them in that direction?

■ In what ways did Lenin's views reflect the specific conditions of Russia?

LENIN | *What Is to Be Done?* | 1902

The history of all countries shows that the working class, exclusively by its own effort, is able to develop only trade union consciousness, i.e., it may itself realize the necessity for combining in unions, for fighting against the employers, and for striving to compel the government to pass necessary labor legislation, etc. The theory of socialism, however, grew out of the philosophic, historical, and economic theories that were elaborated by the educated representatives of the propertied classes, the intellectuals. . . . [I]n Russia . . . it arose as a natural and inevitable outcome of the development of ideas among the revolutionary socialist intelligentsia.

It is only natural that a Social Democrat . . . should conceive of an "organization of revolutionaries" as being more or less identical with an "organization of workers." . . .

[O]n questions of organization and politics, the Economists are forever lapsing from Social Democracy into trade unionism. The political struggle carried on by the Social Democrats is far more extensive and complex than the economic struggle the workers carry on against the employers and the government. Similarly . . . the organization of a revolutionary Social Democratic Party must inevitably *differ* from the organizations of the workers designed for the latter struggle. A workers' organization . . . must be as wide as possible; and . . . it must be as public as conditions will allow. . . . On the other hand, the organizations of revolutionaries must consist first and foremost of people whose profession is that of a revolutionary. . . . Such an organization must of necessity be not too extensive and as secret as possible

I assert:

1. that no movement can be durable without a stable organization of leaders to maintain continuity;

2. that the more widely the masses are spontaneously drawn into the struggle and form the basis of the movement and participate in it, the more necessary is it to have such an organization. . . .

3. that the organization must consist chiefly of persons engaged in revolutionary activities as a profession;

4. that in a country with an autocratic government, the more we restrict the membership of this organization to persons who are engaged in revolutionary activities as a profession and who have been professionally trained in the art of combating the political police, the more difficult will it be to catch the organization. . . .

The centralization of the more secret functions in an organization of revolutionaries will not diminish, but rather increase the extent and the quality of the activity of a large number of other organizations intended for wide membership. . . . [I]n order to "serve" the mass movement we must have people who will devote themselves exclusively to Social Democratic activities, and that such people must *train* themselves patiently and steadfastly to be professional revolutionaries. . . .

Let no active worker take offense at these frank remarks, for as far as insufficient training is concerned, I apply them first and foremost to myself. I used to work in a circle that set itself great and all-embracing tasks; and every member of that circle suffered to the point of torture from the realization that we were proving ourselves to be amateurs at a moment in history when we might have been able to say, paraphrasing a well-known epigram: "Give us an organization of revolutionaries, and we shall overturn the whole of Russia!"

Source: V. I. Lenin, *What Is to Be Done?* (Pamphlet, 1902; Marxists Internet Archive, 1999), https://www.marxists.org/archive/lenin/works/1901/witbd/index.htm.

DOING HISTORY

1. **Defining the socialist vision:** How might you describe the socialist critique of capitalist society and its expectation of the future?

2. **Identifying differences:** What differences in outlook can you identify within the larger socialist movement in Europe during the nineteenth century?

3. **Connecting socialist thinking with the Atlantic revolutions:** To what extent did socialist thinking reflect the concerns of the Atlantic revolutions explored in Chapter 16? In what ways did it diverge from those earlier revolutionary movements?

4. **Considering the appeal of socialism:** To what people might the socialist vision be most appealing? And to whom might it seem threatening?

The Legacy of Karl Marx in the Twenty-First Century

Almost 135 years after the death of Marx, scholars and activists alike continue to debate his relevance in the twenty-first century. Voice 17.1 comes from British educator and author Allan Todd and explores the relationship between recent events and the receptivity to Marxist ideas. In Voice 17.2, Terry Eagleton, a British professor of literature, argues for the continued usefulness of Marxist thinking in contemporary life and society.

- What events or circumstances does Allan Todd believe have shaped postures toward Marx and Marxism in recent decades?

- Why does Terry Eagleton in Voice 17.2 believe that Marx remains relevant in the twenty-first century?

- **Integrating Primary and Secondary Sources:** What evidence from the primary sources might these authors use to support their arguments?

VOICE 17.1

Allan Todd on Marx and Current History | 2016

The opening words of Marx and Engles' *The Communist Manifesto*, first published in 1848, are: "A spectre is haunting Europe, the spectre of communism." Given the visible collapse of most states claiming to be communist, this "spectre" would appear to have been laid to rest. Certainly the failure of attempts in the Soviet Union and Eastern Europe to construct socialism led to a "retreat from Marxism" in the first decades after the collapse of these regimes.

Yet Marx's analysis had claimed that capitalist globalization was bound to lead to periodic and serious economic crises. . . . And indeed the financial crash of 2008 and the global economic crisis of 2011 . . . along with the ecological crises associated with the unrestricted drive for profit suggest that . . . Marx's theories might still have some relevance for the 21st century.

Thus historians such as E. Hobsbawm have argued that the events of 1989–91 and afterwards do not necessarily mark the end of Marxism or communism. They have pointed out that Marxist theory and communist practice arose from conditions of poverty, the destruction of war, and strong desires for liberty, fairness, and equality.

Other commentators have observed that Marxism . . . was in large part an extension of the French Revolution's ideals of "liberty, equality, and fraternity." . . . Movements calling for the full implementation of these ideals continue to emerge around the globe in the 21st century. Thus it may be rather too early for historians to proclaim the death and funeral of communism [Marxism].

Source: Allan Todd, *The Soviet Union and Post-Soviet Russia* (Cambridge: Cambridge University Press, 2016), 294–96.

VOICE 17.2

Terry Eagleton on the Continuing Relevance of Marx | 2011

Very few thinkers . . . have changed the course of actual history as decisively as [Marx]. . . . He transformed our understanding of human history. . . .

Marx was the first to identify the historical object known as capitalism—to show how it arose, by what laws it worked and how it might be brought to an end. . . . Marx unmasked our everyday life to reveal an imperceptible entity known as the capitalist mode of production. . . .

About Marxism as a moral and cultural critique. . . . Alienation, the "commodification" of social life, a culture of greed, aggression, mindless hedonism . . . , the steady hemorrhage of meaning and value from human existence—it is hard to find an intelligent discussion of these questions that is not indebted to the Marxist tradition.

Marxism is a critique of capitalism. . . . It is also the only such critique that has transformed large sectors of the globe. . . . As long as capitalism is in business, Marxism must be as well.

Marx himself predicted a decline of the working class and the steep rise of white collar work. . . . He also foresaw so-called globalization. He is accused of being outdated by champions of a capitalism that is rapidly reverting to Victorian levels of inequality. . . . In our own time, as Marx predicted, inequalities of wealth have dramatically deepened.

Capitalism has brought about great material advances. But though this way of organizing our affairs has had a long time to demonstrate that it is capable of satisfying human demands all around, it seems no closer to doing so than ever.

Source: Terry Eagleton, *Why Marx Was Right* (New Haven, CT: Yale University Press, 2011), x, xi, 2, 3, 8, 10.

Colonial Encounters in Asia, Africa, and Oceania

1750–1950

《 **The Imperial Durbar of 1903** To mark the coronation of British monarch Edward VII and his installation as the emperor of India, colonial authorities in India mounted an elaborate assembly, or durbar. The durbar was intended to showcase the splendor of the British Empire, and its pageantry included sporting events; a state ball; a huge display of Indian arts, crafts, and jewels; and an enormous parade in which a long line of British officials and Indian princes passed by on bejeweled elephants.

In the early twenty-first century the past dramatically resurfaced in both Namibia, a small country in southwest Africa, and in Germany, which had conquered Namibia and ruled it as a colony from 1884 to 1915. In 2013 and again in 2016, angry Namibians had either defaced or forced the removal of several statues that commemorated German soldiers who had been killed while brutally suppressing an uprising in 1904–1907 by the Herero and Nama people. Often called the first genocide of the twentieth century, German efforts to put down that rebellion had killed about 80 percent of the Herero and 50 percent of the Nama. "We as Hereros and we as Namibians don't want German soldiers in front of our State House," declared Uahimisa Kaapehi, one of the leaders of those protests.[1] The push to remove those offending statues came amid sensitive negotiations between Namibia and Germany in which Germany appeared ready to acknowledge its earlier actions as genocide, to issue a formal apology, and to offer financial compensation. In such ways the colonial past has continued to echo more than a century later. ■

For many millions of Africans, Asians, and Pacific islanders, colonial rule—by the British, French, Germans, Italians, Belgians, Portuguese, Russians, or Americans—was the major new element in their historical experience during the long nineteenth century (1750–1900). Of course, no single colonial experience characterized this vast region. Much depended on the cultures and prior history of various colonized people. Policies of the colonial powers sometimes differed sharply and changed over time. Men and women experienced the colonial era differently, as did traditional elites, Western-educated groups, artisans, peasant farmers, and migrant laborers. Furthermore, the varied actions and reactions of such people, despite their oppression and exploitation, shaped the colonial experience, perhaps as much as the policies, practices, and intentions of their temporary European rulers. All of them—colonizers and colonized alike—were caught up in the flood of change that accompanied this new burst of European imperialism.

SEEKING THE MAIN POINT

In what ways did colonial rule transform the societies that it encompassed?

Industry and Empire

Behind much of Europe's nineteenth-century expansion lay the massive fact of its Industrial Revolution, a process that gave rise to new economic needs, many of which found solutions abroad. The enormous productivity of industrial technology and Europe's growing affluence now created the need for extensive raw materials and agricultural products: wheat from the American Midwest and southern Russia; meat from Argentina; bananas from Central America; rubber from Brazil; cocoa and palm oil from West Africa, and much more. This demand radically changed patterns of economic and social life in the countries of their origin.

Guided Reading Question

■ **CHANGE**
In what ways did the Industrial Revolution shape the character of nineteenth-century European imperialism?

Furthermore, Europe needed to sell its own products abroad, since its factories churned out more goods than its own people could afford to buy. By 1840, for example, Britain was exporting 60 percent of its cotton-cloth production, annually sending 200 million yards to Europe, 300 million yards to Latin America, and 145 million yards to India. Part of European and American fascination with China during the nineteenth and twentieth centuries lay in the enormous market potential represented by its huge population. Much the same could be said for capital, for European investors often found it more profitable to invest their money abroad than at home. Between 1910 and 1913, Britain was sending about half of its savings overseas as foreign investment.

Wealthy Europeans also saw social benefits to foreign markets because they kept Europe's factories humming and its workers employed. The English imperialist Cecil Rhodes confided his fears to a friend in the late nineteenth century:

> Yesterday I attended a meeting of the unemployed in London and having listened to the wild speeches which were nothing more than a scream for bread, I returned home convinced more than ever of the importance of imperialism. . . . In order to save the 40 million inhabitants of the United Kingdom from a murderous civil war, the colonial politicians must open up new areas to absorb the excess population and create new markets for the products of the mines and factories.[2]

Thus imperialism promised to solve the class conflicts of an industrializing society while avoiding revolution or the serious redistribution of wealth.

Landmarks for Chapter 18

1775	1800	1825	1850	1875	1900	1925	1950

EUROPE AND UNITED STATES

1750–1900
Europe's Industrial Revolution

1820s
Quinine isolated and mass-produced

1846–1848
Mexican–United States War

1850–1900
Scientific racism and
social Darwinism prominent

1862
Development of Gatling gun, a hand-driven machine gun

1875–1900
Intensification of European rivalries
over African territories

1898 Spanish-American War

AFRICA

1830s France invades Algeria

1869 Opening of Suez Canal

1875–1900
European conquest of Africa

1890s–1908
King Leopold's reign of terror in the Congo

1896
Ethiopia defeats Italy at Battle of Adowa

1899–1902 Boer War

1904–1905
Maji Maji rebellion in German East Africa

ASIA/PACIFIC

1757–1858 East India Company governs India

1788 Initial European settlement of Australia

1830s–1870
Cultivation system in
Netherlands East Indies

1857–1858
Indian Rebellion against rule of British East India Company

1858–1947
British government rules India

1858–1893 French conquest of Indochina

1898
United States acquires Hawaii and Philippines

1910
Japanese annexation of Korea

Colonial Rivalries This image shows Africa as a sleeping giant, while various European countries stake their rival claims to parts of the continent. It was published in 1911 in *Puck*, a British magazine of humor and satire. ("The Sleeping Sickness" by Gordon Ross [1873-1946], from *Puck*, 1911/Library of Congress, Prints and Photographs Division, LC-DIG-ppmsca-27783)

But what made imperialism so broadly popular in Europe, especially in the last quarter of the nineteenth century, was the growth of mass nationalism. By 1871, the unification of Italy and Germany intensified Europe's already competitive international relations, and much of this rivalry spilled over into the struggle for colonies or economic concessions in Asia, Africa, and Pacific Oceania. Colonies and spheres of influence abroad became symbols of "Great Power" status for a nation, and their acquisition was a matter of urgency, even if they possessed little immediate economic value. After 1875, it seemed to matter, even to ordinary people, whether some remote corner of Africa or some obscure Pacific island was in British, French, or German hands. Imperialism, in short, appealed on economic and social grounds to the wealthy or ambitious, seemed politically and strategically necessary in the game of international power politics, and was emotionally satisfying to almost everyone. It was a potent mix!

If the industrial era made overseas expansion more desirable or even urgent, it also provided new means for achieving those goals. Steam-driven ships moving through the new Suez Canal, completed in 1869, allowed Europeans to reach distant Asian, African, and Pacific ports more quickly and predictably and to penetrate interior rivers as well. The underwater telegraph made possible almost instant communication with far-flung outposts of empire. The discovery of quinine to prevent malaria greatly reduced European death rates in the tropics. Breech-loading rifles and machine guns vastly widened the military gap between Europeans and everyone else.

Industrialization also occasioned a marked change in the way Europeans perceived themselves and others. In earlier centuries, Europeans had defined others largely in religious terms. "They" were heathen; "we" were Christian. With the advent of the industrial age, however, Europeans developed a secular arrogance that fused with or in some cases replaced their notions of religious superiority. They had, after all, unlocked the secrets of nature, created a society of unprecedented wealth, and used both to produce unsurpassed military power. These became the criteria by which Europeans judged both themselves and the rest of the world.

By such standards, it is not surprising that their opinions of other cultures dropped sharply. The Chinese, who had been highly praised in the eighteenth century, were reduced in the nineteenth century to the image of "John Chinaman"—weak, cunning, obstinately conservative, and, in large numbers, a distinct threat, represented by the "yellow peril" in late nineteenth-century European thinking. African societies, which had been regarded even in the slave-trade era as nations and their leaders as kings, were demoted in nineteenth-century European eyes to the status of tribes led by chiefs as a means of emphasizing their "primitive" qualities.

Peoples of Pacific Oceania and elsewhere could be regarded as "big children," who lived "closer to nature" than their civilized counterparts and correspondingly distant from the high culture with which Europeans congratulated themselves. Upon visiting Tahiti in 1768, the French explorer Bougainville concluded: "I thought I was walking in the Garden of Eden."[3] Such views could be mobilized to criticize the artificiality and materialism of modern European life, but they could also serve to justify the conquest of people who were, apparently, doing little to improve what nature had granted them. Writing in 1854, a European settler in Australia declared: "The question comes to this; which has the better right—the savage, born in a country, which he runs over but can scarcely be said to occupy . . . or the civilized man, who comes to introduce into this . . . unproductive country, the industry which supports life?"[4]

Increasingly, Europeans viewed the culture and achievements of Asian and African peoples through the prism of a new kind of racism, which is sometimes called **scientific racism**. Although physical differences had often been a basis of fear or dislike, in the nineteenth century Europeans increasingly used the prestige and apparatus of science to support their racial preferences and prejudices. Phrenologists, craniologists, and sometimes physicians used allegedly scientific methods and numerous instruments to classify the size and shape of human skulls and concluded, not surprisingly, that those of whites were larger and therefore more advanced. Nineteenth-century biologists, who classified the varieties of plants and animals, applied these notions of rank to varieties of human beings as well. The result was a hierarchy of races, with the whites on top and the less developed "child races" beneath them. Race, in this view, determined human intelligence, moral development, and destiny. "Race is everything," declared the British anatomist Robert Knox

Guided Reading Question

....

■ **CHANGE**

What contributed to changing European views of Asians and Africans in the nineteenth century?

PROGRESSIVE DEVELOPMENT OF MAN.—(2) EVOLUTION ILLUSTRATED WITH THE SIX CORRESPONDING LIVING FORMS.

European Racial Images This nineteenth-century chart, depicting the "Progressive Development of Man" from apes to modern Europeans, reflected the racial categories that were so prominent at the time. It also highlights the influence of Darwin's evolutionary ideas as they were applied to varieties of human beings.

in 1850. "Civilization depends on it."[5] Furthermore, as the germ theory of disease took hold in nineteenth-century Europe, it was accompanied by fears that contact with "inferiors" threatened the health and even the biological future of more advanced or "superior" peoples.

These ideas influenced how Europeans viewed their own global expansion. Almost everyone saw it as inevitable, a natural outgrowth of a superior civilization. For many, though, this viewpoint was tempered with a genuine, if condescending, sense of responsibility to the "weaker races" that Europe was fated to dominate. "Superior races have a right, because they have a duty . . . to civilize the inferior races," declared the French politician Jules Ferry in 1883.[6] That **civilizing mission** included bringing Christianity to the heathen, good government to disordered lands, work discipline and production for the market to "lazy natives," a measure of education to the ignorant and illiterate, clothing to the naked, and health care to the sick, all while suppressing "native customs" that ran counter to Western ways of living. In European thinking, this was "progress" and "civilization."

A harsher side to the ideology of imperialism found expression in **social Darwinism**. Its adherents applied Charles Darwin's evolutionary concept of "the survival of the fittest" to human society. This outlook suggested that European dominance inevitably led to the displacement or destruction of backward peoples or "unfit" races. Such views made imperialism, war, and aggression seem both natural and progressive, for weeding out "weaker" peoples of the world would allow the "stronger" to flourish. These were some of the ideas with which industrializing and increasingly powerful Europeans confronted the peoples of Asia and Africa in the nineteenth century.

A Second Wave of European Conquests

If the sixteenth- and seventeenth-century takeover of the Americas represented the first phase of European colonial conquests, the century and a half between 1750 and 1900 was a second and quite distinct round of that larger process. Now it was focused in Asia, Africa, and Oceania rather than in the Western Hemisphere. And it featured a number of new players—Germany, Italy, Belgium, the United States, and Japan—who were not at all involved in the earlier phase, while the Spanish and Portuguese now had only minor roles. In general, Europeans preferred informal control, which operated through economic penetration and occasional military intervention but without a wholesale colonial takeover. Such a course was cheaper and less likely to provoke wars. But where rivalry with other European states made it impossible or where local governments were unable or unwilling to cooperate, Europeans proved more than willing to undertake the expense and risk of conquest and outright colonial rule.

Once established in a region, they frequently took advantage of moments of weakness in local societies to strengthen their control. "Each global drought was the green light for an imperialist landrush," wrote one scholar when examining the climatic instability that caused monsoon rains across Asia and parts of Africa to repeatedly fail in the second half of the nineteenth century.[7] Nowhere was this more evident than in Africa, where, for instance, a drought in the southern part of the continent in 1877 coincided with British success in reining in Zulu independence, and famine in Ethiopia from the late 1880s on coincided with Italian efforts to subdue the Horn of Africa.

The construction of these new European empires in the Afro-Asian world, like empires everywhere, involved military force or the threat of it. Increasingly in the nineteenth century, Europeans possessed overwhelming advantages in firepower, derived from the recently invented repeating rifles and machine guns. Nonetheless, Europeans had to fight, often long and hard, to create their new empires, as countless wars of conquest attest. In the end, though, they prevailed almost everywhere, largely against adversaries who did not have machine guns or in some cases any guns at all.

Thus were African, Asian, and Oceanic peoples of all kinds incorporated within one or another of the European empires. Gathering and hunting bands in Australia, agricultural village societies or chiefdoms on Pacific islands and in parts of Africa, pastoralists of the Sahara and Central Asia, residents of states large and small, and virtually everyone in the large and complex civilizations of India and Southeast Asia — all of them alike lost the political sovereignty and freedom of action they had previously exercised. For some, such as Hindus governed by the Muslim Mughal Empire, it was an exchange of one set of foreign rulers for another. But now all were subjects of a European colonial state.

The passage to colonial status occurred in various ways. For the peoples of India and Indonesia, colonial conquest grew out of interaction with European trading firms, which were authorized to conduct military operations and exercise political and administrative control over large areas. The British East India Company, rather than the British government directly, played the leading role in the colonial takeover of South Asia. The fragmentation of the Mughal Empire and the absence of any overall sense of cultural or political unity both invited and facilitated European penetration. A similar situation of many small and rival states assisted the Dutch acquisition of Indonesia. However, neither the British nor the Dutch had a clear-cut plan for conquest. Rather, in India it evolved slowly as local authorities and European traders made and unmade a variety of alliances with local states over roughly a century (1750–1850). In Indonesia, a few areas held out until the early twentieth century (see Map 18.1).

For most of Africa, mainland Southeast Asia, and the Pacific islands, colonial conquest came later, in the second half of the nineteenth century, and rather more

Guided Reading Question

■ COMPARISON
In what different ways was colonial rule established in various parts of Africa and Asia?

MAPPING HISTORY

Map 18.1 Colonial Asia in the Early Twentieth Century

By the early twentieth century, several of the great population centers of Asia had come under the colonial control of Britain, the Netherlands, France, the United States, or Japan.

READING THE MAP: Which Southeast Asian kingdom maintained its independence from European colonial powers?

INTERPRETING THE MAP: What geographical and political barriers made direct confrontations between the British Empire in South Asia and the Chinese Empire unlikely?

abruptly and deliberately than in India or Indonesia. The "**scramble for Africa**," for example, pitted half a dozen European powers against one another as they partitioned the entire continent among themselves in only about twenty-five years (1875–1900). (See Working with Evidence: Colonial Conquest, page 816, for various perspectives on the "scramble.") European leaders themselves were surprised by the intensity of their rivalries and the speed with which they acquired huge territories, about which they knew very little.

That process involved endless but peaceful negotiations among the competing Great Powers about "who got what" and extensive and bloody military action, sometimes lasting decades, to make their control effective on the ground. It took the French sixteen years (1882–1898) to finally conquer the recently created West African empire led by Samori Toure. Among the most difficult to subdue were those decentralized societies without any formal state structure. In such cases, Europeans confronted no central authority with which they could negotiate or that they might decisively defeat. It was a matter of village-by-village conquest against extended resistance. As late as 1925, one British official commented on the process as it operated in central Nigeria: "I shall of course go on walloping them until they surrender. It's a rather piteous sight watching a village being knocked to pieces and I wish there was some other way, but unfortunately there isn't."[8] Another very difficult situation for the British lay in South Africa, where they were initially defeated by a Zulu army in 1879 at the Battle of Isandlwana. And twenty years later, in what became known as the Boer War (1899–1902), the Boers, white descendants of the earlier Dutch settlers in South Africa, fought bitterly for three years before succumbing to British forces (see Map 18.2). The colonial conquest of Africa was intensely resisted.

Europeans and Americans had been drawn into the world of Pacific Oceania during the eighteenth century through exploration and scientific curiosity, by the missionary impulse for conversion, and by their economic interests in sperm whale oil, coconut oil, guano, mineral nitrates and phosphates, sandalwood, and other products. Primarily in the second half of the nineteenth century, these entanglements morphed into competitive annexations as Britain, France, the Netherlands, Germany, and the United States, now joined by Australia, claimed control of all the islands of Oceania (see Map 18.1). Chile too, in search of valuable guano and nitrates, entered the fray and gained a number of coastal islands as well as Rapa Nui (Easter Island), the easternmost island of Polynesia.

The colonization of the South Pacific territories of Australia and New Zealand, both of which were taken over by the British during the nineteenth century, was more similar to the earlier colonization of North America than to contemporary patterns of Asian and African conquest. In both places, conquest was accompanied by large-scale European settlement and diseases that reduced native numbers by 75 percent or more by 1900. Like Canada and the United States, these became settler colonies, "neo-European" societies in the Pacific. Aboriginal Australians constituted only about 2.4 percent of their country's population in the early twenty-first century, and the indigenous Maori were a minority of about 15 percent in New Zealand. In other previously isolated regions as well—Polynesia, Amazonia, Siberia—disease took a terrible toll on peoples who lacked immunities to European pathogens. For example, the population of Hawaii declined from around 142,000 in 1823 to only 39,000 in 1896. Unlike these remote areas, most African and Asian regions shared with Europe a broadly similar disease environment and so were less susceptible to the pathogens of the conquerors.

Elsewhere other variations on the theme of imperial conquest unfolded. The westward expansion of the United States, for example, overwhelmed Native American populations and involved the country in an imperialist war with Mexico. Seeking

1900, French establish their authority in Northern Sahara

1911, Morocco partitioned between France and Spain

SPANISH MOROCCO

Algiers

TUNISIA

Tripoli

Mediterranean Sea

MOROCCO

IFNI

Agadir

Cairo

Suez Canal

RIO DE ORO

ALGERIA

LIBYA (TRIPOLI)

1911–1912, annexed by Italy from Ottoman Empire

EGYPT

Nile R.

MAURITANIA

1908–1909, conquered by France

1909–1911, Wadai conquered by France

Red Sea

FRENCH WEST AFRICA

1900–1903, British conquer northern Nigeria

ANGLO-EGYPTIAN SUDAN

ERITREA

FRENCH SOMALILAND

Niger R.

SENEGAL

GAMBIA

1906, insurrection in Sokoto

Adowa

BRITISH SOMALILAND

PORTUGUESE GUINEA

GOLD COAST

NIGERIA

Wadai

1898, Battle of Omdurman

Fashoda

1896, Ethiopia defeats Italy

SIERRA LEONE

Bagirmi

CAMEROON (KAMERUN)

ABYSSINIA (ETHIOPIA)

LIBERIA

TOGO

1904–1905, Germans suppress insurrection

ITALIAN SOMALILAND

1900, uprising; British suppress Ashantis

1904, insurrection in southern Nigeria

Congo R.

UGANDA

BRITISH EAST AFRICA (KENYA)

1899–1900, Mohammed ben Abdullah clashes with British, Italians, Ethiopians

SPANISH GUINEA (RIO MUNI)

French Congo

BELGIAN CONGO

GERMAN EAST AFRICA

ZANZIBAR

1905, uprising

CABINDA

1905, Maji Maji uprising

ATLANTIC OCEAN

NYASALAND

ANGOLA

1902, 1907, uprisings

NORTHERN RHODESIA

MOZAMBIQUE

MADAGASCAR

0 250 500 miles
0 250 500 kilometers

GERMAN SOUTHWEST AFRICA

SOUTHERN RHODESIA

BECHUANALAND

Transvaal

British
French
German
Italian
Portuguese
Belgian
Spanish
Independent African states

1904–1908, uprising by Herero people

Orange Free State

Natal

SWAZILAND

1896, Shona, Ndebele uprising

INDIAN OCEAN

1903, Hottentot uprising

UNION OF SOUTH AFRICA

BASUTOLAND

1899–1902, Boer War

1904, Bambatha uprising

Cape Town

MAPPING HISTORY

Map 18.2 Conquest and Resistance in Colonial Africa

By the early twentieth century, the map of Africa reflected the outcome of the scramble for Africa, a conquest that was heavily resisted in many places.

READING THE MAP: In what regions of Africa were British colonies concentrated? Where were French colonies concentrated?

INTERPRETING THE MAP: Compare this map with Map 21.3. To what extent did the colonial period of African history provide the framework for the political boundaries of postcolonial Africa?

territory for white settlement, the United States practiced a policy of removing, sometimes almost exterminating, Indian peoples. On the "reservations" to which Indians were confined and in boarding schools to which many of their children were removed, reformers sought to "civilize" the remaining Native Americans, eradicating tribal life and culture, under the slogan "Kill the Indian and Save the Man."

Japan's takeover of Taiwan and Korea bore marked similarities to European actions, as that East Asian nation joined the imperialist club. Russian penetration of Central Asia brought additional millions under European control as the Russian Empire continued its earlier territorial expansion. Filipinos acquired new colonial rulers when the United States took over from Spain following the Spanish-American War of 1898. Some 13,000 freed U.S. slaves, seeking greater freedom than was possible at home, migrated to West Africa, where they became, ironically, a colonizing elite in the land they named Liberia.

Ethiopia and Siam (Thailand) were notable for avoiding the colonization to which their neighbors succumbed. Those countries' military and diplomatic skills, their willingness to make modest concessions to the Europeans, and the rivalries of the imperialists all contributed to these exceptions to the rule of colonial takeover in East Africa and Southeast Asia. Ethiopia, in fact, considerably expanded its own empire, even as it defeated Italy at the Battle of Adowa in 1896.

These broad patterns of colonial conquest contained thousands of separate encounters as the target societies of Western empire builders were confronted with decisions about how to respond to encroaching European power in the context of their local circumstances. Many initially sought to enlist Europeans in their own internal struggles for power or in their rivalries with neighboring states or peoples. As pressures mounted and European demands escalated, some tried to play off imperial powers against one another, while others resorted to military action. Many societies were sharply divided between those who wanted to fight and those who believed that resistance was futile. After extended resistance against French aggression, the nineteenth-century Vietnamese emperor Tu Duc argued with those who wanted the struggle to go on:

> Do you really wish to confront such a power with a pack of [our] cowardly soldiers? . . . With what you presently have, do you really expect to dissolve the enemy's rifles into air or chase his battleships into hell?[9]

Still others negotiated, attempting to preserve as much independence and power as possible. The rulers of the East African kingdom of Buganda, for example, saw opportunity in the British presence and negotiated an arrangement that substantially enlarged their state and personally benefited the kingdom's elite class.

Under European Rule

In many places and for many people, incorporation into European colonial empires was a traumatic experience. Especially for small-scale societies, the loss of life, homes, cattle, crops, and land was devastating. In 1902, a British soldier in East Africa described what happened in a single village: "Every soul was either shot or bayoneted. . . . We burned all the huts and razed the banana plantations to the ground."[10]

For the Vietnamese elite, schooled for centuries in Chinese-style Confucian thinking, conquest meant that the natural harmonies of life had been badly disrupted, that "water flowed uphill." Nguyen Khuyen (1835–1909), a senior Vietnamese official, retired to his ancestral village to farm and write poetry after the French conquest, expressing his anguish at the passing of the world he had known. Many others also withdrew into private life, feigning illness when asked to serve in public office under the French.

Cooperation and Rebellion

Although violence was a prominent feature of colonial life both during conquest and after, various groups and many individuals willingly cooperated with colonial authorities to their own advantage. Many men found employment, status, and security in European-led armed forces. The shortage and expense of European administrators and the difficulties of communicating across cultural boundaries made it necessary for colonial rulers to rely heavily on a range of local intermediaries. Thus Indian princes, Muslim emirs, and African rulers, often from elite or governing families, found it possible to retain much of their earlier status and many of their privileges while gaining considerable wealth by exercising authority, legally and otherwise, at the local level. For example, in French West Africa, an area eight times the size of France and with a population of about 15 million in the late 1930s, the colonial state consisted of just 385 French administrators and more than 50,000 African "chiefs." Thus colonial rule rested on and reinforced the most conservative segments of colonized societies.

Both colonial governments and private missionary organizations had an interest in promoting a measure of European education. From this process arose a small Western-educated class, whose members served the colonial state, European businesses, and Christian missions as teachers, clerks, translators, and lower-level administrators. A few received higher education abroad and returned home as lawyers, doctors, engineers, or journalists. As colonial governments and business enterprises became more sophisticated, Europeans increasingly depended on the Western-educated class at the expense of the more traditional elites.

If colonial rule enlisted the willing cooperation of some, it provoked the bitter opposition of many others. Thus periodic rebellions, both large and small, erupted in colonial regimes everywhere. The most famous among them was the **Indian Rebellion of 1857–1858**, which was triggered by the introduction into the colony's military forces of a new cartridge smeared with animal fat from cows and pigs. Because Hindus venerated cows and Muslims regarded pigs as unclean, both groups viewed the innovation as a plot to render them defiled and to convert them to Christianity. Behind this incident were many groups of people with a whole series of grievances generated by the British colonial presence: local rulers who

Guided Reading Question

••••••••••••••••••••••••••••••••

■ **EXPLANATION**

Why might subject people choose to cooperate with the colonial regime? What might prompt them to violent rebellion or resistance?

had lost power, landlords deprived of their estates or their rent, peasants overtaxed and exploited by urban moneylenders and landlords alike, unemployed weavers displaced by machine-manufactured textiles, and religious leaders outraged by missionary preaching. A mutiny among Indian troops in Bengal triggered the rebellion, which soon spread to other regions of the colony and other social groups. Soon much of India was aflame. Some rebel leaders presented their cause as an effort to revive an almost-vanished Mughal Empire and thereby attracted support from those with strong resentments against the British. Although it was crushed in 1858, the rebellion greatly widened the racial divide in colonial India and eroded British tolerance for those they viewed as "nigger natives" who had betrayed their trust. Moreover, the rebellion convinced the British government to assume direct control over India, ending the era of British East India Company rule in the subcontinent. Fear of provoking another rebellion also made the British more conservative and cautious about deliberately trying to change Indian society.

Colonial Empires with a Difference

At one level, European colonial empires were but the latest in a very long line of imperial creations, all of which had enlisted cooperation and experienced resistance from their subject peoples, but the nineteenth-century European version of empire was distinctive in several remarkable ways. One was the prominence of race in distinguishing rulers as "superior" to the ruled, as the high tide of scientific racism in Europe coincided with the acquisition of Asian and African colonies. In East Africa, for example, white men expected to be addressed as *bwana* (Swahili for "master"), whereas Europeans regularly called African men "boy." Particularly affected by European racism were those whose Western education and aspirations most clearly threatened the racial divide. For example, a proposal in 1883 to allow Indian judges to hear cases involving whites provoked outrage and massive demonstrations among European inhabitants of India.

In those colonies that had a large European settler population, the expression of racial distinctions was much more pronounced than in places such as Nigeria, which had few permanently settled whites. The most extreme case was South Africa, where a large European population and the widespread use of African labor in mines and industries brought blacks and whites into closer and more prolonged contact than elsewhere. The racial fears that were aroused resulted in extraordinary efforts to establish race as a legal, not just a customary, feature of South African society. This racial system provided for separate "homelands," educational systems, residential areas, public facilities, and much more. In what was eventually known as apartheid, South African whites attempted the impossible task of creating an industrializing economy based on cheap African labor while limiting African social and political integration in every conceivable fashion.

A further distinctive feature of nineteenth-century European empires lay in the extent to which colonial states were able to penetrate the societies they governed.

Guided Reading Question

■ **COMPARISON**
What was distinctive about European colonial empires of the nineteenth century?

European Master and Indian Servants This image, dating to 1812, shows a young European gentleman attended by multiple servants in colonial India. It illustrates the exalted status available to quite ordinary Europeans in a colonial setting as well as the sharp racial divide separating Europeans and Indians. (Historia/REX/Shutterstock)

Centralized tax-collecting bureaucracies, new means of communication and transportation, imposed changes in landholding patterns, integration of colonial economies into a global network of exchange, public health and sanitation measures, and the activities of missionaries—all of this touched the daily lives of many people far more deeply than in earlier empires. Not only were Europeans foreign rulers, but they also bore the seeds of a very different way of life, which grew out of their own modern transformation.

Nineteenth-century European colonizers were extraordinary as well in their penchant for counting and classifying their subject people. With the assistance of anthropologists and missionaries, colonial governments collected a vast amount of information, sought to organize it "scientifically," and used it to manage the unfamiliar, complex, varied, and fluctuating societies that they governed. In India, the British found in classical texts and Brahmin ideology an idealized description of the caste system, based on the notion of four ranked and unchanging varnas, that made it possible to bring order out of the immense complexity and variety of caste as it actually operated. Thus the British invented or appropriated a Brahmin version of "traditional India" that they favored and sought to preserve, while scorning as "non-Indian" the new elite who had been educated in European schools and were enthusiastic about Western ways of life. This view of India reflected the great influence of Brahmins on British thinking and clearly served the interests of this Indian upper class.

Likewise, within African colonies Europeans identified, and sometimes invented, distinct tribes, each with its own clearly defined territory, language, customs, and chief. The notion of a "tribal Africa" expressed the Western view that African societies were primitive or backward, representing an earlier stage of human development. It was also a convenient idea, for it reduced the enormous complexity and fluidity of African societies to a more manageable state and thus made colonial administration easier.

Gender too entered into the efforts of Europeans to define both themselves and their newly acquired subject peoples. European colonizers—mostly male—took pride in their "active masculinity" while defining the "conquered races" as soft, passive, and feminine. Indian Bengali men, wrote a British official in 1892, "are disqualified for political enfranchisement by the possession of essentially feminine characteristics."[11] By linking the inferiority of women with that of people of color, imperialists joined gender ideology and race prejudice in support of colonial rule. But the intersection of race, gender, and empire was complex and varied. European men in the colonies often viewed their own women as the bearers and emblems of civilization, "upholding the moral dignity of the white community" amid the darkness of inferior peoples.[12] As such, European women had to be above reproach in sexual matters, protected against the alleged lust of native men by their separation from local African or Asian societies. Furthermore, certain colonized people, such as the Sikhs and Gurkhas in India, the Kamba in Kenya, and the Hausa in Nigeria, were gendered as masculine or "martial races" and targeted for recruitment into British military or police forces.

Finally, the colonial policies of Europeans contradicted their own core values and their practices at home to an unusual degree. While nineteenth-century Britain and France were becoming more democratic, their colonies were essentially dictatorships, offering perhaps order and stability, but certainly not democratic government, because few colonial subjects were participating citizens. Empire, of course, was wholly at odds with European notions of national independence, and ranked racial classifications went against the grain of both Christian and Enlightenment ideas of human equality. Furthermore, many Europeans were distinctly reluctant to encourage within their colonies the kind of modernization — urban growth, industrialization, individual values, religious skepticism — that was sweeping their own societies. They feared that this kind of social change, often vilified as "detribalization," would encourage unrest and challenge colonial rule. As a model for social development, they much preferred "traditional" rural society, with its established authorities and social hierarchies, though shorn of abuses such as slavery and *sati* (widow burning). Such contradictions between what Europeans embraced at home and what they practiced in the colonies became increasingly apparent to many Asians and Africans and played a major role in undermining the foundations of colonial rule in the twentieth century.

Ways of Working: Comparing Colonial Economies

Colonial rule affected the lives of its subject people in many ways, but the most pronounced change was in their ways of working. The colonial state — with its power to tax, to seize land for European enterprises, to compel labor, and to build railroads, ports, and roads — played an important role in these transformations. Even more powerful was the growing integration of colonized societies into a world economy that increasingly demanded their gold, diamonds, copper, tin, rubber, coffee, cotton, sugar, cocoa, and many other products. But the economic transformations born of these twin pressures were far from uniform. Various groups — migrant workers and cash-crop farmers, plantation laborers and domestic servants, urban elites and day laborers, men and women — experienced the colonial era differently as their daily working lives underwent profound changes.

To various degrees, old ways of working were eroded almost everywhere in the colonial world. Subsistence farming, in which peasant families produced largely for their own needs, diminished as growing numbers directed at least some of their energies to working for wages or selling what they produced for a cash income. That money was both necessary to pay taxes and school fees and useful for buying the various products—such as machine-produced textiles, bicycles, and kerosene—that the industrial economies of Europe sent their way. As in Europe, artisans suffered greatly when cheaper machine-manufactured merchandise displaced their own handmade goods. A flood of inexpensive textiles from Britain's new factories ruined the livelihood of tens of thousands of India's handloom weavers. Iron smelting largely disappeared in Africa, and occupations such as blacksmithing and tanning lost ground. Furthermore, Asian and African merchants, who had earlier handled the trade between their countries and the wider world, were squeezed out by well-financed European commercial firms.

Economies of Coercion: Forced Labor and the Power of the State

Many of the new ways of working that emerged during the colonial era derived directly from the demands of the colonial state. The most obvious was required and unpaid labor on public projects, such as building railroads, constructing government buildings, and transporting goods. In French Africa, all "natives" were legally obligated to do "statute labor" for ten to twelve days a year, a practice that lasted through 1946. It was much resented. A resident of British West Africa, interviewed in 1996, bitterly recalled this feature of colonial life: "They [British officials] were rude, and they made us work for them a lot. They came to the village and just rounded us up and made us go off and clear the road or carry loads on our heads."[13]

The most infamous cruelties of forced labor occurred during the early twentieth century in the **Congo Free State**, then governed personally by King Leopold II of Belgium. Private companies in the Congo, operating under the authority of the state, forced villagers to collect rubber, which was much in demand for bicycle and automobile tires, with a reign of terror and abuse beginning in the 1890s that cost millions of lives. One refugee from these horrors described the process:

> We were always in the forest to find the rubber vines, to go without food, and our women had to give up cultivating the fields and gardens. Then we starved. . . . We begged the white man to leave us alone, saying we could get no more rubber, but the white men and their soldiers said "Go. You are only beasts yourselves. . . ." When we failed and our rubber was short, the soldiers came to our towns and killed us. Many were shot, some had their ears cut off; others were tied up with ropes round their necks and taken away.[14]

Eventually such outrages were widely publicized in Europe, where they created a scandal, forcing the Belgian government to take control of the Congo in 1908 and ending Leopold's private control of the colony and his reign of terror.

Guided Reading Question

■ **CONNECTION**
How did the policies of colonial states change the economic lives of their subjects?

A variation on the theme of forced labor took shape in the so-called **cultivation system** of the Netherlands East Indies (Indonesia) during the nineteenth century. Peasants were required to cultivate 20 percent or more of their land in cash crops such as sugar or coffee to meet their tax obligation to the state. Sold to government contractors at fixed and low prices, those crops, when resold on the world market, proved highly profitable for Dutch traders and shippers as well as for the Dutch state and its citizens. According to one scholar, the cultivation system "performed a miracle for the Dutch economy," enabling it to avoid taxing its own people and providing capital for its Industrial Revolution.[15] It also enriched and strengthened the position of those "traditional authorities" who enforced the system, often by using lashings and various tortures, on behalf of the Dutch. For the peasants of Java, however, it meant a double burden of obligations to the colonial state as well as to local lords. Many became indebted to moneylenders when they could not meet those obligations. Those demands, coupled with the loss of land and labor now excluded from food production, contributed to a wave of famines during the mid-nineteenth century in which hundreds of thousands perished.

On occasion, the forced cultivation of cash crops was successfully resisted. In German East Africa, for example, colonial authorities in the late nineteenth century imposed the cultivation of cotton, which seriously interfered with production of local food crops. Here is how one man remembered the experience:

Colonial Violence in the Congo Horrific photos of mutilated children had an important impact on public opinion about imperial rule in the Congo Free State. They came to symbolize widespread abuses, including murders, rapes, starvation, and the burning of villages, associated with efforts to obtain supplies of wild rubber for use in industrialized societies. (Universal History Archive/Getty Images)

> The cultivation of cotton was done by turns. Every village was allotted days on which to cultivate. . . . After arriving you all suffered very greatly. Your back and your buttocks were whipped and there was no rising up once you stooped to dig. . . . And yet he [the German] wanted us to pay him tax. Were we not human beings?[16]

Such conditions prompted a massive rebellion in 1904–1905, known as Maji Maji, and persuaded the Germans to end the forced growing of cotton. Thus the actions of colonized peoples could alter or frustrate the plans of the colonizers.

Economies of Cash-Crop Agriculture: The Pull of the Market

Many Asian and African peoples had produced quite willingly for an international market long before they were enclosed within colonial societies. They offered for trade items such as peanuts and palm oil in West Africa, cotton in Egypt, spices in Indonesia, and pepper and textiles in India. In some places, colonial rule created conditions that facilitated and increased **cash-crop production** to the advantage of local farmers. British authorities in Burma, for example, acted to encourage rice production among small farmers by ending an earlier prohibition on rice exports, providing irrigation and transportation facilities, and enacting land tenure laws that facilitated private ownership of small farms. Under these conditions, the population of the Irrawaddy Delta boomed, migrants from Upper Burma and India poured into the region, and rice exports soared. Local small farmers benefited considerably because they were now able to own their own land, build substantial houses, and buy imported goods. For several decades in the late nineteenth century, standards of living improved sharply, and huge increases in rice production fed millions of people in other parts of Asia and elsewhere. It was a very different situation from that of peasants forced to grow crops that seriously interfered with their food production.

But that kind of colonial development, practiced also in the Mekong River delta of French-ruled Vietnam, had important environmental consequences. It involved the destruction of mangrove forests and swamplands along with the fish and shellfish that supplemented local diets. New dikes and irrigation channels inhibited the depositing of silt from upstream and thus depleted soils in the deltas of these major river systems. And, unknown to anyone at the time, this kind of agriculture generates large amounts of methane gas, a major contributor to global warming.

Profitable cash-crop farming also developed in the southern Gold Coast (present-day Ghana), a British territory in West Africa. Unlike in Burma, it was African farmers themselves who took the initiative to develop export agriculture. Planting cacao trees in huge quantities, they became the world's leading supplier of cocoa, used to make chocolate, by 1911. Cacao was an attractive crop because, unlike cotton, it was compatible with the continued production of foods and did not require so much labor time. In the early twentieth century, it brought a new prosperity to many local farmers. But that success brought new problems in its wake. A shortage of labor fostered the employment of former slaves as dependent and exploited workers and also generated tensions between the sexes when some men married women for their labor power but refused to support them adequately. Moreover, the labor shortage brought a huge influx of migrants from the drier interior parts of West Africa, generating ethnic and class tensions. Another problem was that many colonies came to specialize in one or two cash crops, creating an unhealthy dependence when world market prices dropped. Thus African and Asian farmers were increasingly subject to the uncertain rhythms of the international marketplace as well as to those of weather and climate.

Guided Reading Question

....

■ **CHANGE**
How did cash-crop agriculture transform the lives of colonized peoples?

Economies of Wage Labor: Migration for Work

Yet another new way of working in colonial societies involved wage labor in some European enterprise. Driven by the need for money, by the loss of land adequate to support their families, or sometimes by the orders of colonial authorities, millions of colonial subjects across Asia, Africa, and Oceania sought employment in European-owned plantations, mines, construction projects, and homes. Often this required migration to distant work sites, many of them overseas. In this process, colonized migrants were joined by millions of Chinese, Japanese, and others who lived in more independent states. Together they generated vast streams of migration that paralleled and at least equaled in numbers the huge movement of Europeans during the nineteenth and early twentieth centuries. For Europeans, Asians, and Africans alike, the globalizing world of the colonial era was one of people in motion. (See the Snapshot on long-distance migration below.)

The African segment of this migratory stream moved in several directions. For much of the nineteenth century, the Atlantic slave trade continued, funneling well over 3 million additional people to the Americas, mostly to Brazil. As the slave trade diminished and colonial rule took shape in Africa, internal migration mounted within or among particular colonies. More than in Asia, Africans migrated to farms or plantations controlled by Europeans because they had lost their own land. In the settler colonies of Africa—Algeria, Kenya, Southern Rhodesia (Zimbabwe), and South Africa, for example—permanent European communities, with the help of colonial governments, obtained huge tracts of land, much of which had previously been home to African societies. A 1913 law in South Africa legally defined 88 percent of the land as belonging to whites, who were then about 20 percent of the population. Much of highland Kenya, an enormously rich agricultural region that was home to the Gikuyu and Kamba peoples, was taken over by some 4,000 white farmers. In such places, some Africans stayed on as "squatters," working for the new landowners as the price of remaining on what

SNAPSHOT   Long-Distance Migration in an Age of Empire, 1846–1940

The age of empire was also an age of global migration. Beyond the three major patterns of long-distance migration shown here, shorter migrations within particular regions or colonies set millions more into motion.

Origins	Destination	Numbers
Europe	Americas	55–58 million
India, southern China	Southeast Asia, Indian Ocean rim, South Pacific	48–52 million
Northeast Asia, Russia	Manchuria, Siberia, Central Asia, Japan	46–51 million

Data from Adam McKeown, "Global Migration, 1846–1940," *Journal of World History* 15, no. 2 (2004): 156.

had been their own land. Others were displaced to "native reserves," limited areas that could not support their growing populations, and many were thus forced to work for wages on European farms. Most notably in South Africa, such reserved areas, known as Bantustans, became greatly overcrowded: soil fertility declined, hillsides were cleared, forests shrank, and erosion scarred the land. This kind of ecological degradation was among the environmental consequences of African wage labor on European farms and estates.

The gold and diamond mines of South Africa likewise set in motion a huge pattern of labor migration that encompassed all of Africa south of the Belgian Congo. With skilled and highly paid work reserved for white miners, Africans worked largely as unskilled laborers at a fraction of the wages paid to whites. Furthermore, they were recruited on short-term contracts, lived in all-male prison-like barracks that were often surrounded by barbed wire, and were forced to return home periodically to prevent them from establishing a permanent family life near the mines.

Asians too were in motion and in large numbers. Some 29 million Indians and 19 million Chinese migrated variously to Southeast Asia, the South Pacific, East and South Africa, the Caribbean islands, or the lands around the Indian Ocean basin.

Economic Change in the Colonial World These workers on a Ceylon tea plantation in the early twentieth century are moving sacks of tea into a drying house in preparation for export. The Lipton label on the bags is a reminder of the role of large-scale foreign investment in the economic transformations of the colonial era. (Hulton Deutsch/Getty Images)

All across Southeast Asia in the later nineteenth and early twentieth centuries, huge plantations sprouted that were financed from Europe and that grew sugarcane, rubber, tea, tobacco, sisal (used for making rope), and more. Impoverished workers by the hundreds of thousands came from great distances (India, China, Java) to these plantations, where they were subject to strict control, often housed in barracks, and paid poorly, with women receiving 50 to 75 percent of a man's wage. Disease was common, and death rates were at least double that of the colony as a whole. In 1927 in southern Vietnam alone, one in twenty plantation workers died. British colonial authorities in India facilitated the migration of millions of Indians to work sites elsewhere in the British Empire—Trinidad, Jamaica, Fiji, Malaysia, Ceylon, South Africa, Kenya, and Uganda, for example—with some working as indentured laborers, receiving free passage and enough money to survive in return for five to seven years of heavy labor. Others operated as independent merchants. Particularly in the Caribbean region, Indian migration rose as the end of slavery created a need for additional labor. Since the vast majority of these Asian migrants were male, gender ratios were altered in the islands and in their countries of origin, where women faced increased workloads.

Mines were another source of wage labor for many Asians. In the British-ruled Malay States (Malaysia), tin mining accelerated greatly in the late nineteenth century, and by 1895 that colony produced some 55 percent of the world's tin. Operated initially by Chinese and later by European entrepreneurs, Malaysian tin mines drew many millions of impoverished Chinese workers on strictly controlled three-year contracts. Appalling living conditions, disease, and accidents generated extraordinarily high death rates.

Beyond Southeast Asia, Chinese migrants moved north to Manchuria in substantial numbers, encouraged by a Chinese government eager to prevent Russian encroachment in the area. The gold rushes of Australia and California also attracted hundreds of thousands of Chinese, who often found themselves subject to sharp discrimination from local people, including recently arrived European migrants. For example, Dennis Kearney, who led a California anti-immigrant labor organization with the slogan "The Chinese must go," was himself an Irish-born immigrant. Canada, Australia, New Zealand, and the United States all enacted measures to restrict or end Chinese immigration in the late nineteenth century.

A further destination of African and Asian migrants lay in the rapidly swelling cities of the colonial world—Lagos, Nairobi, Cairo, Calcutta, Rangoon, Batavia, Singapore, Saigon. Racially segregated, often unsanitary, and greatly overcrowded, these cities nonetheless were seen as meccas of opportunity for people all across the social spectrum. Traditional elites, absentee landlords, and wealthy Chinese businessmen occupied the top rungs of Southeast Asian cities. Western-educated people everywhere found opportunities as teachers, doctors, and professional specialists, but more often as clerks in European business offices and government bureaucracies. Skilled workers on the railways or in the ports represented a working-class elite, while a few labored in the factories that processed agricultural goods

Guided Reading Question

■ **CHANGE**
What kinds of wage labor were available in the colonies? Why might people take part in it? How did doing so change their lives?

or manufactured basic products such as beer, cigarettes, cement, and furniture. Far more numerous were the construction workers, rickshaw drivers, food sellers, domestic servants, prostitutes, and others who made up the urban poor of colonial cities. In 1955, a British report on life in Nairobi, the capital of Kenya, found that low wages, combined with the high cost of housing and food, "makes family life impossible for the majority."[17] After a half century of colonial rule, it was quite an admission.

Women and the Colonial Economy: Examples from Africa

If economic life in European empires varied greatly from place to place, even within the same colony, it also offered a different combination of opportunities and hardships to women than it did to men, as the experience of colonial Africa shows.[18] In precolonial Africa, women were almost everywhere active farmers, with responsibility for planting, weeding, and harvesting in addition to food preparation and child care. Men cleared the land, built houses, herded the cattle, and in some cases assisted with field work. Within this division of labor, women were expected to feed their own families and were usually allocated their own fields for that purpose. Many were also involved in local trading activity. Though clearly subordinate to men, African women nevertheless had a measure of economic autonomy.

As the demands of the colonial economy grew, women's lives increasingly diverged from those of men. In colonies where cash-crop agriculture was dominant, men often withdrew from subsistence production in favor of more lucrative export crops. Among the Ewe people of southern Ghana, men almost completely dominated the highly profitable cacao farming, whereas women assumed nearly total responsibility for domestic food production. In neighboring Ivory Coast, women had traditionally grown cotton for their families' clothing, but when that crop acquired a cash value, men insisted that cotton grown for export be produced on their own personal fields. Thus men acted to control the most profitable aspects of cash-crop agriculture and in doing so greatly increased the subsistence workload of women. One study from Cameroon estimated that women's working hours increased from forty-six per week in precolonial times to more than seventy by 1934.

Further increasing women's workload and differentiating their lives from those of men was labor migration. As growing numbers of men sought employment in the cities, on settler farms, or in the mines, their wives were left to manage the domestic economy almost alone. In many cases, women also had to supply food to men in the cities to compensate for very low urban wages. They often took over such traditionally male tasks as breaking the ground for planting, milking the cows, and supervising the herds, in addition to their normal responsibilities. In South Africa, where the demands of the European economy were particularly heavy, some 40 to 50 percent of able-bodied adult men were absent from the rural areas, and women headed 60 percent of households. In Botswana, which supplied much male labor to South Africa, married couples by the

Guided Reading Question

■ CHANGE
How were the lives of African women altered by colonial economies?

1930s rarely lived together for more than two months at a time. Increasingly, men and women lived in different worlds, with one focused on the cities and working for wages and the other on village life and subsistence agriculture.

Women coped with these difficult circumstances in a number of ways. Many sought closer relations with their families of birth rather than with their absent husbands' families, as would otherwise have been expected. Among the Luo of Kenya, women introduced laborsaving crops, adopted new farm implements, and earned some money as traders. In the cities, they established a variety of self-help associations, including those for prostitutes and for brewers of beer.

The colonial economy sometimes provided a measure of opportunity for enterprising women, particularly in small-scale trade and marketing. In some parts of West Africa, women came to dominate this sector of the economy by selling foodstuffs, cloth, and inexpensive imported goods, while men or foreign firms controlled the more profitable wholesale and import-export trade. Such opportunities sometimes gave women considerable economic autonomy. By the 1930s, for example, Nupe women in northern Nigeria had gained sufficient wealth as itinerant traders that they were contributing more to the family income than their husbands and frequently lent money to them. Among some Igbo groups in southern Nigeria, men were responsible for growing the prestigious yams, but women's crops—especially cassava—came to have a cash value during the colonial era, and women were entitled to keep the profits from selling them. "What is man? I have my own money" was a popular saying that expressed the growing economic independence of such women.[19]

At the other end of the social scale, women of impoverished rural families, by necessity, often became virtually independent heads of household in the absence of their husbands. Others took advantage of new opportunities in mission schools, towns, and mines to flee the restrictions of rural patriarchy. Such challenges to patriarchal values elicited various responses from men, including increased accusations of witchcraft against women and fears of impotence. Among the Shona in Southern Rhodesia, and no doubt elsewhere, senior African men repeatedly petitioned the colonial authorities for laws and regulations that would criminalize adultery and restrict women's ability to leave their rural villages. The control of women's sexuality and mobility was a common interest of European and African men.

Women and Peanut Production in Gambia In this photograph from the British colony of Gambia in West Africa, women are threshing peanuts, separating the nuts from the plants on which they grow. Throughout the colonial era, peanuts were the colony's major export crop, and women were heavily involved in their production. (Popperfoto/Getty Images)

Assessing Colonial Development

Beyond the many and varied changes that transformed the working lives of millions in the colonial world lies the difficult and highly controversial question of the overall economic impact of colonial rule on Asian and African societies. Defenders, both then and now, praise it for jump-starting modern economic growth, but numerous critics cite a record of exploitation and highlight the limitations and unevenness of that growth.

Amid the continuing debates, three things seem reasonably clear. First, colonial rule served, for better or worse, to further the integration of Asian and African economies into a global network of exchange, now centered in Europe. In many places, that process was well under way before conquest imposed foreign rule, and elsewhere it occurred without formal colonial control. Nonetheless, it is apparent that within the colonial world far more land and labor were devoted to production for the global market at the end of the colonial era than at its beginning. Many colonized groups and individuals benefited from their new access to global markets—Burmese rice farmers and West African cocoa farmers, for example. Others were devastated. In India, large-scale wheat exports to Britain continued unchecked—or even increased—despite a major drought and famine that claimed between 6 and 10 million lives in the late 1870s. A colonial government committed to free market principles declined to interfere with those exports or to provide much by way of relief. One senior official declared it "a mistake to spend so much money to save a lot of black fellows."[20]

Second, Europeans could hardly avoid conveying to the colonies some elements of their own modernizing process. It was in their interests to do so, and many felt duty bound to "improve" the societies they briefly governed. Modern administrative and bureaucratic structures facilitated colonial control; communication and transportation infrastructure (railroads, motorways, ports, telegraphs, postal services) moved products to the world market; schools trained the army of intermediaries on which colonial rule depended; and modest health care provisions fulfilled some of the "civilizing mission" to which many Europeans felt committed. These elements of modernization made an appearance, however inadequately, during the colonial era.

Third, nowhere in the colonial world did a major breakthrough to modern industrial society occur. When India became independent after two centuries of colonial rule by the world's first industrial society, it was still one of the poorest of the world's developing countries. The British may not have created Indian poverty, but neither did they overcome it to any substantial degree. Scholars continue to debate the reasons for that failure: was it the result of deliberate British policies, or was it due to the conditions of Indian society? The nationalist movements that surged across Asia and Africa in the twentieth century had their own answer. To their many millions of participants, colonial rule, whatever its earlier promise, had become an economic dead end, whereas independence represented a grand opening to new and more hopeful possibilities. Taking off from a famous teaching of

Guided Reading Question

■ **CHANGE**

Did colonial rule bring "economic progress" in its wake?

Jesus, Kwame Nkrumah, the first prime minister of an independent Ghana, declared, "Seek ye first the political kingdom,
and all these other things [schools, factories, hospitals, for
example] will be added unto you."

PRACTICING HISTORICAL THINKING

In what different ways did the colonial
experience reshape the economic lives of
Asian and African societies?

Believing and Belonging: Identity and Cultural Change

Beyond profound economic transformations, the experience of colonial rule—its
racism, its exposure to European culture, its social and economic upheavals—also
generated new patterns of identity within Asian, African, and Oceanic societies.
Millions of people underwent substantial and quite rapid changes in what they
believed and in how they defined the communities to which they belonged. Those
new ways of believing and belonging echoed long after European rule had ended.

Education

For an important minority, it was the acquisition of Western education, obtained
through missionary or government schools, that generated a new identity. To previously illiterate people, the knowledge of reading and writing of any kind often
suggested an almost magical power. Within the colonial setting, it could mean an
escape from some of the most onerous obligations of living under European control, such as forced labor. More positively, it meant access to better-paying positions
in government bureaucracies, mission organizations, or business firms and to the
exciting imported goods that their salaries could buy. Moreover, education often
provided social mobility and elite status within colonized peoples' own communities and an opportunity to achieve, or at least approach, equality with whites
in racially defined societies. An African man from colonial Kenya described an
encounter he had as a boy in 1938 with a relative who was a teacher in a mission
school:

> Aged about 25, he seems to me like a young god with his smart clothes and
> shoes, his watch, and a beautiful bicycle. I worshipped in particular his bicycle
> that day and decided that I must somehow get myself one. As he talked with
> us, it seemed to me that the secret of his riches came from his education, his
> knowledge of reading and writing, and that it was essential for me to obtain
> this power.[21]

Many such people ardently embraced European culture, dressing in European
clothes, speaking French or English, building European-style houses, getting married in long white dresses, and otherwise emulating European ways. Some of the
early Western-educated Bengalis from northeastern India boasted about dreaming in English and deliberately ate beef, to the consternation of their elders. In a

**Guided Reading
Question**
....
■ **CHANGE**
What impact did Western
education have on colo-
nial societies?

well-known poem titled "A Prayer for Peace," Léopold Senghor, a highly educated West African writer and political leader, enumerated the many crimes of colonialism and yet confessed, "I have a great weakness for France." Asian and African colonial societies now had a new cultural divide: between the small numbers who had mastered to varying degrees the ways of their rulers and the vast majority who had not. Literate Christians in the East African kingdom of Buganda referred with contempt to their "pagan" neighbors as "those who do not read."

Many among the Western-educated elite saw themselves as a modernizing vanguard, leading the regeneration of their societies in association with colonial authorities. For them, at least initially, the colonial enterprise was full of promise for a better future. The Vietnamese teacher and nationalist Nguyen Thai Hoc, while awaiting execution in 1930 by the French for his revolutionary activities, wrote about his earlier hopes: "At the beginning, I had thought to cooperate with the French in Indochina in order to serve my compatriots, my country, and my people, particularly in the areas of cultural and economic development."[22] Senghor too wrote wistfully about an earlier time when "we could have lived in harmony [with Europeans]."

In nineteenth-century India, Western-educated men organized a variety of reform societies that drew inspiration from the classic texts of Hinduism while seeking a renewed Indian culture that was free of idolatry, caste restrictions, and other "errors" that had entered Indian life over the centuries. Much of this reform effort centered on improving the status of women. Thus reformers campaigned against *sati*, the ban on remarriage of widows, female infanticide, and child marriages, while advocating women's education and property rights. For a time, some of these Indian reformers saw themselves working in tandem with British colonial authorities. One of them, Keshub Chunder Sen, addressed his fellow Indians in 1877: "You are bound to be loyal to the British government that came to your rescue, as God's ambassador, when your country was sunk in ignorance and superstition. . . . India in her present fallen condition seems destined to sit at the feet of England for many long years, to learn western art and science."[23]

Those who held such hopes for the modernization of their societies within a colonial framework would be bitterly disappointed. Europeans generally declined to treat their Asian and African subjects—even those with a Western education—as equal partners in the enterprise of renewal. The frequent denigration of Asian and African cultures as primitive, backward, uncivilized, or savage certainly rankled, particularly among the well educated. "My people of Africa," wrote the West African intellectual James Aggrey in the 1920s, "we were created in the image of God, but men have made us think that we are chickens, and we still think we are; but we are eagles. Stretch forth your wings and fly."[24] In the long run, the educated classes in colonial societies everywhere found European rule far more of an obstacle to their countries' development than a means of achieving it. Turning decisively against a now-despised foreign imperialism, they led the many struggles for independence that came to fruition in the second half of the twentieth century.

The Educated Elite Throughout the Afro-Asian world of the nineteenth century, the European presence generated a small group of people who enthusiastically embraced the culture and lifestyle of Europe. Here King Chulalongkorn of Siam poses with the crown prince and other young students, all of them impeccably garbed in European clothing. (Hulton Deutsch/Getty Images)

Religion

Religion too provided the basis for new or transformed identities during the colonial era. Most dramatic were those places where widespread conversion to Christianity took place, such as Pacific Oceania and especially non-Muslim Africa. Some 10,000 missionaries had descended on Africa by 1910; by the 1960s, about 50 million Africans, roughly half of the non-Muslim population, claimed a Christian identity. The attractions of the new faith were many. As in the Americas centuries earlier, military defeat shook confidence in the old gods and local practices, fostering openness to new sources of supernatural power that could operate in the wider world now impinging on Oceanic and African societies. Furthermore, Christianity was widely associated with modern education, and, especially in Africa, mission schools were the primary providers of Western education. The young, the poor, and many women—all of them oppressed groups in many African societies—found new opportunities and greater freedom in some association with missions. Moreover, the spread of the Christian message was less the work of European missionaries than of those many thousands of African teachers, catechists, and pastors who brought the new faith to remote villages as well as the local communities that begged for a teacher and supplied the labor and materials to build a small church or school. In Oceania, local authorities, such as those in Fiji, Tonga, and Hawaii, sought to strengthen their position by associating with Christian missionaries, widely regarded as linked to the growing influence of European or American power in the region. In many of these small island societies, mission Christianity with its schools, clinics, political counsel, and new social conventions provided a measure of social cohesion for peoples devastated by disease and other disruptions that accompanied Western incursions.

Guided Reading Question
....

■ **CHANGE**
What were the attractions of Christianity within some colonial societies?

But missionary teaching and practice also generated conflict and opposition, particularly when they touched on gender roles. A wide range of issues focusing on the lives of women proved challenging for missionaries and spawned opposition from converts or potential converts. Female nudity offended Western notions of modesty. Polygyny contradicted Christian monogamy, though such prescriptions sat uneasily beside the biblical testimony that Old Testament figures such as Abraham, Jacob, David, and Solomon all had multiple wives. And the question of what male converts should do with their additional wives was always difficult. To many missionaries, bride wealth made marriage seem "a mere mercantile transaction." Marriages between Christians and non-Christians remained problematic. Sexual activity outside of monogamous marriage often resulted in disciplinary action or expulsion from the church. Missionaries' efforts to enforce Western gender norms were in part responsible for considerable turnover in the ranks of African church members.

Among the more explosive issues that agitated nascent Christian communities in colonial Kenya was that of **female circumcision**, the excision of a pubescent girl's clitoris and adjacent genital tissue as a part of initiation rites marking her coming-of-age. To the Gikuyu people, among whom it was widely practiced, it was a prerequisite for adult status and marriage. To missionaries, it was physically damaging to girls and brought "unnecessary attention . . . to the non-spiritual aspects of sex."[25] When missionaries in 1929 sought to enforce a ban on the practice among their African converts, outrage ensued. Thousands abandoned mission schools and churches, but they did not abandon Christianity or modern education. Rather, they created a series of independent schools and churches in which they could practice their new faith and pursue their educational goals without missionary intrusion. Some recalled that the New Testament itself had declared that "circumcision is nothing and uncircumcision is nothing." Accordingly, wrote one angry convert to a local missionary, "Has God spoken to you this time and informed you that those who circumcise will not enter in to God's place? It is better for a European like you to leave off speaking about such things because you can make the Gospel to be evil spoken of."[26]

As elsewhere, Christianity in Africa soon adapted to local cultural patterns. This **Africanization of Christianity** took many forms. Within mission-based churches, many converts continued using protective charms and medicines and consulting local medicine men, all of which caused their missionary mentors to speak frequently of "backsliding." Other converts continued to believe in their old gods and spirits but now deemed them evil and sought their destruction. Furthermore, thousands of separatist movements established a wide array of independent churches that were thoroughly Christian but under African rather than missionary control and that in many cases incorporated African cultural practices and modes of worship. It was a twentieth-century "African Reformation."

In India, where Christianity made only very modest inroads, leading intellectuals and reformers began to define their region's endlessly varied beliefs, practices, sects, rituals, and philosophies as a more distinct, unified, and separate religion, now known as **Hinduism**. It was in part an effort to provide for India a religion wholly equivalent to Christianity, "an accessible tradition and a feeling of historical worth when faced with the humiliation of colonial rule."[27] To **Swami Vivekananda** (1863–1902), one of nineteenth-century India's most influential religious figures, as well as others active in reform movements, a revived Hinduism, shorn of its distortions, offered a means of uplifting the country's village communities, which were the heart of Indian civilization. It also served to distinguish a "spiritual East" from a "materialistic West." (See Zooming In: Vivekananda, a Hindu Monk in America, page 810.)

The Missionary Factor Among the major change agents of the colonial era were the thousands of Christian missionaries who brought not only a new religion but also elements of European medicine, education, gender roles, and culture. Here is an assembly at a mission school for girls in New Guinea in the early twentieth century. (Library of Congress, Prints and Photographs Division, LC-USZ62 46884)

This new notion of Hinduism provided a cultural foundation for emerging ideas of India as a nation, but it also contributed to a clearer sense of Muslims as a distinct community in India. Before the British takeover, little sense of commonality united the many diverse communities who practiced Islam—urban and rural dwellers; nomads and farmers; artisans, merchants, and state officials. But the British had created one set of inheritance laws for all Muslims and another set for all Hindus; in their census taking, they counted the numbers of people within these now sharply distinguished groups; and they allotted seats in local councils according to these artificial categories. As some anti-British patriots began to cast India in Hindu terms, the idea of Muslims as a separate community that was perhaps threatened by the much

Guided Reading Question

■ **CHANGE**
How and why did Hinduism emerge as a distinct religious tradition during the colonial era in India?

Vivekananda, a Hindu Monk in America

The modern colonial era is associated with the "westernization" of the peoples of Asia, Africa, and the Middle East. Less frequently noticed has been traffic in the other direction, as Eastern, and especially Indian, religious culture penetrated Europe and the Americas. At his cabin on Walden Pond in the mid-1840s, Henry David Thoreau remarked, "In the morning I bathe my intellect in the stupendous . . . philosophy of the Bhagavad Gita . . . in comparison with which our modern world and its literature seem puny and trivial."[28]

A more seminal moment in the coming of Indian spirituality to the United States occurred in Chicago during September 1893. The occasion was the World's Parliament of Religions, an interfaith gathering that drew representatives from many of the world's religious traditions. The man who made the most vivid impression at the conference was a handsome

Swami Vivekananda.

thirty-year-old Hindu monk known as Swami Vivekananda. Appearing in an orange robe and a yellow turban and speaking fluent and eloquent English, he had only recently arrived from India, where he had received an excellent European education as well as a deep immersion in Hindu philosophy and practice.

In his initial speech to the parliament on its opening day, Vivekananda declared, "I am proud to belong to a religion which has taught the world both tolerance and universal acceptance. . . . We accept all religions as true." He concluded with a plea that the parliament might mark the end of sectarianism, fanaticism, and persecution "between persons wending their way to the same goal."

In further speeches at the parliament and in subsequent travels around

photo: Roland and Sabrina Michaud/akg-images

larger number of Hindus began to make sense to some who practiced Islam. In the early twentieth century, a young Hindu Bengali schoolboy noticed that "our Muslim school-fellows were beginning to air the fact of their being Muslims rather more consciously than before and with a touch of assertiveness."[29] Here were the beginnings of what became in the twentieth century a profound religious and political division within the South Asian peninsula.

"Race" and "Tribe"

In Africa as well, intellectuals and ordinary people alike forged new ways of belonging as they confronted the upheavals of colonial life. Central to these new identities were notions of race and ethnicity. By the end of the nineteenth century, a number of African thinkers, familiar with Western culture, began to define the idea of an **"African identity."** Previously, few if any people on the continent had regarded themselves as Africans. Rather, they were members of particular local communities, usually defined by language; some were also Muslims; and still others inhabited the country, Vivekananda expressed the major themes of his modernized Hindu outlook: that all human beings possess a divine nature; that awakening to that nature can be pursued through a variety of paths; and that spiritual practice and realization are far more important than dogma or doctrine. He argued that the disciplines of the mind and body that derived from Hindu tradition represented a psychological, experimental, and almost scientific approach to spiritual development and certainly did not require "conversion" to an alien faith. On occasion, he was sharply critical of Christian missionaries for their emphasis on conversion. "The people of India have more than religion enough," he declared. "What they want is bread." He described England as "the most prosperous Christian nation in the world with her foot on the neck of 250 million Asiatics."

Vivekananda emerged from the parliament a sensation and a celebrity, widely acclaimed but also widely criticized. His critique of Christian missionaries offended many. More conservative Christians objected to his assertion of the equality of all religious traditions. "We believe that Christianity is to supplant all other religions," declared the leading organizer of the parliament.

Vivekananda's time in the United States represented India speaking back to the West. After a century of European missionary activity and colonial rule in his country, he was declaring that India could offer spiritual support to a Western world mired in materialism and militarism. He proclaimed, "The whole of the Western world is a volcano which may burst tomorrow. . . . Now is the time to work so that India's spiritual ideas may penetrate deep into the West."[30]

In exposing Americans to Indian spirituality, Vivekananda's followers did not seek converts, but invited participants to apply Hindu principles and practices within their own religious traditions. They also spoke about Jesus with great respect and displayed his image along with that of the Buddha and various Hindu sacred figures. In the early twentieth century, these ideas attracted a modest following among Americans who were disillusioned with the superficiality of modern life as well as with the rigidity of Christian doctrine and the many divisions and conflicts among Christian churches. In the 1960s and later, interest in Eastern religion exploded in the West as hundreds of Indian teachers arrived, many of them bearing the same universal message that Vivekananda had presented in Chicago. The growing numbers of Americans who claim to be "spiritual but not religious" are following in the path of that orange-robed monk.

QUESTION

What accounts for the appeal of Vivekananda's message, and what accounts for opposition to it?

some state or empire. Now, however, influenced by the common experience of colonial oppression and by a highly derogatory European racism, well-educated Africans began to think in broader terms, similar to those of Indian reformers who were developing the notion of Hinduism. It was an effort to revive the cultural self-confidence of their people by articulating a larger, common, and respected "African tradition," equivalent to that of Western culture.

This effort took various shapes. One line of argument held that African culture and history in fact possessed the very characteristics that Europeans exalted. Knowing that Europeans valued large empires and complex political systems, African intellectuals pointed with pride to the ancient kingdoms of Axum/Ethiopia, Mali, Songhay, and others. C. A. Diop, a French-educated scholar from Senegal, insisted that Egyptian civilization was in fact the work of black Africans. Reversing European assumptions, Diop argued that Western civilization owed much to Egyptian influence and was therefore derived from Africa. Black people, in short, had a history of achievement fully comparable to that of Europe and therefore deserved just as much respect and admiration.

Guided Reading Question

■ **CHANGE**
In what ways were "race" and "tribe" new identities in colonial Africa?

An alternative approach to defining an African identity lay in praising the differences between African and European cultures. The most influential proponent of such views was **Edward Blyden** (1832–1912), a West African born in the West Indies and educated in the United States who later became a prominent scholar and political official in Liberia. Blyden accepted the assumption that the world's various races were different but argued that each had its own distinctive contribution to make to world civilization. The uniqueness of African culture, Blyden wrote, lay in its communal, cooperative, and egalitarian societies, which contrasted sharply with Europe's highly individualistic, competitive, and class-ridden societies; in its harmonious relationship with nature as opposed to Europe's efforts to dominate and exploit the natural order; and particularly in its profound religious sensibility, which Europeans had lost in centuries of attention to material gain. Like Vivekananda in India, Blyden argued that Africa had a global mission "to be the spiritual conservatory of the world."[31]

In the twentieth century, such ideas resonated with a broader public. Hundreds of thousands of Africans took part in World War I, during which they encountered other Africans as well as Europeans. Some were able to travel widely. Contact with American black leaders, such as Booker T. Washington, W. E. B. DuBois, and Marcus Garvey, as well as various West Indian intellectuals further stimulated among a few a sense of belonging to an even larger pan-African world. Such notions underlay the growing nationalist movements that contested colonial rule as the twentieth century unfolded.

For the vast majority, however, the most important new sense of belonging that evolved from the colonial experience was not the notion of "Africa"; rather, it was the **idea of "tribe"** or, in the language of contemporary scholars, that of ethnic identity. African peoples, of course, had long recognized differences among themselves based on language, kinship, clan, village, or state, but these were seldom clearly defined. Boundaries fluctuated and were hazy; local communities often incorporated a variety of culturally different peoples. The idea of an Africa sharply divided into separate and distinct "tribes" was in fact a European notion that facilitated colonial administration and reflected Europeans' belief in African primitiveness. For example, when the British began to rule the peoples living along the northern side of Lake Tanganyika, in present-day Tanzania, they found a series of communities that were similar to one another in language and customs but that governed themselves separately and certainly had not regarded themselves as a distinct "tribe." It was British attempts to rule them as a single people, first through a "paramount chief" and later through a council of chiefs and elders, that resulted in their being called, collectively, the Nyakyusa. A tribe had been born. By requiring people to identify their tribe on applications for jobs, schools, and identity cards, colonial governments spread the idea of tribe widely within their colonies.

New ethnic identities were not simply imposed by Europeans, for Africans themselves increasingly found ethnic or tribal labels useful. This was especially true in rapidly growing urban areas. Surrounded by a bewildering variety of people and in a setting where competition for jobs, housing, and education was very intense, migrants to the city found it helpful to categorize themselves and others in larger ethnic terms. Thus, in many colonial cities, people who spoke similar languages, shared a common culture, or came from the same general part of the country began to think of themselves as a single people—a new tribe. They organized a rich variety of ethnic or tribal associations to provide mutual assistance while in the cities and to send money back home to build schools or clinics. Migrant workers, far from home and concerned about protecting their rights to land and to their wives and families, found a sense of security in being part of a recognized tribe, with its chiefs, courts, and established authority.

The Igbo people of southeastern Nigeria represent a case in point. Prior to the twentieth century, they were organized in a series of independently governed village groups. Although they spoke related languages, they had no unifying political system and no myth of common ancestry. Occupying a region of unusually dense population, many of these people eagerly seized on Western education and moved in large numbers to the cities and towns of colonial Nigeria. There they gradually discovered what they had in common and how they differed from the other peoples of Nigeria. By the 1940s, they were organizing on a national level and calling on Igbos everywhere to "sink all differences" to achieve "tribal unity, cooperation, and progress of all the Igbos." Fifty years earlier, however, no one had regarded himself or herself as an Igbo. One historian summed up the process of creating African ethnic identities in this way: "Europeans believed Africans belonged to tribes; Africans built tribes to belong to."[32]

REFLECTIONS

Who Makes History?

Winners may write history, but they do not make history, at least not alone. Dominant groups everywhere—slave owners, upper classes, men generally, and certainly colonial rulers—have found their actions constrained and their choices limited by the sheer presence of subordinated people and the ability of those people to act. Europeans who sought to make their countries self-sufficient in cotton by requiring colonized Africans to grow it generally found themselves unable to achieve that goal. Missionaries who tried to impose their own understanding of Christianity in the colonies found their converts often unwilling to accept missionary authority or the cultural framework in which the new religion was presented. In the twentieth century, colonial rulers all across Asia and Africa found that their most highly educated subjects became the leaders of those movements seeking to end colonial rule. Clearly, this was not what they had intended.

In recent decades, historians have been at pains to uncover the ways in which subordinated people—slaves, workers, peasants, women, the colonized—have been able to act in their own interests, even within the most oppressive conditions. Historians of women's lives, for example, have sought to show women not only as victims of patriarchy but also as historical actors in their own right. Likewise, colonized people in any number of ways actively shaped the history of the colonial era. On occasion, they resisted and rebelled; in various times and places, they embraced, rejected, and transformed a transplanted Christianity; many eagerly sought Western education but later turned it against the colonizers; women both suffered from and creatively coped with the difficulties of colonial life; and everywhere people created new ways of belonging. None of this diminishes the hardships, the enormous inequalities of power, or the exploitation and oppression of the colonial experience. Rather, it suggests that history is often made through the struggle of unequal groups and that the outcome corresponds to no one's intentions.

Perhaps we might let Karl Marx have the last word on this endlessly fascinating topic: "Men make their own history," he wrote, "but they do not make it as they please nor under conditions of their own choosing." In the colonial experience of the nineteenth and early twentieth centuries, both the colonizers and the colonized "made history," but neither was able to do so as they pleased.

Second Thoughts

What's the Significance?

scientific racism, 785
civilizing mission, 786
social Darwinism, 786
scramble for Africa, 788
Indian Rebellion of 1857–1858, 792
Congo Free State, 796
cultivation system, 797
cash-crop production, 798
female circumcision, 808
Africanization of Christianity, 808
Hinduism, 809
Swami Vivekananda, 809
African identity, 810
Edward Blyden, 812
idea of "tribe," 812

Big Picture Questions

1. In what ways did colonial rule rest on violence and coercion, and in what ways did it elicit voluntary cooperation or generate benefits for some people?

2. In what respects were colonized people more than victims of colonial conquest and rule? To what extent could they act in their own interests within the colonial situation?

3. Was colonial rule a transforming, even a revolutionary, experience, or did it freeze or preserve existing social and economic patterns? What evidence can you find to support both sides of this argument?

4. **Looking Back:** How would you compare the colonial experience of Asian and African peoples during the long nineteenth century to the earlier colonial experience in the Americas?

Next Steps: For Further Study

A. Adu Boahen, *African Perspectives on Colonialism* (1987). An examination of the colonial experience by a prominent African scholar.

Adam Hochschild, *King Leopold's Ghost* (1999). A journalist's evocative account of the horrors of early colonial rule in the Congo.

Douglas Peers, *India under Colonial Rule* (2006). A concise and up-to-date exploration of colonial India.

Bonnie Smith, ed., *Imperialism* (2000). A fine collection of documents, pictures, and commentary on nineteenth- and twentieth-century empires.

Heather Streets-Salter and Trevor R. Getz, *Empires and Colonies in the Modern World: A Global Perspective* (2016). A highly readable survey of empires and colonies from the early modern period to the twenty-first century.

Margaret Strobel, *Gender, Sex, and Empire* (1994). A brief account of late twentieth-century historical thinking about colonial life and gender.

"Colonial Identities," Annenberg Learner, Bridging World History, Unit 21, http://www.learner.org/courses/worldhistory/unit_main_21.html. Provides text, primary and secondary sources, images, and videos to explore the question of identity during the colonial era via clothing.

Saul David, "Slavery and the 'Scramble for Africa,'" BBC History, http://www.bbc.co.uk/history/british/abolition/scramble_for_africa_article_01.shtml. An examination of how abolitionism and the end of slavery in the nineteenth century shaped British interests in the colonization of Africa.

Colonial Conquest: The Scramble for Africa

The centerpiece of Europe's global expansion during the nineteenth century occurred in the so-called scramble for Africa, during which a half dozen or so European countries divided up almost the entire continent into colonial territories (see Map 18.2, page 790). The "scramble" took place very quickly (between roughly 1875 and 1900), surprising even the European leaders who initiated it, as well as the many African societies that suddenly found themselves confronting highly aggressive and well-armed foreign forces. It is remarkable that the entire partition of Africa took place without any direct military conflict between the competing imperial countries. But in establishing their control on the ground, Europeans faced widespread African resistance, making the scramble an extremely bloody process of military conquest. The sources that follow illustrate some of the distinctive features of the scramble for Africa as well as the differing ways in which it was perceived and represented.

SOURCE 18.1 Competition and Conquest ▶

As the scramble for Africa got under way in earnest in the 1880s and 1890s, it became a highly competitive process. French designs on Africa, for example, focused on obtaining an uninterrupted east-west link from the Red Sea to the Atlantic Ocean. But the British, entrenched in Egypt and in control of the Suez Canal, were determined that no major European power should be allowed to control the headwaters of the Nile on which Egypt depended. Those conflicting goals came to a head in 1898, when British forces moving south from Egypt met a French expedition moving northeast from the Atlantic coast of what is now Gabon. That encounter took place along the Nile River at Fashoda in present-day Sudan, threatening war between France and Great Britain. In the end, negotiations persuaded the French to withdraw.

Source 18.1, the cover of a French publication, shows the commander of the French expedition, Jean-Baptiste Marchand, who gained heroic stature by leading his troops on an epic journey across much of Africa for more than eighteen months.

■ How did the artist portray Marchand? How might a British artist have portrayed him?

■ What does this source suggest about the role of violence in the scramble for Africa?

■ Notice the large number of African troops among Marchand's forces. What does that suggest about the process of colonial conquest? Why might Africans have agreed to fight on behalf of a European colonial power?

■ How do you understand the fallen soldier lying between Marchand's legs?

CHARLES TICHON | *Commandant Marchand across Africa* | 1900

SOURCE 18.2 "Pacification" in East Africa

In European eyes, conquest was frequently termed "pacification," with the goal of ending all active resistance to colonial authorities. For African communities, it often meant devastating violence. Source 18.2 provides a vivid example of what the scramble for Africa meant at the level of a single village. It comes from the diary of a young British soldier who took part in the takeover of what is now Kenya.

- What posture did this soldier take toward this military action?

- How might this experience be described from the viewpoint of one of the surviving young women?

- How does the violence depicted in this account differ from that shown in Source 18.1?

RICHARD MEINERTZHAGEN | *A Small Slaughter* | 1902

I have performed a most unpleasant duty today. I made a night march to the village at the edge of the forest where the white settler had been so brutally murdered the day before yesterday. Though the war drums were sounding throughout the night, we reached the village without incident and surrounded it. By the light of the fires, we could see savages dancing in the village, and our guides assured me that they were dancing around the mutilated body of the white man.

I gave orders that every living thing except children should be killed without mercy. I hated the work and was anxious to get through with it.

So soon as we could see to shoot we closed in. Several of the men tried to break out but were immediately shot. I then assaulted the place before any defense could be prepared. Every soul was either shot or bayoneted, and I am happy to say that there were no children in the village. They, together with the younger women, had already been removed by the villagers to the forest. We burned all the huts and razed the banana plantations to the ground.

Source: R. Meinertzhagen, *Kenya Diary* (London: Oliver and Boyd, 1957), 51–52.

∎ ∎ ∎

SOURCE 18.3 From Cape to Cairo ▶

Nowhere did the vaulting ambition of European colonial powers in Africa emerge more clearly than in the British vision of a north-south corridor of British territories along the eastern side of the continent stretching from South Africa to Egypt, or in the popular phrase of the time, "from the Cape to Cairo." A part of this vision was an unbroken railroad line running the entire length of the African continent. That grand idea was popularized by Cecil Rhodes, a British-born businessman and politician who made a fortune in South African diamonds and became an enthusiastic advocate of British imperialism. Source 18.3, an 1892 cartoon published in the popular British magazine of satire and humor named *Punch*, shows Rhodes bestriding the continent with one foot in Egypt and the other in South Africa.

- Is this famous image criticizing or celebrating Rhodes's Cape-to-Cairo dream? Explain your reasoning.

- What does this source suggest about the purpose of the Cape-to-Cairo scheme and the means to achieve it?

- How did the artist portray the African continent? What does the absence of African people suggest?

The Rhodes Colossus | 1892

THE RHODES COLOSSUS
STRIDING FROM CAPE TOWN TO CAIRO.

■ ■ ■

SOURCE 18.4 Ethiopia and the Scramble for Africa

The East African state of Ethiopia played an intriguing role during the scramble, for alone in all of Africa, it successfully resisted incorporation into a European empire. But Ethiopia also participated in the scramble, almost doubling the size of the country at the expense of neighboring peoples. Source 18.4A presents a letter written in 1891 from the Ethiopian emperor Menelik II to the great powers of Europe announcing his outlook and intentions as the scramble for Africa picked up speed. This warning, however, did not prevent the Italians from claiming a protectorate over Ethiopia, an action that led to war. Source 18.4B records Menelik's call to arms in 1895 as that war unfolded. The famous Battle of Adowa, which followed in 1896, marked a decisive victory for Ethiopia over the Italians. Ethiopia had preserved its independence, becoming a symbol of African resistance and bravery. The people forcibly incorporated into a growing Ethiopian empire, no doubt, saw things differently.

■ How would you summarize Menelik's goals as expressed in Source 18.4A?

■ How does Menelik try to distinguish his kingdom from others in Africa? In what ways does he try to appeal to European sensibilities?

■ On what basis does Menelik appeal to his people to mobilize against the Italians in Source 18.4B?

SOURCE 18.4A
MENELIK II | *Letter to the European Great Powers* | 1891

Being desirous to make known to our friends the Powers (Sovereigns) of Europe the boundaries of Ethiopia, we have addressed also to you (your Majesty) the present letter.

These are the boundaries of Ethiopia: [Then follows a detailed description of Ethiopia's boundaries.]

While tracing today the actual boundaries of my Empire, I shall endeavour, if God gives me life and strength, to re-establish the ancient frontiers (tributaries) of Ethiopia up to Khartoum, and as far as Lake Nyanza with all the Gallas.

Ethiopia has been for fourteen centuries a Christian island in a sea of pagans. If powers at a distance come forward to partition Africa between them, I do not intend to be an indifferent spectator.

As the Almighty has protected Ethiopia up to this day, I have confidence He will continue to protect her, and increase her borders in the future. I am certain He will not suffer her to be divided among other Powers.

Formerly the boundary of Ethiopia was the sea. Having lacked strength sufficient, and having received no help from Christian Powers, our frontier on the sea coast fell into the power of the Muslim-man [Muslims].

At present we do not intend to regain our sea frontier by force, but we trust that the Christian Powers, guided by our Saviour, will restore to us our sea-coast line, at any rate, certain points on the coast.

Source: Mohamed Osman Omar, *The Scramble in the Horn of Africa* (New Delhi: Somali Publications, 2001), 143.

SOURCE 18.4B
MENELIK II │ *Mobilization Proclamation* │ 1895

Enemies have now come upon us to ruin our country and to change our religion. Our enemies have begun the affair by advancing and digging into our country like moles. With the help of God, I will not deliver my country to them. Today, you who are strong, give me your strength, and you who are weak, help me by prayer. Men of my country, up to now I believe I have never wronged you and you have never caused me sorrow. If you refuse to follow me, beware. You will hate me, for I shall not fail to punish you. I swear in the name of Mary that I shall never accept any plea of pardon. . . . Meet me at Were Illu [the place of assembly for Menelik's forces], and may you be there by the middle of [October]. So says Menelik, elect of God, king of kings.

Source: Quoted in Rick Duncan, *Man, Know Thyself* (Bloomington, IN: XLibris, 2013), 1:330.

■ ■ ■

SOURCE 18.5 Empire Building in North Africa ▶

In North Africa, the primary European rivalries for territory involved Great Britain, which occupied Egypt in 1881; France, which came to control Tunisia, Algeria, and Morocco; and Italy, which seized Libya in 1912. Source 18.5 portrays two of these rivals—Britain, on the right, and France, on the left—toasting one another while standing on piles of skeletons. This image appeared in the Cairo *Punch*, a British-owned magazine in Egypt published in Arabic, probably around 1910.

This image refers specifically to two incidents. On the British side, the cartoon evokes a 1906 quarrel between British soldiers hunting pigeons and local villagers of Denshway that resulted in the death of one of the soldiers. In response, outraged British authorities hanged several people and flogged dozens of others. The following year in Morocco, French civilians building a small railway near the harbor of Casablanca dug up parts of a Muslim cemetery, "churning up piles of bones." When attacks against European laborers followed, killing eight, the French bombarded the Arab quarter of the city, with many casualties—European and Arab alike—in the fighting that ensued. Both incidents stimulated nationalist feelings in these two North African countries.

■ What references to the incidents described here can you find in Source 18.5?

■ The British and French generally saw themselves as rivals in the scramble for Africa. How are they portrayed here?

■ What posture toward colonial rule does this image reflect? While the artist remains unknown, do you think it more likely to have been an Egyptian or a European?

British and French in North Africa | ca. 1910

• • •

SOURCE 18.6 **An African American Voice on the Scramble for Africa**

Writing in 1915, shortly after the outbreak of World War I, the African American scholar and activist W. E. B. DuBois reflected on the scramble for Africa, arguing that it was a leading cause of the war.

- How does DuBois characterize the process of the scramble?

- With which of the earlier sources does the tone of his essay most clearly resonate?

- What connection does DuBois see between the partition of Africa and World War I?

W. E. B. DuBOIS │ *The African Roots of War* │ 1915

Africa is a prime cause of this terrible overturning of civilization [World War I]....

The Berlin Conference to apportion the rising riches of Africa among the white peoples met on the fifteenth day of November, 1884 ... and before the Berlin Conference had finished its deliberations, [Germany] had annexed ... an area over half as large again as the whole German Empire in Europe. Only in its dramatic suddenness was this undisguised robbery of the land of seven million natives different from the methods by which Great Britain and France got four million square miles each, Portugal three quarters of a million, and Italy and Spain got smaller but substantial areas.

The methods by which this continent has been stolen have been contemptible and dishonest beyond expression. Lying treaties, rivers of rum, murder, assassination, mutilation, rape, and torture have marked the progress of Englishman, German, Frenchman, and Belgian on the dark continent....

The present world war is, then, the result of jealousies engendered by the recent rise of armed [nations] ... whose aim is the exploitation of the wealth of the world mainly outside the European circle of nations ..., and particularly in Africa....

[I]n the minds of yellow, brown, and black men the brutal truth is clearing: a white man is privileged to go to any land where advantage beckons and behave as he pleases; the black or colored man is being more and more confined to those parts of the world where life for climatic, historical, economic, and political reasons is most difficult to live and most easily dominated by Europe for Europe's gain.

Source: W. E. B. DuBois, "The African Roots of War," *Atlantic Monthly* (May 1915), 707–8, 712.

DOING HISTORY

1. **Distinguishing viewpoints:** From what different perspectives do these sources represent the scramble for Africa? What criticisms of the scramble can you read in them?

2. **Portraying Africans and Europeans:** In what different ways are Europeans and Africans portrayed in these sources?

3. **Considering motives:** Scholars have sometimes argued that the scramble for Africa was driven less by concrete economic interests than by emotional, even romantic, notions of national grandeur and personal adventure. In what ways do these sources support or challenge this interpretation?

4. **Considering moral visions:** How do these sources deal with issues of morality or visions of right and wrong?

The Invasion of Africa

Two major issues have informed historians' inquiry about the scramble for Africa—the motives of the Europeans and the responses of Africans. Voice 18.1 deals with the first of these issues. It comes from British historian Thomas Pakenham's award-winning history of the scramble. In Voice 18.2 the West African scholar A. Adu Boahen, a pioneer in the field of African history, addresses the second problem.

- What range of European motivations underlay the scramble for Africa according to Voice 18.1?

- How does Boahen in Voice 18.2 classify African responses to the European intrusion, and why does he believe Africans were unable to maintain their independence?

- **Integrating Primary and Secondary Sources:** How might Pakenham (Voice 18.1) use Sources 18.1 and 18.3 to substantiate his argument? In which of his three categories of African response to the scramble might Boahen place Menelik in Source 18.4?

VOICE 18.1

Thomas Pakenham on European Motivations | 1992

Why this undignified rush by the leaders of Europe to build empires in Africa? . . . [T]hey all conceived the crusade in terms of romantic nationalism. To imperialism—a kind of race nationalism—they brought a missionary zeal. Not only would they save Africa from itself. Africa would be the saving of their own countries.

At first, European governments were reluctant to intervene. But to most people in their electorates, there seemed a real chance of missing something. . . . There were dreams of El Dorado, of diamond mines and goldfields crisscrossing the Sahara. There might be new markets out there in this African Garden of Eden and tropical groves where golden fruit could be plucked by willing brown hands. . . .

[O]verseas empire would sooth the *amour proper* [self-esteem] of the French army, humiliated by its collapse in the Franco-Prussian war. And it would no less bolster the pride of the political *parvenus* [newcomers] of Europe [recently united Germany and Italy] . . . and what about a place in the sun for emigrants? . . .

In Britain . . . there was growing resentment toward the intruders. . . . Britain had pioneered the exploration and evangelization of Central Africa and she felt a proprietary right to most of the continent. . . . As the only great maritime empire, she needed to prevent her rivals obstructing the steamer routes to the East, via Suez and the Cape.

Source: Thomas Pakenham, *The Scramble for Africa* (New York: Avon Books, 1992), xxi–xxiii.

VOICE 18.2

A. Adu Boahen on African Strategies | 1987

Africans devised three main strategies [for responding to the scramble]. . . . [First] some African rulers readily submitted to the European invaders . . . either because they became aware of the futility and cost of confronting the imperialists or . . . because they themselves urgently needed European protection.

The second main strategy adopted . . . was that of alliance. . . . These African rulers sought to achieve the very sovereignty of their state, and what they saw themselves doing was not collaborating but rather allying with the incoming invaders to achieve this national end.

The third strategy . . . was confrontation . . . and an overwhelming majority of the Africans adopted the military option. [Boahen then discusses why this option failed.] Most of these African armies were non-professional and not properly trained. . . . African armies were, in many cases, numerically inferior to European armies. . . . Most of the armies of the European imperialists consisted of African soldiers. . . . Above all, technologically and logistically, African armies were at a great disadvantage.

[And] no African state was strong enough economically to have sustained any protracted warfare. . . . Most African rulers failed to form . . . alliances [among themselves]. Not only did this weaken them militarily, but it also enabled European imperialists to play one African power against the other. . . . It was above all . . . because the Europeans had the maxim gun and the Africans did not that an overwhelming number of African states lost their independence.

Source: A. Adu Boahen, *African Perspectives on Colonialism* (Baltimore, MD: Johns Hopkins University Press, 1987), 39–57.

From "Le Petit Journal," 1898, lithograph by Henri Meyer (1844–1899)/Private Collection/Roger-Viollet, Paris, France/Bridgeman Images

CHAPTER
19

Empires in Collision

Europe, the Middle East, and East Asia

1800–1900

"Several centuries ago, China was strong. . . . In over 100 years after the 1840 Opium War, China suffered immensely from aggression, wars and chaos."[1] Speaking in early 2017, Chinese president Xi Jinping thus reminded his listeners of Britain's nineteenth-century violent intrusion into China's history bearing shiploads of highly addictive opium. This conflict marked the beginning of what the Chinese still describe as a "century of humiliation." In official Chinese thinking, it was only the victory of the Chinese Communist Party that enabled China to finally escape from that shameful past. Memories of the Opium War remain a central element of China's "patriotic education" for the young, serving as a warning against uncritical admiration of the West and providing a rejoinder to any Western criticism of China. Almost 180 years after that clash between the Chinese and British empires, the Opium War retains an emotional resonance for many Chinese and offers a politically useful tool for the country's government. ■

C hina was among the countries that confronted an aggressive and industrializing West while maintaining its formal independence, unlike the colonized areas discussed in Chapter 18. So too did Japan, the Ottoman Empire, Persia (now Iran), Ethiopia, and Siam (now Thailand). Latin America also falls in this category (see "The Industrial Revolution and Latin America in the Nineteenth Century" in Chapter 17). These states avoided outright incorporation into European colonial empires, retaining some ability to resist European aggression and to reform or transform

« **Carving Up the Pie of China** In this French cartoon from the late 1890s, the Great Powers of the day (from left to right: Great Britain's Queen Victoria, Germany's Kaiser Wilhelm, Russia's Tsar Nicholas II, a female figure representing France, and the Meiji emperor of Japan) participate in dividing China, while a Chinese figure behind them tries helplessly to stop the partition of his country.

their own societies. But they shared with their colonized counterparts the need to deal with four dimensions of the European moment in world history. First, they faced the immense military might and political ambitions of the major imperial powers. Second, they became enmeshed in networks of trade, investment, and sometimes migration that arose from an industrializing and capitalist Europe to generate a new world economy. Third, they were touched by various aspects of traditional European culture, as some among them learned the French, English, or German language; converted to Christianity; or studied European literature and philosophy. Fourth, they too engaged with the culture of modernity—its scientific rationalism; its technological achievements; its belief in a better future; and its ideas of nationalism, socialism, feminism, and individualism. In those epic encounters, they sometimes resisted, at other times accommodated, and almost always adapted what came from the West. They were active participants in the global drama of nineteenth-century world history, not simply its passive victims or beneficiaries.

At the same time, these societies were dealing with their own internal issues. Population growth and peasant rebellion wracked China; internal social and economic changes eroded the stability of Japanese public life; the great empires of the Islamic world shrank or disappeared; rivalry among competing elites troubled Latin American societies. China, the Ottoman Empire, and Japan provide a range of experiences, responses, and outcomes and many opportunities for comparison, as they navigated this era of colliding empires.

SEEKING THE MAIN POINT

What differences can you identify in how China, the Ottoman Empire, and Japan experienced Western imperialism and responded to it? How might you account for those differences?

Reversal of Fortune: China's Century of Crisis

In 1793, just a decade after King George III of Britain lost his North American colonies, he received yet another rebuff, this time from China. In a famous letter to the British monarch, the Chinese emperor Qianlong (chyan-loong) sharply rejected British requests for a less restricted trading relationship with his country. "Our Celestial Empire possesses all things in prolific abundance," he declared. "There was therefore no need to import the manufactures of outside barbarians." Qianlong's snub simply continued the pattern of the previous several centuries, during which Chinese authorities had strictly controlled and limited the activities of European missionaries and merchants. But by 1912, little more than a century later, China's long-established imperial state had collapsed, and the country had been transformed from a central presence in the global economy to a weak and dependent participant in a European-dominated world system in which Great Britain was the major economic and political player. It was a stunning reversal of fortune for a country that in Chinese eyes was the civilized center of the entire world—in their terms, the Celestial Empire or the Middle Kingdom.

Landmarks for Chapter 19

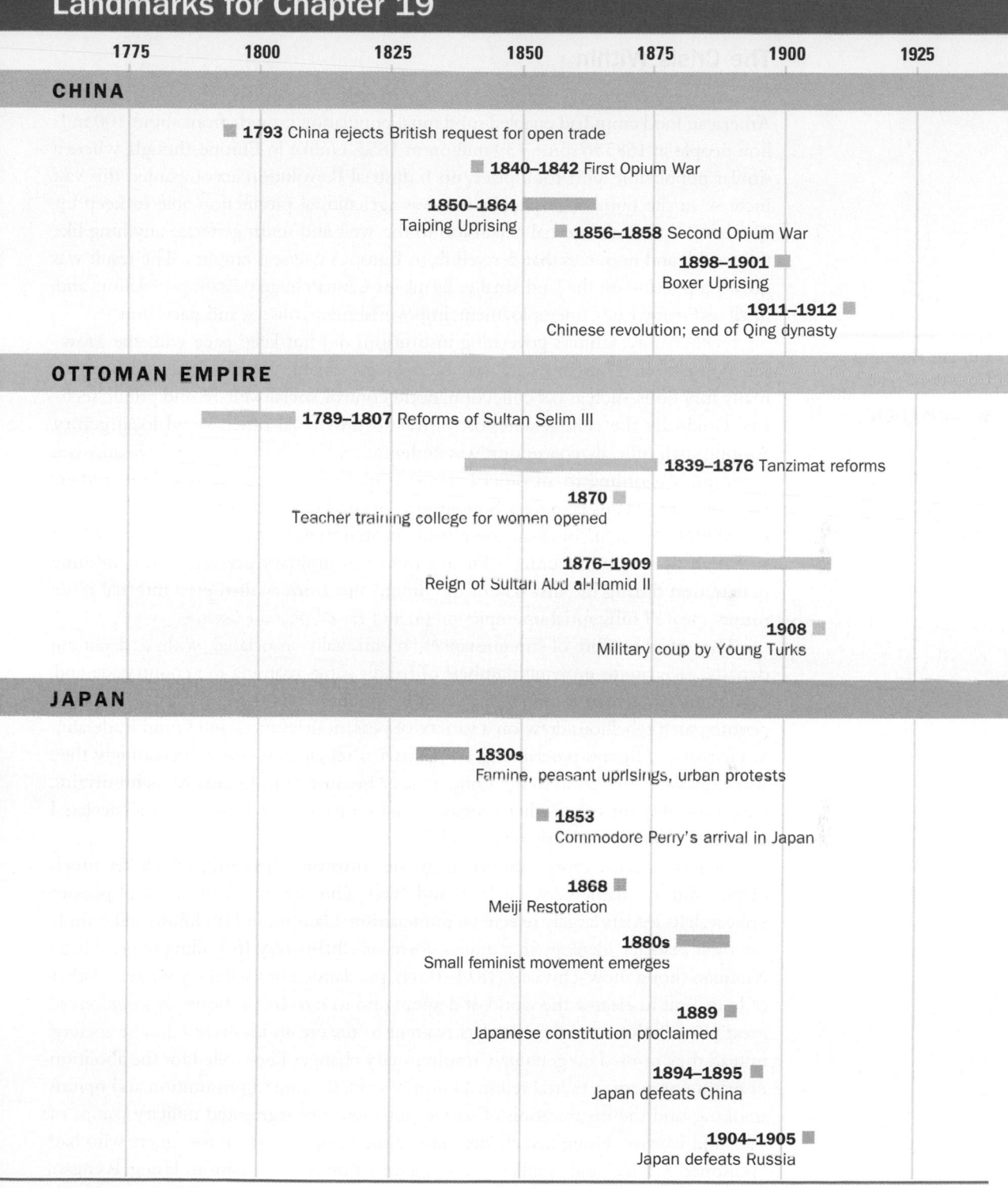

| | 1775 | 1800 | 1825 | 1850 | 1875 | 1900 | 1925 |

CHINA

1793 China rejects British request for open trade

1840–1842 First Opium War

1850–1864
Taiping Uprising

1856–1858 Second Opium War

1898–1901
Boxer Uprising

1911–1912
Chinese revolution; end of Qing dynasty

OTTOMAN EMPIRE

1789–1807 Reforms of Sultan Selim III

1839–1876 Tanzimat reforms

1870
Teacher training college for women opened

1876–1909
Reign of Sultan Abd al-Hamid II

1908
Military coup by Young Turks

JAPAN

1830s
Famine, peasant uprisings, urban protests

1853
Commodore Perry's arrival in Japan

1868
Meiji Restoration

1880s
Small feminist movement emerges

1889
Japanese constitution proclaimed

1894–1895
Japan defeats China

1904–1905
Japan defeats Russia

The Crisis Within

In some ways, China was the victim of its own earlier success. Its robust economy and American food crops had enabled substantial population growth, from about 100 million people in 1685 to some 430 million in 1853. Unlike in Europe, though, where a similar population spurt took place, no Industrial Revolution accompanied this vast increase in the number of people, nor was agricultural production able to keep up. Neither did China's internal expansion to the west and south generate anything like the wealth and resources that derived from Europe's overseas empires. The result was growing pressure on the land, smaller farms for China's huge peasant population, and, in all too many cases, unemployment, impoverishment, misery, and starvation.

Furthermore, China's governing institutions did not keep pace with the growing population. Thus the state was increasingly unable to effectively perform its many functions, such as tax collection, flood control, social welfare, and public security. Gradually the central state lost power to provincial officials and local gentry. Among such officials, corruption was endemic, and harsh treatment of peasants was common. According to an official report issued in 1852, "Day and night soldiers are sent out to harass taxpayers. Sometimes corporal punishments are imposed upon tax delinquents; some of them are so badly beaten to exact the last penny that blood and flesh fly in all directions."[2] Finally, European military pressure and economic penetration during the first half of the nineteenth century disrupted internal trade routes, created substantial unemployment, and raised peasant taxes.

This combination of circumstances, traditionally associated with a declining dynasty, gave rise to growing numbers of bandit gangs roaming the countryside and, even more dangerous, to outright peasant rebellion. Beginning in the late eighteenth century, such rebellions drew on a variety of peasant grievances and found leadership in charismatic figures proclaiming a millenarian religious message. Increasingly they also expressed opposition to the Qing dynasty because of its foreign Manchu origins. "We wait only for the northern region to be returned to a Han emperor," declared one rebel group in the early nineteenth century.[3]

China's internal crisis culminated in the **Taiping Uprising**, which set much of the country aflame between 1850 and 1864. This was a different kind of peasant upheaval. Its leaders largely rejected Confucianism, Daoism, and Buddhism alike, finding their primary ideology in a unique form of Christianity. Its leading figure, Hong Xiuquan (hong show-chwaan) (1814–1864), proclaimed himself the younger brother of Jesus, sent to cleanse the world of demons and to establish a "heavenly kingdom of great peace." Nor were these leaders content to restore an idealized Chinese society; instead they insisted on genuinely revolutionary change. They called for the abolition of private property, a radical redistribution of land, the end of prostitution and opium smoking, and the organization of society into sexually segregated military camps of men and women. Hong fiercely denounced the Qing dynasty as foreigners who had "poisoned China" and "defiled the emperor's throne." His cousin, Hong Rengan, developed plans for transforming China into an industrial nation, complete with railroads, health insurance for all, newspapers, and widespread public education.

Guided Reading Question

▪ **CAUSATION**
What accounts for the massive peasant rebellions of nineteenth-century China?

Among the most revolutionary dimensions of the Taiping Uprising was its posture toward women and gender roles. This outlook reflected its origins among the minority Hakka people of southern China, where women were notably less restricted than Confucian orthodoxy prescribed. During the uprising, Hakka women, whose feet had never been bound, fought as soldiers in their own regiments, and in liberated regions, Taiping officials ordered that the feet of other women be unbound. The Taiping land reform program promised women and men equal shares of land. Women were now permitted to sit for civil service examinations and were appointed to supervisory positions, though usually ones in which they exercised authority over other women rather than men. Mutual attraction rather than family interests was promoted as a basis for marriage.

None of these reforms were consistently implemented during the short period of Taiping power, and the movement's leadership demonstrated considerable ambivalence about equality for women. Hong himself reflected a much more traditional understanding of elite women's role when he assembled a large personal harem and declared: "The duty of the palace women is to attend to the needs of their husbands; and it is arranged by Heaven that they are not to learn of the affairs outside."[4] Nonetheless, the Taiping posture toward women represented a sharp challenge to long-established gender roles and contributed to the hostility that the movement generated among many other Chinese, including women.

Taiping Uprising Western powers generally supported the Qing dynasty during the Taiping Uprising and even provided it with some military support. This image shows a group of the Taiping rebels and a British soldier they have captured. (Private Collection/Peter Newark Military Pictures/Bridgeman Images)

With a rapidly swelling number of followers, Taiping forces swept out of southern China and established their capital in Nanjing in 1853. For a time, the days of the Qing dynasty appeared to be over. But divisions and indecisiveness within the Taiping leadership, along with their inability to link up with several other rebel groups also operating separately in China, provided an opening for Qing dynasty loyalists to rally and by 1864 to crush this most unusual of peasant rebellions. Western military support for pro-Qing forces likewise contributed to their victory. It was not, however, the imperial military forces of the central government that defeated the rebels. Instead provincial military leaders, fearing the radicalism of the Taiping program, mobilized their own armies, which in the end crushed the rebel forces.

Thus the Qing dynasty was saved, but it was also weakened as the provincial gentry consolidated their power at the expense of the central state. The intense conservatism of both imperial authorities and their gentry supporters postponed any resolution of China's peasant problem, delayed any real change for China's women, and deferred vigorous efforts at modernization until the communists came to power in the mid-twentieth century. More immediately, the devastation and destruction occasioned by this massive civil war seriously disrupted and weakened China's economy. Estimates of the number of lives lost range from 20 to 30 million. In human terms, it was the most costly conflict in the world during the nineteenth century, and it took China more than a decade to recover from its devastation. China's internal crisis in general and the Taiping Uprising in particular also provided a highly unfavorable setting for the country's encounter with a Europe newly invigorated by the Industrial Revolution.

Western Pressures

Nowhere was the shifting balance of global power in the nineteenth century more evident than in China's changing relationship with Europe, a transformation that registered most dramatically in the famous **Opium Wars**. Derived from Arab traders in the eighth century or earlier, opium had long been used on a small scale as a drinkable medicine; it was regarded as a magical cure for dysentery and described by one poet as "fit for Buddha."[5] It did not become a serious problem until the late eighteenth century, when the British began to use opium, grown and processed in India, to cover their persistent trade imbalance with China. By the 1830s, British, American, and other Western merchants had found an enormous, growing, and very profitable market for this highly addictive drug. From 1,000 chests (each weighing roughly 150 pounds) in 1773, China's opium imports exploded to more than 23,000 chests in 1832. (See Snapshot, page 833.)

By then, Chinese authorities recognized a mounting problem on many levels. Because opium importation was illegal, it had to be smuggled into China, thus flouting Chinese law. Bribed to turn a blind eye to the illegal trade, many officials were corrupted. Furthermore, a massive outflow of silver to pay for the opium reversed China's centuries-long ability to attract much of the world's silver supply, and this imbalance caused serious economic problems. Finally, China found itself with many millions of addicts—men and women, court officials, students preparing for exams, soldiers going into combat, and common laborers seeking to overcome the pain

Addiction to Opium Throughout the nineteenth century, opium imports created a massive addiction problem in China, as this photograph of an opium den from around 1900 suggests. Not until the early twentieth century did the British prove willing to curtail the opium trade from their Indian colony. (Hulton Deutsch/Getty Images)

SNAPSHOT Chinese/British Trade at Canton, 1835–1836

What do these figures suggest about the role of opium in British trade with China? Calculate opium exports as a percentage of British exports to China, Britain's trade deficit without opium, and its trade surplus with opium. What did this pattern mean for China?

	Item	Value (in Spanish dollars)
British Exports to Canton	Opium	17,904,248
	Cotton	8,357,394
	All other items (sandalwood, lead, iron, tin, cotton yarn and piece goods, tin plates, watches, clocks)	6,164,981
	Total	32,426,623
British Imports from Canton	Tea (black and green)	13,412,243
	Raw silk	3,764,115
	Vermilion	705,000
	All other goods (sugar products, camphor, silver, gold, copper, musk)	5,971,541
	Total	23,852,899

Data from Hsin-Pao Chang, ed., *Commissioner Lin and the Opium War* (New York: W. W. Norton, 1970), 226–27.

and drudgery of their work. Following an extended debate at court in 1836 on whether to legalize the drug or crack down on its use, the emperor decided on suppression. An upright official, **Commissioner Lin Zexu** (lin zuh-SHOO), led the campaign against opium use as a kind of "drug czar." (See Zooming In: Lin Zexu, page 834.) The British, offended by the seizure of their property in opium and emboldened by their new military power, sent a large naval expedition to China, determined to end the restrictive conditions under which they had long traded with that country. In the process, they would teach the Chinese a lesson about the virtues of free trade and the "proper" way to conduct relations among countries. Thus began the first Opium War (1840–1842), in which Britain's industrialized military might proved decisive. The Treaty of Nanjing, which ended the war in 1842, largely on British terms, imposed numerous restrictions on Chinese sovereignty and opened five ports to European traders. Its provisions reflected the changed balance of global power that had emerged with Britain's Industrial Revolution. To the Chinese, that agreement represented the first of the "**unequal treaties**" that seriously eroded China's independence by the end of the century.

But it was not the last of those treaties. Britain's victory in a second Opium War (1856–1858) was accompanied by the brutal vandalizing of the emperor's exquisite Summer Palace outside Beijing and resulted in further humiliations. Still more ports were opened to foreign traders. Now those foreigners were allowed to travel

Guided Reading Question

■ **CONNECTION**
How did Western pressures stimulate change in China during the nineteenth century?

Lin Zexu: Confronting the Opium Trade

When the Chinese emperor decided in 1838 on firm measures to suppress the opium trade, he selected Lin Zexu to enforce that policy.[6] Born in 1785, Lin was the son of a rather poor but scholarly father who had never achieved an official position. Lin, however, excelled academically, passing the highest-level examinations in 1811 after two failed attempts and then rising rapidly in the ranks of China's bureaucracy. In the process, he gained a reputation as a strict and honest official; he was immune to bribery, genuinely concerned with the welfare of the peasantry, and unafraid to confront the corruption and decadence of rich and poor alike.

And so in December of 1838, after some nineteen personal audiences with the emperor, Lin found himself in Canton, the center of the opium trade and the only Chinese city legally open to foreign merchants. He was facing the greatest challenge of his professional life. Undertaken with the best of intentions, his actions were unable to prevent a war with

Commissioner Lin Zexu ordering the destruction of opium.

Britain, which propelled the country into a century of humiliating subservience to an industrializing Europe and forced growing numbers of Chinese to question their vaunted civilization.

In established Confucian fashion, Lin undertook his enormous task with a combination of moral appeals, reasoned argument, political pressure, and coercion, while hoping to avoid outright armed conflict. It was an approach that focused on both the demand and supply sides of the problem. In dealing with Chinese opium users, Lin emphasized the health hazards of the drug and demanded that people turn in their supplies of opium and the pipes used to smoke it. By mid-1839, he had confiscated some 50,000 pounds of the drug, together with over 70,000 pipes, and arrested some 1,700 dealers. Hundreds of local students were summoned to an assembly where they were invited to identify opium distributors and to suggest ways

photo: Pictures from History/The Image Works

freely and buy land in China, to preach Christianity under the protection of Chinese authorities, and to patrol some of China's rivers. Furthermore, the Chinese were forbidden to use the character for "barbarians" to refer to the British in official documents. Following later military defeats at the hands of the French (1885) and Japanese (1895), China lost control of Vietnam, Korea, and Taiwan. By the end of the century, the Western nations plus Japan and Russia had all carved out spheres of influence within China, granting themselves special privileges to establish military bases, extract raw materials, and build railroads. Many Chinese believed that their country was being "carved up like a melon" (see Map 19.1 and the chapter-opening photo).

Coupled with its internal crisis, China's encounter with European imperialism had reduced the proud Middle Kingdom to dependency on the Western powers as it became part of a European-based "**informal empire**," an area dominated by Western powers but retaining its own government and a measure of independence.

of dealing with the problem. Opium-using officials became the target of investigations, and five-person teams were established to enforce the ban on opium smoking on one another.

Lin applied a similar mix of methods to the foreign suppliers of opium. A moralistic appeal to Queen Victoria argued that the articles the English imported from China—silk, tea, and rhubarb—were all beneficial. "By what right," he asked, "do [the barbarians] use this poisonous drug to injure Chinese people?" He pointedly reminded Europeans that new regulations, applying to Chinese and foreigners alike, fixed the penalty for dealing in opium at "decapitation or strangling." Then he demanded that foreign traders hand over their opium, and without compensation. When the merchants hesitated, Lin tightened the screws, ordering all Chinese employed by foreigners to leave their jobs and blockading the Europeans in their factories. After six weeks of negotiations, the Europeans capitulated, turning over some 3 million pounds of raw opium to Lin Zexu.

Disposing of the drug was an enormous task. Workers, stripped and searched daily to prevent looting, dug three huge trenches into which they placed the opium mixed with water, salt, and lime and then flushed the concoction into the sea. (See the image in this feature, which shows the commissioner overseeing this process.) Lin also offered a sacrifice to the Sea Spirit, apologizing for introducing this poison into its domain and "advising the Spirit to tell the creatures of the water to move away for a time." He informed the emperor that throngs of local people flocked to witness the destruction of the opium. And foreigners too came to observe the spectacle. Lin reported, "[The foreigners] do not dare to show any disrespect, and indeed I should judge from their attitudes that they have the decency to feel heartily ashamed."

Had Lin been correct in his appraisal, history would have taken a very different turn. But neither Lin nor his superiors anticipated the response that these actions provoked from the British government. They were also largely unaware that European industrial and military advances had decisively shifted the balance of power between China and the West. Arriving in 1840, a British military expedition quickly demonstrated its superiority and initiated the devastating Opium War that marked Lin's policies in Canton as a failure.

As a punishment for his unsatisfactory performance, the emperor sent Lin to a remote post in western China. Although his career rebounded somewhat after 1845, he died in 1850 while on the way to an appointment aimed at suppressing the Taiping rebellion. While his reputation suffered in the nineteenth century, it recovered in the twentieth as an intensely nationalist China recalled his principled stand against Western imperialism.

QUESTIONS

How might Lin Zexu have handled his task differently or more successfully? Or had he been given an impossible mission?

China was no longer the center of civilization to which barbarians paid homage and tribute, but just one weak and dependent nation among many others. The Qing dynasty remained in power, but in a weakened condition, which served European interests well and Chinese interests poorly. Restrictions imposed by the unequal treaties clearly inhibited China's industrialization, as foreign goods and foreign investment flooded the country largely unrestricted. Chinese businessmen mostly served foreign firms, rather than developing as an independent capitalist class capable of leading China's own Industrial Revolution.

The Failure of Conservative Modernization

Chinese authorities were not passive in the face of their country's mounting internal and external crises. Known as "**self-strengthening**," their policies during the 1860s and 1870s sought to reinvigorate a traditional China while borrowing

MAPPING HISTORY

Map 19.1 China and the World in the Nineteenth Century

As China was reeling from massive internal upheavals during the nineteenth century, it also faced external assaults from Russia, Japan, and various European powers. By the end of the century, large parts of China were divided into spheres of influence, each affiliated with one of the major industrial powers of the day.

READING THE MAP: Which imperial powers created spheres of influence in China that were adjacent to territories that they already controlled? Which created spheres of influence that were geographically separate from their existing territories?

INTERPRETING THE MAP: How might you compare the success of Japanese and European colonialism in Asia?

cautiously from the West. An overhauled examination system, designed to recruit qualified candidates for official positions, sought the "good men" who could cope with the massive reconstruction that China faced in the wake of the Taiping rebellion. Support for landlords and the repair of dikes and irrigation helped restore rural social and economic order. A few industrial factories producing textiles and steel were established, coal mines were expanded, and a telegraph system was initiated. One Chinese general in 1863 confessed his humiliation that "Chinese weapons are far inferior to those of foreign countries."[7] A number of modern arsenals, shipyards, and foreign-language schools sought to remedy this deficiency.

Self-strengthening as an overall program for China's modernization was inhibited by the fears of conservative leaders that urban, industrial, or commercial development would erode the power and privileges of the landlord class. Furthermore, the new industries remained largely dependent on foreigners for machinery, materials, and expertise. And they served to strengthen local authorities, who largely controlled those industries, rather than the central Chinese state.

The general failure of "self-strengthening" became apparent at the end of the century, when China suffered a humiliating military defeat by Japan (1894–1895). This failure was only confirmed when an antiforeign movement known as the **Boxer Uprising** (1898–1901) erupted in northern China. Led by militia organizations calling themselves the Society of Righteous and Harmonious Fists, the "Boxers" killed numerous Europeans and Chinese Christians and laid siege to the foreign embassies in Beijing. When Western powers and Japan occupied Beijing to crush the rebellion and imposed a huge payment on China as a punishment, it was clear that China remained a dependent country, substantially under foreign control.

No wonder, then, that growing numbers of educated Chinese, including many in official elite positions, became highly disillusioned with the Qing dynasty, which was both foreign and ineffective in protecting China. By the late 1890s, such people were organizing a variety of clubs, study groups, and newspapers to examine China's desperate situation and to explore alternative paths. The names of these organizations reflect their outlook—the National Rejuvenation Study Society, Society to Protect the Nation, and Understand the National Shame Society. They admired not only Western science and technology but also Western political practices that limited the authority of the ruler and permitted wider circles of people to take part in public life. They believed that only a truly unified nation in which rulers and ruled were closely related could save China from dismemberment at the hands of foreign imperialists. Despite the small number of women who took part in these discussions, traditional gender roles became yet another focus of opposition. No one expressed that issue more forcefully than Qiu Jin (1875–1907), the rebellious daughter of a gentry family who started a women's journal, arguing that liberated women were essential for a strong Chinese nation, and became involved in revolutionary politics. (For more on Qiu Jin, see Working with Evidence, Source 19.3, page 859.) Thus was born the immensely powerful force of Chinese nationalism, directed alike against Western imperialists, the foreign Qing dynasty, and aspects of China's traditional culture.

Guided Reading Question

■ **CONNECTION**
What strategies did China adopt to confront its various problems? In what ways did these strategies reflect China's own history and culture as well as the new global order?

The Qing dynasty response to these new pressures proved inadequate. A flurry of progressive imperial edicts in 1898, known as the Hundred Days of Reform, was soon squelched by conservative forces. More extensive reform in the early twentieth century, including the end of the old examination system and the promise of a national parliament, was a classic case of too little too late. (See Working with Evidence: China: On the Brink of Change, page 857.) In 1912 the last Chinese emperor abdicated as the ancient imperial order that had governed China for two millennia collapsed, with only a modest nudge from organized revolutionaries. This **Chinese revolution of 1911–1912** marked the end of a long era in China's long history and the beginning of an immense struggle over the country's future.

The Ottoman Empire and the West in the Nineteenth Century

Like China, the Islamic world represented a highly successful civilization that felt little need to learn from the "infidels" or "barbarians" of the West until it collided with an expanding and aggressive Europe in the nineteenth century. Unlike China, though, Islamic civilization had been a near neighbor to Europe for 1,000 years. Its most prominent state, the Ottoman Empire, had long governed substantial parts of southeastern Europe and had posed a clear military and religious threat to Europe in the sixteenth and seventeenth centuries. But if its encounter with the West was less abrupt than that of China, it was no less consequential. Neither the Ottoman Empire nor China fell under direct colonial rule, but both were much diminished as the changing balance of global power took hold; both launched efforts at "defensive modernization" aimed at strengthening their states and preserving their independence; and in both societies, some people held tightly to old identities and values, even as others embraced new loyalties associated with nationalism and modernity.

"The Sick Man of Europe"

In 1750, the Ottoman Empire was still the central political fixture of a widespread Islamic world. From its Turkish heartland in Anatolia, it ruled over much of the Arab world, from which Islam had come. It protected pilgrims on their way to Mecca, governed Egypt and coastal North Africa, and incorporated millions of Christians in the Balkans. Its ruler, the sultan, claimed the role of caliph, successor to the Prophet Muhammad, and was widely viewed as the leader, defender, and primary representative of the Islamic world. But by the middle, and certainly by the end, of the nineteenth century, the Ottoman Empire was no longer able to deal with Europe from a position of equality, let alone superiority. Among the Great Powers of the West, it was now known as "**the sick man of Europe**." Within the Muslim world, the Ottoman Empire, once viewed as "the strong sword of Islam," was unable to prevent region after region — India, Indonesia, West Africa, Central Asia — from falling under the control of Christian powers.

The Ottoman Empire's own domains shrank considerably at the hands of Russian, British, Austrian, and French aggression (see Map 19.2). In 1798, Napoleon's invasion of Egypt, which had long been a province of the Ottoman Empire, was a particularly stunning blow. A contemporary observer, Abd al-Rahman al-Jabarti, described the French entry into Cairo:

> The French entered the city like a torrent rushing through the alleys and
> streets without anything to stop them, like demons of the Devil's army. . . .
> And the French trod in the Mosque of al-Azhar with their shoes, carrying
> swords and rifles. . . . They plundered whatever they found in the mosque. . . .

MAPPING HISTORY

Map 19.2 The Contraction of the Ottoman Empire
Foreign aggression and nationalist movements substantially diminished the Ottoman Empire during the nineteenth century, but they also stimulated a variety of efforts to revive and reform Ottoman society.

READING THE MAP: Aside from North Africa, where did the Ottoman Empire lose the most territory between 1800 and 1913?

MAKING CONNECTIONS: Compare this map with Map 13.4: The Ottoman Empire. How does the Ottoman Empire in 1800 compare to the empire in 1566? Had the empire already lost major territories before 1800, or does much of the decline seem to have occurred between 1800 and 1913?

They treated the books and Quranic volumes as trash. . . . Furthermore, they soiled the mosque, blowing their spit in it, pissing and defecating in it. They guzzled wine and smashed bottles in the central court.[8]

When the French left, a virtually independent Egypt pursued a modernizing and empire-building program of its own during the early and mid-nineteenth century and on one occasion came close to toppling the Ottoman Empire itself.

Beyond territorial losses to stronger European powers, other parts of the empire, such as Greece, Serbia, Bulgaria, and Romania, achieved independence based on their own surging nationalism and support from the British or the Russians. The continued independence of the core region of the Ottoman Empire owed much to the inability of Europe's Great Powers to agree on how to divide it up among themselves.

Behind the contraction of the Ottoman Empire lay other problems. As in China, the central Ottoman state had weakened, particularly in its ability to raise necessary revenue, as provincial authorities and local warlords gained greater power. Moreover, the Janissaries, once the effective and innovative elite infantry units of Ottoman military forces, lost their military edge, becoming a highly conservative force within the empire. The technological and military gap with the West was clearly growing.

Economically, the earlier centrality of the Ottoman and Arab lands in Afro-Eurasian commerce diminished as Europeans achieved direct oceanic access to the treasures of Asia. Competition from cheap European manufactured goods hit Ottoman artisans hard and led to urban riots protesting foreign imports. Furthermore, a series of agreements, known as capitulations, between European countries and the Ottoman Empire granted Westerners various exemptions from Ottoman law and taxation. Like the unequal treaties with China, these agreements facilitated European penetration of the Ottoman economy and became widely resented. Such measures eroded Ottoman sovereignty and reflected the changing position of that empire relative to Europe. So too did the growing indebtedness of the Ottoman Empire, which came to rely on foreign loans to finance its efforts at economic development. By 1881, its inability to pay the interest on those debts led to foreign control of much of its revenue-generating system, while a similar situation in Egypt led to its outright occupation by the British. Like China, the Ottoman Empire had fallen into a position of considerable dependency on Europe.

Reform and Its Opponents

The leadership of the Ottoman Empire recognized many of its problems and during the nineteenth century mounted increasingly ambitious programs of "defensive modernization" that were earlier, more sustained, and far more vigorous than the timid and halfhearted measures of self-strengthening in China. One reason perhaps lay in the absence of any internal upheaval, such as the Taiping Uprising in China, which threatened the very existence of the ruling dynasty. Nationalist revolts on the empire's periphery, rather than Chinese-style peasant rebellion at the center, represented the primary internal crisis of nineteenth-century Ottoman history.

Guided Reading Question

■ CHANGE

What lay behind the decline of the Ottoman Empire in the nineteenth century?

Guided Reading Question

■ CHANGE

In what different ways did the Ottoman state respond to its various problems?

Nor did the Middle East in general experience the explosive population growth that contributed so much to China's nineteenth-century crisis. Furthermore, the long-established Ottoman leadership was Turkic and Muslim, culturally similar to its core population, whereas China's Qing dynasty rulers were widely regarded as foreigners from Manchuria.

Ottoman reforms began in the late eighteenth century when Sultan Selim III (r. 1789–1807) sought to reorganize and update the army, drawing on European advisers and techniques. Even these modest innovations stirred the hostility of powerful factions among both the *ulama* (religious scholars) and the elite military corps of Janissaries, who saw them in conflict with both Islam and their own institutional interests. Opposition to his measures was so strong that Selim was overthrown in 1807 and then murdered. Subsequent

Ottoman Modernization Railroads were a major element in Ottoman modernization efforts. This photograph shows a celebration in Medina, Arabia, of the opening in 1908 of the Hejaz rail line from Damascus. Part of the larger Ottoman railroad network, the Hejaz line linked Constantinople more firmly to the empire's Arab domains. It also facilitated the movement of Muslim pilgrims undertaking the *hajj* in Mecca and, potentially, the movement of Ottoman troops as well. Financed substantially by German banks, the Hejaz rail line connected to the more famous Berlin to Baghdad railway, constructed at the same time and also with German funding. (Granger, NYC—All rights reserved)

sultans, however, crushed the Janissaries and brought the ulama more thoroughly under state control than elsewhere in the Islamic world.

Then, in the several decades after 1839, more far-reaching reformist measures, known as **Tanzimat** (tahn-zee-MAHT) (reorganization), took shape as the Ottoman leadership sought to provide the economic, social, and legal underpinnings for a strong and newly recentralized state. Factories producing cloth, paper, and armaments; modern mining operations; reclamation and resettlement of agricultural land; telegraphs, steamships, railroads, and a modern postal service; Western-style law codes and courts; new elementary and secondary schools—all of these new departures began a long process of modernization and westernization in the Ottoman Empire.

Even more revolutionary, at least in principle, were changes in the legal status of the empire's diverse communities, which now gave non-Muslims equal rights under the law. An imperial proclamation of 1856 declared:

> Every distinction or designation tending to make any class whatever of the subjects of my Empire inferior to another class, on account of their religion, language or race shall be forever effaced. . . . No subject of my Empire shall be hindered in the exercise of the religion that he professes. . . . All the subjects

of my Empire, without distinction of nationality, shall be admissible to public employment.

This declaration represented a dramatic change that challenged the fundamentally Islamic character of the state. Mixed tribunals with representatives from various religious groups were established to hear cases involving non-Muslims. More Christians were appointed to high office. A mounting tide of secular legislation and secular schools, drawing heavily on European models, now competed with traditional Islamic institutions.

Although Tanzimat-era reforms did not directly address gender issues, they did stimulate modest educational openings for women, mostly in Istanbul, with a training program for midwives in 1842, a girls' secondary school in 1858, and a teacher training college for women in 1870. Furthermore, the reform-minded class that emerged from the Tanzimat era generally favored greater opportunities for women as a means of strengthening the state, and a number of upper- and middle-class women were involved in these discussions. During the 1870s and 1880s, the prominent female poet Sair Nigar Hanim held weekly "salons" in which reformist intellectuals of both sexes participated.

The reform process raised profound and highly contested questions. What was the Ottoman Empire, and who were its people? Were they Ottoman subjects of a dynastic state, Turkish citizens of a national state, or Muslim believers in a religiously defined state? For decades, the answers oscillated, as few people wanted to choose decisively among these alternative identities.

Guided Reading Question

··

■ **COMPARISON**
In what different ways did various groups define the Ottoman Empire during the nineteenth century?

To those who supported the reforms, the Ottoman Empire was an inclusive state, all of whose people were loyal to the dynasty that ruled it. This was the outlook of a new class spawned by the reform process itself—lower-level officials, military officers, writers, poets, and journalists, many of whom had a modern Western-style education. Dubbed the **Young Ottomans**, they were active during the middle decades of the nineteenth century, as they sought major changes in the Ottoman political system itself. They favored a more European-style parliamentary and constitutional regime that could curtail the absolute power of the sultan. Only such a political system, they felt, could mobilize the energies of the country to overcome backwardness and preserve the state against European aggression. Known as Islamic modernism, such ideas found expression in many parts of the Muslim world in the second half of the century. Muslim societies, the Young Ottomans argued, needed to embrace Western technical and scientific knowledge, while rejecting its materialism. Islam in their view could accommodate a full modernity without sacrificing its essential religious character. After all, the Islamic world had earlier hosted impressive scientific achievements and had incorporated elements of Greek philosophical thinking.

In 1876, the Young Ottomans experienced a short-lived victory when **Sultan Abd al-Hamid II** (r. 1876–1909) accepted a constitution and an elected parliament, but not for long. Under the pressure of war with Russia, the sultan soon suspended the reforms and reverted to an older style of despotic rule for the next thirty years, even renewing the claim that he was the caliph, the successor to the Prophet and the protector of Muslims everywhere.

Opposition to this revived despotism soon surfaced among both military and civilian elites known as the **Young Turks**. Largely abandoning any reference to Islam, they advocated a militantly secular public life, were committed to thorough modernization along European lines, and increasingly thought about the Ottoman Empire as a Turkish national state. "There is only one civilization, and that is European civilization," declared Abdullah Cevdet, a prominent figure in the Young Turk movement. "Therefore we must borrow western civilization with both its rose and its thorn."[9]

A military coup in 1908 finally allowed the Young Turks to exercise real power. They pushed for a radical secularization of schools, courts, and law codes; permitted elections and competing parties; established a single Law of Family Rights for all regardless of religion; and encouraged Turkish as the official language of the empire. They also opened modern schools for women, including access to Istanbul University; allowed women to wear Western clothing; restricted polygamy; and permitted women to obtain divorces in some situations. Women established a number of publications and organizations, some of them linked to British suffrage groups. In the western cities of the empire, some women abandoned their veils.

But the nationalist Turkish conception of Ottoman identity antagonized non-Turkic peoples and helped stimulate Arab and other nationalisms in response. For some, a secular nationality was becoming the most important public loyalty, with Islam relegated to private life. Nationalist sentiments contributed to the complete disintegration of the

The First Ottoman Constitution This Ottoman-era postcard celebrates the short-lived constitutional period of 1876–1878 and the brief political victory of the Young Ottoman reformers. The country is represented by an unveiled woman being released from her chains, while an angel carries a banner inscribed with the slogan of the French Revolution: liberty, equality, fraternity. ("The Ottoman Constitution, December 1895." Color postcard, artist unknown/ Visual Connection Archive)

Ottoman Empire following World War I, but the secularizing and westernizing principles of the Young Turks informed the policies of the Turkish republic that replaced it.

Outcomes: Comparing China and the Ottoman Empire

By the beginning of the twentieth century, both China and the Ottoman Empire, recently centers of proud and vibrant civilizations, had experienced the consequences of a rapidly shifting balance of global power. Now they were "semi-colonies" within the "informal empires" of Europe, although they retained sufficient independence for their governments to launch catch-up efforts of defensive modernization, the Ottomans earlier and the Chinese later. But neither was able to create the industrial economies or strong states required to fend off European intrusion and restore their former status in the world. Despite their diminished power, however, both China and the Ottoman Empire gave rise to new nationalist conceptions of society that were initially small and limited in appeal but of great significance for the future.

In the early twentieth century, that future witnessed the end of both the Chinese and Ottoman empires. In China, the collapse of the imperial system in 1912 was followed by a vast revolutionary upheaval that by 1949 led to a communist regime within largely the same territorial space as the old empire. By contrast, the collapse of the Ottoman Empire following World War I led to the creation of the new but much smaller nation-state of Turkey in the Anatolian heartland of the old empire, which lost its vast Arab and European provinces.

China's twentieth-century revolutionaries rejected traditional Confucian culture far more thoroughly than the secularizing leaders of modern Turkey rejected Islam. Almost everywhere in the Islamic world, including Turkey, traditional religion retained its hold on the private loyalties of most people and later in the twentieth century became a basis for social renewal in many places. Islamic civilization, unlike its Chinese counterpart, had many independent centers and was never so closely associated with a single state. Furthermore, it was embedded in a deeply religious tradition that was personally meaningful to millions of adherents, in contrast to the more elitist and secular outlook of Confucianism. Many Chinese, however, retained traditional Confucian values such as filial piety, and Confucianism has made something of a comeback in China over the past several decades. Nonetheless, Islam retained a hold on its civilization in the twentieth century rather more firmly than Confucianism did in China.

PRACTICING HISTORICAL THINKING

In what ways were the histories of China and the Ottoman Empire similar during the nineteenth century? And how did they differ?

The Japanese Difference: The Rise of a New East Asian Power

Like China and the Ottoman Empire, the island country of Japan confronted the aggressive power of the West during the nineteenth century. This threat took shape as U.S. commodore Matthew Perry's "black ships" steamed into Tokyo Bay in 1853 and forcefully demanded that this reclusive nation open up to more "normal" relations with the world. However, the outcome of that encounter differed sharply from the others. In the second half of the nineteenth century, Japan undertook a radical transformation of its society — a "revolution from above," according to some historians — that turned it into a powerful, modern, united, industrialized nation. It was an achievement that neither China nor the Ottoman Empire was able to duplicate. Far from succumbing to Western domination, Japan joined the club of imperialist countries by creating its own East Asian empire at the expense of China and Korea. In building a society that was both modern and distinctly Japanese, Japan demonstrated that modernity was not a uniquely European phenomenon. This "Japanese miracle," as some have called it, was both promising and ominous for the rest of Asia.

The Tokugawa Background

For 250 years prior to Perry's arrival, Japan had been governed by a shogun (a military ruler) from the Tokugawa family who acted in the name of a revered but powerless emperor who lived in Kyoto, 300 miles away from the seat of power in Edo (Tokyo). The chief task of this Tokugawa shogunate was to prevent the return of civil war among some 260 rival feudal lords, known as daimyo, each of whom had a cadre of armed retainers, the famed samurai warriors of Japanese tradition.

Based on their own military power and political skills, successive shoguns gave Japan more than two centuries of internal peace (1600–1850). To control the restive daimyo, they required these local authorities to create second homes in Edo, the country's capital, where they had to live during alternate years. When they left for their rural residences, families stayed behind, almost as hostages. Nonetheless, the daimyo, especially the more powerful ones, retained substantial autonomy in their own domains and behaved in some ways like independent states, with separate military forces, law codes, tax systems, and currencies. With no national army, no uniform currency, and little central authority at the local level, **Tokugawa Japan** was "pacified . . . but not really unified."[10] To further stabilize the country, the Tokugawa regime issued highly detailed rules governing the occupation, residence, dress, hairstyles, and behavior of the four hierarchically ranked status groups into which Japanese society was divided — samurai at the top, then peasants, artisans, and, at the bottom, merchants.

During these 250 years of peace, much was changing within Japan in ways that belied the control and orderliness of Tokugawa regulations. For one thing, the samurai, in the absence of wars to fight, evolved into a salaried bureaucratic or administrative class amounting to 5 to 6 percent of the total population, but they remained fiercely devoted to their daimyo lords and to their warrior code of loyalty, honor, and self-sacrifice.

More generally, centuries of peace contributed to a remarkable burst of economic growth, commercialization, and urban development. Entrepreneurial peasants, using fertilizers and other agricultural innovations, grew more rice than ever before and

Guided Reading Question

■ **CHANGE**

In what ways was Japan changing during the Tokugawa era?

engaged in a variety of rural manufacturing enterprises as well. By 1750, Japan had become perhaps the world's most urbanized country, with about 10 percent of its population living in sizable towns or cities. Edo, with perhaps a million residents, was among the world's largest cities. Well-functioning networks of exchange linked urban and rural areas, marking Japan as an emerging market economy. The influence of Confucianism encouraged education and generated a remarkably literate population, with about 40 percent of men and 15 percent of women able to read and write. Although no one was aware of it at the time, these changes during the Tokugawa era provided a solid foundation for Japan's remarkable industrial growth in the late nineteenth century.

Such changes also undermined the shogunate's efforts to freeze Japanese society in the interests of stability. Some samurai found the lowly but profitable path of commerce too much to resist. "No more shall we have to live by the sword," declared one of them in 1616 while renouncing his samurai status. "I have seen that great profit can be made honorably. I shall brew *sake* and soy sauce, and we shall prosper."[11] Many merchants, though hailing from the lowest-ranking status group, prospered in the new commercial environment and supported a vibrant urban culture, while not a few daimyo found it necessary, if humiliating, to seek loans from these social inferiors. Thus merchants had money, but little status, whereas samurai enjoyed high status but were often indebted to inferior merchants. Both resented their positions.

Despite prohibitions to the contrary, many peasants moved to the cities, becoming artisans or merchants and imitating the ways of their social betters. A decree of 1788 noted that peasants "have become accustomed to luxury and forgetful of their status." They wore inappropriate clothing, used umbrellas rather than straw hats in the rain, and even left the villages for the city. "Henceforth," declared the shogun, "all luxuries should be avoided by the peasants. They are to live simply and devote themselves to farming."[12] This decree, like many others before it, was widely ignored.

More than social change undermined the Tokugawa regime. Corruption was widespread, to the disgust of many. The shogunate's failure to deal successfully with a severe famine in the 1830s eroded confidence in its effectiveness. At the same time, a mounting wave of local peasant uprisings and urban riots expressed the many grievances of the poor. The most striking of these outbursts left the city of Osaka in flames in 1837. Its leader, Oshio Heihachiro, no doubt spoke for many ordinary people when he wrote:

> We must first punish the officials who torment the people so cruelly; then we must execute the haughty and rich Osaka merchants. Then we must distribute the gold, silver, and copper stored in their cellars, and bands of rice hidden in their storehouses.[13]

From the 1830s on, one historian concluded, "there was a growing feeling that the *shogunate* was losing control."[14]

American Intrusion and the Meiji Restoration

It was foreign intervention that brought matters to a head. Since the expulsion of European missionaries and the harsh suppression of Christianity in the early seventeenth century, Japan had deliberately limited its contact with the West to a single port, where only the Dutch were allowed to trade. (See "Asians and Asian Commerce" in Chapter 14.) By the early nineteenth century, however, various European countries and the United States were knocking at the door. All were turned away, and even shipwrecked sailors or whalers were expelled, jailed, or executed. As it happened, it was the United States that forced the issue, sending Commodore Perry in 1853 to demand humane treatment for castaways, the right of American vessels to refuel and buy provisions, and the opening of ports for trade. Authorized to use force if necessary, Perry presented his reluctant hosts with, among other gifts, a white flag for surrender should hostilities follow.

In the end, the Japanese avoided war. Aware of what had happened to China as a result of resisting European demands, Japan agreed to a series of unequal treaties with various Western powers. That humiliating capitulation to the demands of the "foreign devils" further eroded support for the shogunate, triggered a brief civil

The Black Ships of the United States The initial occasion for serious Japanese reflection on the West occurred in 1853–1854, in the context of American commodore Matthew Perry's efforts to "open" Japan to regular commercial relationships with the United States. His nine coal-fired steamships, belching black smoke and carrying a crew of some 1,800 men and more than 100 mounted cannons, became known in Japan as the "black ships." Created around 1854, this image represents perhaps the best known of many such Japanese depictions of the American warships. (Granger, NYC — All rights reserved)

war, and by 1868 led to a political takeover by a group of young samurai from southern Japan. This decisive turning point in Japan's history was known as the **Meiji Restoration**, for the country's new rulers claimed that they were restoring to power the young emperor, then a fifteen-year-old boy whose throne name was Meiji (MAY-jee), or Enlightened Rule. Despite his youth, he was regarded as the most recent link in a chain of descent that traced the origins of the imperial family back to the sun goddess Amaterasu. Having eliminated the shogunate, the patriotic young men who led the takeover soon made their goals clear—to save Japan from foreign domination not by futile resistance, but by a thorough transformation of Japanese society drawing on all that the modern West had to offer. "Knowledge shall be sought throughout the world," they declared, "so as to strengthen the foundations of imperial rule."

Japan now had a government committed to a decisive break with the past, and it had acquired that government without massive violence or destruction. By contrast, the defeat of the Taiping Uprising had deprived China of any such opportunity for a fresh start, while saddling it with enormous devastation and massive loss of life. Furthermore, Japan was of less interest to Western powers than either China, with its huge potential market and reputation for riches, or the Ottoman Empire, with its strategic location at the crossroads of Asia, Africa, and Europe. The American Civil War and its aftermath likewise deflected U.S. ambitions in the Pacific for a time, further reducing the Western pressure on Japan.

Modernization Japanese-Style

These circumstances gave Japan some breathing space, and its new rulers moved quickly to take advantage of that unique window of opportunity. Thus they launched a cascading wave of dramatic changes that rolled over the country in the last three decades of the nineteenth century. Like the more modest reforms of China and the Ottoman Empire, Japanese modernizing efforts were defensive, based on fears that Japanese independence was in grave danger. Those reforms, however, were revolutionary in their cumulative effect, transforming Japan far more thoroughly than even the most radical of the Ottoman efforts, let alone the limited "self-strengthening" policies of the Chinese.

The first task was genuine national unity, which required an attack on the power and privileges of both the daimyo and the samurai. In a major break with the past, the new regime soon ended the semi-independent domains of the daimyo, replacing them with governors appointed by and responsible to the national government. The central state, not the local authorities, now collected the nation's taxes and raised a national army based on conscription from all social classes.

Thus the samurai relinquished their ancient role as the country's warrior class and with it their cherished right to carry swords. The old Confucian-based social order with its special privileges for various classes was largely dismantled, and almost all Japanese became legally equal as commoners and as subjects of the emperor.

Guided Reading Question

■ **CHANGE**
In what respects was Japan's nineteenth-century transformation revolutionary?

Limitations on travel and trade likewise fell as a nationwide economy came to parallel the centralized state. Although there was some opposition to these measures, including a brief rebellion of resentful samurai in 1877, it was on the whole a remarkably peaceful process in which a segment of the old ruling class abolished its own privileges. Many, but not all, of these displaced elites found a soft landing in the army, bureaucracy, or business enterprises of the new regime, thus easing a painful transition.

Accompanying these social and political changes was a widespread and eager fascination with almost everything Western. Knowledge about the West—its science and technology; its various political and constitutional arrangements; its legal and educational systems; its dances, clothing, and hairstyles—was enthusiastically sought out by official missions to Europe and the United States, by hundreds of students sent to study abroad, and by many ordinary Japanese at home. Western writers were translated into Japanese. "Civilization and Enlightenment" was the slogan of the time, and both were to be found in the West. The most prominent popularizer of Western knowledge, Fukuzawa Yukichi, summed up the chief lesson of his studies in the mid-1870s—Japan was backward and needed to learn from the West: "If we compare the knowledge of the Japanese and Westerners, in letters, in technique, in commerce, or in industry, from the largest to the smallest matter, there is not one thing in which we excel. . . . In Japan's present condition there is nothing in which we may take pride vis-à-vis the West."[15]

After this initial wave of uncritical enthusiasm for everything Western receded, Japan proceeded to borrow more selectively and to combine foreign and Japanese elements in distinctive ways. For example, the Constitution of 1889, drawing heavily on German experience, introduced an elected parliament, political parties, and democratic ideals, but that constitution was presented as a gift from a sacred emperor descended from the sun goddess. The parliament could advise, but ultimate power, and particularly control of the military, lay theoretically with the emperor and in practice with an oligarchy of prominent reformers acting in his name. Likewise, a modern educational system, which achieved universal primary schooling by the early twentieth century, was laced with Confucian-based moral instruction and exhortations of loyalty to the emperor. Christianity made little headway in Meiji Japan, but Shinto, an ancient religious tradition featuring ancestors and nature spirits, was elevated to the status of an official state cult. Japan's earlier experience in borrowing massively but selectively from Chinese culture perhaps served it better in these new circumstances than either the Chinese disdain for foreign cultures or the reluctance of many Muslims to see much of value in the infidel West.

Like their counterparts in China and the Ottoman Empire, some reformers in Japan—male and female alike—argued that the oppression of women was an obstacle to the country's modernization and that family reform was essential to gaining the respect of the West. Fukuzawa Yukichi, who was widely read, urged an end to concubinage and prostitution, advocated more education for girls, and called for gender equality in matters of marriage, divorce, and property rights. But most male reformers understood women largely in the context of family life, seeing them as "good wife, wise mother." By the 1880s, however, a small feminist movement arose, demanding—and modeling—a more public role for women. Some even sought the right to vote at a time when only a small fraction of men could do so. A leading feminist, Kishida Toshiko, not yet twenty years old, astonished the country in 1882 when she undertook a two-month speaking tour during which she addressed huge audiences. Only "equality and equal rights," she argued, would allow Japan "to build a new society." Japan must rid itself of the ancient habit of "respecting men and despising women."

While the new Japanese government included girls in its plans for universal education, it was with a gender-specific curriculum and in schools segregated by sex. Any thought of women playing a role in public life was harshly suppressed. A Peace Preservation Law of 1887, in effect until 1922, forbade women from joining political parties and even from attending meetings where political matters were discussed. The Civil Code of 1898 accorded absolute authority to the male head of the family, while grouping all wives with "cripples and disabled persons" as those who "cannot undertake any legal action." To the authorities of Meiji Japan, a serious transformation of gender roles was more of a threat than an opportunity.

At the core of Japan's effort at defensive modernization lay its state-guided industrialization program. More than in Europe or the United States, the government itself established a number of enterprises, later selling many of them to private investors. It also acted to create a modern infrastructure by building railroads, creating a postal service, and establishing a national currency and banking system. From the 1880s on, the Japanese government developed a distinctive form of "labor-intensive industrialization" that relied more heavily on the country's abundant workforce and less on the replacement of labor by machinery and capital than in Western Europe or North America.[16] By the early twentieth century, Japan's industrialization, organized around a number of large firms called *zaibatsu*, was well under way. The country became a major exporter of textiles, in part as a way to pay for needed imports of raw materials, such as cotton, owing to its limited natural resources. Soon the country was able to produce its own munitions and industrial goods as well. Its major cities enjoyed mass-circulation newspapers, movie theaters, and electric lights. All of this was accomplished through its own resources and without the massive foreign debt that so afflicted Egypt and the Ottoman Empire. No other country outside of Europe and North America had been able to launch its own Industrial Revolution in the nineteenth century. It was a distinctive feature of Japan's modern transformation.

Less distinctive, however, were the social results of that process. Taxed heavily to pay for Japan's ambitious modernization program, many peasant families slid into poverty. Their sometimes-violent protests peaked in 1883–1884 as the Japanese countryside witnessed infanticide, the sale of daughters, and starvation.

While state authorities rigidly excluded women from political life and denied them adult legal status, they badly needed female labor in the country's textile

Japan's Modernization This wood print shows Commodore Perry's gift of a small-scale train to the Japanese in 1853. In Japan, as in Europe, railroads quickly became a popular symbol of the country's modernization. (Woodblock print, 1858, by Ando or Utagawa Hiroshige [1797-1858]/Private Collection/Bridgeman Images)

industry, which was central to Japan's economic growth. Accordingly, the majority of Japan's textile workers were young women from poor families in the country-side. Recruiters toured rural villages, contracting with parents for their daughters' labor in return for a payment that the girls had to repay from their wages. That pay was low and their working conditions were terrible. Most lived in factory-provided dormitories and worked twelve or more hours per day. While some committed suicide or ran away and many left after earning enough to pay off their contracts, others organized strikes and joined the anarchist or socialist movements that were emerging among a few intellectuals. One such woman, Kanno Sugako, was hanged in 1911 for participating in a plot to assassinate the emperor. Efforts to create unions and organize strikes, both illegal in Japan at the time, were met with harsh repression even as corporate and state authorities sought to depict the company as a family unit to which workers should give their loyalty, all under the beneficent gaze of the divine emperor.

Japan and the World

Japan's modern transformation soon registered internationally. By the early twentieth century, its economic growth, openness to trade, and embrace of "civilization and enlightenment" from the West persuaded the Western powers to revise the unequal treaties in Japan's favor. This had long been a primary goal of the

Japanese Women Workers Young women were prominent in Japan's emerging textile industry. The women in this photograph from a silk factory around 1900 are spinning silk threads from raw cocoons. (Pictures from History/Bridgeman Images)

Guided Reading Question

■ **CONNECTION**
How did Japan's relationship to the larger world change during its modernization process?

Meiji regime, and the Anglo-Japanese Treaty of 1902 now acknowledged Japan as an equal player among the Great Powers of the world.

Not only did Japan escape from its semi-colonial entanglements with the West, but it also launched its own empire-building enterprise, even as European powers and the United States were carving up much of Asia, Africa, and Pacific Oceania into colonies or spheres of influence. It was what industrializing Great Powers did in the late nineteenth century, and Japan followed suit, in part to compensate for the relative poverty of its natural resource base. A successful war against China (1894–1895) established Japan as a formidable military competitor in East Asia, replacing China as the dominant power in the region. Ten years later in the **Russo-Japanese War** (1904–1905), which was fought over rival imperial ambitions in Korea and Manchuria, Japan became the first Asian state to defeat a major European power. Through those victories, Japan also gained colonial control of Taiwan and Korea and a territorial foothold in Manchuria. And in the aftermath of World War I, Japan acquired a growing influence in China's Shandong Peninsula and control over a number of Micronesian islands under the auspices of the League of Nations.

Japan's entry onto the broader global stage was felt in many places (see Map 19.3). It added yet one more imperialist power to those already burdening a beleaguered China. Defeat at the hands of Japanese upstarts shocked Russia and triggered the 1905 revolution in that country. To Europeans and Americans, Japan was now an economic, political, and military competitor in Asia.

In the world of subject peoples, the rise of Japan and its defeat of Russia generated widespread admiration among those who saw Japan as a model for their own modern development and perhaps as an ally in the struggle against imperialism.

Map 19.3 The Rise of Japan
As Japan modernized after the Meiji Restoration, it launched an empire-building program that provided a foundation for further expansion in the 1930s and during World War II.

Some Poles, Finns, and Jews viewed the Russian defeat in 1905 as an opening for their own liberation from the Russian Empire and were grateful to Japan for the opportunity. Despite Japan's aggression against their country, many Chinese reformers and nationalists found in the Japanese experience valuable lessons for themselves. Thousands flocked to Japan to study its achievements. Newspapers throughout the Islamic world celebrated Japan's victory over Russia as an "awakening of the East" that might herald Muslims' own liberation. Some Turkish women gave their children Japanese names. Indonesian Muslims from Aceh wrote to the Meiji emperor asking for help in their struggle against the Dutch, and Muslim poets wrote odes in his honor. The Egyptian nationalist Mustafa Kamil spoke for many when he declared: "We are amazed by Japan because it is the first Eastern government to utilize Western civilization to resist the shield of European imperialism in Asia."[17]

Those who directly experienced Japanese imperialism in Taiwan or Korea no doubt had a less positive view, for its colonial policies matched or exceeded the brutality of European practices. In the twentieth century, China and much of Southeast Asia suffered bitterly under Japanese imperial aggression. Nonetheless, both the idea of Japan as a liberator of Asia from the European yoke and the reality of Japan as an oppressive imperial power in its own right derived from the country's remarkable modern transformation and its distinctive response to the provocation of Western intrusion.

REFLECTIONS

Success and Failure in History

Beyond describing what happened in the past and explaining why, historians often find themselves evaluating the events they study. When they make judgments about the past, notions of success and failure frequently come into play. Should Europe's Industrial Revolution and its rise to global power be regarded as a success? If so, does that imply that other civilizations were failures? Should we consider Japan more successful than China or the Ottoman Empire during the nineteenth century? Three considerations suggest that we should be very careful in applying these ideas to the complexities of the historical record.

First, and most obviously, is the question of criteria. If the measure of success is national wealth and power, then the Industrial Revolution surely counts as a great accomplishment, at least for some. But if preservation of the environment, spiritual growth, and the face-to-face relationships of village life are more highly valued, then industrialization, as Gandhi argued, might be more reasonably considered a disaster. Certainly the expectation of endless economic growth, which derived from the Industrial Revolution, has been a primary factor in generating the climate changes that threaten modern society in the twenty-first century.

Second, there is the issue of "success for whom?" British artisans who lost their livelihood to industrial machines as well as Japanese women textile workers who suffered through the early stages of industrialization might be forgiven for not appreciating the "success" of their countries' transformation, even if their middle-class counterparts and subsequent generations benefited. In such cases, issues of both social and generational justice complicate any easy assessment of the past.

Third, and finally, success is frequently associated with good judgment and wise choices, yet actors in the historical drama are never completely free in making their decisions, and none, of course, have the benefit of hindsight, which historians enjoy. Did the leaders of China and the Ottoman Empire fail to push industrial development more strongly, or were they not in a position to do so? Were Japanese leaders wiser and more astute than their counterparts elsewhere, or did their knowledge of China's earlier experience and their unique national history simply provide them with circumstances more conducive to modern development? Such questions regarding the possibilities and limitations of human action have no clear-cut answers, but they might caution us about any easy assessment of success and failure.

Second Thoughts

What's the Significance?

Taiping Uprising, 830
Opium Wars, 832
Commissioner Lin Zexu, 833
unequal treaties, 833
informal empire, 834
self-strengthening, 835
Boxer Uprising, 837
Chinese revolution of 1911–1912, 838
"the sick man of Europe," 838
Tanzimat, 841
Young Ottomans, 842
Sultan Abd al-Hamid II, 842
Young Turks, 843
Tokugawa Japan, 845
Meiji Restoration, 848
Russo-Japanese War, 852

Big Picture Questions

1. "The response of each society to European imperialism grew out of its larger historical development and its internal problems." What evidence might support this statement?

2. "Deliberate government policies were more important than historical circumstances in shaping the history of China, the Ottoman Empire, and Japan during the nineteenth century." How might you argue for and against this statement?

3. What kinds of debates, controversies, and conflicts were generated by European intrusion within each of the societies examined in this chapter?

4. **Looking Back:** How did the experiences of China, the Ottoman Empire, Japan, and Latin America, all of which retained their independence despite much European pressure, differ from those of Africa, India, Southeast Asia, and Pacific Oceania, which fell under formal colonial rule?

Next Steps: For Further Study

Carter V. Finley, *The Turks in World History* (2004). A study placing the role of Turkish-speaking peoples in general and the Ottoman Empire in particular in a global context.

Marius B. Jansen, *The Making of Modern Japan* (2002). A well-regarded account of Japan since 1600 by a leading scholar.

Stephen R. Platt, *Autumn in the Heavenly Kingdom: China, the West, and the Epic Story of the Taiping Civil War* (2012). A dramatic account of the Taiping Rebellion and the role of the West in it.

Jonathan D. Spence, *The Search for Modern China* (1999). Probably the best single-volume account of Chinese history from about 1600 through the twentieth century.

E. Patricia Tsurumi, *Factory Girls: Women in the Thread Mills of Meiji Japan* (1990). An examination of the lives of women in Japan's nineteenth-century textile factories.

Arthur Waley, *The Opium War through Chinese Eyes* (1968). An older classic that views the Opium War from various Chinese points of view.

"The Meiji Revolution," directed by Alex Gibney, The Annenberg CPB Project, 1992, https://www.youtube.com/watch?v=gURiHVTJX4A. A well-produced documentary on the rise of modern Japan, featuring major scholars in the field.

Shirvan Neftchi, "The Decline of the Ottoman Empire," The Caspian Report, http://www.youtube.com/watch?v=T-SUlb4rwls. A ten-minute video that offers an interpretation of the declining fortunes of the Ottoman Empire.

China: On the Brink of Change

By the end of the nineteenth century, growing numbers of thoughtful Chinese recognized that their country was in crisis. A decisive military defeat in a war with Japan (1894–1895) represented a further humiliation to a country already reduced to a semi-colonial dependent of various European powers. And the Boxer rebellion (1898–1901) disclosed a virulent antiforeign and anti-Christian outlook even among rural people. This upheaval demonstrated—once again—the ability of China's vast peasant population to make its presence felt in the political life of the country, as it had in the Taiping Uprising of the 1850s and 1860s (see "The Crisis Within" earlier in this chapter). Its outcome—foreign occupation of Beijing and large reparation payments from China's government—revealed China's continuing weakness relative to European powers and Japan.

In this context, many educated Chinese began to consider various alternatives to the status quo. Some sought reform of various kinds, aimed at preserving the Qing dynasty regime. And several such projects were initiated: ending the traditional civil service examination system, modernizing the military, having consultations about a constitution, and creating elected provincial assemblies. Other voices were more revolutionary, seeking to replace dynastic China with a new society and political system altogether. The climax of this process occurred in 1912 with the collapse of the Qing dynasty and the end of several millennia of imperial rule. The sources that follow provide a glimpse of the various possibilities that awaited China on the brink of dramatic transformation.

SOURCE 19.1 Toward a Constitutional Monarchy

Among the leading advocates of reform in the aftermath of China's defeat by Japan was Kang Youwei (1858–1927), a brilliant Confucian scholar and political thinker. Understanding Confucius as a reformer, he argued that the emperor could be an active agent for China's transformation while operating in a parliamentary and constitutional setting. With its emphasis on human goodness, self-improvement, and the moral example of superiors, Confucianism could provide a framework for real change even as it protected China from "moral degeneration" and an indiscriminate embrace of Western culture. In an appeal to the emperor in early 1898, Kang Youwei spelled out his understanding of what China needed.

- In what ways does Kang Youwei express a Confucian outlook, and in what respects does he show an awareness of a larger world?

- What obstacles to reform does Kang Youwei identify?

- Why does he advocate the Russia of Peter the Great and Meiji Japan as models for China rather than Western Europe and the United States?

KANG YOUWEI | *An Appeal to Emperor Guangxu* | 1898

A survey of all states in the world will show that those states that undertook reforms became stronger while those states which clung to the past perished. . . . If Your Majesty, with your discerning brilliance, observes the trends in other countries, you will see that if we can change, we can preserve ourselves; but if we cannot change, we shall perish. . . .

It is a principle of things that the new is strong but the old is weak. . . . [T]here are no institutions that should remain unchanged for a hundred years. Moreover our present institutions are but unworthy vestiges of the Han, Tang, Yuan, and Ming dynasties. . . . [T]hey are the products of fancy writing and corrupt dealing of the petty officials rather than the original ideas of the ancestors. To say that they are ancestral institutions is an insult to the ancestors. Furthermore institutions are for the purpose of preserving one's territories. Now that the ancestral territory cannot be preserved, what good is it to maintain the ancestral institutions? . . .

Nowadays the court has been undertaking some reforms, but the action of the emperor is obstructed by the ministers, and the recommendations of the able scholars are attacked by old-fashioned bureaucrats. If the charge is not "using barbarian ways to change China," then it is "upsetting ancestral institutions." . . . I beg Your Majesty to make up your mind and to decide on the national policy.

After studying ancient and modern institutions, Chinese and foreign, I have found that . . . ancient times were different from today. I hope that Your Majesty will daily read Mencius [a famous Confucian writer] and follow his example of loving the people . . . but it should be remembered that the [present] age of universal unification is different from that of sovereign nations. . . . As to the republican governments of the United States and France and the constitutional governments of Britain and Germany, these countries are far away and their customs are different from ours. . . . Consequently I beg Your Majesty to adopt the purpose of Peter the Great of Russia as our purpose and to take the Meiji Reform of Japan as the model of our reform. The time and place of Japan's reforms are not remote and her religion and customs are somewhat similar to ours. Her success is manifest; her example can be followed.

Source: Wm. Theodore de Bary and Richard Lufrano, eds., *Sources of Chinese Tradition: From 1600 through the Twentieth Century* (New York: Columbia University Press, 2000), 269–70.

■ ■ ■

SOURCE 19.2 Resistance to Change

A growing reform movement also triggered conservative opposition, rooted in particular understandings of China's Confucian tradition. These brief excerpts from more traditionally oriented Chinese scholars illustrate that opposition.

■ What specific values or principles are evoked in these excerpts?

■ How might Kang Youwei respond to them?

Conservative Reactions after the Sino-Japanese War | **late 19th / early 20th century**

From Zeng Lian: "The state (dynasty) belongs to the ancestors; the emperor merely maintains the dynasty for them. He cannot change the permanent laws laid down by the ancestors."

From Chu Chengbo: ". . . [O]ur trouble is not that we lack good institutions, but that we lack upright minds. If we seek to reform institutions, we must first reform men's minds. Unless all men of ability assist each other, good laws become mere paper documents; unless those who supervise them are fair and enlightened, the venal will end up occupying the places of the worthy. . . ."

From Ye Dehui: "An examination of the causes of success and failure in government reveals that in general the upholding of Confucianism leads to good government and the adoption of foreignism leads to disorder. . . . Confucianism represents the supreme expression of justice in the principles of Heaven and the hearts of men."

Source: Wm. Theodore de Bary and Richard Lufrano, eds., *Sources of Chinese Tradition: From 1600 through the Twentieth Century* (New York: Columbia University Press, 2000), 274–75, 279–80.

■ ■ ■

SOURCE 19.3 Gender, Reform, and Revolution

Among those seeking to change China, the question of women's roles in society frequently arose. The most well-known advocate for women was Qiu Jin (1875–1907). Born into a well-to-do family with liberal inclinations and married to a much older man at age eighteen, she was distinctly unsatisfied in such a conventional life and developed a growing feminist awareness, sometimes dressing in men's clothes and Western styles. In 1903, Qiu Jin left her husband and children to pursue an education in Japan, selling her jewelry to finance the trip. Returning to China in 1906, she started a women's magazine, the *Chinese Women's Journal*, which was a strong advocate for women's independence and education. Soon Qiu Jin became active in revolutionary circles. For her role in an abortive plot to overthrow the Qing dynasty, she was arrested, tortured, and beheaded in 1907 at the age of thirty-two. The selection that follows comes from her most famous appeal for the rights of women.

■ How does Qiu Jin describe the difficulties that faced Chinese women?

■ How does she account for these sad conditions?

■ What does she advocate as a remedy for the problems she identifies? Does she seem to have a political agenda?

■ To what extent do you think she was writing from personal experience?

QIU JIN │ *Address to Two Hundred Million Fellow Countrywomen* │ **1904**

Alas, the most unfairly treated things on this earth are the two hundred million who are born as Chinese women. We consider ourselves lucky to be born to a kind father. If we are unlucky, our father will be an ill-tempered and unreasonable person who . . . will resent us and say things like "she's eventually going to someone else's family" and give us cold and contemptuous looks. When we grow a few years older, without bothering to ask us our thoughts, they will bind our tender, white and natural feet with a strip of cloth. . . . In the end, the flesh is mangled and the bones broken, all so that relatives, friends and neighbors can say, "the girl from so and so's family has tiny feet."

When the time comes (for the parents) to select a husband . . . , the daughter's parents will go along with any proposal as long as his family is rich and powerful. . . . On the wedding day, one will sit in the brightly decorated bridal sedan chair barely able to breathe. When we arrive at the new home, if the husband is . . . no good, her family will blame it "on our wrong conduct in a previous life," or simply "bad luck." If we dare complain, or otherwise try to counsel our husbands, then a scolding and beating will befall us. Others who hear of the abuse will say: "She is a woman of no virtue. She does not act as a wife should!" Can you believe such words? . . . Further inequities will follow if the husband dies. The wife will have to wear a mourning dress for three years and will not be allowed to remarry. Yet, if the wife dies, the husband only needs to wear a blue (mourning) braid. Some men find even that unbecoming and do not bother to wear it at all. Even when the wife has only been dead for three days, he can go out and cavort and indulge himself. . . . In the beginning, Heaven created all people with

no differences between men and women. . . . Why are things so unjust? Everyday these men say, "We ought to be equal and treat people kindly." Then why do they treat women so unfairly and unequally as if they were African slaves?

A woman has to learn not to depend on others, but to rely on herself instead. . . . Why can't we reject footbinding? Are they afraid of women being educated, knowledgeable, and perhaps surpassing them? Men do not allow us to study. We must not simply go along with their decision without even challenging them. . . .

However, from now on I hope we can leave the past behind us and focus on our future. . . . If you have a decent husband who wants to establish a school, do not stop him. If you have a fine son who wishes to study abroad, do not stop him. . . . If you have a son, send him to school. Do the same for your daughter and never bind her feet. If you have a young girl, the best choice would be for her to attend school, but even if she is unable to attend schools, you should teach her to read and write at home. If you come from a family of officials that has money, you should persuade your husband to establish schools and factories and do good deeds that will help common people. If your family is poor, you should work hard to help your husband. . . . These are my hopes. All of you are aware that we are about to lose our country. Men can scarcely protect themselves. How can we rely on them? We must revitalize ourselves. Otherwise all will be too late when the country is lost. Everybody! Everybody! Please keep my hopes alive!

Source: David G. Atwill and Lurong Y. Atwill, *Sources in Chinese History* (Upper Saddle River, NJ: Prentice Hall, 2010), 140–41.

■ ■ ■

SOURCE 19.4 **Cutting the Queue**

Another sign of changing times in late nineteenth-century China was the growing frequency with which more radical Chinese men began to cut or hide their *queue*, the long braided tail of hair that descended from their largely shaved heads. That hairstyle had been forcibly imposed by Manchu rulers of the Qing dynasty and had been periodically resisted since the seventeenth century. From the mid-1890s on, cutting the queue became a symbol of opposition to the Qing dynasty, of a favorable attitude toward modernization, and of a commitment to substantial political change in China. Source 19.4 provides an illustration from 1911 of this radical political action.

■ How do you imagine the responses to this event of the various figures visible in the image? Notice especially the man in the lower left with his hands upraised and the man in Western dress in the lower right.

■ How does the public setting for this event shape your understanding of its significance? Keep in mind also that earlier in its history, the Qing dynasty had applied the death penalty for those cutting their queue.

The Modernization of China | **1911**

Historia/REX/Shutterstock

■ ■ ■

SOURCE 19.5 **Toward Revolution**

While some advocates for change pressed for various reforms within the framework of Qing dynasty China, others felt that the millennia-old monarchy itself had to be overthrown if China was to modernize and prosper as a nation. Among them was Wang Jingwei, a political figure who had studied in Japan and later joined the revolutionary movement. When the Chinese government in 1908 announced plans for developing a quite conservative constitution, Wang Jingwei wrote a ferocious rebuttal, excerpted in Source 19.5. At the time, he was in prison awaiting execution for his revolutionary activities.

■   Why does Wang Jingwei believe that an effective constitutional government can be achieved only after a revolution?

■   What kind of revolution does he prescribe?

■   How might Kang Youwei respond to this revolutionary manifesto?

WANG JINGWEI | *We Want a Republic, Not a Constitutional Monarchy* | **April 25, 1910**

The constitutionalists say that . . . the establishment of a constitutional monarchy will lead to the establishment of a good government. But we revolutionaries emphatically do not share this optimism. . . . [U]nless the monarchal power is destroyed, there is no way of eliminating the existing state system and replacing it with something new.

For several thousand years China has practiced nothing but autocracy. . . . The state power is vested with the monarch, and officials on all levels, central or local, are merely his servants or slaves, whom he can order to whatever he pleases. Suddenly enchanted with the good name of constitution, this autocratic China decided to promote one.

It is our belief that only under a constitutional government established in the wake of a revolution can the principles of nationalism and democracy be carried out. . . .

Speaking of [China's] relations with the outside world, we cannot but feel frightened and alarmed; she is so weak that her chance of survival, for all practical purposes, has become very slim indeed. Knowing her impending peril, how can any Chinese enjoy peace of mind . . . ?

[W]ith a constitutional government scheduled to be established, everyone believes that all of China's problems, foreign and domestic, will be automatically resolved. Like a man who has taken hallucinatory drugs, we are fascinated with appearance at the expense of reality.

Neither will the situation improve nor can she be rejuvenated unless there is a basic change in political structure. The time for making this change is very late, but by no means too late.

Source: Wang Ching-wei, "We Want a Republic, Not a Constitutional Monarchy," in Dun J. Li, *China in Transition: 1517–1911* (New York: Van Nostrand Reinhold, 1969), 319–24.

■ ■ ■

SOURCE 19.6 The Chinese Revolution of 1911

In late 1911 and early 1912, more than 2,000 years of Chinese imperial history came to an inglorious end amid the confused maneuverings of various revolutionary groups, Qing dynasty loyalists, and constitutional reformers. The young boy-emperor Puyi abdicated the imperial throne, and power passed to a prominent military leader, Yuan Shikai. Revolutionary ideas had penetrated the ranks of both officers and soldiers in China's modernizing "New Army," which had been in the making since 1901. Source 19.6, from a French newspaper of 1911, provides a visual account of the evolution of the Chinese military, with figures on the left representing older and now outdated Qing dynasty units, and those on the right depicting the modernized forces of the New Army that were so instrumental in the revolution of 1911. As it happened, those dramatic events were but the prelude for a far deeper and more violent revolutionary transformation of China in the half century that followed. At the time, however, they marked a momentous turning point for an ancient civilization poised at the edge of a tumultuous upheaval.

- ■ What distinguishes these two groups of military men from one another?

- ■ What does the image imply about their attitudes toward one another?

- ■ How might the authors of the other sources respond to the 1911 revolution?

About the Insurrectional Movement in China | 1911

Private Collection/© Look and Learn/Bridgeman Images

DOING HISTORY

1. **Defining obstacles to change:** What hindrances to China's effective transformation are stated or implied in these sources?

2. **Assessing outcomes:** What do these sources contribute to an understanding of the eventual collapse of the Qing dynasty?

3. **Assessing goals:** "China as a culture and a political system must be destroyed in order to preserve China as a nation." To what extent would the creators of these sources have agreed or disagreed with this statement?

4. **Identifying differences:** Imagine a conversation among the authors of the written sources in this collection. What points of agreement might they find? What conflicts would likely arise among them?

The Sino-Japanese War of 1894–1895

The war between China and Japan during 1894–1895, fought largely over control of Korea, signaled a radical reversal in the historical relationship of these two East Asian countries. It also marked major turning points in the internal development of both countries. Voice 19.1, from two Chinese historians, David and Yurong Atwill, describes the significance of that war for China, while historian James Huffman does the same for Japan in Voice 19.2.

- In what ways was the Sino-Japanese War devastating for China?

- What impact did the Sino-Japanese War have on Japan?

- **Integrating Primary and Secondary Sources:** What evidence from the primary sources might support the Atwills' conclusion that the Sino-Japanese War "marks the beginning of the end for the Qing dynasty"?

VOICE 19.1

David and Yurong Atwill on the Significance of the War for China | 2010

[N]o military loss affected the Qing court and the Chinese populace quite as much as their defeat at the hands of the Japanese. . . . For centuries China had sat at the center of a vast tributary network, with neighboring countries acknowledging China's dominant military, political and commercial importance. . . . Contemporary observers all assumed Japan would be defeated quickly. It was a horrible shock to China when Japan not only routed Chinese troops dispatched to Korea, but with devastating precision devastated China's navy. These defeats dealt a savage blow to China's national pride. . . .

If the war eroded China's confidence, the peace was excruciating. With the Treaty of Shimonoseki, Japan proved itself fully as capable as its European counterparts at extracting concessions, indemnities, and territories. The Chinese public, who had been sheltered from the Qing's lack of military modernization, were whipped into a frenzy over the defeats and were further enraged at [China's] submissive acceptance of Japan's peace terms. While the Qing dynasty survived for another fifteen years, it would never recover psychologically from the humiliation it received at the hands of the Japanese. This truly marks the beginning of the end for the Qing dynasty.

Source: David G. Atwill and Yurong Y. Atwill, *Sources in Chinese History* (Upper Saddle River, NJ: Prentice Hall, 2010), 89–90.

VOICE 19.2

James L. Huffman on the Significance of the War for Japan | 2010

More important than the victory . . . , was the explosion of patriotic fervor the war ignited at home. "The excitement generated among the Japanese people was beyond imagination," the commentator Ubukata Toshiro recalled. . . . By war's end, Japan had become a different place; proud of defeating Asia's giant, confident in its military might, thirsty for more territory.

The postwar years saw a rush of support for this vision of strength, even as Japan's cities became both modern and massive. . . . In part, that reflected a rise in industry—and city jobs—as the Sino-Japanese War indemnity poured more than 300 million yen into the economy. . . . When Japan provided roughly half of the international force that put down China's Boxer Rebellion in 1900, and then shared handsomely in the indemnity, the pride that had marked the Sino-Japanese War was reignited.

Source: James L. Huffman, *Japan in World History* (Oxford: Oxford University Press, 2010), 86, 88.

The Long Twentieth Century

1900–present

THE BIG PICTURE

The Long Twentieth Century: A New Period in World History?

The years since 1900, or perhaps a little earlier, appear to many historians as a new and distinct phase of the human journey, in large part because the pace of change has so sharply accelerated during this relatively brief time. The world wars during the first half of the twentieth century were far more destructive than earlier conflicts, and the development of nuclear weapons has provided humankind a completely unprecedented capacity for destruction. Both fascism and communism challenged established

PHOTOS: left, "West Africa Awakes" (gouache on paper) by Angus McBride (1931-2007)/Look and Learn (A & B Images)/Private Collection/Bridgeman Images; center, Peter Langer/Design Pics/UIG/Bridgeman Images; right, Image created by Reto Stockli, Nazmi El Saleous, and Marit Jentoft-Nilsen, NASA GSFC

Western values as they presented new political ideologies to the world. The architecture of global politics changed several times—from a world dominated by European imperial powers, to one structured around the rivalry of two superpowers among some 200 independent states, and by the end of the twentieth century to a global system with one military superpower and a widening array of other centers of economic, military, and political influence.

Beneath the surface of these dramatic events, more significant and enduring processes likewise accelerated at an unprecedented rate. Industrialization quickly became a genuinely global phenomenon, accompanied by a massive increase in energy consumption and overall wealth, a soaring population, and rapid urbanization. Furthermore, long-distance migration mixed the world's peoples in novel ways, generating new social patterns and cultural identities. Feminists mounted an unprecedented attack on patriarchal attitudes and practices, while religious fundamentalists renewed their faith, often in opposition to established political and religious authorities.

But the most fundamental of these processes involved an extraordinary and mounting human impact on the environment. The well-known world historian David Christian has written that "the big story of the twentieth century is how one species began to dominate the energy and resources of the biosphere as a whole."[1] By the late twentieth century, that dominance had taken humankind well into what many scientists have been calling the Anthropocene era, the age of man, in which human activity is leaving an enduring and global mark on the geological, atmospheric, and biological history of the planet itself. All of this has been part of an astonishing and sometimes disorienting rate of change in human life.

A further distinctive feature of the human story during the past 100 years or so lies in an increasingly thick network of connectedness or entanglement that we commonly refer to as "globalization." It found expression in the worldwide empires of major European powers, in a great increase of international trade and investment, in the flow of ideas and cultural patterns around the world, in the large-scale movements of people, and in the global spread of diseases. War, economic crises, communism, fundamentalism, feminism, and the warming of the planet all operated on a global scale. The speed with which this globalizing world took shape and the density of the connections it forged—these too arguably mark the past century or more as a new era in world history.

But if speed and change mark the past century or so, there were also elements of continuity with the more distant past. Interaction among distinct societies, civilizations, and regions has a very long history. "Contact with strangers possessing new and unfamiliar skills," wrote world historian William McNeill, has long been "the principal factor promoting historically significant social change."[2] In that sense, modern globalization has an ancient pedigree. Furthermore, the collapse of empires during the past century resonates with the dissolution of many earlier empires. Technological innovation too has been a feature of human societies since the beginning, and human activity has left its mark on the planet since our gathering and hunting ancestors decimated a number of large animal species. Billions of people continue to operate in the tradition of long-established religions. Not everything has been new since 1900.

And even if world historians emphasize global networks and connections, what was local, regional, and particular continued to matter. Communism may have been a global phenomenon, but its Russian, Chinese, and Cuban variants were hardly identical. Feminism in the Global North certainly differed from that of the Global South. Economic globalization elicited both a warm embrace among corporate and technological elites and bitter rejection from those whose livelihoods and values were threatened by global linkages. Family, village, city, and nation remain deeply meaningful communities even in an interconnected world. Not everything has been global in this most recent era of world history.

In recounting this history, the four chapters of Part 6 do emphasize what was new, what was rapidly changing, and what was global, but with an eye on what persisted from the past and what was unique to particular places. Chapters 20 and 21 highlight the major events or "milestones" of this era. Thus Chapter 20 focuses on the first half of the twentieth century: the world wars, the Great Depression, the rise of fascist and authoritarian movements and states, and the beginnings of communism in Russia and China, all of this cast in a global context. Chapter 21 then carries this narrative of events from roughly 1950

to 2018. It examines the postwar recovery of Europe, the Soviet Union, and Japan; the emergence of a distinctive Chinese communism; the cold war; the end of European empires in Asia and Africa; the emergence of dozens of new states on the global stage; the demise of communism; and international tensions in the quarter century since the end of the cold war.

With these "milestones" of the past century in mind, Chapters 22 and 23 turn to the larger and perhaps even more consequential processes occurring beneath the surface of major public events. Chapter 22 treats the enormous acceleration of technological innovation as a decisive driver of a deeply interconnected world economy and of pervasive social change. Chapter 23 then turns the spotlight on the explosive growth of human numbers, on the movement of many people to the cities and to new lives abroad, and on the cultural transformations that accompanied modern life during the past century. The chapter—and the book—conclude by examining the enormous and continuing impact of human activity on the entire biosphere, which represents by far the most significant long-term process of this new era and the most critical challenge of the next century.

The accelerating changes of this globalizing century have elicited a wide range of responses. Some individuals and communities welcomed changes that brought them unheard-of levels of material comfort and opportunities for an enriched personal life. Others resisted, denied, or sought to endure and adapt to changes that produced loss, disappointment, impoverishment, and sometimes horror beyond imagination. Reflecting on the flux and flow of this tumultuous era allows all of us—historians and students of history alike—to assess these recent transformations of the human condition, to locate ourselves in this torrent of change, and to ponder what lies ahead.

Landmarks in World History (ca. 1900–present)

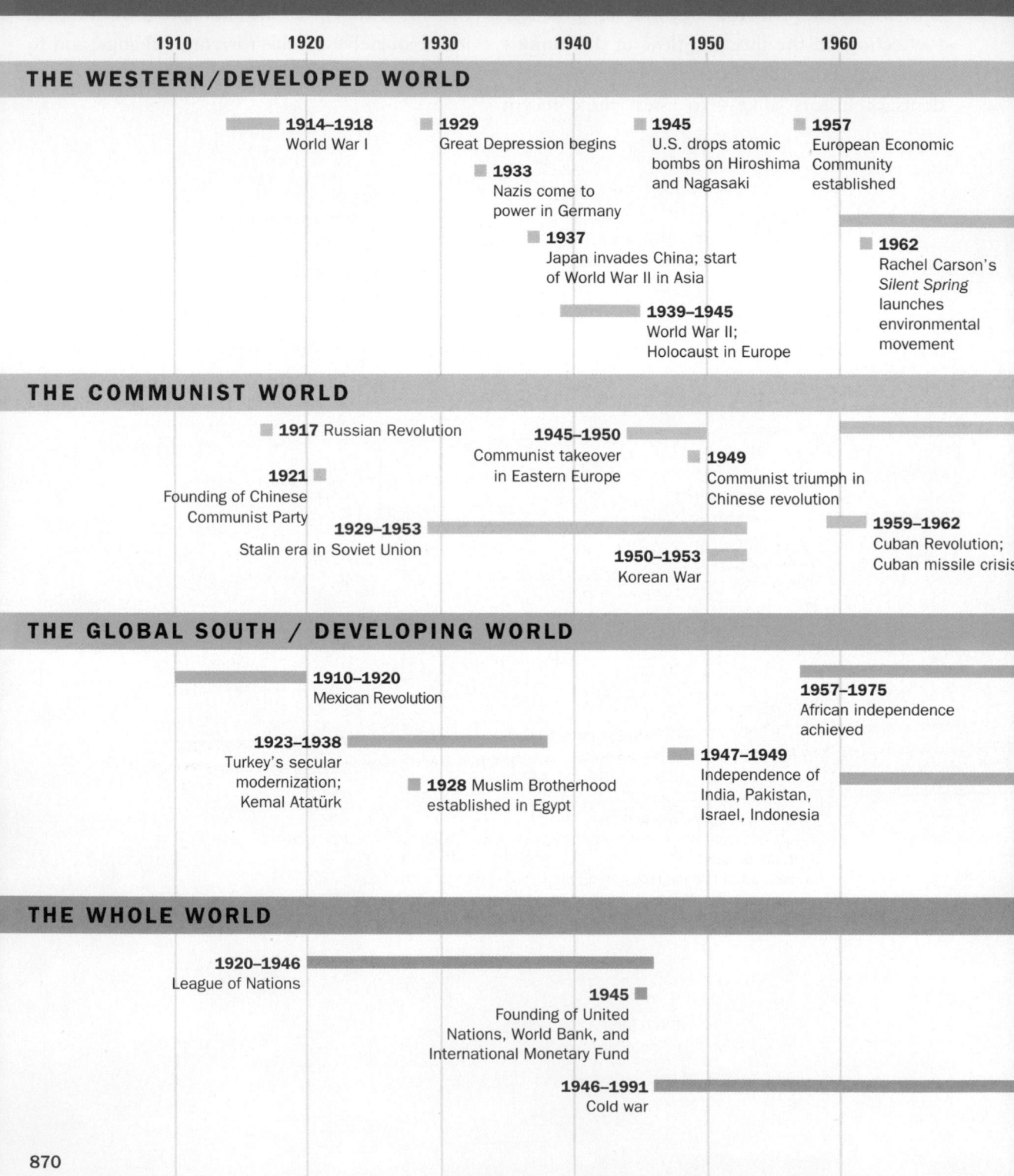

| | 1910 | 1920 | 1930 | 1940 | 1950 | 1960 |

THE WESTERN/DEVELOPED WORLD

1914–1918
World War I

1929
Great Depression begins

1933
Nazis come to
power in Germany

1937
Japan invades China; start
of World War II in Asia

1939–1945
World War II;
Holocaust in Europe

1945
U.S. drops atomic
bombs on Hiroshima
and Nagasaki

1957
European Economic
Community
established

1962
Rachel Carson's
Silent Spring
launches
environmental
movement

THE COMMUNIST WORLD

1917 Russian Revolution

1921
Founding of Chinese
Communist Party

1929–1953
Stalin era in Soviet Union

1945–1950
Communist takeover
in Eastern Europe

1950–1953
Korean War

1949
Communist triumph in
Chinese revolution

1959–1962
Cuban Revolution;
Cuban missile crisis

THE GLOBAL SOUTH / DEVELOPING WORLD

1910–1920
Mexican Revolution

1923–1938
Turkey's secular
modernization;
Kemal Atatürk

1928 Muslim Brotherhood
established in Egypt

1947–1949
Independence of
India, Pakistan,
Israel, Indonesia

1957–1975
African independence
achieved

THE WHOLE WORLD

1920–1946
League of Nations

1945
Founding of United
Nations, World Bank, and
International Monetary Fund

1946–1991
Cold war

870

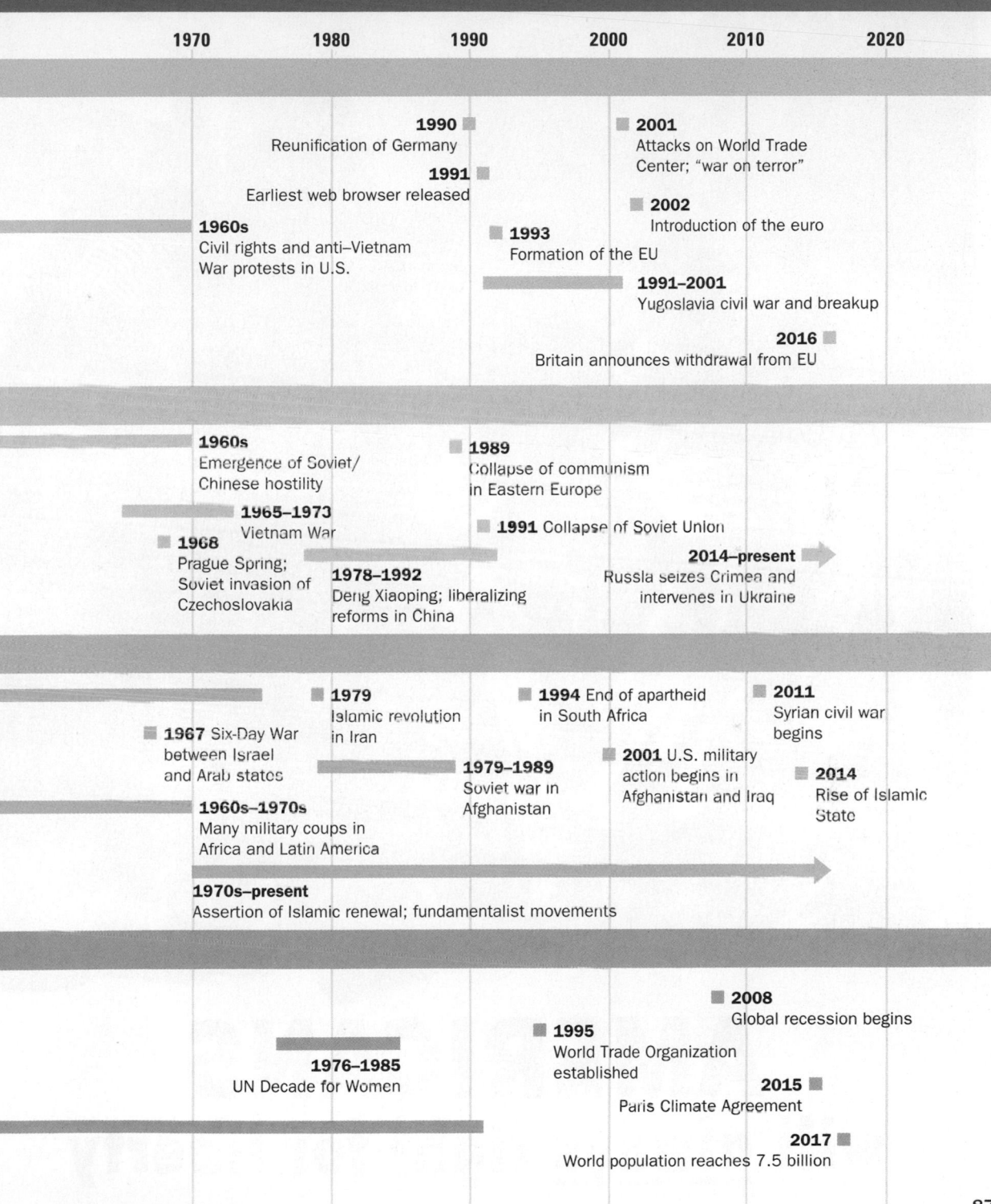

1970   1980   1990   2000   2010   2020

1990 Reunification of Germany

1991 Earliest web browser released

1960s Civil rights and anti–Vietnam War protests in U.S.

1993 Formation of the EU

2001 Attacks on World Trade Center; "war on terror"

2002 Introduction of the euro

1991–2001 Yugoslavia civil war and breakup

2016 Britain announces withdrawal from EU

1960s Emergence of Soviet/ Chinese hostility

1965–1973 Vietnam War

1968 Prague Spring; Soviet invasion of Czechoslovakia

1978–1992 Deng Xiaoping; liberalizing reforms in China

1989 Collapse of communism in Eastern Europe

1991 Collapse of Soviet Union

2014–present Russia seizes Crimea and intervenes in Ukraine

1967 Six-Day War between Israel and Arab states

1960s–1970s Many military coups in Africa and Latin America

1979 Islamic revolution in Iran

1979–1989 Soviet war in Afghanistan

1994 End of apartheid in South Africa

2001 U.S. military action begins in Afghanistan and Iraq

2011 Syrian civil war begins

2014 Rise of Islamic State

1970s–present Assertion of Islamic renewal; fundamentalist movements

1976–1985 UN Decade for Women

1995 World Trade Organization established

2008 Global recession begins

2015 Paris Climate Agreement

2017 World population reaches 7.5 billion

1778   # 1943

AMERICANS
will <u>always</u> fight for liberty

Milestones of the Past Century

War and Revolution

1900–1950

"The First World War was described at the time as the war to end all wars. It did nothing of the sort." So said UN secretary general Ban Ki-moon at an event in 2014 marking one hundred years since the outbreak of that global conflict. And in 2017, the one-hundredth anniversary of the Russian Revolution, Russian president Vladimir Putin offered a largely negative commentary on that event. "Could we not have evolved by way of gradual and consistent forward movement," he asked, "rather than at a cost of destroying our statehood and the ruthless fracturing of millions of human lives."[1] ■

However they are evaluated, these two immense upheavals—World War I and the Russian Revolution—initiated a chain of events that shaped much of world history during the past century. They were followed by the economic meltdown of the Great Depression, by the rise of Nazi Germany and the horror of the Holocaust, and by an even bloodier and more destructive World War II, a struggle that encompassed much of the world. Among the major outcomes of that war was the Chinese revolution, which brought a modern communist party to power in that ancient land. Within the colonial world of Africa, Asia, and the Middle East, these events set in motion processes of change that would shortly put an end to Europe's global empires. It was, to put it mildly, an eventful half century, and many of its developments had their origins in the First World War and the Russian Revolution.

《 The United States and World War II The Second World War and its aftermath marked the decisive emergence of the United States as a global superpower. In this official 1943 poster, U.S. soldiers march forward to "fight for liberty" against fascism while casting a sideways glance for inspiration at the ragged colonial militiamen of their Revolutionary War.

The First World War: A European Crisis with a Global Impact, 1914–1918

Since 1500, Europe had assumed an increasingly prominent position on the global stage, reflected in its military capacity, its colonial empires, and its Scientific and Industrial Revolutions (see Map 20.1). That unique situation provided the foundation for Europeans' pride, self-confidence, and sense of superiority. In 1900, few could have imagined that this "proud tower" of European dominance would lie shattered less than a half century later. The starting point in that unraveling was the First World War.

SEEKING THE MAIN POINT

In what ways were the world wars and the Depression motors of global change?

Origins: The Beginnings of the Great War

Europe's modern transformation and its global ascendancy were certainly not accompanied by a growing unity or stability among its own peoples—in fact, quite the opposite. The historical rivalries of its competing nation-states further sharpened as both Italy and Germany joined their fragmented territories into two major new powers around 1870. A powerful and rapidly industrializing Germany, seeking its "place in the sun," was a particularly disruptive new element in European political life, especially for the more established powers, such as Britain, France, and Russia. Since the defeat of Napoleon in 1815, a fragile and fluctuating balance of power had generally maintained the peace among Europe's major countries. By the early twentieth century, that balance of power was expressed in two rival alliances, the Triple Alliance of Germany, Italy, and the Austro-Hungarian Empire and the Triple Entente of Russia, France, and Britain. Those commitments, undertaken in the interests of national security, transformed a relatively minor incident in the Balkans (southeastern Europe) into a conflagration that consumed almost all of Europe.

That incident occurred on June 28, 1914, when a Serbian nationalist assassinated the heir to the Austro-Hungarian throne, Archduke Franz Ferdinand. To the rulers of Austria-Hungary, the surging nationalism of Serbian Slavs was a mortal threat to the cohesion of their fragile multinational empire, which included other Slavic peoples as well. Thus they determined to crush it. But behind Austria-Hungary lay its far more powerful ally, Germany; and behind tiny Serbia lay Russia, with its self-proclaimed mission of protecting other Slavic peoples. Allied to Russia were the French and the British. Thus a system of alliances intended to keep the peace created obligations that drew these Great Powers of Europe into a general war by early August 1914 (see Map 20.2).

The outbreak of **World War I** was something of an accident, in that none of the major states planned or predicted the archduke's assassination or deliberately sought a prolonged conflict, but the system of rigid alliances made Europe vulnerable to that kind of accident. Moreover, behind those alliances lay other factors that

Guided Reading Question

■ **EXPLANATION**

What elements of Europe's nineteenth-century history contributed to the First World War?

Landmarks for Chapter 20

| | **1910** | **1920** | **1930** | **1940** | **1950** | **1960** |

GLOBAL DEVELOPMENTS

1914–1918 World War I

1919 Treaty of Versailles

1920
League of Nations established

1929–1939 The Great Depression

1937–1945 World War II

1945
UN, World Bank, International
Monetary Fund established

1945–1950
Beginnings of cold war

THE WESTERN WORLD

1917 U.S. joins World War I

1922–1943
Mussolini in power in Italy

1933–1943 New Deal in the U.S.

1933–1945
Hitler in power in Germany

1939–1945 The Holocaust

1936–1940
Italy, Germany, Japan form Axis alliance

THE COMMUNIST WORLD

1917 Russian Revolution

1921 Chinese Communist Party established

1929–1953
Stalin in power in Soviet Union

1945–1950
Imposition of communism
in Eastern Europe

1949
Chinese Communist Party
comes to power

THE COLONIAL/DEVELOPING WORLD

1910–1920
Mexican Revolution

1911
Collapse of Qing dynasty China

1918–1920
Collapse of Ottoman Empire

1945–1950: Israel,
Indonesia, and India
establish independence

ALASKA
GREENLAND
CANADA
UNITED
STATES
PACIFIC
OCEAN
MEXICO
ATLANTIC
OCEAN
GUIANAS
SOUTH
AMERICA

- Russian Empire
- Under colonial rule
- British dominions
- Europe
- Independent,
  European-derived states
- Semi-colonial regions

0   1,500   3,000 miles
0   1,500   3,000 kilometers

MAPPING HISTORY

Map 20.1 The World in 1914

A map of the world in 1914 shows an unprecedented situation in which one people—
Europeans or those of European descent—exercised enormous control and influence over
virtually the entire planet.

contributed to the eruption of war and shaped its character. One of them was a
mounting popular nationalism (see "Nations and Nationalism" in Chapter 16). The
rulers of the major countries of Europe saw the world as an arena of conflict and
competition among rival nation-states. Schools, mass media, and military service
had convinced millions of ordinary Europeans that their national identities were
profoundly and personally meaningful. The public pressure of these competing

READING THE MAP: Identify the two countries that were fully independent in 1914 and were not European-derived states that had once been European colonies.

MAKING CONNECTIONS: Compare this map to Map 14.2: The Global Silver Trade, which depicts European colonial empires in the seventeenth century. On which continents did direct European colonial control expand or decline?

nationalisms allowed statesmen little room for compromise and ensured widespread popular support, at least initially, for the decision to go to war. Many men rushed to recruiting offices, fearing that the war might end before they could enlist, and celebratory parades sent them off to the front. For conservative governments, the prospect of war was a welcome occasion for national unity in the face of the mounting class- and gender-based conflicts in European societies.

Map 20.2 Europe on the Eve of World War I

Despite many elements of common culture, Europe in 1914 was a powder keg, with its major states armed to the teeth and divided into two rival alliances. In the early stages of the war, Italy changed sides to join the French, British, and Russians.

Also contributing to the war was an industrialized militarism. Europe's armed rivalries had long ensured that military men enjoyed great social prestige, and most heads of state wore uniforms in public. All of the Great Powers had substantial standing armies and, except for Britain, relied on conscription (compulsory military service) to staff them. Furthermore, each of the major states had developed elaborate "war plans" that spelled out in great detail the movement of men and materials that should occur immediately upon the outbreak of war. Such plans created a hair-trigger mentality since each country had an incentive to strike first so that its particular strategy could be implemented on schedule and without interruption or surprise. The rapid industrialization of warfare generated an array of novel weapons, including submarines, tanks, airplanes, poison gas, machine guns, and barbed wire. This new military technology contributed to the staggering casualties of the war, including some 10 million deaths, the vast majority male; perhaps twice that number were wounded, crippled, or disfigured. For countless women, as a result, there would be no husbands or children.

Europe's imperial reach around the world likewise shaped the scope and conduct of the war. It funneled colonial troops and laborers by the hundreds of thousands into the war effort, with men from Africa, India, China, Southeast Asia, Australia, New Zealand, and Canada taking part in the conflict. British and French forces seized German colonies in Africa and the South Pacific. Japan, allied with Britain, took various German possessions in China and the Pacific and demanded territorial and economic concessions from China itself. The Ottoman Empire, which entered the conflict on the side of Germany, became the site of intense military actions and witnessed an Arab revolt against Ottoman Turkish control. Finally, the United States, after initially seeking to avoid involvement in European quarrels, joined the war in 1917 when German submarines threatened American shipping. Thus the war, though centered in Europe, had global dimensions and certainly merited its title as a "world war."

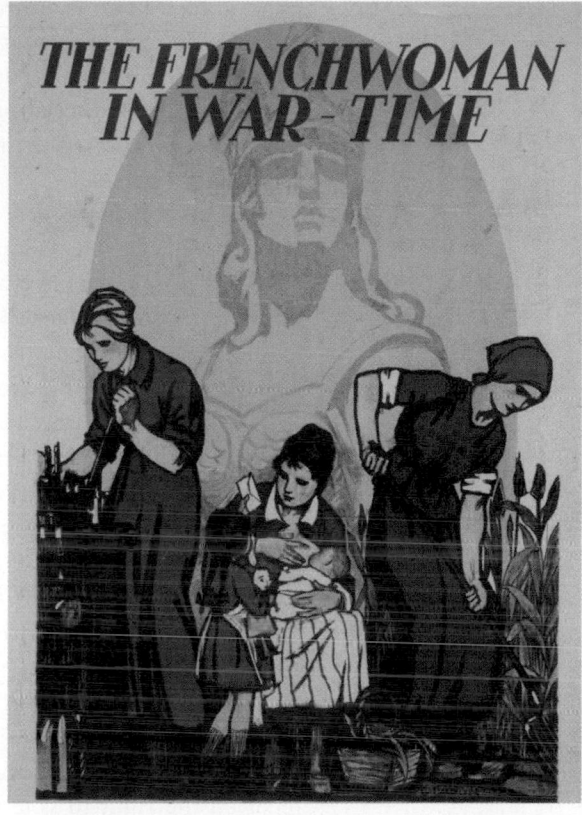

Women and the Great War World War I temporarily brought a halt to the women's suffrage movement as well as to women's activities on behalf of international peace. Most women on both sides actively supported their countries' war efforts, as suggested by this French wartime poster, showing women contributing to the war effort in industrial, agricultural, and domestic settings. (Library of Congress, Prints and Photographs Division, LC-USZC2-4067)

Outcomes: Legacies of the Great War

The Great War shattered almost every expectation. Most Europeans believed in the late summer of 1914 that "the boys will be home by Christmas," but instead the war ground relentlessly on for more than four years before ending in a German defeat in November 1918. Moreover, it had become a "**total war**," requiring the mobilization of each country's entire population. Thus the authority of governments expanded greatly. As the German state, for example, assumed further control over the economy, its policies became known as "war socialism," thus continuing a long-term strengthening of state power across much of Europe. Vast propaganda campaigns sought to arouse citizens by depicting a cruel and inhuman enemy who killed innocent children and violated women. Labor unions agreed to suspend strikes and accept sacrifices for the common good, while women, replacing the men who had left the factories for the battlefront, temporarily abandoned the struggle for the vote.

Guided Reading Question

....

■ **CHANGE**
In what ways did World War I mark new departures in the history of the twentieth century?

No less surprising were the longer-term outcomes of the war. In the European cockpit of that conflict, unprecedented casualties, particularly among elite and well-educated groups, and physical destruction, especially in France, led to a widespread disillusionment among intellectuals with their own civilization. For many, the war seemed to mock the Enlightenment values of progress, tolerance, and rationality, and some began to doubt that the West was superior or that its vaunted science and technology were unquestionably good things. In the most famous novel to emerge from the war, the German veteran Erich Remarque's *All Quiet on the Western Front*, one soldier expressed what many no doubt felt: "It must all be lies and of no account when the culture of a thousand years could not prevent this stream of blood being poured out."

The aftermath of war also brought substantial social and cultural changes to ordinary Europeans and Americans. Women were urged to leave the factory work they had taken up during the war and return to their homes, where they would not compete against returning veterans for "men's jobs." Nonetheless, the war had loosened the hold of tradition in various ways. Enormous casualties promoted social mobility, allowing the less exalted to move into positions previously dominated by the upper classes. As the war ended, suffrage movements revived and women received the right to vote in a number of countries—Britain, the United States, Germany, the Soviet Union, Hungary, and Poland—in part perhaps because of the sacrifices they had made during the conflict. Young middle-class women, sometimes known as "flappers," began to flout convention by appearing at nightclubs, smoking, dancing, drinking hard liquor, cutting their hair short, wearing revealing clothing, and generally expressing a more open sexuality. Technological innovations, mass production, and pent-up demand after the austerities of wartime fostered a new consumerism, particularly in the United States, encouraging those who could to acquire cars, washing machines, vacuum cleaners, electric irons, gas ovens, and other newly available products. Radio and the movies now became vehicles of popular culture, transmitting American jazz to Europe and turning Hollywood stars into international celebrities.

The war also transformed international political life. From the collapse of the German, Russian, and Austro-Hungarian empires emerged a new map of Central Europe with an independent Poland, Czechoslovakia, Yugoslavia, and other nations (see Map 20.3). Such new states were based on the principle of "national self-determination," a concept championed by U.S. president Woodrow Wilson, but each of them also contained dissatisfied ethnic minorities who claimed the same principle. By the **Treaty of Versailles**, which formally concluded the war in 1919, Germany lost its colonial empire and 15 percent of its European territory, was

Map 20.3 Europe and the Middle East after World War I

The Great War brought into existence a number of new states that were carved out of the old German, Austro-Hungarian, Russian, and Ottoman empires. Turkey and the new states in Europe were independent, but those in the Middle East — Syria, Palestine, Iraq, and Transjordan — were administered by Britain or France as mandates of the League of Nations.

READING THE MAP: In which regions were new countries created in the aftermath of World War I?

MAKING CONNECTIONS: Compare Map 20.3 with Map 20.2: Europe on the Eve of World War I. At the conclusion of World War I, which states ceded significant territories to create new states in Europe?

required to pay heavy reparations to the winners, had its military forces severely restricted, and was required to accept sole responsibility for the outbreak of the war. All of this created immense resentment in Germany. One of the country's many demobilized and disillusioned soldiers declared in 1922: "It cannot be that two million Germans should have fallen in vain. . . . No, we do not pardon, we demand—vengeance."[2] His name was Adolf Hitler, and within two decades he had begun to exact that vengeance.

The Great War generated profound changes in the world beyond Europe as well. During the conflict, Ottoman authorities, suspecting that some of their Armenian subjects were collaborating with the Russian enemy, massacred or deported an estimated 1 million Armenians. Although the term "genocide" had not yet been invented, some historians have applied it to those atrocities, arguing that they established a precedent on which the Nazis later built. The war also brought a final end to a declining Ottoman Empire, creating the modern map of the Middle East, with the new states of Turkey, Syria, Iraq, Transjordan, and Palestine. Thus Arabs emerged from Turkish rule, but many of them were governed for a time by the British or French, as "mandates" of the League of Nations (see Map 20.3). Conflicting British promises to both Arabs and Jews regarding Palestine set the stage for an enduring struggle over that ancient and holy land. And in the world of European colonies, the war echoed loudly. Millions of Asian and African men had watched Europeans butcher one another without mercy, had gained new military skills and political awareness, and returned home with less respect for their rulers and with expectations for better treatment as a reward for their service. To gain Indian support for the war, the British had publicly promised to put that colony on the road to self-government, an announcement that set the stage for the independence struggle that followed. In East Asia, Japan emerged strengthened from the war, with European support for its claim to take over German territory and privileges in China. That news enraged Chinese nationalists, particularly among the young, and pushed many of them into a more revolutionary posture, as it seemed to signify the continuation of an arrogant imperialist attitude among Europeans toward the Chinese people.

Furthermore, the First World War brought the United States to center stage as a global power. Its manpower had contributed much to the defeat of Germany, and its financial resources turned the United States from a debtor nation into Europe's creditor. When the American president Woodrow Wilson arrived in Paris for the peace conference in 1919, he was greeted with an almost religious enthusiasm. His famous Fourteen Points seemed to herald a new kind of international life, one based on moral principles rather than secret deals and imperialist machinations. Particularly appealing to many was his idea for the League of Nations, a new international peacekeeping organization committed to the principle of "collective security" and intended to avoid any repetition of the horrors that had just ended. Wilson's idealistic vision largely failed, however. Germany was treated more harshly than he had wished. National self-determination in the multiethnic states of Europe and elsewhere was very difficult, and Wilson's rhetoric inspired hopes in the colonies that could not be immediately fulfilled. In his own country, the U.S. Senate refused to join the League, which was established in 1920, fearing that Americans would be forced to bow to "the will of other nations." That refusal seriously weakened the League of Nations as a vehicle for Wilson's new international order.

The Russian Revolution and Soviet Communism

Among the most significant outcomes of World War I was the beginning of world communism, which played such an enormous role in the history of the twenti- eth century. Modern communism found its political and philosophical roots in nineteenth-century European socialism, inspired by the teachings of Karl Marx. Most European socialists had come to believe that they could achieve their goals peacefully and through the democratic process, but not so in Russia, where democ- racy barely existed. Many Russian socialists therefore advocated uncompromising revolution as the only possible route to a socialist future. That revolution occurred during World War I in 1917. (For the background to the Russian Revolution, see "Russia: Industrialization and Revolution" in Chapter 17.)

The catalyst for the **Russian Revolution** was World War I, which was going very badly for the Russians. Under this pressure the accumulated tensions of Russian society exploded. Workers—men and women alike, along with the wives of soldiers—took to the streets to express their outrage at the incompetence and privileges of the elites. Activists organized demonstrations, published newspapers, and plotted revolution. By early 1917, Tsar Nicholas II had lost almost all support and was forced to abdicate the throne, thus ending the Romanov dynasty, which had ruled Russia for more than three centuries. What followed was a Provisional Government, led by major political figures from various parties. But the Russian Revolution had only begun.

The tsar's abdication opened the door for a massive social upheaval. Ordinary soldiers, seeking an end to a terrible war and despising their upper-class officers, deserted in substantial numbers. In major industrial centers such as St. Petersburg and Moscow, new trade unions arose to defend workers' interests, and some workers seized control of their factories. Grassroots organizations of workers and soldiers, known as soviets, emerged to speak for ordinary people. Peasants, many of whom had been serfs only a generation or two earlier, seized landlords' estates, burned their manor houses, and redistributed the land among themselves. Non-Russian nation- alists in Ukraine, Poland, Muslim Central Asia, and the Baltic region demanded greater autonomy or even independence (see Map 21.1, page 924).

This was social revolution, and it provided an environment in which a small socialist party called the Bolsheviks was able to seize power by the end of 1917 under the leadership of its determined and charismatic leader, Vladimir Ilyich Uly- anov, more commonly known as **Lenin**. In the desperate circumstances of 1917, his party's message—an end to the war, land for the peasants, workers' control of factories, self-determination for non-Russian nationalities—resonated with an

Guided Reading Question

■ **CHANGE**
What factors contributed to the Russian Revolu tion and the victory of the Bolsheviks?

ЭЛЕКТРОФИКАЦИЯ и КОНТР-РЕВОЛЮЦИЯ

The Russian Civil War through Bolshevik Eyes This Bolshevik poster from 1921, titled "Electrification and Counterrevolution," presents a communist view of the civil war that followed the Russian Revolution. It shows a worker bringing electricity and more generally the light of modernity and progress to a backward country, while depicting his opponents, which include a priest, a general, and a businessman, as seeking to extinguish that light. (The New York Public Library/Art Resource, NY)

increasingly rebellious public mood, particularly in the major cities.

A three-year civil war followed in which the Bolsheviks, now officially calling their party "communist," battled an assortment of enemies — tsarist officials, landlords, disaffected socialists, and regional nationalist forces, as well as troops from the United States, Britain, France, and Japan, all of which were eager to crush the fledgling communist regime. Remarkably, the Bolsheviks held on and by 1921 had staggered to victory over their divided and uncoordinated opponents. They renamed their country the Union of Soviet Socialist Republics (USSR or Soviet Union) and set about its transformation. For the next twenty-five years, the Soviet Union remained a communist island in a capitalist sea.

Once they had consolidated power and resolved their leadership struggles, Russian communists soon began the task of constructing a socialist society under the control of Joseph **Stalin** (1878–1953), who emerged as the principal Soviet leader by the late 1920s. To Stalin and communists generally, building socialism meant first of all the modernization and industrialization of a backward Russian society. They sought, however, a distinctly socialist modernity with an emphasis on social equality and the promotion of cultural values of selflessness and collectivism.

Those imperatives generated a political system thoroughly dominated by the Communist Party. Top-ranking party members enjoyed various privileges but were expected to be exemplars of socialism in the making by being disciplined, selfless, and utterly loyal to their country's Marxist ideology. The party itself penetrated society in ways that Western scholars called "totalitarian," for other parties were forbidden, the state controlled almost the entire economy, and political authorities ensured that the arts, education, and the media conformed to approved ways of thinking. Mass organizations for women, workers, students, and various professional groups operated under party control, with none of the independence that characterized civil society in the West.

In the rural areas, building socialism meant the end of private ownership of land and **collectivization of agriculture**. Between 1928 and 1933, peasants were forced, often against great resistance, into large-scale collective farms, which were supposedly more productive and better able to utilize modern agricultural machinery than

Guided Reading Question

■ **DESCRIPTION**
What were the major features of Soviet communism during the Stalin era?

the small family farms that had emerged from the revolution. Stalin singled out the richer peasants, known as *kulaks* (koo-LAHKS), for exclusion from the new collective farms. Some were killed, and many others were deported to remote areas of the country. With little support or experience in the countryside, the urban activists who enforced collectivization were viewed as intrusive outsiders in Russian peasant villages. A terrible famine ensued, with some 5 million deaths from starvation or malnutrition.

In the cities, the task was rapid industrialization. The Soviet approach to industrial development, so different from that of the capitalist West, involved state ownership of property, centralized planning embodied in successive five-year plans, priority to heavy industry, massive mobilization of the nation's human and material resources, and intrusive Communist Party control of the entire process. For a time, it worked. During the 1930s, while the capitalist world floundered amid the massive unemployment of the Great Depression, the Soviet Union largely eliminated unemployment and constructed the foundations of an industrial society that proved itself in the victory over Nazi Germany in World War II. In addition, the USSR achieved massive improvements in literacy rates and educational opportunities, allowing far greater social mobility for millions of people than ever before. As in the West, industrialization fostered rapid urbanization, exploitation of the countryside to provide resources for modern industry in the cities, and the growth of a privileged bureaucratic and technological elite intent on pursuing their own careers and passing on their new status to their children.

Mobilizing Women for Communism As the Soviet Union mobilized for rapid economic development in the 1930s, women entered the workforce in great numbers. Here two young women are mastering the skills of driving a tractor on one of the large collective farms that replaced the country's private agriculture. (Sovfoto/Getty Images)

Despite its totalitarian tendencies, the communist society of the Soviet Union was laced with conflict. Under Stalin's leadership, those conflicts erupted in a search for enemies that terribly disfigured Soviet life. An elastic concept of "enemy" came to include not only surviving remnants from the prerevolutionary elites but also, and more surprisingly, high-ranking members and longtime supporters of the Communist Party, who allegedly had been corrupted by bourgeois ideas, as evidenced by their opposition to some of Stalin's harsh policies. Refracted through the lens of Marxist thinking, these people became "class enemies" who had betrayed the revolution and were engaged in a vast conspiracy, often linked to foreign imperialists, to subvert the socialist enterprise and restore capitalism.

That process culminated in the Terror, or the Great Purges, of the late 1930s, which enveloped tens of thousands of prominent communists, including virtually all of Lenin's top associates, and millions of more ordinary people. Based on suspicious associations in the past, denunciations by colleagues, connections to foreign countries, or simply bad luck, such people were arrested, usually in the dead of night, and then tried and sentenced either to death or to long years in harsh and remote labor camps known as the gulag. A series of show trials publicized the menace that these "enemies of the people" allegedly posed to the country and its revolution. Close to 1 million people were executed between 1936 and 1941. An additional 4 or 5 million were sent to the gulag, where they were forced to work in horrendous conditions and died in appalling numbers. Such was the outcome of the world's first experiment with communism.

Capitalism Unraveling: The Great Depression

While the Soviet Union was constructing the world's first communist society, the capitalist world languished in the **Great Depression**, which began with an abrupt stock market crash in October 1929 and then lasted for a decade. If World War I represented the political collapse of Europe, this economic catastrophe suggested that Western capitalism was likewise failing, as Marx had predicted. All across the Euro-American heartland of the industrialized capitalist world, this vaunted economic system seemed to unravel. For the rich, it meant contracting stock prices that wiped out paper fortunes almost overnight. Banks closed, and many people lost their life savings. Investment dried up, world trade dropped by 62 percent within a few years, and businesses contracted or closed. Unemployment soared everywhere, and in both Germany and the United States it reached 30 percent or more by 1932 (see Snapshot: Comparing the Impact of the Depression, page 887). Vacant factories, soup kitchens, bread lines, shantytowns, and beggars came to symbolize the human reality of this economic disaster.

This economic breakdown began in the United States, which had experienced a booming economy during the 1920s. By the end of that decade, its farms and factories were producing more goods than could be sold, either at home or abroad. Meanwhile, a speculative stock market frenzy had driven up stock prices to an unsustainable level. When that bubble burst in late 1929, its ripple effects quickly encompassed the industrialized economies of Europe, which were intimately connected to the United States through ties of trade, debt, and investment.

Much as Europe's worldwide empires had globalized the Great War, so too its economic linkages globalized the Great Depression. Countries or colonies tied to exporting one or two products were especially hard-hit. Colonial Southeast Asia, the world's major rubber-producing region, saw the demand for its primary export drop dramatically as automobile sales in Europe and the United States were cut in half. In Britain's West African colony of the Gold Coast (present-day Ghana), farmers who had staked their economic lives on producing cocoa for the world market were badly hurt by the collapse of commodity prices. Latin American countries saw the value of their exports cut by half, generating widespread unemployment

Guided Reading Question

■ **CONNECTION**
In what respects was the Great Depression a global phenomenon?

SNAPSHOT   Comparing the Impact of the Depression

As industrial production dropped during the Depression, unemployment soared. Yet the larger Western capitalist countries differed considerably in the duration and extent of this unemployment. Note especially the differences between Germany and the United States. How might you account for this difference?

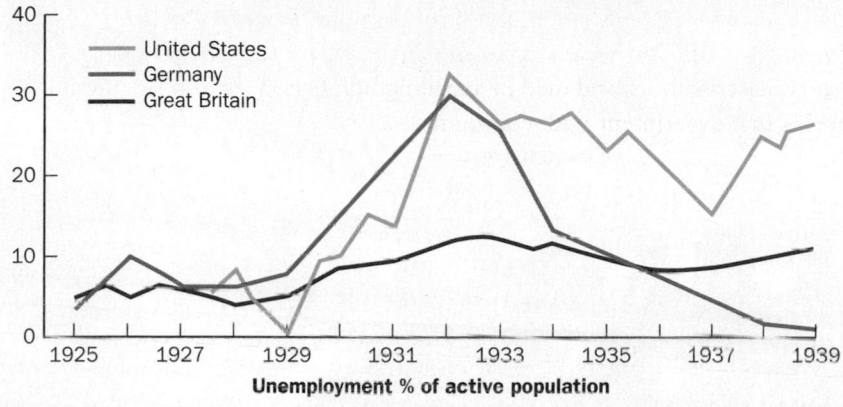

Unemployment % of active population

Adapted from Lynn Hunt et al., *The Making of the West: Peoples and Cultures* (Boston: Bedford/St. Martin's, 2001), 1024.

---

and social tensions. In response to these problems, governments sought to steer their economies away from exports toward producing for the internal market, a policy known as import substitution. In Mexico, the Depression opened the way to reviving the principles of the Mexican Revolution under the leadership of Lázaro Cárdenas (1934–1940), who pushed land reform, favored Mexican workers against foreign interests, and nationalized an oil industry dominated by American capital.

The Great Depression also sharply challenged the governments of industrialized capitalist countries. The apparent failure of a market economy to self-correct led many people to look twice at the Soviet Union. There, the dispossession of the propertied classes and a state-controlled economy had generated an impressive economic growth with almost no unemployment in the 1930s, even as the capitalist world was reeling. No Western country opted for the dictatorial and draconian socialism of the Soviet Union, but in Britain, France, and Scandinavia, the Depression energized a "democratic socialism" that sought greater regulation of the economy and a more equal distribution of wealth through peaceful means and electoral politics. The Great Depression, like the world wars, strengthened the power of the state.

The United States illustrated this trend as President Franklin Roosevelt's New Deal (1933–1942) took shape, permanently altering the relationship among government, the private economy, and individual citizens. The New Deal involved immediate programs of public spending (for dams, highways, bridges, and parks);

Contrasts of the Great Depression This 1937 *Life* magazine image by famed photographer Margaret Bourke-White shows black victims of a flood in Louisville, Kentucky, standing in a breadline during the Depression while behind them rises a billboard depicting a happy and prosperous white family. (Margaret Bourke-White/The LIFE Picture Collection/Getty Images)

longer-term reforms, such as the Social Security system, the minimum wage, and various relief and welfare programs; support for labor unions; and subsidies for farmers. A mounting number of government agencies marked a new degree of federal regulation and supervision of the economy.

Ultimately, none of the New Deal's programs worked very well to end the Great Depression. Not until the massive government spending required by World War II kicked in did economic disaster abate in the United States. The most successful efforts to cope with the Depression came from unlikely places—Nazi Germany and an increasingly militaristic Japan.

Democracy Denied: The Authoritarian Alternative

Despite the victory of the democratic powers in World War I—Britain, France, and the United States—their democratic political ideals and their cultural values celebrating individual freedom came under sharp attack in the aftermath of that bloody conflict. One challenge derived from communism, which was initiated in the Russian Revolution of 1917. In the 1920s and 1930s, however, the more immediate challenge to the victors in the Great War came from highly authoritarian, intensely nationalistic, territorially aggressive, and ferociously anticommunist regimes, particularly those that took shape in Italy, Germany, and Japan. (See Working with Evidence: Ideologies of the Axis Powers, page 911.) The common political goals of these three countries drew them together by 1936–1937 in an alliance directed against the Soviet Union and international communism. In 1940, they solidified their relationship in a formal military alliance, creating the so-called Axis powers. Within this alliance, Germany and Japan clearly stand out, though in quite different ways, in terms of their impact on the larger patterns of world history, for it was their efforts to "establish and maintain a new order of things," as the Axis Pact put it, that generated the Second World War both in East Asia and in Europe.

European Fascism

Between 1919 and 1945, a new political ideology, known as **fascism**, found expression across parts of Europe. While communists celebrated class conflict as the driving force of history, for fascists it was the conflict of nations. Fascism was intensely nationalistic, seeking to revitalize and purify the nation and to mobilize its people for some grand task. Its spokesmen praised violence against enemies as a renewing force in society, celebrated action rather than reflection, and placed their faith in a charismatic leader. Fascists also bitterly condemned individualism, liberalism, feminism, parliamentary democracy, and communism, all of which, they argued, divided and weakened the nation. In their determination to overthrow existing regimes, they were revolutionary; in their embrace of traditional values and their opposition to much of modern life, however, they were conservative or reactionary.

Such ideas appealed to aggrieved people all across the social spectrum. In the devastation that followed the First World War, the numbers of such people grew substantially. Some among the middle and upper classes felt the rise of socialism and communism as a dire threat; small-scale merchants, artisans, and farmers feared the loss of their independence to either big business or socialist revolution; demobilized soldiers had few prospects and nursed many resentments; and intellectuals were appalled by the materialism and artificiality of modern life. Such people had lost faith in the capacity of liberal democracy and capitalism to create a good society and to protect their interests. Some among them proved a receptive audience for the message of fascism. Fascist or other highly authoritarian movements appeared in many European countries, such as Spain, Romania, and Hungary, and some in Latin America, but it was in Italy and Germany that such movements achieved prolonged power in major states, with devastating consequences for Europe and the world.

The fascist alternative took shape first in Italy. That nation had become a unified state only in 1870 and had not yet developed a thoroughly industrialized economy or a solidly democratic culture. The First World War gave rise to resentful veterans,

Guided Reading Question

■ CHANGE
In what ways did fascism challenge the ideas and practices of European liberalism and democracy?

many of them unemployed, and to patriots who believed that Italy had not gained the territory it deserved from the Treaty of Versailles. During the serious economic downturn after World War I, trade unions, peasant movements, and various communist and socialist parties threatened the established social order with a wave of strikes and land seizures.

Into this setting stepped a charismatic orator and a former journalist with a socialist background, Benito **Mussolini** (1883–1945). With the help of a private army of disillusioned veterans and jobless men known as the Black Shirts, Mussolini swept to power in 1922 amid considerable violence, promising an alternative to communism, order in the streets, an end to bickering party-based politics, and the maintenance of the traditional social order. That Mussolini's government allegedly made the trains run on time became evidence that these promises might be fulfilled.

In Mussolini's thinking, fascism was resolutely anticommunist, "the complete opposite . . . of Marxist socialism," and equally antidemocratic. "Fascism combats the whole complex system of democratic ideology, and repudiates it," he wrote. At the core of Mussolini's fascism was his conception of the state. "Fascism conceives of the State as an absolute, in comparison with which all individuals and groups are relative, only to be conceived of in their relation to the State." The state was a conscious entity with "a will and a personality" that represented the "spirit of the nation." Its expansion in war and empire building was "an essential manifestation of vitality."

Mussolini's government suspended democracy and imprisoned, deported, or sometimes executed opponents. Italy's fascist regime also disbanded independent labor unions and peasant groups as well as all opposing political parties. In economic life, a "corporate state" took shape, at least in theory, in which workers, employers, and various professional groups were organized into "corporations" that were supposed to settle their disagreements and determine economic policy under the supervision of the state.

Culturally, fascists invoked various aspects of traditional Italian life. Though personally an atheist, Mussolini embraced the Catholic culture of Italy in a series of agreements with the Church, known as the Lateran Accords of 1929, that made the Vatican a sovereign state and Catholicism Italy's national religion. In fascist propaganda, women were portrayed in highly traditional domestic terms, particularly as mothers creating new citizens for the fascist state, with no hint of equality or liberation. Nationalists were delighted when Italy invaded Ethiopia in 1935, avenging the embarrassing defeat that Italians suffered at the hands of Ethiopians in 1896. In the eyes of Mussolini and fascist believers, all of this was the beginning of a "new Roman Empire" that would revitalize Italian society and give it a global mission. (See Working with Evidence, Source 20.1, page 911.)

Hitler and the Nazis

Far more important in the long run was the German expression of European fascism, which took shape as the **Nazi Party** under the leadership of Adolf **Hitler**

(1889–1945). In many respects, it was similar to its Italian counterpart. Both espoused an extreme nationalism, openly advocated the use of violence as a political tool, generated a single-party dictatorship, were led by charismatic figures, despised parliamentary democracy, hated communism, and viewed war as a positive and ennobling experience.[3] The circumstances that gave rise to the Nazi movement were likewise broadly similar to those of Italian fascism, although the Nazis did not achieve national power until 1933. Germany too was a new European nation, lacking a long-term democratic tradition. As in Italy, resentment about the Treaty of Versailles was widespread, especially among unemployed veterans. Fear of socialism or communism was prevalent among middle- and upper-class groups. But it was the Great Depression that provided the essential context for the victory of German fascism. The German economy largely ground to a halt in the early 1930s amid massive unemployment among workers and the middle class alike. Everyone demanded decisive action from the state.

The Faces of European Fascism Benito Mussolini (left) and Adolf Hitler came to symbolize fascism in Europe in the several decades between the two world wars. In this photograph from September 1937, they are reviewing German troops in Munich during Mussolini's visit to Germany, a trip that deepened the growing relationship between their two countries. (Luce/Getty Images)

This was the context in which Adolf Hitler's National Socialist, or Nazi, Party gained growing public support. Its message expressed an intense German nationalism cast in terms of racial superiority, bitter hatred for Jews as an alien presence, passionate opposition to communism, a determination to rescue Germany from the humiliating requirements of the Treaty of Versailles, and a willingness to decisively tackle the country's economic problems. All of this resonated widely, enabling the Nazis to win 37 percent of the vote in the election of 1932. The following year, Hitler was legally installed as the chancellor of the German government. Thus a weak democratic regime that never gained broad support gave way to the Third Reich.

Once in power, Hitler moved quickly to consolidate Nazi control of Germany. All other political parties were outlawed; independent labor unions were ended; thousands of opponents were arrested; and the press and radio came under state control. Far more thoroughly than Mussolini in Italy, Hitler and the Nazis established their control over German society.

By the late 1930s, Hitler apparently had the support of a considerable majority of the population, in large measure because his policies successfully brought Germany

Guided Reading Question
....
■ **COMPARISON**
What was distinctive about the German expression of fascism? How were Nazis able to gain widespread popular support?

out of the Depression. The government invested heavily in projects such as superhighways, bridges, canals, and public buildings and, after 1935, in rebuilding and rearming the country's diminished military forces. These policies drove down the number of unemployed Germans from 6.2 million in 1932 to fewer than 500,000 in 1937. Two years later Germany had a labor shortage. Erna Kranz, a teenager in the 1930s, later remembered the early years of Nazi rule as "a glimmer of hope . . . not just for the unemployed but for everybody because we all knew that we were downtrodden. . . . It was a good time . . . there was order and discipline."[4] Millions agreed with her.

Other factors as well contributed to Nazi popularity. Like Italian fascists, Hitler appealed to rural and traditional values that many Germans feared losing as their country modernized. In Hitler's thinking and in Nazi propaganda, Jews became the symbol of the urban, capitalist, and foreign influences that were undermining traditional German culture. Thus the Nazis reflected and reinforced a broader and long-established current of anti-Semitism that had deep roots in much of Europe. In his book *Mein Kampf* (My Struggle), Hitler outlined his case against the Jews and his call for the racial purification of Germany in vitriolic terms. (See Working with Evidence, Source 20.2, page 913.)

Far more than in Italy or elsewhere, this insistence on a racial revolution was a central feature of the Nazi program. Upon coming to power, Hitler implemented policies that increasingly restricted Jewish life. Soon Jews were excluded from universities, professional organizations, and civil employment. In 1935, the Nuremberg Laws ended German citizenship for Jews and forbade marriage or sexual relations between Jews and Germans. On the night of November 9, 1938, known as Kristallnacht ("Night of Crystal" or "Night of Broken Glass"), persecution gave way to terror, when Nazis smashed and looted Jewish shops. Such actions made clear the Nazis' determination to rid Germany of its Jewish population, thus putting into effect the most radical element of Hitler's program. Still, it was not yet apparent that this "racial revolution" would mean the mass killing of Europe's Jews. That horrendous development emerged only in the context of World War II.

Beyond race, gender too figured prominently in Nazi thought and policies. While Soviet communists sought to enroll women in the country's industrialization effort, Nazis wanted to limit women largely to the home, removing them from the paid workforce. To Hitler, the state was the natural domain of men, while the home was the realm of women. "Woman in the workplace is an oppressed and tormented being," declared a Nazi publication. Concerned about declining birthrates, Italy and Germany alike promoted a cult of motherhood, glorifying and rewarding women who produced children for the state. Accordingly, fascist regimes in both countries generally opposed abortion, contraception, family planning, and sex education, all of which were associated with feminist thinking. Yet such an outlook did not necessarily coincide with conservative or puritanical sexual attitudes. In Germany, a state-sponsored system of brothels was initiated in the mid-1930s, for it was assumed that virile men would be promiscuous and that soldiers required a sexual outlet if they were to contribute to the nation's military strength.

Also sustaining Nazi rule were massive torchlight ceremonies celebrating the superiority of the German race and its folk culture. In these settings, Hitler was the mystical leader, the Führer, a mesmerizing orator who would lead Germany to national greatness and individual Germans to personal fulfillment.

If World War I and the Great Depression brought about the political and economic collapse of Europe, the Nazi phenomenon represented a rejection of some of the values—rationalism, tolerance, democracy, human equality—that for many people had defined the core of Western civilization since the Enlightenment. On the other hand, Nazis claimed the legacy of modern science, particularly in their concern to classify and rank various human groups. Thus they drew heavily on the "scientific racism" of the late nineteenth century and its expression in phrenology, which linked the size and shape of the skull to human behavior and personality (see "Industry and Empire" in Chapter 18). Moreover, in their effort to purify German society, the Nazis reflected the Enlightenment confidence in the perfectibility of humankind and in the social engineering necessary to achieve it.

By 1940, the European political landscape had altered dramatically from what it had been just a few decades earlier. At the beginning of the twentieth century, major European countries had embraced largely capitalist economies and to varying degrees

The Ideal Nazi Family This painting by Wolfgang Willrich, a prominent Nazi artist, portrays the highly romanticized Nazi image of an ideal Aryan family. They have four children; most are dressed in plain peasant-style clothing; the mother wears her hair in a bun and does not use makeup; they live in a rural agricultural setting; the boy is wearing a Hitler Youth uniform; and all of them are blonde, with athletic bodies and ruddy complexions. (bpk Bildagentur/Art Resource, NY)

increasingly democratic political systems with multiple parties and elected parliaments. But by the time World War II broke out, Europe's largest country, the Soviet Union, had altogether rejected capitalism in favor of a state-controlled economy and a political system dominated by a single communist political party. The fascist states of Germany and Italy likewise dismantled multiparty democracies, replacing them with highly authoritarian dictatorships. While they retained major private ownership of property, the state played a large role in economic affairs. Communist and fascist states alike rejected the individualistic liberalism of the remaining democracies, celebrating the collective identities of "class" in the case of the Soviet Union and of nation or race in Italy and Germany.

Japanese Authoritarianism

In various ways, the modern history of Japan paralleled that of Italy and Germany. All three were newcomers to Great Power status, with Japan joining the club of industrializing and empire-building states only in the late nineteenth century as its sole Asian member (see "The Japanese Difference" in Chapter 19). Like Italy and Germany, Japan had a rather limited experience with democratic politics, for its elected parliament was constrained by a very small electorate (only 1.5 million men in 1917) and by the exalted position of a semi-divine emperor and his small coterie of elite advisers. During the 1930s, Japan too moved toward authoritarian government and a denial of democracy at home, even as it launched an aggressive program of territorial expansion in East Asia. But in sharp contrast to Italy and Germany, Japan's participation in World War I was minimal, and its economy grew considerably as other industrialized countries were consumed by the European conflict. At the peace conference ending that war, Japan was seated as an equal participant, allied with the winning side of democratic countries such as Britain, France, and the United States.

During the 1920s, Japan seemed to be moving toward more democratic politics and Western cultural values. Universal male suffrage was achieved in 1925, and a two-party system began to emerge. Supporters of these developments, mostly urban and well-to-do, generally embraced the dignity of the individual, free expression of ideas, and greater gender equality. Education expanded; an urban consumer society developed; middle-class women entered new professions; and young women known as *moga* (modern girls) sported short hair and short skirts, while dancing with *mobo* (modern boys) at jazz clubs and cabarets. To such people, the Japanese were becoming global citizens and their country was becoming "a province of the world" as they participated increasingly in a cosmopolitan and international culture.

In this environment, the accumulated tensions of Japan's modernizing and industrializing processes found expression. "Rice riots" in 1918 brought more than a million people into the streets of urban Japan to protest the rising price of that essential staple. Union membership tripled in the 1920s as some factory workers began to think in terms of entitlements and workers' rights rather than the benevolence of their employers. In rural areas, tenant unions multiplied, and disputes with landowners increased amid demands for a reduction in rents. A mounting women's movement advocated a variety of feminist issues, including suffrage and the end of legalized prostitution. "All the sleeping women are now awake and moving," declared Yosano Akiko, a well-known poet, feminist, and social critic in 1911. A number of "proletarian (working class) parties"—the Labor-Farmer Party, the Socialist People's Party, and a small Japan Communist Party—promised in various ways to promote radical social change.

For many people in established elite circles—bureaucrats, landowners, industrialists, military officials—all of this was both appalling and alarming, suggesting echoes of the Russian Revolution of 1917. As in Germany, however, it was the impact of the Great Depression that paved the way for harsher and more authoritarian action. That worldwide economic catastrophe hit Japan hard. Shrinking world demand for silk impoverished millions of rural dwellers who raised silkworms. Japan's exports fell by half between 1929 and 1931, leaving a million or

Guided Reading Question

■ **COMPARISON**
How did Japan's experience during the 1920s and 1930s resemble that of Germany, and how did it differ?

more urban workers unemployed. Many young workers returned to their rural villages only to find food scarce, families forced to sell their daughters to urban brothels, and neighbors unable to offer the customary money for the funerals of their friends. In these desperate circumstances, many began to doubt the ability of parliamentary democracy and capitalism to address Japan's "national emergency." Such conditions energized a growing movement in Japanese political life known as Radical Nationalism or the **Revolutionary Right**. Expressed in dozens of small groups, it was especially appealing to younger army officers. The movement's many separate organizations shared an extreme nationalism, hostility to parliamentary democracy, a commitment to elite leadership focused around an exalted emperor, and dedication to foreign expansion. The manifesto of one of those organizations, the Cherry Blossom Society, expressed these sentiments clearly in 1930:

> As we observe recent social trends, top leaders engage in immoral conduct, political parties are corrupt, capitalists and aristocrats have no understanding of the masses, farming villages are devastated, unemployment and depression are serious. . . . The rulers neglect the long term interests of the nation, strive to win only the pleasure of foreign powers and possess no enthusiasm for external expansion. . . . The people are with us in craving the appearance of a vigorous and clean government that is truly based upon the masses, and is genuinely centered around the Emperor.[5]

In sharp contrast to developments in Italy and Germany, however, no right-wing or fascist party gained wide popular support in Japan, and no such party was able to seize power. Nor did Japan produce any charismatic leader on the order of Mussolini or Hitler. People arrested for political offenses were neither criminalized nor exterminated, as in Germany, but instead were subjected to a process of "resocialization" that brought the vast majority of them to renounce their "errors" and return to the "Japanese way." Japan's established institutions of government were sufficiently strong, and traditional notions of the nation as a family headed by the emperor were sufficiently intact, to prevent the development of a widespread fascist movement able to take control of the country.

In the 1930s, though, Japanese public life clearly changed in ways that reflected the growth of right-wing nationalist thinking. The military in particular came to exercise a more dominant role in Japanese political life, reflecting the long-standing Japanese respect for the samurai warrior class. Censorship limited the possibilities of free expression, and a single news agency was granted the right to distribute all national and most international news to the country's newspapers and radio stations. Established authorities also adopted many of the ideological themes of the Revolutionary Right. In 1937, the Ministry of Education issued a new textbook, *Cardinal Principles of the National Entity of Japan*, for use in all Japanese schools (see Working with Evidence, Source 20.4, page 916). That document proclaimed the Japanese to be "intrinsically quite different from the so-called citizens of Occidental [Western] countries." Those nations were "conglomerations of separate individuals" with "no deep foundation between

The Growth of Japanese Militarism This poster celebrating the Japanese navy was created by the National Defense Women's Association in 1938. It reflects the increasing role of the military in Japanese national life and seeks to encourage female support for it. (Pictures from History/Bridgeman Images)

ruler and citizen to unite them." In Japan, by contrast, an emperor of divine origin related to his subjects as a father to his children. It was a natural, not a contractual, relationship, expressed most fully in the "sacrifice of the life of a subject for the Emperor."

The state's success in quickly bringing the country out of the Depression likewise fostered popular support. As in Nazi Germany, state-financed credit, large-scale spending on armaments, and public works projects enabled Japan to emerge from the Depression more rapidly and more fully than major Western countries. "By the end of 1937," noted one Japanese laborer, "everybody in the country was working."[6] By the mid-1930s, the government increasingly assumed a supervisory or managerial role in economic affairs. Private property, however, was retained, and the huge industrial enterprises called *zaibatsu* continued to dominate the economic landscape.

Although Japan during the 1930s shared some common features with fascist Italy and Nazi Germany, it remained, at least internally, a less repressive and more pluralistic society than either of those European states. Japanese intellectuals and writers had to contend with government censorship, but they retained some influence in the country. Generals and admirals exercised great political authority as the role of an elected parliament declined, but they did not govern alone. Political prisoners were few and were not subjected to execution or deportation as in European fascist states. Japanese conceptions of their racial purity and uniqueness were directed largely against foreigners rather than an internal minority. Nevertheless, like Germany and Italy, Japan developed extensive imperial ambitions. Those projects of conquest and empire building collided with the interests of established imperial powers such as the United States and Britain, launching a second, and even more terrible, global war.

A Second World War, 1937–1945

World War II, even more than the Great War, was a genuinely global conflict with independent origins in both Asia and Europe. Dissatisfied states in both continents sought to fundamentally alter the international arrangements that had emerged from World War I. Many Japanese, like their counterparts in Italy and Germany, felt stymied by Britain and the United States as they sought empires that they regarded as essential for their national greatness and economic well-being.

The Road to War in Asia

World War II began in Asia before it occurred in Europe. In the late 1920s and the 1930s, Japanese imperial ambitions mounted as the military became more powerful in Japan's political life and as an earlier cultural cosmopolitanism gave way to more nationalist sentiments. An initial problem was the rise of Chinese nationalism, which seemed to threaten Japan's sphere of influence in Manchuria, acquired by Japan after the Russo-Japanese War of 1904–1905. Acting independently of civilian authorities in Tokyo, units of the Japanese military seized control of Manchuria in 1931 and established a puppet state called Manchukuo. This action was condemned by China, the United States, and the League of Nations alike, but there was no effective military response to the Japanese aggression. The condemnation, however, prompted Japan to withdraw from the League of Nations and in 1936 to align more closely with Germany and Italy. By that time, relations with an increasingly nationalist China had deteriorated further, leading to a full-scale attack on heartland China in 1937 and escalating a bitter conflict that would last another eight years. **World War II in Asia** had begun (see Map 20.4).

As Japan's war against China unfolded, the view of the world held by Japanese authorities and many ordinary people hardened. Increasingly, they felt isolated, surrounded, and threatened. Anti-Japanese immigration policies in the United States convinced some Japanese that racism prevented the West from acknowledging Japan as an equal power. Furthermore, Japan was quite dependent on foreign and especially American sources of strategic goods — oil, for example — even as the United States was becoming increasingly hostile to Japanese ambitions in Asia. Moreover, Western imperialist powers — the British, French, and Dutch — controlled resource-rich colonies in Southeast Asia. Finally, the Soviet Union, proclaiming an alien communist ideology, loomed large in northern Asia. To growing numbers of Japanese, their national survival was at stake.

Thus in 1940–1941, Japan extended its military operations to the French, British, Dutch, and American colonies of Southeast Asia — Malaya, Burma, Indonesia, Indochina, and the Philippines — in an effort to acquire those resources that would free it from dependence on the West. In carving out this Pacific empire, the Japanese presented themselves as liberators and modernizers, creating an "Asia for Asians" and freeing their continent from European and American dominance. Experience soon showed that Japan's concern was far more for Asia's resources than for its liberation and that Japanese rule exceeded in brutality even that of the Europeans.

A decisive step in the development of World War II in Asia lay in the Japanese attack on the United States at Pearl Harbor in Hawaii in December 1941. Japanese authorities undertook that attack with reluctance and only after negotiations to end American hostility to Japan's empire-building enterprise proved fruitless and an American oil embargo was imposed on Japan in July 1941. In the face of this hostility, Japan's leaders felt that the alternatives for their country boiled down to either an acceptance of American terms, which they feared would reduce Japan to

Guided Reading Question

■ **COMPARISON**
How did the origins of World War II in Asia and Europe resemble one another, and how did they differ?

Map 20.4 World War II in Asia and the Pacific

Japanese aggression temporarily dislodged the British, French, Dutch, and Americans from their colonial possessions in Asia, while inflicting vast devastation on China. Much of the American counterattack involved "island hopping" across the Pacific until the dropping of the atomic bombs on Hiroshima and Nagasaki finally prompted the Japanese surrender in August 1945.

a second- or third-rank power, or a war with an uncertain outcome. Given those choices, the decision for war was made more with foreboding than with enthusiasm. A leading Japanese admiral made the case for war in this way in late 1941: "The government has decided that if there were no war the fate of the nation is sealed. Even if there is a war, the country may be ruined. Nevertheless a nation that does not fight in this plight has lost its spirit and is doomed."[7]

As a consequence of the attack on Pearl Harbor, the United States entered the war in the Pacific, beginning a long and bloody struggle that ended only with the use of atomic bombs against Hiroshima and Nagasaki in 1945. Since Japan was allied with Germany and Italy, the Pearl Harbor action also joined the Asian theater of the war with the ongoing conflict in Europe into a single global struggle that pitted Germany, Italy, and Japan (the Axis powers) against the United States, Britain, and the Soviet Union (the Allies).

The Road to War in Europe

If Japan was the dissatisfied power in Asia, Nazi Germany occupied that role in Europe. As a consequence of their defeat in World War I and the harsh terms of the Treaty of Versailles, many Germans harbored deep resentments about their country's position in the international arena. Taking advantage of those resentments, the Nazis pledged to rectify the treaty's perceived injustices. Thus, to most historians, the origins of **World War II in Europe** lie squarely in German aggression, although with many twists and turns and encouraged by the initial unwillingness of Britain, France, or the Soviet Union to confront that aggression forcefully. If World War I was accidental and unintended, World War II was deliberate and planned—perhaps even desired—by the German leadership and by Hitler in particular.

Slowly at first and then more aggressively, Hitler rearmed the country for war as he also pursued territorial expansion, annexing Austria and the German-speaking parts of Czechoslovakia. At a famous conference in Munich in that year, the British and the French gave these actions their reluctant blessing, hoping that this "appeasement" of Hitler could satisfy his demands and avoid all-out war. But it did not. On September 1, 1939, Germany unleashed a devastating attack on Poland, triggering the Second World War in Europe, as Britain and France declared war on Germany. Quickly defeating France, the Germans launched a destructive air war against Britain and in 1941 turned their war machine loose on the Soviet Union. By then, most of Europe was under Nazi control (see Map 20.5).

The Second World War was quite different from the first. It was not welcomed with the kind of mass enthusiasm across Europe that had accompanied the opening of World War I in 1914. The bitter experience of the Great War suggested to most people that only suffering lay ahead. The conduct of the two wars likewise differed. The first war had quickly bogged down in trench warfare that emphasized defense, whereas in the second war the German tactic of *blitzkrieg* (lightning war) coordinated the rapid movement of infantry, tanks, and airpower over very large areas.

Such military tactics were initially successful and allowed German forces, aided by their Italian allies, to sweep over Europe, the western Soviet Union, and North Africa. The tide began to turn in 1942 when the Soviet Union absorbed the German onslaught and then began to counterattack, slowly and painfully moving westward

Map 20.5 World War II in Europe and Africa
For a brief moment during World War II, Nazi Germany came close to bringing all of Europe and North Africa under its rule. Then in late 1942, the Allies began a series of counterattacks that led to German surrender in May 1945.

toward the German heartland. The United States, with its enormous material and human resources, joined the struggle against Germany in 1942 and led the invasion of northern France in 1944, opening a long-awaited second front in the struggle against Hitler's Germany. Years of bitter fighting ensued before these two huge military movements ensured German defeat in May 1945.

Consequences: The Outcomes of a Second Global Conflict

The Second World War was the most destructive conflict in world history, with total deaths estimated at around 60 million, some six times that of World War I. More than half of those casualties were civilians. Partly responsible for this horrendous toll were the new technologies of warfare—heavy bombers, jet fighters, missiles, and atomic weapons. Equally significant, though, was the almost complete blurring of the traditional line between civilian and military targets, as entire cities and whole populations came to be defined as the enemy. Nowhere was that blurring more complete than in the Soviet Union, which accounted for more than 40 percent of the total deaths in the war—probably around 25 million, with an equal number made homeless and thousands of towns, villages, and industrial enterprises destroyed. In China as well, perhaps 15 million deaths and uncounted refugees grew out of prolonged Chinese resistance and the shattering Japanese response, including the killing of every person and every animal in many villages. Within a few months, during the infamous Rape of Nanjing in 1937–1938, some 200,000 to 300,000 Chinese civilians were killed and often mutilated, and countless women were sexually assaulted. Indiscriminate German bombing of British cities and the Allied firebombing of Japanese and German cities likewise reflected the new morality of total war, as did the dropping of atomic bombs on Hiroshima and Nagasaki, which in a single instant vaporized tens of thousands of people. This was total war with a scale, intensity, and indiscriminate brutality that exceeded even the horrors of World War I. (See Zooming In: Hiroshima, page 902.)

A further dimension of total war lay in governments' efforts to mobilize their economies, their people, and their propaganda machines even more extensively than before. Colonial resources were harnessed once again. The British in particular made extensive use of colonial troops and laborers from India and Africa. Japan compelled several hundred thousand women from Korea, China, and elsewhere to serve the sexual needs of Japanese troops as so-called comfort women, who often accommodated twenty to thirty men a day.

As in World War I, though on a much larger scale, the needs of the war drew huge numbers of women into both industry and the military. In the United States, "Rosie the Riveter" represented those women who now took on heavy industrial jobs, which previously had been reserved for men. In the Soviet Union, women constituted more than half of the industrial workforce by 1945 and almost completely dominated agricultural production. Soviet women also participated actively in combat, with some 100,000 of them winning military honors. A much smaller percentage of German and Japanese women were mobilized for factory work, but a Greater Japan Women's Society enrolled some 19 million members, who did volunteer work and promised to lay aside their gold jewelry and abandon extravagant weddings. As always, war heightened the prestige of masculinity, and given the immense sacrifices that men had made, few women were inclined to directly challenge the practices of patriarchy immediately following the war.

Guided Reading Question

■ **COMPARISON**
How did World War II differ from World War I?

Hiroshima

"If the radiance of a thousand suns were to burst at once into the sky. That would be the splendor of the Mighty One."[8] This passage from the Bhagavad Gita, an ancient Hindu sacred text, occurred to J. Robert Oppenheimer, a leading scientist behind the American push to create a nuclear bomb, as he watched the first successful test of a nuclear weapon in the desert south of Santa Fe, New Mexico, on the evening of July 16, 1945. Years later, he recalled that another verse from the same sacred text had also entered his mind: "I am become Death, the Destroyer of Worlds." And so the atomic age was born amid Oppenheimer's thoughts of divine splendor and divine destruction.

Several weeks later, the whole world became aware of this new era when American forces destroyed the

A mother and child, victims of Hiroshima, on the floor of a makeshift hospital, two months after the attack.

photo: AP Images

Japanese cities of Hiroshima and Nagasaki with nuclear bombs. The U.S. government decided to use this powerful new weapon partially to hasten the end of World War II, but also to strengthen the United States' position in relation to the Soviet Union in the postwar world. Whether the bomb was necessary to force Japan to surrender is a question of some historical debate. What is not in dispute was the horrific destruction and human suffering wrought by the two bombs. The centers of both cities were flattened, and as many as 80,000 inhabitants of Hiroshima and 40,000 of Nagasaki perished almost instantly from the force and intense heat of the explosions.

Among the most haunting outcomes of the war was the **Holocaust**. The outbreak of war closed off certain possibilities, such as forced emigration, for implementing the Nazi dream of ridding Germany of its Jewish population. It also brought millions of additional Jews in Poland and the Soviet Union under German control and triggered among Hitler's enthusiastic subordinates various schemes for a "final solution" to the Jewish question. From this emerged the death camps that included Auschwitz, Treblinka, and Sobibór. Altogether, some 6 million Jews perished in a technologically sophisticated form of mass murder that set a new standard for human depravity. Millions more whom the Nazis deemed inferior, undesirable, or dangerous—Russians, Poles, and other Slavs; Gypsies, or the Roma; mentally or physically handicapped people; homosexuals; communists; and Jehovah's Witnesses—likewise perished in Germany's efforts at racial purification.

Although the Holocaust was concentrated in Germany, its significance in twentieth-century world history has been huge. It has haunted postwar Germany in particular and the Western world in general. How could such a thing have occurred in a Europe bearing the legacy of both Christianity and the Enlightenment? More

The harrowing accounts of survivors offer some sense of the suffering that followed. Iwao Nakamura, a schoolboy in Hiroshima who lived through the attack, recalled "old people pleading for water, tiny children seeking help, students unconsciously calling for their parents." He remembered that "there was a mother prostrate on the ground, moaning with pain but with one arm still tightly embracing her dead baby."[9] But for many of these survivors, the suffering had only begun. It is estimated that by 1950 as many as 200,000 additional victims had succumbed to their injuries, especially burns and the terrible effects of radiation. Cancer and genetic deformations caused by exposure to radiation continue to affect survivors and their descendants today.

Human suffering on a massive scale was a defining feature of total war during the first half of the twentieth century. In this sense, the atomic bomb was just the latest development in an arms race that drew on advances in manufacturing, technology, and science to create ever more horrific weapons of mass destruction. But no other weapon from that period was as revolutionary as the atomic bomb, which made use of recent discoveries in theoretical physics to harness the fundamental forces of the universe for war. The subsequent development of those weapons has cast an enormous shadow on the world ever since.

That shadow lay in a capacity for destruction previously associated only with an apocalypse of divine origin. Now human beings have acquired that capacity. A single bomb in a single instant can obliterate any major city in the world, and the detonation of even a small fraction of the weapons in existence today would reduce much of the world to radioactive rubble and social chaos. The destructive power of nuclear weapons has led responsible scientists to contemplate the possible extinction of our species—by our own hands. It is hardly surprising that the ongoing threat of nuclear war has led many survivors of the Hiroshima and Nagasaki bombings to push for a world free of nuclear weapons by highlighting the human suffering that they cause. In a speech to a United Nations Special Session on Disarmament in 1982, Senji Yamaguchi, a survivor of the Nagasaki bombing, pleaded, "Please look closely at my [burnt] face and hands. . . . We, atomic bomb survivors, are calling out. I continue calling out as long as I am alive: no more Hiroshima, no more Nagasaki, no more war, no more [victims of nuclear attacks]."[10]

QUESTION

How might you define both the short- and long-term outcomes of the Hiroshima bombing?

specifically, it sent many of Europe's remaining Jews fleeing to Israel and gave urgency to the establishment of a modern Jewish nation in the ancient Jewish homeland. That action outraged many Arabs, some of whom were displaced by the arrival of the Jews, and has fostered an enduring conflict in the Middle East. Furthermore, the Holocaust defined a new category of crimes against humanity—genocide, the attempted elimination of entire peoples.

On an even larger scale than World War I, this second global conflict rearranged the architecture of world politics. As the war ended, Europe was impoverished, its industrial infrastructure shattered, many of its great cities in ruins, and millions of its people homeless or displaced. Within a few years, this much-weakened Europe was effectively divided, with its western half operating willingly under an American security umbrella and the eastern half subject to Soviet control, but less willingly. It was clear that Europe's dominance in world affairs was finished. Not only had the war weakened both the will and the ability of European powers to hold on to their colonies, but it had also emboldened nationalist and anticolonial movements everywhere (see "Toward Independence in Asia and Africa" in Chapter 21). Japanese victories in Southeast Asia had certainly damaged European prestige. Furthermore, tens of thousands of Africans had fought for the British or the French, had seen white people die, had enjoyed the company of white women, and had returned home with very different ideas about white superiority and the permanence of colonial rule. Colonial subjects everywhere were very much aware that U.S. president Franklin Roosevelt and British prime minister Winston Churchill had solemnly declared in 1941 that "we respect the right of all peoples to choose the form of government under which they will live." Increasingly, Asian and African leaders demanded that such principles should apply to them as well.

The horrors of two world wars within a single generation prompted a renewed interest in international efforts to maintain the peace in a world of competing and sovereign states. The chief outcome was the United Nations (UN), established in 1945 as a successor to the moribund League of Nations. As a political body dependent on agreement among its most powerful members, the UN proved more effective as a forum for international opinion than as a means of resolving the major conflicts of the postwar world, particularly the Soviet/American hostility during the cold war decades. Further evidence for a growing internationalism lay in the creation in late 1945 of the World Bank and International Monetary Fund, whose purpose was to regulate the global economy, prevent another depression, and stimulate economic growth, especially in the poorer nations. What these initiatives shared was the dominant presence of the United States, as the half century following the end of World War II witnessed its emergence as a global superpower. This was among the major outcomes of the Second World War and a chief reason for the remarkable recovery of a badly damaged and discredited Western civilization.

> **PRACTICING HISTORICAL THINKING**
>
> Is it more useful to view the two world wars as separate and distinct conflicts or as a single briefly interrupted phenomenon?

Communist Consolidation and Expansion: The Chinese Revolution

Yet another outcome of World War II lay in the consolidation and extension of the communist world. The Soviet victory over the Nazis, though bought at an unimaginable cost in blood and treasure, gave immense credibility to that communist regime and to its leader, Joseph Stalin. Whatever atrocities he had committed, many in the Soviet Union credited Stalin with leading the country's heroic struggle against Nazi aggression. Furthermore, Stalin also presided over a major expansion of communist control in Eastern Europe, much of which was occupied by Soviet forces as the war ended. He insisted that Soviet security required "friendly" governments in the region to permanently end the threat of invasion from the West. Stalin also feared that large-scale American aid for Europe's economic recovery, which began in 1948, sought to incorporate Eastern Europe into a Western and capitalist economic network. Thus he acted to install fully communist governments, loyal to himself, in Poland, East Germany, Czechoslovakia, Hungary, Romania, and

Bulgaria. Backed by the pressure and presence of the Soviet army, **communism in Eastern Europe** was largely imposed from the outside rather than growing out of a domestic revolution, as had happened in Russia itself. The situation in Yugoslavia differed sharply from the rest of Eastern Europe. There a genuinely popular communist movement had played a leading role in the struggle against Nazi occupation and came to power on its own with little Soviet help. Its leader, Josef Broz, known as Tito, openly defied Soviet efforts to control Yugoslav communism, claiming that "our goal is that everyone should be master in his own house."

In Asia too communism took root after World War II. Following Japan's defeat, its Korean colony was partitioned, with the northern half coming under Soviet and therefore communist control. In Vietnam, a much more locally based communist movement, active since the mid-1920s under the leadership of **Ho Chi Minh** (1890–1969), embodied both a socialist vision and Vietnamese nationalism as it battled Japanese, French, and later American invaders and established communist control first in the northern half of the country and after 1975 throughout the whole country. The victory of the Vietnamese communists spilled over into neighboring Laos and Cambodia, where communist parties took power in the mid-1970s.

Far and away the most striking expansion of communism occurred in China, where that country's Communist Party triumphantly seized power in 1949. As in Russia, that victory came on the heels of war and domestic upheaval. But the **Chinese Revolution of 1949**, which was a struggle of decades rather than a single year, was far different from its earlier Russian counterpart. The Chinese imperial system had collapsed in 1911, under the pressure of foreign imperialism, its own inadequacies, and mounting internal opposition (see "The Failure of Conservative Modernization" in Chapter 19). Unlike in Russia, where intellectuals had been discussing socialism for half a century or more before the revolution, the ideas of Karl Marx were barely known in China in the early twentieth century. Not until 1921 was a small Chinese Communist Party (CCP) founded, aimed initially at organizing the country's minuscule urban working class.

Over the next twenty-eight years, that small party, with an initial membership of only sixty people, grew enormously, transformed its strategy, found a charismatic leader in **Mao Zedong** (1893–1976), engaged in an epic struggle with its opponents, fought the Japanese heroically, and in 1949 emerged victorious as the rulers of the world's most populous country. That victory was all the more surprising because the CCP faced a far more formidable foe than the weak Provisional Government over which the Bolsheviks had triumphed in Russia. That opponent was the **Guomindang** (GWOH-mihn-dahng) (Nationalist Party), which governed China after 1928. Led by a military officer, Chiang Kai-shek, that party promoted a measure of modern development (railroads, light industry, banking, airline services) in the decade that followed. However, the impact of these achievements was limited largely to the cities, leaving the rural areas, where most people lived, still impoverished. The Guomindang's base of support was also narrow, deriving from urban elites, rural landlords, and Western powers.

Guided Reading Question

■ **CHANGE**
How did the Chinese Communist Party win popular support?

Mao Zedong and the Long March An early member of China's then-minuscule Communist Party, Mao rose to a position of dominant leadership during the Long March of 1934–1935, when beleaguered communists from southeastern China trekked to a new base area in the north. This photograph shows Mao on his horse during that epic journey. (© Collection J.A. Fox/Magnum Photos)

Whereas the Bolsheviks had found their primary audience among workers in Russia's major cities, Chinese communists, in a striking adaptation of European Marxism, increasingly looked to the country's peasant villages for support. But Chinese peasants did not rise up spontaneously against their landlords, as Russian peasants had. Instead, years of guerrilla warfare, experiments with land reform in areas under communist control, and the creation of a communist military force to protect liberated areas slowly gained for the CCP a growing measure of respect and support among China's peasants, particularly during the 1930s. In the process, Mao Zedong, the son of a prosperous Chinese peasant family and a professional revolutionary since the early 1920s, emerged as the party's leader. A central event in Mao's rise to prominence was the Long March of 1934–1935, when beleaguered communist forces in southern China made a harrowing but successful retreat to a new base area in the northwest of the country, an epic journey of some 5,600 miles that soon acquired mythical dimensions in communist lore.

To recruit women for the revolution, communists drew on a theoretical commitment to their liberation and in the areas under their control established a Marriage Law that outlawed arranged or "purchased" marriages, made divorce easier, and gave women the right to vote and own property. Women's associations enrolled hundreds of thousands of women and promoted literacy, fostered discussions of women's issues, and encouraged handicraft production such as making clothing, blankets, and shoes, so essential for the revolutionary forces. But resistance to such radical measures from more traditional rural villagers, especially the male peasants and soldiers on whom the communists depended, persuaded the party leaders to modify these measures. Women were not permitted to seek divorce from men on active military duty. Women's land deeds were often given to male family heads and were regarded as family property. Female party members found themselves limited to work with women or children.

It was Japan's brutal invasion of China that gave the CCP a decisive opening, for that attack destroyed Guomindang control over much of the country and forced it to retreat to the interior, where it became even more dependent on conservative landlords. The CCP, by contrast, grew from just 40,000 members in 1937 to more than 1.2 million in 1945, while the communist-led People's Liberation Army mushroomed to 900,000 men, supported by an additional 2 million militia troops. Much of this growing support derived from the vigor with which the CCP waged war against the Japanese invaders. Using guerrilla warfare techniques learned in the struggle against the Guomindang, communist forces established themselves behind enemy lines and, despite periodic setbacks, offered a measure of security to many Chinese faced with Japanese atrocities. The Guomindang, by contrast, sometimes seemed to be more interested in eliminating the communists than in actively fighting the Japanese. Furthermore, in the areas it controlled, the CCP reduced rents, taxes, and interest payments for peasants; taught literacy to adults; and mobilized women for the struggle. As the war drew to a close, more radical action followed. Teams of activists encouraged poor peasants to "speak bitterness" in public meetings, to "struggle" with landlords, and to "settle accounts" with them.

Thus the CCP frontally addressed both of China's major problems—foreign imperialism and peasant exploitation. It expressed Chinese nationalism as well as a demand for radical social change. It gained a reputation for honesty that contrasted sharply with the massive corruption of Guomindang officials. It put down deep roots among the peasantry in a way that the Bolsheviks never did. And whereas the Bolsheviks gained support by urging Russian withdrawal from the highly unpopular First World War, the CCP won support by aggressively pursuing the struggle against Japanese invaders during World War II. In 1949, four years after the war's end, the Chinese communists swept to victory over the Guomindang, many of whose followers fled to Taiwan. Mao Zedong announced triumphantly that "the Chinese people have stood up."

REFLECTIONS

War and Remembrance: Learning from History

When asked about the value of studying history, most students respond with some version of the Spanish-born philosopher George Santayana's famous dictum: "Those who cannot remember the past are condemned to repeat it." At one level, this notion of learning from the "lessons of history" has much to recommend it, for there is, after all, little else except the past on which we can base our actions in the present. And yet historians in general are notably cautious about drawing particular lessons from the past and applying them to present circumstances.

For one thing, the historical record is sufficiently rich and complex to allow many people to draw quite different lessons from it. The world wars of the twentieth century represent a case in point, as writer Adam Gopnik has pointed out:

> The First World War teaches that territorial compromise is better than full-scale war, that an "honor-bound" allegiance of the great powers to small nations is a recipe for mass killing, and that it is crazy to let the blind mechanism of armies and alliances trump common sense. The Second teaches that searching for an accommodation with tyranny by selling out small nations only encourages the tyrant, that refusing to fight now leads to a worse fight later on. . . . The First teaches us never to rush into a fight, the Second never to back down from a bully.[11]

Did the lessons of the First World War lead Americans to ignore the rise of fascism until the country was directly threatened by Japanese attack? Did the lessons of World War II contribute to unnecessary wars in Vietnam and Iraq? There are no easy answers to such questions, for the lessons of history are many, varied, and changing.

Behind any such lesson is the common assumption that history repeats itself. This too is a notion to which historians bring considerable skepticism. They are generally more impressed with the complexity and particularity of major events such as wars rather than with any clear-cut "laws" or patterns of historical development. Thus historians are often reluctant to speculate about the future based on drawing lessons from the past.

That reluctance is also grounded in historians' awareness of the unexpected outcomes of the wars of the past century. Few people in 1914 anticipated the duration and carnage of World War I. The Holocaust was literally unimaginable when Hitler took power in 1933 or even at the outbreak of the Second World War in 1939. Who would have expected an American defeat at the hands of the Vietnamese? And suicide bombings by Islamic radicals have been a novel and unpredictable development in the history of warfare. History repeats itself most certainly only in its unexpectedness.

Second Thoughts

What's the Significance?

World War I, 874
total war, 879
Treaty of Versailles, 880
Russian Revolution, 883
Lenin, 883
Stalin, 884

Big Picture Questions

1. What explains the disasters that befell Europe in the first half of the twentieth century?

2. To what extent did the two world wars settle the issues that caused them? What legacies for the future did they leave?

3. In what ways did Europe's internal conflicts between 1914 and 1945 have global implications?

4. In what ways did communism have an impact on world history in the first half of the twentieth century?

5. **Looking Back:** In what ways were the major phenomena of the first half of the twentieth century—world wars, communist revolutions, the Great Depression, fascism, the Holocaust, the emergence of the United States as a global power—rooted in earlier times?

Next Steps: For Further Study

Michael Burleigh, *The Third Reich: A New History* (2001). A fresh and thorough look at the Nazi era in Germany's history.

Sheila Fitzpatrick, *The Russian Revolution* (2008). The third edition of what has become a classic overview of the Russian Revolution.

John Keegan, *The Second World War* (2005). A comprehensive account by a well-known scholar.

Bernd Martin, *Japan and Germany in the Modern World* (1995). A comparative study of these two countries' modern history and the relationship between them.

Mark Mazower, *Dark Continent* (2000). A history of Europe in the twentieth century that views the era as a struggle among liberal democracy, fascism, and communism.

Michael S. Nieberg, *Fighting the Great War: A Global History* (2006). An exploration of the origins and conduct of World War I.

Dietman Rothermund, *The Global Impact of the Great Depression, 1929–1939* (1996). An examination of the origins of the Depression in America and Europe and its impact in Asia, Africa, and Latin America.

Adam Tooze, *The Deluge: The Great War and the Remaking of the Global Order 1916–1931* (2014). An exploration of the new global order that took shape in the tumultuous period from the closing years of World War I to the Great Depression.

Michael Duffy, ed., First World War.com, http://www.firstworldwar.com, 2009. A website rich with articles, documents, photos, diaries, and more that illustrate the history of World War I.

Jewish Virtual Library, "The Holocaust," http://www.jewishvirtuallibrary.org/jsource/holo .html. A wealth of essays, maps, photographs, and timelines that explores the Holocaust and the context in which it arose.

Ideologies of the Axis Powers

Even more than the Great War of 1914–1918, the Second World War was a conflict of ideas and ideologies as well as a struggle of nations and armies. The ideas of the losing side in that war, repellant as they were to their enemies and probably to many people today, had for a time attracted considerable support. Described variously as fascist, authoritarian, right-wing, or radically nationalist, the ideologies of the Axis powers — Italy, Germany, and Japan — differed in tone and emphasis. But they shared a repudiation of mainstream Western liberalism and democracy, an intense hatred of Marxist communism, and a desire for imperial expansion. The sources that follow provide a sample of this thinking as it took shape in those three countries.

SOURCE 20.1 Italian Fascism: Creating a New Roman Empire ▶

Empire was central in the thinking of Italy's Benito Mussolini and his understanding of fascism. "For Fascism," he wrote, "the growth of Empire, that is to say the expansion of the nation, is an essential manifestation of vitality, and its opposite a sign of decadence."[12] And for Mussolini, the model for empire was decidedly Roman. Following the conquest of Ethiopia in 1936, he triumphantly celebrated "the reappearance of empire on the fated hills of Rome." "Italy finally has its own empire," he proclaimed. "An empire of civilization and of humanity for all the populations of Ethiopia. This is in the tradition of Rome. . . ."[13] One year later, marking the first anniversary of that victory, the image in Source 20.1 was on the cover of school exercise books. Mussolini appears in the foreground in military uniform including a combat helmet, while in the background looms a famous national monument commemorating the unification of Italy in 1871. Located near the heart of ancient Rome, this monument used classical architectural and sculptural styles to evoke the revival of Italy's glorious past. The golden winged figure, busy inscribing the date of the empire's foundation on a tablet, is Victoria, the Roman goddess of victory, widely revered in Roman armies and worshipped by returning generals. The caption reads: "In the first year of the foundation of the Empire, the Italian people renew the victorious Duce [Mussolini] with fervent testimonies of gratitude and devotion."

- Why might the artist have chosen to present Mussolini in the context of the ancient Roman Empire?

- Why might Mussolini want to link his recent conquest of Ethiopia with the nineteenth-century reunification of Italy?

■ What does the arrangement of the image suggest about how Mussolini wanted to be viewed? What attitudes or postures does this portrayal of Mussolini project?

School Exercise Book Celebrating Italy's Victory over Ethiopia | 1937

Nel primo annuale della fondazione dell' Impero, il popolo Italiano, rinnova al Duce vittorioso ardenti testimonianze di gratitudine e devozione.

■ ■ ■

SOURCE 20.2 **Hitler on Nazism**

The ideology of German Nazism found its classic expression in Adolf Hitler's *Mein Kampf* (My Struggle), written while he was briefly imprisoned in 1923. Armed with these ideas, Hitler assumed the leadership of Germany in 1933.

■ What larger patterns in European thinking do Hitler's ideas reflect, and what elements of European thought does he reject? Consider in particular his use of social Darwinism, then an idea with wide popularity in Europe.

■ How does Hitler distinguish between Aryans and Jews? How does he understand the role of race in human affairs?

■ What kind of political system does Hitler advocate?

ADOLF HITLER │ *Mein Kampf (My Struggle)* │ **1925–1926**

There are truths that are so obvious that they are not seen, or at least not recognized, by ordinary people. . . . In the struggle for daily bread the weak and sickly, as well as the less resolute, succumb, while in the struggle of the males for the female only the healthiest is granted the right or opportunity to propagate. . . . However little Nature wishes that the weaker mate with the stronger, even less does she desire the blending of a higher race with a lower. . . . All great cultures of the past collapsed only because the originally creative race died off from the poisoning of their blood. . . .

Those who want to live, must also fight, and those who will not fight in this world of eternal struggle do not deserve to live. . . . All that we see before us today of human culture, all the achievements of art, science, and technology, is almost exclusively the creative product of the Aryan race. . . . [H]e alone was the founder of all higher forms of humanity, and thus represents the very prototype of all that we understand by the word "human." He is the Prometheus of mankind from whose bright forehead the divine spark of genius has always sprung. . . .

Everything in this world that is not of good race is chaff. All occurrences in world history, for better and for worse, are simply the expression of the racial instinct for self-preservation. . . .

The Jew represents the most formidable opponent of the Aryan. . . . Because the Jew . . . has never possessed a culture of his own, the foundations of his intellectual work have always been provided by others. . . . If the Jews were alone in this world, not only would they suffocate in filth and offal, but they would also seek, in their hate-filled struggles, to cheat and to destroy each another. . . . [T]he Jew is led by nothing more than the naked egoism of the individual. . . .

The black-haired Jewish youth, satanic joy in his face, lurks in wait for the unsuspecting girl whom he defiles with his blood, thus stealing her from her people. He uses every means to taint the racial foundations of the people he has set out to subjugate. . . . And thus he tries to systematically lower the racial level [of a people] by the continuous poisoning of individuals. . . . He has found, in the organized masses of Marxism, the weapon that allows him . . . to subjugate and to "govern" the peoples with a dictatorial and brutal fist. . . .

If we mentally review all the reasons for the German collapse [defeat in World War I], the ultimate and most decisive remains the failure to recognize the racial problem and especially the Jewish menace. . . . The lost purity of the blood is enough to destroy the inner happiness [of a people] forever . . . the consequences of which can never be eliminated from body and from spirit. . . . All really significant symptoms of decay from the prewar period can be traced back to racial causes. . . .

. . . [T]he state is a means to an end. Its purpose lies in the preservation and advancement of a society of physically and spiritually homogenous beings. . . . States that do not serve this purpose are misbegotten, indeed they are monstrosities. . . .

The highest purpose of the folkish state is therefore concern for the preservation of those original cultural-bestowing racial elements that create the beauty and dignity of higher humanity. We, as Aryans, conceive of the state simply as the living organism of a nation that not only ensures the preservation of the nation, but through the development of its spiritual and intellectual abilities leads it to the highest freedom. . . .

This world is surely moving toward a great revolution. And the only question is whether it will rebound to the salvation of Aryan mankind or to the profit of the eternal Jew. . . .

. . . [T]he folkish state must accordingly free the political leadership . . . entirely from the parliamentarian principle of majority or mass rule, and instead absolutely guarantee the right of the personality. . . . The best state constitution and state form is the one with the instinctual certainty to raise the best minds of the national community to leading prominence and influence. . . . There will be no majority decisions, only responsible individuals, and the word "counsel" will be restored to its original meaning. Every man will have advisers by his side to be sure, but the decision will be made by one man. . . .

With respect to the feasibility of these ideas, I beg you not to forget that the parliamentary principle of democratic majority rule has not always governed mankind, but rather is to be found only in the briefest periods of history, which are invariably eras of decay of peoples and states.

Source: Adolf Hitler, *Mein Kampf. Zwei Bände in einem Band,* translated by Sarah Panzer (München: Zentralverlag der NSDAP, 1943), 311, 312–313, 316, 317, 324, 329, 330, 331, 357, 359, 360, 433, 434, 475, 500, 501, 502.

■ ■ ■

SOURCE 20.3 Nazi Anti-Semitism ▶

Hatred of Jews was central to Nazi ideology. This image, which served as the cover of a Nazi publication titled *Der Ewige Jude* (The Eternal Jew), summed up many of the themes in Nazi anti-Semitism.

■ How does this image illustrate Hitler's understanding of Jews as expressed in Source 20.2?

■ Notice particular aspects of the image: the coins in the man's right hand, the whip in his left hand, the map of Russia with a hammer and sickle. What does each of these suggest about the Nazi case against the Jews?

■ Notice also the general appearance and dress of the figure. What does this contribute to the image of Jews that Nazis are trying to convey?

H. SCHLUTER | *Der Ewige Jude (The Eternal Jew)* | 1937

akg-images

. . .

SOURCE 20.4 **The Japanese Way**

In the Japanese language, the word *kokutai* is an evocative term that refers to the national essence or the fundamental character of the Japanese nation and people. Drawing both on long-established understandings and on recently developed nationalist ideas, the Ministry of Education in 1937 published a small volume, widely distributed in schools and homes throughout the country, titled *Kokutai No Hongi* (*Cardinal Principles of the National Entity of Japan*). That text, excerpted in Source 20.4, defined the uniqueness of Japan and articulated the philosophical foundation of its authoritarian regime. When the Americans occupied a defeated and devastated Japan in 1945, they forbade the further distribution of the book.

■ According to *Cardinal Principles*, what is *kokutai*? How does the document define the national essence of Japan? How do its authors compare Japan to the West?

■ What was the ideal role of the individual in Japanese society?

■ Why do you think the American occupation authorities banned the document?

Cardinal Principles of the National Entity of Japan | 1937

[T]he foreign ideologies imported into our country are in the main ideologies of the [European] Enlightenment. . . . The views of the world and of life that form the basis of these ideologies . . . lay the highest value on, and assert the liberty and equality of, individuals. . . .

We subjects [of the Japanese emperor] are intrinsically quite different from the so-called citizens of the Occidental [Western] countries. . . .

Our country is established with the Emperor. . . . For this reason, to serve the Emperor and to receive the Emperor's great august Will as one's own is the rationale of making our historical "life" live in the present. . . .

Loyalty means to reverence the Emperor as [our] pivot and to follow him implicitly. . . . Hence, offering our lives for the sake of the Emperor does not mean so-called self-sacrifice, but the casting aside of our little selves to live under his august grace and the enhancing of the genuine life of the people of a State. . . . An individual is an existence belonging to the State and her history, which forms the basis of his origin, and is fundamentally one body with it. . . .

We must sweep aside the corruption of the spirit and the clouding of knowledge that arises from setting up one's "self" and from being taken up with one's "self" and return to a pure and clear state of mind that belongs intrinsically to us as subjects, and thereby fathom the great principle loyalty. . . .

Indeed, loyalty is our fundamental Way as subject, and is the basis of our national morality. Through loyalty are we become Japanese subjects; in loyalty do we obtain life and herein do we find the source of all morality.

Source: J. O. Gauntlett, trans., and R. K. Hall, ed., *Kokutai No Hongi* (*Cardinal Principles of the National Entity of Japan*) (Cambridge, MA: Harvard University Press, 1949), 52, 80–83.

■ ■ ■

SOURCE 20.5 **Japanese Imperialism**

Empire was a major theme in Japanese ideology of the 1930s and 1940s. It began to be put into practice in the early 1930s, when Japanese forces seized parts of north-eastern China, calling it Manchukuo. Source 20.5 presents a Japanese propaganda poster, created in 1933, showing anti-Japanese Manchurians in hell (on the left), while pro-Japanese supporters (on the right) enjoy a blissful paradise.

■ What contrasts can you identify between the two panels? How does the imagery in both panels enhance the message of the poster? What kinds of figures dominate each panel of the image, and what are they doing?

■ To whom might this image be directed?

■ How does this portrayal of Japanese empire building compare with that of Italian imperialism in Source 20.1?

Japanese Propaganda Poster of Manchuria under Japanese Occupation | 1933

ullstein bild/Getty Images

DOING HISTORY

1. **Making comparisons:** What broad similarities and differences in outlook can you identify among these sources? What aspects of the Japanese *Cardinal Principles* text might Hitler have viewed with sympathy, and what parts of it might he have found distasteful or offensive?

2. **Criticizing the West:** In what ways did Mussolini, Hitler, and the authors of *Cardinal Principles* find fault with mainstream Western societies and their political and social values?

3. **Considering ideas and action:** To what extent did the ideas articulated in these sources find expression in particular actions or policies of political authorities?

4. **Placing sources in context:** To what extent were the ideas in these sources new and revolutionary? In what respects did they draw on long-standing traditions? In what ways did they embrace modern life, and what aspects of it did they reject? Have these ideas been completely discredited, or do they retain some resonance in contemporary political discourse?

Anti-Semitism

Because hatred and fear of Jews were central to Nazi ideology, the history of anti-Semitism and its relationship to the Holocaust have loomed large in historians' efforts to understand the Nazi phenomenon. Voice 20.1, by historian Beth A. Griech-Polelle, shows how anti-Semitism created a sense of Jews as radically "other" and threatening. Voice 20.2, derived from a highly controversial book by Daniel Goldhagen, an American author and former Harvard professor of government, argues that "eliminationist anti-Semitism," seeking the physical removal of Jews from Germany, was not a uniquely Nazi outlook, but permeated German life and culture.

- In what ways did anti-Semitism define Jews as radically "other"?

- Why does Goldhagen believe that a widespread German anti-Semitism motivated the Holocaust? What alternative explanations does he reject?

- **Integrating Primary and Secondary Sources:** How might these two historians use Sources 20.2 and 20.3 to support their arguments?

VOICE 20.1

Beth A. Griech-Polelle on Anti-Semitism Creating "Otherness" | 2017

In this "Us" vs "Them" world, insiders are told that their very existence is threatened by an enemy who seeks to define, pollute, and destroy the coherence of "us." The threatening imagery of "the Jew" . . . was built up over the course of centuries. Destructive legends, myths, and stereotypes all contributed to a type of acceptable language about Jews that enabled Hitler to play on well-established tropes. Images of the "diabolical, cunning" Jew could be used to instill fear and anxiety and could serve as an explanation as to why an average German person felt stymied in their personal and professional development. They were told repeatedly that the enemy, the Jew, was standing in their way of creating a peaceful harmonious society. . . . In order for the German people to live, Jews had to die. . . .

The "other" is portrayed in language that suggests Jews are dirty, foreign, corrupt, corrupting, and never to be trusted. They are depicted as being in league with the devil, perpetrating every evil known to mankind. . . . Germans had to attack Jews in a kind of preemptive strike. . . . The Germans were only acting in self-defense to protect themselves from an imagined future annihilation. . . .

The image of "the Jew" was now a figure standing outside of history, an eternal enemy of "us."

Source: Beth A. Griech-Polelle, *Anti-Semitism and the Holocaust* (London: Bloomsbury Academic, 2017), 1–2.

VOICE 20.2

Daniel Goldhagen on the Uniqueness of German Anti-Semitism | 1997

The Holocaust was the defining aspect of Nazism, but not only of Nazism. It was also the defining feature of German society during its Nazi period. No significant aspect of German society was untouched by anti-Jewish policy. . . . The program's first parts, namely the systematic exclusion of Jews from German economic and social life, were carried out in the open, under approving eyes, and with the complicity of virtually all sectors of German society from the legal, medical and teaching professions, to the churches, both Catholic and Protestant, to the gamut of economic, social and cultural groups and associations. . . . Hundreds of thousands of Germans contributed to the genocide and . . . the vast concentration camp system. . . . [M]illions knew of the mass slaughter. . . . The killings met with general understanding, if not approval. . . .

[A]nti-Semitism moved many thousands of "ordinary" Germans . . . to slaughter Jews. Not economic hardship, not the coercive means of a totalitarian state, not social psychological pressure, not invariable psychological propensities, but ideas about Jews that were pervasive in Germany, and had been for decades, induced ordinary Germans to kill unarmed defenseless Jewish men, women and children by the thousands, systematically and without pity.

Source: Daniel J. Goldhagen, *Hitler's Willing Executioners* (New York: Viking Books, 1997), 8–9.

"West Africa Awakes" (gouache on paper) by Angus McBride (1931–2007)/Look and Learn (A & B Images)/Private Collection/Bridgeman Images

Milestones of the Past Century

A Changing Global Landscape

1950–present

"Today marks exactly twenty years since the dawn of freedom and democracy in our country," declared South African president Jacob Zuma on April 27, 2014. "We gained equal citizenship in the land of our birth."[1] It was the twentieth anniversary of the end of apartheid and white domination as well as the election of the highly regarded Nelson Mandela as the country's first African leader. But not everyone was ready to celebrate. The activist Archbishop Desmond Tutu said: "I am glad that [Mandela] is dead. . . . I didn't think there would be disillusionment so soon."[2] He was referring to widespread corruption in official circles and frustration with the slow pace of movement toward overcoming the poverty and inequalities of the apartheid era. ■

《 African Independence Achieved This poster depicts an Independence Day celebration in the new West African nation of Ghana in 1957. Its exuberance reflects the sense of great achievement that came with the defeat of colonial rule and the immense hopes for the future that independence promised.

The end of European empires and the arrival of many newly independent nations on the global stage marked a dramatic change in the political landscape of the world in the second half of the twentieth century. So too did the continuing struggles of their people to create stable, unified, and prosperous societies. But this epic transformation intersected with other profound changes during the more than seventy years that followed World War II. A devastated Europe rebuilt its modern economy and moved toward greater union. Communism expanded its reach into Eastern Europe, China, Southeast Asia, and Cuba. A cold war between the United States and the Soviet Union, both of them armed with nuclear weapons of unprecedented destructive power, structured much of international life until the communist experiment largely collapsed at the end of the twentieth century. By the early twenty-first century, China had become a powerful and prominent player in the global arena, while the Middle East emerged as a center of conflict and instability.

SEEKING THE MAIN POINT

In what ways has the architecture of global political life changed in the decades since the end of World War II?

These are among the major milestones of world history during the past seven decades. Each of them had roots in the past, and each had a profound impact on many millions of people. Together they transformed the texture of human life all across the planet.

Recovering from the War

The tragedies that afflicted Europe in the first half of the twentieth century — fratricidal war, economic collapse, the Holocaust — were wholly self-inflicted, and yet that civilization had not permanently collapsed. In the twentieth century's second half, Europeans rebuilt their industrial economies and revived their democratic political systems. Three factors help to explain this astonishing recovery. One is the apparent resiliency of an industrial society, once it has been established. The knowledge, skills, and habits of mind that enabled industrial societies to operate effectively remained intact, even if the physical infrastructure had been substantially destroyed. Thus even the most terribly damaged countries — Germany, the Soviet Union, and Japan — had largely recovered by 1960, amid a worldwide economic boom during the 1950s.

Guided Reading Question

■ **CHANGE**
What enabled Europe, the Soviet Union, and Japan to recover from the devastation of war?

A second factor lay in the ability of the major Western European countries to integrate their recovering economies, putting aside some of their prickly nationalism in return for enduring peace and common prosperity. That process took shape during the 1950s, giving rise to the **European Economic Community** (EEC), established in 1957, whose members reduced their tariffs and developed common trade policies. Over the next half century, the EEC expanded its membership to include almost all of Europe, including many former communist states. In 1994, the EEC was renamed the European Union, and in 2002 twelve of its members, later increased to seventeen, adopted a common currency, the euro (see Map 21.1). All of this sustained Europe's remarkable economic recovery and expressed a larger European identity.

A third element of European recovery lay in the United States, which emerged after 1945 as the dominant center of Western civilization and a global superpower. An early indication of the United States' intention to exercise global leadership took shape in its effort to rebuild and reshape shattered European economies. Known as the **Marshall Plan**, that effort funneled into Europe some $12 billion (roughly $121 billion in 2017 dollars), together with numerous advisers and technicians. It was motivated by some combination of genuine humanitarian concern, a desire to prevent a new depression by creating overseas customers for American industrial goods, and an interest in undermining the growing appeal of European communist parties. This economic recovery plan, along with access to American markets, was

Landmarks for Chapter 21

| 1950 | 1960 | 1970 | 1980 | 1990 | 2000 | 2010 | 2020 |

THE COLD WAR

1949–1955 Formation of NATO and Warsaw Pact as rival military alliances

1950–1953 Korean War

1955–1975 Vietnam War

1962 Cuban missile crisis

1979–1989 Soviet war in Afghanistan

1991 End of cold war

WESTERN WORLD

1948–1952 Marshall Plan for European recovery

1957 European Economic Community established

1990 German reunification

1994 EU established

2016 British vote to exit from EU

COMMUNIST WORLD

1949–1976 Mao Zedong rules China

1959 Cuban Revolution

1978–1989 Deng Xiaoping reforms in China

1987 Gorbachev reforms begin in Soviet Union

1989 Collapse of Eastern European communism

1991 Collapse of Soviet Union

COLONIAL/DEVELOPING WORLD

1947 Independence of India

1959–1990 Military governments in Africa and Latin America

1957 Independence of Ghana

1979 Iranian revolution

1994 End of apartheid in South Africa

2011 Beginning of Syrian civil war

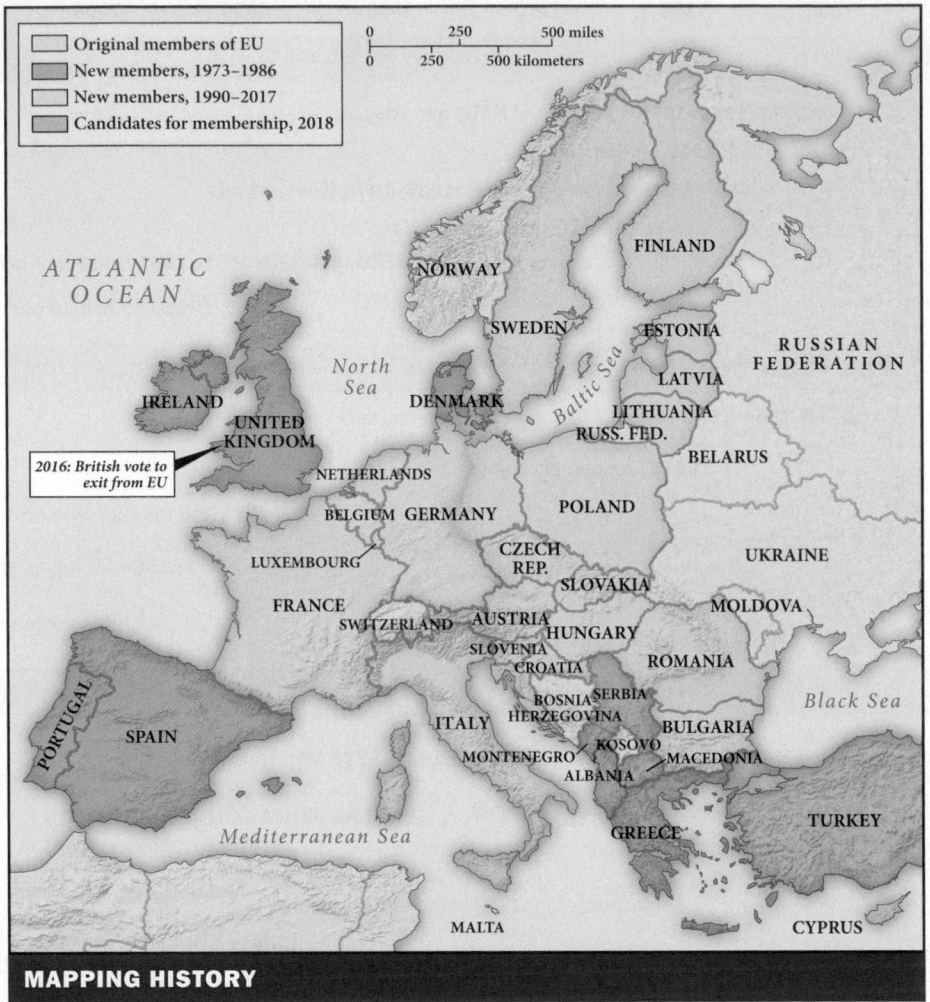

Original members of EU
New members, 1973–1986
New members, 1990–2017
Candidates for membership, 2018

0   250   500 miles
0   250   500 kilometers

MAPPING HISTORY

Map 21.1 The Growth of European Integration

During the second half of the twentieth century, Europeans gradually put aside their bitter rivalries and entered into various forms of economic cooperation with one another, although these efforts fell short of complete political union. This map illustrates the growth of what is now called the European Union (EU).

READING THE MAP: How would you describe the growth of the European Union? Where did it start, and into which regions did it expand? What explains the number of new members after 1990 in Eastern and Southeastern Europe?

INTERPRETING THE MAP: Why might Russia have found the recent growth of the European Union threatening to its interests?

successful beyond all expectations. Between 1948 and the early 1970s, Western European economies grew rapidly, generating a widespread prosperity and improving living standards. Beyond economic assistance, the American commitment to Europe soon came to include political and military security against the distant possibility of renewed German aggression and the more immediate communist threat from the Soviet Union. Thus was born the military and political alliance known as the North Atlantic Treaty Organization (NATO) in 1949. It committed the United States and its nuclear arsenal to the defense of Europe against the Soviet Union, and it firmly anchored West Germany within the Western alliance. It also allowed Western Europe to avoid heavy military expenditures.

A parallel process in Japan, which was under American occupation between 1945 and 1952, likewise revived that country's devastated but already industrialized economy. In the two decades following the occupation, Japan's economy grew remarkably, and the nation became an economic giant on the world stage. The democratic constitution imposed on Japan by American occupation authorities required that "land, sea, and air forces, as well as other war potential, will never be maintained." This meant that Japan, even more so than Europe, depended on the United States for its military security.

Recovery in the Soviet Union, so terribly damaged by the war, occurred under very different conditions from that of Japan and Western Europe. The last years of Stalin's rule (1945–1953) were extraordinarily harsh, with no tolerance for dissent of any kind. One result was a huge and growing convict labor force of 3 to 4 million people who provided a major source of cheap labor for the recovery effort. Furthermore, that program was a wholly state-planned effort that favored heavy industry, agricultural production, and military expenditure at the expense of basic consumer goods, such as shoes and clothing. But Stalin's regime did gain some popular support by substantially lowering the price of bread and other essentials. Finally, the Soviet Union benefited greatly from its seizure of industrial complexes, agricultural goods, raw materials, gold, and European art from Germany, Poland, and elsewhere. Viewed as looting or plunder in the West, this appropriation in Soviet eyes was seen as the "spoils of war" and justified by the massive damage, both human and material, that the Nazi invasion had caused in the USSR. By the mid-1950s, economic recovery was well under way.

Communism Chinese-Style

While Europe, Japan, and the Soviet Union were emerging from the chaos of World War II, China was likewise recovering from decades of civil war and from its devastating struggle against Japanese imperialism. And it was doing so under the direction of the Chinese Communist Party and its leader Mao Zedong. In a longer-term perspective, China's revolution represented the real beginning of that country's emergence from a century of imperialist humiliation and semi-colonial rule, the development of a distinctive Chinese approach to modern development,

Guided Reading Question
....
■ **COMPARISON**
What was distinctive about the Chinese experience of communism compared to that of the Soviet Union?

The Great Leap Forward This Chinese poster from 1960 celebrates both the agricultural and industrial efforts of the Great Leap Forward. The caption reads: "Start the movement to increase production and practice thrift, with foodstuffs and steel at the center, with great force!" The great famine that accompanied this "great leap" belied the optimistic outlook of the poster. (Stefan R. Landsberger Collections/International Institute of Social History, Amsterdam/www.chineseposters.net)

and its return to a position of prominence on the global stage.

As a communist country, China began its task of "building socialism" in a very different international environment than its Soviet counterpart had experienced. In 1917 Russian Bolsheviks faced a hostile capitalist world alone, while Chinese communists, coming to power over thirty years later, had an established Soviet Union as a friendly northern neighbor and ally. Furthermore, Chinese revolutionaries had actually governed parts of their huge country for decades, gaining experience that the new Soviet rulers had altogether lacked, since they had come to power so quickly. And the Chinese communists were firmly rooted in the rural areas and among the country's vast peasant population, while their Russian counterparts had found their support mainly in the cities.

If these comparisons generally favored China in its efforts to "build socialism," in economic terms that country faced even more daunting prospects than did the Soviet Union. Its population was far greater, its industrial base far smaller, and the availability of new agricultural land far more limited than in the Soviet Union. China's literacy and modern education, as well as its transportation network, were likewise much less developed. Even more than the Soviets, Chinese communists had to build a modern society from the ground up.

Building a Modern Society

Initially China sought to follow the Soviet model of socialist modernization, though with important variations. In sharp contrast to the Soviet experience, the collectivization of agriculture in China during the 1950s was a generally peaceful process, owing much to the close relationship between the Chinese Communist Party and the peasantry that had been established during three decades of struggle. China, however, pushed collectivization even further than the Soviet Union did, particularly in huge "people's communes" during the **Great Leap Forward** in the late 1950s. It was an effort to mobilize China's enormous population for rapid development and at the same time to move toward a more fully communist society with an even greater degree of social equality and collective living. (See Working with Evidence, Source 21.2, page 959.)

China's industrialization program was also modeled on the earlier Soviet experience, with an emphasis on large-scale heavy industries, urban-based factories, centralized planning by state and party authorities, and the mobilization of women for the task of development. As in the Soviet Union, impressive economic growth followed, as did substantial migration to the cities and the emergence of a bureaucratic elite of planners, managers, scientists, and engineers (see Snapshot). And both countries favored urban over rural areas and privileged an educated, technically trained elite over workers and peasants. Stalin and his successors largely accepted

SNAPSHOT China under Mao, 1949–1976

The following table reveals some of the achievements, limitations, and tragedies of China's communist experience during the era of Mao Zedong.

Steel production	from 1.3 million to 23 million tons
Coal production	from 66 million to 448 million tons
Electric power generation	from 7 million to 133 billion kilowatt-hours
Fertilizer production	from 0.2 million to 28 million tons
Cement production	from 3 million to 49 million tons
Industrial workers	from 3 million to 50 million
Scientists and technicians	from 50,000 to 5 million
"Barefoot doctors" posted to countryside	1 million
Annual growth rate of industrial output	11 percent
Annual growth rate of agricultural output	2.3 percent
Total population	from 542 million to 1 billion
Average population growth rate per year	2 percent
Per capita consumption of rural dwellers	from 62 to 124 yuan annually
Per capita consumption of urban dwellers	from 148 to 324 yuan annually
Overall life expectancy	from 35 to 65 years
Counterrevolutionaries killed (1949–1952)	between 1 million and 3 million
People labeled "rightists" in 1957	550,000
Deaths from famine during Great Leap Forward	30 million to 45 million
Deaths during Cultural Revolution	500,000
Officials sent down to rural labor camps during Cultural Revolution	3 million or more
Urban youth sent down to countryside	17 million (1967–1976)

Such figures are often highly controversial. See Maurice Meisner, *Mao's China and After* (New York: Free Press, 1999), 413-25; and Roderick MacFarquhar, ed., *The Politics of China* (Cambridge: Cambridge University Press, 1997), 243-45.

these inequalities, while Mao certainly did not. Rather, he launched recurrent efforts to combat these perhaps inevitable tendencies of any industrializing process and to revive and preserve the revolutionary spirit that had animated the Communist Party during its long struggle for power.

By the mid-1950s, Mao and some of his followers had become persuaded that the Soviet model of industrialization was leading China away from socialism and toward new forms of inequality, toward individualistic and careerist values, and toward an urban bias that favored the cities at the expense of the countryside. The Great Leap Forward of 1958–1960 marked Mao's first response to these distortions of Chinese socialism. It promoted small-scale industrialization in the rural areas rather than focusing wholly on large enterprises in the cities; it tried to foster widespread and practical technological education for all rather than relying on a small elite of highly trained technical experts; and it envisaged an immediate transition to full communism in the "people's communes" rather than waiting for industrial development to provide the material basis for that transition. The Great Leap, however, generated a national catastrophe and an unprecedented human tragedy that temporarily discredited Mao's radicalism. Administrative chaos, disruption of marketing networks, and bad weather combined to produce a massive famine, the worst in human history according to some scholars, that killed some 30 million people or more between 1959 and 1962, dwarfing the earlier Soviet famine.

Nonetheless, in the mid-1960s, Mao launched yet another campaign—the Great Proletarian **Cultural Revolution**—to combat the capitalist tendencies that he believed had penetrated even the highest ranks of the Communist Party itself. The Cultural Revolution also involved new efforts to bring health care and education to the countryside and to reinvigorate earlier attempts at rural industrialization under local rather than central control. In these ways, Mao struggled, though without great success, to overcome the inequalities associated with China's modern development and to create a model of socialist modernity quite distinct from that of the Soviet Union.

Eliminating Enemies

China under Mao, like the Soviet Union under Stalin, found itself caught up in a gigantic search for enemies beginning in the 1950s. In the Soviet Union, that process occurred under the clear control of state authorities. In China, however, it became much more public, escaping the control of the leadership, particularly during the most intense phase of the Cultural Revolution (1966–1969). Convinced that many within the Communist Party had been seduced by capitalist values of self-seeking and materialism, Mao called for rebellion against the Communist Party itself. Millions of young people responded, and, organized as Red Guards, they set out to rid China of those who were "taking the capitalist road." Following gigantic and ecstatic rallies in Beijing, they fanned out across the country and attacked local party and government officials, teachers, intellectuals, factory managers, and others they defined as enemies. Many were "sent down" to the countryside for hard physical labor and to "learn from the peasants." Others were humiliated, beaten, and sometimes killed. (See Working with Evidence, Source 21.6, page 966.) Rival revolutionary groups soon began fighting with one another, violence erupted throughout the country, and civil war threatened China. Mao was forced to call in the military to restore order and Communist Party control. Both the Soviet Terror and the Chinese Cultural Revolution badly discredited the very idea of socialism and contributed to the ultimate collapse of the communist experiment at the end of the century.

East versus West:
A Global Divide and a Cold War

Not only did communist regimes bring revolutionary changes to the societies they governed, but their very existence launched a global conflict that restructured international life and touched the lives of almost everyone, particularly in the twentieth century's second half. That rift had begun soon after the Russian Revolution when the new communist government became the source of fear and loathing to many in the Western capitalist world. The common threat of Nazi Germany temporarily made unlikely allies of the Soviet Union, Britain, and the United States, but a few years after World War II ended, that division erupted again in what became known as the **cold war**. Underlying that conflict were the geopolitical and ideological realities of the postwar world. The Soviet Union and the United States were now the world's major political and military powers, replacing the shattered and diminished states of Western Europe, but they represented sharply opposed views of history, society, politics, and international relations. In retrospect, conflict seemed almost inevitable, as both sides felt they were riding the tides of historical progress.

Military Conflict and the Cold War

The initial arena of the cold war was Eastern Europe, where Soviet insistence on security and control clashed with American and British desires for open and democratic societies with ties to the capitalist world economy. What resulted were rival military alliances. The **North Atlantic Treaty Organization (NATO)**, created in 1949, brought the United States and various West European countries together to defend themselves against the threat of Soviet aggression. Then in 1955 the **Warsaw Pact** joined the Soviet Union and East European communist countries in an alliance intended to provide a counterweight to NATO and to prevent Western influence in the communist bloc. These alliances created a largely voluntary American sphere of influence in Western Europe and an imposed Soviet sphere in Eastern Europe. The heavily fortified border between Eastern and Western Europe came to be known as the Iron Curtain. Thus Europe was bitterly divided. But

Map 21.2 The Global Cold War

The cold war witnessed a sharp division between the communist world and the Western democratic world. It also divided the continent of Europe; the countries of China, Korea, Vietnam, and Germany; and the city of Berlin. In many places, it also sparked crises that brought the nuclear-armed superpowers of the United States and the USSR to the brink of war, although in every case they managed to avoid direct military conflict between themselves. Many countries in Africa and Asia claimed membership in a Non-Aligned Movement that sought to avoid entanglements in cold war conflicts.

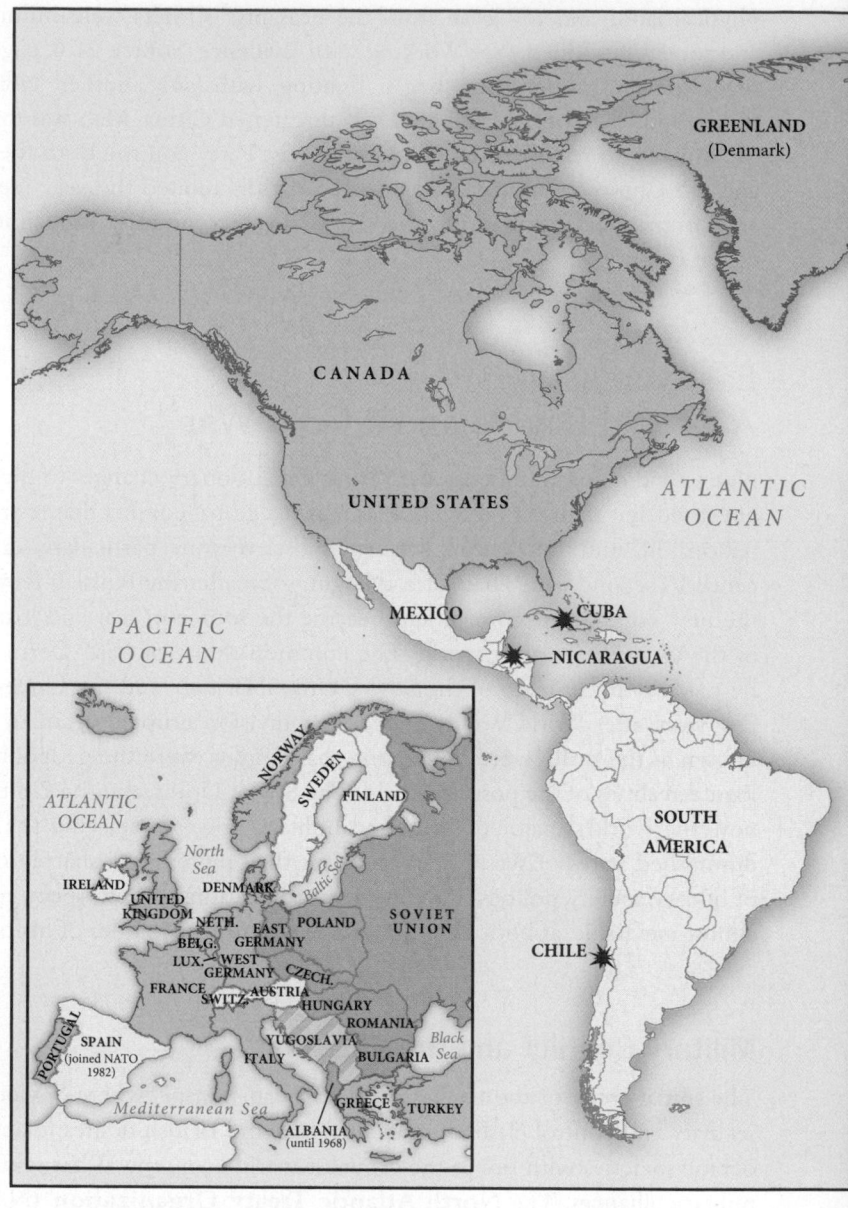

Guided Reading Question

■ CHANGE

In what different ways was the cold war expressed and experienced?

although tensions flared across this dividing line, particularly in Berlin, no shooting war occurred between the two sides (see Map 21.2).

By contrast, the extension of communism into Asia—China, Korea, and Vietnam—globalized the cold war and occasioned its most destructive and prolonged "hot wars." A North Korean invasion of South Korea in 1950 led to both Chinese and American involvement in a bitter three-year conflict (1950–1953),

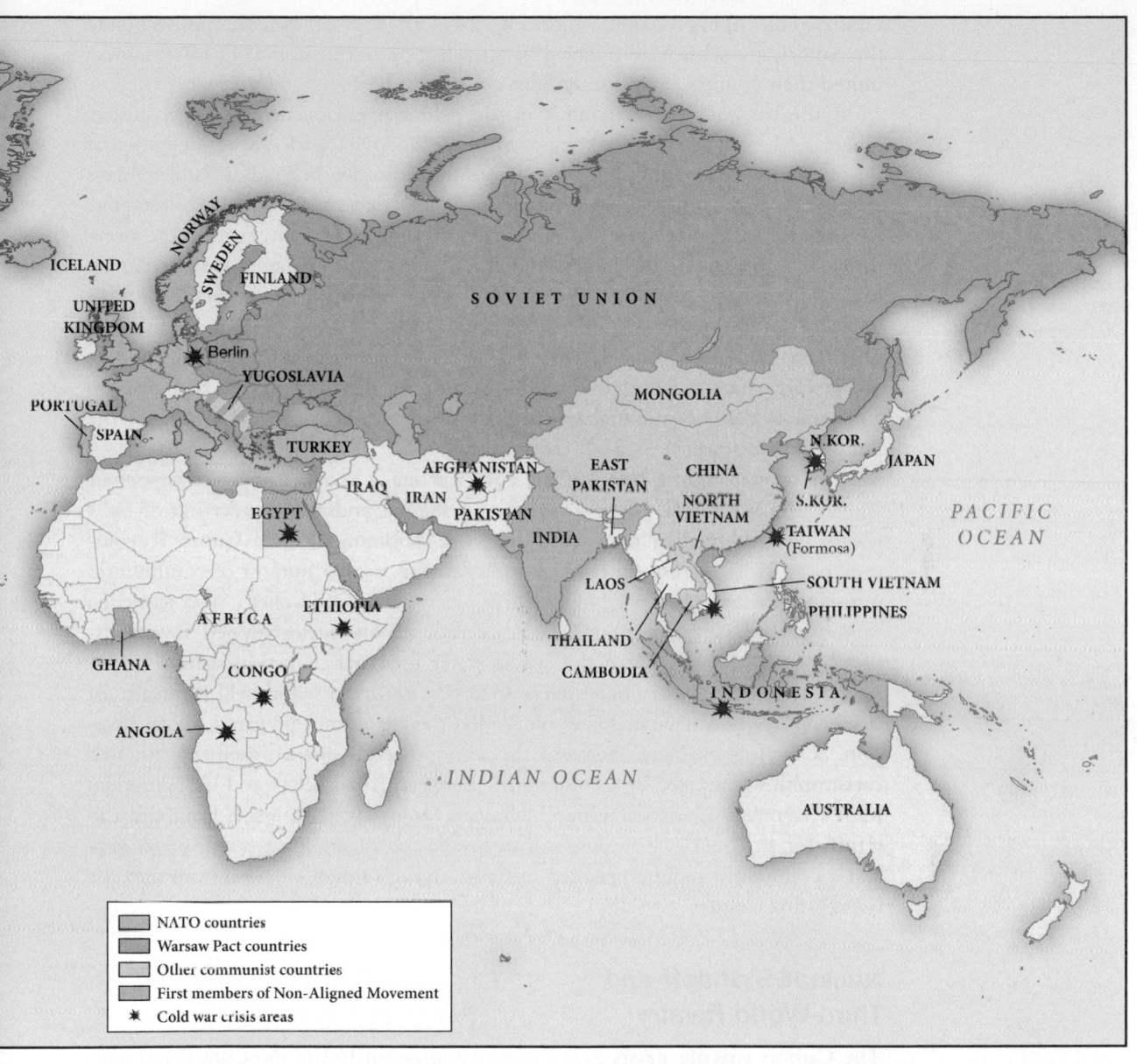

which ended in an essential standoff that left the Korean peninsula still divided in the early twenty-first century. Likewise in Vietnam, military efforts by South Vietnamese communists and the already communist North Vietnamese government to unify their country prompted massive American intervention in the 1960s. To American authorities, a communist victory would open the door to further communist expansion in Asia and beyond. Armed and supported by the Soviets and

Chinese and willing to endure enormous losses, the Vietnamese communists bested the Americans, who were hobbled by growing protest at home. The Vietnamese united their country under communist control by 1975.

A third major military conflict of the cold war era occurred in Afghanistan, where a Marxist party had taken power in 1978. Soviet leaders were delighted at this extension of communism on their southern border, but radical land reforms and efforts to liberate Afghan women soon alienated much of this conservative Muslim country and led to a mounting opposition movement. Fearing the overthrow of a new communist state and its replacement by Islamic radicals, Soviet forces intervened militarily and were soon bogged down in a war they could not win. For a full decade (1979–1989), that war was a "bleeding wound," sustained in part by U.S. aid to Afghan guerrillas. Under widespread international pressure, Soviet forces finally withdrew in 1989, and the Afghan communist regime soon collapsed. In Vietnam and Afghanistan, both superpowers painfully experienced the limits of their power.

The most haunting battle of the cold war era was one that never happened. The setting was Cuba, where a communist regime under the leadership of Fidel Castro had emerged by the early 1960s. (See Zooming In: The Cuban Revolution, page 934.) Intense American hostility to this nearby outpost of communism prompted the Soviet leader Nikita Khrushchev (KROOSH-chef), who had risen to power after Stalin's death in 1953, to secretly deploy nuclear-tipped Soviet missiles to Cuba, believing that this would deter further U.S. action against Castro. When the missiles were discovered in October 1962, the world held its breath for thirteen days as American forces blockaded the island and prepared for an invasion. A nuclear exchange between the superpowers seemed imminent, but that catastrophe was averted by a compromise between Khrushchev and U.S. president John F. Kennedy. Under its terms, the Soviets removed their missiles from Cuba in return for an American promise not to invade the island. That promise was kept and a communist regime persisted in Cuba, though much changed, well into the twenty-first century.

Nuclear Standoff and Third-World Rivalry

The **Cuban missile crisis** gave concrete expression to the most novel and dangerous dimension of the cold war—the arms race in nuclear weapons. An initial American monopoly on those weapons prompted the Soviet Union to redouble its efforts to acquire them, and in 1949 it succeeded. Over the next forty years, the world moved from a mere handful of nuclear weapons to a global arsenal of close to 60,000 warheads. Delivery systems included submarines, bomber aircraft, and missiles that could rapidly propel numerous warheads across whole continents and oceans with accuracies measured in hundreds of feet. During those decades, the

The Hydrogen Bomb During the 1950s and early 1960s, tests in the atmosphere of ever larger and more sophisticated hydrogen bombs made images of enormous fireballs and mushroom-shaped clouds the universal symbol of these weapons, which were immensely more powerful than the atomic bombs dropped on Japan. The American test pictured here took place in 1957. (Photo courtesy of National Nuclear Security Administration/Nevada Site Office)

entire world lived in the shadow of weapons whose destructive power is scarcely within the bounds of human imagination.

Awareness of this power is surely the primary reason that no shooting war of any kind occurred between the two superpowers, for leaders on both sides knew beyond any doubt that a nuclear war would produce only losers and utter catastrophe. Already in 1949, Stalin had observed that "atomic weapons can hardly be used without spelling the end of the world."[3] Particularly after the frightening Cuban missile crisis of 1962, both sides carefully avoided further nuclear provocation, even while continuing the buildup of their respective arsenals. Moreover, because they feared that a conventional war would escalate to the nuclear level, they implicitly agreed to sidestep any direct military confrontation at all.

Still, opportunities for conflict abounded as the U.S.-Soviet rivalry spanned the globe. Using military and economic aid, educational opportunities, political pressure, and covert action, both sides courted countries emerging from colonial rule. The Soviet Union aided anticolonial and revolutionary movements in many places, including South Africa, Mozambique, Vietnam, and Cuba. Cold war fears of communist penetration prompted U.S. intervention, sometimes openly and often secretly, in Iran, the Philippines, Guatemala, El Salvador, Chile, the Congo, and elsewhere. In the process the United States frequently supported anticommunist but corrupt and authoritarian

The Cuban Revolution

"You Americans must realize what Cuba means to us old Bolsheviks," declared a high-ranking Soviet official, Anastas Mikoyan, in 1960. "We have been waiting all our lives for a country to go communist without the Red Army. It has happened in Cuba, and it makes us feel like boys again."[4] The triumph of the Cuban revolutionaries must have been exhilarating for communists everywhere because it occurred in such an unlikely place. Located just ninety miles from Florida, Cuba had been a virtual protectorate of the United States in the decades following its independence from Spain in 1902. Moreover, U.S. companies had long exerted considerable influence over the weak and corrupt Cuban government and dominated key sectors of the economy, including sugar, the island's most important export. Nonetheless, Fidel Castro, son of a wealthy sugar plantation owner, led a successful popular insurrection that transformed Cuba into a Marxist socialist state just off the southern coast of the United States.

The armed revolt began disastrously. In 1953, the Cuban army defeated Castro and 123 of his supporters

Fidel Castro fighting in the mountains of Cuba in 1957.

when they attacked two army barracks in what was their first major military operation. Castro himself was captured, sentenced to jail, and then released into exile. However, fortunes shifted in 1956, when Castro slipped back into Cuba and succeeded in bringing together many opponents of the current regime in an armed nationalist insurgency dedicated to radical economic and social reform. Upon seizing power in 1959, Castro and his government acted decisively to implement their revolutionary agenda. Within a year, they had effectively redistributed 15 percent of the nation's wealth by granting land to the poor, increasing wages, and lowering rents. In the following year, the new government nationalized the property of both wealthy Cubans and U.S. corporations. Many Cubans, particularly among the elite, fled into exile. "The revolution," declared Castro, "is the dictatorship of the exploited against the exploiters."[5]

photo: Private Collection/Peter Newark American Pictures/Bridgeman Images

regimes. However, neither superpower was able to completely dominate its supposed allies, many of whom resisted the role of pawns in superpower rivalries. Some countries, such as India, took a posture of nonalignment in the cold war, while others tried to play off the superpowers against each other. Indonesia received large amounts of Soviet and Eastern European aid, but that did not prevent it from destroying the Indonesian Communist Party in 1965, killing half a million suspected communists in the process. When the Americans refused to assist Egypt in building the Aswan Dam in the mid-1950s, that country developed a close relationship with the Soviet Union. Later, in 1972, Egypt expelled 21,000 Soviet advisers, following disagreements over the extent of Soviet military aid, and again aligned more clearly with the United States.

Economic and political pressure from the United States followed, culminating in the Bay of Pigs, a failed invasion of the island in 1961 by Cuban exiles with covert support from the U.S. government. American hostility pushed the revolutionary nationalist Castro closer to the Soviet Union, and gradually he began to think of himself and his revolution as Marxist. In response to Cuban pleas for support against American aggression, the Soviet premier Khrushchev deployed nuclear missiles on the island, sparking the Cuban missile crisis. While the compromise reached between the two superpowers resulted in the withdrawal of the missiles, it did include assurances from the United States that it would not attack Cuba.

In the decades that followed, Cuba sought to export its brand of revolution beyond its borders, especially in Latin America and Africa. Che Guevara, an Argentine who had fought in the Cuban Revolution, declared, "Our revolution is endangering all American possessions in Latin America. We are telling these countries to make their own revolution."[6] Cuba supported revolutionary movements in many regions; however, none succeeded in creating a lasting Cuban-style regime.

The legacy of the Cuban Revolution has been mixed. The new government devoted considerable resources to improving health and education on the island. By the mid-1980s, Cuba possessed both the highest literacy rate and the lowest infant mortality rate in Latin America. Over the same period, life expectancy increased from fifty-eight to seventy-three years, putting Cuba on a par with the United States. Living standards for most improved as well.

Indeed, Cuba became a model for development in other Latin American countries.

However, earlier promises to establish a truly democratic system never materialized. Castro declared in 1959 that elections were unneeded because "this democracy . . . has found its expression, directly, in the intimate union and identification of the government with the people."[7] The state placed limits on free expression and arrested opponents or forced them into exile. Cuba has also failed to achieve the economic development originally envisioned at the time of the revolution. Sugar remains its chief export crop, and by the 1980s Cuba had become almost as economically dependent on the Soviet Union as it had been upon the United States. Desperate consequences followed when the Cuban economy shrank by a third following the collapse of the Soviet Union.

Like communist experiments in the Soviet Union and China, Cuba experienced real improvements in living standards, especially for the poor, but these gains were accompanied by sharp restraints on personal freedoms and mixed results in the economy. Such have been the ambivalent outcomes of many revolutionary upheavals.

QUESTIONS

Compare the Cuban Revolution to those in Russia and China. What are the similarities and differences? How might you assess the successes and failures of the Cuban Revolution?

The Cold War and the Superpowers

World War II and the cold war provided the context for the emergence of the United States as a global superpower. Much of that effort was driven by the perceived demands of the cold war, during which the United States spearheaded the Western effort to contain a worldwide communist movement that seemed to be advancing. By 1970, one writer observed, "the United States had more than 1,000,000 soldiers in 30 countries, was a member of four regional defense alliances and an active participant in a fifth, had mutual defense treaties with 42 nations, was a member of 53 international organizations, and was furnishing military or economic aid to nearly 100 nations across the face of the globe."[8] Sustaining this immense international effort was a flourishing U.S. economy and an increasingly middle-class society. The United States was the only major industrial country to escape the physical devastation of war on its own soil. As World War II ended with Europe, the Soviet Union, and Japan in ruins, the United States was clearly the world's most productive economy.

On the communist side, the cold war was accompanied by considerable turmoil within and among the various communist states. In the Soviet Union, the superpower of the communist world, the mid-1950s witnessed devastating revelations of Stalin's many crimes, shocking the communist faithful everywhere. And in Hungary (1956–1957), Czechoslovakia (1968), and Poland (early 1980s), various reform movements registered sharp protest against highly repressive and Soviet-dominated communist governments.

Many in the West had initially viewed world communism as a monolithic force whose disciplined members meekly followed Soviet dictates in cold war solidarity against the West. And Marxists everywhere contended that revolutionary socialism would erode national loyalties as the "workers of the world" united in common opposition to global capitalism. Nonetheless, the communist world experienced far more bitter and divisive conflict than did the Western alliance, which was composed of supposedly warlike, greedy, and highly competitive nations.

In Eastern Europe, Yugoslav leaders early on had rejected Soviet domination of their internal affairs and charted their own independent road to socialism. Fearing that reform might lead to contagious defections from the communist bloc, Soviet forces actually invaded their supposed allies in Hungary and Czechoslovakia to crush such movements, and they threatened to do so in Poland. Such actions gave credibility to Western perceptions of the cold war as a struggle between tyranny and freedom and badly tarnished the image of Soviet communism as a reasonable alternative to capitalism.

Even more startling, the two communist giants, the Soviet Union and China, found themselves sharply opposed, owing to territorial disputes, ideological differences, and rivalry for communist leadership. In 1960, the Soviet Union backed away from an earlier promise to provide China with the prototype of an atomic bomb and abruptly withdrew all Soviet advisers and technicians who had been assisting Chinese development. By the late 1960s, China on its own had developed a modest nuclear capability, and the two countries were at the brink of war, with the Soviet Union hinting at a possible nuclear strike on Chinese military targets. Beyond this central conflict, communist China in fact went to war against communist Vietnam in 1979, even as Vietnam invaded communist Cambodia. Nationalism, in short, proved more powerful than communist solidarity, even in the face of cold war hostilities with the capitalist West.

Despite its many internal conflicts, world communism remained a powerful global presence during the 1970s, achieving its greatest territorial reach. China was emerging from the chaos of the Cultural Revolution, while the Soviet Union had matched U.S. military might. Despite American hostility, Cuba remained a communist outpost in the Western Hemisphere, with impressive achievements in education and health care for its people and a commitment to supporting revolutionary movements in Africa and Latin America. Communism triumphed in Vietnam, dealing a major setback to the United States. A number of African countries also affirmed their commitment to Marxism. Few people anywhere expected that within two decades most of the twentieth century's experiment with communism would be gone.

Toward Freedom: Struggles for Independence

From an American or Soviet perspective, cold war struggles dominated international life from the 1940s through the early 1990s. But viewed from the world of Asia and Africa, a rather different global struggle was unfolding. Its central focus was colonial rule, subordination, poverty, and racism. Variously called the struggle for independence or **decolonization**, that process marked a dramatic change in the world's political architecture, as nation-states triumphed over the empires that had structured much of the world's political life in the nineteenth and early twentieth centuries. It mobilized millions of people, thrusting them into political activity and sometimes into violence and warfare. Decolonization signaled the declining legitimacy of both empire and race as a credible basis for political or social life. It promised not only national freedom but also personal dignity, opportunity, and prosperity.

In 1900, European colonial empires in Africa, Asia, the Caribbean region, and Pacific Oceania appeared as enduring features of the world's political landscape. Well before the end of the twentieth century, they were gone. The first major breakthroughs occurred in Asia and the Middle East in the late 1940s, when the Philippines, India, Pakistan, Burma, Indonesia, Syria, Iraq, Jordan, and Israel achieved independence. The decades from the mid-1950s through the mid-1970s were an age of African independence as colony after colony, more than fifty in total, emerged into what was then seen as the bright light of freedom. During the 1970s, many of the island societies of Pacific Oceania—Samoa, Fiji, Tonga, the Solomon Islands, Kiribati—joined the ranks of independent states, almost entirely peacefully and without much struggle as the various colonial powers willingly abandoned their right to rule. Hawaiians, however, sought incorporation as a state within the United States, rather than independence. Finally, a number of Caribbean societies—the Bahamas, Barbados, Belize, Jamaica, Trinidad, and Tobago—achieved independence during the 1960s and 1970s, informed by a growing awareness of a distinctive Caribbean culture. Cuba, although formally independent since 1902, dramatically declared its rejection of American control in its revolutionary upheaval in 1959. By 1983 the Caribbean region hosted sixteen separate independent states.

The End of Empire in World History

At one level, this vast process was but the latest case of imperial dissolution, a fate that had overtaken earlier empires, including those of the Assyrians, Romans, Arabs, and Mongols. But never before had the end of empire been so associated with the mobilization of the masses around a nationalist ideology. More comparable perhaps was that earlier decolonization in which the European colonies in the Americas had thrown off British, French, Spanish, or Portuguese rule during the late eighteenth and early nineteenth centuries (see "Comparing Atlantic Revolutions" in Chapter 16). Like their earlier counterparts, the new nations of the mid-to-late twentieth century claimed an international status equivalent to that of their former rulers. In the Americas, however, many of the colonized people were themselves of European origin, sharing much of their culture with their colonial rulers. In that respect, the freedom struggles of the twentieth century were very different, for they not only asserted political independence but also affirmed the vitality of their cultures, which had been submerged and denigrated during the colonial era.

The twentieth century witnessed the demise of many empires. The Austrian and Ottoman empires collapsed following World War I, giving rise to a number of new states in Europe and the Middle East. The Russian Empire also unraveled, although it was soon reassembled under the auspices of the Soviet Union. World War II ended the German and Japanese empires. African and Asian movements for independence shared with these other end-of-empire stories the ideal of national self-determination. This novel idea—that humankind was naturally divided into distinct peoples or nations, each of which deserved an independent state of its own—was loudly proclaimed by the winning side of both world wars. It gained a global acceptance, particularly in the colonial world, during the twentieth century and rendered empire illegitimate in the eyes of growing numbers of people.

Empires without territory, such as the powerful influence that the United States exercised in Latin America, likewise came under attack from highly nationalist governments. An intrusive U.S. presence was certainly one factor stimulating the Mexican Revolution, which began in 1910. One of the outcomes of that upheaval was the nationalization in 1937 of Mexico's oil industry, much of which was owned by American and British investors. Similar actions accompanied Cuba's revolution of 1959–1960 and also occurred in other places throughout Latin America and elsewhere. National self-determination and freedom from Soviet control likewise lay behind the Eastern European revolutions of 1989. The disintegration of the Soviet Union itself in 1991 brought to an inglorious end one of the last major territorial empires of the twentieth century and the birth of fifteen new national states. China's Central Asian empire, however, remained intact despite considerable resistance in Tibet and elsewhere. Although the winning of political independence for Europe's African and Asian colonies was perhaps the most spectacular challenge to empire in the twentieth century, that process was part of a larger pattern in modern world history (see Map 21.3).

Toward Independence in Asia and Africa

As the twentieth century closed, the end of European empires seemed in retrospect almost inevitable, for colonial rule had lost any credibility as a form of political order. What could be more natural than for people to seek to rule themselves? Yet at the beginning of the century, few observers were predicting the collapse of these empires, and the idea that "the only legitimate government is national self-government" was not nearly so widespread as it subsequently became. How might historians explain the rapid collapse of European colonial empires and the emergence of a transformed international landscape with dozens of new nation-states?

One approach focuses attention on fundamental contradictions in the entire colonial enterprise. The rhetoric of Christianity, Enlightenment thought, and material progress sat awkwardly with the realities of colonial racism, exploitation, and poverty. The increasingly democratic values of European states ran counter to the essential dictatorship of colonial rule. The ideal of national self-determination was profoundly at odds with the possession of colonies that were denied any opportunity to express their own national character. The enormously powerful force of nationalism, having earlier driven the process of European empire building, now played a major role in its disintegration. From this perspective, colonial rule dug its own grave because its practice ran counter to established European values of democracy and national self-determination.

But why did this "fatal flaw" of European colonial rule lead to independence in the post–World War II decades rather than earlier or later? Here, historians have found useful the notion of "conjuncture": the coming together of several separate developments at a particular time. At the international level, the world wars had weakened Europe while discrediting any sense of European moral superiority. Both the United States and the Soviet Union, the new global superpowers, generally opposed the older European colonial empires, even as they created empire-like international relationships of their own. Meanwhile, the United Nations provided a prestigious platform from which to conduct anticolonial agitation. Within the colonies, the dependence of European rulers on the cooperation of local elites, and increasingly on Western-educated men, rendered those empires vulnerable to the withdrawal of that support. All of this contributed to the global illegitimacy of empire, a novel and stunning transformation of social values that was enormously encouraging to anticolonial movements everywhere.

At the same time, social and economic processes within the colonies themselves generated the human raw material for anticolonial movements. By the early twentieth century in Asia and the mid-twentieth century in Africa, a second or third generation of Western-educated elites, largely male, had arisen throughout the colonial world. These young men were thoroughly familiar with European culture; they were deeply aware of the gap between its values and its practices; they no longer viewed colonial rule as a vehicle for their peoples' progress as their fathers had; and they increasingly insisted on immediate independence. Moreover, growing numbers of ordinary people—women and men alike—were receptive to this message. Veterans of the world wars; young people with some education but few jobs commensurate with their expectations; a small class of urban workers who were increasingly aware of their exploitation; small-scale female traders resentful of European privileges; rural dwellers who had lost land or suffered from forced labor; impoverished and insecure newcomers to the cities—all of these groups had reason

Guided Reading Question

■ **CHANGE**
What international circumstances and patterns of social change contributed to the end of European colonial empires in Africa and Asia?

PORTUGAL   SPAIN   ITALY   TURKEY

MALTA 1964 CYPRUS 1960 SYRIA
From G.B.   1944
TUNISIA   LEBANON 1944   IRAQ
1957   ISRAEL 1948 JORDAN   1932   IRAN
MOROCCO   1946
1956
ALGERIA   LIBYA   EGYPT   KUWAIT 1961
1962   1951   1922   BAHRAIN 1971
WESTERN   QATAR 1971
SAHARA   UNITED ARAB
(Morocco) 1975   EMIRATES 1971
From Spain
MAURITANIA   ERITREA   YEMEN P.D.R. OF
1960   MALI   NIGER   1950   YEMEN 1967
1960   1960   CHAD SUDAN Federated with Ethiopia
SENEGAL   1960   1956   DJIBOUTI 1977
1960
GAMBIA   BURKINA
1965   FASO   ETHIOPIA
GUINEA   1960   NIGERIA   1941
GUINEA- 1958   1960   CENTRAL
BISSAU   IVORY   AFR. REP.   SOMALIA
1974   COAST   1960   UGANDA   1960
SIERRA   1960   BENIN CAMEROON   1962
LEONE   1960   1960   DEMOCRATIC KENYA
1961 LIBERIA GHANA TOGO   REP. OF CONGO 1963
1820s   1957 1960   1960
GABON   RWANDA 1962   SEYCHELLES
SÃO TOMÉ   1960   1976
AND PRINCIPE EQUATORIAL   BURUNDI 1962
1975 From Portugal GUINEA   TANZANIA
1968 From Spain   1964
REP. OF   COMOROS
CONGO   1975
1960   MALAWI
ATLANTIC   ANGOLA   1964
OCEAN   1975   ZAMBIA   MADAGASCAR
1964   1960
ZIMBABWE
1980   MOZAMBIQUE
NAMIBIA 1985   1974
From South Africa BOTSWANA   MAURITIUS
1966   1968
SWAZILAND 1968   From Great Britain
SOUTH
AFRICA   LESOTHO 1966
(Republic 1961;
black majority rule, 1994)

1960 Year of independence
      Belgium
      France
      Great Britain
      Italy
      Netherlands
      Portugal
      United States
      Other

MAPPING HISTORY

Map 21.3 The End of Empire in Africa and Asia

In the second half of the twentieth century, under pressure from nationalist movements, Europe's Asian and African empires dissolved into dozens of new independent states, dramatically altering the structure of international life.

to believe that independence held great promise. And as populations grew across the colonial world, the pressure of numbers enhanced these grievances.

Such pressures increasingly placed colonial rulers on the defensive. As the twentieth century wore on, these colonial rulers began to plan—tentatively at

SOVIET
UNION

AFGHANISTAN

PAKISTAN
1947

CHINA

NORTH
KOREA
1948   From Japan

SOUTH
KOREA
1948

JAPAN

INDIA
1947

MYANMAR
(BURMA)
1948

LAOS
1949

NORTH VIETNAM
1954

PACIFIC
OCEAN

Unified 1975

PAKISTAN 1947
(BANGLADESH 1971)

CAMBODIA
1954

SOUTH VIETNAM
1954

PHILIPPINES
1946

SRI LANKA
(CEYLON)
1948

BRUNEI 1984
From Great Britain

MALAYSIA 1963

PAPUA
NEW GUINEA
1975
From Australia

SINGAPORE 1965

INDONESIA 1949

INDIAN
OCEAN

EAST TIMOR
From Portugal, 1975;
From Indonesia, 2002

0   500   1,000 miles

0   500   1,000 kilometers

READING THE MAP: Which European colonial power gave up its colonies late in the decolonization process?

MAKING CONNECTIONS: Compare this map with Maps 18.1 and 18.2. To what extent did the colonial era provide the framework for the postcolonial political boundaries of Africa, South Asia, and Southeast Asia?

first—for a new political relationship with their Asian and African subjects. The colonies had been integrated into a global economic network, and local elites were largely committed to maintaining those links. In these circumstances, Europeans could imagine retaining profitable economic interests in Asia, Africa, and Oceania

Military Struggles for Independence While many colonies won their independence through peaceful political pressure, others found it necessary to adopt a military strategy. This photograph shows an assembly of Algerian fighters from the National Liberation Front (NLF) in 1960. Established in 1954, the NLF was the major nationalist organization in Algeria that led the country to independence from France in 1962 following a bitter and violent eight-year struggle. (Kharbine-Tapabor/REX/Shutterstock)

without the expense and trouble of formal colonial governments. Deliberate planning for decolonization included gradual political reforms; investments in railroads, ports, and telegraph lines; the holding of elections; and the writing of constitutions. To some observers, it seemed as if independence was granted by colonial rulers rather than gained or seized by anticolonial initiatives.

But these reforms, and independence itself, occurred only under considerable pressure from mounting nationalist movements. Creating such movements was no easy task. Leaders, drawn everywhere from the ranks of the educated few and almost always male, organized political parties, recruited members, plotted strategy, developed an ideology, and negotiated with one another and with the colonial state. The most prominent among them became the "fathers" of their new countries as independence dawned—Gandhi and Nehru in India, Sukarno in Indonesia, Ho Chi Minh in Vietnam, Nkrumah in Ghana, and Mandela in South Africa. In places where colonial rule was particularly intransigent—settler-dominated colonies such as Algeria, Kenya, and Rhodesia and Portuguese territories, for example—leaders also directed military operations and administered liberated areas. While such movements drew on memories of earlier, more localized forms of resistance, nationalist leaders did not seek to restore a vanished past. Rather, they looked forward to joining the world of independent nation-states, to membership in the United Nations, and to the wealth and power that modern technology promised.

A further common task of the nationalist leadership involved recruiting a mass following, and to varying degrees, they did. Millions of ordinary men and women joined Gandhi's nonviolent campaigns in India; tens of thousands of freedom fighters waged guerrilla warfare in Algeria, Kenya, Mozambique, and Zimbabwe; in West Africa workers went on strike and market women joined political parties, as did students, farmers, and the unemployed.

But struggles for independence were rarely if ever cohesive movements of uniformly oppressed people. More often, they were fragile alliances representing different classes, ethnic groups, religions, or regions. Beneath the common goal of independence, they struggled with one another over questions of leadership, power, strategy,

Guided Reading Question

....

■ **CHANGE**
What divisions or conflicts accompanied struggles for independence in Asia and Africa?

ideology, and the distribution of material benefits, even as they fought and negotiated with their colonial rulers. Sometimes the relationship between nationalist leaders and their followers was fraught with tension. One such Indonesian leader, educated in Holland, spoke of his difficulty in relating to the common people: "Why am I vexed by the things that fill their lives, and to which they are so attached? Why are the things that contain beauty for them . . . only senseless and displeasing for me? We intellectuals here are much closer to Europe or America than we are to the primitive Islamic culture of Java and Sumatra."[9] In colonial Nigeria, the independence movement took shape as three major political parties, each of them identified primarily with a particular ethnic group, Igbo, Yoruba, or Hausa. Thus the very notion of "national self-government" posed obvious but often contentious questions: What group of people constituted the "nation" that deserved to rule itself? And who should speak for it?

India's independence movement, which found expression in the **Indian National Congress** or Congress Party, provides a compelling example of these divisions and controversies. Its primary leader, **Mohandas Gandhi**, rejected modern industrialization as a goal for his country, while his own chief lieutenant, Jawaharlal Nehru, thoroughly embraced science, technology, and industry as essential to India's future. Nor did everyone accept Gandhi's nonviolent philosophy or his inclusive definition of India as embracing all religions, regions, and castes. Some believed that Gandhi's efforts to improve the position of women or untouchables were a distraction from the chief task of gaining independence. Whether to participate in British-sponsored legislative bodies prior to complete independence also became a divisive issue. Furthermore, a number of smaller parties advocated on behalf of particular regions or castes.

By far the most serious threat to a unified movement derived from the growing divide between the country's Hindu and Muslim populations. As a distinct minority within India, some Muslims feared that their voice could be swamped by numerically dominant Hindus, despite Gandhi's inclusive sensibility. Some Hindu politicians confirmed those fears when they cast the nationalist struggle in Hindu religious terms, hailing their country, for example, as a goddess, Bande Mataram (Mother India). This approach, as well as Hindu efforts to protect cows from slaughter, antagonized Muslims. Their growing skepticism about the possibility of a single Indian state found expression in the **Muslim League**, whose leader, Muhammad Ali Jinnah (JIN-uh), argued that those parts of India that had a Muslim majority should have a separate political status. They called it Pakistan, the land of the pure. In this view, India was not a single nation, as Gandhi had long argued. Jinnah put his case succinctly: "The Muslims and Hindus belong to two different religious philosophies, social customs, and literatures. They neither intermarry nor interdine [eat] together and, indeed, they belong to two different civilizations."[10] With great reluctance and amid mounting violence, Gandhi and the Congress Party finally agreed to partition as the British declared their intention to leave India after World War II.

Thus colonial India became independent in 1947 as two countries—a Muslim Pakistan, itself divided into two wings 1,000 miles apart, and a mostly Hindu India

Mahatma Gandhi on the Salt March The most widely recognized and admired figure in the global struggle against colonial rule was Mohandas Gandhi, often known as Mahatma, or "Great Soul." He is shown here with his granddaughter Ava (left) and his personal physician Dr. Sushila Nayar (right). (Bettmann/Getty Images)

governed by a secular state. Dividing colonial India in this fashion was horrendously painful. A million people or more died in the communal violence that accompanied partition, and some 12 million refugees moved from one country to the other to join their religious compatriots. Gandhi himself, desperately trying to stem the mounting tide of violence, refused to attend the independence celebrations. Only a year after independence, he was assassinated by a Hindu extremist. The great triumph of independence, secured from the powerful British Empire, was overshadowed by the great tragedy of violent partition.

Beyond their internal divisions, nationalist movements seeking independence differed sharply from one another. In some places, that struggle, once begun, produced independence within a few years, four in the case of the Belgian Congo. Elsewhere it was measured in decades. Nationalism had surfaced in Vietnam in the early 1900s, but the country achieved full political independence only in the mid-1970s, having fought French colonial rulers, Japanese invaders during World War II, and U.S. military forces in the 1960s and 1970s, as well as Chinese forces during a brief war in 1979. And the struggle in South Africa was distinctive in many ways. It was not waged against a distant colonial power, but against a white settler minority representing about 20 percent of the population that had already been granted independence from Great Britain in 1910. It took place in a mature industrialized and urbanized nation and in the face of the world's most rigid and racially repressive regime, known as apartheid. These factors help to explain why South Africa gained its "independence" from colonial oppression only in 1994.

Tactics too varied considerably. In many places, such as West Africa, nationalists relied on peaceful political pressure—demonstrations, strikes, mass mobilization, and negotiations—to achieve independence. Elsewhere armed struggle was required. Eight years of bitter guerrilla warfare preceded Algerian independence from France in 1962.

While all nationalist movements sought political independence for modern states, their ideologies and outlooks also differed. Many in India and the Islamic world viewed their new nations through the prism of religion, while elsewhere more secular outlooks prevailed. In Indonesia an early nationalist organization, the Islamic Union, appealed on the basis of religion, while later groups espoused Marxism. Indonesia's primary nationalist leader, Sukarno, sought to embrace and reconcile these various outlooks. "What is Sukarno?" he asked. "A nationalist? An Islamist? A Marxist? . . . Sukarno is a mixture of all these isms."[11] Nationalist movements led by communist parties, such as those in Vietnam and China, sought major social transformations as well as freedom from foreign rule, while those in most of Africa focused on ending racial discrimination and achieving political independence with little concern about emerging patterns of domestic class inequality.

However it was achieved, the collapse of colonial rule and the emergence of these new nations onto the world stage as independent and assertive actors have been distinguishing features of world history in this most recent century.

After Freedom

Having achieved the long-sought status of independent nation-states, how would those states be governed? And how would they undertake the tasks of nation building and modern development? Those were the questions that confronted both the former colonies and those already independent, such as China, Thailand, Ethiopia, Iran, Turkey, and Central and South America. Together they formed the bloc of nations known variously as the third world, the developing countries, or the Global South.

All across the developing world, efforts to create a new political order had to contend with a set of common conditions. Populations were exploding, and expectations for independence ran very high, often exceeding the available resources. Many developing countries were culturally very diverse, with little loyalty to a central state. Nonetheless, public employment mushroomed as the state assumed greater responsibility for economic development. In conditions of widespread poverty and weak private economies, groups and individuals sought to capture the state, or parts of it, both for the salaries and status it offered and for the opportunities for private enrichment that public office provided.

This was the formidable setting in which developing countries had to hammer out new political systems. The range of that effort was immense: Communist Party control in China, Vietnam, and Cuba; multiparty democracy in India and South Africa; one-party democracy in Mexico, Tanzania, and Senegal; military regimes for a time in much of Latin America, Africa, and the Middle East; personal dictatorships in Iraq, Uganda, and the Philippines. In many places, one kind of political system followed another in kaleidoscopic succession.

As colonial rule drew to a close, European authorities in many places attempted to transplant democratic institutions to colonies they had long governed with such a heavy and authoritarian hand. They established legislatures, permitted elections, allowed political parties to operate, and in general anticipated the development of constitutional, parliamentary, multiparty democracies similar to their own.

It was in India that such a political system established its deepest roots. There Western-style democracy, including regular elections, multiple parties, civil liberties,

Guided Reading Question
....
■ **COMPARISON**
To what extent did Western-style political democracy take root in the developing countries?

and peaceful changes in government, has been practiced almost continuously since independence. Elsewhere in the colonial world, democracy proved a far more fragile transplant. Among the new states of Africa, for example, few retained their democratic institutions beyond the initial post-independence decade. Many of the apparently popular political parties that had led the struggle for independence lost mass support and were swept away by military coups. When the army took power in Ghana in 1966, no one lifted a finger to defend the party that had led the country to independence only nine years earlier. Other states evolved into one-party systems, and still others degenerated into corrupt personal tyrannies or "Big Man" dictatorships. Freedom from colonial rule certainly did not automatically generate the internal political freedoms associated with democracy.

Across much of Africa, economic disappointments, class resentments, and ethnic conflicts provided the context for numerous military takeovers. By the early 1980s, the military had intervened in at least thirty of Africa's forty-six independent states and actively governed more than half of them. Army officers swept aside the old political parties and constitutions and vowed to begin anew, while promising to return power to civilians and restore democracy at some point in the future.

A similar wave of military interventions swept over Latin America during the 1960s and 1970s, leaving Brazil, Argentina, Peru, Chile, Uruguay, Bolivia, the Dominican Republic, and other countries governed at times by their military officers. However, the circumstances in Latin America were quite different from those in Africa. While military rule was something new and unexpected in Africa, Latin American armed forces had long intervened in political life. The region had also largely escaped the bitter ethnic conflicts that afflicted so many African states, though its class antagonisms were more clearly defined and expressed. Furthermore, Latin American societies in general were far more modernized and urbanized than those of Africa. And while newly independent African states remained linked to their former European rulers, long-independent Latin American states lived in the shadow of a dominant United States. "Poor Mexico," bemoaned Porfirio Díaz, that country's dictator before the Mexican Revolution, "so far from God and so close to the United States."

The late twentieth century witnessed a remarkable political reversal, a **globalization of democracy**, that brought popular movements, multiparty elections, and new constitutions to many countries all around the world. This included the end of military and autocratic rule in Spain, Portugal, and Greece as well as the stunning rise of democratic movements, parties, and institutions amid the collapse of communism in the Soviet Union and Eastern Europe. But the most extensive expression of this global reemergence of democracy lay in the developing countries. By 2000, almost all Latin American countries had abandoned their military-controlled regimes and returned to some form of democratic governance. So too did most African states previously ruled by soldiers, dictators, or single parties. In Asia, authoritarian regimes, some long established, gave way to more pluralistic and participatory political systems in South Korea, Taiwan, Thailand, the Philippines, Iraq, and Indonesia. And in 2011, mass movements in various Arab countries—Tunisia, Egypt, Libya, Syria, Bahrain, Yemen—challenged or ended the hold of entrenched, corrupt, and autocratic rulers, while proclaiming their commitment to democracy, human dignity, and honest government. What might explain this global pattern and its expression in the Global South in particular?

One factor surely was the untethering of the ideas of democracy and human rights from their Western origins. By the final quarter of the twentieth century, democracy increasingly was viewed as a universal political principle to which all could aspire rather than an alien and imposed system deriving from the West. Democracy, like communism, feminism, modern science, and Christianity, was a Western import that took root in a globalizing world and partly lost its association with the West. It was therefore increasingly available as a vehicle for social protest in the rest of the world.

Perhaps the most important internal factor favoring a revival of democracy lay in the apparent failure of authoritarian governments to remedy disastrous economic situations, to raise standards of living, to provide jobs for the young, and to curb pervasive corruption. The oppressive and sometimes brutal behavior of repressive governments humiliated and outraged many. Furthermore, the growth of civil society with its numerous voluntary groups provided a social foundation, independent of the state, for demanding change. Disaffected students, professionals, urban workers, religious organizations, women's groups, and more joined in a variety of grassroots movements, some of them mobilized through social media, to insist on democratic change as a means to a better life. Such movements found encouragement in the demands for democracy that accompanied the South African struggle against apartheid and the collapse of Soviet and Eastern European communism. And the end of the cold war reduced the willingness of the major industrial powers to underwrite their authoritarian client states.

But the consolidation of democratic practice was an uncertain and highly variable process. Some elected leaders, such as Hugo Chávez in Venezuela, Vladimir Putin in Russia, and Recip Erdogan in Turkey, turned authoritarian once in office. Even where parliaments existed, they were often quite circumscribed in their powers. Outright electoral fraud tainted democratic institutions in many places, while established elites and oligarchies found it possible to exercise considerable influence even in formal democracies, and not only in the Global South. Chinese authorities brutally crushed a democratic movement in 1989. The Algerian military sponsored elections in 1992 and then abruptly canceled them when an Islamic party seemed poised to win. And the political future of the Arab Spring remained highly uncertain, as a military strongman became a civilian politician and returned to power in Egypt in 2014 and Syria degenerated into brutal civil war. Nonetheless, this worldwide revival of democracy represented the globalization of what had been a Western idea and the continuation of the political experiments that had begun with independence.

PRACTICING HISTORICAL THINKING

The two major international conflicts of the second half of the twentieth century involved the cold war struggle between the communist and capitalist worlds and the anticolonial struggles of Afro-Asian peoples against the Western imperial powers. How might you compare these two conflicts, and how did they intersect with one another?

The End of the Communist Era

As the emergence of dozens of "new nations" from colonial rule reshaped the international political landscape during the second half of the twentieth century, so too did the demise of world communism during the last quarter of that century. It effectively ended the cold war, diminished the threat of a nuclear holocaust, and marked the birth of another twenty or so new nation-states.

Surprisingly enough, the communist era came to an end far more peacefully than it had begun. That ending might be viewed as a drama in three acts. Act One began in China during the late 1970s, following the death of its towering revolutionary leader **Mao Zedong** in 1976. Over the next several decades, the CCP gradually abandoned almost everything that had been associated with Maoist communism, even as the party retained its political control of the country. Act Two took place in Eastern Europe in the "miracle year" of 1989, when popular movements toppled despised communist governments one after another all across the region. The climactic act in this "end of communism" drama occurred in 1991 in the Soviet Union, where the entire "play" had opened seventy-four years earlier. There the reformist leader Mikhail Gorbachev (GORE-beh-CHOF) had come to power in 1985 intending to revive and save Soviet socialism from its accumulated dysfunctions. Those efforts, however, only exacerbated the country's many difficulties and led to the political disintegration of the Soviet Union on Christmas Day 1991. The curtain had fallen on the communist era.

Behind these separate stories lay two general failures of the communist experiment, measured both by communists' own standards and by those of the larger world. The first was economic. Despite their early successes, communist economies by the late 1970s showed no signs of catching up to the more advanced capitalist countries. The highly regimented Soviet economy in particular was largely stagnant; its citizens were forced to stand in long lines for consumer goods and complained endlessly about their poor quality and declining availability. This was enormously embarrassing, for it had been the proud boast of communist leaders everywhere that they had found a better route to modern prosperity than their capitalist rivals. Furthermore, these unflattering comparisons were increasingly well known, thanks to the global information revolution. They had political and national security implications as well, for economic growth, even more than military capacity, was increasingly the measure of state power and widely expected among the general population as consumerism took hold around the world. The second failure was moral. The horrors of Stalin's Terror and the gulag, of Mao's Cultural Revolution, of something approaching genocide in communist Cambodia—all of this wore away at communist claims to moral superiority over capitalism. Moreover, this erosion occurred as global political culture more widely embraced democracy and human rights as the universal legacy of humankind, rather than the exclusive possession of the capitalist West. In both economic and moral terms, the communist path to the modern world was increasingly seen as a road to nowhere.

Communist leaders were not ignorant of these problems, and particularly in China and the Soviet Union, they moved aggressively to address them. But their approach to doing so varied greatly, as did the outcomes of those efforts. Thus, much as the Russian and Chinese revolutions differed and their approaches to building socialism diverged, so too did these communist giants chart distinct paths during the final years of the communist experiment.

Guided Reading Question

....

■ **COMPARISON**
In what different ways was the erosion of communism experienced in China and the Soviet Union?

Beyond Mao in China

In China the reform process took shape under the leadership of **Deng Xiaoping** (dung shee-yao-ping), who emerged as China's "paramount leader" in 1976, following the death of Mao Zedong. Particularly dramatic were Deng's dismantling of the country's system of collectivized farming and a return to something close to small-scale private agriculture. Impoverished Chinese peasants eagerly embraced these new opportunities and pushed them even further than the government had intended. Industrial reform proceeded more gradually. Managers of state enterprises were given greater authority and encouraged to act like private owners, making many of their own decisions and seeking profits. China opened itself to the world economy and welcomed foreign investment in "special enterprise zones" along the coast, where foreign capitalists received tax breaks and other inducements. Local governments and private entrepreneurs joined forces in thousands of flourishing "township and village enterprises" that produced food, clothing, building materials, and much more.

The outcome of these reforms was stunning economic growth and a new prosperity for millions. Better diets, lower mortality rates, declining poverty, massive urban construction, and surging exports—all of this accompanied China's state-directed rejoining of the world economy and contributed to a much-improved material life for millions of its citizens. China was the rising economic giant of the twenty-first century. That economic success provided the foundation for China's emergence as one of the Great Powers of the new century, able to challenge American dominance in eastern Asia and the Pacific.

After Communism in China Although the Communist Party still governed China in the early twenty-first century, communist values of selflessness, community, and simplicity had been substantially replaced for many by Western-style consumerism. This New Year's Good Luck poster from 1993 illustrates the new interest in material wealth in the form of American dollars and the return of older Chinese cultural patterns represented by the traditional gods of wealth, happiness, and longevity. The caption reads: "The gods of wealth enter the home from everywhere." (Zhejiang People's Art Publishing House/Stefan R. Landsberger Collections/International Institute of Social History, Amsterdam/www .chineseposters.net)

On the other hand, the country's burgeoning economy also generated massive corruption among Chinese officials, sharp inequalities between the coast and the interior, a huge problem of urban overcrowding, terrible pollution in major cities, and periodic inflation as the state loosened its controls over the economy. Urban vices such as street crime, prostitution, gambling, drug addiction, and a criminal underworld, which had been largely eliminated after 1949, surfaced again in China's booming cities. Nonetheless, something remarkable had occurred in China: a largely capitalist economy had been restored, and by none other than the Communist Party itself. Mao's worst fears had been realized, as China "took the capitalist road."

Although the party was willing to abandon many communist economic policies, it was adamantly unwilling to relinquish its political monopoly or to promote democracy at the national level. "Talk about democracy in the abstract," Deng Xiaoping declared, "will inevitably lead to the unchecked spread of ultra-democracy and anarchism, to the complete disruption of political stability, and to the total failure of our modernization program. . . . China will once again be plunged into chaos, division, retrogression, and darkness."[12] Such attitudes associated democracy with the chaos and uncontrolled mass action of the Cultural Revolution. Thus, when a democracy movement spearheaded by university and secondary school students surfaced in the late 1980s, Deng ordered the brutal crushing of its brazen demonstration in Beijing's Tiananmen Square before the television cameras of the world.

The Collapse of the Soviet Union

A parallel reform process unfolded quite differently in the USSR under the leadership of **Mikhail Gorbachev**, beginning in the mid-1980s. Like Deng Xiaoping in China, Gorbachev was committed to aggressively tackling the country's many problems—economic stagnation, a flourishing black market, public apathy, and cynicism about the party. His economic program, launched in 1987 and known as *perestroika* (per-uh-STROI-kuh) (restructuring), paralleled aspects of the Chinese approach by freeing state enterprises from the heavy hand of government regulation, permitting small-scale private businesses called cooperatives, offering opportunities for private farming, and cautiously welcoming foreign investment in joint enterprises.

But in cultural and political affairs, Gorbachev moved far beyond Chinese reforms. His policy of *glasnost* (GLAHS-nohst) (openness) now permitted an unprecedented range of cultural and intellectual freedoms. In the late 1980s, glasnost hit the Soviet Union like a bomb. Newspapers and TV exposed social pathologies—crime, prostitution, child abuse, suicide, elite corruption, and homelessness—that previously had been presented solely as the product of capitalism. "Like an excited boy reads a note from his girl," wrote one poet, "that's how we read the papers today."[13] Plays, poems, films, and novels that had long been buried "in the drawer" were now released to a public that virtually devoured them. Films broke the ban on nudity and explicit sex.

Soviet history was also reexamined as revelations of Stalin's crimes poured out of the media. The Bible and the Quran became more widely available, atheistic propaganda largely ceased, and thousands of churches and mosques were returned to believers and opened for worship. And beyond glasnost lay democratization and a new parliament with real powers, chosen in competitive elections. When those elections occurred in 1989, dozens of leading communists were rejected at the polls. In foreign affairs, Gorbachev moved to end the cold war by making unilateral cuts in Soviet military forces, engaging in arms control negotiations with the United States, and refusing to intervene as communist governments in Eastern Europe were overthrown.

But almost nothing worked out as Gorbachev had anticipated. Far from strengthening socialism and reviving a stagnant Soviet Union, the reforms led to its further weakening and collapse. In a dramatic contrast with China's booming economy, the Soviet Union spun into a sharp decline as its planned economy was dismantled before a functioning market-based system could emerge. Inflation mounted; consumer goods were in short supply, and ration coupons reappeared; many feared the loss of their jobs. Unlike Chinese peasants, few Soviet farmers were willing to risk the jump into private farming, and few foreign investors found the Soviet Union a tempting place to do business.

Furthermore, the new freedoms provoked demands that went far beyond what Gorbachev had intended. A democracy movement of unofficial groups and parties now sprang to life, many of them seeking a full multiparty democracy and a market-based economy. They were joined by independent labor unions, which actually went on strike, something unheard of in the "workers' state." Most corrosively, a multitude of nationalist movements used the new freedoms to insist on greater autonomy, or even independence, from the Soviet Union. In the face of these mounting demands, Gorbachev resolutely refused to use force to crush the protesters, another sharp contrast with the Chinese experience.

Events in Eastern Europe intersected with those in the Soviet Union. Gorbachev's reforms had lit a fuse in these Soviet satellites, where communism had been imposed and maintained from outside. If the USSR could practice glasnost and hold competitive elections, why not Eastern Europe as well? This was the background for the "miracle year" of 1989. Massive demonstrations, last-minute efforts at reforms, the breaching of the Berlin Wall, the surfacing of new political groups—all of this and more overwhelmed the highly unpopular communist regimes of Poland, Hungary, East Germany, Bulgaria, Czechoslovakia, and Romania, which were quickly swept away. This success then emboldened nationalists and democrats in the Soviet Union. If communism had been overthrown in Eastern Europe, perhaps it could be overthrown in the USSR as well. Soviet conservatives and patriots, however, were outraged. To them, Gorbachev had stood idly by while the political gains of World War II, for which the Soviet Union had paid in rivers of blood, vanished before their eyes. It was nothing less than treason.

A brief and unsuccessful attempt to restore the old order through a military coup in August 1991 triggered the end of the Soviet Union and its communist

Breaching the Berlin Wall In November 1989, anticommunist protesters broke through the Berlin Wall dividing the eastern and western sections of the city, even as East Berlin citizens joyfully entered their city's western zone. That event has become an iconic symbol of the collapse of communism in Eastern Europe and heralded the reunification of Germany and the end of the cold war, which had divided Europe since the late 1940s. (Tom Stoddart/Reportage via Getty Images)

regime. From the wreckage there emerged fifteen new and independent states, following the internal political divisions of the USSR. Arguably the Soviet Union had collapsed less because of its multiple problems and more from the unexpected consequences of Gorbachev's efforts to address them. The Soviet collapse represented a unique phenomenon in the world of the late twentieth century. Simultaneously, the world's largest state and its last territorial empire vanished; the world's first Communist Party disintegrated; a powerful command economy broke down; an official socialist ideology was repudiated; and a forty-five-year global struggle between the East and the West ended, at least temporarily. In Europe, Germany was reunited, and a number of former communist states joined NATO and the European Union, ending the division of the continent. At least for the moment, capitalism and democracy seemed to triumph over socialism and authoritarian governments. In many places, the end of communism allowed simmering ethnic tensions to explode into open conflict. Beyond the disintegration of the Soviet Union, both Yugoslavia and Czechoslovakia fragmented. Chechens in Russia, Abkhazians in Georgia, Russians in the Baltic states and Ukraine, Tibetans and Uighurs in China—all of these minorities found themselves in opposition to the states in which they lived.

After Communism

As the twenty-first century dawned, the communist world had shrunk considerably from its high point just three decades earlier. In the Soviet Union and Eastern Europe, communism had disappeared entirely as the governing authority and dominant ideology. In the immediate aftermath of the Soviet collapse, Russia experienced a sharply contracting economy, widespread poverty and inequality, and declining life expectancy. Not until 2006 did its economy recover to the level of 1991. China had largely abandoned its communist economic policies as a market economy took shape, spurring remarkable economic growth. Like China, Vietnam and Laos remained officially communist, even while they pursued Chinese-style reforms, though more cautiously. Even Cuba, which was beset by economic crisis in the 1990s after massive Soviet subsidies ended, allowed small businesses, private food markets, and tourism to grow, while harshly suppressing opposition political groups. Cubans were increasingly engaged in private enterprise, able to buy and sell cars and houses, and enthusiastically embracing mobile phones and computers. In 2015 diplomatic relations with the United States were restored after more than a half century of hostility between the two countries. An impoverished and highly nationalistic North Korea, armed with nuclear weapons, remained the most unreformed and repressive of the remaining communist countries. But either as a primary source of international conflict or as a compelling path to modernity and social justice, communism was effectively dead. The brief communist era in world history had ended.

The end of the cold war and the thorough discrediting of communism, however, did not usher in any extended period of international tranquility as many had hoped, for the rivalries of the Great Powers had certainly not ended. As the bipolar world of the cold war faded away, the United States emerged as the world's sole superpower, but Russia and China alike continued to challenge American dominance in world affairs. Russian president Vladimir Putin deeply resented the loss of his country's international stature after the breakup of the Soviet Union and what he regarded as U.S. efforts to intrude upon Russia's legitimate interests. Issues such as the eastward expansion of NATO, Russia's intervention in the Ukraine and its outright annexation of the Crimea, rival involvements in Syria's civil war, and Russian meddling in American elections had brought the relationship of Russia and the United States by 2016 to something resembling cold war era hostility, though without the sharp ideological antagonism of that earlier conflict. And the rising economic and military power of China generated many tensions in its relationship with the United States and Japan as China sought to assert its interests and influence in East Asia, the South China Sea, and the global economic arena.

Beyond the antagonisms among the major world powers, the Middle East emerged as a vortex of instability and conflict that echoed widely across the world. The struggles between the new Jewish state of Israel, granted independence in 1948,

Guided Reading Question
....
■ **CHANGE**
In what ways did international life change following the end of the communist era?

The Middle East, ca. 2000

and the adjacent Palestinian Muslim territories generated periodic wars and upheavals that have persisted into the post–cold war era. Both near neighbors, such as Syria, Jordan, Turkey, and Egypt, as well as distant powers, such as the United States and Russia, have been drawn into the **Israeli-Palestinian Conflict** on both sides. The **Iranian revolution** of 1979 established a radically Islamist government in that ancient land, helped to trigger a long and bloody war with neighboring Iraq during the 1980s, posed a serious threat to Israel, and launched a continuing rivalry with Saudi Arabia for dominant influence in the region. Iran's alleged efforts to acquire nuclear weapons capability generated widespread efforts to forestall that possibility, which came to fruition in a contentiously negotiated international agreement in 2015.

But the most globally unsettling and novel aspect of post–cold war international life has been the proliferation of "terrorist" attacks undertaken by radical Islamist groups such as the Taliban, al-Qaeda, Boko Haram, and the Islamic State or by individuals inspired by their message. (See "Religion and Global Modernity" in Chapter 23.) The random character of these attacks, their unpredictability, and their targeting of civilians have generated immense fear and insecurity in many places. In terms of their international consequences, the most significant of these attacks was that launched against several U.S. targets, including the World Trade Center, in September of 2001, for that event prompted large-scale U.S. military intervention and prolonged wars in both Afghanistan and Iraq. In both places old regimes were replaced by new ones amid enormous and continuing conflict and carnage. But the United States has certainly not been the sole target of terrorist violence. Many European and Russian cities have experienced such attacks in the twenty-first century, and terrorism has claimed far more victims in the Islamic world itself, as Islamic radicals have sought to oust what they view as corrupt and un-Islamic governments. Thus terrorism and the so-called war on terrorism have become a global issue in the post–cold war era.

A final source of international tension deriving from the Middle East has been the flood of refugees from war-torn and economically desperate societies in the region and adjacent African states, many of them headed for Europe. The **Syrian civil war**, beginning in 2011, had by itself generated over 12 million refugees by mid-2016, with about 1 million seeking asylum in Europe, almost 5 million relocated to Turkey and other neighboring countries, and another 6.5 million displaced within Syria. That conflict became thoroughly internationalized as Russia, the United States, and various Muslim governments and radical groups took sides. It also sharpened the regional rivalry between Iran and Saudi Arabia, which contained both an ethnic

Persian/Arab dimension and a religious Shia/Sunni element.

Beyond the Middle East, conflicts between India and Pakistan, between North Korea and its various neighbors, and between China and Taiwan continued to roil the waters of international life. That all of these countries except Taiwan possessed nuclear weapons compounded the potential dangers of these conflicts. Furthermore, the East-West struggles of the cold war era gave way to tension between the wealthy countries of the Global North and the developing countries of the Global South, led by such emerging powers as India, Indonesia, Brazil, Mexico, and South Africa. And any number of civil wars or ethnically based separatist movement

The Syrian Refugee Crisis Among the most wrenching aspects of the Syrian civil war were the millions of refugees that it generated, many of them fleeing to Turkey or Europe and winding up in refugee camps. This photograph shows an anguished woman arriving on the Greek island of Lesbos, having survived a hazardous crossing of the Aegean Sea from Turkey in late 2015. Five other migrants had died during that crossing. (DIMITAR DILKOFF/Getty Images)

ments took shape in Yugoslavia, Rwanda, Russia, Ukraine, Myanmar (Burma), Iraq, Somalia, Afghanistan, and Libya, among other places.

The pattern of global military spending in the postcommunist era reflected all of these continuing or emerging tensions in international life. After a brief drop during the 1990s, global military spending rose during the early twenty-first century to exceed cold war levels by 2010. The United States led this global pattern, with sharp spending increases after the attacks of 2001, as the "war on terror" took hold. Although the United States accounted for roughly 35 to 40 percent of this spending in the twenty-first century, China has steadily increased its military budget during this time and is now second only to the United States in expenditures for war. Clearly, no prolonged period of international stability and no lasting "peace dividend" accompanied the passing of the cold war into history.

REFLECTIONS

To Judge or Not to Judge

Should historians or students of history make moral judgments about the people and events they study? On the one hand, some would argue, scholars do well to act as detached and objective observers of the human experience. The task is to describe what happened and to explain why things turned out as they did. Whether we approve or condemn the outcomes of the historical process is, in this view, beside the point. On the other hand, all of us, scholars and students alike, stand somewhere. We are members of particular cultures; we have values and outlooks on the world that inevitably affect the way we think about the past. Perhaps it is better to recognize and acknowledge these realities than to pretend to some unattainable objectivity that places us above it all. Furthermore, making judgments is a way of caring about the past, of affirming our continuing relationship with those who have gone before us.

The question of making judgments informs historical analysis of everything from the Agricultural Revolution of 12,000 years ago to the events and processes of the past century. Consider as an example the communist phenomenon. In a United States lacking a major socialist tradition, sometimes saying anything positive about communism or even noting its appeal to millions of people has brought charges of whitewashing its crimes. Within the communist world, even modest criticism was usually regarded as counterrevolutionary and was largely forbidden and harshly punished. Certainly few observers were neutral in their assessment of the communist experiment.

Were the Russian and Chinese revolutions a blow for human freedom and a cry for justice on the part of oppressed people, or did they simply replace one tyranny with another? Was Stalinism a successful effort to industrialize a backward country or a ferocious assault on its moral and social fabric? Did Chinese reforms of the late twentieth century represent a return to sensible policies of modernization, a continued denial of basic democratic rights, or an opening to capitalist inequalities, corruption, and acquisitiveness? Passionate debate continues on all of these questions.

Communism, like many human projects, has been an ambiguous enterprise. On the one hand, communism brought hope to millions by addressing the manifest injustices of the past; by providing new opportunities for women, workers, and peasants; by promoting rapid industrial development; and by ending Western domination. On the other hand, communism was responsible for mountains of crimes—millions killed and wrongly imprisoned; massive famines partly caused by radical policies; human rights violated on an enormous scale; lives uprooted and distorted by efforts to achieve the impossible.

Studying communism challenges our inclination to want definitive answers and clear moral judgments. Can we hold contradictory elements in some kind of tension? Can we affirm our own values while acknowledging the ambiguities of life, both past and present? Doing so is arguably among the essential tasks of growing up and achieving a measure of intellectual maturity. In that undertaking, history can be helpful.

Second Thoughts

What's the Significance?

European Economic Community, 922

Marshall Plan, 922

Great Leap Forward, 926

Cultural Revolution, 928

cold war, 929

North Atlantic Treaty Organization (NATO), 929

Warsaw Pact, 929

Big Picture Questions

1. What was the global significance of the cold war?
2. How would you compare the historical experiences of India and China since World War II?
3. In what ways did the struggle for independence shape the agenda of developing countries in the second half of the twentieth century?
4. "The end of communism was as revolutionary as its beginning." Do you agree with this statement?
5. **Looking Back:** To what extent did the struggle for independence and the post-colonial experience of African and Asian peoples in the twentieth century parallel or diverge from that of the earlier "new nations" in the Americas in the eighteenth and nineteenth centuries?

Next Steps: For Further Study

Archie Brown, *The Rise and Fall of Communism* (2009). A global overview of the communist phenomenon in the twentieth century by a respected scholar.

Timothy Check, *Mao Zedong and China's Revolutions* (2002). A collection of documents about the Chinese revolution and a fine introduction to the life of Mao.

Frederick Cooper, *Africa since 1940* (2002). A readable overview of the coming of independence and efforts at development by a leading historian of Africa.

John L. Gaddis, *The Cold War: A New History* (2005). An overview by one of the most highly regarded historians of the cold war.

Ramachandra Guha, *India after Gandhi: The History of the World's Largest Democracy* (2007). A thoughtful account of India's first six decades of independence.

Michael H. Hunt, *The World Transformed: 1945 to the Present* (2015). An accessible survey of world history since World War II.

John Isbister, *Promises Not Kept* (2006). A well-regarded consideration of the obstacles to and struggles for development in the Global South.

Jan C. Jansen and Jurgen Osterhammel, *Decolonization: A Short History* (2017). An up-to-date survey of the end of empire in the twentieth century considered as a global process.

Noah Morowitz (writer and producer), "Mahatma Gandhi: Pilgrim of Peace," 1997, https://www.youtube.com/watch?v=ibagACLb-6s. A celebratory documentary surveying the life of Gandhi.

"Soviet Archives Exhibit," http://www.ibiblio.org/expo/soviet.exhibit/entrance.html. A rich website from the Library of Congress, focusing on the operation of the Soviet system and relations with the United States.

WORKING WITH EVIDENCE

Mao's China

Within the communist world of the twentieth century, the experience of Chinese people was distinctive, particularly during the decades when Mao Zedong led the country (1949–1976). The sources that follow provide a glimpse into those tumultuous decades, at times hopeful for some and at other times tragic for many.

SOURCE 21.1 Revolution in Long Bow Village

The Chinese revolution occurred in thousands of separate villages as Communist Party activists called "cadres" encouraged peasants to "speak the bitterness" of their personal experience, to "struggle" with their landlords, and to "settle accounts" with them. Source 21.1 provides a brief account of one such struggle as it unfolded in Long Bow Village in northern China in 1948. It was written by the American farmer and activist William Hinton, who had worked in China with the U.S. government during World War II and later with the United Nations. He personally observed and took part in the events he describes.

- What grievances found expression as peasants challenged landlords and husbands in Long Bow Village?

- In what specific ways did these gatherings take shape?

- What change in consciousness had occurred in the course of these events? How might you imagine the conversations that occurred at the New Year's feast that evening or following the women's gathering?

WILLIAM HINTON | *Confronting Landlords and Husbands* | 1948

There was no holding back. . . . So vicious had been Ching-ho's practices and so widespread his influence that more than half the families in the village had scores to settle with him. Old women who had never spoken in public before stood up to accuse him. Even Li Mao's wife—a woman so pitiable she hardly dared look anyone in the face—shook her fist before his nose and cried out, "Once I went to glean wheat on your lands but you cursed me . . . and beat me. Why did you seize the wheat I had gleaned?" Altogether over 180 opinions were raised. Ching-ho had no answer to any of them. He stood there with his head bowed. . . . When the committee of our [Peasant] Association met to figure up what he owed, it came to 400 bags of milled grain. . . .

That evening all the people went to Ching-ho's courtyard to help take over his property. We went in to register his grain and altogether found . . . only a quarter of what he owed us. Right then and there we decided to call another meeting. People said he must have a lot of silver dollars. . . .

958

We called him out of the house and asked him what he intended to do since the grain was not nearly enough. He said, "I have land and house."

"But all this is not enough," shouted the people. So then we began to beat him. Finally he said, "I have 40 silver dollars under the *k'ang*." We went in and dug it up. The money stirred up everyone. We beat him again. He told us where to find another hundred after that. But no-one believed that this was the end of his hoarding. We beat him again and several militiamen began to heat an iron bar in one of the fires. . . .

Altogether we got $500 from Ching-ho that night. . . . We were tired and hungry. . . . So we decided to eat all of things that Ching-ho had prepared to pass the New Year.

All said, "In the past we never lived through a happy new year, because he always asked for his rent and interest then and cleaned our houses bare. This time we'll eat what we like."

[*The revolution in Long Bow also encouraged women to confront abusive husbands. When one of those women registered a complaint against her husband, the local Women's Association took action.*]

In front of this unprecedented gathering of determined women, a demand was made that Man-ts'ang explain his actions. Man-ts'ang, arrogant and unbowed, readily complied. He said that he beat his wife because she went to [political] meetings and "the only reason women go to meetings is to gain a free hand for flirtations and seduction."

This remark aroused a furious protest from the women assembled before him. Words soon led to deeds. They rushed at him from all sides, knocked him down, kicked him, tore his clothes, scratched his face, pulled his hair, and pummelled him until he could no longer breathe. . . .

"Stop. I'll never beat her again," gasped the panic stricken husband. . . . From that day onward, Man-ts'ang never dared beat his wife and from that day onward his wife became known to the whole village by her maiden name, Ch'eng Ai-lien, instead of simply by the title of Man-ts'ang's wife, as had been the custom since time began.

Source: William Hinton, *Fanshen* (New York: Random House, 1966), 137–38, 158.

■ ■ ■

SOURCE 21.2 **A Vision of the New China** ▶

In the eyes of its leaders, the Chinese Communist Party's victory in 1949 by no means meant the end of the struggle with enemies. Former landowners and capitalists had to be confronted, as did those within the Communist Party who had become infected with "bourgeois values" such as materialism, careerism, and individualism and were suspected of opposition to some of Mao's radical policies. What the party called the "Four Olds"—old customs, cultures, habits, and ideas—had to be destroyed so that a wholly "new world" might take shape. Source 21.2, a poster from the Cultural Revolution era (1966–1976), effectively presented the major features of this imagined new society. Its caption urged everyone to "encourage late marriage, plan for birth, and work hard for the new age."

■ How does this poster define the "new age" to which the Chinese Communist Party was beckoning its people?

■ What kind of gender relationships does the poster favor?

■ What elements of prerevolutionary Chinese life might be included in the "Four Olds," which had to be rooted out?

■ The caption also speaks of "encouraging late marriage and planning for birth." What might such values contribute to creating the "new age"?

Poster: "Work Hard for a New Age" | **1970s**

提倡晚婚 计划生育 为实现新时期的总任务而奋斗

武汉市武昌区计划生育领导小组

• • •

SOURCE 21.3 **Socialism in the Countryside** ▶

The centerpiece of Mao's plans for the vast Chinese countryside lay in the "people's communes." Established during the Great Leap Forward in the late 1950s, these were huge political and economic units intended to work the land more efficiently and collectively, to undertake large-scale projects such as building dams and irrigation systems, to create small-scale industries in rural areas, and to promote local self-reliance. They were also intended to move China more rapidly toward genuine communism by eliminating virtually every form of private property and emphasizing social equality and shared living. Commune members ate together in large dining halls, and children were cared for during the day in collective nurseries rather than by their own families. Source 21.3A contains Mao's vision of these communes, expressed at a party conference in 1958, while Source 21.3B shows a highly idealized image of one such commune in a poster created in 1958 under the title "The People's Communes Are Good."

The actual outcomes of the commune movement departed radically from its idealistic goals. Economic disruption occasioned by the creation of communes contributed a great deal to the enormous famines of the late 1950s and early 1960s, in which many millions perished. Furthermore, efforts to involve the peasants in iron and steel production through the creation of much-heralded "backyard furnaces," illustrated in Source 21.3B, proved a failure. Most of the metal produced in these primitive facilities was of poor quality and essentially unusable. Such efforts further impoverished the rural areas, as peasants were encouraged to contribute their pots, pans, and anything made of iron to the smelting furnaces.

- What do these sources suggest about the long-term goals of the Chinese Communist Party leadership?

- What aspects of Mao's description of communal life are illustrated in the poster? One of Mao's chief goals was to overcome the sharp division between industrial cities and the agricultural countryside. How is this effort expressed in these sources?

SOURCE 21.3A
MAO ZEDONG | *On Communes* | 1958

The characteristics of the people's communes are (1) big and (2) public. [They have] vast areas of land and abundant resources [as well as] a large population; [they can] combine industry, agriculture, commerce, education and military affairs as well as farming, forestry, animal husbandry, sideline production and fisheries—being "big" is terrific. [With] many people, there's lots of power. [We say] public because they contain more socialism . . . [and] they will gradually eradicate the vestiges of capitalism—for example the eradication of private plots and private livestock rearing and the running of public mess halls, nurseries, and tailoring groups so that all working women can be liberated. They will implement a wage system and agricultural factories [in which] every single man, woman, old person and youth receives his own wage, in contrast to the former [system of] distribution to the head of household. . . . This eradicates the patriarchal system and the system of bourgeois rights. Another advantage of [communes] being public is that labor efficiency can be raised. . . .

Source: Roderick MacFarquhar, Timothy Cheek, and Eugene Wu, eds., *The Secret Speeches of Chairman Mao* (Cambridge, MA: Council on East Asian Studies/Harvard University, 1989), 431.

SOURCE 21.3B

Poster: "The People's Communes Are Good" | 1958

Shanghai Educational Publishing House/Stefan R. Landsberger Collections/International Institute of Social History, Amsterdam/www.chineseposters.net

• • •

SOURCE 21.4 Women, Nature, and Industrialization ▶

Among the core values of Maoist communism were human mastery over the natural order, rapid industrialization, and the liberation of women from ancient limitations and oppressions in order to mobilize them for the task of building socialism. Source 21.4, a 1970 poster, illustrates these values. Its caption reads: "Women hold up half of heaven, and, cutting through rivers and mountains, change to a new attitude."

■ In what ways does this poster reflect Chinese communism's core values?

■ How is the young woman in this image portrayed? What does the expression on her face convey? Notice her clothing and the shape of her forearms, as well as the general absence of a feminine figure. Why do you think she is portrayed in this largely sexless fashion? What does this suggest about the communist attitude toward sexuality?

■ What does this image suggest about how the party sought to realize gender equality? What is the significance of the work the young woman is doing? What is the "new attitude" to which the caption refers?

■ Notice the lights that illuminate a nighttime work scene. What does this suggest about attitudes toward work and production?

Poster: "Women Hold Up Half of Heaven" | 1970

妇女能顶半边天　管教山河换新颜

Private Collection/Bridgeman Images

SOURCE 21.5 The Cult of Mao ▶

A central feature of Chinese communism, especially during the Cultural Revolution of 1966–1976, was the growing veneration, even adoration, of Chairman Mao. Portraits, statues, busts, and Mao badges proliferated. Everyone was expected to read repeatedly the "Red Treasured Book," which offered a selection of quotations from Mao's writings, believed to facilitate solutions to almost all problems, both public and private. Many families erected "tablets of loyalty" to Mao, much like those previously devoted to ancestors. People made pilgrimages to "sacred shrines" associated with key events in his life.

During the Cultural Revolution, millions of young people, organized as Red Guards and committed to revolutionary action, flocked to Beijing, where enormous and ecstatic rallies allowed them to catch a glimpse of their beloved leader and to unite with him in the grand task of creating communism in China. Source 21.5, a poster created in 1968, depicts such a rally. Its caption reads: "The reddest, reddest, red sun in our heart, Chairman Mao, and us together." Following such events, these young people fanned out across the country to attack Mao's alleged enemies, those who were "taking the capitalist road." (See "Communism Chinese Style.")

- What relationship between Mao and his young followers does the poster suggest? Why might some scholars have seen a quasi-religious dimension to that relationship?

- How do you understand the significance of the "Red Treasured Book" of quotations from Mao, which the young people are waving?

- How might you account for the unbridled enthusiasm expressed by the Red Guards? Can you think of other comparable cases of such mass enthusiasm?

Poster: "Chairman Mao and Us Together" | 1968

我們心中最紅最紅的紅太阳毛主席和我們在一起

■ ■ ■

SOURCE 21.6 Experiencing the Cultural Revolution

As the Cultural Revolution unfolded, teachers and other intellectuals became a particular target of the young revolutionary Red Guards, who publicly humiliated, tortured, or killed those they believed to be enemies of Mao and the revolution. Source 21.6 contains an account of such confrontations or "struggle meetings." It was written by Gao Yuan some twenty years after it occurred. Some of the victims of these confrontations committed suicide to escape the horror that befell them.

- What actions did the Red Guards take toward their teachers? What were the actions intended to accomplish?

- How might you imagine the motivations of those who participated in these sessions?

GAO YUAN | *Born Red* | 1987

The list of accusations grew longer by the day: hooligans and bad eggs, filthy rich peasants and son-of-a-bitch landlords, bloodsucking capitalists and neo-bourgeoisie . . . counterrevolutionaries . . . imperialist running dogs and spies. Students stood in the role of prosecutor, judge, and police. No defense was allowed. Any teacher who protested was certainly a liar.

The indignities escalated as well. Some students cut or shaved teachers' hair into curious patterns. The most popular was the yin-yang cut, which featured a full head of hair on one side and a clean shaven scalp on the other. Some said this style represented Chairman Mao's theory of the "unity of opposites." It made me think of the punishments of ancient China, which included shaving the head, tattooing the face, cutting off the nose or feet, castration, or dismemberment by five horse-drawn carts.

At struggle meetings, students would often force teachers into the "jet-plane" position. Two people would stand on either side of the accused, push him to his knees, pull back his head by the hair, and hold his arms out in back like airplane wings. We tried it on each other and found it caused great strain on the back and neck. . . .

A few students even argued that we should use a bit more force. After all, weren't many of these bad eggs Kuomintang and American agents? . . .

A young teacher from a worker's family was charged with emphasizing academics over politics and a young woman of poor peasant origin was criticized for wearing high heels, proof that she had betrayed her class. Each apologized in a public meeting.

Source: Gao Yuan, *Born Red* (Stanford, CA: Stanford University Press, 1987), 53–55.

DOING HISTORY

1. **Analyzing communist intentions:** Based on these sources, how would you describe the kind of society that the Chinese Communist Party sought to create in China during Mao's lifetime?

2. **Distinguishing image and reality:** Based on these sources and the chapter narrative, to what extent do these sources accurately represent the successes of Maoist communism? What insights do they shed on its failures?

3. **Defining audience and appeal:** To whom do you think these sources were directed? What appeal might they have for the intended audience?

4. **Noticing change:** How could you use these sources to define the dramatic changes that transformed China since 1949? How might a traditional Chinese official from the nineteenth century respond to them?

Assessing Mao

The towering significance of Mao Zedong in China's recent history has led to no end of effort to assess his role and legacy. By some mysterious mathematical reckoning, the Chinese Communist Party declared him 70 percent correct and 30 percent wrong. Historians too have weighed in on the question. Voice 21.1 by Maurice Meisner, a prominent historian of modern China, highlights Mao's role as a modernizing figure in China's history, while lamenting his limitations as a builder of democratic socialism. In Voice 21.2, the Dutch historian of China, Frank Dikotter, proclaims Mao's responsibility for perhaps the greatest famine in world history, which emerged from the Great Leap Forward.

■ In what respects was Mao a successful modernizer and a failed builder of socialism according to Meisner?

■ How does Dikotter explain the "great famine" of 1958–1962?

■ **Integrating Primary and Secondary Sources:** How might the primary sources in this feature be used to support or challenge the arguments of Meisner and Dikotter?

VOICE 21.1

Maurice Meisner on Mao, Modernization, and Socialism | 1999

Mao Zedong was far more successful as an economic modernizer than as a builder of socialism. . . . Between 1952 . . . and 1977, the output of Chinese industry increased at an average annual rate of 11.3 percent, as rapid a pace of industrialization as has ever been achieved by any country in a comparable period in modern world history. . . . [T]he Maoist era was the time of China's modern industrial revolution. . . . It is a record that compares favorably with comparable stages in the industrialization of Germany, Japan and Russia. . . . Maoist industrialization proceeded without benefit of foreign loans or investment. . . . The near doubling of average life expectancy over the quarter century of Mao's rule . . . offers dramatic statistical evidence for the material and social gains that the Communist revolution brought to the great majority of the Chinese people.

More questionable . . . is his lingering, if tarnished, image as the builder of a socialist society. . . . As industrial development proceeded, new bureaucratic and technological elites emerged. The rural areas were exploited for the benefit of the cities. . . . And industrial values of economic rationality and bureaucratic professionalism became the dominant social norms, subordinating the socialist goals [of equality, selflessness, service to the collective]. . . . The Maoist state machine became increasingly separated from the society it ruled . . . and the division between rulers and ruled became ever more pronounced. . . . Maoism . . . was not a doctrine that recognized popular democracy as both the necessary means to realize socialism and one of its essential ends as well.

Source: Maurice Meisner, *Mao's China and After* (New York: Free Press, 1999), 414–15, 417–19, 421–22.

VOICE 21.2

Frank Dikotter on Mao's Great Famine | 2011

Between 1958 and 1962 China descended into hell. Mao Zedong . . . threw his country into a frenzy with the Great Leap Forward, an attempt to catch up with and overtake Britain in less than 15 years. By unleashing China's greatest asset, a labor force that was counted in the hundreds of millions, Mao thought he could catapult his country past its competitors. . . . In pursuit of a utopian paradise, everything was collectivized as villagers were herded together in giant communes which heralded the advent of communism. People in the countryside were robbed of their work, their home, their land, their belongings, and their livelihood. Food, distributed by the spoonful in collective canteens according to merit, became a weapon to force people to follow the party's every dictate. Irrigation campaigns forced up to half the villagers to work for weeks on end on giant water conservancy projects, often far from home, without adequate food and rest. The experiment ended in the greatest catastrophe the country had ever known, destroying tens of millions of lives. . . . [A]t least 45 million people died unnecessarily between 1958 and 1962. . . .

[A] vision of promised abundance . . . also inflicted unprecedented damage on agriculture, trade, industry, and transportation. Pots, pans, and tools were thrown into backyard furnaces to increase the country's steel output, which was seen as one of the magic markers of progress.

Livestock declined precipitously . . . despite extravagant schemes for giant piggeries that would bring meat to every table. . . . As everyone cut corners in the relentless pursuit of higher output, factories spewed out inferior goods. . . . Corruption seeped into the fabric of life, tainting everything from soy sauce to hydraulic dams.

Source: Frank Dikotter, *Mao's Great Famine* (London: Bloomsbury, 2011), xi–xiii.

CHAPTER
22

Global Processes

Technology, Economy, and Society

1900–present

The lives of three young Indonesians in the early twenty-first century reflect the changing conditions of a globalized world. The first, Memey, was a young uneducated widow from Java who was caught up in sex work in neighboring Malaysia in a desperate effort to support her young child.[1] The second, Samysuddin, was a fisherman who found his livelihood threatened as coral reefs degraded in the face of global warming and fish became scarce.[2] The third was M. Arle Kurniawan, a twenty-one-year-old engineer who won first place and a $7,000 prize in an international technology competition sponsored by General Electric.[3] ■

For all three of these young Indonesians, life in the early twenty-first century was shaped not so much by war, revolution, or liberation struggles, but by powerful though less visible processes such as migration and sex trafficking for Memey, climate change and impoverishment for Samysuddin, and technological innovation and economic globalization for Kurniawan. And so it has been for billions of others during the past century. Therefore, the two final chapters of Part 6 turn the historical spotlight away from the dominant events of the past century, recounted in Chapters 20 and 21, to focus more explicitly on such immensely transformative processes, all of which have played out on a deeply interconnected global stage.

《 Technological Globalization This image of three young Ecuadorian women in Quito huddled around a cell phone illustrates the very rapid global spread of this new communication technology since it was first introduced in 1973. By 2015, some 80 percent of Ecuadorians had an active mobile phone subscription.

Technology: The Acceleration of Innovation

Behind both the major events and the global processes of the past century lies the decisive power of technological innovation. Technological breakthroughs—such as electrical grids, antibiotics, nuclear weapons, airplanes, automobiles, cell phones, and the Internet—occurred largely within Western Europe, the United States, and Japan, where the Industrial Revolution had first taken shape during the nineteenth century. The accumulated wealth and experience derived from this early industrialization enabled these countries to maintain their momentum as the primary source of global innovation well into the twentieth century.

Particularly after World War II, a potent combination of universities, governments, and large corporations relentlessly drove the process of technological development. University-based scientific research provided the foundational knowledge from which all manner of technical applications emerged. Governments enmeshed in wars and concerned about national security developed weaponry, medicine, communications, aircraft, rocketry, and computing that often had civilian applications. And large corporations, eager for profits and motivated to create or meet consumer demand, invested heavily in new products.

Thanks to the deepening linkages of globalization, many of these innovations spread rapidly to the rest of the world. By the end of the twentieth century, major industrial enterprises had been established in Mexico and Brazil, China and Vietnam, and India and Indonesia. About 45 percent of Nigerians were Internet users and 82 percent had access to mobile phone service in 2015. Some of these countries—China and India, for example—were making their own contribution to global technological development, even as vast disparities in access to technology remained firmly entrenched.

Generating Energy: Fossil Fuel Breakthroughs

Access to the stored energy of fossil fuels—coal, oil, and natural gas—has provided the foundation of the modern world economy, beginning with the Industrial Revolution in the nineteenth century. But it was the twentieth century that became the **age of fossil fuels** as their consumption skyrocketed. (See Figure 22.1.) Coal production increased by some 700 percent during that century, and in its second half oil overtook coal as the dominant source of energy. Natural gas became a growing element in the energy equation in the latter decades of the century. And beyond fossil fuels, the energy contained within the nucleus of atoms, as well as that derived from wind, flowing water, and sunlight, added modestly to global energy consumption. Nonetheless, by 2000 fossil fuels still provided about 80 percent of the energy that powered the world economy.

Technological innovations allowed humankind to turn the potential energy of fossil fuels into useful energy. One such innovation involved the generation of electricity, the basic principles of which were discovered in the early nineteenth century

Guided Reading Question

■ **CHANGE**
What was new about energy production in the twentieth century?

Landmarks for Chapter 22

1900   1920   1940   1960   1980   2000   2020

THE DEVELOPED INDUSTRIAL WORLD / GLOBAL NORTH

1882–1920
Electric grids developed in industrial countries

1908
Mass production of
automobiles begins

1940s Earliest digital computers

1960
Birth control pill
approved in U.S.

1960s Second-wave feminism begins

1991
Earliest web browser released

1999
Seattle protests against the WTO

2016
Britain's exit from EU announced

2017
U.S. withdraws from Trans-Pacific Partnership

THE DEVELOPING WORLD / GLOBAL SOUTH

1920–1940 Land reform in Mexico

1923–1938
Women's
emancipation
in Turkey

1970s
Developing countries demand
"new international economic order"

1978–2013
Rapid economic growth in China

1979 Islamic revolution in Iran

1980–2014
China's one-child family policy

2004
Morocco's Family Law Code
advances women's rights

THE WHOLE WORLD

1929–1940 The Great Depression

1930s–1970
Green Revolution technologies
developed and applied

1945–1970
Postwar economic boom

1975
United Nations: International Women's Year

2006
UN Convention on the Elimination of All Forms of
Discrimination against Women ratified by 183 nations

in Great Britain. The subsequent development of coal-, oil-, or gas–fired power
stations, alternating current, transformers, and batteries permitted electricity to be
generated on a commercial scale, moved across great distances, and stored.

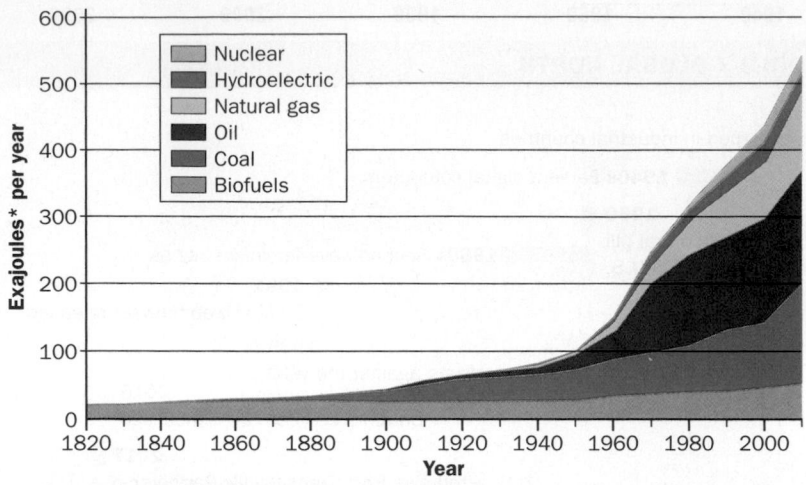

*An exajoule is a large-scale unit of energy.

Figure 22.1 Sources of World Energy Consumption, 1820–2010
It was access to fossil fuels that allowed world energy production to skyrocket during the twentieth century. (Gail Tverberg, OurFiniteWorld.com, from https://ourfiniteworld.com/2012/03/12/world-energy-consumption-since-1820-in-charts)

This more widespread availability of electricity was the product of electric grids, which generated power and transmitted it widely to homes and businesses. The development of such grids began in the late nineteenth century in the already industrialized countries, but it spread rapidly in capitalist, communist, colonial, and developing countries alike. By 2014, some 85 percent of the world's population had access to electricity, though not always reliably. Europe, Russia, North America, and Japan achieved 100 percent electrification first, but China, North Africa, Latin America, and parts of India achieved or approached that figure in the early twenty-first century.[4] By any historical standard, global electrification represents a very rapid transition to new ways of living.

Electrification lit up the world, especially at night, and much more cheaply than oil or gas lighting, allowing students to study, people to play, and employees to work around the clock. Electric motors powered all manner of industrial machinery far more productively than steam engines, and they made possible a vast array of consumer goods. Electrification became a crucial component of all economic development planning.

Another breakthrough in the generation of useful energy via fossil fuels was the gasoline- or oil-driven internal combustion engine, pioneered in the late nineteenth century in Western Europe and applied widely throughout the world in the twentieth century. That innovation created a huge new industry that became central to modern economic life; it led to a sharp decline in the use of horses; it enabled the far more rapid and efficient movement of goods and people, transforming the patterns of daily life for much of humankind; and it has been a potent source of the greenhouse gases that have driven climate change. Together, electricity and the internal combustion engine have enormously increased the energy available to humankind, even as access to that energy has favored the most highly industrialized economies. (See Map 22.1.)

Harnessing Energy: Transportation Breakthroughs

Nowhere did this new availability of energy register more dramatically than in the technology of transportation, which built upon the revolutionary development of railroads and steamships in the nineteenth century. To those innovations, the

Guided Reading Question

■ **CHANGE**
How did electricity and the internal combustion engine transform human life during the past century?

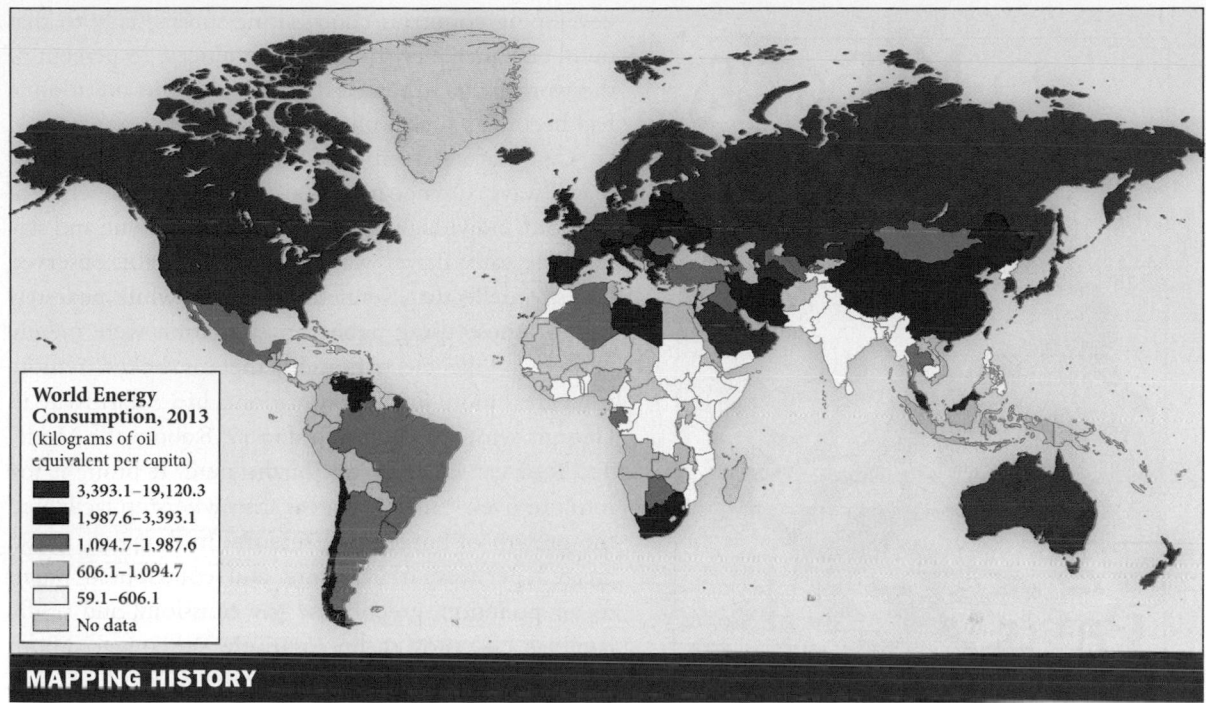

**World Energy
Consumption, 2013**
(kilograms of oil
equivalent per capita)

- 3,393.1–19,120.3
- 1,987.6–3,393.1
- 1,094.7–1,987.6
- 606.1–1,094.7
- 59.1–606.1
- No data

MAPPING HISTORY

Map 22.1 World Energy Consumption per Capita, 2013
While global energy production soared during the past century, access to that energy remained highly uneven in the early twenty-first century when measured on a per person basis. (Data from World Bank)

READING THE MAP: Which continents used the least amount of energy per capita in 2013?

MAKING CONNECTIONS: Compare this map with Map 20.1: The World in 1914. What might you infer about the legacy of colonialism by comparing relative energy consumption in 2013 in former imperial countries and their colonies?

twentieth century added cars, buses, and trucks; containerized shipping and super-tankers; airplanes and air freight. This was the technological infrastructure that has made possible the surging movement of goods and people in the globalized world of recent times. By the early twenty-first century, the planet was densely criss-crossed on land by roads, railways, and pipelines, on the seas by shipping routes, and in the air by flight patterns.

Among these transportation technologies, none achieved a greater social and cultural impact than the automobile. In 1900, there were only about 10,000 cars in the global inventory, all of them expensive luxury items for the rich and most of them driven by steam or electric power. But the growing availability of cheap gasoline established the internal combustion engine as the means of propulsion for cars for the next century. It was Henry Ford's Model T, initially built in 1908, that launched the democratization of the automobile and made the United States the first country to market cars for the masses, followed by European countries and Japan after World War II. By 2010, the world had over 1 billion cars, with

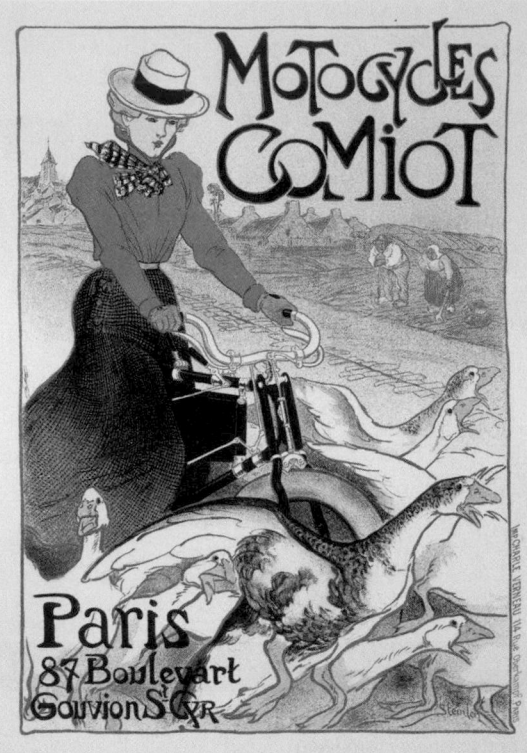

A French Motorcycle Among the early uses of the internal combustion engine was a French petroleum-powered tricycle, illustrated in this 1899 poster and said to be "a means of transportation for everyone." In an apparent celebration of technological progress, the stylish and modern young woman rider scatters a flock of geese as she zooms past an old peasant couple in the background. In this image, modernity and progress trump both nature and tradition. (Lithograph by Alexandre Theophile Steinlen [1859–1923]/Private Collection/The Stapleton Collection/Bridgeman Images)

developing countries contributing substantially to that number. China and India alone produced 28 percent of the world's cars in that year. The age of the automobile had become a global phenomenon.

Cars have shaped modern society and culture in many ways. Ownership of a car conveyed a sense of freedom, individuality, personal empowerment, and status. The early driver was a mounted knight, observed British intellectual Kenneth Boulding, while pedestrians and those using public transportation were merely peasants.[5] Like electrification, the car linked remote rural areas more firmly into national life. A farmwife in Georgia wrote to Henry Ford in 1918 about the Model T: "Your car lifted us out of the mud. It brought joy into our lives."[6] In urban areas, car ownership facilitated the growth of burgeoning suburbs. In doing so, it also created pervasive traffic jams and contributed much to air pollution, greenhouse gas emissions, and traffic fatalities. Like most technologies, the car conveyed both great benefits and heavy costs, but the world's love affair with the automobile has shown few signs of waning.

Harnessing Energy: Communication and Information Breakthroughs

The past century has also witnessed a flurry of innovations in communication and information that have transformed life for almost everyone. The modern **communication revolution**, like that of transportation, began in the nineteenth century with the telegraph and telephone, both of them using electricity to transmit information along a wire. In the twentieth century, innovation piled on innovation: vacuum tubes, transistors, integrated circuits, microprocessors, and fiber-optic cables. These novel technologies enabled radios, motion pictures, televisions, and most recently computers, cell phones, and the Internet. While these technologies and products were initially created in the West or Japan, they have taken root globally in less than a century, albeit unevenly. Radios have spread most widely, with over 75 percent of households in developing countries having access to a radio in 2012. TV coverage is more variable but surprisingly widespread. In much of Latin America, North Africa, the Middle East, and East Asia, 90 percent or more of households had a TV in the early twenty-first century. Internet access has soared globally since the introduction of web browsers in 1991, connecting slightly over half of the world's population by 2017. The availability of cell phones has also spread very rapidly since the first mobile call in 1973 and the first smart phone in 1992. In much of Africa, for example, close to 80 percent of adults had access to a cell phone in 2015, allowing much of the continent to avoid installing more expensive land lines.

These communication technologies have reshaped human life across the planet and have spawned numerous debates about their consequences. Radio enabled even remote villagers to become aware of national and international events, even as it empowered authoritarian and democratic governments alike. Hitler's minister of propaganda, Joseph Goebbels, claimed in 1933 that "it would not have been possible for us [Nazis] to take power or to use it in the ways we have without the radio."[7] And Franklin Roosevelt used his radio "fireside chats" to reassure the American public during the Depression and World War II. But radio also challenged governments that sought to restrict their people's access to information. The availability of short-wave radio broadcasts from Europe and the United States eroded the capacity of the Soviet regime to monopolize the mass media and contributed to the collapse of Communist Party rule in the Soviet Union. Television and the movies have generated a particularly sharp debate. Supporters have praised their ability to inform, educate, and entertain, but critics fear that American or Western domination of the media might erode local or national cultures, regret the generally low cultural level of TV programming, lament the effects of TV violence on children, and argue about the portrayal of women, minorities, Muslims, and others.

The impact of personal computers and their numerous uses (the Internet, e-mail, social media, cell phones) has been pervasive and contested ever since they began to be widely available, at least in the West, during the 1980s. They made possible virtually unlimited access to information, enabling people the world over to participate creatively in this technological revolution. Education in many parts of the world has been transformed as online courses, "smart" classrooms, and digital books have proliferated, while computer science has become a major new field of study. Computer applications have become central to almost every aspect of business and economic life, spawning entirely new industries and forms of commerce. In many African countries, mobile banking has allowed millions to

Guided Reading Question
....
■ CHANGE
What impact has modern communication technology had on the world of the past century?

Computers and Camels The global penetration of computer technology is illustrated in this 2012 image of two Tunisian Bedouins consulting their laptop in the Sahara Desert. (Philippe Liccac/Godong/UIG/akg-images)

access financial services, with some 61 percent of Kenyans using their cell phones for this purpose. Online commerce has grown rapidly in the twenty-first century. China has become the world's largest e-commerce country, with its Internet giant, the Alibaba Group, replacing Walmart as the world's leading retailer in 2014.

Computer applications have also transformed personal life as online dating has spread to urban areas all around the world. Internet pornography has also become pervasive, though it is legally banned in China, India, the Islamic world, and elsewhere. Facebook, launched in 2004, had connected some 2.234 billion active users, over 25 percent of the world's population, to an array of "friends" by 2018. Recreation also has been transformed as computer-based gaming has spread globally, with China emerging as the largest video game market in the world.

Beyond their many advantages, these information technologies have generated anxieties and criticism. Individuals fear being bullied by peers, monitored and controlled by governments, and manipulated by corporations able to track their buying preferences. Debate has arisen as to whether the Internet facilitates or undermines personal relationships. Hacking of government records and corporate secrets has raised concerns about cyber-warfare, while the entire complex system remains vulnerable to outages, sabotage, and natural disaster.

Harnessing Energy: Military Breakthroughs

A final example of accelerated innovation lies in technologies of destruction. The late nineteenth-century development of high-power explosives such as dynamite as well as machine guns found application in World War I, along with other new technologies such as submarines, tanks, poison gas, radio, and military aircraft. World War II refined and enhanced these technologies, while adding radar, computers, jet engines, battle tanks, fighter aircraft, aircraft carriers, and atomic bombs to the mix. The cold war generated ever-more-sophisticated nuclear weapons, from enormous hydrogen bombs to smaller tactical nuclear weapons. New means of delivering them also emerged using ballistic missiles launched from airplanes, land-based silos, or submarines with almost pinpoint accuracies. At the height of the cold war and ever since, we have been able to imagine, realistically, a nuclear war that would result in instant death for tens of millions of people, the collapse of modern civilization, and perhaps the extinction of the human species. Military technologies, of course, have also had numerous civilian spin-offs, including radar, nuclear power plants, the Internet, space exploration, and communication satellites.

The Global Economy: The Acceleration of Entanglement

Accelerating technological innovation decisively shaped the world economy of the past century, enabling what we now refer to as **economic globalization**. Precisely when this most recent phase of global connectivity began is a matter of some dispute among historians. (See Controversies: Debating Globalization, page 980.) But almost all scholars agree that the seven decades following World War II have marked an extraordinary surge in economic globalization. A central element of that process has been the spread of industrialization among the peoples of the Global South.

The Globalization of Industrialization: Development in the Global South

As decolonization, independence, and revolution rolled over much of Africa, Asia, and Latin America, economic development and industrialization became everywhere a central priority. It was an essential promise of all revolutions and independence struggles, and it was increasingly the standard by which people measured and granted legitimacy to their governments.

Achieving economic development, however, was no easy or automatic task for societies sharply divided by class, religion, ethnic group, and gender and facing explosive population growth. In many places, colonial rule had provided only the most slender foundations for modern development, as new nations often came to independence with low rates of literacy, few people with managerial experience, a weak private economy, and little industrial infrastructure. Furthermore, the entire effort occurred in a world split by rival superpowers and economically dominated by the powerful capitalist economies of the West.

Beyond these difficulties lay the vexing question of what strategies to pursue. Should state authorities take the lead, or was it wiser to rely on private enterprise and the market? Should industrial production be aimed at the domestic market in an "import substitution" approach, or was it more effective to specialize in particular products, such as cars, clothing, or electronics, for an export market?

For developing countries, it was an experimental process, and the outcomes varied considerably. (See Snapshot, page 986.) In general, East Asian countries that produced products primarily for export have had the strongest record of economic growth. South Korea, Taiwan, Singapore, and Hong Kong were dubbed **Asian Tigers** or newly industrialized countries. Following the death of Mao Zedong in 1976, China soon became a spectacular economic success story, boasting the most rapid economic growth in the world by the end of the twentieth century while replacing Japan as the world's second-largest economy and edging up on the United States. In the 1990s, Asia's other giant, India, opened itself more fully to the world market and launched rapid economic growth with a powerful high-tech sector and major steel, chemical, automotive, and pharmaceutical industries. Oil-producing countries reaped a bonanza when they were able to demand much higher prices for that essential commodity in the 1970s and after. By 2016, Mexico, Turkey, Malaysia, Thailand, Vietnam, India, and Indonesia numbered in the top twenty of the most competitive manufacturing countries, with China ranking number one. Limited principally to Europe, North America, and Japan in the nineteenth century,

Guided Reading Question

■ **COMPARISON**
What variations in global industrial development have been apparent during the past century?

Debating Globalization

By the early 1990s, "globalization" had become a buzzword among scholars, journalists, and ordinary people alike because it succinctly captured something of the deeply connected and entangled world of the late twentieth century. The economists, sociologists, and political scientists who first embraced the term presented "globalization" as novel and unprecedented: the world was becoming "a single place," and human history was entering a wholly new era of global connectedness and global consciousness.

World historians, however, were not so sure about the novelty of "globalization." They had, after all, long traced patterns of interaction, communication, and exchange among distant regions and civilizations: the Silk Road commercial networks across Eurasia; the movement of technologies and disease; the transcontinental spread of Buddhism, Christianity, and Islam; the making of an Atlantic world linking Europe, Africa, and the Americas; and the globe-spanning empires of Europe. Did all of this count as "globalization," pushing its origins deep into the past?

Yet another controversy involved the "drivers" of globalization. For some, they were impersonal forces—"the inexorable integration of markets, nation-states, and technologies"—according to leading journalist Thomas Friedman. In such a view, no one was in control, and the process, once begun, was inevitable and unstoppable. Others believed that powerful economic elites and political leaders, acting from a free market ideology, deliberately shaped policies (such as low tariffs) and institutions (the World Trade Organization, for example) that opened the door to corporate globalization.

The economic outcomes of recent globalization have also generated much debate. Did globalization increase or reduce inequality? Answers depend very much on what is being measured. If the measure is income, most economists think that inequality on a global level has substantially increased. One study concluded that the per capita income gap between the United States and various regions of the Global South roughly tripled since 1960.[8] The rich were getter richer much faster than the poor were gaining income.

But if the measure of economic outcomes involves "quality of life indicators," the picture changes considerably. Average global life expectancy, for example, more than doubled since 1900, reaching 71.4 years in 2014. Thus many countries in the Global South now approach the 79-year life span of U.S. citizens: China, 76 years; Iran, 75; Brazil, 74; India, 68. Even poorer countries have dramatically increased their life expectancies, with sub-Saharan African rates improving from 40 years in 1960 to 59 years in 2014.[9] Clearly, despite growing inequality in income, inequality in longevity has lessened. So which is the more important measure of inequality: income measured in dollars or life expectancy measured in years?

Yet another controversy involves the impact of globalization on nation-states. Many elements of the globalized world have arguably diminished the ability of nation-states to act freely in their own interests—agreements favoring free trade and the power of huge transnational corporations, for example. The more enthusiastic advocates of globalization have imagined a future in which the nation-state has vanished, or at least greatly weakened, in the face of global flows of people, capital, goods, services, and ideas.

Others, however, view such opinions as exaggerated. It was, after all, the decisions of some states that created a free trade international system after World War II, even as other states, especially in the communist bloc, refused to take part in it. And what states create they can also change. China joined the World Trade Organization in

industrialization and modern economic growth had become a global phenomenon by the early twenty-first century.

But not everywhere. In most of Africa, much of the Arab world, and parts of Asia—regions representing about one-third of the world's population—there was little sign of rapid economic development and frequent examples of declining standards of living since the end of the 1960s. Between 1980 and 2000, the average

2001 after decades of declining to take part in the global marketplace; the United Kingdom decided in 2016 to leave the European Union; the Trump administration in the United States announced American withdrawal from the Trans-Pacific Partnership agreement in early 2017. Even developing countries have some leverage. Both Mexico and Cuba have nationalized American industries in their countries in the twentieth century. And the oil-producing states of the Middle East upended the global markets in the late 1970s when they dramatically raised the price of oil. All of this testifies to the continuing power of state action to shape the world economy.

Cultural globalization too prompted debate and controversy. Has the world become more culturally homogeneous in the global age? Many feared that the answer was "yes" as "cultural imperialism" in the shape of westernization or Americanization swept the planet, displacing many established cultural patterns and ways of living. The prevalence of English and modern science; the popularity of McDonald's, blue jeans, Barbie dolls, and American films; shopping malls and Western-style consumerism across the world; cell phones and the Internet—all of this and much more suggested the emergence of a "global culture."

But perhaps globalization produces or reinforces cultural difference as well as commonality. The rise of Islamic fundamentalism represented strong resistance to the intrusion of Western secular culture. French efforts to prevent the importation of too many American films or TV programs and to prohibit the wearing of headscarves by Muslim women likewise reflected a desire to preserve major elements of French national culture in an age of globalization. A proliferation of ethnic nationalist movements articulated demands to ensure the integrity of particular and local cultures. Furthermore, a phenomenon known as "glocalization" refers to the process by which foreign products or practices are adapted to local cultural patterns. Yoga in the West often became a form of exercise or relaxation, losing much of its original spiritual significance, while McDonald's restaurants in India and China now include various rice-based menu offerings.

Globalization is commonly regarded as a still-unfolding process leading to an uncertain destination, often called "globality" or "entanglement on a global scale." Two prominent historians have recently contested this understanding, arguing that "globality" has long been a "done deal," a condition already achieved. The question then is not whether to participate in this globalized world, but rather "how to change in order to keep pace with, hold out against, or adapt to a world of continuous and inescapable interactivity."[10]

And yet, is it possible to imagine global connections unraveling? Is globalization really a "done deal"? Various events of the early twenty-first century have caused many to wonder: something close to a global economic collapse in 2008; the exit of Great Britain from the European Union; the election of Donald Trump promising that "Americanism not globalism will be our credo"; the reaction against immigration in the United States and Western Europe; and the rise of assertive nationalist movements in much of Europe, Turkey, Iran, China, India, and elsewhere. Does this mean that globalization is in retreat? The debate continues, as it does for almost everything related to globalization.

QUESTIONS TO CONSIDER

1. How might you describe in your own words the major debates and controversies that are associated with the concept of globalization? Can you think of other questions that arise from the use of this term?

2. How do you think the authors of this book have answered those questions in Chapter 22? Or have they avoided doing so?

income in forty-three of Africa's poorest countries dropped by 25 percent, pushing living standards for many below what they had been at independence. But in the early twenty-first century, a number of African countries began to experience encouraging economic growth, an expanding middle class with some money to spend, and more international investment. Some observers began to speak about "Africa Rising."

Scholars and politicians alike argue about the reasons for such sharp differences in economic performance. Variables such as geography and natural resources, differing colonial experiences, variations in regional cultures, the degree of political stability and social equality, state economic policies, population growth rates, and varying forms of involvement with the world economy—all of these have been invoked to explain the widely diverging trajectories among developing countries.

Re-globalization: Deepening Economic Connections

Accompanying the worldwide spread of modern development and industrial growth was a tightening network of global economic relationships that cut across the world's separate countries and regions, binding them together more closely, but also more contentiously, during the second half of the twentieth century. This was the economic face of globalization. (See Controversies: Debating Globalization, page 980.) In some respects, it was a "re-globalization," for the aftermath of World War I and the Great Depression had wreaked havoc on an increasingly globalized world economy. International trade, investment, and labor migration dropped sharply as major states turned inward, favoring high tariffs and economic autonomy, in the face of a global economic collapse. In this context, what occurred after World War II signaled a renewal and a great acceleration of earlier trends that had linked the economies of the world more tightly together.

The capitalist victors in World War II, led by the United States, were determined to avoid any return to the kind of economic contraction and nationalist excesses that had followed World War I. At a conference in Bretton Woods, New Hampshire, in 1944, they forged a set of agreements and institutions (the World Bank and the International Monetary Fund [IMF]) that laid the foundation for postwar globalization. This "**Bretton Woods system**" negotiated the rules for commercial and financial dealings among the major capitalist countries, while promoting relatively free trade, stable currency values linked to the U.S. dollar, and high levels of capital investment.

Guided Reading Question

■ **CONNECTION**

In what ways have global economic linkages deepened during the past century, and with what impact?

By the 1970s, leading figures in capitalist countries such as the United States and Great Britain, as well as in major international lending agencies such as the World Bank, increasingly viewed the entire world as a single market. This approach to the world economy, widely known as neoliberalism, favored the reduction of tariffs, the free global movement of capital, a mobile and temporary workforce, the privatization of many state-run enterprises, the curtailing of government efforts to regulate the economy, and both tax and spending cuts. In this view, the market, operating both globally and within nations, was the most effective means of generating the holy grail of economic growth. As communism collapsed by the end of the twentieth century, "capitalism was global and the globe was capitalist."[11]

Such policies, together with major changes in transportation and communication technology, accompanied a dramatic quickening of global economic transactions after World War II, expressed in the accelerating circulation of both goods and capital. World trade, for example, skyrocketed from a value of some $57 billion in 1947 to about $18.3 trillion in 2012. In wealthy countries and for elites everywhere, increasing global trade meant access to the goods of the world. In varying degrees, it also meant employment. In the United States in 2008, exports supported some 10 million jobs and represented about 13 percent of its gross domestic product (GDP). Many developing countries, however, were far more dependent on exports, usually raw materials and agricultural products. Ghana, for example, relied on exports for 44 percent of its GDP in 2014, mostly gold, cocoa beans, and

Containerized Shipping The growth of global trade has been facilitated by containerized shipping, a highly mechanized process of moving goods that requires far fewer workers and has substantially reduced transportation costs. This photograph illustrates that process as it occurred in the Chinese port of Qingdao in mid-2017. (STR/Getty Images)

timber products. Cocoa alone supported some 700,000 farming families. Mounting trade entangled the peoples of the world to an unprecedented degree.

Economic entanglement was financial as well as commercial. "Foreign direct investment," whereby a firm in, say, the United States opens a factory in China or Mexico, exploded after 1960 as companies in rich countries sought to take advantage of cheap labor, tax breaks, and looser environmental regulations in developing countries. Money also surged around the planet as investors and financiers annually spent trillions of dollars purchasing foreign currencies or stocks likely to increase in value and often sold them quickly thereafter, with unsettling consequences. The personal funds of individuals likewise achieved a new mobility as international credit cards took hold almost everywhere.

Central to the acceleration of economic globalization have been huge global businesses known as **transnational corporations** (TNCs), which produce goods or deliver services simultaneously in many countries. Toyota, the world's largest automaker in 2016, sold cars around the world and had manufacturing facilities in some twenty-eight countries on five continents. Burgeoning in number since the 1960s, TNCs such as Royal Dutch Shell, Sony, and General Motors often were of such an enormous size and had such economic clout that their assets and power dwarfed that of many countries. By 2000, 51 of the world's 100 largest economic units were in fact TNCs, not countries. In the permissive economic climate of recent decades, such firms have been able to move their facilities quickly from place to place in search of the lowest labor costs or the least restrictive environmental regulations. During one five-year period, for example, Nike closed twenty factories and opened thirty-five others, often thousands of miles apart.

Growth, Instability, and Inequality

The impact of these tightening economic linkages has prompted enormous debate and controversy. (See Controversies: Debating Globalization.) Amid the swirl of contending opinion, one thing seemed reasonably clear: economic globalization accompanied, and arguably helped generate, the most remarkable spurt of economic growth in world history. On a global level, total world output grew from a value of $7 trillion in 1950 to $73 trillion in 2009 and on a per capita basis from $2,652 to $10,728.[12] While world population quadrupled, or increased by a factor of 4, during the twentieth century, the output of the world economy grew by a factor of 14 and industrial output by a factor of 40. This represents an immense, rapid, and unprecedented creation of wealth with a demonstrable impact on human welfare. Everywhere people lived longer. Global average life expectancy has more than doubled since 1900, approaching an average of about seventy years in 2012. Everywhere, far fewer children died before the age of five: in 1960 the global average was 18.2 percent; in 2015, 4.3 percent. And everywhere more people were literate. Some 80 percent of adults could read and write at some level by 2000, while only 21 percent could do so in 1900. The UN Human Development Report in 1997 concluded that "in the past 50 years, poverty has fallen more than in the previous 500."

Far more problematic have been the instability of this emerging world economy and the distribution of the immense wealth it has generated. Amid overall economic growth, periodic crises and setbacks have shaped recent world history. Soaring oil prices in 1973–1974 resulted in several years of economic stagnation for many industrialized countries, great hardship for many developing countries, and an economic windfall for oil-producing countries. Inability to repay mounting debts triggered a major financial crisis in Latin America during the 1980s and resulted in a "lost decade" in terms of economic development. Another financial crisis in Asia during the late 1990s resulted in the collapse of many businesses, widespread unemployment, and political upheaval in Indonesia and Thailand. And in 2008 an inflated housing market—or "bubble"—in the United States collapsed, triggering millions of home foreclosures, growing unemployment, the tightening of credit, and declining consumer spending. Soon this crisis rippled around the world. Iceland's rapidly growing economy collapsed almost overnight as three major banks failed, the country's stock market dropped by 80 percent, and its currency lost more than 70 percent of its value—all in a single week. In Sierra Leone, some 90 percent of the country's diamond-mine workers lost their jobs. Impoverished Central American and Caribbean families, dependent on money sent home by family members working abroad, suffered further as those remittances dropped sharply. Contracting economies contributed to debt crises in Greece, Italy, and Spain and threatened to unravel European economic integration. Whatever the overall benefits of globalization, economic stability and steady progress were not among them.

Nor did globalization resolve the problem of inequality. (See Snapshot, page 986.) Despite substantial gains in life expectancy, infant mortality, literacy, and the reduction of poverty, economic inequality on a global level has been stubbornly persistent and by some measures growing. In 1870 the average per capita income in the world's ten richest countries was six times that of the ten poorest countries. By 2002 that ratio was 42 to 1.[13] That gap has been evident, often tragically, in great disparities in incomes, medical care, availability of clean drinking water, educational and employment opportunities, access to the Internet, and dozens of other ways. It has shaped the life chances of practically everyone. Even among developing countries, great inequalities were apparent. The oil-rich economies of the Middle East had little in common with the banana-producing countries of Central America. The rapidly industrializing states of China, India, and South Korea had quite different economic agendas than impoverished African countries.

Economic globalization has contributed to inequalities not only among countries and regions, but also within individual nations, rich and poor alike. In the United States, for example, income inequality has sharply increased since the late 1970s. The American economy shed millions of manufacturing jobs, with some companies moving their operations to Asia or Latin America, where labor costs were lower. More important, however, was automation. The U.S. steel industry, for example, lost 75 percent of its workforce between 1962 and 2005, while producing roughly the same amount of steel. This left many American workers in the lurch, forcing them to work in the low-wage service sector, even as other Americans were growing prosperous in emerging high-tech industries. Globalization divided Mexico as well. The northern part of the country, with close business and manufacturing ties to the United States, grew much more prosperous than the south, which was a largely rural agricultural area and had a far more slowly growing economy. China's rapid economic growth likewise fostered mounting inequality between its rural households and those in its burgeoning cities, where income by 2000 was three times that of the countryside. Economic globalization may have brought people together as never before, but it has also divided them sharply.

Pushback: Resistance to Economic Globalization

The movement toward a thoroughly entangled world economy was accompanied by much conflict, criticism, resistance, and protest from those who felt unfairly treated, left behind, or overwhelmed by a tsunami of change in a globalizing process they could not control. One expression of this resistance derived from the Global South. As the East/West division of capitalism and communism faded, differences between the rich nations of the Global North and the developing countries of the Global South assumed greater prominence in world affairs. Highly contentious issues have included the rules for world trade, availability of and terms for foreign aid, representation in international economic organizations, the mounting problem of indebtedness, and environmental and labor standards. In the 1970s, for example,

SNAPSHOT   Global Development and Inequality, 2011

This table shows thirteen commonly used indicators of "development" and their variations in 2011 across four major groups of countries defined by average level of per capita income. In which areas has the Global South most nearly caught up with the Global North?

Gross National Income per Capita with Sample Countries	Low Income: $995 or Less (Congo, Kenya, Ethiopia, Afghanistan, Myanmar)	Lower Middle Income: $996–$3,945 (India, China, Egypt, Algeria, Indonesia, Nigeria)	Upper Middle Income: $3,946–$12,195 (Mexico, Brazil, Turkey, Russia, Iran)	Upper Income: $12,196 or More (USA, Western Europe, Japan, South Korea, Australia)
Life expectancy: M/F in years	58/60	66/70	68/75	77/83
Deaths under age 5 per 1,000 live births	120	60	24	7
Deaths from infectious disease: %	36	14	11	7
Access to toilets: %	35	50	84	99
Years of education	7.9	10.3	13.8	14.5
Literacy rate: %	66	80	93	99
Population growth: % annual	2.27	1.27	.96	.39
Urban population: %	27	41	74	78
Cell phones per 100 people	22	47	92	106
Internet users per 100 people	2.3	13.7	29.9	68.3
Personal computers per 100 people	1.2	4.3	11.9	60.4
Cars per 1,000 people	5.8	20.3	125.2	435.1
Carbon dioxide emissions: metric tons per capita	1	3	5	13

Data from "Map Supplement," *National Geographic* (Washington, DC: National Geographic Society, March 2011).

a large group of developing countries joined together to demand a "new international economic order" that was more favorable to the poor countries, though the effort met with little success. Developing countries have often contested protectionist restrictions on their agricultural exports imposed by the rich countries seeking to safeguard their own politically powerful farmers.

In the 1990s a growing popular movement, featuring a highly critical posture toward globalization, emerged as an international coalition of political activists, concerned scholars and students, trade unions, women's and religious organizations, environmental groups, and others, hailing from rich and poor countries alike. Though reflecting a variety of viewpoints, that opposition largely agreed that market-driven corporate globalization had lowered labor standards, fostered ecological

Guided Reading Question

■ **CONFLICT**

What criticisms of economic globalization have emerged, and from what sources did they derive?

degradation, prevented poor countries from protecting themselves against financial speculators, ignored local cultures, disregarded human rights, and enhanced global inequality, while favoring the interests of large corporations and rich countries.

This movement appeared dramatically on the world's radar screen in 1999 in Seattle at a meeting of the **World Trade Organization (WTO)**. An international body representing 149 nations and charged with negotiating the rules for global commerce and promoting free trade, the WTO had become a major target of globalization critics. "The central idea of the WTO," argued one such critic, "is that *free trade*—actually the values and interests of global corporations—should supersede all other values."[14] Tens of thousands of protesters from all over the world descended on Seattle in what became a violent, chaotic, and much-publicized protest. Such protests stimulated the creation in 2001 of the World Social Forum, an annual gathering of alternative globalization activists to coordinate strategy, exchange ideas, and share experiences, under the slogan "Another world is possible."

Local activists in various places likewise resisted the impact of globalization. In 1994 in southern Mexico, peasant resentment boiled over against the Mexican

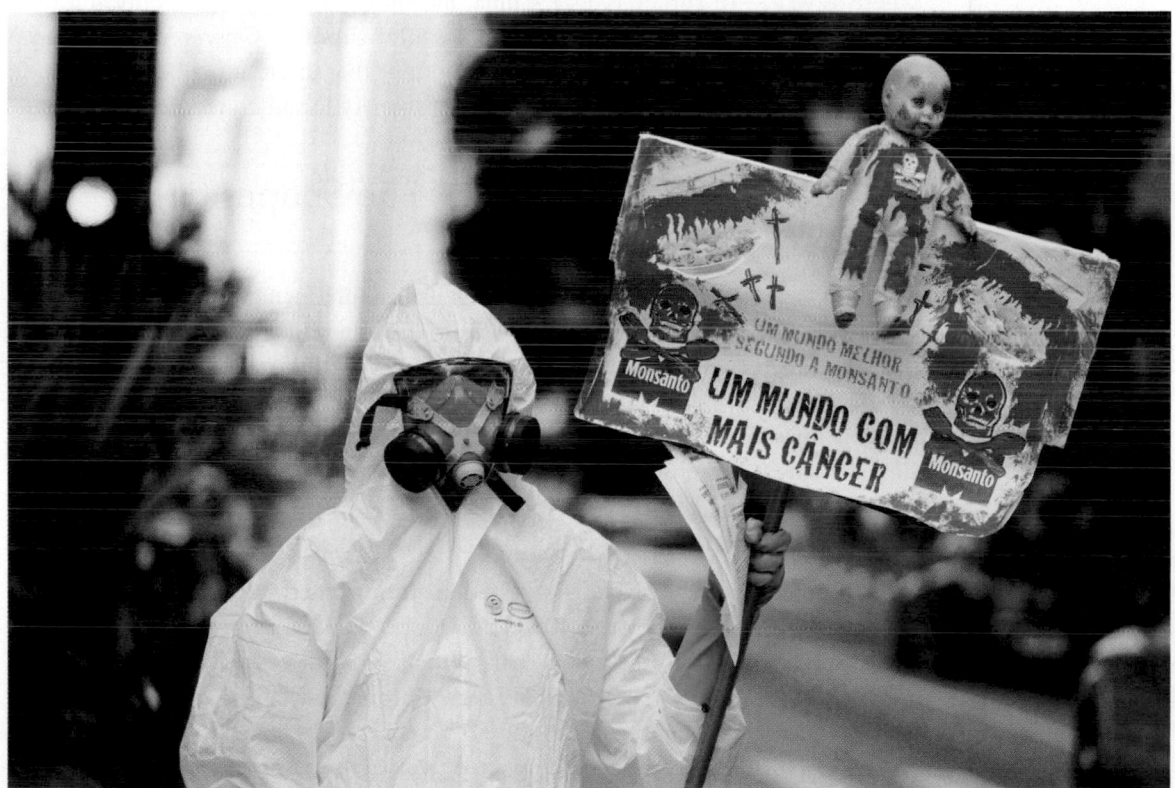

Anti-Globalization Protest A demonstrator in São Paulo, Brazil, in 2013, part of a worldwide protest against the biotech giant Monsanto, holds a sign reading: "A better world according to Monsanto is a world with more cancer." (Nelson Antoine/AP Images)

government and its privatizing of communally held land, which was related to the country's recent entry into the **North American Free Trade Agreement (NAFTA)**. The leader of this peasant upheaval referred to globalization as a "process to eliminate that multitude of people who are not useful to the powerful." Likewise in southern India, activist farmers during the late 1990s organized protests against the opening of Kentucky Fried Chicken outlets as well as against the giant American chemical corporation Monsanto, uprooting and burning fields where Monsanto grew genetically modified cotton.

Opposition to globalization also emerged from more conservative circles, especially after the sharp economic downturn beginning in 2008. Britain's vote in 2016 to leave the European Union clearly represented a backlash against globalization, even as movements hostile to a more united Europe gained support in many countries. So too did the U.S. election of 2016, in which all of the candidates expressed reservations about international trade agreements as threatening American jobs. The most vociferous voice was that of the winner, Donald Trump, who in early 2017 withdrew the United States from the Trans-Pacific Partnership trade agreement and demanded a renegotiation of NAFTA with Mexico and Canada. Elsewhere as well—in Turkey, Russia, China, and India, for example—political leaders increasingly appealed to national pride and cultural purity. Observers wondered if this represented a rejection of earlier assumptions that international cooperation in reducing trade barriers fostered peace and prosperity for all concerned.

Producing and Consuming: The Shapes of Modern Societies

Technological innovation and economic globalization during the past century have dramatically reshaped human societies around the world. Further contributing to this reshaping of social structures have been the actions of state authorities through their laws, regulations, and policies. Broad global patterns such as the declining role of peasant farmers and the growing role of middle-class professionals found expression in many variations across the multiple divides of the modern world.

Life on the Land: The Decline of the Peasantry

Guided Reading Question

···

■ **CHANGE**
What global social changes have accompanied economic globalization?

A little over 20 percent of the world's population farmed full time in 2000, a dramatic drop from 66 percent in 1950 and around 80 percent in many preindustrial agricultural societies. In the second half of the twentieth century, the farming population declined by 80 percent in Western Europe and Japan, around 60 percent in the United States and Canada, and 50 percent or more in many parts of Latin America, North Africa, and Southwest Asia. In communist Eastern Europe, the Soviet Union, and China, similar declines occurred a little later and especially when collectivization was abandoned after the late 1980s. One historian has described this development as "the death of the peasantry," which has allowed "an absurdly tiny percentage" of the population "to flood . . . the world with untold quantities of food."[15]

What caused this dramatic decline? A major factor was mechanization, as machinery such as tractors and combines made farmers more productive, earlier in North America and Australia and later elsewhere in the world. Furthermore, many farmers in the Global North and some regions of the Global South (India, Argentina, and Brazil) also embraced Green Revolution innovations, including chemical fertilizers and new types of seed, that were initially developed between the 1930s and the late 1960s. By the 1970s a corn farmer in the United States was between 100 and 1,000 times more productive than his nineteenth-century counterpart, but costs were also much higher as expenditures on machinery, fertilizer, and diesel fuel soared. Both family farmers and managers for agribusiness companies had to master often complex new farming practices. Describing the impact of technology on his work, Ken Grimsdell, whose company raised crops in the Midlands of England, noted in 2015: "A tractor can be controlled by satellite, drones can fly over a crop, record pictures and send them back to the office. The technology has made for better farming."[16] It also made for fewer farmers.

Many of the most mechanized and efficient farms in the world remained dependent on seasonal labor at crucial moments in the agricultural year. The work of migrant laborers, often organized into teams that moved from place to place, was intense, repetitive, and sometimes dangerous, especially as the use of toxic pesticides increased with the Green Revolution. Migrant workers typically were outsiders in the communities where they worked and in the United States were often undocumented or possessed temporary work visas. Nevertheless, this difficult life attracted millions of Latin American and Caribbean migrants to the fields of the United States and similar numbers of Eastern Europeans to the farms of Western Europe following the enlargement of the European Union in the early twenty-first century.

Ever cheaper transportation costs created an increasingly global market for food, forcing farmers, often on different continents, to compete with each other. Trade deals exposed small-scale farmers in the Global South to the mechanized and heavily subsidized farming industries of the Global North. In 1994, NAFTA allowed corn from the United States to flood the Mexican market, forcing 2 million small farmers in Mexico to abandon its cultivation. In 2006, Tirso Alvares Correa worried that no one would be left to work land that his family had tilled for generations. "Free trade has been a disaster for us. . . . Corn from abroad is taking a toll. . . . We can't sell our corn anymore."[17] Some displaced farmers found work on large estates geared toward raising crops like avocados for export. Many others immigrated to the United States, with some finding work on American farms.

While farmers as a percentage of the population declined dramatically in the second half of the twentieth century, some 27 percent of the world's population, about 1.8 billion people, still earned their living from the land in 2006, more than the total world population in 1850. Most remained small-scale or subsistence cultivators, and in some regions farming populations grew rapidly, paralleling the growth of population generally. In Africa the number of full-time farmers nearly doubled between 1960 and 2000. Land reform movements also served to keep people on the land. In Mexico, for example, "land to the tiller of the soil" was a powerful rallying cry of the Mexican Revolution of 1910 in a country where some 97 percent of the land was owned by 1 percent of the population. Enshrined in a new constitution, land reform laws redistributed about half the total land to those who farmed between 1920 and 1940. Meanwhile, in the communist world, collectivization movements in the Soviet Union from the 1920s and in Eastern Europe and China in the immediate aftermath of World War II also had the effect of employing large numbers in agriculture even as collectives brought an end to private ownership of land. Nonetheless, after millennia during which 80 percent or more of people toiled on the land, the past century has witnessed those who farm shrink to a distinct minority of humankind.

The Changing Lives of Industrial Workers

The opening decades of the twentieth century brought considerable changes to the lives of millions who labored in factories. American industry pioneered the moving production line and "scientific management" that broke down more complex activities into simple steps. While increasing productivity substantially, these changes fundamentally altered the pace and nature of factory work. More jobs became repetitive and boring. The moving assembly line removed nearly all control over the pace of work from those who performed it. Some employers, like the car manufacturer Henry Ford, offered better pay and somewhat shorter hours to his workers to entice them into his factories, while union movements and social reformers pressed for worker's rights, sometimes through strikes. Elements of these American innovations spread to factories in Europe, the Soviet Union, and to a lesser extent Japan by the 1930s.

In many heavily unionized industries, the two-day weekend became standard by the 1920s and along with higher wages created a growing culture of leisure and consumption, often called **consumerism**. In summarizing this development, one scholar has stated that "industrial cities became places of leisure as well as labor."[18] Shopping at department stores and attending movies or sporting events emerged as popular pastimes among working-class families, who also increasingly purchased prepared foods rather than cooking. Fish and chips (French fries) became a particular favorite of the British working class, with over 30,000 shops across the country offering this new convenience food by the 1920s.

Plant closures during the Great Depression significantly disrupted the lives of factory workers, as did World War II through the rationing and physical destruction of wartime. But the shortage of wartime labor drew women into factories across the industrialized world in unprecedented numbers and also allowed them to fill positions traditionally reserved for men. After the war many women were forced to abandon the factories altogether or at least abandon "male" jobs. In the 1950s and 1960s, stable and well-paid workforces often represented by strong unions typified the industrial sectors of Japan, the United States, and Western Europe. After decades of depression and wartime scarcity, industrial workers everywhere reacted to the good times by embracing consumerism. By 1970 nearly all urban households in Japan owned the "big three"—a television, washing machine, and refrigerator. Between 1945 and 1960 companies in the United States quadrupled their collective advertising expenditure, reflecting the buying power of the American worker. Europeans consumed more but also emphasized leisure, as one month of paid annual vacation became standard in many industries. In the communist world, large factory workforces enjoyed similar job security, even if their economies proved unable to produce the variety of consumer goods available to workers elsewhere.

Further changes awaited factory workers in the later twentieth century. Liberalization of global trade, automation and robots, relocation of factories to places with cheaper labor costs, and the rapid growth of manufacturing in the Global South—all of this led to the decline or "rusting out" of many well-established industrial centers in parts of Western Europe and the United States and the displacement of many less-skilled workers. As the former Soviet Union and China opened up to global trade in the 1990s, many state-owned manufacturing enterprises collapsed or fell into decline, displacing many workers, even as a new factory working class formed in China's coastal regions, where foreign investors had created new industrial operations. Closure of factories around the world tore at the social fabric of communities and led many to seek better employment opportunities elsewhere. Speaking in 2015 about his two teenage daughters, Mark Semande, a former worker at the closed Maytag

Closed Factories and Displaced Industrial Workers As automation and outsourcing swept across the industrialized West, factories closed, employees lost their jobs, communities were disrupted, and protests ensued. Workers at a Goodyear tire plant in northern France responded to the company's plans to close the facility, eliminating some 1,000 jobs, by holding two managers hostage and setting fire to numerous tires in early 2014. (Denis Charlet/Getty Images)

appliance plant in Galesburg, Illinois, mused: "Maybe they could find jobs and live in the community but not if they want to do as well as [my wife and I]."[19] Nonetheless, in some heavily industrialized regions, new, more efficient automated manufacturing allowed factories to survive and compete in the global market, but with far fewer and more highly skilled workers.

Even as manufacturing declined in many of its traditional heartlands in the later twentieth century, it took root and thrived in new regions. Between 1980 and 2007 the global manufacturing workforce grew from 1.9 to 3.1 billion people, offering many new employment opportunities, especially in the developing world. Countries competed to attract manufacturers, luring them with weak labor laws, low wages, tax incentives, and special **export-processing zones (EPZs)** where international companies could operate with expedited building permits, exemptions from certain taxes and customs duties, and other benefits.

Many of the conditions for workers remained much as they had been during the first Industrial Revolution. Women made up an important part of the global industrial workforce and typically earned less than men. At the turn of the twenty-first century, around 74 percent of the workers in the Philippine's EPZs were women who earned on average 54 percent of what their male counterparts did. Also mirroring the first Industrial Revolution, workers frequently labored in dangerous conditions that resulted in tragedies like the collapse of the Rana Plaza garment factory in Bangladesh in April 2013, which killed 1,135 workers and injured a further 2,500. In some regions like South Africa during the apartheid era or China during the 1980s and 1990s, migrants from the countryside who worked in industrial zones commonly lacked official residency and work privileges, limiting their ability to oppose the demands of their employers and access services like education or health care. But as manufacturing became established in new regions, workers often voiced dissatisfaction and sought better pay and working conditions. In Brazil, South Africa, and South Korea, labor movements emerged within a generation of the auto industry establishing major production facilities.

The Service Sector and the Informal Economy

Beyond farm and factory, employment opportunities grew significantly in service industries, sales, and the knowledge economy, which included government, medicine, education, finance, communication, information technology, and media. Growth in these areas was driven in part by an emerging consumerism and increasing population and was encouraged by new communication and computation technologies, including the typewriter, telephone, and later the computer and the Internet. Some of these **service sector** enterprises employed highly educated, well-paid workers such as doctors, computer coders, and bankers, but many more were lower-skilled, lower-paid occupations such as cleaners, shopkeepers, taxi drivers, secretaries, and typists. Everywhere race and gender pay differentials existed, with jobs gendered female—manicurist, nurse, teacher—paying less than those gendered male—plumber, bank manager, engineer.

The last decades of the twentieth century witnessed a trend toward less stable employment in service industries and the knowledge economies of more developed regions as employers outsourced jobs to freelancers, independent contractors, contract workers, and temporary staffing agencies. Advances in telecommunications and the Internet allowed companies to relocate jobs in the service industry (call centers, data entry) and knowledge economy (computer coding, editing) to lower-wage countries. At the opening of the twenty-first century, zero-hour contracts, which required employees to be on call without any guarantee of work, grew more common in the retail sector, and new ride-sharing apps competed with taxi firms. In what has been described as the new "gig economy," jobs came with greater flexibility for workers but also less security, fewer fringe benefits, looser relationships with employers, and often longer workdays.

The **informal economy** (or "shadow" economy), which operated "off the books" and largely outside government regulation and taxation, grew rapidly as fewer employees worked in stable, permanent jobs. This growth occurred most notably in the Global South, where new immigrants to rapidly expanding cities often found employment as day laborers or small-scale traders and lived in crowded shantytowns, but it was also evident in the Global North. Greece's black market reached 20 to 25 percent of its total economy in 2017, and in the United States, an estimated $2 trillion of unreported income in 2012 suggested a substantial shadow economy. The expansion of such informal economies over the past several decades has led some scholars to conclude that the stable and well-defined workplaces in the mid-twentieth-century industrialized North were an aberration rather than a new norm in the world of work.

Global Middle Classes and Life at the Top

A prosperous middle class in the Global North was a defining feature of the twentieth century. By the 1950s factory workers, tradesmen, and increasing numbers of service, sales, clerical, and knowledge economy workers came to view themselves as "middle class," for they were earning stable wages that allowed them to live comfortably, own their homes, and secure access to health care, education, entertainment, and travel. In much of the Global South, "middle class" was defined differently — as those households earning significantly above the poverty line but less than the highest earners in their communities. In most developing countries, a large middle class of this kind only emerged at the opening of the twenty-first century. But by 2009, an estimated 1.8 billion people globally were "middle class."[20] The shifting of manufacturing and some service and knowledge economy employment to the Global South was an important driver in this remarkable growth.

However, at the opening of the twenty-first century, many in the global middle class felt that their position in society was insecure or under threat. In Europe, the United States, Japan, and other places in the industrial north, the middle class as a proportion of society has been stagnant or shrinking since the 1970s, and the living standards of many declined even as economic growth continued in these

Middle-Class Life in Nigeria One sign of an emerging middle class in the Global South was the proliferation of malls and huge retail outlets such as this Shoprite store, located in the new Delta Mall in Warri, Nigeria. Shoprite is Africa's largest food retailer, selling food, liquor, household goods, and small appliances. A recent customer commented: "A middle-class person can come into this mall and feel a sense of belonging."[22] (Glenna Gordon/© The New York Times/Redux)

regions. As one Chicago steelworker whose plant shut down in the 1980s put it: "I'm working harder, making less money, got less of a future."[21] Less secure employment, the loss of manufacturing jobs, immigration, and the decline of labor unions have all taken their toll on the middle class, sparking populist political backlashes such as Britain's announced exit from the European Union in 2016 and the election of President Donald Trump in the United States. In the Global South as well, many in the middle class find their positions precarious. More than 60 percent of the middle class in Bolivia, Brazil, Chile, and Mexico work precariously within the informal economy, often running their own very small businesses.

The last several decades also produced economic winners. Never before had the richest 1 percent controlled so much wealth as they did at the opening of the twenty-first century. In 2016 an OXFAM study concluded that the eight richest people in the world possessed roughly the same amount of wealth as the poorest 3.5 billion. The gap between the pay of top executives and employees at major firms has widened dramatically. One commentator in 2011 described it as "The Winner-Take-Most Economy" where a small number of "superstar" performers enjoyed most of the newly generated wealth.[23]

The richest 1 percent looked very different in 2000 than a century earlier. More were self-made, with fewer having inherited their wealth. In the West and some other places, the globalization and deregulation of the financial industry from the 1980s on allowed some in the banking, private equity, and hedge fund industries to make fortunes even as a series of financial bubbles and collapses made finance more risky. At the same time, the remarkable growth of high tech and especially Internet businesses made billionaires out of a lucky few. Some 1 percenters from the Global South made their fortunes following decolonization by taking over the structures of the state, often through direct corruption, as in Nigeria, where billions in oil revenues were siphoned off into the personal accounts of officials. Similarly, following the collapse of the Soviet Union, well-connected individuals who frequently had held elite positions in the former regime purchased state assets on the cheap, becoming billionaires in the process.

The newly enriched rubbed shoulders with one another and with more traditional elites while living global lifestyles almost unimaginable to the rest. Owning multiple houses in desirable locations—London, Dubai, Hong Kong, New York—and moving between them on private jets or on luxury yachts established their place in the new elite, as did participation in exclusive gatherings like the annual DAVOS summit in Switzerland. More so than in the past, the superrich possessed a shared international outlook, educational background, and experiences that made them a self-conscious global class. "A person in Africa who runs a big African bank and went to Harvard Business School has more in common with me than he does with his neighbors, and I have more in common with him than I do with my neighbors," observed the private equity banker Glen Hutchins.[24] At the opening of the twenty-first century, humankind had never been so collectively wealthy. That wealth lifted billions out of poverty and created a growing global middle class, but it also accumulated in the hands of a privileged few, creating an unprecedentedly wealthy global plutocracy.

Getting Personal: Transformations of Private Life

The public face of social life, expressed in work, class, income, and wealth, has a more private counterpart, experienced in marriage, family, sexuality, and gender roles. These elements of personal life also changed dramatically amid the technological and economic transformations of the past century. Increasingly, individuals had to makes choices about intimate matters that were previously regarded as determined by custom or law—who to marry, how many children to bear, when to begin sexual activity, and what it meant to be male or female. Amid much diversity and variation, many people the world over have experienced and celebrated those changes as liberation from ancient constraints and social oppression, while many others have felt them as an assault on the natural order of things and a threat to ways of living sanctioned by religion and traditional moral codes. These diverse reactions have driven matters long considered private or unspeakable into the public sphere of controversy, debate, and political action.

Modernity and Personal Life

Among the agents of change in personal life, none have been more fundamental than the multiple processes widely associated with modernity—science and technology, industrialization and urbanization, and globalization and migration. Consider, for example, their impact on family life, experienced earlier and most fully in the industrialized societies of Europe, North America, and Japan, but also more recently in the Global South.

As industrial and urban life took hold across the world during the past two centuries, large business enterprises and the state took over functions that families

Guided Reading Question

■ CHANGE

In what ways has personal or private life been transformed over the past century?

had previously performed. Production moved from family farms and workshops to factories, offices, and large-scale agricultural enterprises, and opportunities for work outside the home beckoned to growing numbers of women as well as men. Education became the task of state-run schools rather than families, and the primary role of children became that of student rather than worker. Families increasingly functioned primarily to provide emotional and financial security in a turbulent and rapidly changing world. In this setting, modern families became smaller as children were increasingly seen as economic burdens and as both men and women married later. Furthermore, family life grew less stable as divorce became far more frequent and the stigma attached to it diminished. Modern life also witnessed an increasing variety of family patterns across the world: patriarchal families of several generations living together; small nuclear families of mother, father, and children; single-parent families, usually headed by women; unmarried couples living together, sometimes with children and often without; blended families as a result of second marriages; polygamous families; and gay and lesbian families.

These broad patterns of change in family life at the global level hid a great deal of diversity. While family size has dropped sharply in much of Asia and Latin America during the past century, it has remained quite high in sub-Saharan Africa, where women in the early twenty-first century produced on average 5 children during their reproductive years, compared to a global average of 2.5. Divorce rates too varied widely in the early twenty-first century, with 50 percent or more of marriages ending in divorce in the United States, France, Spain, Cuba, Hungary, and the Czech Republic, compared to much lower rates in Chile (3 percent), Brazil (21 percent), Egypt (17 percent), Iran (22 percent), and South Africa (17 percent). Since the mid-1990s, China has experienced a dramatic increase in divorce, prompting the Chinese government to intervene to address the issue. Most of the world's marriages during the past century have involved one man and one woman, though polygamy remains legal in much of Africa and the Islamic Middle East, while same-sex marriages have gained a measure of acceptance at least in some cultures in recent decades. While the past century has generally favored free choice or "love" marriages, many families in India and elsewhere still arrange marriages for their children.

Modern life has also deeply impacted sexuality. Technologies of contraception—condoms, IUDs, diaphragms, and above all "the pill"—have allowed many people to separate sexual life from reproduction. Especially since the 1960s, this has contributed to the emergence of a highly sexualized public culture in many parts of the world, expressed in advertising and in an enormous pornography industry with a global reach. One investigator reported on a remote village in the West African country of Ghana: "The village has no electricity, but that doesn't stop a generator from being wheeled in, turning a mud hut into an impromptu porn cinema."[25] Sex tourism has also become big business, with major destinations in Thailand, Indonesia, the Philippines, Columbia, Brazil, and the Netherlands. Movies, TV, newspapers, and magazines openly display or discuss all manner of sexual topics that would have been largely forbidden in public discourse only a century ago: premarital sex, homosexuality, gay marriage, LGBT rights, sexually transmitted diseases, birth control, abortion, teen pregnancy, and much more. Sex education in schools has spread globally to varying degrees, while provoking sharp controversy in many places.

Sex, in short, has come out of the closet during the past century. Unsurprisingly, this has been associated with a considerable increase in premarital sex in many parts of the world, with the vast majority of Americans and Europeans participating in such activity by the late 1960s. A rapidly industrializing China has witnessed the frequency of premarital sex skyrocket since 1989, approaching levels in the United States.

But all of this has occurred in the face of much controversy and opposition. The hierarchies of the Catholic Church and many fundamentalist or evangelical Christian leaders have remained steadfastly opposed to the "sexual revolution" of the past century, even as many of their parishioners participate in it. Despite the sexual revolution, over 90 percent of Muslims in Indonesia, Jordan, Pakistan, Turkey, and Egypt found premarital sex unacceptable in the early twenty-first century, while fewer than 10 percent of the people in France, Germany, and Spain felt the same way.[26] Greater openness and assertiveness among gays and lesbians have triggered legal action against them, especially in Africa, where many countries have passed harsh antigay legislation, citing the AIDS crisis, a defense of traditional marriage, and the supposedly "un-African" character of homosexuality.

The State and Personal Life

States too have shaped personal life in the past century, as they grew more powerful and intrusive and as matters of marriage, family, gender, and sexuality became ever more entangled with politics. Nazi Germany, for example, prohibited birth control and rewarded large families during the 1930s in an effort to produce as many "good Germans" as possible. At the same time, they sterilized or executed those deemed "undesirable" and forbade marriage or sexual relations between Jews and Germans to prevent "contamination" of the Aryan race. For similar racial reasons, South Africa under the apartheid regime legally prohibited both sexual relationships and marriage between whites and nonwhites. In the aftermath of World War II, the Soviet Union sharply limited access to all contraception in an effort to rebuild a population devastated by war.

But as concerns about population growth mounted in the 1970s and beyond, some states moved to limit the numbers of their people. Acting under a state of emergency, the government of India sterilized some 11 million men and women between 1975 and 1977, using a combination of incentives and compulsion to gain consent. China pursued population control on an even larger scale through its **one-child family policy**, which lasted from 1980 until 2014. Under the pressure of financial incentives and penalties and intense pressure from local authorities, over 300 million women "agreed" to have IUD devices implanted, over 100 million were sterilized, and many were forced to undergo abortions.

China's One-Child Family China's vigorous efforts to limit its population growth represented a radical intrusion of state power into the private lives of its people. It was accompanied by a massive propaganda effort, illustrated by this urban billboard. (Barry Lewis/Alamy)

Communist regimes intervened in personal life in other ways as well. Among the earliest and most revolutionary actions of the new communist government in the Soviet Union were efforts at liberating and mobilizing women. Almost immediately upon coming to power, communist authorities in the Soviet Union declared full legal and political equality for women; marriage became a civil procedure among freely consenting adults; divorce was legalized and made easier, as was abortion; illegitimacy was abolished; women no longer had to take their husbands' surnames; pregnancy leave for employed women was mandated; and women were actively mobilized as workers in the country's drive to industrialization. (See Zooming In: Anna Dubova, a Russian Woman, and the Soviet State, page 1000.) During the 1920s, a special party organization called the **Women's Department** (Zhenotdel) organized numerous conferences for women, trained women to run day-care centers and medical clinics, published newspapers and magazines aimed at a female audience, provided literacy and prenatal classes, and encouraged Muslim women to take off their veils.

Elsewhere as well, states acted in favor of women's rights and gender equality, most notably in Turkey, a thoroughly Muslim country, during the 1920s and 1930s. Turkey had emerged as an independent state, led by Kemal Atatürk, from the ashes of the Ottoman Empire following World War I. In Atatürk's view, the emancipation of women was a cornerstone of the new Turkey and a mark of the country's modernization. In a much-quoted speech, he declared:

> If henceforward the women do not share in the social life of the nation . . .
> we shall remain irremediably backward, incapable of treating on equal terms
> with the civilizations of the West.[27]

Thus polygamy was abolished; women were granted equal rights in divorce, inheritance, and child custody; and in 1934 Turkish women gained the right to vote and hold public office, a full decade before French women gained that right. Public beaches were opened to women, and Atatürk encouraged them to discard the veil or head covering, long associated with Muslim piety, in favor of Western styles of dress. As in the early Soviet Union, this was a state-directed feminism, responsive to Atatürk's modern views, rather than reflecting popular demands from women themselves.

But what the state granted to women, the state could also take away, as it did in Iran in the years following that country's Islamic revolution in 1979. The country's new Islamic government, headed by the Ayatollah Khomeini, moved to sharply tighten religiously inspired restrictions on women, while branding feminism and women's rights as a Western evil. By 1983, all women were required to wear loose-fitting clothing and the head covering known as hijab, a regulation enforced by roving groups of militants, or "revolutionary guards." Sexual segregation was imposed in schools, parks, beaches, and public transportation. The legal age of marriage for girls, set at eighteen under the prerevolutionary regime, was reduced to nine with parental consent. Married women could no longer file for divorce or attend school. Yet, despite such restrictions, many women supported the revolution and over the next several decades found far greater opportunities for employment and higher education than before. By the early twenty-first century, almost 60 percent of university students were women, women's right to vote remained intact, and some loosening of earlier restrictions on women had become apparent.

Feminism and Personal Life

A third source of change in personal life during the past century derived from social movements committed to liberation from ancient patterns of inequality and oppression. No expression of this global culture of liberation held a more profound potential for social change than feminism, for it represented a rethinking of the most fundamental and personal of all human relationships—that between women and men. Although feminism had begun in the West in the nineteenth century, it became global in the twentieth, as organized efforts to address the concerns of women took shape across the world.

Western feminism had lost momentum as an organized movement by the end of the 1920s, when many countries in Western Europe and North America had achieved women's suffrage. But it revived in the 1960s with a quite different agenda as women's participation in the paid workforce mounted rapidly. In France, for example, *The Second Sex*, by the writer and philosopher Simone de Beauvoir, appeared in 1949 arguing that women had historically been defined as "other," or deviant from the "normal" male sex. The book soon became a central statement of a reviving women's movement. Across the Atlantic, millions of American women responded to Betty Friedan's book, *The Feminine Mystique* (1963), which disclosed the identity crisis of educated women, unfulfilled by marriage and motherhood. Some adherents of this **second-wave feminism** took up the equal rights agenda of their nineteenth-century predecessors, but with an emphasis now on employment and education rather than voting rights. A more radical expression of American feminism, widely known as "women's liberation," took broader aim at patriarchy as a system of domination, similar to those of race and class. One manifesto from 1969 declared:

> We are exploited as sex objects, breeders, domestic servants, and cheap labor.
> We are considered inferior beings, whose only purpose is to enhance men's

Guided Reading Question

■ **COMPARISON**

In what different ways has modern feminism found expression?

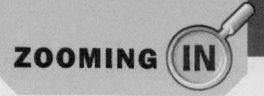
Anna Dubova, a Russian Woman, and the Soviet State

A 1941 image of a woman factory worker in Moscow.

photo: Library of Congress, Prints and Photographs Division, LC-USW33-024241-C (P&P)

Born into a large peasant family near Smolensk in western Russia in 1916, Anna Dubova lived through the entire communist period in her country.[28] Her experience illustrates the impact of state policies on the life of one individual seeking to navigate a communist system.

Anna was one of fourteen children, of whom seven survived. Her family was dominated by a strict, hardworking, and highly religious father, who was choirmaster of the local church. Anna's father was suspicious of the communists when they came to power the year after Anna's birth, but her grandmother was more forthright. "The forces of the Antichrist have triumphed," she declared. Nonetheless, her father accepted an appointment in 1922 as chairman of the village soviet, the new communist organ of local government. During the 1920s, the village and Anna's family flourished under Lenin's New Economic Policy, which briefly permitted a considerable measure of private enterprise and profit making. Her father even opened a small shop in the village, where he sold goods purchased in the city.

By 1928, however, everything changed as the Soviet regime, now under Joseph Stalin's leadership, abruptly moved to collectivize agriculture and root out *kulaks*, supposedly wealthy peasants who were thought to bear the germ of a hated capitalism. Because of her father's shop, the family was labeled as kulak and their property was confiscated. "I remember so well how Mama sat and cried when they took away the cow," Anna recalled years later. The family forestalled their expected deportation to the far north of the Soviet Union only by promising Anna, then just thirteen, in marriage to the local Communist Party secretary. The marriage never took place, however, and the family was forced to leave. Later, Anna was permitted to join her older sister in Moscow, but approval for that much-coveted move

lives. . . . Because we live so intimately with our oppressors, we have been kept from seeing our personal suffering as a political condition.[29]

Thus liberation for women meant becoming aware of their own oppression, a process that took place in thousands of consciousness-raising groups across the United States. Favoring direct action, some of these women disrupted the Miss America contest of 1968 while disposing of girdles, bras, high-heeled shoes, tweezers, and other "instruments of oppression" in a Freedom Trashcan. They also brought into open discussion issues involving sexuality, insisting that free love, lesbianism, and celibacy should be accorded the same respect as heterosexual marriage.

Yet another strand of Western feminism emerged from women of color. For many of them, the concerns of white, usually middle-class, feminists were hardly relevant to their oppression. Black women had always worked outside the home and came at a very high price. Anna recalled, "I had to write out an official statement that I renounced my parents, that I no longer had any ties with them."

Thus Anna, a rural teenager, joined millions of other peasants who flocked to the city to pursue new opportunities that became available as the Soviet Union launched its industrialization drive. In Moscow, she gained a basic education, a vocation in cake decorating, which she enjoyed, and a brief stint as a mechanic and chauffeur, which she detested. All the while the shadow of her kulak label followed her. Had it been discovered, she could have lost her job and her permission to live in Moscow. And so she married a party activist from a poor peasant family, she explained years later, "just so I could cover up my background." Her husband drank heavily, leaving her with a daughter when he went off to war in 1941.

In the Soviet Union, the late 1930s witnessed the Terror when millions of alleged "enemies of the people" were arrested and hauled off to execution or labor camps. Anna recalled what it was like: "You'd come home and they'd say, Yesterday they took away Uncle Lesha. . . . You'd go to see a girlfriend, they'd say, We have an empty room now; they've exiled Andreitsev." Like most people not directly involved, Anna believed in the guilt of these people. And she feared that she herself might be mistakenly accused, for those with a kulak label were particular targets of the search for enemies.

Beyond her kulak background, Anna also felt compelled to hide a deep religious sensibility derived from her childhood. She remembered the disappearance of the village priest, the looting of the churches, and the destruction of icons. And so she never entered a church or prayed in front of others. But she wore a cross under her clothing. "I never stopped [believing]," she recalled. "But I concealed it. Deep down . . . I believed." Nor did she ever seek to join the Communist Party, though it may well have advanced her career prospects and standard of living.

In the decades following World War II and especially after Stalin's death in 1953, Anna's life seemed to stabilize. She entered into a thirty-year relationship with a man and found satisfying work in a construction design office, though the lack of higher education and party connections prevented her from moving into higher-paid jobs. Looking back on her life, she regretted the communist intrusion, particularly in its Stalinist phase, into what she remembered as a happy childhood. She had come to value, perhaps nostalgically, the life of a peasant over that of an urban worker. She reflected, "[As a peasant,] I would have lived on the fruits of my labor. . . . [Instead,] I've lived someone else's life."

QUESTIONS

In what ways did state policies shape Anna's life? To what extent was she able to construct her own life within that system?

---

so felt little need to be liberated from the chains of homemaking. Whereas white women might find the family oppressive, African American women viewed it as a secure base from which to resist racism and poverty. Solidarity with black men, rather than separation from them, was essential in confronting a racist America.

As women mobilized across Asia, Africa, and Latin America, they too faced very different situations than did white women in the United States and Europe. The predominant issues for **feminism in the Global South**—colonialism, racism, poverty, development, political oppression, and sometimes revolution—were not always directly related to gender. To many African feminists in the 1970s and later, the concerns of their American or European sisters were too individualistic, too focused on sexuality, and insufficiently concerned with issues of motherhood, marriage, and poverty to be of much use. Furthermore, they resented Western feminists' insistent interest in cultural matters such as female genital mutilation and polygamy, which sometimes echoed the concerns of colonial-era missionaries and administrators. Western feminism could easily be seen as a new form of cultural imperialism.

During the colonial era, much of women's political activity was aligned with the struggle for independence. Later, women's movements in the Global South took shape around a wide range of issues. In the East African country of Kenya, a major form of mobilization was the "women's group" movement. Some 27,000 small associations of women, an outgrowth of traditional self-help groups, provided support for one another during times of need, such as weddings, births, and funerals, and took on community projects, such as building water cisterns, schools, and dispensaries. Some groups became revolving loan societies or bought land or businesses. One woman testified to the sense of empowerment she derived from membership in her group:

> I am a free woman. I bought this piece of land through my group. I can lie on it, work on it, keep goats or cows. What more do I want? My husband cannot sell it. It is mine.[30]

Elsewhere, other issues and approaches predominated. In the North African Islamic kingdom of Morocco, a more centrally directed and nationally focused feminist movement targeted the country's Family Law Code, which still defined women as minors. In 2004, a long campaign by Morocco's feminist movement, often with the help of supportive men and a liberal king, resulted in a new Family Law Code that recognized women as equals to their husbands and allowed them to initiate divorce and to claim child custody, all of which had previously been denied.

In Chile, a women's movement emerged as part of a national struggle against the military dictatorship of General Augusto Pinochet, who ruled the country from 1973 to 1990. Because they were largely regarded as "invisible" in the public sphere, women were able to organize extensively, despite the repression of the Pinochet regime. From this explosion of organizing activity emerged a women's movement that crossed class lines and party affiliations. Poor urban women by the tens of thousands organized soup kitchens, craft workshops, and shopping collectives, all aimed at the economic survival of their families. Smaller numbers of middle-class women brought more distinctly feminist perspectives to the movement and argued pointedly for "democracy in the country and in the home." This diverse women's movement was an important part of the larger national protest that returned Chile to democratic government in 1990.

Perhaps the most impressive achievement of feminism in the twentieth century was its ability to project the "woman question" as a global issue and to gain international recognition for the view that "women's rights are human rights." Like slavery and empire before it, patriarchy lost at least some of its legitimacy during this most recent century. Feminism registered as a global issue when the United Nations (UN), under pressure from women activists, declared 1975 as International Women's Year and the next ten years as the Decade for Women. By 2006, 183 nations, though not the United States, had ratified a UN Convention on the Elimination of All Forms of Discrimination against Women, which committed them to promote women's legal equality, to end discrimination, to actively encourage women's development, and to protect women's human rights. Clearly, this international attention to women's issues set a global standard to which feminists operating in their own countries could aspire.

But feminism generated a global backlash among those who felt that its agenda undermined family life, the proper relationship of men and women, and civilization generally. To Phyllis Schlafly, a prominent American opponent of equal rights for women, feminism was a "disease" that brought in its wake "fear, sickness, pain, anger, hatred, danger, violence, and all manner of ugliness."[31] In the Islamic world, Western-style feminism, with its claims of gender equality and open sexuality, was highly offensive to many and fueled movements of religious revivalism that invited or compelled women to wear the veil and sometimes to lead highly restricted lives. The Vatican, some Catholic and Muslim countries, and at times the U.S. government took strong exception to aspects of global feminism, particularly its emphasis on reproductive rights, including access to abortion and birth control. Many African governments and many African men defined feminism of any kind as "un-African" and associated with a hated colonialism. Feminist support for gay and lesbian rights only solidified opposition to women's rights activists within socially conservative circles internationally. Thus feminism was global as the twenty-first century dawned, but it was very diverse and much contested.

> ### PRACTICING HISTORICAL THINKING
>
> Which was more important in shaping the history of the past century: impersonal forces (such as technological innovation or economic change) or the deliberate actions of human beings (such as social movements and government policies)?

REFLECTIONS

History in the Middle of the Stream

Historians are usually more at ease telling stories that have clear endings, such as those that describe ancient Egyptian civilization, the Atlantic slave trade, or the French Revolution. There is a finality to these stories and a distance from them that makes it easier for historians to assume the posture of detached observers, even if their understandings of those events change over time. Finality, distance, and detachment are harder to come by when historians are describing the events and processes of the past century, for many of these stories are clearly unfinished. Technological innovation, population growth, globalization, and climate change—all of these are ongoing processes, their outcomes unknown and unknowable. In dealing with such matters, historians write from the middle of the stream, often uncomfortably, rather than from the banks, where they might feel more at ease.

In part, that discomfort arises from questions about the future that such issues inevitably raise. Should historians speculate about "what's next?" when the processes they describe in the past bump up against the present and future? Many people expect that some understanding of the past gives historians a unique insight into what is coming next. But historians themselves are often rather cautious about predictions because they are so aware of the unexpectedness and surprising quality of historical change. Fifty years ago, who could have anticipated the Internet or China's massive industrial growth?

And yet questions about the future are legitimate and important. Present-day issues and their possible futures encourage historians to look at the past in different ways. It is surely no accident that women's history and environmental history have flourished in recent decades, as feminism and environmentalism have achieved global prominence. And for individuals seeking guidance about the future, history is just about the only guide we have. As the nineteenth-century Danish philosopher Søren Kierkegaard remarked: "Life can only be understood backward, but it is lived forward." So, like everyone before us, we stumble on, both individually and collectively, largely in the dark, using analogies from the past, tentatively, as we make our way ahead.

These vast uncertainties about the future provide a useful reminder that although we know the outcomes of earlier human stories—the Asian and African struggles for independence, for example—those who lived that history did not. Such awareness can perhaps engender in us a measure of humility and greater sympathy with those whose lives we study. However we may differ from our ancestors across time and place, we share with them an immense ignorance about what the future holds.

Second Thoughts

What's the Significance?

age of fossil fuels, 972
communication revolution, 976
economic globalization, 978
Asian Tigers, 979
Bretton Woods system, 982
transnational corporations, 983
World Trade Organization (WTO), 987
North American Free Trade Agreement (NAFTA), 988
consumerism, 990
export-processing zones (EPZs), 992
service sector, 992
informal economy, 993
one-child family policy (China), 997
Women's Department, 998
second-wave feminism, 999
feminism in the Global South, 1001

Big Picture Questions

1. How did the energy and technology revolutions impact economic development during the past century?
2. What have been the costs and benefits of globalization for the world economy and the lives of workers since 1900?
3. What social, political, and cultural norms were challenged by women in the twentieth century?
4. How have the global developments examined in this chapter shaped your own life and community?
5. **Looking Back:** To what extent did the processes discussed in this chapter (energy and technological change, globalization, and feminism) have roots in the more distant past? In what respects did they represent something new?

Next Steps: For Further Study

The Cambridge World History, vol. 6: *Production, Consumption and Connection 1750–Present,* edited by J. R. McNeill and Kenneth Pomeranz (2015). An extensive collection of essays by leading figures in their fields.

Nayan Chanda, *Bound Together: How Traders, Preachers, Adventurers, and Warriors Shaped Globalization* (2007). An engaging, sometimes humorous, long-term view of the globalization process.

Sebastian Conrad, *What Is Global History?* (2016). A short introduction to the concepts of global history and globalization.

Chrystia Freeland, *Plutocrats: The Rise of the New Global Super-Rich and the Fall of Everyone Else* (2012). An insightful look at the lives and lifestyles of the 1 percent.

Jeffry A. Frieden, *Global Capitalism: Its Fall and Rise in the Twentieth Century* (2006). A thorough, thoughtful, and balanced history of economic globalization.

Michael Hunt, *The World Transformed* (2015). A thoughtful global history of the second half of the twentieth century.

Bonnie G. Smith, ed., *Global Feminisms since 1945* (2000). A series of essays about feminist movements around the world.

Jörn Barkemeyer and Jan Künzl, "Globalization," WissensWerte, 2011, https://www.youtube.com/watch?v=3oTLyPPrZE4. A brief eight-minute animated primer on the causes and consequences of globalization by two German filmmakers who produce video clips dealing with contemporary political themes.

"Women in Wartime," http://www.iwm.org.uk/history/women-in-wartime. A website of the British Imperial War Museum illustrating the impact of war on the lives of British women in the twentieth century.

Global Feminism

With its focus on equal rights and opportunities for women, modern feminism has challenged the most ancient and perhaps deeply rooted of human inequalities—that of patriarchy or the dominance of men over women. Beginning in Western Europe and the United States during the nineteenth century, it was born in the context of democratic gains for men from which women were excluded. Like science, industrialism, socialism, and electoral democracy, feminism was a Western cultural innovation that acquired a global reach during the most recent century.

In doing so, feminism has found expression in many voices, giving rise to much controversy and many questions within feminist circles. How relevant has mainstream Western feminism been to women of color in the West and in the developing countries? To what extent do all women share common interests? In what ways do differences of class, race, nation, religion, sexual orientation, and economic condition generate quite distinct feminist agendas? How important is sexual freedom to the feminist cause? What tactics are most effective in realizing the varying goals of feminists? The documents that follow provide a sample of the divergent voices in which global feminism has been articulated during the past century.

SOURCE 22.1 Western Feminism in the Twenty-First Century ▶

In the West, where modern feminism had begun, a new phase of that movement took shape during the 1960s and after. Moving well beyond the earlier focus on suffrage and property rights, "second-wave" feminists gave voice to a wide range of new issues: the value of housework, discrimination in the workplace, media portrayal of women, sexuality and the family, reproductive rights, lesbianism, violence against women, pornography, and prostitution.

At the opening of the twenty-first century, Western feminists continued to advance a broad agenda, as reflected in the two images that constitute Source 22.1. Source 22.1A depicts a 2012 slutwalk in London protesting against rape culture. This march was one of many around the world, the first of which occurred in Canada in 2011 when a policeman told a group of students that in order to avoid being raped "women should avoid dressing like sluts." Source 22.1B documents a 2017 protest in Toulouse, France, that advocated for women's rights in the workplace, another major goal of modern Western feminism. The banner in the foreground reads, "Precarious, underpaid, harassed. It's enough!"

■ What strategies are these protesters employing to secure the changes that they advocate for?

■ What do the issues raised by participants and the types of protest depicted in these images reveal about Western feminism in the first decades of the twenty-first century?

SOURCE 22.1A

A Slutwalk Protest in London │ 2012

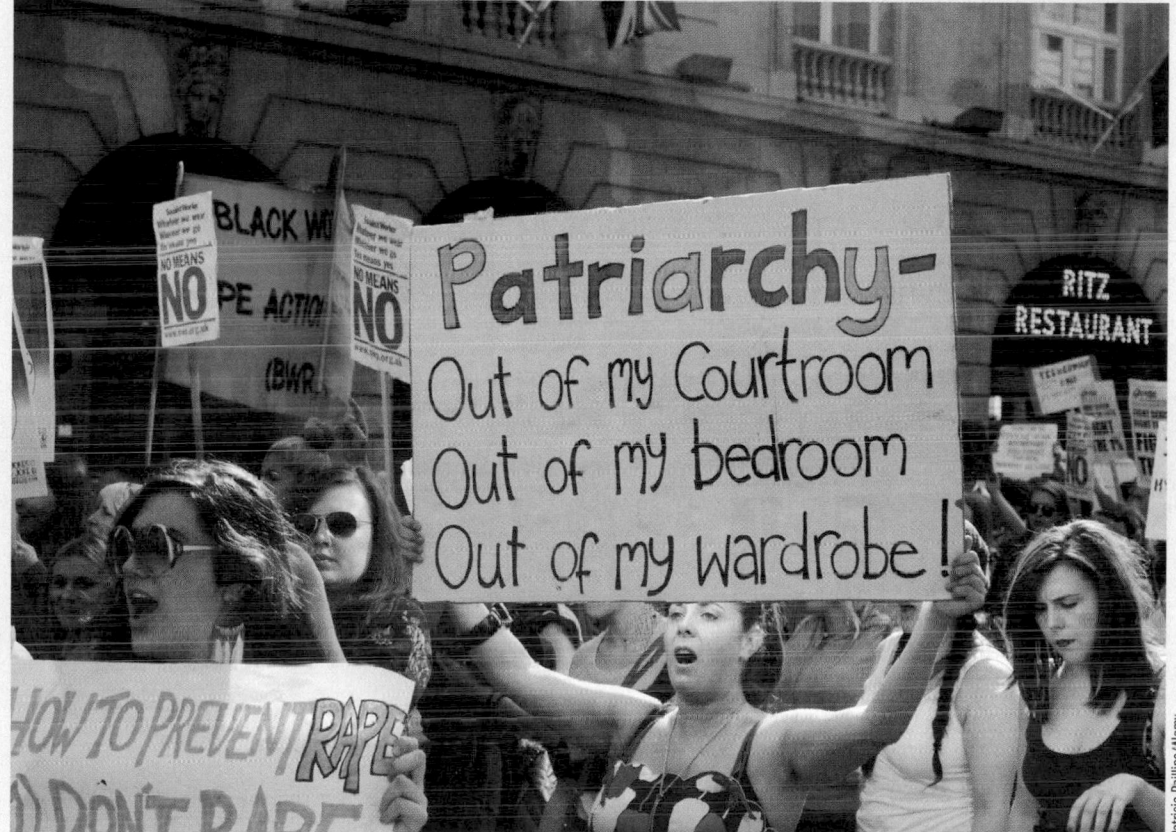

SOURCE 22.1B

A Demonstration for Women Workers' Rights in Toulouse, France | 2017

PRÉCARISÉES, SOUS PAYÉES, HARCELÉES,
Y'EN A ASSEZ !

cgt

NurPhoto/Getty Images

• • •

SOURCE 22.2 Black American Feminism

Within North American feminism, a distinctive voice arose among women of color—especially blacks and Hispanics. Many among them resented the claims of white, middle-class feminists to speak for all women and objected to the exclusive prominence given to gender issues. Capitalism, race, class, and compulsory hetero-sexuality, they insisted, combined with patriarchy to generate an interlocking system of oppression that was unique to women of color. Such a perspective is reflected in the 1977 statement of the Combahee River Collective, a black feminist organization.

■ What similarities and differences in perspective can you identify between this document and the images in Source 22.1?

■ What issues divide black and white feminists in the United States?

■ What difficulties have black American feminists experienced in gaining support for their movement?

■ On what basis might this statement generate opposition and controversy?

COMBAHEE RIVER COLLECTIVE | *A Black Feminist Statement* | 1977

We are a collective of Black feminists who have been meeting together since 1974. . . . [W]e are actively committed to struggling against racial, sexual, heterosexual, and class oppression . . . based upon the fact that the major systems of oppression are interlocking. . . .

[W]e find our origins in the historical reality of Afro-American women's continuous life-and-death struggle for survival and liberation. . . . Black women have always embodied an adversary stance to white male rule. . . . Black feminist politics also have an obvious connection to movements for Black liberation, particularly those of the 1960s and 1970s. . . . It was our experience and disillusionment within these liberation movements, as well as experience on the periphery of the white male left, that led to the need to develop a politics that was anti-racist, unlike those of white women, and anti-sexist, unlike those of Black and white men. . . . [A]s we developed politically we [also] addressed ourselves to heterosexism and economic oppression under capitalism. . . .

Although we are feminists and Lesbians, we feel solidarity with progressive Black men and do not advocate the fractionalization that white women who are separatists demand. . . . We struggle together with Black men against racism, while we also struggle with Black men about sexism. . . . We are socialists because we believe that work must be organized for the collective benefit of those who do the work and create the products, and not for the profit of the bosses. . . . We need to articulate the real class situation of persons . . . for whom racial and sexual oppression are significant determinants in their working/economic lives. . . . No one before has ever examined the multilayered texture of Black women's lives. . . . "Smart-ugly" crystallized the way in which most of us had been forced to develop our intellects at great cost to our "social" lives. . . . We have a great deal of criticism and loathing for what men have been socialized to be in this society . . . [b]ut we do not have the misguided notion that it is their maleness, per se — i.e., their biological maleness — that makes them what they are.

The major source of difficulty in our political work is that we are . . . trying . . . to address a whole range of oppressions. . . . We do not have racial, sexual, heterosexual, or class privilege to rely upon. . . . The psychological toll of being a Black woman and the difficulties this presents in reaching political consciousness and doing political work can never be underestimated. . . . As an early group member once said, "We are all damaged people merely by virtue of being Black women." . . . The material conditions of most Black women would hardly lead them to upset both economic and sexual arrangements that seem to represent some stability in their lives. . . . Accusations that Black feminism divides the Black struggle are powerful deterrents to the growth of an autonomous Black women's movement.

The inclusiveness of our politics makes us concerned with any situation that impinges upon the lives of women, Third World and working people. . . . One issue that is of major concern to us and that we have begun to publicly address is racism in the white women's movement. . . . Eliminating racism in the white women's movement is by definition work for white women to do, but we will continue to speak to and demand accountability on this issue. . . .

Source: Zillah R. Eisenstein, ed., *Capitalist Patriarchy and the Case for Socialist Feminism* (New York: Monthly Review Press, 1979), 362–72.

■ ■ ■

SOURCE 22.3 Communist Feminism ▶

Following the Russian Revolution of 1917, the communist Soviet Union was the site of a remarkable experiment in state-directed feminism. (See "The State and Personal Life" earlier in this chapter.) Early on women were granted full legal and political equality with men, divorce was legalized, and pregnancy leave was mandated for employed women. As part of a determined drive to industrialize the country, authorities also sought to liberate women from household responsibilities so that they could work outside the home. This poster from 1949 advertises the support available to Soviet women who chose to pursue careers in industry. The poster caption reads, "The broad development of a network of nursery schools, kindergartens, dining rooms and laundries will provide for the participation of women in socialist construction."

■ How would you describe the woman in the center of the poster? What do you think that the artist wanted to convey about her?

■ How are the specific services promised to women in the poster text depicted in the image? How might state provision of these services alter the daily life and family dynamics of working women?

■ Compare this image of a female communist worker with the one depicted in Source 21.4, the Chinese poster "Women Hold Up Half of Heaven," on page 962. What similarities can you identify?

■ How might the protesters in Source 22.1B react to this poster?

Soviet Poster Advertising Support for Women Workers │ 1949

. . .

SOURCE 22.4 Islamic Feminism

Beyond the Western world and the communist world, modern feminism has also found expression in the developing countries (see "Feminism and Personal Life" earlier in this chapter). Nowhere has this provoked greater controversy than in the Islamic world. For a few women, exposure to Western gender norms and liberal thought has occasioned the abandonment of Islam altogether. Far more common have been efforts to root gender equality in both personal and public life within the traditions of Islam. Such was the argument of Benazir Bhutto, several times the prime minister of Pakistan, in a speech delivered to a United Nations conference on women in 1995.

■ What message does Bhutto feel that her election and the election of other female Muslim heads of state provide to Muslim women everywhere?

■ How does she account for the manifest inequality of women in so many Muslim societies?

■ How might you compare Bhutto's case for feminism with those of Westerners and communists in the preceding documents?

BENAZIR BHUTTO | *Politics and the Muslim Woman* | 1995

I stand before you not only as a Prime Minister but as a woman and a mother proud of her cultural and religious heritage, a woman sensitive to the obstacles to justice and full participation that still stand before women in almost every society on earth. As the first woman ever elected to head an Islamic nation, I feel a special responsibility towards women's issues and towards all women. And as a Muslim woman, I feel a special responsibility to counter the propaganda of a handful that Islam gives women a second-class status. This is not true. Today the Muslim world boasts three women Prime Ministers, elected by male and female voters on our abilities as people, as persons, not as women. Our election has destroyed the myth built by social taboo that a woman's place is in the house, that it is shameful or dishonourable or socially unacceptable for a Muslim woman to work. Our election has given women all over the Muslim world moral strength to declare that it is socially correct for a woman to work and to follow in our footsteps as working women and working mothers. Muslim women have a special responsibility to help

distinguish between Islamic teachings and social taboos spun by the traditions of a patriarchal society. . . .

In distinguishing between Islamic teachings and social taboos, we must remember that Islam forbids injustice; injustice against people, against nations, against women. It shuns race, colour, and gender as a basis of distinction amongst fellow men. It enshrines piety as the sole criteria for judging humankind. It treats women as human beings in their own right, not as chattels. A woman can inherit, divorce, receive alimony and child custody. Women were intellectuals, poets, jurists and even took part in war. The Holy Book of the Muslims refers to the rule of a woman, the Queen of Sabah. The Holy Book alludes to her wisdom and to her country being a land of plenty. The Holy Prophet (peace be upon him) himself married a working woman. And the first convert to Islam was a woman, Bibi Khadija. Prophet Muhammad (peace be upon him) emphatically condemned and put an end to the practice of female infanticide in pre-Islamic Arabia. The Holy Quran reads:

When news is brought to one of them, of the birth of a female (child),
his face darkens and he is filled with inward grief what shame does he
hide himself from his people because of the bad news he has had.
Shall he retain it on sufferance and contempt, or bury it in the dust.
Ah! what an evil choice they decide on
(Surah Al-Nahl, Ayat 57, 58, 59)

Ladies and gentlemen! How true these words ring even today.

How many women are still "retained" in their families "on sufferance and contempt" growing up with emotional scars and burdens. How tragic it is that the pre-Islamic practice of female infanticide still haunts a world we regard as modern and civilized. Girl children are often abandoned or aborted. Statistics show that men now increasingly outnumber women in more than 15 Asian nations. Boys are wanted. Boys are wanted because their worth is considered more than that of the girl. Boys are wanted to satisfy the ego: they carry on the father's name in this world. Yet too often we forget that for Muslims on the Day of Judgement, each person will be called not by their father's name but by the mother's name. . . . And it [the aborting or killing of female babies] continues, not because of religion in the case of Pakistan, but because of social prejudice. The rights Islam gave Muslim women have too often been denied.

Source: United Nations, Fourth World Conference on Women, September 4, 1995, http://www.un.org/esa/gopher-data/conf/fwcw/conf/gov/950904202603.txt, made available by the United Nations.

■ ■ ■

SOURCE 22.5 Mexican Zapatista Feminists

Mexican feminists, like those in much of Latin America, have operated in societies shaped by widespread poverty, sharp class inequalities, racial and ethnic conflict, and frequently authoritarian or corrupt governments. Thus feminists have often sought to address the ways in which multiple sources of oppression, not only gender relations, affect both women and men. Such was the case in the Zapatista rebellion that erupted in 1994 among the Maya people in the Chiapas region of southern Mexico. It was a protest against a long history of injustice and impoverishment for indigenous peoples. Women activists within this largely peasant movement had to confront the sexist attitudes of their male comrades as well as an oppressive Mexican government that marginalized its Maya citizens. Although they usually rejected the "feminist" label, these women articulated their demands in an Indigenous Women's Petition (Source 22.5A) and succeeded in embedding their concerns in a Women's Revolutionary Law (Source 22.5B).

■ How would you describe the issues that these documents articulate? How do they reflect class, ethnic, and gender realities of Mexican life?

■ Should these documents be regarded as feminist? Why or why not? Why might Zapatista women be reluctant to call themselves feminists?

■ Which of these demands might provoke the strongest male resistance? Why?

■ With which of the previous feminist sources might Zapatista women be most sympathetic?

SOURCE 22.5A

Indigenous Women's Petition | March 1, 1994

We, Indigenous campesino women, demand the immediate solution to our urgent needs, which the government has never resolved:

A: Childbirth clinics with gynecologists....

B: That child care facilities be built in the communities.

C: We ask the government to send sufficient food for the children in all rural communities including: milk, cornflour, rice, corn, soy, oil, beans, cheese, eggs, sugar, soup, oats, etc.

D: That kitchens and dining halls be built for the children in the communities....

E: We demand the construction of community corn dough mills and tortillerías based on the number of families in each community.

F: That they give us poultry, rabbit, sheep and pig farm projects, and also that we be provided with technical assistance and veterinarians.

G: We ask for bakery projects, which include the provision of ovens and ingredients.

H: We want artisan workshops to be built, equipped with machinery and raw materials.

I: Markets in which to sell our crafts at fair prices.

J: That schools be built where women can get technical training.

K: That there be preschools and maternal schools in rural communities, where children can play and grow in a morally and physically healthy way.

L: That as women we have sufficient transportation for the products we produce in our various projects.

Source: *Zapatistas! Documents of the New Mexican Revolution (December 31, 1993–June 12, 1994)* (New York: Autonomedia, 1994), 243, accessed January 9, 2018, http://lanic.utexas.edu/project/Zapatistas/Zapatistas_book.pdf.

SOURCE 22.5B

The Women's Revolutionary Law | January 1, 1994

[T]aking into account the situation of the woman worker in Mexico, the revolution supports their just demands for equality and justice in the following Women's Revolutionary Law.

First: Women, regardless of their race, creed, color or political affiliation, have the right to participate in the revolutionary struggle in a way determined by their desire and capacity.

Second: Women have the right to work and receive a just salary.

Third: Women have the right to decide the number of children they will have and care for.

Fourth: Women have the right to participate in the affairs of the community and hold positions of authority if they are freely and democratically elected.

Fifth: Women and their children have the right to primary attention in matters of health and nutrition.

Sixth: Women have the right to an education.

Seventh: Women have the right to choose their partner, and are not to be forced into marriage.

Eighth: Women shall not be beaten or physically mistreated by their family members or by strangers. Rape and attempted rape will be severely punished.

Ninth: Women will be able to occupy positions of leadership in the organization and hold military ranks in the revolutionary armed forces.

Source: *Zapatistas! Documents of the New Mexican Revolution (December 31, 1993–June 12, 1994)* (New York: Autonomedia, 1994), 38–39, accessed January 9, 2018, http://lanic.utexas.edu/project/Zapatistas/Zapatistas_book.pdf.

DOING HISTORY

1. **Identifying similarities:** What common concerns animate these sources?

2. **Defining differences:** What variations or conflicting feminist perspectives can you identify in these sources? What accounts for those differences?

3. **Considering change over time:** How do you think nineteenth-century Western feminists would have responded to each of these twentieth-century statements (see "Feminist Beginnings" in Chapter 16)?

4. **Evaluating global feminism:** What aspects of global feminism were most revolutionary, liberating, or threatening to established authorities and ways of living? To what extent do you think the goals of these varying feminist efforts have been realized?

Feminism: Tensions and Resistance

The globalization of the feminist movement after 1960 has transformed its scope and impact while also creating new tensions both within the movement and in the wider society. The two historians' voices that follow offer broad assessments of feminism. In Voice 22.1 Merry Wiesner-Hanks examines the movement's globalization after 1960 and the tensions that emerged among feminists. In Voice 22.2 Peter Stearns explores the different countercurrents that have resisted feminism since the 1960s.

■ According to Voice 22.1, what roles did the United Nations play in the modern feminist movement?

■ What motivations for opposing some goals of international feminism does Voice 22.2 identify?

■ **Integrating Primary and Secondary Sources:** How might Wiesner-Hanks and Stearns use the sources in this feature to support their overviews of the modern global feminist movement?

VOICE 22.1

Merry Wiesner-Hanks on International Feminism | 2011

By the 1960s, women in many parts of the world were dissatisfied with the pace at which they were achieving political and legal equality, and a second-wave women's movement began, often termed the "women's liberation movement." Women's groups pressured for an end to sex discrimination in hiring practices, pay rates, inheritance rights, and the granting of credit, they opened shelters for battered women, day care centers, and rape crisis centers, and pushed for university courses on women, and laws against sexual harassment. In Western countries they pushed for abortion rights, and in India they mobilized against dowries and dowry-related deaths. By the early 1970s, advocates of rights for homosexuals had also mobilized in many countries, sponsoring demonstrations, political action campaigns, and various types of self-help organizations. The United Nations declared 1975–1985 to be the International Decade for Women, and meetings discussing the status of women around the world

were held under UN auspices in Mexico City (1975), Copenhagen (1980), Nairobi (1985), and Beijing (1995). These meetings were sometimes divisive, pointing out the great differences in women's concerns around the world, with sexual orientation and female genital cutting often the most explosive issues. The official Platform for Action of the Beijing Conference sought to avoid some of these divisions by calling for a general "empowerment of women," noting that this would mean different things in different areas of the world.

Source: Merry E. Wiesner-Hanks, *Gender in History: Global Perspectives*, 2nd ed. (Oxford: Wiley Blackwell, 2011), 157–58.

VOICE 22.2

Peter Stearns on Resistance to Global Feminism | 2015

Two related trends emerged. The first . . . was the resurgence of religious and other conservatism, often directed explicitly against changes in gender relations. . . . Islamic, Hindu and many Christian fundamentalists all urged more traditional gender hierarchy and the importance of female modesty. . . .

Equally interesting, if less important numerically, was the growing group of women's leaders who objected to international standards because they were too Western and too individualistic. These were people who wanted women to have an active voice in their lives and societies but who did not find the international formulas persuasive. An Indian women's magazine thus objected to global consumerism on the grounds that it tended to force women to waste time and effort on personal beauty in the hope of finding and keeping men. Far better, in terms of real women's interests, was the Indian custom of arranged marriages, which made the Western appearances game irrelevant. . . .

Finally . . . at the grass-roots level, many ordinary women sought to effect compromise, using new standards to a degree but combining them with older goals. Thus a grandmother in Kenya talks of the importance of education for women, so they can fend for themselves, and also accepts new levels of birth control. But beneath this interestingly cosmopolitan surface she hopes not for individual fulfillment for her granddaughters, but for a revived family cohesion in which different generations of women will take care of each other, regardless of what the men do. International influences have had some effect here, but more on the means by which goals were to be met than on the purposes themselves.

Source: Peter N. Stearns, *Gender in World History*, 3rd ed. (New York: Routledge, 2015), 194–95.

CHAPTER
23

Global Processes

Demography, Culture, and the Environment

1900–present

In the early twenty-first century, a forty-five-year-old vegetable grower named Omar Imma Assayar moved with his wife and ten children from their rural village in the West African country of Chad to the capital city of N'Djamena. While living in the village, he had to get up early and carry his produce to the market in the city by bicycle. "My life is easier now," he explained. "I live right next to the market. I have more time to be with my family, and I can get a better price for my vegetables as well. . . . My one big wish is for my children to go to school."[1] ■

Omar and his family have both witnessed and participated in some of the major drivers of world history during the past century. His ten children have contributed to the enormous increase in human numbers. In moving to the capital of Chad, Omar joined millions of others in Africa, Asia, and Latin America who are seeking a better life in the city. In his desire to educate his children, he has also taken part in the vast expansion of literacy that has swept the planet during the past century. Not far from his new home is Lake Chad, which has shrunk drastically in response to climate change and overuse, linking his country to global patterns of environmental degradation. The life of this single individual then is connected to the global processes that conclude this account of the human journey during the twentieth century and beyond—massive population growth, widespread movement of people, changing patterns of cultural identity, and unprecedented human impact on the environment that sustains us all.

《 One World This composite NASA photograph, showing both the earth and the moon, reveals none of the national, ethnic, religious, or linguistic boundaries that have long divided humankind. Such pictures have both reflected and helped create a new planetary consciousness among growing numbers of people.

More People: Quadrupling Human Numbers

From about 1.65 billion people in 1900, world population soared to approximately 7.6 billion in 2018. In little more than a century, the human species had more than quadrupled its numbers. It had taken humankind several hundred thousand years to reach 1 billion people in the early nineteenth century. That number then reached 2 billion in roughly 1930, 3 billion in 1960, 4 billion in 1975, 5 billion in 1987, 6 billion in 1999, and 7 billion by 2012. The speed and extent of this twentieth-century **population explosion** have no parallel in the human past or in the history of primate life on the planet.[2] Equally striking is the distribution of this massive growth, as some 90 percent of it occurred in the developing countries of Asia, Africa, the Middle East, and Latin America. (See Snapshot: World Population Growth, 1950–2100, page 1022.) A striking shift in the demographic weight of the world's various peoples was clearly under way, with more to come in the twenty-first century.

The explanation for this massive demographic change lies in lower death rates. In 1945 roughly 20 people died each year for every 1,000 people in the world's population. By 2014 that figure was 8.[3] Infant mortality has dropped even more quickly, especially since the 1960s. New medical technologies such as antibiotics, disinfectants, vaccines, and x-rays played a major role in this unprecedented change. Many governments, including colonial regimes, as well as international agencies such as the United Nations, established public health programs to push improved sanitation and clean drinking water, while widening access to medical services. Various mosquito control measures sharply reduced death from malaria and yellow fever, while extensive vaccination campaigns eradicated smallpox by 1977.

As populations grew, innovations in agriculture enabled food production globally to keep up with, and even exceed, growing human numbers. A new "**Green Revolution**" greatly increased agricultural output through the use of tractors and mechanical harvesters; the massive application of chemical fertilizers, pesticides, and herbicides; and the development of high-yielding varieties of wheat and rice. All of this sustained the enormous population growth in developing countries.

By the end of the twentieth century, the rate of global population growth had begun to slow, as birth rates dropped all around the world. This transition to fewer births had occurred first in the more industrialized countries, where birth control measures were widely available, women were educated and pursuing careers, and large families were economically burdensome. By 1983, in a dozen or more countries in Europe, population growth had stopped altogether and then began to decline in a number of places. More recently, this pattern began to take hold in developing countries as well, associated with urbanization, with growing educational opportunities for girls, and with vigorous family-planning programs in many places. China's famous one-child family policy, introduced in 1980, was the most dramatic of these efforts. Nonetheless, the world's population has continued to rise and according to UN projections is expected to reach 9.7 billion in 2050 and 11.2 billion in 2100.

SEEKING THE MAIN POINT

How has technology shaped the demographic, cultural, and environmental changes of the past century?

Guided Reading Question

■ **CHANGE**
What specific factors allowed the human population to grow rapidly over the last century?

Landmarks for Chapter 23

| 1950 | 1960 | 1970 | 1980 | 1990 | 2000 | 2010 | 2020 |

THE WHOLE WORLD

1948 UN Universal Declaration of Human Rights

1960 Human population reaches 3 billion

1977 Smallpox eradicated

2007 50 percent of human population in towns/cities

2015 Paris Climate Agreement

ca. 1981 Beginning of AIDS epidemic

2018 Human population reaches 7.6 billion

THE GLOBAL NORTH

1962 Rachel Carson's *Silent Spring* launches modern environmentalism

1986 Chernobyl nuclear disaster

1992 Collapse of Grand Banks cod fishery

2001 Terrorist attack on World Trade Center

2017 U.S. announces withdrawal from Paris Climate Agreement

THE GLOBAL SOUTH

1949 Apartheid in South Africa

ca. 1965 Beginning of widespread deforestation in Amazon basin

1979 Iranian revolution

ca. 1990 Growing prominence of Indian Bollywood films

ca. 1980 Beginning of massive Chinese migration to coastal cities

2004–2005 Amman Message of a more tolerant Islam

1988 Al-Qaeda established

2014 Rise of the Islamic State

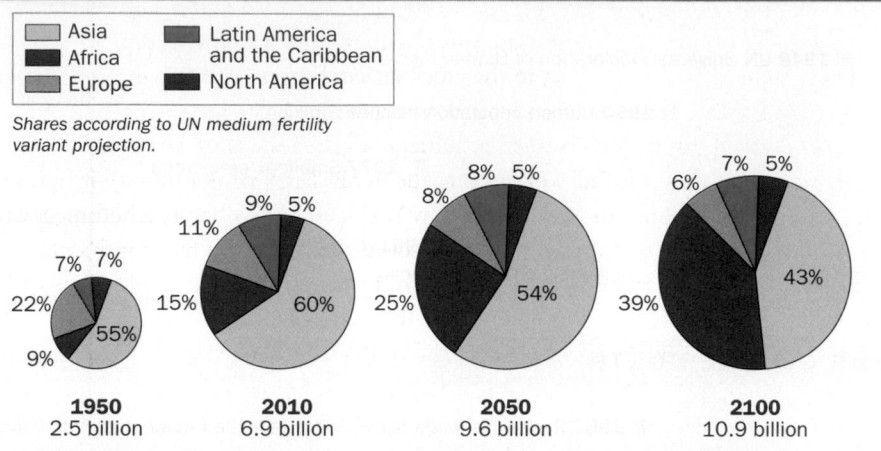

SNAPSHOT World Population Growth, 1950–2100 (projected)

Asia
Africa
Europe
Latin America and the Caribbean
North America

Shares according to UN medium fertility variant projection.

1950
2.5 billion

2010
6.9 billion

2050
9.6 billion

2100
10.9 billion

The European Environment Agency

People in Motion: Patterns of Migration

Growing numbers meant more people on the move. Transportation technology—steamships, trains, buses, cars, trucks, airplanes—has facilitated this vast circulation of people as well as goods. So has war, famine, climate change, poverty, industrialization, and urban growth. For millions of individuals, those decisions to move led to wrenching separations, exhilarating possibilities, immense disappointments, social conflicts, and new identities.

To the Cities: Global Urbanization

In the early twenty-first century, humankind reached a remarkable, though largely unnoticed, milestone. For the first time more people around the world lived in towns and cities than in the countryside. Although urban populations had been slowly increasing for centuries, it was massive **global urbanization**, the explosive growth of cities after 1900, that made the world an "urban place."[4] City-dwellers made up 15 percent of the world's population in 1900 and about 25 percent in 1950 before doubling again to 50 percent by 2007.

Mechanized farming and the Green Revolution had reduced the need for rural labor even as population was growing rapidly, pushing many to migrate to cities. Opportunities for employment in manufacturing, commerce, government, and the service industry drew such people to urban centers, where life expectancies were rising because of improving infrastructure and health care. "These shifts in population,"

PRACTICING HISTORICAL THINKING

What was the relationship (cause and effect) between human population growth and human migration during the past century?

wrote historian Michael Hunt, "stripped villages of healthy young men and young, unmarried women. Their departure tore the social fabric of villages, leaving wives, young children, and the elderly behind to struggle to preserve the tattered threads of economic and social life amidst a diminished circle of kin and compatriots."[5]

The timing of this movement to the cities varied. Europe and North America led the way, with about half their populations urbanized by 1950. Latin America, Africa, and Asia followed this general pattern in subsequent decades. And many of the urban centers to which they moved were unprecedentedly large **megacities** with populations of over 10 million. In 1950, only New York and Tokyo had reached megacity status, but by 2017 the world counted thirty-seven such cities on five continents.

This general trend of global urbanization hid a number of variations. The world wars and the Depression in the first half of the century slowed the growth of cities, especially in the industrialized world. World War II in particular damaged or destroyed innumerable cities in Western Europe, the Soviet Union, and East Asia. But some areas well away from conflict zones, such as Latin America, witnessed rapid urban growth. After 1945, the postwar economic boom led to the revival and growth of cities in Western Europe, parts of Asia, and North America. But in the communist world, where centralized command economies prevailed, migration to cities was sharply restricted. Passports and residency permits regulated migration in the Soviet Union, while in China the government created a household registration system in 1958 to limit movement of rural workers to cities. Communist governments, however, still embraced urban living, with over 1,000 new planned cities built in Eastern Europe and the Soviet Union in the aftermath of World War II.

From the 1970s, the decline in manufacturing in some regions of the developed world prompted many industrial cities to reinvent themselves as hubs for education, health care, logistics, information technology, and other services. And as industrialization took hold in the Global South after 1950, cities grew at around twice the rate of already industrialized regions. In the 1980s, the Chinese government loosened residency restrictions that had kept much of the population in the countryside, unleashing an unprecedented wave of urban migrants, so that by 2015, 56 percent of China's population lived in cities, dramatically up from 26 percent in 1990. Everywhere, cities attracted primarily young people from the countryside looking for better job prospects and educational, social, and cultural opportunities.

Even the most modern, well-managed cities had profound impacts on the environment, as large concentrations of people consumed huge amounts of food, energy, and water and in turn emitted enormous amounts of sewage, garbage, carbon dioxide, and toxic substances. Certainly, the poorly serviced slums and loosely regulated manufacturing enterprises of many cities across the planet created ecological disasters that destroyed the environment and damaged the health of residents, while elite neighborhoods boasted safe water, sewage systems, electricity, and fire and police services. On a per person basis, however, city living sometimes reduced electricity consumption and carbon emissions because public transportation, energy-efficient residences, and smaller families lessened the impact of humans on the environment.

Guided Reading Question

■ COMPARISON
What different patterns of urbanization were apparent during the past century?

Slums and Skyscrapers The enormous disparities that have accompanied urbanization in Latin America and elsewhere are illustrated in this photograph from São Paulo, Brazil. (Florian Kopp/imageBROKER/AGE Fotostock)

Everywhere, wealth was concentrated in cities, but inequality was all the more apparent because the rich and poor often lived in close proximity, with luxury apartment buildings, office blocks, and malls overlooking slums and shantytowns. Improvements in public and private transport in the twentieth century allowed cities to spread out as never before. In the early twentieth century some cities, like Munich, Chicago, Sydney, and Cape Town, had large middle-class suburban communities composed of single-family houses, and after mid-century similar communities developed in cities across the globe where incomes and transportation networks allowed. In other cities, like Jakarta, Rio de Janeiro, Nairobi, and Lagos, rapid urban sprawl was driven primarily by recent arrivals who settled in slums on empty pieces of land with few public services, often at the edges of cities or in marginal spaces like steep hillsides or areas prone to flooding. In 2006, a visitor described the Kibera slum in Nairobi as "a squeezed square mile . . . home to nearly one million people. . . . Most of them live in one-room mud or wattle huts or in wooden or basic stone houses often windowless. . . . The Kenyan state provides the huge, illegal sprawl with nothing—no sanitation, no roads, no hospitals. It is a massive ditch of mud and filth, with a brown dribble of a stream running through it."[6] Clearly population growth and the rise of cities did not solve, and probably exacerbated in many places, the problem of urban poverty.

Moving Abroad: Long-Distance Migration

While most "people in motion" traveled to nearby cities, a growing number moved abroad. (See Map 23.1.) Older patterns of migration, from Europe to the Americas, for example, continued and even accelerated in the early twentieth century, but migration patterns changed as the century progressed. (For earlier patterns of migration, see "Europeans in Motion" in Chapter 17 and "Economies of Wage Labor: Migration for Work" in Chapter 18.) The number of migrants from Africa and Latin America grew significantly, while Europe, earlier a leading source of long-distance emigrants, instead became an important destination for immigrants. From the 1920s on, the percentage of female migrants steadily grew, and in 2016 women constituted nearly half of all international migrants.

During the twentieth century states increasingly sought to control the flow of migrants across their borders, requiring travelers to possess passports and creating numerous administrative categories to describe migrants—asylum seekers, guest workers, refugees, tourists, students, climate refugees, illegals, and undocumented persons. Since World War II, these efforts to regulate borders have helped create enormous increases in refugees as desperate individuals find routes for flight shut off, leaving many millions living in refugee camps, often for generations. The situation of Abdallah Hajji, a Somalian refugee in Kenya in 2016, was typical of displaced people around the world: "I arrived . . . in 1994, since then I never moved out of here. I can't return because it's not safe now."[7]

The twentieth century also witnessed new patterns of human migration driven by war, revolution, the end of empire, and the emergence of new nation-states—many of which proved less tolerant of ethnic minorities than the empires that they replaced. The collapse of the Ottoman Empire following World War I prompted a large-scale exchange of populations as over a million Greek Orthodox Christians from Turkey relocated to Greece, while some 400,000 Turkish-speaking Muslims living in Greece moved in the other direction. Fleeing anti-Semitism, fascism, and the Holocaust, Jews immigrated to what is now Israel in large numbers, generating in the process a flow of Palestinian refugees to settlements in neighboring countries. Indian independence from Britain in 1947 resulted in the partition of the region along sectarian lines, forcing millions to migrate. In Rwanda, massacres by Hutus in July 1994 required over a million Tutsis to flee their homes, while the ultimate victory of the Tutsis sparked an even larger exodus of Hutus. Still other peoples moved as refugees fleeing violence or political oppression in places such as Vietnam, Cambodia, Sudan, Uganda, Cuba, Haiti, Iraq, Afghanistan, and Syria.

Perhaps the most significant pattern of global migration since the 1960s has featured a vast movement of people from the developing countries of Asia, Africa, and Latin America to the industrialized world of Europe and North America, with smaller flows to Australia and the oil rich states of the Persian Gulf. Pakistanis, Indians, and West Indians moved to Great Britain; Algerians and West Africans to France; Turks and Kurds to Germany; Filipinos, Koreans, Cubans, Mexicans, and Haitians to the United States; and Egyptians, Pakistanis, Bangladeshis, and smaller numbers of highly skilled Westerners to the Persian Gulf states.

Much of this involved **labor migration**, as people moved, often illegally and with few skills, to escape poverty in their own lands, drawn by a belief that employment opportunities and a better future awaited them in the developed countries. Often their journeys have been dangerous, as migrants have confronted long treks through burning deserts in the American Southwest or braved dangerous crossings of the Mediterranean Sea to Europe in rickety and overcrowded vessels. Many depended on expensive and sometimes unreliable human smugglers. Smaller numbers of highly skilled and university-trained people, such as doctors and computer scientists, came in search of professional opportunities less available in their own countries.

Guided Reading Question

■ **CONNECTION**
How did patterns of international migration change during the past century, and with what results?

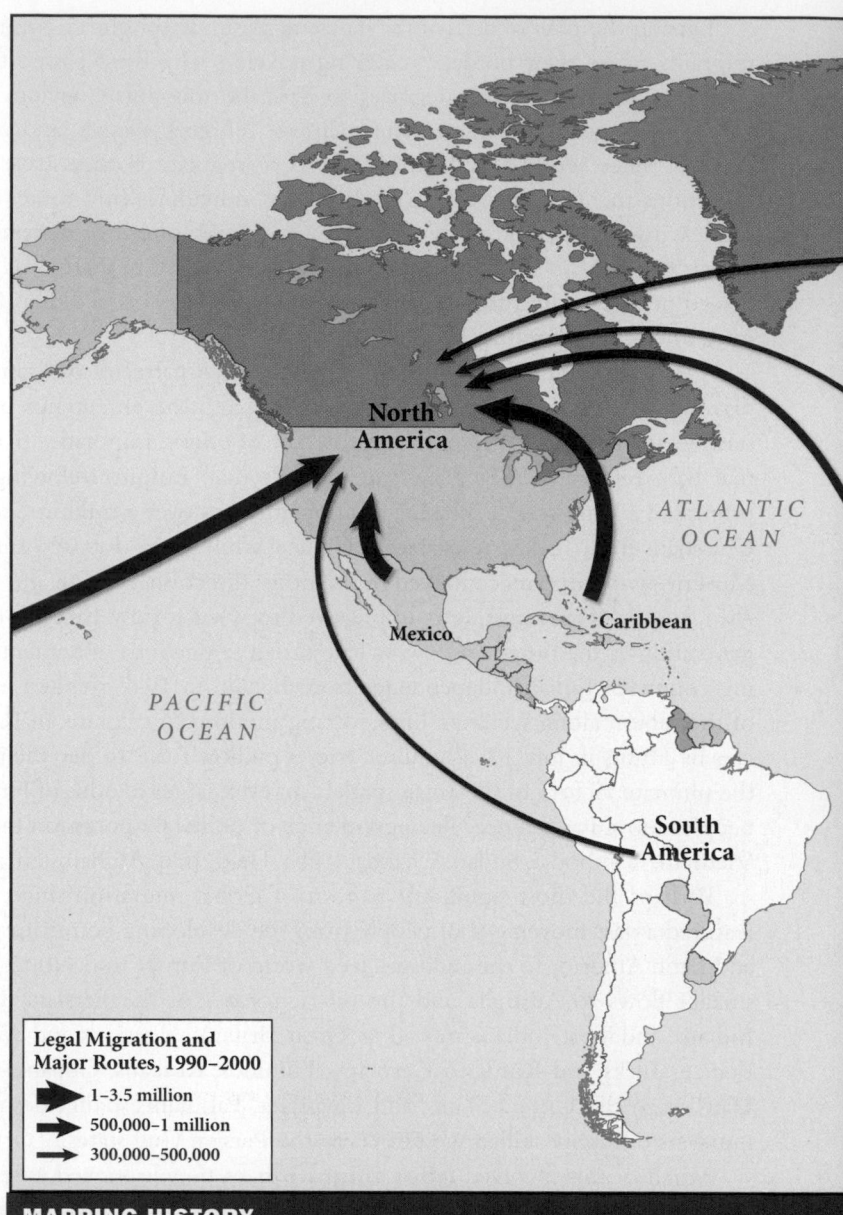

Legal Migration and
Major Routes, 1990–2000

➤ 1–3.5 million

➤ 500,000–1 million

➤ 300,000–500,000

MAPPING HISTORY

Map 23.1 Global Migration Patterns, 1990–2005

The late twentieth and early twenty-first centuries witnessed a large-scale movement of people, primarily from the Global South to the Global North.
(Data from United Nations, World Bank, 2005; OEDC, 2001)

READING THE MAP: Which regions produced the most emigrants? Which regions received the most immigrants? ➡

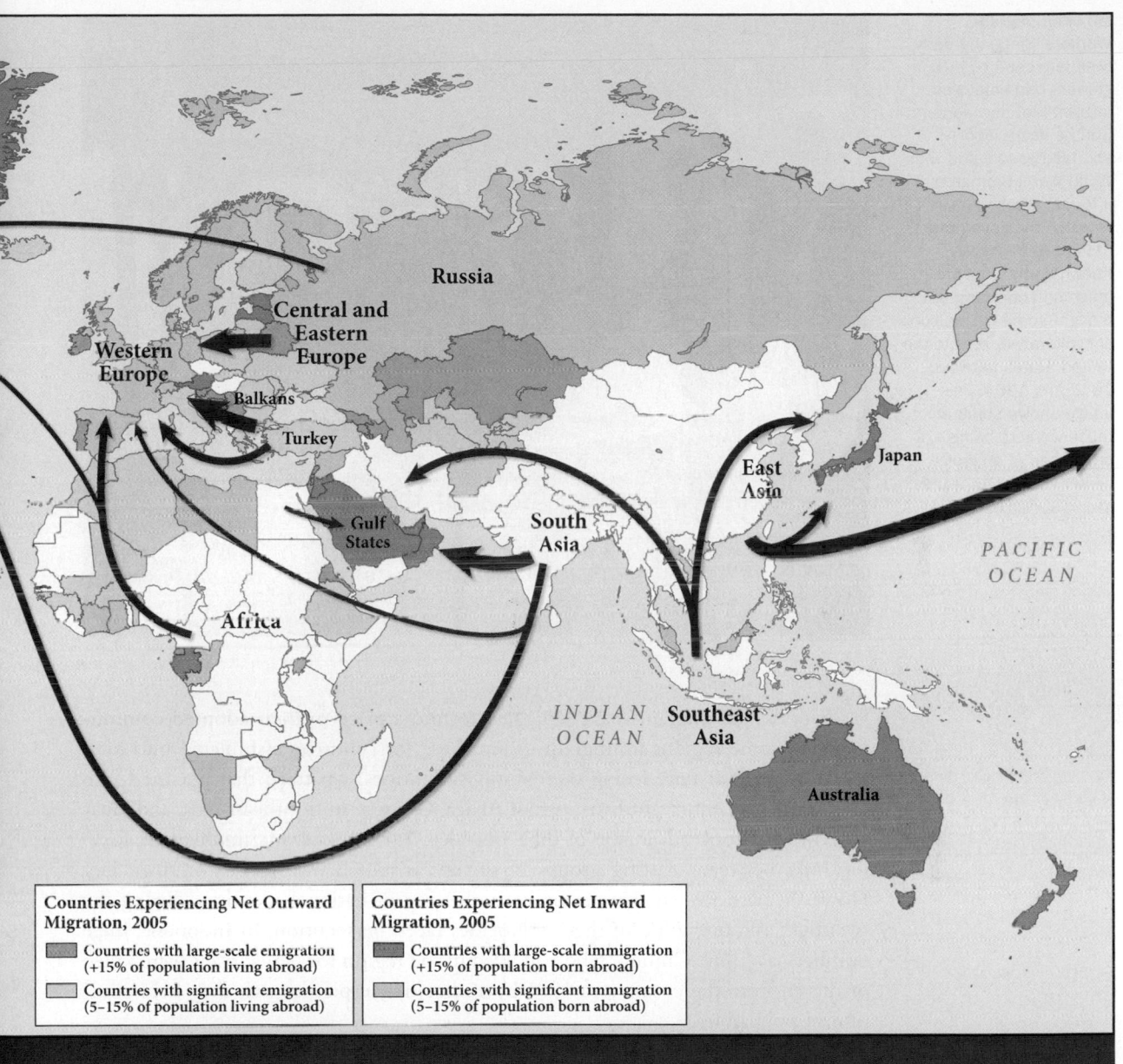

Countries Experiencing Net Outward Migration, 2005

◼ Countries with large-scale emigration (+15% of population living abroad)

◻ Countries with significant emigration (5–15% of population living abroad)

Countries Experiencing Net Inward Migration, 2005

◼ Countries with large-scale immigration (+15% of population born abroad)

◻ Countries with significant immigration (5–15% of population born abroad)

MAKING CONNECTIONS: Does this map offer any evidence to support the idea that migration patterns at the end of the twentieth century were still influenced by older links between Europe and its overseas empires?

Mexican Migrant Workers Since the early twentieth century, U.S. growers had employed migrant Mexican workers. But the acute labor shortage associated with World War II prompted a formal agreement between the governments of the two countries. Known as the Bracero (migrant labor) program, it brought some 4.5 million agricultural workers to the United States between 1942 and 1964. This image shows some of these workers being processed at a labor center in Hidalgo, Texas, in 1959. (AP/REX/Shutterstock)

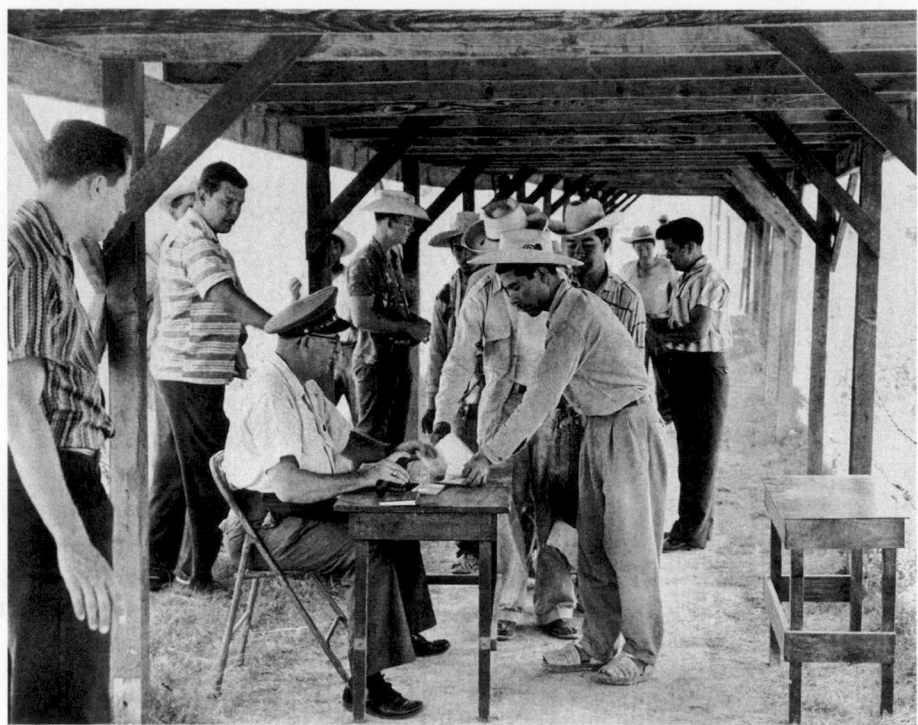

Everywhere migrants have struggled to find a place in their adopted communities. In some regions immigrant groups have for centuries assimilated into local societies without fully losing their distinct identities, a pattern that persisted into the twentieth century. Indians in East Africa, Chinese in Southeast Asia, and Japanese in Peru took advantage of their outsider status to become middlemen, forging links between existing groups in society as merchants, traders, or financiers. However, with the emergence or strengthening of national identities during the twentieth century, some of these minorities faced persecution. In Indonesia, huge numbers of ethnic Chinese who had lived in the region for generations were killed or driven from the country in 1965 by authorities suspicious that they held communist sympathies.

The most important countries of arrival for twentieth-century migrants—the United States, Canada, Australia, and, since the 1960s, Western Europe—all expected that immigrants would assimilate into their societies by adopting the language, political values, and cultural norms of the host society. Many migrants agreed, viewing assimilation as a pathway to better economic opportunities and social status even if it often took several generations for a migrant family to fully integrate into the host society. Despite this pressure toward assimilation, migrants also maintained aspects of their homelands' cultures, some of which were embraced by their new communities. Immigrants often opened eateries featuring dishes from their countries of origin, such as a Mexican tamale food truck in Los Angeles, an Indian curry house in London, or a Chinese noodle café in Sydney.

The expectation of migrant assimilation in the West also brought tensions and conflict, particularly over cultural integration. In France, for instance, the immigration of Muslims, mostly from North Africa, has sparked controversy over women's clothing. A French law in 2004 forbade the practice of wearing headscarves in public schools on the grounds that it compromised the secularism of French education and represented the repression of women. But many Muslim women strongly objected to the law, arguing that it undermined their freedom of religion and violated their cultural traditions. As one woman put it, "France is supposed to be a free country. Nowadays women have the right to take their clothes off but not put them on."[8] In the United States large-scale migration in recent decades from Latin America has led some to demand that English be designated the official language of the country. More recently, fears that immigrants openly hostile to Western values might bring terrorism to host societies have led to calls to limit or refuse admission to refugees from some Islamic countries. At the same time, other voices have advocated the benefits of multiculturalism for the globalized and knowledge-based societies and economies of the twenty-first century.

A final category of long-distance migrants has encompassed those engaged in short-term travel. International tourist arrivals grew from 25 million in 1950 to 988 million in 2011. Businesspeople in search of profits and students in search of education have crisscrossed the world in large numbers. These travelers have participated in "an unprecedented new era of transnational ties and mobility" that is only a few decades old.[9]

Microbes in Motion: Disease and Recent History

People in motion have carried not only their cultures but also their microbes. Everywhere growing populations, urban living, and unprecedented mobility created more efficient pathways for deadly diseases to mutate and spread across the globe. Even before the emergence of commercial air travel, the early twentieth century witnessed the worst pandemic in human history when three waves of an **influenza pandemic** swept across the globe in 1918 and 1919, carried by demobilized soldiers, refugees, and other dislocated people returning home from World War I. One American army doctor at a base just outside of Boston reported: "We used to go down to the morgue and look at the boys laid out in long rows. It beats any sight they ever had in France after a battle."[10] Between 50 and 100 million people died in the pandemic—five to ten times more than perished on the battlefields of World War I.

Another new pathogen, human immunodeficiency virus (HIV), which causes acquired immune deficiency syndrome (AIDS), sparked a second global pandemic beginning in the 1980s. Unlike the influenza virus of 1918, **HIV/AIDS** spread primarily through sexual contact, contaminated blood products, or the sharing of

HIV/AIDS: A Global Pandemic From its place of origin in West Central Africa in the early twentieth century, HIV/AIDS has spread widely since the 1980s to become a global pandemic. This billboard from Mumbai, India, in 2015 illustrates the global presence of that disease and global efforts to contain it. (Ahmed Divyakant Solanki/EPA/REX/Shutterstock)

needles by intravenous drug users. Nonetheless, the disease has spread rapidly across the globe. In 2016 nearly 37 million people lived with HIV, while tens of millions have died since the 1980s of AIDS or its complications. In sub-Saharan Africa, where the disease first emerged—and where nearly 70 percent of those currently infected reside—the disease was spread in part by long-distance truck drivers and the commercial sex workers they frequented on their travels. However, the connected world that facilitated its spread also produced treatments, which have transformed this disease from a major killer into a serious but chronic and manageable disease for those with access to the latest medicines.

Modern communication meant that in the twentieth century reports of new diseases spread faster than ever before. Concerned communities and their governments took action to try to keep diseases out or limit their spread by ordering measures like border checks and quarantines. Recognizing the potentially destabilizing economic, social, and political effects of pandemics, governments created both national and international institutions, like the World Health Organization, to help coordinate efforts to combat disease within national borders and beyond. In the early twenty-first century, new threats—severe acute respiratory syndrome (SARS), the Ebola virus, and the Zika virus, among others—prompted large-scale international efforts to identify, track, and stop their spread. Thus, while the twentieth century saw humankind mobilize its resources as never before to combat deadly pandemics, the more connected and urbanized world of recent times has left us more vulnerable to such outbreaks than in the past.

Cultural Identity in an Entangled World

Large and impersonal global processes (industrialization, migration, and urbanization, for example) have had a profound and personal impact at the level of individual identity—how people define the communities to which they belong, the religions with which they affiliate, and even the food they eat, the clothes they wear, and the music they enjoy. Certainly older patterns of cultural identity have been challenged as individuals have come up against people and cultures quite different from their own. Secular ideas and values were often at odds with traditional religious outlooks; feminist ideas confronted patriarchal assumptions; socialist or communist thinking undermined the legitimacy of deeply rooted social hierarchies. Among the identities in question during the past century, those of political and religious loyalty loomed large.

Race, Nation, and Ethnicity

Nineteenth-century Europe gave rise to an elaborate ideology of "race" as a fundamental distinction among human communities based on allegedly permanent biological characteristics. (See "Industry and Empire" in Chapter 18.) But it was in the twentieth century that such ideas achieved their greatest prominence, shaping individual behavior, institutional practices, and government policies alike. Three societies in particular stand out as openly racist regimes: Nazi Germany, the southern United States from the 1890s to the 1950s, and apartheid-era South Africa. All of them officially sanctioned explicitly racist ideologies, prohibited marriage across racial lines, legislated extreme forms of social segregation, denied all political rights to Jews or blacks, and deliberately kept Jews or blacks in poverty.

In many other places, race was a pervasive reality, though perhaps racist thinking was less officially endorsed. Racial distinctions and white supremacy were prominent in European thinking and central features within all of the European colonies in Africa and Asia, generating in turn a new racial awareness among many colonized people. Aime Cesaire, a poet from the French island of Martinique in the Caribbean region, coined the term "negritude," which he defined in 1939 as "the simple recognition of the fact that one is black."[11] Black, Indian, and mixed-race people in Latin America clearly experienced discrimination and disadvantage in relationship to whites or Europeans, even in the absence of legal constraints.

Guided Reading Question

■ **CHANGE**
In what ways have racial, national, and ethnic identities found expression during the past century?

During the second half of the twentieth century, race lost much of its public legitimacy as a social distinction, discredited in part by the horrors of the Nazi regime. As the American author Barbara Ehrenreich put it: "Hitler gave race a bad name." Furthermore, scholars thoroughly debunked the connection between biology and culture or behavior, which was so central to racial thinking. But perhaps most importantly, the sharp critique of white bigotry and discrimination that accompanied the surging independence movements across Asia and Africa made overt racism globally illegitimate. The 1948 UN Declaration of Human Rights inscribed this rejection of racism as a new global moral standard, even as it persisted in practice in many places.

Even more pervasive than race as a form of individual identity and political loyalty has been that of nationalism, and the two have sometimes overlapped. Loyalty to national states and their presumed interests drove the world wars of the past century and undermined empires around the globe. But if nation-states and national loyalties largely triumphed during the past century, they also faced challenges. Pan-African and pan-Arab aspirations beckoned to those seeking a larger identity and loyalty, though they never achieved an effective political expression. The European Union did give concrete political meaning to a broader European identity in the aftermath of two disastrous wars, though by the early twenty-first century the Union appeared shaky in the face of rising nationalist sentiments and the British decision to withdraw. Globalization too challenged national loyalties as visions of a world without borders and destructive national rivalries appealed to many. The League of Nations and the United Nations gave expression to such visions. The growth of international economic linkages as well as an increasing global awareness of problems common to all of humankind generated for some a sense of global citizenship, a cosmopolitan feeling of being at home in the world as a whole. Pictures of the earth viewed from the moon or outer space—a beautiful but solitary planet in an immense cosmos—came to symbolize this one-world sensibility. Any number of transnational organizations—the Red Cross, Amnesty International, sister-city projects, a vast array of international professional, charitable, and scientific groups—have also articulated a distinctly international outlook.

If globalization represented an external challenge to national loyalties and existing nation-states, a serious internal challenge took shape as ethnically based separatist movements. Most of the world's states, after all, contained several, and sometimes many, culturally distinct peoples. Such peoples readily adopted the rhetoric and logic of nationalism, arguing that they too deserved some separate political status such as greater autonomy or full independence. Under the pressure of such movements, a number of states have in fact disintegrated. British India dissolved immediately upon independence into a Muslim Pakistan and largely Hindu India. In the early 1990s, Czechoslovakia and Yugoslavia fragmented, the former peacefully and the latter amid great violence. In northeastern Africa, Eritrea seceded from Ethiopia in 1993, and in 2011 South Sudan claimed independence from the Republic of Sudan, both of them following decades of civil war. Even where a separate state was not achieved, ethnic separatist movements have threatened the integrity of existing nation-states. Scotland has sought to exit from the United Kingdom, Quebec from Canada, Tibet from China, the Basques from Spain, Igbo-speaking peoples from Nigeria, and the Moro people from the Philippines. Many Russians living in eastern Ukraine would prefer annexation by Russia, and many Kurds living in Iraq, Iran, Syria, and Turkey aspire to an independent Kurdistan.

Ethnic Cleansing in Vukovar, Croatia The disintegration of the multiethnic state of Yugoslavia in southeastern Europe during the 1990s gave rise to numerous violent conflicts among its various ethnic groups. This photograph shows Croatians making their way through the rubble of the city of Vukovar, from which some 20,000 of them had been expelled by Serbian troops. The city was almost completely destroyed and largely "cleansed" of its non-Serb population. (© Ron Haviv/VII/Redux)

These various cultural identities—racial, national, ethnic, and global—have become politically and personally meaningful for much of the world's population even as they have mixed and mingled in many ways. German nationalism in the Nazi era found expression in racial terms. Some people found it possible to embrace both an ethnic heritage and loyalty to a larger nation with little contradiction, as many Irish, Italians, Hispanics, and African Americans have done in the United States. A sense of global citizenship, in the struggle against climate change, for example, remains compatible with loyalty to a particular country.

Popular Culture on the Move

Related to these cultural and political identities have been the many elements of popular culture that have increasingly permeated social life during the past century. They too have been on the move around the world in a process widely known as **cultural globalization**. It has been a many-sided phenomenon, with the heaviest currents moving from the West to the rest of the world. From the 1920s on,

Hollywood films have been a major cultural export of the United States. Western music, including classical, jazz, rock and roll, and rap, has gained large audiences across the planet. By the late twentieth century, the United States accounted for roughly 75 percent of world TV programming exports. All of this has shaped patterns of taste globally. When American TV was introduced into Fiji in the 1990s, bulimia and anorexia among teenage girls soon increased substantially, as girls sought to acquire the slender body style of their TV favorites.

Guided Reading Question

....

■ **CONNECTION**

What elements of popular culture have moved globally during the past century?

Beyond film, TV, and music, other elements of Western culture have gained widespread acceptance around the world. English has become a world language, with a billion or more people able to use it at some level, particularly within educated and elite circles. Western sports such as soccer, cricket, basketball, and baseball have an international presence. In 2015, more than 36,000 McDonald's restaurants in over 100 countries served 69 million people daily. And Western fashions—jeans, suits and ties, miniskirts, white wedding dresses—have become common in many places, sometimes losing their direct association with the West.

All of this has been driven by the dominance of the West in world affairs over the past several centuries and the impulse of many to imitate the ways of the powerful. But the assimilation of Western cultural forms has also come to symbolize modernity, inclusion in an emerging global culture, and sometimes liberation or rebellion, especially among the young. Such a sensibility informed Kemal Atatürk's desire for "civilized, international dress" for Turkish men when he sought to impose Western-style clothing on them during the 1920s and 1930s. The outlook was similar for liberated young women in Japan who imitated the dress style of Western "flappers" during the same time. They were *moga* or "modern girls" whose country was becoming a "province of the world."

The global spread of Western culture has raised fears in many places about cultural homogenization or cultural imperialism threatening local or national cultures, values, and traditions. Like other forms of globalization, the cultural variant of this larger process has witnessed not only enthusiastic embrace but also pushback, much of which has targeted the outsized American influence in the world. Communist Party officials in the Soviet Union, for example, were suspicious of the growing popularity of American jazz and later rock and roll. Associating these musical forms with Western individualistic values of spontaneity, open sexuality, and opposition to authority, they tried periodically to suppress them, though without much success.

In the Islamic world, pushback against cultural "contamination" from the West has been particularly prominent, especially in religiously fundamentalist circles. The Ayatollah Khomeini, architect of Iran's Islamic revolution, strongly expressed this outlook:

> Just what is the social life we are talking about? Is it those hotbeds of immorality called theatres, cinemas, dancing, and music? Is it the promiscuous presence in the streets of lusting young men and women with arms, chests, and thighs bared? Is it the ludicrous wearing of a hat like the Europeans or the imitation of their habit of wine drinking . . . [or] the disrobed women to

be seen on the thoroughfares and in swimming pools? . . .[12]

Efforts to protect national languages have also prompted resistance to cultural globalization. The French Academy, for example, has long been on the lookout for English terms that have crept into general usage while urging their replacement by French equivalents. Chinese authorities have sought to require foreign firms to use Chinese terms for their products, and in 2012 over 100 Chinese scholars urged the removal of English words from a prominent Chinese dictionary.

But the cultural flows of the past century have moved in many directions, not simply outward from the United States and Europe. In exchange

Yoga in the United States The cultural dimension of globalization is illustrated in the spread of yoga, a mind-body practice from India that has become a part of global culture. This photo shows an outdoor yoga class held in New York's Time's Square to celebrate the summer solstice in 2017. (Brazil Photo Press/Alamy)

for Big Macs, Americans and Europeans received Chinese, Indian, Thai, Mexican, and Ethiopian cuisine. Yoga, originally a mind-body practice of Indian origin, took hold widely in the West and elsewhere, losing much of its earlier association with spiritual practice and becoming a form of exercise or relaxation. India's huge film industry, known as Bollywood, had a major cultural impact in the Soviet Union, Western Europe, the United States, and Latin America. India-based Ayurvedic medicine and traditional Chinese medicine, including acupuncture, have become widely used "alternative" medical treatment in Europe and North America. Japanese and Chinese martial arts have attracted numerous participants in the West and have been featured in many highly popular films. Latin American telenovelas or "soap operas" have enthralled audiences around the world. Korean popular culture, including TV dramas, movies, and music, has taken hold widely in East and Southeast Asia. Congolese music, sometimes blended with Latin American dance rhythms, spread widely throughout Africa and by the 1980s attracted eager audiences in Europe as well. Jamaican-based reggae music has extended around the world, while its superstar Bob Marley became an international icon. In short, cultural traffic in the entangled world of the past century has moved in many directions.

Religion and Global Modernity

Among the various expressions of cultural identity during the past century, religion has often provoked perhaps the deepest personal response among individuals and has provided a potent source of identity in social and political life. Some of

Religion and Soviet Communism This postcard from the 1930s illustrates Soviet hostility to religion as it depicts a Soviet worker against the background of modern industrial life smashing the symbols of Muslim, Christian, and Jewish religion. (Postcard by Boris Grigorievich Klinch [also Garri Petrushanskii] [1892–1946]/Private Collection/Photo © Tobie Mathew Collection/Bridgeman Images)

these responses were highly critical of religion, while others affirmed and sought to renew or revitalize religious belief and practice.

On the critical side, many of the most "advanced" thinkers of the past several hundred years—Enlightenment writers in the eighteenth century, Karl Marx in the nineteenth, and many academics and secular-minded intellectuals in the twentieth— believed that religion was headed for extinction in the face of modernity, science, communism, or globalization. In some respects, that prediction seemed to come true during the twentieth century and beyond. Soviet authorities, viewing religion as a backward-looking bulwark of an exploiting feudal or capitalist class, closed many churches and seminaries, promoted atheism in public education, prohibited any display of religion in public or the media, and denied believers access to better jobs and official positions. In several modernizing Islamic countries, the role of religion in public life was sharply restricted. Kemal Atatürk in Turkey sought to relegate Islam to the personal and private realm, arguing that "Islam will be elevated, if it will cease to be a political instrument." (See Working with Evidence, Source 23.1, page 1054.)

Even without such state action, religious belief and practice during the past century declined sharply in the major European countries such as Britain, France, Italy, and the Netherlands. A recent poll found that in 2014 almost 23 percent of Americans defined themselves as religiously unaffiliated, while only 36 percent claimed to attend religious services every week.[13] Moreover, the spread of a scientific culture around the world persuaded small minorities everywhere, often among the most highly educated, that the only realities worth considering were those that could be measured with the techniques of science. To such people, all else was superstition, born of ignorance.

Nevertheless, the far more prominent trends of the last century have involved the further spread of major world religions, their resurgence in new forms, their opposition to elements of a secular and global modernity, and their political role as a source of community identity and conflict. Contrary to earlier expectations, religion has played an unexpectedly powerful role in this most recent century.

Buddhism, Christianity, and Islam had long functioned as transregional cultures and continued to do so in the twentieth century. Buddhist ideas and practices such as meditation found a warm reception in the West, and Buddhism has been reviving in China since the 1970s. Christianity of various kinds spread widely in non–Muslim Africa and South Korea, less extensively in parts of India, and after 1975 was growing even in China. By 2016 Christianity was no longer a primarily European or North American religion, as some 62 percent of its adherents lived in Asia, Africa, Oceania, and Latin America. Islam too continued its centuries-long spread in Asia and Africa, while migrants from the Islamic world have planted their religion solidly in the West, constructing over 2,000 mosques in the United States by 2010. Sufi mystical practices have attracted the attention of many in the West who have grown disillusioned with conventional religion.

Religious vitality in the twentieth century was expressed also in the vigorous response of those traditions to the modernizing and globalizing world. One such response has been widely called **religious fundamentalism**—a militant piety hostile to secularism and religious pluralism—that took shape to some extent in every major religious tradition. Many features of the modern world, after all, appeared threatening to established religion. The scientific and secular focus of global modernity challenged the core beliefs of religion, with its focus on an unseen realm of reality. Furthermore, the social upheavals connected with capitalism, industrialization, imperialism, and globalization thoroughly upset customary class, family, and gender relationships that had long been sanctified by religious tradition.

To such threats deriving from a globalized modern culture, fundamentalism represented a religious response, characterized by one scholar as "embattled forms of spirituality . . . experienced as a cosmic war between the forces of good and evil."[14] The term "fundamentalism" came from the United States, where religious conservatives in the early twentieth century were outraged and threatened by many recent developments: the growth of secularism; critical and "scientific" approaches to the Bible; Darwin's concept of evolution; liberal versions of Christianity that emphasized ethical behavior rather than personal salvation; the triumph of communism in the Soviet Union, which adopted atheism as its official doctrine; and postwar labor strikes that carried echoes of the Russian Revolution to many conservatives.

Feeling that Christianity itself was at stake, they called for a return to the "fundamentals" of the faith, which included a belief in the literal truthfulness of the scriptures, in the virgin birth and physical resurrection of Jesus, and in miracles. After World War II, American Protestant fundamentalists came to oppose political liberalism and "big government," the sexual revolution of the 1960s, homosexuality and abortion rights, and secular humanism generally. From the 1970s on, they entered the political arena as the "religious right," determined to return America to a "godly path."

In the very different setting of independent India, another fundamentalist movement—known as **Hindutva** (Hindu nationalism)—took shape during the 1980s. Like American fundamentalism, it represented a politicization of religion within a democratic context. To its advocates, India was, and always had been, an essentially Hindu land, even though it had been overwhelmed in recent centuries by Muslim invaders, then by the Christian British, and most recently by the secular

Guided Reading Question
....
■ **COMPARISON**
What do the various "fundamentalist" movements have in common?

state of the post-independence decades. The leaders of modern India, they argued, and particularly its first prime minister, Jawaharlal Nehru, were "the self-proclaimed secularists who . . . seek to remake India in the Western image," while repudiating its basically Hindu religious character. The Hindutva movement took political shape in an increasingly popular party called the Bharatiya Janata Party (BJP), promoting a distinctly Hindu identity in education, culture, and religion. Muslims in particular were sometimes defined as outsiders, potentially more loyal to a Muslim Pakistan than to India. The BJP's sweeping victory in national elections in 2014 raised questions about how its Hindu nationalism would fare in twenty-first-century India.

Nowhere were fundamentalist religious responses to political, social, and cultural change more intense or varied than within the Muslim world. Conquest and colonial rule; awareness of the huge technological and economic gap between Islamic and European civilizations; the disappearance of the Ottoman Empire, long the chief Islamic state; elite enchantment with Western culture; the retreat of Islam for many to the realm of private life—all of this had sapped the cultural self-confidence of many Muslims by the mid-twentieth century. Political independence for former colonies certainly represented a victory for Islamic societies, but it had given rise to major states—Egypt, Pakistan, Indonesia, Iraq, Algeria, and others—that pursued essentially Western and secular policies of nationalism, socialism, and economic development, often with only lip service to an Islamic identity.

Even worse, these policies were not very successful. Vastly overcrowded cities with few services, widespread unemployment, pervasive corruption, slow economic growth, a mounting gap between the rich and poor—all of this flew in the face of the great expectations that had accompanied the struggle against European domination. Despite formal independence, foreign intrusion still persisted. Israel, widely regarded as an outpost of the West, had been reestablished as a Jewish state in the very center of the Islamic world in 1948. In 1967, Israel inflicted a devastating defeat on Arab forces in the Six-Day War and seized various Arab territories, including the holy city of Jerusalem. Furthermore, broader signs of Western cultural penetration persisted—secular schools, alcohol, Barbie dolls, European and American movies, miniskirts, and more. (See Zooming In: Barbie and Her Competitors in the Muslim World, page 1040.) Yet another example of Western-style modernity derived from the largely secular leader of independent Tunisia, Habib Bourguiba (president 1959–1987), who argued against the veil for women and polygamy for men and even discouraged his people from fasting during Ramadan.

To all of these failed policies and Western intrusions, many Muslims objected strongly. An emerging fundamentalist movement argued that it was the departure from Islamic principles that had led the Islamic world into its sorry state, and only a return to the "straight path of Islam" would ensure a revival of Muslim societies. To politically militant Islamists, this meant the overthrow of those Muslim governments that had allowed these tragedies and their replacement by regimes that would purify Islamic practice while enforcing Islamic law and piety in public life. One of the leaders of an Egyptian Islamist group put the matter succinctly:

Guided Reading Question

■ **CHANGE**

What factors help to explain the rise of Islamic fundamentalism? In what different ways was it expressed?

We have to establish the Rule of God's Religion in our own country first, and to make the Word of God supreme. . . . There is no doubt that the first battlefield for jihad is the extermination of these infidel leaders and to replace them by a complete Islamic Order.[15]

Islamic fundamentalists won a significant victory in 1979 when the Iranian revolution chased out the country's long-reigning monarch, the shah of Iran. The leader of the revolution, the Ayatollah Khomeini, believed that the purpose of government was to apply the law of Allah as expressed in the *sharia*. Thus all judges now had to be competent in Islamic law, and those lacking that

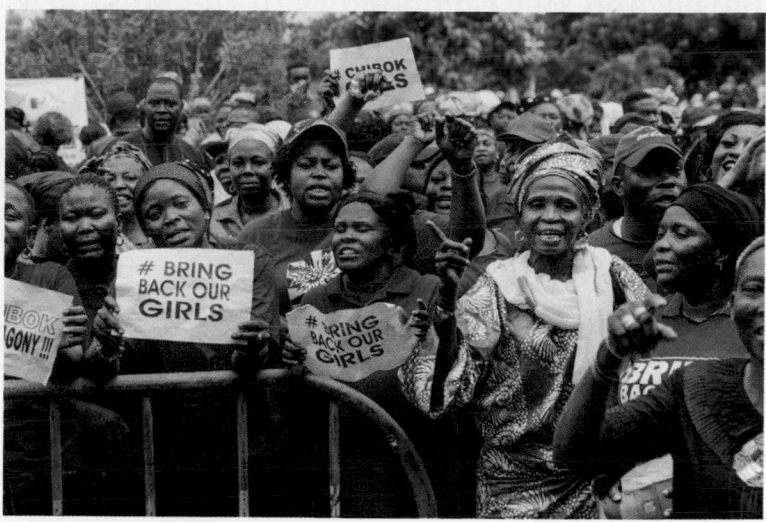

Confronting Islamic Radicalism The Nigerian Islamic radical group Boko Haram ("Western influence is a sacrilege") has waged a violent campaign of terror in support of a highly restrictive version of sharia law, killing thousands and displacing millions in northeastern Nigeria. In 2014 the group abducted over 200 schoolgirls, prompting this demonstration in Lagos to "bring back our girls." (Xinhua/Alamy)

qualification were dismissed. The secular law codes under which the shah's government had operated were discarded in favor of those based solely on Islamic precedents. The new government soon closed some 200 universities and colleges for two years while textbooks, curricula, and faculty were "purified" of un-Islamic influences. Elementary and secondary schools, largely secular under the shah, now gave priority to religious instruction and the teaching of Arabic, even as about 40,000 teachers lost their jobs for lack of sufficient Islamic piety. Pre-Islamic Persian literature and history were now out of favor, while the history of Islam and Iran's revolution predominated in schools and the mass media. Sharp restriction of the lives of women represented a major element of this religious revolution. (See Historians' Voices: Perspectives on the Iranian Revolution, page 1065.)

A further expression of **Islamic radicalism** lay in violent attacks, largely against civilian targets, undertaken by radical groups such as al-Qaeda, the Taliban, Boko Haram, and the Islamic State. The most widely known of these attacks occurred on September 11, 2001, when the World Trade Center in New York and other targets were attacked. Subsequent assaults targeted various European and Russian cities, but this kind of terrorist violence was directed far more often and with far greater casualties against targets in the Islamic world itself, including Iraq, Pakistan, Afghanistan, Saudi Arabia, India, Indonesia, Yemen, Somalia, and Nigeria.

Violence, however, was not the only response of Islamic fundamentalists or radicals. All over the Muslim world, from North Africa to Indonesia, Islamic renewal movements spawned organizations that operated legally to provide social

Barbie and Her Competitors in the Muslim World

"I think every Barbie doll is more harmful than an American missile," declared Iranian toy seller Masoumeh Rahimi in 2002. To Rahimi, Barbie's revealing clothing, her shapely appearance, and her close association with Ken, her longtime unmarried companion, were "foreign to Iran's culture."[16] Thus Rahimi warmly welcomed the arrival in 2002 of Sara and Dara, Iranian Muslim dolls meant to counteract the negative influence of Barbie, who had long dominated Iran's toy market. Created by the Iranian government, Sara and her brother, Dara, represented eight-year-old twins and were intended to replace Barbie and Ken, the sale of which the authorities had officially banned in the mid-1990s because they represented a "Trojan horse" for Western values. Sara came complete with a headscarf to cover her hair in modest Muslim fashion and a full-length white chador enveloping her from head to toe. She and her brother were described

A Syrian girl examining Fulla dolls at a toy store in Damascus in 2005.

photo: Khaled al-Hariri/Reuters/Newscom

as helping each other solve problems, while looking to their loving parents for guidance, hardly the message that Barbie and Ken conveyed.

In 2003, a toy company based in Syria introduced Fulla, a doll depicting a young Muslim woman about the same age as Barbie, perhaps a grown-up version of Sara. Dressed modestly in a manner that reflected the norms of each national market, Fulla was described by her creator as representing "Muslim values." Unlike Barbie, with her boyfriend and a remarkable range of careers, including astronaut and president of the United States, Fulla was modeled on the ideal traditional Arab woman. She interacted with male family members rather than a boyfriend and was depicted only as a teacher or a doctor, both respected professions for

services—schools, clinics, youth centers, legal-aid societies, financial institutions, publishing houses—that the state offered inadequately or not at all. Islamic activists took leadership roles in unions and professional organizations of teachers, journalists, engineers, doctors, and lawyers. Such people embraced modern science and technology but sought to embed these elements of modernity within a more distinctly Islamic culture. Some served in official government positions or entered political life and contested elections where it was possible to do so. The Algerian Islamic Salvation Front was poised to win elections in 1992, when a frightened military government intervened to cancel them, an action that plunged the country into a decade of bitter civil war. Egypt's Muslim Brotherhood did come to power peacefully in 2012, but it was removed by the military a year later amid widespread protests against its policies.

Militant fundamentalism has certainly not been the only religious response to modernity and globalization within the Islamic world. (See Working with Evidence: Contending for Islam, page 1054.) Considerable debate among Muslims has raised questions about the proper role of the state; the difference between the eternal women in the Islamic world. But she did share an eye for fashion with Barbie. Underneath her modest outer dress, Fulla wore stylish clothing, although it was less revealing than that of her American counterpart, and, like Barbie, she chose from an extensive wardrobe, sold separately of course. "This isn't just about putting the hijab [a head-scarf covering a woman's hair and chest] on a Barbie doll," Fawaz Abidin, the Fulla brand manager, noted. "You have to create a character that parents and children want to relate to."[17]

Fulla proved far more popular than Sara among Muslim girls, becoming one of the best-selling dolls in the Islamic world. In part, the adoption by Fulla's creators of West-ern marketing techniques, similar to those that had been used to promote Barbie for decades, lay behind the doll's remarkable success. Fulla-themed magazines appeared on newsstands, and commercials advertising Fulla dolls and their accessories permeated children's television stations in the Muslim world. "When you take Fulla out of the house, don't forget her new spring abaya [a long, robe-like full-body covering]!" admonished one advertisement. Fulla's image was used to market an endless number of other licensed products, including branded stationery, backpacks, prayer rugs, bikes, and breakfast cereals, all in trademark "Fulla pink." In this respect, Fulla and Barbie shared a great deal. Despite Fulla's success, Barbie has continued to enjoy a loyal following in the region, in part because of her exotic qualities. "All my friends have Fulla now, but I still like Barbie the best," one ten-year-old Saudi girl stated. "She has blonde hair and cool clothes. Every single girl in Saudi looks like Fulla. . . . What's so special about that?"

The widespread availability of Barbie in the Muslim world provides one small example of the power of global commerce in the world of the early twenty-first century. But Sara and Fulla illustrate resistance to the cultural val-ues associated with this American product. Still, Sara, Fulla, and Barbie had something in common: nearly all were manufactured in East Asian factories. Indeed, the same factories frequently manufactured the rival dolls. This triangular relationship of the United States, the Muslim world, and East Asia symbolized the growing integration of world economics and cultures as well as the divergences and conflicts that this process has generated. These linked but contrasting patterns involve much more than dolls in the early twenty-first century, for they define major fea-tures of the world we all share.

QUESTIONS

What can Barbie, Sara, and Fulla tell us about the glo-balized world of the twenty first century? What different values and sensibilities do they convey?

---

law of God (sharia) and the human interpretations of it; the rights of women; the possibility of democracy; and many other issues. In 1996, Anwar Ibrahim, a major political and intellectual figure in Malaysia, insisted:

> Southeast Asian Muslims . . . would rather strive to improve the welfare of the women and children in their midst than spend their days elaborately defin-ing the nature and institutions of the ideal Islamic state. They do not believe it makes one less of a Muslim to promote economic growth, to master the information revolution, and to demand justice for women.[18]

In 2004 and 2005 scholars from all major schools of Islamic thought gathered in Amman, the capital of Jordan. They issued the "Amman Message," which called for Islamic unity, condemned terrorism, forbade Muslims from declaring one another as "apostate" or nonbelievers, and emphasized the commonalities shared by Mus-lims, Christians, and Jews.

Within other religious traditions as well, believers found various ways of responding to global modernity. A number of liberal and mainstream Christian groups spoke to the ethical issues arising from economic globalization and climate change. Many Christian organizations, for example, were active in agitating for debt relief for poor countries and the rights of immigrants. Adherents of "liberation theology," particularly in Latin America, sought a Christian basis for action in the areas of social justice, poverty, and human rights, while viewing Jesus as liberator as well as savior. In Asia, a growing movement known as socially engaged Buddhism addressed the needs of the poor through social reform, educational programs, health services, and peacemaking action during times of conflict and war. In short, religious responses to global modernity were articulated in many voices.

Humankind and the Environment: Entering the Anthropocene Era

The fossil fuel revolution and rapid technological innovation; industrialization and economic growth; urbanization and consumerism; population growth and migration; nationalism and global citizenship — all of these accelerating global processes of the past century connect with what is surely the most distinctive feature of that century: the human impact on the environment. As environmental historian J. R. McNeil put it: "This is the first time in human history that we have altered ecosystems with such intensity, on such a scale, and with such speed. . . . The human race, without intending anything of the sort, has undertaken a gigantic uncontrolled experiment on the earth."[19]

The Global Environment Transformed

By the early twenty-first century, that "experiment" had acquired a name: the **Anthropocene era** or the age of man. Many scientists and environmental historians now use this term to designate the contemporary era since the advent of the Industrial Revolution and more dramatically since 1950. It emphatically calls attention to the enduring impact of recent human activity on the planet. Species extinctions; mounting carbon dioxide emissions and climate change; the depletion of groundwater reserves; accumulating radioactive isotopes in the earth's surface; the enlargement of deserts; dead zones in the oceans; the prevalence of concrete and plastics — these and other environmental changes, all of them generated by human actions, will be apparent to archeologists many thousands of years in the future, should they be around to reflect on them. A prominent geologist recently declared: "We are the dominant geologic force shaping the planet. It's not so much river or ice or wind anymore. It's humans."[20]

As geologists reckon time, humankind has been living for the past 12,000 years in the **Holocene era**, a warmer and often a wetter period that began following the end of the last ice age. During this Holocene era, environmental conditions were uniquely favorable for human thriving. It was, according to prominent earth scientist Johan Rockstrom, a "Garden of Eden" era, providing "a stable equilibrium

Guided Reading Question

■ **CHANGE**
What evidence might support the notion that the earth has moved into the "age of man"?

of forests, savannahs, coral reefs, grasslands, fish, mammals, bacteria, air quality, ice cover, temperatures, fresh water availability, and productive soils."[21] These conditions enabled the development of agriculture, significant population growth, and the creation of complex civilizations. Human activity during the Holocene era certainly transformed the environment in many ways, as plants and animals were domesticated, as native vegetation and forests gave way to agricultural fields and grazing land, as soils were eroded or became salty, as cities grew, and in many other ways. However, these environmental impacts were limited, local, and sometimes temporary.

That began to change as industrialization and population growth took hold first in Europe, North America, and Japan during the nineteenth century, in the Soviet Union during the 1930s, and then after 1950 in many other parts of the world. Everywhere, the idea of economic growth or "development" as something possible and desirable took hold, in capitalist, communist, and developing countries alike. Unlike in earlier times, human impact on the environment has become pervasive, global, and permanent, eroding the "Garden of Eden" conditions of the Holocene era.

Among the chief indicators of the emerging "age of man" were multiple transformations of the landscape.[22] The growing numbers of the poor and the growing consumption of the rich led to the doubling of cropland and pasturelands during the twentieth century. By 2015, some 40 percent of the world's land area was used to produce food for humans and their domesticated animals, whereas in 1750 that figure was only 4 percent.

As grasslands and swampland contracted, so too did the world's forests. Since the mid-1960s, about 20 percent of the Amazon rainforest has been cut down to make way for timbering and farming, more than had been lost since the beginning of European colonization over four centuries ago. The most dramatic deforestation took place in tropical regions of Latin America, Africa, and Southeast Asia, even as some reforestation took hold in Europe, North America, and Japan. Furthermore, huge urban complexes have transformed the landscape in many places into wholly artificial environments of concrete, asphalt, steel, and glass. China alone lost some 6.7 million hectares of farmland, over 5 percent of its available agricultural land, to urban growth between 1996 and 2003.[23]

These human incursions reduced the habitat available to wild plants and animals, leading to the extinction of numerous species and declining biodiversity. Extinction is of course a natural phenomenon, but by the early twenty-first century the pace of species extinction had spiked far beyond the natural or "background rate" because of human interventions in the form of agriculture, lumbering, and urban growth. Tropical rain forest habitats, home to a far richer diversity of species than more temperate environments, were particularly susceptible to human intrusion.

This loss of biodiversity extended to the seas of the world as well. Fishing with industrial-style equipment has led to the collapse or near collapse of fisheries around the world. The 1992 breakdown of the Grand Banks cod fishery off the coast of Newfoundland persuaded the Canadian government to place a moratorium on further fishing in that area. By the early 1960s, most whale species were on the verge of extinction, though many have begun to recover as restrictions on whaling have been put in place. "For the first time since the demise of the dinosaurs 65 million years ago," wrote the director of the World Wildlife Federation, "we face a global mass extinction of wildlife."[24]

The global spread of modern industry, heavily dependent on fossil fuels, generated dramatic changes in the air, water, soil, and atmosphere, with profound impacts on human life. China's spectacular economic growth since the 1980s, fueled largely by coal, resulted in an equally spectacular pall of air pollution in its major cities. In 2004, the World Bank reported that 12 of the world's 20 most polluted cities were in China. Degradation of the world's rivers, seas, and oceans has also mounted, as pesticides, herbicides, chemical fertilizers, detergents, oil, sewage, industrial waste, and plastics have made their way from land to water. By the 1960s, Lake Erie in the United States was widely reported as "dead." The Great Pacific Garbage Patch, an area of about 7 million square miles in the North Pacific, has trapped an enormous quantity of debris, mostly plastics, endangering oceanic food webs and proving deadly to creatures of the sea, which ingest or become entangled in this human garbage. Industrial pollution in the Soviet Union rendered about half of the country's rivers severely polluted by the late 1980s, while fully 20 percent of its population lived in regions defined as "ecological disasters." The release of chemicals known as chlorofluorocarbons thinned the ozone layer, which protects the earth from excessive ultraviolet radiation, before an international agreement put an end to the practice.

In other ways as well, human activity has left a lasting mark on the planet during the past century. Radioactive residue from the testing of nuclear weapons and from the storage of nuclear waste produced by power plants can remain detectable for tens or hundreds of thousands of years. Mining has also created a vast underground network of shafts and tunnels and above-ground scarring of open pit mines and quarries. As the demand for water to serve growing populations, industries, and irrigation needs increased by 900 percent during the twentieth century, many of the planet's aquifers have become

Urban Pollution in Beijing   Deriving from auto exhausts, coal burning, and dust storms, the air pollution in China's capital city of Beijing has long been horrendous. In this photograph from early 2014, teenagers wear face masks to protect themselves from inhaling the noxious particles in the air. Many thousands of people across the globe die daily from the long-term effects of air pollution. (Rolex Dela Pana/EPA/REX/Shutterstock)

substantially depleted. A number of large cities—Beijing, Mexico City, Bangkok, Tokyo, Houston, Jakarta, and Manila—have been measurably sinking over the past century due in part to groundwater depletion. All of these environmental changes deriving from human activity will be apparent to our descendants for a long time to come.

Changing the Climate

By the early twenty-first century, **climate change** had become the world's most pressing environmental issue. Since the Industrial Revolution took hold in Western Europe, higher concentrations of carbon dioxide and methane, generated by the burning of fossil fuels, as well as nitrous oxide derived largely from fertilizers, began to accumulate in the atmosphere, slowly at first and then much more rapidly after 1950. These so-called greenhouse gases act as a blanket around the world, limiting the escape of infrared energy from the earth's surface and so warming the planet. Carbon dioxide concentrations have increased by 43 percent since 1750, reaching 410 parts per million (ppm) by early 2017, a level well beyond the 350 ppm generally considered "safe" and greater than at any time during the over 200,000 years of human life on the planet. (See Figure 23.1 and Figure 23.2.) Average global temperature during this time increased by 1°C or more, and sixteen of the seventeen warmest years on record have all occurred since 2000. While this temperature increase may seem numerically small, its consequences have already been substantial, and projections into the near future of the twenty-first century are frightening.

Scientists have associated this warming of the planet with all manner of environmental changes. One of them involves the accelerating melting of glaciers and polar ice caps. Arctic temperatures, unprecedented in the past 44,000 years, have been melting glaciers and sea ice at record levels. Coupled with expanded sea volumes

Guided Reading Question
....
■ **CHANGE**
In what specific ways has global warming affected life on earth?

Figure 23.1 Carbon Dioxide Concentrations, 1750–2017
Rising concentrations of carbon dioxide in the atmosphere have been matched by a marked increase in global temperatures. (Scripps Institution of Oceanography at the University of California San Diego)

**Figure 23.2
Distribution of
Total World Carbon
Dioxide Emissions,
1850–2011**

The various regions or
countries of the world
have contributed very
unevenly to carbon dioxide
emissions over the past
160 years. By 2014,
however, industrializing
Asian economies had
become major emitters,
with China responsible for
some 30 percent of global
carbon dioxide discharges
into the atmosphere in
that year. (World Resources Institute)

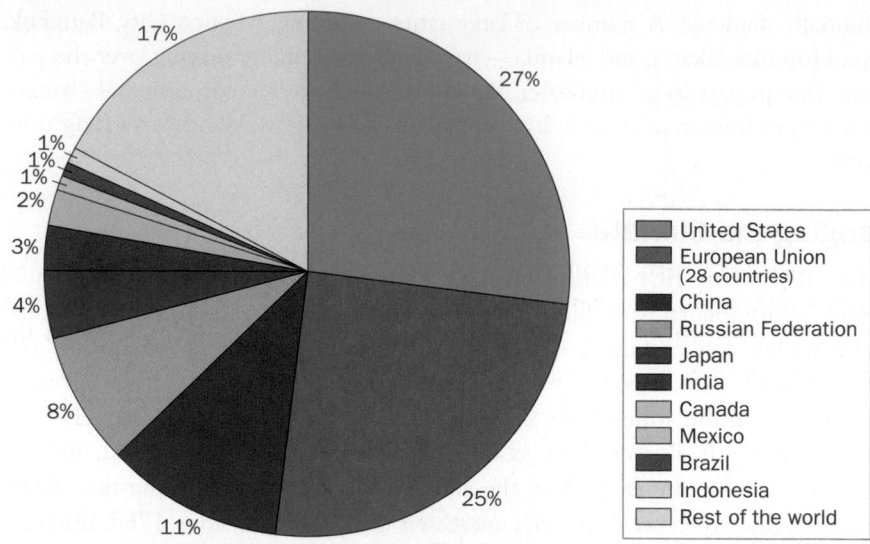

United States
European Union
(28 countries)
China
Russian Federation
Japan
India
Canada
Mexico
Brazil
Indonesia
Rest of the world

as the oceans warm, this rapid melting has raised sea levels by roughly 8.5 inches
since 1850. Particularly threatened have been a number of small island nations in
Oceania — Tuvalu and Kiribati in particular. Coastal communities everywhere have
become more vulnerable to storm surges. Low-lying regions of Bangladesh and the
Philippines already flood almost every year and more catastrophically during particularly powerful storms, which seem to occur with increasing frequency and power
as the planet warms. The first decade of the twenty-first century witnessed eight
Category 5 hurricanes in the Atlantic Ocean, the most for any decade on record.

While global warming has exacerbated storms and rainfall in some regions, it
has increased the prevalence and duration of droughts in others. Since the 1970s,
droughts have been longer and more extreme in parts of Africa, the Middle East,
southern Asia, and the western United States. In 2010 and 2011 extreme weather
conditions characteristic of global warming — droughts, dust storms, fires, heavy
rainfall — afflicted many grain-producing regions of the world, including Canada,
Russia, China, Argentina, and Australia, causing a sharp spike in grain prices on
the world market. The Middle East and North Africa, heavily dependent on grain
imports, experienced sharply rising food prices, arguably aggravating social unrest
and contributing to the political protests of the Arab Spring. In various parts of
Africa, surging populations, record high temperatures, and prolonged drought have
generated crop failures, devastation of livestock herds, and local conflicts over land
and water. These pressures have turned many into "climate refugees," migrating to
urban areas or northward toward Europe.

Climate change has also disrupted many aquatic ecosystems, as the world's
oceans and lakes have become warmer and more acidic, absorbing some 25 percent

of human-generated carbon dioxide. While this absorption has limited the extent of atmospheric warming to date, the resulting carbonic acid has damaged any number of marine organisms with calcium shells, such as oysters, clams, sea urchins, and plankton, and places entire aquatic food chains in jeopardy. The world's coral reefs have been especially vulnerable. Record high oceanic temperatures in 2016 killed 67 percent of the coral in some areas of Australia's Great Barrier Reef. "The coral was cooked," declared one of the scientists studying this phenomenon.[25]

Nor have land-based communities of living organisms been spared the impact of global warming. Drier conditions, for example, have meant more forest fires. Those in the western United States have increased fourfold since 1970, and the fire season has been extended by more than two months. Both plants and animals adapted to a particular temperature range were forced to migrate or die as temperatures increased. In Ethiopia, this has meant that mosquitos bearing malaria have migrated higher up the country's mountains, bringing the disease to people who never knew it before. Warmer temperatures in western North America have enabled bark beetles, which cause great damage as they feed on the bark and wood of trees, to survive the less intense winters and move to new environments. They have killed over 70,000 square miles worth of trees in recent decades. Polar bears have become an iconic image of the impact of global warming, as the sea ice on which they depend vanishes.

Clearly climate change as a marker of the Anthropocene era is in its early stages, with more, much more, to follow, if these emissions continue more or less unchecked. Projections to the year 2100, although subject to much dispute and controversy, paint a bleak picture: there will be carbon dioxide concentrations of 600 ppm and up, temperature increases of 1.8°C to 4°C, massive melting of glaciers and sea ice with sea level rise in the range of 2.5 to 6 feet; millions of homes and hundreds of cities at least partially under water, drought and falling food production in parts of Africa leading to mass migrations, widespread species extinction of up to half of earth's higher life forms by one estimate, and frequent international conflicts over dwindling fresh water supplies. Under these conditions, serious observers have begun to speak about the possibility of a major collapse of modern civilization. Widening awareness of both current conditions and future possibilities has energized the environmental movements of the twenty-first century.

Protecting the Planet: The Rise of Environmentalism

Long before climate change emerged as a global issue, a growing awareness of ecological damage and a desire to counteract it accompanied human entry into the Anthropocene era.[26] In the late eighteenth and early nineteenth centuries, Romantic English poets such as William Blake and William Wordsworth denounced the industrial era's "dark satanic mills," which threatened the "green and pleasant land" of an earlier England. In opposing the extension of railroads, the British writer John Ruskin declared in 1876 that "the frenzy of avarice is daily drowning our sailors, suffocating our miners, poisoning our children and blasting the cultivable surface of England into a treeless waste of ashes."[27] Another element in early environmentalism, especially prominent in the United States and Germany, derived from a concern with deforestation, drought, and desertification as pioneering settlers, lumbermen, miners, and the owners of colonial plantations inflicted terrible damage on the woodlands and pasturelands of the world. Articulated primarily by men of science often working in the colonial world, this approach sought to mobilize scientific expertise and state control to manage, contain, and tame modern assaults on the environment.

Protecting remaining wilderness areas was yet another piece of early environmentalism. The first international environmental conference, held in London in 1900, aimed at preserving African wildlife from voracious European hunters. In the United States it was the opening of the west to European settlers that threatened the natural order. "With no eye to the future," wrote naturalist John Muir in 1897, "these pious destroyers waged interminable forest wars . . . , spreading ruthless devastation ever wider and further. . . . Wilderness is a necessity . . . not only as fountains of timber and irrigating rivers, but as fountains of life."[28] This kind of sensibility found expression in the American national parks, the first of which, Yellowstone, was established in 1872.

These early examples of environmental awareness were distinctly limited, largely a product of literary figures, scientists, and some government officials. None of them attracted a mass following or elicited a global response. But "**second-wave environmentalism**," beginning in the 1960s, certainly did. It began, arguably, with the publication in 1962 of Rachel Carson's *Silent Spring*, which exposed the chemical contamination of the environment with a particular emphasis on the use of pesticides. The book struck a chord with millions, triggering environmental movements on both sides of the Atlantic. Ten years later, the Club of Rome, a global think tank, issued a report called *Limits to Growth*, which warned of resource exhaustion and the collapse of industrial society in the face of unrelenting economic and population growth. Soon a mounting wave of environmental books, articles, treatises, and conferences emerged in Europe and North America, pushing back in various ways against the postwar emphasis on "development," consumerism, and unending economic growth. That sensibility was aptly captured in the title of a best-selling book by British economist E. F. Schumacher in 1973, *Small Is Beautiful*.

But what most clearly distinguished second-wave environmentalism was widespread grassroots involvement and activism. By the late 1990s, millions of people in North America, Europe, Japan, Australia, and New Zealand had joined one of the rapidly proliferating environmental organizations, many of them local. The issues addressed in these burgeoning movements were many and various: pollution, resource depletion, toxic waste, protecting wildlife habitats, nuclear power and nuclear testing, limiting development, and increasingly at the top of the agenda in the twenty-first century, climate change. Beyond particular issues, proponents of "deep ecology" argued that human beings should no longer be considered central but

Guided Reading Question

∎ **COMPARISON**

In what different ways has environmentalism been expressed?

understood as occupying a place of equivalence with other species. Those supporting an "environmental justice" outlook were more concerned with the impact of environmental devastation on the poor, minorities, and developing countries. This social justice perspective informed Pope Francis's 2015 environmental encyclical, which commanded global attention, as the world's most prominent Christian leader called for humankind to "care for our common home."

The tactics of these movements were as varied as the issues they addressed. Much attention was given to public education and to lobbying governments and corporations, often through professionally run organizations. In Germany, New Zealand, and Australia, environmentalists created Green parties, which contested elections and on occasion shared power. Teach-ins, demonstrations, street protests, and various local actions also played a role in the strategies of environmental activists.

In the communist world, environmentalism was constrained by highly authoritarian states that were committed to large-scale development. In the late 1980s, the Chinese government, for example, sharply repressed groups critical of the enormous Three Gorges Dam project across the Yangzi River. By the early twenty-first century, however, a grassroots environmental movement had taken root in China, expressed in hundreds of private groups and in state-sponsored organizations as well. Many of these sought to ground their activism in Buddhist or Daoist traditions that stressed the harmony of humankind and the natural order. In the Soviet Union during the 1970s and after, environmentalists were able to voice their concerns about the shrinking of the Aral Sea, pollution threats to Lake Baikal in Siberia, and poor air quality in many cities. After the nuclear disaster at Chernobyl in 1986, Gorbachev's policy of *glasnost* allowed greater freedom of expression as environmentalist concerns became part of a broader challenge to communism and Russian domination.

Quite quickly, during the 1970s and 1980s, environmentalism also took root in the Global South, where it frequently assumed a distinctive character compared to the more industrialized countries. There it was more locally based, with less connection to global issues or large national organizations than in the West; it involved more poor people in direct action rather than in political lobbying and corporate strategies; it was more concerned with issues of food security, health,

Environmentalism in Action Australian climate activists spell out 350 on the steps of the Sydney Opera House, pointing to the goal of limiting CO_2 concentrations in the atmosphere to 350 parts per million. The event occurred in October 2009 as part of an international day of protest about global warming. (CulturalEyes -- AusGS2/Alamy)

and basic survival than with the rights of nature or wilderness protection; and it was more closely connected to movements for social justice. Thus, whereas Western environmentalists defended forests where few people lived, the Chikpo, or "tree-hugging," movement in India sought to protect the livelihood of farmers, artisans, and herders living in areas subject to extensive deforestation. A massive movement to prevent or limit the damming of India's Narmada River derived from the displacement of local people; similar anti-dam protests in the American Northwest were more concerned with protecting salmon runs.

In the Global South, this "environmentalism of the poor" took shape in various ways, often in opposition to the gigantic development projects of national governments. Residents of the Brazilian Amazon basin, facing the loss of their livelihood to lumbering interests, ranchers, and government road-building projects, joined hands and directly confronted workers sent to cut down trees with their chainsaws. When the Thai government sought to create huge eucalyptus plantations, largely to supply Japanese-owned paper mills, Buddhist teachers, known as "ecology monks," mobilized peasants to put their case to public officials. In the Philippines, coalitions of numerous local groups mobilized large-scale grassroots movements against foreign-owned mining companies. Kenya's Green Belt Movement organized groups of village women to plant millions of trees intended to forestall the growth of deserts and protect the soil.

By the early twenty-first century, environmentalism had become a matter of global concern and had prompted action at many levels. A growing market for solar and wind power helped drive its cost sharply lower, moving it closer to being competitive with conventional forms of electric generation like coal. Governments acted to curtail pollution and to foster the use of renewable energy sources, sometimes by putting a price on carbon-based fuels through "cap and trade" systems or a carbon tax. Germany, for example, increased the proportion of its electricity from renewable sources from 6.3 percent in 2000 to 32 percent in 2016. China has enacted a large body of environmental laws and regulations, has invested heavily in solar power, and in 2017 announced plans to close 100 coal-fired power plants. Brazil and Canada derive the bulk of their electricity from renewables, primarily hydropower. Some 6,000 national parks in over 100 countries served to protect wildlife and natural beauty. Many businesses found it commercially useful and therefore profitable to brand themselves as "green." Reforestation programs were under way in China, Honduras, Kenya, and elsewhere. International agreements have come close to eliminating the introduction of ozone-depleting substances into the atmosphere. And after extensive negotiations, the **Paris Climate Agreement** of 2015 committed some 195 countries, 700 cities, and many companies to reduce greenhouse gas emissions sufficiently to avoid a 2°C increase in global temperatures. Furthermore, millions of individuals altered their ways of life, agreeing to recycle, to install solar panels, to buy fuel-efficient cars, to shop in local markets, and to forgo the use of plastic bags.

But resistance has also surfaced, partly because moving toward a clean energy economy would require lifestyle adjustment for citizens in the Global North and for elites everywhere. Powerful and entrenched interests in fossil fuel industries likewise generate resistance. In 2017 the new Trump administration in the United States began to partially dismantle existing climate change regulations and stunned the world by announcing American withdrawal from the Paris agreement.

Furthermore, large-scale international agreement on global warming has come up against sharp conflicts between the Global North and South. Both activists and governments in the developing countries have often felt that Northern initiatives to address atmospheric pollution and global warming would curtail their industrial development, leaving the North/South gap intact. A Malaysian official put the dispute succinctly: "The developed countries don't want to give up their extravagant lifestyles, but plan to curtail our development."[29]

More than any other widespread movement, global environmentalism came to symbolize a focus on the common plight of humankind across the artificial boundaries of nation-states. It also marked a challenge to modernity itself, particularly its overriding commitment to endless growth and consumption. The ideas of sustainability and restraint, certainly not prominent in any list of modern values, entered global discourse and marked the beginnings of a new environmental ethic. This change in thinking, although limited, was perhaps the most significant achievement of global environmentalism.

REFLECTIONS

World History and the Making of Meaning

Among the most distinctive features of human life is our penchant for meaning. We seek to infuse almost every action and activity with some larger significance, and we are most apt to fall into despair when we are unable to do so. A large part of the historian's task involves identifying and describing the multiple meanings that individuals and societies have ascribed to their world and to their behavior in the past. For example, world historians notice and compare the various ways that humans have given meaning to the communities they create. Many small village-based societies have viewed themselves in terms of kinship, feeling themselves bonded by a relationship to a common ancestor. To distinguish themselves from neighboring "barbarians," Chinese thought of their country as the "middle kingdom," radiating "civilization" to their less fortunate neighbors. Americans have defined the United States as a "city set upon a hill," a melting pot, or the "land of the free." All such understandings are the product of human imagination, intended to provide some larger meaning to social and political life, even as those identities change over time.

But historians do more than record the meanings that have arisen in the course of the human journey. Historians themselves also create meaning as they give definition to the human past. World historians, for example, have sometimes pointed out a broad trend toward greater social complexity and more connectivity among regions and peoples during the course of our history. They give some meaning to human tragedies such as slavery, war, and genocide by explaining their origins and development. The notion of an "Anthropocene era," increasingly used by historians, provides a distinctive character to the past century or so.

In these ways historians seek to impose some shape and significance on the chaos of random events, ensuring that the human story becomes more than "one damned thing after another." Some might argue that any such "shape" is an illusion, an artificial product of human self-serving. Certainly historians' formulations are endlessly contested and debated. But we are apparently impelled to seek pattern or structure in the past. An infinite array of miscellaneous historical "facts" is neither satisfying nor useful.

The study of world history can also be helpful for each of us as we seek to make meaning in our own lives. As we witness the broad contours of the human journey and learn more about the wider world, we can more readily locate ourselves individually in the larger stream of that story. In short, world history provides context, which is so essential to the creation of meaning. If we base our understanding of the world only on what we personally experience in our own brief and limited lives, we render ourselves both impoverished and ineffective.

World history opens a marvelous window into the unfamiliar. It confronts us with the "ways of the world," the whole panorama of human achievement, tragedy, and sensibility. It allows us some modest entry into the lives of people far removed from us in time and place. And it offers us company for the journey of our own lives. Pondering the global past with a receptive heart and an open mind can assist us in enlarging and deepening our sense of self. In exposing us to the wider experience of "all under Heaven," as the Chinese put it, world history can aid us in constructing more meaningful lives. That is among the many gifts that the study of the global past offers to us all.

Second Thoughts

What's the Significance?

population explosion, 1020

Green Revolution, 1020

global urbanization, 1022

megacities, 1023

labor migration, 1025

influenza pandemic, 1029

HIV/AIDS, 1029

cultural globalization, 1033

religious fundamentalism, 1037

Hindutva, 1037

Islamic radicalism, 1039

Anthropocene era, 1042

Holocene era, 1042

climate change, 1045

second-wave environmentalism, 1048

Paris Climate Agreement, 1050

Big Picture Questions

1. In what ways has population growth shaped the movement of people and the human impact on the environment?
2. How have cultural patterns evolved over the past century? What broader processes have contributed to those cultural changes?
3. To what extent do the changes described in these last two chapters justify considering the past century a new phase of world history?
4. **Looking Back:** How have the technological and economic changes explored in the previous chapter shaped the demographic, cultural, and environmental processes discussed in this chapter?

Next Steps: For Further Study

Karen Armstrong, *The Battle for God* (2000). A comparison of Christian, Jewish, and Islamic fundamentalism in historical perspective.

Wolfgang Behringer, *A Cultural History of Climate* (2010). Places contemporary issues of climate change in a broad world historical context.

Ian Law, *Racism and Ethnicity: Global Debates, Dilemmas, Directions* (2010). A broad historically grounded and global survey of the intersection of racial and ethnic identities.

J. R. McNeill, *Something New under the Sun: An Environmental History of the Twentieth-Century World* (2001). A much-acclaimed global account of the rapidly mounting human impact on the environment during the most recent century.

Rainer Munz and Albert Reiterer, *The Overcrowded World: Global Population and International Migration* (2009). Two German scholars place population growth, urbanization, and migration in a broad world historical context, but with an emphasis on the past century.

Jan Nederveen Pieterse, *Globalization and Culture: Global Mélange* (2015). Explores the cultural dimension of recent globalization within a longer historical context.

NASA, "Global Climate Change," https://climate.nasa.gov/. A NASA website full of articles, essays, images, and videos related to climate change.

"Overpopulation: The Human Explosion Explained," produced by Kurzgesagt, a Munich-based YouTube channel and design studio, https://www.youtube.com/watch?v=QsBT5EQt348. A thoughtful and informed animated film that describes and explains the recent and spectacular increase in human numbers.

Contending for Islam

Over the past century, the growing intrusion of the West and of modern secular culture into the Islamic world has prompted acute and highly visible debate among Muslims. Which ideas and influences flowing from the West could Muslims safely utilize, and which should they decisively reject? Are women's rights and democracy compatible with Islam? To what extent should Islam find expression in public life as well as in private religious practice? The sources that follow show something of these controversies while illustrating sharp variations in the understanding of Islam.

SOURCE 23.1 A Secular State for an Islamic Society

Modern Turkey emerged from the ashes of the Ottoman Empire after World War I, adopting a distinctive path of modernization, westernization, and secularism under the leadership of Mustafa Kemal Atatürk (see "Religion and Global Modernity" earlier in the chapter). Such policies sought to remove Islam from any significant role in public life, restricting it to the realm of personal devotion. They included abolition of the caliphate, by which Ottoman rulers had claimed leadership of the entire Islamic world. In a speech delivered in 1927, Atatürk explained and justified these policies, which went against the grain of much Islamic thinking.

- On what grounds did Atatürk justify the abolition of the caliphate?

- What additional actions did he take to remove Islam from a public or political role in the new Turkish state?

- What can you infer about Atatürk's view of Islam?

- How did Atatürk's conception of a Turkish state differ from that of Ottoman authorities? In what ways did he build upon Ottoman reforms of the nineteenth century? (See "The Ottoman Empire and the West in the Nineteenth Century" in Chapter 19.)

MUSTAFA KEMAL ATATÜRK | *Speech to the General Congress of the Republican Party* | 1927

[Our Ottoman rulers] hoped to unite the entire Islamic world in one body, to lead it and to govern it. For this purpose, [they] assumed the title of Caliph [successor to the Prophet Muhammad]. . . . It is an unrealizable aim to attempt to unite in one tribe the various races existing on the earth, thereby abolishing all boundaries. . . .

If the Caliph and the Caliphate were to be invested with a dignity embracing the whole of Islam . . . , a crushing burden would be imposed on Turkey. . . . [Furthermore], will Persia or Afghanistan, which are [Muslim] states, recognize the authority of the Caliph in a single matter? No, and this is quite justifiable, because it would be in contradiction to the independence of the state, to the sovereignty of the people.

[The current constitution] laid down as the first duty of the Grand National Assembly that "the prescriptions of the Shari'a [Islamic law] should be put into force. . . ." [But] if a state, having among its subjects elements professing different religions and being compelled to act justly and impartially toward all of them . . . , it is obliged to respect freedom of opinion and conscience. . . . The Muslim religion includes freedom of religious opinion. . . . Will not every grown-up person in the new Turkish state be free to select his own religion? . . . When the first favorable opportunity arises, the nation must act to eliminate these superfluities [the enforcement of sharia] from our Constitution. . . .

Under the mask of respect for religious ideas and dogmas, the new Party [in opposition to Atatürk's reformist plans] addressed itself to the people in the following words: "We want the re-establishment of the Caliphate; we are satisfied with the religious law; we shall protect the Medressas [Islamic schools], the Tekkes [places for Sufi worship], the pious institutions, the Softahs [students in religious schools], the Sheikhs [Sufi masters], and their disciples. . . . The party of Mustapha Kemal, having abolished the Caliphate, is breaking Islam into ruins; they will make you into unbelievers . . . they will make you wear hats." Can anyone pretend that the style of propaganda used by the Party was not full of these reactionary appeals? . . .

Gentlemen, it was necessary to abolish the fez [a distinctive Turkish hat with no brim], which sat on our heads as a sign of ignorance, of fanaticism, of hatred to progress and civilization, and to adopt in its place the hat, the customary headdress of the whole civilized world, thus showing that no difference existed in the manner of thought between the Turkish nation and the whole family of civilized mankind. . . . [Thus] there took place the closing of the Tekkes, of the convents, and of the mausoleums, as well as the abolition of all sects and all kinds of [religious] titles. . . .

Could a civilized nation tolerate a mass of people who let themselves be led by the nose by a herd of Sheikhs, Dedes, Seids, Tschelebis, Babas, and Emirs [various religious titles]? . . . Would not one therewith have committed the greatest, most irreparable error to the cause of progress and awakening?

Source: *A Speech Delivered by Ghazi Mustapha Kemal, October 1927* (Leipzig: K. F. Koehler, 1929), 377–79, 591–93, 595–98, 717, 721–22.

■ ■ ■

SOURCE 23.2 **Toward an Islamic Society**

Even as Kemal Atatürk was seeking to remove Islam from the public life of Turkey, a newly formed Muslim organization in Egypt was strongly advocating precisely the opposite course of action. Founded in 1928 by impoverished schoolteacher Hassan al-Banna (1906–1949), the Muslim Brotherhood argued in favor of "government that will act in conformity to the law and Islamic principles." As the earliest mass movement in the Islamic world advocating such ideas, the Brotherhood soon attracted a substantial following, including many poor urban residents recently arrived from the countryside. Long a major presence in Egyptian political life, the Brotherhood has frequently come into conflict with state authorities and briefly came to power in 2012. In 1936, it published a pamphlet, addressed to Egyptian and other Arab political leaders, that spelled out its views about the direction toward which a proper Islamic society should move.

■ How does this document define the purposes of government?

■ How does the Muslim Brotherhood understand the role of Islam in public life?

■ To what extent was this document anti–Western in its orientation? What posture does it advocate toward capitalism and economic development?

■ How might Kemal Atatürk respond to these views?

THE MUSLIM BROTHERHOOD | *Toward the Light* | 1936

After having studied the ideals which ought to inspire a renascent nation on the spiritual level, we wish to offer, in conclusion, some practical suggestions....

I. In the political, judicial, and administrative fields:

1st. To prohibit political parties and to direct the forces of the nation toward the formation of a united front;

2nd. To reform the law . . . [to] be entirely in accordance with Islamic legal practice;

5th. To propagate an Islamic spirit within the civil administration...

6th. To supervise the personal conduct of officials . . .

9th. Government will act in conformity to the law and to Islamic principles; . . . The scheduling of government services ought to take account of the hours set aside for prayer. . . .

II. In the fields of social and everyday practical life:

2nd. To find a solution for the problems of women, a solution that will allow her to progress and which will protect her while conforming to Islamic principles.

3rd. To root out clandestine or public prostitution and to consider fornication as a reprehensible crime. . .

4th. To prohibit all games of chance (gaming, lotteries, races, golf)

5th. To stop the use of alcohol and intoxicants

6th. To . . . educate women, to provide quality education for female teachers, school pupils, students, and doctors;

7th. To develop an educational program for girls different than the one for boys

8th. Male students should not be mixed with female students

10th. To close dance halls; to forbid dancing;

11th. To censor theater productions and films;

12th. To supervise and approve music;

14th. To confiscate malicious articles and books as well as magazines displaying a grotesque character or spreading frivolity;

16th. To change the hours when public cafes are opened or closed

19th. To bring to trial those who break the laws of Islam, who do not fast, who do not pray, and who insult religion;

21st. Religious teaching should constitute the essential subject matter to be taught in all educational establishments and faculties;

24th. . . . Absolute priority to be given to Arabic over foreign languages;

25th. To study the history of Islam, the nation, and Muslim civilization;

27th. To combat foreign customs

29th. To safeguard public health . . . increasing the number of hospitals, doctors, and out-patient clinics;

30th. To call particular attention to the problems of village life (administration, hygiene, water supply, education, recreation, morality).

III. The economic field:

1st. Organization of the zakat tax [an obligatory payment to support the poor] according to Islamic precepts

2nd. To prevent the practice of usury [charging interest on loans]

3rd. To facilitate and to increase the number of economic enterprises and to employ the jobless . . . ,

4th. To protect workers against monopoly companies, to require these companies to obey the law, the public should share in all profits;

5th. Aid for low-ranking employees and enlargement of their pay, lowering the income of high-ranking employees; . . .

7th. To encourage agricultural and industrial works, to improve the situation of the peasants and industrial workers[.]

Source: Hassan al-Banna, "Towards the Light," in Robert Landen, *The Emergence of the Modern Middle East* (New York: Van Nostrand Reinhold, 1970), 261–64.

. . .

SOURCE 23.3 Two Images of Islamic Radicalism ▶

By the late twentieth century, the most widely publicized face of Islam, at least in the West, derived from groups sympathetic to the views of the Muslim Brotherhood—Iran's revolutionary government, Saudi Arabia, and radical Islamist organizations such as al-Qaeda, the Islamic State, Boko Haram, and Hamas. These photographs illustrate two dimensions of Islamic radicalism. Its violent face is horrifically expressed in Source 23.3A, which shows a group of teenage Islamic State militants preparing to execute twenty-five Syrian prisoners in a Roman amphitheater in Palmyra in May 2015. That execution was carried out. On the other hand, Source 23.3B illustrates the kind of social services often provided by radical Islamist groups, such as the Palestinian militant organization Hamas, which governs the small territory of Gaza on the eastern coast of the Mediterranean Sea. The computer classroom pictured was part of a school established by Hamas, which was later destroyed in fighting between Hamas and Israeli forces.

■ Why might the Islamic State choose children to perform executions? Why might they have chosen the ruins of a Roman amphitheater as the site for this event?

■ What does the computer classroom suggest about the posture of Hamas to the modern world? Notice also the English textbook on the table.

■ What do these contrasting images suggest about the appeal of Islamic radicalism?

SOURCE 23.3A

The Violent Face of Islamic Radicalism │ 2015

Pictures from History/Newscom

SOURCE 23.3B

The Peaceful Face of Islamic Radicalism | 2015

© Abed Rahim Khatib: 2015/Flash90/Redux

• • •

SOURCE 23.4 **The Sufi Alternative**

In sharp contrast to the Islamic secularists like Atatürk or Islamic radicals or fundamentalists such as the Muslim Brotherhood stand the Sufis, gathered in multiple "orders" or "brotherhoods" all across the Islamic world and beyond it. Sufism has long represented the more spiritual or mystical dimension of Islam. While most Sufis participate in conventional Islamic practices, they are generally more sharply focused on interior spiritual experience than on the precise prescriptions of the law. For this reason, they have on occasion come into conflict with mainstream and especially "fundamentalist" Muslims, who view them as a threat to established religious authorities, as potential heretics for their openness to non-Islamic practices, and as "idolaters" for their veneration of Sufi masters and their shrines. They have also resisted the legalistic prescriptions of Islamic radicals. In many parts of the Islamic world, Sufis have been persecuted, their practices suppressed, and their places of worship attacked.

Others, however, view the Sufis as counteracting the appeal of Islamic radicals committed to violence. According to the prominent Iranian Sufi scholar Seyyed

Nasr, "Sufism is the most powerful antidote to the religious radicalism called fundamentalism. . . . Its influence is immense; Sufism has kept alive the inner quality of ethics and spiritual virtues, rather than a rigid morality . . . and it provides access to knowledge of the divine reality."[30] This was the message that India's prime minister Narendra Modi delivered to the Sufi World Forum in Delhi in 2016. That it came from a prominent Hindu figure in India made the message all the more striking, given the historical tension between Muslims and Hindus.

- Why might Islamic fundamentalists such as those in the Muslim Brotherhood find Sufism "un-Islamic"?

- Why might a Hindu prime minister of India make a very public speech praising Sufism and Islam?

- What elements of Sufism do Prime Minister Modi and Seyyed Nasr believe can serve as an "antidote" to Islamic radicalism?

Narendra Modi | *Sufism and Islamic Radicalism* | 2016

At a time when the dark shadow of violence is becoming longer, you [Sufis] are the noor, or the light of hope. . . . And, you represent the rich diversity of the Islamic civilization that stands on the solid bedrock of a great religion. . . . It is a civilization that reached great heights by the 15th century in science, medicine, literature, art, architecture and commerce. . . . It set, once again, an enduring lesson of human history: it is through openness and enquiry, engagement and accommodation, and respect for diversity that humanity advances, nations progress and the world prospers. . . . And, this is the message of Sufism, one of the greatest contributions of Islam to this world.

From its origins in Egypt and West Asia, Sufism travelled to distant lands, holding aloft the banner of faith and the flag of human values, learning from spiritual thoughts of other civilisations, and attracting people with the life and message of its saints. . . . In the different settings of Saharan Africa or in Southeast Asia, in Turkey or in Central Asia, in Iran or India, Sufism reflected the universal human desire to go beyond the practice and precepts of religion for a deeper unity with the Almighty. . . .

For the Sufis, therefore, service to God meant service to humanity. In the words of Khwaja Moinuddin Chishti [the thirteenth-century Persian founder of a major Sufi order], of all the worships, the worship that pleases the Almighty God the most is the grant of relief to the humble and the oppressed. . . . In a beautiful imagery of human values, he said, human beings must have the affection of the Sun, the generosity of the river and the hospitality of the earth, because they benefit us all, without discrimination and distinction among people. . . . And, its humanism also upheld the place and status of women in society.

Above all, Sufism is a celebration of diversity and pluralism, expressed in the words of Hazrat Nizamuddin Auliya [a fourteenth-century Indian Sufi master], that every people has its own path of truth, beliefs and focus of reverence. . . . Sufism is the voice of peace, co-existence, compassion and equality; a call to universal brotherhood.

Sufism became the face of Islam in India, even as it remained deeply rooted in the Holy Quran, and Hadiths. . . . Just as it once came to India, today Sufism from India has spread across the world.

Indeed, when terrorism and extremism have become the most destructive force of our times, the message of Sufism has global relevance. . . . Every year, we spend over 100 billion dollars on securing the world from terrorism, money that should have been spent on building lives of the poor. . . . [W]e must reject any link between terrorism and religion. Those who spread terror in the name of religion are anti-religious. . . . And, we must advance the message of Sufism that stands for the principles of Islam and the highest human values.

Source: NDTV, "Full Text of PM Narendra Modi's Speech at World Sufi Forum," March 17, 2016, http://www.ndtv.com/india-news/full-text-of-pm-narendra-modis-speech-at-world-sufi-forum-1288303.

■ ■ ■

SOURCE 23.5 Progressive Islam

All across the Islamic world, many Muslims argued that they could retain their distinctive religious sensibility while embracing democracy, women's rights, technological progress, freedom of thought, and religious pluralism. Such thinkers were following in the tradition of nineteenth-century Islamic modernism (see "Reform and Its Opponents" in Chapter 19), even as they recalled earlier centuries of Islamic intellectual and scientific achievement and religious tolerance. That viewpoint was expressed in a pamphlet composed in 2009 by a leading American Muslim scholar, translator, and teacher, Kabir Helminski. He was listed then as one of the 500 most influential Muslims in the world.

■ Against what charges does Helminski seek to defend Islam? How does this document reflect the experience of 9/11?

■ In what ways are his views critical of radical, or "fundamentalist," ideas and practices?

■ How does this document articulate the major features of a more progressive or liberal Islam? What kinds of arguments does the author employ to make his case?

■ To whom might these arguments appeal? How might Hassan al-Banna or Kemal Atatürk respond to these views?

KABIR HELMINSKI | *Islam and Human Values* | 2009

If the word "Islam" gives rise to fear or mistrust today, it is urgent that American Muslims clarify what we believe Islam stands for in order to dispel the idea that there is a fundamental conflict between the best values of Western civilization and the essential values of Islam. . . .

Islamic civilization, which developed out of the revelation of the Qur'an in the seventh century, affirms the truth of previous revelations, affirms religious pluralism, cultural diversity, and human rights, and recognizes the value of reason and individual conscience. . . .

[One issue] is the problem of violence. . . . Thousands of Muslim institutions and leaders, the great majority of the world's billion or more Muslims, have unequivocally condemned the hateful and violent ideologies that kill innocents and violate the dignity of all humanity. . . .

Islamic civilizations have a long history of encouraging religious tolerance and guaranteeing the rights of religious minorities. The Qur'an explicitly acknowledges that the diversity of religions is part of the Divine Plan and no religion has a monopoly on truth or virtue. . . .

Jerusalem, under almost continuous Islamic rule for nearly fourteen centuries, has been a place where Christians and Jews have lived side by side with Muslims, their holy sites and religious freedom preserved. Medieval Spain also created a high level of civilization as a multi-cultural society under Islamic rule for several centuries. The Ottoman Empire, the longest lived in history, for the more than six centuries of its existence encouraged ethnic and religious minorities to participate in and contribute to society. It was the Ottoman sultan who gave sanctuary to the Jews expelled from Catholic Spain. India was governed for centuries by Muslims, even while the majority of its people practiced Hinduism. . . .

[T]he acceptance of Islam must be an act of free will. Conversion by any kind of coercion was universally condemned by Islamic scholars. . . . There are many verses in the Qur'an that affirm the actuality and even the necessity of diversity in ways of life and religious belief.

In general, war is forbidden in Islam, except in cases of self-defense in response to explicit aggression. If there is a situation where injustice is being perpetrated or if the community is being invaded, then on a temporary basis permission is given to defend oneself.

[I]n recent decades . . . an intolerant ideology has been unleashed. A small minority of the world's one and a half billion Muslims has misconstrued the teachings of Islam to justify their misguided and immoral actions. It is most critical at this time for Muslims to condemn such extreme ideologies and their manifestations. It is equally important that non–Muslims understand that this ideology violates the fundamental moral principles of Islam and is repugnant to the vast majority of Muslims in the world. . . . So-called "suicide-bombers" did not appear until the mid-1990s. Such strategies have no precedent in Islamic history. The Qur'an says quite explicitly: *Do not kill yourselves* [4:29]. . . .

Muslims living in pluralistic societies have no religious reasons to oppose the laws of their own societies as long as they are just, but rather are encouraged to uphold the duly constituted laws of their own societies. . . . Islam and democracy are compatible and can coexist because Islam organizes humanity on the basis of the rule of law and human dignity. . . . The only principle of political governance expressed in the Qur'an is the principle of Consultation (Shura), which holds that communities will "*rule themselves by means of mutual consultation*" [Surah 42:38].

An American Muslim scholar, Abdul Aziz Sachedina, expresses it this way: "Islam does not encourage turning God into a political statement since humans cannot possess God. . . ."

[T]here is nothing in the Qur'an that essentially contradicts reason or science. . . . Repeatedly the Qur'an urges human beings to "reflect" and "use their intelligence."

Islam is not an alien religion. It does not claim a monopoly on virtue or truth. It follows in the way of previous spiritual traditions that recognized One Spirit operating within nature and human life. It continues on the Way of the great Prophets and Messengers of all sacred traditions.

Source: Selections from Kabir Helminski, *Islam and Human Values*, unpublished pamphlet, 2009.

■ ■ ■

SOURCE 23.6 **Debating the Burqa** ▶

Among the contested issues in the Islamic world, none have been more prominent than those involving the lives—and the bodies—of women. The revolutionary Islamist government of Iran, for example, insisted on and enforced "good hijab" for women, which meant compulsory head covering and very conservative and modest attire. But the issue has surfaced in Europe as well. A prominent British Muslim woman, Saira Khan, called for banning the burqa, the head-to-toe covering worn by some Muslim women, in public places. "The veil is simply a tool of oppression," she declared. "The burkha is the ultimate visual symbol of female oppression. It is the weapon of radical Muslim men who want to see Sharia law on Britain's streets, and would love women to be hidden, unseen and unheard. It is totally out of place in a civilised country."[31]

When the French government in 2011 began to enforce a law forbidding the concealment of the face in public, it was widely understood to be a prohibition of the burqa. To many French people, the burqa represented a security risk and violated the secularism of French life, while banning it prevented women from being forced by their families to wear it. But the new law prompted considerable protest in many places. One such protestor outside Notre Dame Cathedral in Paris said: "We view this ban as an assault on our human rights."[32] Source 23.6 shows a group of Muslim women in Britain, clad in black burqas, protesting the law outside the French embassy in London.

■ Based on the signs, how might you summarize the women's objections to the French ban on burqas?

■ Why might this kind of dress for women be highly objectionable to many in France and elsewhere in Europe?

■ How do you imagine that ordinary French people would respond to these signs?

Protests in London against French Ban of Face Concealment | 2011

Peter Macdiarmid/Getty Images

DOING HISTORY

1. **Understanding the issues:** What issues might arise in a conversation among people holding the various perspectives represented here? Can you identify any areas of agreement? On which points would they probably never agree?

2. **Comparing Islamic modernists:** How do you think Kemal Atatürk would have responded to later Islamic modernists such as Kabir Helminski and perhaps Saira Khan?

3. **Comparing Islamic radicals:** How might the authors of the Muslim Brotherhood declaration of 1936 respond to the actions of Hamas and the women protesting the French ban on burqas?

4. **Explaining variations:** What accounts for the very different understandings of Islam that are reflected in these sources?

Perspectives on the Iranian Revolution

The Iranian revolution of 1979 gave rise to a religiously inspired government that has sought to inscribe Islamist principles in the political, economic, and social fabric of a major Middle Eastern nation. In Voice 23.1, Francis Robinson, a prominent British historian of the Islamic world, describes the modern Islamic renewal movements that provide the larger context for the Iranian revolution. Then in Voice 23.2, John Esposito, a highly regarded American scholar of modern Islam, reflects on the specific conditions that gave rise to the Iranian revolution.

- How does Francis Robinson in Voice 23.1 explain the appeal of Islamist renewal movements since the 1970s?

- According to John Esposito in Voice 23.2, what conditions within Iran provided the raw material for revolution?

- **Integrating Primary and Secondary Sources:** How might both of these authors use the primary sources to illustrate or support their arguments?

VOICE 23.1

Francis Robinson on Islamic Renewal Movements | 1996

A powerful movement of religious renewal has animated all parts of the Muslim world since the eighteenth century. . . .

Since the 1970s the desire to effect renewal has been more powerfully expressed in the Islamist movements. Often led by western-educated professionals and run by university students, these movements have aimed to fill the vacuum created by the failures of the state at the local level in cities and towns through much of the Islamic world. By providing schools, clinics, welfare, and psychological support, they have served the needs of urban communities disrupted by the penetration of the modern state and the international economy. They have also attracted the millions who have flocked to the cities in recent decades from the countryside. The rhetoric of these movements is profoundly opposed to western culture and western power. Their programmes, which start from the premise that the Quran and the holy law are sufficient for all human circumstances, aim to establish an Islamic system to match those of capitalism or socialism. They are to be implemented by seizing power in the modern nation state. This understanding of Islam as a system, an ideology is new in

Islamic history. So too . . . is the complete merger between religion and political power.

Islamist movements . . . have brought Islam closer to the centre of political identity of Muslim peoples. In some places, such as Iran . . . , they have taken power.

Source: Francis Robinson, *The Cambridge Illustrated History of the Islamic World* (Cambridge: Cambridge University Press, 1996), 292, 293, 296.

VOICE 23.2

John Esposito on the Source of the Iranian Revolution | 1999

Iran [in 1979] captured the imagination of many throughout the Muslim world and the West. . . . A seemingly modern, enlightened and invincible shah was overthrown by a movement led by an ayatollah [a high-ranking religious scholar] in exile in France. Intellectuals, merchants, students, and journalists as well as clergy mobilized under the banner of Islam. Islam was . . . also a symbol of protest for all who opposed the shah. . . . Islamic symbols, rhetoric, and institutions provided the infrastructure for organization, protest, and mobilization of a coalition of forces calling for reform and in the end for revolution. . . .

Although the shah's modernization program did improve the lot of many, the benefits of modernization tended to favor disproportionately a minority of elites and urban centers. Economic, educational and military reforms were not accompanied by political liberalization. Traditional merchants and religious leaders . . . were alienated by the shah's religious and economic reforms. State control of religious affairs . . . and a tilt toward western markets and the corporate sector threatened their interests, authority, and power. Many modern educated academics, professionals, and journalists increasingly expressed concerns over the excessive dependence of Iran on the West. . . . Some . . . spoke of the dangers of "Westoxification," an excessive dependence on the West that threatened to rob Iranians of their independence and cultural identity. These were issues that resonated across many sectors of society.

Source: John Esposito, *The Oxford History of Islam* (Oxford: Oxford University Press, 1999), 661–62.

Notes

Prologue

1. See David Christian, *Maps of Time* (Berkeley: University of California Press, 2004).
2. Voltaire, *Treatise on Toleration*, chap. 22.
3. See David Christian, "World History in Context," *Journal of World History* 14, no. 4 (December 2003): 437–58.

Chapter 1

1. Richard Rainsford, "What Chance, the Survival Prospects of East Africa's Last Hunting and Gathering Tribe the Hadzabe, in a Gameless Environment?," Information about Northern Tanzania, March 1997, http://www.ntz.info/gen/b00473.html.
2. What follows comes from Sally McBreatry and Alison S. Brooks, "The Revolution That Wasn't: A New Interpretation of the Origin of Modern Human Behavior," *Journal of Human Evolution* 39 (2000): 453–563.
3. Charles V. Langlois and Charles Seignobos, *Introduction to the Study of History*, translated by G. G. Berry (New York: Holt, 1898), 17.
4. David Christian, Cynthia Stokes Brown, and Craig Benjamin, *Big History: Between Nothing and Everything* (New York: McGraw-Hill, 2014), 2.
5. William H. McNeill, "History and the Scientific Worldview," *History and Theory* 37, no. 1 (1998): 12.
6. Christian et al., *Big History*, 4.
7. David Christian, *Maps of Time: An Introduction to Big History* (Berkeley: University of California Press, 2004), 1–5.
8. Fred Spier, *Big History and the Future of Humanity* (West Sussex: Wiley-Blackwell, 2011), 132; David Christian, *Maps of Time* (Berkeley: University of California Press, 2004), 143.
9. Richard B. Lee, *The Dobe Ju/'hoansi* (New York: Harcourt Brace, 1993), 58.
10. J. C. Beaglehole, *The Journals of Captain James Cook* (Cambridge: Hakluyt Society, 1968), 1:399.
11. Inga Clendinnen, *Dancing with Strangers* (Cambridge: Cambridge University Press, 2005), 159–67.
12. Steven Pinker, *The Better Angels of Our Nature* (New York: Viking, 2011), 47–52.
13. Marshall Sahlins, *Stone Age Economics* (London: Tavistock, 1972), 1–39.
14. Christopher Ehret, *The Civilizations of Africa* (Charlottesville: University of Virginia Press, 2002), chap. 2.
15. Marija Gimbutas, *The Language of the Goddess* (San Francisco: HarperCollins, 1989), 316–18.
16. Neil Roberts, *The Holocene: An Environmental History* (Oxford: Blackwell, 1998), 116.
17. Nina V. Federoff, "Prehistoric GM Corn," *Science* 302 (November 2003): 1158.
18. Andrew Sherrat, "The Secondary Exploitation of Animals in the Old World," *World Archeology* 15, no. 1 (1983): 90–104.
19. Tom Standage, *A History of the World in Six Glasses* (New York: Walker, 2005), chaps. 1, 2; Li Zhengping, *Chinese Wine* (Cambridge: Cambridge University Press, 2011), 1–3.
20. Yuval Noah Harari, *Sapiens: A Brief History of Humankind* (New York: HarperCollins, 2015), chap. 5.
21. Anatoly M. Khazanov, *Nomads and the Outside World* (Madison: University of Wisconsin Press, 1994), 15.
22. Ian Hodder, "Women and Men at Catalhoyuk," *Scientific American* 15, no. 1 (2005): 35–41.
23. Marija Gimbutas, *The Language of the Goddess* (New York: Harper and Row, 1989), xix.
24. "Cultural Information," Jinta Desert Art, accessed May 9, 2017, http://www.jintaart.com.au/culinfo.html.
25. Josephine Flood, "Linkage between Rock-Art and Landscape in Aboriginal Australia," in *The Figured Landscape of Rock-Art*, edited by Christopher Chippindale and George Nash (Cambridge: Cambridge University Press, 2004), 197.

Chapter 2

1. Bryan Nelson, "Becoming One with Nature," Mother Nature Network, http://www.mnn.com/earth-matters/wilderness-resources/photos/7-people-who-gave-up-on-civilization-to-live-in-the-wild-0.
2. Charles C. Mann, *1491: New Revelations of the Americas before Columbus* (New York: Alfred A. Knopf, 2005), 174–91.
3. Jonathan Mark Kenoyer, *Ancient Cities of the Indus Valley Civilization* (Oxford: Oxford University Press, 1998), 83–84.
4. David Christian, *A History of Russia, Central Asia and Mongolia* (Oxford: Blackwell, 1998), 114.
5. Robert Carneiro, "A Theory of the Origin of the State," *Science* 169 (1970): 733–38.
6. Susan Pollock, *Ancient Mesopotamia* (Cambridge: Cambridge University Press, 1999), 48.
7. *The Epic of Gilgamesh*, translated and edited by Benjamin R. Foster (New York: W. W. Norton, 2001), 10, tablet 1: 226–32.
8. James Legge, trans., *The Chinese Classics* (London: Henry Frowde, 1893), 4:171–72.
9. Margaret Ehrenberg, *Women in Prehistory* (London: British Museum, 1989), 107.
10. Sherry Ortner, "Is Female to Male as Nature Is to Culture?," in *Women, Culture, and Society*, edited by Michelle Rosaldo and Louise Lamphere (Stanford, CA: Stanford University Press, 1974), 67–88.
11. Gerda Lerner, *The Creation of Patriarchy* (New York: Oxford University Press, 1986), 70.
12. I Samuel 8: 11–17.

13. Steven Pinker, *The Better Angels of Our Nature* (New York: Viking, 2011), chaps. 2, 3.

14. Hammurabi, *The Code of Hammurabi King of Babylon,* edited by Robert Francis Harper (Chicago: University of Chicago Press, 1904), http://oll.libertyfund.org/titles/1276#Harper_0762_26.

15. Adolf Erman, *The Literature of the Ancient Egyptians,* translated by Aylward M. Blackman (London: Methuen, 1927), 136–37.

16. Henri Frankfort et al., *Before Philosophy: The Intellectual Adventure of Ancient Man* (Baltimore: Penguin Books, 1963), 39, 138.

17. Quoted in Peter Stearns et al., *World Civilizations* (New York: Longman, 1996), 1:30.

18. See Clive Ponting, *A Green History of the World* (New York: St. Martin's Press, 1991), chap. 5.

19. K. J. W. Oosthoek, "The Role of Wood in World History," Environmental History Resources, 1998, http://www.eh-resources.org/wood.html#_ednrefl.

20. James B. Pritchard, ed., *Ancient Near Eastern Texts Relating to the Old Testament* (Princeton, NJ: Princeton University Press, 1969), 647–48.

21. Miriam Lichtheim, *Ancient Egyptian Literature* (Berkeley: University of California Press, 1975), 1:25–27.

22. M. J. Rowlands et al., eds., *Center and Periphery in the Ancient World* (Cambridge: Cambridge University Press, 1987), 59.

23. Marvin Harris, ed., *Cannibals and Kings* (New York: Vintage, 1978), 102.

24. Kenoyer, *Ancient Cities of the Indus Valley Civilization,* 84.

25. Gregory L. Possehl, *The Indus Civilization: A Contemporary Perspective* (Walnut Creek, CA: AltaMira Press, 2002), 114.

Part 2

1. Colin Ronan and Joseph Needham, *The Shorter Science and Civilization in China* (Cambridge: Cambridge University Press, 1978), 58.

Chapter 3

1. Cullen Murphy, *Are We Rome? The Fall of an Empire and the Fate of America* (Boston: Houghton Mifflin, 2007).

2. J. M. Cook, *The Persian Empire* (London: J. M. Dent, 1983), 76.

3. George Rawlinson, trans., *The Histories of Herodotus* (London: Dent, 1910), 1:131–40.

4. Erich F. Schmidt, *Persepolis I: Structures, Reliefs, Inscriptions,* Oriental Institute Publications 68 (Chicago: University of Chicago Press, 1953), 63.

5. Quoted in Anthony N. Penna, *The Human Footprint* (Oxford: Wiley-Blackwell, 2010), 151.

6. Quoted in Thomas R. Martin, *Ancient Greece from Prehistoric to Hellenistic Times* (New Haven, CT: Yale University Press, 1996), 86.

7. Christian Meier, *Athens* (New York: Metropolitan Books, 1993), 93.

8. Arrian, *The Campaigns of Alexander,* translated by Aubrey de Selincourt, revised by J. R. Hamilton (London: Penguin, 1971), 395–96.

9. Stanley Burstein, *The Hellenistic Period in World History* (Washington, DC: American Historical Association, 1996), 12.

10. Norman F. Cantor, *Antiquity* (New York: HarperCollins, 2003), 25.

11. Paul Halsall, "Early Western Civilization under the Sign of Gender," in *A Companion to Gender History,* edited by Teresa A. Meade and Merry E. Wiesner-Hanks (London: Blackwell, 2004), 293–94.

12. Keith W. Taylor, *The Birth of Vietnam* (Berkeley: University of California Press, 1983), 334.

13. Roger Boesche, *The First Great Political Realist: Kautilya and His Arthashastra* (Lanham, MD: Lexington Books, 2002), 17.

14. Stanley Wolpert, *A New History of India* (New York: Oxford University Press, 1993), 90.

15. Zhengyuan Fu, *Autocratic Tradition and Chinese Politics* (New York: Cambridge University Press, 1993), 188.

Chapter 4

1. "Birthday of Confucius celebrated with grand ceremony . . . ," Embassy of the People's Republic of China in Australia, September 29, 2009, http://au.china-embassy.org/eng/xw/t608286.htm.

2. Quoted in Arthur Waley, *Three Ways of Thought in Ancient China* (Garden City, NY: Doubleday, 1956), 159–60.

3. Nancy Lee Swann, trans., *Pan Chao: Foremost Woman Scholar of China* (New York: Century, 1932), 111–14.

4. Kam Louie and Morris Low, *Asian Masculinities* (London: Routledge, 2003), 3–6.

5. Quoted in Huston Smith, *The Illustrated World's Religions* (San Francisco: HarperCollins, 1994), 123.

6. Robert Marks, *China: Its Environment and History* (Lanham, MD: Rowman and Littlefield, 2012), 94–95.

7. Lao-tzu, *Tao Te Ching,* translated by James Legge, in *Sacred Books of the East* (Oxford: The Clarendon Press, 1891), 39:122.

8. Catherine Clay et al., *Envisioning Women in World History* (New York: McGraw-Hill, 2009), 1:67–77.

9. Quoted in Karen Andrews, "Women in Theravada Buddhism," Institute of Buddhist Studies, accessed November 21, 2017, http://www.bhikkhuni.net/women-in-theravada-buddhism/.

10. A. L. Basham, *The Wonder That Was India* (London: Sidgwick and Jackson, 1967), 309.

11. Isaiah 1:11–17.

12. Plato, *Apologia,* translated by Benjamin Jowett (1891).

13. Hippocrates, *On the Sacred Disease,* translated by Francis Adams, Internet Classics Archive, accessed February 2, 2012, http://classics.mit.edu/Hippocrates/sacred.html.

14. Karl Jaspers, *The Origin and Goal of History* (New Haven, CT: Yale University Press, 1953).

15. See, for example, Robert N. Bellah, "What Is Axial about the Axial Age?" *European Journal of Sociology* 46, no. 1 (2005): 69–89.

16. Jaspers, *The Origin and Goal of History,* 6.

17. See Iain Provan, *Convenient Myths* (Waco, TX: Baylor University Press, 2013), 2–3, 41.

18. Galatians 3:28.

19. Ephesians 5:22–23; 1 Corinthians 14:35.

20. "The Martyrdom of Saints Perpetua and Felicitas," *Frontline,* "From Jesus to Christ," PBS, April 1998, http://www.pbs.org/wgbh/pages/frontline/shows/religion/maps/primary/perpetua.html.

21. Robert Sider, "Early Christians in North Africa," *Coptic Church Review* 19, no. 3 (1998): 2.

22. Quoted in Mary Ann Rossi, "Priesthood, Precedent, and Prejudice: On Recovering the Women Priests of Early Christianity," *Journal of Feminist Studies* 7, no. 1 (1991): 73–94.

23. Chai-Shin Yu, *Early Buddhism and Christianity* (Delhi: Motilal Banarsidass, 1981), 211.

24. Peter Frankopan, *The Silk Roads: A New History of the World* (New York: Vintage, 2017), 9.

Chapter 5

1. Quoted in Lydia Polgreen, "Business Class Rises in Ashes of Caste System," *New York Times*, September 10, 2010.

2. Po Chu-I, "After Passing the Examination," in *More Translations from the Chinese*, by Arthur Waley (New York: Alfred A. Knopf, 1919), 37.

3. Quoted in Michael Lowe, *Everyday Life in Early Imperial China* (New York: Dorset, 1968), 38.

4. Li Shen, "Old Style," Selected Poems from T'ang Dynasty, accessed May 25, 2017, http://www.shigeku.org/xlib /lingshidao/hanshi/tang1.htm.

5. Orlando Patterson, *Slavery and Social Death* (Cambridge, MA: Harvard University Press, 1982).

6. A. L. Basham, *The Wonder That Was India* (London: Sidgwick and Jackson, 1967), 152.

7. Sarah Pomeroy et al., *Ancient Greece* (New York: Oxford University Press, 1999), 63, 239.

8. R. Zelnick-Abramovitz, *Not Wholly Free* (Leiden: Brill, 2005), 337, 343.

9. I Peter 2:18.

10. Quoted in Brent D. Shaw, *Spartacus and the Slave Wars: A Brief History with Documents* (Boston: Bedford/St. Martin's, 2001), 145.

11. Shaw, *Spartacus and the Slave Wars*, 143.

12. Milton Meltzer, *Slavery: A World History* (New York: Da Capo Press, 1993), 189.

13. Judith Bennett, *History Matters: Patriarchy and the Challenge of Feminism* (Philadelphia: University of Pennsylvania Press, 2006), chap. 4.

14. Quoted in Bret Hinsch, *Women in Early Imperial China* (Oxford: Rowman and Littlefield, 2002), 155.

15. Nancy Lee Swann, trans., *Pan Chao: Foremost Woman Scholar of China* (New York: Century, 1932), 111–14.

16. Quoted in Valerie Hansen, *The Open Empire* (New York: Norton, 2000), 183–84; see also Thomas Barfield, *The Perilous Frontier* (Cambridge: Blackwell, 1989), 140.

17. Aristotle, *Politica*, translated by H. Rackham, Loeb Classical Library, no. 264 (Cambridge, MA: Harvard University Press, 1932), 1254b10–14.

18. Sarah B. Pomeroy, *Spartan Women* (Oxford: Oxford University Press, 2002), 63.

19. Anton Powell, "Dining Groups, Marriage, Homosexuality," in *Sparta*, edited by Michael Whitby (New York: Routledge, 2002), 93.

20. Quoted in "The Destruction of Pompeii, 79 AD," EyeWitness to History, 1999, www.eyewitnesstohistory.com/pompeii.htm.

Chapter 6

1. "Morales Becomes Head of a Pluri-national State Blessed by Aymara Gods," *MercoPress*, January 22, 2010, http://en.mercopress .com/2010/01/22/morales-becomes-head-of-a-pluri-national -state-blessed-by-aymara-gods.

2. Roderick J. McIntosh, *Ancient Middle Niger* (Cambridge: Cambridge University Press, 2005), 10.

3. Roderick J. McIntosh, *The Peoples of the Middle Niger* (Oxford: Blackwell, 1998), 177.

4. Richard E. W. Adams, *Ancient Civilizations of the New World* (Boulder, CO: Westview Press, 1997), 53–56; T. Patrick Culbert, "The New Maya," *Archeology* 51, no. 5 (1998): 47–51

5. George L. Cowgill, "The Central Mexican Highlands . . . ," in *The Cambridge History of the Native Peoples of the Americas*, vol. 2, pt. 1, "Mesoamerica," edited by Richard E. W. Adams and Murdo J. MacLeod (Cambridge: Cambridge University Press, 2000), 289.

6. Scott Norris, "Mummy of Tattooed Woman Discovered in Peru Pyramid," *National Geographic News*, May 16, 2006, http://news .nationalgeographic.com/news/2006/05/mummy-peru.html.

7. Gordon F. McEwan, *The Inca: New Perspectives* (New York: W. W. Norton, 2008), 39–41.

8. Christopher Ehret, *The Civilizations of Africa* (Charlottesville: University of Virginia Press, 2002), 175.

9. David Schoenbrun, "Gendered Themes in Early African History," in *A Companion to Gender History*, edited by Teresa Meade and Merry Wiesner-Hanks (Oxford: Blackwell, 2004), 253–56.

10. See Jan Vansina, *Paths in the Rainforest* (Madison: University of Wisconsin Press, 1990), 95–99.

11. David Hurst Thomas, *Exploring Ancient Native America* (New York: Routledge, 1999), 137–42.

12. Brian M. Fagan, *Ancient North America* (London: Thames and Hudson, 2005), 475.

13. Quoted in Lynda Norene Shaffer, *Native Americans before 1492* (Armonk, NY: M. E. Sharpe, 1992), 70.

14. Steven R. Fischer, *A History of the Pacific Islands* (New York: Palgrave Macmillan, 2013), 37. This section draws heavily on Fischer, chaps. 1, 2; Ian Campbell, *Worlds Apart* (Cambridge: Cambridge University Press, 2011), chaps. 1, 2; and Matt K. Matsuda, *Pacific Worlds* (Cambridge: Cambridge University Press, 2012), chaps. 1, 2.

15. Campbell, *Worlds Apart*, 48.

16. Terry L. Hunt, "Rethinking the Fall of Easter Island," *American Scientist* 94, no. 5 (September/October 2006), 412–19.

17. David W. Phillipson, *Foundations of an African Civilization: Aksum and the Northern Horn 100 BC–AD 1300* (Woodbridge, Suffolk: James Currey, 2012), 143.

Chapter 7

1. Nayan Chanda, *Bound Together* (New Haven, CT: Yale University Press, 2007), 35–36.

2. William J. Bernstein, *A Splendid Exchange* (New York: Grove Press, 2008), 58–66; Proverbs 7:17–18.

3. Quoted in Patricia Buckley Ebrey, *The Inner Quarters* (Berkeley: University of California Press, 1993), 150.

4. Seneca the Elder, *Declamations* (Cambridge: Harvard University Press, 1999), 1:374–75.

5. Liu Xinru, "Silks and Religion in Eurasia, A.D. 600–1200," *Journal of World History* 6, no. 1 (1995): 25–48.

6. Boccaccio, *The Decameron*, translated by M. Rigg (London: David Campbell, 1921), 1:5–11.

7. Kenneth McPherson, *The Indian Ocean* (Oxford: Oxford University Press, 1993), 15.

8. Janet L. Abu-Lughod, *Before European Hegemony* (Oxford: Oxford University Press, 1989), 269.

9. McPherson, *Indian Ocean*, 97.

10. This section draws heavily from Craig A. Lockard, *Southeast Asia in World History* (Oxford: Oxford University Press, 2009), chaps. 2, 3. See also Victor Lieberman, *Strange Parallels* (Cambridge: Cambridge University Press, 2009), chaps. 1, 7.

11. Kenneth R. Hall, *Maritime Trade and State Development in Early Southeast Asia* (Honolulu: University of Hawaii Press, 1985), 101.

12. M. C. Horton and T. R. Burton, "Indian Metalwork in East Africa: The Bronze Lion Statuette from Shanga," *Antiquities* 62 (1988): 22.

13. Ross Dunn, *The Adventures of Ibn Battuta* (Berkeley: University of California Press, 1986), 124.

14. Christopher Ehret, *The Civilizations of Africa* (Charlottesville: University of Virginia Press, 2002), 255.

15. Richard W. Bulliet, *The Camel and the Wheel* (New York: Columbia University Press, 1990), 8. This feature largely derives from this book.

16. Nehemia Levtzion and Jay Spaulding, eds., *Medieval West Africa: Views from Arab Scholars and Merchants* (Princeton, NJ: Marcus Wiener, 2003) 5.

17. David Schoenbrun, "Gendered Themes in Early African History," in *A Companion to Gender History*, edited by Teresa Meade and Merry Wiesner-Hanks (Oxford: Blackwell, 2004), 263.

18. Quoted in John Iliffe, *Africans: The History of a Continent* (Cambridge: Cambridge University Press, 1995), 75–76.

19. J. R. McNeill and William McNeill, *The Human Web* (New York: W. W. Norton, 2003), 160.

20. Li Rongxi, trans., *A Biography of the Tripitaka Master of the Great Ci'en Monastery of the Great Tang Dynasty* (Berkeley, CA: Numata Center for Buddhist Translation, 1995), 31.

Chapter 8

1. Tom Phillips, "China's Xi Jinping Says Paris Climate Deal Must Not Be Allowed to Fail," *The Guardian*, January 18, 2017.

2. Quoted in Mark Elvin, *The Retreat of the Elephants* (New Haven, CT: Yale University Press, 2004), 19.

3. Mark Elvin, *The Pattern of the Chinese Past* (London: Eyre Methuen, 1973), 55.

4. Samuel Adshead, *Tang China: The Rise of the East in World History* (New York: Palgrave, 2004), 30.

5. William McNeill, *The Pursuit of Power* (Chicago: University of Chicago Press, 1984), 50.

6. See "The Attractions of the Capital," in *Chinese Civilization: A Sourcebook*, edited by Patricia Buckley Ebrey (New York: Free Press, 1993), 178–85.

7. Marco Polo, *The Travels of Marco Polo*, translated by Henry Yule (Toronto: General, 1993), 2:185.

8. Jack Kelly, *Gunpowder: Alchemy, Bombards, and Pyrotechnics: The History of the Explosive That Changed the World* (New York: Basic Books, 2005), 4. Much of this feature is derived from this book.

9. J. R. McNeill and William H. McNeill, *The Human Web* (New York: W. W. Norton, 2003), 123.

10. Quoted in Francesca Bray, *Technology and Gender: Fabrics of Power in Late Imperial China* (Berkeley: University of California Press, 1997), 116.

11. Patricia Buckley Ebrey, *The Inner Quarters* (Berkeley: University of California Press, 1993), 207.

12. Ebrey, 37–43.

13. Ebrey, 6.

14. Burton Watson, trans., *Records of the Grand Historian of China*, rev. ed. (New York: Columbia University Press, 1993), 2:144–45, as quoted in Thomas J. Barfield, "Steppe Empires, China, and the Silk Route," in *Nomads in the Sedentary World*, edited by Anatoly M. Khazanov and Andre Wink (New York: Routledge, 2001), 237.

15. Quoted in Edward H. Shafer, *The Golden Peaches of Samarkand* (Berkeley: University of California Press, 1963), 28.

16. Susan Mann, "Women in East Asia," in *Women's History in Global Perspective*, edited by Bonnie Smith (Urbana: University of Illinois Press, 2005), 2:53–56.

17. Quoted in McNeill, *Pursuit of Power*, 40.

18. John K. Fairbank et al., *East Asia: Tradition and Transformation* (Boston: Houghton Mifflin, 1978), 353.

19. Arnold Pacey, *Technology in World Civilization* (Cambridge, MA: MIT Press, 1991), 50–53.

20. McNeill, *Pursuit of Power*, 24–25.

21. Quoted in Arthur F. Wright, *Studies in Chinese Buddhism* (New Haven, CT: Yale University Press, 1990), 16.

22. Arthur F. Wright, *Buddhism in Chinese History* (Stanford, CA: Stanford University Press, 1959), 36–39.

23. Quoted in Wright, *Buddhism in Chinese History*, 67.

24. Quoted in Eric Zurcher, *The Buddhist Conquest of China* (Leiden: E. J. Brill, 1959), 1:262.

25. Quoted in Robert Marks, *China: Its Environment and History* (Lanham, MD: Rowman and Littlefield, 2012), 139–40.

26. Edwin O. Reischauer, *Ennin's Travels in Tang China* (New York: Ronald Press, 1955), 221–24.

27. "Ma Yuan — Song Dynasty," China Online Museum, http://www.chinaonlinemuseum.com/painting-ma-yuan-6.php.

28. David Hinton, *Existence: A Story* (Boulder, CO: Shambhala, 2016), 3.

Chapter 9

1. "Religion in Sierra Leone," *The Economist*, May 31, 2014.

2. Reza Aslan, *No God but God* (New York: Random House, 2005), 14.

3. Quoted in Karen Armstrong, *A History of God* (New York: Ballantine Books, 1993), 146.

4. Quran 1:5 and 41:53.

5. Quran 9:71.

6. "Prophet Muhammad's Farewell Sermon," IslamiCity, accessed November 28, 2014, http://www.islamicity.com/articles /Articles.asp?ref=ic0107-322.

7. Quoted in Fred M. Donner, *Muhammad and the Believers* (Cambridge, MA: Harvard University Press, 2010), 114. The preceding section draws on chapter 3.

8. Richard Bulliet, *Conversion to Islam in the Medieval Period* (Cambridge, MA: Harvard University Press, 1979), 33.

9. Quoted in Bertold Spuler, *The Muslim World*, vol. 1, *The Age of the Caliph* (Leiden: E. J. Brill, 1960), 29.

10. Bernard Lewis, *Islam and the West* (New York: Oxford University Press, 1993), 157.

11. Quoted in Patricia Crone, "The Rise of Islam in the World," in *Cambridge Illustrated History of the Islamic World*, edited by Francis Robinson (Cambridge: Cambridge University Press, 1996), 14.

12. Many of these stories are summarized from accounts in Imam Jamal Rahman, *Sacred Laughter of the Sufis* (Woodstock, VT: Skylight Paths, 2014).

13. Quran 4:34.

14. Quoted in Judith Tucker, "Gender and Islamic History," in *Islamic and European Expansion*, edited by Michael Adas (Philadelphia: Temple University Press, 1993), 46.

15. Ria Kloppenborg and Wouter Hanegraaf, eds., *Female Stereotypes in Religious Traditions* (Leiden: E. J. Brill, 1995), 111.

16. Quoted in William T. de Bary, ed., *Sources of Indian Tradition* (New York: Columbia University Press, 1958), 2:355–57.

17. Quoted in Nikki R. Keddie, "Women in the Middle East since the Rise of Islam," in *Women's History in Global Perspective*, edited by Bonnie G. Smith (Urbana: University of Illinois Press, 2005), 81.

18. Ross Dunn, *The Adventures of Ibn Battuta* (Berkeley: University of California Press, 1986), 300.

19. Jane I. Smith, "Islam and Christendom," in *The Oxford History of Islam*, edited by John L. Esposito (Oxford: Oxford University Press, 1999), 317–21.

20. Richard Eaton, "Islamic History as Global History," in Adas, *Islamic and European Expansion*, 12.

21. Francis Robinson, "Knowledge, Its Transmission and the Making of Muslim Societies," in Robinson, *Cambridge Illustrated History of the Islamic World*, 230.

22. Robinson, 215.

23. Donner, *Muhammad and the Believers*, 179.

Chapter 10

1. Louisa Lim, "In the Land of Mao, a Rising Tide of Christianity," *All Things Considered*, NPR, July 19, 2010, http://www.npr.org /templates/story/story.php?storyId=128546334.

2. This section relies heavily on Diarmaid MacCulloch, *Christianity: The First Three Thousand Years* (New York: Viking, 2010), chap. 8.

3. Quoted in Ray Riegert and Thomas Moore, eds., *The Lost Sutras of Jesus* (Berkeley, CA: Ulysses Press, 2006), 103.

4. Quoted in Deno John Geanakoplos, *Byzantium: Church, Society, and Civilization Seen through Contemporary Eyes* (Chicago: University of Chicago Press, 1984), 389.

5. Quoted in Geanakoplos, *Byzantium*, 143.

6. Quoted in Geanakoplos, *Byzantium*, 369.

7. Quoted in Patrick J. Geary, *Before France and Germany* (New York: Oxford University Press, 1988), 79.

8. Quoted in Stephen Williams, *Diocletian and the Roman Recovery* (London: Routledge, 1996), 218.

9. Peter Brown, *The Rise of Western Christendom* (London: Blackwell, 1996), 305.

10. Quoted in John M. Hobson, *The Eastern Origins of Western Civilization* (New York: Cambridge University Press, 2004), 113.

11. Clive Ponting, *A Green History of the World* (New York: St. Martin's, 1991), 121–23.

12. Quoted in Richard C. Hoffman, "Economic Development and Aquatic Ecosystems in Medieval Europe," *American Historical Review* 101, no. 3 (1996): 648.

13. Judith M. Bennett, *A Medieval Life* (Boston: McGraw-Hill, 1998).

14. Bonnie Anderson and Judith Zinsser, *A History of Their Own* (Oxford: Oxford University Press, 2000), 1:393–94.

15. Christopher Tyerman, *Fighting for Christendom: Holy Wars and the Crusades* (Oxford: Oxford University Press, 2004), 16.

16. Quoted in Elizabeth Hallam, *Chronicles of the Crusades* (New York: Welcome Rain, 2000), 127.

17. Quoted in Peter Watson, *Ideas* (New York: Harper, 2006), 319.

18. Quoted in Jean Gimple, *The Medieval Machine* (New York: Holt, 1976), 178.

19. Quoted in Stuart B. Schwartz, ed., *Victors and Vanquished* (Boston: Bedford/St. Martin's, 2000), 147.

20. Quoted in Carlo Cipolla, *Before the Industrial Revolution* (New York: Norton, 1976), 207.

21. Quoted in S. Lilley, *Men, Machines, and History* (New York: International, 1965), 62.

22. See Toby Huff, *The Rise of Early Modern Science* (Cambridge: Cambridge University Press, 1993).

23. Quoted in Edward Grant, *Science and Religion from Aristotle to Copernicus* (Westport, CT: Greenwood Press, 2004), 158.

24. Quoted in L. Thorndike, *A History of Magic and Experimental Science* (New York: Columbia University Press, 1923), 2:58.

25. Quoted in Edward Grant, *God and Reason in the Middle Ages* (Cambridge: Cambridge University Press, 2001), 70.

26. Quoted in Grant, *Science and Religion*, 228–29.

27. Marcia L. Colish, *Medieval Foundations of the Western Intellectual Tradition* (New Haven, CT: Yale University Press, 1997), 128.

Chapter 11

1. Jehangir S. Pocha, "Mongolia Sees Genghis Khan's Good Side," *New York Times*, May 10, 2005.

2. Giovanni Carpini, *The Story of the Mongols*, translated by Erik Hildinger (Boston: Braden, 1996), 54.

3. Quoted in Peter B. Golden, "Nomads and Sedentary Societies in Eurasia," in *Agricultural and Pastoral Societies in Ancient and Classical History*, edited by Michael Adas (Philadelphia: Temple University Press, 2001), 73.

4. Anatoly Khazanov, "The Spread of World Religions in Medieval Nomadic Societies of the Eurasian Steppes," in *Nomadic Diplomacy, Destruction and Religion from the Pacific to the Adriatic*,

edited by Michael Gervers and Wayne Schlepp (Toronto: Joint Center for Asia Pacific Studies, 1994), 11.

5. Quoted in J. Otto Maenchen-Helfer, *The World of the Huns* (Berkeley: University of California Press, 1973), 14.

6. Carter Finley, *The Turks in World History* (Oxford: Oxford University Press, 2005), 28–37.

7. Finley, 40.

8. David Christian, *A History of Russia, Central Asia, and Mongolia* (London: Blackwell, 1998), 1:385.

9. Quoted in Christian, 389.

10. Stephen Turnbull, *The Mongol Invasions of Japan, 1274 and 1281* (Oxford: Osprey, 2010). This feature is derived largely from this book.

11. Jack Weatherford, *Genghis Khan and the Making of the Modern World* (New York: Crown, 2004), 86.

12. Chinggis Khan, "Letter to Changchun," in E. Bretschneider, *Mediaeval Researches from Eastern Asiatic Sources* (London: Kegan, Paul, Trench, Trübner, 1875), 1:37–39.

13. Thomas T. Allsen, *Mongol Imperialism* (Berkeley: University of California Press, 1987), 6.

14. Chinggis Khan, "Letter to Changchun," 38.

15. Quoted in Weatherford, *Genghis Khan*, 111.

16. Thomas J. Barfield, *The Nomadic Alternative* (Englewood Cliffs, NJ: Prentice Hall, 1993), 166.

17. Quoted in Christian, *History of Russia*, 1:425.

18. Quoted in David Morgan, *Medieval Persia* (London: Longman, 1988), 79.

19. Morgan, 82.

20. Guity Nashat, "Women in the Middle East," in *A Companion to Gender History*, edited by Teresa A. Meade and Merry E. Wiesner-Hanks (London: Blackwell, 2004), 243.

21. Charles J. Halperin, *Russia and the Golden Horde* (Bloomington: Indiana University Press, 1985), 126.

22. Charles H. Halperin, "Russia in the Mongol Empire in Comparative Perspective," *Harvard Journal of Asiatic Studies* 43, no. 1 (1983): 261.

23. Thomas Allsen, *Culture and Conquest in Mongol Eurasia* (Cambridge: Cambridge University Press, 2001), 211.

24. Quoted in Allsen, 121.

25. George Nathaniel Curzon, *Problems of the Far East* (London: Longmans, Green, 1894), vi.

26. Yuval Noah Harari, *Sapiens: A Brief History of Humankind* (New York: HarperCollins, 2015), 191.

27. William Skidelsky, "Niall Ferguson: 'Westerners Don't Understand How Vulnerable Freedom Is,'" *The Observer*, February 19, 2011, accessed May 22, 2017, https://www.theguardian.com /books/2011/feb/20/niall-ferguson-interview-civilization.

28. John Aberth, *The First Horseman: Disease in Human History* (Upper Saddle River, NJ: Pearson/Prentice Hall, 2007), 18.

29. Quoted in John Aberth, *The Black Death: The Great Mortality of 1348–1350* (Boston: Bedford/St. Martin's, 2005), 84–85.

30. Michael Dols, *The Black Death in the Middle East* (Princeton, NJ: Princeton University Press, 1977), 212, 223.

31. Quoted in John Aberth, *A Knight at the Movies: Medieval History on Film* (New York: Routledge, 2003), 225.

32. Quoted in Aberth, *Black Death*, 72.

33. Quoted in Dols, *Black Death in the Middle East*, 67.

34. Andre Gunder Frank, *ReOrient: Global Economy in the Asian Age* (Berkeley: University of California Press, 1998), 256.

35. Arnold Pacey, *Technology in World Civilization* (Cambridge, MA: MIT Press, 1990), 62.

36. Quoted in Golden, "Nomads and Sedentary Societies," 72–73.

37. Quoted in Gregory Guzman, "Were the Barbarians a Negative or Positive Factor in Ancient and Medieval History?" *Historian* 50 (August 1988): 558–72.

38. Quoted in Barfield, *Nomadic Alternative*, 3.

Chapter 12

1. Winona LaDuke, "We Are Still Here: The 500 Year Celebration," *Sojourners*, October 1991.

2. Jonathan Marcantoni, "Columbus Day . . . Is Complicated," October 9, 2015, http://www.latinorebels.com/2015/10/09 /in-defense-of-columbus-day/.

3. Brian Fagan, *Ancient North America* (London: Thames and Hudson, 2005), 503.

4. Quoted in Charles C. Mann, *1491: New Revelations of the Americas before Columbus* (New York: Alfred A. Knopf, 2005), 334.

5. Louise Levanthes, *When China Ruled the Seas* (New York: Simon and Schuster, 1994), 175.

6. Christine de Pisan, *The Book of the City of Ladies*, translated by Rosalind Brown-Grant (New York: Penguin Books, 1999), pt. 1, p. 1.

7. Frank Viviano, "China's Great Armada," *National Geographic*, July 2005, 34.

8. Quoted in C. R. N. Routh, *They Saw It Happen in Europe: An Anthology of Eyewitnesses' Accounts of Events in European History, 1450–1600* (Oxford: Blackwell, 1965), 386.

9. Quoted in John J. Saunders, ed., *The Muslim World on the Eve of Europe's Expansion* (Englewood Cliffs, NJ: Prentice Hall, 1966), 41–43.

10. Leo Africanus, *History and Description of Africa* (London: Hakluyt Society, 1896), 824–25.

11. Quoted in Craig A. Lockhard, *Southeast Asia in World History* (Oxford: Oxford University Press, 2009), 67.

12. Quoted in Patricia Risso, *Merchants and Faith* (Boulder, CO: Westview Press, 1995), 49.

13. Quoted in Stuart B. Schwartz, ed., *Victors and Vanquished* (Boston: Bedford/St. Martin's, 2000), 8.

14. Quoted in Michael E. Smith, *The Aztecs* (London: Blackwell, 2003), 108.

15. Smith, 220.

16. Quoted in Miguel Leon-Portilla, *Aztec Thought and Culture*, translated from the Spanish by Jack Emory Davis (Norman: University of Oklahoma Press, 1963), 7.

17. For a summary of this practice among the Aztecs and Incas, see Karen Vieira Powers, *Women in the Crucible of Conquest* (Albuquerque: University of New Mexico Press, 2005), chap. 1.

18. Powers, 25.

19. Louise Burkhart, "Mexica Women on the Home Front," in *Indian Women of Early Mexico*, edited by Susan Schroeder et al. (Norman: University of Oklahoma Press, 1997), 25–54.

20. The "web" metaphor is derived from J. R. McNeill and William H. McNeill, *The Human Web* (New York: W. W. Norton, 2003).

21. Quoted in Rosamund E. Mack, *Bazaar to Piazza* (Berkeley: University of California Press, 2002), 1.

22. Jerry Brotton, *The Renaissance Bazaar: From the Silk Road to Michaelangelo* (Oxford: Oxford University Press, 2006), 51.

23. Brotton, 51.

Chapter 13

1. See Kevin Meerschaert, "U.S. Sen. Nelson Says Putin Wants to Rebuild Russian Empire," *WJCT News*, March 17, 2014, http://news.wjct.org/post/us-sen-nelson-says-putin-wants-rebuild-russian-empire; and Asli Aydintasbas, "Rebuilding the Turkish Empire: Fantasy or Reality?" *The Caravan*, April 17, 2013, http://www.hoover.org/research/rebuilding-turkish-empire-fantasy-or-reality.

2. Quoted in Thomas E. Skidmore and Peter H. Smith, *Modern Latin America* (New York: Oxford University Press, 2001), 15.

3. George Raudzens, ed., *Technology, Disease, and Colonial Conquest* (Boston: Brill Academic, 2003), xiv.

4. Quoted in Noble David Cook, *Born to Die: Disease and the New World Conquest* (Cambridge: Cambridge University Press, 1998), 202.

5. Quoted in Cook, 206.

6. Quoted in Charles C. Mann, *1491: New Revelations of the Americas before Columbus* (New York: Alfred A. Knopf, 2005), 56.

7. Geoffrey Parker, *Global Crisis* (New Haven, CT: Yale University Press, 2013), chap. 15.

8. Quoted in Charles C. Mann, *1493: Uncovering the New World Columbus Created* (New York: Alfred A. Knopf, 2011), 165.

9. Felipe Fernandez-Armesto, "Empires in Their Global Context," in *The Atlantic in Global History*, edited by Jorge Canizares-Esguerra and Erik R. Seeman (Upper Saddle River, NJ: Prentice Hall, 2007), 105.

10. Quoted in Alejandro Lugo, *Fragmented Lives; Assembled Parts* (Austin: University of Texas Press, 2008), 53.

11. Quoted in Anthony Padgen, "Identity Formation in Spanish America," in *Colonial Identity in the Atlantic World, 1500–1800*, edited by Nicholas Canny and Anthony Padgen (Princeton, NJ: Princeton University Press, 1987), 56.

12. Quoted in James Lockhart and Stuart B. Schwartz, *Early Latin America* (Cambridge: Cambridge University Press, 1983), 206.

13. Mary Prince, *The History of Mary Prince* (1831; Project Gutenberg, 2006), http://www.gutenberg.org/ebooks/17851.

14. Kevin Reilly et al., eds., *Racism: A Global Reader* (Armonk, NY: M. E. Sharpe, 2003), 136–37.

15. Benjamin Wadsworth, *The Well-Ordered Family* (1712), 39.

16. Willard Sutherland, *Taming the Wild Fields: Colonization and Empire on the Russian Steppe* (Ithaca, NY: Cornell University Press, 2004), 223–24.

17. Quoted in Michael Khodarkovsky, *Russia's Steppe Frontier* (Bloomington: Indiana University Press, 2002), 216.

18. Khodarkovsky, 222.

19. Geoffrey Hosking, "The Freudian Frontier," *Times Literary Supplement*, March 10, 1995, 27.

20. Peter Perdue, *China Marches West: The Qing Conquest of Central Eurasia* (Cambridge, MA: Harvard University Press, 2005), 10–11.

21. Quoted in P. Lewis, *Pirs, Shrines, and Pakistani Islam* (Rawalpindi, Pakistan: Christian Study Centre, 1985), 84.

22. Quoted in Stanley Wolpert, *A New History of India* (New York: Oxford University Press, 1993), 160.

23. Lewis Melville, *Lady Mary Wortley Montagu: Her Life and Letters* (Whitefish, MT: Kessinger, 2004), 88.

24. Jane I. Smith, "Islam and Christendom," in *The Oxford History of Islam*, edited by John Esposito (Oxford: Oxford University Press, 1999), 342.

25. Charles Thornton Forester and F. H. Blackburne Daniell, *The Life and Letters of Ogier Ghiselin de Busbecq* (London: C. Kegan Paul, 1881), 1:405–6.

26. Jean Bodin, "The Rise and Fall of Commonwealths," Chapter VII, Constitution Society, accessed February 21, 2012, http://www.constitution.org/bodin/bodin_4.htm.

Chapter 14

1. Jacob Wheeler, "From Slave Post to Museum," *Christian Science Monitor*, December 31, 2002.

2. M. N. Pearson, ed., *Spices in the Indian Ocean World* (Aldershot, UK: Valorium, 1996), xv.

3. Quoted in Paul Lunde, "The Coming of the Portuguese," *Saudi Aramco World*, July/August 2005, 56.

4. Quoted in Patricio N. Abinales and Donna J. Amoroso, *State and Society in the Philippines* (Lanham, MD: Rowman and Littlefield, 2005), 50.

5. Quoted in Craig A. Lockard, *Southeast Asia in World History* (Oxford: Oxford University Press, 2009), 85.

6. Anthony Reid, *Southeast Asia in the Age of Commerce, 1450–1680* (New Haven, CT: Yale University Press, 1993), 2:274, 290.

7. Anthony Reid, *Charting the Shape of Early Modern Southeast Asia* (Chiang Mai, Thailand: Silkworm Books, 1999), 227.

8. Quoted in Adam Clulow, "Like Lambs in Japan and Devils outside Their Land: Diplomacy, Violence, and Japanese Merchants in Southeast Asia," *Journal of World History* 24, no. 2 (2013): 343.

9. Kenneth Pomeranz and Steven Topik, *The World That Trade Created* (Armonk, NY: M. E. Sharpe, 2006), 28.

10. Makrand Mehta, *Indian Merchants and Entrepreneurs in Historical Perspective* (Delhi: Academic Foundation, 1991), 54–58.

11. Andre Gunder Frank, *ReOrient: Global Economy in the Asian Age* (Berkeley: University of California Press, 1998), 131.

12. Quoted in Richard von Glahn, "Myth and Reality of China's Seventeenth Century Monetary Crisis," *Journal of Economic History* 56, no. 2 (1996): 132.

13. Quoted in Pomeranz and Topik, *The World That Trade Created*, 165.

14. Quoted in John Hemming, *The Conquest of the Inca* (New York: Harcourt, 1970), 372.

15. Dennis O. Flynn and Arturo Giraldez, "Born with a 'Silver Spoon,'" *Journal of World History* 6, no. 2 (1995): 210.

16. Quoted in Mark Elvin, *The Retreat of the Elephants* (New Haven, CT: Yale University Press, 2004), 37.

17. Quoted in Robert Marks, *The Origins of the Modern World* (Lanham, MD: Rowman and Littlefield, 2002), 81.

18. See John Richards, *The Endless Frontier* (Berkeley: University of California Press, 2003), pt. 4. Much of this section is drawn from this source.

19. Quoted in Elspeth M. Veale, *The English Fur Trade in the Later Middle Ages* (Oxford: Clarendon Press, 1966), 141.

20. Quoted in Herbert Milton Sylvester, *Indian Wars of New England* (Cleveland, 1910), 1:386.

21. Quoted in Timothy Brook, *Vermeer's Hat: The Seventeenth Century and the Dawn of the Global World* (London: Bloomsbury, 2008), 44.

22. Quoted in Richards, *Endless Frontier*, 499.

23. Richards, 504.

24. Quoted in Jeff Crane, *The Environment in American History* (New York: Routledge, 2015), 68.

25. Pamela McVay, *Envisioning Women in World History* (New York: McGraw-Hill, 2009), 86.

26. These figures derive from the Trans-Atlantic Slave Trade Database, accessed December 26, 2017, http://www.slavevoyages.org/assessment/estimates.

27. Quoted in Charles E. Curran, *Change in Official Catholic Moral Teaching* (Mahwah, NJ: Paulist Press, 2003), 67.

28. David Brion Davis, *Challenging the Boundaries of Slavery* (Cambridge, MA: Harvard University Press, 2003), 13.

29. Quoted in Bernard Lewis, *Race and Slavery in the Middle East* (New York: Oxford University Press, 1990), 52–53.

30. Audrey Smedley, *Race in North America* (Boulder, CO: Westview Press, 1993), 57.

31. Kevin Reilly et al., eds., *Racism: A Global Reader* (Armonk, NY: M. E. Sharpe, 2003), 131.

32. Quoted in Donald R. Wright, *The World and a Very Small Place in Africa* (Armonk, NY: M. E. Sharpe, 1997), 109–10.

33. John Thornton, *Africa and Africans in the Making of the Atlantic World* (Cambridge: Cambridge University Press, 1998), 72.

34. Thomas Phillips, "A Journal of a Voyage Made in the Hannibal of London in 1694," in *Documents Illustrative of the History of the Slave Trade to America*, edited by Elizabeth Donnan (Washington, DC: Carnegie Institute, 1930), 399–410.

35. Erik Gilbert and Jonathan T. Reynolds, *Africa in World History* (Upper Saddle River, NJ: Pearson Educational, 2004), 160.

36. Anne Bailey, *African Voices in the Atlantic Slave Trade* (Boston: Beacon Press, 2005), 153–54.

37. This account is based largely on Thomas Bluett, *Some Memoirs of the Life of Job . . .* (London, 1734), http://docsouth.unc.edu/neh/bluett/bluett.html/; and James T. Campbell, *Middle Passages* (New York: Penguin Books, 2007), 1–14.

38. Francis Moore, *Travels into the Inland Parts of Africa* (London, 1755), 146–47.

39. James Grehan, "Smoking and 'Early Modern' Sociability: The Great Tobacco Debate in the Ottoman Middle East (Seventeenth to Eighteenth Centuries)," *American Historical Review* 111, no. 5 (2006): 1352–77.

40. Edwards Forbes Robinson, *Coffee Houses in England* (London: Kegan, Paul, Trench, Trübner & Co., 1893), 163.

41. Brook, *Vermeer's Hat,* 140.

Chapter 15

1. Andrew Rice, "Mission from Africa," *New York Times Magazine*, April 8, 2009; "African Missionaries Take Religion to the West," *Church Shift*, August 7, 2006, http://www.churchshift.org/in-the-press/70-african-missionaries-take-religion-to-the-west.

2. Quoted in Armin Siedlecki and Perry Brown, "Preachers and Printers," *Christian History*, Issue 118 (2016): 22.

3. Glenn J. Ames, *Vasco da Gama: Renaissance Crusader* (New York: Pearson/Longman, 2005), 50.

4. Quoted in Marysa Navarro et al., *Women in Latin America and the Caribbean* (Bloomington: Indiana University Press, 1999), 37.

5. Quoted in James Rinehart, *Apocalyptic Faith and Political Violence* (New York: Palgrave Macmillan, 2006), 42.

6. Quoted in Nicolas Griffiths, *The Cross and the Serpent* (Norman: University of Oklahoma Press, 1996), 263.

7. Richard M. Eaton, "Islamic History as Global History," in *Islamic and European Expansion*, edited by Michael Adas (Philadelphia: Temple University Press, 1993), 25.

8. Patricia Buckley Ebrey, ed. and trans., *Chinese Civilization: A Sourcebook* (New York: Free Press, 1993), 257.

9. Robert Bly and Jane Hirshfield, trans., *Mirabai: Ecstatic Poems* (Boston: Beacon Press, 2004), ix–xi.

10. Quoted in Steven Shapin, *The Scientific Revolution* (Chicago: University of Chicago Press, 1996), 66.

11. This section draws heavily on Toby E. Huff, *The Rise of Early Modern Science* (Cambridge: Cambridge University Press, 2003), 48, 52, 76.

12. Huff, *Rise of Early Modern Science*, 339.

13. Huff, 76.

14. Jerome Cardano, *The Book of My Life*, translated by Jean Stoner (London: J. M. Dent, 1931), 189.

15. Quoted in Shapin, *Scientific Revolution*, 28.

16. Quoted in Shapin, 61.

17. Quoted in Andrew Lossky, *The Seventeenth Century: Sources in Western Civilization* (New York: Free Press, 1967), 72.

18. Quoted in Shapin, *Scientific Revolution*, 33.

19. Quoted in Shapin, 68.

20. For this observation, see Clifford R. Backman, *The Cultures of the West: A History* (Oxford: Oxford University Press, 2013), 473.

21. Pope John Paul II, "Faith Can Never Conflict with Reason," *L'Osservatore Romano*, November 4, 1992.

22. Quoted in Lossky, *Seventeenth Century*, 88.

23. David C. Lindberg and Ronald L. Numbers, "Beyond War and Peace: A Reappraisal of the Encounter between Christianity and Science," *Perspectives on Science and Christian Faith* 39, no. 3 (1987): 140–49.

24. H. S. Thayer, ed., *Newton's Philosophy of Nature: Selections from His Writings* (New York: Hafner Library of Classics, 1953), 42.

25. Immanuel Kant, "What Is Enlightenment?" translated by Peter Gay, in *Introduction to Contemporary Civilization in the West* (New York: Columbia University Press, 1954), 1071.

26. Voltaire, *Treatise on Tolerance* (1763), chap. 22, http://www.constitution.org/volt/tolerance.htm.

27. Quoted in Margaret C. Jacob, *The Enlightenment* (Boston: Bedford/St. Martin's, 2001), 103.

28. Quoted in Karen Offen, *European Feminisms, 1700–1950* (Stanford, CA: Stanford University Press, 2000), 39.

29. Quoted in Toby E. Huff, *Intellectual Curiosity and the Scientific Revolution* (Cambridge: Cambridge University Press, 2010), 48.

30. Joanna Waley-Cohen, *The Sextants of Beijing* (New York: W. W. Norton, 1999), 105–14.

31. Benjamin A. Elman, *On Their Own Terms: Science in China, 1550–1900* (Cambridge, MA: Harvard University Press, 2005).

32. Quoted in David R. Ringrose, *Expansion and Global Interaction, 1200–1700* (New York: Longman, 2001), 188.

33. Gauvin Alexander Bailey, *Art on the Jesuit Missions in Asia and Latin America* (Toronto: University of Toronto Press, 1999), 102–4.

34. John W. O'Malley et al., *The Jesuits* (Toronto: University of Toronto Press, 1999), 381.

Part 5

1. William H. McNeill, "*The Rise of the West* after 25 Years," *Journal of World History* 1, no. 1 (1990): 7.

Chapter 16

1. Quoted in Keith M. Baker, "A World Transformed," *Wilson Quarterly* (Summer 1989): 37.

2. Quoted in Thomas Benjamin et al., *The Atlantic World in the Age of Empire* (Boston: Houghton Mifflin, 2001), 205.

3. Quoted in Jack P. Greene, "The American Revolution," *American Historical Review* 105, no. 1 (2000): 96–97.

4. Quoted in Greene, "American Revolution," 102.

5. Quoted in Susan Dunn, *Sister Revolutions* (New York: Faber and Faber, 1999), 11, 12.

6. Quoted in Dunn, *Sister Revolutions*, 9.

7. Quoted in Lynn Hunt et al., *The Making of the West* (Boston: Bedford/St. Martin's, 2003), 625.

8. Quoted in Lynn Hunt, ed., *The French Revolution and Human Rights* (Boston: Bedford, 1996), 123.

9. Bonnie S. Anderson and Judith P. Zinsser, *A History of Their Own* (New York: Harper and Row, 1988), 283.

10. Hunt, *French Revolution*, 29.

11. From James Leith, "Music for Mass Persuasion during the Terror," copyright James A. Leith, Queen's University Kingston.

12. Franklin W. Knight, "The Haitian Revolution," *American Historical Review* 105, no. 1 (2000): 103.

13. Quoted in David P. Geggus, *Haitian Revolutionary Studies* (Bloomington: Indiana University Press, 2002), 27.

14. John Charles Chasteen, *Born in Blood and Fire* (New York: W. W. Norton, 2006), 103.

15. Peter Winn, *Americas: The Changing Face of Latin America and the Caribbean* (Berkeley: University of California Press, 2006), 83.

16. Quoted in Thomas E. Skidmore and Peter H. Smith, *Modern Latin America* (New York: Oxford University Press, 2001), 33.

17. Quoted in David Armitage and Sanjay Subrahmanyam, eds., *The Age of Revolutions in Global Context, c. 1760–1840* (New York: Palgrave Macmillan, 2010), xxiii.

18. James Walvin, "The Public Campaign in England against Slavery," in *The Abolition of the Atlantic Slave Trade*, edited by David Eltis and James Walvin (Madison: University of Wisconsin Press, 1981), 76.

19. Michael Craton, "Slave Revolts and the End of Slavery," in *The Atlantic Slave Trade*, edited by David Northrup (Boston: Houghton Mifflin, 2002), 200.

20. Joseph Dupuis, *Journal of a Residence in Ashantee* (London: Henry Colburn, 1824), 162–64.

21. Eric Foner, *Nothing but Freedom* (Baton Rouge: Louisiana State University Press, 1983).

22. Quoted in Daniel Moran and Arthur Waldron, eds., *The People in Arms: Military Myth and National Mobilization since the French Revolution* (Cambridge: Cambridge University Press, 2003), 14.

23. Barbara Winslow, "Feminist Movements: Gender and Sexual Equality," in *A Companion to Gender History*, edited by Teresa A. Meade and Merry E. Wiesner-Hanks (London: Blackwell, 2004), 186.

24. Quoted in Claire G. Moses, *French Feminism in the Nineteenth Century* (Albany: SUNY Press, 1984), 135.

25. Raden Adjeng Kartini, *Letters of a Javanese Princess* (New York: W. W. Norton, 1964). Unless otherwise noted, all quotes come from this source.

26. Quoted in Jooste Cote, "Raden Ajeng Kartini," in *Gender, Colonialism and Education*, edited by Joyce Goodman and Jayne Martin (London: Woburn Press, 2002), 204.

Chapter 17

1. http://news.xinhuanet.com/english/2017-06/05/c_136342098.htm.

2. https://citifmonline.com/2017/06/07/webster-university-holds-public-lecture-on-africa-china-relations/.

3. Edmund Burke III and Kenneth Pomeranz, eds., *The Environment and World History* (Berkeley: University of California Press, 2009), 41.

4. Gregory T. Cushman, *Guano and the Opening of the Pacific World* (Cambridge: Cambridge University Press, 2013), chaps. 1–3.

5. Ricardo Duchesne, *The Uniqueness of Western Civilization* (Leiden: Brill, 2011).

6. Eric Jones, *The European Miracle: Environments, Economics and Geopolitics in the History of Europe and Asia* (Cambridge: Cambridge University Press, 1981).

7. Kenneth Pomeranz, *The Great Divergence* (Princeton: Princeton University Press, 2000); Pier Vries, "Are Coal and Colonies Really Crucial?" *Journal of World History* 12 (2001): 411.

8. Peter Stearns, *The Industrial Revolution in World History*, 3rd ed. (Boulder, CO: Westview, 2007), 47.

9. Eric Hopkins, *Industrialization and Society* (London: Routledge, 2000), 2.

10. Joel Mokyr, *The Lever of Riches* (New York: Oxford University Press, 1990), 81.

11. Eric Hobsbawm, *Industry and Empire* (New York: New Press, 1999), 58. This section draws heavily on Hobsbawm's celebrated account of British industrialization.

12. Samuel Smiles, *Thrift* (London: John Murray, 1875), 30–40.

13. Quoted in Bonnie S. Anderson and Judith P. Zinsser, *A History of Their Own* (New York: Harper and Row, 1988), 2:131.

14. Much of this feature draws from E. P. Thompson, *The Making of the English Working Class* (New York: Vintage Books, 1966).

15. Hobsbawm, *Industry and Empire*, 65.

16. Peter Stearns and John H. Hinshaw, *Companion to the Industrial Revolution* (Santa Barbara, CA: ABC–CLIO, 1996), 150.

17. Quoted in Herbert Vere Evatt, *The Tolpuddle Martyrs* (Sydney: Sydney University Press, 2009), 49.

18. Hobsbawm, *Industry and Empire*, 171.

19. Dirk Hoeder, *Cultures in Contact* (Durham, NC: Duke University Press, 2002), 331–32.

20. Carl Guarneri, *America in the World* (Boston: McGraw-Hill, 2007), 180.

21. Quoted in Hoeder, *Cultures in Contact*, 318.

22. John Charles Chasteen, *Born in Blood and Fire* (New York: W. W. Norton, 2006), 181.

23. Peter Bakewell, *A History of Latin America* (Oxford: Blackwell, 1997), 425.

24. Michael Adas, *Machines as the Measure of Men* (Ithaca, NY: Cornell University Press, 1990).

Chapter 18

1. Norimitsu Onishi, "A Colonial-Era Wound Opens in Namibia," *New York Times*, January 21, 2017, accessed July 30, 2017, https://www.nytimes.com/2017/01/21/world/africa/namibia-germany-colonial.html.

2. Quoted in Heinz Gollwitzer, *Europe in the Age of Imperialism* (London: Thames and Hudson, 1969), 136.

3. Quoted in Steven Roger Fischer, *A History of the Pacific Islands* (New York: Palgrave Macmillan, 2013), 112.

4. Charles Griffith, *The Present State and Prospects of the Port Phillips District . . .* (Dublin: William Curry and Company, 1845), 169.

5. Robert Knox, *Races of Man* (Philadelphia: Lea and Blanchard, 1850), v.

6. Quoted in Ralph Austen, ed., *Modern Imperialism* (Lexington, MA: D. C. Heath, 1969), 70–73.

7. Mike Davis, *Late Victorian Holocausts: El Niño Famines and the Making of the Third World* (New York: Verso, 2001), 12.

8. Quoted in John Iliffe, *Africans: The History of a Continent* (Cambridge: Cambridge University Press, 1995), 191.

9. Quoted in Nicholas Tarling, "The Establishment of Colonial Regimes," in *The Cambridge History of Southeast Asia*, edited by Nicholas Tarling (Cambridge: Cambridge University Press, 1992), 2:76.

10. R. Meinertzhagen, *Kenya Diary* (London: Oliver and Boyd, 1957), 51–52.

11. Mrinalini Sinha, *Colonial Masculinity* (Manchester: Manchester University Press, 1995), 35; Jane Burbank and Frederick Cooper, *Empires in World History* (Princeton, NJ: Princeton University Press, 2010), 308–9.

12. Nupur Chaudhuri, "Clash of Cultures," in *A Companion to Gender History*, edited by Teresa A. Meade and Merry E. Wiesner-Hanks (London: Blackwell, 2004), 437.

13. Quoted in Donald R. Wright, *The World and a Very Small Place in Africa* (Armonk, NY: M. E. Sharpe, 2004), 170.

14. Quoted in Scott B. Cook, *Colonial Encounters in the Age of High Imperialism* (New York: HarperCollins, 1996), 53.

15. D. R. SarDesai, *Southeast Asia: Past and Present* (Boulder, CO: Westview Press, 1997), 95–98.

16. Quoted in G. C. K. Gwassa and John Iliffe, *Records of the Maji Maji Rising* (Nairobi: East African, 1967), 1:4–5.

17. Quoted in Basil Davidson, *Modern Africa* (London: Longman, 1983), 79, 81.

18. This section draws heavily on Margaret Jean Hay and Sharon Stichter, eds., *African Women South of the Sahara* (London: Longman, 1984), especially chaps. 1–5.

19. Quoted in Robert A. Levine, "Sex Roles and Economic Change in Africa," in *Black Africa*, edited by John Middleton (London: Macmillan, 1970), 178.

20. Quoted in Davis, *Late Victorian Holocausts*, 37.

21. Josiah Kariuki, *Mau Mau Detainee* (London: Oxford University Press, 1963), 5.

22. Quoted in Harry Benda and John Larkin, *The World of Southeast Asia* (New York: Harper and Row, 1967), 182–85.

23. Quoted in William Theodore de Bary, *Sources of Indian Tradition* (New York: Columbia University Press, 1958), 619.

24. Quoted in Edward W. Smith, *Aggrey of Africa* (London: SCM Press, 1929).

25. Robert Strayer, *The Making of Mission Communities in East Africa* (London: Heinemann, 1978), 137.

26. Strayer, *The Making of Mission Communities*, 139.

27. C. A. Bayly, *The Birth of the Modern World* (Oxford: Blackwell, 2004), 343.

28. Unless otherwise noted, this essay and all the quotes derive from Philip Goldberg, *American Vedas* (New York: Harmony Books, 2010), 47–66; and Diana L. Eck, *A New Religious America* (New York: HarperCollins, 2001), 94–104.

29. Nirad Chaudhuri, *Autobiography of an Unknown Indian* (London: John Farquharson, 1968), 229.

30. Quoted in William Theodore de Bary, *Sources of Indian Tradition* (New York: Columbia University Press, 1958), 652.

31. Edward Blyden, *Christianity, Islam, and the Negro Race* (Edinburgh: Edinburgh University Press, 1967), 124.

32. John Iliffe, *A Modern History of Tanganyika* (Cambridge: Cambridge University Press, 1979), 324.

Chapter 19

1. Xi Jinping, "Xi Jinping: UN Climate Deal 'Must Not Be Derailed,'" *Climate Home News*, January 19, 2017, http://www.climatechangenews.com/2017/01/19/xi-jinping-un-climate-deal-must-not-be-derailed/.

2. Dun J. Li, ed., *China in Transition, 1517–1911* (New York: Van Nostrand Reinhold, 1969), 112.

3. Quoted in Jonathan D. Spence, *The Search for Modern China* (New York: W. W. Norton, 1999), 169.

4. Quoted in Vincent Shih, *The Taiping Ideology: Its Sources, Interpretations, and Influences* (Seattle: University of Washington Press, 1967), 73.

5. Barbara Hodgson, *Opium: A Portrait of the Heavenly Demon* (San Francisco: Chronicle Books, 1999), 32.

6. This account of Lin Zexu draws from Jonathan D. Spence, *The Search for Modern China* (New York: W. W. Norton, 1999); and Arthur Waley, *The Opium War through Chinese Eyes* (London: George Allen and Unwin, 1968).

7. Quoted in Teng Ssu and John K. Fairbanks, eds. and trans., *China's Response to the West* (New York: Atheneum, 1963), 69.

8. Quoted in Magali Morsy, *North Africa: 1800–1900* (London: Longman, 1984), 79.

9. Quoted in M. Sukru Hanioglu, *The Young Turks in Opposition* (New York: Oxford University Press, 1995), 17.

10. Marius B. Jansen, *The Making of Modern Japan* (Cambridge, MA: Harvard University Press, 2002), 33.

11. Quoted in Carol Gluck, "Themes in Japanese History," in *Asia in Western and World History*, edited by Ainslie T. Embree and Carol Gluck (Armonk, NY: M. E. Sharpe, 1997), 754.

12. Quoted in S. Hanley and K. Yamamura, *Economic and Demographic Change in Pre-Industrial Japan* (Princeton, NJ: Princeton University Press, 1977), 88–90.

13. Quoted in Harold Bolitho, "The Tempo Crisis," in *The Cambridge History of Japan*, vol. 5, *The Nineteenth Century*, edited by Marius B. Jansen (Cambridge: Cambridge University Press, 1989), 230.

14. Kenneth Henshall, *A History of Japan* (New York: Palgrave, 2004), 67.

15. Quoted in James L. McClain, *Japan: A Modern History* (New York: W. W. Norton, 2002), 177.

16. Kaoru Sugihara, "Global Industrialization: A Multipolar Perspective," in *The Cambridge World History* (Cambridge: Cambridge University Press, 2015), 7:117.

17. Quoted in Renée Worringer, *Ottomans Imagining Japan* (New York: Palgrave Macmillan, 2014), 59.

Part 6

1. David Christian et al., *Big History* (New York: McGraw-Hill, 2014), 283.

2. William McNeill, "*The Rise of the West* after 25 Years," *Journal of World History* 1, no. 1 (1990): 2.

Chapter 20

1. UN Secretary General, "Remarks to General Assembly . . . ," July 8, 2014, https://www.un.org/sg/en/content/sg/speeches /2014-07-08/remarks-general-assembly-commemoration -100th-anniversary-outbreak; meeting of the Valdai Discussion Club, October 19, 2017, http://en.kremlin.ru/events/president /news/55882.

2. Quoted in John Keegan, *The First World War* (New York: Vintage Books, 1998), 3.

3. Stanley Payne, *History of Fascism, 1914–1945* (Madison: University of Wisconsin Press, 1995), 208.

4. Quoted in Claudia Koonz, *Mothers in the Fatherland* (New York: St. Martin's Press, 1987), 75.

5. James L. McClain, *Japan: A Modern History* (New York: W. W. Norton, 2002), 414.

6. Quoted in Marius B. Jansen, *The Making of Modern Japan* (Cambridge, MA: Harvard University Press, 2000), 607.

7. Quoted in Jansen, 639.

8. Quoted in Robert Jungk, *Brighter Than a Thousand Suns: A Personal History of the Atomic Scientists* (New York: Harcourt Brace, 1958), 201.

9. Quoted in Merry E. Wiesner-Hanks et al., *Discovering the Global Past*, 3rd ed. (Boston: Houghton Mifflin, 2007), 422.

10. Quoted in Exordio Blog, "Draft shows that in the UN survivor of the atomic bomb tended bridges over political differences," http://www.exordio.com/blog/biografias/borrador-muestra -que-en-la-onu-sobreviviente-de-la-bomba-atomica-tendio -puentes-sobre-diferencias-politicas.html#axzz53Qipu8CG.

11. Adam Gopnik, "The Big One: Historians Rethink the War to End All Wars," *New Yorker*, August 23, 2004, 78.

12. Benito Mussolini, *The Political and Social Doctrine of Fascism* (London: Hogarth Press, 1933), 25.

13. Quoted in Christopher Kelly, *The Roman Empire* (Oxford: Oxford University Press, 2006), 124.

Chapter 21

1. Aaron Yakinyebi, "South Africa Celebrates . . . ," *International Business Times*, May 2, 2014, http://www.ibtimes.co.uk/south -africa-celebrates-20th-anniversary-since-end-apartheid-1446321.

2. NPR, "South Africa Celebrates . . . ," April 27, 2014, http:// www.npr.org/sections/thetwo-way/2014/04/27/307427490 /south-africa-marks-20-years-of-democracy.

3. Quoted in John L. Gaddis, *The Cold War: A New History* (New York: Penguin Press, 2005), 57.

4. Quoted in Dean Rusk, *As I Saw It* (New York: Norton, 1990), 245.

5. Quoted in Frank Mankiewicz and Kirby Jones, *With Fidel: A Portrait of Castro and Cuba* (New York: Ballantine Books, 1976), 83.

6. Quoted in Paul Mason, *Cuba* (New York: Marshall Cavendish, 2010), 14.

7. Quoted in Peter Roman, *People's Power: Cuba's Experience with Representative Government* (Lanham, MD: Rowman and Littlefield, 2003), 63.

8. Ronald Steel, *Pax Americana* (New York: Viking Press, 1970), 254.

9. Quoted in Craig A. Lockard, *Southeast Asia in World History* (Oxford: Oxford University Press, 2009), 138–39.

10. Quoted in Stanley Wolpert, *A New History of India* (Oxford: Oxford University Press, 1993), 331.

11. Quoted in J. D. Legge, *Sukarno: A Political Biography* (New York: Praeger, 1972), 341.

12. Deng Xiaoping, "The Necessity of Upholding the Four Cardinal Principles in the Drive for the Four Modernizations," in *Major Documents of the People's Republic of China* (Beijing: Foreign Language Press, 1991), 54.

13. Quoted in Abraham Brumberg, *Chronicle of a Revolution* (New York: Pantheon Books, 1990), 225–26.

Chapter 22

1. "Put Yourself in My Shoes," United Nations Office on Drugs and Crime, http://www.unodc.org/unodc/en/frontpage/2012 /November/put-yourself-in-my-in-my-shoes-a-human -trafficking-victim-speaks-out.html.

2. Climate and Migration Coalition, "Moving Stories: Indonesia," September 26, 2013, http://climatemigration.org.uk /moving-stories-indonesia/.

3. http://www.gereports.com/post/77131235083/jet-engine -bracket-from-indonesia-wins-3d-printing/.

4. International Energy Agency, "World Energy Outlook," 2015, http://www.worldenergyoutlook.org/resources /energydevelopment/energyaccessdatabase/; The World Bank, "World Development Indicators," http://databank.worldbank .org/data/reports.aspx?source=2&series=EG.ELC.ACCS. ZS&country=.

5. Vaclav Smil, *Transforming the Twentieth Century* (New York: Oxford University Press, 2006), 2:266.

6. Douglas Brinkley, *Wheels for the World* (New York: Viking, 2003), 118.

7. Maja Adena et al., "Radio and the Rise of the Nazis in Pre-War Germany," *The Quarterly Journal of Economics* 130, no. 4 (2015): 2.

8. Jason Hickel, "Global Inequality May Be Much Worse Than We Think," *The Guardian*, April 8, 2016.

9. The World Bank, "Life Expectancy at Birth," http://data .worldbank.org/indicator/SP.DYN.LE00.IN.

10. Charles Bright and Michael Geyer, "Benchmarks of Globalization," in *A Companion to World History*, edited by Douglas Northrup (New York: Wiley-Blackwell, 2012), 290.

11. Jeffrey Frieden, *Global Capitalism* (New York: W. W. Norton, 2006), 476.

12. "Gross World Product, 1950–2009," in *World on the Edge*, by Lester R. Brown (New York: W. W. Norton, 2011).

13. Branko Milanovic, "Global Income Inequality: What It Is and Why It Matters," United Nations Department of Economic and Social Affairs, 2006, 9, www.un.org/esa/desa/papers/2006 /wp26_2006.pdf.

14. Quoted in Frieden, *Global Capitalism*, 459.

15. Eric Hobsbawm, *The Age of Extremes: A History of the World, 1914–1991* (New York: Vintage, 1996), 289, 290, 292.

16. John Vidal, "Hi-Tech Agriculture Is Freeing the Farmer from His Fields," *The Guardian*, October 20, 2015, accessed February 4, 2017, https://www.theguardian.com/environment/2015 /oct/20/hi-tech-agriculture-is-freeing-farmer-from-his-fields.

17. Amy Clark, "Is NAFTA Good for Mexico's Farmers?" CBS Evening News, July 1, 2006, accessed February 4, 2017, http:// www.cbsnews.com/news/is-nafta-good-for-mexicos-farmers/.

18. Merry Wiesner-Hanks, *The Concise History of the World* (Cambridge: Cambridge University Press, 2015), 308.

19. Binyamin Appelbaum, "Perils of Globalization When Factories Close and Towns Struggle," *New York Times*, May 17, 2015, accessed February 8, 2017, https://www.nytimes.com/2015/05 /18/business/a-decade-later-loss-of-maytag-factory-still -resonates.html?_r=0.

20. The Organisation for Economic Co-operation and Development (OECD) defined middle class as living in a household with a daily per capita income of between 10 and 100 U.S. dollars; Homi Kharas, *The Emerging Middle Class in Developing Countries*, Working Paper No. 285 (Paris: OECD, 2009), 6.

21. Studs Terkel, *The Great Divide: Second Thoughts on the American Dream* (New York: Pantheon, 1988), 175.

22. Norimitsu Onishi, "Nigeria Goes to the Mall," *New York Times*, January 5, 2016.

23. Chrystia Freeland, "The Rise of the New Global Elite," *The Atlantic*, January/February 2011, accessed February 4, 2017,

https://www.theatlantic.com/magazine/archive/2011/01 /the-rise-of-the-new-global-elite/308343/.

24. Quoted in Chrystia Freeland, *Plutocrats: The Rise of the New Global Super-Rich and the Fall of Everyone Else* (New York: Penguin, 2012), 59.

25. Tim Samuels, "Africa Goes Hardcore," *The Guardian*, August 30, 2009.

26. "Global Views on Premarital Sex 2013," Statista, https://www .statista.com/statistics/297288/global-views-on-premarital-sex/.

27. Quoted in Patrick B. Kinross, *Ataturk: A Biography of Mustafa Kemal* (New York: Morrow, 1965), 390.

28. Barbara Engel and Anastasia Posadskaya-Vanderbeck, eds., *A Revolution of Their Own* (Boulder, CO: Westview Press, 1998), 17–46.

29. Quoted in Sarah Shaver Hughes and Brady Hughes, *Women in World History* (Armonk, NY: M. E. Sharpe, 1997), 2:268.

30. Quoted in Wilhelmina Oduol and Wanjiku Mukabi Kabira, "The Mother of Warriors and Her Daughters: The Women's Movement in Kenya," in *Global Feminisms since 1945*, edited by Bonnie G. Smith (London: Routledge, 2000), 111.

31. Phyllis Schlafly, *The Power of the Christian Woman* (Cincinnati: Standard Publishers, 1981), 117.

Chapter 23

1. BBC, "Chad Urban Migrant's Story," http://news.bbc.co.uk/2 /shared/spl/hi/picture_gallery/06/africa_chad_urban_migrant0s _story/html/2.stm.

2. J. R. McNeill, "Energy, Population and Environmental Change since 1750," in J. R. McNeill and Kenneth Pomeranz, *The Cambridge World History* (Cambridge: Cambridge University Press, 2015), vol. 7, part 1, pp. 63–67.

3. World Bank, "Death Rate, Crude," http://data.worldbank.org /indicator/SP.DYN.CDRT.IN.

4. David Clark, *Urban World/Global City* (London: Routledge, 1996), 1.

5. Michael H. Hunt, *The World Transformed: 1945 to the Present*, 2nd ed. (New York: Oxford University Press, 2016), 443.

6. Gareth McLean, "Where We're Headed," *The Guardian*, April 1, 2006.

7. https://kanere.org/2016/12/31/quotes-of-the-month-for -august-october-december-edition, accessed January 20, 2018.

8. Lizzy Davis, "The Young French Women Fighting to Defend the Full Face Veil," *The Guardian*, January 31, 2010.

9. Jose C. Moya and Adam McKeown, *World Migration in the Long Twentieth Century* (Washington, DC: American Historical Association, 2011), 39.

10. http://www.pbs.org/wgbh/americanexperience/features /primary-resources/influenza-letter/.

11. Quoted in John J. Simon, "Aime F. Cesaire: The Clarity of Struggle," *Monthly Review* 60 (2008): 2.

12. *Sayings of Ayatollah Khomeini* (New York: Bantam Books, 1980), 4.

13. Pew Research Center, "America's Changing Religious Landscape," 2015, http://www.pewforum.org/2015/05/12/americas-changing -religious-landscape/.

14. Karen Armstrong, *The Battle for God* (New York: Alfred A. Knopf, 2000), xi.

15. Quoted in John Esposito, *Unholy War* (Oxford: Oxford University Press, 2002), 63.

16. "Muslim Dolls Tackle 'Wanton' Barbie," BBC News, March 5, 2002, http://news.bbc.co.uk/2/hi/middle_east/1856558.stm.

17. Quoted in Katherine Zoepf, "Barbie Pushed Aside in Mideast Cultural Shift. Little Girls Obsessed with Fulla in Scarf," *International Herald Tribune*, September 22, 2005, 2. The passages concerning Fulla are largely drawn from this article.

18. Quoted in John Esposito and John Voll, *Makers of Contemporary Islam* (New York: Oxford University Press, 2001), 193.

19. J. R. McNeill, *Something New under the Sun* (New York: W. W. Norton, 2001), 3–4.

20. Ker Than, "The Atomic Age Ushered In the Anthropocene, Scientists Say," *Smithsonian.com*, January 7, 2016, http://www .smithsonianmag.com/science-nature/scientists-anthropocene -officially-thing-180957742/.

21. Johan Rockstrom et al., *Big World, Small Planet* (New Haven, CT: Yale University Press, 2015), 33.

22. This section draws heavily on the work of John McNeill, a leading environmental historian. See McNeill, "Energy, Population," 72–77; and McNeill, *Something New*.

23. George J. Gilboy and Eric Heginbotham, "The Latin Americanization of China," *Current History*, September 2004, 258.

24. "Sixth Wildlife Mass Extinction May Happen in 2020, Experts Say," *Nature World News*, November 27, 2016, http://www .natureworldnews.com/articles/30805/20161027/year-2020 -era-wildlife-mass-extinction.htm.

25. Hywel Griffith, "Great Barrier Reef Suffered Worst Bleaching on Record in 2016, Report Finds," *BBC News*, November 28, 2016, http://www.bbc.com/news/world-australia-38127320.

26. See Ramachandra Guha, *Environmentalism: A Global History* (New York: Longmans, 2000).

27. Quoted in Guha, 14.

28. Quoted in Guha, 50, 53.

29. Quoted in Shiraz Sidhva, "Saving the Planet: Imperialism in a Green Garb," *UNESCO Courier*, April 2001, 41–43.

30. Quoted in Jane Lampman, "Sufism May Be Powerful Antidote to Islamic Extremism," *Christian Science Monitor*, December 5, 2007.

31. Saira Khan, "Why I, as a British Muslim Woman, Want the Burkha Banned from Our Streets," *Daily Mail*, June 24, 2009.

32. Peter Allen, "Burka Ban," *Daily Mail.com*, April 11, 2011.

Acknowledgments

Chapter 1

Source 1.2: "The Rainbow Serpent Awakens" from http://www.expedition360 .com/australia_lessons_literacy/2001/09/dreamtime_stories_the_rainbow .html. Used by permission of BullyFish Books LLC.

Source 1.4: Excerpts from *Time Before Morning: Art and Myth of the Australian Aborigines,* pages 215–219, by Louis A. Allen. Copyright © 1975 by Louis A. Allen. Reprinted by permission of HarperCollins Publishers.

Chapter 2

Excerpt beginning "Come then, Enkidu to ramparted Uruk" from *The Epic of Gilgamesh,* translated by Benjamin R. Foster. Copyright © 2001 by W. W. Norton & Company. Used by permission of W.W. Norton & Company, Inc. This selection may not be reproduced, stored in a retrieval system, or transmitted in any form or by any means without the prior written permission of the publisher.

Excerpt beginning "He has come unto us" from Adolf Erman, *The Literature of the Ancient Egyptians,* by Adolf Erman, translated by Aylward M. Blackman. Copyright © 1927 by Methuen Publishing Ltd, 1927. Reproduced by permission of Taylor & Francis Books UK.

Excerpt beginning "In those Days" from James B. Pritchard, editor, *Ancient Near Eastern Texts Relating to the Old Testament* by James Bennett Pritchard. Reproduced with permission of Books on Demand in the format Book via Copyright Clearance Center.

Chapter 4

Source 4.5: "Sunita the Outcaste" (Thag 12.2), translated from the Pali by Thanissaro Bhikkhu. Access to Insight (Legacy Edition). November 30, 2013, http://www.accesstoinsight.org/tipitaka/kn/thag/thag.12.02.than .html. Used by permission of Thanissaro Bhikkhu.

Chapter 5

Source 5.4: From *Daily Life in Ancient Rome: A Sourcebook,* by Brian Harvey. Copyright © 2016 Hackett. Reprinted with permission of Hackett Publishing Company, Inc. All rights reserved.

Voice 5.1: From Mary Beard, "Pompeii Exhibition" *The Telegraph,* April 10, 2017. © Telegraph Media Group Limited 2017.

Chapter 8

Excerpt beginning "A tumbled confusion" from Mark Elvin, *The Retreat of the Elephants* (New Haven, CT: Yale University Press, 2004). Copyright © 2004 by Mark Elvin. Used by permission of Yale University Press.

Excerpt beginning "Ever since the Western horsemen" from *The Golden Peaches of Samarkand: A Study of T'ang Exotics,* by Edward H. Schafer, © 1985 by the Regents of the University of California. Published by the University of California Press.

Source 8.4A: Li Po, "Zazen on Ching-t'ing Mountain" from *Crossing the Yellow River: Three Hundred Poems from the Chinese,* translated by Sam Hamill. Copyright © 2000 by Sam Hamill. Reprinted with the permission of The Permissions Company, Inc., on behalf of Tiger Bark Press, www .tigerbarkpress.com.

Source 8.4B: Li Po, "Drinking Alone with the Moon," from *The Jade Mountain.* Print usage: Translated by Witter Bynner, translation copyright © 1929, renewed 1957 by Penguin Random House LLC. Used by permission of Alfred A. Knopf, an imprint of the Knopf Doubleday Publishing Group, a division of Penguin Random House LLC. All rights reserved. Any third party use of this material, outside of this publication, is prohibited. Interested parties must apply directly to Penguin Random House LLC for permission. Electronic usage: Translated by Witter Bynner, translation copyright © 1929, renewed 1957 by Penguin Random House LLC. Used by permission of the Witter Bynner Foundation.

Source 8.4C: Wang Wei, "My Retreat at Mount Zhongnan," from *The Jade Mountain.* Print usage: Translated by Witter Bynner, translation copyright © 1929, renewed 1957 by Penguin Random House LLC. Used by permission of Alfred A. Knopf, an imprint of the Knopf Doubleday Publishing Group, a division of Penguin Random House LLC. All rights reserved. Any third party use of this material, outside of this publication, is prohibited. Interested parties must apply directly to Penguin Random House LLC for permission. Electronic usage: Translated by Witter Bynner, translation copyright © 1929, renewed 1957 by Penguin Random House LLC. Used by permission of the Witter Bynner Foundation.

Source 8.4D: Du Fu, "A View of Taishan," from *The Jade Mountain.* Print usage: Translated by Witter Bynner, translation copyright © 1929, renewed 1957 by Penguin Random House LLC. Used by permission of Alfred A. Knopf, an imprint of the Knopf Doubleday Publishing Group, a division of Penguin Random House LLC. All rights reserved. Any third party use of this material, outside of this publication, is prohibited. Interested parties must apply directly to Penguin Random House LLC for permission. Electronic usage: Translated by Witter Bynner, translation copyright © 1929, renewed 1957 by Penguin Random House LLC. Used by permission of the Witter Bynner Foundation.

Chapter 9

Source 9.4: From *Muhammad and the Believers: At the Origins of Islam* by Fred M. Donner, Cambridge, Mass.: The Belknap Press of Harvard University Press, Copyright © 2010 by Fred M. Donner.

Source 9.6: From Caliph Ali, Letter to Malik Ashtar, 658 C.E., in Paul Salahuddin Armstrong (ed.), "Caliph Ali's Letter to Malik Ashtar." Used by permission of Paul Salahuddin.

Chapter 11

Source 11.1B: From Paul Kahn, *The Secret History of the Mongols: The Origins of Chingis Khan* (San Francisco: North Point Press, 1984). Copyright © 1984 by Paul Kahn. Reprinted by permission of the author.

Chapter 12

Excerpt beginning "Truly do we live on Earth" from *Aztec Thought and Culture: A Study of the Ancient Nahuatl Mind,* by Miguel Leon-Portilla. Reproduced with permission of the University of Oklahoma Press in the format Republish in a book via Copyright Clearance Center.

Source 12.5: From Norman Housely, *Documents of the Later Crusades, 1274–1580,* published 1996 by St. Martin's Press, reproduced with permission of Palgrave Macmillan.

Chapter 13

Source 13.3A: From *Louis XIV* by Robert Campbell. Copyright © 1993 Taylor and Francis. Reproduced by permission of Taylor & Francis Books UK.

Source 13.4: From *Incas of Pedro de Cieze de Leon,* by Pedro de Cieze de Leon. Reproduced with permission of University of Oklahoma Press in the format Republish in a book via Copyright Clearance Center.

Chapter 14

Excerpt beginning "Rarer, too, their timber grew" from Mark Elvin, *The Retreat of the Elephants* (New Haven, CT: Yale University Press, 2004). Copyright © 2004 by Mark Elvin. Used by permission of Yale University Press.

Source 14.7: From *Vermeer's Hat: The Seventeenth Century and the Dawn of the Global World,* by Timothy Brook. Copyright © 2008 by Timothy Brook. Bloomsbury Press, an imprint of Bloomsbury Publishing Inc. Used by permission of Bloomsbury Publishing and Penguin Canada, a division of Penguin Random House Canada Limited.

Chapter 15

Excerpt beginning "What I paid" from *Mirabai*, translated by Robert Bly and Jane Hirshfield. Copyright © 2004 by Robert Bly and Jane Hirshfield. Reprinted by permission of Beacon Press, Boston.

Source 15.2: From *Book of Chilam Balam of Chumayel* by University of Oklahoma Press. Reproduced with permission of University of Oklahoma Press in the format Republish in a book via Copyright Clearance Center.

Chapter 19

Source 19.1: From *Sources of Chinese Tradition: From 1600 Through the Twentieth Century,* edited by Wm. Theodore de Bary and Richard J. Lufrano.

Reproduced with permission of Columbia University Press in the format Republish in a book via Copyright Clearance Center.

Source 19.2: From *Sources of Chinese Tradition: From 1600 Through the Twentieth Century,* edited by Wm. Theodore de Bary and Richard J. Lufrano. Reproduced with permission of Columbia University Press in the format Republish in a book via Copyright Clearance Center.

Chapter 21

Source 21.1: From *Fanshen: A Documentary of Revolution in a Chinese Village,* by William Hinton. Reproduced with permission of Monthly Review Press in the format Republish in a book via Copyright Clearance Center.

Chapter 22

Source 22.2: From Zillah R. Eisenstein, ed., *Capitalist Patriarchy and the Case for Socialist Feminism* (New York: Monthly Review Press, 1979). Used by permission of Zillah Eisenstein.

Chapter 23

Source 23.5: From Kabir Helminski, "Islam and Human Values," unpublished pamphlet, 2009. Used by permission of the author.

Glossary

Abbasid caliphate An Arab dynasty of caliphs (successors to the Prophet) who governed much of the Islamic world from its capital in Baghdad beginning in 750 C.E. After 900 C.E. that empire increasingly fragmented until its overthrow by the Mongols in 1258.

Abd al-Hamid II Ottoman sultan (r. 1876–1909) who accepted a reform constitution but then quickly suppressed it, ruling as a despotic monarch for the rest of his long reign.

abolitionist movement An international movement that condemned slavery as morally repugnant and contributed much to ending slavery in the Western world during the nineteenth century; the movement was especially prominent in Britain and the United States beginning in the late eighteenth century.

African diaspora The global spread of African peoples via the slave trade.

African identity A new way of thinking about belonging that emerged by the end of the nineteenth century among well-educated Africans; it was influenced by the common experience of colonial oppression and European racism and was an effort to revive the cultural self-confidence of their people.

Africanization of Christianity Process that occurred in non-Muslim Africa, where many who converted to Christianity sought to incorporate older traditions, values, and practices into their understanding of Christianity; often expressed in the creation of churches and schools that operated independently of the missionary and colonial establishment.

age of fossil fuels Twentieth-century shift in energy production with increased use of coal and oil, resulting in the widespread availability of electricity and the internal combustion engine; a major source of the greenhouse gases that drive climate change.

Akbar The most famous emperor of India's Mughal Empire (r. 1556–1605); his policies are noted for their efforts at religious tolerance and inclusion.

Alexander the Great A ruler of Macedonia who unified the Greek city-states and during a ten-year military expedition (334–323 B.C.E.) conquered Egypt, the Persian Empire, and part of northwest India, creating a vast Greek empire.

Alexandria A cosmopolitan Egyptian city established by Hellenistic rulers, with a population of half a million people; a major avenue for the spread of Greek culture and learning.

Almoravid Empire Emerging out of an Islamic reform movement among the Sanhaja Berber pastoralists in the eleventh century, the Almoravid Empire incorporated a large part of northwestern Africa and southern Spain. The empire collapsed by the mid-twelfth century.

American Revolution Successful rebellion against British rule conducted by the European settlers in the thirteen colonies of British North America, starting in 1776; a conservative revolution whose success preserved property rights and class distinctions but established republican government in place of monarchy.

American web A term used to describe the network of trade that linked parts of the pre-Columbian Americas; although less densely woven than the Afro-Eurasian trade networks, this web nonetheless provided a means of exchange for luxury goods and ideas over large areas.

al-Andalus Arabic name for Spain, most of which was conquered by Arab and Berber forces between 711 and 718 C.E. Muslim Spain represented a point of encounter between the Islamic world and Christian Europe.

Angkor Wat The largest religious structure in the premodern world, this temple was built by the powerful Angkor kingdom (located in modern Cambodia) in the twelfth century C.E. to express a Hindu understanding of the cosmos centered on a mythical Mount Meru, the home of the gods in Hindu tradition. It was later used by Buddhists as well.

Anthropocene era A recently coined term denoting the "age of man," in general since the Industrial Revolution and more specifically since the mid-twentieth century. It refers to the unprecedented and enduring impact of human activity on the atmosphere, the geosphere, and the biosphere.

Arabian camel Introduced to North Africa and the Sahara in the early centuries of the Common Era, this animal made trans-Saharan commerce possible by 300 to 400 C.E.

Aristotle A Greek philosopher (384–322 B.C.E.); student of Plato and teacher of Alexander the Great.

Ashoka The most famous ruler of India's Mauryan Empire (r. 268–232 B.C.E.), who converted to Buddhism and tried to rule peacefully and with tolerance.

Asian Tigers Nickname for the East Asian countries of South Korea, Taiwan, Singapore, and Hong Kong, which experienced remarkable export-driven economic growth in the late twentieth century.

Aspasia A foreign resident in Athens (ca. 470–400 B.C.E.) who was famed for her learning and wit. She was the partner of the statesman Pericles.

Athenian democracy A radical form of direct democracy in which most of the free males of Athens were able to vote in the Assembly and officeholders were chosen by lot.

Augustus A title that implied divine status for Octavian (r. 27 B.C.E.–14 C.E.), who emerged as sole ruler of the Roman state at the end of an extended period of civil war.

Aurangzeb Mughal emperor (r. 1658–1707) who reversed his predecessors' policies of religious tolerance and attempted to impose Islamic supremacy. (pron. ow-rang-ZEHB)

Austronesian migrations The last phase of the great human migration that established a human presence in every habitable region of the earth. Austronesian-speaking people settled the Pacific islands and Madagascar in a series of seaborne migrations that began around 3,500 years ago.

Axum Second-wave era kingdom of East Africa in present-day Eritrea and northern Ethiopia with a highly productive plow-based farming system; an early adopter of Christianity. (pron. AX-uhm)

Aztec Empire Major state that developed in what is now Mexico in the fourteenth and fifteenth centuries; dominated by the semi-nomadic Mexica, who had migrated into the region from northern Mexico.

Banpo An early agricultural village in northern China dating to around 6,000 years ago. It consisted of approximately 45 thatched buildings that housed an estimated 500 people. Archeological evidence suggests millet, pigs, and dogs had been domesticated, and diets were supplemented with wild plants, animals, and fish.

Bantu migration Gradual movement of Bantu-speaking peoples, beginning in ca. 3000 B.C.E., from their homeland in what is now southern Nigeria and the Cameroons into most of eastern and southern Africa by ca. 400 C.E. The agricultural techniques and ironworking technology of Bantu-speaking farmers gave them an advantage over the gathering and hunting peoples they encountered.

Ban Zhao A major female Confucian author of China (45–116 C.E.) whose works explore the implications of Confucian thinking for women. (pron. bahn jow)

Benin West African kingdom (in what is now Nigeria) whose strong kings for a time sharply limited engagement with the slave trade.

Bhagavad Gita A great Hindu epic text that conveyed the message that ordinary people could find spiritual fulfillment by selflessly performing the ordinary duties of their lives. (pron. BUH-guh-vahd GEE-tuh)

bhakti **movement** Meaning "worship," this Hindu movement began in south India and moved northward between 600 and 1000 C.E.; it involved the intense adoration of and identification with a particular deity through songs, prayers, and rituals. (pron. BAHK-tee)

Black Death A massive pandemic that swept through Eurasia in the early fourteenth century, spreading along the trade routes within and beyond the Mongol Empire and reaching the Middle East and Western Europe by 1347. Associated with a massive loss of life.

Blyden, Edward (1832–1912) Prominent West African scholar and political leader who argued that each civilization, including that of Africa, has its own unique contribution to make to the world.

Boxer Uprising Antiforeign movement (1898–1901) led by Chinese militia organizations, in which large numbers of Europeans and Chinese Christians were killed. It resulted in military intervention by Western powers and the imposition of a huge payment as punishment.

Bretton Woods system Name for the agreements and institutions (including the World Bank and the International Monetary Fund) set up in 1944 to regulate commercial and financial dealings among the major capitalist countries.

British East India Company Private trading company chartered by the English around 1600, mainly focused on India; it was given a monopoly on Indian Ocean trade, including the right to make war and to rule conquered peoples.

British textile industry The site of the initial technological breakthroughs of the Industrial Revolution in eighteenth-century Britain, where multiple innovations transformed cotton textile production, resulting in an enormous increase in output.

bushido The "way of the warrior," referring to the martial values of the Japanese samurai, including bravery, loyalty, and an emphasis on death over surrender. (pron. boo-shee-doh)

Byzantine Empire The surviving eastern Roman Empire and one of the centers of Christendom during the medieval centuries. The Byzantine Empire was founded at the end of the third century, when the Roman Empire was divided into eastern and western halves, and survived until its conquest by Muslim forces in 1453.

caesaropapism A political-religious system in which the secular ruler is also head of the religious establishment, as in the Byzantine Empire.

Cahokia The dominant center of an important Mississippi valley mound-building culture, located near present-day St. Louis, Missouri; flourished from about 900 to 1250 C.E.

Caral The largest of some twenty-five urban centers that emerged in the Norte Chico region along the central coast of Peru from 3000 B.C.E. to 1800 B.C.E.

cash-crop production Agricultural production of crops for sale in the market rather than for consumption by the farmers themselves; operated at the level of both individual farmers and large-scale plantations.

Çatalhüyük An early agricultural village and archeological site in what is now Turkey; flourished between 7400 and 6000 B.C.E. With a settled population of several thousand people, the village displayed few signs of class or gender inequality. (pron. cha-TAHL-hoo-YOOK)

caudillos Military strongmen who seized control of a government in nineteenth-century Latin America, and were frequently replaced. (pron. kow-DEE-yos)

Central Asian / Oxus civilization A major First Civilization that emerged around 2200 B.C.E. in Central Asia in the Oxus or Amu Darya River valley in what is now northern Afghanistan and southern Turkmenistan. An important focal point for a Eurasian-wide system of intellectual and cultural exchange, it faded away by about 1700 B.C.E.

Chaco Phenomenon Name given to a major process of settlement and societal organization that occurred in the period 860–1130 C.E. among the peoples of Chaco canyon, in what is now northwestern New Mexico; the society formed is notable for its settlement in large pueblos and for the building of hundreds of miles of roads, the purpose of which is not known.

Charlemagne Ruler of the Carolingian Empire (r. 768–814) who staged an imperial revival in Western Europe. (pron. SHAHR-leh-mane)

Chavín An Andean town strategically located between the western coast and eastern rain forests that was the center of a large Peruvian religious movement from around 900 to 200 B.C.E. (pron. cha-BEEN)

chiefdom A societal grouping governed by a chief who typically relies on generosity, ritual status, or charisma rather than force to win obedience from the people.

China's economic revolution A major rise in prosperity that took place in China under the Song dynasty (960–1279), which was marked by rapid population growth, urbanization, economic specialization, the development of an immense network of internal waterways, and a great increase in industrial production and technological innovation.

China's scholar-gentry class A term used to describe members of China's landowning families, reflecting their wealth from the land and the privileges that they derived as government officials.

Chinese Buddhism Buddhism was China's only large-scale cultural borrowing before the twentieth century; it entered China from India in the first and second centuries C.E. but only became popular in 300 to 800 C.E. through a series of cultural accommodations. At first supported by the state, Buddhism suffered persecution during the ninth century but continued to play a role in Chinese society alongside Confucianism and Daoism.

Chinese revolution of 1911–1912 The collapse of China's imperial order, officially at the hands of organized revolutionaries but for the most part under the weight of the troubles that had overwhelmed the imperial government for the previous century.

Chinese Revolution of 1949 An event that marks the coming to power of the Chinese Communist Party under the leadership of Mao Zedong, following a decades-long struggle against both domestic opponents and Japanese imperialism.

chu nom A variation of Chinese writing developed in Vietnam that became the basis for an independent national literature; "southern script."

Church of the East An early theologically and organizationally distinct Christian church based in Syria and Persia but with followers in southern India and Central Asia.

civilizing mission A European understanding of empire that emphasized Europeans' duty to "civilize inferior races" by bringing Christianity, good government, education, work discipline, and production for the market to colonized peoples, while suppressing "native customs," such as polygamy, that ran counter to Western ways of living.

climate change The warming of the planet largely caused by higher concentrations of "greenhouse gases," generated by the burning of fossil fuels. It has become the most pressing environmental issue of the early twenty-first century.

Clovis culture The earliest widespread and distinctive culture of North America, dating to about 13,000 years ago; named for a particular kind of projectile point, initially found near the city of Clovis, New Mexico.

Code of Hammurabi A series of laws publicized at the order of King Hammurabi of Babylon that reveals much about the social order of Mesopotamian civilization. (pron. hahm-moo-RAH-bee)

cold war Geopolitical and ideological conflict between communist regimes and capitalist powers after World War II, spreading from Eastern Europe through Asia; characterized by the avoidance of direct military conflict between the USSR and the United States and an arms race in nuclear weapons.

collectivization of agriculture Communist policies that ended private ownership of land by incorporating peasants from small family farms into large-scale collective farms. Implemented forcibly in the Soviet Union (1928–1933), it led to a terrible famine and 5 million deaths; a similar process occurred much more peacefully in China during the 1950s.

Columbian exchange The enormous network of transatlantic communication, migration, trade, and the transfer of diseases, plants, and animals that began in the period of European exploration and colonization of the Americas.

communication revolution Modern transformation of communication technology, from the nineteenth-century telegraph to the present-day smart phone.

communism in Eastern Europe Expansion of post–World War II communism to Poland, East Germany, Czechoslovakia, Hungary, Romania, and Bulgaria, imposed with Soviet pressure rather than growing out of domestic revolution.

Condorcet The Marquis de Condorcet (1743–1794) was a French philosopher who argued that society was moving into an era of near-infinite improvability and could be perfected by human reason.

Confucianism The Chinese philosophy first enunciated by Confucius, advocating the moral example of superiors as the key element of social order.

Congo Free State A private colony ruled personally by Leopold II, king of Belgium; it was the site of widespread forced labor and killing to ensure the collection of wild rubber; by 1908 these abuses led to reforms that transferred control to the Belgian government.

Constantinople New capital for the eastern half of the Roman Empire; Constantinople's highly defensible and economically important site helped ensure the city's cultural and strategic importance for many centuries.

consumerism A culture of leisure and consumption that developed during the past century or so in tandem with global economic growth and an enlarged middle class; emerged first in the Western world and later elsewhere.

Copernicus, Nicolaus (1473–1543) Polish mathematician and astronomer who was the first to argue in 1543 for the existence of a sun-centered, helping to spark the Scientific Revolution.

Cortés, Hernán Spanish conquistador who led the expedition that conquered the Aztec Empire in modern Mexico.

Counter-Reformation An internal reform of the Catholic Church in the sixteenth century stimulated in part by the Protestant Reformation; at the Council of Trent (1545–1563), Catholic leaders clarified doctrine, corrected abuses and corruption, and put a new emphasis on education and accountability.

Crusades A term used to describe the "holy wars" waged by Western Christendom, especially against the forces of Islam in the eastern Mediterranean from 1095 to 1291 and on the Iberian Peninsula into the fifteenth century. Further Crusades were also conducted in non-Christian regions of Eastern Europe from about 1150 on. Crusades could be declared only by the pope; participants swore a vow and received in return an indulgence removing the penalty for confessed sins.

Cuban missile crisis Major standoff between the United States and the Soviet Union in 1962 over Soviet deployment of nuclear missiles in Cuba; the confrontation ended in compromise, with the USSR removing its missiles in exchange for the United States agreeing not to invade Cuba.

cultivation system System of forced labor used in the Netherlands East Indies in the nineteenth century; peasants were required to cultivate at least 20 percent of their land in cash crops, such as sugar or coffee, for sale at low and fixed prices to government contractors, who then earned enormous profits from resale of the crops.

cultural globalization The global spread of elements of popular culture such as film, language, and music from various places of origin, especially the spread of Western cultural forms to the rest of the world; has come to symbolize modernity, inclusion in global culture, and liberation or rebellion. It has prompted pushback from those who feel that established cultural traditions have been threatened.

Cultural Revolution China's Great Proletarian Cultural Revolution was a massive campaign launched by Mao Zedong in the mid-1960s to combat the capitalist tendencies that he believed reached into even the highest ranks of the Communist Party; the campaign threw China into chaos.

Dahomey West African kingdom in which the slave trade became a major state-controlled industry. (pron. deh-HOH-mee)

Daoism A Chinese philosophy / popular religion that advocates a simple and unpretentious way of living and alignment with the natural world, founded by the legendary figure Laozi. (pron. dow-ism)

Declaration of the Rights of Man and Citizen Charter of political liberties, drawn up by the French National Assembly in 1789, that proclaimed the equal rights of all male citizens; the declaration gave expression to the essential outlook of the French Revolution and became the preamble to the French constitution completed in 1791.

decolonization Process in which many African and Asian states won their independence from Western colonial rule, in most cases by negotiated settlement and in some cases through violent military confrontations.

Deng Xiaoping (1904–1997) Leader of China from 1976 to 1997 whose reforms dismantled many of the distinctly communist elements of the Chinese economy. (pron. dung shee-yao-ping)

dependent development Term used to describe Latin America's economic growth in the nineteenth century, which was largely financed by foreign capital and dependent on European and North American prosperity and decisions; also viewed as a new form of colonialism.

devshirme A term that means "collection or gathering"; it refers to the Ottoman Empire's practice of removing young boys from their Christian subjects and training them for service in the civil administration or in the elite Janissary infantry corps. (pron. devv-shirr-MEH)

Dream of the Red Chamber, The Book written by Cao Xueqin that explores the life of an elite family with connections to the court; it was the most famous popular novel of mid-eighteenth-century China.

Dreamtime A complex worldview of Australia's Aboriginal people that held that living humans exist in a vibration or echo of ancestral happenings.

Dutch East India Company Private trading company chartered by the Netherlands around 1600, mainly focused on Indonesia; it was given a monopoly on Indian Ocean trade, including the right to make war and to rule conquered peoples.

Eastern Orthodox Christianity Branch of Christianity that developed in the eastern part of the Roman Empire and gradually separated, mostly on matters of practice, from the branch of Christianity dominant in Western Europe; noted for the subordination of the Church to political authorities, a married clergy, the use of leavened bread in the Eucharist, and a sharp rejection of the authority of Roman popes.

economic globalization The deepening economic entanglement of the world's peoples, especially since 1950; accompanied by the spread of industrialization in the Global South and extraordinary economic growth following World War II; the process has also generated various forms of inequality and resistance as well as increasing living standards for many.

Egypt One of the earliest civilizations in world history, with a three-thousand-year history as an intact state ruled by pharaohs. It became part of an international political system that included Babylon and Mesopotamia.

Empress Wu China's only female ruler (r. 690–705 C.E.), who patronized scholarship and worked to elevate the position of women.

Epic of Gilgamesh Mesopotamia's ancient epic poem dating to around 2000 B.C.E.

Ethiopian Christianity Emerging in the fourth century with the conversion of the rulers of Axum, this Christian church proved more resilient than other early churches in Africa. Located in the mountainous highlands of modern Ethiopia, it was largely cut off from other parts of Christendom and developed traditions that made it distinctive from other Christian churches.

European Economic Community An alliance formed in 1957 by six West European countries dedicated to developing common trade policies and reduced tariffs; it gradually developed into the larger European Union.

European Enlightenment European intellectual movement of the eighteenth century that applied the principles of the Scientific Revolution to human affairs and was noted for its commitment to open-mindedness and inquiry and the belief that knowledge could transform human society.

European Renaissance A "rebirth" of classical learning that is most often associated with the cultural blossoming of Italy in the period 1350–1500 and that included not just a rediscovery of Greek and Roman learning but also major developments in art, as well as growing secularism in society. It spread to Northern Europe after 1400.

export-processing zones (EPZs) Areas where international companies can operate with tax and other benefits, offered as an incentive to attract manufacturers.

fascism Political ideology that considered the conflict of nations to be the driving force of history; marked by intense nationalism and an appeal to post–World War I discontent. Fascists praised violence against enemies as a renewing force in society, celebrated action rather than reflection, and placed their faith in a charismatic leader. Fascists also bitterly condemned individualism, liberalism, feminism, parliamentary democracy, and communism.

female circumcision The excision of a pubescent girl's clitoris and adjacent genital tissue as part of initiation rites marking her coming-of-age; missionary efforts to end the practice sparked a widespread exodus from mission churches in colonial Kenya.

feminism in the Global South Mobilization of women across Asia, Africa, and Latin America; distinct from Western feminism because of its focus on issues such as colonialism, racism, and poverty, rather than those exclusively related to gender.

Fertile Crescent Region sometimes known as Southwest Asia that includes the modern states of Iraq, Syria, Israel/Palestine, Jordan, and southern Turkey; the earliest home of agriculture and some of the first civilizations.

feudalism A highly fragmented and decentralized society in which power was held by the landowning warrior elite. In this highly competitive system, lesser lords and knights swore allegiance to greater lords or kings and thus became their vassals, frequently receiving lands and plunder in return for military service.

foot binding The Chinese practice of tightly wrapping girls' feet to keep them small, prevalent in the Song dynasty and later; an emphasis on small size and delicacy was central to views of female beauty.

French Revolution Massive upheaval of French society (1789–1815) that overthrew the monarchy, ended the legal privileges of the nobility, and for a time outlawed the Catholic Church. The French Revolution proceeded in stages, becoming increasingly radical and violent until the period known as the Terror in 1793–1794, after which it became more conservative, especially under Napoleon Bonaparte (r. 1799–1815).

Fulbe West Africa's largest pastoral society, whose members gradually adopted Islam and took on a religious leadership role that led to the creation of a number of new states by the nineteenth century. (pron. FULB)

fur trade A global industry in which French, British, and Dutch traders exported fur from North America to Europe, using Native American labor and with great environmental cost to the Americas. A parallel commerce in furs operated under Russian control in Siberia.

Galileo (1564–1642) An Italian scientist who developed an improved telescope in 1609, with which he made many observations that undermined established understandings of the cosmos. (pron. gal-uh-LAY-oh)

Gandhi, Mohandas (1869–1948) Often known as "Mahatma" or "Great Soul," the political leader of the Indian drive for independence from Great Britain; rejected the goal of modern industrialization and advocated nonviolence.

General Crisis The near-record cold winters experienced in much of China, Europe, and North America in the mid-seventeenth century, sparked by the Little Ice Age; extreme weather conditions led to famines, uprisings, and wars.

Ghana An early and prominent state within West African civilization. With a reputation for great riches, Ghana flourished between 750 and 1076 and was later absorbed into the larger Kingdom of Mali.

globalization of democracy Late twentieth-century political shift that brought popular movements, multiparty elections, and new constitutions to countries around the world.

global urbanization The explosive growth of cities after 1900, caused by the reduced need for rural labor and more opportunities for employment in manufacturing, commerce, government, and the service industry.

Göbekli Tepe A ceremonial site in southeastern Turkey comprising twenty circles made up of large carved limestone pillars. The site, which dates to almost 12,000 years ago, was built by gatherers and hunters who lived at least part of the year in settled villages. (pron. goh-BEHK-lee TEH-peh)

Gorbachev, Mikhail (1931–) Leader of the Soviet Union from 1985 to 1991 whose efforts to reform the USSR led to its collapse. (pron. GORE-beh-CHOF)

Great Depression Worldwide economic contraction that began in 1929 with a stock market crash in the United States and continued in many areas until the outbreak of World War II.

Great Dying Term used to describe the devastating demographic impact of European-borne epidemic diseases on the Americas; in many cases, up to 90 percent of the pre-Columbian population died.

Great Jamaica Revolt Slave rebellion in the British West Indies (1831–1832) inspired by the Haitian Revolution, in which around 60,000 slaves attacked several hundred plantations; the discontent of the slaves and the brutality of the British response helped sway the British public to support the abolition of slavery.

Great Leap Forward Communist push for collectivization that created "people's communes" and aimed to mobilize China's population for rapid development.

Great Zimbabwe A powerful state in the southern African interior that apparently emerged from the growing trade in gold to the East African coast; flourished between 1250 and 1350 C.E.

Greco-Persian Wars A half century of intermittent conflict (499–449 B.C.E.) between the Greek city-states and the Persian Empire. During two major Persian invasions of Greece, in 490 B.C.E. and 480 B.C.E., the Persians were defeated on both land and sea.

Greco-Roman slavery In the Greek and Roman world, most slaves were captives from war, slave raiding, and piracy (and their descendants); manumission was common. Among the Greeks, household service was the most common form of slavery, but slavery was entrenched in all areas of Roman society except the military.

Greek rationalism A secularizing system of scientific and philosophic thought that developed in classical Greece in the period 600 to 300 B.C.E.; it emphasized using human reason to understand the world in nonreligious terms.

Green Revolution Innovations in agriculture during the twentieth century, such as mechanical harvesters, chemical fertilizers, and the development of high-yielding crops, that enabled global food production to keep up with, and even exceed, growing human numbers.

gunpowder A Chinese invention that came about during the ninth century. A mix of saltpeter, sulfur, and charcoal, it was originally created by Daoist alchemists seeking to discover an elixir of immortality. Ultimately, though, it revolutionized global military affairs.

Guomindang The Chinese Nationalist Party led by Chiang Kai-shek that governed from 1928 until its overthrow by the communists in 1949. (pron. GWOH-mihn-dahng)

Gupta Empire An era of Indian civilization from 320 to 550 C.E. that witnessed considerable political unity, cultural flourishing, and thriving trade.

Haitian Revolution The only fully successful slave rebellion in world history; the uprising in the French Caribbean colony of Saint Domingue (later renamed Haiti, which means "mountainous" or "rugged" in the native Taino language) was sparked by the French Revolution and led to the establishment of an independent state after a long and bloody war (1791–1804). Its first leader was Toussaint Louverture, a former slave.

Han dynasty The Chinese dynasty (206 B.C.E.–220 C.E.) that emerged after the Qin dynasty collapsed, establishing political and cultural patterns that lasted into the twentieth century.

hangul A phonetic alphabet developed in Korea in the fifteenth century in a move toward greater cultural independence from China. (pron. HAHN-gool)

Hangzhou China's capital during the Song dynasty, with a population at its height of more than a million people.

Hellenistic era The period from 323 to 30 B.C.E. in which Greek culture spread widely in the Middle East and parts of India in the cities and kingdoms ruled by Alexander's political successors.

helots The dependent, semi-enslaved class of ancient Sparta whose social discontent prompted the militarization of Spartan society.

Hidalgo-Morelos rebellion Socially radical peasant rebellion in Mexico (1810) led by the priests Miguel Hidalgo and José Morelos.

hijra The "journey" of Muhammad and his original followers from Mecca to Yathrib (later Medina) in 622 C.E.; the journey marks the starting point of the Islamic calendar. (pron. HIJJ-ruh)

Hinduism A religion based on the many beliefs, practices, sects, rituals, and philosophies in India; in the thinking of nineteenth-century Indian reformers, it was expressed as a distinctive tradition, an Indian religion wholly equivalent to Christianity.

Hindutva A Hindu nationalist movement that became politically important in India in the 1980s; advocated a distinct Hindu identity and decried government efforts to accommodate other faith communities, particularly Islamic.

Hitler, Adolf (1889–1945) Leader of the German Nazi Party and Germany's head of state from 1933 until his death.

HIV/AIDS A pathogen that spreads primarily through sexual contact, contaminated blood products, or the sharing of needles; after sparking a global pandemic in the 1980s, it spread rapidly across the globe and caused tens of millions of deaths.

Ho Chi Minh (1890–1969) Leader of the Vietnamese communist movement that established control first in the north and then the whole of Vietnam after 1975.

Holocaust Name commonly used for the Nazi genocide of Jews and other "undesirables" in German society.

Holocene era A warmer and often a wetter period that began approximately 12,000 years ago following the end of the last ice age. These environmental conditions were uniquely favorable for human thriving and enabled the development of agriculture, significant population growth, and the creation of complex civilizations.

Holy Roman Empire A loose confederation of regional states, centered on what is now Germany but stretching from Denmark to Rome and the borders of France to Poland. From its beginning in the early ninth century, it was headed by an emperor, but in practice regional states proved effective in limiting his power.

Hopewell culture A common name for the Mississippi valley mound-building culture, after an archeological site in Ohio. Significant for the wide variety of artifacts found in elaborate burial mounds.

House of Wisdom An academic center for research and translation of foreign texts that was established in Baghdad in 830 C.E. by the Abbasid caliph al-Mamun.

Hulegu Grandson of Chinggis Khan who became the first il-khan (subordinate khan) of Persia. (pron. HE-luh-gee)

idea of "tribe" A new sense of clearly defined ethnic identities that emerged in twentieth-century Africa, often initiated by Europeans intent on showing the primitive nature of their colonial subjects, but widely adopted by Africans themselves as a way of responding to the upheavals of modern life.

ideology of domesticity A set of ideas and values that defined the ideal role of middle-class women in nineteenth-century Europe, focusing their activity on homemaking, child rearing, charitable endeavors, and "refined" activities as the proper sphere for women.

Igbo People whose lands were east of the Niger River in what is now southern Nigeria in West Africa. They built a complex society that rejected kingship and centralized statehood, while relying on other institutions to provide social coherence. (pron. EE-boh)

Inca Empire The Western Hemisphere's largest imperial state in the fifteenth and early sixteenth centuries. Built by a relatively small community of Quechua-speaking people (the Incas), the empire stretched some 2,500 miles along the Andes Mountains, which run nearly the entire length of the west coast of South America, and contained perhaps 10 million subjects.

Indian National Congress The political party led by Mahatma Gandhi that succeeded in bringing about Indian independence from Britain in 1947.

Indian Ocean commercial network The massive, interconnected web of commerce in premodern times between the lands that bordered the Indian Ocean (including East Africa, India, and Southeast Asia); the network was transformed as Europeans entered it in the centuries following 1500.

Indian Rebellion of 1857–1858 Massive uprising of much of India against British rule caused by the introduction to the colony's military forces of a new cartridge smeared with animal fat from pigs and cows, which caused strife among Muslims, who regarded pigs as unclean, and Hindus, who venerated cows. It came to express a variety of grievances against the colonial order.

Indus Valley civilization A major civilization that emerged in what is now Pakistan during the third millennium B.C.E., in the valleys of the Indus and Saraswati rivers, noted for the uniformity of its elaborately planned cities over a large territory.

influenza pandemic The worst pandemic in human history, caused by three waves of influenza that swept across the globe in 1918 and 1919, carried by demobilized soldiers, refugees, and other dislocated people returning home from World War I; between 50 million and 100 million people died in the pandemic.

informal economy Also known as the "shadow" economy; refers to unofficial, unregulated, and untaxed economic activity.

informal empires Term commonly used to describe areas that were dominated by Western powers in the nineteenth century but retained their own governments and a measure of independence (e.g., China).

Iranian revolution Establishment of a radically Islamist government in Iran in 1979; helped trigger a war with Iraq in the 1980s.

Iroquois Iroquois-speaking peoples in what is now New York State; around the fifteenth century they formed a loose alliance based on the Great Law of Peace, an agreement to settle disputes peacefully through a council of clan leaders.

Islamic radicalism Movements that promote strict adherence to the Quran and the sharia, often in opposition to key elements of Western culture. Particularly prominent since the 1970s, such movements often present themselves as returning to an earlier expression of Islam. Examples include the Iranian revolution, Taliban, al-Qaeda, and Islamic State.

Israeli-Palestinian Conflict Struggle between the Jewish state of Israel and the adjacent Palestinian Muslim territories that has generated periodic wars and upheavals since 1948.

jatis The thousands of occupationally based social groups, each associated with a *varna*, that became the primary cells of social life in the Indian caste system.

Jesuits in China Series of Jesuit missionaries from 1550 to 1800 who, inspired by the work of Matteo Ricci, sought to understand and become integrated into Chinese culture as part of their efforts to convert the Chinese elite, although with limited success.

Jesus of Nazareth A peasant/artisan "wisdom teacher" and Jewish mystic (ca. 4 B.C.E.–29 C.E.) whose life, teachings, death, and alleged resurrection gave rise to the new religion of Christianity.

Jesus Sutras The written product of Nestorian Christians living in China, these texts articulate the Christian message using Buddhist and Daoist concepts.

jizya Special tax paid by *dhimmis* (protected but second-class subjects) in Muslim-ruled territory in return for freedom to practice their own religion.

Judaism The monotheistic religion developed in the Middle East by the Hebrews, emphasizing a sole personal god (Yahweh) with concerns for social justice.

kaozheng Literally, "research based on evidence"; Chinese intellectual movement whose practitioners were critical of conventional Confucian philosophy and instead emphasized the importance of evidence and analysis, applied especially to historical documents.

Khanate of the Golden Horde The Russian name for the incorporation of Russia into the Mongol Empire in the mid-thirteenth century; known to Mongols as the Kipchak Khanate.

Khubilai Khan Grandson of Chinggis Khan who ruled China from 1271 to 1294. (pron. koo-buh-l'eye kahn)

Kievan Rus A culturally diverse civilization that emerged around the city of Kiev in the ninth century C.E. and adopted Christianity in the tenth, thus linking this emerging Russian state to the world of Eastern Orthodoxy.

laboring classes The majority of Britain's nineteenth-century population, which included manual workers in the mines, ports, factories, construction sites, workshops, and farms of Britain's industrializing and urbanizing society; this class suffered the most and at least initially gained the least from the transformations of the Industrial Revolution.

labor migration The movement of people, often illegally, into another country to escape poverty or violence and to seek opportunities for work that are less available in their own countries.

Labour Party British working-class political party established in the 1890s and dedicated to reforms and a peaceful transition to socialism, in time providing a viable alternative to the revolutionary emphasis of Marxism.

Latin American export boom Large-scale increase in Latin American exports (mostly raw materials and foodstuffs) to industrializing countries in the second half of the nineteenth century, made possible by major improvements in shipping; the boom mostly benefited the upper and middle classes.

Latin American revolutions Series of risings in the Spanish and Portuguese colonies of Latin America (1808–1825) that established the independence of new states from European rule but that for the most part retained the privileges of the elites despite efforts at more radical social change by the lower classes.

Legalism A Chinese philosophy distinguished by an adherence to clear laws with vigorous punishments.

Lenin (1870–1924) Born Vladimir Ilyich Ulyanov, leader of the Russian Bolshevik (later Communist) Party in 1917, when it seized power.

Lin Zexu, Commissioner Royal official charged with ending the opium trade in China; his concerted efforts to seize and destroy opium imports provoked the Opium Wars. (pron. lin zuh-SHOO)

Little Ice Age A period of unusually cool temperatures from the thirteenth to nineteenth centuries, most prominently in the Northern Hemisphere.

lower middle class Social stratum that developed in Britain in the nineteenth century and that consisted of people employed in the service sector as clerks, salespeople, secretaries, police officers, and the like; by 1900, this group comprised about 20 percent of Britain's population.

Luther, Martin (1483–1546) German priest who issued the Ninety-Five Theses and began the Protestant Reformation with his public criticism of the Catholic Church's theology and practice.

madrassas Formal colleges for higher instruction in the teachings of Islam as well as in secular subjects like law, established throughout the Islamic world beginning in the eleventh century.

Mahayana Buddhism "Great Vehicle," the popular development of Buddhism in the early centuries of the Common Era, which gives a much greater role to supernatural beings and to compassion and proved to be more popular than original (Theravada) Buddhism.

maize An ancient version of corn, first domesticated in southern Mexico by 4000 to 3000 B.C.E. This ancestor of corn was a mountain grass that looks nothing like today's corn or maize. Selective adaptation of this plant over thousands of years allowed for the development of sustainable agriculture in Mesoamerica and elsewhere.

Malacca Muslim port city that came to prominence on the waterway between Sumatra and Malaya in the fifteenth century C.E.; it was the springboard for the spread of a syncretic form of Islam throughout the region.

Mali A prominent state within West African civilization; it was established in 1235 C.E. and flourished for several centuries. Mali monopolized the import of horses and metals as part of the trans-Saharan trade; it was a large-scale producer of gold; and its most famous ruler, Mansa Musa, led a large group of Muslims on the pilgrimage to Mecca in 1324–1325.

mana **and** *tapu* Religious concepts in Oceania; people or objects became sacred through a spiritual energy or power (mana) that was kept pure with ritual restrictions (tapu), which came into English as "taboo."

Manila The capital of the colonial Philippines, which by 1600 had become a flourishing and culturally diverse city; the site of violent clashes between the Spanish and Chinese.

Mao Zedong (1893–1976) Chairman of China's Communist Party and de facto ruler of China from 1949 until his death.

maroon societies / Palmares Free communities of former slaves in remote regions of South America and the Caribbean; the largest such settlement was Palmares in Brazil, which housed 10,000 or more people for most of the seventeenth century.

Marshall Plan Huge U.S. government initiative to aid in the post–World War II recovery of Western Europe that was put into effect in 1948.

Marx, Karl (1818–1883) The most influential proponent of socialism, Marx was a German expatriate in England who advocated working-class revolution as the key to creating an ideal communist future.

maternal feminism Movement that claimed that women have value in society not because of an abstract notion of equality but because women have a distinctive and vital role as mothers; its exponents argued that women have the right to intervene in civil and political life because of their duty to watch over the future of their children.

Mauryan Empire The first and largest of India's short experiments with a large-scale political system (326–184 B.C.E.), it encompassed all but the southern tip of the Indian subcontinent. (pron. MORE-yuhn)

Maya civilization A major civilization of Mesoamerica known for the most elaborate writing system in the Americas and other intellectual and artistic achievements; flourished from 250 to 900 C.E.

megacities Very large urban centers with populations of over 10 million; by 2017, there were thirty-seven such cities on five continents.

megafaunal extinction The dying out of a number of large animal species, including the mammoth and several species of horses and camel. Occurred around 11,000 years ago, at the end of the Ice Age in North America. The extinction may have been caused by excessive hunting or by the changing climate of the era.

Meiji Restoration The political takeover of Japan in 1868 by a group of young samurai from southern Japan. The samurai eliminated the shogun and claimed they were restoring to power the young emperor, Meiji. The new government was committed to saving Japan from foreign domination by drawing upon what the modern West had to offer to transform Japanese society. (pron. MAY-jee)

mercantilism The economic theory that governments served their countries' economic interests best by encouraging exports and accumulating bullion (precious metals such as silver and gold); helped fuel European colonialism.

Meroë City in southern Nubia that was the center of Nubian civilization between 300 B.C.E. and 100 C.E.; had a reputation for great riches and was culturally distinct from Egypt. (pron. MER-oh-ee)

mestizo A term used to describe the mixed-race population of Spanish colonial societies in the Americas, most prominently the product of unions between Spanish men and Native American women. (pron. mehs-TEE-zoh)

Mexican Revolution Long and bloody war (1910–1920) in which Mexican reformers from the middle class joined with workers and peasants to overthrow the dictator Porfirio Díaz and create a new, much more democratic political order.

middle-class society British social stratum developed in the nineteenth century, composed of small businessmen, doctors, lawyers, engineers, teachers, and other professionals required in an industrial society; politically liberal, they favored constitutional government, private property, free trade, and social reform within limits; had ideas of thrift, hard work, rigid morality, "respectability," and cleanliness.

Ming dynasty Chinese dynasty (1368–1644) that succeeded the Yuan dynasty of the Mongols; noted for its return to traditional Chinese ways and restoration of the land after the destructiveness of the Mongols.

Mirabai (1498–1547) One of India's most beloved bhakti poets, she transgressed the barriers of caste and tradition.

Moche An important regional civilization of northern Peru, governed by warrior-priests; flourished from around 100 to 800 C.E. (pron. MOH-chee)

Modun Great ruler of the Xiongnu Empire (r. 210–174 B.C.E.) who exacted tribute from other Central Asian pastoral peoples as well as China itself, forcing Han dynasty emperor Wen to acknowledge the Xiongnu Empire as an equal.

Mohenjo Daro / Harappa Major cities of the Indus Valley civilization, both of which flourished around 2000 B.C.E. (pron. moe-hen-joe DAHR-oh) / (pron. hah-RAHP-uh)

Mongol world war Term used to describe half a century of military campaigns, massive killing, and empire building pursued by Chinggis Khan and his successors in Eurasia after 1209.

Mound Builders Members of a number of cultures that developed east of the Mississippi River in what is now the United States and that are distinguished by their large earthen mounds; most widespread between 200 B.C.E. and 1250 C.E.

Mughal Empire A successful state founded by Muslim Turkic-speaking peoples who invaded India and provided a rare period of relative political unity (1526–1707); their rule was noted for efforts to create partnerships between Hindus and Muslims. (pron. MOO-guhl)

Muhammad (570–632 C.E.) The Prophet and founder of Islam whose religious revelations became the Quran, bringing a radically monotheistic religion to Arabia and the world.

mulattoes Term commonly used for people of mixed African and European blood.

Muslim League Political group formed in response to the Indian National Congress in India's struggle for independence from Britain; the League's leader, Muhammad Ali Jinnah, argued that regions of India with a Muslim majority should form a separate state called Pakistan.

Mussolini, Benito (1883–1945) Charismatic leader of the Italian Fascist Party who came to power in 1922 and ruled until his death.

Napoleon Bonaparte French head of state and general (r. 1799–1815); Napoleon preserved much of the French Revolution under a military dictatorship and was responsible for the spread of revolutionary ideals through his conquest of much of Europe.

nationalism The focusing of citizens' loyalty on the notion that they are part of a "nation" with a unique culture, territory, and common experience, which merits an independent political life; first became a prominent element of political culture in nineteenth-century Europe and the Americas.

Nazi Party German political party that established a fascist state dedicated to extreme nationalism, territorial expansion, and the purification of the German state.

Neolithic Revolution The "new stone age," referring to the introduction of agriculture in societies that had long survived with a gathering and hunting economy.

Newton, Isaac (1642–1727) English scientist whose formulation of the laws of motion and mechanics is regarded as the culmination of the Scientific Revolution.

Niger Valley civilization Distinctive city-based civilization that flourished from about 300 B.C.E. to about 900 C.E. in the floodplain of the middle Niger and that included major cities like Jenne-jeno; the Niger Valley civilization is particularly noteworthy for its apparent lack of centralized state structures, having been organized instead in clusters of economically specialized settlements.

Norte Chico A region along the central coast of Peru, home to an early civilization that developed from 3000 B.C.E. to 1800 B.C.E.

North American Free Trade Agreement (NAFTA) Free trade agreement between the United States, Mexico, and Canada, established in 1984.

North Atlantic Treaty Organization (NATO) A military alliance, created in 1949, between the United States and various European countries; largely aimed at defending against the threat of Soviet aggression during the cold war.

Nubia A region to the south of Egypt in the Nile Valley, noted for its development of a separate civilization with an alphabetic writing system and a major ironworking industry by 500 B.C.E.

Nubian Christianity Emerging in the fifth and sixth centuries in the several kingdoms of Nubia to the south of Egypt, this Christian church thrived for six hundred years but had largely disappeared by 1500 C.E., by which time most of the region's population practiced Islam.

Olmec civilization An early civilization that developed along the coast of the Gulf of Mexico around 1200 B.C.E. and possibly created the first written language in the Americas.

one-child family policy (China) Chinese policy of population control that lasted from 1980 to 2014; used financial incentives and penalties to promote birth control, sterilization, and abortions in an effort to limit most families to a single child.

Opium Wars Two wars fought between Western powers and China (1840–1842 and 1856–1858) after China tried to restrict the importation of foreign goods, especially opium; China lost both wars and was forced to make major concessions.

"the original affluent society" Term coined to describe Paleolithic societies, which are regarded as affluent not because they had so much but because they wanted or needed so little.

Ottoman Empire Major Islamic state centered on Anatolia that came to include the Balkans, parts of the Middle East, and much of North Africa; lasted in one form or another from the fourteenth to the early twentieth century.

Ottoman seizure of Constantinople The city of Constantinople, the capital and almost the only outpost left of the Byzantine Empire, fell to the army of the Ottoman sultan Mehmed II "the Conqueror" in 1453, an event that marked the end of Christian Byzantium.

Paleolithic era The long period during which human societies sustained themselves through gathering, hunting, and fishing without the practice of agriculture. Such ways of living persisted well after the advent of agriculture in many places.

Paleolithic settling down The process by which some Paleolithic peoples moved toward permanent settlement in the wake of the last Ice Age. Settlement was marked by increasing storage of food and accumulation of goods, as well as growing inequalities in society.

Paris Climate Agreement An international agreement negotiated in 2015 among some 195 countries, 700 cities, and many companies to reduce greenhouse gas emissions sufficiently to avoid a 2°C increase in global temperatures. The United States withdrew from the agreement in 2017.

pastoral society Based on an alternative kind of food-producing economy focused on the raising of livestock, pastoral societies emerged in the Afro-Eurasian world where settled agriculture was difficult or impossible. Pastoral peoples often led their animals to seasonal grazing grounds rather than settling permanently in a single location.

patriarchy A social system in which women have been made subordinate to men in the family and in society; often linked to the development of plow-based agriculture, intensive warfare, and private property.

Paul, Saint An early convert and missionary (ca. 6–67 C.E.) and the first great popularizer of Christianity, especially to Gentile (non-Jewish) communities.

pax Romana The "Roman peace," a term typically used to denote the stability and prosperity of the early Roman Empire, especially in the first and second centuries C.E.

Peloponnesian War The Greek civil war (431–404 B.C.E.) that followed the Greco-Persian Wars, with Sparta defending city-state independence against Athenian dominance; the war left the Greeks in a state of distrust and disunity.

Perpetua Christian martyr (181–203 C.E.) from an upper-class Roman family in Carthage. Her refusal to renounce her faith made her an inspiration for other early Christians.

Persian Empire A major empire of the second-wave era that expanded from the Iranian plateau to incorporate the Middle East from Egypt to India; flourished from around 553 to 330 B.C.E.

Philippines (Spanish) An archipelago of Pacific islands colonized by Spain in a relatively bloodless process that extended for the century or so after 1565, a process accompanied by a major effort at evangelization; the Spanish named them the Philippine Islands in honor of King Philip II of Spain.

piece of eight The standard Spanish silver coin used by merchants in North America, Europe, India, Russia, West Africa, and China.

Pillars of Islam The five core requirements of the Quran: the belief in one God, regular prayer, charitable giving, fasting during Ramadan, and a pilgrimage to Mecca (if financially and physically possible).

Plato A Greek philosopher (429–348 B.C.E.) who famously sketched out a design for a good society in *The Republic*.

pochteca Professional merchants among the Aztecs who undertook large-scale trading expeditions in the fifteenth century C.E. (pron. pohch-TEH-cah)

Pohnpei Micronesian island dubbed the "Venice of the Pacific" where a complex urban construction made of coral and stone served as the ceremonial, administrative, and burial center.

population explosion An extraordinarily rapid growth in human population during the twentieth century that quadrupled human numbers in little more than a century. Experienced primarily in the Global South.

Potosí City that developed high in the Andes (in present-day Bolivia) at the site of the world's largest silver mine and that became the largest city in the Americas, with a population of some 160,000 in the 1570s.

Progressives Followers of an American political movement (progressivism) in the period around 1900 that advocated reform measures such as wages-and-hours legislation to correct the ills of industrialization.

Protestant Reformation Massive schism within Christianity that had its formal beginning in 1517 with the German priest Martin Luther; the movement was radically innovative in its challenge to church authority and its endorsement of salvation by faith alone, and also came to express a variety of political, economic, and social tensions.

Qing expansion The growth of Qing dynasty China during the seventeenth and eighteenth centuries into a central Asian empire that added a small but important minority of non-Chinese people to the empire's population and essentially created the borders of contemporary China.

Qin Shihuangdi Literally "first emperor from the Qin"; Shihuangdi (r. 221–210 B.C.E.) forcibly reunited China and established a strong state that governed, often brutally, according to a Legalist philosophy. (pron. chin shee-HUANG-dee)

Quran Also transliterated as Qur'án and Koran, this is the most holy text of Islam, which records the words of God through revelations given to the Prophet Muhammad.

religious fundamentalism Occurring within all the major world religions, fundamentalism is a self-proclaimed return to the alleged "fundamentals" of a religion and is marked by a militant piety, exclusivism, and a sense of threat from the modern secular world.

Revolutionary Right (Japan) Also known as Radical Nationalism, this was a movement in Japanese political life during the Great Depression that was marked by extreme nationalism, a commitment to elite leadership focused around the emperor, and dedication to foreign expansion.

ritual purity and pollution The idea that members of higher Indian castes must adhere to strict regulations limiting or forbidding their contact with "polluted" objects and members of lower castes to preserve their own caste standing and personal purity.

Robespierre, Maximilien (1758–1794) Leader of the French Revolution during the Terror; his Committee of Public Safety executed tens of thousands of enemies of the revolution until he was arrested and guillotined. (pron. ROHBS-pee-air)

Roman Catholic Church Western European branch of Christianity that gradually defined itself as separate from Eastern Orthodoxy, with a major break occurring in 1054 C.E. that still has not been overcome. By the eleventh century, Western Christendom was centered on the pope as the ultimate authority in matters of doctrine. The Church struggled to remain independent of established political authorities.

Russian Empire A Christian state centered on Moscow that emerged from centuries of Mongol rule in 1480; by 1800, it had expanded into northern Asia and westward into the Baltics and Eastern Europe.

Russian Revolution Massive revolutionary upheaval in 1917 that overthrew the Romanov dynasty in Russia and ended with the seizure of power by communists under the leadership of Lenin.

Russian Revolution of 1905 Spontaneous rebellion that erupted in Russia after the country's defeat at the hands of Japan in 1905; the revolution was suppressed, but it forced the government to make substantial reforms.

Russo-Japanese War (1904–1905) Fought over rival ambitions in Korea and Manchuria, this conflict ended in a Japanese victory, establishing Japan as a formidable military competitor in East Asia. The war marked the first time that an Asian country defeated a European power in battle, and it precipitated the Russian Revolution of 1905.

Safavid Empire Major Turkic empire established in Persia in the early sixteenth century and notable for its efforts to convert its people to Shia Islam. (pron. SAH-fah-vid)

Sand Roads A term used to describe the routes of the trans-Saharan trade, which linked interior West Africa to the Mediterranean and North African world.

scientific racism A new kind of racism that emerged in the nineteenth century that increasingly used the prestige and apparatus of science to support European racial prejudices and preferences.

Scientific Revolution The intellectual and cultural transformation that shaped a new conception of the material world between the mid-sixteenth and early eighteenth centuries in Europe; instead of relying on the authority of religion or tradition, its leading figures believed that knowledge was acquired through rational inquiry based on evidence, the product of human minds alone.

scramble for Africa The process by which European countries partitioned the continent of Africa among themselves in the period 1875–1900.

Sea Roads The world's largest sea-based system of communication and exchange before 1500 C.E. Centered on India, it stretched from southern China to eastern Africa.

secondary products revolution The series of technological changes that began ca. 4000 B.C.E. as people in the Eastern Hemisphere began to use their domesticated animals in new ways, such as for their milk, wool, and manure. Also involved learning to ride horses and camels and using animals to pull carts, plows, and chariots.

second-wave environmentalism A movement that began in the 1960s and triggered environmental movements in Europe and North America. It was characterized by widespread grassroots involvement focused on issues such as pollution, resource depletion, protection of wildlife habitats, and nuclear power.

second-wave feminism Women's rights movement that revived in the 1960s with a different agenda than earlier women's suffrage movements; second-wave feminists demanded equal rights for women in employment and education, women's right to control their own bodies, and the end of patriarchal domination.

self-strengthening China's program of internal reform in the 1860s and 1870s, based on vigorous application of traditional principles and limited borrowing from the West.

Seljuk Turkic Empire An empire of the eleventh and twelfth centuries, centered in Persia and present-day Iraq. Seljuk rulers adopted the Muslim title of *sultan* (ruler) as part of their conversion to Islam.

service sector Industries like government, medicine, education, finance, and communication that have grown due to increasing consumerism, population, and communication technologies.

settler colonies Imperial territories in which Europeans settled permanently in substantial numbers. Used in reference to the European empires in the Americas generally and particularly to the British colonies of North America.

shamans Persons believed to be especially skilled at dealing with the spirit world, often by means of trances induced by psychoactive drugs.

sharia Islamic law, dealing with political, economic, social, and religious life. It literally translates as "a path to water," which is considered the source of all life. (pron. shah-REE-ah)

Shotoku Taishi Japanese statesman (572–622) who launched the drive to make Japan into a centralized bureaucratic state modeled on China; he is best known for issuing the Seventeen Article Constitution in 604 C.E., which lays out the principles of this reform.

"the sick man of Europe" Western Europe's description of the Ottoman Empire in the nineteenth and early twentieth centuries, based on the empire's economic and military weakness and its apparent inability to prevent the shrinking of its territory.

Siddhartha Gautama (the Buddha) The Indian prince whose exposure to human suffering led him to develop a path to Enlightenment, which became the basis for the emerging religious tradition of Buddhism; lived ca. 566–ca. 486 B.C.E. (pron. sidd-ARTH-uh gow-TAHM-uh)

signares The small number of African women who were able to exercise power and accumulate wealth through marriage to European traders.

Sikhism Religious tradition of northern India founded by Guru Nanak (1469–1539); combines elements of Hinduism and Islam and proclaims the brotherhood of all humans and the equality of men and women.

Silk Roads Land-based trade routes that linked many regions of Eurasia. They were named after the most famous product traded along these routes.

Silla kingdom The first ruling dynasty to bring a measure of political unity to the Korean peninsula (688–900). (pron. SHEE-lah)

"silver drain" Term often used to describe the siphoning of money from Europe to pay for the luxury products of the East, a process exacerbated by the fact that Europe had few trade goods that were desirable in Eastern markets; eventually, the bulk of the world's silver supply made its way to China.

social Darwinism An outlook that suggested that European dominance inevitably led to the displacement or destruction of backward peoples or "unfit" races; this view made imperialism, war, and aggression seem both natural and progressive.

socialism in the United States Fairly minor political movement in the United States; at its height in 1912, it gained 6 percent of the vote for its presidential candidate.

Socrates The first great Greek philosopher (469–399 B.C.E.), whose constant questioning of conventional thinking led to his death sentence from an Athenian jury.

"soft gold" Nickname used in the early modern period for animal furs, highly valued for their warmth and as symbols of elite status.

Song dynasty The Chinese dynasty (960–1279) that rose to power after the Tang dynasty. During the Song dynasty, an explosion of scholarship gave rise to Neo-Confucianism, and a revolution in agricultural and industrial production made China the richest and most populated country on the planet.

Songhay Empire Major Islamic state of West Africa that formed in the second half of the fifteenth century. (pron. song-GAH-ee)

Spartacus A Roman gladiator who led the most serious slave revolt in Roman history in 73 B.C.E.

Srivijaya A Malay kingdom that dominated the critical choke point in Indian Ocean trade at the Straits of Malacca between 670 and 1025 C.E. Like other places in Southeast Asia, Srivijaya absorbed various cultural influences from India. (pron. SREE-vih-juh-yuh)

Stalin, Joseph (1878–1953) Leader of the Soviet Union from the late 1920s until his death.

Stanton, Elizabeth Cady (1815–1902) Leading figure of the early women's rights movement in the United States. At the first Women's Rights Convention in Seneca Falls, New York, in 1848, she drafted a statement paraphrasing the Declaration of Independence, stating that men and women were created equal.

steam engine The great breakthrough of the Industrial Revolution, the coal-fired steam engine provided an almost limitless source of power and could be used to drive any number of machines as well as locomotives and ships; the introduction of the steam engine allowed a hitherto unimagined increase in productivity and made the Industrial Revolution possible.

Sufism An understanding of the Islamic faith that saw the worldly success of Islamic civilization as a distraction and deviation from the purer spirituality of Muhammad's time. By renouncing the material world, meditating on the words of the Quran, chanting the names of God, using music and dance, and venerating Muhammad and various "saints," Sufis pursued an interior life, seeking to tame the ego and achieve spiritual union with Allah.

Sui dynasty Ruling dynasty of China (589–618) that effectively reunited the country after several centuries of political fragmentation. This unity was solidified through the extension of canals economically linking northern and southern China, but harsh leadership and futile efforts to conquer Korea eventually prompted the overthrow of the dynasty.

Sumer The region in the southern reaches of Mesopotamia between the Tigres and Euphrates rivers, mostly in present-day Iraq. Home to an early civilization that arose around 3500 B.C.E. to 3000 B.C.E., this area likely gave rise to the world's earliest written language.

Swahili civilization An East African civilization that emerged in the eighth century C.E. as a set of commercial city-states linked into the Indian Ocean trading network. Combining African Bantu and Islamic cultural patterns, these competing city-states accumulated goods from the interior and exchanged them for the products of distant civilizations.

Syrian civil war Conflict beginning in 2011 that generated over 12 million refugees and asylum seekers by mid-2016 and engaged both regional and world powers on various sides of the conflict.

Taiping Uprising Massive Chinese rebellion against the ruling Qing dynasty that devastated much of the country between 1850 and 1864; it was based on the millenarian teachings of Hong Xiuquan.

Taki Onqoy Literally, "dancing sickness"; a religious revival movement in central Peru in the 1560s whose members preached the imminent destruction of Christianity and of the Europeans and the restoration of an imagined Andean golden age.

Tang dynasty Ruling dynasty of China (618–907) noted for its openness to foreign cultural influences. Together with its successor, the Song dynasty, it represented a golden age of arts and literature and established patterns of Chinese life that endured into the twentieth century.

Tanzimat Important reform measures undertaken in the Ottoman Empire beginning in 1839; the term "Tanzimat" means "reorganization." (pron. tahn-zee-MAHT)

Temujin (Chinggis Khan) Birth name of the Mongol leader better known as Chinggis Khan (1162–1227), or "universal ruler," a name he acquired after unifying the Mongols. (pron. TEM-oo-chin)

Teotihuacán The largest city of pre-Columbian America, with a population between 125,000 and 150,000; seemingly built to a plan in the Valley of Mexico, Teotihuacán flourished between 300 and 600 C.E., during which time it governed or influenced much of the surrounding region. The name Teotihuacán is an Aztec term meaning "city of the gods." (pron. tay-uh-tee-wah-KAHN)

Theravada Buddhism "Teaching of the Elders," the early form of Buddhism according to which the Buddha was a wise teacher but not divine; emphasizes practices rather than beliefs. (pron. THAIR-ah-VAH-dah)

Thirty Years' War Catholic-Protestant struggle (1618–1648) that was the culmination of European religious conflict, brought to an end by the Peace of Westphalia and an agreement that each state was sovereign, authorized to control religious affairs within its own territory.

"three obediences" In Chinese Confucian thought, the notion that a woman is permanently subordinate to male control: first to her father, then to her husband, and finally to her son.

Timbuktu A major commercial city of West African civilization and a noted center of Islamic scholarship and education by the sixteenth century.

Timur Turkic warrior, also known as Tamerlane, whose efforts to restore the Mongol Empire in the late fourteenth and early fifteenth centuries devastated parts of Persia, Russia, and India. His successors created a vibrant elite culture drawing on both Turkic and Persian elements, especially in the city of Samarkand. Timur's conquests represent the last major military success of Central Asian pastoral peoples.

Tokugawa Japan A period of internal peace in Japan (1600–1850) that prevented civil war but did not fully unify the country; led by military rulers, or shoguns, from the Tokugawa family, who established a "closed door" policy toward European encroachments.

Tonga Islands Polynesian state with a central royal court, specialized craftsmen, and widespread military and commercial influence in the central Pacific.

total war War that requires each country involved to mobilize its entire population in the effort to defeat the enemy.

trading post empire Form of imperial dominance based on control of trade through military power rather than on control of peoples or territories.

transatlantic slave system Between 1500 and 1866, this trade in human beings took an estimated 12.5 million people from African societies, shipped them across the Atlantic in the Middle Passage, and deposited some 10.7 million of them in the Americas as slaves; approximately 1.8 million died during the transatlantic crossing.

transnational corporations Global businesses that produce goods or deliver services simultaneously in many countries; growing in number since the 1960s, some have more assets and power than many countries.

trans–Saharan slave trade A fairly small-scale commerce in enslaved people that flourished especially from 1100 to 1400, exporting West African slaves across the Sahara for sale in Islamic North Africa.

Treaty of Versailles The 1919 treaty that officially ended World War I; the immense penalties it placed on Germany are regarded as one of the causes of World War II.

tribute system A set of practices that required a show of subordination from all non-Chinese authorities and

the payment of tribute — products of value from their countries — to the Chinese emperor. In return, China would grant trading rights to foreigners and offer gifts even more valuable than the tribute itself.

Tupac Amaru Leader of a Native American rebellion in Peru in the early 1780s, claiming the last Inca emperor as an ancestor.

Turkic peoples Turkic speakers from Central Asia, originally nomads, who spread westward, creating a series of nomadic empires between 552 and 965 C.E. Having converted to Islam between the tenth and fourteenth centuries, Turkic peoples carried that faith into new lands, most notably the Christian Byzantine Empire, and became a politically powerful presence in the Islamic world.

ulama Islamic religious scholars, both Sunni and Shia, who shaped and transmitted the core teachings of Islamic civilization.

Umayyad caliphate Family of caliphs who ruled the Islamic world from 661 to 750 C.E., expanding the Arab Empire and creating a ruling class of Arab military aristocrats. (pron. oo-MEYE-ahd)

umma The community of all believers in Islam, bound by common belief rather than territory, language, or tribe. (pron. OOM-mah)

unequal treaties Series of nineteenth-century treaties in which China made major concessions to Western powers.

Upanishads Indian mystical and philosophical works written between 800 and 400 B.C.E. (pron. oo-PAHN-ee-shahds)

Uruk The largest city of ancient Mesopotamia, with a population around 50,000 in the third millennium B.C.E. (pron. OOH-rook)

varnas The four inherited ranked social classes of the Indian caste system.

Vedas The earliest religious texts of India, a collection of ancient poems, hymns, and rituals that were transmitted orally before being written down ca. 600 B.C.E. (pron. VAY-duhs)

Venus figurines Paleolithic carvings of the female form, often with exaggerated breasts, buttocks, hips, and stomachs.

vertical integration Control of a variety of ecological zones (and thus a variety of crops and animals) in areas with diverse climates and competing cities, chiefdoms, and states; common in Mesoamerican and Andean civilizations.

Vindication of the Rights of Woman Written by Mary Wollstonecraft, this tract was one of the earliest expressions of feminist consciousness.

Vivekananda (1863–1902) Leading religious figure of nineteenth-century India; advocate of a revived Hinduism and its mission to reach out to the spiritually impoverished West.

Vladimir of Kiev Grand prince of Kiev whose conversion to Orthodox Christianity in 988 C.E. led to the incorporation of an emerging Russian state into the sphere of Eastern Orthodoxy.

Voltaire The pen name of François-Marie Arouet (1694–1778), a French writer whose work is often taken as a model of the Enlightenment's outlook; noted for his deism and his criticism of traditional religion.

Wahhabi Islam Major Islamic movement led by the Muslim theologian Muhammad Ibn Abd al-Wahhab (1703–1792) that advocated an austere lifestyle and strict adherence to the Islamic law; became an expansive state in central Arabia.

Wang Mang A Han court official who usurped the throne and ruled from 8 C.E. to 23 C.E.; noted for his Confucian-inspired reform movement that included the breakup of large estates.

Wang Yangming Influential Ming thinker (1472–1529) who argued that anyone could achieve a virtuous life by introspection and contemplation, without the extended education and study of traditional Confucianism.

Wari and Tiwanaku Two states that flourished between 400 and 1000 C.E. in the interior highlands of the Andean region. At their height, they possessed urban capitals with populations in the tens of thousands and productive agricultural systems. (pron. wah-ree)

Warsaw Pact A military alliance between the Soviet Union and communist states in Eastern Europe, created in 1955 as a counterweight to NATO; expressed the tensions of the cold war in Europe.

West African civilization A series of important states that developed in the region stretching from the Atlantic coast to Lake Chad in the period 500 to 1600 C.E. Developed in response to the economic opportunities of trans-Saharan trade (especially control of gold production), it included the states of Ghana, Mali, Songhay, and Kanem, as well as numerous towns and cities.

Western Christendom Western European branch of Christianity, also known as Roman Catholicism, that gradually defined itself as separate from Eastern Orthodoxy, with a major break occurring in 1054 C.E.; characterized by its relative independence from the state and its recognition of the authority of the pope.

Women's Department A distinctive organization, known as Zhenotdel, within the Communist Party of the Soviet Union that worked to promote equality for women in the 1920s with conferences, publications, and education.

World Trade Organization (WTO) An international body representing 149 nations and charged with negotiating the rules for global commerce and promoting free

trade; its meetings have been the site of major anti-globalization protests since 1999.

World War I The "Great War" (1914–1918), in essence a European civil war with a global reach that was marked by massive casualties, trench warfare, and mobilization of entire populations. It triggered the Russian Revolution, led to widespread disillusionment among intellectuals, and rearranged the political map of Eastern Europe and the Middle East.

World War II in Asia A struggle to halt Japanese imperial expansion in Asia, fought by the Japanese against primarily Chinese and American foes.

World War II in Europe A struggle to halt German imperial expansion in Europe, fought by a coalition of allies that included Great Britain, the Soviet Union, and the United States.

Xiongnu Empire An imperial creation of nomadic steppe peoples who inhabited lands north of China. In the third and second centuries B.C.E., this empire stretched from Manchuria to Central Asia, establishing a model for later Turkic and Mongol empires.

Yap An island in western Micronesia that developed ceremonial tributary relationships with surrounding islands based in part on fear of Yapese sorcery.

yasak Tribute that Russian rulers demanded from the native peoples of Siberia, most often in the form of furs.

Yellow Turban Rebellion A massive Chinese peasant uprising around 184 B.C.E. that was inspired by Daoist teachings; it aimed to establish a new golden age of equality, harmony, and common ownership of property.

Young Ottomans Group of would-be reformers in the mid-nineteenth-century Ottoman Empire that included lower-level officials, military officers, and writers; they urged the extension of westernizing reforms to the political system.

Young Turks Movement of Turkish military and civilian elites that advocated a militantly secular public life and a Turkish national identity; came to power through a coup in 1908.

Yuan dynasty (China) Mongol dynasty initiated by Khubilai Khan that ruled China from 1271 to 1368.

Zheng He Great Chinese admiral who commanded a huge fleet of ships in a series of voyages in the Indian Ocean that began in 1405. Intended to enroll distant peoples and states in the Chinese tribute system, those voyages ended abruptly in 1433 and led to no lasting Chinese imperial presence in the region. (pron. JUHNG-huh)

Zoroastrianism Persian monotheistic religion founded by the prophet Zarathustra and emphasizing free will and the choice between good and evil. (pron. zohr-oh-ASS-tree-ahn-i'zm)

Index

About the Authors

Robert W. Strayer (Ph.D., University of Wisconsin) brings wide experience in world history to the writing of *Ways of the World*. His teaching career began in Ethiopia, where he taught high school world history for two years as part of the Peace Corps. At the university level, he taught African, Soviet, and world history for many years at the College at Brockport: State University of New York, where he received the Chancellor's Awards for Excellence in Teaching and for Excellence in Scholarship. In 1998 he was visiting professor of world and Soviet history at the University of Canterbury in Christchurch, New Zealand. Since moving to California in 2002, he has taught world history at the University of California, Santa Cruz; California State University, Monterey Bay; and Cabrillo College. He is a long-time member of the World History Association and served on its Executive Committee. He has also participated in various AP World History gatherings, including two years as a reader. His publications include *Kenya: Focus on Nationalism, The Making of Mission Communities in East Africa, The Making of the Modern World, Why Did the Soviet Union Collapse?*, and *The Communist Experiment*.

Eric W. Nelson (D.Phil., Oxford University) is a professor of history at Missouri State University. He is an experienced teacher who has won a number of awards, including the Missouri Governor's Award for Teaching Excellence in 2011 and the CASE and Carnegie Foundation for the Advancement of Teaching Professor of the Year Award for Missouri in 2012. His publications include *Layered Landscapes: Early Modern Religious Space across Faith and Cultures, The Legacy of Iconoclasm: Religious War and the Relic Landscape of Tours, Blois and Vendôme*, and *The Jesuits and the Monarchy: Catholic Reform and Political Authority in France*.